The

Complete

HOME
LEARNING
SOURCEBOOK

ALSO BY REBECCA RUPP

Red Oaks and Black Birches

Blue Corn and Square Tomatoes

Everything You Never Learned About Birds

Good Stuff: Learning Tools for All Ages

Committed to Memory: How We Remember and Why We Forget

The
Complete
HOME
LEARNING
SOURCEBOOK

**The Essential Resource Guide for
Homeschoolers, Parents,
and Educators
Covering Every Subject
from Arithmetic to Zoology**

REBECCA RUPP

Three Rivers Press, NEW YORK

NOTES ON HOW TO USE THIS BOOK

1. Prices and shipping charges are subject to continual change. Always check with the source before placing an order.

2. Since individual children vary so greatly, age recommendations for educational resources are always difficult. Parents/teachers should always review items for content and safety before use.

3. In most cases, sources have been listed for all reviewed items. Books can generally be obtained through bookstores or through the public library, which stock both recent publications and out-of-print selections. Many bookstores will perform searches for out-of-print books, often for free, though sometimes for a minimal charge.

4. See page xii for User's Guidelines.

◆

Copyright © 1998 by Rebecca Rupp
www.rebeccarupp.com

Published by Three Rivers Press, 201 East 50th Street, New York, New York 10022.
Member of the Crown Publishing Group.
Portions of this work were previously published in *Good Stuff* by Rebecca Rupp published by Home Education Press in 1993.

Random House, Inc. New York, Toronto, London, Sydney, Auckland
www.randomhouse.com

THREE RIVERS PRESS and colophon are trademarks of Crown Publishers, Inc.

Printed in the United States of America
Design by Meryl Sussman Levavi/digitext, inc.

Library of Congress Cataloging-in-Publication Data
Rupp, Rebecca.
The complete home learning sourcebook : the essential resource
guide for homeschoolers, parents, and educators covering every
subject from arithmetic to zoology / Rebecca Rupp.
Includes bibliographical references and index.
1. Home schooling—United States—Handbooks, manuals, etc.
I. Title
LC40.R83   1998
371.04'2—dc21   98-38440
CIP

ISBN 0-609-80109-0
10 9 8 7 6 5 4 3 2 1
First Edition

FOR RANDY AND OUR SONS

AND FOR TERRY AND RON AND THEIRS

ACKNOWLEDGMENTS

Writing a book is never a one-person affair—and never more so than in this case. I am indebted to the many people who contributed information and advice during the assembly of this book—with very special gratitude for the help of Joe Spieler and John Thornton; Ayesha Pande, Alexia Brue, Andrea Connolly Peabbles, and Justine Valenti, my editors at Crown; Terry Deloney, fellow homeschooler and infinitely supportive pen pal; my husband, Randy, who never has doubts about our educational choices; and our three sons, Joshua, Ethan, and Caleb, who are all strong, good-looking, and above average.

CONTENTS

USER'S GUIDELINES

Next to each description of the resources reviewed in this book are icons denoting the appropriate age range of the resource as well as the format (e.g. book, Web site, hands-on kit).

AGE GUIDELINES: The boxes with numbers denote the appropriate age range for each resource. These are approximations based on the author's experience and will obviously differ from student to student. Examples:

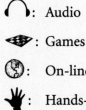: appropriate for children ages 5 to 8

: appropriate for children over 13

: a tool for parents and teachers

FORMAT GUIDELINES: Each resource is also identified by its format. Listed and defined below are the various icons you'll see throughout book:

⌒ : Audio	◆ : Curriculum	▯ : Software
◆ : Games	⬛ : Kit	▱ : Magazine
◉ : On-line resource	▬ : Video	◼ : Catalog
✋ : Hands-on activity	▨ : Book	

These symbols give you the ability to scan the margins in search of resources for specific ages and in specific formats. For example, 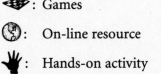 denotes a book appropriate for students ages 6 to 10. Or, 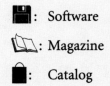 indicates a Web site suitable for students over 13. 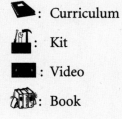 means that the resource is a catalog useful to parents and teachers.

TO SCHOOL OR
NOT TO SCHOOL

Never ask someone to do for you what you
can do for yourself.

THOMAS JEFFERSON

Choosing a mode of education is one of the most difficult decisions parents make for their children. Which is best, we all agonize: public school, private school, alternative school, homeschool? Should they go to preschool? Should they try Montessori school or Waldorf school? Which system will best enable our kids to grow up healthy, happy, ethical, self-sufficient, tolerant, mannerly, compassionate, and intellectually above average?

The answer, frustrating for those seeking a reproducible formula, seems to be all of the above. Children succeed in any number of learning environments. There simply is no one best way of education; there is instead a multitude of best ways—and what defines "best" is often a matter of subjective judgment. How do you define success? As a high-paying job? As social popularity? As intellectual accomplishment? As a satisfied mind?

In the end, for all our well-meaning choices, it won't even be our judgment that matters. Our kids inevitably will have the final say. What did they think of their educational experience? Did we, their parents, make the right decisions? "If it weren't for you," they'll begin, casting their minds back to these essential formative years, and we can only hope that the end of sentence will be gratefully positive.

Our three children—now teenagers—have never been to school. They have instead been educated entirely at home, a process that, over the years, has been alternately fascinating, frustrating, exciting, stressful, and deeply rewarding. It has not, however, been quite what we expected. Homeschooling, as it turns out, is not at all the same as school at home. Randy, my husband, and I had envisioned, when we first set out into uncharted educational territory, a learning process not unlike the one we had both experienced in our many years of public school: a logical and well-rounded progression from counting games and basal readers to higher mathematics and English literature. What we got were disorderly obsessions with Baroque music, glassblowing, particle physics, Egyptian archaeology, rocket models, telescopes, submarines, Shakespearean tragedy, and ant farms. One kid refused to learn the multiplication tables. One balked at geography, another at cursive handwriting. One spent months reading nothing but *The Encyclopedia of Fish*. Our sons, Josh, Ethan, and Caleb, all vociferously opinionated from day one, have always had distinctive educational agendas of their own. Homeschooling, for all of us, has been a learning process.

Our decision to homeschool has also had far broader implications than we had originally anticipated, permeating all aspects of our joint and separate lives. When we formally announced our plan to homeschool the boys (to doubtful friends and disapproving

relatives), we thought we were making a single simple decision: "Should Joshua start kindergarten this September?" In retrospect, however, that simple answer—"No"—signaled a whole battery of decisions and choices. For each homeschooling family, hard upon the heels of that "No" follows a list of closely linked questions: What kind of lifestyle do you want to pursue? What values do you feel are important for your family? What is your idea of an ideal family relationship? What are your views on independence and self-reliance versus social cooperation and community involvement? What kinds of responsibilities should the state have toward the nation's children? What are your responsibilities as a parent? What constitutes an education? How is learning best accomplished? And twenty years from now, when your youngest sets out to tackle the world, just where do you yourself want to be?

Homeschooling, twentieth-century style, is a relatively new trend in education. Nearly twelve years ago, as we approached the non-entry of our eldest child into kindergarten, homeschooling was the rare province of the educational rebel, the ornery oddball, and those leftover free spirits from the sixties blithely raising their offspring on communal peacock farms in the mountains outside Sacramento. Nowadays the movement—reportedly some one and a half million strong—has entered the mainstream. Homeschoolers a decade ago who announced their educational practices in public were greeted with "What's *that*?" and "Is it legal?" Now, with homeschooling legal in all fifty states, its practitioners are more likely to hear "Why, so are we"—or so is my sister-in-law, mailperson, dentist, or next-door neighbor.

Reasons for homeschooling are as varied and individual as the participants themselves. A sizable contingent of families homeschools for religious—most prominently, fundamentalist Christian—reasons. Others cite dissatisfaction with their local school systems, determination to maintain family interdependence and closeness, or a firm belief in the benefits of small-scale individualized instruction.

"When all our kids were in school," wrote the parents of five from Texas, "the schools controlled our lives. We didn't have time to do any of the things we felt were important as a family—we were always transporting one of the kids to one activity or another." "We didn't like the school peer pressure," another parent said. "We had a vision of Jenny at twelve, wearing black fishnet stockings and hanging around on the street corner next to the 7-Eleven. We wanted to give her a chance to develop her own interests, without being forced into a mold by the crowd." "I decided to homeschool after my first look at the elementary-school playground," one mother explained. "All asphalt and not a green leaf in sight; kids pushing and screaming. I couldn't stand the thought." "When our oldest son was nearing school age," wrote a mother from Wisconsin, "we realized that once he started school, we'd only really get to see him on Sundays. The school bus schedule had him leaving the house every day at 7 A.M. and not getting home again until 4 in the afternoon. My husband works late in the evenings and on Saturdays. It was just too little family time." "We wanted our kids to learn *our* concept of right and wrong, not their teacher's," said a parent from Massachusetts. "Our daughter's third-grade teacher was very opinionated and all of that came home to roost. Some things *should* be done; others *should not* be allowed—and we didn't always agree." "I taught first and second grades for several years," wrote a homeschooling mother from Tennessee, "and it's astounding how much more you can do with two children than with twenty-five." "Homeschooling fosters the innate joy of learning," stated an Arizona father, "and returns strength to the family."

Some parents choose to homeschool from the very beginning. Others make their decisions following unhappy experiences with the public schools, variously describing emotional, physiological, and intellectual miseries—everything from temper tantrums to tummy aches to chronic academic boredom. "Our son was bright and creative at home," wrote a North Dakota mother, "but was classified as learning disabled and a behavior problem at school. The school system worked well for our older daughter, but simply failed for Sean. Once free of the stress created in the classroom environment, however, he learned very well. He now reads and writes competently, and has developed a good self-image and high level of self-confidence. He also has time at home to pursue his own areas of interest." Sean, nine, seconded the motion: "I didn't like having to sit at a desk all the time and getting yelled at by teachers," he wrote. "And

I didn't like having to do the same thing over and over again until I got it just right."

The freedom to pursue personal interests is a—if not *the*—major advantage of homeschooling. Nothing is so motivating as love. A kid who enjoys gardening, for example, will absorb volumes of botanical information without visible effort; a kid enthralled by Shakespeare will remember every plot of every play, a vast array of arcane vocabulary words, and an amazing amount of Elizabethan history. All this is a joy to watch; this is education as we all dream it could and should be. Still, providing raw materials, enriching supplements, background information, appropriate field trips, and—when needed—instructions and explanations is challenging and time-consuming. Homeschooling is often a matter of having a great many intellectual plates in the air.

"What exactly *do* you do all day?" a friend from Missouri, with two children in private school, once asked. I found it a difficult question to answer. *Which* day? The day we spent rigging pulleys and pendulums to the beams in the living-room ceiling for physics experiments? The day we built and flew kites? The day we did nothing but lie in front of the woodstove reading *The Hobbit*? Approaches to homeschooling vary widely from family to family. Some families hold a highly structured school at home, complete with desks, textbooks, blackboard, and an introductory Pledge of Allegiance to the American flag. Others are completely unstructured, providing no formal instruction but plenty of enrichment, keeping themselves available to answer kids' questions and supply help when needed. We fall somewhere in between these two extremes. Though we've never had a strictly structured school day, we do have certain agreed-upon hours when we get together to do "school": assorted collective activities covering, over the course of each week, all the academic disciplines and whatever extras catch the boys' fancy. When the boys were younger, homeschool generally took place from eight or nine in the morning until lunchtime; and the afternoons were left relatively open, for field trips, extracurricular classes, outdoor play, continuation of the morning's projects (if wildly successful), or relaxed free time.

We have never used a packaged curriculum: given our kids' eclectic interests, we've found it easier—and more enjoyable—to invent our own. When the boys were younger, we based our educational program in part on the calendar, centering studies and projects around birthdays of famous persons, historical anniversaries, and unusual holidays. As they grew older, we concentrated for longer periods on specific topics or interests, creating detailed multidisciplinary unit studies. Unit studies are in-depth investigations of a specialized subject—say, elephants, electricity, China, or Thomas Jefferson—in which the chosen topic is approached from a number of different angles. A study unit on China, for example, might involve listening to traditional Chinese music, reading Chinese folktales, raising silkworms, experimenting with Chinese calligraphy, locating China on the world map and identifying its major geographical features, researching the history of the famous Great Wall, building a Chinese-style kite, learning to use a Chinese abacus, and cooking a Chinese meal. Depending on the ages and interest levels of the participating kids, unit studies can last anywhere from several days to months.

For information on packaged curricula, unit studies, and calendar-based studies, see Curricula, Lesson Plans, and How-tos, page 17.

From my homeschool journal:

◆ February 10, 1989. Josh is eight; Ethan, six; and Caleb, four.

In honor of Thomas Edison's upcoming birthday, we began the morning with a short biography of Edison by Robert Quackenbush, What Has Wild Tom Done Now? *(see page 564)—and discussed Edison's inventions. Questions from the boys: "What's a phonograph?" "What does the inside of a lightbulb look like?" "How come some lightbulbs are brighter than others?" I got out a clear glass lightbulb so that the boys could see what it looked like inside: "That wire is the tungsten part, right?"*

We then moved on to a stack of kid-picked picture books, ending with a Let's-Read-and-Find-Out science book, Paul Showers's Hear Your Heart *(see page 312). The boys, intrigued, listened to each other's hearts, my heart, the cat's heart, and the dogs' hearts with a stethoscope. A thrill. We then outlined a model heart on the floor with blocks, showing all four chambers, and strung pieces of blue yarn (veins) and red yarn (arteries)*

between the heart and the "body" and the "lungs," these last represented by labeled pieces of furniture. The boys then pretended to be red blood cells—they made themselves RBC labels with big circles of red construction paper and circulated through our model system, collecting oxygen tokens from the lungs (a chair) and dropping them off at the body (the kitchen table), before returning, via blue yarn veins, to the right atrium of the heart. I sat in a corner yelling BEAT! at intervals, which signaled all the blood cells to change places. "How big is a red blood cell?" "How fast do they go in your arteries?" "How many do you have in your whole body?" "Can red blood cells die?" "How does a red blood cell carry oxygen? Does the oxygen just stick to it in little bunches?"

We played a math game described in Family Math *(see page 173) on estimation, which had the boys grab handfuls of dried beans from a jar, guess how many were in their hands, and then count and compare. I thought they might be bored with this, but they enjoyed it—kept it up for half an hour. They next tried squashing the beans with a hammer, grinding the beans in the nut grinder, and throwing the beans in the fire to see if they would pop like popcorn (no). They finally tried real popcorn, which did pop nicely in the hot ashes. This led to a discussion of how the Indians might have originally discovered popcorn.*

This afternoon, to great excitement, a new toy (educational resource) arrived. It's called a "Poliopticon"; with it, by screwing together assorted tubes and lenses, kids can make a microscope, telescope, binoculars, kaleidoscope, and pocket magnifier. The boys pounced on the instruction manual and built everything, figuring out which lens combinations make things look closer and which make things look far away. They examined, among other things, salt crystals, ground pepper, a dead fly, birds at the bird feeder, and the trees across the driveway.

Bed book: several chapters of Charlie and the Great Glass Elevator *by Roald Dahl.*

◆ December 14, 1989

Today is astronomer Tycho Brahe's birthday, which we celebrated with the help of home-written interactive workbooks. We read a short account of Tycho's life: the boys found him fascinating, with his metal nose (he lost his real one in a student duel) and his private observatory, an island castle named Uraniborg. The boys drew detailed diagrams of their own island observatories, which definitely rivaled Tycho's. We covered Tycho's astronomical theories and discoveries: his observation of an eclipse (we read a book about eclipses, drew diagrams of lunar and solar eclipses, and demonstrated both with a couple of rubber balls and a flashlight); his study of comets; his theory about planets orbiting the sun; his observation of a supernova in the constellation Cassiopeia in 1572. We drew pictures of the solar system, showing orbits of the planets and comets. Explained how meteor showers occur when the Earth's orbit crosses the a comet's path. (The peak of the Geminid meteor shower is tonight; the boys plan to stay up and watch.) The boys did connect-the-dots Cassiopeia puzzles in their "Astro-Dots" puzzle books; and we read the stories of Cassiopeia, Andromeda, Perseus, and the sea monster; and of Castor and Pollux (Gemini), their beautiful sister Helen, and the Trojan War.

The boys then made themselves a set of tinfoil noses and set off to fight duels.

◆ **January 7, 1992. Josh is ten; Ethan, nine; Caleb, seven.**

We're doing a study unit on the New England states. Today we started with Connecticut, which we located on the United States map, variously pinpointing Hartford, the Connecticut River, and Long Island Sound. ("How come it's called a sound?") Read the history of Connecticut's state song—"Yankee Doodle"—and sang several verses. "Yankee Doodle," uncut, has ninety-something verses; we found a book that listed every one of them. Looked up the Connecticut state bird (the robin) in the Peterson field guide and colored robin pictures in Fifty Favorite Birds (see page 335) coloring books. Ethan's robin is very accurate ("They're not really red"); Caleb's robin is an imaginative yellow and purple.

Read the story of Connecticut's Charter Oak, and the boys made a lot of tea-dyed antique paper, supposedly to make their own charters, but actually they made treasure maps.

We invented a "Famous People of Connecticut" card game, covering Nathan Hale, Eli Whitney, P. T. Barnum, Samuel Colt, Benedict Arnold, and Mark Twain. Josh, who has read Twain's A Connecticut Yankee in King Arthur's Court, told everybody about it.

Read a short biography of P. T. Barnum, measured heights of Tom Thumb, the giantess Anna Swan, and Jumbo the elephant, and compared them on a bar graph. Much interest in midgets ("Why don't they grow?"), bearded ladies ("How?"), giants ("How big can they get?"), and Siamese twins. Explained the biology of each.

Josh read Mother West Wind's Children (Thornton Burgess) to himself; Ethan and Caleb wrote in their journals.

Bed book: several chapters of Mossflower by Brian Jacques.

◆ **September 5, 1995. Josh is fourteen; Ethan twelve; and Caleb, ten.**

We began the day with an impassioned discussion of current events, based on articles from yesterday's New York Times, on censorship of school library books and immigration policy reform.

Then moved on to science: we're doing a unit on optics. Initially we experimented with a collection of assorted glass lenses and a gelatin lens-casting kit (Edible Optics from Edmund Scientific) (see page 395), with which the kids cast convex and concave lenses using petri plates, watch glasses, and Jell-O. (With the leftovers, we added bananas and made dessert.) We covered the definitions of concave and convex lenses, positive and negative lenses, focal length, focal point, and nearsightedness and farsightedness (this last all the boys had down, having studied the eye section of the A.D.A.M. computer program) (see page 316). Drew and labeled diagrams illustrating all of the above. Then, using "The Eyes Have It" kit from the Wild Goose Company (see page 315), the boys built model convex and concave lenses (using washers, microscope slides, and water) and demonstrated their magnifying/reducing abilities; also made a model light-and-dark-detecting "simple eye," tried a compound eye viewer, and experimented with optical illusions. The optical illusions were a hit—the kids went through two packs of optical illusion cards and finally figured out how to see "perceived depth images"—the kinds of illusions shown in the Magic Eye books. Caleb produced the Magic Eye book he got last Christmas, and everybody, including me, leafed gleefully through it, seeing images. Discussed eye spots in primitive animals, the structure of the complex human eye, the genetic control of eye development, and patterns of eye *color inheritance. Tested visual acuity with Snellen eye chart and learned numerical explanation of 20/20 vision. (Ethan has it.) Tested for astigmatism. (Josh and I have it.)*

Writing: the boys started autobiography projects. Today everybody wrote about their very earliest memories. We discussed childhood amnesia and the biology of memory formation and storage.

History: over lunch, read and discussed a chapter in Joy Hakim's Liberty for All? *(see page 453) about nineteenth-century urbanization of America. Josh and Caleb both find the Hakim books fascinating; Ethan stead-fastly insists that he hates history, but he does hang around to participate in the discussions, so it can't be all bad.*

Afternoon: Saxon math lessons (see page 177) for each boy. Josh read Saki's "The Open Window"; Ethan read "Wishes" in Natalie Babbitt's The Devil's Story-book; *and Caleb read three chapters in Jane Werner Watson's version of* The Iliad and the Odyssey. *Latin for Josh; Japanese for Ethan and Caleb.*

Pottery class 3:30–5:30. Today Josh made a spectacular bowl; Ethan spent nearly the entire two hours making a mug handle; and Caleb decorated some of his earlier pots, plus made a bowl and a plate. Sarah, their instructor, says they are impressive on the potter's wheel.

Evening: reading by Josh and Caleb; Ethan on the computer, teaching himself computer programming. We're also watching A Town Like Alice *on videotape, a story of World War II Malaysia and postwar Australia. Caleb follows all the action on the world map.*

Now, as teenagers, the boys handle "school" pretty much on their own, though we spend considerable time preparing educational materials, tracking down resources, reviewing the kids' work, offering suggestions, and asking questions. We compose assignment lists, which sound more intimidating than they really are, with input from each boy. These, I find, are useful for keeping track of who's doing what when; with the boys now going in several different directions, this isn't as easy as it used to be. (A suggestion that the boys maintain their own educational records was firmly squashed. "That's not the kind of thing I put in my journal," said Ethan.) I spend at least one (official) hour of individual time with each boy each day, reviewing the previous day's work, discussing interests, problems, and ideas for future studies, and providing explanations when wanted. The boys cooperate on or share certain projects—joint unit studies, games, book or current event discussions, field trips, video classes. For others, they work alone. Often they do the things that appear on their lists; sometimes they don't. "Don't worry, Mom; I'll get to it tomorrow," says Josh, heading purposefully for the computer. "I've just read *Othello* and I have a great idea for a short story. Want to read it when I'm finished?"

◆ **May 21, 1997**

Josh's List:

1. *Math: Do today's Saxon math lesson. You had a couple of mistakes on yesterday's sheet—take a look at them; if you don't understand what you did wrong, see me.*

    Try "And He Built a Crooked House" by Robert Heinlein in Fantasia Mathematica. *(Sci fi math. I think you'll like it.)*

2. *Latin: Last two exercises in* Oxford Latin Course *chapter (see page 704) and continue work in* Artes Latinae *(see page 703).*

3. *Literature: I know you're still reading Robert Fagles's translation of* The Iliad. *Try these two chapters in David Denby's* Great Books *(see page 74): "Homer I" and "Homer II." I think you'll find them interesting.*

4. *Science: Remember to measure the caterpillars in your butterfly-raising project. Enter the numbers in your lab notebook, calculate the average, and plot it on the growth graphs.*

    Anatomy pages and worksheet.

    Stargazing again tonight if it's clear.

5. *It's my turn to give you* one word *for your essay/story topic. Your word is . . .* Griffin. *Good luck. (Caleb gave me one: it's* Kooshball.*)*

6. *World history: Watch next video lesson in series.*

7. *Remember to practice the piano.*

Ethan's List:

1. *Today's Saxon math lesson.*

2. *Spelling/grammar review sheets.*

3. *Reading: Next chapter in Bob Berman's* Secrets of the Night Sky *(see page 254). (It's on satellites.) If it's a clear night tonight, let's go spot some.*

4. *Writing: Your* one word *for your essay/story topic today is . . .* Penguin.

5. *Science: Anatomy pages and worksheet.*

   Read "The Roadrunner Triumphs Again" in Jay Ingram's The Science of Everyday Life. *Do physics workbook on gravity/acceleration. Includes calculations and experiments. (You'll need a partner or two.)*

6. *World history: Next video lesson in series.*

7. *Japanese: Next exercise in* hiragana *workbook; review cassette tapes.*

8. *Don't forget to practice your violin.*

Caleb's List:

1. *Saxon math lesson. You left out a couple on yesterday's sheet—let's go over them.*

2. *Read biography of Edgar Allan Poe in* The Lives of the Writers *(see page 87) and "The Telltale Heart" in* The Collected Stories of Edgar Allan Poe. *(Highly recommended by Josh.)*

   Make sure you enter Poe in your Timeline Book.

3. *Writing: Your* one word *for today's essay/story is* Pineapple.

4. *Science: Anatomy pages and worksheet.*

   Stargazing again tonight if it's clear: want to set up the telescope?

5. *Japanese: next exercise in* hiragana *workbook; review cassette tapes.*

6. *World history: Next video lesson.*

   Next chapter in Practical Archaeology; *continue interactive workbook.*

7. *Practice piano/violin.*

Selecting a course of study is the easiest part of the homeschool process. "Let's study bugs!" one child will say brightly, appearing at the back door with a grasshopper penned in a Mason jar. "Is this a male or a female? How does he hop? Does he have muscles? Are grasshoppers the same as crickets?" The subsequent steps, however—(1) tracking down appropriate books, reference materials, and resources, and (2) paying for them—are more challenging.

How much does home education cost? Homeschool expenses, depending on your children's interests—microscopy, calligraphy, bassoon playing—can range from not much to intimidatingly substantial.

The average homeschool family, according to the National Home Education Research Institute (see page 10), spends an annual $546 per child. By this yardstick, during the 1988–1989 school year, which we spent in Missouri, we were close to financially average, spending about $1,800 on the children's education. Around $800 of this went for extracurricular classes: an art course, swimming lessons, and gymnastics lessons. We spent about $400 on books; $250 on science supplies, educational games, and math manipulatives; and $200 on arts and crafts supplies. The remainder included video rentals, kids' magazine subscriptions, and computer software. The total didn't include the cost of field trips, which, according to my journal, included multiple visits to the science center and art museum, two canoe trips, three cave tours, a fossil-hunting expedition, visits to the zoo, two plays and a children's concert, several story hours at the library, and visits to the St. Louis Arch, the Daniel Boone House, the Cahokia Indian Mounds, Mark Twain's House in Hannibal, the Chicago Museum of Industry and Technology, and Lincoln's House in Springfield, Illinois.

These days our annual costs are higher. The boys' collective book bills average about $1,000; violin and piano lessons and orchestra memberships run about $2,000; the winter ski program costs about $200. Not all activities are so pricey, however, and creative money-savers for homeschoolers are plentiful. Foremost among these is the public library, an unending source of literature, information, free enrichment programs, and—if you desperately need something they don't have—book searches and interlibrary loans. Many museums and historical sites do not charge admission; and most communities have a wealth of unexpected learning opportunities that cost nothing: the local veterinary clinic, for example, or post office, newspaper office, apple orchard, dairy farm, sawmill, horse stable, or fire station.

The family field trip, a staple of most homeschooling programs, is (usually) an excellent learning experience and (usually) fun and can constitute anything from a major weeklong expedition to the Smithsonian or Yellowstone National Park, to a quick hike (armed with bread crusts and field guide) to the duck pond down the road. Our considerable experience with field trips, however, indicates that all are not created equal.

Large field trips, attended by an entire homeschool support group, can be a blast, but they are generally nowhere near as educationally rewarding as trips taken by one or two families on their own. Large groups get mass impersonal lectures and suffer from intergroup social distractions. (The kids yell, squirm, giggle, and tussle with each other.) Small groups get individual attention and a chance to ask questions; they can take their time, spending as much or as little as interest demands; and they provide plenty of relaxed opportunities for parent-child interaction and discussion.

We've also found that, no matter how worthwhile the field trip, too much of a good thing can backfire. Many of our most rewarding learning experiences have taken place in the breathing spaces, the times when our family simply sits and does nothing but talk: under a tree on a picnic blanket, on the rug in front of the woodstove, around the kitchen table. And sometimes kids just need undisturbed time alone, to think, to assimilate, to mull things over, to daydream.

Which brings us to the bottom line: every home is a learning center. No matter what educational choices you make for your children, all families, in one way or another, homeschool. All parents, of whatever educational philosophy, are their children's first and most influential teachers. Homeschooling comes in many shapes, sizes, and creative permutations. Those who teach French and algebra at the kitchen table are homeschooling. Those who read their kids bedtime stories, help them build airplane models or birdhouses, teach them how to fish, knit, or ride a bicycle, or explain the difference between the big hand and the little hand on the clock are homeschooling too.

GETTING STARTED

LAWS AND REGULATIONS

Parents who decide to teach their children full-time at home must, in theory, be in compliance with state law. Homeschooling is legal everywhere in the United States, but requirements vary from state to state, ranging from the comfortably permissive to the stringently restrictive. For new homeschoolers, a local homeschool

support group is generally a reliable source for information and advice about specific regulations and compliance strategies. For addresses and names of helpful persons or organizations, contact the **American Homeschool Association,** Box 3142, Palmer, AK 99645-3142; (509) 486-2477; e-mail AHAonline@aol.com; Web site: www.home-ed-press.com/AHA/aha.html. The AHA maintains state-by-state lists of homeschool support groups and an up-to-date portfolio of information on state laws and regulations. Often copies of state homeschooling regulations can also be obtained directly from your State Department of Education.

BOOKS

School Rights: A Parent's Legal Handbook and Action Guide
Thomas Condon and Patrician Wolff; Macmillan General Reference, 1996

School Rights summarizes the legal rights of parents in regard to many different educational issues, among them teacher competency, testing, curriculum content, tracking, special education, bilingual education, sexual discrimination, racial and religious problems, and homeschooling. The book includes case studies and step-by-step guidelines for taking action.

ORGANIZATIONS: LEGAL SUPPORT

Home School Legal Defense Association
For an annual membership fee, the Home School Legal Defense Association (HSLDA) offers legal advice and, if necessary, professional representation in court to homeschooling families. The organization also tracks federal legislation on homeschooling and family rights issues. The HSLDA, while it purports to represent all homeschoolers, is strongly conservative and has been involved in considerable political lobbying, promoting an agenda that may be uncongenial to many homeschool groups and families.

Annual family membership, $100, including subscription to a bimonthly newsletter, *The Home School Court Report*
Home School Legal Defense Association

Box 3000
Purcellville, VA 20134
(540) 338-5600
Web site: www.hslda.org

National Association for the Legal Support of Alternative Schools

The National Association for the Legal Support of Alternative Schools (NALSAS) is an information and legal service center that researches, coordinates, and supports legal actions involving alternative education, including homeschooling. The organization publishes a quarterly newsletter on legal issues and alternative education, the *National Coalition News.*

Annual membership, $35; a subscription to the *National Coalition News* (4 issues), $20
National Association for the Legal Support of Alternative Schools
Box 2823
Santa Fe, NM 87501
(505) 471-6928

ORGANIZATIONS: GENERAL

Alliance for Parental Involvement in Education (AllPIE)

AllPIE is a nonprofit organization that promotes parental involvement in education in all learning environments: public schools, private schools, and homeschools. The group publishes assorted information pamphlets, two newletters (*Options in Learning* and *New York State Home Education News*), and a book and resources catalog; sponsors educational workshops and seminars; and maintains a Web site with links to other education-related resources on-line.

Box 59
East Chatham, NY 12060-0059
(518) 392-6900
e-mail: ALLPIESR@aol.com
Web site: www.croton.com/allpie

American Homeschool Association (AHA)

AHA maintains an extensive on-line resource file of state-by-state legal information, local and national support group listings (with addresses and telephone

numbers), and recommended books and resources for home educators. It also publishes a monthly on-line newsletter.

Box 1125
Republic, WA 99166-1125
(509) 486-2477
e-mail: AHAonline@aol.com
Web site: www.home-ed-press.com/AHA/aha.html

Family Learning Exchange (FLEx)

The Family Learning Exchange is devoted to natural learning, family learning, and homeschooling. The group maintains an extensive Web site, with answers to frequently asked questions about homeschooling, listings of state, national, and international support groups, links to other homeschool resource sites, and an on-line newsletter.

Box 5629
Lacey, WA 98509-5629
(360) 491-5193
e-mail: FmlyLrngEx@aol.com
Web site: www.FLExOnline.org

Also see **FLEx Online** (page 22).

Family Unschoolers Network (F.U.N.)

F.U.N. provides information and support for homeschoolers, unschoolers, and self-directed learners. It publishes an excellent quarterly newsletter of educational essays and resource reviews, the *F.U.N. News,* and a book and resource catalog, *F.U.N. Books,* and maintains an extensive Web site with links to other homeschool resources.

1688 Belhaven Woods Ct.
Pasadena, MD 21122-3727
(410) 360-7330
e-mail: FUNNews@MCIMail.com
Web site: members.aol.com/FUNNews/index.htm

Also see *F.U.N. News* (page 10) and *F.U.N. Books* (page 25).

Holt Associates

Holt Associates, founded by innovative educator John Holt, is a national organization that stresses the natural ability of children to learn without a formal curriculum or a structured "school at home." The group publishes a bimonthly homeschooling magazine, *Growing Without Schooling,* and a free book catalog, *John Holt's Bookstore,* and provides a consultation service (call for rates) for home educators.

2269 Massachusetts Ave.

Cambridge, MA 02140

(617) 864-3100/fax (617) 864-9235

e-mail: holtgws@aol.com

Web site: www.holtgws.com

Also see *Teach Your Own* (page 14), *Growing Without Schooling* (page 11), and **John Holt's Bookstore** (page 26).

National Challenged Homeschoolers Associated Network (NATHHAN)

NATHHAN is a network of families who have children with special developmental or physical needs. The group publishes a newsletter of information and resources.

Annual family membership, $25.

5383 Alpine Rd. SE

Olalla, WA 98359

(253) 857-4257

National Home Education Research Institute (NHERI)

A nonprofit organization dedicated to accumulating facts and figures about homeschooled students and their families. NHERI publishes a number of booklets, fact sheets, and information packets for homeschoolers, as well as a quarterly journal, *The Home School Researcher.*

Box 13939

Salem, OR 97309

(503) 364-1490/fax (503) 364-2827

e-mail: mail@nheri.org

Web site: www.nheri.org

National Homeschool Association (NHA)

The NHA promotes freedom of choice in education, providing support and advice to homeschoolers nationwide. The organization disseminates general information about homeschooling and related political issues and maintains a homeschool referral service, which helps new homeschoolers connect with local contact persons or support groups. The NHA also publishes a quarterly newsletter.

Annual family membership, $15; a Homeschool Information Resource packet, $4

Box 290

Hartland, MI 48353-0290

(513) 772-9580

Web site: www.alumni.caltech.edu/~casner/nha

MAGAZINES: PARENTING, HOMESCHOOLING, AND EDUCATION

The Drinking Gourd

P/T A multicultural homeschooling magazine featuring informational articles, teaching hints, letters, and resource reviews.

Single issues $4; annual subscription (6 issues), $18

The Drinking Gourd

Box 2557

Redmond, WA 98073

(206) 836-0336

e-mail: TDrnkngGrd@aol.com

Early Childhood Today

P/T Targeted at early childhood teachers, *ECT* includes curriculum activities, projects suggestions, teaching advice, and reviews of new products for preschoolers.

Annual subscription (8 issues), $29.95

Early Childhood Today

Box 54814

Boulder, CO 80322

(303) 604-1464 or (800) 544-2917

F.U.N. News

P/T F.U.N. is the acronym of the Family Unschoolers Network, a warmhearted organization "that believes learning should be fun for the whole family." "Unschooling" is an open-ended participatory approach to learning in which the educational program is tailored to the interests of the children rather than restricted to a formal curriculum. Your child, for example, poring over the encyclopedia, looks up and exclaims, "Kangaroos! This is really interesting. Do we have any books about them?" You hop in the car and take the child to the library, where you check out a stack of books on kangaroos, wallabies, koala bears, Captain Cook, the Great Barrier Reef, and the art of the Australian aborigines. You've got it: you're unschooling.

F.U.N. News is a collection of informative articles, accounts of personal experiences, news notes, readers' letters, and resource reviews and addresses.

Annual subscription (4 issues), $8
F.U.N. News
1688 Belhaven Woods Ct.
Pasadena, MD 21122-3727
e-mail: 619-3098@MCImail.com
Web site: members.aol.com/FUNNews/index.html
See *F.U.N. Books* (page 25).

Growing Without Schooling

GWS was established in 1977 by author/educator John Holt, whose books—among them *How Children Learn* and *How Children Fail*—were a radical departure from accepted educational dogma, introducing a new concept of child-led learning. The magazine, dedicated to Holt's philosophy, includes homeschooling news updates, informational articles, interviews with prominent persons in education-related fields, book and resource reviews, letters from readers, and a regional directory of homeschooling families.

Single issues, $6; annual subscription (6 issues), $25
Holt Associates
2269 Massachusetts Ave.
Cambridge, MA 02140
(617) 864-3100/fax (617) 864-9235
e-mail: holtgws@aol.com
Web site: www.holtgws.com
See **John Holt's Bookstore** (page 26).

Home Education Magazine

A national 60+-page bimonthly homeschooling magazine, filled with informational articles, news updates, book and resource reviews, legal and philosophical debates, teaching suggestions, personal stories, and letters from readers. Also included: a list of pen pals for both kids and adults and a regional directory of support groups and homeschool organizations. *HEM* also publishes a free 24-page "Homeschooling Information and Resource Guide" for new homeschoolers.

Annual subscription (6 issues), $24
Home Education Magazine
Box 1587
Palmer, AK 99645-1587
(907) 746-1336 or (800) 236-3278/fax (907) 746-1335
e-mail: HomeEdMag@aol.com
Web site: www.home-ed-press.com

Homeschooling Today

A bimonthly magazine for Christian homeschool families, including personal and informational essays, resource suggestions, and activities for students of all ages.

Annual subscription (6 issues), $19.99
Homeschooling Today
Box 1608
Ft. Collins, CO 80522-1608
(954) 962-1930
e-mail: hstodaymag@aol.com.

Instructor

A teacher's magazine published in two editions, either for primary (K–3) or intermediate (4–6+) grade levels. Each edition includes general articles on teaching techniques, book and product reviews, activity suggestions, contest information, and poetry. Each issue also contains a complete integrated study unit with an accompanying pull-out poster.

Annual subscription (8 issues), $19.95
Instructor
Box 53896
Boulder, CO 80322-3896
(800) 544-2917

The Mailbox

The "idea magazine for teachers," filled with teaching suggestions, lesson plans, and activities. Published in four different editions for preschool, kindergarten, primary grades (1–3), and intermediate grades (4–6).

Annual subscription (6 issues), $24.95
The Mailbox
Box 51955
Boulder, CO 80322
(800) 334-0298
Web site: theeducationcenter.com

Mothering

Mothering, the "Magazine of Natural Family Living," includes articles on pregnancy and birth, parenting, family life, children's health issues, learning resources, alternative education, and homeschooling.

Annual subscription (6 issues), $18.95

Mothering

Box 1690

Santa Fe, NM 87505-1690

(800) 984-8116

e-mail: mother@ni.net

Practical Homeschooling

Informational articles, detailed product reviews, lesson plans, and teaching hints for Christian homeschoolers. A regular column, "A Day At Our House," describes a "typical" day in the lives of different homeschool families.

Annual subscription (6 issues), $19.95

Practical Homeschooling

Home Life

Box 1250

Fenton, MO 63026-1850

(800) 346-6322/fax (314) 343-7203

e-mail: PHSCustSvc@aol.com

Web site: www.home-school.com

Teacher Magazine

The magazine, targeted at professional educators, covers political issues and current research in education. Included are book and resource reviews, "On the Web," which lists and describes educational Web sites, and "For Your Students," which lists contests, scholarships, and internships.

Annual subscription (8 issues), $17.94

Teacher Magazine

Box 2090

Marion, OH 43301

(800) 728-2753/fax (740) 382-5866

Web site: www.edweek.org

Teacher's Helper

Reproducible pages of activities for thematic study units, variously appropriate for kids in kindergarten, grade 1, grades 2–3, or grades 4–5.

Annual subscription (4 issues), $16.95

Teacher's Helper

Box 51110

Boulder, CO 80322

(800) 334-0298

Web site: theeducationcenter.com

The Teaching Home

Articles, activities, and teaching tips suitable solely for dedicated Christian fundamentalists.

Annual subscription (6 issues), $15

The Teaching Home

Box 20219

Portland, OR 97294

(503) 253-9633/fax (503) 253-7345

Books: Alternative and Home Education

Alternatives in Education

Mark and Helen Hegener, eds.; Home Education Press, 1992

A collection of articles on the many and varied educational alternatives available to those unhappy with the public schools. Topics covered include diverse philosophies of education, the politics of alternative education, personal accounts of homeschooling experiences, Waldorf and Montessori schools, and alternative education for high school– and college-aged students.

The Art of Education

Linda Dobson; Holt Associates, 1997

This thought-provoking book is divided into two major parts. Part One, "Wisdom of the Art," covers the philosophies of home and public education; various chapters discuss the process of "natural learning," provide a checklist for developing a personal educational philosophy, and counter the top five (negative) myths about homeschooling. Part Two, "Benefits of the Art," describe the many advantages of family-centered education for the kids, their parents, and their communities and lists "A Dozen Simple Starting Points" for persons eager to give it a try.

The Dan Riley School for a Girl: An Adventure in Home Schooling

Dan Riley; Houghton Mifflin, 1994

A year in the life of a very California homeschooler. Dan Riley, English teacher, removed his 13-year-old daughter from school for a year because he felt her peer-group-centered social life was hindering her academic development. The book describes their innovative academic program and gives an account of the ups and downs of homeschooling daily life.

Deschooling Our Lives

Matt Hern, ed.; New Society Publishers, 1996

Twenty-six authors discuss creative alternatives to the present public school system. Chapter titles include "Instead of Education" by John Holt, "The Public School Nightmare: Why Fix a System Designed to Destroy Individual Thought?" by John Taylor Gatto, "Homeschooling as a Single Parent" by Heather Knox, and "Dinosaur Homeschool" by Donna Nichols-White.

Family Matters: Why Homeschooling Makes Sense

David Guterson; Harcourt Brace Jovanovich, 1992

An excellent presentation of the pros, cons, and practices of homeschooling by a high school English teacher whose own children are taught at home.

The Home School Source Book

Donn Reed; Brook Farm Books, 1991

A large and wonderful collection of essays, opinions, reviews, and resources for homeschoolers. One of my all-time favorites.

The Homeschool Reader

Mark and Helen Hegener, eds.; Home Education Press, 1995

A collection of articles that have appeared in past issues of *Home Education Magazine*, categorized by topic. Included are pieces on beginning homeschooling, general approaches to home education, home teaching of reading/writing, science/math, history/geography, and the arts, advanced learning, and networking.

Homeschooling for Excellence

David and Micki Colfax; Warner Books, 1988

The story of the Colfax family, whose four sons, homeschooled on an isolated mountaintop ranch in California, ended up at Harvard. The book describes the Colfax's educational philosophy, methods, and everyday experiences.

The Homeschooling Handbook: From Preschool to High School, a Parent's Guide

Mary Griffith; Prima Publishing, 1997

A comprehensive soup-to-nuts guide to the homeschooling process. Chapter titles include "Does Homeschooling Really Work, or What Do We Tell the Grandparents?"; "Legal Stuff, or Can We Really *Do* This?"; "Structure, or Can We Wear Our Pajamas to School?"; "Evaluation and Record-Keeping, or How Do We Know They're Learning?"; "Money and Other Practical Matters"; and "Finding Learning Resources."

Homeschooling: A Patchwork of Days

Nancy Lande; WindyCreek Press, 1996

Curious about what homeschoolers do all day? Lande's book is a collection of descriptions of a typical day's occupations by 30 homeschooling families.

The Parents' Guide to Alternatives in Education

Ronald E. Koetzsch; Shambhala, 1997

An overview of many different forms of alternative education, among them Montessori schools, Waldorf schools, Friends schools, multiple intelligences education, teenage liberation, and homeschooling. Included under each are lists of resource addresses and supplementary reading suggestions.

Raising Lifelong Learners: A Parent's Guide

Lucy Calkins with Lydia Bellino; Addison-Wesley, 1997

"Teaching is always a mystery," writes Calkins. Still, *Raising Lifelong Learners* attempts to clarify matters for parents, children's first, most important—and often most nervous—teachers. The book is filled with suggestions for encouraging those qualities that best make children independent learners: curiosity, imagination, perseverance, thoughtfulness. A series of appendices covers common educational decisions parents must make for their children, including how to select a preschool or kindergarten, how to evaluate a school curriculum, and how to approach classroom testing and assessment.

Schooling At Home: Parents, Kids, and Learning

Anne Pedersen and Peggy O'Mara, eds.; John Muir Publications, 1992

An excellent collection of 30 articles on homeschooling, compiled by the editors of *Mothering* magazine. Articles are grouped into four major categories: "Thoughts on Learning," "Legal Issues," "Ways of Learning in the Home," and "Home Schooling Stories."

Taking Charge Through Home Schooling: Personal and Political Empowerment

M. Larry Kaseman and Susan D. Kaseman; Koshkonong Press, 1991

The decision to homeschool can constitute much more than a homegrown educational program; it can also lead to a clarification of political and social values and beliefs. The Kasemans discuss the implications of the homeschooling movement for individuals and for American society at large.

Teach Your Own: A Hopeful Path for Education

John Holt; Delacorte Press, 1989

Teach Your Own describes how children—who, Holt points out, are natural learners—can be allowed to learn in their own way outside of schools. The book is filled with general information about homeschooling and anecdotes about families in the process of "teaching their own."

BOOKS: HOME EDUCATION FOR KIDS

The Day I Became an Autodidact

Kendall Hailey; Delacorte Press, 1989

An autodidact is a "self-taught person," which is what Kendall Hailey became when she left school at 16. The book is a delightful account of life, literature, and intellectual growth.

I Am a Home Schooler

Julie Voetberg; Albert Whitman & Co., 1995

A picture-book account of the daily life of a 9-year-old homeschooler, from morning prayers through daily lessons, field trips, serendipitous learning opportunities, and social activities. Illustrated with photographs. For 6–10-year-olds.

The Teenage Liberation Handbook: How to Quit School and Get a Real Life and Education

Grace Llewellyn; Element, 1997

This is a book for teenagers—particularly for teenagers who are unhappy in school—showing them how they can break free of the system and educate themselves. The book, chattily written and filled with questions, comments, and opinions from real-life teenagers, covers reasons for making the decision to leave school, how to go about it, how to acquire a first-rate education on your own, and how to experience the working world, through jobs, apprenticeships, internships, and volunteering. Lots of suggestions, anecdotes, and information.

BOOKS: PUBLIC SCHOOLING, PRO AND CON

Compelling Belief: The Culture of American Schooling

Stephen Arons; University of Massachusetts Press, 1986.

An account of the ongoing battle between parents and government over the control of children's education, both in the public schools and at home.

Deschooling Society

Ivan Illich; HarperCollins, 1983

When children are "schooled," Illich states, they begin to confuse teaching with learning, test scores and promotions with education, and graduation with competence. Furthermore, the authoritarian school culture predisposes students to accept the pronouncements of governmental bureaucracies rather than to think for themselves. "School is the advertising agency," writes Illich, "which makes you believe that you need the society as it is." His solution: to dismantle the current school system, replacing it with a network of "learning webs," freely accessible to self-motivated learners.

*Dumbing Us Down: The Hidden
Curriculum of Compulsory Schooling*

John Taylor Gatto; New Society Publishers, 1992

A passionate argument for the restructuring of the public schools by an experienced New York schoolteacher. At the heart of the public school system, warns Gatto, is a "hidden curriculum" inherent to the organization of the schools that teaches confusion, hierarchy, indifference, emotional and intellectual dependency, provisional self-esteem, and intimidation. "Mass-schooling," writes Gatto, "damages children."

*The End of Education: Redefining
the Value of School*

Neil Postman; Alfred A. Knopf, 1995

Postman's response to the current educational crisis is to restore substance to the curriculum. The schools, according to him, rather than giving children an education, teach them a series of mechanical tricks essential for getting a job, mastering modern technology, and functioning as consumers in the public marketplace. A good education, in contrast, necessarily provides children with critical-thinking capacities and a viable world view. Postman suggests several means by which this might be accomplished.

The Graves of Academe

Richard Mitchell; Fireside, 1987

A witty, learned, and thought-provoking attack on the educational establishment and teachers' colleges. Any proposal to improve the present system, Mitchell states caustically, is met by a predictable response from the educational authorities: "Whatever we do will require more money, more teachers, more administrators, and more mandated courses in education."

*Inside American Education: The Decline,
the Deception, the Dogmas*

Thomas Sowell; The Free Press, 1993

An extensively researched account of the political and social agendas that underlie many of the current problems of American education.

Insult to Intelligence

Frank Smith; Heinemann, 1991

The insult to intelligence is the "drill and kill" style of teaching—often with standardized tests in mind—that so sadly dominates the public-school curricula. Smith discusses how kids do (and don't) learn, the ideal uses of computers, and some solutions to the problems of classroom education.

CLASSES AND CORRESPONDENCE SCHOOLS

Calvert School

A complete education-in-a-package for kids in grades K–8, with step-by-step teachers' manuals, textbooks, workbooks, and supplementary materials. The program covers reading (including phonics and literature), spelling/vocabulary, writing/composition, grammar, math, science, poetry, history, geography, and art. Along with the basic program, Calvert also offers assorted extras, including "Video Lessons for the First Grade" (40 lessons on three videocassettes, in the fields of art appreciation, language arts, mathematics, music, physical education, and science), "Melody Lane," 32 music appreciation lessons on video for kids in grades K–3 (titles include "The String Family," "Introduction to Rhythm," "Songs From Other Countries," "Make Your Own Instruments," and "Mozart"), "Discovering Art," a 32-lesson video art series, and French and Spanish lessons on audiocassettes. These supplemental courses are available separately. Calvert courses in general, however, can be purchased only as a full-package deal. (You can't, for example, buy just the second-grade science course; you have to purchase the entire second-grade curriculum.) Along with Calvert enrollment, families have the option of signing up for Calvert's Advisory Teaching Service, in which a Calvert teacher corrects each child's tests and assignment papers, sends letters of evaluation and encouragement, awards grades, maintains records, and sends out a completion certificate when the child finishes the course.

Courses, $300 to $500

Calvert School

105 Tuscany Rd.

Baltimore, MD 21210

(410) 243-6030/fax (410) 366-0674

Web site: www.jhu.edu/~calvert

Clonlara School

The Clonlara School Home Based Education Program, for kids in grades K–12, includes—in a big green looseleaf notebook—instructions for complying with your state homeschooling regulations; a grade-appropriate curriculum, with instructions for using and personalizing it; information on keeping records, which can be kept on file at the school; mathematics and communications skills (reading, writing, speaking, listening) guidebooks; a catalog of texts and learning resources; and standardized testing information (tests and a scoring service are available through the school). Each enrolled family is also assigned a support teacher, who maintains the family's file and provides assistance and support as needed. "As needed" is a crucial phrase: Clonlara supplies just as much input as a family wants. The Clonlara program encourages children to pursue their own interests and exercise their own learning styles. "Real world" learning is emphasized: the Clonlara high school curriculum, for example, calls for 120 hours of community service.

For secondary students, Clonlara also offers "Compuhigh": assorted high school courses accessible on-line, among them algebra, American government, collaborative writing, and earth science.

> Annual enrollment, $475 per family (any number of kids), including a subscription to *The Learning Edge*, a bimonthly newsletter
> Clonlara School Home Based Education Program
> 1289 Jewett
> Ann Arbor, MI 48104
> (313) 769-4515
> Web site: www.grfn.org/education/clonlara

Curriculum Services

Complete educational programs for kids in grades K–12, covering all the subjects required by the public schools and using "materials published for public schools." The basic first-grade program, for example, includes a math worktext, science and social studies texts and workbooks, three phonics-based readers with accompanying workbooks, phonics, spelling, and grammar worktexts, and a handwriting workbook. For homeschoolers who favor "school at home."

> Programs, $285 to $329
> Curriculum Services
> 26801 Pine Ave.
> Bonita Springs, FL 34135
> (941) 992-6381/fax (941) 992-6473
> e-mail: hscurric@peganet.com

Keystone National High School

Keystone offers a complete high school curriculum by correspondence course. Students can enroll in the full diploma program, which requires the completion of 21 credits for graduation, or they may take individual courses. The school provides all necessary materials (textbooks, workbooks, and learning guides), evaluates tests, maintains records, and provides an Advisory Teaching Service to answer parental questions.

> Tuition, $150 per credit (plus shipping and handling)
> Keystone National High School
> School House Station
> 420 W. Fifth St.
> Bloomsburg, PA 17815
> (800) 255-4937/fax (717) 784-2129
> e-mail: info@keystonehighschool.com
> Web site: www.keystonehighschool.com

Oak Meadow School

Integrative learning programs for students of all ages, from kindergarten through grade 12. "Our curricula," explains the school catalog, "include assignments that not only require children to read, write, and think, but also to paint, draw, play music, write poetry, build things, and learn through experience." Curricula for kids in grades K–4 include weekly lessons in English, math, science, social studies, art, crafts, and music; for kids in grades 5–8, there's a comprehensive syllabus for each major subject. The high school program includes a long list of individual course offerings, from which students must complete 20 units to obtain a high school diploma. For each grade level or high school course, books, workbooks, and supplementary materials are included.

There are several Oak Meadow enrollment options, or without enrolling in the school, parents can simply order Oak Meadow materials to use in conjunction with home programs.

Curriculum packages, $150 to $300

Oak Meadow School

Box 740

Putney, VT 05346

(802) 387-2021/fax (802) 387-5108

Web site: www.oakmeadow.com

The Teaching Company

College and high school courses on video- or audiocassettes. High school classes, taught by "the best high school teachers in America," include world history, basic math, algebra, geometry, and chemistry.

Courses, $100 to $200

The Teaching Co.

7405 Alban Station Ct., Suite A107

Springfield, VA 22150-2318

(800) 832-2412

Upattinas School and Resource Center

Upattinas School, dedicated to "non-compulsory, non-coercive learning," offers an Independent Home Program for homeschooling families. The program includes curriculum advice and consultation, record evaluation, and required testing. The school does not offer correspondence courses or provide a standardized curriculum, but individual curriculum packets are available for each academic subject.

Curriculum packets, $35 each; fees per student for nonenrolled homeschoolers, $50 for evaluation and portfolio review, $35 for testing, $50 per hour for consultation

Upattinas School

429 Greenridge Rd.

Glenmore, PA 19343

(610) 458-5138

Web site: www.chesco.com/upattinas

CURRICULA, LESSON PLANS, AND HOW-TOS

Amanda Bennett's Unit Study Adventures

The Unit Study Adventures is a series of ready-to-use unit studies, each of which is designed to occupy children of all ages (pre-K through grade 12) for five to six weeks of creative learning activities. Titles in the series include "Baseball," "Computers," "Elections," "Gardens," "Oceans," "Electricity," and "Pioneers." Each includes background material, activity and project suggestions, reading lists, and Internet resources. The studies are written from a Christian perspective but can be adapted for secular homeschool programs.

Unit Study Adventures, $14 each

Holly Hall Publications

255 South Bridge St.

Box 254

Elkton, MD 21921

(888) 669-4693/fax (410) 392-0354

Web site: www.unitstudy.com.

A Bigger World

An interdisciplinary curriculum on CD-ROM for middle and high school students. Each year of the curriculum (still a work in progress) consists of eight unit studies in which central themes—for example, astronomy, geology, or ancient Rome—are approached from a range of different perspectives, variously incorporating math, history, science, art, music, and literature. The unit studies pair an informative illustrated text with a series of multimedia exercises, including animations, photographs, diagrams, demonstrations, interactive lessons, and student quizzes. The text—which is designed to be printed out and clipped in a notebook—contains clearly presented general information, excerpts from primary sources, discussion questions, instructions for student projects and experiments, reading lists, and lists of related Internet sites.

The first of the unit studies, *Stars and Stories* (see page 265), centers around astronomy. Students, for example, identify the constellations and track the movements of stars and planets, read Greek and Egyptian myths, study trigonometry and coordinate graphing and apply this knowledge to astronomical measurement and mapping, and investigate the physics of motion, the history of celestial navigation, and the archaeology of the Minoan civilization on Crete. Other first-year unit studies include *Architecture and Physics, Mathematics and Music,* and *Geology and Geography.*

A challenging and creatively integrated approach to learning.

Wildridge Software, Inc.
Wildridge Farm Rd.
Box 61
Newark, VT 05871
(888) 244-4379/fax (802) 467-3442
e-mail: ABIGGERWORLD@wildridge.com
Web site: www.wildridge.com

Birthday a Day

Stephen Currie; Good Year Books, 1996

A collection of very short, cartoon-illustrated biographies, one for each day of the year, with suggestions for accompanying simple projects. Among the persons featured (each with a birth—not death—date, and place of birth) are Louis Braille, Rosa Parks, Elizabeth Blackwell, Neil Armstrong, and Jackson Pollock. The book is recommended for kids in grade 3 and up. It's a good jumping-off point, but you'll need to supplement the abbreviated biographies with information from other sources.

Celebrations Around the World: A Multicultural Handbook

Carole S. Angeli; Fulcrum, 1996

A month-by-month listing of holidays, celebrations, and festivals from all over the world. Explanatory background information is included for each entry, and there are lists of related activities and projects for many. Appendices include related reading suggestions and international recipes.

A Charlotte Mason Education

Catherine Levison; Charlotte Mason Communiqué-tions, 1996

A 92-page how-to manual summarizing Charlotte Mason's educational philosophy and methods for those who don't want to plow through the 2,400-page *Original Homeschooling Series* (see below).

Charlotte Mason's Original Homeschooling Series

Charlotte Mason; Charlotte Mason Research and Supply Company, 1993

This six-volume series was originally written in the 19th century by British educator Charlotte Mason, and it remains popular among many homeschoolers today. The series describes, in 2,400 pages, Mason's educational philosophy and methods, which emphasize child-centered self-education and self-discipline. Some of Mason's methods can benefit any modern homeschool program. For example, she stresses the use of "living books"—that is, primary sources—rather than simplified interpretations. She encourages narration—that is, having children repeat back what they have just learned in their own words—as a means of solidifying knowledge and testing comprehension, and she urges the maintenance of a detailed nature diary and an annotated history timeline by each student. The series includes suggestions and instructions for teaching all academic subjects, from grades 1–12.

One caution: Mason's educational program is firmly rooted in the Christian religion, which will not appeal to all homeschoolers, and many of her instructional recommendations are out-of-date. Her science methods, in particular, are severely limited.

See *A Charlotte Mason Education* (left) and the **Charlotte Mason Education Home Page** (page 22).

The Compleat Teacher's Almanack: A Daily Guide to All 12 Months of the Year

Dana Newmann; Fine Communications, 1997

Happenings, holidays, birthdays, resources, and related projects and activities for every day of the year. For each month there's a day-by-day list of historical birthdays and anniversaries, a list of quotations related to the month's activities, descriptions of the month's interesting events, with detailed descriptions of suggested projects, and month-related language arts, science, math, and arts and crafts activities. In September, for example, Newmann presents information about and suggestions for celebrating Better Breakfast Month, the patenting of the first roll-film camera, California's entry into the Union, National Hispanic Week, and the start of Magellan's round-the-world voyage.

By the same author, also see *The Early Childhood Almanac* (Center for Applied Research in Education, 1998), which lists activities for every month of the year for kids aged 3–7, including recipes, songs, poems, arts and crafts, and field trip suggestions.

Comprehensive Curriculum of Basic Skills Series

American Education Publishing

This is a series of fat, color-illustrated workbooks, one for each grade from kindergarden through grade 6, each providing a full year's curriculum in the "basic skills": namely, reading, math, English, comprehension, study skills, spelling and writing, citizenship, and environmental science. Each book is consumable—that is, users write in it—and includes tests, and, in the back, an answer key. The lessons are mostly standard workbook fare: true/false, fill-in-the-blank, cross out the answer that does not belong, circle the correct answer, and the like.

The books do, however, give a good picture of what the public school expects at each elementary grade level, and the exercises are good practice for standardized tests.

Books, $10.95 to $19.95; also available at bookstores
American Education Publishing
150 E. Wilson Bridge Rd., Suite 145
Columbus, OH 43085
(614) 848-8866/fax (614) 848-8868

Core Knowledge Series

E. D. Hirsch Jr., ed.; Doubleday

The Core Knowledge Series comprises seven books outlining a core curriculum of essential knowledge that kids should assimilate from kindergarten through sixth grade. Each book lists the required fundamentals in math, science, history, geography, language arts, technology, and the arts for each grade level and includes many age-appropriate book excerpts and illustrations, among them photographs, maps, and prints. Books are variously titled *What Your Kindergartener (First-Grader, Second-Grader,* etc.) *Needs to Know: Preparing Your Child for a Lifetime of Learning.*

Also see *Cultural Literacy: What Every American Needs to Know* (right) and *A First Dictionary of Cultural Literacy: What Our Children Need to Know* (page 20).

Creative Projects for Independent Learners

Janet Caudill Banks; CATS Publications, 1995

A curriculum guide for grades 3–8, filled with creative projects for kids to tackle on their own or in small cooperative groups. Examples include literature-based activities, research challenges, and "writing across the curriculum."

Cultural Literacy: What Every American Needs to Know

E. D. Hirsch Jr.; Vintage, 1988

Hirsch argues that a cohesive society can exist only when its citizens share a common pool of background knowledge, which he refers to as "cultural literacy." The book includes a 50-plus-page alphabetical list of the "core knowledge" that literate Americans should know. See *A First Dictionary of Cultural Literacy: What Our Children Need to Know* (page 20) and the **Core Knowledge Series** (left).

Doing the Days: A Year's Worth of Creative Journaling, Drawing, Listening, Reading, Thinking, Arts & Crafts for Children 8–12

Lorraine M. Dahlstrom; Free Spirit Publishing, 1994

Nearly 1,500 activities, projects, and journaling ideas for young writers based on the calendar year.

See, by the same author, *Writing Down the Days* (page 22) and **Journals and Diaries** (page 152).

Endangered Minds: Why Children Don't Think and What We Can Do About It

Jane M. Healy; Simon & Schuster, 1990

How children's brains develop, how kids acquire language, reasons for attention deficits and learning disabilities, the effects of television and video games on critical-thinking processes, and suggestions for parents and teachers on methods for enhancing creativity, literacy, and mental skills.

Family Learning: How to Help Your Children Succeed in School by Learning at Home

William F. Russell; First World, 1997

"There's a difference," writes Russell, "between *learning* and *schooling*." The book is a 350+-page treasury of information, creative activities, games, discussion questions, and project suggestions, all intended to maximize learning, stimulate curiosity, and promote understanding. The text is divided into seven major sections, variously covering language arts, math, science, geography and astronomy, history, daily living, and character development. Each chapter includes a list of "Useful Family Resources."

5 12 A First Dictionary of Cultural Literacy: What Our Children Need to Know

E. D. Hirsch Jr., ed.; Houghton Mifflin, 1996

A 350+-page alphabetical listing of necessary knowledge for kids, with explanations, definitions, and illustrations.

Also see the **Core Knowledge Series** (page 19) and *Cultural Literacy: What Every American Needs to Know* (page 19).

P/T Frames of Mind: The Theory of Multiple Intelligences

Howard Gardner; Basic Books, 1983

Cognitive scientist Howard Gardner argues that "intelligence" is not one single lumpish entity but an assemblage of separate components. Psychological and biological studies suggest that there are at least seven different kinds of intelligences—linguistic, musical, logical-mathematical, spatial, bodily-kinesthetic, and personal (which includes both self-knowledge and understanding of others)—which each individual possesses in different degrees. The predominance of different forms of intelligence has marked implications for each child's preferred learning styles and optimal educational approaches.

Also see *In Their Own Way* (right).

3 9 Happy Birthday, Grandma Moses: Activities for Special Days Throughout the Year

Clare Bonfanti Braham and Maria Bonfanti Esche; Chicago Review Press, 1995

A month-by-month listing of over 100 special days with accompanying creative hands-on activities, targeted at celebration-loving 3–9-year-olds. For each holiday, the authors include background information, complete instructions for associated projects, and related age-appropriate reading suggestions. Featured special days include both such popular celebrations as Chinese New Year, George Washington's Birthday, Cinco de Mayo, and Flag Day, and such lesser-known holidays as Babe Ruth's birthday, National Magic Day, Space Week, and the Japanese Tanabata Star Festival. Participating readers, for example, cook up a batch of green eggs on Dr. Seuss's birthday, play Ladybug Bingo

on Rachel's Carson's birthday, and make sunflower mosaics on Vincent van Gogh's birthday.

P/T How to Write a Low Cost/No Cost Curriculum for Your Home-School Child

Borg Hendrickson; Mountain Meadow Press, 1995

"If you follow all the steps included in this book," states the introduction, "you will write a well-structured curriculum for your child—complete with philosophies, lifelong aims, general learning goals, and learning objectives. It will look professional; it will be exceptionally usable; yet it will allow you all the teaching flexibility you want." The book includes useful worksheets for parents, a state-by-state list of academic requirements, and a list of "Typical Grade-Level Subjects" with descriptions, suggestions for translating your curriculum into daily lessons, and record-keeping ideas.

P/T In Their Own Way

Thomas Armstrong; J. P. Tarcher, 1988

The author links the theory of multiple intelligences (see *Frames of Mind,* left) to children's individual learning styles. The "in their own way" of the title indicates the unique way in which each child learns. Children with marked linguistic aptitudes, for example, are happiest learning from books, while kids with strong musical or bodily kinesthetic skills learn more effectively using audio resources or approaches that emphasize physical movement. Armstrong discusses how to identify a child's individual learning style and suggests appropriate techniques for maximizing learning.

4 6 Kindergarten at Home

Cheryl Gorder; Blue Bird Publishing, 1997

257 activities for preschool and kindergarten-aged kids, each with a stated educational goal or purpose, a materials list, simple teaching hints, and complete instructions. Kids, for example, make pudding paint, design a musical instruments poster, play charades, make a body drawing, set up a lemonade stand, and construct a 1–10 number line and a color wheel.

5 13 KONOS Curriculum

The KONOS Curriculum, published in three fat volumes, covers all school topics required for grades K–8 through a multifaceted series of unit studies, filled with hands-on projects, activities, and reading lists. The KONOS approach, explain the authors, emphasizes the "Five D's"—Do, Discover, Dramatize, Dialogue, and Drill—which add up to an active involvement in learning. Unit studies are designed so that several children of different ages can participate at the same time. Sample topics include the eye, birds, bees, kings and queens, and Daniel Boone.

The curriculum, targeted at Christian homeschool families, groups the unit studies around such "godly character traits" as attentiveness, obedience, honor, generosity, courage, and cooperation. History is taught from a "Christian World View" and science is evolution-free. Each unit study, however, includes a wealth of suggestions and activities; families who approach education from a secular perspective can adapt most to suit their own needs.

> Each volume, $85
> KONOS, Inc.
> Box 250
> Anna, TX 75409
> (972) 924-2712/fax (972) 924-2733
> Web site: www.konos.com

Playing Smart: A Parent's Guide to Enriching, Offbeat Learning Activities for Ages 4–14

Susan K. Perry; Free Spirit Publishing, 1990

Detailed instructions for many creative projects and learning activities, with supplementary resource and reading lists. Chapter titles include "Journal Journeys," "Photography: More Than Meets the Eye," "Dirt, Worms, Bugs, and Mud: Kids in the Garden," "Mind Snacks: Recipes for Kitchen Learning," "Cultural Diversity: It's All Relative," and "The Junior Psychologist."

School's Out: Resources for Your Child's Time

Joan M. Bergstrom; Ten Speed Press, 1990

This book is targeted at conventionally schooled children who spend a substantial portion of each weekday in a public or private school. A child's out-of-school hours, however, Bergstrom states, may be more significant than those spent in school, providing time to read, pursue hobbies, learn new skills, volunteer, participate in household chores and projects, and share in family field trips. *School's Out* includes suggestions for organizing time, encouraging positive work habits, and dealing with television viewing and computer games. It also contains a wealth of ideas for mind-expanding activities (athletic, cultural, civic, and outdoor) and interesting places to visit. Useful for all.

TRISMS

TRISMS ("Time Related Integrated Studies for Middle School") is a history-centered curriculum for students in grade 6 through high school. Volume I, for kids in grades 6–8, takes a biographical approach to history, variously covering scientists, inventions, explorers, and language arts. As students proceed through the curriculum, moving from 3000 B.C. to the present day, they are expected to construct their own annotated timelines, to read—and write a weekly book report on—a work of historical fiction, and to maintain separate "coursebooks" for scientists, inventors, and explorers, each containing all daily assignments, including completed "questionnaires" and maps (reproducible copies are provided). For each scientist studied, for example, students fill out a standard questionnaire listing the scientist's name, nationality, year of birth and death, his/her noted achievements and their significance, and an "interesting bit of trivia."

The curriculum is organized into a block of 36 weeks, including detailed lesson plans. Supplementary reading lists, research projects, and essays are suggested for older students.

Volume II, for students in grades 9–12, is an in-depth multidisciplinary study of history from prehistory to the Middle Ages; Volume III (in preparation) will cover the Renaissance and Reformation to the present.

TRISMS is not a complete curriculum—it does not include math or laboratory science—but its history-based approach to learning is varied and appealing.

> Each volume, $100
> TRISMS
> 5710 E. 63rd Pl.
> Tulsa, OK 74136
> Linda Thornhill (918) 585-2778 or Sally Barnard (918) 491-6826
> Web site: www.trisms.com

Trust the Children: An Activity Guide for Homeschooling and Alternative Learning

Anna Kealoha; Celestial Arts, 1995

While *Trust Your Children* begins with a brief introduction to alternative learning philosophies and homeschooling, the bulk of the text covers creative games, projects, activities, and teaching techniques in the fields of art, music, math, language arts, history, physical education, the natural sciences, social relations, and spiritual development. The book also includes a section of assessments and evaluations, with a number of useful checklists.

World Book Educational Products

World Books publishes a small booklet titled "Typical Course of Study: Kindergarten Through Grade 12," which lists, year by year, the concepts that children are typically expected to master in the fields of social studies, science, language arts, health and safety, and mathematics.

Booklet, free
World Book Educational Products
Box 980
Orland Park, IL 60462
(708) 873-1533

Writing Down the Days: 365 Creative Journaling Ideas for Young People

Lorraine M. Dahlstrom; Free Spirit Publishing, 1990

Creative writing ideas for every day of the year, each based on an interesting historic event. Events include the invention of bingo, the return of the swallows to Capistrano, National Mustard Day, and the Battle of the Little Bighorn.

See, by the same author, *Doing the Days: A Year's Worth of Creative Journaling, Drawing, Listening, Reading, Thinking, and Arts & Crafts for Children Ages 8–12* (page 19), and **Writing: Journals and Diaries** (page 152).

ON-LINE RESOURCES FOR HOME EDUCATORS

American Montessori Consulting

An on-line newsletter for parents and educators interested in the teaching methods and materials of innovative educator Maria Montessori. The Montessori system, geared to the natural progression of early childhood development, allows children to learn at their own pace through a close interaction with their learning environment. The site also includes resource reviews; links to other sites of interest to kids, parents, or teachers; and an on-line book service.

members.aol.com/amonco/amonco.html

See **Montessori for Moms** (page 24) and **Michael Olaf's Essential Montessori** (page 26).

Charlotte Mason Home Education Page

Articles, resources, a discussion forum, and links to other Web pages related to the educational philosophy and methods of 19th-century educator Charlotte Mason.

members.aol.com/beeme1/index.html

See **A Charlotte Mason Education** (page 18) and **Charlotte Mason's Original Homeschooling Series** (page 18).

Eclectic Homeschool Online

Informational articles, resource reviews, legal information, lists of state organizations and support groups for homeschoolers, and links to other homeschool-related sites. This site also includes many useful educational materials that can be downloaded: weekly and daily lesson forms, calendar pages, graph paper, chore charts, and blank timelines.

www.eho.org

Education Home Page

Links to many general education sites, teaching publications and educational journals, and professional educational organizations. The site also includes a "Kids' Corner," with connections to many educational sites for children.

www.columbia.edu/~sss31@columbia.edu

Family.Com

Information on parenting and family issues, including health, food, travel, computing, and learning, as well as online activities for children, links to many good kids' web sites, and electronic greeting cards.

www.family.com

FLEx Online

An on-line journal of natural learning, family learning, and homeschooling, support group and conference news, "Questions and Answers About Homeschooling," an on-line book service, and links to other homeschool sites.

www.FLExOnline.org

See **Family Learning Exchange** (page 9).

France & Associates

An on-line education software supplier with a multitude of links to general homeschooling information, including lists of Web sites, interviews with educators and homeschoolers, and news updates, homeschooling book lists and reviews, and "WebTopics," lists of reviewed Web sites for kids that are centered, unit-study-style, around a single theme. Examples include "The Brain," "Aviation," "Tour the World," and "Egyptian Archaeology."

www.dimensional.com/~janf

Gill Family Homeschooling

Essays, resources, information, and articles about homeschooling.

pw2.netcom.com/~nemesise/hmschling.html

The High School Homeschool Page

Targeted at high school–aged homeschoolers. The site includes questions and answers about high school at home, lists of educational objectives for teens, information about colleges and universities that accept homeschoolers, articles and essays on homeschooling teenagers, and links to related Internet sites.

www.cis.upenn.edu/~brada/homeschooling.html

Home Education Mailing List

Includes answers to common questions about homeschooling, a homeschooling resource guide, and the "mailing list," which functions as a massive homeschool discussion group. Send a message to the list and it will be forwarded to all list subscribers for feedback, comment, and controversy.

home-ed-request@world.std.com

Home Educator's Resources Online (HERO)

An on-line "Home Schooler's Handbook," answers to "Frequently Asked Questions" about homeschooling, links to homeschooling family Web pages, lists of books, resource suppliers, national and regional homeschool organizations, and homeschool publications.

www.mscomm.com/~snowline/hero/hero.htm

Home's Cool

A creative collection of essays on homeschooling (for example, "Why homeschooling will save the world" and "Reinventing Western Civilization with a Swiss Army Knife and strands of parachute silk"), plus links to other homeschooling sites.

www.vvm.com/~birons/homecool.htm

Homeschool Cyber-News

An excellent on-line newsletter, which includes schedules for homeschool conferences, workshops, and on-line chat sessions, resource reviews, descriptions of educational Web sites, and letters from readers about their homeschool experiences.

www.home-school.com/CyberNews/HSCN.html

Homeschool World

This site, maintained by the publishers of *Practical Homeschooling,* includes homeschool news and legal updates, informational articles, book and resource reviews, lists of educational suppliers, "Daily Devotions," children's lesson plans and activities, and links to homeschool publications and homeschool-related Web sites.

www.home-school.com

See *Practical Homeschooling* (page 12).

The Homeschool Zone

An extensive collection of links to areas of interest to parents, teachers, and homeschoolers: support group listings, homeschool Web pages, newsletters, chat sessions, correspondence schools and distance learning organizations, college information, and interesting educational sites for kids.

www.homeschoolzone.com

Homeschooling at the Mining Company

 Articles, essays, and links to "up-to-date, reviewed" homeschool sites. Sample article titles include "Beginning to Homeschool," "And What About College?," "Common Objections to Homeschooling," and "What Is Unschooling?"

homeschooling.miningco.com

Jon's Homeschool Resource Page

Interesting and opinionated essays; helps for beginning homeschoolers; links to homeschool newsletters, magazines, resources, and other home-school-related Web sites; and much more. A great starting point for information seekers.

www.midnightbeach.com/hs

Montessori for Moms

And Dads. The site discusses ways of incorporating Montessori methods into homeschool programs for young children (ages 2–5). Included are descriptions of Montessori materials and sample lesson plans.

www.primenet.com/~gojess/mfm/mfmhome.htm

See **American Montessori Consulting** (page 22) and **Michael Olaf's Essential Montessori** (page 26).

The National Academy for Child Development

The NACD is an international organization devoted to helping kids (and adults) reach their full potential. The site includes research and news articles, information on learning disabilities and special needs, and many resources of interest to home educators.

www.nacd.org

ParentNews

Articles and advice on parenting, book and movie reviews, information on children's health issues, homework helps, and a large number of links to interesting Web sites ordered by academic subject, from "Art," "Biographies," and "Biology" to "World Governments" and "Writers."

parent.net

Web Resources for the Home-Based Educator

An innovative collection of resources for homeschoolers and others, including connections to "B.J. Pinchbeck's Homework Helper," "Kid's Web," and the "Index of Resources for Historians."

www.integralink.com/homeschool.html

Yahoo!—Home Schooling

A large and comprehensive list of homeschool-related Internet resources, including information on discussion forums, programs, and conferences, home-school supply companies, lesson plans and curricula, publications, organizations, and much more.

www.yahoo.com/Education/K_12/Alternative/Home_Schooling

EDUCATIONAL SUPPLIES AND LEARNING MATERIALS

Across the Curriculum

A creative catalog of fiction and nonfiction books related by theme. Among the subject headings are "The Solar System," "Prehistoric Life," "African-Americans," "Our Bodies," "Under the Water," "Where in the World," "Early Americans," "Transportation," "Weather," and "Ancient Civilizations."

World Almanac Education
Box 94556
Cleveland, OH 44101-4556
(800) 321-1147/fax (800) 321-1149

American Home School Publishing

A large list of educational products from more than 40 popular publishers, most at discount prices.

5310 Affinity Ct.
Centreville, VA 22020
(703) 266-0348 or (800) 684-2121/fax (703) 266-2921
e-mail: Web@ahsp.com
Web site: www.doubled.com/ahsp

Animal Town

An exceptional catalog of cooperative games, toys, books, and kits. Games include "Dam Builders," "Save the Whales," and "Nectar Collector" (see Science), some of our boys' all-time favorites.

Box 757
Greenland, NH 03840
(800) 445-8642/fax (603) 430-0334
Web site: www.animaltown.com

Aristoplay Ltd.

A catalog of terrific games, among them "Made for Trade" (see page 482), "True Math" (see page 193), and "The Play's the Thing" (see page 95).

450 S. Wagner Rd.
Ann Arbor, MI 48103

(800) 634-7738 or (888) GR8-GAME

fax (734) 995-4611

Web site: www.aristoplay.com

Childcraft
Toys, games, puzzles, and kits.

Box 1811

Peoria, IL 61656-1811

(800) 631-5657

Creative Home Teaching
A 100+-page newsprint catalog of learning resources in a range of academic disciplines. A large proportion of Christian-slanted materials; most are identified as such.

Box 152581

San Diego, CA 92105

(619) 263-8633

Dover Publications, Inc.
Ask for the complete Children's Book Catalog: over 1,300 books and activity books for kids, most under $5. Included are science and history coloring books; presidential family paper dolls; puzzle, stencil, sticker, and maze books; origami project books; and cut-and-assemble paper-building projects of all kinds.

31 E. Second Street

Mineola, NY 11501

EDC Publishing
The American publisher of the popular Usborne books, attractively illustrated and information-crammed paperbacks in a wide range of fields, among them early learning, arts and crafts, science, history, and foreign languages. Catalog, $2; customers receive a $2 rebate on first order.

Box 470663

Tulsa, OK 74147-0663

(800) 475-4522

Web site: www.edcpub.com

The Education Connection
A 45-page newsprint catalog of varied learning materials, including resources for art appreciation, a large assortment of kids' biographies, and math manipulatives. A source for the Core Knowledge Series (see page 19) and the Comprehensive Curriculum of Basic Skills workbooks (see page 19).

Box 1417

Tehachapi, CA 93581

(800) 863-3828/fax (805) 822-7984

Web site: www.educationconnection.com

Educational Insights
The catalog offers a variety of learning materials in all academic fields; the company is best known, however, for its line of electronic learning games, notably GeoSafari (see page 428), and MathSafari (see page 191).

16941 Keegan Ave.

Carson, CA 90746

(310) 884-2000 or (800) 933-3277

Web site: edin.com

F.U.N. Books
A catalog of books, activity books, kits, games, and other learning resources from the Family Unschoolers Network.

1688 Belhaven Woods Ct.

Pasadena, MD 21122-3727

fax/voice mail: (410) 360-7330

e-mail: FUNNews@MCImail.com

Web site: members.aol.com/FUNNews

See *F.U.N. News* (page 10) and **Family Unschoolers Network** (page 9).

Genius Tribe
Unusual and innovative resources for "unschoolers and other free people" from Grace Llewellyn, author of *The Teenage Liberation Handbook* (see page 14).

Box 1014

Eugene, OR 97440-1014

(541) 686-2315

Geode Educational Options
A highly creative collection of books and resources. The complete catalog can be accessed through the company's Web site. (A partial catalog is available through the mail.)

309 W. Union St.

West Chester, PA 19382

(610) 692-0413 or (800) 807-9051

Web site: www.geodeopt.com

Good Apple

Thematic study units and interactive student activity books in a variety of subjects, including language arts and literature, social studies, math, and creative thinking.

4350 Equity Dr.

Box 2649

Columbus, OH 43216

(800) 321-3106

Hewitt Homeschooling Resources

Learning resources recommended a Christian interdenominational organization. Many catalog materials are appropriate for persons of all philosophies; history and science books, however, have a strong religious bias.

Box 9

Washougal, WA 98671-0009

(360) 835-8708

The Home School Books and Supplies

A 50+-page newsprint catalog in small print (no illustrations, few descriptions, just titles) that offers a wide selection of workbooks, activity books, and books. There are pages, for example, packed with kids' biographies, Usborne books, and classic works of literature in inexpensive paperback editions. Christian-slanted materials are identified.

104 S. West Ave.

Arlington, WA 98223

(360) 435-0376 or (800) 788-1221/fax (360) 435-1028

Web site: www.TheHomeSchool.com

Home School Supply House

Books and resources for all academic disciplines.

Box 2000

Beaver, UT 84713

(801) 438-1254 or (800) 772-3129

John Holt's Bookstore

Books, activity books, games, toys, and videos for homeschooling parents and kids.

2269 Massachusetts Ave.

Cambridge, MA 02140-1226

(617) 864-3100/fax (617) 864-9235

e-mail: holtgws@aol.com

Web site: www.holtgws.com

See **Holt Associates** (page 9) and *Growing Without Schooling* (page 11).

Kids & Things

High-quality books, science kits, art and craft kits, and building sets.

Box 14607

Madison, WI 53714-0607

(800) 243-0464

Lakeshore Learning Materials (preschool and elementary resources)

Lakeshore 1-2-3

(elementary resources)

Lakeshore Basics & Beyond

(middle and high school resources)

Three fat, colorful catalogs of books, workbooks, games, toys, art and craft supplies, and manipulatives for kids of all ages.

2695 E. Dominguez St.

Carson, CA 90749

(310) 537-8600 or (800) 421-5354/fax (310) 537-5403

Web site: www.lakeshorelearning.com

The Learning Home

A small newsprint catalog of learning materials, including books, activity books, math manipulatives, geography puzzles, and science and social studies materials.

5573 Ashbourne Rd.

Baltimore, MD 21227-2813

(410) 536-5990/fax (410) 242-7826

e-mail: learninghome@aol.com

Web site: members.aol.com/learninghome/index.html

Michael Olaf's Essential Montessori

A superb catalog of creative and high-quality learning resources for infants to age 12.

Box 1162

Arcata, CA 95518

(707) 826-1557/fax (707) 826-2243

MindWare

An innovative assortment of brain-boosting games, puzzles, and books, all chosen for their ability to build problem-solving skills and enhance creative thinking.

2720 Patton Rd.
Roseville, MN 55113
(612) 639-1161 or (800) 999-0398/fax (888) 299-9273

The Sycamore Tree

A fat, tightly packed newsprint catalog of varied learning resources for students of all ages. Christian materials are marked with a little fish icon.

2179 Meyer Pl.
Costa Mesa, CA 92627
(714) 642-6750 or (800) 779-6750
e-mail: 75767.1417@compuserve.com
Web site: www.sycamoretree.com

Timberdoodle Company

Varied learning materials for kids of all ages; a particularly good source for the Fischertechnik "engineer-quality" building kits, which are terrific. Christian materials are generally identified; Timberdoodle's life science materials, for example, are suitable only for fundamentalists.

E. 1510 Spencer Lake Rd.
Shelton, WA 98584
(360) 426-0672 or (800) 478-0672
Web site: www.timberdoodle.com

Troll Learn & Play

Toys, puzzles, kits, books, art materials, and learning resources—among them a laminated write-on/wipe-off world map and a "Magnetic Story Tales Set," with which kids combine bright-colored magnetized words and pictures to make their own stories.

45 Curiosity Lane
Box 1822
Peoria, IL 61656-1822
(800) 247-6106

Turn Off the TV Family Game Catalog

An excellent selection of games and craft kits, all chosen with an eye toward promoting family togetherness.

Box 4162
Bellevue, WA 98009
(800) 949-8688/fax (425) 558-7564
Web site: www.turnoffthetv.com

Worldwide Games

Many games of all kinds for persons of all ages.

Box 517
Colchester, CT 06415-0517
(800) 888-0987/fax (800) 566-6678
Web site: www.worldwidegames.com

Young Explorers

Educational games, science kits, and many kinds of creative building sets with which kids can make anything from a stone pyramid to a working clock, a solar-powered helicopter, and a robotic power claw.

825 S.W. Frontage Rd.
Ft. Collins, CO 80522
(800) 239-7577 or (800) 777-8817/fax (970) 484-8067
Web site: www.youngexplorers.summitlearning.com

Zephyr Press

A catalog of creative books, interactive workbooks, games, puzzles, and kits, all centering around the theory of multiple intelligences and the concept of an integrated curriculum.

3316 N. Chapel Ave.
Box 66006
Tucson, AZ 85728-6006
(520) 322-5090 or (800) 232-2187/fax (520) 323-9402
e-mail: neways2learn@zephyrpress.com
Web site: www.zephyrpress.com

ELECTRONIC MEDIA

All technological change is a Faustian
bargain. For every advantage a new
technology offers, there is always a
corresponding disadvantage.

NEIL POSTMAN

One of the greatest changes in our homeschool program over the past decade has been brought about by the home computer. Within weeks of our acquisition of a computer, our kids went from computer-ignorant to computer-literate to computer-addicted—all in the time it took me to figure out the definition of "RAM" and the position of the Escape key. If there's anything that clearly demonstrates the phenomenal ability of the young to learn on their own, it's the computer. Kids are experts at self-directed learning. Match the relative electronic know-how of the average twelve-year-old and the average forty-year-old and you'll see what I mean.

As an educational tool, the computer has many and marvelous possibilities, from creative software programs to access to the information-laden Internet. Advocates claim that computer use boosts overall student achievement, promotes collaborative learning and teamwork, ensures the technological competence of the future workforce, and broadens students' worldviews through global interconnections. Positive though this all sounds, the computer and its culture also have their downsides. Opponents—or at least those who view this explosively expanding new technology with caution—point out that computers are far from being a universal panacea for educational problems; in fact these multifaceted machines may decrease reading skills, stifle creativity, limit imagination, and promote social isolation.

The truth probably lies somewhere in between. Computers, like any other technology, can be put to a range of uses, from excellent to lousy. (Think of television, the hot technology of the fifties and sixties, which can be made to deliver either soap operas and Saturday morning cartoons or historical documentaries, science programs, and National Geographic specials.) Most computer owners, in the relatively few years since the personal computer has become accessible to families, have discovered that an on-screen presentation of information does not necessarily mean educational worth or success.

That all said, our family has been generally delighted with the computer. Joshua, an enthusiastic writer whose handwriting is on the slovenly side, blossomed when he got his hands on a word processor. Ethan, hooked on science, has tracked down immense amounts of information on the Internet, connected to assorted physics and chemistry tutorials, and communicated with science professionals willing to answer questions, give advice, and help solve problems. Caleb, a fantasy book fan, has linked up to discussion groups filled with like-minded readers. This year Josh has started taking college classes on-line. Ethan, fascinated with the physical workings of computers, is teaching himself computer programming.

While the word processor and the Internet have been definite pluses, when it comes to educational software programs, we've had mixed experiences: some notable successes, some equally notably failures. A sample success story: our kids loved the Carmen Sandiego programs, among them *Where in the World is Carmen Sandiego?* (see page 435) and *Where in the U.S.A. is Carmen Sandiego?* (see page 435), clever and graphically attractive games in which players follow geographical clues to pursue a gang of zanily innovative crooks. The boys played these repeatedly, enjoyed them consistently, and learned a good deal of geography from them. A failure, or at best, partial success story: They also enjoyed *Oregon Trail* (see page 536), a creative historical simulation in which players, as members of a westward-rolling nineteenth-century wagon train, travel across the country to settle in the Oregon Territory. Unfortunately, in our hands, this game did not pack much of an educational punch. The boys adroitly tended to skip all the worthwhile information contained in the game in favor of on-screen hunting, which involved the arcade-style shooting of animals. Thus they all learned that wagon trains needed to be supplied with food and that no hunter can carry a whole buffalo home singlehanded, but that was about it. In other words, kids do not necessarily learn the lessons that we think they are—or ought to be—learning from educational software programs. Sometimes what looks like an exercise in American history turns out to be a chance to practice hand-eye coordination. *Caveat emptor.*

One great advantage of the family computer over the family television set is its ability to further interactive learning. Media specialists point out that kids in front of a TV screen are passive learners, able only to watch and absorb, while kids in front of a computer screen are undeniably part of the action. Though this is a potentially terrific benefit, again there are qualifiers: the educational worth of the interactive experience depends on what the computer user is interacting *with*, and how. One of our earlier software purchases was a popular reading readiness program called *Reader Rabbit* (see page 63), an assortment of attractively animated games in which, after a given number of correct phonetic responses, users were rewarded by watching a little bunny do a dance or a colorful train chug its way out of the station. The interaction, however, consisted primarily of fill-in-the-blank-style workbook exercises; our kids—who quickly lost interest in the bunny—never found these activities challenging or intellectually stimulating. *Rabbit,* in our house, was shelfware.

In contrast, a program called *The Even More Incredible Machine* (see page 401) was an interactive gold mine. In *Machine,* players, using an assortment of often positively peculiar components, attempt to assemble a machine that will solve a certain problem. By aligning an eclectic combination of falling bowling balls, exploding cannons, trampolines, and lighted candles, for example, they are challenged to turn on a light or drop a goldfish into a bowl of water. Users put all the pieces together; then click to watch their creation in operation. The puzzles become increasingly complex as players proceed in the game—and the level of required interactivity is clearly mind-broadening, thought provoking, and fascinating. Kids hone their problem-solving skills while learning a lot of basic physics.

The bottom line: using a computer in an educational program is not difficult; but using a computer *well* is less straightforward and takes some effort. Like books, games, and packaged study units, some computer software programs are inspirationally effective, and others are repetitive and dull. Unfortunately, telling the difference between the two from catalog descriptions or the blurb on the back of the box is often difficult to impossible. Most of us, in the first flush of computer ownership, have acquired examples of what one user calls "shelfware": stuff that looked good but ended up sitting, rejected and unused, on a bottom bookshelf. There is no totally foolproof solution to this problem; however, it can be at least reduced by reading software reviews (see page 32) or, where possible, viewing program demonstrations.

For homeschoolers—especially for those of us who live fifteen miles from the nearest library in a state given to snowstorms—the home computer is an invaluable resource, an indefatigable supplier of information, and a welcome link to the very wide outer world. In our homeschool program, it's the Mother of All Tools. Persons who lack a home computer, however—some sixty-two percent of families with children under eighteen, by one estimate—should remember that it's just a tool.

It's not a book or a symphony; it's not a cageful of crickets or an exciting conversation; it's not a walk in the woods or a carpentry project; and it's not a garden or a model rocket launch or a watercolor painting. And it's certainly not, in and of itself, an education.

COMPUTERS AND SOFTWARE

CATALOGS

Broderbund
ALL Software for kids, including the popular *Carmen Sandiego* titles and the *Living Books* series.
Broderbund
500 Redwood Blvd.
Novato, CA 94948
(800) 474-8840 or (415) 382-4684
Web site: www.broderbund.com

Computer Curriculum Corporation
5 18 An 18-page catalog of educational software titles for kids in grades K–12.
CCC
1287 Lawrence Station Rd.
Sunnyvale, CA 94089
(800) 455-7910 or (408) 745-6270
Web site: www.cccnet.com

Computer Learning Foundation
P/T A 24-page catalog of books and materials on using technology with children.
Computer Learning Foundation
Box 60007
Palo Alto, CA 94306-0007
(415) 327-3347
Web site: www.computerlearning.org

Davidson and Associates
ALL Educational software for kids in preschool through grade 12, including the *JumpStart* early learning series and *Math Blaster* series.
Davidson and Associates
Box 2961
Torrance, CA 90503
(800) 542-4240/fax (818) 246-8412
Web site: www.education.com

Edmark Corporation
3 12 A 16-page catalog of educational software for kids of preschool age through grade 8.

Edmark Corp.
Box 97021
Redmond, WA 98073
(800) 362-2890/fax (425) 556-8430
e-mail: edmarkteam@edmark.com
Web site: www.edmark.com

Educational Resources

A 250+-page catalog of educational software in all academic subjects for kids in grades K–12; also hardware and computer accessories.

Educational Resources
1550 Executive Dr.
Elgin, IL 60123-9330
(708) 888-8300 or (800) 624-2926/fax (708) 888-8499
Web site: www.edresources.com

Educational Software Institute
Master Resource Guide

A 700+-page catalog of books, software programs, CD-ROMs, laser discs, and videos. Free to educators.

Educational Software Institute
4213 S. 94th St.
Omaha, NE 68127
(800) 955-5570/fax (402) 592-2017
e-mail: order@edsoft.com
Web site: www.edsoft.com/esi

Educorp

A large collection of excellent CD-ROM programs for kids of all ages, including encyclopedias, atlases, foreign language programs, and many selections in the fields of literature, music, art, religion, history, geography, science, math, and early learning.

Educorp
12 B W. Main St.
Elmsford, NY 10523
(914) 347-2464 or (800) 843-9497/fax (914) 347-0217
e-mail: service@educorp.com
Web site: www.educorp.com

Edunetics Corporation

Educational software for kids in grades 3–12, including the *Rediscover Science* and *Rediscover Math* series.

Edunetics Corp.
1600 Wilson Blvd.
Arlington, VA 22209
(800) 290-3958
Web site: www.edunetics.com

The Edutainment Catalog

A wide variety of educational and entertaining software from the best publishers for kids of all ages. The catalog includes everything from preschool activities to physics.

The Edutainment Catalog
Box 21210
Boulder, CO 80308
(800) 338-3844/fax (800) 226-1942
e-mail: teccat@tecdirectinc.com
Web site: www.edutainco.com

Learn Technologies Interactive/
The Voyager Company

Very creative interactive CD-ROMs for persons of all ages, among them such children's art appreciation programs as *With Open Eyes* and *Fun With Architecture*.

Learn Technologies Interactive/The Voyager Co.
Box 2284
S. Burlington, VT 05417
(888) 292-5584
Web site: voyager.learntech.com/cdrom

The Learning Company

Educational software for kids of all ages in the fields of math, social studies, language arts, and science, including the *Reader Rabbit* reading titles and *Oregon Trail*.

The Learning Company
6760 Summit Dr. N
Minneapolis, MN 55430-4003
(800) 685-6322/fax (612) 569-1551
Web site: www.learningco.com

Microsoft

Educational software for kids in grades K–12 covering a wide range of academic subjects.

Microsoft
One Microsoft Way
Redmond, WA 98052-6399
(800) 426-9400 or (800) 555-4K12
Web site: www.microsoft.com/k-12

⬛5 18 Mindscape

Educational software, including *Mavis Beacon Teaches Typing* and the *Grolier Multimedia Encyclopedia*.

Mindscape
88 Rowland Way
Novato, CA 94945
(800) 231-3088 or (415) 397-9900
Web site: www.mindscape.com/education.html

⬛P/T Resources and Sevices for Technology-Using Educators

A free catalog from the International Society for Technology in Education (ISTE), published three times annually. Each issue lists over 200 books, journals, newsletters, and resource materials on technology in education.

ISTE
480 Charnelton St.
Eugene, OR 97401-2626
(800) 336-5191 or (341) 346-4414
Web site: isteonline.uoregon.edu

⬛ALL Scholastic New Media

A 68-page catalog of educational software covering a range of academic subjects for kids in preschool through grade 12.

Scholastic New Media
2931 E. McCarty St.
Jefferson City, MO 65101
(800) 724-6527
Web site: scholastic.com

⬛ALL Software Spectrum Catalog

A fat catalog listing hundreds of educational software titles for kids of all ages.

Software Spectrum
2140 Merritt Dr.
Garland, TX 75041
(800) 726-3446
Web site: www.swspectrum.com

⬛ALL Sunburst Communications

Education software for preschoolers to adults in such fields as early learning, math, science, and social studies.

Sunburst Communications
101 Castleton St.
Pleasantville, NY 10570
(800) 321-7511
Web site: www.nysunburst.com

⬛5 13 Thomson Learning Tools

Keyboarding and computer literacy software.

Thomson Learning Tools
5101 Madison Rd.
Cincinnati, OH 45227
(800) 824-5179
Web site: www.thomson.com/tltools

⬛5 18 Tom Snyder Productions

A 56-page catalog of educational software for kids in grades K–12.

Tom Snyder Productions
80 Coolidge Hill Rd.
Watertown, MA 02172-2817
(800) 342-0236/fax (617) 926-6222
Web site: www.teachtsp.com

⬛5 18 Zenger Media

A 250+-page catalog of educational CD-ROMs and videos in the fields of world and American history, government, literature, science, and the humanities. An excellent resource for parents and educators.

Zenger Media
10200 Jefferson Blvd.
Box 802
Culver City, CA 90232-0802
(310) 839-2436 or (800) 421-4246/fax (310) 839-2249
or (800) 944-5432
e-mail: access@ZengerMedia.com
Web site: ZengerMedia.com/Zenger

MAGAZINES

Children's Software

⬛P/T A quarterly newsletter of software reviews and associated hints on how to best use computers for education.

Annual subscription (4 issues), $20
Children's Software Press
720 Kuhlman

Houston, TX 77024

(713) 467-8686

Web site: www.ultra.net/jlengel/csp/

Children's Software Revue

Detailed reviews, ratings, and comparisons of software programs and Internet sites for kids aged 2–15.

Annual subscription (6 issues), $24

Children's Software Revue

44 Main St.

Flemington, NJ 08822

(800) 993-9499/fax (908) 284-0405

Web site: www.childrenssoftware.com

Electronic Learning

Articles on the role of technology in education, the use of computers in K–12 classrooms, software reviews, a computer product buyers' guide, and a list of student contests.

Annual subscription (6 issues), $23.95; free to educators

Scholastic Inc.

555 Broadway

New York, NY 10012

(212) 505-4900 or (800) 544-2917

Web site: www.scholastic.com/EL/

FamilyPC

The magazine centers around family use of computers; included are reviews of hardware and software, information about computers and accessories, hints for families on-line, and educational tips.

Annual subscription (12 issues), $14.95

FamilyPC

Box 55411

Boulder, CO 80323

(800) 825-6450

Home PC

Reviews of games and kids' software programs, a buyer's guide, technology news, and an "Ask Dr. P.C." problem-solving column.

Annual subscription (12 issues), $16

Home PC

Box 42021

Palm Coast, FL 32142-0211

(800) 829-0119

Macworld

Feature articles on the world of computing, many software and hardware reviews, technological news updates, and a shopping section, all targeted at a general audience.

Annual subscription (12 issues), $24

Macworld Subscription Services

Box 54529

Boulder, CO 80322

(303) 665-8930

Web site: macworld.com

Multimedia Schools

Feature articles and product reviews of on-line resources, CD-ROM technology, and computer hardware and software for K–12 classrooms.

Annual subscription (5 issues), $38

Information Today

143 Old Marlton Pike

Medford, NJ 08055

(800) 300-9868

Web site: www.onlineinc.com/mmschools

PC Magazine

Reviews, news, general information on computers and computing, and a shopping section, for a general audience.

Annual subscription (22 issues), $49.97

PC Magazine

Box 54093

Boulder, CO 80323-4093

(303) 665-8930

Web site: www.pcmag.com

PC World

Hardware and software reviews, new product reports, and general information on computers and computing, all aimed at the general public.

Annual subscription (12 issues), $21.97

PC World Subscriber Services

Box 55029

Boulder, CO 80322-5029

(800) 234-3498 or (303) 604-1465

Web site: www.pcworld.com

T.H.E. Journal

A magazine of "Technological Horizons in Education," including information on the use of technology in education, classroom collaborations, educational on-line resources, and software reviews.

Annual subscription (12 issues), $29

T.H.E. Journal Subscriptions

150 El Camino Real, Suite 112

Tustin, CA 92780-3670

(714) 730-4011

Web site: www.thejournal.com

Technology and Learning Magazine

Information on how technology helps kids in grades K–12 learn more effectively. The magazine includes articles on educational research, classroom success stories, and software reviews.

Annual subscription (10 issues), $24

Miller Freeman

600 Harrison St.

San Francisco, CA 94107

(800) 607-4410

Web site: techlearning.com

BOOKS FOR ADULTS

The Children's Machine: Rethinking School in the Age of the Computer

Seymour Papert; Basic Books, 1994

Papert, one of the foremost proponents of computers in early education, contends that the schools to date have used computer technology improperly and poorly. While conventional educational programs have long assumed that reading is a necessary prerequisite for acquiring knowledge, Papert argues that computers allow barely literate or preliterate students to explore and master complex concepts. Included are many stories about kids learning with computers in a variety of innovative ways. Papert also gives a pat to video games: these games, fast paced, appealing, and rewarding, are an excellent introduction to the rapid-fire world of computers.

The Complete Sourcebook on Children's Software

Children's Software Revue, 1998

Over 3,000 detailed reviews and ratings of software programs, categorized by topic, for kids aged 2–13, and a resource list of 700 children's software publishers. An excellent reference tool; recommend it to a local library.

$85

Children's Software Revue

44 Main St.

Flemington, NJ 08822

(800) 993-9499/fax (908) 284-0405

Computer Wimp No More: The Intelligent Beginner's Guide to Computers

John Bear and David Pozerycki; Ten Speed Press, 1991

A good starting point for first-time computer buyers, filled with basic information and clear explanations.

Consumer Reports Home Computer Buying Guide

Donna Heiderstadt and the editors of Consumer Reports; Consumer Reports, 1998

Detailed information on buying a computer, covering desktops, notebooks, printers, monitors, modems, scanners, and CD-ROM drives. Also included are a guide to computer brands, a chapter on "Cyberspace" with a section devoted to "Children on the Web," and a glossary of computer terms.

Does Jane Compute? Preserving Our Daughters' Place in the Cyber Revolution

Roberta Furger; Warner Books, 1998

Boys are immersed in computer games and out there surfing the Net—but what about girls? Furger warns of a gender gap in computer education and utilization—four times more boys go on-line than girls; computer software is predominately male-oriented—and suggests methods for ensuring that girls attain adequate computer literacy.

Family Computing from A to Z

Newsweek Interactive Staff; Simon & Schuster, 1997

Detailed reviews of hundreds of educational software titles and kids' web sites; a good resource for parents attempting to integrate the family computer into a home learning program. The book comes with a CD-ROM with samples from many of the reviewed programs.

Minutes of the Lead Pencil Club: Pulling the Plug on the Electronic Revolution

Bill Henderson, ed.; Pushcart Press, 1996

Short essays, poems, quotations, cartoons, and protests from the opposing side of the Computer Revolution. Sample selections include "Pencils" by Gail Lawrence, "Why I Am Not Going to Buy a Computer" by Wendell Berry, "Young Cyber Addicts" by Amy Wu, and "The Myth of Computers in the Classroom" by David Gelernter.

Sympathizers can join the Lead Pencil Club. Acceptance is automatic; simply write The Lead Pencil Club, Box 380, Wainscott, NY 11975.

There is no e-mail address.

School's Out

Lewis J. Perelman; Avon Books, 1992

The new computer and communications technologies have the potential to revolutionize education, says Perelman, who envisions a future in which schools are wholly replaced by "hyperlearning channels," shared by persons of all ages.

Young Kids and Computers: A Parent's Survival Guide

Children's Software Revue, 1998

A guide for getting started with computers, targeted at users aged 2–7. Chapters are organized by age group, from babies through toddlers, preschoolers, kindergartners, and first graders. Each includes teaching suggestions, a "what to expect" section, and an annotated list of software recommendations.

$9.99

Children's Software Revue
44 Main St.
Flemington, NJ 08822
(800) 993-9499/fax (908) 284-0405

BOOKS FOR KIDS

A Computer Dictionary for Kids and Their Parents

Jami Lynne Borman; Barron's Juveniles, 1995

An illustrated dictionary of hundreds of basic computer terms, among them *Internet, cyberspace, CD-ROM, format,* and *folder.* The book also includes a brief history of the computer, charts, diagrams, and cartoon-style drawings, and games and puzzles. Mac and IBM terms are differentiated by color: Mac in red; IBM, appropriately, in blue.

The Cartoon Guide to the Computer

Larry Gonick; HarperPerennial, 1991

A cleverly illustrated introduction to the basics of computers, in three parts: "The Ages of Information," which covers the history of computers; "Logical Spaghetti," which covers information processing, computer languages, and memory; and "Software," which covers Turing machines, algorithms, and the writing of computer programs. Substantive science with a sense of humor. For teenagers.

How Computers Work

Ron White; Ziff Davis Press, 1997

A marvelously illustrated 300+-page trip through the innards of the computer, clearly explaining such mysteries as "How RAM Works," "How a Hard Drive Works," and "How a Microprocessor Works." Readers will learn how a laser printer prints, how a scanner scans, how e-mail functions, and how joysticks, disk drives, and digital cameras function. The book is ostensibly for adults, but computer buffs aged 12 and up will be fascinated. Other titles from in the same format include *How Networks Work* (Frank J. Derfler, Jr. and Les Freed; 1996); *How Virtual Reality Works* (Joshua Eddings, 1994); and *How the World Wide Web Works* (Chris Shipley and Matt Fish, 1996).

Kids' Computer Creations

Carol Sabbeth; Williamson, 1995

Fifty arts and crafts activities for kids aged 4–10 to be done on, with, or for the computer. The book includes basic information about computers and their operation. A "Computer Q & A" section answers such questions as "How does RAM work?" "What's a PC?" and "What's virtual reality?" Kids also learn how to send e-mail and discover the identity of the world's oldest computer (Stonehenge). Projects include making jam jar labels and stationery, constructing a "Mouse House" for a computer mouse, and making a medieval dragon, Christmas ornaments, puzzles, and a pin-the-nose-on-the-clown game.

Kids and Computers Series

Charles A. Jortberg; Abdo & Daughters, 1997

A series of 48-page illustrated books about computers for kids aged 8–12. Titles include *The Big Machines, The Fast Computers, The Super Computers,* and *Virtual Reality and Beyond. The Big Machines,* for example, introduces readers to the computer revolution and describes the many uses of computers in the modern world. *The First Computers* describes the history of the computer, tracing computing machines from Stonehenge to the abacus to Univac. Subsequent volumes describe the history, workings, and uses of different kinds of computers, from the handy laptop to the massive "supercomputer."

Let's Discover Computers! Ready-to-Use Computer Discovery Lessons & Activities for Grades K–3

Barbara R. Hamm; Prentice-Hall, 1997

Lesson plans, with reproducible games, activities, and stories, intended to show young kids what a computer is, how it works, and what can be done with it.

Mousetracks: A Kid's Computer Idea Book

Peggy L. Steinhauser; Tricycle Press, 1997

A 100+-page illustrated collection of activities designed to teach young children how to use graphics and word processing programs. Activities are grouped under a number of kid-appealing topics, including dinosaurs, sports, tropical rain forests, and outer space. Each activity includes simple step-by-step instructions; some can be followed merely by looking at the pictures. For kids aged 4–9.

THE INTERNET

MAGAZINES

Classroom Connect

Books, manuals, videos, lesson plans, and CD-ROMs for kids, parents, and teachers on the Internet. Examples include *The Kid's WebKit,* with which kids aged 7 and up can create their own web sites; *The Space Science Internet CD,* which links kids to a wealth of spectacular on-line space sites; and *WebGuides* on all academic subjects for students in grades K–6 or 7–12. Each *WebGuide* includes reviews of subject-related Web sites and lesson plan suggestions.

Classroom Connect

431 Madrid Ave.

Torrance, CA 90501-1430

(800) 638-1639

Web site: www.classroom.com

Online Educator

The on-line version of the magazine includes an annotated list of "Super Sites" for students, a discussion forum for educators, and samples of "NetLessons" for on-line learners at the elementary, middle school, and high school level. Subscribers to the print or e-mail versions of the *Educator* receive detailed monthly lesson plans and Internet resource reviews.

Annual subscription (12 issues) print, $34.95; e-mail, $24.95

Online Education, Inc.

3131 Turtle Creek Blvd., Suite 1250

Dallas, TX 75219

(800) 672-6988

Web site: www.ole.net/ole

Web Feet

Internet research by subscription. Subscribers receive a three-ring binder with sectional dividers organized by academic subject: "Literature and Language Arts," "History, Archaeology, and Geography," "Psychology, Sociology, and Anthropology," "Arts and Culture," "Mass Communications," "Math and Computer Science," "Biology, Chemistry, and Physics," "Earth Sciences and the Environment," "Business and Economics," "Personal Interests," and "Calendar Connections." Each month they also receive a categorized packet of annotated Web site listings, each with a detailed description and snapshot of the home page. A terrific and time-saving resource for overworked parents, teachers, and librarians.

Annual subscription (notebook and 12 *Web Feet* packets), $66.50

Web Feet
Rock Hill Press
14 Rock Hill Rd.
Bala Cynwyd, PA 19004
(888) ROCKHILL/fax (610) 667-2291
e-mail: info@rockhillpress.com
Web site: www.rockhillpress.com

BOOKS FOR ADULTS

The Book Lover's Guide to the Internet
P/T Evan Morris; Fawcett Books, 1996

A very comfortable introduction to the Internet for beginners, followed by the accounts of the many resources available on-line for bookworms, including literary discussion groups, on-line publishing, and on-line books and bookstores.

Children and the Internet: A Zen Guide for Parents and Educators
Brendan P. Kehoe and Victoria Mixon; Prentice-Hall, 1997

Information on integrating the Internet into educational programs, listings of on-line educational resources, and classroom case studies.

Educator's Internet Yellow Pages
P/T Ron Place, Klaus Dimmler, and Thomas Powell; Prentice-Hall, 1996

A 386-page collection of Web sites for K–12 educators, including general education resources and sites categorized by academic subject, among them "Art," "Computer Science," "Foreign Languages," "Science," and "Social Studies." Lots of addresses; not much description.

Growing Up Digital: The Rise of the Net Generation
Don Tapscott; McGraw-Hill, 1997

"For the first time in history," writes Tapscott, "children are more comfortable, knowledgeable, and literate than their parents about an innovation central to society." The book details the rise of the "Net Generation" and the ways in which kids use computer technology, and discusses the effects of the Internet on kids and society. Included are many quotes and insights from computer-savvy kids. Tapscott thinks the Net Generation is doing just fine.

Internet Directory for Kids & Parents
P/T Barbara Moran; IDG Books Worldwide, 1997

A 384-page reader-friendly guide to the Internet in the Family Computing for Dummies series, which isn't as dumb as it sounds. The books includes the standard introduction to the Internet, information about Internet safety and software screening programs, and a lush collection of annotated site listings, categorized under such headings as sports, toys, student reference materials, family life, and science and nature. An accompanying CD-ROM includes an Internet service provider, a search engine, and links to all sites reviewed.

The Internet and Instruction
Ann E. Barron and Karen S. Ivers; Teacher Ideas Press, 1996

Cross-curricular Internet activities for kids in grades 4–12, arranged by academic subject area.
$26.50
Libraries Unlimited
Box 6633
Englewood, CO 80155-6633
(303) 770-1220 or (800) 237-6124/fax (303) 220-8843
e-mail: lu-books@lu.com
Web site: www.lu.com

The Internet for Teachers
P/T Bard Williams; IDG Books Worldwide, 1996

A volume in the popular For Dummies series, the book explains the how-tos of getting wired, describes many creative ways of using and navigating the Internet, and includes lists of good sites for teachers and students.

The Internet Resource Directory for K–12 Teachers and Librarians: 1996/1997 Edition
P/T Elizabeth B. Miller; Libraries Unlimited, 1997

A thorough annotated collection of Internet resources of educators and students, categorized by academic subject. Updated annually.

Kidnet: The Kid's Guide to Surfing through Cyberspace

Debra Schepp and Brad Schepp; HarperCollins, 1995

Information about computer shopping and on-line services, safety tips, and a large list of recommended sites for kids, categorized by topic. Sites inappropriate for younger browsers are tagged.

The On-line Classroom: Teaching With the Internet

Eileen Giuffre Cotton; ERIC/EDINFO, 1996

The book is divided into two major parts: the first, an introduction to the Internet and its use; the second, a collection of creative lesson plans and activities using the Internet for kids of all ages.

From bookstores or
$22.95
Zenger Media
10200 Jefferson Blvd.
Box 802
Culver City, CA 90232-0802
(310) 839-2436 or (800) 421-4246/fax (310) 839-2249
or (800) 944-5432
e-mail: access@ZengerMedia.com
Web site: ZengerMedia.com/Zenger/

Parenting Online: The Best of the Net for Moms and Dads

Melissa Wolf; Equinox Press, 1998

A large list of good Web sites for parents and kids, categorized by topic. Among these are Homeschooling, Health, Homework Helps, Education, Teens, Baby Stuff, and Travel and Vacations.

Virtual Field Trips

Gail Cooper and Garry Cooper; Teacher Ideas Press, 1997

Internet "field trips" for kids of all ages, from kindergarten through grade 12. The trips are grouped by academic subject. Chapters include "Historic Time Travel," "The Natural World," "Art Museums and Galleries," and "Meet Famous People." For example, young travelers visit Monticello, Fermilab, the bottom of the ocean, and the Seven Wonders of the Ancient World.

$24
Libraries Unlimited
Box 6633
Englewood, CO 80155-6633
(303) 770-1220 or (800) 237-6124/fax (303) 220-8843
e-mail: lu-books@lu.com
Web site: www.lu.com

WebPointers Internet Guide

catbird@webpointers.com; Hope Springs Press, 1997

A creative interactive guide to the Net, with which users of all ages can tour, explore, and experiment on their own. Each two-page chapter includes general information and suggestions—all in conversational compubabble-free style—plus descriptions and lists of particularly appealing Web sites. The book includes a wealth of interesting topics, among them "Do You Have a Web Scholar at Home?" "Great Art's Not to Be Missed," "Bookwire: A Gymnasium for the Mind," "National Geographic Explores the Web," and "Mr. Potato Head Meets Virtual Bubble Wrap."

The book is available as an Electronic Edition (with over 4,000 active hyperlinks), an Email Edition (delivering three new "narrative excursions" to your e-mail each week), or a comprehensive Interactive Edition, which includes both of the above.

278-page Interactive Edition, $29.95 (plus $3 shipping/handling)
Hope Springs Press
849 Hermitage Rd.
Manakin-Sabot, VA 23103
(800) 784-5025
Web site: www.webpointers.com

Wired for Learning

Jane Lasarenko; Que Education & Training, 1997

Internet learning strategies for kids in grades K–12, including instructions for collaborative projects, Internet-based research activities, and on-line publishing.

BOOKS FOR KIDS

Cybersurfer: The Owl Internet Guide for Kids

Nyla Ahmad; Owl Communications, 1996

A zippy illustrated guide to the Net for kids aged 8–13, with basic information, Internet vocabulary definitions, photographs and diagrams, and a large annotated list of appealing Web sites. The book comes with a "Cybersurfer Cyber Blastoff Disk" (Mac/Windows) with links to reviewed sites.

How the Internet Works
Preston Gralla; Ziff Davis Press, 1997

Impressive and colorful graphics and a beautifully clear text explain the inner workings of the Internet, the modem, Web TV, and such Internet tools as Gopher, Telnet, and FTP. The book is intended for an adult audience, but is an excellent resource for motivated computer buffs aged 12 and up.

The Internet for Kids
Dennis Brindell Fradin; Children's Press, 1997

A very simple introduction to the Internet and what it does for readers aged 5–9.

Internet for Kids! A Beginner's Guide to Surfing the Net
Ted Pedersen and Francis Moss; Price Stern Sloan, 1995

A general introduction to Net navigation and terminology for kids aged 9–15, all directed by the knowledgeable CyberSarge of Cyberspace Academy. The book includes step-by-step instructions, projects, safety cautions, and a list of particularly interesting sites.

The Internet for Your Kids
Deneen Frazier, Barbara Kurshan, and Sara Armstrong; Sybex, 1998

An Internet project book for kids aged 9 and up, showing how to conduct on-line research, track down fun game sites, communicate with famous people, enjoy virtual field trips, and construct Web pages.

Kids On-Line: 150 Ways for Kids to Surf the Net for Fun and Information
Marian Salzman and Robert Pondiscio; Camelot, 1995

General information about on-line providers, the rules of "netiquette," homework help-line lists, age-appropriate bulletin board listings and chat rooms, and cautions about the potential dangers of e-mail. By the same authors, see *The Ultimate On-Line Homework Helper* (Camelot, 1996).

Online Kids: A Young Surfer's Guide to Cyberspace
Preston Galla; John Wiley & Sons, 1996

The introduction—"Learning the Basics"—defines cyberspace, explains the ins and outs of navigating the Internet, and discusses the use of chat rooms and e-mail. The bulk of the book, however, is devoted to a descriptive list of "the best and coolest" web sites for kids. Sites are rated on a scale of 1 to 10 according to usefulness and coolness. Categories include homework help, astronomy, computers and software, writing and reading, hobbies, games, and creating your own home page.

Tech Girl's Internet Adventures
Girl Tech; IDG Books Worldwide, 1997

For those who worry that their daughters are being left behind in the increasingly connected world, *Tech Girl* is a girl-friendly introduction to the Internet, with listings of over 200 Web sites of particular appeal to girls aged 8 and up. The book comes with a CD-ROM with which girls can have a go at creating their own personal web pages.

COMPUTER EDUCATION ON-LINE

The Computer Museum Network
A comprehensive site on the history, operations, and uses of computers for kids of all ages from the Boston Computer Museum. Included are interactive exhibits, historical resources, and downloadable educational materials. For example, kids can design their own working robot, participate in an interactive "Networked Puzzle," view a timeline of computer research and development, and investigate such topics as "Robots and Artificial Intelligence," "Networks," and "Software." Educational materials include a series of five study units, each based on a museum exhibit. Among these are "How Does a Computer Work?," "Where Did Computers Come From?," and "Can Computers Think?"

www.net.org

Eclectic Homeschool Computer Department
General information on computers and their use, articles on using computers for homeschooling, and links to related Web sites.

www.eho.org/compdept.htm

Kid's Interactive Home Page Maker

5 9 A very simple "Home Page Maker" for beginners. Kids simply fill in the blanks, choose illustrations, and click to display their newly created page.

www.tiac.net/users/sturner/interact.html

Web Mastery

12 + Detailed information for more advanced computer users on Web style, Web design, and HTML language (and where to learn it). The site includes lists of resources and links for Web designers, including information on the World Wide Web, servers, browsers, and images.

hypernews.org/Hypernews/get/www/html/guides.html

SOFTWARE REVIEWS ON-LINE

CD-ROMs in Primary Education Home Page

P/T Reviews of children's CD-ROMs, including information on how each fulfills the requirements listed in the National Curriculum.

ourworld.compuserve.com/homepages/SE_Bailey

Children's Software Revue

P/T A searchable database of more than 3,000 reviews of children's software programs and 600 software publishers, plus feature articles, links to related software review sites, and a chance to write your own comments and reviews.

www.childrenssoftware.com

LearningWare Reviews

P/T A monthly on-line magazine of detailed educational software reviews, available to subscribers by e-mail. The site includes a sample of the magazine and contact information for a long list of software companies.

Annual subscription (12 issues), $5.95
LearningWare Reviews
1447 E. Country Lane
Tooele, UT 84074
(801) 269-0656
members.aol.com/juline

The PEPsite

P/T Detailed information about children's software programs and a large directory of software publishers. The "PEP" stands for Parents, Educators, and Publishers.

www.microweb.com/pepsite

School House World Village

ALL Educational sofware reviews, information on using and buying computers, games, downloads, a guide to the Web, a list of cool sites for kids, and a little yellow schoolbus that scoots back and forth across the top of the screen.

www.worldvillage.com/wv/school/html/school.htm

SuperKids Educational Software Review

P/T A searchable database of reviews of educational software, new product information, feature articles on technology and education, and an immense alphabetical list of on-line and mail-order educational software sources.

www.SuperKids.com

EDUCATIONAL RESOURCES ON-LINE

American Library Association

ALL The ALA has assembled annotated lists of excellent sites for "Parents and Caregivers," "Home Schooling Families," and "Educators and Librarians," as well as a collection of over 700 terrific educational sites for kids, categorized by subject. Categories include "Arts and Entertainment," "Literature and Language," "People, Past and Present," "Planet Earth and Beyond," and "Science and Technology."

www.ala.org

Armadillo's K–12 WWW Resources

ALL Many Web sites for kids, listed under such categories as "Gifted Education," "Special Education," "Libraries," "Field Trips," and "Internet Tutorials."

chico.rice.edu/armadillo/Rice/k12resources.html

Cyberhaunts for Kids

ALL Lists of good Web sites for kids of all ages, categorized by topic. Among these are "Animals," "Art," "Communications," "Computer Fun," "Literature," "Science," and "Sports."

www.freenet.hamilton.on.ca/~aa937/Profile.html

Educational Hotlists from the Franklin Institute

ALL A fascinating collection of links for curious kids, listed under many subject areas, among them "Africa," "Insects," "American History," "Space Science," and "Weather." The site also includes links to interactive activities, on-line exhibits, and museums.

sln.fi.edu/tfi/hotlists/hotlists.html

ERIC

P/T ERIC—the on-line Educational Resources Information Center—provides a wealth of information for parents and teachers, including a virtual library of lesson plans (listed by subject and age group), education-related "listservs," TV companion guides, and educational Web sites. Also included are a question-and-answer service and a versatile search feature.

ericir.sunsite.syr.edu or www.aspensys.com/eric

Especially for Teachers Learning Areas

P/T Resources on the Internet for teachers, information on the use of technology in the schools, CD-ROM reviews, and many links to student information sites and collaborative projects, categorized by academic subject.

www.eddept.wa.edu.au/centoff/cmis/tea16.htm

Interesting Places for Kids

ALL Includes an introduction to using the Internet and an immense assortment of good sites for children, variously listed under "Art and Literature," "Music," "Science and Math," "Museums," and "Arts and Crafts." Sites that might contain material inappropriate for the very young are tagged.

www.starport.com/places/forKids

Internet for Kids

ALL Helpful hints for kids navigating the Internet, games, a list of good Web sites for kids, and instructions for designing Web pages.

www.internet4kids.com

Internet Public Library

ALL A multifaceted site that includes a special section for kids of all ages (through high school) containing annotated book lists and Web sites grouped under such categories as "Science," "Math," "Art and Music," and "Sports and Recreation."

www.ipl.org

The Kids on the Web

ALL A large assortment of good sites for kids of all ages, along with a page on "Net Safety" and a "Homework Tools" feature, which links users to reference works, atlases, search engines, and question-and-answer forums.

www.zen.org/~brendan/kids.html

KidsConnect

ALL A question-and-answer service for kids in grades K–12 looking for resources on specific subjects or interests. Queries are answered by a library media specialist.

www.ala.org/ICONN/kidsconn.html

Monroe County Public Library

ALL Children's books and Web sites listed according to the Dewey Decimal System of classification. Kids click on "500: Science and Math," for example, and find a list of sample 500 books—all on science and math topics—and related Web sites.

www.monroe.lib.in.us

Telepath—Kids' Links

ALL Games, arts and crafts, homework help, a "Playground" for preschoolers, and a "People, Places, Things" category, which lists links to historical sites, maps, foreign languages, and much more.

www.telepath.com/telepath/kids

Yahooligans

ALL A "Web Guide for Kids" that allows kids to search the best children's sites in many different categories, among them "Around the World," "Computers and Games," "Art Soup," "Science and Oddities," and "The Scoop," which last links users to newspapers, comics, and current events.

www.yahooligans.com

TELEVISION AND VIDEO

When our sons were small, we had no access to television—no cable, no satellite dish, no reception. This meant no Saturday morning cartoons, no kid-targeted commercials, and no gratuitous sex, violence, and evil language; it also meant no *Sesame Street,* no *Reading Rainbow,* and no mind-expanding historical documentaries. Like any technology, television has distinct advantages and disadvantages. For the past two years, we've had it, via satellite dish clamped to the porch roof. So far, it's a plus: there seems to be a great deal of worthwhile programming available and the kids haven't turned into sluggish couch potatoes.

One advantage of our early lack of television, however, may be that none of our boys ever formed the *habit* of television-watching: that is, they don't use television as a time filler. They tend to watch purposefully selected programs; then they turn off the set and proceed to do something else. I wouldn't say that all their television choices are wholly uplifting and laudable, but clearly, in terms of viewing behavior, they're making reasoned decisions. They run the television; the television doesn't run them.

On the other hand, while the boys had relatively little early exposure to televison, they have almost always had access to videos, which have been a valuable supplement to our homeschool program. Many are enriching additions to specific study units—the movie version of *Johnny Tremain,* for example, paired to a study of the Revolutionary War; or *Apollo 13* linked to a study of the space program. Videos that particularly interested the boys were watched repeatedly and enthusiastically quoted; those that didn't appeal usually didn't hold them for more than ten or fifteen minutes, and so at least weren't time wasters. Video, however, is a kid-appealing medium; and our kids generally like movies. When the children were small, we usually screened

video selections beforehand; as the boys grew older, more responsible, and able to exercise critical judgment, their video-watching decisions became almost entirely their own. To tell the truth, however, we've never been particularly restrictive about what the boys watch and read. Our basic guidelines have been "If it scares you, turn it off (or close it)" and "If you don't understand something, ask," both of which worked reasonably well.

Early video favorites included such selections as *The Lion, the Witch, and the Wardrobe; The Phantom Tollbooth; Mrs. Frisby and the Rats of NIMH; The Adventures of Huckleberry Finn;* and *Tuck Everlasting.* Later choices included *The Vikings, The Ten Commandments, The Adventures of Sherlock Holmes,* and *Anne of Green Gables;* later still, *Moby Dick, Roots,* Ken Burns's *Civil War, The Life of Leonardo da Vinci,* and *The Diary of Anne Frank.*

In most cases, videos added to the boys' educational experience. As a rule, however, we tried to see that they read the books first.

CATALOGS

Direct Video
ALL Hundreds of titles, categorized by topic, among these Action/Adventure, Drama, Family/Children, Animation, Star Trek, Sports and Fitness, and Opera, Ballet, and Classical Music.
Direct Video
Box 6565
London, Ontario N5W 5S5, Canada
(800) 461-1651
Web site: www.directvideo.com

Discovery Channel Multimedia
ALL Video titles from programs and miniseries aired on the Discovery Channel.
Discovery Channel Multimedia
Box 1089
Florence, KY 41022
(800) 678-3343
Web site: www.discovery.com

Movies Unlimited
ALL A massive catalog containing over 40,000 reasonably priced videos of all kinds, from black-and-white

classics to National Geographic specials, miniseries, foreign films, exercise tapes, and the very latest films.

Basic catalog, $11.95; subsequent updates are free

Movies Unlimited

3015 Darnell Rd.

Philadelphia, PA 19154

(215) 637-4444 or (800) 4-MOVIES

e-mail: movies@moviesunlimited.com

Web site: www.moviesunlimited.com

PBS Home Video

Video titles from PBS, including both brand-new selections and enduring favorites, such as Ken Burns's *The Civil War,* Lord Kenneth Clark's *Civilisation,* and Carl Sagan's *Cosmos.*

PBS Home Video

1320 Braddock Pl.

Alexandria, VA 22314-1698

(800) 645-4PBS

Web site: www.pbs.org

Schoolmasters Video

Hundreds of inexpensive videos for kids in preschool through grade 9, including how-to videos, sing-alongs, classic folk and fairy tales, Bible stories, sports videos, and science videos.

Schoolmasters Video

745 State Circle

Box 1941

Ann Arbor, MI 48106

(800) 521-2832

Web site: www.school-tech.com

The Video Collection/Wellspring Media

A collection of quality educational videos and video series, many on history, literature, and the arts.

The Video Collection/Wellspring Media, Inc.

Box 2284

South Burlington, VT 05407-2284

(800) 538-5856

Web site: www.videocollection.com

Zenger Media

A 250+-page catalog of educational videos and CD-ROMs in the fields of world and American history, government, literature, science, and the humanities. An excellent resource for parents and educators.

Zenger Media

10200 Jefferson Blvd.

Box 802

Culver City, CA 90232-0802

(310) 839-2436 or (800) 421-4246/fax (310) 839-2249 or (800) 944-5432

e-mail: access@ZengerMedia.com

Web site: ZengerMedia.com/Zenger

Books

Adventures in Video: A Guide to the Best Instructional Videos

Patricia A. Wendling; Arden Press, 1995

An annotated guide to over 2,000 instructional and how-to videos for persons of all ages, classified by topic, with lists of sources and ordering information.

Inside Kidvid: The Essential Parents' Guide to Video

Loretta MacAlpine; Penguin, 1995

Descriptions of over 7,000 recommended children's videos, categorized under feature films, animated feature films, musicals, discovery and learning videos, sports and fitness videos, activity tapes, and storytelling and literature-based videos.

Kick the TV Habit! A Simple Program for Changing Your Family's Television Viewing and Video Game Habits

Steve and Ruth Bennett; Penguin, 1994

Kids watching too much television? The Bennetts summarize the negatives of television overindulgence, among them exposure to racial and sexual stereotypes, desensitization to violence, decreased physical fitness, and increased obesity. Kids who watch too much TV, warn the authors, also participate in less imaginative play and show diminished reading skills. The book suggests remedies for the TV habit, provides guidelines for establishing restricted "viewing goals," and lists a large number of inviting TV-free activities for families.

Kidvid: Fundamentals of Video Instruction

Kaye Black; Zephyr Press

Make your own video movies. The book is a comprehensive guide to video production techniques for

kids in grades 4–12, covering everything from prepro-
duction planning through staging, camera work, and
lighting, to postproduction evaluation.

$25

Zephyr Press

3316 N. Chapel Ave.

Box 66006

Tucson, AZ 85728-6006

(800) 232-2187/fax (520) 323-9402

e-mail: neways2learn@zephyrpress.com

Web site: www.zephyrpress.com

A Parent's Guide to the Best Children's Videos and Where to Find Them

Mary C. Turck; Houghton Mifflin, 1994

Detailed reviews of over 200 videos for kids aged
1–12, with ratings for violence, language, cultural
diversity, and gender sensitivity, plus a list of sources.

The Plug-In Drug: Television, Children, and the Family

Marie Winn; Viking, 1985

A classic on the damage television—the "plug-in
drug"—can inflict on children and families, affecting
learning behavior, personality development, and family interactions.

Remote Control: A Sensible Approach to Kids, TV, and the New Electronic Media

Leonard A. Jason and Libby Kennedy Hanaway; Professional Resource Exchange, 1997

"If the first thing any family member does when
entering the home is to turn on television, that is a problem," states psychologist Leonard Jason. A problem-
solving guide for those who feel their children's lives
have been overwhelmed by the television, the VCR,
video games, or the computer.

Richard Hack's Complete Home Video Companion for Parents: Over 300 Reviews of the Best Videos for Children

Richard Hack; Dove Books, 1995

Detailed reviews of over 300 videos by a professional film critic, with the help of a panel of kid advisors.

Screen Smarts: A Family Guide to Media Literacy

Gloria Degaetano and Kathleen Bander; Houghton
Mifflin, 1996

The authors urge families to develop "media literacy," a reasoned approach to media use based on an
understanding of television's impact on children's
emotional and intellectual development. The book
suggests ways of coping with television negatives—
various chapters, for example, cover on-screen violence, stereotypes, and deceptive advertising—and discusses alternative educational activities.

Stay Tuned! Raising Media-Savvy Kids in the Age of the Channel-Surfing Couch Potato

Jane Murphy and Karen Tucker; Doubleday, 1996

A discussion of responsible television and video
viewing; information on video, television, and learning; suggestions on what and how to watch; accounts of
using videos to trigger meaningful discussions; and
opinionated quotes from parents and kids on their
media experiences.

VIDEO REVIEWS ON-LINE

Cinema Sites

Reviews, previews, games and trivia related to the
movies, news on the film and television business,
information about studios and producers, and sources
for purchasing videos.

www.webcom/~davidaug/Movie_Sites.html

The Movie Mom's Guide to Family Movies and Videos

Many detailed reviews of current and old movies,
available on video and in theaters. Updated weekly.

pages.prodigy.com/moviemom/moviemom.html

The Movie Mom's List of the Best Movies for Families

A long annotated list of the best movies ever for kids,
with detailed descriptions and age recommendations.

pages.prodigy.com/moviemom/list.html

READING

My education was the liberty I had to read indiscriminately and all the time, with my eyes hanging out.

DYLAN THOMAS

I'm not sure how our kids learned to read. Perhaps it was simply a process of osmosis. After all, my husband, Randy, and I both read, continually and obsessively, and the house is overwhelmingly full of books. The boys were raised on stacks of daily picture books, chapter books, and bedtime stories. Each of us has three library cards, one for each of the libraries within reasonable reach. Birthdays bring bookstore coupons. Books are toted along on picnics, in the backpack; carried in the car, to be read aloud on trips; hauled to doctors' and dentists' offices, to be read while waiting in line. Given this literary immersion, Joshua and Caleb—our oldest and youngest—by the age of six or seven simply read, moving imperceptibly from letters to words to sentences to a gleeful grasp of whole books.

Ethan, our second son, however, didn't read. He loved being read *to,* but that was as far as things went. He didn't read at six, seven, or eight, and was just capable—not fluent—at nine and ten. I would like to think that I remained calm about this—a prime advantage of homeschooling, after all, is the freedom to allow children to progress at their own eccentric paces—but my homeschool journals, detailed and devastatingly truthful volumes, indicate otherwise. In private, on paper, I fretted and fussed. When Ethan was a nonreading eight, we acquired a formal reading program: *Teach Your Child to Read in 100 Easy Lessons* (see page 54). The 100 easy lessons are a carefully designed sequence of studies reportedly capable of taking a prereader from literary ground zero to a second-grade reading level in a mere 100 days. The program, said to be appropriate for bright three-and-a-half-year-olds to average five-year-olds, is almost humiliatingly precise: instructions for each lesson include a catechism-like dialogue between teacher/parent and pupil, with the adult's lines helpfully printed in red. Each lesson is intended to take about fifteen to twenty minutes per day. (Real hotshots can do two lessons a day, one in the morning and one in the afternoon, and thus learn to read in fifty days, but we decided not to push it.)

The program nudges beginners into reading in part through the use of a specially designed alphabet, altered such that each symbol has only a single sound and thus all words are spelled regularly. This sensible and simple technique—a pity it's not used in conventional English—helps new readers in the initial bumpy process of word decoding. It is gradually phased out in later lessons, as readers become more skillful and confident. This regular one sound/one symbol pairing clicked nicely with Ethan and he did, in the course of the 100 lessons, learn to read. The stories, to my mind, were no great shakes—"The Dog That Dug," "The Singing Bug," "The Fat Eagle"—but that didn't seem to bother Ethan, and they're certainly no worse that the stuff in the average basal reader.

I must admit—despite the apparent success of the *100 Easy Lessons*—that I've never been a fan of phonics. No child in its right mind, it seems to me, could possibly prefer those lackluster reading readiness workbooks and early readers to honest-to-goodness picture books. Josh, our oldest, was a case in point,

flatly rejecting a phonics-based reading program (starring Tat and Tam, the rams; we checked it out of the public library) in favor of genuine children's literature. While many "recommended readers" are truly vapid little volumes, not all beginner books, of course, are blah. Bobby Lynn Maslen's Bob Books (see page 59), for example, a collection of small bright-colored booklets for very new readers, manage to be funny with a minimal three-letter-word vocabulary. School Zone's Start to Read series (see page 59) includes a number of clever little books for just-beginners, each a mere handful of words in sixteen illustrated pages, among them *Jog, Frog, Jog,* in which an athletic amphibian jogger creatively outwits a pursuing dog, and *Beep, Beep!,* in which the harried driver of a truckload of mattresses contends with a vast herd of road-blocking sheep—and look what the incomparable Dr. Seuss managed to do with fifty-five words, among them "Cat" and "Hat."

From my homeschool journal:

◆ October 25, 1989. Josh is eight; Ethan, six; Caleb, five.

The Bob Books *(see page 59) arrived today—twelve tiny paperbacks packaged together in an envelope, just the sort of thing to appeal to Ethan. They're very simple (sample sentence: "Sam sat."), but the illustrations are funny, and—best of all—Ethan can (sort of) read them. He is very pleased with himself.*

Caleb promptly demanded a set of Bob Books *of his own, so we spent the morning writing and illustrating the* Bad Bob Books, *a series of little stapled pamphlets about a goggle-eyed sheep who eats everything in sight, including trees, bees, a house, a pirate ship, and the moon. (Sample sentence: "No, Bob, no!") Caleb is delighted with these: he colored all the pictures (Bob is pink); then curled up in a chair and read them all over and over again to himself, giggling.*

Josh, our oldest, a natural sight reader, never studied phonics, aside from a hasty day or so of explanation in third grade when—according to the school district in Colorado where we were living at the time—he was required to take a series of standardized (CAT) tests. Josh, for whom letter sounds were clearly something one leaped over as rapidly as possible en route to literature, was not taken with phonics. He managed, lickety-split, to acquire enough barebones information to perform dazzlingly on the verbal section of the CAT test—which, as I recall, spent some pages assessing kids' abilities to differentiate between long and short vowels—and that, he announced, slapping down his pencil, was enough. Clearly it was; and since, subsequently, it seemed foolish to haul Josh away from *The Hobbit, The Borrowers,* or *James and the Giant Peach* to teach him all about "sh" and "ch" sounds, that essentially ended his phonics education.

The phonics versus whole-language question continues to bedevil reading specialists. Phonics proponents favor a method of reading instruction in which kids are taught to decode the language, learning to "sound out" words, letter by letter (or letter group by letter group). Whole-language experts counter that reading fluency is best developed by an immersion in real written language, during which kids learn to decipher word meanings using a combination of best-guess logic and memory skills. (See Learning to Read, page 51.) The conclusion seems to be that most kids need both, in complementary combination: that is, instruction in the underpinnings of the English language—phonics—supplemented with exposure to real books and literary experiences.

Ethan and Caleb did use phonics programs. They began with the Sing, Spell, Read & Write (SSRW) program (see page 54), which teaches letters, sounds, and words through a battery of songs, cut-and-color projects, and games. When this paled, which it eventually did, we alternated or substituted a collection of homemade hands-on phonics workbooks.

From my homeschool journal:

◆ **June 2, 1990. Joshua is nine; Ethan, seven; and Caleb, five.**

I've just written a new set of phonics books for Ethan and Caleb, which are working beautifully on some level or another—that is, I'm not absolutely sure they're learning phonics, *but they're enthusiastically learning* something. *There's a separate booklet for each letter, full of letter-coordinated exercises and projects. In the* A *books, they studied* Ants *under a magnifying glass, fed ants cookie crumbs and watched to see what would happen, read a*

(very short) story about a boy named Al *who had a pet* Ant, *listened to a picture book about Johnny* Appleseed, *made* Apple *dolls,* Apple *monsters, and dried* Apple *rings, cut huge capital* A*'s out of gold paper, pretended to be* Acrobats, *folded paper* Airplanes, *and invented an* Acorn-*finding machine for a forgetful squirrel. The ant project was a spectacular success—they've all been talking about insects ever since. Ethan goes out daily to observe "his" ants and has assembled his own insect-studying kit, complete with magnifying glass, sketchbook, plastic specimen box, and bottle of tempting crumbs. He and Caleb went through the bookcase and picked out all the books on insects that they could find, spent ages looking at the pictures, and demanded that we start reading all of them aloud.*

They're about to move on to the B *booklet, which, I am pleased to say, features* Bees. *(Also making their* Beds, *reading* The Bed Book *by Sylvia Plath* [see page 149], *designing their own magical* Beds, *and making a* Boat *to take in the* Bathtub.*)*

Caleb, somewhere in the midst of all this, learned to read, a process that may or may not have been helped along by phonics. (He largely taught himself, apparently by reading *Calvin and Hobbes* books in bed.) Ethan enjoyed the phonics projects and had no difficulty learning letters and sounds but had a hard time integrating his phonics knowledge with the outrageous irregularities of English spelling. Phonics, he pointed out peevishly, never quite worked: *G* sometimes sounds like *J*, *C* sometimes sounds like *S*, and words like *through, done,* and *some* make no earthly sense whatsoever. A knowledge of phonics did, however, allow him to write, using invented (but logical) spelling. Armed with phonics, he kept journals, wrote letters to friends and relatives, and composed stories and poems, all well before he could read conventional English in anything but a very limited capacity. Without phonics, we would never have seen Ethan's tales of the rocket-building "Pngwin," the evil criminal "Sknk," or the enormous "Se Monstr," or known—by his bold notation on the refrigerator-posted Family Bird List—of his sighting of a "Chikade."

Ethan did not, however, at the completion of Easy Lesson 100, leap lightheartedly into higher literature. His reading skills developed slowly and painfully, and his spelling to this day still leans toward the nightmarishly imaginative. Even now, while his brothers read in bed, Ethan often prefers to listen to audiobooks. Looking back—a practice to which I am particularly prone in moments of doubt—I often wonder how we would handle Ethan's reading differences if we had to do it all over again. Would we do the same thing? Should we have started a formal reading program earlier? Waited longer? There are, of course, no answers: the reading lesson decision, like so many others, is now irrevocable. My guess is that if we had known then what we know now, we might have introduced Ethan early on to a more congenial battery of reading resources. Broderbund's selection of on-screen storybooks, the Living Books series (see page 62), for example, would have delighted Ethan, who is fascinated by computers—as would Renée Fuller's creative Ball-Stick-Bird reading program (see page 52), which is particularly appropriate for science-minded young readers.

Or perhaps—given our daily and nightly group reading sessions, our trips to the library, and constant positive exposure to books—Ethan, in his own good time, would have put written language together on his own in the same manner that he successfully and single-handedly worked out the techniques of arithmetic. Perhaps by eleven or twelve, he would have learned to read anyway, without strenuous parental intervention.

From my homeschool journal:

◆ **June 3, 1990. Joshua is nine;
Ethan, seven; Caleb, five.**

I worry that if Ethan gets more discouraged with the technicalities of reading, he's going to be put off books altogether. That's probably a foolish fear: he dearly loves being read to, and he'll sit for long periods poring over books on subjects that interest him. (Just now, insects, airplanes, and submarines.) Still, the process of deciphering words is clearly a struggle for him.

Caleb is reading simple books pretty well these days. He asks for words all the time—"What does this one say?"—and once he's told, he never seems to forget. Ethan is still doggedly halting along and will ask for the same word over and over without connecting. He doesn't seem bothered by Caleb's burgeoning expertise, however: he's got his own set of skills. Yesterday he completely dismantled Caleb's pedal tractor, repaired the chain and the

steering wheel, and put the whole thing back together again—it now works—and day before yesterday, he got out a collection of electrical odds and ends and figured out how to light three little lightbulbs at the same time, turning them on and off with a switch.

I guess learning styles and paces are just plain different, and that's life.

In the course of our many years of homeschooling, the hardest lesson I've had to learn is patience. Time and again, we've seen the kid who, it seemed, would never *never* master the multiplication tables, spelling, or geography, eventually manage all with insouciant ease. The rule of thumb seems to be that kids can and will learn all they need to know—but not necessarily just when you want them to. Our kids certainly have their own agendas. What was Ethan doing during all that time when I thought he should be learning to read? He built fleets of model airplanes, rockets, robots, and model boats. He took a pottery class; he raised fish; he learned to use the microscope. He collected and identified (pounds and pounds) of rocks; he disassembled, diagrammed, and reassembled an old bicycle. He built a bird feeder. He learned to swim, carve, and use a compass. He honed his chess skills. He planted a garden. He made paper. He built a (very small, but workable) telescope.

Just now, several years and many books later, he's upstairs in his bedroom, practicing his violin. Caleb, sprawled on his stomach in front of the woodstove, is reading "The Telltale Heart" by Edgar Allan Poe; Josh, draped across the neighboring armchair, is reading Shakespeare's *King Lear;* and I, watching and listening to them, can't believe I wasted so much time in groundless worry. Thinking back, I realize that Josh gave me the answer to Ethan's reading dilemma years ago.

"Don't worry about it, Mom," Josh—aged nine—said kindly, after a particularly frustrating afternoon. "He'll get it. Learning is what people are for."

ORGANIZATIONS

American Library Association

The American Library Association (ALA) is primarily for professional librarians, though personal memberships are available. Many ALA publications are available to non-members and are excellent sources of information about books for children. The association publishes a catalog and several periodicals, among them *Booklist,* a large and detailed list of book and electronic media reviews (see page 75), and *Book Links,* a magazine for "adults interested in connecting children with high-quality books" (see pages 69, 75).

The ALA Web site includes on-line versions of both *Booklist* and *Book Links,* as well as "The Librarian's Guide to Cyberspace," which includes links to over 700 good Web sites for kids "and the adults who care about them."

American Library Association
50 E. Huron St.
Chicago, IL 60611
(312) 944-6780 or (800) 545-2433/fax (312) 944-2641
Web site: www.ala.org

International Reading Association

The International Reading Association (IRA) was founded in 1956, just as American schoolchildren entered their 30th year of learning to read with Dick, Jane, Sally, and their perennially running dog, Spot. The association was then and is now devoted to promoting literacy by improving the quality of reading instruction. An annual membership ($30) includes a subscription to *Reading Today,* a bimonthly newspaper featuring news and views on the teaching of reading. Also available, for an additional fee, are four teacher-targeted journals, each containing articles on the practice and theory of teaching reading, literature reviews, and summaries of recent research results: *The Reading Teacher* (preschool and elementary teachers), *Journal of Adolescent and Adult Literacy, Reading Research Quarterly,* and—in Spanish—*Lectura y vida.* The IRA also publishes a catalog, available upon request, of reading-related books and pamphlets, among them overviews of teaching strategies and guides to books and magazines for young readers. The catalog also offers an assortment of inexpensive (and some free) booklets and brochures for parents, including "How Can I Prepare My Young Child for Reading?," "Beginning Literacy and Your Child," "Creating Readers and Writers," and "You Can Help Your Child Connect Reading to Writing."

International Reading Association
800 Barksdale Rd.
Box 8139
Newark, DE 19714-8139
(302) 731-1600, ext 293/fax (302) 731-1057
Web site: www.reading.org

National Council of Teachers of English

Membership in the NCTE—which is not, despite the formal title, restricted to accredited teachers of English—costs $25 a year and brings with it a subscription to *The Council Chronicle,* a newspaper published five times annually with news of the latest policies and practices in English education. For an additional fee, members can receive one of the council's three professional journals—*Language Arts,* for elementary school teachers, *English Journal,* for middle- and high-school teachers, or *College English*—or any of several additional NCTE periodicals, among them *Primary Voices K–6* and *Voices from the Middle,* in which teachers describe successful classroom approaches to various aspects of language arts.

The NCTE also publishes a catalog (available upon request) of books, pamphlets, booklists, audiocassettes, and literary maps. Among these are annotated booklists for kids of all ages, suggestions for teaching literature and language arts, creative writing texts, and authors' biographies.

National Council of Teachers of English
111 W. Kenyon Rd.
Urbana, IL 61801-1096
(217) 328-3870 or (800) 369-NCTE
fax (217) 328-0977
Web site: www.ncte.org

Reading Is Fundamental

RIF is a national nonprofit organization associated with the Smithsonian Institution, which aims to promote reading among American children. It does so through a network of community-based reading programs, operated by book-loving volunteers and funded through schools, parent-teacher associations, libraries, and local businesses. RIF also publishes a short list of books and brochures, prominent among them *The RIF Guide to Encouraging Young Readers* (see page 80).

Reading Is Fundamental, Inc.
600 Maryland Ave. SW, Suite 600
Washington, DC 20024-2569
(202) 287-3220/fax (202) 287-3196

LEARNING TO READ

CATALOGS

Constructive Playthings

An all-purpose catalog of toys, games, and educational materials, including—for pre- and beginning readers—alphabet puzzles, "Match 'n Spell" blocks, magnetic alphabet letters, and multicolored vinyl-coated letters, which can be stuck to tile walls or the sides of the bathtub for a language-enriching bath time.

Constructive Playthings
13201 Arrington Rd.
Grandview, MO 64030-2886
(816) 761-5900 or (800) 832-0572
Web site: www.ustoyco.com

Educational Record Center

The Educational Record Center catalog carries a large selection ("over 2,500 titles in stock") of cassettes, CDs, records, videos, and book-and-tape "read-along" sets on a wide range of subjects for kids of all ages. Included are video versions of many classic storybooks, plus—for very early learners—videos of *Dr. Seuss's ABC, Richard Scarry's Best ABC Video Ever,* and *The Animal Alphabet,* 30 minutes of *National Geographic* wild animal footage accompanied by 27 short alphabetical songs. Cassette tapes include recordings of many favorite picture books (available as book-and-tape sets), collections of phonics songs, and *The Alphabet Operetta,* which includes "an original song for every letter of the alphabet," each highlighting that letter's sound.

Educational Record Center, Inc.
3233 Burnt Mill Dr., Suite 100
Wilmington, NC 28403-2655
(800) 438-1637/fax (888) 438-1637
e-mail: erc-inc.@worldnet.att.net
Web site: www.erc-inc.com

Lakeshore Learning Materials

The catalog includes a wide range of teaching materials, toys, and games for early readers. Among these: sets of plastic, foam, or magnetic letters; alphabet puzzles; alphabet tracing templates; letter and sight-word rubber stamp kits; and lots of simple books for beginners. For hands-on learning, the "Letter of the Week Activities Box" contains five project cards for each letter of the alphabet, one each for art, math, science, language arts, and active play. Under *A,* for example, kids make an ant nest (science) and apple prints (art); under *B,* they build bird feeders; under *C,* they make crayon suncatchers. The even more active game "Alphabet Twist" comes with an enormous letter-patterned floor mat and has kids—at the whirl of a spinner—placing a right hand on a blue *S* and a left foot on a pink *K* while trying not to fall down. For one to six players, with suggestions for several kinds of games.

Lakeshore Learning Materials
2695 E. Dominguez St.
Carson, CA 90749
(310) 537-8600 or (800) 421-5354/fax (310) 537-5403
Web site: lakeshorelearning.com

United Art and Education Supply

A source of simple and inexpensive early-reading-related teaching aids and games for young readers. Among these: a magnetic 9 × 12-inch "Wonderboard" with accompanying set of 132 upper- and lower-case letters; a 24 × 36-inch alphabet floor puzzle (24 easy pieces); "Basic Picture Words" illustrated flash cards; and assorted bingo games for just-beginning book-worms, including "Initial Consonant Bingo," in which players match labeled pictures with consonants, *br* and *st* blends, or *ch, sh, th,* and *wh* digraphs; "Vowel Bingo"; "Rhyming Bingo" and "Basic Sight Words Bingo."

The catalog also carries "Bull's-Eye Activity Cards," available in three sets of 28 cards each, variously teaching the sounds of beginning consonants, long vowels, and short vowels. The Activity Cards are a new twist on old-fashioned flash cards: each has a single colored illustration, accompanied by three letter choices, each with a hole punched under it. Kids poke a finger through the hole under their letter choice—*b,* for

example, is for butterfly—and then flip the card over
to check their answer. The correct hole is circled on the
back of the card.

Catalog, $7.50 to individuals or free to schools

United Art and Education Supply Co., Inc.

Box 9219

Fort Wayne, IN 46899

(219) 478-1121 or (800) 322-3247/fax (219) 478-2249

BOOKS FOR ADULTS

99 Ways to Get Kids to Love Reading
Mary Leonhardt; Three Rivers Press, 1997

Ninety-nine short, sensible, and useful tips for
encouraging readers of all ages, from preschoolers on
up. Some hints for parents of beginners: take your children to libraries and bookstores often, make read-
aloud time fun, play beginning reading games, and
"don't get hung up on the whole-language-versus-
phonics debate."

Any Child Can Read Better: Developing Your
Child's Reading Skills Outside the Classroom
Harvey S. Wiener; Oxford University Press, 1996

Detailed suggestions for ways parents can support
and enhance their children's developing reading skills,
through activities, practice exercises, interactive conversations, and shared reading.
See *Any Child Can Write* (page 136).

Children Learning to Read:
A Guide for Parents and Teachers
Seymour W. Itzkoff; Praeger Publishing, 1996

A thorough explanation of the developmental
stages children pass through on the road to reading,
from the beginnings of baby talk through elementary
school. The author discusses how common educational
practices mesh with the natural stages of child development, reviews the pros and cons of phonics and whole-
language reading instruction, and describes the intimate
relationship between learning to read and learning to
write. Included are many helpful suggestions for parents
and teachers, and a sizable bibliography.

Learning to Read: The Great Debate
Jeanne S. Chall; Harcourt Brace Jovanovich, 1995

The "Great Debate" among reading specialists currently centers around the relative benefits of phonics
and whole-language methods in the teaching of reading. While both approaches have their pros and cons,
Chall stresses the importance of phonics: kids need
technical decoding skills in order to attain reading fluency.

What's Whole in Whole Language?

Kenneth Goodman; Heinemann, 1986

Information about whole-language teaching: what
it is and how it works.

Why Johnny Can't Read: And
What You Can Do About It
Rudolf Flesch; HarperCollins, 1986

First published in the fifties, this is a now classic
defense of phonics.

BOOKS FOR KIDS
ABOUT READING

Benjamin's Book
Alan Baker; Lothrop, Lee & Shepard, 1982

Benjamin, a hamster, struggles to remove his
grubby paw print from a clean book page. A nice way
to show kids how to handle books.

Grover Learns to Read
Dan Elliott; Random House, 1985

Grover doesn't want to learn to read, because he's
afraid that if he learns, his mother won't read to him
anymore. (He learns, and she still does.)

Hey, I'm Reading!: How to Read
for Kids Who Want to Read

Betty Miles; Alfred A. Knopf, 1995

A how-to book for just-beginning readers that
explains, through colorful illustrations and simple language, the process of learning to read.

I Can Read With My Eyes Shut

4/8 Dr. Seuss; Random House, 1978

Young Cat, a kitten-size version of the famous Cat in the Hat, insists that he can read with his eyes shut. The Cat in the Hat, in zany rhyme, shows him all the things he can learn by reading with his eyes open.

I Like Books

4/8 Anthony Browne; Random House, 1997

A book-loving chimp shows kids his many different kinds of favorite books.

Just Open a Book

4/8 P. K. Hallinan; Ideals Children's Books, 1995

A picture-book tour of all the people, places, and things that can be discovered in books.

The Wednesday Surprise

4/8 Eve Bunting; Clarion, 1989

Young Anna has a special surprise for her father's birthday: she has taught her grandmother how to read.

READING PROGRAMS

Alphabetika

3/7 The newly revised Alphabetika, by Nancy Cross Aldrich, is a collection of engaging and varied activities based on the letters of the alphabet. Subtitled "A Homeschool Curriculum for Pre-Primary Age Children," it comes in a floppy blue looseleaf notebook and includes a teaching manual, dictionary word tablet, and manuscript handwriting tablet. As the title implies, the teaching manual runs through the letters of the alphabet one by one, listing for each an assortment of letter-related field trips, picture books, hands-on art, math, and science projects, and snacks. Under *B*, for example, kids are urged to visit a bridge and balance on a teeter-totter at the playground, blow up a balloon (and draw a picture of the lungs), and start a bone collection, build a boat, make a book, and plant bulbs. One suggested snack is blueberry muffins, eaten while reading the classic *B* book *Blueberries for Sal*, by Robert McCloskey. Also included is a brief history of the letter *B* and a featured dictionary word—in this case, *buoyant*.

Users then flip to the *B* page in their Dictionary Word Tablet, which includes space to draw a pair of boats (one buoyant, the other sadly not buoyant), an explanation of the origin of the word *buoyant* (from the Spanish *boyar*, to float), and a short list of other *B* word facts and possible assignments. Examples: An early name for bicycle was *bone-shaker;* a group of bears is called a *sleuth* of bears; how is a flower bulb like a lightbulb?

The Manuscript Handwriting Tablet—one page per letter—is a conventional learn-to-print workbook with a slight twist: letters are based on an oval, which the author feels is a more natural and easily written shape than the familiar "ball and stick."

$35 (plus $5 shipping/handling)
Bookstuff
Box 13773
Portland, OR 97213
Web site: www.iscn.com/bookwork

Ball-Stick-Bird

3/+ A ball (a circle), a stick (a straight line), and a bird (two lines that meet at an angle, like a cartoon sketch of a distant seagull) are forms "so fundamental to the human brain," writes psychologist and child development specialist Renee Fuller, "that even newborns recognize them." Using combinations of these three basic shapes, Fuller explains, just-beginning readers quickly learn all the letters of the alphabet and embark on the road to reading. The multisensory B-S-B approach, with its emphasis on pattern recognition and practice, is also markedly effective for dyslexics, slow learners, and kids with various forms of what educational experts term "learning disabilities."

In the B-S-B system, letters are not, as in conventional alphabet workbooks, taught in strict alphabetical order but are presented in a sequence based on simplicity and frequency of use. Hence *I*—the "Big Stick"—is the first letter young prereaders encounter, followed by *T, O,* and *D*. The reading program itself is contained in ten vividly colorful $8\frac{1}{2} \times 11$-inch paperback books, each 100 to 150 pages long. (Books are sold in sets of five, with accompanying teachers' manuals.) The stories, which kick off as soon as users have mastered their first four letters, teach reading through a zany science fiction epic, starring Vad of Mars, our hero, who has rockets for feet, and his archenemies, the evil Vooroos of Venus, who look like ill-tempered little ghosts. The adventures of Vad, once he acquires a bit of supportive vocabulary, are interesting and thought provoking, dealing with such issues as authoritarianism, overpopulation, and the like. Each story is written as a cliff-hanger, which provides an extra jolt of motivation: young readers must learn the next letter or sound in line in order to find out what happens next.

Ball-Stick-Bird Publications, Inc.

Box 592

Stony Brook, NY 11790

(516) 331-9164

Challenger Phonics Fun

A series of three "Video and Reading" kits, variously narrated by Miss Becky, the quintessential preschool teacher, the Letter Lady, the Professor, and Cowgirl Cory, with backup support from a scattering of heavily rehearsed little kids. This is absolutely standard preschool fare; no amount of perky enthusiasm from the instructors can disguise the fact that this is heavy-handed drill. Volume I includes a 35-minute video; an audiocassette of phonetically worthwhile songs; *My Alphabet Book,* a spiral-bound collection of the lower-case letters of the alphabet on bright-colored pages; and a pair of black-and-white-illustrated workbooks in which users, for example, circle the objects that start with *H,* draw lines under things that start with *F,* find pictures that are alike or different, and learn to blend sounds, forming words like *Sam, ham,* and *jam.*

Volume II ("Vowels and Reading") includes a 45-minute video, an audiocassette, a workbook, and a reader. The reader includes lists of sight words; songs include such catchy numbers as "Ba-Be-Bi-Bo-Bu."

Volume III ("Irregular Vowel Families") has a 46-minute video, a musical audiocassette, a workbook, and a set of Irregular Vowel Families flash cards. Irregular vowel families include such combos as *ough* as in thought and *eigh* as in eight.

Volume I, $114.95; Volume II, $39.95; and Volume III, $49.95, each (plus shipping/handling)

Learning Crew

571 W. 9320 South

Sandy, UT 84070

(800) 477-5551

Hooked on Phonics

This program, tested on first- and second-graders in the California public schools, boosted students' performances a year or more above grade level on standardized tests assessing such language skills as letter and word recognition, word attack (the ability to decipher unfamiliar words), reading vocabulary, and passage comprehension. To accomplish this, participating kids spent a year mastering phonics, through lessons on nine audiocassette tapes, nine accompanying sets of color-coded flash cards, a series of six workbooks, and a "Reading Review Book," which includes short sentences and stories. Learning to read, through Hooked on Phonics, is a very earnest process: the lesson tapes consist of repetitive recitals of sounds, words, and rules, to a monotonous musical background; the workbooks, similarly, pair sounds to endless word lists. Students work their way through page after identical page, finding, for example, the *ur* sound in picture, fracture, fixture, feature, luxury, lecture, and so forth.

Hooked on Phonics Plus adds reading comprehension exercises to the basic phonics program: users move from the phonics tapes and workbooks to a series of "Reading Power" tapes and "Power Builder" stories. There are 100 short stories in the "Power Builder" books, arranged in order of increasing difficulty from the very short and simple through high school–level material. (The first 34, read aloud, are presented on the cassette tapes.) Each selection is followed by a series of reading comprehension questions; all the answers are listed in the accompanying key.

The program is attractively packaged and presented, but it offers a lot more mechanical drudgery than it does joy of reading.

$200

Gateway Educational Products

2900 S. Harbor Blvd.

Santa Ana, CA 92704-6429

(714) 429-2223 or (800) 616-4004

The Reading Lesson

"Dear parent," begins the accompanying Reading Lesson brochure, "Conventional wisdom says that if you teach children the alphabet, buy them picture books, and read to them every night, they will magically start to read. Conventional wisdom is wrong.

Children do not learn to read this way despite these and other well-meaning efforts." Then follow The Reading Lesson rules for teaching reading:

1. Teach lowercase letters first.
2. Teach sounds of the letters, not just the names.
3. Teach families of words.
4. Don't worry about rules of grammar.
5. Teach writing along with reading.
6. Limit the initial reading vocabulary.

The Reading Lesson approach combines both phonics and sight-reading. "Any reading program for young children based solely on phonics," state the authors, "is both boring and incomplete." While a grounding in phonics is useful in that it teaches children how words are made, they continue, reading competence depends on the ability to recognize whole words at a glance. To this end, the program avoids audiotapes (ineffective and distracting) and flash cards (ditto), using instead a collection of four attractive spiral-bound workbooks, each containing five 22-page lessons. Book 1 begins with common letters and sounds, then simple words, then (very) short stories; subsequent books build on the earlier lessons until, by the completion of Book 4, kids are reading (and writing) at a second-grade level. Accompanying computer software (Win/Mac disks or CD-ROMs) and videotapes are also available: both follow the lessons closely, with the added attraction of colorful animation. The Reading Lesson, which comes packaged in a natty purple plastic briefcase, is recommended for kids aged 4 to 7.

Complete program (books, progress chart, and
12 floppy disks), $150
Mountcastle Company
2 Annabel La., Suite 130
San Ramon, CA 94583
(510) 838-4441 or (800) 585-READ

Sing, Spell, Read & Write

Sing, Spell, Read & Write (SSRW) is a "multisensory" program designed to introduce kids to phonics and reading skills. The original SSRW kit (Level 1) is aimed at 5–8-year-olds. It includes—all neatly packaged in a plastic bin that converts into a child-size lap-top desk—17 phonetic readers, 6 audiocassettes, 5 games (phonetic versions of rummy, bingo, and "go fish"), 2 student workbooks ("Off We Go" and "Raceway"), a teacher's manual, and a "treasure chest" full of lots of rewarding little plastic prizes. Kids sing, color, cut, paste, and play their way through 36 lessons, charting their progress by moving a tiny car around the colorful spaces of the "raceway progress chart." (The car is magnetic; the chart posts nicely on the family refrigerator.) Users are allowed to choose a prize from the treasure chest after the successful completion of each lesson. For those teaching more than one child, extra workbooks can be ordered separately. Workbook and reader illustrations are homely, but this doesn't seem to bother most kids. SSRW in general is enjoyable: songs are catchy, activities are varied, and most users learn to read.

Also available: a preschool version of SSRW for 4–5-year-olds, and Level 2 and 3 kits for increasingly advanced students, which cover word meanings and classifications, grammar skills, parts of speech, and creative writing.

International Learning Systems, Inc.
1000 112th Circle N
St. Petersburg, FL 33716
(800) 321-8322/fax (813) 576-8832
Web site: www.singspell.com

Teach Your Child to Read in 100 Easy Lessons

Siegried Engelmann, Phyllis Haddox, and Elaine Bruner; Simon & Schuster, 1983

An entire reading program in one oversize 395-page book. Lesson one begins with simple phonics (*m* and *s* sounds); by lesson 100, kids are reading at a second-grade level. Instructions for parents/teachers are detailed, presented in catechism-like dialogue form with adult lines printed in red. Stories, to the critical adult eye, are unappealing and unimaginative—titles include "The Dog That Dug," "The Singing Bug," and "The Pig Who Liked to Hide"—but our kids liked them well enough to request them as read-alouds. All in all, a solid, sequential, phonics-based approach to reading. Available from bookstores or

Timberdoodle Company
E. 1510 Spencer Lake Rd.

Shelton, WA 98584

(360) 426-0672 or (800) 478-0672

Web site: www.timberdoodle.com

48 The Writing Road to Reading

The Writing Road to Reading program, devised by teacher Romalda Bishop Spalding, combines instruction in speech, spelling, writing, and reading. Many children have difficulty reading, Spalding adherents believe, because they are never taught how written language works. "The core of the method," writes Spalding, "is teaching the *saying* and the *writing* of the sounds used in spoken English. Soon the child learns to combine the sounds into words he knows."

The program is based on the teaching of 70 phonograms, a series of sound/letter units that includes all the letters of the alphabet, plus multiple-letter units such as *ea, ng,* and *ow.* Once the first 54 phonograms have been mastered, manuscript handwriting and spelling begin. ("The teaching of handwriting and written spelling," states Spalding, "should precede reading from books.") Spelling is taught using a list of 1,700 words, ordered by frequency of usage. Spelling lessons are precisely choreographed: the teacher says the word aloud, then has the children say the first syllable of the word (or the first sound of a one-syllable word). The children write this down; then the teacher writes it down for public view. Kids proceed systematically through each word, syllable by syllable and sound by sound. As they do so, they learn, through examples, Spalding's 29 basic rules of spelling. (Rule 2, for example, states: "When c by itself has a sound, it always says 's' if followed by e, i, or y (cent, city, cyclone); otherwise its sound is k (cat, cyclone, music).") Spelling words are recorded in individual spelling notebooks.

Once kids have accumulated a list of 150 spelling words, they begin to read. Reading is never taught, Spalding explains. After a requisite number of hours of phonogram learning and spelling by sequential word analysis, children "simply pick up a book and start reading." The program includes recommendations for reading materials. For kids at the 150-spelling-word mark, Spalding recommends, in order, five "Beginner Books" from Random House: *Ten Apples Up on Top; Green Eggs and Ham; Go, Dog, Go; Put Me in the Zoo;* and *Are You My Mother?*

The complete Spalding program is contained in *The Writing Road to Reading* by Romalda Bishop Spalding (William Morrow, 1990), which includes instructions, reproducible phonogram cards, the ordered 1,700-word spelling list, and a phonogram record. Other materials, available separately, include the phonogram sounds on audiocassette, spelling notebooks, and reading test booklets.

Spalding Education Foundation

15410 N. 67th Ave., Suite 8

Glendale, AZ 85306

(602) 486-5881

ALPHABET BOOKS

Kids love making their own alphabet books. We made many of ours—a letter per page—in spiral-bound or looseleaf notebooks or on sheets of construction paper stapled together. The results weren't precisely professional, but the thrill of reading a book of one's very own outweighs the aesthetic hurdles. Here are a few suggestions based on the projects we tried in our early-reading days:

1. Make a decorated alphabet in which the design of each letter represents the letter's sound. Try an apple-colored *A,* a *B* cut from a brown paper bag, an *F* made from scraps of fur or foil, an *N* from nails, a string *S,* a wooden (try Popsicle sticks) *W,* a black-and-white zebra-striped *Z.*

2. Make an alphabet collage book in which kids cut out or draw pictures of objects representing each letter of the alphabet. These are also terrific vocabulary builders: *A,* the boys explained to me, assembling ours, was not for Spider, as I had initially and nervously believed, but for Arachnid; and B—accompanied by a pop-eyed stick figure with a kite, was for Benjamin Franklin.

3. Photograph the alphabet. Our boys loved a chance to experiment with the camera. Take pictures of objects illustrating the letters from *A* to *Z.* This can be a challenging project; an inspirational trip to the zoo gave us—among others—Alligator, Bear, Camel, Ostrich, Snake, and Zebra.

4. Or photograph a family alphabet. Make a set of large-size letters—white letters on a colored

construction-paper background work well because they show up—and photograph friends and family members holding a letter apiece. We had thought it would be clever, at one point, to coordinate letters to people's names—which worked nicely for such letters as *C* (Caleb posed with his cat), *D* (Daddy), *G* (Grandma), and *M* (Mom)—but collapsed abruptly at *U, X, Y,* and *Z.* If you have a large circle of alphabetical acquaintances, it's something to think about.

5. Invent alphabet poems. Choose a topic—"Food," "Animals," "Vehicles," "Clothes"—and take turns picking one (or more) words that relate to it, in order, for each letter of the alphabet. Our (illustrated) masterpiece, titled "Alphabet Outer Space," begins "Astronauts, Black holes, Challenger, Deathstar, Eclipse . . ." The runner-up, "Camping," includes "Away from home, Backpack, Climbing hills, Deer tracks . . ."

Aardvarks, Disembark!

Ann Jonas; Greenwillow, 1990

The animals exit the ark in alphabetical order, with the double-*a* aardvarks in first place. By the end of the book, there's a line of 132 alphabetized species, including duikers, meerkats, numbats, wallabies, and zerens.

A B Cedar
George Ella Lyon; Orchard Press, 1989

A tree for each letter of the alphabet.

The ABCs of Origami: Paper Folding for Beginners
Claude Sarasas; Charles Tuttle, 1964

Step-by-step instructions for making 26 alphabetically ordered paper animals and objects, from albatross to zebra.

Abracadabra to Zigzag
Nancy Lecourt; Lothrop, Lee & Shepard, 1991

No apples or zebras: in this linguistically eccentric alphabet book, entries are unexpected. M, for example, is for mishmash and L is for lickety-split.

Albert's Alphabet
Leslie Tryon, Atheneum, 1991

Albert, a creative woodworking duck, builds all the letters of the alphabet.

Alison's Zinnia
Anita Lobel; Greenwillow, 1990

An exquisitely illustrated alphabet of little girls and flowers, beginning with Alison, who acquired an amaryllis for Beryl. Flowers are traded alphabetically from girl to girl, finally returning to the beginning, when Zoe gives a zinnia to Alison.

Alligators Always Dress for Dinner
Linda Donigan and Michael Horowitz; Images of the Past, Inc., 1997

The illustrations are eye-catching turn-of-the-century photographs: the elegant alligators on the *A* page come from a 1904 Florida postcard.

Alphabet City
Stephen Johnson; Viking/Penguin, 1996

A photographic tour of the city, with letters popping up everywhere: *A* in a construction worker's sawhorse; *G* in the neck of a lamppost; *P* in a subway railing.

The Alphabet From Z to A:
With Much Confusion on the Way
Judith Viorst; Atheneum, 1994

A backward look at letters for kids who have already learned the alphabet frontward.

Alphabet Soup

Scott Gustafson; Greenwich Workshop, Inc., 1990

Otter moves into a new house with nothing in it but a gigantic soup pot, and promptly sends out invitations to a housewarming party. All 26 alphabetically ordered guests show up with gifts of food, from the Armadillo (asparagus) and the Bear (bread) through the Yak (yams) and the Zebra (zucchini).

The Alphabet Symphony
Bruce McMillan; Greenwillow, 1977

Black-and-white photographs of musical instruments, each of which turns out to contain a letter of the alphabet.

Animalia

Graeme Base; Harry N. Abrams, 1987

A "visual feast" of spectacular alphabetical animal illustrations, from "An Armored Armadillo Avoiding An Angry Alligator" through "Eight Enormous Elephants Expertly Eating Easter Eggs," "Unruly Unicorns Upending Urns of Ultramarine Umbrellas," and "Zany Zebras Zigzagging in Zinc Zeppelins."

Anno's Alphabet: An Adventure in Imagination

Mitsumasa Anno; HarperCollins, 1974

Illustrations show a three-dimensional alphabet of beautifully crafted wooden letters.

Away from Home

Anita Lobel; Greenwillow, 1994

Twenty-six traveling boys tour the alphabet and the world, from Adam (arriving in Amsterdam) to Zachary (zigzagging through Zaandam).

Chicka Chicka Boom Boom

Bill Martin Jr. and John Archambault; Simon & Schuster, 1989

"A told B and B told C, 'I'll meet you at the top of the coconut tree'" begins a catchy rhyming tour of the alphabet, all to the rhythmic refrain of "chicka chicka boom boom."

See **Computer Software: Chicka Chicka Boom Boom** (page 62).

Curious George Learns the Alphabet

H. A. Rey; Houghton Mifflin, 1963

George, the curious little monkey, with the help of the "Man in the Yellow Hat," learns the letters of the alphabet, both upper- and lower-case. Each letter is pictured in the shape of a representative letter word: the *P*s, for example, are penguins; the *K*s, kangaroos.

See **The Curious George Forum** Web site at www.hminet .com/georg

Dr. Seuss's ABC

Dr. Seuss; Random House, 1963

A delightful rhyming romp through the alphabet, from Aunt Annie's alligator to the snoring Zizzer-Zazzer-Zuzz.

See, by the same author, *On Beyond Zebra,* a zany account of the imaginary letters that come after *Z* in the alphabet.

Dr. Seuss's ABC is also available on CD-ROM in the **Living Books** series from Broderbund (see page 62).

Also see the Dr. Seuss Web site, **Seussville,** at www.random house.com/seussville (page 64).

Eating the Alphabet: Fruits and Vegetables from A to Z

Lois Ehlert; Harcourt Brace Jovanovich, 1989

An alphabet based on bright-colored arrangements of fruits and vegetables, from Apple to Zucchini.

Eight Hands Round: A Patchwork Alphabet

Ann W. Paul; HarperCollins, 1991

Twenty-six alphabetically named quilt patterns, starting with Anvil, Buggy Wheel, and Churn.

The Handmade Alphabet

Laura Rankin; Dial, 1991

An American Sign Language alphabet with realistic pictures of sign-forming hands, plus visual cues for each letter. The *G* hand, for example, wears a glove; the *I* hand is touching an icicle; the *V* hand holds a paper valentine.

I Can Be the Alphabet

Marinella Bonini; Viking, 1986

Colorful illustrations of kids in leotards forming the letters of the alphabet with their bodies.

I Spy: An Alphabet in Art

Lucy Micklethwait; Greenwillow, 1992

Based on the old guessing game "I spy with my little eye something beginning with . . ."), the book challenges readers to find alphabetical objects in each of 26 famous paintings from museums around the world. *A* is for Apple, found in René Magritte's *Son of Man,* the wonderful painting of a bowler-hatted gentleman with an immense green apple obscuring his face.

See **I Spy Series** (page 721)

Pigs from A to Z

Arthur Geisert; Houghton Mifflin, 1986

Seven ambitious little pigs attempt to build a tree house. The pigs and seven letters hide on each page.

Q is for Duck

Mary Etling and Michael Folsom; Clarion, 1980

An alphabet guessing game that requires critical-thinking skills. (*Q* is for duck because ducks quack.)

Tomorrow's Alphabet

George Shannon; Greenwillow, 1996

Each letter of the alphabet demonstrates where something comes from: "*A* is for seed—tomorrow's Apple."

The War Between the Vowels and the Consonants

Priscilla Turner; Farrar, Straus & Giroux, 1996

"For as long as any letter could remember," begins this delightful picture book, "Vowels and Consonants had been enemies." However, the alphabetical war ends happily after both sides unite to defeat a common enemy—a chaotic-colored squiggle—and the reconciled letters set off happily to create poems, plays, and even, says the Supreme Commander of the Consonants, "Our memoirs!"

The Z Was Zapped

Chris Van Allsburg; Clarion, 1987

The letters of the alphabet are the stars of a disastrous play in 26 acts. *A* is caught in an avalanche; *B* is badly bitten (by a bear); and luckless *Z*, the grand finale, is zapped by lightning.

ALPHABET POEMS

Alpha Beta Chowder

Jeanne Steig; HarperCollins, 1992

Tongue-twisting and hilarious poems for all 26 letters of the alphabet, featuring, for example, Tactless Toby, who teases Tina with tadpoles in her tapioca, and Penelope, who plummets from her piano stool.

Animal Poems from A to Z

Meish Goldish; Scholastic, 1995

Animal poems for each letter of the alphabet, with related projects and activities.

April, Bubbles, Chocolate: An ABC of Poetry

Lee Bennett Hopkins; Simon & Schuster, 1994.

An alphabetical anthology of poems by such well-known poets as Carl Sandburg, Langston Hughes, Eve Merriam, and Myra Cohn Livingston. *M,* for example, is for Karla Kushkin's "Moon"; *O* is for Ogden Nash's "Octopus."

READERS AND BEGINNER BOOKS

Many children's publishers offer books specifically targeted toward kids just beginning to read on their own. Often these are kept in a special section at the public library; ask your local librarian. Frequently recommended titles include:

P. D. Eastman

Are You My Mother? (Random House, 1988)

Go, Dog, Go (Random House, 1987)

Sam and the Firefly (Random House, 1988)

Michael K. Firth

I'll Teach My Dog 100 Words (Random House, 1973)

Syd Hoff

Danny and the Dinosaur (HarperCollins, 1993)

Arnold Lobel

Days With Frog and Toad (HarperTrophy, 1984)

Frog and Toad All Year (HarperTrophy, 1984)

Frog and Toad Are Friends (HarperCollins, 1979)

Frog and Toad Together (HarperTrophy, 1979)

Grasshopper on the Road (HarperTrophy, 1986)

Mouse Soup (HarperCrest, 1987)

Mouse Tales (HarperTrophy, 1978)

Owl At Home (HarperTrophy, 1982)

Uncle Elephant (HarperTrophy, 1986)

Roy McKie

Snow (Random House, 1987)

Else Homelund Minarik

Father Bear Comes Home (HarperTrophy, 1978)

A Kiss for Little Bear (HarperTrophy, 1984)

Little Bear (HarperTrophy, 1978)

Little Bear's Friend (HarperTrophy, 1984)

Little Bear's Visit (HarperTrophy, 1979)

4/7 Dr. Seuss

The Cat in the Hat (Random House, 1957)

The Cat in the Hat Comes Back (Random House, 1958)

Fox in Socks (Random House, 1965)

Hop on Pop (Random House, 1963)

I Am Not Going to Get Up Today! (Random House, 1988)

Mr. Brown Can Moo! Can You? (Random House, 1970)

One Fish Two Fish Red Fish Blue Fish (Random House, 1981)

P/T *Best Books for Beginning Readers*

Thomas G. Gunning; Allyn & Bacon, 1998

A large annotated list of books for early readers, grouped by reading level from preschool through grade 2, along with information on how to evaluate books by difficulty level and an appendix of graduated word lists.

4/7 Bob Books

The Bob Books, written by primary school teacher Bobby Lynn Maslen, are bright-covered little paperback booklets for barely beginning readers. Each is illustrated with simple, but somehow hysterically funny, black-and-white line drawings. There are 28 Bob Books in all, divided into three sets of increasing (but never very great) difficulty. Set I (12 booklets) feature a pair of buddies named Sam and Mat: Sam has a triangular head; Mat looks somewhat like a doughboy in checkerboard-pattern pants. The activities of Sam and Mat, summed up in very few, very short words per page, aren't much from a adult point of view—"Sam sat. Mat sat on Sam"—but quickly provide new readers with the thrill of reading a whole book by themselves. Sets II and III (8 booklets each) have increasingly longer sentences that contain an occasional challenging nonphonetic word.

Bob Books Publications

Box 633

West Linn, OR 97068

or

Scholastic, Inc.

2931 E. McCarty St.

Jefferson City, MO 65101

(800) 724-6527/fax (573) 635-5881

Web site: www.scholastic.com

4/7 School Zone Start to Read Books

Better-than-average books for just-beginning readers, available at three levels of increasing difficulty. Level 1 titles, which include a mere handful of simple words, include *Up Went the Goat, I Want a Pet, The Gum on the Drum,* and *Jog, Frog, Jog.* Level 2 titles include *Say Good Night, Sue Likes Blue,* and *I Don't Like Peas;* Level 3 titles include *The Raccoon on the Moon, Mouse and Owl,* and *Big, Big Trucks.* There are 10 to 12 titles at each level, all available as illustrated paperbacks.

School Zone Publishing Company

Box 777

Grand Haven, MI 49417

(800) 253-0564/fax (616) 846-6181

Web site: www.schoolzone.com

ACTIVITY BOOKS

3/6 *30+ Games to Get Ready to Read: Teaching Kids At Home and in School*

Toni S. Gould; Walker & Company, 1994

Simple reading-readiness games for preschoolers based on such old favorites as "bingo," "go fish," and "concentration."

Alphabet Antics

ALL Ken Vinton; Free Spirit Publishing, 1996

A collection of creative alphabet activities for learners of all ages. This is not your average "A is for apple" book but a freewheeling tour of the alphabet, with ample opportunities for learning and invention. *Alphabet Antics* begins with a brief cartoon history of the alphabet; then each letter gets four pages all to itself. Under each, from *A* to *Z*, there are several categories of information and proposed activities. "Fun Facts" includes catchy letter-related information: the expression *A-OK*, readers learn, was invented by Project Mercury astronauts in 1961; the *E* in e-mail stands for electronic; *N* is the chemical symbol for nitrogen; and U-boat comes from *unterseeboot,* the

German word for *submarine.* Projects center around literature, art, and creative thinking. Under *F,* for example, the author proposes "*Fracture* a famous story. Rewrite it your way"; and under *I,* "*Illustrate* a famous quotation."

"Find Out About" includes three letter-related lists of people, places, and potpourri: *E* students, for example, are urged to check out, among others, Amelia Earhart, Leif Ericson, Egypt, Ellis Island, eclipses, entomology, and extraterrestrials. Lists of (simple) "Words" and (not-so-simple) "Challenge Words" enhance spelling skills and build vocabulary; "History" traces the origins of each letter (*C* began as the Phoenecian *gimel* which meant *camel*); and "In More Alphabets" pictures each letter in several alphabets, including hand-sign, Braille, Morse Code, semaphore, the International Flag Code, and the NATO code. There's also a picture puzzle for each letter in which kids are challenged to identify objects staring with the featured letter (*R* includes rhinoceros, rook, rain, rabbit, and ricochet) and a quotation by a famous letter-related person. *F,* for example, from Benjamin Franklin, is "Tell me and I forget, teach me and I remember, involve me and I learn."

$19.95 from bookstores or
Free Spirit Publishing, Inc.
400 First Ave. N, Suite 616
Minneapolis, MN 55401-1730
(612) 338-2068
e-mail: help4kids@freespirit.com

Alphabet Art
Judy Press; Williamson, 1998

Art activities for each letter of the alphabet. The book contains detailed instructions for making 26 alphabetical toys and puppets, among them Carlos, a paper-bag cat, Gertrude, a towel-tube giraffe, and Katherine, a paper-plate kangaroo. Also included are letter-related games, puzzles, fingerplays, and book lists.

Cuisenaire Alphabet Book
In this 64-page workbook, designed to be used with Cuisenaire rods (see page 168), each letter of the alphabet is represented by a two-page spread: on the left, a large-size letter, to be covered with rods in a number of different ways; on the right, pictures of familiar objects whose names start with the letter, each to be covered with rods in turn. (*A,* Cuisenaire-style, is for Airplane, Apple tree, and Alligator.) Such hands-on exercises not only teach the letters of the alphabet but also give small learners some useful practice in counting, spatial relationships, and problem-solving. Recommended for kids in kindergarten through grade 4.

Cuisenaire/Dale Seymour Publications
Box 5026
White Plains, NY 10602-5026
(800) 872-1100 or (800) 237-0338
fax (800) 551-RODS
Web site: www.cuisenaire.com or
www.awl.com/dsp

Games for Reading
Peggy Kaye; Pantheon Books, 1984

A collection of 76 games to inspire and assist young readers, designed and tested by an early childhood education specialist. The book is divided into three main parts: Part One describes games and hands-on projects aimed at improving sight vocabulary; Part Two lists games and activities that develop phonics and "sounding-out" skills; and Part Three concentrates on games for enhancing reading comprehension. Sample suggestions include making word posters in which a single featured word is decked out with paint, crayon, stickers, and glitter; making three-dimensional words out of Play-Doh; playing "Word Hunt" in the car or at the supermarket ("Find the word *orange*"); inventing alliterative sentences (as in "Purple penguins pick pineapples"); playing a homemade board game, "Chickens and Whales," to teach kids the sounds *ch, th, sh,* and *wh;* and making jointly written and illustrated family scrapbooks and calendars. Flip through the book, the author encourages, and experiment: choose the games that seem best for your particular child. The key to success, Kaye emphasizes, is fun. "If these games aren't fun, they aren't working."

Tangrams ABC Kit
A collection of 122 tangram puzzles based on the letters of the alphabet, starting with *A* is for acrobat. The 32-page book includes two sets of punch-out tangram pieces.

$3.50
Dover Publications, Inc.
31 E. Second St.
Mineola, NY 11501

GAMES

ABC Game

3 6 This British-made alphabet game is a beauty, based on colorful details from artworks in London's National Gallery. The game consists of 52 big square cards. Half of the cards have a reproduction of a feature from a famous work of art on one side, and the lower-case letter representing the pictured object on the other; the remaining 26 have a lower-case letter on one side, and the letter plus a relevant word on the other. (*P*, for example, is for parrot, from a painting by Joshua Reynolds.) Suggestions are included for using the cards for several different games. Also included is a page showing the complete pictures from which each card detail was taken, with listed titles and artists.

$20
Michael Olaf's Essential Montessori
Box 1162
Arcata, CA 95518
(707) 826-1557/fax (707) 826-2243

Alpha Animals

4 9 This is a board game for young creature lovers. The playing board is a spiral path of green and yellow squares, each labeled with a letter of the alphabet; playing pieces are small plastic animals (gorilla, alligator, elephant, and dolphin). Players hop their pieces through the alphabet letter by letter, naming at each turn an animal whose name begins with that particular letter: Anteater, Bear, Crocodile, Deer, and so on through *Z*. For older players, there's a more challenging twist: for each letter of the alphabet, they must name an animal of a specific class, determined by the role of a die. Roll a one, for example, and you have to come up with a mammal; roll a two, a fish; three, a bird.

Periodically, in their progress through the alphabet, players land on an "Alpha Card" space and must draw a card and answer an animal-related question.

There are two questions per card, one, for younger children, deemed easy; the other more difficult. Examples: "How many humps does a dromedary have?" "What does an icthyologist study?"

For those stumped for a reptile beginning with *J*, the playing instructions booklet contains a helpful alphabetical list of 700 animals.

$24
Aristoplay
450 S. Wagner Rd.
Ann Arbor, MI 48107
(800) 634-7738 or (888) GR8-GAME
fax (313) 995-4611
Web site: www.aristoplay.com

Alphabake

4 8 Debora Pearson; Dutton Children's Books, 1995

This clever kit is a scrumptiously edible alphabet experience. It includes 26 red, yellow, and blue plastic cookie cutters, one for each letter of the alphabet, an aluminum baking sheet, and a kid-friendly cookbook stuffed with cookie recipes.

$16.99 from bookstores or
Childcraft
Box 1811
Peoria, IL 61656-1811
(800) 631-5657/fax (309) 689-3858

Classroom Cooking From A to Z

4 8 This not-just-for-classroom cooking kit takes kids on a terrific food-oriented tour through the alphabet. The kit includes a copy of Lois Ehlert's *Eating the Alphabet* (see page 57), a recipe box crammed with simple, kid-friendly recipes based on the letters of the alphabet (*F* is for Frozen Fruit pops), a set of popsicle molds, 26 alphabet gelatin molds, measuring cups and funnels, a little plastic kitchen scale, and even packets of seeds for growing pizza herbs (*P* is for Planting a Pizza).

$49.95
Lakeshore Learning Materials
2695 E. Dominguez St.
Box 6261
Carson, CA 90749
(310) 537-8600 or (800) 421-5354/fax (310) 537-5403
Web site: www.lakeshorelearning.com

4
8 **Tongue Twisters**

Tongue Twisters is a delightful phonics lotto game. Young players listen to alliterative tongue twisters on audiocassette—for example, "Two tired tigers take a taxi to town"—and then identify the *T* on their lotto board, marking it with a colored plastic counter. The game can be played at two levels: the reversible boards are illustrated on one side (the *T* is accompanied by a pair of yawning tigers emerging from a pale green taxi) for those young enough to need pictorial hints; the opposite side carries only unadorned letters. *Tongue Twisters* is suitable for one to four players, aged 4–8.

From toy and game stores.

COMPUTER SOFTWARE

3
6 **A to Zap**

A screen stacked with colorful alphabet blocks is the gateway to 26 different interactive activities, one for each letter of the alphabet. If kids click on the letter *O*, for example, they hear the spelling of the word *over;* then they help a lop-eared pink bunny rabbit leap over a stack of teetering turtles, aided by a pogo stick, jet pack, or balloon. If they click on *X* they learn to spell *X-ray:* then they click and drag assorted objects to an X-ray screen, which obligingly reveals their insides. Recommended for kids aged 3–6. On CD-ROM for Mac or Windows.

$19.95

Sunburst Communications

101 Castleton St.

Pleasantville, NY 10570

(914) 747-3310 or (800) 786-3155

Web site: www.sunburst.com

3
6 **Chicka Chicka Boom Boom**

The popular alphabet book *Chicka Chicka Boom Boom,* spectacularly expanded into an electronic book on CD-ROM, is narrated by the incomparably rhythmic Ray Charles. As well as listening to the animated text, kids can tackle five different interactive activities or games: learning little songs, for example, for each letter of the alphabet, or designing inventive percussion instruments with which they can play along with the "Chicka Chicka Boom Boom" song. On CD-ROM for Windows.

$29.95

Davidson and Associates

19840 Pioneer Ave.

Torrance, CA 90503

(800) 545-7677/fax (310) 793-0601

Web site: www.davd.com

4
9 **Davidson's Kid Phonics 1 and 2**

Young users learn phonics and hone their reading skills through an animated series of songs, rhymes, and games. In *Kid Phonics 1,* for kids aged 4–7, players first listen to letter sounds and match them to little letter-toting creatures called "Sound Busters," then proceed to more challenging exercises, identifying sounds in words and songs, identifying rhyming words, and choosing the proper words to end nursery rhymes. Correct answers reveal, piece by piece, puzzle-style, a hidden picture from which kids can select individual illustrations and spell their names, again matching sounds to helpful Sound Busters. Similarly, using the Word Builder function, kids can choose from any of 200 colorful pictures and spell the matching word by selecting the proper sequence of letters/sounds. Anybody who gets really stuck can hit the "Show Me" button; an animated tutor appears with helpful hints.

Kid Phonics 2, for 6–9-year-olds, covers spelling, prefixes and suffixes, silent letters, homonyms, and reading comprehension, in a similar musically animated format. On CD-ROM for Mac or Windows.

$39.95

Davidson and Associates

19840 Pioneer Ave.

Torrance, CA 90503

(800) 545-7677/fax (310) 793-0601

Web site: www.davd.com

3
7 **Living Books**

A whole new take on books for kids in the computer age, "electronic books" are on-screen versions of children's storybook favorites, including the original artwork and the original text read aloud, plus any number of imaginative extras: animation, music, sound effects, distinctive voices for each character, games, and the opportunity to explore the book in depth on one's own. In some on-screen storybooks, a click on an illustration or a word in the text elicits new layers of activity or information; others operate more like video movies, with text and pictures coming smoothly to life before the viewer's eyes; and in others, younger observers can insert themselves into the action, characters, and plot lines.

Many publishing houses and software companies now offer interactive books; one excellent source is Broderbund's "Living Books" series. This ever-growing collection of titles, aimed at kids aged 3–7, includes *Dr. Seuss's ABC,* Janell Cannon's *Stellaluna,* Mercer Mayer's *Just Grandma and Me,* Aesop's *The Tortoise and the Hare,* and Marc Brown's *Arthur's Reading Race.* Many of the books can be read in either English or Spanish; readers of *Just Grandma and Me* have a choice of English, Spanish, or Japanese.

Each book, $19.95 to $29.95
Broderbund
Box 6125
Novato, CA 94948-6125
(800) 521-6263
Web site: www.broderbund.com

Reader Rabbit

Reader Rabbit, still a googly animated bunny, has been updated and improved since our early experience with the programs. There is now an entire grade-level-coordinated *Reader Rabbit* series for early learners, covering the basics of beginning reading, math, and thinking skills. *Reader Rabbit's Preschool,* for example, for kids aged 3–5, teaches letters, numbers, and pattern-solving through assorted games and activities involving Rabbit, his friend Mat the Mouse, and a magic carousel. *Reader Rabbit's Interactive Reading Journey Grades K–1* is a complete learn-to-read program for 4–7-year-olds starring Reader Rabbit and Sam the Lion; the program contains 100 interactive lessons teaching phonics and early word skills, 40 electronic storybooks, and a "Record & Playback" feature with which kids can record and then listen to the sounds of their own voices reading aloud. *Reader Rabbit's Interactive Reading Journey Grades 1–2,* for kids aged 5–8, contains 100 interactive reading lessons stressing vocabulary and reading comprehension, and 30 electronic books.

Reader Rabbit titles are available on CD-ROM for Mac or Windows.

$29.95 to $44.95
The Learning Company
6160 Summit Dr. N
Minneapolis, MN 55430-4003
(800) 622-3390/fax (612) 589-1151
Web site: www.learningco.com

ON-LINE RESOURCES

Children's Storybooks Online

Many attractive picture-book tales, including a brightly illustrated alphabet book.

www.magickeys.com/books

Chocolate Milk

A "literary adventure" on the Internet. Kids click on a color illustration to view and listen to a simple story.

www.chocolatemilk.com

The Froggy Page

A delightful Web site devoted to all things frog, including a section of "Froggy Tales," among them "The Frog Prince," Beatrix Potter's "The Tale of Jeremy Fisher," and the American Indian legend "Why Frogs Croak."

frog.simplenet.com/froggy

Grandad's Animal Alphabet Book

An interactive alphabet book with a poem and an animal picture for each letter of the alphabet, from antelope to zebra. There's also a multiple-choice quiz—"Find the Animal Whose Name Begins with D," for example—in which kids are asked to click on the correct animal picture.

www.mrtc.org/~twright/animals/grandad.htm

Literature and Language—Sites for Children

From the American Library Association, a list of recommended literature-related Web sites for kids of all ages. Sites for beginning readers are listed under the category "Favorite Children's Stories."

www.ala.org/parentspage/greatsites/lit.html

The Mother Goose Pages

2 7 An enormous master list of nursery rhymes, grouped both alphabetically and by theme, plus suggestions for fun ways to read the rhymes aloud with children of different ages.

pubweb.acns.nwu.edu/~pfa/dreamhouse/nursery/rhymes.html

Reading Rainbow

4 8 Descriptions of over 100 Reading Rainbow titles with suggestions for accompanying children's activities. The site also includes an annual broadcast schedule, an on-line store, and information about the annual Young Writers and Illustrators Contest.

www.pbs.org/readingrainbow

Seussville

3 8 Interactive games, contests, activities, and an opportunity to chat with the Cat in the Hat. The site is based on the popular Dr. Seuss books; games include "Green Eggs and Ham Picture Scramble," "The Cat's Concentration Game," and "The Lorax's Save the Trees Game."

www.randomhouse.com/seussville

thekids.com

3 11 Illustrated poems, fables, folktales, fairy tales, and adventure stories from all over the world. There's also a place to write your own story on-line.

www.thekids.com

STORYTELLING

"Once upon a time," begins Joshua's high, eager voice, "there was a wizard named Apollo. He was both good and bad. He could turn blood into roses and boulders into elephants. He could turn chickens into butterflies, toys into real things, and dogs into cats. He could turn pineapples into raspberries, pictures into monsters, candles into grizzly bears, glasses into owls, and mugs into soda pop. He could also turn men into werewolves, but he hardly ever did it. Then one day . . ." The story is a recording of a family storytelling session. Joshua was eight years old.

We told stories often when the boys were younger: the home-grown imaginary tales of the Three Green Bears, the Three Little Pigs and the Magic Mouse, or the house that sprouted wings—and the real-life stories of what happened on the day each child was born, of the upsetting night the bat got into the bedroom, of the winter there was a terrible blizzard and no one could leave the house for four days. Sometimes storytelling was a game. We kept a "Storytelling Envelope" in the living room, a fat manila envelope crammed with postcards, photographs, and pictures clipped from magazines: each person in turn drew a selection from the envelope and used it as a story starter. The envelope—we use it for writing project starters too—is still around. A sample handful of its contents turn up a picture clipped from a magazine advertisement of a space-suited astronaut floating two feet above a living-room sofa; a photograph of an immense snowman, complete with three stone eyes and a pair of stick antennae; a playing card illustrated with a photograph of the Hope Diamond; pictures of the Eiffel Tower, a herd of buffalo, and an erupting volcano; a snapshot of Caleb's cat; and a postcard from the Metropolitan Museum of Art illustrated with a geometric abstract by Mondrian.

We still tell stories these days, but most now tend to be reminiscences. This, too, can be a game: for nostalgic story starters, we've made a pack of index cards, each with a single printed word. Storytellers draw a card and "Tell a story about a . . . pet, neighbor, birthday, storm, vacation, accident, camping trip, pair of shoes, wild animal, bicycle, or Halloween costume"—and up pops Joshua's memory of his first hamster, Ethan's recollection of a trip to Disneyland, and Caleb's story of a birthday visit to the zoo.

ORGANIZATIONS

National Storytelling Association

"People are hungry for stories," writes author Studs Terkel. "It's part of our very being. Storytelling is a form of history, of immortality too. It goes from one generation to another." If you're a professional or wanna-be storyteller, an annual membership in the National Storytelling Association (NSA) brings with it a subscription to the bimonthly *Storytelling Magazine,* a periodical stuffed with storytelling news, interviews with successful storytellers, and—the cream—stories, ripe for telling. The NSA also publishes a small catalog of storytelling how-to and suggestion books, including Annette Harrison's *Easy-to-Tell Stories for Young Children* and the National Storytelling Press's *Many Voices: True Tales from America's Past.* Also available are audiocassette recordings of the best tales from the annual National Storytelling Festival.

> Annual membership, $40
> National Storytelling Association
> Box 309
> Jonesborough, TN 37659
> (423) 753-2171 or (800) 525-4514
> e-mail: nsa@tricon.net
> Web site: www.storynet.org

CATALOGS

You don't need anything but imagination to tell a story—which is why they're such fun told by firelight or while sitting in the dark on a summertime back porch—but sometimes a few audiovisual aids add extra pizzazz. Try, for example, using your very own stuffed animals to reenact "Goldilocks and the Three Bears" or a favorite toy train to puff its way up a hill (or across the living room rug) as "The Little Engine That Could." Puppets make wonderful storytelling aids; in our early storytelling days, we made a lot of our own, constructing the characters from colored paper, collage supplies, and glue, and taping them to craft sticks, or decorating simple stitched felt "mittens." Paper, pencils, paints, crayons, and felt-tip pens can also be useful storytelling accompaniments, especially for particularly active listeners. Try having the kids draw along with the first telling of the story; then tell it again, using their finished illustrations. Or invent joint illustrations as you tell the tale: "Jack was a poor boy who lived with his mother in a little square house that looked like *this.* It had a little garden—what do you think they should have in their garden, kids? What color door do you think Jack's house had?"

Storytelling sessions can also be paired with hands-on craft projects, musical selections, or charades. Plant a pot of beans to accompany "Jack and the Beanstalk," play a lullaby while Sleeping Beauty sleeps, or hop around the room like Peter Rabbit.

Lakeshore Learning Materials

The Lakeshore Learning Materials catalog carries a wide assortment of eye-catching props for storytellers. Among these is a storytelling apron: as the story progresses, the storyteller sticks Velcro-backed stuffed characters and objects to the apron, each illustrating some crucial event in the plot. Storytelling kits to accompany the apron are available separately: each consists of a children's book and set of stuffed characters. Eric Carle's *The Very Hungry Caterpillar,* for example, comes with 22 stuffed props, including a skinny caterpillar, a fat caterpillar, a cocoon, a gorgeous multicolored butterfly, and a lot of stuffed fruit.

Also from Lakeshore: several kinds of puppets and a "Fingerplay Mitt Kit," which includes a fuzzy glove with Velcro-tipped fingers, to which can be stuck little Velcro-backed figures from children's songs or stories.

> Lakeshore Learning Materials
> 2695 E. Dominguez St.
> Carson, CA 90749
> (310) 537-8600 or (800) 421-5354/fax (310) 537-5403

Also see **Puppets** (page 777).

MAGAZINES

Storytelling
Faces; December, 1991

Each issue of *Faces* magazine features a different multicultural theme. The December 1991 issue is about storytelling around the world, including articles on the history of storytelling, Chinese storytelling with shadow puppets, international versions of "Cinderella" (900 of them), and storytelling through rap music—plus a retelling of the Arabic tale of the clever storyteller Scheherazade and a "recipe" for telling a story of one's own. Back issues of *Faces* are available.

> $4.50
> Cobblestone Publishing, Inc.
> 30 Grove St.
> Peterborough, NH 03458
> (603) 924-7209 or (800) 821-0115/fax (603) 924-7380

e-mail: custsvc©cobblestone.mv.com

Web site: www.cobblestonepub.com

See *Faces* (page 411).

BOOKS

The following is a list of how-to books for would-be storytellers, including helpful instructions for beginners, descriptions and summaries of good tales to tell, and suggestions for accompanying activities.

Awakening the Hidden Storyteller: How to Build a Storytelling Tradition in Your Family
Robin Moore; Shambhala, 1991

Creative Storytelling: Building Community, Changing Lives
Jack David Zipes; Routledge, 1995

The Family Storytelling Handbook: How to Use Stories, Anecdotes, Rhymes, Handkerchiefs, Paper, and Other Objects to Enrich Your Family Traditions
Anne Pellowski; Macmillan, 1987

The Parent's Guide to Storytelling: How to Make Up New Stories and Retell Old Favorites
Margaret Read MacDonald; HarperCollins, 1995

The Storytelling Handbook: A Young People's Collection of Unusual Tales and Helpful Hints on How to Tell Them
Anne Pellowski; Simon & Schuster, 1995

GAMES

Greek Myths and Legends, New Testament Stories, and Old Testament Stories

These beautifully illustrated card games are played like rummy: players, aged 7 and up, attempt to collect four-card sets, each illustrating one of 13 Greek myths, or Old or New Testament tales. Greek myth cards are stylistically patterned in black and orange. The pictures, reminiscent of the paintings on Greek pottery, represent, among others, the stories of Leda and the Swan, Jason and the Argonauts, Theseus and the Minotaur, and Persephone and Hades. Sample Old Testament cards picture the stories of Noah's Ark, Daniel and the Lions, and Cain and Abel; sample New Testament cards show the Birth of Jesus, the Last Supper, and the Resurrection. The storytelling feature of the game comes into play once a four-card set has been collected: the triumphant collector then challenges the player on his/her left to tell the featured story. An entertaining introduction to traditional stories and storytelling.

> $7 per card game
> Aristoplay
> 450 S. Wagner Rd.
> Ann Arbor, MI 48107
> (800) 634-7738 or (888) GR8-GAME
> fax (734) 995-4611
> Web site: www.aristoplay.com

LifeStories

This addictive board game never fails to absorb our family, plus assorted friends and relations of all ages. "Each of us," reads the "LifeStories" instruction sheet, "has unique stories to tell based on our own life experiences, hopes & dreams." As players hop their pieces around the game board, they do just that: a card which elicits the telling of a story is drawn on each turn. "Tell about one of the traditions in your family." "Tell about a time when you slept outdoors." "Tell about a favorite letter you received." "Recall a story you heard about one of your grandmothers." "Tell a story about a pet or animal."

The game is a storyteller's delight and does, as advertised, "build bridges" among persons of all ages by encouraging the sharing of personal stories.

> $29.95
> Talicor, Inc.
> 8845 Steven Chase Ct.
> Las Vegas, NV 89129
> (800) 433-GAME/fax (702) 655-4366
> Web site: www.talicor.com

Once Upon a Time

In "Once Upon a Time, The Storytelling Card Game," players invent a story using as cues beautifully illustrated cards that show characters, objects, places, and events from classic fairy tales. The story is a group endeavor: the first player begins the tale, placing story cards from his/her hand faceup on the table as the element pictured on the card is mentioned. "A brother and a sister," the story might begin, as the first player lays down the Brother/Sister Card, "lived in a tiny village"—the Village Card—"near a great forest"—the Forest Card. The first player may continue the tale, may pass the story on to the next player if he/she runs out of ideas, or may be interrupted by a player with an Interrupt Card. "In the center of the forest," the interrupter may continue, "was hidden a wonderful treasure"—the Treasure Card—"guarded by fierce and terrible wolves"—the Wolf Card.

The object of the game is to be the first person to play all the cards in his/her hand, while telling a coherent and imaginative story, ending with a Happy Ever After card. Each player is dealt one Happy Ever After card per round, each bearing a possible fairy-tale finale: among them "And there they sit to this very day"; "So everything was restored to its former glory"; "So the spell was broken and they were free"; and (my favorite) "And he listened to his mother's advice from then on."

"Once Upon a Time" is recommended for players of all ages, adapting itself readily to a range of backgrounds, imaginations, and vocabularies. It works equally well for small beginners and for older literary sophisticates. The game includes 112 storytelling cards, 56 Happy Ever After cards, a few blank cards for those who want to add special elements of their own to the action, and a 16-page rule and suggestion booklet.

$15.95

Atlas Games
Box 131233
Roseville, MN 55113
(612) 638-0077/fax (612) 638-0084
e-mail: atlasgames@aol.com

StoryTime Cards

"StoryTime Cards" are seductively pretty. There are 36 cards in the basic pack—big, sturdy, charmingly illustrated, and grouped into four color-coded categories: Characters, Places, Goodies, and Activities. Each card carries a single labeled picture. Places cards, for example, which have sky blue borders, include

"The Woods," "The Moon," "Haunted House," "Secret Hiding Place," "Treehouse," and "Magic Castle." The cards are intended for use as storytelling props, sparking imagination and creativity, providing jumping-off points for your children's or your own story inventions. An included 16-page booklet, "101 Fun Ways to Use StoryTime Cards," gives suggestions for games and learning ideas. Examples: let your child pick a card or two at random and you use them to invent and tell a story, encouraging your child to participate by naming the characters and adding descriptive details. Give a familiar fairy tale a new twist, inspired by your choice of card: try telling the tale of "The Three Little Skunks," for example, or "Goldilocks and the Three Frogs."

Cards are available as basic storytelling sets (Volumes I and II), as add-on 16-card theme sets ("Magical Kingdom," "Under the Sea," "Scared Silly!," and "Pirates!"), and—perhaps the best yet—as a make-your-own activity kit, which includes 8 StoryTime cards and 28 reusable blank cards, to be illustrated and labeled by the kids themselves, using stickers and washable crayons.

StoryTime Creations
Box 19544
Boulder, CO 80308
(800) 55-STORY

TableTalk Conversation Cards

"TableTalk" is the brainchild of St. Louis entrepreneur J. J. Stupp, who got the idea at the family dinner table when then three-year-old daughter Jane asked, "Mother, where do squirrels live?" "Then I stopped and wondered," said Stupp later, "how do people start conversations, what makes it interesting, how can conversations be easier and more fun?" The outcome was the original "TableTalk," a pack of 52 "conversation cards," which come in a little red box, suitable not only for the table but for carrying about in the backpack, coat pocket, or glove compartment of the family car. There are no rules for "TableTalk." "Just pull out a card and read it to everyone at your table. That's it! There are no 'right' or 'wrong' answers. So pick a card and start talking!" These definitely work: the challenge is not to start participants talking but to prevent everybody from talking loudly at once. "TableTalk" topics are intriguing, challenging, and thought-provoking. Try these examples:

> Someday in the distant future, our sun will become a "red giant" and burn the earth to cinders. If you could pick 10 people—living today—to survive this catastrophe and carry on civilization on another planet, whom would you select and why?

> If you could solve any one mystery, which one would you solve and why?

> If you were asked to choose the three best movies ever made, which movies would you select? What was the worst movie you ever saw?

For those talked out on "TableTalk," several new packets of conversation cards are also available: "KidTalk," "AnimalTalk" (which includes one card explaining where squirrels live), "SportsTalk," "BibleTalk" (Old and New Testament versions), "ScienceTalk," "MovieTalk," "ArtTalk," "MusicTalk," and "TravelTalk."

$5.95 each
TableTalk
6 Country Life Acres
St. Louis, MO 63131-1403
(314) 997-5676 or (800) 997-5676/fax (314) 997-3602
Web site: www.tbltalk.com

ON-LINE RESOURCES

Story Resources Available on the Web
ALL Links to storytelling organizations and festivals, storytelling hints and how-tos, and stories of all kinds from all over the world: folktales and legends, multicultural stories, fairy tales, fables, tall tales, and more.

www.cyberenet.net/~sjohnson/stories

The Storytelling Home Page
ALL Links to storytelling organizations and lots of great stories from around the world, including folktales, fairy tales, and classic myths.

members.aol.com/storypage/index.htm

LITERATURE

The fact of knowing how to read is nothing, the whole point is knowing what to read.

JACQUES ELLUL

What to read? There are, unfortunately, no foolproof rules for choosing children's reading material. One kid's all-time favorite book may be ignored—even loathed—by another. Our boys now keep a record of what they read and each list is idiosyncratically individual: I can tell, just by a glance at the first title, who the reader is. Josh, a devotee of the classics, began his latest list with Robert Fagles's translation of *The Iliad;* Caleb, a fantasy fan, started off with Robin McKinley's *The Outlaws of Sherwood;* and Ethan, determinedly technical, jotted down *Mac Programming for Dummies.*

When the boys were small, reading was very much a group affair. A glance back through my journals turns up list after list: all of the *Berenstain Bears* books, repeatedly chosen by Caleb, who loved them; everything we could find by James Stevenson and Chris Van Allsburg, including Ethan's favorite, *The Wreck of the Zephyr;* Rudyard Kipling's *Just-So Stories* and *The Jungle Book;* the entire *Paddington Bear* series; four volumes of *The Borrowers;* Roald Dahl's *James and the Giant Peach* and *The BFG; Mrs. Frisby and the Rats of NIMH; The Reluctant Dragon; The Hobbit; The Sword in the Stone.*

Our kids are teenagers now—or getting close—and their reading choices are almost entirely their own. We make an occasional suggestion—"Just try *Treasure Island,* Caleb; I think you'll like it"—and an occasional mind-broadening assignment—"Ethan! Read this James Thurber story; it's hilarious!"—but reading for the sake of reading is something they do on their own. Every once in a while, though, we still read aloud, just as we did when they were very small—and it's still as warm and wonderful as it was years ago, when they still sat in our laps or leaned their heads against our shoulders.

For parents and teachers searching for suggestions on what to read, children's book review magazines are excellent sources, as are compilations of "Best Books" for children, titles of which are listed below.

From my homeschool journal:

◆ **February 28, 1991. Josh is nine; Ethan, eight; Caleb, six.**

Today we read another selection from the Junior Great Books series (see page 76): "The Goldfish," by Eleanor Farjeon. Josh read the story to himself; then I read it aloud to all three boys and we ran through the suggested discussion questions. It doesn't sound like much on paper, but it was a wild literary success. The boys, all three of them, were interested, enthusiastic, and positively frothing with opinions. The story is about a little goldfish who once lived in the ocean. He was unhappy there because he had grand ambitions: he wanted to marry the moon and possess the world. Finally Neptune took pity on him and lured him into a fisherman's net. The fisherman thought the goldfish was so beautiful that he brought him home to keep as a pet. The goldfish ended up in a fishbowl with a little silver fish for a wife—and was perfectly happy because he thought he now owned the world (the bowl) and was married to the moon (the silver fish). The boys talked and talked about this, spurred on by discussion questions.

Nobody approved of Neptune. "He might have been trying to do good," said Ethan, "but he tricked the goldfish."

"He lied to the goldfish," said Caleb.

"It wasn't exactly a lie," said Ethan. "It's like if a kid asks for a hundred dollars, and his parents say, 'You can have a dollar; that's better for you' and then the kid is happy, but it's not what he really wanted."

"No," said Josh, "it's more like if a kid is really upset about something and his parents lie to make him feel better and then he does feel better. Remember in "Many Moons" how the princess was sick because she wanted the moon? And the jester got her a necklace with a little gold moon on it and then she got better. But it wasn't really the moon."

"But what if you find out later that you've been tricked?" asked Ethan. "Then you feel even worse, because you know people lied to you."

"So some lies can be good lies," said Josh, "and some lies are bad lies."

The deceived goldfish kept resurfacing as a discussion topic all day long, and the boys continued debating him with their father at the dinner table.

REVIEWS AND RECOMMENDATIONS: MAGAZINES

AtoZebra

P/T Reviews of books for kids of all ages, published biannually. The magazine includes detailed reviews by "unstuffy" reviewers, full-color sample pages from picture books, and feature articles about all aspects of children's literature. The paper version of the magazine is paired with an on-line publication (see Web site below).

AtoZebra
Box 5082
Brentwood, TN 37027-5082
e-mail: atozebra@earthlink.net
Web site: www.atozebra.com

Book Links

P/T *Book Links* is a bimonthly magazine published under the auspices of the American Library Association, designed, according to the editorial mission statement, "for teachers, librarians, library media specialists, booksellers, parents, and other adults interested in connecting children with books." For those who fit into one or more of the above categories, the magazine is a rich source of reading ideas for kids in preschool through eighth grade. *Book Links* is essentially an exercise in literary crosslinks and interrelationships: each issue includes a large assortment of bibliographies and book reviews, linking books together by author, illustrator, or subject matter. This is the periodical to reach for if you're looking for assorted books about such topics as quilts, Russia, chemistry, Mozart, Norse mythology, dinosaurs, geometry, grandparents, or pioneers. Each general topic, several of which are covered in each issue, is accompanied by a list—often immense—of related fiction and nonfiction books, plus suggestions for associated hands-on activities. An article on time travel books, for example, in one of my past issues—I save them all—listed over 50 time travel adventure books, an assortment of nonfiction books on the history and science of clocks and timekeeping, and a list of historical books that describe the realities of life long ago.

Book Links also keeps readers abreast of literary awards and competitions, and new book-related publications and resources for parents and teachers.

Annual subscription (6 issues), $24.95

Book Links

434 W. Downer Pl.

Aurora, IL 60506

(630) 892-7465 or (800) 545-2433, ext. 5715

Web site: www.ala.org/BookLinks

See the **American Library Association** (page 48).

Children's Literature

Children's Literature is a monthly newsletter crammed with reviews of recent fiction and nonfiction books for children. The reviews are short—usually only a paragraph or so long—but are thorough; there's enough description in each to give you a feel for the flavor of the book. Books are grouped by recommended age or by theme. An added attraction: if one of the featured volumes catches your fancy, it can be ordered directly through the newsletter, either via the included order form or by dialing (credit card in hand) 1-800-469-2070.

Annual subscription (12 issues), $24 (plus 5% sales tax for Maryland residents)

Children's Literature

7513 Shadywood Rd.

Bethesda, MD 20817

(301) 469-2070 or (800) 469-2070/fax (301) 469-2071

Web site: www.childrenslit.com

The Five Owls

The Five Owls—their logo is four small owlets and one owl adult sitting pudgily on a branch—is published five times annually by the Hamline University Graduate School in St. Paul, Minnesota. It is aimed at "readers who are personally and professionally involved in children's literature," with the express purpose of "advocating books of integrity," those judged "intelligent, beautiful, well-made, and worthwhile in relation to books and literature in general." Reviews are detailed and thoughtful; longer thematic essays compare and contrast numbers of different books, all more or less related to the same subject. One such article, with associated bibliography, brought together some 32 books on water, appropriate for a range of ages, from Alison Shaw's *Until I Saw the Sea: A Collection of Seashore Poems* to Charles Craighead's *The Eagle and the River,* a bird's-eye view story of Wyoming's Snake River, illustrated with photographs; Verna Aardema's Kenyan folktale *Bringing the Rain to Kapiti Plain;* Joanna Cole's charmingly scientific *The Magic Schoolbus at the Waterworks;* and Patricia MacLachlan's *Skylark,* the story of one family's battle with drought on the Western prairie.

Annual subscription (5 issues), $20

Hamline University Graduate School

Hamline University Crossroads Center, MS-C-1924

1536 Hewitt Ave.

St. Paul, MN 55104

(612) 644-7377/fax (612) 641-2956

e-mail: fiveowls@seq.hamline.edu

The Horn Book

The Horn Book, a fat—100+ pages—thorough, and thoroughly worthwhile publication, has been recommending books for children and young adults since 1924. Each issue contains a number of featured academic essays on books and book-related topics, along with—some of us eagerly flip to this first—the "Booklist," some 50 pages of reviews of new children's books, roughly categorized by recommended age. Included categories are "Picture Books," "For Younger Readers," "For Intermediate Readers," "For Older Readers," "Folklore," "Poetry," "Nonfiction," and "Of Interest to Adults." Real prizes—those books that "the majority of reviewers believe to be an outstanding example of its genre"—are marked with a star.

Annual subscription (6 issues), $36

Horn Book, Inc.

11 Beacon St., Suite 1000

Boston, MA 02108

(617) 227-1555 or (800) 325-1170/fax (617) 523-0299

Web site: www.hbook.com

Reviews and Recommendations: Books

A to Zoo: Subject Access to Children's Picture Books

Carolyn W. Lima and John A. Lima; R. R. Bowker, 1993

This is an enormous bright yellow reference volume, over 1,000 pages long, listing some 15,000 picture books generally appropriate for kids from toddlerhood through grade 2. The books, both fiction and nonfiction, are classified by subject: thus, if your small reader is interested in rabbits, tractors, cavepeople, magic, or India, you simply refer to the subject index for a list of picture books dealing with the chosen topic. Alternate indices list books by author, title, and illustrator.

The drawback to *A to Zoo* is lack of text: listed books are not accompanied by plot summaries, which means that you have to guess, based on title. This usually works fairly well, but there are occasional unexpected surprises.

A to Zoo is an expensive personal purchase; luckily it's a standard in most libraries. Look for it in the children's department reference section.

The Best of the Best for Children

Denise Perry Donavin, ed.; Random House, 1992

Over 350 pages of books, magazines, videos, audio resources, computer software, and toys chosen by the American Library Association as "the best of the best" for kids of all ages, from infants to teenagers. Books, each with a short description, are listed in alphabetical order by title and categorized by age group ("Infants and Toddlers," "Preschoolers," "Early Grades," "Middle Graders," and "Teenagers"). Also included: information on purchasing an encyclopedia and recommendations for dictionaries.

Nonbook resources, such as videos and toys, are often accompanied by a list of "Connections": related book titles and other resources intended to expand the original learning experience. For a child enthralled by a toy castle, for example, with its attendant population of knights and dragons, the authors suggest five medieval storybooks, a pair of mathematical software programs with knights-and-castles motifs, two related videos, and an audio performance of Arthurian legends.

Best Books for Beginning Readers

Thomas G. Gunning; Allyn & Bacon, 1997

A 250+-page bibliography of books for very early readers of preschool age through grade 2.

Books for You: An Annotated Booklist for Senior High Schools

Leila Christenbury, ed.; NCTE, 1995

A descriptive book list of the best books of 1990–1994 for young adults, both fiction and nonfiction, grouped under 36 subject headings.

Books Kids Will Sit Still For

Judy Freeman; R. R. Bowker, 1990

Judy Freeman, librarian and lecturer on children's literature, discusses the art of presenting books to children ("My mother's commonsense admonition 'Always read with expression!' was directed to me as a first-grader," writes Freeman, "but it has stood me in good stead.") and briefly reviews over 2,000 "tried-and-true, kid-tested favorites" for reading aloud. The book lists are categorized by age—"Fiction for Preschool–Kindergarten," "Fiction for Kindergarten–Grade 1," and so on through grades 5–6—and by genre: "Folk & Fairy Tales, Myths and Legends," "Poetry, Nonsense, and Language-Oriented Nonfiction," and "Nonfiction and Biography." A detailed subject index in the back (Acting, Adventure, and Africa through Writing, Zebras, and Zoos) groups the listed books by theme. Also see, by the same author, *More Books Kids Will Sit Still For* (R. R. Bowker, 1995).

A Child's Delight

Noel Perrin; Dartmouth College Press, 1997

A collection of delightful essays on the joys of "underappreciated" children's books, among them *The Borrowers, The Railway Children, The Story of Doctor Doolittle,* and *The Planet of Junior Brown.*

Children Talking About Books

Sarah G. Borders and Alice Phoebe Naylor; Oryx Press, 1993

How to get elementary-age children talking about their favorite books, with hints for guiding discussions and a long list of "sure-fire" book choices.

Classics to Read Aloud to Your Children

P/T William F. Russell; Crown, 1984

A generous collection of selections from famous authors, recommended as best bets for reading aloud to kids aged 5–12. The selections are divided into two groups by "listening level": Listening Level I readings are appropriate for kids aged 5 and up; Level II, for kids aged 8 and up. Included are short stories, poems, and excerpts from longer works by such classic writers as Aesop, Cervantes, Shakespeare, Nathaniel Hawthorne, Washington Irving, Jack London, Charles Dickens, Mark Twain, and Arthur Conan Doyle. Also see *More Classics to Read Aloud to Your Children* (Crown, 1986).

See *Classic Myths to Read Aloud* (page 89).

Creative Uses of Children's Literature

P/T Mary Ann Paulin; Library Professional Publications, 1982

Paulin's specialty is the art of making connections through literature. In this vast volume she demonstrates, through innumerable examples, how to introduce young readers to a variety of books by grouping literary selections together by theme. Books can be grouped and regrouped, Paulin points out, in any number of ways: by author, artist, subject, or literary genre (fantasy, science fiction, biography, historical fiction, survival stories, mysteries), by plot, character, or setting, and by the time in which the action takes place. Paulin lists, describes, and connects thousands of children's books and multimedia resources in hundreds of creative categories. Under "Spiders," for example, she discusses some 60 fiction and nonfiction books, poems, and stories about spiders—among them the West African folktales of Anansi the Spider, E. B. White's philosophically enchanting *Charlotte's Web,* and Jane Dallinger's scientifically accurate *Spiders,* illustrated with color photographs. (Also included are suggestions for mind-broadening activities, crafts, and educational projects.) Under "Space Flight," she lists over 60 fiction and nonfiction books, poems, and biographies related to the space program, along with numerous suggestions for videos, audiocassettes, filmstrips, magazines, and hands-on projects. Under "If You Like the *Little House* Books"—Laura Ingalls

Wilder's nine books about growing up on the 19th-century frontier—Paulin lists over 80 additional pioneer-related books, from easy readers to young adult fiction and nonfiction. Paulin's encyclopedic compilations are an invaluable resource for parents whose children—suddenly infatuated with polar bears, the Civil War, or Chinese fairy tales—demand lots more of the same. Also see *More Creative Uses of Children's Literature* (Library Professional Publications, 1992).

Eyeopeners!

P/T Beverly Kobrin; Penguin, 1988

Beverly Kobrin's *Eyeopeners!* is devoted to children's nonfiction. "Why nonfiction?" asks Kobrin. "The adults in kids' lives simply aren't as familiar with nonfiction as they are with fiction. Many hear the negative-sounding term *nonfiction,* think *ugly,* and lose interest." Children, however, though they do adore a good story, are also "fascinated by facts, a fact too often ignored." Hence this guidebook, describing over 500 children's nonfiction books, listed in 62 alphabetical categories stretching from "ABC Books," "Adoption," and "Airplanes" through "Wolves," "Words," and "Zoos." Many of the titles are accompanied by suggestions for related readings and activities. Also see *Eyeopeners II!* (Scholastic, 1995).

The Read-Aloud Handbook

P/T Jim Trelease; Penguin, 1995

"Forty-four percent of our adults never read a book in the course of a year," writes Jim Trelease, "Ten percent of the U.S. public is reading 80 percent of the books." Trelease hopes to combat such grim statistics by encouraging parents and teachers to read aloud to children, thus—by exposing them to the entrancing, interesting, exciting, and moving world of real books—instilling in them the desire to read. Reading skills, the verbal mechanics upon which so many classrooms concentrate so much time, are at best, Trelease states, a necessary evil. The way to open the doors to reading is to show kids its many delights—that is, to open a book and *read.*

The Read-Aloud Handbook covers the whys and how-tos of reading aloud, discusses the uses of home and public libraries, points out the advantages of a television-free home, and provides potential readers with a lengthy annotated list of good books, the "Treasury of Read-Alouds."

The New York Times Parent's Guide to the Best Books for Children

Eden Ross Lipson; Times Books, 1991

Brief reviews of over 1,700 favorite children's books, organized in six categories by reading level: "Wordless Books," "Picture Books," "Story Books," "Early Reading," "Middle Reading," and "Young Adult." Beautifully designed, with lots of black-and-white reproductions of illustrations from the books themselves.

Parents Who Love Reading, Kids Who Don't: How It Happens and What You Can Do About It

Mary Leonhardt; Crown, 1995

The author, a high school English teacher, describes the stages by which children learn to read and gives advice for helping poor or reluctant readers, hints on creating a reader-friendly home, and a long list of reading suggestions for kids aged 9 through high school. Also see *Keeping Kids Reading: How to Raise Avid Readers in the Video Age* (Crown, 1996).

See **99 Ways to Get Kids to Love Reading** (page 51).

Reading Rainbow Guide to Children's Books

Twila C. Liggett and Cynthia Mayer Benfield; Citadel Press, 1996

Reviews of the 101 best books from the popular *Reading Rainbow* television program for 4–9-year-olds.

Worth a Thousand Words: An Annotated Guide to Picture Books for Older Readers

Bette D. Ammon and Gale W. Sherman; Libraries Unlimited, Inc., 1996

"If a picture is worth a thousand words," write the authors, "imagine the value of *many* pictures *plus* a thousand words." The book lists 645 fiction and non-fiction entries in alphabetical order by author's last name. For each book, there is a brief plot summary, followed by a list of suggestions for additional readings, resources, activities, and research projects. To accompany Chris Van Allsburg's *Ben's Dream,* for example, the story of a boy who falls asleep to the sound of rain on the roof and dreams that he and his house are floating past the half-submerged great monuments of the world, the authors suggest reading about Indian dream legends and making hanging "dream catchers," locating all the pictured monuments on a map or globe of the world, and watching a video version of the book.

Those picture books deemed truly extraordinary, including "a combination of sophisticated themes, language, and illustrations" are distinguished by an oversize exclamation point.

REVIEWS AND RECOMMENDATIONS: NOT JUST DEAD WHITE MALES

"What should children read?" High on the list of modern educational controversies is the "Battle of the Books," a pitched battle over reading material centered in many university English departments. Traditionally a thorough grounding in the humanities involved the study of the "Great Books" of Western civilization by those authors who have lately been dubbed "Dead White European Males." Recently many academics have protested this as one-sided Eurocentricity, arguing in favor of a multicultural, nonsexist curriculum that emphasizes the works of women, African-Americans, and authors from all regions of the world. This new slant on the humanities has affected all levels of education, from colleges down to the primary grades.

Neither die-hard traditionalists nor politicized multiculturalists, however, have satisfactorily solved the questions of what students should read. Clearly there are benefits to be gained from both approaches. It would be foolishly shortsighted to eliminate the writings of Western Europeans from the school curriculum, since so many of our political and philosophical traditions derive from their work. Conversely, since we live in a richly multicultural world, it would be equally unacceptable to deprive students of books by and about its peoples. The obvious solution to the "Battle of the Books" is generous compromise. Kids should read it all.

Against Borders: Promoting Books for a Multicultural World

Hazel Rochman; American Library Association Editions, 1993

Many multicultural books listed by theme ("The Perilous Journey," "The Hero and the Monster") or by ethnic group, categorized by appropriate age.

From Hinton to Hamlet: Building Bridges Between Young Adult Literature and the Classics

Sarah K. Herz and Donald R. Gallo; Greenwood Publishing Group, 1996

The authors link modern young adult novels to literary classics, making thematic connections that help kids "build bridges" from the simpler to the more complex literature.

Great Books

David Denby; Simon & Schuster, 1996

The author, well into adult life, returned to college, where he spent a year studying the "Great Books" of Western literature. His experiences with authors, from Homer to Virginia Woolf, and with his classmates are fascinating and may inspire the classically inclined to embark on a similar course of reading.

See the **Great Books Foundation** (page 76).

Great Books for Boys

Kathleen Odean; Ballantine, 1998

Detailed descriptions of over 600 books for boys aged 2–12, including picture books, biographies, mysteries, science fiction and fantasy, technology, poetry, and science and nature.

Great Books for Girls

Katherine Odean; Ballantine, 1997

An annotated list of over 600 books that promote positive female role models and gender equity for girls aged 2–12.

See **Gender Issues** (page 830).

Let's Hear It for the Girls

Erica Baumeister and Holly Smith; Penguin, 1997

Books with themes and protagonists that promote good female role models.

See **Gender Issues** (page 830).

The New Lifetime Reading Plan

Clifton Fadiman and John S. Major; HarperCollins, 1997

A guide to the world's finest literature, updated to include non-Western and women writers. Included are detailed reviews of 133 authors in chronological order, from the anonymous writer of "The Epic of Gilgamesh" and Homer through Chinua Achebe, plus shorter descriptions of 100 additional writers.

Our Family, Our Friends, Our World

Lyn Miller-Lachmann; R. R. Bowker, 1992

An annotated guide to multicultural books for children and teenagers, grouped by age and by geographical area/ethnic group. Included are detailed reviews of over 1,000 books.

Required Reading: Why Our American Classics Matter Now

Andrew Delbanco; Farrar, Straus & Giroux, 1997

Convincing and carefully crafted essays on the importance of classic American writers such as Henry David Thoreau, Herman Melville, Edith Wharton, Richard Wright, Henry Adams, and Harriet Beecher Stowe.

The Western Canon: The Books and School of the Ages

Harold Bloom; Harcourt Brace, 1994

A learned defense of the Western literary tradition in which the author, on intellectual and aesthetic grounds, deplores the inroads of multiculturalism, Afrocentrism, and feminism. The book includes Bloom's list of the essential writings of the Western Canon, for very dedicated and advanced readers.

Reviews and Recommendations: On-Line Resources

AtoZebra

P/T A searchable database of children's book reviews, including a detailed description, a cover photograph, and samples of interior art. Reviews are grouped by category or age group, among these activity books, alphabet books, poetry, picture books, multicultural books, history, and science. Also included are resources for parents, teachers, librarians, and homeschoolers, and reviews of audiobooks, educational games, children's Web sites, and computer software.

www.atozebra.com

Also see *AtoZebra* (page 69).

Book Links

P/T An on-line version of the magazine. Included are reviews and information about children's books, organized thematically, from the American Library Association.

www.ala.org/BookLinks

See **American Library Association** (page 48) and **Book Links** (page 69).

Booklist

P/T The on-line version of the ALA's *Booklist* magazine, with reviews and information about books and electronic media for kids of all ages.

www.ala.org/booklist

See **American Library Association** (page 48).

Book Nook

Book reviews for and by kids categorized by appropriate age group. Users can search for specific books by title, author, publisher, or key word, or can write and post their own book reviews. The site includes a list of books awaiting review.

i-site.on.ca/booknook.html

The WEB

P/T *WEB* stands for "Wonderfully Exciting Books." *The WEB* is a children's literature newsletter of book reviews, essays, and information published at Ohio State University. Articles from back issues can be accessed at the WEB's Web site.

www.armory.com/~web/web.html

Catalogs

"Where is human nature so weak as in the bookstore!" exclaimed Henry Ward Beecher in 1855—a sentiment which holds true to this day and has, in my personal experience, led to the enrichment of bookstores from coast to coast. For those like us who have a hard time adhering to a book budget, a worthwhile and money-saving investment is:

How to Stock a Home Library Inexpensively

P/T Jane Williams; Bluestocking Press, 1995

While developing readers need a generous supply of books, maintaining a household of enthusiastic bookworms can be financially draining. Jane Williams explains how to get the most out of your book budget and lists over 100 sources (including addresses and telephone numbers) for low-priced or discount books.

Bluestocking Press

Box 1014

Placerville, CA 95667

(916) 621-1123 or (800) 959-8586/fax (916) 642-9222

See **Bluestocking Press** (page 447).

Chinaberry

ALL The Chinaberry catalog, all 100+ pages of it, is a gem—a book about books that just happens to double as a mail-order catalog. The books are loosely grouped by reading level. ("Most methods for classifying literature into appropriate age levels are confusing and neglect to take into account the uniqueness of each child," writes Chinaberry's owner.) Chinaberry Level I books are wordless or near-wordless books for the very youngest prereaders. Level II includes picture books, illustrated so that the action in the pictures corresponds to the action in the text, making it easy for small listeners to follow along. Level III books are targeted at kids who can sit through longer stories with fewer illustrations; and Level IV books are suitable as read-alouds for older, interested kids or for intermediate to advanced readers to tackle on their own. It's clear that a good deal of thought goes into each of the (many) selections, and the reviews are little masterpieces.

Chinaberry Books
2780 Via Orange Way, Suite B
Spring Valley, CA 91978
(619) 670-5200 or (800) 776-2242/fax (619) 670-5203

Children's Book-of-the-Month Club

The Children's Book-of-the-Month Club is the junior branch of the better-known Book-of-the-Month Club for adults. It operates in similar fashion: about every three weeks (17 times a year), members receive a catalog of approximately 100 books, suitable for kids from toddlerhood to age 12. One book is the month's featured "Main Selection," which is shipped to you automatically unless you return an enclosed postcard, indicating that you don't want it. Most catalog selections are offered at substantial discounts.

Members can order an introductory starter set (four books for $1 apiece); the membership agreement stipulates that you must then buy at least two books during your first year of membership. After that, it's your choice.

Children's Book-of-the-Month Club
Camp Hill, PA 17012-9852

A Common Reader

The Common Reader catalog, subtitled "A selection of books for readers with imagination," is a creative delight. The 130+-page catalog, though aimed primarily at advanced readers and adults, includes a "For Young Readers" section specifically for kids. For budding classicists, the Common Reader carries all the volumes of the Loeb Classical Library (Greek and Latin texts, with facing English translations); for the slightly less elevated, there are works by P. G. Wodehouse, Don Marquis, James Thurber, and Mark Twain. There are books for the scientist, the artist, the opera buff, the mystery lover, the mathematician, and the just plain curious. The catalog also carries a small, but superb, assortment of videos, from the daunting *King Lear,* with Sir Lawrence Olivier in the title role, to Nick Park's hilarious "claymation" animations starring Wallace, a zanily impractical inventor, and his perspicacious dog, Gromit.

A Common Reader
141 Tompkins Ave.
Pleasantville, NY 10570
(800) 832-7323
Web site: www.commonreader.com

Great Books Foundation

The Chicago-based Great Books Foundation sponsors three excellent reading programs for children and young adults: the Junior Great Books Read-Aloud Program for kids in kindergarten and grade 1; the Junior Great Books Series, for second- through ninth-graders, and the Introduction to Great Book Series, for readers in grades 10–12. The programs are designed to encourage interpretive reading (or listening) and critical-thinking skills. Participants read a Great Books selection and then engage in a "shared inquiry discussion," during which, under the direction of a group leader, they clarify and consolidate their opinions of the text. This sounds stuffier than it is in practice: the reading selections are excellent and thought provoking, and the suggested discussion questions listed in the accompanying Leader's Guides do generate spirited debate.

There are four three-volume sets of stories in the Read-Aloud Program (titled the *Dragon, Sailing Ship, Sun,* and *Pegasus* series). Each volume contains three stories; examples include "The Frog Prince," by the Brothers Grimm; "The Tale of Two Bad Mice," by Beatrix Potter; and "Chestnut Pudding," an Iroquois folktale. Selections for the Junior Great Books Program are numbered by grade level (Series 2 through 9); those for the Introduction to Great Books Program are packaged in three single-volume series. Series 2 books, for example, include "Jack and the Beanstalk," Rudyard Kipling's "How the Camel Got His Hump," and Hans Christian Andersen's "The Emperor's New Clothes"; Series 5 readers tackle Randall Jarrell's "The Bat-Poet" and Oscar Wilde's "The Happy Prince"; Series 8 readers read excerpts from the works of Maya Angelou, Mark Twain, and Amy Tan. More advanced students, in the Introduction to Great Books Program, read "The Melian Dialogue," by Thucydides; "Of Civil Government," by John Locke;

and "A Room of One's Own," by Virginia Woolf. And much more.

Single copies of student texts, teachers' texts, and leaders' guides are available to the general public; only trained Great Books Discussion Leaders, who have completed a formal Foundation-sponsored leader training course, are allowed to purchase books in quantity.

The Great Books Foundation
35 E. Wacker Dr., Suite 2300
Chicago, IL 60601-2298
(800) 222-5870/fax (312) 407-0334
Web site: www.greatbooks.org

The Home School Books and Supplies Catalog

The catalog is 60 pages of no-frills newsprint, with no descriptions or illustrations, but it includes a substantial list of inexpensive books for kids, roughly grouped in age-appropriate categories. Includes classics, abridged classics, and "almost classics," popular series books, historical fiction and nonfiction, and biographies.

The Home School Books and Supplies
104 S. West Ave.
Arlington, WA 98223
(360) 435-0376 or (800) 788-1221/fax (360) 435-1028
Web site: www.TheHomeSchool.com

Learning Links

A catalog of "literature-based reading programs" for kids in kindergarten through grade 12. Included are theme-based book collections, study guides, and a large list of inexpensive editions of individual books, many of which are also available on audiocassette or video.

Learning Links, Inc.
2300 Marcus Ave.
New Hyde Park, NY 11042
(516) 437-9071 or (800) 724-2616/fax (516) 437-5392
Web site: www.learninglinks.com

Novel Units

Novel Units are teachers' guides for specific works of literature, intended to expand upon the initial reading experience with activities that promote reading comprehension, writing skills, and analytical thinking.

Users make plot timelines and story maps, play vocabulary games, discuss crucial questions raised by the text, and do book-related art projects. Over 400 *Novel Units* are available, for well-known books variously suitable for kids in grades 1–12. The books themselves, in inexpensive paperback editions, are also available from *Novel Units.* The company also offers books on audiocassette and video, and a large number of Spanish-language materials.

Novel Units
Box 1461
Palatine, IL 60078
(800) 424-2084/fax (847) 776-0500 or (847) 776-5214

Sundance

Sundance publishes three catalogs of literature-based learning materials, variously appropriately for pre-K–grade 6 students, middle-school students, or students in grades 7–12. Hundreds of books, in inexpensive paperback editions, plus study guides, audiocassettes, and videos.

Sundance
Box 1326
Littleton, MA 01460-9936
(800) 343-8204/fax (800) 456-2419
Web site: www.sundancepub.com

WHERE TO BUY ON-LINE

Amazon Books

Over a million and a half available titles. Users can search for specific selections by title, author, or subject. Selections are cross-indexed, and many listings are accompanied by descriptions or copies of reviews. And all are sold at a tempting discount.

www.amazon.com

Barnes and Noble Booksellers

Over 500,000 titles, many discounted.

www.barnesandnoble.com

Book Stacks

Over 500,000 titles, most with big discounts.

www.books.com

Bookwire Index to Children's Booksellers

🌐 **ALL** Links to an enormous list of sources of books for kids.

www.bookwire.com/index/ChildrensBooksellers.html

Cherry Valley Books

🌐 **ALL** Books for kids, young adults, and parents, listed by subject category. Every entry includes a brief description.

www.cherryvalleybooks.com

Just for Kids Bookstore

🌐 **ALL** Thousands of books for and about kids, listed by age and subject category. A few in-depth reviews.

www.just-for-kids.com

Scholastic's Internet Center

🌐 **5 18** Access to a wide range of materials from Scholastic, Inc., including the "Ultimate Education Store," a source of books and educational materials for kids in grades K–12.

www.scholastic.com

LITERARY MAGAZINES

Babybug

📖 **0 2** A magazine in board-book form—the pages are heavy-duty cardboard with rounded edges—for the very small, aged 6 months–2 years.

Annual subscription (9 issues), $32

The Cricket Magazine Group

Box 7434

Red Oak, IA 51591-4434

(800) 827-0227

Web site: www.cricketmag.com

Cricket

📖 **9 14** *Cricket,* the flagship publication of this excellent line of children's literary magazines, is aimed at readers aged 9–14. Each monthly issue is about 60 pages long, crammed with stories and folktales, nonfiction science and nature articles, poems, puzzles, and contests, all supplemented with colorful illustrations. All are also superbly written—*Cricket* beats the bushes for high-quality children's authors and illustrators—plus

there's a bright little bug at the bottom of the pages that defines any potentially sticky vocabulary words. The popularity of *Cricket*—doubtless accompanied by the pleas of *Cricket* readers' younger brothers and sisters—eventually led to the publication of comparable literary magazines targeted at younger audiences.

Annual subscriptions (12 issues), $32

The Cricket Magazine Group

Box 7434

Red Oak, IA 51591-4434

(800) 827-0227

Web site: www.cricketmag.com

See *Babybug* (left), *Spider* (page 79), and *Ladybug* (below).

Ladybug

📖 **2 6** A well-done magazine of simple stories and activities for kids aged 2–6, from the publishers of *Cricket.*

Annual subscription (12 issues), $32

The Cricket Magazine Group

Box 7434

Red Oak, IA 51591-4434

(800) 827-0227

Web site: www.cricketmag.com

Nexus

📖 **13 +** Each issue of *Nexus,* the "interdisciplinary magazine for students," centers around a different work of literature, from which it branches off creatively into the fields of history, art, music, and science. The magazine is intended, explains the publisher, to promote cross-curriculum thinking skills, enhancing students' abilities to recognize and appreciate connecting themes and patterns in different academic disciplines. Each color-illustrated 32-page issue contains 12 to 13 short articles, with associated questions, projects, and activities. The "*Romeo and Juliet* and the Renaissance" issue, for example, includes articles on Shakespeare's theater, Renaissance fashion, Shakespearean word games, Renaissance art, Italian family feuds, Leonardo da Vinci's inventions, Galilean astronomy, and Renaissance imitative counterpoint music. The "*Lion in Winter* and the Middle Ages" issue includes pieces on Gothic architecture, the Crusades, the Magna Carta, the feudal system, Gregorian chants, falconry, medieval medicine, Arab astronomy, and the physics of the crossbow.

Nexus, appropriate for high school–aged students, is published three times annually, in October, January, and April.

> Individual issues, $6 each (plus $1.25 shipping/handling)
> Pallas Communications, Inc.
> 5017 Archmere Ave.
> Cleveland, OH 44144

Shoofly

Shoofly is an audiomagazine for listeners aged 3–7, published quarterly on cassette tape and "dedicated to the celebration of contemporary children's poetry and literature." Each tape is 45 to 60 minutes long and contains an imaginative mix of songs, stories, and poems—including, in the first several issues, a miniseries starring a brown-and-white puppy named Grummel and a host of friends and acquaintances, including Shipmunk, a vociferous and politically active female chipmunk.

> Annual subscription (4 issues), $29.95 (plus $3.95 shipping/handling); back issues from the catalog, $9.95 apiece
> *Shoofly*
> Box 1237
> Carrboro, NC 27510
> (800) 919-9989

Spider

A literary magazine for kids aged 6–9, from the publishers of *Cricket.* Stories, poems, puzzles, nonfiction articles, and colorful illustrations.

> Annual subscription (12 issues), $32
> The Cricket Magazine Group
> Box 7434
> Red Oak, IA 51591-4434
> (800) 827-0227
> Web site: www.cricketmag.com

Storyworks

A literary magazine for upper-elementary school readers (grades 3–5) from Scholastic. The magazine offers read-aloud plays, fictional stories and folktales,

and "integrated reading and writing activities," plus—twice a year—collections of illustrated trading cards picturing authors, illustrators, and well-known literary characters.

Also available from Scholastic is the 48-page "Storyworks Activity Book," *Getting Into Books,* with suggested activities based on popular features from the magazine, plus 45 literary trading cards.

> Magazine, published monthly during the school year (6 annual issues), $5.50 (10 or more subscriptions)
> Scholastic, Inc.
> 2931 E. McCarty St.
> Jefferson City, MO 65101
> (800) 631-1586
> Web site: www.scholastic.com/classmag/sworks.htm

ACTIVITY BOOKS

Better Than Book Reports

Christine Boardman Moen; Scholastic, 1994

A collection of literature-associated activities for readers in grades 2–6 to be used in lieu of the traditional book report. Instead of "I liked this book because . . . ," kids make book maps, book-based greeting cards, personal dictionaries, and much more.

Jackdaw Literature Collection

Jackdaw Publications (see page 445) publishes several portfolios centering around the lives and times of famous literary figures. Each includes an assortment of background "Broadsheet Essays" by a literary historian, plus a collection of historical document reproductions, pictures, and other items from the period. The *Charles Dickens* portfolio, for example, includes six illustrated essays on Dickens by historian Ivor Brown ("Charles Dickens," "The Man with a Pen," "Crime and Punishment," "Hard Times," "In America," and "The Actor") and 14 historical documents, including pages from the original serialized publication of *The Pickwick Papers,* a portrait sketch of Charles Dickens, a letter from Dickens to his sister-in-law, a chapter plan for an issue of *David Copperfield,* and a ticket to a reading by Charles Dickens. Other portfolios include "The Brontës," "Shakespeare's Theater," "Young Shakespeare," and

"Nathaniel Hawthorne." Portfolios include a study guide with reproducible student worksheets.

> Each portfolio, $37
> Jackdaw Publications
> Box 503
> Amawalk, NY 10501
> (800) 789-0022/fax (800) 962-9101

Learning Through Literature: Over 500 Activities for 21 Children's Books

Mary Jane Butner, Jane Ann Peterson, and Janice Mark Sieplinga; Scott, Foresman, 1991

Hands-on activities to accompany and enhance 21 well-known picture books, suitable for kids of preschool age through grade 2. For each book—among them Robert Lawson's *Make Way for Ducklings,* Norman Bridwell's *Clifford: The Big Red Dog,* and Leo Lionni's *Frederick*—are listed games, songs, poems, and simple hands-on math and science projects, plus reproducible student worksheets.

Literary Trivia: Fun and Games for Book Lovers

Richard Lederer; Vintage Books, 1994

Anecdotes, fascinating and unusual facts, and addictive quizzes about well-known books for teenagers and up.

My Reading List

Emily Ellison; Longstreet Press, 1995

A "personal reading record" for kids aged 4–8. Children maintain an ongoing booklist and get a spiffy reward sticker for each completed book.

Quizzes for 220 Great Children's Books

Polly Jeanne Wickstrom; Teacher Ideas Press, 1996

More Quizzes for Great Children's Books

Polly Jeanne Wickstrom and James Mark Wickstrom; Teacher Ideas Press, 1996

This pair of oversize paperbacks is the foundation of the "Quest Motivational Reading Program," targeted at readers in grades 3–8, in which kids earn points and letter grades for reading books and passing true/false and multiple-choice quizzes on the material they have just read. Each listed book is assigned a point value on the basis of length and a letter value (*A–E*) on the basis of reading difficulty. An *A* book, for example, is appro-priate for kids in grades 3–4; an *E* book, for kids in grades 7–8. Beverly Cleary's *Ramona the Pest,* Judy Blume's *Superfudge,* and Richard and Florence Atwater's *Mr. Popper's Penguins* all rate an *A;* Charles Dickens's *A Tale of Two Cities* and Mark Twain's *The Adventures of Huckleberry Finn* both rate an *E.* Point values, letter values, and quiz scores are eventually all combined to determine a final total score. For home learners, the authors suggest that participants "be given a goal for attaining a certain number of points"; then the progress of individual readers can be charted through personal reading diaries.

The books selected for the Quest Motivational Reading Program are excellent, including works by Louisa May Alcott, Lloyd Alexander, Eleanor Estes, Marguerite Henry, E. Konigsberg, Scott O'Dell, Robert Louis Stevenson, Laura Ingalls Wilder, and many more. The quizzes, which make up the bulk of the books, are the stuff of the reading comprehension sections on standardized tests. True/false statements based on Frances Hodgson Burnett's *The Secret Garden,* for example, include:

> *Colin never learned to walk on his own.*
> *Mr. Craven's wife died of pneumonia.*
> *Mary and Dickon became good friends.*

My expectations for the reception of such quizzes in our household was low. Our sons, however, got their paws on the books and spent much of one rainy afternoon happily quizzing each other on old favorites. "Josh! In *The Grey King!* 'King Arthur was Bran's real father'—true or false?" So obviously there's more here than first met the suspicious parental eye.

> Available through bookstores or
> Libraries Unlimited
> Box 6633
> Englewood, CO 80155-6633
> (303) 770-1220 or (800) 237-6124
> E-mail: lu-books@lu.com
> Web site: www.lu.com

The RIF Guide to Encouraging Young Readers

Ruth Graves; Doubleday, 1987

The RIF stands for "Reading Is Fundamental"—which premise is the jumping-off point for an impressive collection of kid-friendly activities, all intended to encourage kids from infancy to age 11 to become book lovers and eager readers. Among the suggestions: wear special hats for certain stories (a tin pot, for example, for the tale of Johnny Appleseed); read your way around the world, marking the setting of each book on a world map with stickers or colored pins; make your own family card catalog on index cards; cook the foods featured in certain books (make jam sandwiches, for example, to accompany Russell Hoban's *Bread and Jam for Frances*); make your own bookmarks; invent sequels to your favorite books; design a Halloween monster dictionary.

To ensure that you'll have plenty of material for practicing such literary activities, the book includes an annotated list of 200 favorite children's books. See **Reading Is Fundamental** (page 49).

5
10 *Storybook Stew: Cooking With Books Kids Love*

Suzanne I. Barchers and Peter J. Rauen; Fulcrum, 1996

Kid-friendly recipes and hands-on activities, including art, science, and math projects, paired with favorite storybooks. Young cooks prepare "Appetizers and Accompaniments," "Beverages," "Breads and Cereals," "Cookies," "Desserts," "Fruits and Salads," "Main Dishes," "Meat and Eggs," "Treats," and "Vegetables and Rice," while reading such food-oriented picture books as *Cloudy with a Chance of Meatballs, Blueberries for Sal, Bread and Jam for Frances, One Hundred Hungry Ants, The Story of Johnny Appleseed, A Medieval Feast,* and the cautionary *Berenstain Bears and Too Much Junk Food.*

5
9 *Story S-t-r-e-t-c-h-e-r-s*

Shirley C. Raines and Robert J. Canady; Gryphon House, 1989

The book describes 450 varied activities to enhance and expand upon 90 favorite primary-level storybooks, among them Russell Hoban's *A Baby Sister for Frances,* Charlotte Zolotow's *William's Doll,* Eric Carle's *The Very Hungry Caterpillar,* Dr. Seuss's *Green Eggs and Ham,* and Laura Joffe Numeroff's *If You Give a Mouse a Cookie.* For each book is listed a "Circle Time Presentation," which includes book discussion suggestions—and assorted art, music, science, math, cooking, and creative play projects. After reading *If You Give a Mouse a Cookie,* for example, the preposterous

tale of all the things a mouse will probably ask for to go along with his cookie, kids are encouraged to make mouse drawings or Play-Doh mouse models, to bake chocolate chip cookies, to act out the story of the demanding mouse, and to make a sequence chart, picturing the mouse's many requests in order (first the cookie, then the glass of milk, then the straw . . .). Sequels by the same authors include *More Story S-t-r-e-t-c-h-e-r-s, Even More Story S-t-r-e-t-c-h-e-r-s,* and *450 More Story S-t-r-e-t-c-h-e-r-s for Primary Grades.*

GAMES

12
+ **221B Baker Street**

For Arthur Conan Doyle fans, a game based on the mysteries of Sherlock Holmes. The playing board is a map of London, featuring, among other landmarks, the Boar's Head Inn, the Carriage Depot, the Apothecary, and Scotland Yard. Players, setting out from 221B Baker Street, attempt to solve one of 20 mystery adventures, moving from place to place, and receiving clues—some helpfully genuine, some deceptive red herrings. Once a player feels he or she has cracked a case, he/she races to Scotland Yard to announce the solution.

$25, available from toy and game stores

6
12 **Authors, American Authors, and Children's Authors**

The original "Authors" is now a classic: this rummy-type card game dates to the 19th century. Players collect four-card sets of 13 famous American and British authors: William Shakespeare, Charles Dickens, Washington Irving, Alfred Lord Tennyson, William Makepeace Thackeray, Mark Twain, Louisa May Alcott, Sir Walter Scott, Robert Louis Stevenson, James Fenimore Cooper, Edgar Allan Poe, Nathaniel Hawthorne, and Henry Wadsworth Longfellow. Newer versions include "American Authors" (thirteen 20th-century American writers) and "Children's Authors" (among them A. A. Milne, the Brothers Grimm, Beatrix Potter, and Dr. Seuss). The illustrated cards list four works written by each author.

Each game, $6

U.S. Games Systems, Inc.

179 Ludlow St.

Stamford, CT 06902

(203) 353-8400 or (800) 544-2637

or

Aristoplay

450 S. Wagner Rd.

Ann Arbor, MI 48107

(800) 634-7738 or (888) GR8-GAME

fax (734) 995-4611

Web site: www.aristoplay.com

6 Bookworm

"Bookworm, The Game of Reading and Remembering," is a delightful British-made board game. The illustrated board is based on a turn-of-the-century alphabet book; players, as they hop through the 26 spaces from *A* to *Z*, take turns reading or listening to one of the 112 book cards, each of which carries a passage from a different children's book. Each card includes four reading comprehension questions based on the selection just heard; correct answers allow the players to move extra spaces around the playing board.

The alphabet motif is charming but makes the game appear simpler than it actually is. The book card selections are taken from a wide range of books, chosen from the Opie Collection of Children's Literature at Oxford University, and some excerpts are quite challenging. Represented books include, for example, *Uncle Tom's Cabin* (Harriet Beecher Stowe), *The Swiss Family Robinson* (Johann Wyss), *Swallows and Amazons* (Arthur Ransome), and *The Red Badge of Courage* (Stephen Crane)—as well as *Winnie-the-Pooh* (A. A. Milne), *The Lion, the Witch, and the Wardrobe* (C. S. Lewis), and *The Wind in the Willows* (Kenneth Grahame). An accompanying guide lists all the selected books in alphabetical order by title, with brief summaries of each plot.

$31.95

Worldwide Games

Box 517

Colchester, CT 06415-0517

(800) 888-0987/fax (800) 566-6678

e-mail: service@snswwide.com

Web site: www.snswwide.com

or

Old Game Store

Rte. 11/30

Manchester Center, VT 05255

(802) 362-2756 or (800) 818-GAME

Web site: www.vtweb.com/oldgame

13 Ex Libris

"Ex Libris" is a literary game produced jointly by a most elite duo: the British Library in London and the Bodleian Library in Oxford. The result is creative, mind-broadening, and—in practice—potentially hilarious. "Ex Libris" consists of a pack of 100 cards, each bearing the title, author, and brief plot summary of a well-known novel. Your challenge, as player, is to invent the book's first or last sentence (which one is determined at the beginning of each round by the flip of a shiny British halfpenny)—in the style, if you can manage it, of the real author. The attempts are then collected and gleefully read aloud by an appointed "reader," along with the actual first/last line of the novel (printed on the back of the plot summary card). Players vote on which sentence is the genuine article.

Game selections are weighted toward adult novels (*Islands in the Stream* by Ernest Hemingway, *Brave New World* by Aldous Huxley, *Women in Love* by D. H. Lawrence, *Jude the Obscure* by Thomas Hardy), but also include a generous assortment of classic children's books (*The Adventures of Tom Sawyer, Black Beauty, The House at Pooh Corner, Little Women, James and the Giant Peach, Peter Pan*). Recommended for advanced readers.

$30 from game stores or

Old Game Store

Rte. 11/30

Manchester Center, VT 05255

(802) 362-2756 or (800) 818-GAME

Web site: www.vtweb.com/oldgame

The Game of Peter Rabbit

"The Game of Peter Rabbit" was designed by Beatrix Potter in 1904; reproductions of the original are still produced today by the British Traditional Games Company. The game has all the artistic appeal of the Potter books. The playing board is a map of Mr. McGregor's garden, complete with lettuces, toolshed, watering can, and cucumber frames. Peter Rabbit starts the play by squeezing under the garden gate, leaving the brass buttons from his little blue jacket (12 in all, included) at specified locations along the playing path. The irate Mr. McGregor chases him, attempting to capture Peter by landing on the same square before Peter manages to exit the garden. For players aged 5–8.

$49.95 from game stores, or
Old Game Store
Rte. 11/30
Manchester Center, VT 05255
(802) 362-2756 or (800) 818-GAME
Web site: www.vtweb.com/oldgame

The Hobbit Adventure Boardgame

A board game for Tolkien lovers. Playing pieces are plastic hobbits; the playing board an illustrated map of Middle Earth. The game also includes assorted gold pieces, "life markers," magic talismans, and 142 play-directing cards, listing adventures, rewards, dangers, riddles, rest periods, and—occasionally—encounters with monsters. The object of the play is to move the hobbits across the board, gathering experience, equipment, and information, to confront and defeat the Dragon at Carn Dum. For players aged 8 and up.

Iron Crown Enterprises
Box 1605
Charlottesville, VA 22902
(800) 325-0479
Web site: www.ironcrown.com

Lyle, Lyle Crocodile Game

A memory game based on Bernard Waber's books about lovable Lyle, the crocodile who lives in the family bathtub and eats Turkish caviar. The board is illustrated with the brownstone houses of East Eighty-eighth Street—Lyle's address—with spaces for 17 pairs of memory cards, each with a picture of a character or object from the *Lyle* books. Players turn cards over two at a time, attempting to make matches. For players aged 5–9.

$19.95
Lakeshore Learning Materials
2695 E. Dominguez St.
Carson, CA 90749
(310) 537-8600 or (800) 421-5354/fax (310) 537-5403
Web site: www.lakeshorelearning.com

Wind in the Willows Game

The playing board is an enchanting map of Kenneth Grahame's River. A little green boat starts downstream from the top, and four characters from *The Wind in the Willows*—the Badger, the Toad, the Mole, and the Water Rat—set out from the bottom. The object of the game is to capture the boat by landing on the same square at the same time. For players aged 5–9.

$49.95
Turn Off the TV
Box 4162
Bellevue, WA 98009
(800) 949-8688/fax (425) 558-7564
Web site: www.turnoffthetv.com
or
Old Game Store
Rte. 11/30
Manchester Center, VT 05255
(802) 362-2756 or (800) 818-GAME
Web site: www.vtweb.com/oldgame

BOOKS ON TAPE

AudioEditions

A mix of abridged and unabridged books on cassette, including many selections appropriate for young people: children's fiction, classics, drama, poetry, history, and science.

AudioEditions
Box 6930
Auburn, CA 95604
(800) 231-4261/fax (800) 888-1840
e-mail: bookaudio@aol.com
Web site: www.audioeditions.com

Chinaberry Books

"We're always on the look-out for *extraordinary* story tapes," writes the author of the Chinaberry Books catalog, and their selection of audiocassettes and CDs includes some of the best of the best for kids of all ages.

Chinaberry Books
2780 Via Orange Way, Suite B
Spring Valley, CA 91978
(800) 776-2242/fax (619) 670-5203

Greathall Productions

Jim Weiss of Greathall Productions may be our family's all-time favorite storyteller. We listen, enchanted, time and again: this, you realize, is storytelling in its best incarnation, the sort of storytelling that should take place in the evenings around the kitchen fire while snow falls in the woods outside. Weiss, to date, has issued some 15 story collections, available on either cassette tape or CD. Titles include *Greek Myths* (the tales of King Midas, Hercules, Perseus and Medusa, and Arachne), *King Arthur and His Knights, The Three Musketeers/Robin Hood, Sherlock Holmes for Children* (including "The Mazarin Stone," "The Adventure of the Speckled Band," "The Musgrave Ritual," and "The Adventure of the Blue Carbuncle"), *Tales from Cultures Far and Near, The Jungle Book,* and *Rip Van Winkle/Gulliver's Travels.* All are superb.

> Greathall Productions
> Box 5061
> Charlottesville, VA 22905-5061
> (800) 477-6234

Listening Library

ALL The Listening Library offers a large selection of books, cassette tapes, and study guides, variously appropriate for just-beginning readers through sophisticated teenagers.

> Listening Library, Inc.
> 1 Park Avenue
> Old Greenwich, CT 06870-1727
> (800) 243-4504/fax (800) 454-0606
> e-mail: moreinfo@listeninglib.com
> Web site: www.listeninglib.com

Recorded Books

ALL A wonderful collection of full-text, unabridged audiobooks for kids of all ages. Audiobooks are available for either direct purchase or 30-day rental.

> Recorded Books, Inc.
> 270 Skipjack Rd.
> Prince Frederick, MD 20678
> (800) 638-1304/fax (410) 535-5499
> Web site: www.recordedbooks.com

Yellow Moon Press

ALL The Yellow Moon Press catalog includes recordings of contemporary and traditional poems, songs, and stories, all "directly related to the oral tradition/spoken word." Included are Native American and African folk-tales, Jewish fairy tales, Downeast stories and ballads, Chinese legends, Appalachian mountain tales, frontier stories, Greek myths and legends, and much more.

> Yellow Moon Press
> Box 1316
> Cambridge, MA 02238
> (617) 776-2230/fax (617) 776-8246
> orders (800) 497-4385

BOOKS ON VIDEO

Many great books are available in video versions for kids of all ages. For younger viewers, for example, there are wonderful animated versions of E. B. White's *Charlotte's Web,* Robert O'Brien's *The Rats of NIMH,* Lewis Carroll's *Alice in Wonderland,* Roald Dahl's *James and the Giant Peach* and J. R. R. Tolkien's *The Hobbit,* and excellent adaptations of Frances Hodgson Burnett's *The Secret Garden,* C. S. Lewis's *The Chronicles of Narnia,* and Dick King-Smith's *Babe the Gallant Pig.* Intermediate and older viewers may prefer videos of Louisa May Alcott's *Little Women,* Mark Twain's *The Adventures of Huckleberry Finn,* Robert Louis Stevenson's *Treasure Island,* Jack London's *White Fang,* Herman Melville's *Moby Dick,* Rudyard Kipling's *Captains Courageous,* Alexander Dumas's *The Man in the Iron Mask,* Jules Verne's *20,000 Leagues Under the Sea,* Jane Austen's *Pride and Prejudice,* Charles Dickens's *A Tale of Two Cities,* or Sir Arthur Conan Doyle's stories of Sherlock Holmes. We've only had sporadic access to commercial television over the past years, but we do have a VCR, upon which our boys have watched hours of book-based videos. These are almost always enriching, often inspiring ("That was *great!* I'm going to read the book!"), and even at the worst, interesting. "That wasn't nearly as good as the book. The ending was all wrong. Why did they do that?"

A large selection of such book-based videos is usually available at video rental stores; for other sources, see Catalogs (page 42).

Schoolmasters Video

ALL Over 700 educational videos for kids of all ages, including video versions of many favorite books and assorted instructional (but entertaining) videos covering such early reading skills as letter recognition and phonics.

Schoolmasters Video
745 State Circle
Box 1941
Ann Arbor, MI 48106
(800) 521-2832/fax (313) 761-8711
Web site: www.school-tech.com

9 18 Zenger Media: Resources for the English Classroom

Books, lesson plans, activity books, audiocassettes, computer software, and many literature-based videos, among them plays by Shakespeare, Eugene O'Neill, Arthur Miller, and Tennessee Williams; video versions of such classic novels as Jane Austen's *Pride and Prejudice,* Rudyard Kipling's *Captains Courageous,* and Charles Dickens's *David Copperfield;* and "The American Short Story Collections," a series of video dramatizations of short stories by Eudora Welty, Willa Cather, Richard Wright, Mark Twain, F. Scott Fitzgerald, and many more. For younger viewers, there are video versions of many classic children's stories, among them *Lassie Come Home, The Hobbit, The Secret Garden,* and *The Little Prince.*

Zenger Media
10200 Jefferson Blvd.
Box 802
Culver City, CA 90232-0802
(310) 839-2436 or (800) 421-4246/fax (310) 839-2249
or (800) 944-5432
e-mail: access@ZengerMedia.com
Web site: ZengerMedia.com/Zenger

COMPUTER SOFTWARE

9 13 *Alien Tales*

Alien Tales tests kids' reading comprehension skills and general knowledge of literature by means of a wacky extraterrestrial game show. Assorted plagiaristic aliens (variously green, two headed, orange, or topped with antennae) claim to have written well-known works of literature; human players strive to set the record straight by answering questions or solving puzzles about the book's plot, characters, and author. Kids have the option of reading (or hearing read aloud) an excerpt from the disputed book before plunging into the game show contest. The game show features 30 books, among them *Charlotte's Web, The Wizard of Oz, The Secret Garden,* and *Alice in Wonderland.* Recommended for players aged 9–13. On CD-ROM for Mac or Windows.

$39.95
Broderbund
Box 6125
Novato, CA 94948-6125
(415) 382-4700 or (800) 521-6263
Web site: www.broderbund.com

ON-LINE RESOURCES

4 + Aesop's Fables

Two color-illustrated versions of each tale, one in modern and one in traditional style, all designed by students at the University of Massachusetts.

www.umass.edu/acco/projects/aesop

4 + Aesop's Fables

650+ fables, listed by titles with accompany morals, plus a biography of Aesop and a timeline. Full-text versions of all the fables are available, many with accompanying audio or visual images. The site also includes the fairy tales of Hans Christian Andersen and *A Christmas Carol* by Charles Dickens.

www.pacificnet/~johnr/aesop

ALL Carol Hurst's Children's Literature Site

An excellent resource for children's literature, including links to book reviews, teaching ideas, literature-related activities, theme and cross-curricular studies, and literary articles.

www.carolhurst.com

ALL The Children's Literature Web Guide

Perhaps the best on-line literary site for children, with links to book reviews, book lists, book discussion groups, children's literature organizations, resources for parents, teachers, and students, on-line stories, research guides, and a wealth of other information.

www.acs.ucalgary.ca/~dkbrown

Fairrosa Cyber Library of Children's Literature

Thematic book lists centering around such topics as American tall tales, circus books, the Civil War, and time travel, plus links to many other literature sites, including on-line books, stories, and kids' magazines.

www.igloo-press.com

 The Librarian's Guide to Cyberspace

The American Library Association's link to best Web sites, including an extensive list under "Literature and Language" for children.

www.ala.org

 The Modern English Collection

Many complete texts on-line.

etext.lib.virginia.edu/modeng/medeng0.browse.html

 Project Bartleby Archive

Many complete works of classic authors, including George Bernard Shaw, Eugene O'Neill, Herman Melville, F. Scott Fitzgerald, and Walt Whitman.

www.columbia.edu/acis/bartleby/index.html

ABOUT AUTHORS

 The Brontës: Scenes from the Childhood of Charlotte, Branwell, Emily, and Anne

Catherine Brighton; Chronicle Books, 1994

The picture-book story of the creative young Brontë children growing up on the English moors in the 19th century, their family life, and their invention of the imaginary city of Glass Town.

 Charles Dickens: The Man Who Had Great Expectations

Diane Stanley and Peter Vennema; William Morrow, 1993

A beautifully illustrated biography of Dickens that links his life story to the lives of the people in his books.

The Country Artist: A Story about Beatrix Potter

David R. Collins; Carolrhoda, 1989

A short chapter book about the life of Beatrix Potter, nature artist and author of the classic *Tale of Peter Rabbit*, for middle-grade readers.

Emily

Michael Bedard; Doubleday, 1992

An exquisite picture-book story about a young girl who meets her shy and talented neighbor, the poet Emily Dickinson.

A Fairy Tale Life: A Story About Hans Christian Andersen

Joann Johansen Burch and Liz Monson; Carolrhoda, 1994

A short chapter book about the life of famous Danish storyteller, author of such classic tales as "The Little Mermaid," "Thumbelina," and "The Ugly Duckling."

Glass Town

Michael Bedard; Atheneum, 1997

A picture-book account of the daily lives of the four Brontë children and their invention of the imaginary city of Glass Town.

Great Lives: American Literature

Doris Faber and Harold Faber; Atheneum, 1995

A collection of 30 short, informational biographies of prominent persons in American literature, among them Mark Twain, Louis May Alcott, Jack London, Edgar Allan Poe, Henry Wadsworth Longfellow, and Tennessee Williams. All the basic facts, plus black-and-white photographs and prints.

Invincible Louisa

Cornelia Meigs; Little, Brown, 1968

For intermediate and older readers, this is the Newbery Medal–winning story of the real "Little Women": Louisa May Alcott and her three sisters, Anna, Elizabeth, and May.

Jack London: Wilderness Writer
Edward Beecher Claflin; Kipling Press, 1987

A short and interesting biography of London for intermediate readers, illustrated with photographs, maps, and pen-and-ink sketches.

John Steinbeck
Catherine Reef; Clarion, 1996

A 163-page biography for older readers, illustrated with black-and-white photographs.

Laura Ingalls Wilder: Author of the Little House Books
Carol Greene; Children's Press, 1990

A very short, simple text heavily illustrated with wonderful color and black-and-white photographs.

Lives of the Writers
Kathleen Krull; Harcourt Brace, 1994

Short, but fascinating, biographies of 19 famous authors. Readers discover, for example, that Miguel de Cervantes was captured by Barbary pirates and imprisoned for five years until his family managed to pay his ransom; that Emily Dickinson's favorite game was hide-and-seek; and that Jack London liked to eat "cannibal sandwiches" made of raw beef. Wonderful illustrations by Kathryn Hewitt.

A Man Called Thoreau
Robert Burleigh; Macmillan, 1985

This biographical picture book, illustrated with soft black-and-white sketches, gives much of the flavor of Thoreau's philosophy through short quotes from his writings.

The Man Who Was Poe
Avi; Orchard Books/Franklin Watts, 1989

A fictionalized tale of Edgar Allan Poe. The year is 1848, the place is Providence, Rhode Island, and 11-year-old Edmund is alone in the world. His father has been lost at sea, his mother has disappeared, Aunt Pru, who had been taking care of Edmund and his twin sister, has been drowned—and now Edmund's sister has also vanished, out of a locked room. Edmund, in league with an enigmatic gentleman who calls himself

Auguste Dupin, sets out to find his sister and solve the mystery—which turns out to be a spine tingler, full of mausoleums, wicked stepfathers, stolen gold, and false identities. (Guess who Auguste Dupin really is.)

Mark Twain? What Kind of a Name Is That? A Story of Samuel Langhorne Clemens
Robert Quackenbush; Simon & Schuster, 1984

A short, illustrated biography of Twain, filled with interesting information, plus snappy asides from a pack of cats (Mark Twain loved cats) at the bottom of alternate pages. See, by the same author, *Once Upon a Time: A Story of the Brothers Grimm* (Prentice-Hall, 1985) and *Who Says There's No Man in the Moon? A Story of Jules Verne* (Prentice-Hall, 1985).

Meet the Authors
Deborah Kovacs; Scholastic, 1995

Covers 25 well-known children's authors, among them Avi, Susan Cooper, Paula Fox, Margaret Mahy, Katherine Paterson, Robert Newton Peck, Jane Yolen, and Paul Zindel. Included for each is a brief biography, illustrated with a photograph, a bibliography of published works, and a suggestion for a writing activity. An example, from Susan Cooper: "Think of a character who is going on a perfectly ordinary trip somewhere. Imagine something quite extraordinary that happens to him or her on the way. Make it take the story into a totally different world."

Meet the Authors and Illustrators

Deborah Kovacs and James Preller; Scholastic, 1995

Covers 60 authors/illustrators of children's books, among them Mitsumasa Anno, Aliki Brandenberg, Eric Carle, Steven Kellogg, Ezra Jack Keats, William Steig, Maurice Sendak, and Chris Van Allsburg. Included for each is a brief biography, a bibligraphy of book titles, and a "Do It Yourself!" activity for young writers.

The Return of the Twelves
Pauline Clarke; Dell, 1992

Max and his family have just moved into his great-grandfather's English farmhouse, and there in the attic he finds a set of twelve 150-year-old wooden soldiers—which, mysteriously and magically, come alive. The

Twelves, it turns out, once belonged to the Brontë children and wish to return to their ancestral home, the parsonage at Haworth where the Brontës grew up. Max and his brother and sister help them on their dangerous journey. Excitement, magic, and a little literary history just for good measure.

To the Point: A Story About E. B. White
David R. Collins; Carolrhoda, 1989

For young to intermediate readers, five short chapters about the life of the author of *Charlotte's Web, Stuart Little,* and *The Trumpet of the Swan.*

What the Dickens!
Jane Louise Curry; Margaret K. McElderry, 1991

In 1842, 11-year-old twins whose father runs a boat on Pennsylvania's Juniata Canal discover a Harrisburg bookseller's plot to steal Charles Dickens's newly finished novel while Dickens is on a lecture tour in the United States.

The World of the Little House
Carolyn Strom Collins; HarperCollins, 1996

Includes, in 150 beautifully illustrated pages, a biography of author Laura Ingalls Wilder and historical background on each of her books, complete with maps, house floor plans, hands-on projects, and recipes.

Zora Hurston and the Chinaberry Tree
William Miller; Lee & Low Books, 1994

A simple picture-book biography of author Zora Hurston for younger readers.

Videos About Authors

Any Friend of Nicholas Nickleby Is a Friend of Mine

Based on a Ray Bradbury story, this is the tale of a young boy who wants to be a writer and of a near-magical town in which, just around the corner, you might meet the greats of English literature. About 55 minutes long.

Movies Unlimited
3015 Darnell Rd.
Philadelphia, PA 19154
(215) 637-4444 or (800) 4-MOVIES

E-mail: movies@moviesunlimited.com
Web site: www.moviesunlimited.com
or
Zenger Media
10200 Jefferson Blvd.
Box 802
Culver City, CA 90232-0802
(310) 839-2436 or (800) 421-4246/fax (310) 839-2249
or (800) 944-5432
e-mail: access@ZengerMedia.com
Web site: ZengerMedia.com/Zenger

The Belle of Amherst
Julie Harris plays Emily Dickinson in this marvelous one-woman show. The poet's life is presented through quotations, poems, letters, diaries, and historical artifacts, against a backdrop of the Dickinson home in Amherst, Massachusetts. About 90 minutes long.

Movies Unlimited
3015 Darnell Rd.
Philadelphia, PA 19154
(215) 637-4444 or (800) 4-MOVIES
E-mail: movies@moviesunlimited.com
Web site: www.moviesunlimited.com
or
Zenger Media
10200 Jefferson Blvd.
Box 802
Culver City, CA 90232-0802
(310) 839-2436 or (800) 421-4246/fax (310) 839-2249
or (800) 944-5432
e-mail: access@ZengerMedia.com
Web site: ZengerMedia.com/Zenger

The Famous Authors Series
Biographies of 10 famous authors: Jane Austen, the Brontës, Charles Dickens, George Eliot, William Shakespeare, John Keats, Percy Bysshe Shelley, Virginia Woolf, D. H. Lawrence, and James Joyce. Each biography is half an hour long, presented through narration, period art, portraits, diaries, maps, and quotations.

Series (10 videocassettes), $199.95
PBS Home Video
1320 Braddock Pl.
Alexandria, VA 22314-1698

(800) 645-4PBS/fax (703) 739-8131

Web site: www.pbs.org

CLASSICAL MYTHOLOGY

CATALOGS

Bellerophon Books

[ALL] The catalog contains a large selection of detailed educational coloring and activity books. Of interest to myth lovers are *A Coloring Book of Ancient Greece, A Coloring Book of the Olympics and Other Ancient Games, Gorgons, A Coloring Book of the Trojan War* (*Volumes 1 and 2*), and *A Coloring Book of the Odyssey.*

> Bellerophon Books
> 30 Ancapa St.
> Santa Barbara, CA 93101
> (800) 253-9943

The Writing Company

[9+] This educational catalog includes a varied section of resources for teachers of folklore and mythology, including books, activity books, and workbooks, videos and audiocassettes, posters, and computer software.

> The Writing Company
> 10200 Jefferson Blvd.
> Box 802
> Culver City, CA 90232-0802
> (310) 839-2436 or (800) 421-4246/fax (310) 839-2249
> or (800) 944-5432
> e-mail: access@WritingCo.com
> Web site: WritingCo.com/Writing

BOOKS

Also see **World History** (pages 620 and 629).

 Adventures of the Greek Heroes
[9][12] Mollie McLean and Anne Wiseman; Houghton Mifflin, 1989

For intermediate readers, the stories of Hercules, Perseus, Theseus, Orpheus, Meleager, and Jason and his Argonauts.

 Black Ships Before Troy:
[11+] ***The Story of the Iliad***
Rosemary Sutcliff; Delacorte Press, 1993

The story of the Trojan War in prose, for intermediate to older readers.

 Classic Myths to Read Aloud
[5+] William F. Russell; Crown, 1989

A comprehensive collection of ancient Greek and Roman myths presented in a form just right for bedtime reading.

D'Aulaire's Book of Greek Myths
[8][12] Ingri and Edgar Parin D'Aulaire; Doubleday, 1962

All of Greek mythology in an oversize paperback, colorfully illustrated. By the same authors: *D'Aulaire's Norse Gods and Giants* (Doubleday, 1967).

The Gods and Goddesses of Olympus
[7][11] Aliki; HarperCollins, 1994

An attractively illustrated picture book describing each of the ancient Greek gods and goddesses.

Greek Myths
[8][12] Geraldine McCaughrean; Macmillan, 1993

Sixteen beautifully illustrated myths, among them the tales of Pandora, Persephone, Arachne, Midas, Perseus, Hercules, Jason and the Golden Fleece, Theseus and the Minotaur, and Atalanta. Also by McCaughrean: *The Golden Hoard: Myths and Legends of the World* (McElderry, 1995).

 The Iliad and the Odyssey
[9][12] Jane Werner Watson; Simon & Schuster, 1956

A wonderful adaptation of Homer's stories with glorious Greek-style illustrations. Themes of violence, death, and battle; this is an epic for intermediate to older readers.

It's Greek to Me: Brush Up Your Classics
[ALL] Michael Macrone; HarperPerennial, 1994

A large collection of lighthearted short articles explaining the classical origins of many expressions used today, from "eat your heart out" and "bite the dust" (Homer) and "snake in the grass" (Virgil) to

"Eureka!" (a triumphant and dripping Archimedes). Officially for adults and older readers, but there's something here for everyone to enjoy.

By the same author: *By Jove! Brush Up Your Mythology*, which explains the mythological basis of modern words and phrases, among them *panic, cereal,* and *syringe*.

The Shining Stars: Greek Legends of the Zodiac

Ghislaine Vautier; Cambridge University Press, 1981

Twelve picture-book mythical tales, one for each sign of the Zodiac. Also see *Stories from the Stars: Greek Myths of the Zodiac* (Juliet Sharman-Burke; Abbeville Press, 1998).

Tales of Pan

Mordicai Gerstein; HarperCollins, 1986

A wonderful assortment of stories about the wild goat-legged god from whose name we get our word "panic."

The Trojan Horse: How the Greeks Won the War

Emily Little; Random House, 1988

A gentler and simpler version of the *Iliad* for beginning readers. This is a "Step Into Reading" book, targeted at kids in grades 2–4.

ACTIVITY AND COLORING BOOKS

Bullfinch's Mythology

A more-than-just-a-coloring-book from Running Press, in which brief summaries of classical myths are paired with attractive black-and-white line drawings, suitable for coloring. Available through book stores or, for $8.95, from

Running Press Book Publishers
125 South 22nd St.
Philadelphia, PA 19103
(215) 567-5080 or (800) 345-5359

A Coloring Book of the Odyssey and A Coloring Book of the Trojan War

See **Bellerophon Books** (page 89).

An Elementary Odyssey

David H. Millstone; Heinemann, 1991

A collection of suggestions for teaching Homer to elementary school students, with descriptions of many hands-on and multidisciplinary activities. Examples include making a quilt based on the adventures in the *Odyssey*, writing a letter to one of the characters in a favorite episode, building a model Greek ship or Trojan horse, designing an *Odyssey* board game, making Homeric puppets, diagramming the family tree of the gods and goddesses, drawing a map of Odysseus's travels, writing a Homeric poem or composing a Siren song, and tracing the Greek roots of English words.

GAMES AND HANDS-ON ACTIVITIES

By Jove

"By Jove" is a delightful board game in which players advance through Greek mythology, winning or losing the support of heroes and heroines, gaining favors or suffering punishments from the gods and goddesses, and participating in Jason's quest for the Golden Fleece and Theseus's journey through the Labyrinth to battle the Minotaur. Winner is the first player to acquire a Golden Fleece card, a Minotaur card, and 16 golden (plastic) Greek coins. The board is beautifully illustrated with mythological characters and maps; and the game includes a paperback booklet of Greek myths. An enduring favorite in our family. Recommended for 2 to 6 players, aged 10 and up.

$24
Aristoplay
450 S. Wagner Rd.
Ann Arbor, MI 48107
(800) 634-7738 or (888) GR8-GAME
fax (734) 995-4611
Web site: www.aristoplay.com

6 12 Greek Myths and Legends

A rummy-style card game in which players collect four-card sets, each illustrating one of 13 classic myths, among them the tales of Theseus and the Minotaur, Jason and the Argonauts, Persephone and Hades, and the Labors of Hercules. The cards are beautifully illustrated in black and orange; pictures are reminiscent of scenes on ancient Greek pottery.

$7

Aristoplay

450 S. Wagner Rd.

Ann Arbor, MI 48107

(800) 634-7738 or (888) GR8-GAME

fax (734) 995-4611

Web site: www.aristoplay.com

8 14 National Mythology Exam

Those who think they know their mythology may want to take the National Mythology Exam, administered each spring under the auspices of the American Classical League (see page 703). The exam is offered for students in grades 3–9. Kids in grades 3–4 take a 30-item multiple-choice test; kids in grades 5–9 take the basic exam plus 10 additional questions on a mythological theme; and kids in grades 6–9 must also take a 10-item literary subtest on the *Iliad,* the *Odyssey,* the *Aeneid,* African myths, or native American myths.

Each exam, $10 ($2 if you order 6 or more)

Elementary Teachers of the Classics

American Classical League

Miami University

Oxford, OH 45056-1694

(513) 529-7741/fax (513) 529-7342

e-mail: AmericanClassicalLeague@muohio.edu

8 13 Odyssey

Take the kids on an Odyssey of their very own. This cooperative learning unit from Interact is a multifaceted group "journey" through mythology. Users read assorted classical myths and cooperate to "climb" Mt. Olympus by completing, at each of the mountain's levels, a mythology-related activity, such as turning a myth into a comic strip or making a list of English words with Greek origins. To reach the mountain's peak, kids must complete one major interactive proj-

ect. Examples include performing a mythology puppet show, publishing a mythology newspaper, or painting a mythology mural.

$37

Interact

1825 Gillespie Way, #101

El Cajon, CA 92020

(619) 448-1474 or (800) 359-0961/fax (800) 700-5093

Web site: www.interact-simulations.com

AUDIOVISUAL RESOURCES

5 12 Greathall Productions

Storyteller Jim Weiss has recorded two excellent collections of myths for young listeners. In *Greek Myths,* he tells the stories of King Midas and his disastrous golden touch, Arachne and her weaving challenge to the goddess Athena, Perseus and the snake-haired Medusa, and the Labors of Hercules. In *She and He: Adventures in Mythology,* he recounts the tales of Echo and Narcissus, Pygmalion and Galatea, kindly Baucis and Philemon, and swift-footed Atalanta and her clever husband-to-be, Hippomenes. Available on cassette or CD.

Greathall Productions

Box 5061

Charlottesville, VA 22905-5061

(800) 477-6234

10 + The Odyssey

Storyteller Odds Bodkins has recorded a 4+-hour Homeric retelling of *The Odyssey,* performed in spellbinding fashion with background accompaniment of harp and 12-string guitar. Though fascinating and often beautiful, it's also a harsh and scary story in parts; not recommended for listeners under 10. A 4-cassette or CD set.

$34.95 (cassettes) or $49.95 (CDs)

Rivertree Productions

Box 410

Bradford, NH 03221

(800) 554-1333

e-mail: rivertree@conknet.com

Web site: www.oddsbodkin.com

The Odyssey

The dramatic tale of Odysseus's adventure-filled return from the Trojan War. This video version is a 1997 Hallmark production, with spectacular scenery and an all-star cast. Armand Assante plays Odysseus. 165 minutes.

$92.98
Social Studies School Service
10200 Jefferson Blvd.
Box 802
Culver City, CA 90232-0802
(310) 839-2436 or (800) 421-4246/fax (310) 839-2249
or (800) 944-5432
e-mail: access@SocialStudies.com
Web site: SocialStudies.com

The Odyssey of Troy

An episode on the A&E Channel's *Ancient Mysteries* series, narrated by Kathleen Turner. The hour-long program covers the historical and archaeological aspects of Homer's *Iliad,* including a discussion of Heinrich Schliemann's famous discovery of the ancient city in Turkey that may or may not have been Troy.

$19.95
The Writing Company
10200 Jefferson Blvd.
Box 802
Culver City, CA 90232-0802
(310) 839-2436 or (800) 421-4246/fax (310) 839-2249
or (800) 944-5432
e-mail: access@WritingCo.com
Web site: WritingCo.com/Writing

SHAKESPEARE

CATALOGS

The Writing Company:
Shakespeare Catalog

The Writing Company publishes an impressive catalog of resources for Shakespeare students of all ages, including books about Shakespeare's life and times, abridged and unabridged versions of the plays,

activity books, games, posters, timelines, videos, audiocassettes, and computer software.

The Writing Company
10200 Jefferson Boulevard
Box 802
Culver City, CA 90232-0802
(310) 839-2436 or (800) 421-4246/fax (310) 839-2249
or (800) 944-5432
e-mail: access@WritingCo.com
Web site: WritingCo.com/Shakespeare

BOOKS

The Best of Shakespeare:
Retellings of 10 Classic Plays

E. Nesbit; Oxford University Press, 1997

Delightful storybook-like retellings of ten Shakespearean plays by E. Nesbit, author of such children's classics as *Five Children and It* and *The Phoenix and the Carpet.* Among the plays are *Romeo and Juliet, The Merchant of Venice, The Tempest, Hamlet, Macbeth,* and *As You Like It,* all recounted in child-friendly style for young readers. Illustrated with black-and-white photographs from modern Shakespeare productions.

Discovering Shakespeare Series

Fredi Olster and Rick Hamilton; Smith and Kraus, 1996

The "Discovering Shakespeare" workbooks, each of which centers around a single Shakespearean play, provide background information about plot and characters and give students an easily readable version of the original play. Their objective, explain the authors, was to "tell the story, introduce the characters, and let Shakespeare's ideas come ringing through. The difficulty, of course, is that wonderfully complex language of Shakespeare's. So we decided that the best way to introduce Shakespeare to people who were not familiar with him was . . . to translate him into the vernacular—that is, our equivalent everyday language." Each play is thus presented in an easy-to-follow four-column format: readers can compare vernacular and original versions of the dialogue, supplemented with detailed scene descriptions and stage directions. The books also include instructions for putting on a (simplified) Shakespearean performance. Titles available in the Discovering Shakespeare series include *A Midsummer Night's Dream, Romeo and Juliet,* and *The Taming of the Shrew.*

Smith and Kraus, Inc.

1 Main St.

Box 127

Lyme, NH 03768

(609) 922-5118 or (800) 895-4331

Web site: www.scy.com/ayer

Favorite Tales from Shakespeare

Bernard Miles; Checkerboard Press, 1988

Colorfully illustrated prose versions of well-known Shakespearean plays for children. *Favorite Tales* includes *Macbeth, A Midsummer Night's Dream, Romeo and Juliet, Twelfth Night, Hamlet, Well-Loved Tales, The Tempest, As You Like It, Othello, The Merry Wives of Windsor,* and *Julius Caesar.* "The plays are not easy to read," writes the author. "All I have tried to do is to dig out the stories from which the plays were made and put them back into simple modern language—as a sort of gateway into the magical world of the plays themselves. . . ." See, by the same author, *Well-Loved Tales From Shakespeare* (Rand McNally, 1986).

Ian Pollock's Illustrated King Lear

William Shakespeare; Workman, 1984

The complete and unabridged *King Lear* in high-quality full-color comic book form. "Very valuable for those students initially staggered by Shakespeare," writes Peggy O'Brien of the Folger Shakespeare Library. Also see, in the same series, *Othello,* illustrated by Oscar Zarate, and *Macbeth,* illustrated by Von.

Shakespeare and Macbeth: The Story Behind the Play

Stewart Ross; Viking, 1994

A picture-book account of Shakespeare's writing of the play *Macbeth* and its first performance before King James I at Hampton Court.

Shakespeare Made Easy Series

In the Shakespeare Made Easy books, targeted at high school–aged students, one page shows the play in the original version, while the facing page shows a "translation" in modern English. A "nonthreatening introduction to Shakespeare's immortal works." Ten

plays are available in this series, in inexpensive paperback editions: *Hamlet, Henry IV Part One, Julius Caesar, King Lear, Macbeth, The Merchant of Venice, A Midsummer Night's Dream, Romeo and Juliet, The Tempest,* and *Twelfth Night.*

Barron's Educational Series, Inc.

250 Wireless Blvd.

Hauppage, NY 11788

(516) 434-3311 or (800) 645-3476/fax (516) 434-3723

Web site: barronseduc.com

Shakespeare Stories

Leon Garfield; Houghton Mifflin, 1991

Illustrated prose versions of 12 of Shakespeare's best-known plays, among them *Twelfth Night, King Lear, The Tempest, The Merchant of Venice, Hamlet,* and *Macbeth.* These retellings retain enough of the original dialogue to give readers a feel for Shakespearean language.

Twelfth Night for Kids

Lois Burdett and Christine Coburn; Black Moss, 1994

A version of the play in rhymed couplets for kids in grades 2–4, suitable for performing "on stage" or transforming into a Shakespearean puppet show. The book includes the simplified script of the play, plus suggestions for many related activities.

William Shakespeare's The Tempest

Bruce Colville; Doubleday, 1994

A 40-page prose retelling of the tale for kids in grades 3–6, illustrated with magical oil paintings. Colville uses many quotes from the original text, which gives young readers a feel for Shakespeare's powerful language. Also by Colville in the same format is the equally beautiful *William Shakespeare's A Midsummer Night's Dream.*

BOOKS ABOUT SHAKESPEARE

Bard of Avon

Diane Stanley and Peter Vennema; Morrow Junior Books, 1992

A short, colorfully illustrated oversize biography of Shakespeare: his life, times, and plays. Recommended for kids in grades 4–8, but can be enjoyed by younger listeners.

A Child's Portrait of Shakespeare

Lois Burdett; Black Moss, 1995

A life of Shakespeare in rhyme—"It must have been exciting in the year that Will was five/When the players of the Queen at his village did arrive"—adorably illustrated with colorful drawings by second- and third-graders.

The Friendly Shakespeare

Norrie Epstein; Viking/Penguin, 1993

Subtitled "A Thoroughly Painless Guide to the Best of the Bard," this 550-page tome is a fascinating, factual, and funny account of all things Shakespearean. Among the topics covered are the question of what Shakespeare looked like, with reproductions of the (bald and best-known) Droeshout Engraving and of Pablo Picasso's scribbled portrait; an account of the archaeological excavation of the site of the Globe Theatre (they found a bear's skull); catchy chronological summaries of all the plays ("The Forest of Arden," writes Epstein, under *As You Like It*, "is a sylvan sanatorium for the politically exiled, the lovelorn, and assorted undesirables."); a glossary of Shakespearean insults; photographs of scenes from Shakespearean films and stage productions; and quotes from unrepentant Shakespeare haters, such as George Bernard Shaw, who called Shakespeare's ideas "platitudinous fudge." There's also a summary of the "Who Really Wrote the Plays?" debate and some nice instructions for how to stage a Shakespearean sword fight.

Shakespeare and His Theatre

John Russell Brown; Lothrop, Lee & Shepard, 1982

The illustrated story of the Globe Theatre and the persons who performed in it. The behind-the-scenes details are especially intriguing: there's an account, for example, of a scene in *Cymbeline* in which a small overhead crane lowered from the "heavens" a throne shaped like an eagle carrying the god Jupiter.

William Shakespeare: The Extraordinary Life of the Most Successful Writer of All Time

Andrew Gurr; HarperPerennial, 1995

A fascinating 192-page account of Shakespeare's life and times, illustrated with 300 superb color photographs of Shakespearean reenactors. The pictures give readers an enthralling look at what life was really like in Shakespeare's day: imagine photographs of young Shakespeare with his parents, of Queen Elizabeth I attending a performance of *The Merry Wives of Windsor,* of the backstage staff of the Globe Theatre. The text is detailed and interesting—the author is an authority on Shakespeare—and is stuffed with information on everything from the plague and the Spanish Armada to the secrets behind the special effects during theater performances. For high school–aged readers.

Will's Quill

Don Freeman; Viking, 1975

A picture-book tale for young readers about Will, the helpful goose who provided William Shakespeare with the quills for writing his famous plays.

ACTIVITY AND COLORING BOOKS

A Children's Macbeth

A coloring book of costumed kids performing various scenes from Shakespeare's *Macbeth*. The pictures are accompanied by a simplified text, which can be used by the dramatically inclined to stage a home version of the play.

$4.95

Bellerophon Books

36 Ancapa St.

Santa Barbara, CA 93101

(800) 253-9943/fax (800) 965-8286

Shakespeare Coloring Book

A history of Shakespeare in black-and-white line drawings ("from the very old Peacham drawing to Ronald Searle's illustrations of Richard Burton as Henry V and Orson Welles as Othello") with an accompanying text.

$4.95

Bellerophon Books

36 Ancapa St.

Santa Barbara, CA 93101

(800) 253-9943/fax (800) 965-8286

Shakespeare's Theatre and Young Shakespeare

Portfolios of materials on the life of Shakespeare and the Elizabethan theater. Each portfolio includes several illustrated historical "Broadsheet Essays" plus an assortment of reproduction historical documents. "Shakespeare's Theatre" includes four illustrated essays ("The Elizabethan Theatre," "The Chamberlain's Men and the Globe Theatre," "The King's Men and a Private Theatre," and "What Was a Performance Like?") and 10 historical documents, including pages from the First Folio editions of 1623, a contract for the building of the Fortune Theatre in 1599, a model of the Globe Playhouse, and an "Inventory of Costumes." "Young Shakespeare" includes seven illustrated essays ("Home," "School," "Shakespeare Learns to Write," "Heroes," "Books," "Games," and "Young Shakespeare Goes to London") and seven documents, among them period maps of London and Westminster, photographs of Elizabethan buildings known to Shakespeare, a page from Holinshed's *Chronicles* (the source of Shakespeare's *Macbeth*), and an engraved portrait of Shakespeare.

Each portfolio (including a study guide and reproducible student worksheets), $37

Jackdaw Publications

Box 503

Amawalk, NY 10501

(800) 789-0022/fax (800) 962-9101

GAMES AND HANDS-ON ACTIVITIES

Elizabethan Costumes Paper Dolls

For those interested in what Shakespeare and his audience wore, this set of paper dolls—one male, one female—includes 16 costumes of the time, complete with doublets, cloaks, plumed hats, farthingales, ruffs, and sweeping velvet gowns.

$3.95

Dover Publications, Inc.

31 East Second St.

Mineola, NY 11501

The Game of Shakespeare

A board game of Shakespeare's plays in which players attempt to move their pieces—chess pawns and knights—around the playing path to the Globe Theater. Each space on the path directs players to make a move based on the plot of one of the plays. Land on Elsinore, for example, and the ghost sends you back to the beginning of "Hamlet"; land in the Forest of Arden, and you meet your true love and win an extra roll of the dice. The game can be played at several levels, from the basic, which requires no knowledge of Shakespeare, to the advanced, in which players are challenged to name characters from each of the plays or to identify the sources of Shakespearean quotations from a pack of 180 Quotation Cards. (In which play, for example, do you find "Brevity is the soul of wit"?) The playing board features eight plays in detail: *The Taming of the Shrew, Romeo and Juliet, King Lear, Hamlet, The Tempest, Macbeth, The Merchant of Venice,* and *Othello.* An accompanying booklet contains plot summaries of all 37 of Shakespeare's plays, a chronology, and a list of quotation sources.

$25

Avalon Hill Game Co.

4517 Harford Rd.

Baltimore, MD 21214

(410) 254-9200 or (800) 999-3222/fax (410) 254-0991

e-mail: AH GAMES@aol.com

Web site: www.avalonhill.com

The Play's the Thing

The Play's the Thing includes a colorful playing board, based on Shakespeare's Globe Theatre, and three packs of cards, each based on a different Shakespearean play: *Hamlet, Romeo and Juliet,* and *Julius Caesar.* Each pack includes a mix of plot cards, which summarize the plot of the play; character cards, describing each of the main characters; and quote cards, listing assorted notable quotations. Players decide which of the three plays they want to perform, then advance their playing pieces, each representing an Elizabethan actor or actress, around the board, attempting to collect sets of matching cards that correspond to "scenes" in the featured play. En route, they variously receive rave reviews ("Queen Elizabeth applauds you!") or suffer stage mishaps ("The plague forces all playhouses to close"), answer questions about the play, recite quotations, imitate characters, or perform very brief dramatic scenes. The instruction manual describes several permutations of the basic game, among them "Don't Quote Me," in which one player reads a quotation and the other guesses the speaker, and "Plot Lines," in which players order the 13 plot cards in the playing pack in correct sequence.

Familiarity with the plots of the plays makes for a richer game experience but is not strictly necessary— the game can be enjoyed by novices as well as seasoned Shakespeare students. For those who have exhausted the potential of *Hamlet, Romeo and Juliet,* and *Julius Caesar,* supplemental card packs are available separately: the "Tragedy" set includes *Macbeth, King Lear,* and *Othello;* "Comedy" includes *As You Like It, A Midsummer's Night's Dream,* and *Twelfth Night. The Play's the Thing* is recommended for players aged 12 and up.

> Master game, $30; supplemental card packs, $12
> Aristoplay
> 450 S. Wagner Rd.
> Ann Arbor, MI 48107
> (800) 634-7738 or (888) 428-GAME/fax (734) 995-4611
> Web site: www.aristoplay.com

Shakespeare Festival

A hands-on program with complete instructions for creating your own Shakespeare Festival. The program, contained in a seven-section looseleaf notebook, is aimed at grades 6–8 school classrooms but adapts well to any enthusiastic group. The notebook is crammed with directions and suggestions, including ideas for making Shakespeare buttons, holding a quotation contest, organizing a Shakespearean parade in costume, designing puppet shows, and throwing a royal Shakespearean banquet.

> Complete program plans, $43
> Interact
> 1825 Gillespie Way, #101
> El Cajon, CA 92020
> (619) 448-1474 or (800) 359-0961/fax (619) 448-6722
> Web site: www.interact-simulations.com

Shakespeare Playing Cards

A double deck of playing cards illustrated with characters and popular quotations from Shakespeare's plays. Pictured characters include Hamlet, Julius Caesar, Lady Macbeth, Cleopatra, King Lear, Portia, and Iago.

> $12.95
> U.S. Games Systems, Inc.
> 179 Ludlow St.
> Stamford, CT 06902
> (203) 353-8400 or (800) 544-2637

AUDIOVISUAL SHAKESPEARE

Audiocassettes

ALL Recorded Books carries a number of unabridged readings of Shakespearean plays on cassette tapes, including *All's Well That Ends Well, As You Like It, Hamlet, Julius Caesar, King Lear, Macbeth, The Merchant of Venice, A Midsummer Night's Dream, Othello, Romeo and Juliet,* and *The Taming of the Shrew.*

> Recorded Books, Inc.
> 270 Skipjack Rd.
> Prince Frederick, MD 20678
> (800) 638-1304/fax (410) 535-5499

Younger listeners, however, will likely prefer storyteller Jim Weiss's *Shakespeare for Children* from Greathall Productions. *Shakespeare for Children* includes the stories of two Shakespearean comedies, *A Midsummer Night's Dream* and *The Taming of the Shrew.* Both are delightful: Weiss adroitly manages to preserve the rich flavor of the original plays while making the plot understandable—and thoroughly enjoyable—for kids.

> Greathall Productions
> Box 5061
> Charlottesville, VA 22905-5061
> (800) 477-6234

Videos

ALL Many excellent film versions of Shakespearean plays are available on videotape, among them recent productions of *Hamlet, Henry V, Much Ado About Nothing,* and *Romeo and Juliet.* All are available from Sundance, along with *Julius Caesar* (starring Charlton Heston and Jason Robards, 1970), *Macbeth* (Orson Wells, 1948), *A Midsummer Night's Dream* (James Cagney, Olivia de Havilland, and Mickey Rooney, 1935), and *The Taming of the Shrew* (Elizabeth Taylor and Richard Burton, 1968).

READING

Sundance

Box 326

Littleton, MA 01460-9936

(800) 343-8204/fax (800) 456-2419

For younger viewers, Schoolmasters Video carries a series of short, animated versions of six Shakespearean plays: *Hamlet, The Tempest, Twelfth Night, Romeo and Juliet, Macbeth,* and *A Midsummer Night's Dream.* Many of the voices are those of members of England's Royal Shakespeare Company. Each video runs 30 minutes.

Schoolmasters Video

745 State Circle

Box 1941

Ann Arbor, MI 48106

(800) 521-2832/fax (313) 761-8711

Web site: www.school-tech.com

ON-LINE SHAKESPEARE

The Complete Works of William Shakespeare

The Complete Works, listed by genre (comedy, tragedy, history, or poetry). The site includes a list of famous Shakespearean quotations, a chronological listing of the plays, discussion areas, and links to many other related resources.

the-tech.mit.edu/Shakespeare/works.html

Shakespeare and the Globe

An on-line guide to the Globe Theatre, past and reconstructed present.

www.rdg.ac.uk/AcaDepts/In/Globe/home.html

GOOD BOOKS

How to know which books are appropriate for which kids? Our own choices were—still are—largely a matter of guesswork; and those guesses seldom revolved around the age recommendations printed so helpfully on the back of the book. Any book-choosing parent knows that there are no typical "grades K–2" aged readers: there are only specific individuals, with indi-

vidual tastes, interests, and senses of humor. Kids also have distinctly different levels of reading ability, which necessarily affects choices of books for them to tackle on their own. For adults attempting to judge difficulty levels of children's books, one helpful source is *Best Books for Beginning Readers* (Thomas G. Gunning; Allyn & Bacon, 1998; see page 59).

Qualitative Assessment of Text Difficulty: A Practical Guide for Teachers and Writers

Jeanne S. Chall, Glenda S. Bissex, Sue S. Conrad, and Susan Harris-Sharples; Brookline Books, 1996

The authors have attempted to come up with a method for assessing text difficulty, based on such factors as vocabulary size, complexity of sentence structure, and requirements for background knowledge, assigning books a reading level, from Level 1—manageable by the average first grader—to Level 13–15 (college). Since it is difficult to compare books across genres, they use several different scales, such as literature, popular fiction, life science, and narrative social studies, on which to assess sample books. On the literature scale, for example, Dr. Seuss's *Green Eggs and Ham* rates a Level 1, Robert Newton Peck's *Soup and Me* a Level 4, Edgar Allan Poe's "The Pit and the Pendulum" a Level 9–10, and Herman Melville's *Billy Budd* a Level 13–15.

Scale or no scale, our boys have been consistently inconsistent, variously reading books deemed too old for them, too young for them, or precisely right—or rejecting the same. Age recommendations can help book buyers make a guess, but the real authority when it comes to text difficulty is always the reader.

FOR YOUNGER READERS

Alastair's Time Machine

Marilyn Sadler; Simon & Schuster, 1986

Alastair Grittle, boy of science, builds a time machine in his basement for Twickadilly's Second Science Competition. It works beautifully, but no one believes him.

Also see, by the same author, *Alastair in Outer Space* (Simon & Schuster, 1985) and *Alastair and the Alien Invasion* (Simon & Schuster, 1994).

Alexander and the Terrible, Horrible, No Good, Very Bad Day

Judith Viorst; Aladdin, 1987

Alexander has a terrible, horrible day: gum sticks in his hair, his teacher fails to appreciate his picture of the invisible castle, his mother forgets to put dessert in his lunchbox, the dentist finds a cavity in his teeth, and he has to wear his railroad train pajamas. (He hates his railroad train pajamas.) His mother explains that some days are like that. Also see, by the same author, *Alexander Who Used to Be Rich Last Sunday* (Aladdin, 1980) and *Alexander Who's Not (Do You Hear Me? I Mean It!) Going to Move* (Atheneum, 1995).

The Amazing Bone

William Steig; Sunburst, 1993

Pearl, a piglet, finds a magical talking bone in the woods on the way home from school. Together they manage to escape from an evil (but dapper) fox, who plans to cook Pearl for dinner. Also see, by the same author, *Amos and Boris* (Sunburst, 1992), *Brave Irene* (Farrar, Straus & Giroux, 1988), *Doctor DeSoto* (Sunburst, 1990), *Solomon and the Rusty Nail* (Farrar, Straus & Giroux, 1987), and *Sylvester and the Magic Pebble* (Aladdin, 1987).

Amelia Bedelia

Peggy Parish; HarperCollins, 1992

Amelia Bedelia is a scatterbrained housekeeper who gets into trouble through her literal interpretations of figures of speech. Asked to "draw the drapes," Amelia sits down with sketch pad and pencil. Luckily all is forgiven because she makes simply delicious pies. There are 12 books in the *Amelia Bedelia* series.

A Bear Called Paddington

Michael Bond; Houghton Mifflin, 1960

Paddington Bear arrives at London's Paddington Station from "Darkest Peru" and is adopted by the Brown family. Paddington is a well-meaning, but highly troublesome, bear, and the endearing stories of his bumbling (and funny) adventures continue through 10 more multichaptered volumes.

The Bed Book

Sylvia Plath; HarperTrophy, 1989

A poetic illustrated account of extraordinary beds, including Acrobat Beds, Submarine Beds, and Jet-Propelled Beds.

Blueberries for Sal

Robert McCloskey; Viking, 1976

Sal and her mother are out picking blueberries; so are a mother bear and her cub. Somehow, to the horror of all concerned, kids and mothers get switched—but all sorts itself out happily at the end. Also see *One Morning in Maine* (Viking, 1976), in which Sal loses a tooth.

Bread and Jam for Frances

Russell Hoban; HarperTrophy, 1993

Frances, an adorable and opinionated little badger, decides to eat nothing for breakfast, lunch, or dinner but her favorite bread and jam. Also see, by the same author, *A Baby Sister for Frances* (HarperTrophy, 1993), *A Bargain for Frances* (HarperCollins, 1992), *Bedtime for Frances* (HarperTrophy, 1995), *Best Friends for Frances* (HarperTrophy, 1994), and *A Birthday for Frances* (HarperTrophy, 1994).

The Cat in the Hat

Dr. Seuss; Random House, 1957

Now a classic; most parents of American preschoolers can probably recite most of it by heart. The rhyming tale of the irrepressible cat in the tall striped hat who drops by to visit and creates havoc. Also see, by the same author, *The Cat in the Hat Comes Back* (Random House, 1958).

The Church Mouse

Graham Oakley; Macmillan, 1980

Arthur, the church mouse, shares the vestry with Sampson, the ginger-colored church cat, who, after years of listening to sermons about love and brotherhood, has taken a vow never to harm mice. In this, the first book of a series, Arthur brings home an obstreperous population of mouse friends and manages to save the church from a burglary. Very cleverly written and illustrated, with a British tongue-in-cheek twist. There are several more titles in the series.

Corduroy
4 8 Don Freeman; Viking, 1976

A feisty little teddy bear wanders away from the toy department in search of his missing overall button and has after-hours adventures in the closed store. There are several more titles about Corduroy, among them *A Pocket for Corduroy* (Viking, 1980).

Cross-Country Cat
4 8 Mary Calhoun; Mulberry, 1986

Henry, an extremely competent Siamese cat, is left behind at the mountain cabin after a family ski vacation. He fashions himself a pair of cross-country skis and manages to trek back to civilization. Also see, by the same author, *Hot-Air Henry* (William Morrow, 1984), in which Henry takes to the skies in a hot-air balloon.

Curious George
4 8 H. A. Rey; Houghton Mifflin, 1994

George, a curious and adventurous little monkey, is captured in Africa and taken home to the big city by the Man in the Yellow Hat. Once there, George's curiosity gets him into all kinds of trouble. The tale of George's many exploits continues through 18 more books.

Donna O'Neeshuck Was Chased By Some Cows
4 8 Bill Grossman; HarperTrophy, 1991

It started one day when Donna, at play, patted a cow on the head. The pat was so successful that Donna, in verse, is soon being chased by pat-demanding cows, mooses, gooses, and sows, to say nothing of horses, bears, a herd of buffalo, and all the people in town.

Do Not Open
4 8 Brinton Turkle; E. P. Dutton, 1993

Miss Moody and her cat, Captain Kidd, find a mysterious purple bottle washed up on the beach, with a warning message scratched on the side: *Do not open.* She opens and releases a nasty genie.

Elbert's Bad Word
4 8 Audrey Wood; Harcourt Brace, 1996

Elbert catches an unprintable word, which loudly escapes, to the horror of all, at a garden party when a croquet mallet falls on his big toe. His mother washes his mouth out with soap, which doesn't help at all; finally the estate gardener, who is also a magician, gives him a wonderful cure.

Everyone Knows What a Dragon Looks Like
4 8 Jay Williams; Aladdin, 1988

All the important officials in the city of Wu claim to know what a dragon looks like, but only Han, the small boy who works as a sweeper at the city gate, believes that a dragon could appear as a small, fat, bald old man.

The 500 Hats of Bartholomew Cubbins
4 8 Dr. Seuss; Random House, 1989

Bartholomew Cubbins politely tries to take off his hat before the king, but more and more hats keep magically appearing on his head, each more wonderful and elaborate than the last. Also see *Bartholomew and the Oobleck* (Random House, 1949), in which the king, bored with the weather, asks the castle magicians to cause something different to fall from the sky. He gets the dreadful green oobleck.

Frederick
4 8 Leo Lionni; Alfred A. Knopf, 1990

Frederick the field mouse doesn't gather seeds for the winter; instead he gathers memories, stories, and poems.

Frog and Toad Together

4 8 Arnold Lobel; HarperTrophy, 1979

Lobel's Frog and Toad may be the most delightful duo in easy readers. Toad is grumpy and disaster-prone: he falls off his sled and loses his buttons; his garden seeds don't grow fast enough; his kite won't fly; his ice-cream cones melt; and he looks silly in his bathing suit. He manages to overcome most of this, though, with the help of his cheerful and level-headed friend Frog. Also see *Frog and Toad Are Friends* (HarperTrophy, 1979), *Frog and Toad All Year* (HarperTrophy, 1984), and *Days With Frog and Toad* (HarperTrophy, 1984).

4 8 George and Martha

James Marshall; Houghton Mifflin, 1974

Five very short stories about two very large friends. George and Martha are a pair of hippos who have a few lessons to learn about the art of getting along with each other.

4 9 The Glorious Flight: Across the Channel With Louis Bleriot

Alice and Martin Provensen; Viking, 1987

The true picture-book tale of Papa Bleriot, father of Alceste, Charmaine, Suzette, Jeannot, and Gabrielle, who finally makes it across the English Channel after a series of airplane disasters.

4 8 Gregory the Terrible Eater

Mitchell Sharmat; Scholastic, 1989

Gregory, a small goat, spurns neckties and newspaper in favor of fruits, vegetables, and other healthy foods. His upset parents take him to a doctor.

4 9 The Jolly Postman, or Other People's Letters

Janet and Allan Ahlberg; Little, Brown, 1986

A birthday invitation to Baby Bear from Goldilocks, an advertising circular to the Wicked Witch, a postcard to the giant from Jack, and more, all tucked into the envelope-like pages of the book, just as delivered by the Jolly Postman. Also see *The Jolly Christmas Postman* (Little, Brown, 1991).

6 9 Jumanji

Chris Van Allsburg; Houghton Mifflin, 1981

Two children find an abandoned board game, "Jumanji," under a tree in the park. As they play it, the game comes alive, complete with lurking lions, hissing snakes, and a destructive band of monkeys. Also see, by the same author, *The Stranger* (Houghton Mifflin, 1986), *The Wreck of the Zephyr* (Houghton Mifflin, 1983), and *The Polar Express* (Houghton Mifflin, 1985).

6 9 Keep the Lights Burning, Abbie!

Peter and Connie Roop; Carolrhoda, 1987

Based on the true story of young Abbie, who has to keep the lighthouse lights burning through a frightening storm while her father has gone to the mainland to buy medicine for her sick mother.

4 8 The Legend of the Indian Paintbrush

Tomie de Paola; Paper Star, 1996

The tale of how the flowering Indian Paintbrush was brought to earth by Little Gopher, who dreams of painting the colors of the sunset on his buckskin canvas. Also see *The Legend of the Bluebonnet* (Paper Star, 1996).

3 8 Little Bear

Else Homelund Minarik; HarperTrophy, 1978

Small, gentle tales of the everyday activities of Little Bear, from his demands for warmer clothes to play in the snow to the account of his imaginary trip to the moon. By the same author, also see *A Kiss for Little Bear* (HarperTrophy, 1984), *Little Bear's Friend* (HarperTrophy, 1984), *Little Bear's Visit* (HarperTrophy, 1979), and *Father Bear Comes Home* (HarperTrophy, 1978).

4 8 Madeline

Ludwig Bemelmans; Puffin, 1996

In an old house in Paris, all covered with vines, live 12 little girls, in two straight lines: 11 are well-behaved small orphans, but the youngest is the rambunctious, red-headed Madeline. There are several sequels.

5 10 Many Moons

James Thurber; Harcourt Brace, 1987

The wonderful tale of Princess Lenore, who falls ill from eating raspberry tarts and will recover only if her father gets her the moon. With the help of the wise and imaginative court jester, he does so.

4 8 Mike Mulligan and His Steam Shovel

Virginia Lee Burton; Houghton Mifflin, 1977

Mike Mulligan and his steam shovel, Mary Ann, bravely set out to dig the cellar for the Popperville Town Hall in just one day. Also see, by the same author, *Katy and the Big Snow* (Sandpiper, 1974).

Ming Lo Moves the Mountain
4 8 Arnold Lobel; Mulberry, 1993

Ming Lo and his wife live miserably in the dark, cold shadow of a looming mountain. With the help of the village wise man, they eventually manage (sort of) to make the mountain move.

Miss Rumphius
5 9 Barbara Cooney; Viking, 1985

Miss Rumphius sets out to see the world and finally, tired of traveling, returns home, determined to do something to make the world more beautiful. And she does. The illustrations are enchanting. Also see *Island Boy* (Puffin, 1991).

Mouse Tales
4 8 Arnold Lobel; HarperTrophy, 1978

An imaginative father mouse puts his seven children to sleep by telling seven clever stories: there's the tale of a testy wishing well that says "Ouch!" when pennies are dropped in it; of a very clean mouse whose overflowing bathtub floods the town; and of a chorus of friendly crickets who sing much too loudly. Also see *Mouse Soup* (HarperTrophy, 1983), in which a quick-thinking mouse, captured by a hungry weasel, manages to talk his way out of the soup pot by telling four stories.

Mufaro's Beautiful Daughters
4 8 John Steptoe; Lothrop, Lee & Shepard, 1987

A retelling of the West African Cinderella tale of Mufaro's two beautiful daughters, one nasty and ambitious, the other generous and kind, who both set out to marry the king.

My Father's Dragon
6 9 Ruth Stiles Gannett; Alfred A. Knopf, 1988

At the urging of a friendly cat, young Elmer Elevator, equipped with a knapsack full of tangerines and lollipops, sets out for Wild Island, where he braves tigers and alligators in order to free a little captive dragon. Sequels include *Elmer and the Dragon* (Alfred A. Knopf, 1987) and *The Dragons of Blueland* (Alfred A. Knopf, 1989).

Paul Bunyan
4 9 Steven Kellogg; William Morrow, 1985

The tall tale of the gigantic lumberjack, his enormous sidekick, Babe the Blue Ox, and their exaggerated adventures. Also see, by the same author, *Pecos Bill* (Mulberry, 1992), *Mike Fink* (William Morrow, 1992), and *Johnny Appleseed* (Mulberry, 1996).

The Quilt Story
4 8 Tony Johnston; Paper Star, 1996

A handmade quilt, stitched with a pattern of falling stars, comforts two generations of little girls moving across the country.

Rabbit Hill
4 8 Robert Lawson; Viking, 1982

Little Georgie the rabbit and all his friends and relations on the Hill are in an uproar because new folks are moving into the long-empty Big House.

The Rainbow Goblins
5 9 Ul de Rico; Thames & Hudson, 1994

The beautifully illustrated story of seven greedy goblins who attempt to gobble all the colors of the rainbow. Also see the sequel, *The White Goblin* (Thames & Hudson, 1996).

Ramona the Pest
4 8 Beverly Cleary; Camelot, 1996

Ramona, one of the funniest and most genuine kids in children's literature, has a bumpy year in kindergarten. A chapter book that makes a great read-aloud for younger brothers and sisters. Caleb at five, often deemed a pest by his older brothers, sympathized and loved it.

The Red Balloon
4 9 Albert Lamorisse; Doubleday, 1978

Pascal, a small boy is Paris, makes friends with a gallant and magical red balloon. Illustrated with delightful color photographs.

Rotten Ralph
4 8 Jack Gantos; Houghton Mifflin, 1980

Ralph is Sarah's bright red, badly behaved, and thoroughly rotten cat, but kindhearted Sarah loves him anyway. There are several sequels, among them *Worse*

Than Rotten Ralph (Houghton Mifflin, 1982), *Happy Birthday, Rotten Ralph* (Sandpiper, 1994), and *Not So Rotten Ralph* (Houghton Mifflin, 1997).

Stone Soup
Marcia Brown; Aladdin, 1987

A version of the classic tale in which a trio of clever soldiers manage to feed themselves and an entire French village with soup made from a single stone.

The Story of Ferdinand
Munro Leaf; Viking, 1977

The perennially endearing story of the peace-loving bull who would rather sit under the cork tree and smell the flowers than fight in the bullring.

The Tale of Peter Rabbit
Beatrix Potter; Frederick Warne, 1987

The enchantingly illustrated story of the disobedient Peter, who wiggles under the gate into Mr. McGregor's garden and nearly doesn't get back out again. There are many other little animal tales by Potter, published in various editions, among them *The Tale of Benjamin Bunny, The Tale of Squirrel Nutkin, The Tale of Mrs. Tiggywinkle, The Tale of Jeremy Fisher,* and *The Tale of Jemima Puddleduck.*

Thy Friend, Obadiah
Brinton Turkle; Viking, 1982

Obadiah, a small Quaker boy with a knack for getting himself into trouble, lives with his large and understanding family in 19th-century Philadelphia. There are several sequels, among them *Obadiah the Bold* (Viking, 1988) and *The Adventures of Obadiah* (Viking, 1988).

Tikki Tikki Tembo
Arlene Mosel; Henry Holt, 1989

Once upon a time in China, first-born sons had very long names. Then one day Tikki tikki tembo-no sa rembo-chari bari ruchi-pip peri pembo fell down the well.

The True Story of the 3 Little Pigs
Jon Scieszka; Puffin, 1996

"I'm the wolf," this hilarious book begins. "Alexander T. Wolf. You can call me Al." This is the story of the three little pigs (rude little porkers) from the Wolf's point of view. He was, it turns out, neither Big nor Bad; he simply wanted to borrow a cup of sugar to make a birthday cake for his dear old granny. With priceless illustrations by Lane Smith.

The Velveteen Rabbit
Margery Williams; Camelot, 1996

The story of a most beloved stuffed bunny who finally, magically, becomes real.

William's Doll
Charlotte Zolotow; HarperTrophy, 1985

William wants a doll. His father gets him, instead, a basketball and an electric train, but finally his sensible grandmother buys him a doll, "so he can practice being a father."

Winnie-the-Pooh
A. A. Milne; Puffin, 1992

The adventures of the plump and muddled Pooh, a Bear of Very Little Brain, Piglet, Owl, Eeyore, the mournful donkey, the brisk busybody Rabbit, and all the other inhabitants of the Enchanted Forest and Hundred-Acre Wood. Also see *The House on Pooh Corner* (Puffin, 1992).

The Worst Person in the World
James Stevenson; Mulberry, 1995

The Worst Person, who eats lemons and lives in a house covered with poison ivy, becomes less crochety after meeting an imperturbably cheerful monster named Ugly. Sequels include *Worse Than the Worst* (Greenwillow, 1994) and *The Worst goes South* (Greenwillow, 1995).

FOR INTERMEDIATE READERS

Abel's Island
William Steig; Farrar, Straus & Giroux, 1986

Abel, a fashionably elegant and wholly urban city mouse, is swept out to sea in a storm and stranded on a desert island. He survives, through ingenuity, imagination, and hard work, and by the time he gets back home again, has learned some valuable lessons about life.

The Adventures of King Midas
7 11 Lynne Reid Banks; Camelot, 1993

A delightful retelling of the classic tale of unhappy King Midas, who foolishly asks that everything he touches be turned to gold. In Banks's version, he gets rid of his golden touch with the help of a mumbo—which, Banks explains, is the proper name for a baby dragon.

Alice's Adventures in Wonderland
7 + Lewis Carroll; St. Martin's Press, 1991

The classic tale of Alice, who tumbles down the world's most famous rabbit hole. This edition includes the wonderful illustrations by Tenniel. The further adventures of Alice are described in the companion volume, *Through the Looking-Glass.*

The Bat-Poet
6 12 Randall Jarrell; HarperTrophy, 1996

Jarrell's bat—"a light brown bat, the color of coffee with cream in it"—is a poet seeking new experiences. He stays awake through the day, writing poems about the new friends he finds there, but his masterpiece, composed just as he falls asleep for the long winter, is about the dark, velvety world of bats.

The BFG
9 12 Roald Dahl; Random House, 1993

Eight-year-old Sophie is plucked out of the orphanage window by the Big Friendly Giant, who roams the world blowing dreams into the windows of sleeping children. Together they manage to defeat an evil band of people-eating giants. The BFG's inventive language, once you get the hang of it, is wonderful, from "snozzcumber" to "scrumdiddlyumptious" to "whizzpopping."

The Bookstore Mouse
8 11 Gary A. Lippincott; Harcourt Brace, 1995

Cervantes, the bookstore mouse, a dedicated consumer of words, falls into a book, where he meets Sigfried, unhappily at work copying manuscripts in a monastery scriptorium. Together they set off on a very wordy adventure, confronting the Jargon Giant and the Censor, a fearful firebreathing dragon who captures poets and troubadors and chains them to the wall of his cave.

The Borrowers
9 12 Mary Norton; Harcourt Brace, 1998

The enchanting story of the Borrowers—Pod, Homily, and their daughter, Arriety—who live under the floor of Great-Aunt Sophy's Victorian mansion. Arriety, flouting Borrower tradition, makes friends with a human boy. Sequels include *The Borrowers Afield* (Harcourt Brace, 1998), *The Borrowers Afloat* (Harcourt Brace, 1998), *The Borrowers Aloft* (Harcourt Brace, 1998), and *The Borrowers Avenged* (Harcourt Brace, 1984).

The Boxcar Children
7 10 Gertrude Chandler Warner; Albert Whitman, 1989

Four orphaned children, afraid of being separated, run away and set up housekeeping in an abandoned boxcar. All ends happily when they are found and adopted by their wealthy grandfather. There are many more books about the Boxcar Children, in which they solve a series of mild mysteries.

Bunnicula
7 10 Deborah Howe and James Howe; Aladdin, 1996

Harold, the family dog, is the narrator of this hilarious tale, in which he and Chester, the overexcitable cat, cope with the arrival of a new pet: Bunnicula, a black-and-white bunny (with fangs) found in a movie theater during a showing of *Dracula*. Also see the sequels, *The Celery Stalks At Midnight* (Avon Books, 1989), *Howliday Inn* (Avon Books, 1996), *Nighty-Nightmare* (Aladdin, 1997), and *Return to Howliday Inn* (Camelot, 1993).

Caddie Woodlawn
8 12 Carol Ryrie Brink; Aladdin, 1990

Caddie, the title character, is a feisty and independent-minded 11-year-old, growing up in the mid-19th century on the Wisconsin frontier. In a subplot, the family must decide whether to leave Wisconsin for England, when the Woodlawn father turns out to be the heir to an aristocratic estate.

The Cat Who Went to Heaven
9 12 Elizabeth Coatsworth; Aladdin, 1990

A poor Japanese artist paints a miraculous picture with the help of his white cat, Good Fortune.

Catwings
7 | 10 Ursula Le Guin; Scholastic, 1990

"Mrs. Jane Tabby could not explain why all of her four children had wings." A charmer for cat lovers about the four winged kittens who leave the dangerous city to find a new safe home. Also see *Catwings Return* (Scholastic, 1991) and *Wonderful Alexander and the Catwings* (Little Apple, 1996).

Charlie and the Chocolate Factory
8 | 12 Roald Dahl; Viking, 1994

Little Charlie Bucket finds a golden ticket in a chocolate bar, which entitles him to a fantastic tour of Willie Wonka's fabulous chocolate factory, along with the other golden-ticket holders, a collection of greedy and dreadful children who all come to deservedly bad ends. Also see the sequel, *Charlie and the Great Glass Elevator* (Viking, 1988).

Charlotte's Web
7 | 11 E. B. White; HarperCollins, 1994

Charlotte, the wise and highly literate spider, befriends and saves the life of Wilbur, the "terrific, radiant, humble" pig. Also see, by the same author, *Stuart Little* (HarperCollins, 1974) and *The Trumpet of the Swan* (HarperTrophy, 1973).

The Chronicles of Narnia
8 | 12 C. S. Lewis; Macmillan, 1950

In *The Lion, the Witch, and the Wardrobe,* the first book of this now classic series, four children pass through the back of a magical wardrobe into Narnia, a wonderful kingdom under the rule of the wicked White Witch who keeps the land in eternal winter (but never Christmas) and uses a magic wand to turn her enemies into stone. The children, with the help of Aslan, the great Lion, overthrow the Witch and become kings and queens of Narnia in a castle by the sea. Other books in the series are *Prince Caspian, The Voyage of the Dawn Treader, The Silver Chair, The Horse and His Boy, The Magician's Nephew,* and *The Last Battle.*

The Cricket in Times Square
8 | 12 George Selden; Yearling, 1970

Chester the very musical cricket is carried in a picnic basket to New York City, where he ends up living in the subway station under Times Square along with friends Harry, a cat, Tucker, a mouse, and Mario, the little boy whose parents run the nearby newstand.

David and the Phoenix
8 | 11 Edward Ormondroyd; Scholastic, 1981

David climbs a mountain and discovers the erudite Phoenix, who offers to take over his education. Together they embark upon a series of adventures with competitive witches, practical-joke-playing leprechauns, aggressive griffins, and a sleepy Sea Serpent—and, with the help of a Banshee, manage to defeat a Phoenix-stalking Scientist.

The Devil's Storybook
9 | 12 Natalie Babbitt; Farrar, Straus & Giroux, 1985

A collection of ten thought-provoking stories, all centering around the activities of the clever, but not always successful, devil. Also see *The Devil's Other Storybook* (Farrar, Straus & Giroux, 1989).

The Doll's House
9 | 12 Rumer Godden; Viking, 1976

The doll's house once belonged to Emily and Charlotte's great-grandmother, as did the dolls: Totty, the brave little farthing doll, who always remembers that she was made from the wood of a strong tree, and the elegant, conceited, and villainous Marchpane.

Encyclopedia Brown: Boy Detective
9 | 12 Donald Sobol; Bantam Skylark, 1985

Ten-year-old Encyclopedia (his real name is Leroy) Brown is the world's greatest boy sleuth. This is the first collection of Encyclopedia Brown mysteries; there are many others. Each is a collection of short, intriguing mysteries.

Freddy the Detective
7 | 11 Walter R. Brooks; Overlook Press, 1997

In this volume, Freddy, the adventuresome and versatile pig, decides to become a detective. With the help of his animal friends on the Bean farm, he brings Simon the rat and his evil gang to justice. There are many books in this humorous series, all starring the unsinkable Freddy.

From the Mixed-Up Files of Mrs. Basil E. Frankweiler

E. L. Konigsberg; Aladdin, 1987

Claudia and Jamie run away from home to live in hiding in the Metropolitan Museum of Art, where they solve a mystery about a little marble angel that may (or may not) have been sculpted by Michelangelo.

Half Magic

Edward Eager; Harcourt Brace, 1989

Four children find a magic coin that grants only half of every wish made upon it, and have a series of (carefully calculated) magical adventures. Also see, by the same author, *Magic by the Lake* (Harcourt Brace, 1989), *Knight's Castle* (Harcourt Brace, 1989), *Seven-Day Magic* (Harcourt Brace, 1995), and *The Time Garden* (Harcourt Brace, 1990).

Harriet the Spy

Louise Fitzhugh; HarperTrophy, 1996

Harriet Welsch, the spy, keeps a private notebook filled with devastatingly honest observations about the people around her. When the notebook falls into the hands of her schoolmates, results are disastrous.

The Hobbit

J. R. R. Tolkien; Houghton Mifflin, 1966

Bilbo, the furry-footed hobbit, sets off with a band of dwarves to battle the dragon Smaug in the Lonely Mountain. Adventure, heroic deeds, valuable lessons, and a wonderful magic ring.

Homer Price

Robert McCloskey; Viking, 1976

Young Homer Price of the small town of Centerburg variously copes with skunks, burglars, an insane automatic doughnut-making machine, a musical mousetrap on wheels, and the world's biggest ball of string. Also see, by the same author, *Centerburg Tales: More Adventures of Homer Price* (Viking, 1977).

The Indian in the Cupboard

Lynne Reid Banks; Camelot, 1991

Omri's tiny toy Indian, when placed inside a magical cupboard, comes alive, bringing excitement, adventure, and great difficulties into Omri's life.

Sequels include *The Return of the Indian* (Avon Books, 1990), *The Secret of the Indian* (Avon Books, 1990), and *The Mystery of the Cupboard* (Camelot, 1996).

Jacob Two-Two and the Dinosaur

Mordecai Richler; McClelland & Stewart, 1995

Jacob Two-Two got his nickname because, as the youngest child in a large family, he has to say everything two times before anyone pays attention to him. The ultimate attention getter, however, is his pet lizard, who turns out to be a pizza-loving *Diplodocus*. Jacob Two-Two is also the hero of *Jacob Two-Two Meets the Hooded Fang* (Random House, 1994), in which Jacob inadvertently insults a grown-up and is sent to prison on Slimer's Isle, a desolate and dreadful place guarded by the Hooded Fang and his pack of wolverines.

James and the Giant Peach

Roald Dahl; Alfred A. Knopf, 1996

James lives with his awful aunts, Spiker and Sponge, until—with the help of a mysterious little man in green—he grows an enormous magical peach and sets off on an adventure with peach's surprising inhabitants: the Spider, the Centipede, the Glow-worm, the Grasshopper, and the Earthworm.

Just-So Stories

Rudyard Kipling; William Morrow, 1996

A collection of classic animal fables, including "How the Rhinoceros Got His Skin," "How The Camel Got His Hump," "How the Leopard Got His Spots," and the wonderful tale of the insatiably curious "Elephant's Child."

Knights of the Kitchen Table

Jon Scieszka; Puffin, 1994

The first of the Time Warp Trio series. From his uncle, a magician, Joe gets a birthday present: *The Book*, which has the power to transport its readers through time. Joe and his two best friends are transported to the days of King Arthur, where they stumble through a series of humorous adventures and bring disaster on their heads by breaking Merlin's window with a baseball. Sequels include *The Not-So-Jolly Roger* (Puffin, 1993), *The Good, the Bad, and the Goofy* (Puffin, 1993), *Your Mother Was a Neanderthal* (Puffin, 1995), and *Tut Tut* (Puffin, 1998), in which the boys variously visit a pirate ship, the Old West, the Stone Age, and ancient Egypt.

Lafcadio, the Lion Who Shot Back
7 11 Shel Silverstein; HarperCrest, 1988

Lafcadio, who likes the sound of the word *hunter*, eats one, takes his rifle, and teaches himself sharpshooting. He then leaves home for the big city, where he becomes the star of Finchfinger's Circus, spends his spare time riding up and down in hotel elevators, and lives on toasted marshmallows and buttermilk. He becomes famous, but not quite happy.

The Littles
7 10 John Peterson; Scholastic, 1993

A short chapter book that tells the story of the Littles, the family of tiny people with tails who live in the walls of the Bigg family's house. Many sequels.

Martin's Mice
7 11 Dick King-Smith; Alfred A. Knopf, 1998

Unbeknownst to his mouse-eating family, Martin keeps pet mice in a bathtub in the attic of the barn. Also see, by the same author, *Harry's Mad* (Alfred A. Knopf, 1997), in which Harry inherits, from an American uncle, an extremely intelligent and adventuresome talking parrot named Madison.

Mary Poppins
8 12 P. L. Travers; Harcourt Brace, 1997

The story of the sharp-tongued and mysteriously magical nanny with the parrot-headed umbrella who blows into Cherry Tree Lane on the East Wind to care for the Banks children: Jane, Michael, and the twins. Individual adventures have a charmingly eerie Victorian flavor, not at all like the saccharine Disney movie interpretation. Also see *Mary Poppins Comes Back* (Harcourt Brace, 1997), *Mary Poppins Opens the Door* (Harcourt Brace, 1997), and *Mary Poppins in the Park* (Harcourt Brace, 1997).

The Mouse and the Motorcycle
8 11 Beverly Cleary; Avon Books, 1996

Ralph (the mouse) encounters Keith, who owns a toy motorcycle, while the boy and his parents are staying at the Mountain View Inn. After a series of exciting escapades and adventures, Keith gives Ralph the motorcycle to keep. Sequels include *Runaway Ralph* (Avon Books, 1991) and *Ralph S. Mouse* (Camelot, 1993). (The *S* is for Smart.)

Mr. Popper's Penguins
7 10 Richard and Florence Atwater; Little, Brown, 1992

Mr. Popper, a housepainter who has always dreamed of going to Antarctica, acquires a pair of penguins. In next to no time, the penguin family has grown to 12, and Mr. Popper decides to support them all by teaching his penguins to perform onstage.

Mrs. Frisby and the Rats of NIMH
8 12 Robert C. O'Brien; Aladdin, 1986

Mrs. Frisby, a widowed field mouse, seeks help from the superintelligent Rats of NIMH, escapees from the laboratories of the National Institute of Mental Health. The rats help her move her home; in return, she gives them information that saves their lives. Also see the sequels, written by the author's daughter, Jane Conly, *Rasco and the Rats of NIMH* (HarperTrophy, 1991) and *R-T, Margaret, and the Rats of NIMH* (HarperCollins, 1991).

Owls in the Family
9 12 Farley Mowat; Dell, 1996

A warm and funny book about Mowat's childhood on the prairies of Saskatchewan and his adoption of a pair of obstreperous owlets, Wol and Weeps. A special treat for young naturalists. By the same author, see *The Dog Who Wouldn't Be* (Bantam Books, 1984).

The Phantom Tollbooth
9 12 Norton Juster; Random House, 1993

Milo passes through the Phantom Tollbooth and ends up in a magical country where he sets out on a quest to find the sisters Rhyme and Reason, thus restoring peace to the warring kingdoms of Dictionopolis and Digitopolis. A creative cast of characters and much brilliant play with words and numbers.

Pippi Longstocking
7 10 Astrid Lindgren; Puffin, 1997

Pippi Longstocking, the strongest and most self-sufficient girl in the world, keeps a horse on the porch and a chest of gold coins under her bed, to the admiration and awe of the children next door. Sequels include *Pippi in the South Seas* (Viking, 1997) and *Pippi Goes on Board* (Viking, 1988).

The Pushcart War
Jean Merrill; Yearling, 1987

The war between the pushcart peddlers and the truckers of New York City is described in journalistic detail, beginning with the fatal Daffodil Massacre, in which the pushcart of Morris the Florist is flattened by a Mammoth Moving Truck. Both hilarious and thought provoking.

The Reluctant Dragon
Kenneth Grahame; Henry Holt, 1988

The dragon wants only to be left alone to sit in his cave and write poetry, but St. George has come to town and the townspeople are demanding a battle. With the help of a peasant boy, an understanding solution is found that satisfies all.

Sarah, Plain and Tall
Patricia MacLachlan; HarperTrophy, 1987

Anna and Caleb's mother has died, so their lonely father writes for a mail-order bride. When Sarah, who describes herself as "plain and tall," arrives from the coast of Maine, she changes all their lives. Also see the sequel, *Skylark* (HarperTrophy, 1997).

The Search for Delicious
Natalie Babbitt; Farrar, Straus & Giroux, 1991

The Prime Minister is writing a dictionary, in which he claims that the definition of *delicious* is fried fish. There the trouble begins: the General of the Armies argues that *delicious* is a mug of beer; the king says apples; and the queen, Christmas pudding. To settle the controversy, young Gaylen is sent out to take a survey of *delicious* definitions throughout the kingdom. Along the way, he has many strange adventures, narrowly avoids a war, and learns the true definition of *delicious*.

The Shrinking of Treehorn
Florence Parry Heide; Holiday House, 1992

Treehorn is dwindling daily, but his oblivious parents pay no attention. Also see, by the same author, *Treehorn's Treasure* (Holiday House, 1981), in which Treehorn's parents refuse to believe that the tree in the backyard is growing dollar bills, and *The Problem with Pulcifer* (Mulberry, 1992), in which Pulcifer's parents take him to a psychiatrist because he stubbornly insists on reading instead of watching television.

The Sign of the Beaver
Elizabeth George Speare; Yearling, 1994

Twelve-year-old Matt, left alone at the family cabin in the Maine wilderness, is attacked by a swarm of wild bees and saved by Saknis, the chief of the nearby Beaver clan. Matt becomes friends with Saknis and his grandson, Attean, and the boys learn much from each other.

Soup
Robert Newton Peck; Yearling, 1979

Soup is the author's imaginative and trouble-prone boyhood friend; the book describes their adventures, escapades, and activities in rural Vermont in the 1920s. Several sequels.

Stone Fox
John Gardiner; HarperTrophy, 1988

The only way to pay off the taxes on his grandfather's farm is for 10-year-old Willy and his dog, Searchlight, to win the dog-sled race. It's a long shot; he'll be racing against the legendary Indian champion, Stone Fox.

The 13 Clocks
James Thurber; Yearling, 1992

The poetic, touching, comic, and linguistically versatile tale of a prince who, with the help of the peculiar Golux, rescues the Princess Saralinda from the cold and evil Duke of Coffin Castle. Also see, by the same author, *The Wonderful O* (Yearling, 1992), *The White Deer* (Harcourt Brace, 1984), *The Great Quillow* (Harcourt Brace, 1994), and *Many Moons* (Harcourt Brace, 1987).

Tintin
Hergé; Little, Brown

This is a text-heavy comic book series, detailing the mystery-solving adventures of Tintin, the boy detective, and his talking dog, Snowy. There are 21 available titles in the series, among them *The Castafiore Emerald, The Calculus Affair,* and *Red Rackham's Treasure.*

The Twenty-One Balloons

William Pène Dubois; Viking, 1986

Professor Sherman is carried by 21 hot-air balloons to the fabulous island of Krakatoa, a land of elaborate restaurants and diamond mines. He arrives just before the island is destroyed in a volcanic explosion.

The Whipping Boy

Sid Fleischman; Troll Associates, 1989

Prince Brat, the spoiled heir to the throne, and Jemmy, his whipping boy, run away from the palace together and stumble into a series of adventures with a gang of outlaws that change both boys' lives and one boy's character for the better.

The Wind in the Willows

Kenneth Grahame; St. Martin's Press, 1995

The classic story of the Water Rat, the Mole, the wise old Badger, and the flighty and obstreperous Mr. Toad, and their adventures along the River and in the Wild Wood. Also see the sequels, in the style of the original book, by William Horwood, which continue the adventures of Grahame's characters: *The Willows in Winter* (St. Martin's Press, 1994) and *Toad Triumphant* (St. Martin's Press, 1996).

The Wish Giver

Bill Brittain; HarperCollins, 1990

The mysterious Wish Giver comes to town and sells wishes, for 50 cents apiece, at the church social, but none of the wishes come true quite as planned.

The Wonderful Flight to the Mushroom Planet

Eleanor Cameron; Little, Brown, 1988

David and Chuck come upon a startling advertisement, printed in green, in the local newspaper: "Wanted: A small space ship about eight feet long, built by a boy, or by two boys, between the ages of eight and eleven." David and Chuck have built just such a spaceship; in it, they take a marvelous trip through space to Basidium, the pale green Mushroom Planet. There are five sequels, including *Stowaway to the Mushroom Planet* (Little, Brown, 1988).

FOR OLDER READERS

Anne of Green Gables

L. M. Montgomery; Scholastic, 1989

The story of everyone's favorite orphan, the red-haired, talkative, and imaginative 11-year-old Anne (spelled with an *e*) who comes to live with Marilla and Matthew Cuthbert on their farm on Prince Edward Island. There are several sequels, among them *Anne of Avonlea* (Scholastic, 1991), *Anne of the Island* (Bantam Books, 1983), and *Anne of Windy Poplars* (Bantam Books, 1984).

The Call of the Wild

Jack London; Simon & Schuster, 1995

Adventure in the days of the Klondike Gold Rush. The hero is a dog, Buck, kidnapped and taken to the Alaskan wilderness where he becomes a sled dog. Also see, by the same author, *White Fang* (Tor Books, 1990).

Cheaper By the Dozen

Frank B. Gilbreth Jr. and Ernestine Gilbreth Carey; Bantam Books, 1987

The hilarious true story of the redheaded Gilbreth family, 12 kids and their parents, both efficiency experts and specialists in the field of "motion study."

Children of Green Knowe

L. M. Boston; Harcourt Brace, 1989

Young Tolly goes to spent the school holidays with his great-grandmother at the ancient family mansion, Green Knowe, and meets there the ghosts of three children who lived in the house in the 17th century. Sequels include *Treasure of Green Knowe, The River at Green Knowe, A Stranger at Green Knowe,* and *An Enemy at Green Knowe* (all Harcourt, Brace, 1989).

The Dark Is Rising Series

Susan Cooper; Aladdin

This series is a marvelous and mostly modern-day tale of the great battle between good and evil, with

READING

roots in the legendary past of King Arthur and Merlin the magician. The main characters are three children, whose lives become entangled in the ancient conflict going on about them. Titles are *Over Sea, Under Stone, Greenwitch, The Dark Is Rising, The Grey King,* and *Silver on the Tree.*

Dealing with Dragons
Patricia C. Wrede; Harcourt Brace, 1990

The feminist Princess Cimorene, who prefers fencing to embroidery, deals efficiently with wizards, witches, djinns, and an enchanted stone prince, and ends up as Chief Cook and Librarian to Kazul, the (female) King of the Dragons. Sequels include *Searching for Dragons* (Harcourt Brace, 1991), *Calling on Dragons* (Harcourt Brace, 1993), and *Talking to Dragons* (Harcourt Brace, 1993).

Dragon's Milk
Susan Fletcher; Aladdin, 1996

Kaeldra's little sister is dying of vermilion fever. To save her sister's life, Kaeldra sets out on a quest to find the Ancient Ones—the dragons—and to beg for some dragon's milk, which can cure the fatal disease. Kaeldra's meeting with the dragons takes on added dimensions when the mother dragon is killed, and Kaeldra strives to save the remaining babies, the draclings. Sequels include *Flight of the Dragon Kyn* (Aladdin, 1997) and *The Sign of the Dove* (Atheneum, 1996).

Fahrenheit 451
Ray Bradbury; Ballantine, 1996

In this future world, all books are banned. The state Firemen are bookburners, and the "Fahrenheit 451" of the title is the temperature at which paper incinerates. Then one Fireman, Montague, actually reads a book—and finds himself an outlaw. Also see, by the same author, *The Martian Chronicles* (Avon Books, 1997), *Something Wicked This Way Comes* (Bantam Books, 1983), and *The Illustrated Man* (Bantam Books, 1992).

The Fifty-First Dragon
Heywood Broun; Creative Education, 1985

Gawaine le Coeur-Hardy is at the bottom of his class at knight school until the Headmaster gives him a magic word (*Rumplesnitz*) guaranteed to protect him from dragons. Gawaine, armed with his magic word, successfully defeats 50 dragons, a school record. Then the Headmaster tells him that there's no such thing as a magic word.

The Gammage Cup
Carol Kendall; Harcourt Brace, 1990

The Minnipins, who live in 12 little villages on a river that runs through a hidden valley, are all very much alike, right down to the color of their cloaks and their front doors (both green). Five Minnipins in the town of Slipper-on-the-Water, however, simply don't fit in: Muggles isn't tidy; Curley Green spends all her time painting pictures; Gummy composes silly poems; Walter the Earl digs under his house looking for ancient artifacts; and Mingy just doesn't like being told what to do. All five are banished from the village—but nonetheless they manage to save the country from invasion and thus change the Minnipin way of thinking forever. Also see the sequel, *The Whisper of Glocken* (Harcourt Brace, 1986).

Ghosts I Have Been
Richard Peck; Yearling, 1987

The story of Blossom Culp, who has second sight, and her adventures in the spirit world, including her meeting with the ghost of young Julian Poindexter, who died in the sinking of the *Titanic*. Also see, by the same author, *The Ghost Belonged to Me* (Puffin, 1997).

Gildaen: The Heroic Adventures of a Most Unusual Rabbit
Emilie Buchwald; Milkweed Editions, 1993

"Gildaen was that rarity among rabbits, an adventurer," begins this wonderful fantasy book, filled with enchantments, heroes, gallant friends, and one very wicked and powerful sorcerer.

The Giver
Lois Lowry; Houghton Mifflin, 1993

Jonas lives in a perfect society, a world in which everyone fits into his or her proper place. Now, as he enters adolescence, the time arrives for Jonas to be assigned his future job in the community—and he is chosen to be the next Receiver, the keeper of all the community's memories. It is a lonely and painful job, and—as Jonas assimilates more and more memories—

he begins to doubt the values with which he has been raised. Finally he makes a difficult and revolutionary decision.

See **Philosophy** (page 807).

The House of Dies Drear
Virginia Hamilton; Aladdin, 1984

A modern black family moves into an old Ohio farmhouse, once a stop on the Underground Railroad. The original owner and two escaping slaves were murdered there, over 100 years ago. An enthralling mystery. Also see the sequel, *The Mystery of Drear House* (Scholastic, 1997).

The House With a Clock in its Walls
John Bellairs; Puffin, 1993

Young Lewis, his uncle Jonathan, a wizard, and next-door-neighbor Mrs. Zimmerman, a witch with a taste for wearing purple, struggle to find and stop the hidden clock designed by an evil sorcerer to end the world. Scary and exciting. There are many titles by the author in the same Gothic vein, among them *The Figure in the Shadows* (Puffin, 1993), *The Letter, the Witch, and the Ring* (Puffin, 1993), and *The Curse of the Blue Figurine* (Puffin, 1996).

The Incredible Journey
Sheila Burnford; Yearling, 1990

Two dogs and a cat set out on a long trek through the Canadian wilderness to find their human family. All ends happily, but they have some hard times along the way, including a battle with a bear.

Island of the Blue Dolphins
Scott O'Dell; Yearling, 1987

Karana, a young Indian girl, survives for years alone on an island off the coast of California, fighting off the wild dogs that killed her younger brother, fashioning weapons, hunting for food, and building a house with a fence of whalebone.

Johnny Tremain
Esther Forbes; Houghton Mifflin, 1992

Now a classic, this is the story of young Johnny Tremain, silversmith's apprentice, who becomes caught up in the Revolutionary War and loses his best friend at the Battle of Lexington and Concord.

Julie of the Wolves
Jean Craighead George; HarperTrophy, 1996

Thirteen-year-old Julie—taking her Eskimo name, Miyax—runs away from the Bureau of Indian Affairs School in Barrow, Alaska, to live in the wilds with the wolves. See also, by the same author, *Julie's Wolf Pack* (HarperCollins, 1997).

The Little Prince
Antoine de Saint-Exupéry; Harcourt Brace, 1982

The mystical story of the Little Prince, who comes to earth from his own tiny planet, leaving behind a sheep and a rose. A multifaceted fable for all ages.

Little Women
Louisa May Alcott; Alfred A. Knopf, 1994

The story of four girls, Meg, Jo, Beth, and Amy, growing up in Massachusetts in the days of the Civil War. There are several sequels, among them *Little Men* (Puffin, 1995) and *Jo's Boys* (Puffin, 1996).

My Side of the Mountain
Jean Craighead George; Viking, 1991

Fifteen-year-old Sam Gribley, tired of overcrowded New York City, heads for the Catskill Mountains where, equipped only with a penknife, a ball of twine, an ax, and some flint and steel, he builds a treehouse and lives for months on his own. See also, by the same author, *On the Far Side of the Mountain* (Puffin, 1991).

Never Cry Wolf
Farley Mowat; Bantam Books, 1983

Naturalist Farley Mowat is sent to investigate reports that wolves are slaughtering the Arctic caribou. He spends months living with and learning to know and love the wolves. Fascinating, funny, and heartbreaking.

The Neverending Story
Michael Ende; E. P. Dutton, 1997

Bastian Balthazar Bux, evading school, discovers a magical book through which he enters the kingdom of Fantastica where he participates in a great quest.

The Once and Future King
T. H. White; Ace Books, 1996

A rich and marvelous retelling of the King Arthur legend in four parts. The first part, "The Sword in the Stone," which tells of the King Arthur's boyhood and his education with his tutor, the wise but slightly confused Merlin, has been published separately and is most suitable for kids. The entire book, however, is wonderful, filled with humor, joy, tragedy, history, and a truly glorious endeavor. Also by T. H. White, see *Mistress Masham's Repose* (Ace Books, 1989), the story of Maria who lives with her nasty governess, Miss Brown, in the vast and crumbling castle of Malplaquet, and who discovers a community of tiny people living on an island. Their ancestors were brought to England from Lilliput by Gulliver. Maria and her friend the Professor must find a way to protect them from Miss Brown and her equally evil crony, the Vicar.

The Prydain Chronicles
Lloyd Alexander; Henry Holt, 1988

The land of Prydain, where the action of these five books takes place, is much like ancient Wales. In the first book of the series, *The Book of Three,* young Taran, Assistant Pig-Keeper, sets out with assorted companions on a quest to destroy the Black Cauldron, used by the evil magician Arawn to conjure up a diabolical army. Subsequent volumes are *The Black Cauldron, The Castle of Llyr, The High King,* and *Taran Wanderer.*

Redwall Series
Brian Jacques; Philomel Books

These heroic, action-packed stories feature the mice of Redwall Abbey, and their friends and allies in Mossflower forest. In *Redwall* (1997), the first book of the series, the mice, led by a young apprentice named Matthias, battle the vicious rat Cluny and his band of evil cutthroats. There are many sequels, among them *Mossflower* (1988), *Mattimeo* (1990), *Martin the Warrior* (1994), and *The Pearls of Lutra* (1998).

The Secret Garden
Frances Hodgson Burnett; Scholastic, 1997

The story of skinny, cross, 11-year-old Mary Lennox, sent from India to live with her guardian in England in his mansion on the Yorkshire Moors. There she finds the way into the secret garden—locked and forgotten for many years—and meets the gentle cottage boy, Dickon, who has a magical way with wild things, and her invalid cousin Colin. Together they make the garden bloom again, and change their own lives in the process.

Shiloh

Phyllis Reynolds Naylor; Atheneum, 1991

Shiloh is an endearing beagle puppy with an abusive owner; when the dog follows 11-year-old Marty Preston home, his parents explain that he cannot keep Shiloh—even though his motives are good—because the dog does not belong to him. Excitement, danger, and a moral dilemma. *Shiloh* led to a lot of passionate debate and discussion around here. Our boys started out insisting that they didn't want to read a dog book. But they got hooked. Sequels include *Shiloh Season* (Atheneum, 1996) and *Saving Shiloh* (Atheneum, 1997).

Sounder
William Armstrong; HarperCollins, 1989

The story centers around a young black boy growing up in the 19th-century South. When his father steals a ham to feed his hungry family, he is arrested and sentenced to heavy labor—and the sheriff shoots the family's great coon dog, Sounder, who drags himself away and vanishes into the woods. Both father and dog eventually come home again, but there's no easy happy ending. The boy is forced to learn to deal with death and change—and eventually to understand a phrase from a book that he reads with his teacher: "Only the unwise think that what has changed is dead."

Treasure Island
Robert Louis Stevenson; Atheneum, 1981

The swashbuckling tale of young Jim Hawkins and his voyage in search of pirate treasure, in company with the villainous (but appealing) Long John Silver. Also see *Kidnapped* (Atheneum, 1982) and *The Black Arrow* (Atheneum, 1987).

Tuck Everlasting

Natalie Babbitt; Farrar, Straus & Giroux, 1988

Ten-year-old Winnie meets the mysterious Tuck family, who have drunk from a spring whose waters give eternal life. A beautiful and thoughtful book.

The Westing Game
Ellen Raskin; Puffin, 1997

The heirs to the fortune of Samuel Westing must compete for their inheritance by solving a series of clues, a contest that proves to be very dangerous indeed.

The White Mountains
John Christopher; Aladdin, 1989

Will lives in a future world that has been enslaved by the Tripods, huge three-legged machines. All humans, at the age of 13, are Capped, fitted with a brain-modifying device that ensures absolute obedience to the Tripods' rule. As the day of Will's Capping approaches, he meets a stranger who urges him to escape and sends him off on the long journey to the White Mountains. Also see the sequels, *The City of Gold and Lead* (Aladdin, 1988) and *The Pool of Fire* (Aladdin, 1988), and the prequel, *When the Tripods Came* (Aladdin, 1990).

The Witch of Blackbird Pond
Elizabeth George Speare; Yearling, 1972

Kit Tyler, sent to live with relatives in Connecticut from her home in Barbados, is lonely and unhappy in the strict Puritan colony until she meets the Quaker, Hannah, known as the "witch of Blackbird Pond."

A Wrinkle in Time
Madeleine L'Engle; Yearling, 1973

One dark and stormy night, Meg Murry, her genius younger brother Charles Wallace, and her scientist mother meet Mrs. Whatsit—who remarks, while putting on her boots, "Speaking of ways, pets, there *is* such a thing as a tesseract." A tesseract is a wrinkle in time, through which Charles Wallace, Meg, and their friend Calvin pass to participate in a great battle between good and evil. Also see the sequels, *A Wind in the Door* (Yearling, 1974), *A Swiftly Tilting Planet* (Yearling, 1981), and *Many Waters* (Yearling, 1987).

"But you've left out so much," my sons said in dismay, reading this list over my shoulder. "What about *A Wizard of Earthsea? Captains Courageous? Watership Down? Babe the Gallant Pig?* What about *Black Beauty?* There's a lot that's not on here."

"It's just a list of suggestions," I said with dignity. "People will add to it as they go along."

"She left out *Robinson Crusoe*," said Josh to Ethan and Caleb.

"*The Legend of Sleepy Hollow*," said Caleb, snickering. "*The Ransom of Red Chief.*"

"*The Brave Little Toaster*," said Ethan.

"Scram," I said. "Go read."

READING

WRITING

Writing is one of the easiest things; erasing
is one of the hardest.

RABBI ISRAEL SALANTER

Our boys generally enjoy creative writing. Josh and Caleb compose almost daily: stories, plays, poems, political essays, letters, journal entries, and anything else that strikes their literary fancy. Even Ethan, whose interest in the written word is limited, keeps a journal and an idea book (heavy in labeled diagrams), communicates by e-mail with assorted acquaintances, and turns out science essays and technological adventure stories. I like to think that this positive take on writing is the product of the imaginative writing projects to which the boys have been exposed since the inception of our homeschool program. On the other hand, since equally imaginative math projects did not instill a comparable affection for arithmetic, I suspect there's something else at work—perhaps simply the fun of self-expression and invention on paper. Just in case, however, here are a few of the writing projects that worked for us.

THE IMAGINATION BOX

Our Imagination Box was a kid-decorated pencil box filled with index cards, on each of which we printed a different idea for a poem, story, or essay. Examples included: "On a walk through the woods, you meet a large golden dragon. What happens?" "The moon is falling into the Pacific Ocean. You are in charge of saving the planet. What are you going to do?" "Imagine that you are a magician's rabbit. What is your life like? Tell about your adventures."

LETTERS

Our attempts at pen pal correspondence have never been too successful—either we faded out, or they did—but the boys, given the right impetus, do write letters. They are, for example, excellent writers of thank-you letters—which have blossomed over the years from the absolute minimum demanded by politeness ("Dear Grandma, Thank you for the book, Love, Josh") into hilarious multipage essays, complete with descriptions, dialogue, and sincere, but dramatic, expressions of gratitude. We also encouraged letter writing by engineering imaginary communications: Caleb for years, for example, kept up a lively, if somewhat acrimonious, correspondence with the tooth fairy's lawyer. Try sending your kids notes from the Easter rabbit, the family pets, an imaginary family of Borrowers who live behind the walls of the kitchen.
See **Letter Writing** (page 155).

NEWSLETTERS

The boys always enjoyed writing and assembling a family newsletter, complete with advertisements, on-the-spot news stories, science reports, comic strips, political commentary, and illustrations. A variant of the newsletter, the "Boys' Bookletter," also popular, was a monthly collection of illustrated book reviews.
See **Journalism and Newspapers** (page 158).

MEMORY BOOKS

The boys keep personal journals—at least sporadically—but we've had the most success with these when, rather than daily accounts of activities, the journals are written as memoirs. During each writing session, each writer describes a chosen memory: "What is the very first thing you can remember? Tell as much as you can about it." "Where was the first house you lived in? What was it like? What was your room like? Describe it." "Think about a visit to Grandma's house. Where was she living? What was her house like? Write down everything you can remember about the visit." "Make a list of all the pets you've ever had. Tell something special about each one."
See **Journals and Diaries** (page 152).

FRACTURED FOLKTALES AND FAIRY TALES

Inspired by such books as Jon Scieszka's *The True Story of the 3 Little Pigs,* William Brooke's *A Telling of the Tales,* and James Finn Garner's *Politically Correct Bedtime Stories*—all retellings of classic tales with new and unexpected twists—the boys have had a blast reinventing children's literature.

TANDEM WRITING

A recent favorite, in which one writer begins a story, writing a paragraph or two; a second then takes over, continuing and altering the plot; and so on, until, at some to-be-decided-upon point, the last person to take a turn invents a conclusion.
See **Boomerang Books** (page 139).

ONE-WORD WRITING

Another recent hit around here. Each person is assigned a single word—*noodle, penguin, mousetrap, balloon*—around or about which he or she must write a story, essay, or poem. We have amassed a fat looseleaf notebook of one-word-inspired works, and I look forward to the next installments, the words for which are *sea cow, protoplasm,* and *Koosh ball.*

While all of the above worked in that they triggered excited participation in writing, other projects came to what can only be called literary bad ends. Formal children's writing programs, in our hands, have often fallen into this undesirable category, largely because they provide so little scope for the imagination. In the process of learning the proper structure of sentences, kids are often given bland examples and asked to produce more of the same, writing descriptions of pencils, sneakers, the living room furniture. The results, unsurprisingly, smack leadenly of technical drudgery.

"The kids in my class," an acquaintance who teaches second grade once told me, "just love group writing. I put a word up on the board—something everybody is familiar with, like *dog*. Then the kids take turns suggesting words and phrases about a dog, like *big* or *brown* or *dogs bark*. Then we put all the words together to make a little story about a dog."

Our kids, however, didn't love group writing. "This is boring," Joshua announced, glaring at our painfully elicited list of appropriate dog words. "I can write my *own* story about a dog. A magic dog with blue fur wings who digs up dinosaur bones."

"A *robot* dog," piped up Ethan, reaching for his pencil, "who sniffs out criminals with his bionic nose."

"I don't like dogs," said Caleb. "and I don't want to write about a dog. Let's read a book about cats."

So we read a book about cats.

HANDWRITING AND PENMANSHIP

Our children—all somewhat slovenly in matters of penmanship—resisted conventional handwriting copybooks, on grounds of repetitive tedium. This disinclination to practice explains the spurts of illegibility that keep cropping up to this day, which problem we have partially avoided by emphasizing "keyboarding skills" (see Typing for Kids, page 119). While penmanship met with a cold reception here, however, everybody was intrigued by calligraphy. Calligraphy is dramatically pretty, and its practitioners, who get to use an appealing array of pens, colored inks, and chisel-tip markers, are soon turning out elaborately lettered cards, signs, messages, mottoes, and more. Especially popular among our children: dinner menus, treasure maps (see page 116), and refrigerator-posted announcements of forthcoming family events.

CALLIGRAPHY BOOKS

Alphabet Art: Thirteen ABCs from Around the World
Leonard Everett Fisher; Macmillan, 1984

Thirteen beautifully drawn alphabets for readers of all ages.

Calligraphy
Don Marsh; North Light Books, 1996

Step-by-step instructions for beginners in four chapters, covering materials, basic strokes, easy-to-learn alphabets, and assorted calligraphy projects. Pre-ruled practice sheets are included.

Calligraphy: From Beginner to Expert
Caroline Young, Chris Lyon, and Paul Sullivan; EDC Publications, 1994

An Usborne instructional guide for calligraphers in grades 7–9, packaged with three calligraphy pens.

Calligraphy Workstation
Manda Hanson and Rita Warren; Price Stern Sloan, 1993

An attractive calligraphy set, including a calligraphy pen with three nibs, six ink cartridges, and 16 practice grids, and an illustrated manual with step-by-step instructions and many project suggestions. Recommended for kids in grades 7 and up.

CALLIGRAPHY SUPPLIES

Calligraphy supplies can be purchased at most arts and craft supply stores, or can be obtained by mail order from the sources below.

Dick Blick Company
Arts and crafts supplies, plus calligraphy pens, inks, markers, papers, and instruction books.
Dick Blick Co.
Box 1267
Galesburg, IL 61402
orders (800) 447-8192; customer service (800) 723-2787; product information (800) 933-2542/fax (800) 621-8293

Sax Arts & Crafts
The catalog, which carries an enormous range of arts and crafts supplies, includes a large selection of calligraphy markers, pens, and inks, calligraphy kits, parchment papers, and instruction booklets.
Catalog, $5
Sax Arts & Crafts

Box 510710

New Berlin, WI 53151

orders (800) 558-6696; customer service (800) 522-4278/fax (414) 784-1176

e-mail: saxarts@execpc.com

Web site: www.artsupplies.com or www.saxarts.com

United Art and Education Supply Company

Arts and crafts supplies, including calligraphy pens, inks, paper, and instruction manuals.

Catalog, $7.50 to individuals; free to schools

United Art and Education Supply Co., Inc.

Box 9219

Fort Wayne, IN 46899

(219) 478-1121 or (800) 322-3247/fax (219) 478-2249

MAKE YOUR OWN TREASURE MAP

Home-style parchment paper for treasure maps is fun to use and simple to make. Crumple a sheet of ordinary white typing paper into a ball; then smooth it out flat. Repeat two or three times. Place the flattened sheet of paper in a shallow pan and cover with coffee or strong tea. Let sit until the paper turns a nice shade of weathered brown (usually about half an hour). Remove from the pan and dry on layers of paper towels or newspaper. For an additional authentic touch—children will need adult supervision here—singe the edges of the paper with a lighted match. Write neatly upon it.

Penmanship Workbooks

We did not use commercial handwriting workbooks in our homeschool program, arguing that we could perfectly well make our own—provided, of course, that we could reproduce copy-worthy examples of the tidy slanted penmanship of our youth, which neither my husband nor I uses anymore. (As it turned out, we couldn't quite, which is why all our sons make funny-looking capital Ds.) At first, we made each boy a personal copybook, with pages of upper- and lower-case letters and simple words. Once they mastered the intricacies of the cursive alphabet, we moved on to more challenging handwriting models, making for each boy what we called a Commonplace Book. The original Commonplace Book was a standby of the 18th- and 19th-century scholar; in it, writers jotted down memoranda, interesting facts, quotations, brief

anecdotes, proverbs, and favorite lines of poetry. (Thomas Jefferson kept one; so did Arthur Conan Doyle's omniscient Sherlock Holmes.) In our versions, quotations, proverbs, and the like—written neatly in classical cursive (except for the Ds) at the top of the page—served as practice exercises, models for the boys to copy. They also occasionally served as starting points for essays and short stories.

Commonplace Book entries were tailored somewhat to the interests of the writer. Josh's book, for example, included quotes from Shakespeare, Thoreau, Twain, and Emerson, and a lot of short poetry selections; Ethan's included a good many facts and figures ("The speed of light is 186,000 miles per second"); and Caleb's contained epigrams from *Poor Richard's Almanack,* limericks, quotes from books about dragons, and—because he had trouble with *f*s—Abraham's Lincoln's "You can fool all the people some of the time, and you can fool some of the people all the time, but you can not fool all the people all of the time." (See Quotations, page 134.)

Penmanship workbook series, featuring varied styles of scripts, are available from many educational supply companies. None, despite competing claims, seems to have marked advantages over the others; and all, according to user affidavits, successfully teach the young how to write. Roughly speaking, the D'Nealian Handwriting Series, below, attempts to facilitate the manuscript-to-cursive transition by teaching beginners to print at a slant, giving their letters little hooks at the bottom, suitable for future cursive connections; the Italic Handwriting Series teaches an elegant quasi-manuscript cursive; and the Spencerian Penmanship Classic Curriculum teaches a classic old-fashioned copperplate.

Most educational supply companies carry assorted penmanship series, among them:

American Home School Publishing

5310 Affinity Ct.

Centreville, VA 22020

(703) 266-0348 or (800) 684-2121/fax (703) 266-2921

e-mail: web@ahsp.com

Web site: www.doubled.com/ahsp

The Home School Books and Supplies

104 S. West Ave.

Arlington, WA 98223

WRITING

(306) 435-0376 or (800) 788-1221/fax (360) 435-1028

Web site: www.TheHomeSchool.com

Home School Supply House

Box 2000

Beaver, UT 84713

(801) 438-1254 or (800) 772-3129

D'Nealian Handwriting Series

Includes manuscript and cursive exercise books, activity books, and practice journals.

Good Year Books

1900 E. Lake Ave.

Glenview, IL 60025

(312) 729-3000 or (800) 628-4480

Italic Handwriting Series

Barbara Getty and Inga Dubay; Portland State University

The series includes eight instructional workbooks, from Book A (kindergarten) through Book G (6th grade to adult), plus a 108-page teacher's manual, an instructional video ("Introduction to Teaching Italic Handwriting"), desk strips picturing manuscript or cursive alphabets, and packets of colored plastic movable italic letters (vowels are blue, consonants red).

Individual books, $5.75 each

Portland State University

Continuing Education Press

Box 1394

Portland, OR 97207

(800) 547-8887, ext. 4891/fax (503) 725-4840

Spencerian Penmanship Classic Curriculum

Mott Media

A series of five student copybooks and a teacher's theory book.

Set, $15; individual copybooks can be purchased separately

Mott Media

1000 E. Huron St.

Milford, MI 48402

(248) 685-8773/fax (248) 685-8776

Zaner-Bloser

The Zaner-Bloser people have simplified the alphabet. Results are presented in the Handwriting With a New Alphabet series, featuring pared-down versions of the traditional manuscript and cursive alphabets. In the simplified alphabet, for example, the manuscript *J* lacks the top crosspiece, many of the cursive capitals have lost their fancy loops, and the cursive capital *Q*—which, in traditional alphabets, looks like the number 2—now looks like a *Q*.

Zaner-Bloser also publishes handwriting books based on the traditional alphabet, and a large range of supplementary materials for young writers, including alphabet desk strips, practice workbooks, "finger-fitting" pens and pencils, and many varieties of red-and-blue-lined handwriting paper tailored to the abilities of different age groups. The company also sells blank books, including "Make-Your-Own" Big Books, writing journals ruled for writers of various ages, story journals (the pages are half lined and half unlined, for text and illustration), and—for brand-new writers—ABC Journals, in which, for each letter of the alphabet, kids trace letters and do letter-related activities.

Zaner-Bloser

2200 W. Fifth Ave.

Box 16764

Columbus, OH 43216-6764

(800) 421-3018/fax (614) 487-2699

Web site: www.zaner-bloser.com

HISTORY OF WRITING

Alphabetics: A History of Our Alphabet

Sally J. Patton; Zephyr Press, 1989

Information and activities based on six alphabets: the pictographs of prehistoric peoples, and the alphabets of the Sumerians, Egyptians, Chinese, Greek, and Romans. A bibliography, categorized by reading level, accompanies each alphabet, and a final section, "The Origin of Each Letter," traces the development of each letter of the modern alphabet.

Zephyr Press

3316 N. Chapel Ave.

Box 66006

Tucson, AZ 85732-3448

(602) 322-5090 or (800) 232-2187/fax (520) 323-9402

e-mail: neways2learn@zephyrpress.com

Web site: www.zephyrpress.com

The 26 Letters

Oscar Ogg; Thomas Y. Crowell, 1948

A chapter book on the history of the alphabet for intermediate and older readers, liberally illustrated in red and black with letters and alphabets from many cultures. Ogg, a calligrapher, covers everything from prehistoric picture writing through the ancient Egyptians, Phoenicians, Greeks, and Romans to Caroline and Gothic scripts and the invention of printing. (Johann Gutenberg, the inventor of movable type, Ogg tells us, adopted his mother's family name, which means "good mountain," instead of retaining his father's family name—Gensfleisch—which means "gooseflesh.") Look for it at the library.

Writing and Printing

Chris Oxlade; Franklin Watts, 1995

A 32-page illustrated history of writing, covering the development of the alphabet, the invention of printing, and papermaking. The book includes instructions for writing-related craft activities. Kids, for example, make a Roman writing tablet, a medieval-style block print and illuminated alphabet, and a quill pen. Also see *Alphabet Antics* (right), **The Development of Writing** (right), and *Word Works* (page 120).

BOOKS ABOUT LEARNING PENMANSHIP

Muggie Maggie

Beverly Cleary; Camelot, 1991

Maggie is a third-grader who digs in her heels when it comes to learning cursive handwriting. She simply doesn't want to learn, and it's largely because she doesn't like doing things just because someone else tells her to. A story of independence and compromise: Maggie is eventually convinced to learn cursive (but when she grows up, she announces, she's going to print all the time).

That's Right, Edie

Johanna Johnston; Putnam, 1966

Edie refuses to learn to write properly—she'd rather scribble—until it turns out that her birthday present is at stake. For readers aged 4–8.

ACTIVITY BOOKS

Alphabet Antics: Hundreds of Activities to Challenge and Enrich Letter Learners of All Ages

Ken Vinton; Free Spirit Publishing, 1996

History, fun facts, vocabulary words, research and hands-on projects, writing suggestions, puzzles, and quotations for each letter of the alphabet.

See **Reading** (page 45).

The Development of Writing

A portfolio of materials on the history of writing, from its earliest beginnings to modern times. The portfolio includes 7 illustrated historical background essays ("Cavemen and Picture Writing," "The Sumerians," "The Egyptians," "The First Alphabet," "The Romans," "Medieval Manuscripts," and "Handwriting Since the Invention of Printing") and 11 historical document reproductions and other resource materials, among them a map locating sites of development of various world languages, a chart showing the evolution of the alphabet, a picture of the Rosetta Stone, a copy of a Greek letter on papyrus, a picture of a Sumerian tablet, a Roman diploma, and illustrative manuscript pages from the 17th, 18th, and 19th centuries.

The portfolio, including a study guide with reproducible student worksheets, $37

Jackdaw Publications

Box 503

Amawalk, NY 10501

(800) 789-0022/fax (800) 962-9101

Draw Write Now

Marie Hablitzel and Kim Stitzer; Barker Creek Publishing

A step-by-step drawing and handwriting course for kids aged 4–8. Book 1 (1994) is subtitled "On the Farm, Kids and Critters, Storybook Characters"; Book 2 (1995), in similar format, is simply designated "A Drawing and Handwriting Course for Kids." In both, kids, armed with pencils, learn to draw simple shapes and print manuscript letters.

See *Word Works* (page 120) and **The History of the Book** (page 145).

TYPING FOR KIDS

6 + *Kids Can Type Too!*

Christine Mountford; Barron's, 1987

A stand-up typing manual, wire-bound along the top edge like a stenographer's notebook, with a foldout base. Each lesson is illustrated with a color-coded keyboard (first fingers touch the purple keys, second fingers touch the green keys, and so on), plus, for extra emphasis, a pair of hands with color-coded fingertips. Each lesson consists of a short typing exercise, concentrating on a different set of keys, to be practiced repeatedly until the student has it down. By the end of the book (lesson 22), students have learned the fingering for all the letters of the alphabet, keyboard numbers and punctuation marks, and the use of the shift key and space bar. The book comes with an assortment of stick-on textured dots, to be placed on the "anchor" and "buoy" keys (*F, J, A,* and *;*) to help beginners keep their fingers in the proper positions.

5 8 *Read, Write & Type!*

A software program in which a talking keyboard and a pair of friendly animated hands, one blue, one yellow, teach beginners letter sounds and keyboarding skills. Kids, in the course of 40 animated lessons, not only learn to type but enhance their writing and reading comprehension skills. Recommended for kids in grades 1–2. On CD-ROM for Mac or Windows.

$29.95

The Learning Company

6160 Summit Dr. N

Minneapolis, MN 55430-4003

(800) 685-6322

Web site: www.learningco.com

10 + *Typing Tutor 7*

Keyboarding skills for kids aged 10 and up. The program includes practice samples from over 100 familiar books; kids who complete each typing exercise get to view an entertaining QuickTime video clip. The program also includes puzzles and three arcade-style games. On CD-ROM for Mac and Windows.

$44.95

Davidson and Associates

19840 Pioneer Ave.

Torrance, CA 90503

(800) 545-7677/fax (310) 793-0601

Web site: www.davd.com

VOCABULARY

BOOKS: NONFICTION

8 12 *A Chartreuse Leotard in a Magenta Limousine*

Lynda Graham-Barber; Hyperion, 1994

A book of eponyms (words derived from people's names) and toponyms (words derived from place names). Included are the stories behind such words as *zeppelin, gypsy, hamburger, cardigan,* and *guppy*—the last after the Reverend Robert John Lechmere Guppy, who first shipped some tiny tropical fish to the British Museum from Trinidad in the late 19th century.

8 + *Go Hang a Salami! I'm a Lasagna Hog! and Other Palindromes*

Jon Agee; Farrar, Straus & Giroux, 1992

Phrases that read the same in both directions, illustrated with clever little cartoons. (Try TODD ERASES A RED DOT.) Also see, by the same author, *So Many Dynamos! & Other Palindromes* (Farrar, Straus & Giroux, 1997).

12 + *Heavens to Betsy! & Other Curious Sayings*

Charles Earle Funk; HarperCollins, 1993

Short, clever, and utterly fascinating accounts of how over 400 familiar expressions originated, including "not worth a hill of beans," "as dead as a dodo," and "hocus pocus." (The source of "Heavens to Betsy!," sad to say, is unknown, though Mr. Funk gives some interesting guesses.) Also see, by the same author, *A Hog On Ice* (HarperCollins, 1985), *Horsefeathers* (HarperCollins, 1994), and *Thereby Hangs a Tale* (HarperCollins, 1993).

13 + *I Hear America Talking: An Illustrated History of American Words and Phrases*

Stuart Berg Flexner; Simon & Schuster, 1976

An immense and irresistible history of the American language, illustrated with period prints and photographs, covering common expressions by topic in alphabetical order. Among them: "Bayous, Creoles, and Cajuns," "Blue Grass, Red Wood, and Poison Ivy," "The Great Depression," "Fanny Farmer and the Level Teaspoon," "Hamburgers," "OK," "Scram, Skedaddle, Take a Powder," and "Uncle Sam." Some Americanisms probably aren't suitable for younger readers, but that shouldn't cause families to bypass this terrific reference.

A sequel with more of the same, *Listening to America* (Simon & Schuster, 1982), explains the history behind another enormous selection of Americanisms, from "Alaska, Seward's Folly, and Eskimos" through "Barnstorming," "Breakfast Food," "Fats, Shorty, Red, and Baldy: Common Nicknames," "Hoboes, Tramps, and Bums," "Pirates, Privateers, and Buccaneers," "It's Raining Cats and Dogs," "ToMAYto or ToMAHto?," and "Western Union."

Ladyfingers and Nun's Tummies: A Lighthearted Look at How Foods Got Their Names

Sarah Barnette; Times Books, 1997

For teenagers and adults, a fascinating history of food names, from the exotic to the everyday. Readers learn, for example, about the origins of graham crackers, rosemary, and hamburgers.

See **Ladyfingers and Nun's Tummies** (page 125).

The Mother Tongue

Bill Bryson; William Morrow, 1990

The story of the English language, aimed at adults and older readers, but there's something interesting here for everyone. There are chapters on the development of language, word origins, pronunciation, the history of dictionaries, proper names, and British versus American English, plus a chapter on swearing, which, though intriguing, is probably inappropriate for younger readers. There's also a wonderful chapter on English spelling, its many awfulnesses, and the number of people who have battled for its simplification and reform, among them Mark Twain, Theodore Roosevelt, and Andrew Carnegie. Also see, by the same author, *Made in America* (Avon Books, 1996), an equally enthralling history of American English.

The Story of English

Robert McCrum, William Cran, and Robert MacNeil; Viking, 1986

A fascinating and comprehensive history of the English language (and companion to the equally fascinating PBS television series) for older readers and adults, though there's much interesting information here for language lovers of all ages. *The Story of English* is also available on video—nearly nine hours of interesting information on five videocassettes.

Book, $22.95; video series, $99.95

Zenger Media

10200 Jefferson Blvd.

Box 802

Culver City, CA 90232-0802

(310) 839-2436 or (800) 421-4246/fax (310) 839-2249 or (800) 944-5422

e-mail: access@ZengerMedia.com

Web site: ZengerMedia.com/Zenger

Too Hot to Hoot

Marvin Terban; Clarion, 1987

An illustrated book of palindrome riddles, beginning with simple three-letter palindromes (*mother*, MOM; *small child*, TOT; *short for Robert*, BOB), then escalating to more difficult four-, five-, and six-letter palindromes and two-word "flip-flop phrases." (Answers are at the end of each chapter.) There's also a chapter on palindromic sentences, which read the same frontward and backward, a chapter about palindromic numbers, and the stories of three famous historical palindromes.

Also see, by the same author, *The Dove Dove: Funny Homograph Riddles* (Clarion, 1988), *Eight Ate: A Feast of Homonym Riddles* (Houghton Mifflin, 1982), *I Think I Thought and Other Tricky Verbs* (Houghton Mifflin, 1984), *In a Pickle and Other Funny Idioms* (Houghton Mifflin, 1983), and *Guppies in Tuxedos: Funny Eponyms* (Houghton Mifflin, 1988).

Word Works: Why the Alphabet Is a Kid's Best Friend

Cathryn Berger Kaye; Little, Brown, 1985

"This book is about words," begins the Introduction, "why we have them, why we need them, how we use them." The next 120+ pages are stuffed with history, facts, puzzles, projects, and activities, all having to do

WRITING

with the wonders of language. Included are accounts of codes and ciphers, the story of American Sign Language, hints for storytellers, information on newspapers and diaries ("Who Was Samuel Pepys?"), directions for putting on your own play, catchy word history segments, and recipes for baking all the letters of the alphabet.

BOOKS: FICTION

Amelia Bedelia
4 8 Peggy Parish; HarperCollins, 1992

The first in a long series about Amelia Bedelia, the housekeeper who takes all figures of speech literally. When told to "put out the light," Amelia hangs the lightbulbs on the clothesline. Fun with everyday sayings and idioms for readers aged 4–8.

A Chocolate Moose for Dinner
4 8 Fred Gwynne; Aladdin, 1988

A little boy interprets figures of speech literally, which leads to humor, confusion, and a vision of a real chocolate moose (not mousse) for dessert. Also see, by the same author, *The King Who Rained* (following).

The King Who Rained
6 9 Fred Gwynne; Aladdin, 1988

A delightful picture-book play on homonyms for elementary-school readers, in which the king did not reign, but rained.

The Phantom Tollbooth
8 12 Norton Juster; Random House, 1993

A superb fantasy book filled with wonderful word and number play, in which Milo, accompanied by Tock the watchdog (he's part clock and he ticks), visits the kingdoms of Dictionopolis and Digitopolis. In the wordy kingdom of Dictionopolis, he ends up eating his words (plus assorted half-baked ideas) at a state banquet and meets a real Spelling Bee. Clever, funny, and delightful. Ostensibly for upper-elementary to middle-school readers, but a treat for all ages.

The Rebellious Alphabet
ALL Jorge Diaz; Henry Holt, 1993

The short picture-book tale of a wicked and illiterate dictator who bans reading and writing. A clever old man trains canaries to deliver printed freedom messages; when these are captured and burned by the dictator's soldiers, the released words form a great black cloud that saves the people. A political and literary fable for readers of all ages.

The Search for Delicious
9 12 Natalie Babbitt; Farrar, Straus & Giroux, 1991

The prime minister is writing a dictionary, but the members of the court cannot agree on a definition for the word *delicious*. (The Queen says *delicious* is Christmas pudding; the king says it's apples; and the General votes for beer.) Gaylen, the prime minister's 12-year-old son, is sent out to take a poll of every citizen in the kingdom in an attempt to discover the true meaning of *delicious*. Eventually, after many adventures, a meeting with a mermaid, and a brush with war, he does. At the end of the book, the court is debating the definition of *golden*.

The Weighty Word Book
9 13 Paul M. Levitt, Douglas A. Burger, and Elissa S. Guralnick; Manuscripts, Ltd., 1990

Twenty-six terrific illustrated short stories, each centering around the definition of a challenging vocabulary word, presented in alphabetical order from *abasement* to *zealot*. Each ends with a memory-prodding pun. For readers aged 10–13.

The Wonderful O
ALL James Thurber; Yearling, 1992

The peaceful island of Ooroo is tyrannized by a pirate named Black who bans the letter *O*. "No longer could the people say Heigh-Ho, Yoohoo, or Yo ho ho, or even plain Hello"—and *book* became *bk*, *Robinhood* became *Rbinhd*, and *moon* became *mn*. There were no more poodles or cellos or pillows or yo-yos, and children went to *schl*. All ends happily, however, when the islanders rally to the greatest of O words: *freedom*.

GAMES

Articulation Family
8 + A board game of words—all kinds of words—for kids and adults. Players move their pieces along a brightly colored playing path while answering chal-

lenging questions about slang, jargon, word definitions, and spelling, or tackling scrambled-word puzzles. The game comes with two sets of question cards, one for players aged 8–12, one for ages 13–adult.

> $26.95
> Worldwide Games
> Box 517
> Colchester, CT 06415-0517
> (800) 888-0987/fax (800) 566-6678
> e-mail: service@snswwide.com
> Web site: www.worldwidegames.com

6 + *ASAP*

A card game of words and letters. Players are challenged to come up with an ice-cream flavor starting with *C*, an animal starting with *G*, or a vegetable starting with *B*.

"ASAP" is recommended for two or more players aged 6–adult.

> $5.95 from game stores or
> Worldwide Games
> Box 517
> Colchester, CT 06415-0517
> (800) 888-0987/fax (800) 566-6678
> e-mail: service@snswwide.com
> Web site: www.worldwidegames.com

8 + *Bethump'd with Words*
Bethump'd with Words Junior

"Bethump'd" is a board game for lovers of English, and its name, appropriately enough, is a quote from the language's greatest practitioner: in William Shakespeare's *King John,* Richard Plantagenet exclaims, "Zounds! I was never so bethump'd with words since I first called my brother's father dad." Each game of "Bethump'd," according to the accompanying rule booklet, "is an enjoyable journey through the origins, history, and evolution of our mother tongue." Players move around an alphabetical playing path, past portraits of various linguistic VIPs (among them Samuel Johnson, Geoffrey Chaucer, Noah Webster, and Mark Twain), attempting to land on each letter of a designated Game Word. The letters of the Word (chosen from the pack of Game Word cards) must be "won" by both landing on the letter's space on the board and correctly answering a question from one of the 1,000+ Question Cards. It's through the Question Cards that

the word *bethumping* occurs: cards are sorted into six levels of difficulty and cover 30 language categories, among them "Acronyms," "Briticisms," "Eponyms," "History," "Homophones," "Idioms," "Nicknames," "Slang," and "Word Origins." A few question examples: "In England, what is a *lift?*" "What common name for *peanut* did English borrow from the African Bantu language?" "What word did Lewis Carroll coin in 1871 by blending the words *chuckle* and *snort?*" "What nickname for a New Zealander is also the name of a small oval fruit of a Chinese gooseberry?"

"Bethump'd With Words" is recommended for two to eight players, teenagers–adults; reasonably language-savvy younger kids, however, should be able to hold their own.

A simpler version of the game, "Bethump'd With Words Junior," is available for kids aged 8–12.

> Mamopalire
> R.R. 1
> Box 122-3
> Warren, VT 05674
> (802) 496-4095/fax (802) 496-4096

8 + *Huggermugger*

Huggermugger means "in secret," which makes sense, since the object of the game is to discover— letter by letter—the identity of a hidden "Mystery Word." Players move about the board, attempting to land on one of the six numbered "arenas," each of which wins them a peek at a corresponding letter in the Mystery Word. (Get to arena 5, for example, and you learn letter 5 of the hidden word.) En route from arena to arena, players must answer word-oriented questions or solve puzzles from the game's 500 question-and-answer cards. These variously involve unscrambling words, giving correct word spellings or definitions, or tackling such miscellaneous challenges as: "List ten words that rhyme with 'shame.'" "What do the initials UNICEF stand for?" "Finish: 'A _____ of a thousand miles must begin with a single step.'"

"Huggermugger" is recommended for two to four players or teams, all adults, but the publishers underestimate the abilities of kids. Those of upper-elementary age and up can handle it. A kid-targeted version of similar format, "Huggermugger, Jr.," is also available. Both can be purchased at toy and game stores.

WRITING

10 *PiQadilly Circus*

An addictive word game inspired by Lewis Carroll's *Alice in Wonderland*; the colorful board looks as if it could have been designed by *Alice*'s original illustrator, Sir John Tenniel. Players advance around the board by constructing words from their hand of letter cards, attempting to reach the "Queen's Table" in the board center without being bumped by an opponent.

$30

Chatham Hill Games, Inc.

Box 253

Chatham, NY 12037

(518) 392-5022 or (800) 554-3039

Web site: www.ocdc.com/Chatham_Hill_Games

10 *Prefix*

A delightful word game designed to build vocabulary, boost verbal creativity, enhance spelling skills, reinforce phonics, and even—in scoring—to give each player some quick practice in mental arithmetic. It's not, however, a thinly disguised grammar lesson: "Prefix" is enjoyable, fast paced, and fun. The heart of the game is four packs of colored cards, each printed with a two- or three-letter prefix. One card is flipped over per round and players, on the included score pads, write down as many words as they can think of that begin with the revealed prefix.

On each turn, the roll of a color-coded die determines which color card is chosen. Colors roughly indicate degree of difficulty: yellow cards are deemed a "modest" challenge; green cards, "moderate"; blue, "monstrous"; and red, "mortifying." Modest yellow cards, for example, prod players to come up with words beginning with *be, so,* and *cr*; brain-wrenching reds demand words beginning with *py, rh,* and *ur.* Players have one minute in which to complete their word lists—the game includes a sand timer—after which they read their lists aloud and compare results. There are set, but simple, rules for scoring—players lose points for duplicate words and for misspellings—and suspicious words are referred to the family dictionary. The person with the highest final score officially wins, but the game in practice has more of a cooperative than competitive flavor, which may come from all that companionable reading aloud.

$29.95 from game stores or

Merriment, Inc.

2140 W. Hubbard St.

Chicago, IL 60612

(312) 942-9420 or (800) 772-4263

12 *Quickword*

A board game of word skills and general knowledge in which players move a token around a colorful triangle-patterned playing path, attempting to be the first to cross off all the required question categories on their scorecards. There are four categories of question cards, grouped according to difficulty. Blue cards are the easiest, requiring players to write down as many words as possible pertaining to an assigned subject: for example, "Anything found at a circus," "Animals found at a zoo," "Chemical elements," or "Members of Congress." Green cards are used in sets of three, for a total list of six topics; the twirl of a spinner then determines the letter of play. Players must give one answer for each topic category, beginning with the selected letter: for example, an "Author or Poet," "Wine or Cheese," "Bird," "Civil War General or Statesman," "Cooking Term," and "Shakespearean Character," all starting with *L.* Pink cards challenge players to come up with as many words as possible that both begin with the letter determined by the spinner and contain the two or more letters shown on the card. With a spinner letter of *B,* for example, plus a pink card requiring the letters *ED,* players might variously produce *bed, breed, bored,* and *buried.* Gray cards are tougher, demanding, for example, six-letter words starting with the letter determined by the spinner, or words that contain the two letters on either side of the spinner, plus one or more letters contained in the word printed on the card. Gray card players thus may end up struggling to find words that contain both a *G* and a *K,* plus at least one of the letters in the word *praise.* They have 90 seconds in which to perform this feat; each "Quickword" round is timed, using the included sand timer. It's an addictive test of linguistic ingenuity, recommended for players aged 12 and up.

$29.95 from game stores or

Aristoplay

450 S. Wagner Rd.

Ann Arbor, MI 48107

(800) 634-7738 or (888) 628-GAME

Web site: www.aristoplay.com

Rhymes & Nyms

A round-robin game of words based on a colorful pack of 52 cards, which variously challenge players to produce rhymes or "nyms" (synonyms, homonyms, or antonyms) for a "starter" word, chosen at random by the dealer. Players are initially dealt 10 cards apiece; the object of the game is to unload all the cards in the hand by giving correct word responses. Each player responds to the word given by the previous player. For the starter word *walk,* for example, player one, discarding a rhyme (*R*) card, may say *talk;* player two, discarding a synonym (*S*) card, responds *speak;* player three, with another rhyme card, says *week;* player four unloads a homonym (*H*) card, with the word *weak;* and the round returns to player one, who discards an antonym (*A*) card, with the word *strong.* And so on. An included instruction sheet describes several variations of the basic game.

Fireside Games
Box 82995
Portland, OR 97282-0995
(503) 231-8990 or (800) 414-8990

Scattergories

A creative game of words in which participants roll a die to determine the key letter of play and are then given a list of categories for which they must come up with a list of words or phrases beginning with the key letter. Players write their answers on the included score pads; points are earned for unique words or phrases that do not match those of other players. The original "Scattergories" is appropriate for older kids and adults; a younger version, "Scattergories Junior," is targeted at kids aged 8–11. Sample kid-style categories include "Wild Animals," "Things You Feed Your Pet," and "Names for a Dog or Cat."

$48.95 from toy and game stores

Symbol Simon

A card game of rebus-style puzzles, in which players translate the pictured symbols into everyday words or phrases. Recommended for two or more players aged 8–adult.

$5.95; available from toy and game stores or
Worldwide Games

Box 517
Colchester, CT 06415-0517
(800) 888-0987/fax (800) 566-6678
e-mail: service@snswwide.com
Web site: www.worldwidegames.com

VOCABULARY ON-LINE

Cool Word of the Day

A new word each day, with definition. Users can also submit their own "cool words," access an on-line thesaurus, or search the Merriam Webster dictionary.

130.63.218.180:80/~wotd

Focusing on Words

Linguistic roots, histories, definitions, synonyms, antonyms, and vocabulary quizzes for advanced word lovers.

www.go-ed.com/el-public/wordfocus/index.html

Fun and Games for Playful Brains: Words

A collection of word games for advanced players based on puns, clerihews, autoantonyms, and scrambled words. There's also a version of Lewis Carroll's "Doublets," in which players, altering one letter at a time, try to transform one word into another.

www.thinks.com
Also see **Word Trek** (page 131).

Hot Rod Your Vocabulary

A word lesson a day. Users first guess the meaning of the featured word, then learn about the word's roots and origins, and finally check their chosen definition through a link to an on-line dictionary.

www.botree.com/vocab

Internet Anagram Server

An anagram is a word or phrase made by rearranging the letters of another word—say turning *lemon* into *melon.* At this site, the computer does all the difficult work for you: type in a word and get back an anagram or list of anagrams. Also included are "Fun Facts" about anagrams and a long list of particularly impressive "Hall of Fame" anagrams.

www.wordsmith.org/anagram/index.html

Jesse's Word of the Day

A word a day, with definition, origin, and comments. Users can also access past words and submit their own word questions.

www.randomhouse.com/jesse

Ladyfingers and Nun's Tummies

The origin of food names. Users click on the highlighted words in the text to learn about Jordan almonds, Tootsie Rolls, Fig Newtons, and many more. The site also includes food word quizzes and links to related sites.

members.iglou.com/barnette

Also see *Ladyfingers and Nun's Tummies* (page 120).

The Palindrome Home Page

Palindromes of all kinds, including simple, foreign-language, name (BOB), and "wordy" (that is, word palindromes, as opposed to letter palindromes).

www.ecst.csuchico.edu/~nanci/Pdromes/index.html

Also see *Go Hang a Salami! I'm a Lasagna Hog! and Other Palindromes* (page 119) and *Too Hot to Hoot* (page 120).

Verbivore

Essays by wordsmith Richard Lederer on word origins, plus links to many related word sites.

pov1.netcom.com/~rlederer/index.html

Where's That From?

A multiple-choice quiz on word origins.

www.intuitive.com:80/origins

A Word a Day

A new vocabulary word every day, along with its definition, occasional historical commentary, and an illustrative quotation.

www.wordsmith.org/awad/index.html

The Word Wizard

Those who join the (free) on-line club have access to listings of recently coined words and their definitions, quotations and their sources, classic insults, and selections from the world's best diaries (what happened on their day *today*). There's also an option for submitting your own word questions.

wordwizard.com

WWWebster Dictionary

Users can type in a word and search for the definition, learn the word of the day, and play assorted word games, variously based on slang, word definitions, word history, or antonyms and synonyms. Also included is the game of "Transform Brainstorm," a puzzle in which players must figure out how to change one word into another by altering letters.

www.m-w.com/netdict.htm

GRAMMAR

BOOKS

A is for Angry: An Animal and Adjective Alphabet

Sandra Boynton; Workman, 1987

An animal and an adjective for each letter of the alphabet. For readers aged 4–7.

The Amazing Pop-Up Grammar Book

Kate Petty; Dutton Children's Books, 1995

Friendly animal characters introduce kids to all the parts of speech in this interactive book, which includes games, puzzles, flaps, wheels, tabs, and explanatory dialogue in cartoon-style balloons. Readers, for example, can create strange creatures by mixing adjectives or search the "Lost and Found" department for the missing possessive case.

A Bundle of Beasts

Patricia Hooper; Houghton Mifflin, 1987

Short, clever poems about collective nouns, among them a smack of jellyfish, a pod of whales, and a murder of crows.

A Cache of Jewels and Other Collective Nouns

Ruth Heller; Paper Star, 1998

A beautifully illustrated picture book that begins "A word that means a collection of things, like a CACHE of jewels for the crowns of kings . . . or a BATCH of bread all warm and brown, is always called a COLLECTIVE NOUN." Heller then takes young readers on a gloriously colorful rhyming tour of assorted collective nouns, among them a gam of green whales, a fleet of purple-sailed chips, a coven of witches, a swarm of bees, and an army of ants. Other books about parts of speech in the same format by Heller include *Behind the Mask: A Book About Prepositions* (Grosset & Dunlap, 1995), *Kites Sail High: A Book About Verbs* (Paper Star, 1998), *Many Luscious Lollipops: A Book About Adjectives* (Paper Star, 1998), *Merry-Go-Round: A Book About Nouns* (Paper Star, 1998), *Mine, All Mine: A Book About Pronouns* (Grosset & Dunlap, 1997), and *Up, Up, and Away: A Book About Adverbs* (Price Stern Sloan, 1993).

6 10 *I Think I Thought and Other Tricky Verbs*
Marvin Terban; Houghton Mifflin, 1984

Many clever examples of irregular verbs for elementary school–aged grammarians, in 64 illustrated pages. See *Your Foot's on My Feet! and Other Tricky Nouns* (below).

4 8 *Slither, Swoop, Swing*
Alex Ayliffe; Viking, 1993

A picture book of verbs for young readers. Each double-page spread describes a different kind of animal movement: *waddle,* for example, is paired with a picture of penguins.

6 10 *Your Foot's on My Feet! and Other Tricky Nouns*
Marvin Terban; Houghton Mifflin, 1986

An illustrated collection of nouns with unconventional plurals for elementary school–aged readers.

ACTIVITY BOOKS

8 18 *Caught' Ya! Grammar With a Giggle*
Jane Bell Kiester; Maupin House, 1993

Kiester's book attempts to apply a "learning by doing" approach to the ins and outs of English grammar, language mechanics, and usage skills. The process is simple, quick—it takes about 10 minutes a day—effective, and fun. A "Caught'ya," explains Kiester, is a sentence or two of an ongoing, silly story, laced with grammatical and spelling errors. Kids are challenged to write the "Caught'ya" as correctly as possible. If they goof, they're caught—"Caught'ya!"—and the teacher helps correct the error. Once the "Caught'ya" is finished, the entire sentence is reviewed and evaluated.

Kiester encourages users to invent their own stories, tailored to tickle the funnybones of their own group of students, and gives advice on how to do so. She also includes three complete sentence-by-sentence tales, variously targeted at kids in grades 3–5 ("The Magic Purple Umbrella"), 6–8 ("Hairy Beast and Friends"), and 9–11 ("Romeo and Juliet Revised"). Each sentence of each story is shown in incorrect and corrected versions, and for each there's a list of the grammatical, spelling, and vocabulary skills emphasized. "While I do not claim that the Caught'ya will, like the proverbial snake oil, cure all the ills of every English class," concludes Kiester, "it certainly does solve a plethora of problems. (Please note correct use of the vocabulary word and give me extra credit.)"

9 + *Editor in Chief*
In this grammatical disaster series, kids learn the rules of English by correcting the errors—always a satisfying process—in short articles written by other people. *Editor in Chief Book A* zeroes in on the grammar skills generally taught in grades 4–5; *Book B* covers grades 6–7; and *Book C,* grades 8 and up. To-be-edited articles, all illustrated, are generally interesting and informational, including short reports, letters, and first-person stories. Each article contains 9 to 15 mistakes in spelling, punctuation, sentence structure, paragraph organization, and the like. Turn the kids loose with a red pencil; then flip to the back of the book for the answers, which include a complete correct version of the original article, plus explanations of all the necessary alterations.

Critical Thinking Press & Software
Box 448
Pacific Grove, CA 93950
(800) 458-4849

8 + *Hajek House*
Teacher Ellen Hajek has devised a grammar program based on the helpful Humpties ("Parts of Speech with 'Eggceptional' Personalities"), a collection of little

WRITING

egg-shaped characters that variously represent nouns, verbs, conjunctions, pronouns, adjectives, adverbs, prepositions, and interjections. The Noun Humpty, for example, the "father of the parts of speech family," is an evilly smirking egg in glasses and top hat; the Verb Humpty (mother) has eyelashes and wiggle lines, suggestive of active dancing; the Conjunction Humpty (the family friend) has a spit curl in the middle of his forehead and arms spread wide, hug-style. In the first book, *Humpties,* targeted at beginning grammar students, kids are given sample sentences in which to identify each new part of speech, matching words to the correct Humpty. Sheets of cutout Humpties are provided for this purpose at the back of the book.

Once users have mastered the introductory Humpties, they're ready for the next book, *Building Sentences with the Humpties,* in which they learn the definitions of simple and compound subjects and predicates, prepositional phrases, and objects, and are taught how to diagram a sentence.

A drawback of the workbooks is the poor quality of the all-black-and-white illustrations: the Humpties are definitely homely, though they can be livened up a bit by coloring. A second negative is the blahness of the sample sentences, which are all standard workbook fare, along the lines of "Bob has a red kite," "I like to eat fish," and "Jane cleans her room thoroughly." (Grammar, never a hot topic around here, goes down better with a little pizzazz, as in "The evil space monster foolishly stepped in the quicksand.")

Hajek's Humpties do, however, straightforwardly cover the grammar basics, and the cut-and-match technique makes for more hands-on interaction than is found in conventional circle-the-verb-type workbooks.

Hajek House
12750 W. Sixth Pl.
Golden, CO 80401
(303) 237-3471

Learning Language Arts Through Literature
6 18 This series of nine color-coded spiral-bound books is intended to teach the rules and skills of written language to kids in grade 1 through high school. The books consist of a collection of weekly lessons, each including a short literature passage for copying or dictation, followed by assorted grammar, spelling, creative writing, and discussion activities.

Literature selections are somewhat uneven in quality. *The Purple Book* (grade 5), for example, includes passages from Richard and Florence Atwater's *Mr. Popper's Penguins,* E. B. White's *The Trumpet of the Swan,* Lois Lenski's *Strawberry Girl,* and Elizabeth Yates's *Amos Fortune, Free Man,* along with a definitely unremarkable retelling of the story of Johnny Appleseed ("The Mission of John Chapman" by Linda Fowler) and excerpts from a mediocre biography of David Livingstone. The series has a Christian orientation, but with a little editing can be adapted to persons who prefer their language arts nondenominational.

Common Sense Press
8786 Hway. 21
Box 1365
Melrose, FL 32666
(904) 475-5757

GAMES

Challenges
8 13 A grammatical card game, splashily illustrated in red, yellow, and blue, in which the cards are divided into four color-coded suits: noun/pronoun, verb, adjective/verb, and conjunction/preposition. Instructions are included for two levels of play: beginners learn the basics of grammar; more advanced players use the cards to build complex and creative (and grammatically correct) sentences.

$12.95
U.S. Games Systems, Inc.
179 Ludlow St.
Stamford, CT 06902
(203) 353-8400 or (800) 544-2637
Also see **Games** (page 121).

AUDIO RESOURCES

Grammar Songs
6 12 Assorted collections of grammar songs, among them *Rock & Learn Grammar, Grammar Grooves,* and *Grammar and Punctuation Songs,* are available from

the Educational Record Center. All feature "contemporary upbeat" music and are accompanied by activity workbooks. Recommended for kids aged 6–12.

Educational Record Center, Inc.

3233 Burnt Mill Dr., Suite 100

Wilmington, NC 28403-2655

(910) 251-1236 or (800) 438-1637/fax (888) 438-1637

e-mail: erc-inc@worldnet.att.net

Web site: www.erc-inc.com

Grammar Songs

"You never forget what you sing!" writes author and English teacher Kathy Troxel, whose book-and-cassette set, *Grammar Songs*, includes musical tributes to verbs ("I'm a verb, verb, verb/I'm an action word"), nouns, sentences, pronouns, adjectives, adverbs, prepositions, capital letters, plurals, commas, quotation marks, and Greek and Latin prefixes. There's even a six-verse song all about apostrophes. An accompanying 68-page workbook includes all the song lyrics, plus written language-usage exercises to accompany each song. Answers, as well as suggestions for additional activities and grammar games, are listed in an included teacher's guide booklet.

Audio Memory Publishing

2060 Raymond Ave.

Signal Hill, CA 90806

(800) 365-SING

Computer Software

Carmen Sandiego Word Detective

Carmen Sandiego and her gang of villains have developed a Babble-On machine, an evil device that turns language into incomprehensible nonsense. Players must deactivate the machine and free their babbling fellow detectives. They do so by solving grammar, spelling, and vocabulary problems and puzzles. The game, which can be played at three levels of difficulty, covers parts of speech, punctuation, sentence structure, spelling, and vocabulary. Included are a list of 10,000 spelling words, 100 basic rules of grammar, and an Electronic Dictionary. On CD-ROM for Mac or Windows.

$34.95

Broderbund

Box 6125

Novato, CA 94948-6125

(800) 521-6263

Web site: www.broderbund.com or www.carmen-sandiego.com

Grammar On-Line

Common Errors in English

Many common grammatical goofs in alphabetical order, from a professor of English at Washington State University. Users learn, for example, the proper usage of such often confused pairs as accept/except and farther/further.

www.wsu.edu:8080/~brians/errors

On-Line English Grammar

A very thorough site for middle school and high school students, including detailed information about all aspects of English grammar, plus many practice tests.

www.edunet.com/english/grammarl

Right Words: Grammar, Punctuation, and Other Tricks of the Trade

A list of helpful grammatical information, including "Sentenced to a Cruel End" (the definition of a complete sentence), "Muddled Sentences" (about misplaced modifiers), and "Capital Punishment" (the proper use of capital letters). Cute titles, but a serious text for teenagers.

www.rightwords.co.nz

Save the Adverb

Includes a detailed definition of *adverb*, a long list of quotations using adverbs, and information on how to campaign to save the adverb (use them in sentences).

www.cs.wisc.edu/~dgarret/adverb

SPELLING

Books

How to Teach Any Child to Spell

Gayle Graham; Common Sense Press, 1995

This small, bright yellow teacher's guide accompanies a larger student spelling notebook, *Tricks of the*

Trade. The gist of Graham's how-to technique is free writing. "Children are forced to *think about spelling* when they write," states Graham. "Write something every day—journals, letters, paragraphs, descriptions, explanations, posters, lists . . ." These written pieces should then be edited and corrected—by the student him/herself—and the misspelled words categorized in the individualized student notebook "according to the syllable patterns of our language."

By the time kids are 8 or 9, Graham suggests, the daily spelling lessons should consist of a five-minute review of phonics, a five-minute review of words from the child's spelling notebook, 10 minutes of oral reading with "penciling"—draw little swoop marks under each syllable of selected words—to enhance visual perception and pattern recognition, and a writing project. Editing of the writing project, in turn, generates new words to be entered in the student's spelling notebook, for the next day's review.

Categorization of student spelling errors, unfortunately, quickly becomes an intimidating process. *How to Teach Any Child to Spell* lists six basic spelling rules (each with listed exceptions), plus four pages of basic phonics rules. These quickly expand in the individualized spelling notebook—you'll need one for each student— into 70+ pages of word categories: "*ce* as in ocean," "*ci* as in special," "*se* as in noise," "*gh* as in spaghetti," "*ue* as in guest," "*yr* as in martyr," and so on. Users are expected to analyze their misspelled words and enter them in the notebooks in the proper categories.

> *How to Teach Any Child to Spell* and *Tricks of the Trade,* respectively, $8 and $12; two-book set, $18
> Common Sense Press
> 8786 Hway. 21
> Box 1365
> Melrose, FL 32666
> (904) 475-5757

A Measuring Scale for Ability in Spelling

ALL Leonard Porter Ayers; Mott Media, 1988

The Ayers scale is designed to pinpoint students' levels of spelling competency. It consists of a series of graded lists of spelling words, in order of difficulty from the very simple to the very challenging. Users simply test their kids on each list; when you reach the list where your kid misses about half the words, that's his/her

grade spelling level. Helpful if you're trying to decide what level commercial spelling program to order.

> Mott Media
> 1000 E. Huron St.
> Milford, MI 48402
> (248) 685-8773/fax (248) 685-8776

Spelling Book

6 12 Edward Fry; Laguna Beach Educational Books, 1992

"It is scientifically proven that English spelling is a mess," begins the Preface to Edward Fry's *Spelling Book.* Still, somehow people learn to spell, and Fry, in 195 sequential lessons, tries to help the process along. The book is a complete spelling curriculum for grades 1–6, teaching a total of 2,985 of our most frequently used words. Each lower-level lesson includes a 10- to 20-word spelling list, sample sentences using the spelling words for students to read or write, and a phonics review. More advanced lessons include a "word study" section, covering suffixes, prefixes, homophones, phonograms, and word origins, and lists of "variant forms" of the basic spelling words. (Variant forms of *apply,* for example, include *applied, applies,* and *applying.*)

> Laguna Beach Educational Books
> 245 Grandview
> Laguna Beach, CA 92651
> (714) 494-4225

Spelling Power Activity Cards

5 18 Beverly L. Adams-Gordon; Castlemoyle Books

Designed to accompany and enhance any spelling program. The cards, all 365 of them, are color coded, sorted into five spelling activity categories, and packaged in a durable plastic filing box. Colors indicate the approximate grade level appropriate to the listed activity: red cards cover grades K–3; blue, 3–6; green, 6–9; and yellow, grade 10 and up.

The five activity categories include "Drill Activities," "Skill Builders," "Writing Prompters," "Dictionary Skills," and "Homonyms & More." Drill Activities lure young spellers into the repetitive practice of assigned spelling words: "dial" your words on the buttons of the telephone; spell your words with letter tiles; play "Spelling Baseball" in which players "pitch" words at each other and move around the bases with each correct spelling. Skill Builders activities deal with the rules of spelling, identifying long and short vowel sounds, properly adding *ed* and *ing* to words that end in a silent *e;* use of abbreviations and capital letters. Writing Prompters include suggestions for short writing projects using assigned spelling words. (Example: "Invent a food that could be named after you. Describe it in three sentences.") Dictionary Skills activities hone in on alphabetization skills and the practical use of the dictionary, including a lot of connect-the-dot puzzles that involve putting words in alphabetical order. Homonyms & More activities concentrate on words that sound alike (but aren't) through assorted matching, multiple-choice, and fill-in-the-blank worksheet-style activities.

Some of the sample activities have religious themes (Card 148: "Rev. Graham proclaimed, 'God remembers all who worship Him.'"), but most are theology-free.

$24.95, including teacher's manual
Castlemoyle Books
15436 42nd Ave. S
Seattle, WA 98188-2215
(206) 439-0248

Spelling Smart!

Cynthia M. Stowe; Center for Applied Research in Education, 1996

A 400+-page spelling program for students in grade 4 and up, targeted at those who have trouble learning to spell through rote memorization. The program encourages students to apply logical thinking skills to spelling in 40 lessons, each concentrating on a different sound or spelling rule. Each lesson follows the same format: new information is presented and discussed; students practice new words from the spelling list and use the words in context, in dictated sentences; and finally, students are encouraged to participate in reinforcing activities, among them word games, short research projects, and reading spelling-word-related books. Also included for each lesson are ready-to-use fill-in-the-blank and categorization worksheets, lists of vocabulary words to define and use in sentences, a "list" project (in lesson one, for example, which concentrates on "short *a*" words, users are challenged make a list of many types of hats), and a creative writing project.

What Rhymes with Eel? A Word-and-Picture Flap Book

Harriet Ziefert; Viking, 1996

A playful lesson in phonics and spelling for kids aged 4–8. Readers lift up flaps, thus converting a boat into a goat, a wheel into an eel, a bear into a pear.

What Rhymes With Snake? A Word-and-Picture Flap Book

Rick Brown; William Morrow, 1994

An interactive lesson in phonics and spelling for beginners, in which readers lift flaps, variously turning a hen into a pen and a goose into a moose.

Words Their Way: Word Study for Phonics, Vocabulary, and Spelling

Donald R. Bear, ed.; Merrill Publishing Company, 1995

A 384-page comprehensive text and sourcebook by and for educators, which covers word recognition and spelling skills exhibited by kids in grades K–12, discusses teaching tools and techniques, and suggests over 250 phonics, vocabulary, and spelling activities in developmental order for kids of all ages.

GAMES

Boggle

The three-minute word game from Parker Brothers for kids aged 8 and up. Players scramble the 16 Boggle letter cubes into the playing grid, then search for as many words as can be found by joining letters horizontally, vertically, diagonally, or all of the above. The longer the word, the more points won. Each round takes a mere three minutes; a sand timer is included. Fast and fun.

Available from toy and game stores.

Scrabble

The classic spelling game in which players use letter tiles to spell interconnected words, crossword puzzle–style, on the game board. Letters are assigned point values depending on their frequency of usage, which means that any word with a *Q, J,* or *Z* in it is bound to be a plum. Can be played by a wide range of ages, especially if you're willing to help younger spellers along with an occasional hint.

Available from toy and game stores.

[12] Word Trek

The original game of "Word Trek" was invented by author/mathematician Lewis Carroll. The game consists of a series of puzzles printed on cards. Each puzzle contains two words with the same number of letters—say, *play a tune* or *good luck*. The trick is to change word one (*play, good*) into word two (*tune, luck*) by changing just one letter at a time or by rearranging existing letters. In a step-by-step process for changing *play* into *tune,* for example, players might first change the *p* into a *c* to make *clay*. Then rearrange the letters to make the word *lacy,* which—by single letter changes—can then go from *lace* to *lane* to *lune* to *tune*. A solution to each puzzle is given on the reverse side of the card, though, the publishers hasten to explain, there are many other correct possibilities. The first person to solve the puzzle says (or shouts, depending on how triumphant he/she feels) "Word Trek!" and thus wins a point. The person with the most points at the end of the game wins. The game includes two decks of cards, with 216 word puzzles. The puzzles aren't easy; the game is recommended for teenagers and up.

$12

Rex Games, Inc.

530 Howard St., Suite 100

San Francisco, CA 94105-3007

(800) 542-6375

Web site: www.rexgames.com

Also see *Fun and Games for Playful Brains* (page 124) and *WWWebster Dictionary* (page 125).

SPELLING ON-LINE

[10] A Spelling Test

Test your skills with a multiple-choice spelling test based on the 50 most commonly misspelled words in English. Users can check their answers at the end. For advanced spellers: among the 50 are such words as *broccoli, irritable,* and *accommodation*.

www.sentex.net/~mmcadams/spelling.html

DICTIONARIES

GENERAL DICTIONARIES

[P/T] *Kister's Best Dictionaries for Adults and Young People: A Comparative Guide*

Kenneth F. Kister; Oryx Press, 1992

General information on dictionaries, instructions for differentiating between good dictionaries and bad, and reviews of some 300 dictionaries, including 132 for adults and 168 for kids.

[ALL] *The Oxford English Dictionary*

Oxford University Press, 1978

The mother of all dictionaries, familiarly known as the *OED*. The full-size version includes 12 enormous volumes, plus four supplements; there's also a heroically reduced version, in three volumes, which comes with a magnifying glass because the print is too tiny to be read by the unaided eye. The content, in both, is enthralling: the *OED* not only lists word origins, definitions, and pronunciations but also traces the history of each included word from its first appearance in written English, using a wealth of intriguing quotations.

[ALL] *When Is a Pig a Hog? A Guide to Confoundingly Related English Words*

Bernice Randall; Budget Book Service, 1997

Has 1,500 comparative word definitions, variously explaining the differences between such seemingly synonymous pairs of words as street and avenue, couch and sofa, and number and numeral.

DICTIONARIES FOR KIDS

[9][12] *The American Heritage Children's Dictionary*

Houghton Mifflin, 1997

An 880-page illustrated dictionary for readers aged 9–12. Also see *The American Heritage Student Dictionary,* for readers aged 11–15.

Cat in the Hat Beginner Book Dictionary

P. D. Eastman; Random House, 1973

Definitions for 1,350 vocabulary words, all illustrated with zany Dr. Seuss characters, for readers aged 4–8.

Eyewitness Visual Dictionary Series

Dorling Kindersley

A series of beautifully illustrated 64-page books for young adults, featuring "exploded view" photographs with all possible parts labeled in detail. Each book in the series centers around a specific theme. Sample titles: *The Visual Dictionary of Buildings* and *The Visual Dictionary of the Human Body*. Other topics include cars, chemistry, dinosaurs, plants, ancient civilizations, and everyday things.

The Kingfisher First Dictionary

John Grisewood, ed.; Kingfisher Books, 1995

Contains 1,500 major entries, 1,000 color graphics, simple definitions, and activities designed to promote dictionary skills.

See *The Kingfisher Illustrated Children's Dictionary* (below).

The Kingfisher Illustrated Children's Dictionary

John Grisewood, ed.; Kingfisher Books, 1994

A 480-page illustrated dictionary/encyclopedia for kids aged 9–12. The book includes 12,000 dictionary entries, 1,000 encyclopedic entries, and 1,000 color illustrations.

The Macmillan Dictionary for Children

Robert B. Costello, ed.; Simon & Schuster, 1997

An excellent 896-page dictionary for readers aged 9–12, including 1,100 color illustrations, word history and synonym boxes for featured words, and detailed instructions for using the dictionary. Also see *The Macmillan First Dictionary* and *The Macmillan Dictionary for Students*, for younger and older readers, respectively.

Merriam-Webster's Elementary Dictionary

Merriam-Webster, 1994

Contains 33,000 entries and 600 color illustrations, for kids in grades 4–6. Also see *Merriam-Webster's School Dictionary*, for kids in grades 6–12.

My Very Own Big Dictionary

Pamela Cote; Houghton Mifflin, 1996

A 40-page illustrated dictionary for kids aged 4–8, with suggestions for dictionary-related activities.

Scholastic Children's Dictionary

Scholastic, 1996

Has 30,000 word entries, with word history, synonym, and suffix and prefix boxes for featured words. For readers aged 9–12.

The Sesame Street Dictionary

Linda Hayward; Random House, 1980

Lists 1,300 words, each with a simple definition, a sentence using the word, and a word-related illustration featuring the familiar *Sesame Street* characters, for readers aged 4–8.

DICTIONARIES ON-LINE

Casey's Snowy Day Reverse Dictionary (and Guru)

The flip side of the dictionary: type in a definition and get back the word—or rather a list of possible words. Users click on each to get a full definition.

www.c3.lanl.gov:8064/cgi/revdict.cgi

Galaxy

A huge number of informational links, organized by category. Under "Reference" are included links to dictionaries, encyclopedias, libraries, and quotation collections.

galaxy.einet.net/galaxy.html

Kids Reference Stuff

Links to English dictionaries, foreign-language dictionaries, thesauri, fact books, encyclopedias, maps, and more.

www.kcstar.com/kids/links/refer.htm

List of Dictionaries

Links to a long list of dictionaries, including English, foreign-language, acronym, rhyming, idiom, specialty, and technical dictionaries.

math-www.uni.paderborn.de/HTML/
Dictionaries.html

Macquarie K*I*D

A "Kids Internet Dictionary," written entirely by kids. Users can browse the dictionary, search for specific words, add a word of their own, or investigate a clickable world map.

www.dict.mq.edu.au/kid.html

OneLook Dictionaries

Well over a million words in 211 dictionaries. Enter a word, hit *look it up,* and find the definition.

www.onelook.com

On-line Rhyming Dictionary

Type in a word—any word—and search for a list of rhymes.

www.link.cs.com.edu/dougb/rhyme-doc.html

WWWebster Dictionary

Word definitions, word games, a word of the day, and many links to other dictionary-related sites.

www.m-w.com/netdict.htm

STYLE MANUALS

The Deluxe Transitive Vampire: A Handbook of Grammar for the Innocent, the Eager, and the Doomed

Karen Elizabeth Gordon; Pantheon, 1993

All the rules of English grammar, demonstrated through hilarious examples paired with doleful Victorian illustrations. "I had moped for five days before I would touch my gruel." "After they removed the leeches, she showed them to the door." And my favorite: "Not only were we naked, crazed, and starving (and far from our warm little homes); we were without any good books as well."

These are books for adults and sophisticated older kids: portions of them are suggestively naughty ("Ogling stevedores is his penchant") and the vocabulary is advanced. All those creative visual images, however, give an extra boost to memory; rules learned from *The Transitive Vampire* are remembered.

Also see, by the same author, *The New Well-Tempered Sentence: A Punctuation Handbook for the Innocent, the Eager, and the Doomed* (Ticknor & Fields, 1993).

The Elements of Style

William Strunk Jr. and E. B. White; Macmillan, 1979

A classic and invaluable manual of language usage for writers of all ages. It includes, in clear and graceful prose, explanations of the basic rules of usage and principles of composition, and a wonderful chapter, "Misused Words and Expressions," which deals with such tricky problems as the frowned-upon split infinitive, the proper use of *shall* versus *will,* and the fatally abused adverb *hopefully.*

Also see *Elements of Style On-line* at www.cc. columbia.edu/acis/bartleby/strunk

The New Fowler's Modern English Usage

R. W. Burchfield, ed.; Oxford University Press, 1996

The first edition was published in 1926; Winston Churchill used it to criticize the grammar in the plans for the Normandy invasion. The latest 800+-page edition, with thousands of alphabetically arranged entries, clears up questions of word usage, spelling, pronunciation, definition, and style. It explains, for example, when *every day* should be spelled as one word and when as two; clarifies the difference between *legal* and *lawful;* and describes, with many literary examples, the correct use of the exclamation point.

Woe Is I: The Grammarphobe's Guide to Better English in Plain English

Patricia T. O'Conner; Putnam, 1996

"A survival guide for intelligent people who probably never have diagrammed a sentence and never will." Chapters in this delightful and useful book include "Woe Is I: Therapy for Pronoun Anxiety," "Plurals Before Swine: Blunders With Numbers," and "Yours Truly: The Possessives and the Possessed." Includes a list of 13 rules for clear and competent writing and a glossary, defining all essential grammatical terms from adjective to vowel.

QUOTATIONS

BOOKS

American Heritage Dictionary of American Quotations

Margaret Miner and Hugh Rawson, eds.; Penguin, 1997

Over 5,000 quotations on 500 topics by such prominent Americans as Abigail Adams, Sojourner Truth, Will Rogers, Benjamin Franklin, Geronimo, and Al Capone.

American Indian Quotations

Howard J. Langer. ed.; Greenwood Publishing Group, 1996

Contains 800 quotations arranged chronologically, with brief biographies of the speakers.

The Beacon Book of Quotations by Women

Rosalie Maggio, ed.; Beacon Press, 1992

Over 5,000 quotations by women past and present, listed by category, from "Absence" and "Absolutes" to "Writing" and "Youth."

Chemical Curiosities: Spectacular Experiments and Inspired Quotes

H. W. Roesky, K. Mockel, and Roald Hoffman; John Wiley & Sons, 1996

A combination of terrific chemical experiments—titles include "Golden Rain," "Lightning Under Water," and "Volcano"—and literary quotations.

Familiar Quotations

John Bartlett; Little, Brown, 1980

A 1,000+-page collection of quotations, arranged in chronological order by author, with a very detailed index.

The Great Thoughts

George Seldes, ed.; Ballantine, 1996

Over 500 pages of quotations from great thinkers, listed in alphabetical order from Abbey and Abelard to Zola and Zwingli.

The Harper Book of Quotations

Robert I. Fitzhenry, ed.; HarperPerennial, 1993

More than 6,500 quotations listed by category, from "Ability and Achievement" through "Youth."

Hodge Podge: A Commonplace Book

J. Bryan III; Atheneum, 1986

A wonderful and eclectic collection of quotes and fascinating facts, listed in alphabetical (rather than chronological) order by subject. Also see, by the same author, *Hodge Podge Two: Another Commonplace Book* (Atheneum, 1989).

See **Commonplace Books** (page 116).

The Oxford Dictionary of Quotations

Oxford University Press, 1980

Nearly 900 comprehensive pages of quotations. I prefer this one to Bartlett's *Familiar Quotations* because names, titles, and keywords are set in boldface type, which makes them easy to read, and the quotations are listed in alphabetical (rather than chronological) order by author, which—presuming you know the author's name—makes them easier to find. The book also includes a comprehensive index of quotations listed by key words.

QUOTATIONS ON-LINE

The Quotation Page

Includes quotes of the day and week, random quotes, keyword search for specific quotations, and links to other quotation-related sites. Users can also submit favorite quotations of their own.

www.starlingtech.com/quotes

Quotations

Nearly 18,000 entries in 30 categories, among them "Wisdom," "Poetry," "Serious Sarcasm," and "The Best of Anonymous."

www.geocities.com/~spanoudi/quote.html

WRITING

CREATIVE WRITING

While creative writing is often considered an exercise in pure imagination—as in short stories, poems, and plays—creativity can find expression in other fields as well. "Writing Across the Curriculum" (WAC) programs encourage students to write not only in formal English classes but also to use writing as a learning tool in all academic subjects, including science, math, history, geography, art, and music. Proponents of such programs explain that writing reinforces lesson material, helps kids assess their level of understanding, and provides a detailed record of individual progress. Often such writing takes place in a student log or journal, in which kids summarize or describe interdisciplinary information: science experiments, math problems and procedures, history projects and discoveries, art and music studies. Kids who find creative writing difficult often blossom in cross-curricular expression.

Our middle son, for example—Ethan, the incipient engineer—first began to enjoy writing as a part of his science education. One aspect of Ethan's science curriculum involves the daily reading of articles from science journals, magazines, or essay collections. Fretting over his underdeveloped writing skills, we suggested that he write short summaries of the information gleaned from his readings to share with his family. The result: an ongoing "Science Reading Journal."

Some useful sources for cross-curricular writers include the following:

Thinking Globally: Writing and Reading Across the Curriculum
Andrew E. Robson; McGraw-Hill, 1997

How to implement a cross-curricular writing program for teenagers and college students, with writing/reading activities from varied academic disciplines. Sample writing project topics include the origin of the universe, plate tectonics, maps, and cultural relativism.

Writing Across the Curriculum in Middle and High Schools
Rhoda J. Maxwell; Allyn & Bacon, 1996

Discusses the process of writing, the advantages of cross-curricular writing, and techniques of journal keeping, with suggestions for using writing in math, science, social studies, art, and music classes.

Writing in Math Class: A Resource for Grades 2–8
Marilyn Burns; Marilyn Burns Educational Associates, 1995

How to use writing to support math learning, ways to incorporate creative writing into a math curriculum, and suggestions for general writing assignments.

Writing Journals: Activities Across the Curriculum/Grades 4–6
Linda Western; Good Year Books, 1995

Suggestions for cross-curricular journals for kids aged 9–12.
See *Responding* (page 141).

ORGANIZATIONS

The Writing Conference
The Writing Conference, Inc., was founded in 1980 to provide services and support for parents and teachers interested in children's writing. The group sponsors an annual contest for young writers, a week-long summer Writing/Literature Camp for kids in grades 6–12, and an annual conference for writing teachers and specialists. The Writing Conference also publishes a small catalog of interesting publications on strategies for teaching writing, *The Writer's Slate*, a journal of original student writing (see page 145), and *The Teacher's Slate*, which includes articles on creative writing by teachers.

The Writing Conference, Inc.
Box 664
Ottawa, KS 66067
(913) 242-0407

CATALOGS

Interact English Catalog
Interact projects stress "learning through involvement," specializing in cooperative learning units and education simulations across a range of academic disci-

plines. The company publishes several catalogs, among them the *Interact English Catalog,* which carries materials suitable for kids in grades 6–12. Among these are several innovative creative writing programs such as *Responding* (see page 141) for cross-curricular writers and the creative essay-writing programs on page 143.

Interact
1825 Gillespie Way, #101
El Cajon, CA 92020
(800) 359-0961/fax (800) 700-5093
Web site: www.interact-simulations.com

The Writing Company

The Writing Company, a division of the Social Studies School Service, publishes a large and varied catalog of materials for writers and readers. The catalog includes books, workbooks, and activity books on journal keeping, script writing, poetry, library research, report writing, journalism, study skills, test preparation, grammar basics, word skills, and much more.

The Writing Company
10200 Jefferson Blvd., Room WR
Box 802
Culver City, CA 90232-0802
(310) 839-2436 or (800) 421-4246/(310) 839-2249 or (800) 944-5432
e-mail: access@SocialStudies.com
Web site: writingco.com/writing

MAGAZINES

The Teacher's Slate
See **The Writing Conference** (page 135).

Writing Teacher

P/T This 48-page magazine for writing teachers (grades K–8) is published five times per year, in September, November, January, March, and May. Features include interviews with writing specialists and articles on the practice and theory of teaching writing, plus pages of "writing warm-ups" for primary- and intermediate-level writers, ready-to-use lesson plans, and reviews of writing resources.

Annual subscription (5 issues), $25

Writing Teacher
Box 791437
San Antonio, TX 78279
(210) 438-4262 or (800) 68-TEACH/(210) 438-4263

BOOKS: NONFICTION

Any Child Can Write

ALL Harvey S. Wiener; Bantam Books, 1990

Subtitled "An At-Home Guide to Enhancing Your Child's Elementary Education," this book is a collection of writing games, exercises, examples, and techniques for developing young writers. Included is a list of writing goals for kids at various public school grade levels from kindergarten through high school (though the author states that "no absolute standards of competence may be established for children in particular grades or at particular ages") and, in an appendix, a list of "One Hundred Ideas for Writing at Home."

Families Writing

ALL Peter R. Stillman; Writer's Digest Books, 1989

How to encourage family writing, plus a lifetime of writing activities for family members of all ages. "The kinds of writing addressed throughout this book have a variety of intents," writes Stillman, "but they have in common a recreational quality; they should be engaging, even fun." For this reason, Stillman continues, "Don't stress correctness over substance in others' writing, offer critiques, issue assignments, refer to anyone's writing as a 'paper,' ask a family member of any age to 'pass in' his or her 'work,' write comment of any kind on a piece of writing without an express request from its author, ever, ever use red ink, circle words, insert question marks, employ such handy-hideous shorthand as 'awk,' 'sp,' or 'expl' . . ."

This is writing for the joy of it, and for those who have been taught to view setting pen to paper in a far different light, Stillman suggests starting small. Jot down lists, for example, of—depending on your age and interests—all the pets you've ever had, with a line or two about each, all the vehicles you've ever owned, each with a short comment, the names of the people in your kindergarten class or childhood neighborhood, your 10 favorite possessions, the 10 most important dates in your life. From there, literary possibilities branch, multiply, and become more challenging. Stillman suggests keeping a round-robin family journal or a joint "Field Notes" book, writing a family newsletter or compiling a family recipe book, recording family stories and traditions, inventing storyboards or writing text to accompany family photographs, or writing—jointly or singly—poetry. Suggestions are peppered with wonderful examples, which make readers itch to grab a pencil and do likewise.

One of my favorite anecdotes in *Families Writing* is Stillman's account of the best Christmas present ever, the gift of a young man who wrote to his grandmother one December:

> Dear Grandma,
>
> This is to wish you a Merry Christmas. Instead of giving you a typical present this year, I promise instead to write you a letter every week.

It was the beginning of a lifelong correspondence. Also see *Write Away: A Friendly Guide for Teenage Writers* (Boynton/Cook, 1995).

GNYS AT WRK

P/T Glenda Bissex; Harvard University Press, 1980

GNYS AT WRK translates as "Genius At Work," and this sign, posted by the author's young son on his bedroom door, eventually developed into an entire doctoral thesis on the process of learning to write. The book is a detailed account of one five-year-old's acquisition of writing skills, tracing his progress from simple invented spellings through the gradual self-correction of mistakes to mastery of conventional spelling by the age of 11.

In Your Own Words: A Beginner's
ALL Guide to Writing

Sylvia Cassedy; HarperTrophy, 1990

Sculptor Michelangelo, writes Sylvia Cassedy, imagined that every block of stone held a finished statue simply waiting to be released. "Ideas for stories and poems," she continues, "are like imprisoned statues" waiting to be liberated by a notebook and pen. Hints and suggestions for releasing such ideas are dis-

cussed in 20 short chapters, covering—with many helpful examples—the writing of myths and hero tales, fantasies, essays and editorials, poems, letters, and reports.

8 + Market Guide for Young Writers

Kathy Henderson; Writer's Digest Books, 1996

Over 300 pages of information and advice on getting published for writers aged 8 and up. The book includes interviews with publishers, editors, and young published writers, instructions on preparing manuscripts for submission, and a long list of markets and contests open to literary kids.

13 + Models for Writers

Alfred Rosa and Paul Eschholz, eds.; St. Martin's Press, 1992

"*Models for Writers,*" state the editors, "offers seventy-four short, lively essays that represent particularly appropriate models for use by beginning college writers." Each of the short essays illustrates a basic principle, purpose, or technique of nonfiction writing, and each is accompanied by a list of discussion questions, a list of vocabulary words, and two suggested writing assignments. The essays collectively cover a wide range of topics, tones, and styles. Among the selections are Helen Keller's "The Most Important Day," Eudora Welty's "The Corner Store," Jack London's "An Eye-Witness Account of the San Francisco Earthquake," David Raymond's "On Being 17, Bright, and Unable to Read," Maya Angelou's "Momma, the Dentist, and Me," Diane Ackerman's "Why Leaves Turn Color in Fall," Stephen King's "Why We Crave Horror Movies," and Tipper Gore's "Hate, Rape, and Rap."

Interesting, challenging, and mind broadening for thoughtful high school students. Our oldest son, who tackled it at 14, loved it.

The Mysteries of Harris Burdick

ALL Chris Van Allsburg; Houghton Mifflin, 1984

An irresistible picture-book door into magical realms of imagination. The book consists of 14 strange and beautiful black-and-white drawings, each with a story title and picture caption. The first picture in the book, for example, shows a boy asleep in bed. His window is open and several small, brightly glowing balls of light are floating through it into the room. Title, on the opposite page, is *Archie Smith, Boy Wonder;* and the picture caption reads, "A tiny voice asked, 'Is he the one?'" Marvelous and mysterious story starters for creative writers of all ages.

The Story in History: Writing Your Way into the American Experience

Margot Fortunato Galt; Teachers & Writers Collaborative, 1992

Innovative approaches to writing "personal and public history," for kids of upper elementary age through adults. Projects include writing a Civil War ballad based on a period photograph, inventing a tall tale, writing about a historic event from the point of view of an animal, and composing a family "Winter Count" based on American Indian tribal histories.

To Be a Writer: A Guide for Young People Who Want to Write and Publish

Barbara Seuling; Twenty-First Century Books, 1997

Helpful instructions for writers, including how to design a plot, develop characters, and compose dialogue and descriptions. Included are lists of contests for young writers, suggestions for writing software, and information about getting published.

What's Your Story? A Young Person's Guide to Writing Fiction

Marion Dane Bauer; Clarion, 1992

The emphasis of this book is on the importance of "knowing your craft": the formal techniques of expanding upon basic ideas, developing characters, plots, and themes, and mastering the basics of grammar, spelling, and punctuation. Imagination is important, the author explains, but creativity can be hampered by a lack of proper language tools. For writers aged 9–13.

Write From the Start

Donald Graves and Virginia Stuart; E. P. Dutton, 1985

"Most adults think children can't write until they successfully complete spelling, punctuation, and grammar exercises," write the authors of *Write From the Start,* "but children can best learn these skills in the context for which they were intended—writing." Most schools,

Graves and Stuart go on to explain, are adherents of the component model of learning: that is, the belief that skills are best acquired by breaking them down into discrete pieces, which are mastered individually before being reassembled into a coordinated whole. Thus writing is often taught as a sequential series of usage skills. Kids first learn to form letters and then words; next they are taught sentence structure and allowed to construct simple sentences from word lists; next, they study punctuation marks and parts of speech. Only at the end of this prolonged process are they encouraged to sit down and compose. By then, for many, it may be too late. "It doesn't take too many years of filling blanks, copying words, diagramming sentences, and ending someone else's story starters," write Graves and Stuart, "before children decide writing is no fun at all."

To combat this, Graves and Stuart propose a program in which kids write right from the start, choosing their own topics, dealing as best they can with English grammar, and "inventing" the spelling of any words they don't know. They cite many examples demonstrating the effectiveness of this technique among elementary school–aged children and include reassuring data indicating that inventive young writers do eventually learn to spell.

Writing Because We Love To: Homeschoolers At Work

Susannah Sheffer; Heinemann, 1992

How to be a helpful and supportive reader of your kids' writing, with many examples of young writers' works.

Writing Down the Bones

Natalie Goldberg; Shambhala, 1986

Helpful hints, encouraging advice, and how-to-start suggestions for people who want to write but find the process difficult or intimidating. Chapter titles include "A List of Topics for Writing Practice," "Writing is Not a McDonald's Hamburger," and "A Tourist in Your Own Town."

Writing From Life

Phyllis Ballata; Mayfield Publishing Company, 1997

"A Hundred Writing Projects" to encourage creative thinking, with associated readings and quotations.

Sample project titles include "On Judging Quality," "The Value of Mistakes," "What Are Stories For?," and "Defining Freedom." Each project includes one or more thought-provoking quotations, assorted suggestions for related writing projects, and a short list of associated readings. The readings—all present in the book—include essays, articles, and poems by such authors as Lewis Thomas, Stephen Jay Gould, Langston Hughes, Emily Dickinson, Mark Twain, and Annie Dillard. A mind-expanding challenge for teenagers.

Young Person's Guide to Becoming a Writer
Janet E. Grant; Free Spirit Publishing, 1991

For kids aged 12 and up who are seriously considering careers in writing. Grant suggests ways for developing and enhancing writing skills and tells how to prepare and present a finished manuscript for publication. Includes projects, useful addresses, and a list of recommended readings.

Books: Fiction

Arthur Writes a Story
Marc Brown; Little, Brown, 1996

Arthur, a bespectacled little aardvark, is given a creative writing assignment by his teacher, Mr. Ratburn. His story, as he listens to the criticism of family and friends, gets funnier with each revision. For readers ages 4–8.

Author's Day
Daniel Pinkwater; Atheneum, 1993

Noted writer Branwell Wink-Porter has been invited to visit an elementary school, where all the students—dressed up in bunny ears for the occasion—think that he is the author of *The Fuzzy Bunny*. Unfortunately, he isn't. For readers aged 4–8.

The Better Brown Stories
Allan Ahlberg; Viking, 1996

The Browns, a set of run-of-the-mill storybook characters, demand a more exciting plot of their author, and continue to make suggestions and changes as the story progresses. For readers aged 9–12.

Daphne's Book
Mary Downing Hahn; Clarion, 1983

Seventh-graders Jessica and Daphne collaborate on a children's picture book for an English creative writing project. While writing and illustrating the book, Jessica learns about Daphne's difficult home life and the girls form a bond. For readers aged 11–13.

If You Were a Writer
Joan Lowery Nixon; Four Winds Press, 1988

Melia wants to be a writer like her mother, but she's having a hard time. Her understanding mother gives her a lot of helpful hints about the process of creative writing. For readers aged 5–8.

Jenny Archer, Author
Ellen Conford; Little, Brown, 1989

A short chapter book in which Jenny, given a school assignment to write the story of her life, produces an exciting autobiography stuffed with fiction and fantasy. Her teacher thinks she's telling lies. For readers aged 7–9.

Nothing Ever Happens on 90th Street
Roni Schotter; Orchard Books, 1997

Eva, a blank notebook in her lap, sits on the steps of her city apartment building, trying to do a class writing assignment about her neighborhood. An eclectic bunch of neighbors, including a dancer, a mousse maker, and a pizza delivery boy, give literary advice. For readers aged 4–8.

Simon's Book
Henrik Drescher; Lothrop, Lee & Shepard, 1983

A delightful picture book in which a young boy goes to bed, leaving an unfinished story on his desk. At night, his drawing pens and bottle of ink come to life, along with the main character of the story: a scary hairy monster. For readers aged 4–8.

Activity Books

Boomerang Books

A Boomerang Book—each an attractive, oversize, comb-bound book—is a joint writing project, designed to be passed back and forth among families and friends. Usually the original book owner fills in the first couple of pages in the book; then he or she passes it on to a friend, who writes and passes it on in turn. By the time the completed book is returned to its owner, some 20 double pages later, it's a unique multiauthor work of art.

Two of the Boomerang Books are specifically intended for young children: *Boomerang Friends,* in which each participant has a page of questions to answer about him/herself, a place to paste a photograph, and a blank page for drawing a picture; and *Boomerang Pets,* featuring two pages of space for stories, photos, and drawings of each participant's pet. For older writers, there's *Mystery Novel,* in which participants collaborate in the invention of a mystery story; and *Remember Me, Remember You,* a cumulative book of memories, thoughts, and reminiscences.

> Boomerang Publications (USA), Inc.
> Box 936
> West Yarmouth, MA 02673
> (800) 838-6848

See **Tandem Writing** (page 114).

Clever Kids Language Skills
World Book, 1996

Clever activities for beginning writers aged 5–7, including making a family dictionary, a family newsletter, and homemade birthday cards.

Games for Writing
Peggy Kaye; HarperCollins, 1995

A large collection of activities for young writers, from "Just for Starters" prehandwriting exercises for small beginners through varied and creative projects for increasingly older kids. Children are encouraged to make popcorn and pretzel letters, to draw story maps based on the movements of the characters in favorite stories, to write fill-in-the-blank "form" stories, and to make their own comic books, board games, and family journals. And much more. There's even a suggestion for composing the longest story ever written on a roll of adding-machine tape.

If You're Trying to Teach Kids How to Write, You've Gotta Have This Book!
Marjorie Frank; Incentive Publications, 1979

A fat, illustrated book crammed with ideas for inspiring kids to try many kinds of writing. There are dozens of ideas for word games: play "Alphabet Antics," in which kids list a word that fits a certain category for each letter of the alphabet ("Animal Names," for example, from alligator to zebra, or "Words That Describe Winter"); invent riddles and tongue twisters; create original titles for items or events, for example, a title for a song to be sung at a blueberry festival, a movie about an outer space mystery, or a Halloween dance. Make word mobiles or framed pictures of decorated favorite words.

Other suggestions include writing stories based on literature selections or newpaper reports based on science experiments; combining writing and art to make "painted poems"; inventing epitaphs and describing dreams; writing directions for unusual activities (try "How To Pet a Lion" or "How To Make a Rainbow"); writing a pictorial history using Polaroid photographs; composing mixed-up fairy tales; or collecting quotations. And much more. Also included are hints for parents and teachers—what to say to reluctant writers, how to criticize painlessly, how to encourage the very young—and a sizable bibliography of books that stimulate writing.

Write From the Edge
Ken Vinton; Free Spirit Publishing, 1997

A delightful book of creative writing projects for kids in grades K–6. The book includes a collection of illustrated (and reproducible) border pages upon which to write or draw, accompanied on facing pages by lists of creative writing suggestions, discussion questions, and thought-provoking quotations. Each project page has a different theme, among them "Castle Towers," "Bugs," "The Solar System," and "Sounds of Music."

Also see *Alphabet Antics* (page 59).

PROGRAMS

Models for Writing

Joanne F. Carlisle; Academic Therapy Publications, 1996

This creative writing program for children in grades 1–3 consists of three 100+-page workbooks, each with plenty of space for writing and drawing, plus an accompanying teacher's guide. *Workbook A,* designed for first-graders, is divided into three major sections: "Getting Started," "Learning About Writing," and "Topics for Writing." Under "Getting Started," kids draw and label pictures of themselves, their families, their friends, and their homes, and are encouraged to use their imaginations to describe the action in pictures or to invent new situations ("Imagine that a frog kissed you and turned you into a mushroom. What happened next?"). Under "Learning About Writing," kids make many kinds of lists, learn to put story events in the proper order, invent endings to a series of simple stories, write descriptions and discuss feelings, and learn the proper format for writing letters and notes. "Topics for Writing" includes story starters and related activities centering around such kid-appealing subjects as birthdays, zoo animals, seasons, bicycles, kites, and pets.

Workbooks B and *C* cover increasingly complex writing concepts: organizing and writing paragraphs, brainstorming, methods of gathering information, linking ideas, speaking with different voices, editing finished work, and writing reports.

Academic Therapy Publications
20 Commercial Blvd.
Novato, CA 94949-6191
(800) 422-7249

Responding

Responding is a cross-disciplinary "write-to-learn" program using a sectioned three-ring binder, in which kids write daily in all subjects. Three kinds of writing are involved: "Initial Responses," which include lecture and reading notes, study questions, and descriptions of step-by-step processes; "Reflective Responses," which include personal reactions, opinions, and annotations; and "Assimilative Responses,"

based upon the previous two, which culminate in formal essays, lab reports, research papers, and creative stories. Notebooks are 140+ pages long, divided into 10 sections, among them language arts, social studies, science, mathematics, foreign language, and computer science. Specific teaching instructions and student handouts are included.

Interact also publishes "Steps," an essay-writing program in three levels, which leads students through the crafting of literature, research, contrast, and problem-solving essays; and "A Writer's Journal," a structured journal-writing program in which students are encouraged to use personal journal entries "to generate creative and academic writings."

Interact
1825 Gillespie Way, #101
El Cajon, CA 92020
(619) 448-1474 or (800) 359-0961/(800) 700-5093
Web site: www.interact-simulations.com

Super Kids Publishing Company

Debbie Robertson and Patricia Barry; Teacher Ideas Press, 1990

A creative writing program in a book, for kids in grades 2–8. The book covers every step of the writing process, from story idea and first draft, through revising, editing, illustrating, printing, and binding. Included are helpful activities, literary models, and story starters.

Wordsmith

A "creative writing course for young people" by Janie Cheaney. "If you had enrolled in a painting course," explains the introduction, "you would probably spend some time in the early classes learning how to hold a brush, how to mix paint, how to stroke the paint onto the canvas. In a similar manner, Parts One and Two of this book will teach you some techniques of writing, or how to use your tools. The third will give you some ideas about what to 'paint,' and how." In other words, *Wordsmith* moves from grammar to composition, first covering the parts of speech, then sentence structure, and finally various kinds of writing techniques. Grammatical examples and writing samples aren't very interesting, but they get the point across, and the instructions are nice and clear.

Writing Strands

ADULT Dave Marks, public school writing teacher and homeschooling parent, founded the National Writing Institute in part out of pure frustration: he felt that the present public school programs simply do not teach children how to write. "Children can, and have for years," writes Marks, "endlessly underlined nouns and verbs and diagrammed sentences and still can't write good sentences and paragraphs." Marks's answer to this dilemma is *Writing Strands,* a seven-level series of instruction and exercise books designed to teach kids, from absolute beginners through high school–aged students, how to write well.

Each book, which addresses readers in a cozy, conversational manner—"It's as though the book is talking to you!" remarked our youngest son—contains about 90 days' worth of writing lessons, each designed to demonstrate or enhance a specific writing skill. Lessons are presented in absolutely complete detail. "It will take you three days to learn," begins lesson 1 in *Writing Strands* Level 3 (recommended for writers in grade 3 and/or grade 7, depending on their previous writing experience):

1. That you can follow directions if you try
2. That following directions sometimes is better than not following directions
3. What goes in a sentence
4. How to write a sentence
5. That you can write good sentences while following directions

Students are then led, step by step, through their three days of assignments, at the end of which they can write simple, correct sentences. They then move on to lesson 2 in which, in sequentially guided fashion, they master complex sentences and paragraphs.

The *Writing Strands* books are thorough, precisely organized, and reader-friendly. They are, however, process manuals, which means that their emphasis is on the mechanics of correct writing, rather than on the richness of language or the joys of creative flair. Literary examples and accompanying assignments tend to be flat and pedestrian. The Level 4 book, for example, targeted at the average eighth-grader, uses as models a paragraph of directions for making a peanut-butter sandwich, a description of a doll, an account of walking to the car in the rain. Assignments include writing descriptions of your living room and of fresh (versus rotten) fruit.

Also available are the *Gentle Steps to Writing Skill* books (Levels 1 and 2), targeted at students with learning disabilities, and the more sophisticated *Writing Nonfiction, Creating Fiction,* and *College Writing* manuals for advanced students.

Writing Strands books, $15 to $20 apiece
National Writing Institute
7946 Wright Rd.
Niles, MI 49120
(616) 684-5375 or (800) 688-5375

COMPUTER SOFTWARE

The Amazing Writing Machine

This is amazingly nice. I have been resistant to kids' creative writing software, insisting grumpily to all about me that the best tools for creative writing are pencil and paper (or, at very most, a turn at the word processor). Kids, I said, positively bubble over with imagination; a machine that spits out all the ideas for them will, ultimately, restrict independent thinking and squash spontaneous invention.

"You're really backward," my kids said.

The Writing Machine provides space and tools for many forms of imaginative writing, from the very basic—templates for stories, letters, poems, essays and journals; kids provide every single bit of the text on their own—to the dramatically embellished. A series of "spin documents" provides a lush assortment of prewritten writing samples that kid can alter and expand to suit themselves; various "tools" allow kids to translate their text into rebus pictures or convert it into one of eight codes (among them Pig Latin), or provide them with "Bright Ideas," including quotations, jokes, story starters, and catchy facts, along the lines of "A cockroach can live for 10 days without a head." There's a library of clip art images, Kid Pix–style stamps and paint tools, a dictionary of rhyming words, a journal (totally private unless you know the access password), and an address book.

Our boys loved it. Recommended for writers aged 6–12. On CD-ROM for Mac or Windows.

$59.95

Broderbund

Box 6125

Novato, CA 94948-6125

(415) 382-4700 or (800) 521-6263

Web site: www.broderbund.com

Davidson's Kid Works Deluxe

Creative writing for younger kids. Type in a story and it appears in big elementary school–style print on lined paper. Included are pictures, stamps, painting tools, and a rebus tool that turns words into pictures (and vice versa). Kids can listen to a written story read back to them by computer, or can record their own dictated stories. Recommended for kids aged 3–9.

On CD-ROM for Mac or Windows.

$39.95

Davidson and Associates

19840 Pioneer Ave.

Torrance, CA 90503

(800) 545-7677/fax (310) 793-0601

Web site: www.davd.com

ON-LINE CREATIVE WRITING

Cyberkids

An on-line site just for kids, with numerous features, among them a chat room, contests, games, movie reviews, links to sites of interest to kids, a "Young Composers" page through which kids can submit original musical compositions or listen to music written by their peers, a "Reading Room," which includes a page for kid-written poetry, and "Kidzeen," an on-line magazine of articles, stories, reviews, and puzzles, all written by kids.

www.cyberkids.com

Cyberteens

A more sophisticated version of Cyberkids (see above) for users aged 13 and up.

www.cyberteens.com

Help Your Child Learn to Write Well

A government educational publication including general information about writing, pointers for supportive parents, and a list of activity suggestions.

www.ed.gov/pubs/parents/Writing/index.html

Ink Spot

A Web site for (adult) children's book writers. The site includes an excellent page for "Young Writers," including articles about writing, advice and helpful hints, lists of markets that publish young writers, links to on-line places to publish, information about young writers' associations and workshops, and a discussion forum.

www.inkspot.com

Kid Story

Kids can publish stories and poems on-line. The site is partitioned by age group, with separate pages for kids, teens, and schools/clubs. Also includes links to many kid-friendly Web sites.

www.kidstory.com

KidPub

Publish your stories on-line. Users can submit their own stories or read those of their peers, selecting from an ever-growing collection. The site also includes a source for e-mail pen pals ("Key Pals"); kids can sign up or search for a "key pal" of their own.

www.kidpub.org/kidpub

The Looking-Glass Gazette

An on-line magazine of creative writing for kids in preschool through age 13. Young writers can submit poems, stories, artwork, and book, music, and movie reviews.

www.cowboy.net/~mharper/LGG.html

MidLink Magazine

An electronic magazine by and for middle school kids. Each monthly issue centers around a theme; kids can submit stories, artwork, poems, articles, and plays. The site also includes links to book-related sites and "The MidLink ABCs," with which kids can research various topics organized alphabetically.

longwood.cs.ucf.edu:80/~MidLink

The Mighty Pen Online Magazine

An electronic magazine for and by young adult authors. Young writers can submit original poems, short stories, essays, nonfiction articles, reviews, and artwork.

pages.prodigy.com/FL/coolie/coolie.html

Researchpaper.com

A terrific on-line source for students writing research papers, including an idea directory through which users can browse by category (art and literature, history, science, business, society), writing helps, discussion groups, and lists of topic-related Web hot spots for gathering information.

www.researchpaper.com

Scriptito's Place

An on-line story contest, plus helpful hints for young writers, story starters, and tips for parents on fostering family creative writing.

members.aol.com/vangarnews/scriptito.html

UBS for Kids

Kids can meet an author on-line, submit their own artwork, stories, poetry, or book reviews for publication, or take a theme-oriented "Web Tour of the Month."

www.mrcoffee.univbkstr.com/kids

Wacky Web Tales

Users first fill in the blanks in a short word list, picking various adjectives, nouns, and verbs; the computer then uses their choices to generate a wacky story. Kids can read their own finished tale or check out stories by others. For writers in grade 4 and up.

www.eduplace.com/tales

Writing Den

An educational site for kids in grades 6–12, targeted at improving reading comprehension and writing skills. The site centers around a featured topic, presented through color photographs, with associated exercises and quizzes designed to enhance vocabulary, reading comprehension, note taking, and writing skills. Users can also access alternative topics in the fields of history, science, and nature, check grammar rules, and receive advice and writing tips. A teacher's guide is included.

www2.actden.com/writ_den

Young Writer On-line

A magazine of creative writing for kids. Young writers can submit poems, fiction and nonfiction stories and articles, essays, drawings, photos, and cartoons.

www.mystworld.com/youngwriter/index.html

Young Writers' Clubhouse

How-tos and FAQs for young writers, on-line chat rooms and critique groups, writing contests, and information about real-life kid authors.

www.realkids.com/club.htm

KID-WRITTEN MAGAZINES

Boodle

This magazine "by kids for kids" is a collection of poems, stories, articles, and (black-and-white) drawings by kids aged about 6–12.

Annual subscription (4 issues), $12

Boodle

Box 1049

Portland, IN 47371

(219) 726-8141

Creative Kids

Creative Kids, "The National Voice for Kids," publishes original work by kids aged 8–14, including poems, songs, cartoons, stories (800–900 words), puzzles, games, editorials, drawings, and plays. The magazine sponsors many creative contests (examples: write the silliest possible limerick; devise a world-improving invention using recyclable materials; choose a mascot for *Creative Kids*) and includes hints and advice for young writers hoping to get published.

Annual subscription (4 issues), $19.95

Creative Kids

Box 8813

Waco, TX 76714-8813

e-mail: Creative_Kids@prufrock.com

Merlyn's Pen
12 18 This high-quality 30-page collection of student work on glossy paper publishes stories, poems, essays, reviews, and artwork. Two versions of the magazine are currently published: the *Senior Edition,* for kids in grades 9–12, and the *Middle School Edition* for kids in grades 6–9.

Annual subscription (4 issues), $17.50

Merlyn's Pen, Inc.

Box 1058

E. Greenwich, RI 02818

(800) 247-2027

Stone Soup
4 13 *Stone Soup,* which has been publishing the best of young people's writing for nearly a quarter of a century, accepts submissions from kids up to age 13, including stories, poems, essays, artwork (in black and white or color), and book reviews. The magazine is published by the Children's Art Foundation.

Annual subscription (5 issues), $26

Stone Soup

Box 83

Santa Cruz, CA 95063

(800) 447-4569

Web site: www.stonesoup.com

The Writer's Slate
5 18 Features writing by kids in grades K–12. Submissions are divided into four categories: "Beginnings" (grades K–3), "Creations" (grades 4–6), "Visions" (grades 7–9), and "Elevations" (grades 10–12).

Annual subscription (3 issues), $12.95

The Writer's Slate

Box 664

Ottawa, KS 66067

(913) 242-0407

Young Voices

8 18 Contains stories, essays, nonfiction articles, black-and-white photographs and drawings, and poetry by kids aged 8–18. The magazine is published by Young

Voices, a nonprofit organization founded to "honor and nurture the artistry of young people."

Annual membership, including a subscription to *Young Voices* (6 issues) and to the *Young Voices News* newsletter (4 issues), $20

Young Voices

Box 2321

Olympia, WA 98507

(360) 357-4683

e-mail: patcha@olywa.net

THE BASICS OF BOOKS

THE HISTORY OF THE BOOK

Book

ALL Karen Brookfield; Alfred A. Knopf, 1993

A volume in the Eyewitness series, covering the history of books from the earliest alphabets and the invention of papermaking through Gutenberg's movable type, the printing press, and modern bookbinding processes. Illustrated with superb color photographs.

Breaking Into Print: Before and After the Invention of the Printing Press

6 10 Stephen Krensky; Little, Brown, 1996

How books were written, before and after the landmark invention of movable type, told through an appealingly interesting and simple text and beautiful illustrations.

Fine Print: A Story About Johann Gutenberg

9 12 Joann Johanson Burch; Carolrhoda, 1992

A short chapter biography of Johann Gutenberg and his landmark invention of movable type for middle-grade readers.

Gutenberg
9 12 Leonard Everett Fisher; Simon & Schuster, 1993

A short picture-book story of Johann Gutenberg and his printing press with impressive and dramatic illustrations. For readers aged 9–12.

5 9 *Gutenberg's Gift*

Nancy Willard; Harcourt Brace, 1996

The story of Johann Gutenberg and the invention of movable type, charmingly told in rhyme. In this version, Gutenberg hurries to perfect his invention so that the first printed Bible will be completed in time for Christmas, as a gift to his wife, Anna.

10 + *The History of Making Books: From Clay Tablets, Papyrus Rolls, and Illuminated Manuscripts to the Printing Press*

Gallimard Jeunesse; Scholastic, 1996

A 48-page interactive history of bookmaking, from the beginnings of writing through modern printing processes. Includes lots of appealing manipulatives, among them stickers, cutout pages, and acetate overlays.

MAKING BOOKS

7 10 *A Book Takes Root: The Making of a Picture Book*

Michael Kehoe; Carolrhoda, 1993

The process of bookmaking, from idea to manuscript to finished product.

5 9 *From Pictures to Words: A Book About Making a Book*

Janet Stevens; Holiday House, 1995

A picture book all about the process of writing and publishing a book, from idea through finished product.

5 9 *How a Book Is Made*

Aliki; HarperTrophy, 1988

Charmingly illustrated, this picture book clearly describes just how a book is made, from the author's writing of the manuscript and the illustrator's drawing of the pictures through the technical processes of printing and binding.

Also see the on-line version of the book, at **www.harper.childrens.com/index.htm**

ACTIVITY BOOKS

5 8 *Is This You?*

Ruth Krauss; Scholastic, 1988

Picture-book instructions for making a 10-page illustrated book all about yourself, for 5–8-year-olds.

6 12 *Making Books (Step-by-Step)*

Charlotte Stowell; Kingfisher Books, 1994

A simple bookmaking guide with which kids, armed with glue, paper, cardboard, and scissors, can make a variety of their own creative books, including classic hardbound books, work folders, and pop-up books.

9 12 *The Young Author's Do-It-Yourself Book: How to Write, Illustrate, and Produce Your Own Book*

Donna Guthrie, Nancy Bentley, and Katy Keck Araskeen; Millbrook Press, 1994

A 64-page start-to-finish guide that shows kids how to write and illustrate a fiction or nonfiction story and then package the result into a finished hardbound book.

POETRY FOR KIDS

Poetry is popular at our house. Our oldest son wears a Dylan Thomas T-shirt; our youngest is a fan of T. S. Eliot's poetically practical cats; and even the middle kid, whose taste in literature runs to computer manuals, admits a sneaking fondness for Ogden Nash. Humorist Jean Kerr, mother of six, wrote in her essay "The Poet and the Peasants": "We have made mistakes with our children, which will undoubtedly become clearer as they get old enough to write their own books. But I would like to be serious for a few minutes about the one thing we did that was right. We taught them not to be afraid of poetry." "The Poet and the Peasants" is a short account of Kerr's home "Culture Hour" program, during which her sons, then aged 2 to 14, learned to memorize, recite, and—eventually—appreciate poetry. The essay appears in Jean Kerr's *Penny Candy* (Doubleday, 1966); it's simultaneously tender, touching, and hysterically funny.

It strikes, with us, a familiar chord. We too have doubtless made mistakes with our children, but

WRITING

depriving them of poetry is not one of them. Even the middle kid, the verbal hard case, is occasionally captured by its wonder, its beauty, and its sudden laughter.

"What's the weather like, Ethan?" I asked one morning some days ago.

"Brillig," my son said.

From my homeschool journal:

◆ **April 4, 1990. Josh is eight; Ethan, seven; Caleb, five.**

This morning we read and discussed a few selected— carefully selected; there aren't all that many that work for little kids—poems from Spoon River Anthology *by Edgar Lee Masters. The boys were fascinated at the idea of tombstone poems. I explained what an epitaph is, and we read a lot of funny ones from an epitaph collection; then looked at pictures of tombstones, all with unusual motifs (and/or epitaphs), from* New England Cemeteries.

The boys, inspired, promptly designed a series of very elaborate tombstones, complete with tunnels, statuary, lights, special effects, and (Ethan's) complex machinery.

◆ **April 5, 1990**

We read a few more Spoon River Anthology *selections this morning, after which the boys wrote/dictated their own Spoon River–style poems. Each kid wrote four or five; Caleb immortalized Captain Kidd (rolled over by a machine and buried in a bat castle); Ethan's included a miner, caught in an avalanche ("In the mines in heaven they have laser blasters"); and Josh's featured a Revolutionary War soldier and an abused British carriage horse (he's been reading* Black Beauty*). I typed all the poems on the word processor and printed them out, and the boys assembled them into books. They cut each poem out and pasted each on a decorated tombstone. The books are impressive (if a trifle morbid); the boys can't wait to show them to their father.*

BOOKS: NONFICTION

Beyond Words: Writing Poems With Children
Elizabeth McKim and Judith W. Steinbergh; Wampeter Press, 1983

This guide for encouraging children to write poetry begins by describing assorted word games and then proceeds gradually to longer and more challenging poetry-writing projects. For an initial icebreaker, McKim and Steinbergh suggest, make a "Word Bowl": a bowl containing many slips of paper, each printed with a word or phrase. (*Beyond Words* includes six pages of Word Bowl words, suitable for copying and cutting up.) Children draw 10 or so words from the bowl and then string them together to form their first poems. Or they may draw a single word—for example, *apple* or *hurricane*—and then compose "firedrill" poems, scribbling down all the associations that come to mind about their word in just one minute.

Calliope
Greta Barclay Lipson and Jane A. Romatowski; Good Apple, 1981

A poetry-writing workbook intended for kids in grades 4–8, in which the authors describe and demonstrate 47 poetic forms and suggest associated projects. Students are encouraged to write initial poems based on their own names, alphabet poems in which the first words of the poem are arranged in ABC order, concrete poems, patchwork poems, cinquains, quatrains, limericks, ballads, parodies, and sonnets. And much more.

Good Apple
Box 299
Carthage, IL 62321
(217) 357-3981 or (800) 435-7234

Created Writing: Poetry from New Angles
Paul Agostino; Prentice-Hall, 1996

Poetry writing for high school students, with analyses of poetic form and content, and many examples of work by students and lesser-known poets.

A Crow Doesn't Need a Shadow: A Guide to Writing Poetry from Nature
Lorraine Ferra and Diane Boardman; Gibbs Smith, 1994

Poetic examples and projects based on the natural world for kids aged 9–12.

Daily Poetry

6 12 Carol Simpson; Good Year Books, 1995

A poem for every week of the school year, each accompanied by teaching suggestions, student activities, and a poem starter to help kids compose a poem of their own. For elementary students.

Getting the Knack: 20 Poetry Writing Exercises

10 + Stephen Dunning and William Stafford; National Council of Teachers of English, 1992

Examples of many kinds of poems, among them headline, letter, recipe, list, and monologue poems, with innovative writing exercises.

How Does a Poem Mean?

13 + John Ciardi; Houghton Mifflin, 1975

How Does a Poem Mean? answers just the question that the title asks—not the more expected "*What* does a poem mean?," the author explains, but *how*. How does the poem make its effect; how does it accomplish what it set out to do? Ciardi approaches the problem from different angles, analyzing and discussing a large and varied collection of poems. Includes study and discussion questions. The book was intended for college students but is appropriate for interested teenagers.

The List Poem

8 + Larry Fagin; Teachers & Writers Collaborative, 1991

The list poem, explains Fagin, a published poet and writing teacher, "is the simplest way for beginners to write poetry." The book gives examples of list poems by poets professional and amateur, and follows them up with many suggestions for list poem projects, appropriate for kids of all ages. Make lists of beautiful things, of ugly things, of things that make you sad or happy, of things you remember, suggests Fagin. Make lists of ingredients for magic spells, of ice-cream flavors, of dreams and wishes, of things that happen in the morning or the middle of the night. Results are delightful. One third-grader's list of "The Most Beautiful Things I Can Think Of" included diamonds, emeralds, rubies, gold, lightning bugs, ladybugs, turkey, chicken, and science.

Pass the Poetry, Please!

ALL Lee Bennett Hopkins; HarperTrophy, 1987

The book includes short biographies of 20 modern poets, among them Gwendolyn Brooks, Robert Frost, Nikki Giovanni, Langston Hughes, John Ciardi, and Shel Silverstein, with a bibliography of books by or about each, plus samples of their work. There's also a section on poetry writing with children and a long list of recommended poetry books and anthologies for young readers.

Poetry A to Z

9 13 Paul B. Janeczko; Simon & Schuster, 1994

A collection of 72 poems appealing to kids aged 9–13, arranged alphabetically by subject or theme, intended to serve as models for poetry-writing projects. Under *H,* for example, Janeczko includes how-to poems (Ralph Fletcher's "How to Make a Snow Angel"), horses, and haiku.

The Practice of Poetry

13 + Robin Behn and Chase Twichell, eds.; HarperPerennial, 1992

A large collection of challenging writing exercises for older writers, each contributed by a published poet. The exercises "are extremely various in approach, style, and content, and cover a great deal of territory." Poet Michael Pettit, for example, focuses on descriptions of one particular member of a group or set, challenging writers to describe "one sparrow in a flock of sparrows, one baby in a nursery of babies, one fish in a barrel of fish, one scream in a stadium of screams." Other suggestions include: write a poem that is simply a list of things, write a poem based on one of a list of pre-Socratic Greek quotations, hold a conversation between two different sides of yourself, make a "Personal Universe Deck" of word cards and use them to write poems, write a 50-line poem that consists of a single, grammatically correct sentence.

Rose, How Did You Get That Red?

9 + Kenneth Koch; Vintage Books, 1990

Subtitled "Teaching Great Poetry to Children," the book encourages young students to read and appreciate the work of famous poets, then to use the poems as inspirational jumping-off points for compositions of

WRITING

their own. After reading and discussing William Blake's "The Tyger," for example, Koch's students wrote poems in which they talked directly to an animal; after reading Wallace Stevens's "Thirteen Ways of Looking at a Black-bird," they wrote poems in which they looked at some ordinary thing in several different ways. The book is divided into 10 chapters, each discussing a poem by a well-known poet, among them John Donne, Walt Whit-man, William Carlos Williams, and Federico García Lorca. Included is an anthology of 60+ additional poems, with accompanying writing project suggestions.

A Surfeit of Similes
Norton Juster; William Morrow, 1989

A delightful illustrated collection of similes, all in rhyme, among them "As pure as an angel/As clever as zippers/As awkward as crutches/As friendly as slip-pers." Read it through and your kids will *never* forget what a simile is.

Wishes, Lies, and Dreams
Kenneth Koch; HarperCollins, 1980

This book describes Koch's method of teaching poetry writing to elementary school students. (The book is coauthored by "The Students of P.S. 61.") "I wanted to find, if I could," writes Koch in the intro-duction, "a way for children to get as much from poetry as they did from painting"—and *Wishes, Lies, and Dreams* lists his tried-and-true collection of tech-niques for inspiring kids to create. Koch's students, for example, wrote "Wish" poems in which every line began with "I wish . . . ," poems in which every line was an imaginative lie ("I was born nowhere," wrote one fourth-grader, "and I live in a tree"), poems about ani-mals, poems in which a color appeared in every line, and "comparison" poems. "A butterfly is like a colorful flying rainbow," wrote one third-grader, and another, "A tiger is like a beating of drums."

Writing Across Cultures
Edna Kovacs; Blue Heron Publishing, 1994

The book is subtitled "A Handbook on Writing Poetry & Lyrical Prose From African Drum Song to Blues, From Ghazal to Haiku, From Villanelle to Zoo." In practice, this translates into 26+ creative poetry forms from all over the world, with examples and sug-gested exercises. Students are encouraged, for example, to experiment with calendar poetry, letter poems, and couplets, to keep illustrated poetry journals, invent leg-ends, chants, and proverbs, and to write 99-word short stories.

BOOKS OF POETRY

The Bed Book
Sylvia Plath; HarperTrophy, 1989

A charming poem, published in picture-book form, about a series of magical beds.

Bone Poems
Jeff Moss; Workman, 1997

Poetry for young paleontologists. Poems about dinosaurs and dinosaur eggs, dinosaur wordplay, and a dinosaur math quiz, plus one very short poem with a very long title.

A Book of Americans
Rosemary and Stephen Vincent Benet; Henry Holt, 1987

A collection of poems about American historical figures from Christopher Columbus, Peregrine White, and Pocahontas through Theodore Roosevelt and Woodrow Wilson.

Consider the Lemming
Jeanne Steig; Farrar, Straus & Giroux, 1990

Giggle-provoking poems featuring not only the luckless lemming but also the penguin, the weasel, the elephant, the parrot, and the fish.

The Dream Keeper and Other Poems
Langston Hughes; Alfred A. Knopf, 1996

A lovely illustrated collection of poems about the African-American experience for young readers.

Hailstones and Halibut Bones
Mary O'Neill; Doubleday, 1990

Twelve illustrated poems for children about a rain-bow assortment of colors. ("Gold is feeling/Like a king . . .")

I'm Nobody! Who Are You!

Emily Dickinson; Stemmer House, 1991

A short, illustrated collection of Dickinson's poems, especially selected for young readers.

Imaginary Gardens

Charles Sullivan, ed.; Harry N. Abrams, 1989

A beautiful book in which poems by well-known poets are illustrated with works of American art, including paintings, prints, photographs, sculptures, pen-and-ink sketches, and even a patchwork quilt.

The Invisible Ladder: An Anthology of Contemporary American Poems for Young Readers

Liz Rosenberg, ed.; Henry Holt, 1996

A powerful collection of poems by such writers as Nikki Giovanni, Allen Ginsberg, Robert Bly, Rita Dove, and Alice Walker. The selections are arranged alphabetically by author, with photographs and brief biographies of each. For readers aged 12 and up.

Joyful Noise

Paul Fleischman; HarperCollins, 1988

An entomological collection of "Poems for Two Voices" on such subjects as grasshoppers, fireflies, book lice, cicadas, honeybees, and house crickets. See, by the same author, *I Am Phoenix* (HarperTrophy, 1989), more poems for two voices, this volume on the world of birds.

Math Talk

Theoni Pappas; World Wide Publishing, 1991

Thoroughly clever mathematical poems for young readers, variously celebrating triangles, prime numbers, squares, Mobius strips, proper fractions, googols, and zero.

A New Treasury of Poetry

Neil Philip, ed.; Stewart, Tabori & Chang, 1990

Contains 288 poems, elegantly illustrated with woodcuts. Included are works by W. B. Yeats, William Carlos Williams, William Blake, Ted Hughes, Christina Tassetti, Gwendolyn Brooks, Dylan Thomas, and many more.

Old Possum's Book of Practical Cats

T. S. Eliot; Harcourt Brace, 1982

Poetic cats for all ages, from the dapper black-and-white Jellicle Cats to Macavity the Mystery Cat and the intimidating Old Deuteronomy.

Opposites

Richard Wilbur; Harcourt Brace, 1991

Delightful illustrated poems that give readers a new view of opposites, as in "What is the opposite of riot?/*It's lots of people keeping quiet.*" Also see, by the same author, *More Opposites* (Harcourt Brace, 1991) and *Runaway Opposites* (Harcourt Brace, 1995).

A Poem a Day

Karen McCosker and Nicholas Albery, eds.; Steerforth Press, 1994

A poem for every day of the year, from Susan Coolidge's "New Every Morning" on January 1 through "Auld Lang Syne" on December 31. A brief paragraph of interesting information about the poem or the poet accompanies each selection. Along with "Richard Cory" by Edwin Arlington Robinson, for example, the poem for January 30, readers learn that the poet's parents had so badly wanted a daughter that their unexpected son remained nameless for six months. The real challenge: readers are supposed to memorize each of the poems.

Poem Stew

William Cole; HarperTrophy, 1983.

Humorous poems in honor of pizza, oysters, lemonade, celery, and potato chips, plus a lament for cold cocoa.

Poetry for Young People Series

Sterling Publications

A series of illustrated 48-page books each featuring the work of a famous poet. Each book includes about 25 poems, both complete short poems and excerpts from longer works, plus beautiful full-page watercolor paintings. Titles in the series include *Emily Dickinson, Robert Frost, Edgar Allan Poe, Carl Sandburg,* and *Walt Whitman.*

WRITING

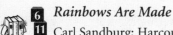

Poetry Out Loud

12 + Robert Alden Rubin, ed.; Algonquin Books, 1993

A collection of poems of all kinds, from the serious and sophisticated to the just plain silly, intended to be read aloud. Each poem is accompanied by fascinating marginal notes about the poet and the poem.

Rainbows Are Made

6 11 Carl Sandburg; Harcourt Brace, 1984

Illustrated Sandburg poems for young readers, among them such favorites as "Buffalo Dusk," "Fog," and "Grass."

The Random House Book of Poetry for Children

5 12 Jack Prelutsky, ed.; Random House, 1983

An excellent illustrated anthology of over 500 poems for young readers, categorized by subject.

Reflections on a Gift of Watermelon Pickle

9 + Stephen Dunning, Edward Lueders, and Hugh Smith, eds.; Lothrop, Lee & Shepard, 1967

An appealing collection of modern verse, including Maxine Kumin's "The Microscope," Carl Sandburg's "Arithmetic," Langston Hughes's "Dreams," and the title poem, by John Tobias, "Reflections on a Gift of Watermelon Pickle Received from a Friend Called Felicity."

Ride a Purple Pelican

5 9 Jack Prelutsky; Mulberry, 1997

A collection of short, delightful poems for small readers, with big colorful illustrations by Garth Williams. ("Bullfrogs, bullfrogs, on parade/Dressed in green and gold brocade . . .") There are many collections of children's poems by Prelutsky, among them *The Dragons Are Singing Tonight* (Greenwillow, 1993).

Sing a Song of Popcorn

5 9 Beatrice Schenk de Regniers, ed.; Scholastic, 1988

A beautiful anthology for younger kids. The book includes over 100 poems in many different styles and themes, with illustrations by nine Caldecott Medal winners, among them Maurice Sendak and Arnold Lobel.

Stopping by Woods on a Snowy Evening

4 8 Robert Frost; E. P. Dutton, 1985

Frost's most beloved poem, enchantingly and snowily illustrated by Susan Jeffers. Collections of Frost poems for young readers include *You Come Too: Favorite Poems for Young Readers* (Henry Holt, 1959) and *A Swinger of Birches: Poetry of Robert Frost for Young People* (Stemmer House, 1982).

Talking to the Sun

9 + Kenneth Koch and Kate Farrell, eds.; Henry Holt, 1985

An anthology of poems from very old to new, illustrated with color photographs of artworks from the Metropolitan Museum. The title poem, Frank O'Hara's "A True Account of Talking to the Sun at Fire Island," for example, is paired with a glorious sunrise painting by Henri Rousseau.

A Visit to William Blake's Inn

6 12 Nancy Willard; Harcourt Brace, 1981

An unusual and delightful collection of poems, illustrated by Alice and Martin Provensen, about a magical inn where a rabbit makes your bed and two dragons bake your bread.

Where the Sidewalk Ends

6 12 Shel Silverstein; HarperCollins, 1974

A hilarious and irresistible collection of verse, written and illustrated by Silverstein. Also see, by the same author, *A Light in the Attic* (HarperCollins, 1981) and *Falling Up!* (HarperCollins, 1996).

Zoo

ALL Ogden Nash; Stewart, Tabori & Chang, 1987

Short and funny poems about animals from the clam, ant, and guppy to the armadillo, grackle, and kangaroo. Also see, by the same author, *Custard and Company* (Little, Brown, 1985), in which the title poem features Custard the pet dragon.

GAMES AND ACTIVITIES

Magnetic Poetry

 ALL Create poems on the family refrigerator. "The Magnetic Poetry Kit" consists of 300 individual magnetized words for stringing together into original compositions. Available in original and supplementary editions, and as "Magnetic Poetry for Kids," which contains simpler words in bigger print.

Available at toy and game stores or
Magnetic Poetry, Inc.
Box 14862
Minneapolis, MN 55414
(800) 720-7269

8 Poetryslam

Scrabble for poets. The game includes a playing board, peppered with double and triple "poem score" squares, and over 700 magnetized words and word endings. Players compete by forming creative interconnecting poetic sentences. These must make reasonable sense, but players are "free to stretch the boundaries of the language." For a more varied game, add-on word kits are available, each containing an additional 800 words and word endings: "Art & Artists," "The Beat Generation," and "Genius." For two to four players, aged 8 and up.

$40 from toy and game stores or
Flax Art & Design
Box 7216
San Francisco, CA 94120-7216
orders (800) 547-7778; customer service (800) 343-3529/fax (800) FLAX-123
e-mail: flaxart@msn.com

Poet's Corner

ALL A pack of 48 purple-bordered cards, each with a quotation from a famous poem on one side, the source of the poem and biographical information and its author on the other. Among the represented poets are William Wordsworth, Pablo Neruda, Dylan Thomas, Carl Sandburg, Sylvia Plath, Emily Dickinson, Langston Hughes, Geoffrey Chaucer, and Sappho. No instructions are included with the deck, but you or your kids will be able to think of something.

Available at game or book stores or
Pomegranate Books
Box 6099
Rohnert Park, CA 94927

ON-LINE POETRY

See **On-Line Creative Writing** (page 143).

13 The Poetry Exchange

 Writers can submit their poems and get feedback from their peers.
bigsky.uoregon.edu/Site/Poetry/index.html

Positively Poetry

ALL Kids of all ages can post their poems on-line.
advicom.net/~e-media/poetry.html

JOURNALS AND DIARIES

BOOKS ABOUT AND FOR JOURNAL WRITING

6 / 12 All About Me
Linda Kranza; Northland Publishing, 1996

A charmingly illustrated write-it-yourself journal filled with thought- and memory-provoking questions and suggestions for young writers. A predominant page tint is pale lavender; our sons pronounced it flatly feminine, but it isn't supposed to be.

12 / + A Book of Your Own: Keeping a Diary or Journal
Carla Stevens; Clarion, 1993

All about the joys of journaling, with many suggestions for different ways of keeping a diary. Included are excerpts from historical and modern-day diaries.

4 / + The Creative Journal for Children
Lucia Capacchione; Shambhala, 1989

A practical guide to journal keeping that can be used both with very small children and kids of upper elementary to junior high age. The book includes 72 creative exercises for young journal keepers, among them suggestions for drawing a self-portrait, making a personal timeline, illustrating feelings, diagramming a family tree, inventing an imaginary friend, describing a dream, and making wishes.

Daily Journals

Carol Simpson; Good Year Books, 1993

Journal-keeping suggestions and activities for kids in grades K–3, with examples of student work.

Doing the Days: A Year's Worth of Creative Journaling, Drawing, Listening, Reading, Thinking, Arts & Crafts for Children Ages 8–12

Lorraine M. Dahlstrom; Free Spirit Publishing, 1994

Has 366 suggestions for daily journal-writing projects, plus over 1,000 other learning activities lined to the calendar. Suggestions are variously based on celebrations and holidays, famous birthdays, and landmark inventions.

Also see *Writing Down the Days: 365 Creative Journaling Ideas for Young People* (page 154).

I'm in the Spotlight

A guided journal that encourages writers aged 7–11 to make an autobiographical "journey of discovery." The book is divided into eight sections, to be completed by the young author: "Me, Myself, & I," "Early Memories," "Family Matters," "Friends, Buddies, Pals," "My Favorite Things," "A Rainbow of Feelings," "School Days, School Days," and "Wishes, Hopes, & Dreams."

$11.95

Dream Tree Press

3836 Thornwood Dr.

Sacramento, CA 95821

(800) 769-9029

Also see *Rainbow Writing* (right).

Journal Keeping with Young People

Barbara Steiner and Kathleen C. Phillips; Teacher Ideas Press, 1991

Many journal-writing ideas for kids of all ages. Suggestions include describing a first memory, designing a perfect house, and creating a character for a story or novel. The book includes a list of supplementary resources.

Make Beliefs

Bill Zimmerman; Guarionex Press, 1989

A 112-page illustrated journal designed to spark the imaginations of young writers and artists. Each page is a "Make Believe" to be filled in—written, drawn, or colored—by the user. Examples: "Make believe rainbows were handed to you. What would you do with them and how would they feel?" "Make believe you could add a new wonder to the world. What would that wonder be?" From bookstores or

$8.50 (plus $1.50 shipping/handling)

Guarionex Press Ltd.

201 W. 77th St., Suite 6AA

New York, NY 10024

(212) 724-5259

Rainbow Writing

Mary Euretig and Darlene Kreisberg; Dream Tree Press, 1992

A fill-it-in-yourself journal, in lollipop-colored oversize paperback, for beginning journal writers. Each month's worth of writing activities includes a calendar to number, assorted encouraging finish-the-sentence exercises ("One new book or story I read this month was _____." "If I could be an animal, I would be a _____." "If I could take a trip anywhere in the world this summer, I would go to _____."), spaces to write personal stories, frames in which to draw pictures, and questions to ask family members and friends, with spaces to record their answers.

$11.95

Dream Tree Press

3836 Thornwood Dr.

Sacramento, CA 95821

(800) 769-9029

Also see *I'm in the Spotlight!* (left).

Totally Private and Personal

Jessica Wilber; Free Spirit Publishing, 1996

A book of journaling ideas for girls and young women, with discussion of different uses of journals, descriptions of the creative forms journals can take, and many suggestions for topics to write about in one's totally private and personal journal. Chapter headings include "Growing Up" and "Feeling Good About Being a Girl."

Writing Down the Days
Lorraine M. Dahlstrom; Free Spirit Publishing, 1990

Creative journaling ideas and activities for each day of the year, from January 1 through December 31. Under March 19, for example, Dahlstrom writes:

> Each year on this day, in San Juan Capistrano, California, the swallows return from their stay in the south. This traditional sign of spring has been observed since 1776 as Swallows Day.
>
> Invent a holiday to celebrate something that you've been doing for a long time. Be outrageous!

Other journaling ideas are based on the founding of the National Weather Service, Michelangelo's birthday, National Tomb-Sweeping Day in Taiwan, and the anniversary of the completion of the transcontinental railroad.

Also see *Doing the Days: A Year's Worth of Creative Journaling, Drawing, Listening, Reading, Thinking, Arts & Crafts for Children Ages 8–12* (page 153).

DIARIES IN LITERATURE

Anne Frank: The Diary of a Young Girl
Anne Frank; Bantam Books, 1993

Possibly the world's most famous diary. The beautifully written story of a young girl's coming of age while in hiding from the Nazis during World War II. Available in several editions, on audiocassettes, and on video.

Catherine, Called Birdy
Karen Cushman; Clarion, 1994

Medieval life through the eyes of Catherine, whose father is determined to marry her off to the richest possible suitor, who, says Catherine, looks like a bearded pig. Catherine is witty, articulate, and delightful; her descriptions of medieval life are fascinating; and the book has a happy ending. For young adults.

Dear America Series
Scholastic

History as seen through the eyes of the young girls who lived it. Each book in this series purports to be the diary kept by a 12- or 13-year-old of the time, detailing troubles, tragedies, joys, triumphs, and the simple ups and downs of everyday life. Each book includes an historical appendix. Titles in the series include *Across the Wide and Lonesome Prairie: The Oregon Trail Diary of Hattie Campbell* (Kristiana Gregory; 1997), *A Journey to the New World: The Diary of Remember Patience Whipple* (Kathryn Lasky; 1996), and *A Picture of Freedom: The Diary of Clotee, A Slave Girl* (Patricia C. McKissack; 1997).

Diary of an Early American Boy
Eric Sloane; Ballantine, 1974

Based on the diary of 15-year-old Noah Blake, living in Connecticut in 1805, and illustrated with Sloane's detailed pen-and-ink drawings of early American buildings and tools.

Harriet the Spy
Louise Fitzhugh; HarperTrophy, 1996

Harriet Welsch writes everything—absolutely everything—down in her journal, which proves disastrous when the notebook is discovered and read by her classmates. By the end of the book, however, Harriet has solved her problems, learned some valuable lessons, and is well on her way to becoming a writer. Funny and touching. For readers aged 9–12.

Keeping Secrets: The Girlhood Diaries of Seven Women Writers
Mary E. Lyons; Henry Holt, 1995

Stories based on the teenage diaries of such writers as Louisa May Alcott, Kate Chopin, and Charlotte Perkins Gilman. For young adults.

Only Opal: The Diary of a Young Girl
Opal Whiteley; Paper Star, 1997

Selections from the diary of six-year-old Opal Whiteley, an orphan, who lived with a foster family in a logging camp in Oregon at the turn of the century.

Opal recorded the details of her days on scraps of paper: her life with her adopted family, her love of nature, her visits to favorite tree (named Michael Raphael), and an account of her pet mouse (Felix Mendelssohn).

Zlata's Diary: A Child's Life in Sarajevo

Zlata Filipovic; Penguin, 1995

Eleven-year-old Zlata Filipovic began her diary in September 1991 in war-torn Bosnia. Also available on audiocassette.

ON-LINE DIARIES

The Diary Project

Kids from around the world submit entries about their personal lives, thoughts, and feelings, under a list of topics, including drugs, families, friends, school, relationships, and the all-purpose "other."

www.diaryproject.com

LETTER WRITING

BOOKS: NONFICTION

Clever Letters: Fun Ways to Wiggle Your Words

Laura Allen; Pleasant Company, 1997

Creative and artistic ideas for young letter writers. The book is divided into six sections: "Clever Lettering," "Top Secret," "Paper Capers," "Writing from the Road," "Super Stationery," and "Signing Off With Style." Kids learn to design marvelously decorated messages, write in secret code or invisible ink, make their own stationery and envelopes, and send "fan" mail in the shape of a face-cooling folded paper fan.

Drift Bottles in History and Folklore

Dorothy B. Francis; Ballyhoo Books, 1990

Letter writing with a special twist for everyone who has ever dreamed of sending or finding a message in a bottle. The history, science, and lore of drift bottles, from the ancient Greeks (who used them to map water currents) through Queen Elizabeth I (who appointed an Official Uncorker of Ocean Bottles) to the present day. Included are instructions for making your own drift bottles and reproducible "Drift Bottle Record" forms on which to note launch location and date, with space to write a special message.

How to Make Pop-Ups

Joan Irvine; William Morrow, 1988

For messages with extra pizzazz, Joan Irvine explains, with easy-to-follow step-by-step instructions on how to make 28 kinds of truly terrific pop-up cards. Users will soon be turning out wide-mouthed frogs, opening flowers, pop-out people, zoo animals in fold-out cages, leaping rabbits and shooting rocket ships, spiraling snakes, flapping doors, and even a fire-breathing dragon.

Also see *How to Make Super Pop-Ups* (Beech Tree Books, 1992), which contains instructions for more and fancier pop-ups, including a foldout Christmas tree, a noise-making robot, a juggler with rotating colored balls, and an entire pop-up castle; and *How to Make Holiday Pop-Ups* (Beech Tree Books, 1996), which contains directions for making cards to celebrate holidays around the world.

The Kid's Address Book

Michael Levine; Perigee Books, 1994

Over 2,000 addresses of organizations, clubs, famous persons, and heads of state for young letter writers. Heavy on sports, popular music, and television.

Messages in the Mailbox: How to Write Letters

Loreen Leedy; Holiday House, 1994

The how-tos of letter writing for kids aged 6–10. The students in Mrs. Gator's class learn the parts of a letter and the many different types of letters and their proper formats, among them thank-you letters, sympathy letters, letters of apology, invitations, fan letters, and letters to the editor.

4/8 *The Post Office Book: Mail and How It Moves*

Gail Gibbons; Trophy Press, 1986

The brightly illustrated story of the mail for readers aged 4–8, from the time the letter is dropped in the mailbox until it reaches its destination. Included are some simple historical facts about the U.S. Post Office.

9/12 *Sincerely Yours: How to Write Great Letters*

Elizabeth James and Carol Barkin; Clarion, 1993

A comprehensive guide to letter writing, including the proper forms for business and friendly letters, the way to address an envelope, suggestions for making your own artistic postcards and stationery, and pen pal sources.

LETTER WRITING IN LITERATURE

5/8 *Casey Over There*

Staton Rabin; Harcourt Brace, 1994

It has been over three months since seven-year-old Aubrey has heard from his brother Casey, a soldier in Europe during World War I, so he writes a letter to the "Honorable Uncle Sam." He gets a personal reply from President Woodrow Wilson.
See **American History** (page 570).

10+ *Daddy-Long-Legs*

Jean Webster; Puffin, 1995

Jerusha Abbott, orphan, is sent to college to be educated as a writer by a mysterious trustee. The story of her life there is told in a lighthearted series of letters from Jerusha (Judy) to her nameless benefactor, whom she nicknames "Daddy-Long-Legs." There's a happy romantic ending. For readers aged 10 and up.

4/8 *Dear Annie*

Judith Caseley; Greenwillow, 1991

Annie takes her box of letters from her grandfather to school. The letters, each with an accompanying picture, tell stories about Annie's six years of life. Her classmates are so fascinated that they decide to begin writing letters to pen pals. For readers aged 4–8.

9/12 *Dear Mr. Henshaw*

Beverly Cleary; Avon Books, 1996

Fourth-grader Leigh Botts writes letters about his many troubles—his parents are divorced; he's struggling to be accepted at a new school—to his favorite author, Mr. Henshaw. For readers aged 9–12.

5/9 *Dear Peter Rabbit*

Alma Flor Ada; Atheneum, 1994

The picture-book tale of the developing relationships among Goldilocks and Baby Bear, and Peter Rabbit and the Three Little Pigs, as told through their letters.
See *The Jolly Postman or Other People's Letters* (below).

12+ *84 Charing Cross Road*

Helene Hanff; Penguin, 1990

The friendly, funny, and touching correspondence between New York author Helene Hanff and the little British bookstore through which she bought volumes of classical literature. For teenagers, who will promptly be inspired to (1) read classical literature and (2) write letters to foreign bookstores.

13+ *Griffin & Sabine: An Extraordinary Correspondence*

Nick Bantock; Chronicle Books, 1991

English artist Griffin Moss receives a postcard from Sabine, a woman he has never met, who lives on a mysterious and remote island. The book traces their developing relationship, through exquisitely illustrated postcards with handwritten messages on the back; then through letters, which arrive in hand-painted envelopes. A wonderful and unusual love story for teenagers. Also see, by the same author, *Sabine's Notebook: In Which the Extraordinary Correspondence of Griffin & Sabine Continues* (Chronicle Books, 1992) and *The Golden Mean: In Which the Extraordinary Correspondence of Griffin & Sabine Concludes* (Chronicle Books, 1993).

4/9 *The Jolly Postman or Other People's Letters*

Janet and Allan Ahlberg; Little, Brown, 1986

The Jolly Postman, on a red bicycle, makes deliveries to well-known storybook characters, and all the letters are right there in the book, folded and tucked in envelopes. Baby Bear gets an apologetic note (and a party invitation) from Goldilocks; the Wicked Witch gets a wicked advertising circular; and the Giant gets a postcard from Jack. Also see *The Jolly Christmas Postman* (Little, Brown, 1991).

7 10 Kate Heads West

Pat Brisson; Simon & Schuster, 1990

The story of Kate's journey through Oklahoma, Texas, Arizona, and New Mexico—with a stop-off at the Grand Canyon and a visit to the World Watermelon Seed Spitting Contest—is told through the letters that Kate writes back home. Also see *Your Best Friend, Kate* (Bradbury Press, 1989), in which Kate tours the mid-Atlantic states, and *Kate on the Coast* (Simon & Schuster, 1992), in which Kate visits the Pacific Coast, Alaska, and Hawaii.

Also see **Literature Links to Geography for Kids** (page 420).

13 + Letters to Julia

Barbara Ware Holmes; HarperCollins, 1997

Fifteen-year-old Liz, who is writing a book about the confusions of life with her divorced parents, submits a chapter to Julia, editor at a publishing company in New York City. A correspondence develops as Liz sends letters and subsequent chapters of her book to Julia, and Julia replies. For readers aged 13 and up.

9 12 Nettie's Trip South

Ann Turner; Aladdin, 1995

In a series of letters home, 10-year-old Nettie, on a visit to Richmond, Virginia, describes life in the pre–Civil War South.

See **American History** (page 539).

8 12 Post Card Passages

Susan Joyce; Peel Productions, 1994

Susan's great-aunt Gladys sends postcards from all over the globe, each with pictures and messages about exotic places and foreign cultures. (Illustrations include color reproductions of the postcards, with the foreign stamps.)

Also see **Literature Links to Geography for Kids** (page 420).

PEN PAL SOURCES

Keypals

A source for e-mail pen pals.
www.kidpub.org/kidpub/keypals

The Letter Exchange

The Letter Exchange offers "friendly conversation through the mail" to people of all ages through a 36-page magazine of pen pal listings published three times yearly. Potential pen pals are listed under 30+ categories, depending on the writer's interests, among them education, hobbies, music, nature/gardening, sports, and writing. There's a kids' corner for young letter writers.

Annual subscription (3 issues), $20; single copies of the magazine, available by mail, $9
The Letter Exchange
Box 6218
Albany, CA 94706

Making Mailbox Memories: Global Pen Friends for Grown-Ups and Kids

All about pen pals and pen pal sources.
Julia Anne Riley
Kindred Spirit Press
Box 682560
Park City, UT 84068-2560

Skipping Stones

Skipping Stones, a "Multicultural Children's Magazine" (see Geography, page 412) includes a "Penpals" column in each issue, listing potential pen pals by country.

Annual subscription (5 issues), $25
Skipping Stones
Box 3939
Eugene, OR 97403
(541) 342-4956

World Pen Pals

A source of pen pals from all over the world.
For an application form, send a stamped self-addressed envelope to
World Pen Pals
1694 Como Ave.
St. Paul, MN 55108

WRITING

On-Line Letter Writing

The Electric Postcard

 ALL Send a postcard by e-mail. Choose an illustrated postcard by category, such as "Paintings," "Photographs," or "Science" (which includes some spectacular NASA images from space), write a message, and e-mail the result to the correspondent of your choice.

postcards.www.media.mit.edu/Postcards

JOURNALISM AND NEWSPAPERS

Books: Nonfiction

Deadline! From News to Newspaper
4 8 Gail Gibbon; Thomas Y. Crowell, 1987

A picture-book account of what goes on behind the scenes at a small-town daily newspaper.

The Furry News: How to Make a Newspaper
5 9 Loreen Leedy; Holiday House, 1990

A bunch of furry animals collaborate to write and edit the stories, lay out the newspaper, and print *The Furry News*. The book includes definitions of essential newspaper words (*headline, byline*) and suggestions to help kids in publishing their own newspapers.

Hot Off the Press: Getting the News Into Print
9 13 Ruth Crisman; Lerner, 1991

The history of newspapers, what's in them, why we read them, how they are distributed, and an account of various careers in journalism and print media for kids aged 9–13.

A Mathematician Reads the Newspaper
13 + John Allen Paulos; Basic Books, 1995

A fascinating and mathematically insightful tour of the newspaper, covering such topics as mathematical sneakiness in advertising, misleading uses of polit-

ical, environmental, and medical statistics, coincidences (do they mean anything?), and the dangers of extrapolation. An informative delight for teenagers and adults.

Also see **Innumeracy** (page 178).

Reading the Sports Page: A Guide to Understanding Sports Statistics
12 + Jeremy R. Feinberg; New Discovery, 1992

An explanation of how to interpret baseball, football, basketball, hockey, and tennis statistics for newspaper-reading sports fans.

Stop the Presses, Nellie's Got a Story! A Story of Nellie Bly
9 12 Robert Quackenbush; Simon & Schuster, 1992

A short illustrated biography of feisty reporter Nellie Bly for middle-grade readers.

What It's Like to Be a Newspaper Reporter
5 9 Janet Craig; Troll Associates, 1990

A short picture book, illustrated with color photographs, in which readers follow a newspaper reporter through the day as he covers assignments, files his story, and goes to press.

Games and Hands-On Activities

It's News to Me!
9 + "It's News to Me!," designed by journalist/educator Barbara Goldman of Pittsburgh, is a board game intended to promote imagination and critical-thinking skills—and to boost interest in reading the newspaper. Each player, according to the game instructions, needs a current issue of the newspaper (sharing works); everything else is provided in the game box. Players proceed around the board, drawing "Press Pass" cards and attempting to complete five journalistic assignments. The first player to polish these off and arrive back at the Editor's Office wins the game. Sample assignments, based on the newspaper in hand: "Pick an article that deals with foreign trade. Name the countries and products involved." "What is the topic of the

paper's Editorial Cartoon?" "Headlines are designed to grab a reader's attention. Choose two that you find most interesting and two that you feel are dull. Jazz up the dull headlines."

A workbook, *News to Use,* a collection of activities for teaching kids about the newspaper, is included in each game. It contains a list of definitions of newspaper terms (masthead, by-line), an explanation of the five essential Ws of a good newspaper story (who, what, where, when, and why), and a large assortment of kid-oriented journalistic projects. "It's News to Me!" is recommended for two to six players, aged 9 and up.

$29 (plus $4 shipping/handling)

Newsline Publications, Inc.

Box 8114

Pittsburgh, PA 15217

(800) 770-2648

Make Your Own Newspaper Kit

The "Make Your Own Newspaper Kit" leads beginning reporters through newspaper publishing process step-by-step. The kit includes an illustrated 48-page how-to book, *Make Your Own Newspaper,* by Ray and Chris Harris, featuring the helpful explanations of Newsnose the Newshound, and five tabloid-size blank copies of a four-page newspaper, *The Reporter,* designed for kids to write and illustrate themselves. *The Reporter* provides a bit of something for everybody: there are spaces for news stories and weather reports, editorial cartoons, reader polls, book and movie reviews, travel guides, sports reports, personal profiles, comics, and classified ads. The kit is recommended for kids aged 7–14, but the layout of *The Reporter* is slanted toward younger people with large printing.

Kit, $9.95 (plus shipping/handling)

In bookstores or

Adams Media Corp.

260 Center St.

Holbrook, MA 02343

(800) 872-5627

The Newspaper Anti-Coloring Book

Susan Striker; Henry Holt, 1992

Creative activities for would-be reporters aged 6 and up. This is part of the Anti-Coloring Book series, which kids illustrate and write themselves. In the newspaper version, users have opportunities to invent news stories, illustrate headline news ("Scientists Create New Species!," "Snowstorm up north inspires a snowperson-building contest!," "New Skyscraper Erected!"), write wedding announcements and obituaries, review the best and worst movies of the year, draw a pair of comic strips, write and illustrate convincing advertisements, and complete a crossword puzzle.

News for Kids

Boomerang!

A monthly children's audiomagazine on 70-minute cassette tapes for 7–12-year-olds. *Boomerang!* is the equivalent of National Public Radio's *All Things Considered* for kids. Included is a "Money" report, in which the economy is explained through the ups and downs of business at Freddie's Baxter's rhubarb-and-banana sandwich stand; "Turning Points," in which a time-traveling reporter interviews famous historical figures; "Natural Wonders," which deals with science, the environment, and nature; and "The Big Idea," the monthly feature story, which explores different sides of current events issues. Past "Big Ideas" have included cults, extraterrestrials, the information superhighway, and gender equality. The tapes also include the wonderful stories of Dave Schmave, the Elevator Man. Each begins with the *whoosh* of the closing elevator door as listeners settle in for a ride.

Annual subscription (12 issues), $43.95; back issues, $5 per tape

Boomerang!

13366 Pescadero Rd.

La Honda, CA 94020

(800) 333-7858

Tomorrow's Morning

A weekly newspaper for kids aged 8–14, including all the news basics: national and world news, feature stories, sports updates, a stock market report, editorials, and kids' letters to the editor.

Annual subscription (52 issues), $24.95

Tomorrow's Morning

Box 338

Vandalia, OH 45377

(800) 607-4410

Also see **Tomorrow's Morning** (right).

4
18 *Weekly Reader*
Classroom newspapers available at nine age-appropriate levels, for kids in preschool through high school. Each illustrated weekly issue covers current events in a variety of fields; also included are quizzes and puzzles.

> Single elementary-level subscriptions (26 issues per year), $24.95; two or more subscriptions, $5.70 to $6.80 apiece, depending on grade level. Single secondary subscriptions (26 issues), $29.95; two or more, $16.50
> Weekly Reader Corp.
> 3001 Cindel Dr.
> Delran, NJ 08370
> (800) 446-3355/fax (609) 786-3360

Weekly Reader also publishes several other student periodicals, including *Current Health, READ,* and *Current Science* (see page 218).

NEWS FOR KIDS ON-LINE

10
+ Children's Express
A news service by and for kids, in which participants submit editorials or news stories on issues of interest. The site also includes a monthly poll question. Most of the stories are by writers aged 12–16.

> www.ce.org

12
+ CNN Interactive
News on-line from the television news channel. *CNN Interactive* is the familiar news channel on-line, with access to up-to-the-minute and past news stories on world and national events, the weather, sports, science and technology, travel, entertainment, medicine, and the environment.

CNN Newsroom and Worldview is a 30-minute commercial-free block of news coverage specifically designed for classrooms: enrolled schools and teachers have permission to videotape the programs off the television. The program schedule is available on-line;

each daily show includes an overview of the day's top news stories plus a special feature on environmental, international, economic, or scientific issues. Also available on-line is a "Classroom Guide," with suggestions for program-related discussion questions and projects.

> For CNN Interactive: www.cnn.com
> For CNN Newsroom and Worldview:
> www.cnn.com/CNN/Programs/CNNnewsroom

13
+ CRAYON
"Create your own newspaper" on-line. While this sounds like a young children's site, it isn't: CRAYON is designed as an Internet news-management tool. Those who want a customized newspaper can select specific news sources or topics—for example, only science and technology stories and sports updates—for a personalized overview of the news. For teenagers and adults.

> crayon.net

ALL KidNews
Submissions by kids from "practically everywhere," categorized as news stories, sports stories, feature articles, reviews, or creative writing (poetry and fiction). The site also includes chat rooms for kids and adults, a pen pal connection, and links to interesting web sites for kids.

> www.vsa.cape.com/~powens/kidnews.html

8
14 Time Magazine for Kids
A kid-targeted version of the adult news magazine, covering people in the news, feature stories, cartoons, games and quizzes, and kids' letters to the editor. A colorful site filled with photographs.

> www.pathfinder.com/@@3w*AOAcAbqsmQkmQ/TFK

8
14 Tomorrow's Morning
The on-line version of the print newspaper, including national and international news, "Oddball Facts," "Historytalk," sports, stories about readers (kids can submit their own by filling out a detailed on-line questionnaire), and "Kid$stock$," a market report on stocks of interest to kids, such as Coca-Cola, Disney, and McDonald's.

> morning.com

WRITING

LIBRARIES

BOOKS

Books and Libraries
Jack Knowlton; HarperCollins, 1991

A short, brightly illustrated history of books and libraries, starting at the very beginning, with 30,000-year-old cave paintings in France. The book then covers the "libraries" of ancient Mesopotamia where the books, written on clay tablets, were stored in baskets; the famous library at Alexandria in Egypt, stocked with 700,000 scrolls; medieval copyists; the invention of the printing press; Benjamin Franklin and the first "subscription library"; Melvil Dewey and the Dewey Decimal System for cataloguing books; and the Library of Congress. The inside covers of the book include a colorful illustrated diagram of the Dewey Decimal System.

Check It Out! A Book About Libraries
Gail Gibbons; Harcourt Brace, 1985

A picture-book explanation of the workings of the public library for young readers.

Find It! The Inside Story at Your Library
Claire McInerney; Lerner, 1989

Describes the various resources and references available at the public library and how to use them, for students aged 9–12.

The Inside-Outside Book of Libraries
Julie Cummins; E. P. Dutton, 1996

A picture-book tour of all kinds of libraries, from the back-roads bookmobile to the Library of Congress. Also featured are a prison library, a shipboard library (onboard the Navy aircraft carrier *Abraham Lincoln*), a branch library in Chinatown, a library for the blind, a tool-lending library, and the Internet ("a library without walls").

Ms. Davison, Our Librarian
Alice K. Flanagan; Children's Press, 1997

A simple, large-print text illustrated with photographs explains just what a librarian does for readers aged 4–8.

LIBRARIES IN LITERATURE

Clara and the Bookwagon
Nancy Smiler Levison; HarperTrophy, 1991

Clara's life on the farm is transformed when the horse-drawn "bookwagon"—the country's first traveling library—arrives at her door. For readers aged 4–8.

The Day They Came to Arrest the Book
Nat Hentoff; Dell, 1983

An activist group wants to remove Mark Twain's *The Adventures of Huckleberry Finn* from the shelves of the school library on the grounds that the book is racist, sexist, and immoral; 17-year-old Barney Roth, editor of the school paper, decides to protest. An interesting and discussion-provoking account of book censorship.

The Library
Sarah Stewart; Farrar, Straus & Giroux, 1995

A delightful picture book that tells—in rhyme—the story of Elizabeth Brown, a redheaded bookworm with thick glasses, who likes nothing better than reading. Elizabeth eventually accumulates so many books that not so much as an inch of space is left in her house—so she donates them all to the town to start a public library.

The Library Dragon
Carmen Agra Deedy; Peachtree Publishing, 1994

The new librarian at Sunrise Elementary School is a dragon—and a very disagreeable one, who won't let the children borrow or even touch the books. Then one day nearsighted Molly Brickmeyer wanders into the library in search of her lost glasses, trips over a bookshelf, and a book falls open into her lap. Molly begins to read aloud—which so enthralls the dragon that the library is opened once again to eager readers.

Library Lil

Suzanne Williams; Dial Books for Young Readers, 1997

A tall tale about a truly larger-than-life librarian who single-handedly converts an entire town to reading. When a storm knocks the electricity out, Lil drags the bookmobile from door to door, delivering a good book to every man, woman, and child. She also defeats a television-watching motorcycle gang, turning them all into avid bookworms. With great illustrations by Steven Kellogg.

Richard Wright and the Library Card

William Miller; Lee & Low Books, 1997

Based on an episode from Wright's autobiography. Young Richard wanted to learn to read but was banned from the library in the South of the 1920s because of his race. Finally, at age 17, he convinced a white man to lend him his library card, and a whole new world opened for him. For readers aged 5–9.

Tomás and the Library Lady

Pat Mora; Alfred A. Knopf, 1997

Young Tomás is the son of migrant workers who follow the ripening crops from Texas to Iowa and spend long days at work in the fields. At night, all listen to Grandfather's wonderful stories. One day, Grandfather tells Tomás that there are many more stories in the library. Tomás, eager to discover them, visits the town library, where a kind librarian introduces him to books (and he, in return, teaches her a bit of Spanish).

ACTIVITY BOOKS

Can You Find It?

Randall McCutcheon; Free Spirit Publishing, 1991

Can You Find It?, subtitled "25 Library Scavenger Hunts to Sharpen Your Research Skills," poses a series of challenges that lures kids into the library reference section. Students track down the answers to definitely out-of-the-ordinary research problems, using card catalogs, microfilm collections, dictionaries, directories, encyclopedias, and more. Sample challenges include hunts for the name of the first R-rated movie, the location of the world's largest shopping mall, and the means of making restaurant reservations in Beijing. Recommended for kids aged 13 and up.

Available through bookstores or
Free Spirit Publishing, Inc.
400 First Ave. N, Suite 616
Minneapolis, MN 55401-1724
(800) 735-7323

Cruising Through Research: Library Skills for Young Adults

John D. Volkman; Teacher Ideas Press, 1998

A series of creative multidisciplinary projects for kids in grades 7–12 that allow them to practice their library research skills. Complete instructions are included for each of the 12 lessons, plus a resource list, reproducible activity sheets, and a bibliography. Kids are introduced to the use of basic reference sources, such as *The World Almanac, The Dictionary of American Biography,* and *Bartlett's Familiar Quotations,* and then led through the process of researching and writing term papers. In a study unit on the Vietnam War, for example, students, using library resources, make a map of Vietnam, identify and listen to music of the war era, comment on poetry written by Vietnam veterans, and produce a research paper on a war-related topic.

The Reference Information Skills Game

Myram Forney Tunnicliff and Susan Sheldon Soenen; Teacher Ideas Press, 1995

The book details a game-style technique for teaching research skills to kids in grades 4–9. Kids, armed with search maps and suggestions, are challenged to solve problems and collect information using a variety of reference materials, from the dictionary and the encyclopedia to computer networks.

ON-LINE LIBRARIES

American Library Association Resources for Parents and Kids

A parent's page with helpful hints for connecting kids to the public library and instilling a love of reading, book lists for kids of all ages, research helps, many links to terrific Web sites for kids, and a parent-and-kid introduction to cyberspace.

www.ala.org/parents/index.html

See **American Library Association** (page 48) and *Book Links* (page 69).

Internet Public Library
ALL Access to reference materials, magazines, newspapers, and on-line texts, plus special sites for "Teens" and "Youth." Under each are age-appropriate links to book lists, resources, and Web sites categorized by academic subject, and an instructive tour of the Dewey Decimal System.

www.ipl.org

KidsConnect
18 A question-answering service for kids in grades K–12 looking for resources on topics of special interest. Users post a question and will receive an answer from a library media specialist within two days. The site also includes links to a wide number of educational sites arranged by category.

www.ala.org/ICONN/kidsconn.html

Monroe County Public Library Children's
ALL Services
Kids can search the Dewey Decimal System for related book titles and Web sites. The site also includes book lists and many informational links for kids, parents, and teachers.

www.monroe.lib.in.us/childrens/childrens_dept.html

MATHEMATICS

Let no one ignorant of geometry enter here.

ABOVE THE DOOR AT PLATO'S ACADEMY

Mathematics—at least, its subset, basic arithmetic—has never been a favorite with our children. We floundered about, in our early homeschool days, attempting to lay our hands on the perfect math program, the one collection of exercise books and manipulatives that would spark interest and generate that delighted revelatory response that accompanies real learning. This mathematical Holy Grail never quite materialized. After numerous false starts, however, we did eventually devise approaches and track down assorted resources that motivated and appealed. The boys, presented with these, moved slowly from an outright loathing of all things arithmetical to cheerful tolerance to—occasionally—positive enthusiasm. Ethan was fascinated by measurements and statistics—he always seemed to know the depth of the Grand Canyon, the top speed of a running cheetah, and the weight of the world's largest watermelon—but he never enjoyed arithmetic exercises; we therefore designed a series of arithmetic workbooks just for him, slanted toward interesting numbers.

Josh and Caleb found math most interesting when approached in a cross-curricular fashion: both liked math in a historical context. We therefore integrated math into their history studies and projects. They graphed the sizes of famous ships, from the *Mayflower* to the *Titanic*; determined the speed of the average Conestoga wagon en route to Oregon; compared Civil War battle statistics; and calculated the circumference of Stonehenge.

From my homeschool journal:

◆ **May 26, 1992. Josh is eleven; Ethan, nine; Caleb, seven.**

Today we began reading Mathematicians Are People, Too *by Luetta and Wilbert Reimer (see page 203). The first chapter is about the Greek mathematician Thales, who managed to measure the height of the Great Pyramid of Cheops by means of a ratio: he determined that the ratio of his own height to the length of his shadow would be the same as the ratio of the pyramid's height to the length of its shadow. We discussed the concept of* ratio, *and the boys were intrigued enough to try some experiments. We thus went outside and determined, by shadow-measuring techniques, the heights of the house, barn, assorted trees, and the outside lamppost. It all seemed to work; we double-checked by measuring the height of the lamppost with the yardstick.*

Ethan: "Does it make a difference that the pyramid was really fat at the bottom? Wouldn't that change the length of its shadow?"

So we compared shadows of (fat) boxes and (skinny) sheets of cardboard, all of the same height.

Answer: No.

Caleb: "How do you measure the height of a mountain?"

Our next project: triangulation.

We first introduced the boys to math through a combination of hands-on manipulatives and workbooks, initially using Cuisenaire rods (see page 168), Mortensen Math materials (see page 176), dice games, and dominoes to launch them into addition, subtraction, multiplication, and division. As the boys, one by one, reached the age of ten or eleven, we began to center our program around the Saxon Math texts (see page 177), which are dull but thorough; under Saxon tutelage, all became increasingly competent in math. Genuine mathematical interest, however, was reserved for supplementary projects, experiments, games, and activities.

A popular approach to math in the schools involves linking mathematical operations to the activities of daily life: stressing the place of math in comparative shopping, for example, or in calculating savings at department store sales, or in figuring tips at restaurants, gasoline mileages, and mortgage rates. While our kids showed little interest in mortgage rates (restaurant tips had some minor appeal), math encountered in a real-world context was generally well (even excitedly) received. The mathematical aspects of science particularly caught their attention and imaginations: all were fascinated by the calculations involved in radioisotope-based dating (Caleb: "You could figure out just how old a mammoth was!"), by the mathematics of satellite launches, by the fractal patterns of sprouting snowflakes, and the logarithmic growth rates of multiplying bacteria.

Other notable successes in our homeschool math program have included:

1. Chess. Our boys all learned to play chess as preschoolers—which was the last time that I managed to defeat any of them—and they've continued to play, becoming increasingly skillful, ever since. Chess, which enhances a battery of spatial, pattern-forming, and logic skills, is an excellent experience for young mathematicians; it's also fun. See Chess, page 205.

2. Math-oriented fiction books. Good—and mathematically mind-expanding—choices are available for kids of all ages. For younger readers, try picture books, such as David Birch's *The King's Chessboard,* Mitsumasa Anno's *The Mysterious Multiplying Jar,* Jon Sciezska's riotous *Math Curse,* or David Schwartz's *How Much Is a Million?,* and older readers won't be able to

resist Norton Juster's *The Phantom Tollbooth*. (And, once they read it, they'll never forget what a dodecahedron is.) See *Books for Kids* (page 180).

3. Very large, very small, and very strange numbers. Our boys were enthralled with the monstrous, the minuscule, and the weird; thus through an anecdotal approach to numbers—as in "There are one quadrillion ants on earth"—everybody learned a great deal about number names, measurement (English and metric), exponents, and scientific notation. (They also picked up a lot of truly bizarre mathematical facts.) Excellent sources for fascinating numerical information include Philip and Phylis Morrison's *Powers of Ten* (see page 200), Russell Ash's *Incredible Comparisons* (see page 200), Theoni Pappas's *Fractals, Googols, and Other Mathematical Tales* (see page 184), and Stephen Strauss's *The Sizesaurus* (see page 201). And there's always the ever-popular *Guinness Book of World Records*.

4. Mathematical art. Try assembling geometric mosaics and tessellations, building three-dimensional geometric shapes, experimenting with homemade Mobius strips, and making your own mathematical board games, counting books, and decorated calendars. Try pendulum painting, make an Archimedean spiral, experiment with compasses and spirographs, build an abacus, make your own sets of tangrams. Our kids, at various ages, enjoyed all of these. Good sources for comparable projects include Carol Vorderman's *How Math Works* (see page 184) and Mary Ann Kohl and Cindy Gainer's *MathArts* (see page 185). See Activity Books (page 183).

5. Graphs. A graph, by formal definition, is the pictorial representation of mathematical information, and our kids have always had soft spots for pictorial representations. They enjoyed translating numerical information into bar graphs, pie charts, and line graphs; they also liked Cartesian graphing, for which we initially used a set of workbooks in which the lists of coordinate points, connected, made nice little pictures. See Activity Resources (page 167).

From my homeschool journal:

◆ **June 19, 1995. Josh is fourteen; Ethan, twelve; Caleb, ten.**

Caleb is learning about exponents and scientific

notation, using Mathematics: A Human Endeavor *by Harold Jacobs (see page 175);* Fractals, Googols, and Other Mathematical Tales *by Theoni Pappas (page 184), and a homemade workbook (by me). He's now able to convert enormous numbers back and forth from decimal to scientific notation and vice versa. Jacobs uses a lot of nice large-number examples (telephone line amplifiers, astronomical distances, the number of molecules of water in the Pacific Ocean), which Caleb finds fascinating. Today we reviewed tera-, peta-, exa-, zepto-, and yocto-meters, with appropriate astronomical examples; then covered centimeters, millimeters, and micrometers, variously determining the lengths of a Goliath beetle and the world's smallest spider, and calculating how big a red blood cell would be if it were 7.7×10^6 meters in diameter instead of 7.7×10^{-6} meters.*

Ethan just finished the Hands-On Equations *(see page 173) introductory algebra program and is in the process of learning how to convert units from one measurement system to another, as in physics (that is, convert speed in miles/hour to centimeters/second). I've made him a workbook on this, using many many real-world numerical examples.*

Josh spent most of the day reading The Brothers Karamozov *(Fyodor Dostoyevsky), emerging from literature long enough to argue that, as a future writer, it is a waste of his time to study math. "Look at Dostoyevsky," said Josh. "Do you think he needed math?"*

I sent Josh to look up Dostoyevsky in the encyclopedia. Josh returned looking gleeful and announced that Dostoyevsky spent three years in engineering school, hated every minute of it, and spent all his time there reading.

I should have made him look up Lewis Carroll.

Today, as teenagers, the boys have advanced into the realm of higher math: algebra, geometry, trigonometry, and (soon) calculus. Our favored texts are by mathematician Harold R. Jacobs, among them *Algebra, Geometry,* and *Mathematics: A Human Endeavor* (see page 175). Jacobs's clear and creative approach to mathematics is rare in the textbook world; his books are interesting, information packed, and delightful.

In any case, we must be doing something right. Caleb can calculate practically anything in his head. All Ethan wanted for his birthday was a graphing calculator. And Josh is reading John Paulos's *Innumeracy*.

GENERAL MATH

ORGANIZATIONS

National Council of Teachers of Mathematics

The National Council of Teachers of Mathematics (NCTM) is a national organization "dedicated to the improvement of the teaching and learning of mathematics." An annual (individual) membership costs $57 and includes a subscription to the organization's newsletter, the NCTM *News Bulletin,* which includes in each issue four pages of reproducible student enrichment activities, and a choice of subscriptions to one of the NCTM's other four periodicals: *Teaching Children Mathematics* (pre-K–elementary grades; 9 issues); *Mathematics Teaching in the Middle School* (6 issues); *Mathematics Teacher* (high school grades; 9 issues); or *Journal for Research in Mathematics Education* (the latest in math education research at all levels; 5 issues). Each periodical includes articles on teaching strategies, curriculum suggestions, reviews of new math materials and resources, and reproducible student activity pages. The NCTM also publishes a catalog of teacher idea books, student activity books, and teaching videos, available upon request.

NCTM
1906 Association Dr.
Reston, VA 20191-1593
(703) 620-9840/fax 476-2970
Web site: www.nctm.org

CATALOGS

Activity Resources

"Teaching isn't telling people things," writes Mary Laycock, whose creative teachers' guides, among them *Fabrics of Mathematics* and (with Peggy McLean) *Weaving Your Way from Arithmetic to Mathematics,* formed the original basis of Activity Resources. "It's asking questions. I want . . . to have kids discover rather than tell them anything. I never want a child told a rule." The 48-page company catalog carries a large assortment of activity books, math games, puzzles, and manipulatives in keeping with this investigative philosophy. Popular themes are math in real life, multicultural math, and multidisciplinary math, in which math concepts are linked to science, art, and literature. (Mary Laycock: "Show me one thing that's not math!")

Among the Activity Resources materials are the *Focus On . . .* workbooks, covering Calculator Math, Pre-Algebra, Geometry, Fractions, Decimals, and Percent. Each workbook is a 60+-page overview of a specific set of math skills, taught through illustrations, puzzles, real-life problems (students learning about percents, for example, calculate sales taxes, interest, and discount savings), and practice exercises. Also included: *Bucky for Beginners,* 64 pages of model-making projects based on the geometry of Buckminster Fuller; *Pholdit,* a series of paper-folding activities introducing kids to geometric solids; *Graphiti,* in which kids learn Cartesian graphing by plotting coordinates and then connecting the points to make pictures; and *Enhance Chance,* a collection of instructions for 45 different dice games designed to reinforce such basic math concepts as whole numbers, place value, fractions, decimals, percents, probability, and logic. And many more.

Activity Resources
Box 4875
Hayward, CA 94541
(510) 782-1300/fax (510) 782-8172

Carolina Mathematics

A catalog of creative math materials, books, games, programs, posters, and activity books for students in middle school through college.

Carolina Biological Supply Co.
2700 York Rd.
Burlington, NC 27215-3398
(910) 584-0381 or (800) 334-5551/fax (800) 222-7112
e-mail: math@carolina.com

Cherry Pi

Simple, versatile, and cheap math materials for elementary students. Products include "Kid Checks" sets: two multicolored packs of 40 checks each, two check registers, and a sheet of suggested activities and ideas. "Make a variety of catalogs or circulars available," reads one, "and give your kids each a pretend $200 balance. Have them 'purchase' several items and write checks for each one. Stress that they shouldn't overdraw the account."

Also available are "Tiles" kits: the tiles are multicolored plastic canvas squares that can be used, along with the illustrated guidebook, to teach basic arithmetic operations, fractions, and pattern formation to kids in grades K–3. All in all, it's a low-key activity-based approach to math, just right for young beginners.

Cherry Pi publishes an annual catalog/newsletter, printed on thrifty brown paper, titled *The Mathematics Brown Bag,* a 25-page collection of teaching hints, games, puzzles, and project instructions; it also includes descriptions, prices, and ordering information for Cherry Pi products.

Catalog, $4; "Kid Checks," $6.50; "Tiles" kits, $15
Cherry Pi Publications
6218 Unity Ave. N
Minneapolis, MN 55429-2309
(612) 535-7474
e-mail: CherryPiMN@aol.com

COMAP

COMAP (the Consortium for Mathematics and its Applications) is a nonprofit organization dedicated to improving the quality of math education by publishing innovative teaching materials. Many of these are affordable self-contained teaching modules, which link mathematical concepts to mathematical applications in the real world. Titles are dull, but content is interesting. Modules for geometry students, for example, include "Rigidity and Braced Grids," which—using the flying buttresses of the Cathedral of Notre-Dame and the metal skeleton of the Statue of Liberty—shows kids how architects use math to determine whether a structure will collapse; and "Knottedness," in which kids study topology, using magic tricks, sailing knots, and Egyptian hieroglyphics.

Annual standard membership, $32, including subscription to the quarterly journal *Consortium,* which includes articles on math in the real world, math teaching ideas, math puzzles and problems, and information on math contests; plus a choice of two COMAP teaching modules or other publications. Membership Plus ($64) includes subscriptions to *Con-*

sortium and *UMAP Journal,* a quarterly collection of new math teaching modules, plus a choice of three COMAP publications
COMAP, Inc.
57 Bedford St., Suite 210
Lexington, MA 02173
(781) 862-7878 or (800) 772-6627

Cuisenaire/Dale Seymour Publications

Most educators, confronted with the name *Cuisenaire,* think Cuisenaire rods: colorful polished sets of wooden (or plastic) rods in graded sizes from 1 to 10 with which kids learn, hands-on, the basic principles of mathematics. The company's 130+-page catalog does carry Cuisenaire rods in many sets of different sizes, along with related activity books, workbooks, and idea books. It also carries an immense assortment of other high-quality mathematical materials, including pattern blocks, hundred number boards, base 10 blocks, multi-link cubes, fraction bars and circles, dice and spinners, calculators, and geoboards, and a wide range of books of all kinds, including math-oriented fiction books, workbooks, activity books, and teachers' guidebooks.

Cuisenaire/Dale Seymour Publications
Box 5026
White Plains, NY 10602-5026
orders (800) 237-0338; customer service (800) 872-1100; fax (914) 328-5487 or (800) 551-RODS
Web site: www.cuisenaire.com or www.awl.com/dsp

Delta Hands-On Math

An excellent and varied collection of mathematical games, puzzles, building kits, books, activity books, and manipulatives of all kinds for kids in grades K–8.
Delta Education
Box 3000
Nashua, NH 03061-3000
(800) 442-5444/fax (800) 282-9560
Web site: www.delta-ed.com

ETA Math Catalog

A 170-page catalog of math books, activity books, kits, games, resources, and manipulatives, listed by category. Included, for example, are materials for "Counting & Sorting," "Measurement," "Math 'n' Literature," "Graphing & Statistics," "Algebra," and "Multicultural Math."

ETA
620 Lakeview Pkwy.
Vernon Hills, IL 60061-5985
(847) 816-5050 or (800) 445-5985/fax (800) ETA-9326
e-mail: info@etauniverse.com
Web site: www.etauniverse.com

Institute for Math Mania

The Vermont-based Institute for Math Mania was founded by educator Rachel McAnallen ("Ms. Math"), and is dedicated to what McAnallen calls the "Carburetor Theory of Mathematics:" "Any mechanic can tell you that you won't learn about a carburetor from a picture. You have to take it apart. Mess around with it." The same, explains McAnallen, applies to math. Let kids "mess around with numbers, collect data, look at patterns, develop formulas. When they've done all that, then they'll begin to see how math works." The institute offers workshops and programs for teachers and students, provides consulting services for educators, and publishes a sizable newsprint catalog stuffed with innovative math games and activity books, polyhedral dice, puzzles, blocks, and teaching guides.

McAnallen, whose overall approach to mathematics education is appealingly playful, and coworker Nancy Segal, publisher of the teaching newsletter *Wonderful Ideas* (see page 170), have devised a number of quick and simple arithmetical games using polyhedral dice, including "Wipe Out," "Pig Out," and "Reach for Fifty": directions for all three, plus a packet of all necessary dice, are available for $5 from the catalog.

McAnallen has also written an introduction to fractions, *Action Fractions!* for kids aged 7 and up. The colorful 40-page text is accompanied by a set of pattern blocks and a trio of fraction hexahedral dice. Using these, kids cover symmetry and pattern-block equations, fractional representations (including "How Many Ways Can You Make a '1'?"), and several fraction-trading and fraction addition/subtraction games.

Entire kit, $18; the book alone, $8
Institute for Math Mania
Box 910
Montpelier, VT 05601-0910
(802) 223-5871 or (800) NUMERAL/fax (802) 223-5871

Summit Learning

A catalog of math resources of all kinds for kids in grades K–9, including manipulatives; dice, card, and board games; measuring apparatus; calculators; teachers' guides; and student workbooks and activity books.

Summit Learning
Box 493
Fort Collins, CO 80522
orders (800) 777-8817
customer service (800) 500-8817

United Art and Education Supply Co.

A source for hands-on math materials, including student clocks and magnetic "learning calendars," play money, geoboards, pattern blocks, tangrams, flash cards, and inexpensive games of Addition, Subtraction, or Multiplication Bingo.

Catalog $7.50 to individuals, free to schools
United Art and Education Supply Co., Inc.
Box 9219
Fort Wayne, IN 46899
(219) 478-1121 or (800) 322-3247/fax (219) 478-2249

MAGAZINES

Dynamath

A math magazine for kids in grades 3–6 from Scholastic, filled with puzzles, games, math-related folktales and stories, information about famous mathematicians, and hands-on activities. Readers learn, for example, how to use fractions to make a perfect tortilla, and how to calculate the amount of food needed for an 800-pound elephant. Each issue includes a practice test.

Annual subscription, $9
Scholastic, Inc.
Scholastic Order Processing
2931 E. McCarty St.
Jefferson City, MO 65101
(800) SCHOLASTIC
Web site: www.scholastic.com
Also see *Math* (page 170).

Games Magazine

A bimonthly collection of clever word games, brain benders, mathematical puzzles, logic problems, and visual challenges, plus reviews of new board games. Good for developing problem-solving skills. Some of the games are appropriate for readers of all ages; the word games usually require mature reading skills.

Games Junior is a younger version of the magazine for kids aged 7 and up.

> Annual subscription (6 issues), $15
> *Games Magazine*
> Box 605
> Mt. Morris, IL 61054-0605
> (800) 827-1256

Also see *Games Magazine Big Book of Games* (page 184).

Journal for Research in Mathematics Education

See **National Council of Teachers of Mathematics** (page 167).

Math

A magazine concentrating on the excitements of real-world math for kids in grades 7–9, from Scholastic. Each issue includes informational articles, puzzles, challenges, and hands-on activities. Readers, for example, learn how baseball sluggers use angles and solve math mysteries with a team of comic book–style heroes.

> Annual subscription (14 issues), $9
> Scholastic Inc.
> Scholastic Order Processing
> 2931 E. McCarty St.
> Jefferson City, MO 65101
> (800) SCHOLASTIC
> Web site: www.scholastic.com

See *Dynamath* (page 169).

The Mathematics Brown Bag

See **Cherry Pi** (page 167).

Mathematics Teacher

See **National Council of Teachers of Mathematics** (page 167).

Mathematics Teaching in the Middle School

See **National Council of Teachers of Mathematics** (page 167).

Teaching Children Mathematics

See **National Council of Teachers of Mathematics** (page 167).

Wonderful Ideas

A 12-page collection of puzzles, projects, contests, and mathematical challenges, published five times annually (September, November, January, March, and May). Most of the mathematical challenges are aimed at kids in grade 3 and up, though some can be handled by younger children—and answers, for frustrated mathematicians of any age, are included. Sample "Wonderful Ideas" include instructions for making geometric models, logic problems, calculator-generated number patterns, and arithmetical puzzles.

> Annual subscription (5 issues), $18; back issues,
> $5 apiece
> *Wonderful Ideas*
> Box 64691
> Burlington, VT 05406-4691
> (800) 92-IDEAS
> e-mail: wondideas@aol.com

See **Institute for Math Mania** (page 169).

PROGRAMS AND INSTRUCTION

All the Math You'll Ever Need

Steve Slavin; John Wiley & Sons, 1989

A self-teaching guide to the basics, for high school students boning up for college and for math-insecure parents trying to keep a jump or two ahead of the kids. Topics covered include multiplication and division; decimals; fractions; percentages; negative numbers; algebraic equations; exponents and square roots; ratios and proportions; basic geometry; rate, time, and distance problems; interest rates; big numbers; statistics; personal finances; and business math. Each chapter includes lots of explanatory examples, sample problems, and self-tests.

Basic College Mathematics

Charles D. Miller, Stanley A. Salzman, and Diana L. Hestwood; HarperCollins College Publishers, 1995

The title sounds intimidating, but the average sixth-grader, with a little parental backup, should be

MATHEMATICS

able to handle it. The book is 700+ pages long, in the course of which it covers basic whole-number operations, multiplying and dividing fractions, adding and subtracting fractions, decimals, ratio and proportion, percent, measurement, geometry, basic algebra, and statistics. Chapters are divided into several sections, each of which includes concise summary statements of objectives, clear explanations and examples, and many problem exercises—there's enough variety and repetition here to provide plenty of practice for those who need it. Each chapter concludes with a list of key terms, a review of all material covered, and a comprehensive test. Answers to selected problems appear in an appendix in the back of the book. Also available is an accompanying "Student Solution Manual," which includes answers to all the rest of the exercise problems and the tests. The *Basic College Mathematics Instructors Edition*—probably not necessary for most homeschool programs—is a duplicate of the student text with answers to all exercises included. More useful, for those who want a little extra support, is the text-based tutorial software, available for either Mac or Windows: the software provides practically unlimited practice problems, detailed solutions upon request, and a reference to relevant text pages.

An excellent, efficient, and cost-effective alternative to other intermediate- to upper-level mathematics programs. Sequels include *Introductory Algebra, Intermediate Algebra, Essentials of Geometry,* and *Trigonometry.*

Available through bookstores or
Bluestocking Press
Box 2030
Shingle Springs, CA 95682-2030
(916) 621-1123 or (800) 959-8586/fax (916) 642-9222

A Collection of Math Lessons Series
Cuisenaire Company, 1993

Titles include *A Collection of Math Lessons From Grades 1 Through 3* (Marilyn Burns and Bonnie Tank), *. . . From Grades 3 Through 6* (Marilyn Burns), and *. . . From Grades 6 Through 8* (Marilyn Burns and Cathy Humphreys). If the phrase "math lessons" triggers an image of endless workbook pages, think again: these unconventional collections describe friendly methods for getting kids to assimilate basic concepts by solving hands-on mathematics problems. The lessons are aimed at small groups of kids in cooperative learning situations. The books are based on classroom experiences—which means several small groups, learning all at once—though the projects are equally successful with one small group at home. Descriptions of each lesson are detailed and conversational, starting with an explanation of the math concept to be taught, and continuing through instructions for introducing and teaching the lesson, with examples of exchanges between teacher and students and samples of student work.

A lesson on introducing multiplication to third-graders begins with a discussion of chopsticks.

"If I were eating a Chinese or Japanese meal and using chopsticks," I asked the children, "how many chopsticks would I need?" They all knew the answer was two.

I continued, "Suppose I invited three friends to dinner, and all four of us were going to eat with chopsticks. How many chopsticks would we need?"

The lesson then continues through making charts of things that come in 2s, 3s, 4s, 5s, 6s, 7s, 8s, 9s, and 10s—in which participating kids had to come up with ways of dividing their chart papers into ten equal columns—and the inventing and illustrating of simple multiplication "stories." "It is important to relate numerical symbols to situations as often as possible," writes Burns. "In this way children can come to understand that the numbers they use fit into contexts and can be explained in relation to something they can describe."

In other hands-on lessons, kids solve probability riddles with bags of colored tiles, estimate numbers with jars of beans, learn number place with popcorn and lentils, and experiment with homemade game spinners. Older students study statistics with Scrabble letters ("Why are *Q* and *Z* worth more points than *E*?"), geometry with "pentominoes" (geometric puzzle pieces), and averages with measurements of their own feet.

Available from bookstores or
Cuisenaire/Dale Seymour Publications
Box 5026
White Plains, NY 10602-5026
(800) 872-1100 or (800) 237-0338/fax (914) 328-5487
or (800) 551-RODS

Web site: www.cuisenaire.com or www.awl.com/dsp

Also see *The I Hate Mathematics! Book* (page 184).

Reston, VA 22091-1593

(800) 235-7566/fax (703) 476-2970

Curriculum and Evaluation Standards for School Mathematics

National Council of Teachers of Mathematics, 1991

This 258-page book lists the famous NCTM curriculum standards that so many commercial mathematics programs have recently hastened to adopt. The book is divided into four major sections: "Curriculum Standards for Grades K–4," "Curriculum Standards for Grades 5–8," "Curriculum Standards for Grades 9–12," and "Evaluation Standards." There are 13 listed standards for the early and middle grades and 14 standards for high school students. Each is described in detail, including expected outcomes, numerous illustrated examples of the kinds of skills kids should demonstrate and problems they should be able to solve, and suggestions for student activities. Grades K–4 curriculum standards, for example, include "Mathematics as Problem Solving," "Mathematics as Communication," "Mathematics as Reasoning," "Mathematical Connections," "Estimation," "Number Sense and Numeration," "Concepts of Whole Number Operations," "Whole Number Computations," "Geometry and Spatial Sense," "Measurement," "Statistics and Probability," "Fractions and Decimals," and "Patterns and Relationships."

The book's fourth section, "Evaluation," discusses student-assessment methods for each standard: that is, what kinds of questions should be asked or problems presented to ensure that students are learning what they're supposed to learn?

If you want to know what the public schools think your kids should know about mathematics, this is the horse's mouth.

The original *Standards* has generated the Addenda to the Standards series, a collection of 22 grade-related books describing teaching strategies, lesson plans, and classroom-tested activities for each of the NCTM standards.

Standards, $25; volumes in the Addenda series, $9.50 to $17

NCTM

1906 Association Dr.

The Easy Way Series

Our first experience with the Easy Way series was *Trigonometry the Easy Way* (Douglas Downing; Barron's, 1990), which we acquired for Ethan, our middle son, when he began studying physics. Ethan, who plunged into physics by way of *Star Trek,* Estes rockets, and model robots, soon ran up against vectors, promptly followed by manipulations involving sine, cosine, and tangent. He needed trigonometry. We discovered *Trigonometry the Easy Way* at our local bookstore, a 310-page oversize paperback with a drawing, graph, or diagram on practically every page—Ethan likes drawings, graphs, and diagrams—and a blurb on the back that claimed it was "A complete trigonometry text in the form of a fantasy novel," and in bigger print, "All the essentials in one clear volume." Seduced, we bought it.

The action of the book takes place in the imaginary kingdom of Carmorra. In chapter 1 ("Angles and Triangles"), it's raining, and the officials of the royal court all have various pressing needs for measuring angles. Readers are thus introduced to angles (right, obtuse, acute, and straight), triangles (equilateral, isosceles, acute, obtuse, and right), and the use of the protractor. In chapter 2 ("Solving Right Triangle Problems"), the royal court calculates the height of a Christmas tree, plans the construction of a ski jump, and helps the court astronomer determine, via triangulation, the distance to a star. Subsequent chapters deal with trigonometric functions and their graphs, radian measure, waves, inverse trigonometric functions, polar coordinates, complex numbers, coordinate rotation and conic sections, and spherical trigonometry. Explanations are clear and well illustrated, and there are practice exercises at the end of each chapter (answers in the back of the book).

Other mathematical books in this series include *Arithmetic the Easy Way, Math the Easy Way, Algebra the Easy Way, Calculus the Easy Way, Geometry the Easy Way,* and *Computer Programming the Easy Way* (Basic, Fortran, or Pascal).

Available through bookstores or

Barron's Educational Series, Inc.

MATHEMATICS

250 Wireless Blvd.

Hauppauge, NY 11788

(516) 434-3311 or (800) 645-3476/fax (516) 434-3723

Web site: barronseduc.com

Everything You Need to Know About Math Homework

Anne Zeman and Kate Kelly; Scholastic, 1994

A brightly illustrated synopsis of elementary school math for kids aged 9–12.

Family Math

Jean Kerr Stenmark, Virginia Thompson, and Ruth Cossey; Lawrence Hall of Science, 1986

The "Family Math" program was developed at the Lawrence Hall of Science (University of California, Berkeley) for "parents and children learning mathematics together." The book *Family Math,* an outgrowth of this program, is a 300+-page collection of activities for kids of all ages, in the categories of arithmetic, geometry, probability and statistics, measurement, estimation, calculators, computers, logical thinking, and careers. For each activity, there's a brief explanation of what the exercise is for and/or how it is related to the academic mathematics curriculum, instructions for how to carry out the project, a list of suggestions for further related activities, a materials list, and a grade-level recommendation.

Sample activities: kids play board and dice games, make their own tangrams and solve tangram puzzles, make a square meter decorated with square decimeters, make a construction-paper fraction kit, learn about ratios and proportions with a recipe for Gorp, and learn Cartesian graphing through games of 'Coordinate Tic-Tac-Toe' and 'Hurkle.'"

For the financially strapped, "*Family Math*" provides reproducible master sheets for many forms of mathematical activities: patterns for tangrams, blank do-it-yourself calendars, graph paper in several grid sizes (plus one- and four-quadrant Cartesian graph paper), coin boards, place value boards, and number charts.

$18

University of California

Attn: LHS Store

Lawrence Hall of Science, #5200

Berkeley, CA 94720-5200

(510) 642-1016/fax (510) 642-1055

Web site: www.lhs.berkeley.edu

Hands-On Equations

This innovative math program, developed by ex-teacher Henry Borenson, teaches kids in grades 3 and up the fundamentals of algebraic equations. Users build equations using a combination of blue and white pawns (which represent x or $-x$) and red and green number cubes, which represent positive or negative integers. The two sides of the equation are arranged on opposite arms of a balance scale, pictured in the student kits on a sturdy laminated plastic mat. Students then solve the equation, by making a series of "legal moves" that add or subtract quantities without altering balance.

The program consists of three increasingly complex levels of algebraic concepts, for a total of 26 lessons. Lessons each include precise step-by-step instructions, which combine hands-on manipulations using pawns and cubes with written practice worksheets. By Level III, kids are comfortable solving equations on the order of $2x - 2(-x + 4) = x + (-2)$. The program is an excellent preparation for a formal algebra class and a great builder of mathematical self-confidence. Younger kids especially get a thrill out of solving impressive adult-style equations.

Complete program, including teachers' manuals for

Levels I, II, and III, student practice worksheets, a

package of pawns and number cubes, and a laminated

balance sheet, $34.95

Hands-On Equations

Borenson and Associates

Box 3328

Allentown, PA 18106

(610) 398-6908 or (800) 993-6284/fax (610) 398-7863

Key Curriculum Press

Key Curriculum Press develops mathematical programs, texts, and materials for students in grades K–12. The company is particularly known for its primary-grade mathematics program, "Miquon Math." It is generally appropriate for kids in grades 1–3, consists of a set of six fat, color-coded workbooks (orange, red, blue, green, yellow, and purple), and is designed to be used with Cuisenaire rods (see page 168). Unlike many workbooks, however, which emphasize repetitive drill and rote memorization of rules, the Miquon books stress problem-solving skills and creative thinking. Users develop a grasp of mathematical basics that is helpful as they progress through higher-level programs.

For older students, Key Curriculum Press is noted for the *Key to . . .* workbook series, inexpensive 3- to 10-book sets on decimals, algebra, percents, fractions, geometry, and measurement, targeted at students in grades 4–12. The workbooks are simple and straightforward, each covering one concept per page, with many examples, demonstrations, illustrations, and practice problems. These series are recommended for younger students who need extra mathematical challenges or for older students who "are intimidated by large textbooks and need additional practice." *Practice* is the definitive key word here; the Key to . . . workbooks primarily provide students with lots of repetitive drill. Nicely done, if you need it.

A more recent Key Curriculum publication series is the "Interactive Mathematics Program" (IMP), developed by a team of mathematics professors, curriculum developers, and educators.

Key Curriculum Press
Box 2304
Berkeley, CA 94702-0304
(800) 995-MATH/fax (800) 541-2442

Math in a Bag

This attractive introductory math program is intended for kids aged 4–8. The bag is bright pink and is filled with oversize Cuisenaire rods (see page 168)—an assortment of colorful wooden rods in graded sizes, made large for easier manipulation by small fingers. The bag comes in a box, along with an 82-page illustrated instruction manual and a short video featuring a pair of wacky purple and orange puppets named Soup and Dice, who demonstrate various "Math in a Bag" teaching/playing techniques. Young users begin their math explorations by simply building with the rods—the instruction book encourages them to make towers, bridges, patterns, and funny faces—and then proceed to constructing graded staircases (putting the blocks in order, from smallest to largest or vice versa),

trains, rectangles, and squares. They then begin to use the blocks to represent simple arithmetical equations, and from there move into the basics of beginning addition, subtraction, multiplication, and division. It's a nice-size program for beginners.

Approximately $25 from toy and game stores; for your closest source, contact
WaterStreet Mathematics Co.
Box 16
Yorklyn, DE 19736
(800) 866-8228

Math-It

This program is essentially a collection of memorize-and-practice games designed to teach basic addition and multiplication facts to kids aged 6 and up. The program includes a pair of instructional audiocassettes, an explanatory softcover book (*Math-It: How Stevie Learned His Math*), and game boards and playing cards for the games of "Addit," which teaches addition facts, "Dubblit," which teaches number doubling, and "Timzit," which teaches the times tables. Kids learn arithmetical procedures and some simple mathematical memory tricks from the manual (such as "To add 9 to a number, you count back one and say *teen*") and then practice their number facts, matching color-coded problem cards to the answers printed on the game board. The goal of the game is to match all the problem cards to their correct answers in under one minute.

Variations on the basic "Math-It" include "Pre-Math-It," for kids aged 4–7, which teaches beginning number skills and addition facts using a set of double-nine dominoes (included), and "Advanced Math-It," for kids in grades 3–8, which reviews basic math concepts and teaches division skills and percentages (through the games of "Dividit" and "Percentit").

"Pre-Math-It," $27.95; "Math-It," $34.95; "Advanced Math-It," $19
The Sycamore Tree
2179 Meyer Pl.
Costa Mesa, CA 92627
information (714) 650-4466; orders (714) 642-6750 or (800) 779-6750
Web site: www.sycamoretree.com

Math Sense Building Blocks Program

A hands-on program designed to introduce basic math concepts to young children or to reinforce and supplement lessons for older students. The heart of the program is a set of 104 Lego-style plastic blocks, color coded by size from 1 unit to 10, plus a yellow hundred-block. An accompanying 68-page manual lists suggested activities for grades 1–6 and includes reproducible student worksheets.

The "Math Sense" program is available in two versions: as the "Math Pack," which includes the teaching manual, blocks, and color-coded dice for game activities, all packaged in a backpack, or as the "Math Bag," which includes blocks and a minimanual, briefly describing teaching techniques, packaged in a zippered bag.

"Math Sense," $38; "Math Bag," $26

Common Sense Press

Box 1365

Melrose, FL 32666

(904) 495-5757

Mathematics: A Human Endeavor

Harold R. Jacobs; W. H. Freeman & Company, 1994

The foreword, by math maven Martin Gardner, opens with a quote from Mark Twain's *Huckleberry Finn*:

Well, three or four months run along, and it was well into the winter, now. I had been to school most all the time, and could spell, and read, and write just a little, and could say the multiplication table up to six times seven is thirty-five, and I don't reckon I could ever get any farther than that if I was to live forever. I don't take no stock in mathematics, anyway.

Browse through enough textbooks and workbooks and it's easy to sympathize with Huck's scornful take on math. Jacobs's book, however, may look and feel like a textbook, but it is far from a textbook as we have all dismally come to known them. Math, Jacobs-style, is taught through puzzles, games, and enthralling real-life examples and comes heavily illustrated with curiosity-provoking pictures, photographs, diagrams, and cartoons. Chapter 1, "Mathematical Ways of Thinking," for example, plunges students into experiments with the behavior of billiard balls, the notorious four-color map problem, and the invention of the Soma cube puzzle (how many cuts does it take to slice a cube into 27 smaller cubes?).

Mathematics: A Human Endeavor is no intellectual lightweight. Chapter headings include such serious mathematical standards as "Number Sequences," "Functions and Their Graphs," "Large Numbers and Logarithms," "Symmetry and Regular Figures," "Mathematical Curves," "Methods of Counting," "The Mathematics of Chance," "An Introduction to Statistics," and "Topics in Topology."

It's not the *what* that raises Jacobs's text so far above the common herd; it's the *how*. Users study binary number sequences through the hexagrams of *I Ching* and Francis Bacon's 17th-century diplomatic cipher; are introduced to functions with the temperature-dependent chirp rate of crickets and to coordinate graphing with the leaping speed of kangaroos; learn about logarithms with the electromagnetic spectrum, the frets on a guitar, the f-stop on a camera, and the Richter scale; and discover permutations by way of the Mad Hatter's tea party, the molecular sequence of DNA, stacks of poker chips, and the notes to "Happy Birthday to You."

Our boys, who view the works of John Saxon with a cold eye, love this book. So do I. Also see Jacobs's *Elementary Algebra* (W. H. Freeman, 1995) and *Geometry* (W. H. Freeman, 1987).

Mathematics Programs Associates

Mathematics Programs Associates (MPA) publishes the "Developmental Mathematics" series, a collection of self-teaching workbooks for children in grades K–8. There are sixteen 80-page workbooks in the series, ranging from Level 1 (counting and simple number concepts) to Levels 15 (advanced fractions) and 16 ("Special Topics," including ratio, proportion, percent, probability, graphs, and number theory). *Developmental Mathematics,* explains its author, Dr. L. George Saad, "covers *all* the arithmetic the child has to learn" and provides a solid foundation upon which all future mathematical knowledge is built.

The "developmental" aspect of Saad's workbook program refers to the series' organizational structure: lessons are carefully arranged to mesh with the logical progression of a child's growing mathematical knowledge. Workbooks thus proceed through four increasingly abstract teaching stages. The new mathematical concept is first presented using simple pictures. ("Children can easily learn with pictures the same way they learn with manipulative materials," writes Saad, though at early levels he suggests enhancing the program with concrete objects, such as plastic counters, beans, marbles, or bottle caps.) Next, pictures are gradually phased out, until the student can perform the new skill, in a guided step-by-step fashion, using numbers alone. Stage 3 is a matter of practice makes perfect: a repetitive series of exercises allows users to hone their skills, improve computational accuracy, and increase speed. In the final stage 4, kids apply their new mathematical skill to real-life problem-solving situations, presented as word problems.

Included with each workbook is a short parents' guide and a "Diagnostic Test," to be taken by the student after completing the workbook.

Mathematics Programs Associates, Inc.

Box 2118

Halesite, NY 11743

(516) 643-9300/fax (516) 643-9301

Mathematics Their Way

Mary Baratta-Lorton; Addison-Wesley, 1995

This 400+-page spiral-bound book contains a complete activity-centered mathematics program for kids in grades K–2. Baratta-Lorton urges parents and teachers to allow kids to absorb math concepts "their way"—that is, through hands-on experimentation with such materials as buttons, bottle caps, tiles, mirrors, cups and jars, blocks, and linking cubes. *Mathematics Their Way* includes instructions and reproducible student worksheets for over 200 math-related activities, covering such topics as counting, pattern formation, sorting and classification, measurement, addition, subtraction, and beginning word problems. An attractive and popular introduction to mathematics. Available through bookstores.

Miquon Math

See **Key Curriculum Press** (page 173).

Mortensen Math

A highly popular manipulative-based math program that uses color-coded plastic blocks in graded

sizes to reinforce a wide range of mathematical principles. The blocks include 10 different-size bars, from units to hundreds. Bars are scored on one side, to indicate equivalent number of units; and are hollow on the other, for use in subtraction problems or to represent negative numbers. Participants in the "Mortensen Math" program will need a double tray of these blocks (the "Combo Kit"), plus an array of workbooks, covering five "Strands" of mathematics: arithmetic, measurement, problem-solving, algebra, and calculus. All workbooks are available in three different levels. There are 10 workbooks in each Strand at each level, for a grand total of 50 workbooks per level. The workbooks are flimsy little newsprint productions, and their content is grindingly repetitive, but users do get the fun of playing with all the little blocks, and workbook-monitoring adults can encourage judicious skipping.

The program is recommended for kids of all ages, from absolute beginners on up; it has had particular success with older students who are floundering due to an inadequate early background in the arithmetical basics. Many combinations of Mortensen manipulatives and workbooks are available, including the "Curriculum Starter Collection" (all the basic blocks, plus fraction bars, multiple bars, and 50 Level 1 workbooks) ($226.50), the "Fun Kit" for preschoolers ($109), the "Algebra Kit" (two trays of blocks, 10 Level 1 Algebra workbooks, and an instructional video) ($89), and the "Fraction Kit" (colored fraction bars, clear fraction overlays, and fraction strips) ($39.95).

Mortensen Math Academic Excellence Institute

2450 Fort Union Blvd.

Salt Lake City, UT 84121

(801) 944-2500 or (800) 338-9939

Real-World Mathematics Through Science Series

Washington Mathematics, Engineering, Science Achievement Group

Integrated science-math lessons for students in grades 6–9 in an innovative series of seven books. Each book is approximately 100 pages long and contains science experiments with related mathematics, writing activities, historical background information, and reproducible worksheets. Titles in the series include *Investigating Apples, Classifying Fingerprints, In the Air,*

M
A
T
H
E
M
A
T
I
C
S

Measuring Earthquakes, In the Pharmacy, Packaging and the Environment, and *Measuring Dinosaurs.*

Available through bookstores or
Carolina Mathematics/Carolina Biological Supply Co.
2700 York Rd.
Burlington, NC 27215-3398
(910) 584-0381 or (800) 334-5551/fax (800) 222-7112
e-mail: math@carolina.com

Saxon Math

Students learn most effectively, according to teacher and textbook author John Saxon, "through gentle repetition extended over a considerable period of time." Hence the Saxon math books, a series of texts, tests, and drill sheets available for kids of kindergarten age through grade 12. All embody the gently repetitious learning technique that Saxon terms "incremental development." This means, in essence, that mathematical concepts are presented sequentially in small, manageable bits, so that each new topic is thoroughly understood before another is introduced. Topics are never discontinued or considered "completed," but are continuously carried from lesson to lesson, gradually increasing in complexity. "This practice has an element of drudgery in it," admits Saxon, "but it has been demonstrated that people who are not willing to practice fundamentals often find success elusive."

The program for kids in grades K–3 consists of a consumable workbook (you'll need one for each participating child), a detailed teacher's manual, and a "meeting book," which provides instructions for daily "opening exercises" featuring a range of practical mathematical skills. Saxon and coworkers strongly recommend the purchase of a set of manipulatives to accompany the K–3 program. Required manipulatives include an arm balance, a student clock, plastic counters, dominoes, a geoboard with rubber bands, a 1–100 number chart, multilink cubes, a teacher's number line, pattern blocks, a ruler, a set of tangrams, a thermometer, and one-inch tiles in four colors.

Middle-grade mathematics materials include, for each grade level, a hardcover textbook, a manual of tests and practice drill sheets, and a separate answer key. *Math 54* is generally recommended for kids in grade 4; *Math 65* for kids in grade 5; *Math 76,* grade 6; and *Math 87,* grade 7. Each contains about 140 lessons.

Secondary texts, also accompanied by test manuals and answer keys, include *Algebra 1/2, Algebra 1* and *2, Advanced Mathematics,* and *Calculus. Algebra 2* includes the equivalent of one semester's study of geometry; *Advanced Mathematics,* "a comprehensive treatment of pre-calculus mathematics," covers algebra, geometry, trigonometry, and mathematical analysis.

The Saxon texts, with their no-nonsense emphasis on practice and repetition, do work. The program has been shown to increase scores on standardized math achievement tests. Placement tests are available for the elementary and middle grades, to allow parents and teachers to determine where best to start potential students in the series. Saxon books are available as "Home Study Kits" for home learners, including student texts, test manuals, and answer keys.

Kits range from about $45 to $90 each
Saxon Publishers
1320 W. Lindsey St.
Norman, OK 73069
(800) 284-7019/fax (405) 360-4205
Web site: www.saxonpub.com

BOOKS ABOUT MATH EDUCATION

Beyond Facts and Flashcards: Exploring Math with Your Kids
Janice R. Mokros; Heinemann, 1996

If reading aloud turns kids into eager readers, what's the equivalent activity for math? Mokros suggests many ways of integrating math into everyday life: in the garden and the kitchen, while doing the laundry, while traveling. She also includes guidelines for evaluating school mathematics programs.

Garbage Pizza, Patchwork Quilts, and Math Magic: Stories About Teachers Who Love to Teach and Children Who Love to Learn
Susan Ohanian; W. H. Freeman & Company, 1994

Accounts of innovative classrooms, creative math projects, and math success.

Humble Pi: The Role Mathematics Should Play in American Education

Michael K. Smith; Prometheus Books, 1994

How important is pure mathematics? Is expertise in math a necessary prerequisite for logical thinking? Smith argues against the prevalence of pure math in school curricula, suggesting that students would be better served by a grounding in practical everyday math skills. Math, says Smith, should be geared to individual interests and career choices. Josh would agree.

Innumeracy: Mathematical Illiteracy and its Consequences

John Allen Paulos; Vintage Books, 1990

"Innumeracy, an inability to deal comfortably with the fundamental notions of number and chance, plagues far too many otherwise knowledgeable citizens," writes John Paulos, and leaves us all defenselessly open to deception, confusion, and unscrupulous exploitation. *Innumeracy,* using many fascinating, if nervous-making, examples, from the federal budget figures to the claims of numerologists, demonstrates the impact of mathematical ignorance in our daily lives.

For older readers and parents who want to impress upon their offspring the importance of a firm grounding in mathematics. By the same author: *Beyond Numeracy: Ruminations of a Numbers Man* (Vintage Books, 1992) and *A Mathematician Reads the Newspaper* (Anchor Books, 1996).

Math Power: How To Help Your Child Love Math, Even If You Don't

Patricia Clark Kenschaft; Addison-Wesley, 1997

How to combat math anxiety and turn kids on to math, using games, conversation, and hands-on activities.

Overcoming Math Anxiety

Sheila Tobias; W. W. Norton, 1994

A book for those who break out in a cold sweat at the sight of a math test. Tobias claims that poor math performance is often a matter of attitude rather than inherent ability, and discusses methods for overcoming math jitters.

BOOKS ABOUT MATH AND NUMBERS

Five Equations That Changed the World

Michael Guillen; Hyperion, 1995

The stories of five famous mathematicians—Isaac Newton, Daniel Bernoulli, Michael Faraday, Rudolf Clausius, and Albert Einstein—and their world-changing mathematical formulae. The book is filled with human interest, fascinating historical facts, and reader-friendly mathematical and scientific explanations. It is intended for an adult audience, but can be enjoyed by teenagers.

The Kids' World Almanac of Amazing Facts About Numbers, Math and Money

Margery Facklam and Margaret Thomas; World Almanac, 1992

A 200+-page collection of facts, figures, fascinating trivia, and numerical tricks. Sample chapters include "Lucky Numbers," "Times and Dates," "Numbers in Sports and Games," and "Signs, Symbols, Scales, and Codes." Readers can identify the Chinese Year of the Dragon, discover the dimensions of a baseball diamond, learn Morse Code, and find out the total number of grains of sand on all earth's beaches.

Math and Music: Harmonious Connections

Trudi Hammel Garland and Charity Vaughan Kahn; Dale Seymour Publications, 1995

The mathematics of music, fascinating for all, and especially for young musicians. Chapters include "The Beat" (the mathematics of rhythm), "The Tone" (frequency and amplitude), "The Tune" (tuning, harmonics, dissonance, and scales), "The Song" (techniques of composition), "The Source" (the workings of different classes of musical instruments), "The People" (important figures in the history of mathematics and music), and "The Curiosities," which discusses such oddities as musical Fibonacci numbers, the mathematics of cricket sound, and the definitions of white, brown, and pink—yes, pink—music. Among the mathematical concepts covered are trigonometric functions, ratios, geometric transformations, and the Golden Ratio.

$13.25

Cuisenaire/Dale Seymour Publications

MATHEMATICS

Box 5026

White Plains, NY 10602-5026

(800) 237-0338 or (800) 872-1100/fax (914) 328-5487

or (800) 551-RODS

Web site: www.cuisenaire.com or awl.com/dsp

Mathematics From the Birth of Numbers

Jan Gullberg; W. W. Norton, 1997

A massive (over 1,000 pages) tome on the history and practice of mathematics, filled with information, explanations, illustrations, and many mathematical formulas. The book covers everything from the naming of numbers to differential equations. An excellent reference work, and much easier to read than it appears at first glance.

Numbers

Richard Phillips; Cambridge University Press, 1994

A marvelous picture-and-information book about numbers, including mathematical, historical, and scientific facts, catchy little anecdotes, problems and puzzles, and creative color illustrations. The book is divided into three sections: in "From 0 to 156," each number is discussed in detail, each getting half a page or so all to itself; in "From 157 to 999," numbers rate only a line or two of mathematical highlights; and in "A Few Large Numbers," Phillips covers a few particularly interesting enormities, including 666, 1,000, a million, a billion, a googol, and infinity.

"Zero," begins the numerical listing lightheartedly, "is the number of months with 39 days, the number of gs in the word *carbuncle* and the number of goal keepers in a game of badminton. It is also the number of cabbages on Mars, the number of hedgehogs who can speak Japanese and the number of fish fingers eaten by William Shakespeare." The author then goes on to discuss John Cage's piano composition *4′33″*, which contains zero notes, the meaning of absolute zero, the invention of zero by Indian mathematicians, the absence of zero from Roman numerals, and our inability, according to the laws of arithmetic, to divide any number by zero. "Try dividing 6 by 0 on a calculator," Phillips invites. "What happens?"

There's more of the same on every page. An addictive and informative book; even the most mathematically resistant readers will find themselves developing a positive affection for numbers.

The Penguin Book of Curious and Interesting Mathematics

David Wells; Penguin, 1997

Over 300 pages of anecdotes, fascinating tidbits of mathematical history, and trivia from a wide range of sources. Readers, for example, learn that over 70 moon craters are named for mathematicians, tackle the oldest math puzzle in the world (from the Egyptian Rhind Papyrus), and discover that the motto above the door of Plato's Academy was "Let no one ignorant of geometry enter here."

The Visual Display of Quantitative Information

Edward R. Tufte; Graphics Press, 1983

A truly beautiful book on the theory and practice of graphs. Included are 250 illustrations of graphs, charts, tables, and other pictorial displays of statistical information, examples of the good, bad, deceptive, confusing, complex, colorful, unusual, and conventional—but all interesting. Included is a "living histogram" of college students, arranged by height on a campus lawn, a reproduction of the first "skyrocketing government debt chart" (Great Britain's, over the course of the Revolutionary War), a 10th-century graph showing the paths of planetary orbits, and a diatribe on the evils of muddling "chartjunk." And, at one point, Tufte proves that one picture is worth precisely 700 words.

Definitely for older students, though younger browsers, with a little adult guidance, will be impressed by the variety and versatility of informational graphics. There's more to life than bar graphs and pie charts. Also see *Envisioning Information* (Graphics Press, 1990) and *Visual Explanations* (Graphics Press, 1997).

$40

Graphics Press

Box 430

Cheshire, CT 06410

(203) 272-9187 or (800) 822-2454/fax (203) 272-8600

Zero to Lazy Eight

Alexander Humez, Nicholas Humez, and Joseph Maguire; Simon & Schuster, 1994

Historical truth, linguistic trivia, mathematical information, and lots of interesting asides about the numbers zero to 13, with an extra chapter ("Lazy

Eight") at the end, all about infinity. Readers encounter, for example, the origin of the phrase "behind the eight ball" (plus the formula for calculating billiard-ball volume), the reason for triskaidekaphobia (fear of the number 13), an explanation of the "pigeonhole principle," and a quick history of secret codes.

The book is intended for adult readers (there are scattered sexual references), but is an excellent source for parents and teachers of enriching mathematical extras for kids of all ages.

BOOKS FOR KIDS: ELEMENTARY MATH CONCEPTS

Anno's Hat Tricks
Akihiro Nozaki and Mitsumasa Anno; Philomel Books, 1985

An introduction to binary logic for the very young, through the medium of the hatter and his collection of red and white hats. The reader him/herself appears in the book, as "Shadowchild," pictured only as a soft gray shadow on the ground. The trick—which gets increasingly trickier as the book progresses—is for Shadowchild to determine the color of his/her own hat by observing the colors of the hats the hatter has given to two visible children, Tom and Hannah. Say, for example, that the hatter has three hats: two red and one white. Tom and Hannah are both pictured in red hats; what color is Shadowchild's? Readers are given a chance to figure it out for themselves; then the text explains how they should have arrived at the correct answer.

Also see *Anno's Counting Book* (page 204), *Anno's Magic Seeds* (below), *Anno's Math Games* (right), *The Mysterious Multiplying Jar* (page 182), and *Socrates and the Three Little Pigs* (page 183).

Anno's Magic Seeds
Mitsumasa Anno; Philomel Books, 1995

Jack meets a wizard who gives him two golden seeds, telling him to bake one and eat it ("You will not be hungry again for a whole year") and to plant the other in the ground. The seed sprouts into a beautiful little blue-flowered plant that bears two seeds. Jack bakes one and plants the other, until finally, one year, he decides to eat something different for a change and

to plant both seeds in the ground. The next summer he gets four seeds; he eats one and plants three. Quickly the story becomes more mathematically challenging, as Jack plants more and more seeds, meets Alice and gets married, gives 2 seeds to each of their 5 wedding guests, sells 60 seeds, stashes 34 seeds in the storehouse. A charmingly illustrated exercise in arithmetic.

See *Anno's Counting Book* (page 204), *Anno's Hat Tricks* (left), *Anno's Math Games* (below), *The Mysterious Multiplying Jar* (page 182), and *Socrates and the Three Little Pigs* (page 183).

Anno's Math Games
Mitsumasa Anno; Paper Star, 1997

A beautifully illustrated 104-page book of thought-provoking puzzles designed to promote creative (and mathematical) thinking in the very young. Chapters include "What is Different?" in which readers identify similarities and differences in groups of familiar objects; and "Putting Together and Taking Apart," in which kids—along with characters Kriss and Kross and their pot of magic glue—learn about "multiplicative classification" and experiment with tangrams. In "Numbers in Order," kids learn about ordinal numbers and play a sequence-forming card game called "Sevens in a Row"; and in "Who's the Tallest?" they discover measurement, comparisons, and graphs.

Sequels include *Anno's Math Games II,* which covers classification, comparison, points, number symbolism, and liquid measures; and *Anno's Math Games III,* which covers topology, triangles, mazes, and concepts of left and right. All are introductions to math, but the major emphasis is on encouraging kids to figure out how to think.

See *Anno's Counting Book* (page 204), *Anno's Hat Tricks* (left), *Anno's Magic Seeds* (left), *The Mysterious Multiplying Jar* (page 182), and *Socrates and the Three Little Pigs* (page 183).

A Cloak for the Dreamer
Aileen Friedman; Scholastic, 1995

A geometric fairy tale. A tailor asks each of his three sons to sew a cloak that can keep out the wind and rain. The first son stitches a cloak of rectangles; the second makes a cloak of triangles; and the dreamy third son makes a cloak of circles.

See *The King's Commissioners* (page 205).

The Doorbell Rang

4 8 Pat Hutchins; Mulberry, 1989

Sam and Victoria have just divided up one dozen freshly baked cookies, when the doorbell starts ringing and visiting friends arrive. With each new guest, the dozen cookies must be divided all over again. An exercise in beginning division.

Eating Fractions

4 8 Bruce Macmillan; Scholastic, 1991

Kids learn about halves, thirds, and quarters by dividing a banana, a bread roll, and a pizza. Simple recipes are included.

Grandfather Tang's Story

4 9 Ann Tompert; Dragonfly, 1997

A Chinese grandfather tells his small granddaughter a story about a pair of magical shape-changing foxes, illustrating the tale with tangram puzzle pieces arranged in the shape of the animal characters. The book includes a reproducible set of tangrams.
Also see **Tangoes** (page 192).

The Greedy Triangle

4 8 Marilyn Burns; Scholastic, 1995

The greedy triangle wants more than just three sides and three angles and wishes for more—and more—each. It becomes in turn a quadrilateral, pentagon, hexagon, heptagon, and octagon before finally deciding that life as a triangle was really the best of all.
Also see Norton Juster's **The Dot and the Line** (page 183).

One Hundred Hungry Ants

5 9 Elinor J. Pinczes; Houghton Mifflin, 1993

A picture-book tale of division. One hundred ants, heading hungrily toward a picnic, are halted by one mathematically minded ant who suggests that they will get the food more efficiently if they split up into ranks. The ants then rearrange themselves into groups of 50, 25, 10, and so on, but by the time they're finally in order, all the picnic food is gone.

By the same author: *A Remainder of One* (Houghton Mifflin, 1995), in which 1 leftover ant rearranges the 25 members of his squadron so that he can march in the big parade.

17 Kings and 42 Elephants

4 8 Margaret Mahy; Dial Books for Young Readers, 1993

A rhyming account of a royal procession through the jungle in which 17 kings share in the care of 42 elephants, which involves some problem-solving skills.

Young Math Books Series

5 10 A series of short picture books from Thomas Y. Crowell, each introducing young readers to a basic principle of mathematics. Titles, of which there are many, include *Angles Are Easy as Pie* (Robert Froman), *Circles* (Mindel and Harry Sitomer), *Fractions Are Parts of Things* (J. Richard Dennis), *The Greatest Guessing Game: A Book About Dividing* (Robert Froman), *Odds and Evens* (Thomas C. O'Brien), *Straight Lines, Parallel Lines, Perpendicular Lines* (Mannis Charosh), *What Is Symmetry?* (Mindel and Harry Sitomer), *Averages* (Jane Jonas Srivastava), *Roman Numerals* (David A. Adler), *Statistics* (Jane Jonas Srivastava), *666 Jellybeans! All That?: An Introduction to Algebra* (Malcolm E. Weiss), and *Zero Is Not Nothing* (Mindel and Harry Sitomer). All are clear, concise, and pleasant to read. They're also, unfortunately, out of print: look for them at your local library.

BOOKS FOR KIDS: UPPER ELEMENTARY MATH CONCEPTS

Arithmetic

ALL Carl Sandburg; Harcourt Brace, 1993

A picture-book version of Sandburg's irreverent poke at arithmetic, which begins "Arithmetic is where numbers fly like pigeons in and out of your head." Illustrations are anamorphic images, which means they are distorted until viewed with a rolled-up piece of reflective Mylar (included).

Half Magic

8 12 Edward Eager; Harcourt Brace, 1989

Four children find a magic token that grants half of every wish made upon it. This makes for some peculiar results and a lot of creative multiplication.

How Much is a Million?

5 9 David Schwartz; Mulberry, 1993

An illustrated introduction to enormous numbers—a million, a billion, and a trillion—under the guidance of Marvelosissimo the Mathematical Magician. "If a goldfish bowl were big enough for a million goldfish," he explains, "it would be large enough to hold a whale" and "If a billion kids made a human tower, they would stand up past the moon."

Also see *If You Made a Million* (Mulberry, 1994) (page 210).

The King's Chessboard
David Birch; Puffin, 1993

The king insists on giving his wise counselor a reward; the counselor finally asks for a single grain of rice, the quantity to be doubled each day for as many days as there are squares on the king's chessboard. The king soon realizes his dreadful mathematical mistake. Also see Demi's *One Grain of Rice: A Mathematical Folktale* (Scholastic, 1997) and, for a Chinese version of the tale, Helena Clare Pittman's *A Grain of Rice* (Skylark, 1996).

Math Curse
Jon Scieszka and Lane Smith; Viking, 1995

"One Monday in math class," begins the young narrator of this riotous picture book, "Mrs. Fibonacci says, 'You know, you can think of almost everything as a math problem.'" And from then on everything she does is a math problem, from getting out of bed in the morning to the apple pie at lunch to social studies class ("1. Estimate how many M&Ms it would take to measure the length of the Mississippi River.") to Rebecca's 24-cupcake birthday party. She breaks the curse at last, in a clever move with fractions, and all is well until the next day in science class, when Mr. Newton says, "You know, you can think of almost everything as a science experiment . . ." Tongue-in-cheek math problems "for ages ">6 to <99."

Melisande
E. Nesbit; Harcourt Brace, 1992

The delightful tale of the princess Melisande, rendered bald by a wicked fairy at her christening. Helped by her father's fairy godmother, Melisande later makes a wish that she had golden hair a yard long that would grow an inch every day and twice as fast every time it was cut. The result—a creative exercise in measurement and multiplication—is disastrous until a solution is found by a mathematically competent prince.

The Mysterious Multiplying Jar
Mitsumasa Anno and Masaichiro Anno; Putnam, 1983

This creative picture book cleverly presents the concept of factorials through a mysterious blue-and-white Oriental jar. The jar, opened, contains an ocean in which are two islands. Each island has two countries; each country has three mountains; on each mountain are four walled kingdoms; within each walled kingdom are five villages. And so on, in a perfectly beautiful multiplication problem, leading up to a phenomenal number of jars.

The Phantom Tollbooth
Norton Juster; Random House, 1993

An infinitely clever and creative fantasy in which young Milo passes through the Phantom Tollbooth to visit the warring countries of Dictionopolis, where he meets the Spelling Bee and has to eat his words at a royal banquet, and Digitopolis, where he meets the Dodecahedron and visits the Mathemagician's number mines. See *The Dot and the Line* (page 183).

Roman Numerals I to MM: Numerabilia Romana Uno ad Duo Mila
Arthur Geisert; Houghton Mifflin, 1996

An irresistible introduction to Roman numerals, illustrated with pictures of cavorting pigs. There really are M pigs on the M page—and a grand total, Mr. Geisert tells us, of MMMMDCCCLXIV pigs in the whole book.

BOOKS FOR KIDS: INTERMEDIATE AND HIGHER-LEVEL MATH CONCEPTS

Archimedes' Revenge: The Joys and Perils of Mathematics
Paul Hoffman; Ballantine, 1997

A reader-friendly tour of modern math, covering such topics as cryptography, the difficulties of building an egg, Turing's machine, and the mathematical aspects of democracy. For motivated teenagers and adults.

MATHEMATICS

The Dot and the Line

Norton Juster; Random House, 1991

The line falls in love with a plump purple dot and, to win her away from his rival, a disorganized squiggle, learns to form squares, triangles, hexagons, parallelograms, polyhedrons, and spectacular curves. Geometry for all ages.

Fantasia Mathematica from The Mathematical Magpie

Clifton Fadiman, ed.; Copernicus, 1997

Originally published in 1958, these are anthologies of stories, essays, poems, cartoons, anecdotes—even a song, titled "The Square of the Hypoteneuse"—by such diverse authors as Lewis Carroll, Arthur C. Clarke, Aldous Huxley, Martin Gardner, Plato, H. G. Wells, and Mark Twain. All have creatively mathematical themes. Both books are fascinating and mind-stretching reads for teenagers.

A Gebra Named Al

Wendy Isdell; Free Spirit Publishing, 1993

Julie, a disgruntled algebra student, is suddenly transported by an Imaginary Number into the Land of Higher Mathematics. There she meets the gebra named Al—a zebralike creature whose stripes are lines of mathematical equations—and the Periodic horses (and their relatives, the Isotopes) who live in the Elemental Forest. Julie and Al travel across the land, passing through the Orders of Operation: the Caves of Parenthesis, the Towers of Exponent, the Field of Multiplication, and the Desert of Division, then crossing the Prime Plain to Addition Mountain and Subtraction Valley. Finally, mathematically and scientifically wiser, Julie reaches the Castle of the Mathematician himself, and returns home. The book lacks the charm of Norton Juster's semi-mathematical fantasy *The Phantom Tollbooth* (see page 182), but older readers will enjoy the cubed food, the "chemistrees" that bear fruits shaped like Bohr atoms, and the howling Wolframs, who serve the power-hungry Tungsten. An accompanying teacher's guide *Using A Gebra Named Al in the Classroom*, includes questions, problems, and activities for reinforcing the mathematical/scientific concepts covered in the novel. Also see *The Chemy Called Al* (page 350).

Socrates and the Three Little Pigs

Mitsumasa Anno and Tsuyoshi Mori; Philomel Books, 1983

Introduces readers to probability theory as Socrates, a big, bad, and hungry wolf, tries to determine which of three houses is most likely to contain three little pigs.

ACTIVITY BOOKS

The Adventures of Penrose— The Mathematical Cat

Theoni Pappas; Worldwide Publishing/Tetra, 1997

Penrose, a charming and intelligent cat, investigates a range of fascinating mathematical topics, among them the mathematics of soap bubbles, triangles, tessellations, Tangrams, and Mobius strips. He also meets a fractal dragon, visits "Nanoworld," and learns to use the abacus. With puzzles, games, and humorous illustrations. For kids aged 9 and up. See *Fractals, Googols, and Other Mathematical Tales* (page 184).

aha! Insight

Martin Gardner; W. H. Freeman & Company, 1978

"It would be a sad day," writes Gardner in his introduction, "if human beings, adjusting to the Computer Revolution, became so intellectually lazy that they lost their power of creative thinking." *aha! Insight* is a collection of brain-stretching puzzles designed to improve just this crucial skill. Puzzles, all illustrated with clever little cartoons, include combinatorial puzzles—that is, puzzles about the ways in which things can be arranged; geometry puzzles; arithmetic puzzles; logic puzzles—which madden me, but at which our oldest son excels—procedural puzzles; and word puzzles. The puzzles are marvelously entertaining, and in the process of solving them, as the author says, "you will find yourself painlessly learning many deep mathematical concepts." Answers are in the back of the book, but you shouldn't peek until you've struggled for a while on your own. Also see Gardner's *aha! Gotcha* (W. H. Freeman, 1982) and *Classic Brainteasers* (Sterling Publications, 1995).

6 12 Fractals, Googols, and Other Mathematical Tales

Theoni Pappas; Wide World Publishing/Tetra, 1993

Complex mathematical ideas lightheartedly presented. Readers learn the difference between three- and two-dimensional shapes when Penrose the cat stumbles into Pancake World, discover topology with Leonhard the Magic Turtle, experiment with base 12 digits with the 12-fingered inhabitants of the planet Dodeka, find out why it's easier to use exponents than to write out a googol, learn about Fibonacci numbers with a very knowledgeable rabbit, read the chatty stories of pi and zero, and watch a fractal dazzle the members of the Shapes Convention. Each imaginative short story is accompanied by an explanatory purple box giving additional mathematical and historical information about the concept described.

Also included: puzzles, projects, and instructions for making your own fractal snowflake and one-sided Mobius strip.

Theoni Pappas is also the author of *The Children's Mathematics Calendar,* an annual illustrated collection of puzzles and problems variously appropriate for kids in grades 1–8. For each month, there's one major mathematical story, puzzle, or project, often starring the mathematically investigative Penrose the Cat, plus short puzzles or problems for each day of the month. Available through bookstores.

See *The Adventures of Penrose—The Mathematical Cat* (page 183).

Games Magazine Big Book of Games

ALL Ronnie Shushan, ed.; Workman, 1984

Unusual brainteasers, logic puzzles, visual challenges, word games, math puzzles, and crosswords. A mind expander for puzzlers of all ages. Also see *Games Magazine Big Book of Games 2* (Workman, 1989).

8 14 How Math Works

Carol Vorderman; Reader's Digest, 1996

This book, in nearly 200 oversize pages, demonstrates "100 ways parents and kids can share the wonders of mathematics." The 100 ways cover a vast number of mathematical topics, roughly grouped by category, among them "Numbers," "Proportions," "Algebra," "Statistics," "Measurement," "Shape," and

"Thinking." Under each is included some reader-friendly explanatory text, assorted short biographies of famous mathematicians, and a wide range of irresistible hands-on projects, targeted at kids aged 8–14. Readers, for example, are shown how to make and manipulate a set of "Napier's bones": numbered rods used in lieu of the calculator in the early 1600s; how to build a single and a double pulley and measure their relative mechanical advantages; how to build a thermometer; and how to play a rousing game of negative-number hopscotch. Kids are encouraged to paint a color wheel, build a working model computer (cardboard), graph the temperature changes in a cup of coffee, tell time with a candle clock, measure the heights of trees with a homemade astrolabe, play a geometric game of "pentominoes," and make an Archimedean spiral. Projects require only readily available materials, such a measuring cups, modeling clay, and poster board, and precise instructions are included for each, illustrated with wonderful color photographs.

9 12 The I Hate Mathematics! Book

Marilyn Burns; Little, Brown, 1976

"Some of the nicest people hate mathematics," Marilyn Burns begins. "Here are some of the things they say: 'I hate mathematics so much it makes me sick!' 'Mathematics is impossible!'" and "Mathematicians have little pig eyes." Before many pages have gone by, however, readers begin to change their minds. The book is a fascinating collection of mathematical concepts, including topology, prime numbers, binary numbers, infinity, enormous numbers ("The Preposterous Googol"), and symmetry ("How Many Sides Does a Banana Have?"). All are presented through a creative collection of mind-bending riddles, hands-on projects, magic tricks, and puzzles. Kids conduct a shoelace survey, calculate the number of combinations and permutations (there's a difference) of 31 ice-cream flavors possible in double-decker ice-cream cones, play games of "Creep," "Poison," "Going Dotty," and "Sprouts," and figure out how many pieces of popcorn it would take to fill a sock drawer.

The I Hate Mathematics! Book is one of the Brown Paper School book series, developed by a group of California teachers, writers, and artists who believe that "learning happens only when it is wanted, that it can happen anywhere, and doesn't require fancy tools." Other mathematically oriented books in the series by Burns include *Math for Smarty Pants* (1982), *The Book of Think (Or How to Solve a Problem Twice Your Size)* (1976), and *This Book is About Time* (1978).

Math for Smarty Pants is another large and clever collection of projects, puzzles, and riddles for kids who don't "feel quite right about hating math." Readers build Wobbly Cubes and write $1 sentences, solve logic puzzles with pizza, and play several twisted versions of tic-tac-toe.

The Book of Think is a bolstering approach to problem-solving strategies, with a lot of puzzling problems to practice on. (Try this one: "Suppose you've got a large bottle with a canary inside. The bottle is sealed and it's on a scale. The canary is standing on the bottom of the bottle. Then the canary starts to fly around inside of it. Does the reading on the scale change?").

This Book Is About Time is an absorbing account of the history and science of all aspects of time, including instructions for such projects as making an Egyptian shadow clock, building a Roman clepsydra, and measuring your sleep cycle.

MathArts
Mary Ann F. Kohl and Cindy Gainer; Gryphon House, 1996

A collection of math-related art activities for 3–6-year-olds. The book includes instructions for 200 math/art projects, reinforcing such early number skills as counting, sorting, pattern formation, sequencing, symmetry, estimating, time, money, and numerals. Sample activities include making paper chains, drawing geometrical sidewalk shapes (for jumping on) with colored chalks, hand-painting (the left hand with a sun, the right with a rainbow), and designing mobiles and paper sculptures. For the truly ambitious, there's one project that involves making 100 decorated refrigerator magnets for counting and simple number manipulations: you'll need 100 baby food jar lids and a lot of patience.

The Math Kit
Ron Van der Meer and Bob Gardner; Charles Scribner's Sons/Macmillan, 1994

The Math Kit, subtitled "A Three-Dimensional Tour Through Mathematics," is a pop-up book to end all pop-up books: an oversize and innovative collection of pop-ups, pullouts, turnable wheels, adjustable graphs, geometrical models, puzzles, and games, all designed to demonstrate crucial mathematical principles. Page 1 opens to a bright white pop-up pyramid: fold down a door in its side and you'll find a scale model of the Statue of Liberty. Adjacent flaps, with colorful portraits of Egyptian gods, open to explain ancient Egyptian number and measurement systems. Subsequent pages are increasingly complex. Included are a foldout set of multiplication tables, a tear-out green-and-yellow wheel that demonstrates equivalent fractions and percents, a pullout number line, and an estimation puzzle involving a green field thick with daisies. There's also a mechanical "balance scale" for solving algebraic equations, a treasure map with movable axes, for the demonstration of Cartesian coordinates, a 3-D geodesic sphere, and a trigonometric toy that shows how calculations involving right triangles can be used to measure the height of a pink house, a green tree, and a peach-colored tower. And a pullout comparison of pictograms, bar charts, and pie charts (yank the tab and they all change at once) and a probability game, using tiny, movable cardboard horses and a pair of (included) minidice.

Appealing as it is, this is not a book for the very young, who may be tempted to tear it apart, but is appropriate for upper-elementary-aged and older mathematicians.

The Math Kit, $35; available through bookstores

Math Wizardry for Kids
Margaret Kenda and Phyllis S. Williams; Barron's, 1995

This 300+-page spiral-bound volume is crammed with projects, games, experiments, information, and explanations for potential young math wizards. There are intriguing activities here for absolutely everybody: history buffs can discover the golden mean of the ancient Greeks; scientists can count their own atoms (if you gain five pounds a year, you're packing on a sextillion new atoms a minute); poets can learn about meter, rhythm, and beat; and northerners can determine the proportions of their own bodies by making mathematical snow angels. Budding private eyes can devise secret codes based on Egyptian hieroglyphics or the Greek alphabet, or try their hands at cracking the code Napoléon used to communicate with his soldiers before the fatal Battle of Waterloo. Sports fans can learn to calculate batting averages; amateur magicians can pick up a repertoire of mind-boggling mathematical tricks. Kids are also encouraged to build an abacus, identify Fibonacci numbers in pine cones, and experiment with numerous mathematical puzzles and multicultural games. The book ends with a splashy grand finale: instructions for throwing a math party, complete with a numbers cake, Mobius strip party favors, and a treasure hunt, during which eager treasure seekers must use maps and compasses.

Available through bookstores or

Barron's Educational Services, Inc.

250 Wireless Blvd.

Hauppage, NY 11788

(516) 434-3311 or (800) 645-3476/fax (516) 434-3723

Web site: barronseduc.com

A Mathematical Mystery Tour
Mark Wahl; Zephyr Press, 1988

The 255 pages of *A Mathematical Mystery Tour* are intended to foster "higher-level thinking processes" through the study of two pivotal concepts not covered in the garden-variety arithmetic class: Fibonacci numbers and the "Golden Ratio." The book is organized around five units: "Living Things Count," in which kids identify Fibonacci numbers in daisies, pinecones, and pineapples, and solve Leonardo da Vinci's multiplying rabbit problem; "The Dance of the Numbers," in which readers practice mathematical manipulations with Fibonacci numbers, largely through puzzles and "magic tricks"; "Finding the Gold," in which kids learn about the Golden Ratio of the ancient Greeks (and its relationship to Fibonacci numbers), study the mathematics of Greek statues, and make a Golden Rectangle puzzle; "Mathematical Artforms," in which the Golden Ratio is discovered in spectacular geometric stars and make-them-yourself Platonic polyhedra; and "Geometry, the Pyramid, and the Moon," in which the Golden Ratio shows up in a model of the Great Pyramid and in a scale model of the Earth and Moon.

The book provides straightforward, easy-to-follow explanations of the concepts involved and is conveniently arranged for home use, alternating student pages with helpful teachers' guides. Student pages are meant to be written upon, workbook-style, which means that you'll need to make copies if you're using the book with several children. The book is accompanied by a student newspaper (each kid should have his/her own), which includes supplementary information, games, and puzzles and an interview with Plato, a quick history of Cheops and his pyramid, and an account of how Eratosthenes, in 231 B.C., managed to measure the circumference of the Earth.

Book, $35; student newspapers, $9.95

Zephyr Press

3316 N. Chapel Ave.

Box 66006

Tucson, AZ 85732-6006

(800) 232-2187/fax (520) 323-9402

e-mail: neways2learn@zephyrpress.com

Web site: www.zephyrpress.com

GAMES AND HANDS-ON ACTIVITIES

24 Game
The original "24 Game"—there are now some seven versions—consists of a stack of 96 two-sided heavy-duty cardboard cards, each printed with a yellow wheel containing four single-digit numbers. The object of the game is to combine these numbers using the four basic operations of arithmetic—addition, subtraction, multiplication, and division—to reach the answer 24. All numbers on the card must be used, but each may be used only once. Thus a solution for a card bearing the numbers 8, 4, 3, and 3, for example, might be: $4 - 3 = 1$; $8 \times 3 = 24$; $24/1 = 24$. Cards are marked with one, two, or three yellow dots indicating level of difficulty: one-dot cards are the easiest; three-dot cards are dillies.

Now also available are "24 Games" in "Add/Subtract," "Multiply/Divide," "Fractions," "Decimals," "Exponents," and "Algebra" editions. "Add/Subtract," recommended for kids aged 5 and up, contains extra-large-size cards for easy handling, in a two-wheel format: users must decide which of the two wheels has the numbers that add or subtract to reach a target number. "Multiply/Divide," recommended for kids aged 7 and older, also has the large-size two-wheel format; users multiply and divide to identify common factors. In "Fractions" and "Decimals" editions, recommended for students in grade 7 and up, users must combine either whole numbers and fractions or whole numbers and decimals using any of the four arithmetical operations to reach a listed target number. In "Exponents" (grades 7–12), players must use one (just one) exponent operation along with the four basics to reach a target total of 24. A card of 7, 27, 1, and 1, for example, might generate the solution: $7^2 = 49$; $1 + 1 = 2$; $49 - 27 = 22$; $22 + 2 = 24$. In "Algebra," students must determine values of x and/or y—which, in combination with three whole numbers and the four arithmetical operations, must again equal 24.

The "24 Games" cost $19.95 apiece
Cusinesaire/Dale Seymour Publications
Box 5026
White Plains, NY 10602-5026
(800) 237-3142 or (800) 872-1100/fax (914) 328-5487 or (800) 551-RODS
Web site: www.cuisenaire.com or www.awl.com/dsp

Abacus

The abacus, invented in ancient times in central Asia, remains a handy mathematical machine to this day—useful as a hands-on counting tool for small children, capable of complex calculations for advanced students. The versatility of the abacus is clearly demonstrated in Jesse Dilson's *The Abacus* (St. Martin's Press, 1968) which comes packaged with a wooden Chinese abacus. The Chinese abacus, Dilson explains, consists of nine vertical columns of seven beads each, divided horizontally into upper ("heaven") and lower ("earth") sections. Heaven contains two of the seven beads; earth, five. (The book also includes instructions for making your own Chinese abacus, using a cigar box.) Clear directions are given for using the abacus for increasingly difficult mathematical operations, from single-digit addition and subtraction through multidigit multiplication and division.

Another version of the abacus, the AL Abacus, consists of 10 horizontal wires each strung with 10 beads, the 5 right-hand beads in one color, the 5 left-hand beads in another. An activities manual (*Activities for the Abacus: A Hands-on Approach to Arithmetic*) and a collection of student worksheets, appropriate for kids in grades K–5, are available to accompany the abacus. Concepts taught include counting, adding, subtracting, place value, multiplication, and division; the activities manual also includes instructions for using the Chinese (two beads in "heaven") and the Japanese (one bead in "heaven") abacus.

AL Abacus, $20; it measures $9\frac{3}{4} \times 8\frac{1}{2}$ inches and is available in three different bead-color combinations
Activities for Learning
21161 York Rd.
Hutchinson, MN 55350
(320) 587-9146
e-mail: ajcotter@hutchtel.net

See **On-Line-Resources: The Abacus: The Art of Calculating with Beads** (page 198).

Athenian Secret

Interact, the California-based company dedicated to promoting "learning through involvement," has devised several cooperative math-oriented simulation programs. Among those is "Athenian Secret," in which kids participate in an ancient Greek treasure hunt, moving about Athens and accumulating Greek drachmas as they solve basic arithmetic problems and puzzles. "Lost Tribe of the Tocowans" reinforces multiplication and division skills, as participants move across the desert in jeeps in search of the mysterious vanished tribe, progressing as they solve math problems and deal with the instructions on the included "Destiny Cards." "Math Quest" sends kids on a tour of four imaginary worlds in search—again—of a treasure. Participants tour Dinosaurland, Fantasyland, Sportsland, and Numberland, solving problems as they go, and plotting their progress on the included Math Quest Map. As increasing numbers and types of problems are mastered, kids graduate from their initial rank of Problem Solver to Calculatrician, Geomagician, Newtonian, and finally Einsteinian.

"Math Quest" is recommended for kids in grades 6–8; "Athenian Secret" and "Lost Tribe of Tocowans," for kids in grades 4–5. "Math Quest" is estimated to require about 20 hours of lesson time; *Athenian Secret* and *Lost Tribe*, about 15. All, while easily adaptable to small student groups, are targeted at large school classes; simulation kits include 35 short student guides, one detailed teacher's guide, and reproducible worksheet materials. "Math Quest" also includes a 22 × 34-inch map of the four Quest lands. A worthwhile experience: home learners might consider coopting a group of interested friends.

"Athenian Secret," $39; "Lost Tribe of Tocowans," $34; "Math Quest," $53

Interact

1825 Gillespie Way, #101

El Cajon, CA 92020

(619) 448-1474 or (800) 359-0961/fax (619) 448-6722

or (800) 700-5093

Web site: www.interact-simulations.com

Configure

A beautifully designed game of mosaic pattern formation. Players, using attractive "marble" tiles in two different shapes and colors, attempt to cover each room in a floor plan of George Washington's homes. The accompanying booklet includes historical and mathematical information (kids learn, for example, how to calculate area) and instructions for four different games. Fun and educational for all.

Available in two versions: the "George Washington's Boyhood Home" set, $29.95; the "Mount Vernon" set, $44.95

Learning Passport Co.

7104 Loch Lomond Dr.

Bethesda, MD 20817

(301) 229-9630 or (800) U-LEARN-2/

fax (301) 229-5940

Web site: www.learningpassport.com

See **George Washington** (page 493).

Dino Math Tracks

A delightful mathematical board game for kids aged 6 and up that won both the approval of our children (and assorted friends) and of the National Council of Teachers of Mathematics, which is no easy feat. To win, each player must move a herd of four dinosaurs from the waterfall at the beginning of the multicolored playing path to the rainbow at the end. The playing path itself is a four-lane road of colored dinosaur tracks—purple, green, yellow, and red—respectively representing the mathematical ones, tens, hundreds, and thousands place. In the simplest version of the game, "Prehistoric Number Roll," players roll four number cubes and then arrange them—in any order they like—in the purple, green, yellow, and red "place value box" at the edge of the board to make a four-digit number. The dinosaurs in the player's herd—each a different color—are then moved the appropriate number of spaces along the appropriately colored track. The red dinosaur, for example, moves the number of space shown by the number cube in the red box along the red track path. First kid to get all his/her animals to the finish wins the game.

"Dino Math Action" adds an extra frill to the basic game; after rolling the number cubes and moving their dinosaurs, players must draw an "Action Number" card and follow its instructions. Examples: "Your red dinosaur skips ahead 2 thousands" or "Your ones dinosaur has a thorn in its foot. Hobble back 2 spaces for help." In "Prehistoric Problem-Solving," the most challenging of the three "Dino Math Tracks" games, players must solve problems on the included "Problem-Solving" cards and follow their instructions. "A flying dinosaur flew 520 kilometers last week and 603 kilometers this week," reads one card, "How far did it fly altogether? Move that many." And another: "Archaeologists must ship 25 tons of dinosaur bones to the museum. If each truck can haul 2 tons, how many trucks do they need? Move that many."

The only quibble concerns the makeup of the dinosaur herds: players have a choice of stegosaurus, triceratops, brontosaurus, or—peculiarly—woolly mammoths. For two to four players aged 6 and up.

$19.95 from toy and game stores

Duo

Mensa, the national organization for the superbrainy, dubbed this one of the best mind games of 1996. The game is a pack of 80 attractive cards, each bearing combinations of three elements: color (orange, blue, purple, or green), number (1, 2, 3, or 4), and symbol (square, triangle, circle, or X). Each player is initially dealt a hand of seven cards; the remainder of the pack is placed facedown in the middle of the playing area. Two cards are drawn and placed faceup, one on either side of the pack. Each player, in turn, tries to play the cards from his/her hand onto the faceup cards, laying down a card that matches at least two out of the three displayed elements. Players can match, for example, color and number—say, a purple 3 on a purple 3—or color and symbol, or number and symbol. First player to unload all of his/her cards wins.

This is more challenging than it sounds. "Duo" reinforces a battery of pattern-forming mathematical skills; it's also addictively fun. Recommended for persons aged 7–adult.

$6.95

U.S. Games Systems, Inc.

179 Ludlow St.

Stamford, CT 06902

(203) 353-8400 or (800) 544-2637

Easy-to-Make 3D Shapes in Full Color
A. G. Smith; Dover Publications, 1989

A hands-on workbook for young geometers, with which kids, by cutting and folding, can construct six attractive polyhedrons. These really are easy to make: users will need only scissors, glue, a ruler, and some sort of sharpish tool for scoring, which makes the shapes fold better. Shapes include a tetrahedron, cube, pentagonal prism, octahedron, cuboctahedron, and icosahedron. All are made of shiny coated poster board (light enough to cut, but still durable), in bright colors. The tetrahedron, for example, is purple and orange; the cube has alternating faces of red, blue, and yellow; and the icosahedron is an attractive yellow and robin's-egg blue.

Workbook, $2.95

Dover Publications, Inc.

31 E. Second St.

Mineola, NY 11501

Hive Alive
"Hive Alive" ("Bee Smart in Math"), a four-level game of mathematical operations, is played on a honeycomb-patterned game board illustrated with googly-eyed black-and-yellow-striped bees. The game includes 120 bright yellow punch-out playing cards; those in use are inserted in small slotted plastic stands to make them stand up during play. Two of these cards, each representing the number 0, are Queen Bees; the rest, a collection of whole numbers, negative numbers, fractions, and decimals, are Worker Bees.

Once equipped with bees, kids are ready to play any one of the four "Hive Alive" games, appropriate for

mathematicians at different levels of expertise: "Primary People," "Fraction Faction," "Droves of Decimals," or "Anything Goes." The game is recommended for two players aged 7 and up.

$12

Aristoplay

450 S. Wagner Rd.

Ann Arbor, MI 48107

(800) 634-7738 or (888) GR8-GAME

fax (734) 995-4611

Web site: www.aristoplay.com

Invicta Mathematical Balance
This is a terrific hands-on math toy—or instructional tool, depending on your age and your attitude. It's a sturdy plastic arm balance, each arm marked off with the numbers 1 through 10. Beneath each number there's a peg, upon which can be hung rectangular plastic weights. Equivalent quantities of weights balance; nonequivalent quantities tilt the scale. A weight on the left-hand 6 peg, for example, can be balanced by several right-hand combinations: 2 weights on the 3 peg, 3 weights on the 2 peg, 1 weight on the 2 and 1 on the 4 peg, and so on. Let the kids fool around with this: either, willy-nilly, they'll figure out the fundamentals of addition, subtraction, multiplication, and division, or the hands-on play will reinforce and reaffirm concepts they already know.

An accompanying instruction book is available, *The Balance Book,* by Lee Jenkins, which describes over 90 balance activities suitable for kids in grades K–8. Our boys, however, resisted adult intervention, preferring to work the thing out on their own.

Alternative balances include the pan balance, which generally sits lower to the ground on a broader base, and in which the balance arms end in shallow trays for holding calibrated weights or counters; and the bucket balance, in which hanging buckets are suspended from each balance arm. Pan balances are probably the simplest for the very small to manipulate: they're generally sturdy, inexpensive, and difficult to knock out of kilter. The same sorts of math exercises—for example, "How many green hexagrams does it take to equal the weight of 30 paperclips?"—can be done with bucket balances, but these have a tendency to bob madly up and down when loaded by preschoolers.

MATHEMATICS

189

Balances, weights, and activity books of several kinds can be ordered from most educational-supply companies, among them

Cuisenaire/Dale Seymour Publications

Box 5026

White Plains, NY 10602-5026

(800) 237-0338 or (800) 872-1100/fax (914) 328-5487

or (800) 551-RODS

Web site: www.cuisenaire.com or www.awl.com/dsp

Delta Education

Box 3000

Nashua, NH 03061-3000

(800) 442-5444/fax (800) 282-9560

Web site: www.delta-ed.com

Learning Wrap-Ups

"Learning Wrap-Ups," which advertise "explosive learning," are packaged in fat little red tubes that look like firecrackers. Each tube contains 10 notched plastic wrap-up strips. One half of the strip is printed with a list of simple math problems; the other half with a scrambled list of answers. The trick is to correctly match the two by wrapping the strip with a length of heavy red string. Kids tuck the string into the notch next to problem one; pull it across the plastic strip to the notch next to the problem's answer; then wrap it around behind the strip to the notch next to problem two; pull it across the strip to the problem's answer, and so on, around and around. To check accuracy, simply flip the strip over: the back is marked with a pattern of lines which—if all your answers are correct—should be perfectly matched by the lines of the wrapped red string.

Mathematical "Learning Wrap-Ups" include "Addition," "Subtraction," "Multiplication," "Division," and "Fractions" sets. Each set, $7.95

The Sycamore Tree, Inc.

2179 Meyer Pl.

Costa Mesa, CA 92627

information (714) 650-4466; orders (714) 642-6750 or (800) 779-6750

Web site: www.sycamoretree.com

M is for Mirror

Duncan Birmingham; Parkwest Publications, 1989

Using the mirror card, which comes stuck in a little slot in the front of the book, kids try to find the "hidden picture" in each of the book's illustrations. Get the mirror in exactly the right place and, via the wonders of symmetry, the wacky bird turns into an umbrella or the piano player becomes an astronomer.

There's a more challenging version for older kids, *The Mirror Puzzle Book* (Marion Walter; Parkwest Publications, 1986), in which each page holds a collection of designs and shapes. One of these, in an upper corner, is designated the "Mirror Master." The trick is to position the mirror on each of the pictures on the page so as to duplicate the Mirror Master. An interesting supplement to studies of pattern and symmetry. Also see Duncan Birmingham's *Look Twice: Mirror Reflections, Logical Thinking* (Parkwest Publications, 1993), another symmetrical challenge for kids aged 4–8.

The Math Chef: Over 60 Math Activities and Recipes for Kids

Joan D'Amico and Karen Eich Drummond; John Wiley & Sons, 1997

The book pairs basic math concepts (metric and English measurement systems, multiplication, division, fractions, percents, and geometry) with easy-to-make recipes. Kids variously discover how many grams are in a pound of potatoes, how to triple a sandwich recipe or cut an applesauce recipe in half, and how to calculate the area of a brownie, the diameter of a cupcake, and the circumference of a pie. Fun and scrumptious math.

Make It Equal

The "Make It Equal" games are based on a pack of cards, each printed with a number from 1 to 10, along with—to help very young players—a corresponding number of countable dots. There are 11 basic "Make It Equal" games, each described in the accompanying bright yellow instruction booklet. All reinforce skills in addition, subtraction, multiplication, and division, and encourage kids to invent creative problem-solving strategies. In "The Operation Game," for example, each player is dealt 10 number cards, faceup. Two cards are chosen from each hand, one designated a *start* and the other a *finish* card. The object of the game is to make a series of equations using all the remaining number cards in the hand, beginning with the *start* card and ending with (and equaling) the *finish* card. Players write each of their equations down as they proceed. At the end of the round, they add up their scores, winning points for each operation sign used. (An addition sign is worth the lowest number of points; a division sign, the highest.)

The "Make It Equal" games were originally designed by teacher Ruth Bell Alexander for her daughter's fourth/fifth-grade class, but they can be played by kids at a wide range of skill levels, from kindergarten through middle school.

> Set (cards and instruction manual), $14.95; additional packs of cards, $5 apiece
> Make It Fun Learning Materials
> 1095 S. Mountain Ave.
> Ashland, OR 97520
> (503) 488-1477

4 *MathSafari*

13 An electronic learning machine from the makers of the earlier "Geosafari" (see page 428). The basic machine, which includes a numerical keyboard and electronic scoreboard, is used with coded spiral-bound lesson books, which slip neatly into place on the display panel. There are 11 lesson books currently available, each containing 40 to 44 single-page lessons, appropriate for students in pre-K through grade 7. Titles include "Ready, Set, Count," "Addition Fun," "Subtraction Fun," "Addition-Subtraction Fun," "Multiplication Fun," "Division Fun," "Fraction Fun," "Fractions, Decimals & Percent Fun," "Algebra," "Geometry," and "Make-Your-Own," this last a series of blank cards upon which users can design their own lessons.

Lessons are attractive, each illustrated with colorful cartoons and photographs that reinforce the mathematical concept under study. "Multiplying by Three," for example, in the "Multiplication Fun" book, is illustrated with stacks of bright green three-leaf shamrocks (plus a leprechaun). The books attempt to give users more than just a fancy form of rote drill. Included are word problems, spatial puzzles, and exercises in selecting the correct mathematical operations, reading graphs, identifying number sequences, and the like.

The machine is appealing to kids: it lights up, plays beeping little bars of music, and buzzes in response to correct or incorrect answers. It can be used by one or two players at a time (or more, in teams, but that tends to get rambunctious); machine settings can be varied for greater or lesser challenge, giving kids anywhere from 1 to 99 seconds to solve the presented problems. "MathSafari" operates on batteries or on an AC adaptor, which must be purchased separately.

In our hands, "MathSafari" had an initial advantage of novelty. Our boys, who nearly always fall for lights and beeps, were briefly seduced into doing a good deal of math. After the first couple of weeks, however, the novelty faded and interest paled. "MathSafari" may be a good investment for determined devotees of electronic games, but when it comes right down to it, there's nothing in the lessons that can't be found in a reasonably good series of workbooks.

> *MathSafari*, $99.95; lesson books, $14.95 each
> Educational Insights
> 16941 Keegan Ave.
> Carson, CA 90746
> (800) 933-3277/fax (310) 605-5048 or (800) 995-0506
> Web site: www.edin.com

5 *Muggins*

+ A two-sided wooden board, four different-colored sets of marbles, and two math games, each playable at different skill levels. Players roll the dice and, based on the mathematical result, place marbles in the appropriately numbered space, variously attempting to create runs, to block an opponent, or to surround a given target number.

> $39.95 from toy and game stores or
> Carolina Mathematics
> Carolina Biological Supply Co.
> 2700 York Rd.
> Burlington, NC 27215-3398
> (910) 584-0381 or (800) 334-5551/fax (800) 222-7112

9 *O! Euclid!*

+ A geometry game for persons aged 9 (or so)–99. "O! Euclid!" consists of an assortment of puzzle cards with which players can assemble 14 geometrical shapes: equilateral, isosceles, and right triangles, and a square, rectangle, parallelogram, trapezoid, pentagon, hexagon, octagon, circle, ellipse, parabola, and hyperbola. Also included are 14 true/false question cards about each shape ("An equilateral triangle . . . is a three-sided polygon. True/False?" "A circle . . . is an arc of 360 degrees. True/False?") and 14 name cards, to be matched to each completed shape puzzle. Rules for four games, at various levels of difficulty, are listed on the accompanying instruction sheet; younger players, however, will simply enjoy doing the puzzles and matching the finished geometrical shapes to their proper names.

> Ampersand Press
> 8040 N.E. Day Rd. W, #5A
> Bainbridge Island, WA 98110
> (206) 780-9015

Set

This award-winning card game, described on the purple box as "the family game of visual perception," is a diabolically clever exercise in mathematical thinking. The game consists of 81 cards, each printed with one of three basic shapes: a diamond, a lozenge, or a fat squiggle. On each card, the shapes appear in different colors (red, green, or purple), numbers (1, 2, or 3), and shadings (solid, outlined, or crosshatched). To play, the dealer lays out 12 cards, faceup, and all the players attempt to identify three cards that make a set: that is, three cards in which each feature (shape, number, color, shading) is either exactly the same or completely different. Three solid red diamonds, one solid purple squiggle, and two solid green lozenges, for example, make a set: color, shape, and number are different on each card, shading on each is the same. Players who identify a set yell "Set!" and remove those three cards from the board; the dealer then adds three new cards and the set-search begins again. Players score one point for each set; person with the most points at the end of the game wins.

One notably nice feature of "Set," from a parental point of view, is that everybody plays at once, which means that nobody has a chance to get bored while waiting for a turn, and the game works equally well for practically any number of players, from one on up. The game, which is considerably more challenging than it appears, is appropriate for persons aged 5–adult, and adult players (I speak from experience) have no advantages over young opponents.

> $13.95, available from toy and game stores or
> Zephyr Press

> 3316 N. Chapel Ave.
> Box 66006
> Tucson, AZ 85728-6006
> (520) 322-5090 or (800) 232-2187/fax (520) 323-9402
> e-mail: neways2learn@zephyrpress.com
> Web site: www.zephyrpress.com

Stack

An innovative strategy dice game for persons aged 6–adult. The large-size version contains six sets of 14 extra-large dice, each in a different eye-catching color (pink, green, yellow, purple, orange, and blue). Each player gets one set; then all players shake their dice up and spill them out (gently) in the center of a flat playing space and the game begins. Players, in turn, make dice stacks by placing one of their dice on top of any matching number (a three on a three, for example) on a die belonging to an opponent. A stack can be two, three, or four dice high. A four-dice stack belongs to the player whose color is on top and is removed from the playing field. At the end of each round, each player gets all stacks with his/her dice on top. Total scores are determined by adding up the (face-up) values of all the dice in each stack; ones, a special case, are worth 10 points. The player with the highest score over 200—only achieved after several rounds of play—wins the game.

> Available in six-, four-, and two-player versions, for
> $24, $18, and $10, respectively, including a net bag for
> storing dice while not in use; individual sets of dice
> may be purchased separately
> Strunk Games
> Box 64
> Eustis, ME 04936
> (800) 669-3315

Tangoes

The first tangram, legend has it, was made of porcelain, created when a butterfingered 10th-century Chinese gentleman named Tan dropped a tile on the floor and broke it into seven pieces. As he struggled to reproduce the original square, the tangram puzzle was born. A 20th-century version of Tan's smashed tile goes by the name of "Tangoes." Each game includes two sets of plastic tangram pieces, one red, one black. Each set consists of a square, a parallelogram, and five triangles.

Using all of these, players are challenged to duplicate 54 puzzle images, pictured on a series of stiff plastic cards. (Solutions are on the back on each card.) Tangrams, according to the National Council of Teachers of Mathematics, develop visual-spatial abilities and problem-solving skills; they're also fun.

"Tangoes" with plastic pieces, $11.95; a deluxe version, in hardwood, $39.95. Extra tangram sets ($2.95) and two sets of additional puzzle cards ($4.95) can be purchased separately
Rex Games, Inc.
2001 California St., Suite 204
San Francisco, CA 94109-4319
(415) 931-8200 or (800) 542-6375/fax (415) 931-8282
See *Grandfather Tang's Story* (page 181).

10 *True Math*

A superbly designed math game in which players hop pawns about a colorful geometric-pattern playing board, attempting to answer questions in six mathematical categories: "Numbers," "Money," "Size & Scale," "Geometry," "Logical Thinking," and "Random Access" (which here means "miscellaneous"). The game includes 300 question cards, each with three creative math questions: 200 of these, in yellow, are True/False cards; 100, in pink, are Genius Cards. The object of the game is to accumulate 50 points worth of correct answers: True/False questions are work 5 points apiece; Genius questions are worth 10, which makes sense, since they're harder.

The "Numbers" category concentrates on questions having to do with computation skills: adding, subtracting, multiplying, dividing, fractions, decimals, negative numbers, Roman numerals, pre-algebra, square numbers, percents, and other exercises in standard arithmetic. Sample questions include: "A human brain weighs up to 3 pounds. The brains of all 100 U.S. Senators total more than 300 pounds—true or false?"

"Money," a topic that unfailingly seems to motivate everyone, includes decimals, making change, budgeting, very large numbers, and a lot of interesting financial trivia. Sample question: "Americans spend $7 billion on blue jeans each year; 21% are made by Levi Strauss. Levi has one-fourth of the market—true or false?"

"Size & Scale" deals with height, weight, volume, area, calories, clothing sizes, speed, time, distance, tem-perature, rock hardnesses, the Periodic Table, and the like, in both metric and English units. Sample question: "If Rumpelstiltskin demanded an ounce of pure gold spun into a fine wire, it would stretch 50 miles long—true or false?"

"Geometry" covers shapes, lines, circles, angles, grids, and other manipulations geometrical. Question: "Jellyfish are not really fish, but they are radially symmetrical—true or false?"

The "Logical Thinking" category includes pattern questions, deductive and inductive reasoning questions, and Boolean logic questions. (Boolean logic is a means of sorting and classifying things, essential in the world of computer science.) Sample questions: "September is the only month with the same number of letters as its order in the year—true or false?" "If you search a computer data base for every article related to 'cats and tigers,' you're really just searching for tigers—true or false?"

"Random Access"—from the computer term *random access memory* (RAM)—includes questions from all of the categories above, plus assorted mathematical oddities intended to promote creative thinking. Try this one: "Super Frosty, a snow figure built in 1988, stood 63.56 feet tall. If it were alive, Super Frosty could peer through the top window of a six-story building—true or false?"

Our boys, rarely enthusiastic over anything with the word *math* in the title, all thoroughly enjoyed this one, busily calculating the heights of Gulliver's Lilliputians and the number of $5 bills pinched in the largest theft in history from the U.S. Mint, and bickering over why 14th-century European castles had cylindrical towers instead of rectangular ones. "True Math" is recommended for two to four players aged 10 and up
$25
Aristoplay
450 S. Wagner Rd.,
Ann Arbor, MI 48107
(800) 634-7738 or (888) GR8-GAME
fax (734) 995-4611
Web site: www.aristoplay.com

6 *Wff 'n Proof Learning Games*

Wff 'n Proof's Resource Strategy Games are "multi-level instructional kits," each including an assortment of games intended to enhance creative thinking and reasoning skills. It seems that they do so successfully: studies show that in classrooms using these games, student absenteeism plummeted, and scores on math achievement and I.Q. tests jumped.

Games in the series include "Equations" ("The Game of Creative Mathematics"), a five-game kit based on the basic operations of arithmetic (addition, subtraction, multiplication, and division), and the use of exponents and roots; "Wff'n Proof" ("The Game of Modern Logic"), a 21-game kit that centers around the rules of inference and logical proofs; "On-Words," a strategic game of word structures; and "On-Sets," a 30-game kit that teaches set theory.

While all have complex possibilities, the kits start simply: beginning games in each kit are appropriate for players as young as 6. If you're not sure that Resource Strategy Games are just the thing for your young mathematicians, try a sample: the first two games from "Wff'n Proof" are packaged separately, as *Wff*, "The Beginner's Game of Logic."

Games, $28 to $33.50; *Wff*, $5.50
Wff 'n Proof Learning Games
1490 South Blvd.
Ann Arbor, MI 48104-4699
(313) 665-2269

5 + Wonder Number Game

The "Wonder Number Game" includes a large multicolored playing board divided into 100 sequentially numbered squares (10 rows of 10), 100 plastic playing chips in four colors (red, white, blue, and yellow), a large-size game spinner, and instructions for about 25 games, variously appropriate for kids aged 5–adult. The board, through an easy-to-read series of symbols, delivers a lot of information about individual numbers. All odd numbers are marked with one dot, and even numbers with two; prime numbers are circled; square numbers are outlined with a colored square. Factor pairs of numbers are shown in the number box in small size; square factors are surrounded by squares, and prime factors are circled. The number 16, for example, a square, is surrounded by a yellow square and has two dots beneath it to indicate that it is an even number (and a multiple of 2). Factors of 16—2, 4, and 8—appear around the edges of the 16 square in smaller print, each enclosed in a small colored box. Each factor's pair (in this case, 8, 4, and 2) appears next to the boxed factor; square factors are outlined with a square, prime factors with a circle. Multiples of 2, 3, 4, 5, 6, 7, 8, and 9 are color coded. A wide range of games can be played on the board, from simple challenges for 5-year-olds to more complex games for teenagers.

A series of lesson plan books based on the "Wonder Number Game" are also available, appropriate for students in grades K–3, 3–6, or 6–8. Each book contains a reproducible black-and-white version of the "Wonder Number" playing board, reproducible student worksheets, and 18 lesson plans. You don't need the boxed game for the lesson activities. The full-size playing board, however, is much more appealing than the workbook version, and the games are not only more fun than the lesson plans but also just as educational.

About $25; individual lesson plan books, about $13
Interactive Dimensions
1825 E. Gaviota Ct.
Simi Valley, CA 93065
(805) 526-7335
Game and lesson books can also be ordered from
Institute for Math Mania
Box 910
Montpelier, VT 05601
(800) 223-5871

4 8 XIT

Pronounced *exit*, this simple card game for small children is designed to teach early number skills. The game consists of a pack of 42 playing cards, each labeled with a numeral from 1 to 6 (in blue) plus a corresponding number of (red) dots. Each player is initially dealt a hand of six cards. On each turn, players roll three dice—one red, one green, and one blue—and discard those cards in their hands that match the numbers on the dice. They then draw a card from the remaining pack. Play continues until one person—the winner—manages to get rid of all his/her cards.

"XIT" is a quick and enjoyable way of teaching beginning counting and matching skills. It is recommended for kids aged 4 and up, but is fast paced enough to hold the attention of older children.

$9, available through toy and game stores or
Old Game Store

Rte. 11/30
Box 1756
Manchester Center, VT 05255-1756
(802) 362-2756 or (800) 818-GAME
Web site: www.vtweb.com/old game

AUDIOVISUAL RESOURCES

The Assistant Professor Video Series

A collection of animated math lessons. The graphics are cute and clever—apple pie–munching ants and sword-wielding samurai, for example, demonstrate the parts of fractions—and the narration is clear and simple. It's also quite determinedly lessonlike, which makes the series somewhat dull to listen to: lines such as "The greater the number of parts we divide something into, the smaller the size of the parts" is hardly likely to have the average fourth-grader sitting on the edge of his/her chair. The videos are attractively presented, however, and all the crucial information is provided. Titles include *Fractions and All Their Parts,* a three-part series defining fractions, explaining equivalent fractions, and demonstrating techniques for adding and subtracting fractions; *All About Angles,* which defines angles and degrees and teaches the use of the protractor; *What Is Area?,* which shows kids how to calculate the areas of rectangles, parallelograms, and triangles; *What Are Variables?,* which teaches kids how mathematical "language" is used to write "sentences"; *The Pythagorean Theorem,* which defines right triangles and explains the use of the famous Theorem; *Which Way Is Minus?,* which discusses negative numbers and their manipulations; *The World of Circles,* which defines circle, radius, diameter, and chord and explains the concept of pi; and *Decimals: To Be Exact,* a two-part set on the function of the decimal point. Most tapes are recommended for math students in grade 4 and up.

> Each tape, about $29.95; packets of reproducible student worksheets with activity suggestions to accompany the tapes are also available
> Allied Video Corporation
> Box 702618
> Tulsa, OK 74170
> (800) 926-5892

Audio Memory Math Songs

Rhyme, rhythm, and melody are powerful memory aids, which is why it's so easy to remember advertising jingles, campfire tunes with multiple verses, and everything ever sung by Raffi or performed on *Sesame Street.* Audio Memory Publishing (their motto: "You never forget what you sing!") capitalizes on this quirk of human memory in a line of fact-filled audiocassettes. Through songs, kids learn addition, subtraction, and multiplication facts. The songs are sung echo-style, with space for repeats by listeners. It's drill, with a musical memory boost.

> Audiocassettes, each accompanied by a sing-along poster of printed arithmetic facts, $9.95 apiece (plus shipping/handling)
> Audio Memory Publishing
> 501 Cliff Dr.
> Newport Beach, CA 92663
> (800) 365-SING

Donald in Mathmagic Land

The "Donald" in the title is Walt Disney's famous duck, the star of this creative 27-minute video. Donald tours Mathmagic Land, learning about the history of math and discovering how math permeates many aspects of daily life. He first meets the mathematicians of ancient Greece (and learns about the mathematics of stringed instruments); then moves magically through space and time to discover the mathematical principles behind cathedrals, baseball diamonds, starfish, and the *Mona Lisa.*

> $14.95
> Movies Unlimited
> 3015 Darnell Rd.
> Philadelphia, PA 19154
> (215) 637-4444 or (800) 4-MOVIES
> e-mail: movies@moviesunlimited.com
> Web site: www.moviesunlimited.com

Educational Record Center

A wide selection of materials with which kids can learn math facts through music on audio- or videocassettes. Take your pick: kids can master math facts through rap, country, rock and roll, or just plain silly songs. (Choose carefully: you might end up listening to a lot of it.)

Educational Record Center, Inc.

3233 Burnt Mill Dr., Suite 100

Wilmington, NC 28403-2655

(800) 438-1637/fax (888) 438-1637

e-mail: erc-inc@worldnet.att.net

Web site: www.erc-inc.com

COMPUTER SOFTWARE

Carmen Sandiego Math Detective

Players set out to infiltrate the secret hideouts of Carmen Sandiego's gang of international criminals and to deactivate Carmen's powerful Quantum Crystallizer. To do so, they must acquire the necessary secret codes that can be obtained only by solving math problems. The game, which can be played at three levels of difficulty, covers basic arithmetic skills, fractions, decimals, percents, geometry, and word problems. On CD-ROM for Mac or Windows.

$34.95

Broderbund

Box 6125

Novato, CA 94948-6125

(415) 382-4700 or (800) 521-6263

Web site: www.broderbund.com or www.carmen-sandiego.com

James Discovers Math

James discovers math from the family kitchen where kids—by clicking on such kitchen furnishings as a bowl of fruit, a refrigerator covered with colorful geometric magnets, a cuckoo clock, a patterned place mat, and a stack of blocks—can join him in 10 mathematical activities. A jar full of pencils, for example, leads to a "Measurement" game in which kids use pencils—dragged into position and placed end to end—to measure the lengths of various (not usually measured) objects, including a snail, an alligator, and a schoolteacher. The fruit bowl leads to a counting activity in which kids, helping out at the fruit shop, fill boxes with different numbers of different kinds of fruits; the stack of (number) blocks leads to addition and subtraction activities; and the cuckoo clock cleverly teaches kids to tell time. The program also includes catchy little sing-along songs, funny animations, and an interactive

story starring James. Recommended for players aged 3–6. Available on CD-ROM for Mac or Windows.

$39.95

Broderbund

Box 6125

Novato, CA 94948-6125

(415) 382-4700 or (800) 521-6263

Web site: www.broderbund.com

The Logical Journey of the Zoombinis

The peace-loving, blue-headed Zoombinis have been conquered by the nasty Bloats and incarcerated on Bloat Island. Players attempt to rescue the Zoombinis, a process that requires the solving of increasingly difficult (but always logical) puzzles. Puzzle solving, whether kids notice it or not, involves such essential mathematical skills as pattern recognition, logic, data analysis, and set theory—and the game is varied, imaginative, and fun. Recommended for players aged 8–12. On CD-ROM for Mac or Windows.

$29.95

Broderbund

Box 6125

Novato, CA 94948-6125

(415) 382-4700 or (800) 521-6263

Web site: www.broderbund.com

Math Blaster Series

Math drill, with spaceships and evil aliens. Basically kids solve problems—of which each program has many—in order to play video-style blast-the-bad-guys arcade games. Our boys promptly figured out that there are plenty of arcade-style games available with which one can blow up the enemy without having to work one's way through assorted addition, subtraction, multiplication, division, fraction, or algebra problems, after which "Math Blaster" fell irretrievably out of favor. There are a number of titles in the "Math Blaster" series, each based on a different galactic adventure story: "Math Blaster Episode 1: In Search of Spot" (ages 6–12), "Math Blaster Epidsode 2: Secret of the Lost City" (ages 8–12), Math Blaster Mystery: The Great Brain Robbery" (ages 10 and up), and "Alge-Blaster 3" (ages 12 and up).

Davidson and Associates

19840 Pioneer Ave.

MATHEMATICS

Torrance, CA 90503

(800) 545-7677/fax (310) 793-0601

Web site: www.davd.com

Math Workshop

This one, despite the no-nonsense title, is not only mathematical but also creative, appealing, and fun, and makes clever use of graphics, animation, video clips, and sound effects. From the main Workshop, kids can access seven different mathematical games, variously teaching basic arithmetical manipulations—addition, subtraction, multiplication, and division, pattern recognition, spatial concepts, shapes, fractions, and equivalencies. Players develop estimation skills, for example, through a series of out-of-the-ordinary measurement challenges: "About how many grapefruits wide is a toilet seat? About how many eggs does a banana weigh?" For each correct answer, a bowling pin drops into position in the Workshop bowling alley; when players have accumulated 10 pins, a gorilla bowls a dramatic strike. Shapes and spatial concepts are taught through a series of puzzles—once players piece them together properly, they view a zany video sequence—and fractions are manipulated in the Rhythm Shop, where kids must cut and paste fractional bars of music into similar-size chunks of sound to create matching rhythms. This completed, the Rhythm Shop plays the resultant tune, to which a colorful little top-knotted bird—the AlgeBird—does a dance. Games are offered at several levels of difficulty. "Math Workshop" is recommended for kids aged 5–10. Available on CD-ROM for Mac or Windows.

$29.95

Broderbund

Box 6125

Novato, CA 94948-6125

(415) 382-4700 or (800) 521-6263

Web site: www.broderbund.com

Millie's Math House

Millie, the owner of the Math House, is a friendly cow, and the House itself contains six attractive games in which young beginners are introduced to the mathematical basics: counting, sizes, and shapes. In the automated Cookie Factory, for example, kids count the proper number of jellybeans to decorate the cookies (if they're wrong, the cookie gets gulped down by a hungry green frog); in the Mouse House game, players combine simple geometric shapes to build a house for an excited family of cheering mice; and in Build-a-Bug, kids create a colorful collection of very strange caterpillars by combining different numbers—from 1 to 10—of ears, eyes, antennae, legs, tails, and decorative spots. Recommended for kids aged 2–5. Available on CD-ROM for Mac or Windows.

$19.95

Edmark Corporation

Box 97021

Redmond, WA 98073

(800) 362-2890/fax (425) 556-8430

e-mail: edmarkteam@edmark.com

Web site: www.edmark.com

The Trig Explorer

An animated trigonometry text. Users can access eight trigonometry topics: "Degrees," "Angles," "Radians (Pi)," "Triangles," "Right Triangles," "Functions," "Plotting," and "Inverse Functions." Under each topic, students can choose among a narrated lesson—the icon is an Einsteinian professor with pointer standing at a blackboard; a demonstration of real-life applications of trigonometric concepts; exercises and problems; or quick reviews of the lesson material. Under "Degrees," for example, kids learn about latitude and longitude; under "Angles," about the operation of a sextant; under "Triangles," about the architectural uses of triangular trusses; and under "Plotting," about sound, radio, and light waves.

"The Trig Explorer," however, is clearly an instructional program, not a game: the text is informationally worthy, but dry; illustrations are attractive and helpful, but, for the most part, absolutely serious. The program could be helped along by a more reader-friendly text with some readily understandable analogies—some of the explanations are a bit too perfunctory for comfort— but this, unfortunately, is a common fault of textbooks. Still, a motivated kid, given "The Trig Explorer," should be able to learn a lot of trigonometry. On CD-ROM for Mac or Windows.

$39.95

Cognitive Technologies Corp.

3601 East West Hwy.

Chevy Chase, MD 20815

(301) 907-3955

Web site: www.cogtech.com/EXPLORER

ON-LINE RESOURCES

The Abacus: The Art of Calculating With Beads

The anatomy of the abacus, how to add and subtract using one, illustrated plans for building an abacus of your own from Lego blocks, view of the world's smallest abacus, and access to the Abacus Museum, a tour of the abacus through the ages, illustrated with color photographs.

www.ee.ryerson.ca:8080/~elf/abacus

See **Abacus** (page 187).

Archimedes and the Crown

A "Eureka story," the first in a planned series of illustrated tales for kids about real scientists and their accomplishments. "Archimedes and the Crown" tells the story of Archimedes and his bathtub, with a clear explanation of the concept of density. The story is linked to a demonstration of how to measure weight.

cyberspc.mb.ca/~dcc/eureka/crown.html

Ask Dr. Math

A wonderful site for math students and educators, with many links to math resources for kids of all ages, math problems and challenges, a list of frequently asked questions (with explanations), and a homework hot line.

forum.swarthmore.edu/dr.math/dr-math.html

Big Sky Telegraph Math Lesson Plans

A long list of math lesson plans, categorized by age group, from elementary school through high school. Topics covered include geometry, money, fractions, metric measures, Roman numerals, and much more. Some sample lesson titles: "Tree Measurement," "Using M&M Cookies to Work with Math Problems," and "Ratio Using Peanut-Butter-and-Jelly Sandwich."

gopher://bvsd.k12.co.us/11/Educational_Resources/
Lesson_Plans/Big%20Sky/math

A Brief History of Algebra

A nicely readable hypertext history of algebra. Topics include the origins of algebra, early English algebra, Boolean algebra, and algebra and computing. Includes links to biographies of famous mathematicians, word definitions, and general mathematical and historical information.

www.comlab.ox.ac.uk/oucl/users/jonathan.bowen/
algebra

Extraordinary Pi

Many many unusual and fascinating facts about pi, plus an explanation of really big numbers, from 100 to the googolplex.

www.users.globalnet.co.uk/~nickjh/Pi.htm

Also see **Pi Through the Ages** (page 199).

Fibonacci Numbers and the Golden Section

Information about Italian mathematician Leonardo Fibonacci and Fibonacci numbers, illustrated examples of Fibonacci numbers in nature, Fibonacci patterns and puzzles, plus an explanation of the "Golden Section" and its appearance in art, architecture, and music.

www.ncs.survey.ac.uk/Personal/R.Knott/Fibonacci/
fib.html

See *A Mathematical Mystery Tour* (page 186).

Fractals

Fractals for elementary and middle school students, including an explanation of what they are with beautiful examples, and instructions for making fractals of your own.

math.rice.edu/~lanius/frac

Gallery of Interactive Geometry

Geometry games and activities on-line. Users can build a rainbow, experiment with the Quasi-Tiler, which generates Penrose tiling patterns, and explore the effects of negatively curved space with a pinball game.

geom.umn.edu/apps/gallery.html

MATHEMATICS

Geometry of the Sphere

Everything you could possibly want to know about the mathematical sphere, including basic information, exercises, formulas, and theorems.

math.rice.edu/~pcmi/sphere.index.html

Great Sites for Math Teachers

Links to a math dictionary, math lesson plans for kids in grades K–12, activities and puzzles, math-related sites on-line, and information about specific math topics.

www.clarifyconnect.com/webpages/terri/sites.html

Helping Your Child Learn Math

An on-line book for parents including a long list of games and activities for kids aged 5–13. Many of these relate math to everyday life at home, at the store, or on the road. Included are lists of math-related books for adults and kids.

www.ed.gov/pubs/parents/Math

I Feel the Need for Speed

An on-line study unit in which kids learn about speed and acceleration by researching famous roller coasters, then designing a roller coaster of their own. There's an accompanying quiz, plus links to many other related sites.

www.cs.rice.edu/~jamerson/roller.html

The Internet Pizza Server

A 45-minute math lesson for kids in grades 8–12. Students make a pizza with their own choice of toppings; then "order" their digitalized creation and perform a series of pizza calculations, determining the areas of pizzas of various sizes and calculating costs and "best buys."

cs.rice.edu/~sboone/lessons/Titles/pizza.html
See **Lessons by Susan Boone** (below).

Lessons by Susan Boone

A series of creative math lessons on-line for kids in grades 8–12, including the "Internet Pizza Server" (above); "Pop Clock," in which kids study probability and predict population trends; "Indy 500," in which they use numbers from the Indianapolis 500 race to determine mean and median speeds; and "Houston Area Real-Time Traffic Report," in which they use Houston travel maps to calculate times required to travel certain distances. There's also an "Internet Scavenger Hunt," which teaches kids how to navigate the Internet.

www.cs.rice.edu/~sboone/Lessons/lptitle.html

The Math Forum

Links to a wealth of math resources, listed by subject, math education issues, and a Student Center, which includes a "Problem of the Week" (by age group) and a monthly "Internet Math Hunt" contest.

forum.swarthmore.edu

Mega-Math

A terrific site from Los Alamos National Laboratory, designed to present new and interesting math ideas to elementary and middle school students. Included are "The Most Colorful Math of All," in which kids tackle the famous four-color map problem; "Untangling the Mathematics of Knots," which includes many hands-on knots activities, among them "Seifert Surfaces," in which kids make bubble makers with knotted wire; and "A Usual Day at Unusual School," in which kids put on a play in which some characters always lie and some always tell the truth. (The trick is to figure out which is which.) There are also color-illustrated stories featuring new math concepts, illustrated explanations of the math behind each activity, and links to other interesting math sites for kids.

www.c3.lanl.gov/mega-math

The Möbius Strip

How to make a Möbius strip and what to do with it. Fun for all.

forum.swarthmore.edu/sum95/math_and/
perspective/perspect.html

Pi Through the Ages

A hypertext history of pi, with links to famous mathematicians and their methods. Users can also see the number pi calculated to 2,000 places.

www-groups.dcs.st-and.ac.uk/~history/HistTopics/
Pi_through_the-ages.html

Polyhedra

 Illustrated instructions for making and experimenting with different kinds of polyhedrons, plus links to other polyhedron-related sites.

forum/swarthmore.edu/sum95/math_and/poly/
polyhedra.html

Symmetry and Pattern: The
Art of Oriental Carpets

Students study symmetry and pattern formation with Oriental carpets. The site includes detailed information about symmetry, a color photograph gallery of Oriental carpets, and links to Islamic art sites and other educational resources.

forum.swarthmore.edu/geometry/rugs

Tesellation Tutorials

What tessellations are, how to make them, on-line activities, and links to related math, history, and geography sites.

forum/swarthmore.edu/sum95/suzanne/tess.intro.html

See **Escher, M. C.** (page 725).

MEASUREMENT

BOOKS

Incredible Comparisons

Russell Ash; Dorling Kindersley, 1996

Though all of us—especially the younger persons among us—continually ask questions such as "How big is it?" and "How fast does it go?," few of us, author Russell Ash explains, can really understand the answers unless we can compare them to something known and familiar: to the weight of a person, for example, or the speed of a car or the height of a house. Ash's book, in 63 heavily and creatively illustrated pages, brings the extraordinary down to earth, comparing the incredible to the commonplace. Each double-page spread deals with a new topic, among them the solar system, the universe, mountains, animal speed, big buildings, and the human body. One illustration, for example, shows a cross-section of the Grand Canyon with six and a half

Empire State Buildings stacked, one on top of the other, inside it; others compare the height of the Eiffel Tower to that of Angel Falls, the world's highest waterfall; and the length of a blue whale to a line of 18 swimming scuba divers. Open this book anywhere; persons of all ages will find it impossible to put down.

By the same author, see *The World in One Day* (page 202).

The Incredible Journey to the Center
of the Atom/The Incredible Journey
to the Edge of the Universe

Trevor Day and Nicholas Harris; Barnes & Noble, 1996

Thirteen illustrated steps from the farthest reaches of the universe to the subatomic particles packed in the nucleus of the atom—or turn the book upside-down and take the trip in reverse, from the infinitesimal quark to the edge of the known universe, 13 billion light-years away. The 13 steps, which include a different text and thus different information in each direction, are "Particle," "Atom," "Molecule," "DNA," "Cell," "Animal," "Soil," "Environment," "Land," "Earth," "Solar System," "Galaxy," and "Universe." Each page connects to the page before and after with see-through "windows," which give readers an additional perspective on size, coming and going.

Measuring Up: Experiments, Puzzles, and
Games Exploring Measurement

Sandra Markle; Atheneum, 1995

Clever hands-on demonstrations of the science and art of measurement for elementary and middle school–aged kids. Book chapters variously cover measuring sizes, distances, quantities, weights, temperatures, volume, perimeter, and area. Kids build clinometers (to measure heights) and odometers (to measure distance), construct rubber-band scales and mobiles, bake fortune cookies and pretzels, compare the heights of basketball players, set out on treasure hunts, and—in the shower—calculate how much water ends up running down the drain.

Powers of Ten: About the Relative
Size of Things in the Universe

Philip Morrison and Phylis Morrison; W. H. Freeman & Company, 1994

M
A
T
H
E
M
A
T
I
C
S

A journey from the most distant quasar (10^{25} m distant) to the subatomic quark (an infinitesimal 10^{-16} m) in 42 steps, each 10 times closer and smaller than the last. Each step in the exponential series is illustrated with a full-color photograph, taken from the film of the same name by Charles and Ray Eames. From remote and nearly empty space, readers move down through galactic clusters, the Milky Way, the solar system, the Earth, and the continent of North America, to an aerial view of metropolitan Chicago, two picnickers in a grassy park, a microscopic view of the skin on the hand of one picnicker, a single cell, DNA, individual atoms, and finally the unseeable subatomic particle (represented by a picture of mysterious colored dots). The scale measurements are defined at the top of each page: 10^{25} meters, for example, is the equivalent of one billion light-years; 10^4 meters, hovering above downtown Chicago, equals 10 kilometers or about 6 miles. An absorbing explanatory text accompanies each photograph, but it's in small print and intended for adult readers. Younger persons, however, will be fascinated by the pictures.

Both book and video are available from
Creative Learning Systems
16510 Via Esprillo
San Diego, CA 92127
(800) 458-2880

The Sizesaurus

Stephen Strauss; Kodansha International, 1995

A witty and wonderful reference book for persons trying to master the multifaceted world of measurement. *The Sizesaurus* is divided into two equally entertaining parts: Part I, "Essays on assays: or, how to make a ruler out of almost anything"; and Part II, "The sizesaurus" itself. Essays cover such topics as how many Big Macs it would take to cover the surface of the Atlantic Ocean, how big was the Big Bang, how many jumping Chinese it would take to start an earthquake, how hot is hell (based on the melting point of brimstone), and—given the number of good children in the world—how many seconds it should take for Santa Claus to jump down a chimney (0.0012156577). Included is a lot of wholly down-to-earth information about the history and science of measurement.

Part II, "The sizesaurus," defines and describes many different forms of measures, from *g* as in gravity through measures of distance, electrical energy, friction, light (you'll learn how many candelas are in a flash of lightning), weight, pH, pressure, radiation, sound, speed, temperature, time, and volume. Measures, listed in both metric and English systems, are presented through tables of intriguing comparisons and illustrated diagrams. A table of comparative speeds, for example, includes figures for the movement of Antarctic glaciers, the pace of the garden snail, the rate at which ketchup pours out of the bottle, and the maximum speed at which the astronauts traveled to the Moon.

An adult book, but invaluable for parents/teachers whose kids insist on knowing the number of quills on a porcupine, the weight of the Statue of Liberty, or the definition of Avogadro's number.

STATISTICS

BOOKS

Averages

Jane Jonas Srivastava; Thomas Y. Crowell, 1975

A simple picture-book explanation of the statistical concepts of average, median, and mean for 6–9-year-olds, charmingly illustrated by Aliki. Also see Srivastava's *Statistics*.

See the **Young Math Books Series** (page 181).

The Cartoon Guide to Statistics

Larry Gonick and Woollcott Smith; HarperPerennial, 1993

Information, explanations, graphs and diagrams, statistical formulas, and lots and lots of clever and comical little pictures. Cartoonist Gonick (a dropout of Harvard Graduate School in mathematics) and Woollcott Smith (a professor of statistics) begin at the very beginning with "What Is Statistics?" and then proceed rapidly through such topics as "Data Description," "Probability," "Random Variables," "A Tale of Two Distributions," "Sampling," and "Experimental Design." A clever approach for advanced students.

In an Average Day

Tom Heynman; Fawcett Columbine, 1991

Heynman details, at the rate of one large-print fact per page, what happens to the average American over the course of the average life. In an average lifetime, for example, each of us eats 4,194 quarts of popcorn, makes 184,702 telephone calls, buys 100 toothbrushes, walks 92,375 miles, and breathes 551,144,160 times. (There are a few sex statistics here and there that parents might want to censor for underage readers.)

In One Day

Tom Parker; Houghton Mifflin, 1984

A day in the life of the United States, in 365 numerical entries. In one day, readers learn, Americans collectively eat 90,000 bushels of carrots and 1,465 miles of licorice twists, build 3,000 new houses, buy 82,000 new mousetraps and 10 tons of aquarium gravel, weave 640 acres of carpet, and write 20,000 letters to the president. Many of the entries are accompanied by unforgettable drawn-to-scale graphics: a person stands next to a towering pile of aspirin, for example, to illustrate the 52 million tablets we collectively swallow each day; a page of 10,000 dots shows how many babies are born daily; and a mammoth head of cauliflower perches next to the heads on Mount Rushmore to illustrate the 750 tons of the stuff that Americans consume each day. An interesting and impressive slant on statistics.

Used Numbers Series

Susan Jo Russell, Rebecca Corwin, and Susan Friel; Dale Seymour Publications

This series of six books is designed to introduce elementary-level students to the techniques of collecting and analyzing real mathematical data. Titles in the series include *Counting: Ourselves and Our Families* (grades K–1), *Sorting: Groups and Graphs* (grades 2–3), *Measuring: From Paces to Feet* (grades 3–4), *Statistics: The Shape of Data* (grades 4–6), *Statistics: Prediction and Sampling* (grades 5–6), and *Statistics: Middles, Means, and In-Betweens* (grades 5–6). Each book contains four to six weeks' worth of project-based lessons, each with detailed instructions and examples of student questions and reactions. Younger

kids count, then sort and group, collections of everyday objects, then learn to display their acquired data in different forms of simple graphs and diagrams. Older kids analyze more complex data using line graphs and stem-and-leaf plots, identify medians and modes, and learn how to predict the statistical accuracy of a sample.

Data-collecting projects include "How long can you hold your breath?," "How many raisins are in a box?," "How many people are in a family?," and "How much taller is a fourth-grader than a first-grader?" Already collected raw numbers are provided for a number of analytical projects (heights of basketball players, weights of zoo lions). Book 5 (*Statistics: Prediction and Sampling*) includes 24 reproducible "Cat Cards," each with the photograph, name, and vital statistics of a different cat, for information gathering and analysis purposes.

Books, $13.95 each from bookstores or
Cuisenaire/Dale Seymour Publications
Box 5026
White Plains, NY 10602-5026
(800) 237-0338 or (800) 872-1100/fax (914) 328-5487
or (800) 551-RODS
Web site: www.cuisenaire.com or www.awl.com/dsp

The World in One Day

Russell Ash; Dorling Kindersley, 1997

A wonderful illustrated statistical overview of everything that happens in a single 24-hour day on earth. The information is organized by topics, among them plants, animals, the human body, food, and waste and recycling.

See **Incredible Comparisons** (page 200)

MATH HISTORY

BOOKS

Fun With Numbers

Massin; Harcourt Brace, 1973

A spectacularly illustrated picture-book history of numbers and counting systems, including Egyptian arithmetic, Sumerian time telling, Julius Caesar's calendar, and an imaginative diagram of the innards of a modern calculator. (It includes conveyor belts, pulleys, and cogs.)

How to Count Like a Martian
Glory St. John; Henry Z. Walck, Inc., 1975

A history of counting systems, from ancient times to the present, and on into the imaginary future. Young readers learn to count like the ancient Egyptians, Babylonians, Mayans, Greeks, Chinese, and Hindus. They also find out how to use an abacus, how to count in binary like a computer, and—just possibly—how to count like a Martian. Symbols of the different number systems are printed in eye-catching red.

The Librarian Who Measured the Earth
Kathryn Lasky; Little, Brown, 1994

A picture-book biography of the Greek mathematician/geographer Eratosthenes and an explanation of how—by a clever calculation involving shadows, angles, and the help of the king's best "bematists" (surveyors trained to walk with absolutely equal steps)—he managed to measure the circumference of the earth. The answer he got was 24,662 miles, a mere 200 miles off.

Mathematical Scandals
Theoni Pappas; Wide World Publishing/Tetra, 1997

Mathematical biographies, with the drama left in. Twenty-one short biographies of famous mathematicians, including Ada Byron Lovelace ("Ada Byron Lovelace's Addiction"), Plato ("Whose Solids Are They Anyway?"), Isaac Newton ("Newton's Apple Never Was"), Jean Baptiste Fourier ("Fourier Cooks His Own Goose"), and René Descartes ("I Sleep Therefore I Think"). Fascinating reading, with lots of quotations and creative illustrations. For older readers.

Mathematicians Are People, Too
Luetta Reimer and Wilbert Reimer; Dale Seymour Publications, 1990

A collection of 15 short, chatty, and thoroughly interesting biographical stories about famous mathematicians, from Thales of Miletus to Srinvasa Ramanujan. (In between: Pythagoras, Archimedes, Hypatia, John Napier, Galileo, Blaise Pascal, Isaac Newton, Leon-hard Euler, Joseph-Louis Lagrange, Sophie Germain, Carl Friedrich Gauss, Evariste Galois, and Emmy Noether.) The stories are attention-holding read-alouds and make excellent jumping-off points for more in-depth studies of mathematical concepts. Unlike *Mathematical Scandals* (above), these are specifically intended for young readers. A sequel, *Mathematicians Are People, Too: Volume 2,* tells the tales of another 12, from Euclid to Ada Lovelace.

Available through bookstores or
Cuisenaire/Dale Seymour Publications
Box 5026
White Plains, NY 10602-5026
(800) 237-0338 or (800) 872-1100/fax (914) 328-5487
or (800) 551-RODS
Web site: www.cuisenaire.com or www.awl.com/dsp

The Story of Numbers and Counting
Anita Ganeri; Evans Brothers, 1996

A history of numbers for kids, from ancient times to the present, covering counting methods and number systems, the history of money, and the invention of counting machines. The book includes a timeline and is illustrated with color photographs and drawings.

The Story of Numbers: How Mathematics Shaped Civilization
John MacLeish; Fawcett Books, 1994

The origin of math systems and concepts and their effects on the growth of civilization worldwide. The book is for teenagers and adults. A good source for those seeking to integrate math history into their educational programs.

MATH AND LITERATURE

Math and Literature Series
Math Solutions Publications

Lesson plans and activity suggestions linking mathematical concepts to popular children's books.

Titles in the series include *Math and Literature: Book One* (Marilyn Burns; 1993) and *Book Two* (Stephanie Sheffield; 1994) for kids in grades K–3; and *Math and Literature* (Rusty Bresser; 1995) for kids in grades 4–6. Lessons are based on such titles as *One Hundred Hungry Ants, The Greedy Triangle,* and *Sam Johnson and the Blue Ribbon Quilt.*

> Cuisenaire/Dale Seymour Publications
> Box 5026
> White Plains, NY 10602-5026
> (800) 237-3142 or (800) 872-1100/fax (914) 328-5487
> or (800) 551-RODS
> Web site: www.cuisenaire.com or www.awl.com/dsp

Math & Stories

Marian R. Bartch; Addison-Wesley, 1995

Math-related hands-on activities and teaching ideas to accompany 29 favorite kid's books, among them *Who Sank the Boat?, Frog and Toad Together, Ox-Cart Man, Jumanji,* and *Anno's Magic Seeds.*

Math Through Children's Literature

Kathryn L. Braddon, Nancy J. Hall, and Dale Taylor; Teacher Ideas Press, 1993

Activities and lesson plans that link works of children's literature to the NCTM mathematics standards. The book includes reproducible worksheets and a large annotated bibliography.

> $23.50
> Libraries Unlimited
> Box 6633
> Englewood, CO 80155-6633
> (303) 770-1220 or (800) 237-6124/fax (303) 220-8843
> e-mail: lu-books@lu.com
> Web site: www.lu.com

Read Any Good Math Lately? Children's Books for Mathematical Learning, K-6

David J. Whitin and Sandra Wilde; Heinemann, 1992

A large listing of popular children's books that demonstrate such mathematical principles as classification, place value, counting, addition, subtraction, multiplication, division, fractions, estimation, big

numbers, geometry, and measurement. A plot summary is included for each book, along with suggestions for projects and activities. Also see, by the same authors, *It's the Story That Counts: More Children's Books for Mathematical Learning* (Heinemann, 1995).

Storytime Mathtime

Patricia Satariano; Dale Seymour Publications, 1993

Hands-on activities, discussion questions, and lesson plans linking basic math concepts to such well-known children's picture books as *Millions of Cats, Caps for Sale,* and *Curious George Rides a Bike.* The books covers patterning skills, logic, basic arithmetic, geometry, measurement, and graphing.

> $13.95
> Cuisenaire/Dale Seymour Publications
> Box 5026
> White Plains, NY 10602-5026
> (800) 237-3142 or (800) 872-1100/fax (914) 328-5487
> or (800) 551-RODS
> Web site: www.cuisenaire.com or www.awl.com/dsp

BOOKS FOR KIDS: COUNTING

Anno's Counting Book

Mitsumasa Anno; HarperTrophy, 1986

An enchanting picture book that teaches the numbers 0 to 12 with the growth of a small village through the months of the year. The book opens (0) with an empty snow scene; by 1, there's one little house, one snowy pine tree, one bridge over the river, one snowman, and one skier; by 7, there are seven buildings, seven pine trees, seven spotted cows, a clothesline hung with seven sheets, and a rainbow striped with seven colors.

See *Anno's Hat Tricks* (page 180), *Anno's Math Games* (see page 180), *Anno's Magic Seeds* (see page 180), *The Mysterious Multiplying Jar* (see page 182), and *Socrates and the Three Little Pigs* (see page 183).

The April Rabbits

David Cleveland; Scholastic, 1993

Learn to count to 29 with rabbits. Robert begins to see mysteriously appearing rabbits. One rabbit shows up on April first, two on April second, and so on, through 29 rabbits (seen tiptoeing down the road with suitcases) on April 29. No rabbits are seen on April 30, and Robert breathes a sigh of relief. Then, on May first, one hippopotamus follows him home.

Counting Cows
Woody Jackson; Harcourt Brace, 1995

Counting backward from 10 to 0, with double-page spreads of Vermont artist Woody Jackson's black-and-white Holsteins.

Counting Wildflowers
Bruce Macmillan; Mulberry, 1995

Kids learn numbers by counting 20 different kinds of American wildflowers in beautiful full-color photographs. One is for one waterlily.

Each Orange Had Eight Slices
Paul Giganti; Mulberry, 1994

A fruity introduction to counting and simple addition.

Frogs Jump
Steven Kellogg; Scholastic, 1996

Readers count animals from 1 to 12 and back again, from 1 jumping frog and 2 diving ducks through 12 whales blowing soap bubbles.

The King's Commissioners
Aileen Friedman; Scholastic, 1995

The King wants to know how many commissioners he has appointed; his Royal Advisors attempt to answer the question by counting by twos and by fives. The confused King's problem is finally solved by his clever daughter, who reaches the answer by counting by tens, and then explains the process of counting by grouping.

One Potato: A Counting Book of Potato Prints
Diane Pomeroy; Harcourt Brace, 1996

Illustrated with colorful potato prints, the book leads young counters from 1 potato through 10 cherries, 50 blackberries, and 100 sunflower seeds. Included are instructions for making your own potato prints.

The Twelve Circus Rings
Seymour Chwast; Harcourt Brace, 1996

Colorful pictures of circus animals and performers illustrate this cumulative counting book, which proceeds, "Twelve Days of Christmas"–style, from the first circus ring (one daredevil on the high wire) to the second (one daredevil and two elephants) up to the overcrowded ring twelve.

12 Ways to Get to 11
Eve Merriam; Aladdin, 1996

The illustrations show 12 combinations that all add up to 11: 9 pine cones + 2 acorns, for example, or 4 flags + 5 rabbits + 1 pitcher of water + 1 bouquet flowers, all pulled out of a magician's hat.

What Comes in 2's, 3's, and 4's?
Suzanne Aker; Aladdin, 1992

A brightly illustrated list of things that come in twos (eyes, ears, feet), threes (tricycle wheels, traffic lights, meals), and fours (table legs, dog and cat paws).

When Sheep Cannot Sleep
Satoshi Kitamura; Farrar, Straus & Giroux, 1988

People count sheep to get to sleep, but what do sheep count? Woolly, an insomniac sheep, sets out on a counting walk, first chasing one butterfly, then watching two ladybugs, and so on.

CHESS

BOOKS

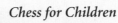
Chess for Children
Ted Nottingham, Bob Wade, and Al Lawrence; Sterling Publications, 1993

A step-by-step introduction to chess using a version of the "Lincolnshire technique," in which beginners practice with one kind of chess piece at a time, slowly adding pieces to the board until they are able to play a complete game of chess. Kids begin by playing the "Pawn Game," using nothing but the pawns. The book includes instructions, diagrams, information on chess history, and brief biographies of famous chess masters.

The Kids' Book of Chess/Book and Chess Set
9 12 Harvey Kidder; Workman, 1990

A bit of chess history, all about each chess piece, and introductory chess strategy for beginning players. A nice basic chess set, with folding board and black and white plastic pieces, accompanies the color-illustrated instruction book.

Maurice Ashley Teaches Chess
8 + The computer, unlike parents and siblings, never gets sick of playing chess; it's also an infinitely patient teacher with—in this case—a sense of humor. Based on the teaching techniques of chess coach Maurice Ashley, this software program—using a lot of clever animations—teaches kids the moves made by each piece and the basics of the game. Once these are mastered, there are chess problems to solve, 10 "master games" to study—all carefully explained by Ashley—and "Play Chess," in which kids play games with the computer, adjusting their electronic opponent to the desired skill level. Recommended for kids aged 6 and up. On CD-ROM for Windows.

$39.95
Davidson and Associates
19840 Pioneer Ave.
Torrance, CA 90503
(310) 793-0600 or (800) 545-7677/fax (310) 793-0601
Web site: www.davd.com

QuickChess
4 12 Chess, for the nervous beginner, can be an intimidating game, with its 16 pieces per player, 64-square board, and complex mathematical strategy. A solution for just such persons is "QuickChess," a pared-down version of traditional chess, designed to teach young children the moves of the game. In "QuickChess," each player has only 10 pieces to contend with—king, queen, bishop, knight, rook, and five pawns—and the game is played on a reassuringly small, 30-square board, attractively checkered in white and bright blue. Rules are clearly explained in the accompanying instruction booklet, *Queen Inja and the Champions of the Galaxy,* in which permissible moves are diagrammed and each

playing piece is given a name and a cartoon superhero persona, such as Bubba the Bishop and Nifty the Knight. (You can ignore these if you're a chess purist and prefer your games plain.) A duplicate set of instructions is laminated onto the back of the board, for those careless types who tend to lose instruction booklets.

"QuickChess," as the name implies, is quick. The average game lasts 10 to 15 minutes, which means that there's enough action in each round to satisfy players with shorter attention spans. The real advantage, however, is not speed, but simplicity: "QuickChess" teaches the fundamentals of chess in an easy-to-grasp manner without sacrificing the tactical realities of the game. A 12-year-old can enjoy it; a 4-year-old can handle it. A variation is "Centre Chess," maddeningly played on a round board.

"QuickChess," $9.95; "Centre Chess," $29.95
Amerigames International
15 Barlow Ave.
Glen Cove, NY 11542
(516) 676-8533

U.S. Chess Federation
The U.S. Chess Federation publishes *School Mates,* a bimonthly magazine for young players, and a catalog of materials for chess lovers of all ages and skills. The catalog includes instruction books and videos, electronic chess games, chess computer software, chess workbooks and puzzle collections, and chess sets in a wide range of prices, from rock-bottom cheap to hideously expensive.

U.S. Chess Federation
3054 Rte. 9W
New Windsor, NY 12553
information (914) 562-8350;
orders (800) 388-KING/fax (914) 561-CHES

CHESS ON-LINE

A History of Traditional Board Games
Information on the history of many traditional games, including chess, "Mancala," backgammon, and Parcheesi.

homepages.which.net/~james.masters/Traditional
Games/TraditionalBoardGames.htm

ECONOMICS FOR KIDS

Mathematics is intended not only to prepare kids for mathematically oriented careers in astrophysics, biochemistry, and accounting, but also to provide them with the numerical skills essential for daily life. This is perhaps best done by simply integrating arithmetic lessons into the day's occupations, encouraging the kids to calculate best buys at the supermarket, to compare sale prices at department stores, and to participate in the formulation of the family budget and the paying of the family bills. Daily living as practiced by us, however, never quite seems to leave room for participatory arithmetic. Our trips to the grocery store are often a matter of snatch-and-run while en route—usually somewhat late—to other appointments; and our personal budgeting and financial record-keeping skills are nothing we want to hold up as models to the impressionable young.

Since our real-life family finances have nothing to offer in the way of consistent and rewarding learning experiences, we devised—when Josh was ten, Ethan eight, and Caleb just turned seven—a hands-on economics program of our own. The result—part game, part slapstick comedy, part mathematical challenge—lasted over three years, was an unfailing source of entertainment, and gave the kids a feel for the process of real-life money management. At the beginning, each boy laid the groundwork for the program by establishing an imaginary home and business, complete with business cards and distinctive logos, diagrammed building plans, pets, and means of transportation. Josh thus became the proprietor of the Black Cat Bookstore (Rare and Old Books); Ethan became a freelance astronomer, supported by a research grant from the National Star Association; and Caleb became the owner of the Movement Robot Store, a small factory devoted to the manufacture of robots, all with amazing abilities.

Props for the program included packets of checks, deposit slips, and transaction record books left over from old banking accounts. We launched the program by providing each business with a wholly imaginary bank balance of $1,000. Thereafter, each week or so, each businessperson received a handful of envelopes, each containing index cards on which were recorded various financial happenings: profits and losses, routine bills, unexpected expenses. The boys deposited money in their checking accounts, made car and insurance payments, paid telephone and electric bills, bought fuel, and paid taxes. They also, weekly, unlike their reprehensible parents, balanced their checkbooks.

Here are a few samples from the weekly envelopes:

JOSH: THE BLACK CAT BOOKSTORE

1. It's the first of the month. The rent on your store is due. Write a check to your Evil Landlord for $400.

2. A book of short stories that you bought for $5 is found to contain a vacation postcard written by Edgar Allan Poe. You sell the book and postcard to a collector for $225. Calculate your profit. Deposit the money in your checking account.

3. You've been making phone calls to your pen pal in Saskatchewan again. Pay the Phone Company $77.95.

ETHAN: ASTRONOMER AT LARGE

1. Your salary check has just arrived from the National Star Association. You made $425.75. Deposit it in your checking account.

2. It's going to be a long, cold winter. You'd better buy some firewood. You buy 5 cords of seasoned hardwood for $75 per cord. How much do you spend? Write a check for the total to Paul Bunyan.

3. A large pinecone fell on your telescope. Repairs cost $56.50. Write a check to the Telescope Repair Shop.

CALEB: THE MOVEMENT ROBOT STORE

1. The Duck Farmers' Collective buys three of your new egg-collecting robots at $100 apiece. Deposit the money in your checking account.

2. Have you been sleeping with the lights on again? You have just received your household electric bill. Pay the Power Company $82.50.

3. It is your dear grandma's birthday. Buy her a purple umbrella and a box of chocolates. Write a check for $22.95 to the Gift Shop.

There are endless permutations of all this: medical and car insurance payments come due; state and federal income taxes must be paid (we made extra copies of the official forms for the boys); donations are made to worthy charities; pets are taken to the vet for rabies shots. The astronomer receives an award for discovering a comet; the Black Cat Bookstore wins a prize for Best Storefront Halloween Decorations; the Movement Robot Store owner invents a poodle-grooming machine that sells like hotcakes when the American Poodle Society holds a meeting in town. There are commercial versions of such business- and consumer-style math games, but none ever had the appeal of our personalized homemade game—or offered quite as much opportunity for player invention and involvement.

Those interested in establishing a similar battery of imaginary businesses need very little in the way of materials. Personalized "checks" can be designed and reproduced by computer printer or copy machine: include kid's name, business name, and address. Any small notebook can serve as a transaction record book. Divide pages into columns for check number, date, transaction description, payment or deposit, and balance. Add envelopes, index cards, and imagination.

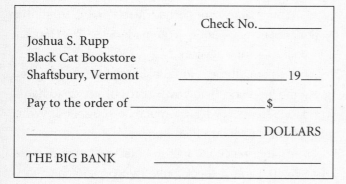

Check No. _____

Joshua S. Rupp
Black Cat Bookstore
Shaftsbury, Vermont _____ 19___

Pay to the order of _____ $_____

_____ DOLLARS

THE BIG BANK _____

ORGANIZATIONS

Academy for Economic Education

The Academy for Economic Education, a nonprofit organization, distributes assorted educational information for young learners, notably the truly delightful *Ump's Fwat: An Annual Report for Young People,* illustrated by Marilyn Sadler. Ump is a business-minded caveperson; the "fwat" is his landmark invention, the Stone Age version of a baseball bat. In combination, they make a clever vehicle for elementary-level explanations of the law of supply and demand, and the concepts of profit, loss, investment, stocks, and dividends.

$3; for an additional $3, there's an accompanying teacher's manual
Academy for Economic Education
125 Nationsbank Center
Richmond, VA 23277
(804) 643-0071

MAGAZINES

7 12 *Faces: Economics*

This multicultural periodical for kids aged 7–12 (see *Faces,* page 411) has published two issues of interest to young economists. The theme of the September 1988 issue, titled "What Is Money?," is historical and unusual money worldwide. Article topics include the "spirit money" of China, the laws of barter in 10th-century Ireland (yearly wages for a shipbuilder: four cows), and the story of the New York Stock Exchange.

The October 1991 issue, "Going to Market," is an overview of the international business world, past and present. Articles cover old English and modern Guatemalan markets, Asian bazaars, auctions, and the world commodities market. Also included is a short biography of Rowland Hussey Macy, founder of Macy's department stores.

Back issues of *Faces* are available at most libraries or $4.50 each from
Cobblestone Publishing, Inc.
30 Grove St.
Peterborough, NH 03458
(603) 924-7209 or (800) 821-0115/fax (603) 924-7380
e-mail: custsvc@cobblestone.mv.com
Web site: www.cobblestonepub.com

9 13 *Zillions: Consumer Reports for Kids*

A splashy bimonthly magazine for young consumers loosely based on the adult magazine *Consumer Reports.* Each issue reviews and evaluates popular products of interest to kids. The magazine also includes general-interest articles on jobs for young people, money management, advertising, and the benefits of educated consumerism. Aimed at a middle school–aged audience.

Annual subscription (8 issues), $16
Zillions
Box 54861

MATHEMATICS

Boulder, CO 80322
(800) 234-2078

BOOKS: NONFICTION

The Annual Report of the United States of America

Meredith E. Bagby; HarperBusiness

The First Annual Report was written in 1994 by Meredith Bagby, then an undergraduate at Harvard College. The book sums up, in 47 crystal-clear pages, the economic, social, and international state of the nation, displayed in straightforward tables and graphs, with a short supportive text. Also included: a two-page summary of the expanded federal budget and a list of the salaries of federal officials. A diagrammed dollar bill on the opening page gives a quick lowdown on where each of our tax dollars go (3 cents to education, 14 cents to welfare, 19 cents to defense, and 14 cents to interest on the national debt). An appendix in the back lists the names of all major government officials, and names, addresses, and telephone numbers of all U.S. Senators and Representatives. Updated annually.

See **On-line National Budget Simulation** (page 214) and **U.S. National Debt Clock** (page 214).

From Gold to Money

Ali Mitgutsh; Carolrhoda, 1985

A simple 24-page picture book explaining where money comes from, beginning with an underground gold mine and ending with the government mint. One of the "Start to Finish Books" (see page 229).

Money

Joe Cribb; Alfred A. Knopf, 1990

Money is a volume in the ever-increasing *Eyewitness* series, a collection of informational books on a wide range of topics, each heavily illustrated with impressive full-color photographs. *Money* covers such topics as the history of coins and paper money, the minting process, counterfeit money, foreign money (past and present), and coin collecting. Included, among many others, are photographs of Greek and Roman coins, American continental bills, German talers, Venetian ducats, Viking pennies, Yukon gambling tokens, Japanese yen, Sudanese ring money, and Spanish pieces of eight.

Money Doesn't Grow on Trees: A Parent's Guide to Raising Financially Responsible Children

Neale S. Godfrey and Carolina Edwards; Simon & Schuster, 1994

A guide to teaching principles of good money management to kids from three through college age. The book begins with a "Financial Personality Type" quiz for kids and adults; then proceeds to discuss money management, savings accounts, budgets, wise consumerism, and the "Terrible T's: Tipping, Taxes, Tickets, Tokens, and Tolls." Includes money management goals for kids of different ages.

The One and Only Common Sense/Cents Series

Neale S. Godfrey; Silver Press, 1995

There are three picture books in this series of money-related books targeted at kids aged 5–9: *Why Money Was Invented; Here's the Scoop: Follow an Ice-Cream Cone Around the World;* and *A Money Adventure: Earning, Saving, Spending, Sharing.* Each is 32 pages long. In *Why Money Was Invented*, the Green$treet$ kids—after finding out that Mr. Bear, the ice-cream truck driver, won't trade ice-cream cones for marbles— learn about trading, bargaining, and the history of money. In *Here's the Scoop* the kids are whizzed around the world, tracking down all the ingredients of an ice-cream cone: to Wisconsin for milk, Costa Rica for sugar, Madagascar for vanilla, Australia for mint, and Brazil for chocolate. A recipe is included for making your own mint chocolate chip ice cream. In *A Money Adventure*, the kids start a frozen fruit pop business, investing money in supplies, advertising, sharing their profits, and opening savings accounts at the local bank.

The Story of Money

Betsy Maestro; Clarion, 1993

"A long time ago," begins this very thorough historical picture book, "there was no such thing as money." Maestro covers early barter systems, the Sumerians and the first metal money, the first coins (from the ancient kingdom of Lydia in Turkey, stamped with lions' heads), the Chinese invention of paper money, American colonial money, modern money, the U.S. Mint, and the Bureau of Engraving and Printing.

 10 + *Whatever Happened to Penny Candy?*
Richard J. Maybury; Bluestocking Press, 1989

This book is one of the best resources we've found for explaining the ins and outs of the economy to children. About 120 pages long in paperback, it consists of a series of short letters written to a curious ninth-grader named Chris by his/her economically savvy Uncle Eric. Uncle Eric begins by defining *coin* and explaining why modern quarters—which, sadly, are no longer true coins—have those little ridges all around the edges. From there, he proceeds to explain inflation, wage/price spirals, recession, and depression, all in readily understandable, reader-friendly bite-size pieces, and finishes up with a supplementary bibliography and a collection of catchy economic quotes by everyone from Laura Ingalls Wilder to Lenin.

Readers also get the scoop on why candy can no longer be bought for a penny at the local corner store. Candy didn't go up, Uncle Eric explains. The penny went down. The book in intended for teenagers, but can be absorbed and enjoyed by younger children. Excellent for reading aloud and discussion. By the same author, also see *The Money Mystery* (Bluestocking Press, 1997) and *The Clipper Ship Strategy* (Bluestocking Press, 1997).

$9.95

Bluestocking Press

Box 2030

Shingle Springs, CA 95682-2030

(916) 621-1123 or (800) 959-8586/fax (916) 642-9222

By the same author, see *Whatever Happened to Justice?* (page 587), *Are You Liberal? Conservative? Or Confused?* (see page 580), *Ancient Rome: How It Affects You Today* (see page 620), and *Evaluating Books: What Would Thomas Jefferson Think About This?*

BOOKS: FICTION

 5 9 *Alexander Who Used to Be Rich Last Sunday*
Judith Viorst; Aladdin, 1980

Alexander blows his only dollar in a series of unfortunate purchases and investments, among them a snake rental. A clever picture book for 5–9-year-olds.

 9 12 *All the Money in the World*
Bill Brittain; HarperCollins, 1992

Quentin captures a leprechaun and wishes for all the money in the world, an act that has unexpectedly far-reaching economic repercussions. A chapter book for 9–12-year-olds.

5 9 *The Berenstain Bears' Trouble With Money*
Stan and Jan Berenstain; Random House, 1983

Brother and Sister Bear start out as spendthrifts but learn to be responsible wage earners and savers. One of the popular Berenstain Bear series, for readers aged 5–9.

5 9 *The Go-Around Dollar*
Barbara Adams; Simon & Schuster, 1992

The picture-book story of a dollar bill, first found abandoned in the park, which changes hands over and over until finally coming to rest, framed, as the first dollar earned at a new store.

6 10 *If You Made a Million*
David M. Schwartz; Mulberry, 1994

A delightful picture-book tour of the world of money making under the tutelage of Marvelosissimo, the starry-robed magician. Busy kids start out earning a penny (for feeding a fish) and work their way up, bit by bit, to earning a million dollars for taming an obstreperous small ogre. ("A million dollars! That's a stack of pennies ninety-five miles high, or enough nickels to fill a school bus, or a whale's weight in quarters.") Topics covered, in lighthearted fashion, include equivalent values of money, checks and checking accounts, bank loans, and interest.

8 12 *Make Four Million Dollars by Next Thursday!*
Stephen Manes; Skylark, 1996

In this short chapter book, Jason Nozzle, in search of his lost allowance, finds an abandoned book in the woods: *Make Four Million Dollar$ By Next Thur$day!* by Dr. K. Pinkerton Silverfish. Following Dr. Silverfish's

MATHEMATICS

hilarious instructions exactly, Jason sets out to become a multimillionaire.

Treehorn's Treasure
Florence Parry Heide; Holiday House, 1981

The leaves on the tree in Treehorn's back yard turn into dollar bills overnight, but nobody believes him when he points this out.

Also see *The Shrinking of Treehorn* (page 107) and *The Problem With Pulcifer* (page 107).

GAMES AND HANDS-ON ACTIVITIES

Allowance Calculator
ALL The "Allowance Calculator Financial Learning System" is intended to teach kids the value of money, the benefits of responsible hard work, and the virtues of saving for established long-term goals. This is all done with a pair of erasable weekly plastic charts (with magnets on the back, suitable for attaching to the family refrigerator) and an *Allowance Calculator* checkbook, which includes 15 professional-looking checks and a transaction record for noting one's personal profits and losses. The charts allow each participating kid to keep track of money earned, through performance of daily listed chores and assignments, or money lost, through nonperformance of the same or other miscellaneous misbehaviors.

Money is earned by completing the chores listed on the upper half of the chart: the pink-and-green Phase I chart, for 4–9-year-olds, lists such responsibilities as making your bed, picking up your room, setting and clearing the table, helping your parents, and going to bed on time; the blue-and-purple Phase II chart, for 10–15-year-olds, includes taking out the trash, doing dishes, feeding pets, and baby-sitting for younger siblings. There are also a couple of blank spaces to be filled in with quirky individualized chores: if you're willing to pay your kids for alphabetizing the family library, washing the family pickup truck, or licking stamps for the family mail-order business, you write it in here. Money is lost by performing any of the evil acts listed on the bottom half of the chart: lying, interrupting, leaving a mess, and neglecting homework are

all penalized, and there's a space for adding on particular sins ("Chasing cats with the tractor") of your own.

Parents fill in amounts of cash they're willing to pay out or deduct for any or all of the above; kids keep track of their daily performances with check marks and, at the end of each day, tote up all amounts earned or lost. A grand total is computed at the end of the week; then the chart is erased with a damp cloth and is ready to be used again. Money can either be handed over in cash or deposited in each child's "checking account," in which case when your kid wants to buy something, he/she writes a check to you for "cash" and records the deduction in his/her transaction record book.

The system was developed by an investment counselor (and father of three) as a means of teaching kids money management; it's also said to lead to a "smoother-running home," which always sounds hopeful to those of us who don't have one.

The "System," which includes Allowance Calculator chart, Goal Reminder chart, and checkbook, $14.95; individual Allowance Calculator charts (one for each kid), $4.95; extra checkbooks, $4
TBSC Learning Systems, Inc.
Box 2493
Grand Rapids, MI 49501-2493
(616) 957-1130 or (800) 209-4800

The Buck Book
ALL Anne Akers Johnson; Klutz Press, 1993

The book, which comes with a crisp new one-dollar bill encased in plastic, is subtitled "All Sorts of Things to Do With a Dollar Bill Besides Spend It." Instructions are included for turning your dollar bill into seven nonmonetary things, among them a bow tie, a jumping frog, and an elephant. The book also includes many interesting snippets of information about the history of the dollar bill.

Available through bookstores or
Klutz Press
2121 Staunton Ct.
Palo Alto, CA 94306
(415) 857-0888

Budget Town from Budget City
Board-game versions of real-life finances. In "Budget Town," players advance their pieces around the

board dealing with amounts of cash up to $130. Players variously acquire money by working overtime, recycling, or accumulating interest on a savings account; they spend it on groceries, transportation, or the paying off of charge account debts.

In "Budget City," life becomes more complicated: players are equipped with cash, credit cards, deposit slips, checks, check and savings register sheets, certificates of deposit (CDs), and budget sheets. As they proceed around the playing board, they deal with grocery and utility bills, rent, transportation costs, and taxes, plus a lot of niggling little necessities such as haircuts, medical checkups, newspaper subscriptions, and trips to the movies. "Budget Town" is recommended for players aged 5 and up; "Budget City," for players aged 8 and up.

"Budget Town," $49; "Budget City," $59
Attainment Co., Inc.
504 Commerce Pkwy.
Verona, WI 53593
(800) 327-4269
Web site: www.attainment-inc.com

Building Toothpick Bridges

Jeanne Pollard; Dale Seymour Publications, 1985

A 10-day project in which kids in small groups act as architectural firms, each contracted to build a strong and economical bridge (from toothpicks) to specified building codes while staying within a fixed budget. Project Day 1 is spent discussing basic principles of bridge design; on Day 2, students form construction companies, assign jobs, and receive $1,500,000 for total building expenses. Subsequent days are spent in designing and constructing bridges, which involves purchasing supplies and keeping accurate financial records. Supplies aren't cheap—toothpicks cost $10,000 apiece (more on Day 8 when inflation generates a price hike) and welding material (white glue) runs $1,000 per bottle capful. On the final day of the project, bridges are tested for strength by suspending weights from a bar placed across the middle; the bridge that holds the most weight (for a period of at least 30 seconds) gets an award.

The book, a 32-page paperback, includes information, instructions, and reproducible student worksheets, bridge planning paper, company checks,

purchase order forms, and balance sheets. Recommended for kids in grades 5–9.

$10.95
Cuisenaire/Dale Seymour Publications
Box 5026
White Plains, NY 10602-5026
(800) 237-3142 or (800) 872-1100/fax (914) 328-5487
or (800) 551-RODS
Web site: www.cuisenaire.com or www.awl.com/dsp

Coin Collecting

For a financial connection to geography and history, try collecting coins. One source for beginning collectors is the Worldwide Treasure Bureau, whose catalog—along with ancient Greek tetradrachms ($1,675 apiece), which are fun to look at—carries an introductory coin set ("50 Coins From 50 Different Countries") for students.

The set, including a labeled illustration sheet, $19.95
Worldwide Treasure Bureau
Box 5012
Visalia, CA 93278-5012
(800) 437-0222/fax (209) 732-3930
For more information on coin-collecting, contact
American Numismatic Society
155th and Broadway
New York, NY 10032
(212) 234-3130

An Income of Her Own

A board game of savvy business practice targeted at girls (but anyone can play) and intended to familiarize participants with the concepts of money management, financial record keeping, legal and tax issues, and business ethics.

$38
Independent Means, Inc.
Box 987
Santa Barbara, CA 93102
(805) 646-1215, (800) 350-2978 or (800) 350-1816
Web site: www.AnIncomeofHerOwn.com

Money: Denarius to Decimal

A portfolio of essays, illustrations, and historical document reproductions. "Money: Denarius to Deci-

M
A
T
H
E
M
A
T
I
C
S

mal" covers the history of money, from the development of the first coins and tokens through the introduction of paper money, early coin design and minting, the adoption of the British decimal system, forgeries, and modern treasury issues.

The portfolio contains four historical "Broadsheet Essays" ("The Beginnings of Money," "The Making of Money," "The Penny," and "The Change to Decimals") and 11 historical documents or resource materials, including a map showing the spread of the dollar, an excerpt from 13th-century Exchequer records listing rules for the making of silver coins, a proposal of 1695 advocating decimal currency, picture sheets of gold and silver coins, and samples of paper money from several countries. The portfolio also includes a study guide with reproducible student worksheets.

$37

Jackdaw Publications

Box 503

Amawalk, NY 10501

(800) 789-0022/fax (800) 962-9101

Moneywise Kids

Two math games in one for kids aged 7 and up. In game one, "Bill Maker," players roll dice in turn, accumulating earnings (in lime green paper dollars). On each turn, players exchange smaller denominations for larger, and roll the dice to earn more, eventually building up to a winning $100 bill.

Game two, "Bill Breaker," is a bit more challenging. Kids roll dice to earn money, with which they purchase "Moneywise Markers," each representing one of life's expensive little essentials: taxes, medical care, housing, clothing, transportation, and food. Markers are drawn from a pool in the center of the playing area, which means that marker-choosing players risk snagging a financial disaster Marker, such as Sick ("Miss a turn or pay $10 if you don't have health care) and Hit a Pot Hole ("Miss a turn or pay $10 if you haven't paid taxes"). "Bill Breaker" costs are in amounts easily managed by young children, which means they are far from realistic—taxes, for example, are a cool $15—but the game does give players a grasp of where money goes and why. Winner is the first person to collect all six Moneywise Markers, plus $100 in savings.

$15

Aristoplay

450 S. Wagner Rd.

Ann Arbor, MI 48107

(800) 634-7738 or (888) GR8-GAME

fax (734) 995-4611

Web site: www.aristoplay.com

Presto Change-O

A board game of saving, spending, and making change, recommended for kids in grades 2–4. The game comes with a lush supply of paper bills and plastic coins; players hop their pawns around the illustrated board—with a picture of a coin-juggling magician in the middle—earning small amounts of money ("Lose a tooth: earn $1.50") and spending it ("Buy a book: spend $1.20"). First player to save $10 wins the game.

$24.95

Educational Insights

16941 Keegan Ave.

Carson, CA 90764

(800) 933-3277/fax (310) 605-5048 or (800) 995-0506

Web site: www.edin.com

AUDIOVISUAL ECONOMICS

The Muffin Market

A model of supply and demand for high school–aged students in which participants run a muffin shop and attempt to make a profit. The study includes a video, a computer simulation, and assorted instructional materials.

Federal Reserve Bank of San Francisco

Public Information

Mail Stop 1110

101 Market St.

San Francisco, CA 94105

(415) 974-2163/fax (415) 974-3341

e-mail: Publications@sf.frb.org

Piggy Banks to Money Markets

A 30-minute video aimed at kids aged 5–12, though more appropriate for viewers at the younger end of the scale. It is attention-grabbing and nicely done, combining narration by money-making (and -spending) kids, animation, and music. Topics covered include "What is money?," "How do you use money?," "How do people get money?," "How can kids make money?," and "What do you do with money when you get it?" All the details are supplied by assorted articulate and ambitious kids, including TJ, who works at his uncle Jack's recycling plant, Dian, who plays the piano at birthday parties, Adam, who throws a yard sale, and Elizabeth, who helps her mother in the garden. TJ has the best line in the show, Uncle Jack's secret of business: "Buy low, sell high, and keep good records."

$14.95
KIDVIDZ
618 Centre St.
Newton, MA 02158
(617) 965-3345

ECONOMICS ON-LINE

A Brief History of Our Nation's Paper Money

The site covers such topics as Colonial and Continental currency, the Free Banking Era, the Civil War, and the National Bank Act, each in a few short paragraphs of text, illustrated with a color photograph of historical paper money.

www.frbsf.org/frbsf/pubs/annualrpt/history.html

EcEd Web

Suggestions and plans for teaching economics to students in grades K–12 to college level, ideas for teaching economics using the Internet, and links to associations of economics educators.

ecedweb.unomaha.edu

Great Economists and Their Times

Short biographies of 10 great economists, among them Adam Smith, Karl Marx, Thorstein Veblen, and John Maynard Keynes, descriptions of the major schools of economic theory, and an economic timeline.

www.frsbf.org/econedu/unfrmd.great/greattimes.html

After working through the lives and times of the great economists (above), students can test their new knowledge with the on-line game "Treasure Hunt," in which they complete a series of fill-in-the-blank questions to unlock keys to the treasure.

www.frbsf.org/econedu/curriculum/treshunt/begin hunt.html

On-Line National Budget Simulation

A site for all who have wanted to get their hands on the national budget. In this simulation, students are asked to cut the 1995 fiscal deficit to get a balanced national budget.

garnet.berkeley.edu:3333/budget/budget.html

See *The Annual Report of the United States of America* (page 209) and **U.S. National Debt Clock** (below).

U.S. National Debt Clock

A study in big numbers. The site shows the size of the national debt at the present time, the estimated population of the United States, and each citizen's personal share of the debt. (Last time I checked, this came to something over $20,000.)

www.brillig.com/debt_cloak

See *The Annual Report of the United States of America* (page 209) and **On-Line National Budget Simulation** (above).

SCIENCE

Science is an astonishment and a delight.

CARL SAGAN

Science illiteracy is said to affect ninety percent of us. Americans, by and large, perform abysmally when asked to produce a definition of DNA, an assessment of the causes of acid rain, or an explanation of why the leaves turn color in fall. In one depressing survey, nearly twenty percent of those questioned insisted that the sun circles around the earth; over sixty percent thought that people coexisted with dinosaurs; and hardly anybody knew what an electron was. American students are repeatedly outstripped by their peers in other developed countries—notably in studious Japan, Korea, and Germany—on science achievement tests.

This collective failure to understand basic scientific concepts has ominous implications for both our national future and our personal lives. The public these days is continually called upon to make science-based decisions. Do power lines cause cancer? Are genetically engineered vegetables dangerous? Is recycling cost-effective? Should we save the spotted owl? Without a solid science education, citizens have little to go on in making these decisions and are prey to buzz words, slogans, and propaganda.

Given the central role of science in today's world, what should constitute an effective science education? The recommended public school course of science study begins with simple general science: kids in the early elementary grades study plants and animals and their habitats, the weather and the seasons of the year, the solar system, magnetism and electricity, light and color, energy and its sources, and simple machines. In the upper elementary and middle school grades, kids investigate the same topics in greater depth, learning about plant and animal classification, human anatomy and physiology, sound, light, and heat, ecology and the environment, and the basics of chemistry, geology, and astronomy. Ninth-grade science typically concentrates on the earth sciences, along with introductory physics and chemistry: kids study the history of the earth, weather and climate, the water cycle, the atmosphere, atomic structure and molecular theory, energy, and simple and complex machines. Tenth-grade science centers around general biology and genetics; eleventh-grade science is usually an intensive course in chemistry; and twelfth-grade science, physics. My husband and I, both educated in this fashion, became scientists, which seems to indicate that the system works.

There's nothing sacred about this structured progression, however, and the truth of the matter is that a genuine interest in stars, spiders, dinosaurs, or rockets will inspire more science learning than any set of textbook exercises. Furthermore, almost any scientific interest inevitably involves a well-rounded range of disciplines. A study of plants, for example—perhaps starting with a windowsill geranium or backyard tomato bush—leads to investigations of plant classification and habitats, plant anatomy and physiology, ecology, chemistry, entomology, and meteorology. "What kind of plant is *this?*" your kids will ask. "What's

a flower press? How do you make one?" "What's inside a seed?" "Where *is* the chlorophyll inside the plant? Is it in the plant's cells?" "If chlorophyll makes leaves green, what kinds of chemicals make flowers blue and red?" "Why do leaves fall off the trees before winter?" "What makes spruce trees sticky?" "How come sequoias don't grow on the East Coast?" "What's an aphid?"

Science, in our at-home program, has been the academic field most subject to intense in-depth enthusiasms. Ethan, our middle son, spent his sixth, seventh, and eighth years obsessed with marine biology, oceanography, and all scientific aspects of water. We read immense numbers of books about the oceans, marine life (large and small), ships (ancient, modern, and famous), submarines, bathyscaphes, and the exploits of Jacques Cousteau. Also included were a massive tome called *The Encyclopedia of Fish*, which Ethan—and only Ethan—adored, and Robert Ballard's books on his undersea discoveries of the *Titanic,* the *Bismarck,* and the Roman *Isis.* We visited aquariums; we raised fish, snails, and hermit crabs; we collected and classified shells. We adopted a whale and listened to audiotapes of whale songs. We watched ocean-related videos— everything from National Geographic specials to *Moby Dick*—and we played endless rounds of ocean-related games (see page 321). We experimented with techniques for mapping the ocean floor and turned out quite a nice contour map using a ruler and a dishpan ocean, filled with continental shelves and underwater mountains made of (horrendous amounts of) modeling clay. Ethan built a model submarine and a working periscope; he studied pond water specimens under the microscope; and we tried to persuade him to try dissecting a fish, but he balked. He and his brothers took a marine biology class at a local science center, where they experimented with water pressure, temperature gradients, and salt concentrations, learned about tides, were allowed to handle sea cucumbers and sea urchins, and got up-close looks at piranhas and electric eels. In the summer, we went snorkeling. This interest went on so long that we began to take it for granted that Ethan would be a marine biologist or oceanographer when he grew up.

Then, abruptly, the fascination with the ocean was gone—replaced by an avid interest in airplanes, aerodynamics, and anything having to do with flight. Airplanes led to rockets; rockets to astronomy; and Ethan's prime interest today is physics, which is why we presently have strings of pulleys hanging from the main beam in the middle of the living room.

Josh, enthralled by entomology, raised butterflies, built a bug-collecting box and populated it with many temporary residents, established an ant farm, dissected a gigantic grasshopper, cultured fruit flies, and bred crickets. This last, an exciting and memorable experiment, had unexpected ramifications: the crickets, ordered from the Carolina Biological Supply Company (see page 221), arrived in a cardboard ice-cream container. When we opened it, crickets erupted hysterically all over the dining room, and the brighter and more alert specimens seized upon this opportunity to vanish forever under the floorboards. There they loudly flourished for months, while we studied their captive mates.

Caleb, our youngest son, went through a dinosaur phase, took a turn through space flight, and then returned to paleontology. His bookcase is full of fossils and a balsa-wood tyrannosaur skeleton teeters next to his bedside lamp.

Science, however, is much more than a collection of facts and figures about submarines, crickets, and dinosaurs. The essence of science is its method. The scientific method—the ordered process of question, hypothesis, experiment, and data analysis by which we discover truths—is one of the greatest achievements of humankind. Using it, we have discovered quarks, quasars, penicillin, planets, and plastic—and ruled out spontaneous generation, Lamarckian evolution, cold fusion, and the theory that the earth is flat. The scientific method is the foundation upon which my husband and I have tried to base our kids' education: the understanding that science at heart is a verb rather than a noun, a process rather than a body of knowledge, a reasoned technique for making sense of the world.

From my homeschool journal:

◆ **April 17, 1990. Josh is eight; Ethan, seven; Caleb, five.**

We started a new unit study today on eggs, using homemade workbooks. The first project centered on what is reputedly the first written description of the hot-air balloon principle: a 2,000-year-old Chinese account of an experiment in which eggshells containing bits of burning tinder were made to rise up into the air. We emptied out some eggshells, and the boys spent over two hours trying to find a way to make them fly. They tried several different kinds of tinder (including paper scraps, a shredded cotton ball, and broken toothpicks), experimented with various sizes of holes in the emptied eggshells, and tried blowing through a straw to direct more air into the eggshell. Josh made a complicated system of fuses leading to the tinder inside his egg; Ethan tried a whole series of eggshells containing gradually increasing amounts of tinder, from a few tiny scraps to a stuffed handful; Caleb tried holding a candle inside his eggshell.

Nobody got an eggshell to so much as twitch, but they came up with a number of hypotheses to explain their failure. "Maybe the Chinese writer used a different-size eggshell—a really tiny egg like a hummingbird egg or a huge egg like an ostrich egg." "Maybe he had a special kind of tinder that burned better than ours did." "Maybe"—Ethan—"he used gunpowder!"

I was tickled with the whole episode. Even though nothing worked as hoped, this was real science: the boys formulated hypotheses, tested them, learned from the results, and went on to try something else. They learned a lot about how scientists operate—plus acquired a firm grasp of the hot-air balloon principle (hot air rises) and discovered that fire needs air to burn.

We made scrambled eggs for lunch.

GENERAL SCIENCE

ORGANIZATIONS

National Science Teachers Association

An organization for professional science teachers and other interested adults. A membership costs between $50 and $100 per year, depending on the number of the association's four professional journals one subscribes to: choices include *Science and Children* (grades K–8), *Science Scope* (5–9), *The Science Teacher* (7–12), and *The Journal of College Science Teaching.* Membership also includes a subscription to *NSTA Reports,* the Association's bimonthly newsletter, and a discount on items from the NSTA catalog. The catalog, available to nonmembers upon request, is a 50+-page collection of science-oriented teaching tools for kids of all ages: books, activity books, curriculum guides, posters, and models.

> NSTA
> 1840 Wilson Blvd.
> Arlington, VA 22201-3000
> (703) 243-7100 or (800) 722-NSTA
> fax (703) 522-6091
> Web site: www.nsta.org

MAGAZINES

Atom

A bimonthly science magazine for kids aged 9–12. Each issue contains several illustrated feature articles on a range of scientific and mathematical topics, such as lightning, whales, infinite numbers, and the geology of the Grand Canyon. Regular departments include "Space Scoop," on astronomical events and missions, "Science Reporter," interviews with scientists and researchers, and "Water World," on oceanographic studies and events. The magazine also carries science news, book and CD reviews, computer and Internet updates, and brain-tickling problems and puzzles.

Cogniz, a sister publication in similar format, targets teenagers.

> Annual subscription to each (6 issues), $25
> New World Publishers
> Box 7216
> Austin, TX 78713-7216
> (888) 397-5264/fax (512) 495-9667
> Web site: www.atom-cogniz.com

Connect

A 20-page magazine of resource ideas, classroom-tested projects and activities, teaching suggestions, and innovative approaches to science and math for kids in grades K–8.

> Annual subscription (5 issues), $20
> Teacher's Laboratory
> Box 6480
> Brattleboro, VT 05302
> (800) 769-6199

See **Teachers' Laboratory** (page 224).

Current Science

Articles, photographs, and suggested hands-on activities for the physical, earth, and life sciences for kids in grade 6 and up, from the publishers of *Weekly Reader* (see page 160).

> A single subscription (26 issues), $29.95; two to nine subscriptions, $16.50 each
> Weekly Reader Corp.
> 3001 Cindel Dr.
> Delran, NJ 08370
> (800) 446-3355

Discover

A monthly magazine stuffed with articles on all aspects of science, from dinosaurs and dolphins to supernovas and subatomic particles, all written by a bevy of talented science writers. Each issue includes five or six feature articles, assorted shorter columns on recent scientific discoveries and advances ("Breakthroughs," "Technology Watch," "Evolution Watch," "Animal Watch," "Health Watch"), and a number of regular departments, among them Bob Berman's "Night Watchman" on astronomical events and phenomena, "Vital Signs" on mysteries of medicine, and "Light Elements," essays on the funny side of science. One annual issue is devoted to the major events of the year in all fields of science. *Discover*'s intended audience is adult, but it is accessible to advanced student readers and a terrific resource for all designers of kids' science programs.

> Annual subscription (12 issues), $34.95
> *Discover*
> Box 420105
> Palm Coast, FL 32142-0105
> (800) 829-9132
> Web site: www.enews.com/magazines/discover

Dragonfly

A science magazine for kids in grades 3–6 from the National Science Teachers Association and Miami University. Each issue centers around a major theme—"Trees," "Flight"—and includes informative articles by research scientists, student essays, poems, and artwork, interviews with professional scientists, and suggestions for student activities. A "Home Companion" with teaching hints and ideas for family projects is included in each issue.

Annual subscription (5 issues), $12.95

NSTA

Box 90477

Washington DC 20090-0477

(800) 722-NSTA

Web site: www.muohio.edu/Dragonfly

Kids Discover

A monthly magazine for kids aged 6 and up, beautifully illustrated with colorful diagrams, drawings, and photographs. Each 20-page issue concentrates on a different topic in the fields of science, history, or geography. Past topics have included the solar system, volcanoes, oceans, the brain, rain forests, weather, light, and endangered species. Basic information, fascinating facts, games and puzzles, and marvelous pictures.

Annual subscription (10 issues), $19.95;

back issues, $3

Kids Discover

Box 54205

Boulder, CO 80322

(800) 284-8276

Muse

A marvelous bimonthly magazine for kids aged 6–14 from the publishers of *Smithsonian* magazine and the kids' literary magazine *Cricket*. The result is a classy and gorgeously illustrated collection of articles on science, technology, history, and art—plus museum news, book reviews, cartoons, contests, and addresses of interesting on-line sites for cyberkids.

Annual subscription (6 issues), $24

Muse

Box 7468

Red Oak, IA 51591-2468

(800) 827-0227

Web site: www.musemag.com

The NewScientist

A fat weekly science journal published in Great Britain. Each issue includes several detailed feature articles, numerous short accounts of recent scientific advances and discoveries, book reviews, and essays. The writing is superb; the information is up-to-the-minute; and the subject matter is wide-ranging.

Intended for adults but thoroughly worthwhile for anyone interested in modern science.

Annual subscription (52 issues), $140

IPC Magazines, Ltd.

King's Reach Tower

Stamford St.

London SE1 9LS, England

Web site: www.newscientist.com

PopSci for Kids

A bimonthly magazine for kids aged 8–13 from the editors of the adult magazine *Popular Science. PopSci* is 33 busy pages long, all heavy on illustration, and all devoted to science, technology, and math. Regular departments include "Really Neat Stuff" (new and inventive games, gizmos, and gadgets), "Ask Ozzie" (science questions from readers, with answers), "New Net" (what's going on in science), "Cyberzone" (kid-written reviews of the latest computer software), and "The Time Machine" (science from way back when). There are also several feature articles in each issue, each devoted to a different scientific topic, plus puzzles, contests, and a bonus poster.

Annual subscription (6 issues), $9.95

PopSci for Kids

Box 5110

Harlan, IA 51593-2610

(800) 323-7070

Quantum

The "Magazine of Math and Science," is a bimonthly publication of the National Science Teachers Association (NSTA) for high school–level physics and math students. Each issue includes four feature articles and assorted regular departments, including math puzzles and challenges ("How Do You Figure?," "At the Black-board," and "Math Investigations") and suggestions for upper-level hands-on experiments ("In the Lab"). This magazine does not adapt well to younger readers; articles assume a solid grasp of advanced math. For kids who have one, it's an excellent and challenging publication.

Annual subscription (6 issues), $25

Quantum

National Science Teachers Association

1840 Wilson Blvd.

Arlington, VA 22201-3000

(800) 722-NSTA

Web site: www.nsta.org

Science News

The "Weekly Newsmagazine of Science," provides up-to-the-minute information on the latest in science research. Each issue is 15 illustrated pages long and includes many short descriptive notes on recent scientific advances and discoveries in the fields of astronomy, biology, physics, earth science, biomedicine, chemistry, environmental science, and behavioral science, plus two longer feature articles on a selected scientific topic. There are also reviews of numerous new reader-friendly science books, which can be ordered directly from the magazine. For teenagers and adults.

Annual subscription (52 issues), $49.50

Science News

Subscription Dept.

Box 1925

Marion, OH 43305

(800) 247-2160

Science Weekly

This magazine is described as a "language arts supplement to the elementary and middle school science curriculum." Each four-page issue is devoted to a single science topic—"Rain Forest," "The Moon," "Wind Power," "Fossils," "Volcanoes"—and includes an informational article, a science-based word puzzle, instructions for a simple hands-on experiment or project, math and critical-thinking challenges, and suggestions for a writing project. The accompanying "Teacher's Notes" include background information, suggestions for additional activities, and a resource list.

Science Weekly is available at seven reading levels, ranging from kindergarten to grades 7–8 (A–F). Issues lean toward the simple, which means that if you think your kid is a competent level C, he/she will probably be happier with level D.

Annual individual subscription (student copy and teacher's notes), $9.95; includes 16 biweekly issues over the course of the conventional school year. Annual "classroom rate" for 20 subscriptions and up, $4.95

Science Weekly, Inc.

Box 70638

Chevy Chase, MD 20813-0638

(301) 680-8804 or (800) 4-WEEKLY/fax (301) 680-9240

Science World

A short, illustrated science magazine for kids in grades 7–9. Feature articles cover the earth, life, and physical sciences; past topics have included sports science, space travel, robotics, and penguins. Each issue includes suggestions for discussion, projects, and hands-on activities.

Annual subscription (14 issues), $7.50

Scholastic, Inc.

Box 7502

Jefferson City, MO 65102

(800) 325-6149

Web site: www.scholastic.com

The Sciences

A bimonthly publication of the New York Academy of Sciences, intended for a general audience. Each issue has several feature articles on a wide range of scientific topics, book reviews, short accounts of recent advances in science, and "Event Horizon: An arbitrary guide to cultural pursuits in the sciences," which includes notes on new scientific gadgets, lists of cyberspace hot spots for science buffs, resources for kids, ongoing museum exhibits, and upcoming science presentations on television.

Annual subscription (6 issues), $21

The Sciences

Subscription Dept.

2 E. 63rd St.

New York, NY 10131-0164

(212) 838-0230 or (800) 843-6927 (Ext. 341)

Scientific American

Each monthly issue includes seven or eight elaborately illustrated feature articles from a wide range of scientific fields, plus several regular departments, among them "Mathematical Recreations," "The Amateur Scientist" (which some of us can cope with sometimes), "Science and the Citizen," "Connections," and "Working Knowledge," which explains the workings of familiar machines and processes. (Past columns have featured the slot machine, the fish ladder, and the process of decaffeinating coffee.) A valuable addition to any high school science program, if not an absolute necessity. Most libraries subscribe.

Annual subscription (12 issues), $34.97

Scientific American

Box 3186

Harlan, IA 51593-2377

(800) 333-1199

Web site: www.sciam.com

The Skeptical Inquirer

The bimonthly "Magazine of Science and Reason," which urges readers to view pseudoscience with a cold and critical eye. Thought provoking, balanced, and down-to-earth.

Annual subscription (6 issues), $32.50

The Skeptical Inquirer

Box 703

Amherst, NY 14226-0703

(800) 634-1610

SuperScience

An illustrated science magazine for kids in grades 3–6. Each issue includes science news, feature articles on many aspects of science, from forensic chemistry to forest fires, and suggestions for hands-on activities.

Annual subscription (8 issues), $5.95

Scholastic, Inc.

Box 7502

Jefferson City, MO 65102

(800) 325-6149

Web site: www.scholastic.com

Catalogs

American Science & Surplus

A marvelous catalog of (mostly) great and (mostly) inexpensive stuff for scientists, inventors, students, tinkerers, practical jokers, and amateur engineers. There are thorough, creative, and often hilarious descriptions of each of the hundreds of catalog items, all printed on recyclable newspaper. Selections range from the just plain bizarre (slimy toy animals that walk down walls, foam-rubber imitation rocks, glow-in-the-dark plastic glasses) to the faultlessly worthwhile (lab glassware, electronic components, science books and kits). Supplies vary; catalog listings change monthly. *American*

Science & Surplus has been a standby of our science program for years: our past finds have included an immense assortment of glass lenses for optical experiments, three sets of lab safety goggles, varied sizes of flasks, beakers, and graduated cylinders, and a bunch of break-your-own geodes. And a lot of really fun quasi-scientific toys. An addictively entertaining catalog.

American Science & Surplus

3605 Howard St.

Skokie, IL 60076

(847) 982-0870/fax (800) 934-0722

Web site: www.sciplus.com

Aves Science Kits

The Aves Company was founded in 1983 to provide science supplies to students in independent-study programs who are often unable to obtain small (one- to three-person) quantities of science materials. If you're not quite up to ordering pickled frogs by the dozen or gibberellic acid by the gallon, this may be an ideal source for you. Aves offers both individual items (laboratory glassware, dissection specimens, chemicals) and packaged biology kits, appropriate for kids in grades 5 or 6 and up. There are over 70 kits currently available, each packaged in a plain no-nonsense little white box, with all necessary supplies and a couple of typewritten instruction sheets included. Sample titles include "Blood Typing," "Enzyme Study," "Fungi Culture Study," "Grasshopper Dissection," "Light Frequency and Plants," "Osmosis and Diffusion," "Radiation and Plants," "Sheep Eye Dissection," and "Soil pH Study."

While these are not the glitzy color graphics–laden kits we're all used to seeing in the bigger commercial catalogs, they cover quite sophisticated science concepts, the experiments work, and the small quantities of included supplies are, in most cases, adequate for about three cooperative young scientists.

Most kits, around $6 (a good buy)

Aves Science Kit Co.

Box 229

Peru, ME 04290

Carolina Biological Supply Company

The catalog is over 1,200 pages long, packed with everything a science educator or student could possibly want: live and preserved specimens, models, kits, books, games, charts, multimedia materials, instruments. Catalog listings are grouped under nine (vast) categories: Biology, Chemistry, Earth and Space Science, Physics, Middle/Junior High Science, Mathematics, Publications, Multimedia, and Apparatus.

The company also publishes a number of specialized catalogs: *K–6 Science, Mathematics* (over 400 items for grades 5 and up), *Biotechnology* (materials for high school and college students), *Science Books and Multimedia,* and *Microscopes.* A superb resource.

> Main catalog, $17.95 (with a coupon for $17.95 off
> any order of $25 or more); free to teachers and science
> professionals
> Carolina Biological Supply Co.
> 2700 York Rd.
> Burlington, NC 27215
> (800) 334-5551/fax (800) 222-7112
> e-mail: carolina@carolina.com

Delta Education/Hands-On Science

A full-color catalog of science supplies, kits, books, and models aimed at students in grades K–8. Catalog items are grouped under a large number of topic-specific categories, from "Animals" and "Aquatic Life" to "Rocketry," "Rocks and Minerals," and "Weather." Delta also produces a series of thematic "Science In a Nutshell" kits. Each is packaged in a tidy turquoise plastic tote box and contains a detailed instruction/ activity book, enough materials for one to three young experimenters to complete several experiments and projects, and a "Student Journal" for notes and record keeping. The kits are generally appropriate for kids in grades 2–6. Sample titles include "Body Basics," "Bubble Science," "Charge It! Static Electricity," "Electrical Connections," "Flight! Gliders to Jets," "Fossil Formations," "Gears At Work," and "Weather Wise."

> Delta Education
> Box 3000
> Nashua, NH 03061-3000
> (800) 442-5444/fax (800) 282-9560
> Web site: www.delta-ed.com

Edmund Scientific Company

A comprehensive 100+-page catalog for "educators, students, and inventors." Catalog items range from the highly sophisticated for advanced scientists,

to simpler kits, toys, models, and manipulatives for beginners. A good source for optical supplies, including a nice line of student microscopes, precision measuring equipment, and science kits for kids at all levels, among them a 1,500-experiment chemistry set, a molecular model-building kit, assorted miniature steam engines, and a build-your-own hot-air balloon.

> Edmund Scientific Co.
> Consumer Science Division
> 101 E. Gloucester Pike
> Barrington, NJ 08007-1380
> (800) 728-6999/fax (609) 573-3292
> e-mail: scientifics@edsci.com
> Web site: www.edsci.com

ETA

Nearly 100 pages of science kits, books, games, posters, models, videos, lab equipment, and the like, much of it unusual and interesting. Materials are categorized under "Fragile Earth," "Life Science," "Magnifiers and Microscopes," "Earth Science," "Measurement," "Space Science," "Physical Science and Technology," "Chemistry," "Lab and Safety Equipment," and "General Science." Included are classification kits for young taxonomists (each kit contains 39 specimens from 13 different species), fossil-hunting kits, crystal-growing kits and rock polishers, weather instruments, robot models, chemistry kits, spectroscopes (10 for $15), and rockets—and much more.

> ETA
> 620 Lakeview Pkwy.
> Vernon Hills, IL 60061
> (800) 445-5985/fax (800) ETA-9326
> e-mail: info@etauniverse.com
> Web site: www.etauniverse.com

Lab-Aids

"Too little laboratory work is done in most science courses," state the administrators of Lab-Aids, Inc., adding that the Lab-Aids science kits are designed to encourage kids to perform laboratory experiments on their own, thus acquiring essential scientific hands-on experience. The company sells well over 100 science kits, variously appropriate for kids in elementary through high school, in the fields of general biology, plant science, biochemistry, genetics, physiology, environmental science, physics, chemistry, and earth science. Titles include "Enzyme Activity Study Kit," "Introduction to Radioactivity and Half-Life Experiment Kit," "Basic Chromatography Kit," "Introduction to pH Measurement Kit," and "Identification of Chemical Reactions Kit."

While the kits are excellent, they are emphatically designed for classroom environments; most assume that you've either got 30 kids or a lot of participating friends. Some, however, are quite adaptable to smaller groups, and, for interested kids, the extra stuff can be a plus. Worth a look. Contact

Lab-Aids, Inc.
17 Colt Ct.
Ronkonkoma, NY 11779
(516) 737-1133

National Teaching Aids

ALL The prime product of this company is a wonderful little device called the Microslide Viewer (see page 272). It looks like a microscope and works (more or less) like a microscope. However, it's much much cheaper than a microscope and—since it's made of heavy-duty plastic—it's next to unbreakable, provided you don't drop a piece of heavy furniture on it. You can also wash it under the faucet if it gets sticky.

The Viewer is designed for observing Microslides, mounted strips of eight different photomicrographs—that is, photographs of specimens taken through actual microscopes. Kids simply stick the Microslide strip in the slot at the top of the Viewer and observe each image through the microscope-style magnifying eyepiece. Images are easy to see: there are a couple of simple adjusting knobs for focusing, plus a white reflector—where the stage is located in an ordinary microscope—that provides plenty of light.

There are nearly 200 Microslide strips available, including many titles for biology, life science, and geology students. Also available: "Astroslides," photographs taken through a telescope for young astronomers (see page 258).

An excellent resource for kids of all ages, from beginners eager for a first microscope experience to advanced students investigating the process of mitosis, frog embryology, or the structure of the chromosome.

Micro-Slide-Viewers, $8; Microslide strip sets, $7 apiece
National Teaching Aids, Inc.
1845 Highland Ave.
New Hyde Park, NY 11040
(516) 326-2555/fax (516) 326-2560

Schoolmasters Science

ALL A 100+-page catalog of lab equipment, science supplies, books, kits, games, models, posters, charts, videos, and CD-ROMs for kids of all ages. Magnetic marbles, solar system mobiles, dinosaur models, rock tumblers, frog hatchery kits, thematic experiment kits, cricket cages, ant farms, and much more.

Schoolmasters Science
745 State Circle
Box 1941
Ann Arbor, MI 48106
(800) 521-2832/fax (313) 761-8711
Web site: www.school-tech.com

Science Kit and Boreal Laboratories

A large and comprehensive catalog for professional educators at all grade levels.

Science Kit and Boreal Laboratories
777 E. Park Dr.
Tonawanda, NY 14150-6784
(716) 874-6020 or (800) 828-7777
Web site: sciencekit.com

Scientific Explorer

Scientific Explorer, Inc., produces a growing line of clever and attractively boxed kits, all designed to nurture "the next generation of inspired scientific explorers." There are several different series of kits. The Explorer series includes coordinated packages of materials and informational instruction booklets for science experiments. The boys' favorite of these, "The Science of Scent," which enthralled our household for two odoriferous days, includes five fragrance oils, plus lots of little bottles, droppers, evaluation sheets, and a detailed booklet of instructions on the sense of smell and the science of perfumes. "Exploring the Ocean" contains a real shark tooth, a chemical light stick, and materials for "deep ocean seascape experiments." "The Nature of Dogs" includes stickers for testing your pet's response to colors and patterns, assorted experimental dog treats, a dog whistle, and a pair of dog eyeglasses. Users find out why dogs love cookies and whether they can see blue skies.

The Expedition series includes materials and guidebooks for science experiments in the field. Titles include "Wilderness Orienteering," "Botany," "Birds," "Seashore," and "Geology." "Botany," for example, has supplies for growing your own carnivorous plant, replicating some of Gregor Mendel's famous genetics experiments with pea plants, constructing an herbarium, and collecting and identifying plant, seed, and pollen samples.

The History of Science series—the most unusual of the company's product line—is a collection of kits designed to introduce kids to famous scientists of the past and to the science of ancient civilizations. Titles include "Sir Isaac Newton," "Galileo," "Charles Darwin," "Ancient Greece," "Ancient Rome," and "Ancient China." Students of Galileo, for example, learn about Galileo's life and work, reproduce simple Galilean physics experiments, and build their own Galilean telescope and thermometer.

Selected kits are also available as "Classroom Packs," each containing materials for up to 25 students, a teacher's booklet, student experiment sheets, and official-looking Certificates of Achievement; or as "Small Group" packs, designed for groups of two to three students.

Individual kits, $12.95 to $23.95; classroom packs, $76; small group packs, $30

Scientific Explorer, Inc.

2802 E. Madison, Suite 114

Seattle, WA 98112

(206) 322-7611 or (800) 900-1182/fax (206) 322-7610

e-mail: sciex@scientificexplorer.com

Web site: www.scientificexplorer.com

Teachers' Laboratory

A small catalog of resources—books, activity guides, measuring instruments, and manipulatives—for students of science, math, and technology in grades K–8. Among the catalog listings is the Early Start series by Roy Richards (Simon & Schuster). Each book, targeted at kids aged 4–10, is 96 pages long, packed with

elaborately illustrated instructions for hands-on activities and projects. Titles in the series include *An Early Start to . . . Technology, the Environment, Ourselves and Evolution, Energy, Science, Nature, Earth and Space,* and *Mathematics.*

The Teachers' Laboratory also publishes *Connect* (see page 218), a 20-page magazine of resource ideas, classroom-tested projects and activities, and new approaches to science and math teaching.

Teachers' Laboratory

Box 6480

Brattleboro, VT 05302

(800) 769-6199/fax (802) 254-5233

TOPS

TOPS isn't just a flattering evaluation; it stands for "Task-Oriented Physical Science," which means multi-lesson modules of coordinated hands-on learning activities for kids in grades 3–10. The modules are extraordinarily clever in that they really do use very simple materials—pennies, tinfoil, tape, clothespins, paper clips, and the like—to demonstrate quite complex scientific concepts.

Modules are available as "Task Cards" for kids in grades 7–12; these contain 16 to 36 individual open-ended experiments, each requiring the collection and analysis of experimental data. There are 23 modules in this format, variously rated as basic, moderate, or challenging. Titles include "Pendulums," "Graphing," "Probability," "Oxidation," "Pressure," "Light," "Sound," "Electricity," and "Machines." In the 16-lesson "Machines," for example, a module of "moderate" difficulty, kids build levers, pulleys, inclined planes, and a wheel-and-axle machine, study gear ratios, experiment with spring scales, and calculate the horsepower involved in climbing a flight of stairs.

"Activity Sheets" modules each include 20 lessons, with more detailed step-by-step instructions for somewhat simpler experiments, plus—for the student—short lists of questions to answer and boxes to illustrate. Accompanying teachers' notes are extremely precise, with directions, explanations, and answers. Titles include "Electricity," "Magnetism," "Green Thumbs: Radishes," "Green Thumbs: Corn and Beans," "Planets and Stars," and "Focus Pocus." This last is a fascinating series of exercises in optics: kids even build their own working microscopes using soda bottles, drinking straws, paper clips, and a dollop of modeling clay.

Modules, $8 to $15
TOPS Learning Systems
10970 S. Mulino Rd.
Canby, OR 97013
(888) 773-9755/fax (503) 266-5200
Web site: www.topscience.org

TransTech

This catalog, published by Creative Learning Systems, carries truly creative building kits—plus books, models, and computer software—for imaginative interactive learning. The name *TransTech* comes from the company motto—"Making Technology Transparent"—which refers not to transforming everything literally into see-through Plexiglas, but to providing materials that make technological concepts clearly understandable. The catalog is a nirvana for budding engineers. Included, for example, are a wide assortment of sophisticated building sets, experimental kits, and components, suitable for building everything from crawling mechanical ants and four-wheel-drive cars to computer-controlled robot arms; a working model of a passive solar house; a small-scale house framing kit (with miter jig, cutting tools, working drawings, and sized balsa-wood "lumber"); and a series of superb activity books dealing with such out-of-the-ordinary topics as origami architecture, homemade holograms, geodesic domes, and hydroponic gardening.

Creative Learning Systems, Inc.
16510 Via Esprillo
San Diego, CA 92127-1708
(800) 458-2880/fax (619) 675-7707
Web site: www.clsinc.com

Ward's Natural Science Establishment

Large and comprehensive catalogs for professional educators at all grade levels, including a biology and an earth sciences catalog.

Ward's Natural Science Establishment, Inc.
Box 92912
Rochester, NY 14692-9012

(800) 962-2660
Web site: www.wardsci.com

Wild Goose Company

Solid science and a wild sense of humor; these people really know kids. Wild Goose sells laboratory equipment, chemicals, activity books, student lab notebooks, posters, and a terrific series of hands-on science kits, most with eye-catching titles: among them "Slime Chemistry," "Crash & Burn Chemistry," "Dit, Dah, Dit," "Volcanoes, Dinosaurs, & Fossils," and "Out to Launch." "MegaLab" kits include all materials to complete 10 or so interesting—and often spectacular—experiments, plus an illustrated instruction/explanation booklet. Our all-time favorite is "Slime Chemistry" (we're not alone; the kit won an Outstanding Toy Award from *Parent's Choice Magazine*), which describes itself as "the art of taking ordinary things like cornstarch, fingernail polish remover, foam cups, glue, food coloring, and borax to make utterly disgusting slime that will ooooze through your fingers." All true; and it's also an excellent introduction to polymer chemistry.

Particularly juicy experiments from the "MegaLab" kits are also available as "ChemShorts": small, inexpensive single-experiment packets possessing a "high degree of intrinsic interest for kids." "How do we know this?" asks the catalog. "Simple. We try the experiment out on a pile of kids. If they do the big Oooh Aaah, the Intrinso-meter gives us two thumbs up." Sample Intrinso-meter high scorers include "FoamMeister," with which young chemists can concoct two forms of stable foams ("ideal for rapid eyeball popping and large colorful messes gleefully exuding out of coffee mugs"), "Fried Peanuts," in which kids observe the phenomenal action of an acetone solvent on polystyrene packing peanuts; and "Snowstorm in a Tube," "Rainbow in a Bottle," and "Smokescreen in a Cap." All tried so far have certainly won an "Oooh Aaah" response around here.

"MegaLabs," about $30; "ChemShorts," $5 to $6
Wild Goose Co.
375 Whitney Ave.
Salt Lake City, UT 84115
(801) 466-1172 or (800) 373-1498/fax (801) 466-1186
Web site: www.wildgoosescience.com

SCIENCE

Books

Building a Popular Science Library Collection for High School to Adult Learners

Gregg Sapp; Greenwood Publishing Group, 1995

A comprehensive annotated bibliography of popular science books in the fields of astronomy, biology, chemistry, mathematics, medicine and health science, natural history, physics, and technology, along with a discussion of the role of popular science in improving science literacy.

The Edge of the Unknown: 101 Things You Don't Know About Science and No One Else Does Either

James Trefil; Houghton Mifflin, 1996

The unsolved questions are the heart of science, and James Trefil discusses 101 of the biggest and best: "What will we do when antibiotics don't work anymore?" "Why can't we build a good electric car?" "Why do people age?" "Will time travel ever be possible?" "How old is the Universe?" Food for thought for the scientists of the future.

Every Teacher's Science Booklist

The Museum of Science and Industry, Chicago; Scholastic, 1995

An annotated bibliography of nearly 900 science books for kids in grades K–8, categorized by topic, plus reviews of 60 science magazines.

Everything You Need to Know About Science Homework

Anne Zeman and Kate Kelly; Scholastic, 1994

For kids in grades 4–6, this book is stuffed with facts, figures, definitions, explanations, and colorful illustrations, charts, and diagrams that provide answers to the "most commonly asked science homework questions." Categories covered include "What's Life All About?", "The Animal Kingdom," "The Plant Kingdom," "Ecology and the Landscapes of Life," "Planet Earth," "Outer Space," and "The Physical World." Whether you're worried about science homework or not, this is a useful science reference for middle-graders. Included, for example, are descriptive taxo-nomic charts, a timeline of geologic eras, Mohs scale, the Richter scale, the Beaufort wind scale, colored diagrams of oceanic and atmospheric layers, a chart of facts and figures about the planets in the solar system, a simplified Periodic Table of Elements, and a Fahrenheit/Celsius conversion scale.

Eyewitness Science Series

Dorling Kindersley

A collection of 64-page visual guides to science topics, each with lush color photographs and illustrations. Titles in the ever-growing series include *Light, Matter, Energy, Force and Motion, Electricity, Chemistry, Ecology, Evolution, Human Body, Electronics,* and *Technology.* The featured scientific topic is covered in a series of double-page spreads, each devoted to a different aspect of the subject at hand. *Electronics,* for example, includes pages on "Electromagnetic waves," "The importance of frequency," "Resistors," "Inductors and transformers," "Oscillators," "Semiconductors," and "Making microchips;" *Chemistry* includes "The first chemists," "Atoms and molecules," "The periodic table," "Chemical reactions," "Acids and bases," "The chemistry of carbon," and "Making synthetic materials." The pictures, as always, are picture-perfect; the text, however, is sketchy.

Free Stuff for Science Buffs

Barry Young; Coriolis Group Books, 1996

A 302-page book stuffed with interesting information and free stuff for young scientists. Most of the free stuff is available on-line; the author provides addresses and descriptions of science-oriented sites on the Internet, World Wide Web, CompuServe, and America Online.

The book is divided into five major sections: "Astronomy," "Atoms," "Weather," "The Earth," and "A Few More Mysteries Explained" (which includes resources on time travel and space flight). Not all of these get equal treatment: over a third of the book is devoted to astronomy. Still, there's a lot to be found: readers discover, for example, where to find on-line instructions for building a kite or a cloud chamber, how to view images from the sea floor or the Hubble Telescope, and whom to contact to find out if your name has been assigned to a hurricane. The book also includes an informative background text and fascinating facts ("Science Bites") in boxes.

From bookstores or

The Coriolis Group

7339 E. Acoma Dr., Suite 7

Scottsdale, AZ 85260

(602) 483-0192

Web site: www.coriolis.com

How Did We Find Out About . . . ? Series
Isaac Asimov; Walker & Company

The late Isaac Asimov has hundreds of excellent popular science books to his credit, among them this series on the history of scientific discovery for kids in grades 5–8. Each book is about 60 pages long, divided into short chapters. For each featured topic, Asimov covers ancient beliefs, historical discoveries, and present-day research information. There are over 30 titles in the series, in a range of scientific disciplines. Examples include *How Did We Find Out About . . . Dinosaurs?*, *Blood?*, *Atoms?*, *Coal?*, *Volcanoes?*, *Life in the Deep Sea?*, *the Speed of Light?*, *DNA?*, *Black Holes?*, *Robots?*, *Earthquakes?*, and *the Beginning of Life?* Challenging material, clearly and comfortably presented.

Let's-Read-and-Find-Out Science Series
HarperTrophy

This series was the brainchild of Dr. Franklyn M. Branley, astronomer and former chairman of the American Museum–Hayden Planetarium, with the help of Dr. Roma Gans, professor emeritus of childhood education at Columbia University. The books are colorful 32-page introductory science volumes for 4–9-year-olds. There are nearly 60 books in the series, by a number of authors. In recent editions, these are classified as either Level 1 or Level 2; Level 1 books are the very simplest volumes, aimed at preschoolers; Level 2 books are more informationally detailed, for kids aged 6–9. Sample titles include *Ant Cities* (Arthur Dorros; 1987), *Danger—Icebergs!* (Roma Gans; 1987), *Flash, Crash, Rumble, and Roll* (Franklyn M. Branley; 1985), *Fossils Tell of Long Ago* (Aliki; 1990), *Gravity is a Mystery* (Franklyn M. Branley; 1986), *A Drop of Blood* (Paul Showers; 1989), *Germs Make Me Sick!* (Melvin Berger; 1995), and *Let's Go Rock Collecting* (Roma Gans; 1997).

We read dozens of these when our boys were small. A excellent resource for beginners.

Magic School Bus Series
Joanna Cole; Scholastic

Ms. Frizzle, the world's best elementary school science teacher, with her outrageous wardrobe and her amazingly versatile school bus, now stars not only in the original *Magic School Bus* books for 6–9-year-olds, but in an easy-to-read series for 5–7-year-olds, a line of hands-on activity books (*The Magic School Bus Science Explorations*), a collection of CD-ROM software programs (for Windows or Mac), and her own PBS television show. In each book, the redoubtable Ms. Frizzle takes her obstreperous class on a fantastic science field trip: the Magic Bus rockets into outer space, shrinks to the size of a red blood cell, drills down to the center of the earth and erupts through a volcano, and dives to the bottom of the ocean. Information is presented through a chatty text, conversational cartoon-style balloons, and kid-written science reports in the margins of each page, printed on what looks like yellow lined notebook paper ("What Is Plankton? by Arnold"; "Why Is Blood Red? by Shirley"). Titles in the series include *The Magic School Bus Lost in the Solar System*, *The Magic School Bus on the Ocean Floor*, and *The Magic School Bus Inside the Earth*.

The *Magic School Bus* books are available from bookstores or

Scholastic, Inc.

2931 E. McCarty St.

Jefferson City, MO 65101

(800) 724-6527

See **Audiovisual General Science:** *The Magic School Bus on Video* (page 242).

National Science Education Standards
National Committee on Science Education Standards and Assessment, National Research Council; National Academy Press, 1996

A detailed description of current recommendations for standards of achievement in science education. Standards are listed by age group (grades K–4, 5–8, and 9–12). The book also discusses reasons for establishing science education standards and means of assessing student achievement. The text is available online at www.nap.edu/readingroom/books/nses

New True Books: Science and Math
Children's Press

A large series of short science books for readers in grades 2–4. Each book is 48 pages long, divided into several very short chapters, all in good-size print with a simple informational text. The books are beautifully illustrated with color photographs, drawings, and diagrams. Books are divided into seven main categories: Animals (sample titles include *African Animals, Dangerous Fish, Koalas, Penguins, Reptiles,* and *Whales and Other Sea Mammals*), Astronomy/Meteorology, Earth Sciences, Environment (sample titles include *Air Pollution, The Greenhouse Effect, The Ozone Hole,* and *Recycling*), Experiments (including *Experiments With Chemistry, Experiments With Electricity,* and *Experiments With Heat*), Human Body, and Plants. There are also single New True volumes listed under Technology (*Internet*) and Math (*Metric System*).

Available through bookstores or
Children's Press
Sherman Turnpike
Danbury, CT 06813
(800) 621-1115/fax (203) 797-3657

The Oxford Children's Book of Science
Charles Taylor and Stephen Pople; Oxford University Press, 1996

A 192-page overview of science for readers aged 9–12 categorized under 22 general topics, among them "Forces of Nature," "Cells and Biology," "Sounds and Music," "Energy," and "Machines." The books is filled with photographs, cutaway diagrams, charts, maps, and graphs; readers view, for example, an enormous snowflake, the Eiffel Tower at night, and a striking lightning bolt.

A Question of Science Series
Carolrhoda

This delightful series of science picture books answers kids' questions about science through an appealing combination of real-life photographs, clever and colorful illustrations, cartoon balloons, and a chatty question-and-answer-style text. Titles in the series include *Can Elephants Drink Through Their Noses?: The Strange Things People Say About Animals at the Zoo* (Deborah Dennard; 1993); *Can You Catch a Falling Star?* (Sidney Rosen; 1995); *Can You Find a Planet?* (Sidney Rosen; 1992); *Can You Hitch a Ride on a Comet?* (Sidney Rosen; 1993); *Do Cats Have Nine Lives? The Strange Things People Say about Animals Around the House* (Deborah Dennard; 1993), *How Far is a Star?* (Sidney Rosen; 1992); *How Wise is an Owl?: The Strange Things People Say about Animals in the Woods* (Deborah Dennard; 1993), *Where Does the Moon Go?* (Sidney Rosen; 1992), and *Where's the Big Dipper?* (Sidney Rosen; 1995). Each book is 32–40 pages long. Recommended for kids in grades K–3.

The Science Book
Sara Stein; Workman, 1980

"*The Science Book,*" writes author Sara Stein, "begins at home and stays there. The living specimens for scientific study are molds and roaches, geraniums, cats, and humans. The dead specimens are logs and lamb chops, leather, and lettuce. Laboratory apparatus isn't more complicated than a flashlight or a jelly jar. Even the chemicals will be familiar and homey: vinegar, bleach, your own saliva." Which doesn't mean that Stein pulls any punches when it comes to the complexities of science: this is the real stuff, clearly and comprehensively explained, in 285 illustrated pages. The book is divided into three sections: "Outsides," which studies behaviors of pests, pets, and people; "Insides," which deals with the innards of protozoans, plants, and animals (including humans); and "Invisibles," which discusses the workings of the senses and the brain. Included, for example, are a chart of "Incredible Rat Statistics" showing how many descendants one pair of breeding rats can generate in a single year (55,070), diagrams showing how a cherry develops and the anatomy of a tree trunk, instructions for growing popcorn, brewing ginger beer, and making a model of your lung, a sound wave demonstration using dominoes, and detailed explanations of light and sight, electricity, and chemical reactions. Under "Insides," there's also a clear account of puberty, sex, and childbirth.

$9.95
Workman Publishing Co.
708 Broadway
New York, NY 10003-9555

(212) 254-5900 or (800) 722-7202/fax (212) 254-8098

Web site: www.workmanweb.com

By the same author, see *The Body Book* (page 311) and *The Evolution Book* (page 304).

The ZScientific Companion

Cesare Emiliani; John Wiley & Sons, 1995

A comprehensive 300+-page overview of basic science for the layperson, covering scientific measurement, physics, astronomy, geology, meteorology, and biology. The book is heavily illustrated with drawings, diagrams, and photographs, and includes tables of essential figures and formulas. Intended to bridge the gap between popular science books and beginning college texts.

Start to Finish Books

Carolrhoda

A collection of small-size 24-page picture books, each tracing the history of some familiar object or phenomenon from "start" to "finish." The books are targeted at kids of preschool age through grade 3. Titles include *From Blossom to Honey* (Ali Mitgutsh; 1987), *From Dinosaurs to Fossils* (Annegert Fuchschuber and Ali Mitgutsh; 1983), *From Egg to Bird* (Marlene Reidel; 1981), *From Sea to Salt* (Ali Mitgutsh; 1985), and *From Tree to Table* (Ali Mitgutsh; 1981).

The Ultimate Visual Dictionary

Dorling Kindersley, 1994

Over 600 pages of elaborately and precisely labeled full-color photographs, pictures, and diagrams. Categories include "The Universe," "Prehistoric Earth," "Plants," "Animals," "The Human Body," "Geology, Geography, and Meteorology," "Physics and Chemistry," "Rail and Road," "Sea and Air," "The Visual Arts," "Architecture," "Music," "Sports," and "Everyday Things." Everything from a cross-section of the sun to a *Tyrannosaurus* skeleton to the innards of a clock, shoe, CD-ROM, and toaster.

Why Can't You Unscramble an Egg? And Other Not Such Dumb Questions About Matter

Vicki Cobb; Lodestar Books, 1990

A humorously illustrated book for kids aged 8–11, providing clear and interesting explanations for not-so-simple questions. The text explains, for example, "Which Weighs More, a Pound of Feathers or a Pound of Gold?," "Why Does an Ice Cube Float?," and "Why Isn't the Earth Egg-Shaped or a Cube?"

Other titles in the same format by Cobb include *Why Doesn't the Sun Burn Out?* (Lodestar, 1990), which deals with such questions as "What Does It Take to Move a Piano?," "How Is a Wound-up Spring Like the Top of a Waterfall?," "How Does a Pot Holder Work?," and "Why Isn't the Sky Green or Yellow?"; *Why Doesn't the Earth Fall Up?* (Lodestar, 1968), which tackles "Why Does a Rolling Ball Stop Rolling?," "Which Falls Faster, A Bowling Ball or a Marble?," and "Why Doesn't the Moon Fall to Earth?"; and *Why Can't I Live Forever?* (Lodestar, 1997), which variously explains why blood is red, why plants are green, and why people can't live forever.

Why Nothing Can Travel Faster than Light . . . and Other Explorations in Nature's Curiosity Shop

Barry E. Zimmerman and David J. Zimmerman; Contemporary Publishing, 1993

A collection of entertainingly readable essays of notably high interest value. Titles include "Of Asteroids and Dinosaurs," "Earth Without a Moon," "Why Is the Sky Blue?," "Is Earth Getting Warmer?," "A World Without Friction," and, of course, "Can Anything Travel Faster than Light?" Also see *Nature's Curiosity Shop: Explorations in the Mysteries and Wonders of Science* (Contemporary Publishing, 1995), which includes "Virtual Reality: A World of Make-Believe," "Heavenly Shadows," "Forensic Medicine" (Part 1 and Part 2), "Superconductivity: The Path of No Resistance," and "Diamonds from Peanut Butter." A hit with our kids.

BOOKS: HISTORY OF SCIENCE

53½ Things That Changed the World: And Some That Didn't

Steve Parker and David West; Millbrook Press, 1995

A cleverly illustrated picture-book history of science, explaining the development of the innovations that have affected human history and their subsequent impacts. Among the 53 things covered are the steam engine, printing press, microscope, telescope, screw, internal combustion engine, satellite, camera, phonograph, microchip, and toilet. The leftover half is fusion power.

Ancient Inventions

Peter James and Nick Thorpe; Ballantine, 1994

A comprehensive and fascinating history of ancient inventions, grouped into 12 general categories, among them "Medicine," "Military Technology," "House and Home," and "Sport and Leisure." Included are accounts of ancient Chinese earthquake detectors, Byzantine flamethrowers, Middle Eastern umbrellas, and Aztec chewing gum. There's also an explicit section on inventions related to "Sex Life," which may require parental guidance. A useful reference book for designers of science history study units.

Asimov's Chronology of Science and Discovery

Isaac Asimov; HarperCollins, 1994

A massive, 800-page chronological history of scientific discovery that is an excellent reference for science programs.

Beakman's Book of Dead Guys and Gals of Science

Luann Colombo; Andrews & McMeel, 1994

This irreverent (but accurate) and graphically creative collection of scientific biographies, covers such science superstars as Copernicus, Galileo, Isaac Newton, Benjamin Franklin, the Montgolfier brothers, Edward Jenner, Maria Mitchell, Thomas Edison, Alexander Graham Bell, Marie Curie, Albert Einstein, Robert Goddard, Louis Leakey, and Philo Farnsworth. For each (dead) subject, there's a bright red-and-green timeline, ordering all the major events of his/her life, illustrations—both color photographs and catchy cartoons—demonstrating his/her most important scientific discoveries, assorted quotations, and a short and engagingly readable explanatory text. Newton's three Laws of Motion, for example, are listed and then dramatically demonstrated by Fuzzy the luckless Crash Dummy on a skateboard; Einstein's famous equation is explained by converting a pastrami sandwich into energy. (Do it and you'll be able to power every city in America for five days.) The book is appropriate for 8–12-year-olds, who will both learn a lot from it and giggle over it.

The Biographical Dictionary of Scientists

Roy Porter, ed.; Oxford University Press, 1994

A hefty reference book listing 1,200 of the world's greatest scientists, with accounts of their lives, accomplishments, and the historical and scientific implications of their work.

Connections

James Burke; Little, Brown, 1995

Fascinating accounts of science history. Burke's books, though written for an adult audience, contain much to interest readers and listeners of all ages. *Connections* traces the historical links that eventually culminated in such landmark inventions as the computer, the airplane, the atom bomb, and the guided rocket. It's an enthralling and unexpected history lesson: the road to the telephone, Burke explains, began with the development of the stirrup, which allowed William the Conqueror to win the Battle of Hastings in 1066.

Also see, by the same author, *The Day the Universe Changed* (Little, Brown, 1995), a similarly multifaceted tour of history, based on the premise that when mankind's view of reality is changed by knowledge—as happened with the invention of the printing press, Newton's discovery of the universal laws of physics, and the publication of the theory of evolution—the world itself changes. The book emphasizes the historical and social implications of scientific discovery.

See **Audiovisual General Science: Connections** (page 241) and **Computer Software: Connections** (page 243).

Galileo's Commandment: An Anthology of Great Science Writing

Edmund Blair Bolles, ed.; W. H. Freeman & Company, 1997

A fascinating collection of science writings, from Herodotus, speculating on "The Creation of Egypt" in 444 B.C., to Carl Sagan and Stephen Jay Gould in the present decade. Included among the authors are Galileo himself, Leonardo da Vinci, Charles Darwin, Isaac Newton, Marie Curie, Bertrand Russell, Richard Feynman, Rachel Carson, and J. B. S. Haldane; topics range over the disciplines of astronomy, biology, chemistry, geology, physics, and psychology. Galileo's commandment, incidentally, is "Contribute to science."

Great Essays in Science
Martin Gardner, ed.; Prometheus Books, 1994

The aim of this book, explains Martin Gardner in the preface, is to present the reader with "a sumptuous feast of great writing—absorbing, thought-disturbing pieces that have something important to say about science and say it forcibly and well." The feast covers 31 authors over a span of 150 years; included are Stephen Jay Gould ("Nonmoral Nature"), Carl Sagan ("Can We Know the Universe? Reflections on a Grain of Salt"), Isaac Asimov ("Science and Beauty"), J. Robert Oppenheimer ("Physics in the Contemporary World"), Rachel Carson ("The Sunless Sea"), Sigmund Freud ("Dreams of the Death of Beloved Persons"), and Albert Einstein (four and a half pages on "E = mc²"). For teenagers and adults.

Great Lives Series
Each volume in the Great Lives Series is a collection of biographies of prominent persons in a specific field, for readers aged 9–13. A number of these books feature the sciences. *Great Lives: Invention and Technology* (Milton Lomack; Charles Scribner's Sons, 1991), for example, includes 27 short biographies of scientists and inventors in alphabetical order from Charles Babbage and Alexander Graham Bell through James Watt, Eli Whitney, and the Wright brothers. *Great Lives: Medicine* (Robert H. Curtis; Atheneum, 1992) includes biographies of Hippocrates, William Harvey, Elizabeth Blackwell, Jonas Salk, and Sigmund Freud; *Great Lives: Nature and the Environment* (Doris and Harold Faber; Macmillan, 1991) includes biographies of John Muir, Rachel Carson, and Jacques Cousteau. All are illustrated with black-and-white prints and photographs.

Great Minds of Science Series
Enslow Publishing

A series of 128-page science biographies for readers aged 10 and up. Each book is illustrated with black-and-white photographs and includes related activity suggestions. Titles include *Albert Einstein: Physicist and Genius* (Joyce Goldenstern; 1995), *Antoine Lavoisier: Father of Modern Chemistry* (Lisa Yount; 1997), *Anton van Leeuwenhoek: First to See Microscopic Life* (Lisa Yount; 1996), *Carl Linnaeus: Father of Classification* (Margaret J. Anderson; 1997), *Charles Darwin: Naturalist* (Margaret J. Anderson; 1994), *Isaac Newton: The Greatest Scientist of All Time* (Margaret J. Anderson; 1996), *The Leakeys: Uncovering the Origins of Humankind* (Margaret Poynter; 1997), *Marie Curie: Discoverer of Radium* (Margaret Poynter; 1994), and *William Harvey: Discoverer of How Blood Circulates* (Lisa Yount; 1994).

The Scientific 100: A Ranking of the Most Influential Scientists, Past and Present
John Simmons; Citadel Press, 1996

Detailed accounts of the lives and accomplishments of the world's 100 greatest scientists, in order of importance, from Newton (no. 1) to Archimedes (no. 100). For teenagers and adults.

They All Laughed: From Light Bulbs to Lasers: The Fascinating Stories Behind the Inventions That Have Changed Our Lives
Ira Flatow; HarperPerennial, 1993

A 238-page collection of short, interesting histories of important inventions and inventors, illustrated with photographs and drawings. Chapter titles include "Whose Light Bulb? Edison in a New Light," "From a Melted Candy Bar to Microwaves," "The Computer That Saved D-Day," and "The Wasp That Changed the World."

The Timetables of Science
Alexander Hellemans and Brian Bunch; Touchstone Books, 1991

A 600-page chronology of "The Most Important People and Events in the History of Science," from the appearance of stone tools to the computer age. Discoveries are categorized by scientific discipline.

The Usborne Book of Scientists from Archimedes to Einstein
Struan Reid and Patricia Fara; Usborne Publishing, 1992

A 48-page illustrated history of science from ancient times to the present day. This is not, as the title suggests, a collection of unrelated biographies: featured scientists are chronologically grouped under the histories of their scientific disciplines. A chapter on early astronomy, for example, "The Earth and the Sun," covers the work of Ptolemy, Copernicus, Tycho Brahe, and Johannes Kepler; "The Fight Against Disease" discusses the work of Edward Jenner, Louis Pasteur, Joseph Lister, and Alexander Fleming; and "Opening Up the Atom" describes the discoveries of Max Planck, Albert Einstein, Ernest Rutherford, and Niels Bohr.

LITERATURE LINKS TO GENERAL SCIENCE: FOR ADULTS

The more mental connections a learner makes, the better new material is retained. Link the study of Bernoulli's principle, for example, to a biography of the Wright brothers, the story of Charles Lindbergh's famous transatlantic flight, the building of model airplanes, and a bird-watching walk, and chances are it will be better remembered than if simply described on a workbook page. This is the rationale behind the many books suggesting ways to connect the study of science to popular children's storybooks.

From my homeschool journal:

◆ **May 17, 1990. Josh is nine; Ethan, seven; Caleb, five.**

We read a picture book this morning titled Ts'ao Chung Weighs an Elephant, about a little Chinese boy who figured out how to weigh an elephant by leading the elephant on board a boat, marking the water level on the side of the boat, then removing the elephant and loading the boat with stones until it sank to the same level. The boys, intrigued, repeated the elephant-weighing experiment in the bathtub, using a plastic toy boat and a can of soup with a paper elephant pasted on the side. We marked the water level on the side of the boat, first empty, then with elephant. Then the boys filled the boat with pebbles until the water-level line matched that reached with the elephant. (Actually, they blew it the first time around and sank the boat due to overenthusiasm.) We then weighed the elephant/soup can and the pebbles on the kitchen scale, thus proving that they weighed exactly the same. Josh: "Hey! This really works!"

6 12 From Butterflies to Thunderbolts: Discovering Science With Books Kids Love

Anthony D. Fredericks; Fulcrum, 1997

Favorite kid's books linked to a wide range of science activities. The books are grouped by subject—for example, "Animals," "Plants," "Earth," "Oceans," "Weather," and "Space." Each book listing includes a detailed description and plot summary, discussion questions, interesting science facts, hands-on projects and activities, field trip suggestions, a bibliography of related readings, and a "Write Away" section, with addresses of organizations and groups that can furnish additional resources or information. Among the featured books are *Miss Rumphius, The Great Kapok Tree, In Coal Country,* and *Bringing the Rain to Kapiti Plain.* Projects include creative dramatics, poetry writing, recipes, arts and crafts, and science experiments. Kids, for example, plant their names in seeds, assemble a desert terrarium, construct and erupt a chemical volcano, and make "fossils" with chicken bones.

8 14 Great Moments in Science: Experiments and Readers Theatre

Kendall Haven; Teacher Ideas Press, 1996

The book links drama and science for kids in grades 4–9. Included are 12 scripts based on major scientific discoveries in the fields of physics, astronomy, biology, rocketry, and genetics, along with instructions for re-creating the experiments featured in each.

8 13 Intermediate Science through Children's Literature: Over Land and Sea

Carol M. Butzow and John W. Butzow; Teacher Ideas Press, 1995

The book links works of children's literature to hands-on activities and projects. Titles include *Sarah, Plain and Tall; Blue Willow; Julie of the Wolves; Island of the Blue Dolphins;* and *The Cay.* The emphasis is on earth and environmental sciences, for kids in grades 4–7.

5 8 Literature-Based Science Activities: An Integrated Approach

Audrey Brainard and Denise H. Wrubel; Scholastic, 1994

Science activities for kids in grades K–3 based on such popular picture books as *Noisy Nora, Make Way* for *Ducklings,* and *A Very Quiet Cricket.* The book includes reproducible student worksheets.

5 12 Science and Stories: Integrating Science and Literature

Hilarie N. Stanton and Tara McCarthy; Good Year Books, 1994

Two volumes, one for grades K–3, one for grades 4–6, each listing 24 children's books with related science projects. The K–3 volume, for example, includes activities related to *The Legend of the Bluebonnet, Katy and the Big Snow,* and *The Mixed-Up Chameleon;* the 4–6 volume includes activities based on *Dragonwings, Call It Courage,* and *Journey to the Planets.*

5 8 Science Through Children's Literature

Carol M. Butzow and John W. Butzow; Teacher Ideas Press, 1988

Over 30 popular children's books, appropriate for kids in grades K–3, are grouped into three major categories: life science, earth and space science, and physical science. The authors give a brief description of each book, followed by a long and varied list of book-related hands-on science activities. After reading Virginia Lee Burton's *Choo Choo* (Houghton Mifflin, 1937), the story of a determined little steam engine, kids experiment with inclined planes, identify different kinds of simple machines, measure their average running speed, make a "speed line" listing—in order—everything from the spider to the family car, and learn just how a steam engine works. Science activities associated with Leo Lionni's *Swimmy,* the story of an inventive little black fish, include studying fish scales under a microscope, making a model water column showing the different types of sea life at each depth, playing "Sea Creature" rummy, making fish prints, and constructing a Japanese fish kite.

6 10 Stepping Stones to Science: True Tales and Awesome Activities

Kendall Haven; Teacher Ideas Press, 1997

Historically accurate science-based stories, paired with discussion questions and related hands-on activities, for kids in grades 2–5.

Also see *Every Teacher's Science Booklist* (page 226) and *Building a Popular Science Library Collection for High School to Adult Learners* (page 226).

LITERATURE LINKS TO GENERAL SCIENCE: FOR KIDS

5 8 101 Science Poems and Songs for Young Learners

Meish Goldish; Scholastic, 1997

Short science-related poems and songs for early elementary–aged kids, with accompanying suggestions for simple hands-on activities.

8 12 Einstein Anderson, Science Detective, Series

Seymour Simon; William Morrow, 1997–98

Einstein (his real name is Adam) Anderson, sixth-grade science whiz, is the star of this series of short chapter books for readers aged 8–12. Each chapter describes a baffling mystery or puzzle, which Einstein—using his wide-ranging knowledge of science—always manages to solve. The stories are fun, informative, and populated with an appealing cast of characters, including Stanley, a continually frustrated high school–aged inventor, and Margaret, Einstein's close friend and fellow superscientist. And there's always a pause in the action—"Can you solve the puzzle?"—to let readers come up with their own hypotheses before they turn the page to hear Einstein's answer. Titles in the series include *The Gigantic Ants & Other Cases, The On-Line Spaceman & Other Cases, The Time Machine & Other Cases,* and *The Invisible Man & Other Cases.*

ACTIVITY BOOKS

4 14 Backyard Scientist Series

Jane Hoffman; Backyard Scientist

The *Backyard Scientist* series by educator Jane Hoffman consists of five little comb-bound books, each a collection of simple hands-on experiments using run-of-the-mill household materials. The first of the books—*The Original Backyard Scientist* and *Backyard Scientist, Series One*—both concentrate on beginning concepts in chemistry and physics, targeted at kids aged 4–12. Both experiments and explanations are very simple: users, for example, dissolve sugar in water, drop balls off ladders, power a paper boat with soap (it's a neat trick demonstrating surface tension), and melt ice cubes. *Backyard Scientist, Series Two,* aimed at 9–14-year-olds, is somewhat more challenging: kids grow crystals on charcoal briquettes, make pH indicators, build a periscope, and experiment with paper chromatography using M&M's. Again, explanations are very short and simple. *Series Three,* for 4–12-year-olds, focuses on the life sciences; *Series Four,* for kids of all ages, is another chemistry and physics collection.

In my experience, the books work best with the very young; and I'd say that an age of 8–9 is probably the cutoff point even for *Series Two,* which is recommended for a group aged 9–14. While some of the experiments are appealing, the text is simply too limited for older kids, who need something meatier.

Backyard Scientist

Box 16966

Irvine, CA 92713-6966

(714) 551-2392/fax (714) 552-5351

The Best of Wonderscience: Elementary Science Activities

James H. Kessler; Delmar, 1997

Over 400 creative hands-on science activities for kids in grades 4–6 from *Wonderscience* magazine (see Chemistry, page 348), chosen to fulfull the National Science Education Standards. The book includes background information, complete instructions for each activity, and color illustrations. Activities are grouped into several thematic categories, including Water, Food Science, Physical Changes, Chemical Changes, Earth and Space Science, Sound, and Light. There's also a guide to science fair projects.

The Best of You Can With Beakman & Jax: A Collection of the Grossest, Weirdest, Coolest Experiments You Can Do

Jok Church; Andrews & McMeel, 1997

Information and fun experiments based on scientific questions posed by curious kids. Science with a sense of humor, illustrated with catchy and colorful graphics. Also see Beakman & Jax on-line at www.beakman.com (see page 246).

Bet You Can't! Science Impossibilities to Fool You

Vicki Cobb and Kathy Darling; Avon Books, 1983

This book is dedicated to P. T. Barnum ("who also believed that there is a sucker born every minute"), and our kids loved it. Cobb and Darling describe 82 impossible tricks, which kids simply can't resist trying. Bet you can't . . . jump forward while holding onto your toes, pop a balloon through a piece of Scotch tape with a pin, blow out a candle through a funnel, keep a match burning over a glass of soda. The boys spent days on these, and then used them all to fool friends, neighbors, and hopelessly gullible parents.

Scientific explanations for all impossibilities are included, which keeps the participants from going nuts.

Boston Children's Museum Activity Book Series

Bernie Zubrowski; William Morrow

Volumes in this illustrated series of books, each about 100 pages long, are filled with hands-on activities and explanations of the relevant scientific principles for kids in grades 3–8. In *Balloons* (1990), for example, kids fool around with homemade inflatable toys (among them a rocket car and a submarine) and study the many properties of air; in *Mirrors* (1992), they experiment with optics; and in *Raceways,* they build roller coasters, ski jumps, and racetracks, with which they investigate acceleration, kinetic energy, and momentum. Other titles include *Blinkers and Buzzers* (1991), *Clocks* (1988), *Mobiles* (1993), *Tops* (1994), *Making Waves* (1994), *Wheels at Work* (1986), *Shadow Play* (1995), *Soda Science* (1997), and *Structures* (1993).

Einstein's Science Parties

Shar Levine and Allison Grafton; John Wiley & Sons, 1994

A scientific alternative to pin-the-tail-on-the-donkey. This book describes 14 science theme parties, categorized by appropriate age group from 4–12, complete with instructions and reproducible invitations. Party titles include "Bubble Blast," "Fossils and Dinos," "Slime Time," and "Eat Your Experiment!"

Explorabook: A Kids' Science Museum in a Book

John Cassidy; Klutz Press, 1992

"Einstein once described himself as being not terribly intelligent, just extremely inquisitive," reads the introduction. "It was in that playful and pestering spirit that the Explorabook was conceived—a celebration of that most human and hopeful trait, curiosity."

For curious young scientists, this book is a blast. It is divided into seven sections: "Magnetism," "Bending Light Waves," "Bacterial Stories," "Light Wave Craziness," "Homemade Science" (which encourages kids to do a lot of peculiar things with balloons and hair dryers), "Bouncing Light Rays" (the first page of this section is printed backward and has to be read with the enclosed mirror), and "Optical Illusions." The book is filled with creative photographs, clever illustrations, instructions for over 50 mind-expanding activities, and a thoroughly fascinating text—plus an attached magnet, a sheet of plastic that acts as a Fresnel lens, two packets of agar ("think of it as bacteria snack food, or maybe fungi brunches"), a sheet of diffraction grating, and a moiré spinner. There's even a science activity ("Gravity Races") on the back cover. For more of the same, also see *Zap Science: A Scientific Playground in a Book* (1997).

Gee Wiz! How to Mix Art and Science, or The Art of Thinking Scientifically

Linda Allison and David Katz; Little, Brown, 1983

This delightful book—dedicated to Galileo and "anybody else who believes that the answers aren't all in books"—stars the Wizard (who knows a lot of tricks, but is excitable, enthusiastic, and easily confused) and Smart Art, a know-it-all kid with a scientific mind. Together, they imaginatively investigate many unusual aspects of science. Sample chapter titles include "Exploding Colors: the science of chromatography," "Fantastic Elastics: building bubbles, observing soap films," and "May the Force Be with You: kinetics and bodies in motion." The dozens of hands-on experiments are marvelous, the explanations are clear and clever, and the illustrations are funny. One of our favorites. For kids aged 9–12.

Great Explorations in Math and Science (GEMS) Series

Lawrence Hall of Science

An excellent series of activity books/teachers' manuals on a wide range of scientific topics from the Lawrence Hall of Science. The books are variously appropriate for kids in preschool through grade 9. Titles include *Hide a Butterfly,* a unit on camouflage and protective coloration for children in preschool to age 5; *Secret Formulas,* in which kids in grades 1–3 make their own paste, toothpaste, soda, and ice cream; and *Oobleck: What Do Scientists Do?* in which kids in grades 4–8 tackle analytical chemistry. For information about GEMS, call (510) 642-7771 or e-mail: GEMS@uclink.berkeley.edu.

$15 to $30
University of California
Attn: LHS Store
Lawrence Hall of Science, #5200
Berkeley, CA 94720-5200
(510) 642-1016/fax (510) 642-1055
Web site: www.lhs.berkeley.edu

How Things Work Series

Reader's Digest

A beautifully designed series of informational books for kids aged 8–14. Each is 192 pages long, filled with background information, catchy anecdotes, capsule biographies of scientists, drawings, diagrams, photographs, and excellent hands-on projects and experiments. Complete instructions are included for each project, illustrated with sequenced color photographs. Titles include *How Science Works* (Judith Hann; 1996), *How the Body Works* (Steve Parker; 1994), *How the Earth Works* (John Farndon; 1992), and *How the Universe Works* (Heather Cooper and Nigel Henbest; 1994).

Magic Mud and Other Great Experiments

Gordon Penrose; Owl Communications, 1996

Gordon Penrose is the real-life moniker of Dr. Zed, star of *OWL/TV,* the award-winning PBS science show for kids. The book, illustrated with a mix of color photographs and hilarious illustrations (including a lot of zany cartoon lab rats), each describe over 20 of Dr. Zed's best and most brilliant science activities. Of these, the making of "Magic Mud"—a gooey suspension of cornstarch and water, with interesting and peculiar properties—is clearly the prize; runners-up, in our home lab, were the impressively effective "Air Banger" (make your own thunder) and the kaleidoscopic "Hall of Mirrors," which is not only pretty but also teaches young scientists how to draw a 60-degree angle. Also see *Dr. Zed's Dazzling Book of Science Activities* (1993) and *Science Fun: Hands-On Science With Dr. Zed* (1998).

See **Audiovisual General Science: *Dr. Zed's Brilliant Science Activities*** (page 242).

Making and Using Scientific Equipment
David E. Newton; Franklin Watts, 1993

Detailed instructions for building a wide range of scientific instruments, among them a water clock, thermometer, spring balance, barometer, anemometer, insect collector, telegraph set, spectroscope, and cloud chamber. Users need some basic carpentry skills. For kids aged 12 and up, with a little parental help.

Also see **General Science On-Line: Fun Science Gallery** (page 245).

The Most Amazing Science Pop-Up Book
Jay Young; HarperFestival, 1994

This creative and highly interactive book contains more pop-up scientific paraphernalia than anyone would believe possible. There's an entire Edison phonograph with a rotatable record (spin it around with your finger and you hear a recitation of "Mary Had a Little Lamb"), a pop-up compass, a pop-up microscope (squeeze the sides to focus), a pop-up pinhole camera, and a dramatic pop-up sundial. There's a distortable mirror, a working kaleidoscope, and a pop-up periscope. The book, however, isn't all glitz and no substance; Young also includes plenty of scientific information, fascinating facts, and supplementary color photographs. The book is sturdy, but not tough enough for the very young; a couple of good yanks could eviscerate it.

Mr. Wizard's Supermarket Science
Don Herbert; Random House, 1980

Don Herbert—"Mr. Wizard"—was the host of a popular NBC children's science show in which, every week for 16 years, two lucky kids got to drop by his house, crammed with fascinating paraphernalia, to mess about with science experiments. This book describes over 100 thoroughly entertaining experiments that can be performed with run-of-the-mill stuff from the grocery store, including cereal boxes, baking soda, gelatin, coffee filters, vinegar and oil, cleaning supplies, picnic supplies, paper towels, silverware, straight pins, and potatoes. Included are short, clear explanations of the scientific principles involved. Also see *Mr. Wizard's Experiments for Young Scientists* (Doubleday, 1990).

Ranger Rick's NatureScope Series
National Wildlife Federation; McGraw-Hill

There are 17 titles in this creative science activity book series, each filled with information, arts and crafts, science experiments and case studies, creative writing projects, songs, games, quizzes, and illustrations. Activities are designed to appeal to kids over a range of ages and skill levels, from kindergarten through grade 8. Titles in the series include *Astronomy Adventures, Digging into Dinosaurs, Diving into Oceans, Endangered Species: Wild and Rare, Geology: The Active Earth, Incredible Insects, Trees Are Terrific,* and *Wild About Weather.* In *Geology: The Active Earth,* for example, kids make a contour map and a geological storybook, study real earthquake date, and make a model of the Earth; in *Wild About Weather,* they learn to calculate windchill factor and measure raindrop size, make a barometer, a cloud chart, and a windsock, write "windblown poetry," and put on a radio play titled "The Weather Zapper."

$12.95 each

McGraw-Hill Co.

Box 548

Black Lick, OH 43004-0548

(800) 262-4729

Web site: www.books.mcgraw-hill.com

Science Around the World
Shar Levine and Leslie Johnstone; John Wiley & Sons, 1996

A scientific journey around the world and through time in 84 pages, for middle-grade scientists. The books swings through Egypt, China, Mexico, Germany, the United Kingdom, Canada, the United States, Russia, and Australia. Each chapter begins with a map, highlighting the featured country's location in the world; then follows historical and scientific background information, capsule biographies of famous scientists, "amazing" science facts, and country-related science projects. Under Egypt, for example, kids build an inclined plane of the sort that was so useful in the construction of the pyramids; under China, they make paper; and under Mexico, a model of the world's earliest suspension bridge. While studying Japan, they experiment with a "shaking table" to test the stability of buildings during earthquakes; while studying the United States, they read about Linus Pauling and test orange juice for the presence of vitamin C. An interesting and multidisciplinary approach to science.

Science Art
Deborah Scheeter; Scholastic, 1997

Arts and crafts projects that interface with such science topics as "Plants and Seeds," "Animal Adaptations," "Sky Watch," "Exploring Energy," and "The Way Liquids Work." Kids, for example, experiment with crystal chemistry; make moon maps, construct kaleidoscopes, whirligigs, and kazoos; make "sink and float sparkle jars"; design pressed flower pictures; make symmetrical paper butterflies; trace silhouettes; and marbleize paper. The book, for kids in grades 2–4, includes explanations of how the topics and activities fulfill the National Science Education Curriculum Standards. Also included are a list of supply sources and instructions for making and using student science journals.

Science Arts: Discovering Science Through Art Experiences
Mary Ann Kohl and Jean Potter; Bright Ring, 1993

Over 130 science-based art projects for kids in preschool through grade 4. Users make dancing paper rabbits, magnetic rubbings, and a paint pendulum, experiment with bottle optics, and "erupt" colors. Each art project is accompanied by a brief explanation of the scientific principle involved.

Science Club Series
William Morrow, 1983

Creative and colorful 48-page collections of better-than-average experiments for 8–12-year-olds. Some of these take extra care and effort, but the results are definitely worth it. *Amazing Air* (Henry Smith), for example, includes instructions for making a fire extinguisher, a fan mobile, a hovercraft, and a Cartesian diver; *Super Motion* (Philip Watson) includes instructions for an elaborate electromagnetic, a magnetic race game, a homemade compass, a spring-powered "bouncing woodpecker," and a paddleboat; *Light Fantastic* (Philip Watson), a cellophane color pyramid, a kaleidoscope, a battery-powered "flashing badge," and a pinhole camera; and *Liquid Magic* (Philip Watson), a soap-powered water skier, milk glue, marbled paper, crystals, and a water thermometer.

The Science Explorer
Pat Murphy, Ellen Klages, Linda Shore, and the staff of the Exploratorium; Henry Holt, 1996

A collection of creative hands-on experiments for families from the San Francisco Exploratorium. Experiments are coded with little clocks that indicate how much time each requires: 15 minutes or less, 15 minutes to an hour, or an hour or more. Experiments are grouped under nine categories in a number of different scientific disciplines: "Blowing, Bouncing, Bursting Bubbles," "It's Colorific," "Seeing the Light," "Seeing Isn't Believing," "Rings, Wings, and Other Flying Things," "Dramatic Static," "Marvelous Music and Astounding Sounds," "Hear Here!," and "Mysterious Mixtures." Each experiment includes a list of necessary materials, an illustrated series of instructions, and a scientific explanation of the results.

Science Is . . .
Susan V. Bosak; Scholastic, 1991

A comprehensive—over 500 pages—collection of experiments, challenges, puzzles, hands-on activities, projects, explanations, and (in little boxes) quotations, definitions, and fascinating facts. The book is divided into 10 major subject areas: "Discovering Science," "Matter & Energy" (physics and chemistry), "The Humans" (physiology, psychology, and sociology), "The Environment," "The Rocks," "The Plants," "Living Creatures," "The Weather," "The Heavens," and "Applying Science." Experiments are further broken down according to time requirements: "Quickies" need little preparation and some take only a few minutes to complete; "Make Time" activities require some planning and additional materials and take about half an hour; and "One Leads to Another" activities require some planning and—since related activities build on each other—may involve considerable time, depending on the interest and enthusiasm of the participants. Lots of information, years of activities, and an extensive bibliography of additional resources.

Science for Every Kid Series
6 12 Janice Van Cleave; John Wiley & Sons

Hands-on science books for kids. There are many titles in the series, among them *Astronomy for Every Kid* (1991), *Biology for Every Kid* (1989), *Chemistry for Every Kid* (1989), *Earth Science for Every Kid* (1991), and *Physics for Every Kid* (1991). Each is a collection of 101 "easy experiments that really work" for kids in grades 2–6. Experiments are laid out cookbook-fashion: there's a statement of purpose, a list of materials, an ordered procedure, a description of the (desired) results, and a very brief scientific explanation of what the completed experiment demonstrated. Experiments are simple and easy but vary in interest and appeal. In the *Earth Science* volume, for example, our boys found erasing pencil marks to demonstrate sand formation, bunching towels together to simulate the growth of mountains, ripping paper towels to demonstrate cleavage lines, and squeezing toothpaste tubes to imitate the action of shield volcanoes to be scientifically pretty bland.

Science Surprises!
8 12 Jean R. Feldman; Center for Applied Research in Education, 1995

Nearly 300 experiments and activities for kids aged 8–12. Kids make a telephone, erupt a volcano, and set out a "bug buffet" to study insect eating habits.

Science Teacher's Almanac
6 12 Julia Moutran; Center for Applied Research in Education, 1992

Lesson plans, experiments, and activities organized by month of the school year, from September through June.

Science Wizardry for Kids
7 12 Margaret Kenda and Phyllis S. Williams; Barron's, 1995

Over 200 hands-on science experiments in a fat, attractive comb-bound book. Activities are divided among 25 categories in the fields of chemistry, physics, meteorology, astronomy, botany, zoology, and human physiology. Users learn to make invisible ink and red-cabbage pH indicator solutions, to build a thermometer, to make "edible glass," to mix up a batch of old-fashioned milk-based paint or modern-style fireplace colors, to make a sun clock, a pendulum, and a barometer, to determine the age of a fish, and to build a cricket garden. And much more.

The Scientific Kid
4 9 Mary Stetten Carson; HarperCollins, 1989

Thirty-five simple science projects for the very young, including making rock-candy lollipops, chemical rockets, and a boomerang, dipping candles, writing messages in invisible ink, and producing your own recycled paper.

GAMES AND HANDS-ON ACTIVITIES

Brain Quest: Science
8 12 Workman

One thousand questions (and answers) for kids in grades 4–6 in seven science categories: "Body & Mind," "Planet Earth," "The Universe," "The Kingdoms," "Life Processes," "Atoms, Etc.," and "Mixed Bag." "Is mayonnaise a solution or an emulsion?" "Do fireflies light up to attract a mate or to find food in the dark?" "Does a beach ball have less mass or more mass than a bowling ball?" The questions are listed on two long, skinny decks of two-sided cards, alternating seven questions on one card, the seven answers on the next. Cards are fastened together in the lower corner by a plastic pin, which keeps them from scattering all over the place if you drop them on the floor of the car.

$9.95 from bookstores or
Workman Publishing Co.
708 Broadway
New York, NY 10003

(212) 254-5900 or (800) 722-7202/fax (212) 254-8098

Web site: www.workmanweb.com

6 Guess It

"At the zoo or watching a nature show," begins the enclosed pamphlet, "can you tell one giant day gecko from another? A scientist can. Two lima beans look alike, right? Not to a scientist. Scientist are trained to see even tiny differences between objects—a slightly more oval shape, a shade lighter color, a nick . . ."

"Guess It" is intended to enhance kids' observation and classification skills, using a collection of detailed color photographs. The game includes 48 cards (the "Subject Cards") with photographs of reptiles, minerals, or leaves on the front, descriptive information on the back. The basic game is a visual version of "20 Questions." The Subject Cards are laid faceup on the table; the "Mystery Cards," smaller-size duplicates of the Subject Cards, are shuffled and one is selected by the Mystery Master. The other players, by asking "yes" or "no" questions, attempt to identify the correct Subject Card match. "Does it have stripes?" "Does it have cube-shaped crystals?" "Does it have legs?" The enclosed instruction booklet lists rules for eight other games, at varying levels of difficulty, that can be played with the cards. Recommended for one to six players aged 6 and up.

$13

Aristoplay

450 S. Wagner Rd.

Ann Arbor, MI 48107

(800) 634-7738 or (888) GR8-GAME/fax (734) 995-4611

Web site: www.aristoplay.com

The Private Eye

ALL *The Private Eye*, at first glance, looks to be an unlikely combination of an oversize paperback book and jeweler's loupe—yes, a jeweler's loupe, that little black monocular magnifier through which experts at Tiffany's scrutinize diamonds. Look a bit closer and this disparate duo begins to make sense. *The Private Eye* is a creative thinking program, designed to encourage science, math, art, writing, and the imagination. "Using *The Private Eye*," reads the book's introduction, "you will walk on the back of a beetle, slide down the throat of a foxglove, wade through the hairs on a bean sprout, and traipse over the back of your own hand. You will visit *other worlds*. You will return more enchanted and wiser and closer to this world—and to yourself—than before you left. You will return a poet, a scientist, an artist."

What this means in actual practice is that kids of all ages are encouraged to examine everyday objects closely, through a jeweler's loupe—a lens with a five-fold (5×) power of magnification. They then attempt to make analogies—to come up with five or 10 things that the object resembles or reminds them of—and to write them down. This both stretches the mind and provides raw material for further writing projects. The next step involves making a detailed drawing of the chosen object while repeatedly observing it through the loupe; in the final step, kids are asked to theorize about their observations in order to answer, scientifically, the question "Why is it like that?"

The Private Eye classroom kit starts kids off with 36 prepared study specimens, collectively known as "The World in a Box." These include a sea urchin, a sand dollar, a seahorse, a chunk of amethyst, an assortment of insects and seed pods, and a tiny starfish. The book, however, encourages participants to go out and collect on their own, and a long list of suggestions for observable items includes a fingerprint, strawberries, popcorn, fish skin, bean sprouts, dandelion fluff, tree bark, and feathers. From these tiny jumping-off points, *The Private Eye* suggests expanded projects: studying electron micrographs, keeping a "Private Eye" journal, planting a garden, taking a bug safari, performing a statistical analysis of dandelion heads. Kids are encouraged to make creative connections: to leap from fingerprints to contour maps to Panamanian *molas*, or from seed pods to Escher tessellations. Lists of associated readings, fiction and nonfiction, are included.

The Private Eye manual by Kerry Ruef, 200+ pages long, is recommended for persons "K–12 through life."

$18.95; accompanying 5× jeweler's loupes, $3.95 apiece (with discounts for quantity orders)

The Private Eye Project

7710 31st Ave. NW

Seattle, WA 98117

(206) 784-8813

Science-by-Mail

8
12
Want a scientist pen pal? The Boston Museum of Science sponsors a correspondence program for young scientists. Participants receive two science activity packs per school year, each with an illustrated activity/information book and enough materials to conduct eight or nine hands-on experiments. Each activity pack centers around a specific scientific theme, such as "Flight," "Simple Machines," or "Weather." The activities culminate in the "Big Challenge," an open-ended project that encourages kids to apply what they've learned and to exercise scientific imagination and creativity. They are helped along the way by a scientist pen pal—a volunteer professional with whom they correspond throughout the year for advice, help, and general information.

> Program, $47 for 1 to 4 kids
> Science-by-Mail
> Museum of Science
> Science Park
> Boston, MA 02114
> (617) 589-0437 or (800) 729-3300/fax (617) 589-0474
> e-mail: sbm@A1.mos.org

The Museum of Science also sponsors a "Science Rental Kit" program, available to home study programs. The kits, designed for one to four participating students, include a teacher's activity guide and all the materials needed to explore a selected scientific topic. Kits for kids aged 4–6 include "Birds," "Dinosaurs," "Insect Investigation," "Sound," and "Tremendous Trees"; kits for ages 6–10 include "Electricity and Magnetism," "Microscopes," "Plants and Seeds," "Simple Machines," "Solar System," and "Weather"; and kits for ages 10 and up include "Ancient Egypt," "Just Add Water," "Prehistory," "Rocks and Minerals," and "Wolves and Humans." The kits rent for $25 per week. For more information, call (800) 722-5487.

ScienceTalk Cards

ALL
A pack of attractive turquoise-blue-and-orange "conversation cards," each intended to get kids, relatives, friends—even visiting dinner guests—talking about science-related themes. Each card includes a brief description of a scientific fact or discovery, followed by a conversation-inspiring question. It's an excellent idea, but many of the cards, rather than initiating discussions about science, simply use a science fact as a jumping-off point into something else entirely. A brief description of the ordering of periodic table, for example, is followed by the questions "Do you have a collection of anything? How do you keep track of, arrange, and display your collection?" A short explanation of black holes is followed by "If you could make one thing disappear forever, what would you choose?"; a description of Archimedes and his famous bathtub discovery by "What is the most exciting thing that has ever happened to you?" With all the interesting and controversial issues in science these days, it seems that "ScienceTalk" could have provided considerably more food for talk.

> $5.95 from toy and game stores or
> TableTalk
> Six Country Life Acres
> St. Louis, MO 63131-1403
> (314) 997-5676 or (800) 997-5676/fax (314) 997-3602
> Web site: www.tbltalk.com

Scientists Card Game

6
+
Play a game of rummy, collecting four-card sets of 13 famous scientists. Each card includes a color portrait and a short description of one of the scientist's most notable achievements. Featured scientists include Aristotle, Galileo, Newton, Leonardo da Vinci, Kepler, Copernicus, Dalton, Darwin, Mendel, Fermi, Pasteur, Marie Curie, and Einstein.

> $6
> Aristoplay
> 450 S. Wagner Rd.
> Ann Arbor, MI 48107
> (800) 634-7738 or (888) GR8-GAME
> fax (734) 995-4611
> Web site: www.aristoplay.com

True Science

10
+
This terrific science board game is designed by Aristoplay, the educational game publishers, in collaboration with the producers of NOVA, the popular television science series. The "True Science" playing board pictures an enormous brain, upon which players hop their pieces from brain cell to brain cell, accumulating points by answering quirky, not-so-quirky, and just

plain fascinating questions in six scientific categories: Physics, Earth, Life, Technology, Science & Society, and Random Access (which last is the "True Science" version of "miscellaneous"). There are 900 science questions in all: 600 of these are true/false questions; the remaining 300—on green "Genius Cards"—require short but knowledgeable answers. Correct answers and clever explanations for all questions are included right there on the cards.

It's undeniably educational, but the real achievement of "True Science," in a world of question-and-answer games that feel like final exams, is that it is genuinely delightful. The game gives players a sense for science as scientists see it: a discipline stuffed with imagination, wonder, and occasional mind-boggling surprises. Try these sample questions:

True or false: Astronauts get shorter in space.
   (FALSE. They get taller. On Earth, gravity compresses your spine, which has soft, squeezable cushions of cartilage between the vertebrae.)

True or false: Giraffe hoofs are really toenails.
   (TRUE. These toenails are the size of dinner plates and can crush the skull of an attacking lion.)

The game is recommended for two to four players aged 10 and up. If you've got more than four players, no problem: just add a couple of extra playing pieces to those provided in the game box. We threw in a couple of pebbles swiped from the family rock collection.

$30
Aristoplay
450 S. Wagner Rd.
Ann Arbor, MI 48107
(800) 634-7738 or (888) GR8-GAME/
fax (734) 995-4611
Web site: www.aristoplay.com

AUDIOVISUAL GENERAL SCIENCE

3-2-1 Classroom Contact
8 12 A video version of the popular series from the Children's Television Workshop, aimed at kids in grades 4–6. The series is accompanied by a "Teacher's Guide" containing 60 step-by-step lesson plans, two for each of the 30 *3-2-1 Contact* programs. The lesson plans have enough material for a 40-minute science lesson, with instructions for discussions, demonstrations, and activities. The series itself includes 30 episodes of *3-2-1 Contact* on videotape, each in special 15-minute editions for school viewing. Sets include Earth Science (7 videos), Life Science (11 videos), Physical Science (8 videos), and Scientific Investigation (4 videos).

Earth Science titles include *Antarctica: Getting to the South Pole, Crystals: They're Habit Forming, Erosion: Earth is Change, Fossils: Remains to be Seen, Ocean Environments: 3-D Sea, Volcanoes: Too Hot to Handle,* and *Water Cycle: Go with the Flow.* Life Science titles are *Animal Vision: Eye of the Beholder, Antarctic Animals: Living on the Edge, Australian Mammals: Life Down Under, Bioelectricity: The Shocking Truth, Classification: The Order of Things, Digestion: The Inside Story, Flying Animals: Winging It, Food Chains: Eat and Be Eaten, Innate and Learned Behavior: How Do They Know?, Social Behavior: Living in Groups,* and *Training Animals: Learning New Tricks.* Physical Science titles include *Air is Matter: Air is There, Friction: Getting a Grip, Generating Electricity: More Power to You, Gravity/Weightlessness: Measuring G's, Light and Color: Living Color, Motion and Forces: Play Ball, Refraction: Facts of Light,* and *Surface Tension: Bubble-ology.* Science Investigation titles include *How Do You Know?: Collect the Data, How Do You Know?: Dig It Up!, How Do You Know?: Experiment!, How Do You Know?: Make a Model.* Or you can simply catch the television program on PBS.

Entire series, including teacher's guide plus 30 videos, $360. Videos purchased individually, $15
GPN
University of Nebraska–Lincoln
Box 80669
Lincoln, NE 68501-0669
(800) 228-4630/fax (402) 472-1785

Connections
10 + A fascinating combination of science and history, in which narrator/author James Burke traces the interconnected chains of occurrences that led to landmark scientific inventions and discoveries. Viewers learn, for

example, what the longbow, the stirrup, and the medieval fair had to do with modern telecommunications systems, and how the ancient Chinese loom led to the computer. Titles in the 10-cassette series include "The Trigger Effect," "Death in the Morning," "Distant Voices," "Faith in Numbers," "Wheel of Fortune," "Thunder in the Skies," "The Long Chain," "Eat, Drink, and Be Merry," "Countdown," and "Yesterday, Today, and Tomorrow." Each episode is about one hour long; all are excellent. *Connections* episodes are still aired on television; call the Discovery Channel at (888) 404-5969 for scheduled times. Sequels on video, *Connections 2* and *3*, are also available.

> $129.95
> Discovery Channel Multimedia
> Box 1089
> Florence, KY 41022
> (800) 678-3343
> Web site: www.discovery.com

Dr. Zed's Brilliant Science Activities

A 30-minute video of particularly appealing hands-on experiments by OWL/TV's zany but thoroughly scientific Dr. Zed.

> $14.99
> Movies Unlimited
> 3015 Darnell Rd.
> Philadelphia, PA 19154
> (215) 637-4444 or (800) 4-MOVIES
> E-mail: movies@moviesunlimited.com
> Web site: www.moviesunlimited.com

See **Activity Books:** *Magic Mud and Other Great Experiments* (page 235).

Eyewitness Video Series

Dorling Kindersley

A large series of beautifully photographed science-and-nature videos, each 30 minutes long. Interesting, informative, and enjoyable for kids of all ages. Titles include *The Jungle, Arctic and Antarctic, Sharks, Birds, Butterflies and Moths, Amphibians, The Skeleton, Trees, Rocks and Minerals, Prehistoric Life,* and *Weather*.

> $12.95 apiece
> Dorling Kindersley Publishing
> 1224 Heil Quaker Blvd.
> LaVergne, TN 37086
> (888) DIALDKP
> Web site: www.dk.com

I'd Like to Be a . . . Science Series

A series of audiocassette and activity book kits. Each kit concentrates on a different scientific specialty. Included are *I'd Like to Be An Astronaut* (or a paleontologist, entomologist, marine biologist, chemist, zoologist, meteorologist, and physicist). The audiocassettes each include 12 catchy songs about the featured scientific subject: aspiring paleontologists, for example, sing about *Tyrannosaurus Rex;* young entomologists sing about metamorphosis. Each also includes a commentary by a professional scientist who tells kids something about his/her career. Tapes are accompanied by a 24-page activity book that contains the lyrics to all the songs, coloring pages, and fascinating fact sheets.

> $10 per set
> Twin Sisters Productions
> 1340 Home Ave., Suite D
> Akron, OH 44310-2570
> (800) 248-TWIN/fax (330) 633-8988
> Web site: www.twinsisters.com

The Magic School Bus on Video

Episodes from the popular PBS television series based on Joanna Cole's *Magic School Bus* books are available on video, with Lily Tomlin as the voice of irrepressible science teacher Ms. Frizzle. Each tape runs about 30 minutes.

> $12.99 to $14.99
> Movies Unlimited
> 3015 Darnell Rd.
> Philadelphia, PA 19154
> (215) 637-4444 or (800) 4-MOVIES
> e-mail: movies@moviesunlimited.com
> Web site: www.moviesunlimited.com

See **The Magic School Bus Series** (page 227).

Mr. Wizard's World Science Video Library

Mr. Wizard, star of a now-classic NBC children's science program, is available on video. Mr. Wizard's World Science Video Library is a collection of 20 tapes, 20 minutes each, appropriate for kids in grades

4–8. Titles include *Simple Machines, Inertia, Gravity, Sound Instruments, Action and Reaction, Fluid Flow, Buoyancy and Displacement, Static and High Voltage Electricity, Light Refraction, Light Instruments, Heat Transfer, Heat: Miscellaneous Topics, Light Reflection, Current Electricity, Change of State, Chemistry in the Kitchen, Chemical Tests, Pressure, Chemical Reactions,* and *Combustion.*

$49.50 each (a lot to pay for 20 minutes). Available to accompany the videos are "Small Group Sets" of scientific materials, suitable for about four kids, including everything needed to perform all the experiments demonstrated in the video, plus a teacher's guide. Sets, $20 to $80

ETA

620 Lakeview Pkwy.

Vernon Hills, IL 60061-9923

(847) 816-5050 or (800) 445-5985/fax (800) ETA-9326

e-mail: info@etauniverse.com

Web site: www.etauniverse.com

A cheaper Mr. Wizard video experience shows Mr. Wizard circa 1956, in the television program that first brought him fame. *Watch Mr. Wizard* (Volume I) concentrates on explosions; Volume II, on the human body. Each runs about 30 minutes.

$14.99 each

Movies Unlimited

3015 Darnell Rd.

Philadelphia, PA 19154

(215) 637-4444 or (800) 4-MOVIES

e-mail: movies@moviesunlimited.com

Web site: www.moviesunlimited.com

Tell Me Why Video Series

A "video encyclopedia" for kids in grades K–5. There are 24 videos in the series, each covering a different science-related theme. Titles include *Space, Earth, and Atmosphere; Gems, Metals, and Minerals; Insects; Fish, Shellfish, and Other Underwater Life; Prehistoric Animals and Reptiles; Anatomy and Genetics;* and *Flight.* Each video runs about 30 minutes.

$19.95 apiece

Carolina Biological Supply Co.

2700 York Rd.

Burlington, NC 27215

(800) 334-5551/fax (800) 222-7112

COMPUTER SOFTWARE

Connections

Based on James Burke's best-selling book (see page 230) and popular television series (see page 241) of the same name, this is a scientific and historical megapuzzle. Players must correctly order scientific innovations throughout history, lining them up in proper sequence in a "chain of connections" at the bottom of the screen. (Click on one of these objects and James Burke himself appears and explains how it works and demonstrates its relationship to other objects in the chain.) There are five levels of increasingly challenging play, plus a helpful hints feature. A real mind stretcher; our 12-year-old has been plugging away at it for weeks. For kids aged 10 and up, mostly up. On CD-ROM for Mac or Windows.

$39.95

Discovery Channel Multimedia

Box 1089

Florence, KY 41022

(800) 678-3343

Web site: discovery.com

The Eyewitness Encyclopedia of Science

This multifaceted program features high-quality graphics, photographs, video clips, and animations. Users can access information in four major scientific categories—life sciences, physics, chemistry, and mathematics. There's also a special astronomy section ("Earth and the Universe"), a periodic table (click on any element for more detailed information), "Who's Who?," with pictures and short biographies of famous scientists, and a science "Quizmaster." Recommended for kids in grades 5 and up. On CD-ROM for Mac or Windows.

$40

Dorling Kindersley Publishing

1224 Heil Quaker Blvd.

LaVergne, TN 37086

(888) DIALDKP

Web site: www.dk.com

Sammy's Science House

Science for just-beginners, from the makers of "Millie's Math House" (see page 197). Sammy is a snake, and a tour of his highly interesting house gives little kids a chance to solve animal classification puzzles at the Sorting Station, whip up a blizzard or a thunderstorm with the Weather Machine, or watch Acorn Pond and its inhabitants change with the seasons. Clicking on one of the Pond scene's residents calls up illustrated pages from the Field Notebook with additional interesting information ("To fatten up for winter, a raccoon may eat 4 pounds of food a day. That equals 16 hamburgers!"). Kids can also practice their sequencing skills by arranging still frames of a movie in order, then setting it in motion (forward or backward). The movies deal with some colorful natural phenomenon: a flower growing from a seed, the sun rising and setting. A delightful introduction to science for kids aged 3–6. On CD-ROM for Mac or Windows.

$40

Edmark Corporation

Box 97021

Redmond, WA 98073

(800) 362-2890/fax (206) 556-8430

e-mail: edmarkteam@edmark.com

Web site: www.edmark.com

Science Court

This CD-ROM series combines a cast of zany characters, a gripping (and funny) courtroom drama, scientific facts, and hands-on activities and experiments to teach kids basic science concepts. Each episode in the series tackles a specific question or problem; kids attempt to reach a verdict, based on presented information, demonstrations, and their own experimental data. Does Clara's secret weight-loss potion really block gravity? Is Mary Murray really the laziest worker at Robocorp? Are UFOs about to invade Earth?

Titles in the series include *Water Cycle, Work & Simple Machines, Gravity, Inertia, Statistics,* and *Sound.* Each CD-ROM comes with a detailed illustrated teacher's manual with instructions, discussion questions, reproducible student worksheets, and an answer key. Optional hands-on science kits, containing all materials for the suggested experiments, are also available. On CD-ROM for Mac/Windows. *Science Court* is now an animated television program on ABC.

Each CD-ROM, $59.95; hands-on science kits, $29.95 to $39.95

Tom Snyder Productions

80 Coolidge Hill Rd.

Watertown, MA 02172-2817

(800) 342-0236/fax (617) 926-6222

Web site: www.teachtsp.com

Science Sleuths

There are two volumes of this science detective program; in each, kids must solve a pair of mysteries—sample titles include "The Mystery of the Blob," "The Mystery of the Exploding Lawnmowers," and "The Mystery of the Biogene Picnic"—using a battery of scientific techniques. Young detectives have access to a "virtual lab" filled with 24 scientific tools and instruments—among them an amazingly powerful microscope—with which they can conduct experiments, plus maps, charts, graphs, an on-line encyclopedia, and a collection of video interviews with crucial witnesses and scientific experts. Each volume includes two mysteries at six levels of difficulty: each level has a different solution.

Science Sleuths Volumes I and *II* is appropriate for kids aged 12 and up. *Science Sleuths Elementary,* geared to kids aged 7–12, has a similar problem-solving format and simpler scientific mysteries. There are 24 different episodes available. All on CD-ROM for Mac or Windows.

Science Sleuths Volumes I and II, $79 each; Science Sleuths Elementary, $39 each

Videodiscovery

1700 Westlake Ave. N, Suite 600

Seattle, WA 98109

(800) 548-3472

Web site: www.videodiscovery.com

GENERAL SCIENCE ON-LINE

Bill Nye the Science Guy

Hands-on activities, fun facts, and a supplementary book list linked to the popular kids' television science series. The site also includes a "Demo of the Day" with complete instructions and the "Top Ten Links" to other science Web sites for kids.

nyelabs.kcts.org

Discovery Channel

The site includes lesson plans for kids of all ages, linked to Discovery Channel programs. Lesson plans are categorized under science, humanities, or social studies. Each plan includes television scheduling information, age recommendations, discussion questions, associated activities, and a vocabulary list.

www.discovery.com

Explore Science: Interactive Science Education

Information, interactive experiments, and games for kids aged 10 and up. Visitors to the site participate in an array of interactive science projects. Kids can breed mice and study genetic inheritance patterns, test their response times, experiment with inclined planes and harmonic motion, learn about plasma physics, and use a virtual prism.

www.explorescience.com

Famous Mistakes Page

Short illustrated accounts of inventions and discoveries that resulted for goofs.

www.mistakes.com/fam.html

Fun Science Gallery

How to build scientific instruments and use them to perform experiments. Included are detailed instructions for building a telescope and a stereoscopic microscope and assembling an herbarium, as well as an explanation of the different kinds of optical instruments and how they work, with accompanying activities. For kids of middle school and high school age.

www.best.com/~funsci

The MAD Scientist Network

A varied science site for kids of all ages. Includes the "MAD Labs," a collection of experiments and hands-on activities categorized by scientific field, a tour of the "Visible Human," an "Ask-a-Scientist" question-and-answer page, and a library of links to other science resources on the World Wide Web.

www.madsci.org

Science Fair Project Resource Guide

How-to activities, samples of successful science fair projects by kids of all ages, idea suggestions, references, resources, and related Web sites.

www.ipl.org/youth/projectguide

Science Learning Network

A large and creative science site, with links to information and activities on many different aspects of science. Users can learn about weather technologies in "Franklin's Forecast," take a tour of a whirligig farm, learn about the science of sports, or perform chemistry experiments. Also includes links to science museums.

www.sln.org

UT Science Bytes

Science information for elementary and secondary students, based on the work of scientists at the University of Tennessee. Each page is designed by a scientist in a different field or specialty. A geologist, for example, provides a description of his own research and a basic overview of geology, with definitions of key terms, maps, photographs, quizzes and puzzles, a supplementary reading list, and links to related Web sites.

loki.ur.utk.edu/ut2kids

Whelmers

Teacher-recommended science activities for kids of all ages, with complete instructions, diagrams, and scientific background information. Activities include "Air Cannon," "Pretzel Predictions," "Density Balloon," and "Potato Float."

mcrel.org/whelmers

The Why Files

Interesting and readily understandable explanations of the science behind stories in the news. The stories are categorized by topic: biology, environmental science, health, and physical science. Each story includes photographs and illustrations, a straightforward text, a supplementary reading list, links to related

Web sites, and quizzes. The site also includes an archive of truly cool science images, from comets and super-novas to crystals and microbes.

whyfiles.news.wisc.edu

8 12 *You Can With Beakman and Jax*

Interactive demonstrations and experiments based on kids' science questions, such as "How does a remote control work?," "What is a magnet?," and "Why do leaves change color in the fall?" Included are links to *Beakman's World,* the popular kids' science television show.

www.beakman.com

Also see *The Best of You Can With Beakman & Jax* (page 234).

SCIENCE MUSEUMS ON-LINE

Exploratorium

ALL The San Francisco Exploratorium on-line. Visitors to the site can dissect a cow's eye, study the science of shadows on a "Lightwalk," or visit "The Learning Studio" to participate in an array of interactive experiments and demonstrations. The site also includes instructions for making home versions of many of the Exploratorium's terrific science exhibits.

www.exploratorium.edu

The Franklin Institute Science Museum

ALL Includes virtual tours of museum exhibits, including a walk-through of the human heart, an investigation of the life and works of institute namesake Benjamin Franklin, and a journey through the universe. The site includes science news stories, science lesson plans for kids of all ages, a visit to an on-line biology class, quizzes and puzzles, and an on-line magazine, the *inQuiry Almanac.* The *Almanac* contains a "Thisday" feature, updated daily, which lists landmark events on this day in history, science, and math; a literary "Word of the Day"; and daily almanac entries.

sln.fi/edu

Miami Museum of Science

ALL Visitors to the site can tour museum exhibits, among them "The Atoms Family," a multifaceted exhibit about atoms and matter, light, energy, and electricity. The site also includes "Science Inquiry Hotlists," links to related sites in such fields as earth and space science, life science, history and nature of science, and physical science.

www.miamisci.org

Museum of Science, Boston

ALL The site includes "Archaeology and the Big Dig," a virtual tour of an American Indian archaeological site on Boston Harbor Island; a view of the world's largest Van de Graaff generator; an exploration of the life and work of Leonardo da Vinci; and an explanation of how a scanning electron microscope works, with views of many unusual objects very close up.

www.mos.org

See **Games and Hands-On Activities: Science-by-Mail** (page 240).

Oregon Museum of Science and Industry

ALL Includes video clips of the museum's famous hairless rats (Princess Gruesome and Cinderella) and "Science Whatzit?," a large collection of kids' questions about science with answers. Examples include "Why is the grass green and the sky blue?," "How does a hologram work and can I make one?," and "What makes an electric eel electric?"

www.omsi.edu

Science Museum of Minnesota

ALL The museum's "Thinking Fountain" includes many on-line science activities for kids, organized alphabetically or by theme. Themes include "Shapes," "Tropical Rainforest," and "Loose Parts," a collection of projects using recycled materials. There are also links to galleries displaying kids' science and art projects.

www.sci.mus.mn.us

Smithsonian Institution

ALL Visitors can search for information on all branches of the natural sciences or tour museum collections on-line. Includes beautiful views of the Smithsonian Gem and Mineral Collection.

www.si.edu

ASTRONOMY

Though entire courses dedicated to astronomy are generally not offered until students reach college, astronomy in the public schools is incorporated into both elementary and secondary science programs. Early-elementary kids learn about the solar system and its planets; upper-elementary and middle school kids study the basics of astronomy, stars and galaxies, the structure of the universe, and space exploration. Since our boys all turned out to be enthusiastic amateur astronomers, astronomical topics occupied a sizable chunk of our homeschool science program, and we studied it in greater than usual depth. We used a combination of home-written workbooks, audiocassette lectures, videos, astronomy magazines, popular science books, and eventually a college textbook (*Astronomy Today* by Eric Chaisson and Steve McMillan; see page 252)—all accompanied by a lot of time spent outside at night, scouring the sky with binoculars, a telescope, and more or less naked (four of us wear glasses) eyes.

We also linked astronomy to history, the arts, mathematics, and literature. The boys read biographies of famous astronomers, made astronomical timelines, and built models of Galileo's first telescope. They built and launched model rockets. They listened to Holst's *The Planets,* admired van Gogh's *Starry Night,* and read Carl Sagan's *Contact,* Gore Vidal's play *Visit to a Small Planet,* and Ray Bradbury's *The Martian Chronicles.* They kept up with astronomy in the news, reading current science articles on space exploration and discoveries. Josh read poems with astronomical subjects, among them Robert P. Tristram Coffin's "Star-Pudding," Frank O'Hara's "Talking to the Sun on Fire Island," and Carl Sandburg's "Early Moon," and wrote a series of his own.

Astronomy is a challenging subject, and none of our three boys approached it in quite the same way. Ethan, who takes astronomy very seriously, is most interested in the physical and mathematical aspects of astronomy, the mechanics of telescopes, and astrophotography; Caleb is fascinated by SETI and the search for extraterrestrial life; and Josh is interested in ancient astronomy and its possible indications of early visitors from outer space. All three are interested in skywatching, a year-round activity that gave all (and their parents) a working knowledge of the night sky. They're also fans of *Star Trek.*

From my homeschool journal:

◆ October 16, 1995. Josh is fourteen; Ethan, twelve; Caleb, eleven.

Started a new set of (homemade) astronomy workbooks today. We covered the electromagnetic spectrum from radio waves to cosmic waves, using scientific notation to compare various wavelengths. The boys made detailed diagrams—gorgeously illustrated with colored pencils—showing the various kinds of waves and their lengths. Discussed relationship between frequency and energy.

◆ October 18, 1995

Covered astrospectroscopy, using the Microslide viewer and sets of Astroslides (see page 258). Explained continuous, absorption, and bright-line spectra and the concept of red shift, using assorted reference books. Covered the structure of the sun, drew diagrams of the sun's inner layers, and defined convection, nuclear fusion, neutrino, plasma, and positron. Caleb demanded explanation of a line from a book of Foxtrot *cartoons: "Plasma man bathes in neutrino water!"*

Calculated the circumference of the sun's core.

Read detailed article "The Life of the Sun" from the NewScientist *magazine.*

Caleb listed all the planets in order; he still remembers the words to a planet song that he learned while studying astronomy five years ago. It has several verses and is sung to the tune of "When Johnny Comes Marching Home."

All three boys read "The Nine Billion Names of God," a science-fiction short story by Arthur C. Clarke about astronomers attempting to catalog all the stars in the universe.

TELESCOPES

Amateur astronomy can range from the rock-bottom cheap to the extremely expensive, depending on the depth of your family's interests, abilities, and pocketbook. At the simplest level, our family—to a person a group of enthusiastic sky watchers—has done pretty well with five pairs of eyes, a flashlight wrapped in red cellophane, and a book of star maps. The eyes are for looking up, the star maps tell you what you're looking at, and the red cellophane preserves your night vision in between. Naked-eye astronomy is fun and friendly, and—with 6,000 visible stars up there every clear night—there's always plenty of material to work on.

A useful gadget for stargazing at the naked-eye level is a planisphere, which is essentially a dial-a-sky wheel, adjustable for the month of the year and time of night, showing the positions of the visible stars. Planispheres, in small and large sizes, are available from astronomical supply companies (see below).

Next step up from the unadorned eye is a set of binoculars. I actually prefer these to the telescope, because they're portable, versatile, and easy to use. Binoculars come in a large range of sizes, usually with defining numbers printed somewhere on the eyepiece: 6 × 25, for example, or 7 × 35. The first number—the 6 or the 7—is the magnifying power of the binoculars; the second number, the 25 or 35, gives the diameter of the objective lenses (the big lenses in the front) in millimeters. The bigger the objectives, the more light enters the binocular tubes, and the brighter and clearer the observed image. There's a trade-off, however: As the objectives get bigger, the binoculars themselves get bigger, heavier, and harder to hold, and may need to be steadied on a tripod. Generally recommended for amateur astronomers is a 7 × 50 binocular, which costs anywhere from $50 to $500, depending on quality.

Acquisition of binoculars opens up a whole new astronomical world. It's fun to explore on your own—just wait until you point those new binoculars at the Pleiades—but you'll get the most out of your instrument by using an astronomical guidebook that specifically lists prime sights visible through binoculars.

Finally, telescopes. Kids can, as I've pointed out, have terrific astronomical experiences without one—but it's undeniably true that some celestial sights are simply out of reach without a telescope. There are three major types of telescopes: refracting telescopes, in which a primary convex lens collects the light and forms an image, which is then magnified by the lens in the eyepiece; reflecting telescopes, in which light is collected by a concave mirror, then bounced off a second mirror and reflected into the eyepiece; and catadioptric telescopes—the best known are the Schmidt-Cassegrains—which use a combination of mirrors and lenses. To view the sky through a refracting telescope, you position yourself at one end and look right straight through the tube, like a pirate peering through a spyglass; with a reflecting telescope, you stand beside the telescope, peeking through an eyepiece positioned perpendicular to the telescope's main tube. Refracting telescopes are noted for their nice, sharp images, and they're easy to take care of; this is probably the telescope of choice for astronomers who are nervous about tinkering with their machines. Reflecting telescopes deliver much brighter images and are somewhat cheaper; their downside is that their mirrors periodically wiggle out of line and require recalibration.

In all telescopes, diameter is the name of the game: generally, the fatter the telescope, the better it is. Diameter determines the light-collecting ability of the objective lens in a refracting telescope or of the mirror in a reflector. The bigger the lens or mirror, the more light is admitted to the instrument, and the better you'll be able to see. Generally recommended for beginners is a 60mm refractor or a 4½-inch reflector, both of which are obtainable in the $100 to $200 price range. Bigger yet becomes increasingly expensive; 80mm refractors and reflecting telescopes with 6- or 8-inch mirrors start around $400 and climb, and Schmidt-Cassegrains—for absolutely serious observers—start around $1,000.

Catalogs provide consumers with a rash of descriptive numbers for each telescope. The *focal length* of the telescope is the distance from the objective lens or the primary mirror to the image it forms; the longer the focal length, the more magnification obtainable with a given eyepiece. More commonly listed is *focal ratio:* the telescope's focal length divided by the diameter of the primary lens or mirror (the aperture). Short-focus telescopes, with focal ratios of f/6 or less, are best for big, broad views of the sky; long-focus scopes, with focal ratios of f/10 or greater, are used for more restricted, high-magnification viewing, best for zeroing in on lunar craters and planetary surfaces. Most beginner telescopes have focal ratios of f/6 or f/8, which are fine for general purposes. *Field of view* is the size of the piece of sky, in degrees, that can be seen through the eyepiece. The bigger this is, the easier it is to locate objects through the telescope, which can be an issue for star-viewing kids. The higher the magnification of the eyepiece, the smaller the field of view.

Magnification is the function of the lens in the telescope's eyepiece. Beginner telescopes usually come with one standard eyepiece; additional eyepieces, capable of different magnifications, can be purchased separately. Eyepieces are sold by focal length, measured in millimeters: the lower the focal length of the eyepiece, the higher the magnification. The *actual* magnification obtained with a given eyepiece, however, depends on the telescope to which it's attached. Magnification is determined by dividing the focal length of the telescope by the focal length of the eyepiece; thus the longer the focal length of the scope, the higher the magnification that the telescope will produce with a given eyepiece. Telescopes are commonly sold with a 25mm eyepiece, which gives a magnification of 28× with a typical 60mm refracting telescope and 40× with a 4-inch reflecting telescope. Recommended is an additional 12mm eyepiece, which ups the magnification to 60× and 85×, respectively.

Magnification, experts warn, is the quantity most likely to deceive new telescope buyers. "High magnification" sounds good in the advertisements, but it's not the defining characteristic of a quality telescope. Too much magnification, in fact, can get you into trouble. Effective magnification is limited by the size of the light-collecting aperture of the telescope—that is, the diameter of the objective lens or primary mirror. The rule of thumb is 60× magnification per inch of aperture—which means 144× max for a 60mm refractor and 240× for a 4-inch reflector. Exceed that level and images seen through your telescope will get progressively dimmer and fuzzier.

A final word on telescope purchase: reputable dealers in astronomical instruments are more reliable (and much more helpful) than the average neighborhood department store. Avoid anything that's either rickety or plastic; the instability will make for a miserable viewing experience, and plastic is optically lousy. A good used telescope, on the other hand, can be an excellent buy; telescopes, unless monumentally abused, don't wear out. An excellent source for used-telescope seekers is the classified ad section in *Astronomy* or *Sky & Telescope* magazines (see page 251).

Sources for Telescopes, Astronomical Instruments, and Supplies

Astronomical Society of the Pacific
390 Ashton Ave.
San Francisco, CA 94112
(800) 335-2624 orders or (800) 962-3412 customer service/fax (415) 337-5205
Web site: www.aspsky.org

Edmund Scientific Company
101 E. Gloucester Pike
Barrington, NJ 08007-1380
(609) 547-8880 or (800) 728-6999/fax (609) 547-3292
e-mail: scientifics@edsci.com
Web site: www.edsci.com

Meade Instruments Corporation
16542 Millikan Ave.
Irvine, CA 92606
(714) 756-2291

Sky Publishing Corporation
Box 9111
Belmont, MA 02178-9111
(800) 253-0245

Telescope & Binocular Center
Box 1815
Santa Cruz, CA 95061-1815
(408) 763-7030 or (800) 447-1001
Web site: www.oriontel.com

Books About Telescopes

Looking Inside Telescopes and the Night Sky
Ron Schultz, Nick Gadbois, and Peter Aschwanden; John Muir Publications, 1992

All about the different kinds of telescopes and how they work, for kids aged 9–12.

Making and Enjoying Telescopes: 6 Complete Projects and a Stargazer's Guide

Robert Miller and Kenneth Wilson; Lark Books, 1995

Background information, detailed instructions, and diagrams for building six amateur telescopes. For teenagers and up.

Star Ware: The Amateur Astronomer's Ultimate Guide to Choosing, Buying, and Using Telescopes and Accessories

Philip S. Harrington; John Wiley & Sons, 1994

A comprehensive 300+-page guide to telescopes and telescope buying, an overview of the telescope market, pointers for viewing the sky through a telescope, and a chapter for telescope builders ("The Homemade Astronomer").

Telescope Power: Fantastic Activities and Easy Projects for Young Astronomers

Gregory L. Matloff; John Wiley & Sons, 1993

An introduction to the telescope and its uses, and instructions for viewing the moon, planets, stars, and the sun. For astronomers aged 9–12.

STAR MAPS AND GUIDES

365 Starry Nights

Chet Raymo; Simon & Schuster, 1992

This is a marvelous book of naked-eye stargazing sights for each night of the year, illustrated with nightly star maps and fascinatingly fleshed out with historical stories and scientific explanations. Work through the whole year, one night at a time, and you and your kids will acquire a thorough astronomical education, enjoying yourselves every step of the way. Our much-used copy has become so tattered that it's now held together by package tape (and somebody, I notice, once upon a time, colored all the January stars with yellow crayon). The book's only drawback is that it lacks an index, which can be maddening if you want to look up something specific, like "Vega," "globular cluster," or "parallax."

Discover the Stars

Richard Berry; Harmony Books, 1987

About telescopes and how to buy one, basic astronomical background information, and 23 seasonal star charts, each with an accompanying text listing highlights of the sky and explaining what you should be able to see with unaided eyes, with binoculars, and with a telescope.

Exploring the Night Sky With Binoculars

Patrick K. Moore; Cambridge University Press, 1996

Explains the different types of binoculars and how they work and gives precise descriptions of astronomical sights visible through binoculars. The book covers double and variable stars, star clusters, nebulae, and galaxies, and all the constellations in alphabetical order. For each constellation, there is a labeled star map and a detailed explanatory text.

Skywatching

David H. Levy; The Nature Company, 1994

A wonderful volume for astronomers of all ages, crammed with information, color graphics, fact boxes and tables, and spectacular photographs. There are seasonal sky charts and detailed maps of all the constellations in alphabetical order, from Andromeda to Vulpecula. Each constellation is accompanied by a descriptive list of its most interesting features, variously visible with the naked eye, binoculars, or a telescope. There's also a chapter on the history of astronomy, capsule biographies of famous astronomers, information on astronomical instruments, explanations of basic astronomical principles, and an illustrated tour of the solar system.

Also see *Advanced Skywatching* (Robert Burnham, Alan Dyer, Robert A. Garfinkle, Martin George, Jeff Kanipe, and David H. Levy; The Nature Company, 1997), which includes more advanced information and very detailed sky maps ("Starhopping Guide").

The Stars: A New Way to See Them

H. A. Rey; Houghton Mifflin, 1980

"This book," begins H. A. Rey, "is meant for people who want to know just enough about the stars to be able to go out at night and find the major constellations, for the mere pleasure of it." Rey's system teaches the constellations by picturing them in a new and more graphically memorable way, showing viewers how to "connect the stars" of the constellations to form shapes more closely resembling the figures those constellations are supposed to represent. Rey's version of Gemini, for example, looks just like a pair of stick-figure twins holding hands—and once you've seen it, it's easy to remember and easy to find in the night sky. The book includes diagrams and descriptions of all the major constellations, a collection of seasonal star charts (shown with and without the little lines delineating the constellations), and a lot of general astronomical information. A great guide for beginners.

A shorter, simpler version of the book, *Find the Constellations,* is available for younger readers.

Star Maps for Beginners

ALL I. M. Levitt and Roy K. Marshall; Simon & Schuster, 1992

Twelve easy-to-use star maps, one for each month of the year.

The Ultimate Guide to the Sky: How to Find the Constellations and Read the Night Sky Like a Pro

John Mosley; Lowell House, 1997

A stargazer's guide for kids aged 9–12. The books lists and describes 88 constellations in alphabetical order and includes star charts for each month of the year.

See **Computer Software: Electronic Planetariums** (page 264).

MAGAZINES

Astronomy

A monthly magazine for astronomy buffs. Each issue includes several major articles on astronomical phenomena and events, reports on recent astronomical discoveries, reviews of new books and products, and the invaluable "Sky Almanac," a detailed description of the sights of each month's sky, complete with a full-color pull-out star map, planetary path map, and moon phase chart.

Annual subscription (12 issues), $35
Astronomy

Box 378
Waukesha, WI 53187-0378
(800) 533-6644
Web site: www.kalmbach.com/astro/astronomy.html

Final Frontier

A bimonthly magazine of space, science, and astronomy, with a touch of science fiction. Includes short reports on the latest in space research, lists of hot spots on the Net for space science buffs, book and software reviews, and "Backyard Universe," a description of seasonal events in the night sky.

Annual subscription (6 issues), $17.95
Final Frontier
Box 16179
North Hollywood, CA 91615-6179
(800) 447-7387
Web site: www.ateg.com

Odyssey

From Cobblestone Publishing, for astronomy-minded kids in grades 4–9. Each 49-page issue centers around a single main topic and includes assorted nonfiction articles, interviews with scientists, terrific photographs and color illustrations, puzzles, games, and suggestions for hands-on activities. Topics for the 1996–97 school year, for example, included "Eclipse!," "Model Rocketry: Hobby and Science," "Looking for Other Earths," "Astrophotography," and "Mapping the Universe."

Annual subscription (9 issues), $24.95
Odyssey
Cobblestone Publishing, Inc.
30 Grove St.
Peterborough, NH 03458-1454
(603) 924-7209 or (800) 821-0115/fax (603) 924-7380
e-mail: custsvc@cobblestone.mv.com
Web site: www.cobblestonepub.com

Sky & Telescope

A monthly astronomy magazine. Each issue includes several articles on astronomical topics, accounts of recent happenings in astronomical research, new product reviews, and a monthly star chart, with detailed descriptions of what can best be seen in the seasonal sky. The magazine also sponsors the "Skyline," a telephone hot line for astronomers, updated weekly on Friday afternoons: call (617) 497-4168 for the latest in skywatching information.

Annual subscription (12 issues), $36

Sky & Telescope
Box 9111
Belmont, MA 02178-9917
(800) 253-0245/fax (617) 864-6117
e-mail: orders@skypub.com
Web site: www.skypub.com

Also see **General Science Magazines** (page 218).

BOOKS ABOUT ASTRONOMY

Astronomy
Kristen Lippincott; Dorling Kindersley, 1995

A volume in the popular Eyewitness Science Series (see page 226), illustrated with terrific color photographs, drawings, diagrams, and models. The book covers astronomical instruments, techniques, history, and landmark discoveries. Most of the information is in the picture captions.

Astronomy Today
Eric Chaisson and Steve McMillan; Prentice-Hall, 1997

If your older kids are seriously interested in astronomy, you might try this. Touted as the best astronomy textbook on the market, this is a well-written and beautifully illustrated college-level text, filled with color photographs, overlays, diagrams, tables, and informational boxes. Chapters cover astronomical history, telescopes, astronomical techniques and measurements, the planets, the sun, stars and their evolution, neutron stars and black holes, galaxies, cosmology, and life in the universe. Each chapter includes a summary, self-test, discussion questions, problems, and suggested projects.

The Beginning of the Earth
Franklyn M. Branley; HarperCollins, 1988

The Big Bang, clearly explained for kids aged 4–9. The book describes the formation of the sun and the planets in the solar system from a massive cloud of gas and dust, billions of years ago.

See the **Let's-Read-and-Find-Out Science Series** (page 227).

The Big Dipper and You
E. C. Krupp; William Morrow, 1989

The history and science of the northern hemisphere's best-known constellation, in 48 illustrated pages. Young readers learn why the handle of the Big Dipper hangs down ("like an icicle") in winter and points up ("like a dipper full of cold lemonade") in summer; that the second (double) star in the Dipper's handle was used by the ancient Persians as a test of eyesight; and that every year, on your birthday, you've not only grown another year older, you've traveled another 583 million miles around the sun. Also see *The Moon and You* (1993).

See *The Comet and You* (below).

The Comet and You
E. C. Krupp; Macmillan, 1985

The history and science of Halley's Comet, filled with fascinating facts, for readers aged 7–11. "A complete trip around the orbit of Halley's Comet is about 7 billion (7,000,000,000) miles. It would take a string of 72 trillion (72,000,000,000,000) hot dogs to go all the way around this path. That's enough for two hot dogs each day for each person now on earth for 22 years."

See *The Big Dipper and You* (above).

Cosmic Questions: Galactic Halos, Cold Dark Matter and the End of Time
Richard Morris; John Wiley & Sons, 1995

An introduction to cosmology for beginners, through 10 frequently asked questions, among them "Is the universe infinite?," "Where did galaxies come from?," and "When did time begin?" The basics of this isn't all that basic. For teenagers and up.

The Dark Side of the Universe: A Scientist Explores the Mysteries of the Cosmos
James Trefil; Anchor Books, 1989

Astronomy, cosmology, and physics, fascinatingly explained for the general public. Chapter titles include "The Big Bang," "Five Reasons Why Galaxies Can't Exist," "Dark Matter: Less Than Meets the Eye," "The Massive Neutrino Caper," and "Is the Universe Controlled by Wimps?" For interested teenagers.

The Friendly Guide to the Universe
Nancy Hathaway; Viking, 1994

All about the universe in 462 pages, divided into short, friendly chunks. The book includes timelines, biographies of famous astronomers (male and female), explanations of astronomical concepts, astronomical anecdotes, scientific and historical facts about astronomical objects, black-and-white illustrations, and quotations from astronomy lovers as diverse as Walt Whitman, Gertrude Stein, Vincent van Gogh, and H. G. Wells. It begins with an "abbreviated" chronology of the universe, from the Big Bang 15 to 20 billion years ago through the formation of galaxies and planets, the discoveries of astronomers, ancient and modern, and on into the distant future when—depending—scientists predict that the universe will either disintegrate or contract back upon itself in a final Big Crunch. Subsequent book sections include "The Solar System," "The Milky Way and Beyond," and "An Album of Stars and Constellations."

Also included is a wonderful story about Theodore Roosevelt who, on camping trips with naturalist William Beebe, would locate the faint smear of the Andromeda Galaxy in the night sky and then recite:

> This is the Spiral Galaxy in Andromeda.
> It is as large as our Milky Way.
> It is one of a hundred million galaxies.
> It is 750,000 light years away.
> It consists of a hundred billion suns, each larger than our sun.

Then Roosevelt would grin his famous grin and announce, "Now I think we are small enough! Let's go to bed."

Seldom is so much information made so clear and so delightful. A terrific resource for educators.

Let's-Read-and-Find-Out Science Series: Astronomy
Franklyn M. Branley; HarperTrophy

The Let's-Read-and-Find-Out series is a large collection of science picture books for 4–9-year-olds. There are many astronomy-related titles in the series, among them *Comets, The Planets in Our Solar System,*

The Moon Seems to Change, Shooting Stars, and *The Sun: Our Nearest Star.* All are short, simple, interesting, and charmingly illustrated.

See the **Let's-Read-and-Find-Out Science Series** (page 227).

The Magic School Bus Lost in the Solar System
Joanna Cole; Scholastic, 1990

Ms. Frizzle's class boards the Magic School Bus for a field trip to the planetarium—and ends up rocketing into outer space. They visit the moon, sun, and each of the planets in the solar system, learning about each as they go. Science facts are presented in the form of kids' science reports in the margins, each printed on lined notebook paper: "Why Do People Feel Weightless in Space? by Phil," "Why Is It So Hot on Venus? by Ralph," "Is Pluto a Real Planet? by Wanda." Finally the bus parachutes back to the schoolyard and the kids, returned to the classroom, make a detailed "Planet Chart" and an elaborate solar system mobile that just might inspire your kids to make one of their own. With delightful illustrations by Bruce Degen.

See **The Magic School Bus Series** (page 227).

Moonwalk: The First Trip to the Moon
Judy Donnelly; Random House, 1989

An easy-to-read account of the *Apollo 11* mission, for kids aged 4–8.

New True Books
Children's Press

The New True Books series, for kids in grades 2–4, includes several astronomy titles. Each book is 48 pages long, divided into very short chapters. The straightforward, large-print text is illustrated with terrific color photographs and drawings. The series includes *Black Holes* and *Comets and Meteor Showers* by Paul Sipiera and volumes on the earth and each of the planets in the solar system by Dennis Fradin.

See **New True Books** (page 228).

The Night Sky Book: An Everyday Guide to Every Night
Jamie Jobb; Little, Brown, 1977

One of the creative Brown Paper School Book series, this excellent overview of astronomy for kids is filled with interesting information, clever illustrations, and many suggestions for hands-on projects. The book is divided into five major sections. "North and Night" covers ways of finding direction using the stars; "Sphere and Here" explains ways of locating yourself on planet Earth; "Noon and Moon" discusses the zodiac, the moon, and using the sky to tell time; "Planets and Orbits" covers the solar system; and "Star and Light" covers meteor showers, constellations, galaxies, and the lives of stars. Instructions are included for playing a game of "Find That Constellation," for making a "Solar System Salad" (you'll need a football field and assorted vegetables, ranging in size from a pea to a cabbage), and for building a night clock, an astrolabe, a solar stone, and a moon bone.

Postcards from Pluto
Loreen Leedy; Holiday House, 1993

A troop of interested kids led by the knowledgeable Dr. Quasar tour all the planets of the solar system, sending informative postcards home from every stop along the way.

A Question of Science Series: Astronomy
Sidney Rosen; Carolrhoda

Astronomical titles in the Question of Science picture-book series include *Can You Find A Planet?* (1992), *Can You Hitch A Ride on a Comet?* (1993), and *How Far Is a Star?* (1992). Each book includes color photographs, humorous illustrations, and a friendly question-and-answer-style text.

See **A Question of Science Series** (page 228).

Secrets of the Night Sky
Bob Berman; William Morrow, 1995

This book is intended for an adult audience but is so reader-friendly that it may appeal to a wide range of ages. (We read it aloud as a group.) It covers all the many fascinations of astronomy, from the aurora borealis to black holes. Chapter titles include "Baa, Baa, Betelgeuse," "Puzzles of the Polestar," "Satellite Season," and "The Andromeda Connection." Want to know how to tell a reconnaissance satellite from a weather balloon

from a UFO? Read Berman. Appendixes discuss telescopes, binoculars, and viewing tips.

Seymour Simon's Astronomy Series
Mulberry

Seymour Simon's superb astronomy books are graphically spectacular. Each 32-page book is illustrated with dazzling color photographs: a computer-enhanced multicolored Saturn; an orange-and-gold erupting volcano on Jupiter's moon Io; the glowing pink rim of the sun's chromosphere, photographed during a lunar eclipse. Titles include *Mercury, Venus, Mars, Jupiter, Saturn, Uranus, Neptune, The Sun, Stars, Galaxies, Our Solar System,* and *Comets, Meteors, and Asteroids.* Each includes a clear informational text, filled with appealing facts. "Think of this," Seymour writes in *The Sun*, "if Earth were the size of a golf ball, then the sun would be a globe about fifteen feet across." Also see *Exploring Space: Using Seymour Simon's Astronomy Books in the Classroom* (Barbara Bourne and Wendy Saul; William Morrow, 1994).

Stargazers
Gail Gibbons; Holiday House, 1992

A brightly illustrated introduction to astronomy for kids aged 4–8. A simple text explains what stars and constellations are and how telescopes work. Also see, by the same author, *The Moon Book* (1998).

BIOGRAPHIES OF ASTRONOMERS

American Astronomers: Searchers and Wonderers
Carole Ann Camp; Enslow Publishing, 1996

Biographies of 10 prominent American astronomers for readers aged 10 and up. Included are Annie Jump Cannon, George Ellery Hale, Edwin Hubble, Maria Mitchell, and Carl Sagan. The book covers the life and work of each, with brief quotations from their writings.

Clyde Tombaugh and the Search for Planet X
Margaret K. Wetterer; Carolrhoda, 1996

An illustrated biography of the discoverer of Pluto, beginning with his childhood (with homemade telescope) in the midwest, for kids aged 7–11.

Edmond Halley, the Man and His Comet
Barbara Hooper Heckart; Children's Press, 1984

A biography of the astronomer who predicted the return of Halley's Comet. For readers aged 9–12.

Edwin Hubble: Discoverer of Galaxies
Claire L. Datnow; Enslow Publishing, 1997

A 128-page account of the life and work of astronomer Edwin Hubble, who discovered that the universe is expanding and calculated the famous Hubble constant. For readers aged 9–12.

Galileo
Leonard Everett Fisher; Macmillan, 1992

A dramatically illustrated picture-book biography of Galileo for kids aged 8–12.

Galileo and the Universe
Steve Parker; Chelsea House, 1995

An excellent biography of Galileo for readers aged 8–12, illustrated with paintings, prints, and photographs. The book covers Galileo's life from his boyhood in Pisa through his landmark discoveries in the physical sciences and astronomy, and his troubles with the church.

Mr. Halley and His Comet
Teresa Dahlquist; Polestar-Nexus, 1986

A rhyming picture-book account of the life and work of astronomer Edmond Halley, famed for predicting the return of the comet that bears his name.

Rocket Man: The Story of Robert Goddard
Tom Streissguth; Carolrhoda, 1995

A short biography of the pioneer rocket scientist who launched his landmark inventions from a Massachusetts cow pasture. For readers aged 9–12.

Rooftop Astronomer: A Story About Maria Mitchell
Stephanie Sammartino McPherson; Carolrhoda, 1990

A 64-page account of the life and work of Maria Mitchell, famed for her discovery of a comet, who became the first woman elected to the American Academy of Arts and Sciences.

The Starry Messenger
Peter Sis; Farrar, Straus & Giroux, 1996

An exquisitely illustrated biography of Galileo for readers aged 6 and up. The book covers the life, work, and world of Galileo through unusual and creative artwork, supplemented by timelines, quotations, and scientific explanations. The book is fascinating on many levels.

What Are You Figuring Now?: A Story About Benjamin Banneker
Jeri Ferris; First Avenue Editions, 1990

A 64-page biography of the black farmer who became a self-taught mathematician, astronomer, and surveyor. Banneker participated in surveying the ground for the city of Washington, D.C., in 1791 and is famed for writing a notably accurate almanac.

LITERATURE LINKS TO ASTRONOMY

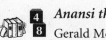
Anansi the Spider: A Tale from the Ashanti
Gerald McDermott; Henry Holt, 1988

A picture-book version of a West African folktale about how the moon came to be.

The Church Mice and the Moon
Graham Oakley; Atheneum, 1974

A hilarious account of Wortlethorpe's Municipal Moon Program, in which two inept scientists attempt to send the two church mice, Arthur and Humphrey, to the moon. The mission fails abysmally. For readers aged 5–10.

Follow the Drinking Gourd
Jeanette Winter; Alfred A. Knopf, 1992

Following the directions in the song "Follow the Drinking Gourd," a black family escapes from slavery and travels north to Canada, navigating by the Big Dipper. For readers aged 4–8. Also see *The Drinking Gourd* (F. N. Monjo; Harpercollins, 1993) and *Follow the Drinking Gourd* (Bernardine Connelly; Simon & Schuster, 1997).

The Lost Children: The Boys Who Were Neglected

Paul Goble; Bradbury Press, 1993

A beautifully illustrated picture-book version of an American Indian legend that tells the story of the Pleiades. Also see, by the same author, *Her Seven Brothers*, the story of the Big Dipper; and *Star Boy*, the story of the Sun Dance.

Many Moons

James Thurber; Harcourt Brace, 1987

The enchanting tale of Princess Lenore, who falls ill from a surfeit of raspberry tarts and refuses to be cured until someone gets her the moon. ("Nobody can get the moon," said the Royal Wizard. "It is 150,000 miles away, and it is made of green cheese, and it is twice as big as this palace.") A delight for all ages.

Meteor!

Patricia Polacco; Paper Star, 1996

A delightful picture-book account of what happens in a quiet country town when a meteor lands in the Gaw family front yard. Based on a true story.

The Shining Stars: Greek Legends of the Zodiac

Ghislaine Vautier; Cambridge University Press, 1989

Color-illustrated versions of Greek legends based on each of the 12 constellations of the zodiac. Also see *Stories from the Stars: Greek Myths of the Zodiac* (Juliet Sharman-Burke; Abbeville Press, 1998).

Star Tales: North American Indian Stories About the Stars

Gretchen Will Mayo; Walker & Company, 1991

An illustrated collection of American Indian tales about the night sky, including stories of the Pleiades, the Big Dipper, Orion's Belt, the Milky Way, and the North Star. Each tale begins with a brief introduction about the Indian tribe from which the story is derived. Also see, by the same author, *More Star Tales* (Walker, 1991).

Tales of the Shimmering Sky: Ten Global Folktales With Activities

Susan Milord; Williamson, 1996

Ten tales about the sky from cultures around the world, with accompanying activities involving arts and crafts, cooking, science, math, history, and games. For kids aged 4–9.

ACTIVITY BOOKS

3-D Galaxy: See the Hidden Pictures in the Stars

William Morrow, 1994

A beautiful "Magic Eye" book in which the constellations appear to pop out of the page and float three-dimensionally in front of the viewer's eyes. For all ages.

Astronomy for All Ages: Discovering the Universe through Activities for Children and Adults

Philip Harrington and Edward Pascuzzi; Globe Pequot Press, 1994

A 210-page collection of activities, background information, and reproducible patterns and study sheets on all aspects of astronomy. The book is divided into six major sections: "The Naked Eye Sky," "The Moon," "The Sun," "The Solar System," "Deep Space," and "Telescopes and Photography." Each activity includes an age recommendation, a statement of lesson objectives, a materials list, scientific and historical background information, and detailed instructions. Sample activities include learning to read a star map, measuring star brightness, using an astrolabe, making a sundial, observing the phases of Venus, and building a reflecting telescope.

Blast Off! Rocketry for Elementary and Middle School Students

Lee Brattland Nielsen; Teacher Ideas Press, 1997

Background information, science experiments, and interdisciplinary activities on rockets for kids aged 9–13. The book even includes a rocket play.

Cosmic Science: Over 40 Gravity-Defying, Earth-Orbiting, Space-Cruising Activities for Kids

Jim Wiese; John Wiley & Sons, 1997

A creative 128-page collection of experiments and astronomical information for kids aged 9–12. Users map the solar system with toilet paper and index cards, make a spaghetti-and-marshmallow model of the constellation Orion, and imitate eating a slice of bread in zero gravity.

Earth, Moon, and Stars

An activity book/teacher's guide in the GEMS series (see page 235) from the Lawrence Hall of Science. This volume, targeted at kids in grades 5–9, is a series of informational astronomy projects. Users, for example, calculate the distance from the earth to the sun, observe and record moon phases, and make models to demonstrate lunar and solar eclipses.

> University of California
> Attn: LHS Store
> Lawrence Hall of Science, #5200
> Berkeley, CA 94720-5200
> (510) 642-1016/fax (510) 642-1055
> Web site: www.lhs.berkeley.edu
> or
> Carolina Biological Supply Co.
> 2700 York Rd.
> Burlington, NC 27215
> (800) 334-5551/fax (800) 222-7112

Exploring the Sky: Projects for Beginning Astronomers

Richard Moeschl; Chicago Review Press, 1993

The book covers the basics of astronomy from early times through *Voyager 2* and the Hubble Telescope, with many creative projects linking astronomy to art, history, philosophy, and literature.

How the Universe Works

Heather Cooper and Nigel Henbest; Reader's Digest, 1994

A marvelously illustrated 160-page information and activity book for kids aged 9–12. The book covers all the basics of astronomy—the solar system, stars, space exploration, and famous astronomers—through creative hands-on projects. (Among them, kids build a model of the Galileo space probe.) Over 1,000 color photographs.

See **How Things Work Series** (page 235).

Janice Van Cleave's Astronomy for Every Kid

Janice Van Cleave; John Wiley & Sons, 1991

Over 100 simple astronomy activities for kids aged 8–12. Also see Janice Van Cleave's *Constellations for Every Kid* (John Wiley & Sons, 1997), which describes 20 of the most recognizable constellations, with instructions for locating them in the night sky.

Life in the Universe Series

A series of books, videos, and informational posters, available separately or packaged as classroom kits, designed to teach kids in grades 3–9 about the search for extraterrestrial intelligence. In "The Science Detectives," for example, for students in grades 3–4, kids accompany astronaut/astronomer Amelia Spacehart in her search for the source of a mysterious extraterrestrial radio signal, learning about the planets in the solar system, the states of matter, the workings of telescopes, and the mathematics of astronomical measurements. Titles for older students include "Project Haystack: The Search for Life in the Galaxy," "The Evolution of a Planetary System," "How Might Life Evolve on Other Worlds?," "The Rise of Intelligence and Culture," and "Life: Here? There? Elsewhere?" The kits were designed by the SETI Institute in company with Teacher Ideas Press.

> Libraries Unlimited
> Box 6633
> Englewood, CO 80155-6633
> (303) 770-1220 or (800) 237-6124/fax (303) 220-8843
> e-mail: lu-books@lu.com
> Web site: www.lu.com

See **Audiovisual Astronomy** (page 263).

Science for Kids: 39 Easy Astronomy Experiments

Robert W. Wood; Tab Books, 1991

Simple but worthwhile experiments for young astronomers. Kids demonstrate eclipses with a golf ball, a softball, and a flashlight, measure the diameters of the sun and moon, build a cross-staff and use it to determine latitude, construct a tin-can planetarium and a refracting telescope, experiment with gravity and centripetal force, and learn to locate the North Star.

Seeing the Sky: 100 Projects, Activities & Explorations in Astronomy

Fred Schaaf; John Wiley & Sons, 1990

A collection of challenging, but absolutely cost-free, projects for naked-eye sky observers, some dealing with fairly complex astronomical concepts. Projects are grouped into 10 categories: "Moon," "Planets," "Stars," "Sunsets and Twilights," "The Blue Sky," "Light Pollution," "Meteors and Comets," "Rainbows, Halos, Coronas, and Glories," "Eclipses," and "Elusive Glows." Each activity includes one to two pages of explanation and background information, followed by a short list of questions for students to tackle.

GAMES AND HANDS-ON ACTIVITIES

Astro-Dots

A connect-the-dots activity book with which pencil-wielding kids can produce 24 pictures of the figures represented by the constellations. Printed stars show the shape of the actual night-sky constellation; each is surrounded by many numbered dots, which turn out a very elaborate classical picture. Directions suggest that users connect the (lettered) stars with one pencil color, the (numbered) dots with another. Also included are six pages of "random star" patterns, which kids can connect to create their own imaginary constellations.

$3.95
Sunstone Publications
Dept. 36
R.D. 3, Box 100A
Cooperstown, NY 13326
or
Michael Olaf's Essential Montessori
Box 1162
1101 H St.
Arcata, CA 95518
(707) 826-1557/fax (707) 826-2243

Astroslides

Astronomy through the Microslide Viewer from National Teaching Aids, Inc. (see page 223). This is an inexpensive microscope-shaped device through which students can view strips of 35mm images, among them "Microslides," photographs taken through a microscope, and "Astroslides," photographs taken through a telescope. Once you get over the idea that you're peering through a microscope to see the stars, this is a wonder-

ful resource for astronomy students. Each Astroslide lesson set includes an informational text folder, which provides background information, astronomical definitions, and instructions, a strip of eight astronomical photographs, and an overlay strip of scales, grids, and references used for making astronomical measurements. The two strips, used in conjunction, allow students to make experimental measurements and perform astronomical calculations. There are ten Astroslide lesson sets available: "Properties of Telescopes," "Measurements in Space," "The Planets," "Probing the Sun's Secrets," "Spectroscopy in Space," "Measuring the Big Bang," "The Birth and Death of Stars," "Galaxies and Nebulae," "Mapping the Stars," and "The Moon."

Micro- (or Astro-) Slide Viewers, $8; Astroslide lesson sets, $7 apiece
National Teaching Aids, Inc.
1845 Highland Ave.
New Hyde Park, NY 11040
(516) 326-2555/fax (516) 326-2560

Constellation Station

A board game for young stargazers aged 9 and up. The game, a nice mix of science and legend, is played on a beautifully illustrated game board. On it, a circular playing path surrounds a starry blue-on-blue map of the night sky. As players move their pieces—little plastic rocket ships—around the board, they identify and "colonize" constellations, marking each acquisition on the sky map with a colored plastic peg. For each constellation, there's an informational Data Card, with a picture of the star group as it appears on the map, and listings of its common name and position in the sky, descriptions of any interesting astronomical features associated with it, and a brief account of its historical or mythological background.

The game can be played at four different levels. Youngest players ("Stargazers") simply locate constellations on the star map; older players ("Skywatchers" and "Astronomers") must be able to state selected facts from the categories on the Data Cards ("Common Name," "Location," "Description," and "History/Myth").

$30
Aristoplay
450 S. Wagner Rd.
Ann Arbor, MI 48107

(800) 634-7738 or (888) GR8-GAME

fax (734) 995-4611

Web site: www.aristoplay.com

Construct-A-Scope

This is a wonderful building kit, with which kids—using an assortment of red and black plastic pieces and screw-in lenses—can make seven optical instruments, including a telescope, binoculars, and a microscope. The kit includes a 20-page instruction and activity booklet.

$45

Delta Education

Box 3000

Nashua, NH 03061-3000

(800) 442-5444/fax (800) 282-9560

Web site: www.delta-ed.com

or

ETA

620 Lakeview Pkwy.

Vernon Hills, IL 60061-9923

(847) 816-5050 or (800) 445-5985/fax (847) 816-5066

or (800) ETA-9326

e-mail: info@etauniverse.com

Web site: www.etauniverse.com

Cut & Fold Paper Spaceships That Fly

Michael Grater; Dover Publications, 1980

Sixteen full-color paper spaceships to cut and fold; all you'll need to add is a paper clip and an occasional scrap of Scotch tape. The spaceships act and fly pretty much like your standard paper airplane, but they look terrific and they all have names like "Orbital Zoom Rider," "Star Cruiser," "Space Sentinental," and "Lunar Freighter."

$2.95

Dover Publications, Inc.

31 E. Second St.

Mineola, NY 11501

Also from Dover: *Cut and Make Space Shuttles* (David Kawami; 8 full-color models), *Cut and Fold Extraterrestrial Invaders That Fly* (Michael Grater; 22 models), *Cut and Assemble UFOs That Fly* (David Kawami; 8 models), and *Cut and Fold Space Stunt Fliers* (Michael Grater; 16 "gravity-defying" models).

$2.95 to $3.50 apiece

Galileo Scientific Explorer Kit

With this history of science kit from Scientific Explorer (see page 223), kids can make their own Galilean telescope. Materials include two glass lenses, a pair of interlocking heavy cardboard tubes in a nice shade of blue, and black sleeves that fit neatly over the tube ends. The finished product is a sturdy spyglass-type telescope (Galileo called it a *perspiculum*), focused by sliding the tubes in and out. It really works, after a fashion, and our youngest son—who made it—still insists on using it for all family astronomy projects.

The kit also includes materials for reproducing Galileo's experiments with gravity, projectiles, and pendulums, and for building a Galilean thermometer, plus a 15-page booklet of instructions, project suggestions, and historical and scientific background information.

$24

Scientific Explorer, Inc.

2802 E. Madison, Suite 114

Seattle, WA 98112

(206) 322-7611 or (800) 900-1182/fax (206) 322-7610

e-mail: sciex@scientificexplorer.com

Web site: www.scientificexplorer.com

The Game of SPACE

The game includes five 36-card packs of letter-coded question cards and a lettered die. S cards have questions on stars; P cards, on planets; A cards, on astronomy in general; C cards, on the constellations; and E cards, on space exploration. The object of the game is to win one card in each letter category by correctly answering questions, thus spelling the word *space*.

Each card lists three questions at increasingly difficult levels of ability: beginner (ages 10 and up), intermediate (ages 13 and up), and advanced (ages 16 to adult). Sample beginner questions include: (S) "What color are the coolest stars?" (P) "Which planet was named for the Roman god of the dead?" (A) "What periodic visitors can be described as 'dirty snowballs'?" (C) "The Big Dipper is part of the constellation Ursa Major. What kind of animal is Ursa Major?" (E) "Who was the first man to observe Earth's moon through a telescope?"

$10.95

Other World Educational Enterprises

Box 6193

Woodland Park, CO 80866-6193

(303) 687-3840

Good Heavens!

A question-and-answer game about comets, meteors, planets, and other heavenly objects and phenomena. Each of the 54 playing cards includes a question, the answer, and a paragraph of additional information. Official rules are included for play, but the cards are also fun for just plain reading aloud, in the car, the dentist's waiting room, or around the kitchen table, while waiting for it to get dark enough for stargazing. Sample questions: "A night sky display of colored light streamers is sometimes seen in arctic regions and as far south as Boston. This phenomenon is called the Northern Lights. What is the scientific name?" "In 1908 a comet struck the earth with a devastating explosion. Where did this happen?"

$9.95 from game stores or

Ampersand Press

750 Lake St.

Port Townsend, WA 98368

(800) 624-4263

Web site: www.ampersandpress.com

History of Space Exploration Coloring Book

Bruce LaFontaine; Dover Publications

The history of space exploration from the launching of Robert Goddard's first liquid-fuel rocket to the moon landing (1969) and the explosion of the space shuttle *Challenger* (1986). The book includes 44 black-and-white illustrations and a brief informational text.

$2.95

Dover Publications, Inc.

31 E. Second St.

Mineola, NY 11501

Moon Exploration Sticker Picture Book

Steven James Petruccio; Dover Publications

Eighteen reusable peel-and-stick stickers of astronauts and space vehicles, to be affixed to a folding laminated backdrop picturing the lunar landscape.

$3.50

Dover Publications, Inc.

31 E. Second St.

Mineola, NY 11501

Newton on the Earth

With this creative science kit, kids build a model of the earth, complete with geologic and atmospheric layers, compare planetary sizes, calculate relative distances to the other planets in the solar system, and learn how to use a sundial. All necessary equipment is included, along with an informational instruction booklet. Appropriate for kids in grades 5–8.

$18

Wild Goose Co.

375 Whitney Ave.

Salt Lake City, UT 84115

(801) 466-1172 or (800) 373-1498/fax (801) 466-1186

Web site: www.wildgoosescience.com

NOVA Spacelab

A space science discovery set filled with materials for hands-on projects and experiments, plus an illustrated instruction manual. Users assemble a solar system mobile and a space shuttle model, locate constellations with a star finder and compass, and learn how astronomers use spectroscopy to study the composition of stars. Recommended for kids in grades 4 and up.

$25

ETA

620 Lakeview Pkwy.

Vernon Hills, IL 60061-9923

(847) 816-5050 or (800) 445-5985/fax (800) ETA-9326

e-mail: info@etauniverse.com

Web site: www.etauniverse.com

Out to Launch

A kit with which interested kids can perform 30 experiments having to do (mostly) with rockets—as well as air pressure, Bernoulli's law, and the basics of aerodynamics. All necessary equipment is included, plus an entertaining instruction booklet. Recommended for kids in grades 2–6 (with cautious adult supervision).

$29.99

Wild Goose Co.

375 Whitney Ave.

Salt Lake City, UT 84115

(801) 466-1172 or (800) 373-1498/fax (801) 466-1186

Web site: www.wildgoosescience.com

Also from Wild Goose: *Bernoulli's Book* (B. K. Hixson), a collection of 25 hands-on experiments for kids in grade 2 and up, all dealing with the basics of air pressure, Newtonian laws of motion, and Bernoulli's law. Patterns for rockets and model airplanes are included.

Project Polaris

A group simulation in which kids—using measurement (length, volume, area, time, and weight) and estimation skills—build a space station (between Orion and Ursa Minor). To do so, they must combat the evil influence of Dastardly Derek, a conniving space business tycoon, and earn "Starbucks" by completing space-related challenge projects in a number of different academic disciplines, among them language arts, art, music, and kinesthetics.

Simulation materials include a detailed teacher's guide with reproducible student handouts and 35 eight-page student guides. The simulation is intended for large numbers of kids—20 to 40 students, in grades 2–6—but can be adapted to smaller groups. It is estimated to take about 15 hours, total.

$34

Interact

1825 Gillespie Way, #101

El Cajon, CA 92020-1095

(619) 448-1474 or (800) 359-0961/fax (619) 448-6722

or (800) 700-5093

Web site: www.interact-simulations.com

Other astronomy-related simulations from Interact include:

"Galaxy," for students in grades 5–9, in which kids attend "Inter-Galactic Space Academy" where they study basic astronomy, spacecraft design, navigation, and galactic history before participating in a space civil war ($29).

"Mars," for grades 5–9, in which students, as members of the World Organization for Space Exploration, set out to explore Mars ($34).

"Space Contracts," which includes enough materials for four one- to two-week units, each "activity

selection" centering around a different set of skills: writing, oral presentations, music, art, kinesthetic projects. Examples: "Invent your own solar system. Name the planets and describe their characteristics. Present as a display or map. Compare your solar system to earth's." For students in grades 5–9 ($34).

Project STAR Kits

The "Project STAR" (the acronym stands for "Science Teaching through its Astronomical Roots") hands-on science materials were developed by the Harvard Smithsonian Center for Astrophysics and tested in classrooms, elementary to college level, around the country. The materials include a collection of innovative activity books, teachers' guides, and kits, most at very affordable prices.

Among these are a "Do-It-Yourself Star Finder Kit," with which kids make their own planispheres, adjustable for any day of the year or time of the night; a "Refracting Telescope Kit," with which kids make their own Galilean telescopes; a "Solar System Scale Model Kit"; a "Light Measurement and Stellar Distance Kit," with which kids determine the luminosity of the sun and investigate the relationship between an object's apparent brightness and its distance; and a "Spectrometer Kit," with which—once it's assembled—kids can see the absorption lines in the sun's spectrum (and in fluorescent desk lamps and street lights). An excellent source for educational astronomy materials.

Learning Technologies, Inc.

40 Cameron Ave.

Somerville, MA 02114

(617) 628-1459 or (800) 537-8703/fax (617) 628-8606

Rockets

Many science and educational supply catalogs carry rockets, as do almost all local hobby stores, but the prime mail-order source is Estes Industries, which has been in the model rocket business since 1958. Best for beginners are the "Starter Sets," which are very easy to assemble and include all necessary equipment: rocket parts, parachute, launch pad, electric launch controller (you supply the batteries), engines, wadding, and igniters. For more advanced rocketeers, Estes offers more complex kits (Skill Levels 1 to 4). The catalog also carries assorted books, manuals, and computer software on model rocketry, and a selection of rocket-based classroom curricula, variously appropriate for kids in grade 2 and up, which include lesson plans and reproducible student worksheets.

Fully equipped "Starter Sets," about $30; single rocket models, generally $5 to $25
Estes Industries
Box 277
1295 H St.
Penrose, CO 81240-0227
(719) 372-6565

Solar System Mobiles

ALL Our solar system mobile, sadly, is a thing of the past. It used to hang elegantly from the ceiling in the boys' room; then someone leaping in forbidden fashion off an upper bunk bed got tangled in Saturn and brought the whole thing down, and we never did get it back together again. While it lasted, however, it was a beauty: the sun (with striking solar flare) and nine planets in glorious color, all artist's renderings of NASA photographs.

Available through most science supply catalogs or
Delta Education
Box 3000
Nashua, NH 03061
(800) 442-5444/fax (800) 282-9560
Web site: www.delta-ed.com
or
Edmund Scientific Co.
101 E. Gloucester Pike
Barrington, NJ 08007-1380
(609) 547-8880 or (800) 728-6999
or
ETA
620 Lakeview Pkwy.
Vernon Hills, IL 60061
(847) 816-5050 or (800) 445-5985/fax (800) ETA-9326
e-mail: info@etauniverse.com
Web site: www.etauniverse.com

Solar System Puzzle

More than just a put-together puzzle, this is an activity kit for kids aged 7 and up. Kids paint all 120 coded puzzle pieces themselves, then assemble them to form a colorful 22 × 28-inch drawn-to-scale portrait of the solar system. Included is an informative *Atlas of the Planets* and all necessary paints and instructions.

$22.50
National Geographic Society
1145 17th St. NW
Washington, DC 20036-4688
(888) CALL-NGS

Solarquest

"Solarquest," subtitled "The Space-Age Real Estate Game," is "Monopoly" for space buffs. Players tour the solar system in rocket ships, attempting to purchase moons, asteroids, space docks, and research stations and to establish fueling stations on each—all with various denominations of "federons," the colorful currency of the Federation League Bank. Players build these space-age real estate empires while fending off the laser attacks of opponents and struggling to keep themselves safely supplied with fuel, which is measured in "hydrons." One player, appointed the Fuel Card Monitor, keeps track of everyone's fuel supply. Run out of hydrons and you're stranded in space and out of the game.

The playing board is pretty; the action is snappy; and after a few rounds of play, young participants will know names, sizes, and statistics for every moon and planet in the solar system. For two to six players, aged 8 to adult.

$30 from toy and game stores or
ETA
620 Lakeview Pkwy.
Vernon Hills, IL 60061-9923
(847) 816-5050 or (800) 445-5985/fax (800) ETA-9326
e-mail: info@etauniverse.com
Web site: www.etauniverse.com

Space Hop

"Space Hop," ("A Game of the Planets") is played on a black grid-patterned board on which is pictured a map of the solar system with a glowing sun in the middle, on a background of cloudy stars. Players move their pieces—little wooden rocket ships—from square to square, attempting to complete missions and earn SNC ("Space Navigation Credit") cards. First player to accumulate 25 SNC points wins. Play begins with each player drawing a "Mission Card," each illustrated with a beautiful astronomical color painting, and solving the listed clue: for example, "Go to the planet which has the hottest surface," "Go to the first planet to be discovered by telescope," and "Go to the smallest planet." (If you don't know the answer, you can find out by means of the "Space Decoder," but using it makes you forfeit a turn.) For two to four players aged 9 and up.

$22.50 from game stores or
Carolina Biological Supply Co.
2700 York Rd.
Burlington, NC 27215
(800) 334-5551/fax (800) 222-7112

Star Hop

"Star Hop" ("The Game of the Cosmos") is similar in format to "Space Hop" (see above), but on a larger scale. The board pictures the entire Milky Way Galaxy, with 40 astronomical destinations labeled, among them Sirius, Polaris, Barnard's Star, Proxima Centauri, and a Cepheid variable, neutron star, supernova, black hole, and quasar. Players follow the instructions on "Star Hop Mission Cards" to earn GNC ("Galactic Navigation Credit") cards. Sample Star Hop Missions include: "Go to the large spiral galaxy which is the most distant object visible with the naked eye," "Go to the binary star system whose large blue member is exchanging long streamers of gas with its smaller companion," and "Go to the object whose gravity is so strong that nothing, not even light, can escape its grip." For two to four players aged 10 and up.

$25 from game stores or
Carolina Biological Supply Co.
2700 York Rd.
Burlington, NC 27215
(800) 334-5551/fax (800) 222-7112

Star Machine

The "Star Machine" is about as close as most of us can come to an at-home planetarium. The machine itself is a roughly soccer ball–size projector, powered by a couple of C batteries and a flashlight bulb. Turned on, in a dark room with a nice smooth ceiling, the machine's master disc projects a skylike display of 31 constellations and 312 stars. A series of plastic "constellation masks" that fit over the master star dome

adjust the display for the proper season of the year. Included is an instruction booklet, an audiocassette of information about the stars and constellations to accompany the "Star Machine" displays, and a tiny red flashlight to use as a pointer.

$34.95
Edmund Scientific Co.
101 E. Gloucester Pike
Barrington, NJ 08007-1380
(800) 728-6999/fax (609) 547-3292
e-mail: scientifics@edsci.com
Web site: www.edsci.com

Ursa Major

Who can resist a chance to sleep out under the stars? While not all of us live in climates conducive to year-round camping—like Vermont, for example, where the seasons are Winter, Mud, and August—anyone with an expanse of blank ceiling (or wall) can take advantage of Ursa Major's "Night Sky Stencils." The stencils are available in two sizes (8 feet or 12 feet in diameter) and for two seasons: each displays 350 stars of either the winter or the summer sky. Users simply tape or tack the stencil to a chosen surface and dab over the stencil's holes (stars) with the included glow-in-the-dark paint. Then remove the stencil, expose the paint briefly to normal light, flick off the switch, and enjoy two hours or so of a glowing (astronomically accurate) starry sky. The paint doesn't show in the daytime; Ursa Major stars can be seen only in the dark, just like the real ones. Kits include stencils, paint, brush, an informational *Night Sky* booklet about the constellations, and a star map.

8-foot stencils, $26; 12-foot stencils, $42
Ursa Major
Box 3368
Ashland, OR 97520
(800) 999-3433

Audiovisual Astronomy

Cosmic Questions: Astronomy from Quark to Quasar

The universe, in a series of eight 45-minute lectures on audiocassettes by Dr. Robert Kirshner of Harvard University. Lecture titles include "A Tour of the Universe," "The Secrets of Starlight," "Force and Motion," "Life and Death of Stars," "Crushed Stars and Strong Gravity," "An Expanding Universe," "Mass in the Universe," and "Will the Universe Expand Forever?" Complex stuff, clearly presented. For teenagers and adults.

> $39.95
> The Teaching Co.
> 7405 Alban Station Ct., Suite A107
> Springfield, VA 22150-2318
> (800) 832-2412

10 *Cosmos*

In this now classic 13-part PBS series, Carl Sagan traces 15 billion years of cosmic evolution, covering the origins of matter, the birth of galaxies and stars, the origins of life on Earth, the history of astronomy, the discovery of the planets, the exploration of Mars, the genetic code, and the marvelous human brain, which manages to appreciate—if not quite comprehend—it all. Titles in the series include "The Shores of the Cosmic Ocean," "One Voice in the Cosmic Fugue," "The Harmony of Worlds," "Heaven and Hell," "Blues for a Red Planet," "Travelers' Tales," "The Backbone of the Night," "Travels in Space and Time," "The Lives of the Stars," "The Edge of Forever," "The Persistence of Memory," "Encyclopaedia Galactica," and "Who Speaks for Earth?" A must for would-be astronomers.

> $149.99 for all 13 episodes on 7 videocassettes
> Public Television Videofinders Collection
> National Fulfillment Center
> Box 27054
> Glendale, CA 91225-7054
> (800) 799-1199
> or
> Movies Unlimited
> 3015 Darnell Rd.
> Philadelphia, PA 19154
> (215) 637-4444 or (800) 4-MOVIES
> e-mail: movies@moviesunlimited.com
> Web site: www.moviesunlimited.com

8 *Life in the Universe Series*

A series of classroom kits designed by the SETI (Search for Extraterrestrial Intelligence) Institute, var-

iously targeted at kids in grades 3–9. Kits include a detailed 200+-page teacher's guide containing multidisciplinary hands-on activities, a 20- to 35-minute video, and an informational poster. Each kit provides information for a four- to six-week study unit. There are six titles in the series.

"The Science Detectives Kit," for kids in grades 3 and up, centers around a space-travel adventure story in which an astronaut searches the solar system for the source of a mysterious radio signal. Kids learn about the solar system, and astronomical techniques and measurements. In "The Evolution of a Planetary System," kids in grades 5 and up study the formation of our own solar system and simulate the development of a system around another star. In "How Might Life Evolve on Other Worlds?," they learn about the evolution of life on earth and simulate the creation of life-forms on other planets; in "The Rise of Intelligence and Culture," they simulate the development of an extraterrestrial civilization. "Life: Here? There? Elsewhere?" concentrates on the search for life on other planets: kids in grades 7 and up study planetology and exobiology, design a spacecraft for life detection of Venus and Mars, and learn about the results of the Viking missions. "Project Haystack: The Search for Life in the Galaxy," for students in grades 8 and up, centers around studies of the scale and structure of the Milky Way Galaxy ("the cosmic haystack"); kids solve problems involved in sending and receiving messages beyond our solar system.

> Kits, $54 to $90; some materials are available
> separately
> Libraries Unlimited
> Box 6633
> Englewood, CO 80155-6633
> (303) 770-1220 or (800) 237-6124/fax (303) 220-8843
> e-mail: lu-books@lu.com
> Web site: www.lu.com
> For sample lessons from the Life in the Universe series, see the Seti Home Page at www.seti.org

COMPUTER SOFTWARE

ELECTRONIC PLANETARIUMS

There are many desktop planetarium programs on the market that can produce acurate pictures of the night sky at any time from anywhere and provide a wealth of information on celestial objects. Examples include *The Sky Astronomy Software, Starry Night Deluxe,* and *Voyager II* (see below).

The Sky Astronomy Software (Version 4.0)

Includes night-sky charts at any time from any location; users can click on any star or celestial object to access detailed descriptions and information. Users also have access to an enormous database of information about celestial objects, a moon-phase calendar, and the orbits of comets and satellites, and they can print out high-quality star charts for use outside with the telescope. The program is available at three levels, with increasing amounts of information. On CD-ROM for Mac or Windows.

> $119 to $249
>
> Telescope & Binocular Center
>
> Box 1815
>
> Santa Cruz, CA 95061-1815
>
> (408) 763-7030 or (800) 447-1001
>
> Web site: www.oriontel.com

Starry Night Deluxe

A planetarium and night-sky simulator that allows users to view the sky at any time, from any location in the solar system. On CD-ROM for Mac.

> $89.95
>
> Sienna Software, Inc.
>
> 105 Pears Ave.
>
> Toronto, Ontario M5R 1S9, Canada
>
> (416) 926-2174
>
> Web site: www.siennasoft.com

Voyager II (Version 2.0)

Includes an immense database of stars, deep-sky objects, and orbiting satellites, satellite-tracking capabilities, and detailed sky maps from any observing site on Earth. On CD-ROM for Mac.

> $119
>
> Telescope & Binocular Center
>
> Box 1815
>
> Santa Cruz, CA 95061-1815
>
> (408) 763-7030 or (800) 447-1001
>
> Web site: www.oriontel.com

OTHER SOFTWARE PROGRAMS

Eyewitness Encyclopedia of Space and the Universe

A marvelous tour of space science. Click on one icon and get the scoop on the Russian space station Mir; click on another and find a biography of Neil Armstrong; hit another and view the moons of Jupiter or the rings of Saturn. The program includes animations, video clips from NASA, 3-D models, and an on-screen planetarium, "Star Dome," that allows viewers to study the night sky from the perspectives of cities all around the globe. On CD-ROM for Mac or Windows.

> $49.95
>
> Dorling Kindersley Publishing
>
> 1224 Heil Quaker Blvd.
>
> LaVergne, TN 37086
>
> (888) DIALDKP
>
> Web site: www.dk.com

Isaac Asimov's Library of the Universe

A multimedia tour of the universe on six CD-ROMs, with over 2,400 images, many computer-generated NASA space photographs. Titles in the series include "Astronomy," "The Inner Planets," "The Outer Planets," "The Solar System," "Space Exploration," and "The Universe." This is the equivalent of a survey course in basic astronomy for high school or beginning college students. Includes quizzes and customized glossaries of terms. On CD-ROM for Mac or Windows.

> $49.95
>
> Telescope & Binocular Center
>
> Box 1815
>
> Santa Cruz, CA 95061-1815
>
> (408) 763-7030 or (800) 447-1001
>
> Web site: www.oriontel.com

Stars and Stories

An interdisciplinary curriculum on CD-ROM for kids aged 13 and up. *Stars and Stories* pairs an illustrated text with a series of multimedia exercises and activities, with which kids learn astronomy through an integrated mix of academic subjects, including math, history, literature, art, and science. The text, nicely readable and illustrated with color photographs and diagrams, includes a glossary, lists of supplementary readings, links to related multimedia activities and Web sites, discussion questions, and detailed instructions for student projects. Text subtitles include "Understanding the Motions of Stars and Planets," "Investigating Deep Space," and "Connecting Astronomy, Mythology, and History." Accompanying multimedia activities include mathematical demonstrations and exercises, animated star charts, a slide show of astronomical photographs, and fill-in-the-blank quizzes.

Users cover astronomy from a range of different perspectives. Kids, for example, read ancient myths about astronomical phenomena, study trigonometry and practice measurement by triangulation, learn about coordinate graphing and scientific notation, and investigate the principles of linear, rotary, and oscillatory motion. They also discover the retrograde motion of the planets, map the Big Dipper, and read about archaological excavations of Minoan sites on Crete. On CD-ROM for Mac or Windows.

> $89.95
> Wildridge Software, Inc.
> Wildridge Farm Rd.
> Box 61
> Newark, VT 05871
> (888) 244-4379
> e-mail: ABIGGERWORLD@wildridge.com
> Web site: www.wildridge.com

Where in Space is Carmen Sandiego?

Using over 1,100 clues to some 32 out-of-the-world locations, kids track archcrook Carmen Sandiego and her band of V.I.L.E. henchcreatures through space, attempting to apprehend the criminals and regain the stolen loot. (Carmen's gang pinches major loot: among others, they make off with the rings of Saturn and the Great Red Spot of Jupiter.) The game includes photographs and video clips from NASA, up-to-date astronomical facts and figures, and celestial mythology. Kids love it. On CD-ROM for Mac or Windows.

> $39.95
> Broderbund
> Box 6125
> Novato, CA 94948-6125
> (800) 521-6263
> Web site: www.broderbund.com or
> www.carmensandiego.com

ASTRONOMY ON-LINE

Astronomy for Kids

Great color graphics and basic information on the sun and the solar system, asteroids, comets, meteorites, stars, galaxies, and space exploration. The site includes a dictionary of astronomical terms and kids' astronomy questions with answers.

> www.frontiernet/~kidpower/astronomy.html

Bradford Robotic Telescope

Register (free) and aim the telescope anywhere you like. The site also includes basic information about the telescope.

> www.eia.brad.ac.uk/btl

Imagine the Universe!

Detailed information and lesson plans from the High-Energy Astrophysics Learning Center. The site covers the structure and evolution of the universe. Individual topics include the electromagnetic spectrum, X-ray astronomy, dark matter, black holes, astronomical instruments and techniques, and current astronomical mysteries to be solved. An interesting site for teenagers.

> imagine.gsfc.nasa.gov

NASA Jet Propulsion Laboratory

The site includes excellent space pictures and video clips, a guide to NASA space missions, past and present, educational resources and programs, and links to astronomical sites and resources categorized under "Planets," "Earth," "Universe," and "Space Technology."

> www.jpl.nasa.gov

National Aeronautics and Space Administration (NASA)

News updates, information about current space missions, educational resources, and a photo archive. The site also includes "Amazing Space Web-Based Activities" for kids, with science challenges and quizzes on stars, the solar system, and space science.

> www.nasa.gov

National Air and Space Museum

Tours of selected exhibits and images from the museum collections, an on-line tour of the solar system, and other educational activities and information, including an illustrated history of the Apollo space program.

www.nasm.si.edu

NEMS Meteorites and Planetary Science

All about meteorites, a photo gallery of meteorites, a meteorite quiz (not for little kids), and links to related meteorite sites.

www.meteorlab.com

The Nine Planets

A tour of the solar system complete with informational text, terrific photographs, and video clips. (Included, for example, is a video of the comet Shoemaker-Levy colliding with Jupiter.)

seds.lpl.arizona.edu/nineplanets/nineplanets/nineplanets.html

Also see "Welcome to the Planets" at stardust.jpl.nasa.gov.planets, a NASA-sponsored multimedia tour of the solar system

SKY Online

Sky and Telescope magazine (see page 251) and *CCD Astronomy* magazine on-line offer tips for backyard astronomers, reviews of astronomy software and equipment, information on comets, meteors, and eclipses, links to related resources, and "What's Up in the Sky?," current sky-watching information and sky charts.

www.skypub.com

Space Telescope Science Institute

Latest pictures and an archive of images from the Hubble Space Telescope.

oposite.stsci.edu

StarChild

 A learning center for young astronomers. Information can be accessed at Level 1, for elementary-aged kids, or Level 2, for middle and high school–aged students. Wonderful graphics, detailed information about the solar system, universe, and space exploration, a glossary of terms, and games, puzzles, and quizzes.

heasarc.gsfc.nasa.gov/docs/StarChild

Stars and Constellations

Lists of the constellations in alphabetical order and by month of the year, interactive sky charts, lists of the 26 brightest and the 26 nearest stars, an alphabetical star catalog, and a "Constellation Quiz." The site also includes links to star myths and legends, a sky tour, a guide to backyard observing, a list of people with constellation names, and information on naming your own star.

www.astro.wisc.edu/~dolan/constellations

U.S. Space Camp

A science-packed summer camp at which kids can experience life as astronauts (or as much as possible without getting off the ground). For more information, contact (800) 63-SPACE.

www.spacecamp.com

Views of the Solar System

Includes images and information on the sun and the planets, moons, comets, asteroids, and meteorites, a history of space science, biographies of astronomers, and a space exploration timeline.

www.hawastsoc.org/solar/homepage.htm

A Virtual Tour of the Sun

Get right inside your very own star.

www.astro.uva.nl.michielb/od95

Windows to the Universe

A terrific and multifaceted site on Earth, the solar system, stars, galaxies, constellations, and the universe for beginning, intermediate, or advanced users. The site includes detailed information and statistics on all the planets in the solar system and their moons, accounts of space missions, biographies of prominent astronomers and space scientists, links to astronomical myths (by subject and culture), space science news updates, and a large archive of statistical data and images.

www.windows.engin.umich.edu

BIOLOGY: Botany, Cell Biology, Entomology, Environmental Science, Evolution, Genetics, The Human Body, Marine Biology/ Oceanography, Microbiology, Ornithology, and Zoology

Biology, in the public school system, is integrated into the science curriculum throughout elementary school, usually culminating in a full-year intensive biology course in tenth grade. Early elementary students learn about plants and animals, their habitats and behaviors, and the basics of biological classification systems. Upper elementary kids usually study plant and animal classification in more detail, covering insects, amphibians, reptiles, fish, birds, and mammals, algae and fungi, plants and trees. They are also introduced to human anatomy and physiology, and to environmental science. Middle school students—typically in seventh grade—study plant and animal cells, and basic heredity and genetics. Tenth-grade biology puts it all together, covering plant and animal classification, microorganisms, plant cells and photosynthesis, animal cells, basic genetics and genetic engineering, human biology, ecology and environmental issues, and disease and disease control.

My husband and I, both cell biologists, found all of the above appealing and we planned, from the very beginning, to emphasize biology in our homeschool program. The boys therefore studied biological topics each year, though seldom in traditional order, since their interests were seldom in step with the traditional course of study. Each boy also preferred different subsets of the biological sciences, and we inevitably concentrated upon these while brushing briefly over others. All the boys were fascinated by the world under the microscope, and all were intrigued by molecular genetics. Josh and Caleb enthusiastically tackled dissection projects; Ethan dissected one frog and pronounced himself done forever. Instead, he enjoyed bird-watching—he liked the binoculars—but rejected botany; found the brain interesting, but not the digestive tract; was enthralled by fish, but nixed reptiles and mammals.

It sounds as though such a conglomeration of diverse interests should make for a disorganized and incomplete science program. In practice, however, this is not true. The sciences and all their branches have many interconnections, and in our experience, depth engenders breadth—that is, an in-depth study of any one thing spreads out to encompass a vast web of related material. Your kid likes fish? That's terrific. You can get anywhere from there.

From my homeschool journal:

◆ May 21, 1990. Josh is nine; Ethan, seven; and Caleb, five.

We spent the early afternoon collecting pond scum from a local pond—also worms, snails, and (Ethan) a small fish. We brought all this home, established a pond scum tank in an old fishbowl, and examined multiple samples under the microscope. The boys were thrilled silly. We identified paramecia, amoebae, algae, and assorted mysterious shrimplike creatures. The boys kept yelling, "Come quick! You have to see this!" The kids also learned to use slides, coverslips, and Pasteur pipettes; reviewed parts of the microscope and practiced focusing.

◆ May 22, 1990

Began the morning with the microscope again, looking at more pond water samples. The find of the day was some spectacular little worms. We managed to identify all the parts of their digestive systems—the worms were transparent—and the boys, fascinated, watched them eating. Also identified lots of algae—which the boys insist on calling "allergy"—more paramecia, little shrimplike creatures with forked tails, and a possible hydra. I didn't see it, but Josh and Ethan drew elaborate pictures showing just what it looked like. It looked like a hydra.

Looked all our miniature animals up in assorted reference books; the boys identified several from the illustrations.

Read Greg's Microscope *by Millicent Selsam (see page 271), a picture book about a little boy and his microscope projects, which gave them a lot of new ideas for samples to examine. ("Let's get some fur from the cat!")*

Spent the afternoon at the creek, collecting even more samples.

MICROSCOPES

We own a microscope. It ranks as one of our major educational purchases, along with the boys' violins, and was, I firmly believe, an equally worthwhile investment. Our microscope was secondhand, but it was still expensive. Good microscopes, unavoidably, are; if your current model only cost $20, either you got the deal of the century or you've got a piece of junk. It's not hard to tell the difference. A good microscope, to begin with, is made of metal, and the heavier, the better. Plastic microscopes, the tempting standbys of toy catalogs, cannot support the precision optics necessary for serious microscopy, and they're so lightweight that viewing of any kind is difficult. If you can pick your microscope up with two fingers, it's too insubstantial for practical purposes; every thump on the table is likely to throw it out of whack.

Most "student" microscopes are monocular, which means that they have a single eyepiece. In lower-grade microscopes, this eyepiece is positioned straight up and down, which makes viewing uncomfortable (or impossible) from a sitting position. Better, especially for shorter microscopists, is an eyepiece set at a 45-degree angle. Ideally, only the eyepiece should slant: the microscope stage—the flat platform that the microscope slides sit on—should remain firmly horizontal. Some microscopes are jointed at the base and can be tilted back to whatever angle suits the viewer.

This sounds user-friendly but is often awkward in practice, since in such cases the stage tilts in company with the eyepiece. This is manageable if you're examining immobile prepared specimens but can be disastrous when studying something sloshy, like pond water.

Binocular microscopes have two eyepieces and are much easier to see through than monocular scopes. The drawback is that they cost considerably more, and many suppliers of student-grade microscopes don't even bother to carry them. The binocular microscope, incidentally, should not be confused with the "stereomicroscope" or dissecting scope. These, though binocular, are intended for large-scale three-dimensional viewing—this is the scope for scientists who want to get a close look at a whole housefly—and their total magnification is generally around 20×.

Total magnification obtainable through a microscope is calculated by multiplying the magnification of the eyepiece by that of the objective lens. Standard eyepieces are 10×, and most student microscopes come with three objective lenses, commonly at 5×, 15×, and 30×. The highest magnification possible with such a microscope is thus 300× (10× times 30×) and this is what suppliers mean when they advertise a "300× microscope." A magnification of 300× will give users a good view of plant and animal cells. For studying bacteria or intracellular structures, you need a magnification of 1000×, which requires a 100× oil-immersion objective. The 100× objective is used with a special synthetic immersion oil, obtainable from scientific supply companies: a drop of this stuff is placed on top of the coverslip on the microscope slide, such that the objective lens, when positioned for viewing, is immersed in the oil. This allows maximum light to pass through the lens, for optimal resolution at high magnification. Some microscopes have interchangeable objectives—the lenses screw out of their casings—such that, if need be, you can buy extras at different magnifications.

On most student microscopes, slides are held in position on the stage by a pair of flat metal clips. To move the slide, you simply reach down and nudge it a bit with your fingers—which can be startlingly disruptive; a nudge, magnified, often translates into a galvanic jolt. You can develop a knack for this with practice, but it's frustrating at first for beginners.

High-quality microscopes avoid this problem altogether: these feature mechanical stages with coaxial controls, such that the movement of the clamped-down slide is controlled by a pair of knobs that move it either vertically or horizontally. For some student microscope models, a mechanical stage can be purchased separately and installed; you simply remove the clips and insert the mechanical stage in the same mounting holes.

Good student microscopes have both coarse and fine focus adjustments; and some have adjustable stops, a desirable feature, which keep users from blithely focusing too far downward and grinding the objective lens into the slide on the stage. (One should, of course, start low and focus *up*, but excited beginners often find that a hard rule to follow.) Good microscopes are also *parfocal*, which means that once a specimen is in focus, you should be able to change magnifications by switching objective lenses without having to refocus each time.

Starter microscopes are usually equipped with a concave mirror beneath the stage, which can be tilted to angle maximum light through specimen, objective, and eyepiece, to the waiting human eye. Such a mirror, all by itself, cannot provide enough light for detailed viewing. High-quality microscopes have built-in illuminators beneath the viewing stage; for lesser models, outside illuminators—you set them up in front of the microscope and direct the light right at the little mirror—can be purchased separately.

Microscope prices are hard to gauge. Roughly speaking, you can get a reasonably good monocular student microscope for somewhere in the range of $150 to $300. An illuminator, if your scope doesn't have one built in, costs anywhere from $20 to $200; additional objectives, $80 to $150.

There are also some microscope alternatives, for families whose finances don't readily run to this kind of cash outlay—or whose children aren't immediately frothing with microscope enthusiasm. Some public and private school science teachers are willing to introduce homeschooled children to the microscope; it's worth an inquiry. If you have friends or fellow support-group members with microscope interests, several families might consider purchasing a microscope jointly. Or—for an inexpensive microscope-style

experience—think about purchasing a Micro-Slide-Viewer (see National Teaching Aids, page 223), through which kids can view a large assortment of excellent photomicrographs.

A final word: as an adult and a cell biologist, I feel that frustrating experiences with poor-quality microscopes can thoroughly discourage potentially interested kids. On the other hand, my brother and I, when we were ten and eight or so, had a little plastic microscope. It was an inflexible monocular model with lousy optics and an undersize substage mirror that we illuminated by taking the shade off my bedside table lamp and tipping it over on its side. Using this thing, we studied pond water organisms, brine shrimp, pollen, bread mold, onion skins, salt crystals, butterfly wings, and anything else we could lay our hands on. We adored it and we had a wonderful time. It was, in retrospect, an awful microscope. But it worked out just fine.

SOURCES FOR MICROSCOPES, ACCESSORIES, AND SUPPLIES

Carolina Biological Supply Company
2700 York Rd.
Burlington, NC 27215
(800) 334-5551/fax (800) 222-7112

Edmund Scientific Company
101 E. Gloucester Pike
Barrington, NJ 08007-1380
(800) 728-6999/fax (609) 547-3292
e-mail: scientifics@edsci.com
Web site: www.edsci.com

Schoolmasters Science
745 State Circle
Box 1941
Ann Arbor, MI 48106-1941
(800) 521-2832/fax (313) 761-8711
Web site: www.school-tech.com

Ward's Natural Science Establishment, Inc.
Box 92912
Rochester, NY 14692-9012

(800) 962-2660

Web site: www.wardsci.com

Books About Microscopes

Close Up: Microscopic Photos of Everyday Stuff

Frank B. Edwards; Firefly Books, 1992

A fascinating collection of electron micrographs of such everyday stuff as dustballs, spiders, and breakfast cereal.

Exploring With the Microscope

Werner Nachtigall; Sterling Publications, 1997

Detailed information on all aspects of microscopy, from how to purchase a first microscope to the ins and outs of photomicroscopy. Illustrated with many color and black-and-white photographs and diagrams. For serious microscopists aged 13 and up.

Extremely Weird Micro Monsters

Sarah Lovett; John Muir Publications, 1996

Colorful photomicrographs of 20 "micro monsters," among them a red blood cell, a head louse, and a spider mite. For each a page of interesting scientific information is included.

See **Extremely Weird Series** (page 339).

Greg's Microscope

Millicent Selsam; HarperTrophy, 1990

An "I-Can-Read" book about a boy who gets a microscope (a monocular model with a mirror) and excitedly looks at all kinds of things through it, from salt from the family kitchen to strands of fur from the family dog.

Guide to Microlife

Kenneth G. Rainis and Bruce J. Russell; Franklin Watts, 1997

A comprehensive 288-page field guide to microorganisms, including monerans, fungi, protists, and microanimals, with background information, descriptions of individual organisms, and terrific photomicrographs. Appendices cover collecting and microscopic techniques. A wonderful reference book for microscopists.

MicroAliens: Dazzling Journeys with an Electron Microscope

Howard Tomb and Dennis Kunkel; Scholastic, 1993

Over 130 marvelous electron micrographs—some at 50,000× magnification—of everything from feathers, fleas, and fungi to human skin and blood cells.

Micromysteries: Stories of Scientific Detection

Gail Kay Haines; Putnam, 1991

This 196-page book contains 13 "mystery" stories, each explaining how microscopic methods were used to solve such scientific puzzles as diabetes, radioactivity, microchips, and superconductors.

The Microscope

Maxine Kumin; HarperCollins, 1984

A short, funny rhyming account of Anton van Leeuwenhoek (don't worry; readers learn how to pronounce it) and his landmark invention of the microscope.

The Microscope Book

Shar Levin and Leslie Johnstone; Sterling Publications, 1997

Step-by-step instructions for interesting microscopy experiments for kids aged 8 and up. The book begins with a clear explanation of how a microscope works and how to use it, in "Light, Lenses, and Microscopes"; then describes many perfectly fascinating experiments for beginners, categorized under "Biology," "Geology," "Forensic Science," and "Food and the Environment." Young microscopists study slices of cork and celery stalks, pond water plants and animals, spiderweb strands, crystals, fingerprints, and growing yeast, and identify fossils in toothpaste. Illustrated with color photomicrographs.

Microscopes

B. K. Hixson and T. J. Hutson; Wild Goose Co.

A three-week course on the use of microscopes for kids in grade 4 and up. Kids learn the proper care of a microscope, names of its parts, operation of microscope optics, and slide preparation techniques. Included are quizzes, puzzles, and a lot of hilarious illustrations.

$8.99

The Wild Goose Co.

375 Whitney Ave.

Salt Lake City, UT 84115

(801) 466-1172 or (800) 373-1498/fax (801) 466-1186

Web site: www.wildgoosescience.com

Microscopes and Telescopes

Fred Wilkin; Children's Press, 1983

A New True Book (see page 228) for kids in grades 2–4 that explains, in several very short chapters, the workings of lenses, microscopes, and telescopes. Illustrated with excellent color photographs.

Pond Water Zoo: An Introduction to Microscopic Life

H. Peter Loewer and Jean Jenkins; Atheneum, 1996

What's inside a drop of pond water, with background information and detailed drawings that enable readers to identify each drop's inhabitants and compare their relative sizes. For kids aged 9–12.

The World of the Microscope

Chris Oxlade and Corinne Stockley; Usborne Publishing, 1989

An illustrated 48-page introduction to the basic techniques of microscopy. Colorful diagrams demonstrate the optical system of a light microscope, the workings of an electron microscope, and the scale of things in the universe (from the length of a light-year to the diameter of a proton); instructions show kids how to make a stereomagnifier, a well slide, and a microtome (with a spool and a razor blade; for making viewably thin slices of specimens). There are descriptions of many potential viewing projects, from feathers, hair, and photographs to mammalian and bacterial cells.

HANDS-ON ACTIVITIES FOR MICROSCOPES

Do You Know Where Your Protozoans Are?

This kit includes cultures of four different protozoans (the company chooses for you), deep-well slides, pipettes, and a plastic 30× student microscope for viewing live wiggling organisms.

$14.95

Carolina Biological Supply Co.

2700 York Rd.

Burlington, NC 27215

(800) 334-5551/fax (800) 222-7112

Carolina Biological Supply also sells a large number of other introductory and specialized kits of live microorganisms for student studies

Focus Pocus

A 20-lesson hands-on activities packet on microscopes, including instructions for making a usable, but very low-powered, microscope from a pair of beverage bottles, a soda straw, and a clothes pin. For kids in grades 3–10.

$15

TOPS Learning Systems

10970 S. Mulino Rd.

Canby, OR 97013

(888) 773-9755/fax (503) 266-5200

Web site: www.topscience.org

For more on TOPS learning modules, see page 224.

Microslide Viewer

A microscope-shaped plastic viewer used for studying mounted strips of photomicrographs (Microslides)—that is, color photographs of specimens taken through a microscope. There are nearly 200 Microslide strips available, covering a wide range of scientific subjects grouped by category. Users get terrific close-up views of bee legs, human red blood cells, influenza virus, and leaf cross-sections. A microscope experience without a microscope.

$8

National Teaching Aids, Inc.

1845 Highland Ave.

New Hyde Park, NY 11040

(516) 326-2555

See **National Teaching Aids, Inc.** (page 223).

Minipond Ecosystem

With the "Minipond Ecosystem" kit, kids can make their own very small pond. The kit includes a plastic minipond container, pond substrate (hay), protozoan mixture, algae mixture, pH test strips, nutrients, and an instruction manual with suggestions for student activities. You will need a microscope to study the denizens of your pond, which are marvelous. Also see the "Algae is NOT Just Pond Scum!" kit, which includes 3 algae specimens, plastic deep-well slides, and a 30× student microscope.

"Minipond" kit, $18; "Algae" kit, $14.95
Carolina Biological Supply Co.
2700 York Rd.
Burlington, NC 27215
(800) 334-5551

PREPARED MICROSCOPE SLIDES

Most science supply companies carry prepared microscope slides, on which the specimens are stained, fixed, and ready for viewing: all you need to do is pop them on the microscope stage and focus.

Carolina Biological Supply Company
Hundreds of prepared microscope slides, available individually or packaged in student sets. The "Basic Science Slide Set," for example, includes six slides (the letter *e*, cork, salt crystals, dust, volcanic ash, and an insect), plus a study guide; the "Beginner's Slide Set" includes 12 slides, plus an instruction manual. Also available for beginners are a series of thematic slide collections, among them the "Nature's Microscopic Beauty Set" (12 particularly gorgeous protists, plants, and animals), the "Burger and Fries Set" (slides show the source material for burger, lettuce, tomato, pickle, bun, and fries, with an explanatory study guide), the "Around the Yard Set" (12 slides of common backyard objects and creatures), the "Life in a Pond Set" (eight pond organisms), and the "Life in the Sea Set" (10 sea organisms, including starfish, seaweed, and shark scales).

Carolina Biological Supply Co.
2700 York Rd.
Burlington, NC 27215
(800) 334-5551/fax (800) 222-7211

Edmund Scientific Company
Sets of prepared slides in 11 categories: "Histology and Zoology," "Botany," "Cell Structures," "Insect Life," "Microorganisms in the Water," "Medical Science," "Vocational Training and Technology," "Foodstuffs,"

"Hobby and Leisure," "Ecology and Environment," and "School Series." Each set includes 10 slides, labeled and beautifully stained in different colors, with an accompanying descriptive manual.

Edmund Scientific Co.
101 E. Gloucester Pike
Barrington, NJ 08007-1380
(800) 728-6999 or (609) 547-8880
e-mail: scientifics@edsci.com
Web site: www.edsci.com

MICROSCOPY ON VIDEO

The Invisible World
Sixty minutes of spectacular photography from National Geographic, revealing secrets of the microscopic world.

$14.99
Movies Unlimited
3015 Darnell Rd.
Philadelphia, PA 19154
(215) 637-4444 or (800) 4-MOVIES
e-mail: movies@moviesunlimited.com
Web site: www.moviesunlimited.com

Video Microscope
This series is a homegrown production by elementary school teacher and video microscopist Warren Hatch of Portland, Oregon. "This video," writes Mr. Hatch of his *Video Microscope 1*, "is not Disney or National Geographic and does not have singing butterflies, dancing centipedes, or computer-generated dazzling synthetic graphics." He's right: it isn't and it doesn't. The opening credits, in fact, are handprinted on sheets of cardboard. Despite the low-tech intro, however, *Video Microscope 1* is a great microscopic show: 91 specimens in 121 minutes, including a painted lady butterfly wing, a hatching harlequin bug, paddling paramecia, a hungry amoeba, salt and sugar crystals, an exciting close-up of a Doritos corn chip, a bird feather, and a smear of human red blood cells. Fascinating stuff, all cosily narrated by Mr. Hatch. (Did you know that painted lady butterflies like prune juice?)

To date, there are 12 *Video Microscope* shows available on tape. All sound interesting: *Video Micro-*

scope 3, for example, includes views of swimming spirochetes, four kinds of beach sand from Hawaii, a computer microchip, a slice of a Styrofoam peanut, and a live slug.

Each tape, $20; $16.00 for three or more

Warren Hatch

1330 S.W. Third Ave., Apt. 703

Portland, OR 97201-6636

(503) 221-7154

MICROSCOPY ON-LINE

Amateur Microscopy on the Web

Includes reviews of microscopes and accessories, a microscopic image gallery, and *Micscape,* an on-line amateur microscopy magazine containing video and still microscopic images, articles about microscopic techniques, and a microscopic "Image of the Month." There's also a kid's page, for junior microscopists.

www.microscopy-uk.org.uk

Dennis Kunkel's Microscopy

A terrific gallery of electron microscope images, among them viruses, bacteria, plants, insects, fungi, and much more. The site includes an informative "About Microscopy" page.

www.pbrc.hawaii.edu/~kunkel

See *MicroAliens* (page 271).

Light Microscopy Page

An introduction to microscopy, including information about the different types of microscopes and their parts, and detailed instructions for setting up and using a microscope. Illustrations with labeled diagrams and photographs.

nsm.fullerton.edu/%7Eskarl/EM/Microscopy/
LightMicroscopy.html

Microscopy Primer

A very thorough introduction to microscopes and microphotography, including a detailed text, diagrams, and photographs.

micro.magnet.fsu.edu/micro/primer.html

Nanoworld Home Page

Includes a gallery of electron micrographs and a Virtual Electron Microscope tour of the Queensland fruit fly.

www.nq.oz.au/nanoworld/nanohome.html

BIOLOGY KITS

Most scientific supply companies (see **General Science Catalogs,** page 221) carry a broad range of experiment kits for young biologists, ranging from the small and simple to the challengingly sophisticated.

Aves Science Kit Company

A large assortment of small, inexpensive biology kits, including several dissection projects, studies of bacteria and protozoans, animal cell studies, and demonstrations of the actions of enzymes and the process of fermentation. Aves kits include enough experimental materials for two or three students, working cooperatively.

$5 to $8

Aves Science Kit Co.

Box 229

Peru, ME 04290

Carolina Biological Supply Company

The massive catalog includes an immense selection of biological kits, specimens, and experimental supplies for studies in the fields of virology, microbiology, zoology, botany, genetics, physiology, and biotechnology.

Main catalog, $17.95

Carolina Biological Supply Co.

2700 York Rd.

Burlington, NC 27215

(800) 334-5551/fax (800) 222-7112

Lab-Aids

Over 70 biology kits in the fields of general biology, plant science, biochemistry, genetics, and physiology. (Some require the use of a microscope.) Sample kit titles include "Osmosis and Diffusion," "Bacteria Study," "Genetic Concepts," "Structure and Function of Mitochondria," and "Basic Blood Typing." Most Lab-

Aids kits are intended for classroom use and contain enough materials for 12 to 15 pairs of students; some, however, are reasonably priced and can be adapted to smaller groups.

Lab-Aids, Inc.

17 Colt Ct.

Ronkonkoma, NY 11779

(516) 737-1133/fax (516) 737-1286

Dissecting Kits

Here's what you get in the standard student dissecting kit: a scalpel, a pair of $4\frac{1}{2}$-inch dissecting scissors, a pair of forceps, a couple of dissecting needles, half a dozen dissecting T pins, a ruler, and an eyedropper. Reasonably good kits come in a little fitted plastic box, the instruments that are supposed to be sharp actually are, and the forceps are metal, not plastic. These generally cost $10 to $15 per set.

Official equipment isn't, strictly speaking, absolutely necessary. You can piece together a reasonable dissecting kit from a handful of household and hardware supplies: most of us can come up with small sharp scissors, tweezers, pins, needles, and single-edged razor blades. An advantage of professional dissecting tools, however, is that they usually work better. The instruments have easy-to-grip handles; and the T pins are large, sturdy, and don't suddenly pop out when you least want them to.

You'll also need a dissecting pan. The standard lab model is a rectangular $11\frac{1}{2} \times 7\frac{1}{2}$-inch aluminum pan filled with black wax. We made our own, using heavy-duty aluminum disposable cake tins from the supermarket and paraffin wax (dyed green, left over from a candlemaking project). Commercial pans are also available with fitted foam rubber pads.

Finally, you'll need specimens. Common first-dissection specimens include an earthworm, crayfish, starfish, clam, fish, and the ever-popular leopard frog, all of which are available from scientific supply houses, packaged in preservative. You'll also need a laboratory dissection manual: these include detailed instructions on how to dissect and labeled diagrams of what you should see as you proceed.

Carolina Biological Supply Company

ALL The catalog carries an immense selection of preserved specimens. Carolina's "Zoology Survey Sets," for example, include 8 to 15 different animal specimens packaged in a single container; "Carolina Anatomy Kits" each contain a single specimen, a dissection manual, a disposable dissection tray, and a storage bag. Anatomy Kit specimens include the frog, dogfish shark, cat, and fetal pig.

Carolina Biological Supply Co.

2700 York Rd.

Burlington, NC 27215

(800) 334-5551

Edmund Scientific Company

ALL The catalog carries a number of preserved specimens and kits, among them a "Specimen Assortment for Dissecting": nine creatures packed in a jar, including an earthworm, clam, sponge, crayfish, starfish, clam, fish, frog, and grasshopper.

Edmund Scientific Co.

101 E. Gloucester Pike

Barrington, NJ 08007-1380

(609) 547-8880 or (800) 728-6999

Also see:

Schoolmasters Science

745 State Circle

Box 1941

Ann Arbor, MI 48106

(800) 521-2832

Dissection is not every young scientist's cup of tea. Two of our children were fascinated and worked their way through a battery of pickled specimens, keeping elaborately illustrated notebooks. The third kid refused to have anything to do with the process. If your kids are interested, but not to the point of hands-on participation, you might try the "Interactive Frog Dissection" on-line (Web site: curry.edschool.virginia.edu/insttech/frog; see page 347). The program is aimed at middle and high school–aged biology students; it includes information, demonstrations, opportunities (on-screen) to practice, and not so much as a whiff of formaldehyde.

For more information on dissection alternatives, see:

Ethical Science Education Coalition

ESEC publishes materials on alternatives to dissection and live-animal experimentation in science classes. Among their publications is a 62-page resource book, *Beyond Dissection: A Sampling of Innovative Teaching Tools for Biology Education,* which lists hundred of creative alternatives for kids like Ethan who don't want to pick up a scalpel.

$2

E.S.E.C.

167 Milk St., #423

Boston, MA 02109-4315

(617) 367-9143

Web site: www.neavs.org/htm/esec.htm

8 + *How to Dissect*

William Berman; Prentice-Hall, 1984

Background information and detailed instructions for dissecting 10 animals, from the earthworm to the fetal pig, and one plant (the gladiolus).

Also see *The Beginner's Guide to Animal Autopsy* (page 339).

GENERAL BIOLOGY ON-LINE

Biology Education Software FAQ

P/T Reviews, evaluations, and ordering information on available biology education software in the fields of ecology and evolution, physiology and neurobiology, and cell biology and genetics.

www.zoology.washington.edu/biosoft

CSU Bioweb

ALL A very large collection of Internet biology resources, searchable by field from agricultural science to zoology.

arnica.csustan.edu

OAC Biology Help Page

12 + Detailed information for middle and high school biology students. General biology topics are covered through a detailed explanatory text, charts, images, diagrams, and worksheets. Topics listed at the site include "Photosynthesis," "Energy and the Cell," "Genetics," "Evolution," and "Ecology."

mss.scbe.on.ca/dsoacbio.htm

A Page for Teachers

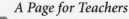 **P/T** Many useful Internet resource links, variously categorized under biology, frogs, animals, dinosaurs, chemistry, the environment, and weather.

www.wartburg.edu/inside/StudentMaintained/biodept/kids/forteachers/teachers.html

BOTANY

Also see **Gardening** (page 824).

BOOKS: NONFICTION

4 8 *A B Cedar: An Alphabet of Trees*

George Ella Lyon; Orchard Books, 1996

A tree for every letter of the alphabet. A delightful introduction to tree identification for young beginners.

5 9 *All About Seeds*

Melvin Berger; Scholastic, 1994

A beginner's introduction to the different kinds of seeds, how seeds are dispersed, and what they need to sprout and grow, with eight seed-related activities.

9 12 *The Amazing Dirt Book*

Paulette Bourgeois; Addison-Wesley, 1990

Kid-friendly information about the science of soil, along with many hands-on projects and activities. Kids, for example, make sand sculptures, footprint casts, "mud cakes," and hydroponic gardens.

5 9 *Ancient Ones: The World of the Old-Growth Douglas Fir*

Barbara Bash; Sierra Club Books, 1994

A richly illustrated informational picture book about the life and environment of the Douglas fir. The book follows the tree throughout its long life, with colorful paintings that give readers a feel for the majestic height of these great trees. By the same author, also see *In the Heart of the Village: The World of the Indian Banyan Tree* (Little, Brown, 1996) and *Tree of Life: The World of the African Baobab* (Sierra Club Books, 1994). See *Desert Giant: The World of the Saguaro Cactus* (page 277).

Crinkleroot's Guide to Knowing Trees
Jim Arnosky; Bradbury Press, 1992

Crinkleroot is a friendly woodsperson with a long white beard, a fringed green jacket, and a walking stick with a carved bear on top. In this informational picture book, he takes readers on a tour of the forest. Included is general information about forests and trees, plus labeled diagrams of the parts of a tree, different kinds of leaves, needles, and cones, and a cross-section of what a tree looks like inside.

By the same author, see *Crinkleroot's Guide to Knowing Birds* (page 331).

Desert Giant: The World of the Saguaro Cactus
Barbara Bash; Little, Brown, 1990

A beautifully illustrated picture-book account of the life and environment of the immense saguaro cactus.

See *Ancient Ones: The World of the Old-Growth Douglas Fir* (page 276).

Eyewitness Series: Botany
Volumes in the Eyewitness series for botanists, include *Plant* (1989) and *Tree* (1988), both by David Burnie, illustrated with superb color photographs and graphics. Each double-page spread concentrates on a different botanical topic. *Plant,* for example, covers "The parts of a plant," "A simple flower dissected," "How a plant is pollinated," "How seeds are spread," "Parasitic plants," and "Living without water." *Tree* topics include "Broadleaved trees," "Coniferous trees," "The tree trunk," "Bark—the outer skin," "Simple leaves," "Compound leaves," "Seeds and nuts," and "From tree to timber." There's an accompanying informational text, most of it in the picture captions.

A Flower Grows
Ken Robbins; Dial, 1990

The life cycle of an amaryllis bulb, which sprouts and produces a truly spectacular flower, illustrated with hand-tinted photographs.

From Seed to Plant
Gail Gibbons; Holiday House, 1991

A beautifully illustrated simple picture-book account of how seeds form and develop into new plants. The book covers the parts of a flower, the process of pollination and seed maturation, the structure of seeds, germination, and plant development, all in simple language, with big bright colored pictures. Included are instructions for a grow-your-own bean plant project.

Green Immigrants: The Plants That Transformed America
Claire Shaver Haughton; Harcourt Brace, 1980

A 400+-page collection of short histories of the many flowers, vegetables, trees, and fruits that have come to America from other parts of the world, arranged in alphabetical order from apple and African violet to yarrow and zinnia. Readers learn that the eucalyptus was picked up in the South Seas by a pirate ship; that the first bananas in North America were served at a Boston dinner party in 1875; and that tumbleweed came to the United States with Russian immigrants who settled in North Dakota. For teenagers and adults, but filled with interesting information for all ages.

How Did We Find Out About Photosynthesis?
Isaac Asimov; Walker & Company, 1989

What photosynthesis is, how it works, and a history of the scientific discoveries that led to its elucidation.

Keepers of Life: Discovering Plants Through Native American Stories and Earth Activities for Children
Michael J. Caduto and Joseph Bruchac; Fulcrum, 1997

This information-filled book links American Indian stories and legends to scientific information and hands-on activities. Stories, grouped by theme, variously cover botany, plant ecology, and the natural history of North American plants. Each story is followed by background information, a list of discussion questions, detailed instructions for hands-on activities, and suggestions for further projects. Also see *Keepers of the Earth: Native American Stories and Environmental Activities for Children* (page 297) and *Keepers of the Animals: Native American Stories and Wildlife Activities for Children.*

Also see **Literature Links to Botany** (page 279).

Let's-Read-and-Find-Out Science Series: Botany

HarperCollins

Plant-related titles in this picture-book science series for 4–9-year-olds (see page 227) include *Be a Friend to Trees* (Patricia Lauber; HarperCollins, 1995) and *Why Do Leaves Change Color?* (Betsy Maestro; HarperCollins, 1994). Simple scientific explanations are accompanied by colorful pictures and diagrams.

Plants That Never Bloom

Ruth Heller; Price Stern Sloan, 1992

Colorful and detailed paintings accompany short rhyming descriptions of such nonbloomers as mushrooms, seaweeds, lichens, and ferns. See, by the same author, *The Reason for a Flower* (Price Stern Sloan, 1992) which, in the same beautiful format, covers the reason for flowers, the process of pollination, and the many different kinds of seeds.

Red Oaks and Black Birches

Rebecca Rupp; Storey Communications, 1990

Twenty informative chapters, each on the science and history of a common North American tree. The book explains why leaves change color, what tannins are good for, how tree rings form, why birchbark makes good canoes, why sycamores make lousy pancake syrup, and why hickory makes good stove wood. Readers also learn the history of chewing gum and the real story behind George Washington's cherry tree. There's even a chapter on the science of Christmas trees.

The Red Poppy

Irmgard Lucht; Hyperion, 1995

A beautifully illustrated picture-book account of the life cycle of a red poppy.

Seeds: Pop, Stick, Glide

Patricia Lauber; Crown, 1991

An account of traveling seeds, illustrated with fascinating photographs: seed pods that explode like tiny bombs, sticky seeds, jelly-coated seeds, winged seeds, wind-borne seeds, and burrs.

Sugaring Time

Kathryn Lasky; Aladdin, 1986

Maple syrup from tree to pancake. The story of a family tapping its trees and making syrup in Vermont, illustrated on every page with black-and-white photographs.

Tiger Lilies and Other Beastly Plants

Elizabeth Ring; Walker & Company, 1996

The stories of such "beastly" animal-named plants as tiger lilies, foxgloves, pussywillows, and skunk cabbage.

The Tree Almanac: A Year-Round Activity Guide

Monica Russo; Sterling Publications, 1994

An introduction to the science of trees for kids aged 6–12, arranged by season of the year. Includes drawings, photographs, a list of tree families with both common and Latin names, and many hands-on projects and activities.

The Visual Dictionary of Plants

Dorling Kindersley, 1992

Sixty-four pages of gorgeous color photographs—including photomicrographs—and drawings, illustrating the parts of plants, inside and out, and their function in such biological processes as photosynthesis, pollination, and germination. The book also includes a detailed survey of the plant kingdom, from the fungi, lichens, and algae, through mosses, ferns, gymnosperms and angiosperms. Absolutely everything is extensively labeled.

See **Eyewitness Visual Dictionary Series** (page 132)

While a Tree Was Growing

Jane Bosveld; Workman, 1997

The illustrated story of one of the world's oldest living trees, a sequoia in the Sierra Nevada Mountains of California. While this tree was growing, the book explains, the Trojan War was fought, Cleopatra was born, Columbus arrived in America, and the Wright brothers took their famous airplane flight. The book pairs a world history timeline with a chronology of the growth of the tree, from seedling to massive adult.

Biographies of Botanists

Here a Plant, There a Plant, Everywhere a Plant, Plant! A Story of Luther Burbank

Robert Quackenbush; Luther Burbank and *Home & Gardens*, 1995

A short, illustrated biography of creative 19th-century botanist Luther Burbank, who developed a white blackberry, a spineless cactus, and the famous Russet Burbank potato.

The Man Who Planted Trees

Jean Giono; Chelsea Green, 1995

The story of Elzeard Bouffier who, over 40 dedicated years, turned a barren region of southern France into a flourishing oak forest by planting 100 acorns a day. An inspiring story, illustrated with woodcuts.

Plant Hunters

Tyler Whittle; Linden Publishing, 1997

An intriguing history of botanists who have traveled the world in search of new plants, from ancient times through the early 20th century. Lots of adventures, hardships, disasters, and incredible plants. For teenagers and up.

The Story of Johnny Appleseed

Aliki; Aladdin, 1987

A charming picture-book version of the life of Johnny Appleseed, who loved animals, wore a tin pot on his head, and planted apple trees wherever he went. Also see *Johnny Appleseed* by Steven Kellogg (Mulberry, 1996) and *Johnny Appleseed* by Reeve Lindbergh (Little, Brown, 1993).

Literature Links to Botany

The Adventures of Treehorn

Florence Parry Heide; Holiday House, 1982

Three delightful tales about the resourceful Treehorn, who is continually ignored by his vague parents. In "Treehorn's Treasure," the leaves on the tree in Treehorn's yard turn into dollar bills, but when he tries to tell people, nobody—including the painter who is painting the family kitchen "Leaf Green"—believes him.

Anno's Magic Seeds

Mitsumasa Anno; Philomel Books, 1995

A mathematical take on botany. Jack meets a wizard who gives him two magical seeds, telling him to eat one and plant the other. The seed sprouts into a lovely blue-flowered plant that bears two golden seeds. Jack plants *both* seeds, grows two plants, and harvests four seeds—of which he eats one and plants three. The story quickly becomes more mathematically complex, all with delightful illustrations.
Also see **Books for Kids** (page 180).

The Giving Tree

Shel Silverstein; HarperCollins, 1986

A large-hearted tree loves a little boy and gives him everything she has until, finally, the boy has grown old and nothing is left of the tree but a stump. The generous tree, however, can still provide a place for the old man to sit down and rest.

The Great Dimpole Oak

Janet Taylor Lisle; Orchard Press, 1987

A 10-year-old boy listens to stories of his town's past beneath the Great Dimpole Oak and helps save the tree when it looks as though it is going to be cut down.

The Great Kapok Tree: A Tale of the Amazon Rain Forest

Lynn Cherry; Harcourt Brace, 1990

A woodchopper at work in the rain forest lies down to take a nap. As he sleeps, all the forest dwellers creep out to plead for the trees, telling him all the good trees do, providing food, homes, shelter. Somehow in his sleep the man hears and understands.
See **Environmental Science** (page 294).

The Legend of the Indian Paintbrush

Tomie de Paola; Paper Star, 1996

Little Gopher, a Plains Indian boy, wants to paint pictures filled with all the colors of the sunset. His scarlet paintbrushes become a beautiful wildflower. Also see, by the same author, *The Legend of the Bluebonnet:*

An Old Tale of Texas (Paper Star, 1996), a Comanche legend about a little girl who sacrifices her most beloved possession to bring rain to her people and is rewarded with the gift of a beautiful blue flower, the Texas bluebonnet.

Pearl Moscowitz's Last Stand
Arthur A. Levine; Tambourine Books, 1993

When Pearl was a little girl, the gingko trees were planted along her city street. Now Pearl has grown up, the neighborhood has changed with the years, filling with interesting multicultural families, and the city has cut down all the trees but one. Feisty Pearl bravely defends the last tree.

The Star Maiden: An Ojibway Tale
Barbara Juster Esbensen; Little, Brown, 1991

A picture-book version of an American Indian legend about a star who longs to live on earth. She gets her wish and becomes the first waterlily.

The Tree in the Trail
Holling C. Holling; Houghton Mifflin, 1990

The history of an ancient cottonwood tree on the Santa Fe trail, beginning with its discovery by a Kansan Indian boy in the early 1600s. The tree witnesses Spanish explorers, French trappers, buffalo hunts, and encampments of mountain men; and it serves as a post office for the westward-traveling wagon trains. A fascinating book, illustrated with paintings, maps, diagrams, and detailed pencil drawings.

COLORING AND STICKER BOOKS

American Wildflowers Coloring Book
Paul E. Kennedy; Dover Publications

Drawings of 44 flowers, among them the fringed gentian and the lady's slipper, all with informational captions. Dover publishes many botanical coloring books; other titles include *The Cactus Coloring Book, The Common Weeds Coloring Book,* and *Trees of the Northeast Coloring Book.*

$2.95 apiece

Dover Publications, Inc.

31 E. Second St.

Mineola, NY 11501

The Botany Coloring Book
Paul Young; HarperPerennial, 1982

A college-level botany class in a book, with detailed information and precise scientific line drawings, for very advanced colorers.

Forests
Bettina Dudley and Helen I. Driggs; Running Press, 1989

A "Fact-Filled Coloring Book" for young tree lovers. The book pairs detailed black-and-white drawings with an interesting and informational text, supplemented with fact boxes and maps. The book is divided into five parts: "How Forests Began," "What Keeps Forests Growing?," "North American Forests," "Forests From the North Pole to the South," and "Forests for the Future." Included is a 17 × 22-inch ready-to-color fold-out poster of rain forest life.

Available from bookstores or

Running Press Book Publishers

125 S. 22nd St.

Philadelphia, PA 19103

(215) 567-5080 or (800) 345-5359

The Ultimate Trees and Flowers Sticker Book
Dorling Kindersley

Over 60 beautiful stickers—from color photographs—of trees, leaves, flowers, fruits, and cones to be matched to the proper place in the descriptive text.

GAMES AND HANDS-ON ACTIVITIES

Aves Science Botany Kits
The company sells many inexpensive experiment kits on botanical topics, each containing enough materials for two or three students. Titles include "Acid Rain and Plant Growth," "Dehydration and Seeds," "Flower Dissection," "Herb Study," "Hydroculture Study," "Light and Seeds," "Light Frequency and Plants," "Nutrients and Plants," "Plant Propagation," "Radiation and Plants," "Root Hair Study," "Soil Type Study," and "Wildflower Study."

$5 to $8

Aves Science Kit Co.

Box 229

Peru, ME 04290

Also see **Lab-Aids** (page 222) and the **Carolina Biological Supply Company** (page 275).

Birch Bark Bric A Brac

A kit of American Indian birchbark crafts, which substitutes a birchbark look-alike in heavy paper for the real thing. The kit includes enough materials for kids to make six craft projects, among them a picture frame, a book, birchbark boxes, and a tiny canoe.

$14.95 from arts and crafts stores or

Creativity for Kids

1802 Central Ave.

Cleveland, OH 44115

(216) 589-4800 or (800) 642-2288/fax (216) 589-4803

Web site: www.creativityforkids.com

Most scientific supply company sells experiment kits for botanical studies. Sources include:

Flower Press

We press flowers in the *Oxford English Dictionary*. Practically anything big, heavy, and flat functions nicely as a flower press, though massive books have always been our favorites. Simply open the book to the middle, slip in a sheet of wax paper, add your plant specimens (carefully spread out), top with more wax paper, close the book, stack a few more volumes on top of it, and wait. This is not precisely the professional method, but it's cheap and it works.

The professional flower press, for serious collectors, consists of a pair of wooden frames between which are layered stacks of blotting-paper driers and corrugated-cardboard ventilators, secured with straps or with screws at the corners. Really good ones generally cost around $40.

Forestry Suppliers, Inc.

Box 8397

Jackson, MS 39284-8397

(800) 647-5368

or less expensive student versions from

Delta Education

Box 3000

Nashua, NH 03061-3000

(800) 442-5444/fax (800) 282-9560

Web site: www.delta-ed.com

or

Edmund Scientific Co.

101 E. Gloucester Pike

Barrington, NJ 08007-1380

(609) 547-8880 or (800) 728-6999

e-mail: scientifics@edsci.com

Web site: www.edsci.com

or

ETA

620 Lakeview Pkwy.

Vernon Hills, IL 60061

(847) 816-5050

(800) 445-5985/fax (800) ETA-9326

e-mail: info@etauniverse.com

Web site: www.etauniverse.com

Goldenrod

A card game of wildflowers. Each card in the deck is illustrated with a beautiful color painting of a wildflower. Instructions are included for four games. The "General Method" is a flower version of rummy, in which players attempt to collect four-card sets of flowers; "Guess" is rummy with an extra twist: players cannot acquire a card from another player until they correctly identify the flower from its picture. For three to five players, aged 5 and up.

$8.95

Carolina Biological Supply Co.

2700 York Rd.

Burlington, NC 27215

(800) 334-5551/fax (800) 222-7112

Green Thumbs

The Green Thumbs TOPS study modules each consist of 20 creative and scientifically thorough lessons for young botanists, using simple and inexpensive equipment. In "Radishes," kids sprout easy-to-grow radish seeds, experimenting with germination conditions and tropisms, and graphing radish growth rates.

In "Corn & Beans," students sprout popcorn and pinto beans, keep daily journals of plant development, graph height and weight gains, study photosynthesis, and learn the difference between a monocot and a dicot. And much more: these modules are packed with activities and information. TOPS is particularly noted for imaginative instructions for building workable scientific apparatus out of practically nothing.

Both "Radishes" and "Corn & Beans" are recommended for kids in grades 3–10. "Radishes," rated as "basic" in difficulty, is more appropriate for kids at the younger end of the scale; "Corn & Beans," rated as "moderate," is more appropriate for middle-grade and older students.

$15

TOPS Learning Systems

10970 S. Mulino Rd.

Canby, OR 97013

(888) 773-9755/fax (503) 266-5200

Web site: www.topscience.org

Juniper

A card game of trees. Each card is illustrated with a color painting of a tree. Some show the tree as a whole; others, close-up details of leaves, flowers, or cones. Instructions are included for four games. The most common is a form of rummy, in which players collect four-card sets of trees in the same group or family: for example, "Oak Family," "Pine Family," "Giant Trees," "Desert Trees," and "Maple Family." For three to five players, aged 5 and up.

$8.95

Carolina Biological Supply Co.

2700 York Rd.

Burlington, NC 27215

(800) 334-5551/fax (800) 222-7112

Leaf & Tree Backyard Explorer Kit

Rona Beame; Workman, 1989

This kit, in a handy plastic envelope, includes a *Leaf & Tree Guide,* with helpful hints for identifying leaves, cones, seedpods, and bark, plus suggestions for year-round leaf- and tree-related hands-on activities, and a *Leaf Collecting Album,* for preserving botanical finds.

$9.95 from bookstores or

Workman Publishing Co.

708 Broadway

New York, NY 10003-9555

(212) 254-5900 or (800) 722-7202/fax (212) 254-8098

Web site: www.workmanweb.com

Natural Collections

A field trip in a box. Collections include "Tree Rings," "Leaves," and "Wildflowers." Each includes an activities booklet with background information and complete instructions for projects. "Tree Rings" contains a slice of a tree, with nice, visible rings for counting; "Leaves" and "Wildflowers" each includes 13 pressed specimens, mounted on cards.

$19.95 each

Educational Insights

16941 Keegan Ave.

Carson, CA 90746

(800) 933-3277/fax (310) 605-5048 or (800) 995-0506

Web site: www.edin.com

Nature Education Kits

Collections of botanical specimens, dried, packaged, and ready to identify. The "Leaf Identification Classroom Kit," for example, includes 39 tree leaves (3 each of 13 species), a leaf identification key, a tree guide, and a teacher's manual; the "Seed Identification Classroom Kit" contains 39 tree seeds (3 each of 13 species), an identification key, a sprouting seed kit and ready-to-grow seeds, and a teacher's guide.

For younger botanists in preschool through grade 4, specimens are packaged in a "Leaf and Seed Games Classroom Kit," which contains 20 leaves, 20 seeds, directions for classifying and identifying, and instructions for eight games.

About $10 to $25 per set

Carolina Biological Supply Co.

2700 York Rd.

Burlington, NC 27215

(800) 334-5551/fax (800) 222-7112

Scientific Explorer Botany Kit

The company sells a series of Expedition Kits (see page 223), among them a Botany Kit. This contains materials for both indoor and out-in-the-field research projects: users grow a carnivorous plant, repeat some of Gregor Mendel's famous genetic experiments with pea plants, construct an herbarium, and collect their own specimens of leaves, seeds, flowers, and pollen. All materials, including seeds, identification charts, and instruction booklets, are included.

$15.95

Scientific Explorer, Inc.

2802 E. Madison, Suite 114

Seattle, WA 98112

(206) 322-7611 or (800) 900-1182/fax (206) 322-7610

e-mail: sciex@scientificexplorer.com

Web site: www.scientificexplorer.com

Wee Enchanted Garden

Combine art, imagination, and a bit of beginning botany. With this kit, kids create a miniature "enchanted" garden in a saucer. The kit includes a 10-inch-diameter saucer, paints for decorating it, potting soil, seeds, rocks, gravel, and garden inhabitants, among them tiny woodland animals and a miniature bark house. Recommended for kids aged 7 and up.

Creativity for Kids

1802 Central Ave.

Cleveland, OH 44115

(216) 589-4800 or (800) 642-2288/fax (216) 589-4803

Web site: www.creativityforkids.com

Wisconsin Fast Plants

The Wisconsin Fast Plants educational materials were developed by Paul Williams, plant pathologist at the University of Wisconsin. The plants, varieties of *Brassica rapa,* develop extremely fast—their entire life cycle, from seed to adult and back to seed again, takes a mere 35 days—which makes them excellent candidates for student botany projects. For beginners, the "Fast Plants Mini Trial Kit" includes seed, soil, fertilizer, an automatic watering system, pollination supplies, stakes, labels, a four-cell foam planter (a quad), and an instruction booklet. Kids pollinate the flowers themselves with a "bee-stick," which consists of a bee's thorax attached to a stick. One bee-stick comes with each kit; extras can be ordered separately. (Or you can order a bag of dried bees and make your own bee-sticks.)

Specialized Fast Plants kits are available for growth and development, nutrition, physiology, tropism, and genetic studies. Many genetic variants of the original parent seed stock are available for studies of inheritance patterns. Various mutations, for example, affect flower or leaf color, plant height, and herbicide resistance.

The "Mini Trial Kit," $6.50; individual student kits, $16.95

Carolina Biological Supply Co.

2700 York Rd.

Burlington, NC 27215

(800) 334-5551/fax (800) 222-7112

PLANT YOUR OWN TREES: SOURCES

Historic Trees

Plant a sapling of a famous historic tree, among them offspring of trees from Mount Vernon, Monticello, or James Madison's Montpelier, Civil War battlefield trees, trees from Thoreau's Walden woods, and trees from the homes of famous American artists, authors, and inventors.

Each tree-planting kit includes a one- to three-foot sapling (with personalized certificate of authenticity), planting materials and instructions, and a one-year replacement guarantee just in case your infant tree doesn't survive. The catalog alone, filled with historical photographs, is fascinating reading.

$35 each

American Forests Famous & Historic Trees

8555 Plummer Rd.

Jacksonville, FL 32219

(800) 320-TREE/fax (800) 264-6869

National Arbor Day Foundation

The foundation offers a catalog of (very small) tree saplings at very low prices and publishes tree-related educational materials and booklets, and a newsletter of tree-related issues, the *Arbor Day News.*

National Arbor Day Foundation

100 Arbor Ave.

Nebraska City, NE 68410

(402) 474-5655

Web site: www.arborday.org

Tree in a Box Set

"Potential" tree in a box is more like it. With this kit, kids can grow six species of trees: American elm, dawn redwood, blue spruce, Douglas fir, red maple, and ponderosa pine. The boxes are each 2½ inches square; each contains a preplanted tree seed in a pot. An included 32-page booklet gives complete instructions on sprouting the seeds and raising the seedlings, plus general scientific and historical information about trees.

$45

Carolina Biological Supply Co.

2700 York Rd.

Burlington, NC 27215

(800) 334-5551/fax (800) 222-7112

BOTANY ON-LINE

CNPS Kids

The kids' page of the California Native Plant Society (CNPS) includes an informative introduction to botany, illustrated with big multicolored diagrams. Kids discover what's inside a flower and learn how pollination works. Includes links to many plant and gardening sites.

www.calpoly.edu/~dchippen

Flowering Plant Gateway

Users explore the three major systems of plant classification, with descriptions and images of examples.

www.isc.tamu.edu/FLORA/cronang.htm

Green and Growing

Includes "From the Ground Up," a detailed lesson plan on the history and present practice of agriculture and food sources worldwide, with activities and worksheets. For kids in middle school and up.

www.gatewest.net/~green

Missouri Botanical Gardens: MBGnet Home

Plant- and environment-related science activities, lesson plans, and contests for kids. Users can also explore six virtual biomes (desert, grasslands, temperate forest, rain forest, tundra, and taiga), learning about the plants, animals, and climate of each.

www.mobot.org/MBGnet

National Garden Association's Growing Ideas

Garden- and plant-based educational activities for kids of all ages.

www.garden.org/nga/EDU/home.html

OAC Biology Help Page

Resources on photosynthesis, including a thorough explanation of the process, with images and text.

mss.scbe.on.ca/dsoacbio.htm

Seeds of Change

A terrific site based on the Smithsonian Institution's "Seeds of Change" exhibit on the plants of the Old and New Worlds. Included is history of many old- and new-world food plants, listed in alphabetical order; detailed instructions for four seasons of garden activities; recipes; suggestions for hands-on learning projects; and seed ordering information.

horizon.nmsu.edu/garden

A Survey of the Plant Kingdoms

A very detailed site on plant classification, with descriptions and definitions of all kingdoms and subdivisions, with illustrations, diagrams, and photographs of representative examples.

www.mancol.edu/science/biolog/plants_new/intro/start.html

The Time-Life Complete Gardener's Encyclopedia

Look up a plant, any plant. The site includes a database of 3,000 North American species.

www.pathfinder.com/@@S3vABQUA1811rCGh/vg/TimeLife/CG/vg_search.html

Virtual Plant Cell

Images, videos, and a descriptive text on the structures and functions of a typical plant cell.

ampere.scale.uiuc.edu/~m-lexa/scripts/cell.cgi

CELL BIOLOGY

In the elementary grades, some simple cell biology is usually included with studies of the human body. Kids learn, for example, that the cell is the basic building block of living things. Cell biology, in secondary school science programs, is generally incorporated into a general biology course, along with some basic biochemistry and genetics.

From my homeschool journal:

◆ **November 21, 1994. Josh is thirteen; Ethan, eleven; Caleb, nine.**

We're still reading (aloud, in a group) Madeline L'Engle's A Wind in the Door, *in which Charles Wallace (1) sees dragons in the garden, and (2) has fallen ill because the farandolae in the mitochondria of his cells are dying. Caleb wanted to know what mitochondria are; Ethan wanted to know if there really is such a thing as farandolae; so we spent the morning doing cell biology. Defined* prokaryote *and* eukaryote *and compared the cellular structures of each; the boys colored and labeled diagrams from* The Biology Coloring Book. *Looked at photomicrographs of various kinds of cells and intracellular structures with the Microslide Viewer. (With particular attention to mitochondria. No farandolae.) Explained what mitochondria are, what they do, how big they are. Made preparations of cheek cells (the boys took scrapings from the inside of their cheeks), stained them with iodine, and examined them under the microscope. Caleb: "What kind of a microscope do you use to see mitochondria? Can you just see them right through the cell membrane?"*

Read and discussed "Organelles as Organisms" from Lives of a Cell *by Lewis Thomas.*

Then went back to reading A Wind in the Door.

Books

Cells Are Us
Fran Balkwill and Mic Rolph; First Avenue Editions, 1994

This is a skinny picture book, illustrated with big bright-colored cartoon-style drawings and diagrams. The picture-book format, however, doesn't mean sparse and simple information; Balkwill and Rolph deal with the challengingly complex. *Cells Are Us*, aimed at readers aged 5–8, is an overview of the many kinds of differentiated cells that make up the human body. "Cells are the 'building blocks' of life. Your body is made of zillions and zillions of them. Each one is so tiny you can't even see it with a magnifying glass. You need a special instrument called a microscope." The book covers DNA, chromosomes, and cell division, and discusses the structure and functions of skin cells, red blood cells, neutrophils, macrophages, and lymphocytes, bone cells, muscle cells, and neurons. See also, by the same authors, *Cell Wars*, for kids aged 7–13, an explanation of the workings of the immune system, with illustrated descriptions of how neutrophils, macrophages, and lymphocytes battle invading viruses and bacteria. The book also tells how vaccination works and explains the blood-clotting process.

From bookstores or
Cold Spring Harbor Laboratory Press
10 Skyline Dr.
Plainview, NY 11803-2500
(800) 843-4388
Web site: www.cshl.org

Life Itself: Exploring the Realm of the Living Cell
Boyce Rensberger; Oxford University Press, 1997

Cell biology for the general public. The book covers the basics of cells, which—just in case you don't appreciate them properly—are marvelous little machines stuffed with genetic blueprints, protein-manufacturing apparatus, and "molecular motors." Rensberger explains how cells grow, function, and divide—and kill, crawl around, digest things, and occasionally spin cancerously out of control. The book also discusses the work of prominent cell biologists and covers current trends in cell biology. Chapter titles include "Molecular Motors," "The Living-Room Cell," "Constructing a Person," and "Pumping Protein."

The Lives of a Cell: Notes of a Biology Watcher
Lewis Thomas; Penguin, 1995

Beautifully written science essays stressing the interrelatedness of life on earth. Topics covered range from the mitochondria inside our cells to social insects to the earth's atmosphere.

Molecular Biology of the Cell

Bruce Alberts, Dennis Bray, Julian Lewis, Martin Raff, and Keith Roberts; Garland Publishing, 1995

An excellent and enormous (1,294 pages) college-level text; a worthwhile investment for serious and advanced science students.

Also see *Molecular Biology of the Cell: The Problems Book* (John Wilson and Tim Hunt; Garland Publishing, 1994), a collection of quizzes and problems based on the text. (Answers and brief explanations are included.)

What's Smaller Than a Pygmy Shrew?

Robert E. Wells; Albert Whitman, 1995

A picture-book tour of all the things that are smaller than the world's smallest mammal, the tiny pygmy shrew: not only worms and bugs but also cells, molecules, atoms, and subatomic particles. An excellent first answer to the question "What are animals made of?"

GAMES AND HANDS-ON ACTIVITIES

The Cell Game

This board game teaches kids about basic cell structure and function. The game includes four game boards, two with diagrammatic illustrations of animal cells, two with representations of plant cells. The aim of the game is to complete the pictured cell by accumulating essential organelles and molecules through such activities as synthesis, parasitism, respiration, and (if you're a plant) photosynthesis. The game contains organelle and molecule tokens, and a deck of "Cell Event" cards. For two to four players, high school age and up.

$32.95

Carolina Biological Supply Co.
2700 York Rd.
Burlington, NC 27215
(800) 334-5551/fax (800) 222-7112

CELL BIOLOGY ON-LINE

Cells Alive!

Impressive color graphics, animation, and video clips of bacteria and mammalian cells, with an explanatory text. Topics include "Making Antibodies" and "How Big?," which compares sizes of viruses, bacteria, and human cells.

www.cellsalive.com

Introduction to Cell Biology

An on-line introduction to cell biology, suitable for high school or college students. The illustrated text covers such topics as the definition of a cell, cell components, different kinds of cells, and cell division.

lenti.med.umn.edu/~mwd/cell.html

OAC Biology Help Page

Links to many topics, including "Energy and the Cell," which covers cell metabolism through images, charts, worksheets, and text, and "Genetics," which includes detailed information about cell division (mitosis and meiosis).

mss.scbe.on.ca/dsoacbio.htm

Virtual Cell

Still images, movies, and explanatory text on the structure and function of a typical plant cell.

ampere.scale.uiuc.edu/~m-lexa/scripts/cell.cgi

Yale Center for Cell Imaging

A very detailed on-line manual of microscopy techniques and a library of terrific photomicrographs of cells, bacteria, and viruses, with accompanying descriptions.

info.med.yale.edu/cellimg

ENTOMOLOGY

One morning some years ago—when Josh was nine, Ethan seven, and Caleb five—we set out after breakfast to inspect a massive ant nest that the boys had discovered in the woods behind the house. We brought with us some scraps of leftover breakfast French toast, which the boys felt would make ideal ant food, a magnifying glass, and (a mistake) the dog. The ant nest was a scientific treasure trove. We spent hours crouched around and over it. The boys offered French toast: one ant discovered it, then another, then a bucket brigade of ants, grabbing crumbs in a steady stream. The boys tried moving the French toast, building a barrier between toast and ants, putting out distracting alternative pieces of toast. More ants were identified, apparently uninterested in toast, exploring the neighborhood, moving grains of sand, disposing of the bodies of dead companions. The dog, disgracefully digging, turned up an underground chamber of ant eggs and hysterical ant nursemaids. The boys fizzed with ant questions, ant observations, ant stories. They examined ants under the magnifying glass. Caleb learned to spell *ant*.

Ant interest, high for several days, gradually faded, to be replaced by other things (penguins, paper airplanes, knights and castles, dinosaurs); the ant-digging dog was forgiven; life moved on. Real learning experiences, however, are never wasted and never really lost. When Josh, our oldest son, turned 15, he wanted a trilobite, a pair of boots, and a fountain pen for his birthday. And E. O. Wilson's *Journey to the Ants*. And an ant farm.

ORGANIZATIONS

Young Entomologists' Society

The Young Entomologists' Society (Y.E.S.) is a group "for minibeast enthusiasts of all ages." The society publishes a catalog of books (fiction and nonfiction), field guides, science kits, videos, computer software, stuffed creatures, puzzles, models, toys, posters, and T-shirts for bug enthusiasts, as well as a bimonthly magazine, *Insect World*, targeted at readers aged 5–12, and the *Y.E.S. Quarterly*, a journal of amateur entomology for readers aged 12 and up.

> Annual youth membership (aged 18 and under), $8; member's annual subscription to *Insect World* (6 issues), $10. Available to new youth members is "Junior Bugologist Package" ($30), which includes membership fees, a subscription to *Insect World*, a copy of *Going Buggy: A Directory to North American Insect Zoos, Butterfly Houses, Museums, and Insect Fairs*, an activity book, a "bug" pencil, and a color-your-own insect poster

Young Entomologists' Society, Inc.
1915 Peggy Pl.

Lansing, MI 48910-2553
(517) 887-0499
e-mail: YESbugs@aol.com

CATALOGS

Insect Lore Products

ALL A catalog of materials for young entomologists, including books, models, kits, activity books, games, posters, puzzles, and videos. Insects may be their favorites, but the catalog includes resources for nature lovers of all interests and ages.

Insect Lore Products
Box 1535
Shafter, CA 93263
(800) LIVE-BUG
Web site: www.insectlore.com

BOOKS

Alien Empire: An Exploration of the Lives of Insects

Christopher O'Toole; Diane Publishing, 1995

A fascinating 224-page "Exploration of the Lives of Insects" with 250 spectacular close-up color photographs and an informational text emphasizing the ecological role of insects.

Backyard Buddies Series

Michael Elsohn Ross; Carolrhoda, 1996

A series of creature-centered science activity books for kids in grades 1–4. *Cricketology*, *Rolypolyology*, *Snailology*, and *Wormology* feature, respectively, crickets, pill bugs, snails, and earthworms. Each illustrated 48-page volume explains where to find and how to keep the featured creatures and includes instructions for simple activities and experiments designed to help kids learn more about their backyard subjects. The books include color photographs, humorous drawings, and a comfortable chatty text. "Most folks don't get too excited about watching a jar of mayonnaise or peanut butter," writes Ross, "but spying on a jar of crickets can be more entertaining than reading a cereal box." Absolutely.

The Bug Book
6 **12** Robin Bernard; Scholastic, 1996

Background information, hands-on activities, and literature links for elementary-aged bug students.

Bugs
4 **9** Nancy Winslow Parker and Joan Richards Wright; William Morrow, 1988

A clever picture book with a double-page format. The left-hand page pairs a cheerful illustration with a two-line rhyme ("What chirped as Nick walked through the thicket?/A cricket"). On the right is a detailed labeled drawing of the featured bug and a paragraph of descriptive scientific information. The book covers 16 familiar insects, among them the flea, the mosquito, the roach, the firefly, and the dragonfly.

Bugwise: Thirty Incredible Insect Investigations and Arachnid Activities
9 **12** Pamela M. Hickman; Addison-Wesley, 1991

Ninety-six illustrated pages of information and surprising facts about insects. Hands-on projects include making a terrarium, a cricket cage, and a firefly lantern, attracting moths, and building a bug-catching model pitcher plant.

The Butterfly Book: The Kids Guide to Attracting, Raising, and Keeping Butterflies
ALL Kersten Hamilton; John Muir Publications, 1997

An illustrated 40-page how-to book; fun for all ages.
See **Butterfly Garden** (page 292).

Creepy Crawlies and the Scientific Method: Over 100 Hands-On Science Experiments for Children
8 **12** Sally Kneidel; Fulcrum, 1993

Over 200 pages of bug-oriented projects and activities, with scientific information and reproducible data and record charts.

Extremely Weird Insects
6 **+** Sarah Lovett; John Muir Publications, 1992

Each double-page spread includes a terrific close-up color photograph of the featured weird insect on the right; a page of explanatory text, including some extremely weird facts, and illustrations on the left. The book covers 21 peculiar creatures, including the multi-colored harlequin bug, the shield stinkbug, the flat-faced katydid, and the giant Australian stick.
See **Extremely Wierd Series** (page 339).

The Icky Bug Alphabet Book
3 **7** Jerry Pallotta; Charlesbridge Publishing, 1993

An alphabet book for preschool-aged naturalists, illustrated with elaborate full-color paintings. For each letter of the alphabet, there's a bug painting plus a few lines of simple scientific text. Also see, by the same author, *The Butterfly Alphabet Book* (1995) and *The Icky Bug Counting Book* (1992), which pairs colorful bug illustrations and information with the numbers 0 through 26.
See **Animal Alphabet Series** (page 339).

The Insect Almanac: A Year-Round Activity Guide

8 **13** Monica Russo; Sterling Publications, 1992

A general introduction to insect classification and life cycles, followed by a season-by-season list of hands-on activities, including how to watch, catch, and keep a wide variety of insects. For kids in grades 3–7.

Let's-Read-and-Find-Out Science Series: Insects
4 **9** *Ant Cities* (Arthur Dorros; 1987) includes wonderful cross-sectional pictures of the many little rooms and tunnels inside an ant hill, information about unusual kinds of ants—such as the leaf-cutting ants who tend underground mushroom gardens—and instructions for making an ant farm in a jar. *Chirping Crickets* (Melvin Berger; 1998) covers the life cycle of the friendly cricket, with a clear explanation of why and how crickets chirp. *Fireflies in the Night* (Judy Hawes; 1991) gives young readers the scoop on fireflies (which aren't flies but beetles). Included is a simple explanation of the chemical reaction that causes fireflies to light up in the dark and a lot of interesting general information about firefly behaviors. (The ancient Chinese used firefly lanterns.)

The Magic School Bus Inside a Beehive
7 **11** Joanna Cole; Scholastic, 1996

Ms. Frizzle's science class sets off to visit a beekeeper, but the visit is more than they bargained for: the Magic School Bus shrinks to bee size, develops black-and-yellow stripes, and sprouts wings, and the kids get a tour of the inside of a beehive. There they learn how bees make honey and beeswax and observe the complex cooperative structure of hive society. Also see, by the same author, *The Magic School Bus Gets Ants in its Pants* (1996), in which the startled science class follows a group of ants into the depths of an ant nest and learns all about ant society and life underground.

Nature Watch Series: Insects
Heiderose and Andreas Fischer-Nagel; Carolrhoda

The series is a collection of informational 48-page books illustrated with large-size color photographs. Each title concentrates on a different plant or animal subject. Insect-related titles include *The Housefly* (1990), *Life of the Butterfly* (1987), *Life of the Honeybee* (1986), and *Life of the Ladybug* (1986).

The Lerner Publishing Group
1251 Washington Ave. N
Minneapolis, MN 55401
(800) 328-4929/fax (800) 332-1132

Pet Bugs: A Kid's Guide to Catching and Keeping Touchable Insects
Sally Kneidel; John Wiley & Sons, 1994

A 128-page informational instruction book on how to find and catch 25 (safe to touch) common insects, including the chirping cricket and the frothing spittlebug, with interesting information about each. Chapter titles include "Bugs That Eat Other Bugs," "Bugs That Look Like Something They're Not," and "Bugs That Live and Work in Groups."

Pets in a Jar: Collecting and Caring for Small Wild Animals
Seymour Simon; Viking, 1988

How to care for ants and butterflies, as well as snails, toads, worms, and starfish.

ENTOMOLOGY AND LITERATURE

Anansi the Spider: A Tale from the Ashanti
Gerald McDermott; Henry Holt, 1987

A picture-book African folktale about Anansi the Spider and his six sons (and how the moon came to be). For kids aged 4–8.

Charlotte's Web
E. B. White; HarperCollins, 1952

The story of Wilbur, the radiant humble pig, and his friend Charlotte, the wise and literate spider who saves his life. A classic for all ages.

The Cricket in Times Square
George Selden; Farrar, Straus & Giroux, 1983

Chester the cricket is inadvertently transported to New York City, where he ends up living in a subway station under Times Square. There he makes friends with Harry (a cat), Tucker (a mouse), and Mario, a small boy whose parents run a newsstand, and displays his great musical talent. For readers aged 9–12.

James and the Giant Peach
Roald Dahl; Alfred A. Knopf, 1996

James, an orphan, is condemned to live with his dreadful aunts, Spiker and Sponge, until he grows an enormous magical peach and sets off on a wonderful worldwide journey with the peach's inhabitants: a spider, a centipede, a glowworm, a grasshopper, and an earthworm. For kids aged 8–12.

Joyful Noise: Poems for Two Voices
Paul Fleischman; HarperCollins, 1988

Illustrated poems for two readers, all about insects. Titles include "Grasshoppers," "Fireflies," "Honeybees," and "House Crickets."

Two Bad Ants
Chris Van Allsburg; Houghton Mifflin, 1988

A cache of sparkling and delectable crystals (sugar) has been discovered, and a group of worker ants sets out to fetch some for their queen. The mission goes well for all but two bad ants, who decided to stay behind and eat their fill. They make it home again only after a series of catastrophic adventures with cups of coffee, toasters, running water faucets, and a deceptively safe-looking electrical outlet. Wonderful illustrations.

The Very Hungry Caterpillar
Eric Carle; Philomel Books, 1991

The caterpillar munches its way through a huge number of fruits and other foods until at last, stuffed, it spins a cocoon and turns into a beautiful double-page-size butterfly. For preschoolers. Also see Carle's *The Very Busy Spider* (Philomel Books, 1995), *The Very Quiet Cricket* (Putnam, 1997), and *The Grouchy Ladybug* (HarperCollins, 1996)

Why Mosquitoes Buzz in People's Ears
Verna Aardema; Dial, 1975

An African tale in which Mosquito tells a dreadful lie that finally results in the sun's not rising. Once the animals figure out whose fault this was, Mosquito is punished—and ends up buzzing in people's ears from then on. For kids aged 4–8.

COLORING AND PAPER-CRAFTS BOOKS

Insects
Helen I. Driggs and George S. Glenn; Running Press

A "fact-filled coloring book" containing 60 black-line drawings with an accompanying kid-friendly text. Topics covered include "Building a Bug" (with a detailed labeled picture of a grasshopper), "Buggy Eyes," with an illustration of how an insect sees a toad, "Magical Metamorphosis," with drawings of caterpillar, pupa, and adult swallowtail butterfly, and "Dining on Wood," with a cross-section of an African termite mound.

$8.95 from bookstores or
Running Press Book Publishers
125 South 22nd St.
Philadelphia, PA 19103
(215) 567-5080 or (800) 345-5359/fax (800) 453-2884

The Insects Coloring Book
Jan Sovak; Dover Publications

The Insects Coloring Book includes drawings of 45 insects, including the elephant stag beetle (a pair are shown, battling, on the book's cover), the black widow spider, the tarantula, the earwig, and the flea, with descriptive captions. Also see, by the same author, *The Butterflies Coloring Book*, which includes black-line drawings of 43 species, including monarch, buckeye, white admiral, and ruddy daggerwing butterflies.

$2.95 each

Dover Publications, Inc.
31 E. Second St.
Mineola, NY 11501

Origami Insects
Robert D. Lang; Dover Publications

Step-by-step instructions for 20 entomological paper-folding projects. Users can turn out an origami treehopper, butterfly, grasshopper, dragonfly, praying mantis, and tarantula. Recommended for intermediate to advanced paper folders.

Dover Publications, Inc.
31 E. Second St.
Mineola, NY 11501

The Ultimate Bug Sticker Book
Dorling Kindersley, 1994

Sixty wonderful color photographs of bugs in sticker form, to be stuck in the proper spaces in the related text.

$6.95
Dorling Kindersley Publishing
1224 Heil Quaker Blvd.
LaVergne, TN 37086
(888) DIALDKP
Web site: www.dk.com

GAMES AND HANDS-ON ACTIVITIES

The Ant Book and See-Through Model
Luann Colombo; Andrews & McMeel, 1994

The kit, which comes in a plastic dome-shaped case, includes a 48-page illustrated book of ant information, *The Ant Book,* plus a giant-size model ant. The ant's exoskeleton is clear plastic, the better for viewing the internal organs that make an ant work. The parts of the model snap together (no glue needed, unless you break something).

$14.95 from bookstores

Ant Farms
In the most popular version of the commercial ant farm, sand is layered between a pair of see-through

plastic panes, which are clamped securely together in a green plastic framework with supporting stand. (Included, just above the sand for decorative effect, is a little two-dimensional scene of green plastic farm buildings, which the ants ignore.) The farm package includes sand, an instructional handbook, and a pre-paid mail-order coupon for ants.

The farm-sponsored ant shipment does not include a queen, so the colony has a limited lifespan. Still, the ants, installed in their farm, are wonderful to watch as they burrow, tunnel, excavate, forage for food, and dump trash. The farm, which is advertised as "unbreakable," is infinitely reusable; replacement sand and ant colonies are available separately. Our boys were delighted with their farm, which operated flawlessly. Friends, however, tell me that *their* farm was subject to great escapes: periodically they would get up in the morning to find the farm tunnels empty and the ants making themselves at home in the kitchen cupboards.

Ant farms come in two basic sizes. "Regular" measures $8\frac{1}{2} \times 6$ inches; "Giant," 10×15 inches. About $11 and $20, respectively

Available from most science supply stores and catalogs
or
Edmund Scientific Co.
101 E. Gloucester Pike
Barrington, NJ 08007-1380
(609) 547-8880 or (800) 728-6999
e-mail: scientifics@edsci.com
Web site: www.edsci.com
or
Insect Lore Products
Box 1535
Shafter, CA 93263
(800) LIVE-BUG
Web site: www.insectlore.com

The Bug Book and Bottle
Hugh Danks; Workman, 1987

The kit consists of a clear plastic bottle with a ventilated green plastic top for the capture and observation of interesting specimens, plus an accompanying field guide and activity book that includes instructions for capturing, identifying, and briefly keeping 24 different bugs.

$9.95
Workman Publishing Co.
708 Broadway
New York, NY 10003-9555
(212) 254-5900 or (800) 722-7202/fax (212) 254-8098
Web site: www.workmanweb.com

The Bug Game
A matching and memory card game for players aged 3 and up. The game includes 44 cards, illustrated with big color paintings of 22 bugs and other backyard creatures, among them a water beetle, dragonfly, bee, ant, snail, spider, and butterfly. It takes two cards to make a complete bug picture. Smallest players can simply use the cards as simple puzzles, finding the proper matching pairs. Older kids can play versions of "Concentration," in which all the cards are turned facedown and players take turns flipping over two at a time, attempting to find matches; or "Go Fish," in which players take turns asking others for a match to a card held in their hands.

$13.95
Carolina Biological Supply Co.
2700 York Rd.
Burlington, NC 27215
(800) 334-5551/fax (800) 222-7112

Build Your Own Bugs Book and Rubber Stamp Kit
Joshua Morris Publishing, for Reader's Digest Young Families, Inc., 1995

With this informational 32-page book, by Dennis Schatz, and the accompanying 29 bug-part stamps, kids can create eight bugs—including monarch butterflies, ladybugs, and spiders—and any number of imaginary entomological creations.

$14.95 from bookstores or
Carolina Biological Supply Co.
2700 York Rd.
Burlington, NC 27215
(800) 334-5551/fax (800) 222-7112

Busy With Bugs
A kit for artistic bug lovers. *Busy With Bugs* contains enough materials for kids to create eight zany

wooden bugs, complete with wings, wire legs and antennae, iridescent paints, beads, and googly eyes.

Also see *Spider Science,* with which kids can make a furry stuffed spider and a collection of spider magnets and try their hands at weaving a web. Both are recommended for kids aged 7 and up.

$14.95 from toy and game stores or
Creativity for Kids
1802 Central Ave.
Cleveland, OH 44115
(216) 589-4800 or (800) 642-2288/fax (216) 589-4803
Web site: www.creativityforkids.com

The Butterfly Game

A butterfly-shaped board game that traces the life cycle of the butterfly. Players begin as striped caterpillars and proceed around a leaf-patterned playing path, eventually turning into beautiful butterflies. The board flips over to reveal a full-color monarch butterfly poster. For players aged 4 and up.

$11.95
Insect Lore Products
Box 1535
Shafter, CA 93263
(800) LIVE-BUG

Butterfly Garden

The garden is a big fold-and-assemble cardboard box with see-through windows on three sides; the butterflies are beautiful black-and-orange painted ladies. Users send away for caterpillars, which arrive in a plastic container, complete with food. Kids watch the (very hungry) caterpillars gorge themselves for several days, then climb to the top of the bottle, hang head-down, and spin cocoons. The about-to-be butterflies can then be transferred to the "garden" where, after about 10 days, they hatch. Butterfly-feeding equipment is included in the kit (they get sugar water–saturated cotton wicks), and the adult butterflies can be studied in captivity or, in season, released to the great outdoors.

A small "Butterfly Garden," with a coupon for five caterpillars, about $22; a larger "school" garden, with a coupon for 33 caterpillars, about $48
Edmund Scientific Co.
101 E. Gloucester Pike
Barrington, NJ 08007-1380

(800) 728-6999
e-mail: scientifics@edsci.com
Web site: www.edsci.com
or
Insect Lore Products
Box 1535
Shafter, CA 93262
(800) LIVE-BUG
Web site: www.insectlore.com

Insect Eye

The Carolina Biological Supply Company calls this a "prism viewer." It's an inexpensive little plastic viewer fitted with a dioptic prism; peek through it and you see multiple (right-side-up) images, which is exactly how a compound-eyed insect sees the world. Cheap, fun, and available from most science supply catalogs and toy stores.

Insect House Kit

A build-your-own temporary habitat for captured fireflies, ladybugs, bumblebees, praying mantises, and company. The kit includes all necessary materials for building a $4\frac{1}{2} \times 7\frac{1}{2}$-inch insect house: precut wood pieces, wire screen, hardware, and a cork (for sealing the entrance/exit), plus a magnifying glass for studying the visiting house guests. Recommended for kids aged 7 and up.

$12 from arts and crafts stores
For a local source, contact:
Curiosity Kits
Box 811
Cockeysville, MD 21030
(410) 584-2605 or (800) 584-KITS/fax (410) 584-1247
e-mail: Ckitsinc@aol.com

Live Bugs

Real live insect specimens are available from many scientific supply companies. These are variously available as adults, infants, and eggs; and many can be ordered as "kits," which include housing, food, and all other necessary materials, plus background information and instructions. Interested kids can raise house crickets, hissing cockroaches, ladybird beetles, silkworms, praying mantises, and many more. Sources include

Carolina Biological Supply Co.
2700 York Rd.

Burlington, NC 27215

(800) 334-5551/fax (800) 222-7112

or

Insect Lore Products

Box 1535

Shafter, CA 93262

(800) LIVE-BUG

Web site: www.insectlore.com

Nectar Collector

An exquisitely designed board game of bee life. The players move their pieces—gold or silver bees—around the concentric layers of the board attempting to gather enough nectar, represented by amber-colored beads, to fill their honeycombs, before racing to reach the Queen Bee in her purple-curtained royal chamber at the very center of the board. The game includes an informational booklet about bees, but players learn almost as much just by moving through the many levels of the game, from "Apple Orchard" to "Alfalfa Field" to "Wedding Flight" to "Bear Raid." Recommended for two to four players aged 8 and up.

> $27.50
> Animal Town
> Box 757
> Greenland, NH 03840
> (800) 445-8642/fax (603) 430-0334

Audiovisual Entomology

Little Creatures Who Run the World

This 60-minute video from *NOVA* features the world of ants, with impressive right-up-close photography of ants at home and abroad. The ants cooperate to build amazing underground cities, establish an impressive social structure, and wage vicious warfare against their enemies. With commentary by master myrmecologist Edward O. Wilson.

> $19.95
> Movies Unlimited
> 3015 Darnell Rd.
> Philadelphia, PA 19154
> (215) 637-4444 or (800) 4-MOVIES
> e-mail: movies@moviesunlimited.com
> Web site: www.moviesunlimited.com

Computer Software

The House is Bugged!

The house, all six rooms of it, from the basement to the bathroom, is full of bugs. Players must capture and identify all of them, nabbing each and transporting the specimen to the lab, when they uncover information about its behavior, habitat, life cycle, and more. The program includes video clips of 48 insects. On CD-ROM for Mac or Windows.

> $89.95
> Sunburst Communications
> 101 Castleton St.
> Box 40
> Pleasantville, NY 10570
> (800) 321-7511/fax (914) 747-4109
> Web site: www.sunburst.com

SimAnt

Young myrmecologists can design their own ant colonies, fight battles with enemy ants, and fend off (or fall prey to) predatorial ant lions. On CD-ROM for Mac or Windows.

> $14.95
> Electronic Arts
> Box 7530
> San Mateo, CA 94403
> (800) 245-4525
> Web site: www.maxis.com

Entomology On-Line

Beekeeping

Color photographs and detailed information on honeybees, honey, and beekeeping, with many links to related sites.

> ourworld.compuserve.com/homepages/Beekeeping

BugWatch

Lots of bugs. The site is organized according to insect taxonomy; users click on a labeled color picture of a representative insect—among them ant, butterfly, wasp, and fly—for information about the taxonomic group, close-up color photographs, and descriptions.

> bugwatch.com/bugindex.html

The Butterfly WebSite

🌐 **ALL** Information on butterfly gardening, ecology, and education, and an enormous gallery of color pictures.

mgfx.com/butterfly

Children's Butterfly Site

🌐 **ALL** A beautiful gallery of color photographs, a life cycle of the monarch coloring page, answers to frequently asked questions about butterflies, and a list of butterfly-related books and videos.

www.mess.usgs.gov/Butterfly.html

The Insects Home Page

🌐 **10+** Pictures and information about many kinds of insects, arthropods, and spiders, basic information on insect anatomy and classification, sources for entomology supplies, links to entomological groups and societies, and a glossary of terms.

info.ex.ac.uk/~gjlramel/six.html

The Yuckiest Site on the Internet

🌐 **ALL** Features "Bug World," a very personal look at the life of the cockroach; "Worm World," a fascinating survey of earthworms, leeches, tapeworms, and planarians; and "Your Gross and Yucky Body," which explains burps, spit, and other yucky human functions. Well done, clever, and interesting.

www.nj.com/yucky

ENVIRONMENTAL SCIENCE

It's hard to find a kid anywhere who is *not* interested in life in the great outdoors. The nature walk—through state and national parks, at the local Audubon Society preserve, around the pond down the road, through the fields and woods beyond our own backyard—has always been a staple of our homeschool program. The kids, depending on time of year, state of current interests, and quality of parental preplanning, set out equipped with binoculars, magnifying glasses, sketch pads, notebooks, cameras, and collecting bottles—or with nothing but a granola bar, grabbed on the way out the door, if it's a particularly beautiful day and we're particularly eager to get ourselves out in it. Over the years, the boys have watched the building of a beaver dam, identified wildflowers, captured insects, raised tadpoles, crickets, and butterflies, made casts of deer tracks, adopted a whale and a wolf, and fed—continually—the birds. They've also responsibly recycled glass, plastic, aluminum, tin cans, and newspaper, participated in projects to pick up roadside litter, and volunteered at the local Humane Society.

Many organizations, private and public, sponsor wildlife and environmental programs for kids: check local science museums, parks, nature societies. Or track down neighborhood experts. Through our local veterinarian, we met a woman who rescues and treats injured racing pigeons. By volunteering at a local museum, we met an enthusiastic birder who leads early morning bird walks (kids welcome). Our dental hygienist raises turtles and likes to show them off. The vegetable farm down the road has started raising hydroponic tomatoes and is friendly to interested viewers. Friends in the town just south of us have neighbors who own a llama farm. Opportunities for education surround all of us; sometimes it just takes a phone call or a question or two to find out where they are.

ORGANIZATIONS

The Children's Rainforest U.S.

This group sponsers several programs to preserve the rain forests. They also publish a 30-page guide for educators, *Rainforests: Educational Resources,* which lists books, videos, and other materials on rain forest topics.

Guide, $4

The Children's Rainforest U.S.

Box 936

Lewiston, ME 04243-0936

(207) 784-1069

Earth Foundation

The foundation sponsors the "Race to Rescue" campaign, in which schoolchildren participate to collect funds for a number of worldwide conservation programs. It also publishes a small curriculum and resource catalog.

> Earth Foundation
> 5151 Mitchelldale, Suite B-11
> Houston, TX 77092
> (713) 686-WILD
> e-mail: EarthFound@aol.com

The National Audubon Society

Many environmental protection projects, especially for birds.

> Annual membership, including a subscription to the monthly magazine, *Audubon,* $20
> The National Audubon Society
> 700 Broadway
> New York, NY 10003
> Web site: www.igc.org/audubon

The Nature Conservancy

The Nature Conservancy sponsors worldwide conservation projects, including an "adopt-an-acre" program for persons interested in working to save the world's rain forests. They also publish a booklet, the "Rainforest Report," which includes suggestions for kids' fund-raising projects and related rain forest activities, information about the rain forests, news on rain forest conservation projects, and teacher resource lists.

> The Nature Conservancy
> 1815 N. Lynn St.
> Arlington, VA 22209
> (800) 84-ADOPT
> Web site: www.tnc.org

Rainforest Preservation Fund

For $25, concerned persons can save an acre of rain forest.

> An informative brochure, $1
> Rainforest Preservation Fund
> Box 820308
> Fort Worth, TX 76182
> (800) 460-RAIN
> e-mail: rpf.flash.net
> Web site: www.flash.net/~rpf

The Sierra Club

Founded by naturalist John Muir in 1892, the Sierra Club today continues to work to preserve the environment. It sponsors many projects and programs nationwide.

> The Sierra Club
> 85 Second St., Second Floor
> San Francisco, CA 94105-3441
> (415) 977-5500
> Web site: www.sierraclub.org

MAGAZINES

Falcon for Kids

An excellent bimonthly magazine for kids about the environment, wildlife, and the outdoors. Each illustrated issue includes puzzles, projects, news, several feature articles on wildlife topics from dinosaurs and caribou to ferrets and frogs, and a sheet of detachable wildlife trading cards. Each card has a color photograph of a plant or animal on the front, basic information—food, size, habitat, characteristics, common and scientific names, and range—on the back.

> Annual subscription (6 issues), $14.95
> *Falcon for Kids*
> Box 15936
> N. Hollywood, CA 91615-9781
> (800) 582-2665

Ranger Rick

From the National Wildlife Federation, this is an excellent high-quality source of good natural history and environmental articles for kids. Included are nonfiction articles, interviews, first-person accounts of kids' outdoor adventures, games, and puzzles. *Ranger Rick* is targeted at 6–12-year-olds. Also see *Your Big Backyard,* for 3–5-year-olds.

> Annual subscription (12 issues) to *Ranger Rick,* about $15; *Your Big Backyard* (12 issues), about $12
> National Wildlife Federation
> 8925 Leesburg Pike
> Vienna, VA 22184
> (800) 588-1650
> Web site: www.nwf.org/nwf

Young Environmentalist's Action Newsletter

A newsletter for kids interested in writing letters to combat environmental threats.

Annual subscription, $12

Global Response Newsletter

Box 7490

Boulder, CO 80306-7280

(303) 444-0306

Also see **General Science Magazines** (page 218).

Books

50 Simple Things Kids Can Do to Save the Earth

The EarthWorks Group; Scholastic, 1990

The book is divided into eight major sections. "What's Happening" gives readers some background information on such crucial environmental problems as acid rain, air pollution, the greenhouse effect, and the depletion of the ozone layer; "Eco-Experiments" includes directions for seven hands-on projects, including recycling newspapers and testing the effects of acid rain. In between are listed 50 earth-saving activities for kids, under the headings "Guarding Our Buried Treasures," "Preserving Our Oceans, Rivers, Lakes, and Streams," "Protecting Animals," "Keeping the Earth Green," "Spending Energy Wisely," and "Spreading the Word." For each of the activities, there's a "Take A Guess" environmental quiz, a description of the problem, and a list of things kids can do to help. The book also includes addresses of many environmental organizations.

Beastly Neighbors: All About Wild Things in the City, or Why Earwigs Make Good Mothers

Mollie Rights; Little, Brown, 1981

A creative approach to nature in the city. Beastly neighbors—including cockroaches, ant, worms, weeds, mice, rats, and birds—are introduced through a chattily informative text and many appealing activities. Urban naturalists try pollinating flowers, teaching a cockroach to navigate a homemade maze, building a bird feeder, and—in the footsteps of Charles Darwin—studying the response of earthworms to music. The book also deals with such ecological issues as pollution, recycling, community projects, and city gardening.

Bottle Biology

Paul Williams; Kendall/Hunt Publishing, 1994

A 127-page collection of ways to use recyclable containers—notably the ever-popular plastic soda bottle—to study environmental science. Users, for example, create a model rain forest, make a spider habitat, and learn about composting. For kids in grade 2 and up.

The author is the developer of the Wisconsin Fast Plants materials (see page 283); the book interfaces well with the Fast Plants projects. Each chapter includes scientific background information and teaching suggestions, as well as detailed instructions for activities.

The Cartoon Guide to the Environment

Larry Gonick and Alice Outwater; HarperPerennial, 1996

All the main topics of environmental science covered through 240 pages of clever text and humorous little cartoons. The authors explain the water and air cycles, food webs, plant and animal communities, population growth, pollution, deforestation, global warming, the ozone hole, energy sources, and recycling.

Earth Book for Kids: Activities to Help Heal the Earth

Linda Schwartz; The Learning Works, 1990

The book is divided into several sections of related activities and projects: "Energy, Resources, and Recycling," "Air, Land, and Water," "Plant and Animal Habitats," and "More Ways to Make Every Day Earth Day." Sample activities include making paper, calculating phosphate levels in detergents, building a trash sculpture, inventing an environmental coat of arms, designing an environmental board game, and organizing an aluminum can drive. Also included: facts, figures, and a list of addresses of activist organizations.

Earth Child: Games, Stories, Activities, Experiments & Ideas About Living Lightly on Planet Earth

Kathryn Sheehan and Mary Waidner; Council Oak Distribution, 1994

A 300+-page compendium of environmental information and activities for elementary and middle school–aged kids.

Keepers of the Earth: Native American Stories and Environmental Activities for Children

Michael J. Caduto and Joseph Bruchac; Fulcrum, 1997

Keepers of the Earth links American Indian stories and legends from many tribes to environmental information and hands-on activities. Stories are grouped by theme ("Water," "Wind and Weather," "Plants and Animals"). Each is followed by scientific background information, discussion questions, detailed instructions for assorted activities, and suggestions for further projects.

Also see *Keepers of the Animals: Native American Stories and Wildlife Activities for Children* (1997), a similarly information-filled resource for young wildlife biologists, linking multidisciplinary activities to 24 American Indian legends about animals.

Both books are illustrated with black-and-white photographs and drawings. For kids of all ages.

See **Literature Links to Environmental Science** (right) and *Keepers of Life: Discovering Plants Through Native American Stories and Earth Activities for Children* (page 277).

Oil Spill!

Melvin Berger; HarperCollins, 1994

A picture-book explanation of oil spills and their consequences for kids aged 5–9. The book, which begins with the *Exxon Valdez* disaster, covers the ecological damage done by oil, the effects of spills on marine and seashore plants and wildlife, and modern technologies for cleaning up spills.

One Small Square Series

Donald M. Silver; Scientific American

Each detailed 48-page book, beautifully illustrated by Patricia J. Wynne, covers the life in one small square of an ecosystem: plants, animals, and their interactions. Included are how-to suggestions for conducting your own outdoor explorations. Titles in the series include *One Small Square: Backyard, Pond, Woods, Seashore, Cave, Cactus Desert, Arctic Tundra,* and *African Savanna.* For naturalists aged 7–12.

Ozone Hole

Darlene R. Stille; Children's Press, 1991

A simple explanation of the causes and effects of ozone depletion for kids aged 6–9. The book is divided into very short, large-print chapters, illustrated with color photographs.

Recycle! A Handbook for Kids

Gail Gibbons; Little, Brown, 1992

A simple picture-book explanation of several ways of recycling, for kids in grades K–3.

Where Does the Garbage Go?

Paul Showers; HarperCollins, 1994

An illustrated explanation of recycling and waste disposal for readers aged 5–9.

LITERATURE LINKS TO ENVIRONMENTAL SCIENCE FOR ADULTS

Bringing the World Alive

 The Orion Society

An annotated bibliography of children's picture books on ecology and the natural world.

$6

The Orion Society
195 Main St.
Great Barrington, MA 01230

Who's Endangered on Noah's Ark?

Glenn McGlathery and Norma J. Livo; Teacher Ideas Press, 1992

Each section of the book covers a different endangered animal, with associated books, folktales, and multidisciplinary activities. Among the featured animals are wolves, tigers, elephants, California condors, spotted owls, and alligators. For kids in grades K–12.

$22

Libraries Unlimited
Box 6633
Englewood, CO 80155-6633
(303) 770-1220 or (800) 237-6124/fax (303) 220-8843
e-mail: lu-books@lu.com
Web site: www.lu.com

LITERATURE LINKS TO ENVIRONMENTAL SCIENCE: FOR KIDS

BAAA
9+ David Macauley; Houghton Mifflin, 1985

"There is no record of when the last person disappeared," begins this thought-provoking picture book. The people are gone, the cities deserted—and sheep take over the earth. One day, by mistake, a young lamb accidentally turns on a television set. By watching television, the sheep learn to talk and eventually become more and more like people. As time goes on, the sheep population (now fully dressed and civilized) grows rapidly, food supplies dwindle, riots break out, and some sheep turn to crime. All of human history repeats itself: soon there are only two sheep left. Then they, too, disappear. Then a fish crawls up on shore. . . . It's not a cheerful book, but it's a definite discussion starter.

The Great Kapok Tree
5-9 Lynn Cherry; Harcourt Brace, 1990

A beautifully illustrated rain forest picture book. A man chopping down trees in the rain forest lies down to take a nap. As he sleeps, all the rain forest inhabitants, from the boa constrictor to a small Indian boy, take turns telling him about all the good the trees do and asking him not to destroy their forest. Somehow the man hears their words: when he awakes, he shoulders his ax and walks away, leaving the trees in peace.

Just a Dream
7-10 Chris Van Allsburg; Houghton Mifflin, 1990

Walter has no interest in taking care of the world around him until one night he has a frightening dream: he wakes up in the far future and finds the world a grimy trash pile. The trees are gone; the oceans are polluted; the air is thick with smog; cars cram the highways; and people and buildings cover every inch of open ground. Walter wakes up a wiser boy and changes his slothful ways.

The Lorax
4-9 Dr. Seuss; Random House, 1971

In spite of the Lorax, who speaks for all the natural world, the Once-ler and his relations chop down all the fluffy-topped "truffula" trees and build smoke-belching factories to turn them into "thneeds," a hot-selling item that looks like an insane turtleneck sweater. Finally the water is polluted, the trees cut down, and the birds and animals—and even the Lorax himself—are gone. The last Once-ler, sorry for all that has happened, passes on the very last truffula seed.

The Wump World
5-9 Bill Peet; Houghton Mifflin, 1981

The fuzzy and adorable Wumps, happily munching grass in their world of green meadows and crystal-clear rivers, are driven underground by invading Pollutians, who arrive in spaceships from the planet Pollutus. The Pollutians, equipped with heavy machinery, soon destroy the beautiful Wump world, covering it with huge cities and immense factories, spouting black smoke into the air and dumping trash into the rivers. Finally, when things have become miserable enough, the Pollutians decamp, and the Wumps, creeping back above ground once again, are horrified at the destruction. After wandering for miles through the abandoned cities, however, they find a remaining grassy meadow. There's hope that the environment will eventually be restored, the book concludes, but the Wump world will never be quite the same.

BIOGRAPHIES OF ENVIRONMENTALISTS

First Books: American Conservationists
8-12 Peter Anderson; Franklin Watts, 1995

A series of 64-page biographies for kids in grades 4–6, illustrated with color photographs. Titles include *Aldo Leopold: American Ecologist, Gifford Pinchot: American Forester, Henry David Thoreau: American Naturalist, John James Audubon: Wildlife Artist,* and *John Muir: Wilderness Prophet.*

Great Lives: Nature and the Environment
10+ Doris Faber and Harold Faber; Macmillan, 1991

A collection of short biographies of 26 naturalists and environmentalists, among them Henry David Thoreau, John Muir, John James Audubon, Rachel Carson, Jacques Cousteau, and Theodore Roosevelt. Illustrated with black-and-white photographs.

Listening to Crickets: A Story about Rachel Carson

Candice F. Ransom; Carolrhoda, 1993

A short biography of environmentalist Rachel Carson, author of *Silent Spring*, for kids aged 9–12.

A Man Named Thoreau

Robert Burleigh; Atheneum, 1985

A picture-book biography of Henry David Thoreau, illustrated with soft black-and-white pencil sketches.

Muir of the Mountains

William O. Douglas; abridged reissue from Sierra Club Books, 1994

A detailed biography of John Muir for kids aged 10 and up.

Of Things Natural, Wild, and Free: A Story about Aldo Leopold

Marybeth Lorbiecki; Carolrhoda, 1993

A short chapter biography of the American naturalist for kids aged 9–12.

GAMES AND HANDS-ON ACTIVITIES

A Beautiful Place

A simple cooperative board game for kids aged 5–8. The players move their pieces around a sun-and-cloud-patterned board, making the earth a "beautiful place" by performing good deeds: recycling, saving energy, planting a tree, feeding the birds. For each good act, they remove a puzzle piece (of a polluted dead landscape) or a pollution marker from the center of the board, revealing the picture of the beautiful country underneath.

$18.50
Animal Town
Box 757
Greenland, NH 03840
(800) 445-8642/fax (603) 430-0334

Dam Builders

A beautifully illustrated cooperative board game for lovers of beavers. The players, as beavers, move around the board gathering sticks from the forests to build a dam, lodge, and a supply of stored food for winter. To succeed, they must evade hungry wolves, forest fires, floods, and the tree-flattening depredations of a bulldozer sponsored by the environmentally insensitive "Corps." Included is an informational booklet about beavers. One of our very favorites.

$26
Animal Town
Box 757
Greenland, NH 03840
(800) 445-8642/fax (603) 430-0334

Into the Forest

"Nature's Food Chain Game" for two to six players aged 7 and up. The game is played with a pack of color-illustrated cards, each picturing a plant or animal found in a typical temperate zone forest. The cards list both what the animal eats and is eaten by. There are several ways to play the game, but the simplest is much like "War": players lay cards down simultaneously, faceup; if one card "eats" the other, that player wins the "eaten" card. The Owl card, for example, eats the Mouse card; the Bobcat card eats the Rabbit card. Player with the most cards at the end of the game wins.

$15.95 from game stores or
Ampersand Press
750 Lake St.
Port Townsend, WA 98368
(800) 624-4263
Web site: www.ampersandpress.com
A less expensive version of the game, "Predator," is also available from Ampersand for $9.95; the cards, illustrated with small black-and-white pictures, aren't as pretty, but the end result is the same

Marsh Master

This delightful ecologically based board game is recommended for kids aged 8 and up. The game includes 20 pairs of beautifully illustrated "Species Cards," bearing the names and pictures of a wetlands plant or animal: these are shuffled and arranged face-down next to the playing board. Each player in turn flips over two cards, trying to make a matched pair. Once a match is made, the successful player places the cards on the board in the appropriate habitat: lake, river, pond, stream, or marsh. Also during each turn, players roll the dice and advance the "Arnold Pathetic" playing piece around the outer edge of the board. Arnold is an exercise in ecological incorrectness: on various squares, he dumps trash in the pond, squashes a lady's slipper, litters, carves his initials on a tree, scares baby ducks, and throws a rock at a muskrat. (To even things up, he also gets stung by a bee and chased by a moose, gets sunburned, and falls in the mud, each of which causes him to lose a turn.) The trick is to get all the Species Cards in place before Arnold makes it all the way around the board. An informational booklet lists scientific names, descriptions, and assorted information about each of the featured species.

$28 (plus $3.75 shipping/handling)—and 5% sales tax for Vermonters
Great Blue Productions
Box 194
Pittsford, VT 05763
(802) 483-6437

Oh Wilderness

A card game of "backcountry lore" for young campers, hikers, naturalists, and picnickers. The game includes 60 question-and-answer cards in four categories: "Wilderness Skills," "Wildlife," "Plants," and "Land and Sky." Each card carries three questions (with answers). Playing rules are included for competitive card games; the cards are also fun for just reading aloud in turn, with or without a campfire. Sample question: "When wading a stream with the help of a walking stick, should you plant the stick upstream or downstream from you?"

$9.95 from game stores or
Ampersand Press
750 Lake St.
Port Townsend, WA 98368
(800) 624-4263
Web site: www.ampersandpress.com

Papermaking Kits

Recycle the Sunday newspaper and the junk mail into brand-new paper. There are a number of kits on the market, for making either recycled sheet paper or paper casts. Basically, in each, paper is shredded and beaten into pulp in a kitchen blender, then formed into sheets using a mold and deckle (a wooden frame with inset screen) or pressed into clay molds to make embossed designs. This is a terrific project for kids of almost all ages. One caution: kits tend to picture finished hand-made papers in a range of gorgeous pastel colors; if your primary source of recyclables is newspaper, however—as ours was and is—the end result is not pink, snow-white, or lavender but an inevitable tattletale gray. (Still, gray is nice, and you can always decorate it.)

Papermaking kits are available from most toy and craft stores or
HearthSong
6519 N. Galena Rd.
Box 1773
Peoria, IL 61656-1773
(800) 325-2502
or
S & S Arts & Crafts
Box 513
Colchester, CT 06415-0513
(800) 243-9232
or
Sax Arts & Crafts
Box 510710
New Berlin, WI 53151
orders (800) 558-6696
customer service (800) 522-4278

Scientific Explorer Tracker Field Series

With this series of field activity kits, kids make plaster casts of animal tracks and learn about the animals that made them. Each kit includes a paw print replica, materials for making a track cast, and an informational tracking guide. Kits include "Bobcat," "Red Fox," "Striped Skunk," and "Snowshoe Hare."

$12.95 each
Scientific Explorer, Inc.
2802 E. Madison, Suite 114
Seattle, WA 98112

(206) 322-7611 or (800) 900-1182/fax (206) 322-7610

e-mail: sciex@scientificexplorer.com

Web site: www.scientificexplorer.com

Solar Energy Kits

A number of kits are available for exploring aspects of solar energy. The "Solar Electricity Kit" includes a solar cell array, a miniature motor, a propeller, and an optical illusion disc, plus a 12-page manual with explanations and instructions for several projects; the "Solar Panel Kit" contains eight modular solar cells that kids can assemble to make output panels to power electronic devices such as calculators, plus a motor, fan blade, lead wire, mounts, and an instruction booklet; the "Solar Power Kit," which comes in a can, includes materials for making a solar-powered airplane, a solar wind tower, and a solar-powered UFO. Among our favorites is the "Solar Shuttle"—an immense black balloon (the catalog calls it a "dirigible") which, when inflated and exposed to sunlight, rises impressively skyward. The "Solar Shuttle," blown up, is about 10 feet long. Shuttles come packaged in pairs.

Solar Electricity Kit, $11.95; Solar Panel Kit, $19.95; Solar Power Kit, $14.95; Solar Shuttle, $8.95 per pair

Edmund Scientific Co.

101 E. Gloucester Pike

Barrington, NJ 08007-1380

(800) 728-6999

e-mail: scientifics@edsci.com

Web site: edsci.com

Multiactivity solar power kits, with which kids can experiment with parabolic reflectors, solar energy collection, and solar water heaters; solar-powered car kits; and solar ovens, with which kids can cook their own hotdogs are also available from

Delta Education

Box 3000

Nashua, NH 03061-3000

(800) 442-5444/fax (800) 282-9560

Web site: delta-ed.com

or

ETA

620 Lakeview Pkwy.

Vernon Hills, IL 60061

(800) 445-5985/fax (800) ETA-9326

e-mail: info@etauniverse.com

Web site: www.etauniverse.com

AUDIOVISUAL ENVIRONMENTAL SCIENCE

Banana Slug String Band

Catchy, funny, and scientific songs about the environment, including "Dirt Made My Lunch" and the "Solar Energy Shout." Several song collections are available. Titles include "Dirt Made My Lunch," "Adventures on the Air Cycle," "Songs for the Earth," "Slugs At Sea," "Singing in Our Garden," and "Penguin Parade."

Tapes, $10; accompanying songbooks, $4

Banana Slug String Band

La Honda, CA 94020

or

Carolina Biological Supply Co.

2700 York Rd.

Burlington, NC 27215

(800) 334-5551/fax (800) 222-7112

The Evergreens: Gentle Tales of Nature

"The Evergreens" is a collection of four nature stories on audiocassette for listeners aged 3–6, narrated by master storyteller Odds Bodkins, to an accompaniment of guitar, Celtic harp, and kalimba. Included are "The Evergreens" from Denmark, the Iroquois legend "The Woman Who Fell From the Sky," Aesop's fable "The Wind and the Sun," and a Bhutanese tale, "The Lion Makers."

Also see "The Earthstone: A Musical Adventure Story," a two-cassette parable about ecological balance with musical accompaniment for kids aged 5 and up.

Rivertree Productions, Inc.

Box 410

Bradford, NH 03221

(603) 938-5120 or (800) 554-1333

e-mail: rivertree@conknet.com

Web site: www.oddsbodkin.com

Lyrical Life Science Volume 2: Mammals, Ecology, and Biomes

Science through songs, each set to a well-known folk, patriotic, or camp tune. The result is simultanously informational, scientifically accurate, and memorable, and the conjunction of traditional songs and biological topics is inherently hilarious. You can't resist trying these. "Ungulates: The Hoofed Mammals" to the tune of "Home on the Range": "Two orders to know/You can tell by their toe/Having hoofs which can help them run well . . ." "Bats" to the tune of "Take Me Out to the Ball Game:" "Bats are the flying mammals/Features designed for flight/Chiroptera is the order's name/Refers to the hands covered with flight membranes . . ."

"Lyrical Life Science Volume 2," in 16 songs, covers the major orders within the vertebrate class Mammalia, general ecology (to the tune of "Sweet Betsy From Pike"), and biomes ("Get Along Little Dogies"). Included in the set are an audiocassette and a 112-page illustrated softcover science text with detailed information about the science concepts behind the songs, all the song lyrics, and sheet music. Also available is an optional student workbook.

Cassette tape and text, about $20; with student workbook, $25

Lyrical Learning

8008 Cardwell Hill

Corvallis, OR 97330

(541) 754-3579

Computer Software

Eyewitness Encyclopedia of Nature

Information on over 250 animals and plants, with superb color graphics, plus special sections on prehistoric life, microorganisms, climate, food webs, and the environment. On CD-ROM for Mac or Windows.

$39.95

Dorling Kindersley Publishing

1224 Heil Quaker Blvd.

LaVergne, TN 37086

(888) DIALDKP

Web site: www.dk.com

SimEarth
SimIsle

In "SimEarth," kids get to create and manage an entire planet; in "SimIsle," to design and protect the environmental balance on a group of rain forest islands.

In both cases, an educational power trip for kids aged 10 and up. On CD-ROM for Mac or Windows.

$14.95 each

Electronic Arts

Box 7530

San Mateo, CA 94403

(800) 245-4525

Web site: www.maxis.com

Environmental Science On-Line

Eddy the Eco-Dog

The interactive illustrated adventures of Eddy the Eco-Dog, a seven-foot-tall surfer dog with a blue nose, who attempts to solve a crime committed by the nasty Polly Pollution. The site also includes activities and coloring pages.

www.eddytheeco-dog.com

Kids' Action Rainforest Network

A gallery of rain forest artwork, questions and answers about the rain forest, and information text with color photographs describing the people, plants, and animals of the rain forest, and a list of ways kids can help save this threatened environment.

www.ran.org/kids_action

Marlborough's Biomes Page

Information, color photographs, and related Internet resources on a range of biomes, including tundra, temperate deciduous forest, desert, and tropical rain forest.

www.marlborough.la/ca.us/depts/science/biomes.html

National Wildlife Federation

Activities from *Ranger Rick* magazine and information on environmental issues and endangered animals.

www.nwf.org/kids

Renewable Energy Project

An illustrated kid-written site about energy sources, including nuclear, hydroelectric, tidal, geothermal, solar, and wind energy.

www.rmplc.co.uk/eduweb/sites/dcastle/renew.html

EVOLUTION

The word *evolution* these days tends to arouse emotions rather than reason. Well over half the population finds the idea an abomination, in direct opposition to biblically based religious beliefs. The theory of evolution, however, is central to modern biology and no good science education is complete without it.

Also see **World History: Prehistoric Peoples** (page 606).

BOOKS

The Adventures of Charles Darwin
Peter Ward; Cambridge University Press, 1982

The story of Charles Darwin—"The Beetle Man"—as told by young George Carter, cabin boy on the H.M.S. *Beagle.* The book is 108 pages long, divided into short chapters. Chapter titles include "A ducking for Mr. Darwin," "Grasshoppers, lizards, and kingfishers," "Mr. Darwin gets ants in his pants," and "Galapagos, giant tortoises, and sea dragons." It reads like a good adventure story—which is what the original expedition was.

The Beagle and Mr. Flycatcher: A Story of Charles Darwin
Robert Quackenbush; Prentice-Hall, 1983

A humorously illustrated 36-page biography of Darwin for young readers. Charles, to the despair of his father, a doctor, liked nothing but watching birds, playing with his dogs, and collecting rocks and beetles—until he got a (nonpaying) job as a naturalist on board the H.M.S. *Beagle.* He then set off for five years of scientific adventures (and seasickness): he captured a cuttlefish in the Cape Verde Islands, collected beetles in Brazil, ate (by mistake) a rare species of ostrich, collected shellfish fossils in the Andes, and rode 300-pound turtles in the Galapagos Islands. The book covers his return home, his marriage, his development of the theory of evolution, and the publication of *The Origin of Species.*

Charles Darwin and Evolution
Steve Parker; Chelsea House, 1995

A short biography of Charles Darwin, heavily illustrated with photographs, paintings, and drawings. The book tells the story of Darwin's life, including his famous round-the-world voyage on board the *Beagle,* and explains how his research led to the theory of evolution.

Darwin for Beginners
Jonathan Miller and Borin Van Loon; Pantheon Books, 1990

A 176-page historical account of the theory of evolution, heavily and wittily illustrated with cartoons. The book covers the scientific discoveries and hypotheses leading up to Darwin's landmark theory, and discusses recent advances that have led to modifications of Darwin's original ideas. "Beginners" means "beginning students of evolution"; the book is for older readers.

Ever Since Darwin
Stephen Jay Gould; W. W. Norton, 1992

Stephen Jay Gould's essays are an excellent education in the principles of evolution and natural history. Essays in this, one of his earlier books, are grouped under such categories as "Darwiniana," "Human Evolution," "Patterns and Punctuations in the History of Life," and "Theories of the Earth." For teenagers and adults.

Evolution
Joanna Cole; HarperTrophy, 1989

A simple explanation of evolution for readers aged 5–9. Cole covers the ordering of fossils in rock strata (there's a lovely multicolored diagram, correlating animal and plant life in rock layers to geologic time periods), Darwin and the theory of evolution, with clear explanations of the descent of modern animals from ancient common ancestors, and the evolution of human beings. With delightful illustrations by Aliki.

Evolution
Linda Gamlin; Dorling Kindersley, 1993

A volume in the Eyewitness Science series (see page 226). The book includes 64 pages of color photographs and drawings, plus a brief descriptive text, most of it in the picture captions. Each double-page spread covers one evolution-related topic, among them "Jean-Baptiste de Lamarck," "Extinct animals," "Charles Darwin," "Fossil evidence," "The age of the Earth," "How new species are formed," "Gregor Mendel," and "Solving the DNA puzzle."

The Evolution Book
Sara Stein; Workman, 1986

Thorough, informational, illustrated, and interesting. Stein covers four billion years of earth history through an interesting text, fact boxes, and many creative hands-on activities and experiments. At "4000 Million Years Ago," for example, kids make model molecules and learn about protein synthesis; at "500 Million Years Ago," they make an underwater view box and a crayfish trap; at "1 Million Years Ago," they cook a caveperson-style meal, make goldenrod dye, and—a really ambitious project—try tanning an animal skin. (Full instructions included.) The evolutionary progression through time is correlated to the hours of the day (dawn, noon, dusk), which enables readers to appreciate just how short a time human beings have been around. A terrific resource for kids aged 10–14.

$12.95, from bookstores or
Workman Publishing Co.
708 Broadway
New York, NY 10003-9555
(212) 254-5900 or (800) 722-7202/fax (212) 254-8098
Web site: www.workmanweb.com

From So Simple a Beginning: The Book of Evolution
Philip Whitfield; Macmillan, 1993

A 220-page illustrated overview of four billion years of life on earth, including a detailed explanation of the development of evolutionary theory. The book includes 400 illustrations and diagrams, among them many full-color full-page photographs.

How Dinosaurs Came to Be
Patricia Lauber; Simon & Schuster, 1996

The evolution of the dinosaurs for readers aged 9–12. The book explains the reasons for the rise and fall of dominant animal groups over time, leading from the amphibians of the Permian era to the dinosaurs of the Jurassic.

Inherit the Wind
Jerome Lawrence and Robert E. Lee; Bantam Books, 1982

Inherit the Wind, though inspired by the Scopes Trial of 1925, is not history but theater. While very little of the play's dialogue was taken from the transcripts of the actual trial, the greater issues involved are all there as, in a small town in summer, a schoolteacher goes on trial for teaching the theory of evolution, and two great lawyers collide over the right of a man to think.

For a video version of the play see Audiovisual Evolution (page 306).

Life Story
Virginia Lee Burton; Houghton Mifflin, 1989

The picture-book history of life on earth, presented as a play in five acts. An introductory "Cast of Characters" lists "Leading Animals" and "Leading Plants" in order of appearance; then the curtain rises upon a prologue, covering the beginnings of the galaxy and solar system. The five acts are the Paleozoic, Mesozoic, and Cenozoic eras, "Recent Life," and "Most Recent Life," each with an explanatory text and illustrations showing the new arrivals on the scene.

Teaching About Evolution and the Nature of Science
Working Group on Teaching Evolution; National Academy of Sciences Press, 1998

An excellent review of the debate over the teaching of evolution in the public schools, an overview of the theory, a selection of challenging activities for teaching about evolution, and a guide to selecting instructional materials. Chapter titles include "Why Teach Evolution?," "Major Themes in Evolution," and "Frequently Asked Questions About Evolution and the Nature of Science." Suggested activities cover natural selection, common descent, geological changes over time, and the process of scientific inquiry.

$15.95
National Academy Press
2101 Constitution Ave. NW
Lockbox 285
Washington, DC 20055
(202) 334-3313 or (800) 624-6242
Web site: www.nap.edu/bookstore

Yellow and Pink

William Steig; Farrar, Straus & Giroux, 1988

A delightful and imaginative debate about the origin of life, conducted by a pair of puzzled puppets, one painted yellow and one painted pink. "Someone must have made us," Pink said. "How could anyone make something like me, so intricate, so perfect?" Yellow asked. Yellow argues that over millions of years a series of accidents "just happened," finally producing a finished puppet; Pink protests steadfastly that all these accidents seem most unlikely. Finally a mustached man who needs a haircut—the puppet maker—comes out of the house, picks up Yellow and Pink, and tucks them under his arm.

"'Who is this guy?' Yellow whispered in Pink's ear. Pink didn't know." A thought-provoking picture book.

GAMES AND HANDS-ON ACTIVITIES

Charles Darwin Scientific Explorer Kit

The kit evades the question of evolution, concentrating on Darwin's accomplishments as a groundbreaking naturalist. Included are supplies for in-the-field sample collecting, biodiversity cards for creating wildlife profiles, wildflower seeds and pots, and an informational booklet that describes Darwin's life and scientific accomplishments and provides detailed instructions for hands-on experiments.

$24

Scientific Explorer, Inc.

2802 E. Madison, Suite 114

Seattle, WA 98112

(206) 322-7611 or (800) 900-1182

Web site: http://www.scientificexplorer.com

Human Evolution Coloring Book

Adrienne L. Zihlman; Barnes & Noble, 1982

A very detailed coloring book in the Coloring Concepts series, suitable for high school and college students. The book is divided into five major sections: "Introduction to Evolution," "Genetics and Evolution," "Characteristics of Living Primates," "Primate Evolution," and "Fossil Evidence for Human Evolution." Each section is arranged as a series of double-page spreads, the left-hand page an explanatory text with precise coloring instructions, the right a scientific illustration. Users color, for example, a timeline of earth history, pictures of Darwin's finches, a diagram demonstrating DNA molecular structure and the genetic code, a "Family Tree of Living Apes," a portrait of Lucy, and a bar graph showing evolutionary changes in the size of the primate brain. There are 111 illustrations in all. A thorough account of the subject for very competent colorers.

Our Amazing Ancestors Science Kit

A collection of hands-on activities designed to teach kids about human evolution. Kids paint model skulls, make plaster casts of primitive stone tools and weapons, create an evolutionary time chart, make cave paintings, and play a game based on early human migrations.

$24.95

Young Explorers

825 S.W. Frontage Rd.

Box 493

Ft. Collins, CO 80522

(800) 239-7577 or (800) 777-8817/fax (970) 484-8067

Web site: www.youngexplorers.summitlearning.com

The Trial of John Scopes

An "American History Re-Creation" in which kids study and reenact the famous "Monkey Trial" that took place in 1925 in Dayton, Tennessee. The unit generally requires three to four hours of class time, including an introductory presentation of background information, the actual reenactment, and a posttrial discussion and summary period. Participants variously portray the defendant, John Scopes, the key attorneys, William Jennings Bryan and Clarence Darrow, the judge, witnesses, and jury.

Unit materials include 35 eight-page student guides, a teacher's manual, and reproducible student handouts, including descriptions of each role in the trial performance. The unit is intended for a large class of kids (the jury, for example, can expand to accommodate large numbers of actors); it can also adapt to smaller groups.

$39

Interact

1825 Gillespie Way, #101

El Cajon, CA 92020-1095

(619) 448-1474 or (800) 359-0961

fax (619) 448-6722 or (800) 700-5093

Web site: www.interact-simulations.com

AUDIOVISUAL EVOLUTION

In Search of Human Origins

A three-part *NOVA* series hosted by anthropologist Donald Johansen, discoverer of the famous ancient hominid fossil known as Lucy. The series, which includes "In Search of Lucy," "Surviving in Africa," and "The Creative Revolution," covers Johansen's landmark find and the other discoveries leading to modern theories of human evolution. Each videotape is about one hour long.

The set, $59.99

Movies Unlimited

3015 Darnell Rd.

Philadelphia, PA 19154

(215) 637-4444 or (800) 4-MOVIES

e-mail: movies@moviesunlimited.com

Web site: www.moviesunlimited.com

Inherit the Wind

Inherit the Wind, made into a movie in 1960, is available on video. The black-and-white film, which stars Spencer Tracy and Fredric March as the opposing lawyers, is brilliant, moving, and thought provoking.

$19.95

Movies Unlimited

3015 Darnell Rd.

Philadelphia, PA 19154

(215) 637-4444 or (800) 4-MOVIES

e-mail: movies@moviesunlimited.com

Web site: www.moviesunlimited.com

EVOLUTION ON-LINE

Enter Evolution

Explanation of evolutionary theory and portraits, and brief biographies of prominent evolutionary theorists such as Charles Lyell and Charles Darwin.

www.ucmp.berkeley.edu/history/evolution.html

Human Prehistory

An informative text, color graphics and photographs of artifacts, and biographies of prominent researchers. Users view stone tools, cave paintings, and the Lucy skeleton.

users.hol.gr/%7Edilos/prehis.htm

Institute of Human Origins

An illustrated explanation of recent scientific discoveries contributing to the theory of human evolution, a collection of anthropological photographs, and a field school.

www.asu.edu/clas/iho

The Talk.Origin Archive

A site devoted to the creationism/evolution controversy, with essays, illustrations, and links to related sites.

www.talkorigins.org

GENETICS

In a typical school science program, heredity and genetics are first introduced in the middle school grades; then covered in more depth in tenth-grade biology, along with cell biology and molecular genetics.

From my homeschool journal:

◆ **March 10, 1994. Josh is twelve; Ethan, eleven; Caleb, nine.**

The boys have been interested in the Human Genome Project—we've been discussing it at the dinner table—so today started a study unit on genetics. We first read and discussed DNA Is Here to Stay *by Fran Balkwill and Mic Rolph (see page 307). Looked at photomicrographs of chromosomes using a Microslide Viewer (see page 223); checked out structural diagrams of the DNA helix in assorted reference texts. Explained DNA and its structure and the boys made two-dimensional paper models of DNA, using different colors for A, C, G, T, and the sugar-phosphate backbone. They then collaborated on building a plastic model of the DNA helix from a science kit; everybody got the idea, even though the model tended to pop apart when bent into proper helical shape.*

Books

The Cartoon Guide to Genetics

Larry Gonick and Mark Wheelis; HarperPerennial, 1991

The story of genetics in over 200 pages of hilarious (but scientifically solid) little pictures, covering sexual reproduction, the Mendelian laws of inheritance, mutations, X-linked characteristics, DNA structure and replication, protein synthesis, gene regulation, "jumping" genes, and genetic engineering. A wonderful way to learn about genetics; try it on your teenagers.

DNA Is Here to Stay

Fran Balkwill and Mic Rolph; First Avenue Editions, 1994

This brightly illustrated picture book is recommended for readers aged 9–15. The book covers the structure and function of DNA, clearly explaining the genetic code and the process by which DNA directs the synthesis of all the body's proteins. Also see, by the same authors, *Amazing Schemes Within Your Genes*, which concentrates on the 23 pairs of human chromosomes, covering the genetic code and DNA-directed protein synthesis, patterns of inheritance, and genetic mutations, which lead to such inherited diseases as cystic fibrosis and sickle-cell anemia. Difficult information, beautifully presented.

From bookstores or
Cold Spring Harbor Laboratory Press
10 Skyline Dr.
Plainview, NY 11803-2500
(800) 843-4388
Web site: www.cshl.org

Genetic Engineering: Progress or Peril?

Linda Tagliaferro; Lerner, 1997

A concise explanation of genetics and the genetic engineering process, accompanied by balanced discussions of the technique's present and possible future uses. Chapter titles include "What is Genetic Engineering?," "Transgenic Plants: Seeds of Hope or Discontent?," "Engineering Humans," "Should We Patent Life?," and "Who Should Regulate Genetic Engineering?" For readers aged 11 and up.

Molecular Biology of the Gene

James D. Watson, Alan M. Weiner, and Nancy H. Hopkins; Addison-Wesley, 1988

This is *the* essential text for molecular and cell biologists, by Nobel laureate James Watson and coauthors. The book, 1,100+ pages long, covers everything from Gregor Mendel's 19th-century investigations of heredity to modern cancer research. Chapter titles include "A Chemist's Look at the Bacterial Cell," "The Genetic Code," "Recombinant DNA at Work," "The Molecular Biology of Development," and "The Genetic Basis of Cancer." The book is intended for a college-level audience.

The Science of Jurassic Park and the Lost World, or, How to Build a Dinosaur

Rob De Salle and David Lindley; Basic Books, 1997

So just how likely is it that scientists could extract dinosaur DNA from blood in the gut of a mosquito embedded in amber over 60 million years ago? The book clearly explains the processes of DNA sequencing, genome assembly, and cloning, and points out that the making of a dinosaur isn't quite as simple as it looked in the movie *Jurassic Park*. A fascinating read for teenagers and for parents whose dinosaur-obsessed kids have lots of difficult questions.

They Came From DNA

Billy Aronson; W. H. Freeman & Company, 1994

Alien scientist Skreeg 402 is yarkolized to Earth to find out just how Earth creatures are made. He ends up in the town dump, where he uses a series of improbable and hilarious clues to determine what DNA is and how it functions to make human beings what they are. The tongue-in-cheek science-fiction story is interlaced with real science, clearly explained, with lots of clever illustrations showing what DNA is, how it replicates, how it serves as a template for protein synthesis, and how it is organized in chromosomes. The book is divided into four main sections, each with "Evidence" collected and a "Conclusion" reached. Titles include "How Does DNA Get into Earth Creatures' Cells?," "How Does DNA Control What People Are?," "How Does DNA Change a Species Over Time?," and—a very short final note—"How Can DNA Transform a Space Creature?" Genetics through science fiction for kids aged 9–14.

Understanding DNA and Gene Cloning: A Guide for the Curious

Karl Drlica; John Wiley & Sons, 1997

Over 300 pages of in-depth information, illustrated with black-and-white diagrams. The book is divided into four major sections: "Basic Molecular Genetics," "Manipulating DNA," "The New Molecular Genetics," and "Human Genetics." Each chapter is followed by a list of questions for review and discussion. For teenagers with a solid science background.

GAMES AND HANDS-ON ACTIVITIES

Bacterial DNA Extraction Kit

A kit with which kids can isolate the DNA from bacteria (*Escherichia coli*) cells. The process involves breaking the bacterial cell walls with detergent and winding up the released DNA—it's long, stringy, sticky stuff—on a spooling rod. The kit includes bacteria and suspension medium, detergent, pipettes, measuring cups, and spooling rods; users have to come up with their own hot-water baths and 95 percent ethanol. Also included is a booklet of instructions and background information.

> Student Kit (enough stuff for a group of 30), $32; or a Teacher Demonstration Kit (for individual use), $12
> Carolina Biological Supply Co.
> 2700 York Rd.
> Burlington, NC 27215
> (800) 334-5551/fax (800) 222-7112

Clone

An interactive simulation from Interact in which kids participate in a congressional debate on what it means to be a human being. The time is 20 years in the future, and the public has just discovered the existence of two cloned beings (Eugene and Eugenia). The clones and the molecular biologist responsible for their "birth" have been called as witnesses before a Senate subcommittee on human experimentation. Kids, as clones, scientists, senators, and citizens argue the pros and cons of human genetic engineering.

Simulation materials include a 28-page teacher's guide, 35 eight-page student guides, reproducible worksheets and handouts, including "affirmative and negative position papers," role descriptions, judging rules, and score cards, and models for the definition of "human being," among them Carl Sagan's list of "15 Human Characteristics." For kids in grade 8 and up.

> $34
> Interact
> 1825 Gillespie Way, #101
> El Cajon, CA 92020-1095
> (619) 448-1474 or (800) 359-0961/fax (619) 448-6722
> or (800) 700-5093
> Web site: www.interact-simulations.com

DNA Isolation Lab

This is a molecular biology "Lab in a Box" kit, with which kids can extract the DNA from onion cells. You'll need to supply your own onion, a no. 6 Melitta coffee filter, a blender, and a refrigerator; the kit includes the necessary reagents, test tubes, and a plastic pipette.

> $12
> ETA
> 620 Lakeview Pkwy.
> Vernon Hills, IL 60061
> (847) 816-5050 or (800) 445-5985/fax (800) ETA-9326
> e-mail: info@etauniverse.com
> Web site: www.etauniverse.com

DNA Models

Build your own double helix by connecting color-coded plastic balls, representing purines, pyrimidines, phosphate groups, and sugars. The whole thing is flexible, so that it can be twisted into helical shape once assembled. Available from many scientific supply companies.

> $6.95
> Aves Science Kit Co.
> Box 229
> Peru, ME 04290
> or
> $10.95
> Lab-Aids, Inc.
> 17 Colt Ct.
> Ronkonkoma, NY 11779
> (516) 737-1133

DNA Puzzle Kit

The kit includes color-coded cardboard pieces (you punch them out) representing ribose and deoxyribose units, nucleotide bases, amino acids, tRNA units, and ribosomes. Kids can use these to study DNA and RNA structure, and the processes of DNA replication, transcription, and protein synthesis. Student worksheets and an instructional guide are included. The reusable kit contains enough materials for one or two students.

$37.50
Carolina Biological Supply Co.
2700 York Rd.
Burlington, NC 27215
(800) 334-5551/fax (800) 222-7112

DNA/RNA Simulation Kit

The "DNA Simulation Kit" allows kids to study DNA structure and replication. The "RNA Simulation Kit" allows kids to model mRNA synthesis (transcription) and protein synthesis (translation). Both include color-coded plastic beads, connectors, and detailed instruction booklets. Student kits contain enough materials for one to three kids.

$12.95
Carolina Biological Supply Co.
2700 York Rd.
Burlington, NC 27215
(800) 334-5551/fax (800) 222-7112

Double-Talking Helix Blues

Joel and Ira Herskowitz; Cold Spring Harbor Laboratory Press, 1993

This 32-page picture book and audiocassette set is about the molecular basis of heredity. Information is delivered in rap-type rhyme: ". . . the point of this story, I'll tell you right now/Did you ever sit down and think about how/It is that each time a baby's born/It's a baby—not a rabbit or an ear of corn?" The 12-minute tape features the authors, who happen to be identical twins, performing the "Double Talking Helix Blues" song; words are found in the accompanying illustrated text. The combination is recommended for "young people (8 and up) and adults who are curious about how they and their relatives became the unique individuals they are."

$20
Cold Spring Harbor Laboratory Press
10 Skyline Dr.
Plainview, NY 11803-2500

(800) 843-4388/fax (516) 349-1946
e-mail: cshpress@cshl.org

Hands-On Genetics Kit

The kit contains all the materials for a six-week experiment on inheritance patterns in *Drosophila melanogaster*, the fruit fly. Kids raise and mate cultures of winged (normal) and wingless fruit flies and study the offspring of the first and second generations to trace the inheritance of the wingless gene. The wingless gene is recessive; thus if all goes well, all the first-generation hybrid flies should be winged. Since they all carry one copy of the wingless gene, however, flies of the second generation should be a mix of winged and wingless in a ratio of 3:1.

The kit contains culture vials and stoppers, culture medium, an anesthetizer, a magnifying glass, detailed instruction manuals, and a mail-in postcard for starter fruit fly cultures.

$35
The Nature Company
Box 188
Florence, KY 41022
(800) 227-1114
or
Carolina Biological Supply Co.
2700 York Rd.
Burlington, NC 27215
(800) 334-5551/fax (800) 222-7112

Human Chromosomes Kits

Want to see what the chromosomes inside your cells look like? Try "Human Biophoto Sheets," each an $8\frac{1}{2} \times 11$-inch photomicrograph of the 46 human chromosomes, stained to show distinct banding patterns. Several kinds of Biophotos are available, including normal male and female and assorted abnormalities. "Human Chromosome Kits" include several different Biophoto Sheets, karyotype forms, student guidebooks, and a teacher's manual. Kids cut out the chromosomes from the photomicrographs and arrange them, in ordered pairs from largest to smallest, to form a karyotype.

"Human Biophoto Sheets" alone are available in pads of 30 for $5; "Human Chromosome Kits," which contain enough material for 30 kids, $30

Carolina Biological Supply Co.
2700 York Rd.
Burlington, NC 27215
(800) 334-5551/fax (800) 222-7112

GENETICS ON-LINE

10 **+** *Beginner's Guide to Molecular Biology*
A short course on-line, with informational text and big colorful diagrams. The guide covers cell structure, chromosomes and DNA, RNA and protein synthesis, protein structure, and molecular engineering. The site also includes updates on molecular biology in the news.

www.res.bbsrc.ac.uk/molbio.guide

12 **+** *Cytogenetics Image Gallery*
An explanation of "What is a chromosome?" and a picture gallery of chromosome spreads and karyotypes from normal humans and persons with various genetic abnormalities.

www.pathology.washington.edu/Cytogallery

12 **+** *Human Genome Project Information*
The Human Genome Project is a concerted effort to sequence and catalog all the DNA in the human genome, thus assembling a complete genetic formula for a human being. This site describes the project and explains the science behind it. Also included are a dictionary of genetics terms and an instructional "Primer on Molecular Genetics" for students.

www.ornl.gov/TechResources/Human_Genome/home.html

THE HUMAN BODY

In the typical school science program, human anatomy and physiology are usually first introduced in the early elementary grades in very simple form, often as part of a "health" class. Kids in kindergarten through grade three learn about the parts of the body, the importance of brushing teeth, and a bit about disease prevention. The human body generally enters the science curriculum in fourth or fifth grade, and human biology is studied in tenth-grade general biology classes.

From my homeschool journal:

◆ **February 14, 1990. Josh is eight; Ethan, seven; Caleb, five.**

Valentine's Day. The boys made piles of cut-paper hearts in every possible color and Ethan made a framed Valentine for the mantelpiece. Our science project for the day was the heart, using home-written workbooks. We discussed the heart as a muscle and demonstrated how big it is (size of a fist) and how hard it works, using the tennis ball squeeze test. (None of us succeeded at rapid tennis ball squeezing.) Discussed William Harvey and his research on the circulation of the blood. Then we played a game of circulation, in which the boys took turns playing the parts of heart, lungs, or red blood cell. We set this up in the living room, stringing red yarn from chair to chair to represent arteries, and blue yarn to represent veins. The red blood cell was pumped (well, shoved) from the heart to the lungs, where he collected an oxygen token; then he ran back to the heart and was pumped (shoved) to a hungry cell, where he dropped off the oxygen token; then he returned to the heart along a blue yarn vein, to be pumped to the lungs again. The boys thought this was great fun and took turns playing all parts.

They listened to their hearts with a stethoscope (see page 316), discussed the pulse and its relationship to heartbeat, and took their pulse rates before and after exercising.

We used a chart from Linda Allison's Blood and Guts *(see page 311) to examine the relationship between heart rate and life span. ("So do people who live to be very, very old have slower heartbeats than people who die young?")*

Colored diagrams of arteries and veins with felt-tipped pens; discussed characteristics and functions of each. The boys identified their own arteries, veins, and capillaries (under tongue, inside eye). They then studied a diagram of the heart, identified its various parts, figured out the blood pathways, discussed valves, and learned a bit about heart attacks.

Then we tried to build our pumping heart model which, completed, is supposed to pump red fluid through a series of clear plastic chambers and tubes. We only got the thing partially together—the tubing is simply awful to attach, so the boys couldn't do much and ended up simply watching me struggle. Not an ideal project.

Read a book on the history of Valentine's Day during lunch.

Books

3-D Kid

Robert Margulies and Roger Culbertson; W. H. Freeman & Company, 1995

A 3-D book and brightly colored foldout wall chart of a kid's body, with all organs and systems labeled, including bones, muscles, digestive organs, heart, and blood vessels.

Blood and Guts: A Working Guide to Your Own Insides

Linda Allison; Little, Brown, 1976

A delightful kid-friendly guide to human physiology. "You are many things," the book begins. "You are miles of blood vessels, billions of cells, hundreds of muscles, thousands of hairs, quarts of blood. You are a system of levers, pumps, and bellows. You are electrical charges and chemical reactions. You are a furnace, filters, and a fancy computer with a vast memory bank." The book is divided into 14 chapters, each devoted to one body system, and is stuffed with interesting information, clever illustrations, and many many hands-on projects. Readers, for example, can make skin prints and map the backs of their hands, dissect a soup bone, a lamb heart, and a chicken leg, build a stethoscope, a model arm, and a model lung, identify the blind spots in their eyes and experiment with stereo vision, make a "matchstick pulse meter," and perform a stress test.

The Body Book

Sara Stein; Workman, 1992

A creative—and very thorough—exploration of the human body, for kids aged 11 and up. The book is nearly 300 pages long, packed with illustrations, photographs, fact boxes, diagrams, and a lot of complex scientific information, very clearly presented, which is no mean trick. Includes straightforward information on sex, sexually transmitted diseases, and the benefits of condoms, so be prepared.

$11.95, bookstores or
Workman Publishing Co.
708 Broadway
New York, NY 10003-9555
(212) 254-5900 or (800) 722-7202/fax (212) 254-8098
Web site: www.workmanweb.com

Bones, Bodies, and Bellies

Diane A. Vaszily and Peggy K. Perdue; Good Year Books, 1993

Information and activities on the human body for kids aged 8–12 in 96 illustrated pages.

Brain Facts

Society for Neuroscience, 1990

The illustrated 32-page "Primer on the Brain and the Nervous System" is published under the auspices of the national Society for Neuroscience with the aim of educating the general public about neurological research. The book covers the structure and function of the neuron, brain development, sensation and perception, learning and memory, and movement, as well as recent major advances in brain research, ongoing research challenges, diagnostic techniques, and potential therapies. For high school–aged readers.

$2.50 (plus $1.50 shipping/handling)
Brain Facts
Society for Neuroscience
11 Dupont Circle NW, Suite 500
Washington, DC 20036
(202) 462-6688

Brain Surgery for Beginners: And Other Major Operations for Minors

Steve Parker and David West; Millbrook Press, 1995

A humorously illustrated 62-page anatomy book filled with information, diagrams, and cartoon-style pictures. Included is a brief history of brain surgery and an explanation of how the brain works.

Cow Eyes, Beef Hearts, & Worms

A hands-on tour of the human body in 35 experiments, covering heart, lungs, nerves, kidneys, muscles, and the five senses. Illustrations include detailed drawings of a cow eye, a beef heart, and a worm.

$7.99

Wild Goose Co.

375 Whitney Ave.

Salt Lake City, UT 84115

(801) 466-1172 or (800) 373-1498/fax (801) 466-1186

Dem Bones

Bob Barner; Chronicle Books, 1996

A picture book, illustrated with personable instrument-playing skeletons, in which the words to the old song ("Toe bone connected to da foot bone") is paired with simple scientific information ("The foot bones are the basement of your skeleton. The twenty-two bones in your foot support the entire weight of your body"). At the end, there's a splashy double-page spread of a whole human skeleton, with the major bones labeled. For readers aged 4–8.

Discover Bones: Explore the Science of Skeletons

Lesley Grant; Addison-Wesley, 1992

Over 40 creative activities on the science of bones (including the central role of bones in archaeology and paleontology), plus games, art projects, and a lot of interesting and unusual information.

How the Body Works

Steve Parker; Reader's Digest, 1994

Background information, fact boxes, capsule biographies of prominent scientists, and 100 creative hands-on activities, all illustrated with over 900 color photographs, drawings, and diagrams. For kids aged and up.

See **How Things Work Series** (page 235).

How to Read Your Mother's Mind

James M. Deem; Bantam Books, 1996

A cleverly illustrated explanation of extrasensory perception (ESP) for kids aged 9–12. The author discusses the different kinds of ESP (clairvoyance, telepathy, precognition), points out ways of analyzing and evaluating the evidence, and suggests experiments with which kids can test their own powers of ESP. Humorous cartoons add to the information in the text.

How You Were Born

Joanna Cole; Mulberry, 1994

For curious kids wondering where they—or their soon-to-be baby brother or sister—come from, a simple and straightforward explanation of how a baby develops and is born, illustrated with black-and-white photographs. This is embryology, childbirth, and early child development, not sex; there's a mention that eggs are made in a woman's ovaries and sperm in a man's testes, but no explanation of how the two get together. Young children aren't especially interested in this, explains Cole in the introduction; if they ask, she recommends giving them only as much information as they seem to want at the time.

Also see **Sex Education** (page 832).

Let's-Read-and-Find-Out Science Series: Human Body

HarperTrophy

A collection of short, simple, colorfully illustrated picture books on a wide variety of science topics for readers aged 4–9 (see page 227). Volumes on the human body include: *A Drop of Blood* (Paul Showers; 1989), *Hear Your Heart* (Paul Showers; 1987), *Oxygen Keeps You Alive* (Franklyn M. Branley; 1972), *The Skeleton Inside You* (Philip Balestrino; 1989), *You Can't Make a Move Without Your Muscles* (Paul Showers; 1982), *What Happens to a Hamburger* (Paul Showers; 1987), *Your Five Senses* (Aliki; 1990), and *Your Skin and Mine* (Paul Showers; 1991).

The Magic School Bus Inside the Human Body

Joanna Cole; Scholastic, 1990

Ms. Frizzle, a most out-of-the-ordinary science teacher, takes her class on a trip to the science museum. En route she presses a strange little button and the Magic School Bus shrinks, spins through the air, and is swallowed. The surprised class then tours the human body—from digestive system to bloodstream, through the heart and lungs, and to the brain. Science information appears in the form of kid-written reports in the margins: "Blood Goes Round and Round" by Michael; "Your Brain is Always Working" by Alex; "Muscles Move Your Bones" by Tim.

See the **Magic School Bus Series** (page 227).

Ouch! A Book About Cuts, Scratches, and Scrapes

Melvin Berger; Lodestar Books, 1991

A simple picture book about how your body heals cuts, scratches, and skinned knees. For readers aged 4–9.

Understanding Your Brain

Rebecca Treays; Usborne Publishing, 1995

A 32-page overview of brain structure and function for kids aged 8 and up, illustrated with lots of humorous little cartoons, colorful diagrams, and photographs. "Your brain," the book begins, "is just over 1 kg (nearly 3 lbs) of gooey, slimy, wobbly, gelatinous stuff which smells of blue cheese. It sounds revolting, but it is the most vital organ in your body." Subsequent sections cover "Brain Parts," "What's Inside?" (including "What Does a Neuron Look Like?" and "How Do Neurons Carry Messages?"), "Baby Brains," "Intelligence," "Eyesight," "Memory," "Staying the Same" (including "Central Heating" and "Monitoring the Blood"), "Consciousness," "Mental Illness," "Drugs," "Animal Brains," "Computer Brains," and "Brains in History."

$6.95 from bookstores or
EDC Publishing
Box 470663
Tulsa, OK 74147-0663
(800) 331-4418

Why I Cough, Sneeze, Shiver, Hiccup, and Yawn

Melvin Berger; HarperCrest, 1987

A picture-book explanation of all of the above, plus blink.

COLORING BOOKS AND WORKBOOKS

Anatomy Coloring Workbook

I. Edward Alcamo; Random House, 1997

A very detailed 290-page coloring book for teenagers and college students. The book is divided into 12 chapters, each covering a different anatomical system. Each double-page spread includes a precisely labeled diagram—all 23 muscles of the lower arm, for example—and an explanatory text.

Gray's Anatomy Coloring Book

Freddy Stark; Running Press, 1991

Human anatomy through 60 clearly labeled black-line diagrams and a kid-friendly text. Insets of whole-body diagrams on each page show the positions of the particular body part or system featured; and fact boxes give readers the biological scoop on yawns, hiccups, growling stomachs, and that strange "pins and needles" feeling you get when your foot falls asleep. The book covers everything from the muscles of the face to the pit of the stomach to the bones of the toes. All anatomical terms are clearly defined. For kids aged 9 and up.

$8.95 from bookstores or
Running Press Book Publishers
125 S. 22nd St.
Philadelphia, PA 19103
(215) 567-5080 or (800) 345-5359

The Human Brain Coloring Book

M. C. Diamond, A. B. Scheibel, and L. M. Elson; Barnes & Noble, 1985

This fat, softcover text on the physiology and function of the brain, contains—on alternate pages—detailed black-and-white diagrams and drawings to be precisely colored. The book covers a lot of complex scientific information. Recommended for very advanced colorers. Also see *A Colorful Introduction to the Anatomy of the Human Brain: A Brain and Psychology Coloring Book* (John Pinel and Maggie Edwards; Allyn & Bacon, 1998).

Inside Brian's Brain

Nancy Margulies; Zephyr Press

An interactive color-illustrated comic book—kids fill in the blanks as they read—that explains the biology and operations of the human brain. For kids in grades 6–12. You'll need one book per student; the books are available only in packs of 5. (But you can always give the extras away.)

$16 per pack
Zephyr Press
3316 N. Chapel Ave.
Box 66006
Tucson, AZ 83728-6006
(800) 232-2187/fax (520) 323-9402

e-mail: neways2learn@zephyrpress.com

Web site: www.zephyrpress.com

GAMES AND HANDS-ON ACTIVITIES

The Body Book: Easy-to-Make Hands-On Models That Teach

Donald M. Silver and Patricia J. Wynne; Scholastic, 1995

Step-by-step instructions and patterns for making paper models of the systems and organs of the human body, plus lesson plans and supplementary learning activities. For kids aged 8–12.

The Bones Book and Skeleton

Stephen Cumbaa; Workman, 1992

The kit includes a 26-piece model human skeleton and an illustrated 64-page informational book (*The Bones Book* by vertebrate paleontologist Stephen Cumbaa), nicely packaged in a bell jar–shaped plastic case. The skeleton pieces, in bone-colored plastic, snap together and are easy to assemble; *The Bones Book* includes a labeled diagram of the human skeleton (front and back views), and a lot of clearly presented information about bones and the human body in general. Chapter titles include "Bone Basics," "The Great Connectors: The Spine and Spinal Cord," "Where Two Bones Meet: Joint Efforts," and "Fractures, Pulls, Twists, and Sprains." Recommended for kids aged 6–12.

$14.95 from book or toy stores or
Workman Publishing Co.
708 Broadway
New York, NY 10003-9555
(212) 254-5900 or (800) 722-7202/fax (212) 254-8098
Web site: www.workmanweb.com

The Bones and Skeleton Game Book

Karen C. Anderson and Stephen Cumbaa; Workman, 1993.

An interactive introduction to the human skeleton (plus) for kids in grade 3 and up. The illustrated 96-page book includes hands-on activities, challenges, experiments, puzzles, quizzes, and a lot of interesting information.

$7.95 from bookstores or
Workman Publishing Co.

708 Broadway

New York, NY 10003-9555

(212) 254-5900 or (800) 722-7202/fax (212) 254-8098

Web site: www.workmanweb.com

The Brain Kit

The kit includes a four-piece plastic model of the brain, in pale pink, suitable for coloring or painting, a collection of reproducible student activity sheets, a labeled color diagram of the brain, and 35 illustrated activity cards, each on a different brain-related topic. The activity cards include a brief explanatory text and instructions for a number of hands-on activities. Students, for example, test their reaction times, experiment with phrenology, test their short-term memories, compare drawings done with the right and left sides of the brain, invent an intelligence test, play the "Brain Drain Game," complete their own series of labeled brain diagrams, and learn about scientific theories of dreaming. Recommended for kids in grades 5–12.

$29.95
Zephyr Press
3316 N. Chapel Ave.
Box 66006
Tucson, AZ 85728-6006
(800) 232-2187/fax (520) 323-9402
e-mail: neways2learn@zephyrpress.com
Web site: www.zephyrpress.com

Circulation

The board pictures a pudgy and transparent human body, patterned with red (arterial) and blue (venous) blood vessel pathways. The object of the game is to circulate: players compete to be the first to transport food and oxygen throughout the system, while collecting and eliminating waste products, and fending off "Germ Attacks." Periodically they also have to cope with unexpected "Emergency Card" events: "You have a splinter in your foot. RUSH a white blood cell to your left leg. Leave it in the capillaries to help prevent infection." For two to four players, aged 10 and up.

$27 from game stores or
Carolina Biological Supply Co.
2700 York Rd.
Burlington, NC 27215
(800) 334-5551/fax (800) 222-7112

Cut and Make a Human Skeleton

A. G. Smith; Dover Publications

All the pieces and instructions for making a 16½-inch tall cardboard human skeleton. Recommended for older model makers; some of the manipulations—involving glue, needle, and thread—are too tricky for the very young.

$4.50

Dover Publications, Inc.

31 E. Second St.

Mineola, NY 11501

Eldoncards

"Eldoncards" give kids a quick and easy way of typing their own blood—though not precisely trouble-free, since you get the blood by jabbing your finger with one of those nasty little sterile lancets. Each Eldoncard includes panels pretreated with monoclonal antisera. Students simply moisten the panels, jab their fingers, place droplets of blood on the four prongs of the kit's mixing comb, and mix the blood samples with the antisera on the card. Results show up in a few minutes. If the blood cells coagulate in the presence of the antiserum, you've got a positive response; kids will be able to tell if their blood is Type A, B, AB, or O, and Rh positive or negative. (You'll know; the results are obvious. The card also includes a control panel—no antisera—for comparison purposes.)

The sticking point, unfortunately, is just that: nobody likes a stab in the finger. In our first round with Eldoncards, I bravely supplied the blood for everybody, which wasn't precisely the point of the experiment. In round two, however, impressed by my courageous example, the kids consented to a finger stick and tested themselves.

$2.05

Carolina Biological Supply Co.

2700 York Rd.

Burlington, NC 27215

(800) 334-5551/fax (800) 222-7112

The Eyes Have It

A terrific activity kit that centers around the workings of the eye. Kids compare concave and convex lenses (made with a washer, a smear of petroleum jelly, and a drop of water), build a very simple eye of the sort found in planaria and millipedes (it detects only light and dark), experiment with an insect-style compound eye, study optical illusions, make a flip book and a pinhole camera, learn about visual purple, and dissect a cow eye. All materials are included, along with an informational instruction booklet.

$29.99

Wild Goose Co.

375 Whitney Ave.

Salt Lake City, UT 84115

(801) 466-1172 or (800) 373-1498/fax (801) 466-1186

Web site: www.wildgoosescience.com

Human Body Action Pack

Steve Parker; Dorling Kindersley, 1995

The pack, an attractive collection of information and hands-on activities, includes a 47-piece build-it-yourself model of the human skeleton with movable joints, poster charts of the developing human body, activity cards with instructions for activities to test body functions, flap cards demonstrating how the circulatory, respiratory, skeletal, and muscular systems work (you lift the flap to see what things look like inside), a packet of facsimile historical documents on the scientific study of the human body, and an informational guidebook.

$17.95 from bookstores or

Dorling Kindersley Publishing

1224 Heil Quaker Blvd.

LaVergne, TN 37086

(888) DIALDKP

Web site: www.dk.com

The Rubber Stamp Bones and Book Set

Joshua Morris Publishing for Reader's Digest Young Families, Inc.

The set includes 28 rubber stamps of bones, an ink pad, and a booklet of information and finish-the-picture bone puzzles. Users, for example, stamp out a set of underground bones for a paleontologist to find, and complete assorted skeletons, stamping in the rib cage, the pelvis, or the feet. For kids aged 6 and up.

$10 from book and toy stores.

SomeBody

An anatomy game for kids aged 6–10. Players learn the names, locations, and functions of the parts of the body by answering the questions on the included question cards ("Which BODY PART has 4 chambers and pumps blood through your body?"), then peeling the (infinitely reusable) labeled vinyl pictures of each body part off the "Body Parts" sheet and sticking them onto the body board—an outline of a chunkily cheerful kid with all his/her insides showing. Younger players can simply play the game as a puzzle, matching vinyl body parts to their outlined shapes on the body board. Each game includes four boards and four sheets of peelable body parts.

$24

Aristoplay

450 S. Wagner Rd.

Ann Arbor, MI 48107

(800) 634-7738 or (888) GR8-GAME

fax (734) 995-4611

Web site: www.aristoplay.com

The Stethoscope Book and Kit

Linda Allison and Tom Ferguson; Addison-Wesley, 1991

The kit includes an easy-to-assemble stethoscope and an informational 64-page booklet stuffed with stethoscope-related activities.

$12.95 from bookstores

COMPUTER SOFTWARE

A.D.A.M.: The Inside Story

"A.D.A.M." is spelled with periods because it's an abbreviation: it stands for "Animated Dissection of Anatomy for Medicine." The program is based on a medical school anatomy key (but is much friendlier). In it, users get a detailed tour of the human body, study a male or female adult, front, back, and—layer by layer—inside. (Supervising parents have options to choose skin colors and to slap concealing fig leaves over sex organs.) The "Family Scrapbook" feature is an overview of human anatomy narrated by "Adam" and "Eve," which includes over four hours of animations, videos, and information, covering all aspects of human body function from burping to snoring. Anatomy students can select among 12 major body systems (cardiovascular, digestive, endocrine, immune, integumentary, lym-

phatic, muscular, nervous, reproductive, respiratory, skeletal, and urinary). There are also six anatomical puzzles to solve. Interesting, worthwhile, and entertaining without being silly. Recommended for kids aged 10 and up. On CD-ROM for Mac or Windows.

$40

A.D.A.M. Software, Inc.

1600 River Edge Pkwy., Suite 800

Atlanta, GA 30328

(619) 549-0222 or (800) 408-2326

The Ultimate Human Body

A multimedia guide to the workings of the human body from Dorling Kindersley, with terrific color photographs, animations, and audio clips. Also includes a glossary of anatomical terms and phrases and an informative reader-friendly text. On CD-ROM for Mac or Windows.

$54.95

Dorling Kindersley Publishing

1224 Heil Quaker Blvd.

LaVergne, TN 37086

(888) DIALDKP

Web site: www.dk.com

AUDIOVISUAL HUMAN BODY

The Brain

This three-part series covers the development, structure, and functions of the human brain through computer-generated animations and interviews with researchers and patients. Each episode is about 90 minutes long. "Evolution and Perception" covers the evolution of the brain, sensory perception, and imaging techniques for brain studies; "Matter Over Mind" covers theories of consciousness and their relation to the biochemistry of the brain; and "Memory and Renewal" covers the process of memory, largely through the stories of persons who have suffered various forms of memory loss due to brain damage.

$49.95

PBS Home Video

1320 Braddock Pl.

Alexandria, VA 22314-1698

(800) 645-4PBS

9 *The Incredible Human Machine*
A marvelously photographed tour of the human body from *National Geographic*.

$14.95

Movies Unlimited

3015 Darnell St.

Philadelphia, PA 19154

(215) 637-4444 or (800) 4-MOVIES

e-mail: movies@moviesunlimited.com

Web site: www.moviesunlimited.com

THE HUMAN BODY ON-LINE

12 *Guided Tour: Visible Human Project*
Has 9,000 digitalized sections of a human body with a clickable interface that explains anatomical details. Users learn about the project and view animations that explain how two-dimensional sections can be used to study three-dimensional objects.

www.madsci.org/~lynn/VH

12 *Inner Body*
Interactive human anatomy, with a detailed anatomy tutorial. Users click on pictured systems for more detail. The site includes informational text, labeled diagrams, and animations.

www.InnerBody.com

9 *Neuroscience for Kids*
A terrific site where kids can learn all about the brain and the nervous system. Kids can explore the brain and nervous system through great graphics and a kid-friendly hypertext, ask questions of the experts, and access links to related resources on the Internet.

weber.u.washington.edu/~chudler/neurok.html

MARINE BIOLOGY/ OCEANOGRAPHY

Kids generally learn about the oceans and their denizens in upper-elementary science programs; marine biology and oceanography, however, are usu-ally not integral parts of the secondary school curriculum. We spent a lot of time studying both when the boys were of elementary school age, primarily because Ethan, our middle son, was intensely interested in all things marine.

From my homeschool journal:

◆ **January 3, 1990. Josh is eight; Ethan, seven; Caleb, five.**

We began the morning with the "Seashells Discovery Collection," which was a great hit: the boys sorted, played with, and studied all the specimens in the collection, discussing the difference between univalves and bivalves, how royal purple dye comes from murex, how starfish eat clams, and fighting conches. Identified conch, cockle, clam, murex, moon snail, barnacle, mussel, cowrie, coral, sea fan, sand dollar, sand biscuit, abalone, starfish, and sundial shell. The boys then took off into a sea fantasy game in which all the shells (etc.) were active characters. The attacking starfish were the bad guys, to be defeated by the murexes with their purple paralyzing poison.

We read Augusta Goldin's The Bottom of the Sea (see page 318), which they found largely dull, but they did learn the definitions of continental shelf, continental slope, seamount, and guyot, and discovered what echo sounders and fathometers do. With all this in mind, the boys then built a model sea bottom out of clay in a big tin dishpan. The model included a continental shelf and slope, trenches, guyots, volcanic islands, underwater caves, sunken meteors, and a toy submarine. We then flooded the model and "mapped" the sea bottom by measuring the water depth with a ruler, recording the results on graph paper. It worked beautifully, though used enormous amount of clay.

ORGANIZATIONS

Whale Adoption Project

A surefire introductory attention grabber for the study of oceanography—at least it worked for us—is to adopt your own ocean-dwelling whale. Whale adoption costs about $20, which goes to support whale conservation projects and cetological research. Adopters get to choose from a list of named whales, after which

317

they receive an official adoption certificate, a photograph of the chosen adoptee (ours shows only the tail), a whale migration map, which allows you to predict where your whale might be at different times of the year, and a quarterly newsletter, *Whalewatch*.

Whale Adoption Project
International Wildlife Coalition
70 E. Falmouth Hwy.
East Falmouth, MA 02536
(508) 548-8328

BOOKS

The Bottom of the Sea
4 8
Augusta Goldin; Thomas Y. Crowell, 1966

Goldin explains undersea geography and how oceanographers study it, and defines such useful terms as *fathom, continental shelf, seamount, trench,* and *ridge.* For readers aged 4–8.

Drift Bottles in History and Folklore
8 12
Dorothy B. Francis; Ballyhoo Books, 1990

Who can resist a message in a bottle? This unusual history is stuffed with stories about floating bottles: Benjamin Franklin used them to map the Gulf Stream; Queen Elizabeth I, who appointed an Official Uncorker of Ocean Bottles, used them for naval intelligence. Included are instructions for making your own drift bottles and reproducible message cards (of great help to retrieving hydrographers) to tuck inside.

Exploring the Titanic
8 12
Robert D. Ballard; Scholastic, 1993

Exploring the Titanic describes "how the greatest ship ever lost—was found" in 64 illustrated pages. The book, written on a middle grade reading level, is thoroughly fascinating—with an unavoidable tinge of the ghoulish, which always, I must admit, spurs our children's interest. The book includes the history of the *Titanic,* complete with period photographs, a multi-colored cross-sectional diagram of the ship that occupies four full pages, and a detailed account of Robert Ballard's discovery of the sunken ship. Included are diagrams of the tiny submarine, *Alvin,* and underwater robot, *Jason,* and some chilling underwater photographs. Eerie, but enthralling.

Of similar format and appeal are Ballard's *Exploring the Bismarck* (1991), the tale of Hitler's famous battleship and its discovery; and *The Lost Wreck of the Isis* (1990), the account of the discovery and exploration of a sunken Roman merchant ship. Included is a fictionalized story of the ship's voyage, circa A.D. 355. For younger readers, see *The Titanic Lost . . . and Found* by Judy Donnelly (Random House, 1987), a Step Into Reading book for kids in grades 2–3.

Extremely Weird Fishes
6 +
Sarah Lovett; John Muir Publications, 1992

Each weird fish gets a double-page spread: on the right, a close-up color photograph; on the left, illustrations, scientific information, and unusual facts. The book covers general information about fish, and 21 weird fish, among them the spiny-toothed parrot fish, the stonefish, the mudskipper, the leafy sea dragon, and the burrfish.
See **Extremely Weird Series** (page 339).

Eyewitness Series: Ocean
9 12
Alfred A. Knopf

Several of the Eyewitness books feature ocean-related topics. In each 64-page volume, the featured topic is surveyed through many impressive color photographs, drawings, and diagrams, accompanied by informational captions. Titles include *Fish* (Steve Parker; 1990), *Seashore* (Steve Parker; 1989), *Shark* (Miranda MacQuitty; 1989), *Shell* (Alex Arthur; 1989), and *Whale* (Vassili Papastavrou; 1993).

Follow the Water From Brook to Ocean
4 9
Arthur Dorros; HarperTrophy, 1993

This picture book follows the journey of water from snowy mountaintop to ocean, through brooks, streams, and rivers, over waterfalls and dams. The book briefly discusses the ways in which people use water, the dangers of water pollution, and the ways in which water changes the earth, hollowing canyons and building deltas.

The Magic School Bus on the Ocean Floor
7 11
Joanna Cole; Scholastic, 1992

Ms. Frizzle's class has taken a trip to the beach. Ms. Frizzle, togged out in red sneakers trimmed with anchors, drives the Magic School Bus straight into the surf and down to the bottom of the sea. The class learns a good deal of ocean science, visiting everything from hot-water vents to coral reefs, and returns home via gigantic surfboard. Back home they do a series of dry-land ocean projects, including making a labeled ocean chart, a fishy food-chain mobile, and a balloon jellyfish, all of which look like fun. Giggle-provoking illustrations by Bruce Degen.

See the **Magic School Bus Series** (page 227).

My Visit to the Aquarium
Aliki; HarperCollins, 1993

A charmingly illustrated introduction to marine life through a child's visit to the public aquarium. For readers aged 4–8.

The Ocean Book: Aquarium and Seaside Activities and Ideas for All Ages
Center for Marine Conservation; John Wiley & Sons, 1989

Puzzles, projects, games, science experiments, and information for kids in grades K–6. Topics covered include the geography of the world's oceans, the water cycle, currents and tides, ocean animals, food chains, adaptation to life in the oceans, ecosystems, undersea exploration, and water pollution.

Oceans
Seymour Simon; William Morrow, 1990

A 32-page photo-essay on the world's oceans. Spectacular color photographs and clearly presented scientific information for young readers.

Oceans for Every Kid
Janice Van Cleave; John Wiley & Sons, 1996

Information, activities, and quizzes on all aspects of oceanography. Users cover, for example, features of the ocean floor, depth determination, waves, tides, water pressure, why the ocean is salty, the effect of oceans on weather, and ocean life. Experiments use simple, readily obtainable materials.

Sea Searcher's Handbook
Monterey Bay Aquarium; Roberts Rinehart Publishers, 1996

Over 90 hands-on activities and 100 detailed black-and-white illustrations of marine plants and animals, for kids aged 5 and up. Information is categorized by marine ecosystem: rocky shore, sandy shore, wetlands, kelp forest, open sea, deep-sea canyons. Each section includes a "Field Guide" of drawings and descriptions of typical animal and plant life. Activities include making squid and jellyfish costumes (for the jellyfish, you'll need a clear plastic umbrella and a lot of ribbon), cleaning up an experimental oil spill, solving ocean crossword puzzles, and playing "Fish Bingo."

Whales in the Classroom Series
Singing Rock Press

This ongoing series of books about oceanography by author/biologist Larry Wade targets kids aged 10–14. The first volume in the series, *Oceanography* (1992), is an informational illustrated manual on ocean science, covering life on the ocean floor, ocean currents and upwellings, marine communities, plankton, and marine ecology. The book includes interviews with marine biologists and oceanographers, a foldout to-be-illustrated mural of marine ecosystems, a foldout to-be-completed depth chart based on echo sounding data, and multitudinous science and math challenges, map exercises, puzzles, and quizzes.

Volume 2 in the series, *Getting to Know the Whales* (1995), covers whale evolution and anatomy, whale life, whale research, and conservation programs. Included are interviews with whale biologists, and scientific and mathematical challenges. Kids, for example, calculate the real-life lengths of whales from drawn-to-scale illustrations, calculate average whale dive times, plot whale migration paths on a map, and determine whale travel speeds and population sizes.

Singing Rock Press
Box 1274
Minnetonka, MN 55345
(612) 935-4910

Where the Waves Break: Life at the Edge of the Sea
Anita Malnig; Carolrhoda, 1987

The reason for tides, and descriptions of the many kinds of plant and animal life found in tidal pools or along the beach: starfish, snails, brittle stars, sea urchins, sand dollars, sponges, sea squirts. Illustrated with magical color photographs.

LITERATURE LINKS TO MARINE BIOLOGY/OCEANOGRAPHY: FOR ADULTS

The World of Water: Linking Fiction to Nonfiction

Phyllis J. Perry; Teacher Ideas Press, 1995

The book links popular fiction titles to informative nonfiction science books, all on the theme of water. The book is divided into five major subject areas, variously covering ships, diving, marine life, survival, and the ocean environment. Includes discussion questions and suggestions for activities and projects. Targeted at kids in grades 5–9.

LITERATURE LINKS TO MARINE BIOLOGY/OCEANOGRAPHY: FOR KIDS

20,000 Leagues Under the Sea

Jules Verne

Illustrated Junior Library; Grosset & Dunlap, 1996

Step Into Classics; Random House, 1994

Troll Illustrated Classics (Raymond James); Troll Associates, 1990

Jules Verne's wonderful classic in which a French professor on board an American frigate is investigating a mysterious sea monster. The monster turns out to be a submarine, under the command of the brilliant (but mad) Captain Nemo. Drama and high adventure on and beneath the seas. Many versions are available, some in simplified form for less advanced readers. The Illustrated Junior Library edition is a challenging 424 pages long; the Step Into Classics edition, 95 pages; the Troll Illustrated Classics a much condensed 47 pages.

Amos & Boris

William Steig; Sunburst, 1992

Amos the mouse is swept off the deck of his boat one beautiful night. His life is saved by Boris the whale and the two become close friends. Later, when Boris is beached after a storm, Amos gets a chance to return the favor. For readers aged 4–8.

Call It Courage

Armstrong Sperry; Aladdin, 1990

Mafatu, a 12-year-old Polynesian boy, sets out alone to conquer his terrible fear of the sea and to win the respect of his people. A splendid tale of courage for kids aged 10 and up.

Do Not Open

Brinton Turkle; E. P. Dutton, 1993

Miss Moody is a beachcomber who lives in a little cottage by the ocean with her cat. One day they discover a mysterious bottle in the sand with a message on it: Do not open. A delightful picturebook for kids aged 4–8.

Moby Dick

Herman Melville

Oxford Illustrated Classics Series; Oxford University Press, 1997

Many versions are available of the classic tale of Captain Ahab and his nemesis, Moby Dick, the great white whale. This well-done 103-page condensation by Geraldine McCaughrean is for readers aged 9–12.

Seabird

Holling C. Holling; Houghton Mifflin, 1978

Young Ezra carves a little ivory seagull after the bird saves his ship in a storm at sea. The bird becomes a mascot through four generations of Ezra's seafaring family, passing from whaling ship to clipper ship to steamship to airplane. For readers aged 9–12.

The Seashore Book

Charlotte Zolotow; HarperTrophy, 1994

A little boy who has never seen the seashore asks his mother to tell him about it. She describes it so beautifully that readers can almost hear the seagulls and feel the splash of cold water. With lovely watercolor illustrations. For readers aged 4–8.

Swimmy

Leo Lionni; Alfred A. Knopf, 1991

The story of a clever little fish who finds a way to protect himself and his friends from threatening bigger fish: camouflage. For readers aged 4–8.

The Voyage of the Frog

11 Gary Paulsen; Yearling, 1990

Fourteen-year-old David inherits a sailboat—the *Frog*—from his uncle and sets out to fulfill his uncle's last wish: to scatter his ashes in the sea wind. Then David gets caught in a sudden violent storm and must survive on the ocean for days on his own. For readers aged 11 and up.

The Wreck of the Zephyr

6 12 Chris Van Allsburg; Houghton Mifflin, 1983

A magically eerie tale of a boy who wants to be the best sailor in the world. Then a storm blows his boat to a town where the sailors use special sails that enable their boats to fly. Exquisite illustrations.

COLORING AND PAPER-CRAFTS BOOKS

Coral Reef Coloring Book

6 Ruth Soffer; Dover Publications

Black-line drawings of life on the coral reef, including pictures of parrot fish, damselfish, octopi, and a lot of wonderful coral. Other ocean-related coloring books from Dover include *Seashore Life Coloring Book, Shells of the World Coloring Book, Strange Creatures of the Sea Coloring Book,* and *Whales and Dolphins Coloring Book.*

$2.95
Dover Publications, Inc.
31 E. Second St.
Mineola, NY 11501

The Marine Biology Coloring Book

13 Thomas M. Niesen; Barnes & Noble, 1982

This coloring book is so booklike that it deserves mention all by itself. It takes itself seriously too. You color the pictures with "coloring instruments" (the author recommends colored pencils or felt-tip pens) and you do so according to precise coloring instructions.

The book includes 96 "plates" of very detailed scientific drawings, picturing sea life large and small,

inside and out, in cross- and longitudinal sections. Each page of illustrations is accompanied by an equally detailed page of text. The book begins with a general explanation of tides (users' color maps, moons, and planets), followed by a series of composite pictures showing the animal and plant life in various ocean zones ("Coastal Wetlands," "Sandy Beach," "Kelp Bed"). The bulk of the book then covers the anatomy and behavior of individual specimens (or related groups of specimens) of marine life, including, for example, marine worms, coelenterates, mollusks, gastropods, bony fish, elasmobranch fish, and marine mammals. A lot of information for definitely advanced colorers.

Oceans

9 12 Diane M. Tyler and James C. Tyler; Running Press, 1990

A "fact-filled" coloring book in the Start Exploring series. Each double-page spread includes, on the right, a black-line drawing for coloring, and, on the left, an interesting informational text. Covers the ocean from the deep sea to coral reefs and tidal pools.

$8.95 from bookstores or
Running Press Book Publishers
125 South 22nd St.
Philadelphia, PA 19103
(215) 567-5080 or (800) 345-5359/fax (800) 453-2884

Origami Sea Life

9 John Montroll and Robert R. Lang; Dover Publications

The book includes instructions for making 38 ocean-related paper-folding projects, among them an origami tadpole, barracuda, lobster, and sailfish.

Dover Publications, Inc.
31 E. Second St.
Mineola, NY 11501

GAMES AND HANDS-ON ACTIVITIES

Deep Sea Diver

8 A cooperative board game in which divers descend from a ship at the top of the vertical playing board down to the depths of the ocean. The object of the game is to retrieve sunken treasure and archaeological artifacts from the ocean floor, while evading entangling seaweed, coral, sharks, and lurking octopi.

> Animal Town
> Box 757
> Greenland, NH 03840
> (800) 445-8642/fax (603) 430-0334

🖐 13 + *Floating and Sinking*

A learning module of hands-on activities and experiments for students in grades 7–12. A single booklet includes general teaching information, test questions (and answers), very detailed teachers' notes, and 24 reproducible student task cards. Users are supposed to copy the cards, cut them out, and tape one copy of each to the top of a piece of lined notebook paper, then assemble all 24 into a student booklet. Each task card includes instructions for an experiment and a series of questions or challenges based on the experimental results. Experiments in the "Floating and Sinking" module cover such principles as liquid densities, specific gravity, displacement of water and Archimedes' principle, the effects of salt concentration and temperature on buoyancy, and the use of a hydrometer. All experiments use only very simple equipment: kids make their own arm balances, spring scales, and hydrometers out of straws, wire, clay, paper cups, and discarded film cannisters.

> $11
> TOPS Learning Systems
> 10970 S. Mulino Rd.
> Canby, OR 97013
> (888) 773-9755/fax (503) 266-5200
> Web site: www.topscience.org

See **TOPS** (page 224).

10 + *The Game of OCEAN*

A question-and-answer card game for two to eight players, aged 10 and up. The object of the game is to win enough cards to spell the word *ocean*. Players accomplish this by correctly answering questions in five ocean-related categories: oceanography, circulation, ecology, animals, and navigation. Which card category the question is read from is determined on each turn by the roll of a letter-coded die.

Sample beginner questions include "What highly prized jewels are produced by oysters?," "What ocean did Balboa sight after crossing the Isthmus of Panama?," and "Which ocean is nearly equal in size to all the others combined?" Sample advanced questions, some of which are dillies, include "What two factors determine the density of seawater found at or near the surface?" and "What gas do corals combine with calcium to form limestone reefs and atolls?" The instruction booklet describes three variations on the basic game, for play with large groups.

> $10.95
> Other Worlds Educational Enterprises
> Box 6193
> Woodland Park, CO 80866
> (719) 687-3840

8 + *Krill*

Krill are the little shrimplike creatures that are the staple of the blue-whale diet—and food is what this card game is all about. With an illustrated deck of 77 cards, "Krill" teaches players who eats (or gets eaten by) what in the Antarctic Ocean marine community. A "Blue Whale" card, for example, takes a "Krill" card; a "Leopard Seal" card takes a "Penguin" card; an "Albatross" card takes a "Squid." An unforgettable introduction to the marine food chain. Recommended for two to six players aged 8 and up.

> $9.95 from game stores or
> Ampersand Press
> 750 Lake St.
> Port Townsend, WA 98368
> (800) 624-4263
> Web site: www.ampersandpress.com

4 8 *Ocean Lotto*

The game includes four playing boards, each with nine color photos of sea creatures, and 36 matching playing cards. Kids pair the cards with the pictures on their boards. The pictures—which include sea urchins, coral, orcas, sea otters, sharks, and dolphins—are terrific. For players aged 4–8.

> $9.95
> Delta Education
> Box 3000
> Nashua, NH 03061-3000
> (800) 442-5444
> or
> Carolina Biological Supply Co.
> 2700 York Rd.

Burlington, NC 27215

(800) 334-5551

The Prehistoric Ocean: An Explorer's Kit

The kit contains two prehistoric shark teeth embedded in a block of clay: a five-inch-long replica of a great white shark's tooth 25 million years old, and a (smaller, but genuine) fossil shark tooth 16 million years old. Kids soak the clay block in water, then unearth the teeth with the included scraping tool. An accompanying 64-page book, *Prehistoric Oceans: An Explorer's Guide* by Warren Allmon, includes information about the denizens of ancient seas and the geography of ancient oceans.

$18.95 from book in toy stores or

Running Press Book Publishers

125 S. 22nd St.

Philadelphia, PA 19103

(215) 567-5080 or (800) 345-5359/fax (800) 453-2884

Save the Whales

A beautifully illustrated board game in which players collaborate to save eight species of whale—bowhead, blue, gray, humpback, fin, right, sperm, and orca—from such evils as pollution, oil spills, and whaling ships. The playing pieces are cast-metal replicas of real whales; the object of the game is to move each safely around the board until it reaches its place in the open ocean. "Old Father Neptune" and "Dawn O'Day" cards variously provide good luck, bad luck, and interesting information about whales and the threats to their survival. Some of the game cards have a distinct antiscience bias: if you believe that all scientists are maliciously intent on the destruction of the planet, you'll be fine here; otherwise, you'll have some fuel for discussion and debate.

$39

Animal Town

Box 757

Greenland, NH 03840

(800) 445-8642/fax (603) 403-0334

Sea Monkeys Ocean Zoo

These aren't really monkeys and they're not going to look anything like the little cartoon creatures shown on the package label. They're brine shrimp. The kit includes a small clear plastic aquarium, sea monkey eggs, food, water purifier, and an instructional handbook. Monkeys/shrimp are cavorting about within three to five days and can be observed through the magnifying bubbles set in the walls of the aquarium. They're even better under a microscope.

Available from most scientific supply stores and catalogs. Sources include:

Edmund Scientific Co.

101 E. Gloucester Pike

Barrington, NJ 08007-1380

(800) 728-6999

or

Carolina Biological Supply Co.

2700 York Rd.

Burlington, NC 27215

(800) 334-5551

or

Insect Lore Products

Box 1535

Shafter, CA 93263

(800) LIVE-BUG

Sea Shells

Sea shells, for those who live too far from the seashore to pick up their own, can be purchased from nature and science supply companies. Shells and other specimens are available individually or packaged in collections or kits. Carolina Biological Supply, for example, carries dried specimens of corals, sponges, sand dollars, starfish, sea urchins, and barnacle clusters, as well as many assorted shell collections. Delta Education sells a "Hands-On Explorations: Shells" kit that includes three pounds of shells, 10 magnifying glasses, and a kid's field guide to shells; Educational Insights sells a "Seashell Nature Adventure" kit, which contains 21 shell specimens and an activity guidebook.

Carolina Biological Supply Co.

2700 York Rd.

Burlington, NC 27215

(800) 334-5551/fax (800) 222-7112

or

Delta Education

Box 3000

Nashua, NH 03061-3000

(800) 442-5444/fax (800) 282-9560

Web site: www.delta-ed.com

or

Educational Insights

16941 Keegan Ave.

Carson, CA 90746

(800) 933-3277/fax (310) 605-5048 or (800) 995-0506

Web site: www.edin.com

Seashore Expedition Kit

You have to supply the seashore; the kit contains everything else. Included are informational activity booklets, a shell chart for identifying specimens, a collecting net, specimen bottles and bags, a pipette, and a magnifying glass.

$15.95

Scientific Explorer, Inc.

2802 E. Madison, Suite 114

Seattle, WA 98112

(206) 322-7611 or (800) 900-1182/fax (206) 322-7610

e-mail: sciex@scientificexplorer.com

Web site: www.scientificexplorer.com

Shello

Bingo, with seashells. The game includes 25 real shells mounted on cards, 25 "Shello" game cards (labeled with shell names), 250 plastic tokens, and a master shell identification list.

$39.95

Carolina Biological Supply Co.

2700 York Rd.

Burlington, NC 27215

(800) 334-5551/fax (800) 222-7112

Voyagers: The Lure of the Sea

A question-and-answer game of the ocean for players aged 10 and up. Players roll a sea-blue die to determine whether they answer an *L* ("Land Ho!"), *U* ("Under Sail!"), or *O* ("Overboard!") question; at least two of each must be answered to complete the game mission. Questions, all on the beautifully illustrated "Ship's Log" cards, include, for example: "Do you know the life span of a great white shark?" and "About how many species of palm trees may be found on tropical islands? 150 / 1500 / 15,000?"

From toy and game stores or

Voyagers

Box 87

Essex, CT 06426

(860) 767-3317

AUDIOVISUAL MARINE BIOLOGY/OCEANOGRAPHY

Eyewitness: Marine Biology/Oceanography

Video versions of the Eyewitness books (see page 318) include *Fish, Seashore, Shark,* and *Shell.* Each runs about 30 minutes and includes scientific information, interesting narration, and wonderful color photography.

$12.95 each

Dorling Kindersley Publishing

1224 Heil Quaker Blvd.

LaVergne, TN 37086

(888) DIALDKP

Web site: www.dk.com

Whales of the World

Eleven songs about whales for kids, interspersed with recordings of actual whale songs and sounds.

NorthSound, NorthWord Press, Inc.

Box 1360

Minocqua, WI 54548

(800) 336-6398

e-mail: nwpinc@newnorth.net

COMPUTER SOFTWARE

Odell Down Under

Kids become fish in this marine life simulation game—or any one of 60 sea creatures, including sharks and electric eels. The trick is to create a creature of the proper size, color, cleverness, and speed to stay alive and move to the top of the food chain, thus becoming the Ruler of the Great Barrier Reef. Colorful animation. Recommended for kids aged 8–12.

$34.95

The Learning Company

6160 Summit Dr. N

Minneapolis, MN 55430-4003

(800) 622-3390/fax (612) 589-1151

Web site: www.learningco.com

Orcas in Our Midst

A multidisciplinary study of whales on CD-ROM. Through color photographs, video clips, scientific data, text, and links to related Internet sites, kids study whale behavior and biology, perform calculations based on whale population dynamics and ranges, learn to identify individual whales, read myths and legends about whales, and follow the investigations of modern whale researchers. The program combines science, math, environmental studies, and creative writing. On CD-ROM for Mac.

$99.95

Sunburst Communications
101 Castleton St.
Box 40
Pleasantville, NY 10570
(800) 321-7511/fax (914) 747-4109
Web site: www.sunburst.com

The Voyage of the Mimi

Interactive CD-ROMs and fascinating videotapes detail the voyage of the *Mimi,* a scientific research expedition during which the young crew has exciting adventures at sea while learning about whales, navigation, ocean survival skills, sea life, and much more. A sequel, *The Second Voyage of the Mimi,* centers around an archaeological expedition to discover a lost Maya city. There are many varied software programs, video collections, books, and resource guides based on the voyages. A complete "Voyages of the Mimi" catalog is available.

Sunburst Communications
101 Castleton St.
Box 40
Pleasantville, NY 10570
(800) 321-7511/fax (914) 747-4109
Web site: www.sunburst.com

The Water Planet

An entire oceanography and marine biology program on CD-ROM. The program includes over 2,000 color photographs, ranging from satellite images of the world's oceans to photomicrographs of plankton, as well as audio and video clips and a detailed text. The program covers plate tectonics, the seafloor, the chemical and physical properties of water, ocean structure, tides, currents, ocean habitats, sea life, and oceanographic explorations. On CD-ROM for Windows.

$199

Videodiscovery, Inc.

1700 Westlake Ave. N, Suite 600
Seattle, WA 98109-3012
(206) 285-5400 or (800) 548-3472/fax (206) 285-9245
Web site: www.videodiscovery.com

MARINE BIOLOGY/ OCEANOGRAPHY ON-LINE

The Conchologist's Information Network

All about shells, including information about marine, freshwater, and terrestrial shells, an on-line course for shell lovers ("Conchology 101"), and a special kids' area, with interesting shell facts, poems, stories, hands-on activities and science experiments, and a shell quiz.

erato.acnatsci.org:80/conchnet

Coral Forest

Maps showing the locations of the world's coral reefs, sample lesson plans from a teacher's guide titled "Diversity of Life on the Coral Reef," and information on coral reef environmental campaigns and projects.

www.blacktop.com/coralforest

Life in the Ocean

An excellent site for young marine biologists. Included is a simplified cross-section of the ocean showing the various "life zones" with photographs of the marine organisms that live in each, from just beneath the ocean's surface to the deepest levels.

encarta.msn.com/schoolhouse/oceans/oceans.asp

Monterey Bay Aquarium On-Line

A virtual tour of the aquarium's exhibits, including a trip through a kelp forest; activities for kids of all ages; and a student oceanography club.

www.mbayaq.org

Ocean Planet Home Page

An on-line version of the "Ocean Planet" exhibit from the Smithsonian National Museum of Natural History. Users learn about ocean science and famous "sea people" through a combination of text, graphics, color photographs, and audio clips.

seawifs.gsfc.nasa.gov/ocean_planet.html

Oceanography Links

Links to many oceanography-related Internet sites.

www.ocgy.ubc.ca/links

VIMS Marine Education

A tour of the VIMS Aquarium, a marine science careers page, information and on-line resources about marine science for kids and teachers, and answers to frequently asked questions.

www.vims.edu.adv/ed

Whale Watching Web

Photographs of whales, sounds of whales, and information about whales.

www.physics.helsinki.fi/whale

WhaleNet

Information on tagged whales and maps showing their locations, whale photographs, whale-related student activities, and an on-line adoption program.

whale.wheelock.edu

Wonders of the Seas

All about marine animals, including sponges, cnidarians, mollusks, and echinoderms, through graphics, photographs, and an informational text.

www.oceanicresearch.org/lesson.html

Woods Hole Oceanographic Institution

General oceanographic information and links to other related sites.

www.whoi.edu/index.html

MICROBIOLOGY

In the typical school science curriculum, microbiology is studied in tenth-grade general biology classes; and some aspects of the subject are taught in health classes in the lower grades.

From my homeschool journal:

◆ September 28, 1995. Josh is fourteen; Ethan, twelve; Caleb, eleven.

We started a study unit on bacteriology. First reviewed the five kingdoms of living things (Monera,
Protista, Fungi, Plantae, and Animalia). Discussed structure of bacterial cells and the differences between prokaryotes and eukaryotes, using assorted reference books. Covered different kinds of bacteria, three basic shapes of bacteria (cocci, bacilli, spirilla), and the mechanism of action of penicillin.

Read about anthrax in Wayne Biddle's A Field Guide to Germs *(see page 327).*

Looked at photomicrographs of bacteria and viruses using the Microslide Viewer (see page 223). Compared sizes of bacteria and viruses.

Looked bacteria up using Science Encyclopedia computer software (see page 243).

◆ September 29, 1995

Reviewed information on bacteria from yesterday. Read "Robert Koch: The Disease Fighter" in Paul de Kruif's Microbe Hunters *(see page 328). Discussed Koch's one germ/one disease theory and its proof, and his work with anthrax, tuberculosis, and cholera. Looked up all three diseases in* A Field Guide to Germs. *Caleb: "What about those strains of tuberculosis that are resistant to antibiotics? How do you treat them?"*

Drew diagrams of viruses; looked at photomicrographs of viruses with the Microslide Viewer; read about viral structure and reproduction.

Read article from The NewScientist *magazine (see page 219) about using bacteria to break down and dispose of old rocket fuel.*

BOOKS

Bacteria and Viruses

Leslie Jean LeMaster; Children's Press, 1985

Introduces kids in grades 2–4 to the world of microorganisms. The book is divided into very short, simple chapters ("What Are Bacteria?," "What Are Viruses?," "What Is Immunity?"), illustrated with color photographs. These are wonderful-looking, but a tad confusing if you don't know just what you're looking at: the book is vague about magnification, which means that beginners don't get much sense of the relative sizes of bacterial colonies on agar plates and individual bacteria and viruses under the microscope.

13 + *A Field Guide to Germs*
Wayne Biddle; Henry Holt, 1995

Wayne Biddle's book covers some 70 nasty microbes, in alphabetical order, from "adenovirus" to "Zika fever." Each gets two to four pages of reader-friendly explanation and discussion: a bit of science, a bit of history, a few catchy statistics, and an occasional black-and-white illustration or apt quotation. We've learned, while galloping eagerly through the guide, that during the Civil War almost as many soldiers died of dysentery (*Shigella dysenteriae*) as were killed in combat, that George Washington may have died of diphtheria, and that, while Mozart suffered through smallpox and survived, Pocahontas died of it. We've also discovered that squirrels can carry bubonic plague, and that a hungry tick can be dislodged by dousing it with whisky. This book is not aimed at children, but at teenagers and question-inundated parents ("What's polio?" "What's measles?"), who will find it a valuable, informational, and irresistibly interesting resource.

4 7 *Germs! Germs! Germs!*
Bobbi Katz; Cartwheel Books, 1996

Germs as flashy cartoon monsters and a short rhyming text describing their habits, for readers aged 4–7.

4 8 *Germs Make Me Sick!*
Melvin Berger; HarperCrest, 1995

A simple, illustrated explanation of bacteria, viruses, contagion, and immunity, for readers aged 4–8. Most bacteriologists would take issue with Berger's assertion that bacteria "are really very small plants," but you can elaborate on that later.

12 + *Microbes, Bugs, and Wonder Drugs: Potions to Penicillin, Aspirin to Addiction*
Fran Balkwill and Mic Rolph, with Victor Darley-Usmar; Portland Press, 1995

A 128-page account of the science of drugs, including the stories of antibiotics, vaccines, anti-cancer medications, and allergy treatments. For readers aged 12 and up.

6 10 *The Smallest Life Around Us*
Lucia Anderson; Crown, 1987

Microbiology for beginners, in which young readers get a pleasantly balanced look at the world of microbes (good and bad). The book includes instructions for eight simple experiments, in which young scientists grow and investigate molds, yeasts, and bacteria.

12 + *When Plague Strikes: The Black Death, Smallpox, AIDS*
James Cross Giblin; HarperCollins, 1995

The science and history of three diseases with global effects: the "Black Death" or bubonic plague, smallpox, and AIDS. Fascinating reading for kids aged 12 and up.

BIOGRAPHIES OF MICROBIOLOGISTS

10 + *Great Lives: Medicine*
Robert H. Curtis; Atheneum, 1992

A collection of short biographies of 38 influential scientists with accomplishments in the field of medicine, among them Louis Pasteur, Marie Curie, Jonas Salk, Hippocrates, Albert Schweitzer, Elizabeth Blackwell, Sigmund Freud, William Harvey, and Wilhelm Röentgen.

10 13 *Louis Pasteur: Disease Fighter*
Linda Wasmer Smith; Enslow Publishing, 1997

A 128-page biography of the French microbiologist for readers aged 10–13, covering his life and accomplishments, among them the development of a rabies vaccine and the discovery of the process of pasteurization.

9 12 *Louis Pasteur and Germs*
Steve Parker; Chelsea House, 1995

A 32-page biography of Pasteur for readers aged 9–12, illustrated with photographs, drawings, and prints. The book includes both the story of Pasteur's life and explanations of his scientific achievements.

Louis Pasteur: Young Scientist
Francene Sabin; Troll Associates, 1983

A short biography of Pasteur for readers aged 6–9, concentrating on the scientist's childhood and young adulthood.

Microbe Hunters
Paul de Kruif; Harcourt Brace, 1996

A classic history of microbiology and microbiologists, including the exciting tales of the scientific battles against rabies, cholera, diphtheria, yellow fever, and malaria. Chapter titles include "Leeuwenhoek: First of the Microbe Hunters," "Pasteur: And the Mad Dog," "Bruce: Trail of the Tsetse," and "Walter Reed: In the Interest of Science—and for Humanity!" Fascinating reading for teenagers.

GAMES, HANDS-ON ACTIVITIES, AND SUPPLEMENTARY MATERIALS

Lyrical Life Science Volume 1
This is music for biologists: 11 informational science songs set to the tunes of familiar folk melodies, patriotic tunes, and campfire songs. The songs, on audiocassette, begin with "The Scientific Method" (to the tune of "Dixie") and proceed through "Invertebrates" ("Clementine"), "Genetics" ("Shortnin' Bread"), and "Viruses" ("Yankee Doodle") to our very favorite, "Oh Bacteria," sung to the tune of "Oh Susanna." It begins: "Oh, lacking any nucleus, you do have a cell wall . . ."

The tape is accompanied by a 92-page illustrated text, which includes music and lyrics to all the songs, plus, for each song topic, a chapter of scientific information. There's also a 40+-page workbook of fill-in-the-blanks and matching quizzes; this isn't quite so appealing, but it's optional.

"Lyrical Life Science" is recommended for kids in the middle grades, but the songs—who can resist "Oh Bacteria"?—are for all ages.

The complete text, tape, and workbook set, $25; text and tape only, $20
Lyrical Learning
8008 Cardwell Hill

Corvallis, OR 97330
(503) 754-3579

Microbiology: 49 Science Fair Projects
H. Steven Dashefsky; McGraw-Hill, 1994

Experiments and project suggestions for kids aged 10 and up.

Pioneers in Medicine Card Game
A rummy game in which players attempt to collect four-card sets featuring 13 medical "pioneers," among them Anton van Leeuwenhoek, Paracelsus, Louis Pasteur, Hippocrates, Galen, Florence Nightingale, and Elizabeth Blackwell.

About $6
Michael Olaf's Essential Montessori
Box 1162
1101 H St.
Arcata, CA 95521
(707) 826-1557/fax (707) 826-2243
or
ETA
620 Lakeview Pkwy.
Vernon Hills, IL 60061
(708) 816-5050 or (800) 445-5985

MICROBIOLOGY ON-LINE

Bugs in the News!
The "bugs" are bacteria and viruses. The site includes a long list of feature articles on bugs ("What's a virus?" "What's microbiology?" "What's *E. coli*?" "What's penicillin?"), each with an informational text and links to images.

falcon.cc.ukans.edu/~jbrown/bugs.html

Cells Alive!
A lot of information on bacteria, with color graphics, animations, photomicrographs, and an explanatory text. Topics covered include "Bacterial Motility," "Dividing Bacteria," and "How Big?," which demonstrates differences in size among viruses, bacteria, and human cells.

www.cellsalive.com

Yale Center for Cell Imaging
Many terrific photomicrographs of viruses, bacteria, and human cells, with descriptions.

info.med.yale.edu/cellimg

ORNITHOLOGY

On our refrigerator every year we post a "Bird-Watcher's Record Sheet." While this sounds scientifically formal, in practice it tends to be a scrawled-upon sheet of notebook paper, covered with names and dates, in pencil, pen, and excited Magic Marker. The list has evolved over the years, from the days when much smaller boys recorded sightings of "Red Berd" and "Chikade," to more recent detailings of scientific names, sexes, and locations. (On the other hand, on this year's list I notice that some scientifically suspect person claims to have seen a pterodactyl.) The refrigerator list is a great way to get your kids thinking about, looking for, and looking at the birds. Add a field guide and a backyard bird feeder and you're well on your way to an ornithological education.

FIELD GUIDES

A field guide is an illustrated bird identification manual, which includes descriptions of bird appearances, calls, and behaviors, and—usually—maps showing the bird's geographical range or distribution. A good field guide is essential equipment for all serious—and even not-so-serious—birders. A number of guides are designed specifically for kids: these are generally shorter and simpler than the adult guides, with bigger pictures. Our experience indicates, however, that if you're in the market for a field guide, go for an adult model. Kids, with a little adult help, quickly learn to use them effectively, and they contain a lot more information and a *lot* more birds.

Among the most popular are the Peterson guides, by ornithologist Roger Tory Peterson, and the Audubon guides. Both are excellent. Titles include: *The Audubon Society Field Guide to North American Birds: Volume I* (John Bull and John Farrand Jr.; Alfred A. Knopf, 1977), *The Audubon Society Field Guide to North American Birds: Volume II* (Miklos D. F. Udvardy; Alfred A. Knopf, 1977), *A Field Guide to the Birds East of the Rockies* (Roger Tory Peterson; Houghton Mifflin, 1980), and *A Field Guide to West-ern Birds* (Roger Tory Peterson; Houghton Mifflin, 1961).

Also see:

The Birder's Handbook: A Field Guide to the Natural History of North American Birds
Paul R. Ehrlich, David S. Dobkin, and Darryl Wheye; Fireside, 1988

This is an intimidatingly fat (nearly 800 pages) paperback with next to no pictures, but it's an informational gem. The left-hand side of each double-page spread contains descriptive listings of individual birds—646 species in all—including information on common and scientific names, habitat, breeding, courtship displays, nests and eggs, diet, and biological notes. A key indicates which page the bird appears on in seven different popular field guides. Readers are also given a list of scientific references relating to the bird (included in the bibliography) and are referred to essays relevant to the bird.

The 250 short essays, which appear on the right-hand side of the pages, are on general bird-related topics—for example, "Eggs and Their Evolution," "Molting," "What Do Birds Hear?," and "Wing Shapes and Flight." Each essay is cross-referenced to other associated essays. Also included are many short biographies of prominent bird biologists, among them John James Audubon, Spencer Fullerton Baird, Konrad Lorenz, Roger Tory Peterson, Nikolaas Tinbergen, and Alexander Wilson. A superb reference.

Everybody's Everywhere Backyard Bird Book
Klutz Press, 1992

An 86-page spiral-bound guide to 28 common backyard birds, illustrated with color photographs, with an attached Audubon birdcall.

Golden Guides
Herbert S. Zim, ed.; Golden Press/Western Publishing Company

A large series of small-size field guides for beginners of all ages. All are 160 pages long, illustrated with color paintings. Titles include *Birds, Butterflies and Moths, Fishes, Flowers, Fossils, Insects, Mammals, Reptiles and Amphibians, Rocks and Minerals, Seashells of the World, Stars, Trees,* and *Weather.*

6 10 *Peterson First Guides*
Houghton Mifflin

A series of short, simple, illustrated identification books just for kids. There are many volumes in the series, among them *Birds, Fishes, Reptiles and Amphibians, Insects,* and *Mammals.* All are small, easy to read, and tuck nicely into a backpack.

ORGANIZATIONS AND PROGRAMS

Cornell Laboratory of Ornithology

The Cornell Laboratory of Ornithology is an international center for bird research and conservation. It welcomes amateur members and volunteers—who form the mainstay of lab-sponsored bird population studies. An annual membership ($30) includes a subscription to the lab's quarterly magazine, *Living Bird,* and to *Birdscope,* a newsletter reporting on current lab research projects.

The lab also offers a "Home Study Course in Bird Biology," the equivalent of a college-level course in introductory ornithology. The class, in nine lessons, covers bird anatomy, behaviors, development, and relationships with humans. Student progress is monitored through worksheets: participants fill these out upon completion of each lesson and send them back to the lab for assessment. The Home Study Course costs about $165; the price includes an annual membership in the lab.

Cornell Laboratory of Ornithology
159 Sapsucker Woods Rd.
Ithaca, NY 14850
(607) 254-2444

The National Audubon Society

The prominent national organization for bird lovers and environmentalists. An annual membership, which includes an annual subscription to the society's magazine, *Audubon,* and free admission to all Audubon Nature Centers, costs $20.

National Audubon Society
700 Broadway
New York, NY 10003
Web site: www.igc.org/audubon

BOOKS

9 12 *The Amazing Egg Book*
Margaret Griffin and Deborah Seed; Addison-Wesley, 1990

The history, lore, and science of eggs, with many puzzles, fact boxes, and hands-on activities, including making your own egg dyes, testing the strength of eggshells, painting with egg-yolk paints, and making eggshell Christmas ornaments.

9 12 *Bird*
David Burnie; Alfred A. Knopf, 1988

An Eyewitness book, 64 pages long, with typical and terrific Eyewitness photographs. Each double-page spread covers a different bird-related topic, among them "From bird to dinosaur," "The wing," "The structure of feathers," "Feet and tracks," "Beaks," "Making a nest," "Extraordinary eggs," and "Watching birds."

4 8 *The Bird Alphabet Book*
Jerry Pallotta; Charlesbridge Publishing, 1990

A bird for every letter of the alphabet, each illustrated with a colorful painting. *J,* for example, is for jacana; *K* for kiwi; and *P* for puffin.
See the **Animal Alphabet Series** (page 339).

5 9 *Birdsong*
Audrey Wood; Harcourt Brace, 1997

An illustrated picture book in which children from different places across the United States discover 14 birds—among them the crow, the owl, and the city pigeon—and learn about their habitats and distinctive calls and songs.

9 12 *Birdwise*
Pamela Hickman; Addison-Wesley, 1988

Interesting information and 40 hands-on activities having to do with birds. Included are instructions for making a milk-carton or Popsicle-stick birdhouse, a hummingbird feeder, and a gull mobile, suggestions for several kinds of bird feeders, directions for making birdbaths (water and dust), and a bird board game, "It's a Bird's Life," that gives players "a glimpse at the good and bad things that a bird may face during its first year of life."

Crinkleroot's Guide to Knowing Birds

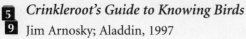

Jim Arnosky; Aladdin, 1997

Beginning birding with Crinkleroot, who has a gnomelike beard and a vast knowledge of nature. Readers learn to identify common birds and discover how a bird grows, how to tell males from females, where to look for birds, and how to attract them to their own backyards. Also see *Crinkleroot's 25 Birds Every Child Should Know* (Simon & Schuster, 1993). By the same author, see *Crinkleroot's Guide to Knowing Trees* (page 277).

Ducks Don't Get Wet

Augusta Goldin; HarperTrophy, 1989

All about ducks for 4–9-year-olds. The illustrated book covers duck behavior and different kinds of ducks and explains why ducks don't get wet. Included are instructions for a couple of simple experiments using oil, water, and feathers.

Everything You Never Learned About Birds

Rebecca Rupp; Storey Communications, 1995

Bird science, history, lore and hands-on projects for persons aged 9 and up. The book is divided into six chapters, each concentrating on a different bird topic: "A Bird is Born" (all about eggs), "Inner Bird, Outer Bird" (bird anatomy and feathers), "Soar Like an Eagle, Flap Like a Duck" (the science of bird flight and migration), "Dinner With the Birds" (bird eating habits and digestion), "The Daily Bird" (nests, songs, pecking order), and "Name That Bird!" (taxonomy and identification). Readers also learn about Peru's "Bridge of Eggs," discover how the enormous Andean condor gets airborne (it jumps off a cliff), find out which bird builds a nest with rubber boots, and learn how a pink flamingo is like a blue whale. Stuffed with colorful photographs, diagrams, charts, and humorous drawings.

An Exceptional Examination of Exemplar Experiments for Exciting Teaching With Eggs

Alfred De Vito; Creative Ventures, 1982

Over 40 hands-on experiments with eggs for kids in grades 6–12. Make egg shampoo, construct an egg thermometer and a candle-driven traveling-egg machine, calculate the mass of an egg, experiment with egg pendulums, build an incubator for fertilized eggs, whip up a batch of mayonnaise.

$9.95
NSTA Science Store
1840 Wilson Blvd.
Arlington, VA 22201-3000
(800) 722-NSTA

Extremely Weird Birds

Sarah Lovett; John Muir Publications, 1992

Profiles of 21 extremely weird birds. Each gets a double-page spread: on the right, a terrific close-up color photograph; on the left, illustrations and interesting scientific information. Among the included weird birds are the Atlantic puffin, the macaroni penguin, the blue-footed booby, the hoatzin, and the harpy eagle. See the **Extremely Weird Series** (page 339).

Feathers for Lunch

Lois Ehlert; Voyager Picture Books, 1996

The rhyming story of a house cat who wants a bird for lunch. Readers meet 12 common North American birds and learn to identify each one. The cat gets nothing to eat but feathers. For readers aged 3–7.

Flute's Journey: The Life of a Wood Thrush

Lynne Cherry; Gulliver Books, 1997

The birds fly south for the winter—but what happens to them along the way and where do they go? This richly illustrated picture book describes the southern journey of Flute, a little wood thrush, from Maryland to Costa Rica and back again, then nest building with his mate, Feather, and their struggles to raise their young. All the trials of modern bird life, for readers aged 6–9.

Let's-Read-and-Find-Out Science Series: Birds

Illustrated science picture books for kids aged 4-9 (see page 227). *Falcons Nest on Skyscrapers* (Priscilla Belz Jenkins; HarperTrophy, 1996) details the life of a peregrine falcon in the wild and describes the falcon's near extinction by the pesticide DDT; included is a list of places to contact for information about falcon watches. *How Do Birds Find Their Way?* (Roma Gans; HarperCollins, 1996) discusses the various theories of bird migration; and *A Nest Full of Eggs* (Priscilla Belz Jenkins; HarperCollins, 1995) explains how birds develop inside eggs and how bird parents care for their young.

The Robins in Your Backyard

Nancy Carol Willis; Cucumber Island Storytellers, 1997

A simple picture-book introduction to birds through descriptions of the life of the American robin. The book follows a baby robin from hatching until it leaves the nest. Detailed colored-pencil illustrations. For readers aged 4–8.

She's Wearing a Dead Bird on Her Head!

Kathryn Lasky; Hyperion, 1995

The story of the founding of the Audubon Society. The society was founded in response to the fashion industry, which, in the late 19th century, was destroying world bird populations in the search for decorative feathers and plumes for ladies' hats.

Urban Roosts: Where Birds Nest in the City

Barbara Bash; Sierra Club Books, 1990

A lovely picture book filled with information about such city-dwelling birds as pigeons, sparrows, finches, barn owls, chimney swifts, crows, and peregrine falcons. The illustrations are big colorful paintings, showing many unexpected nesting places. House wrens, readers learn, will make themselves at home in any cavity: a glove hanging on a clothesline, an old shoe, the hole in the center of a ball of twine. There they build their nests using all matter of found materials, not only grasses and leaves but Kleenex, candy wrappers, Band-Aids, paper clips, and—occasionally—dollar bills.

What Makes a Bird a Bird?

May Garelick; Mondo Publishing, 1995

Just what does make a bird a bird? Flight? But, the author explains, butterflies, bats, and flying fish fly too—and some birds, like ostriches and penguins, can't fly. Through such a series of questions and examples,

the author goes through a simple process of classification, eventually leading to the crucial characteristic that makes a bird a bird: feathers. Also see Ruth Heller's *Chickens Aren't the Only Ones* (page 339).

BIOGRAPHIES OF ORNITHOLOGISTS: FOR KIDS

Birds in the Bushes: A Story About Margaret Morse Nice

Julie Dunlap; Carolrhoda, 1996

Margaret Nice loved birds from the time she was a little girl. Though her research was ignored for many years because she had no professional credentials, she eventually published a book based on her bird-watching records and became a spokesperson for environmental issues. For readers aged 9–13.

John James Audubon

Joseph Kastner; Harry N. Abrams, 1992

A 92-page biography of the artist-naturalist, filled with catchy anecdotes and solid historical information about Audubon's life and career. Illustrated with full-color reproductions of Audubon's work. For readers aged 11 and up.

John James Audubon: American Artist

Peter Anderson; Franklin Watts, 1996

A short biography of the artist and naturalist for readers aged 9–12.

LITERATURE LINKS TO ORNITHOLOGY

Elisabeth the Birdwatcher

Felice Holman; Macmillan, 1963

Elisabeth builds a bird feeder, battles a persistent feeder-raiding squirrel, and learns a lot about backyard birds. For kids aged 4–8.

Harry's Mad

Dick King-Smith; Alfred A. Knopf, 1997

Harry inherits a very clever, articulate, and adventurous parrot named Madison—Mad, for short—from an uncle in America. For readers aged 8–11.

How the Guinea Fowl Got Her Spots: A Swahili Tale of Friendship

Barbara Knutson; First Avenue Editions, 1991

A picture-book version of an African folktale explaining how the guinea fowl got the concealing spots that keep it safe from predators—such as hungry lions.

The Hummingbird King: A Guatemalan Legend

Argentina Palacios; Troll Associates, 1993

The picture-book legend tells the story of a young Mayan chief who was befriended by a hummingbird, and explains the origin of the gorgeously feathered quetzal.

Ka-ha-si and the Loon

Terri Cohlene; Watermill Press, 1990

An Eskimo legend about a young boy who, with the help of a magical loon, saves his people in a time of trouble. The book includes an informational appendix on the Eskimo tribes of the far north, illustrated with maps and photographs.

The Little Brown Jay: A Tale from India

Elizabeth Claire; Mondo Publishing, 1995

An illustrated Indian legend in which the jay helps a beautiful princess and receives a wonderful reward.

The Magpies' Nest

Joanna Foster; Clarion, 1995

A picture-book version of an English folktale explaining why different kinds of birds make different kinds of nests—all under the tutelage of Mother and Father Magpie. The book includes labeled drawings of the varied nests featured in the story.

Make Way for Ducklings

Robert McCloskey; Viking, 1976

The picture-book classic about the determined mother duck who—with the help of the police department—leads her band of ducklings safely through the busy streets of Boston. For readers aged 4–8.

Mr. Popper's Penguins

Richard and Florence Atwater; Little, Brown, 1992

Mr. Popper, a housepainter with an interest in Antarctic research, gets a penguin as a present from Admiral Drake, polar explorer. The penguin gets a mate (from the Mammoth City Aquarium) and the pair produce a large family of small penguins. The Poppers turn their cellar into a freezing plant, complete with ice castle and pond, but soon the expense becomes too much. To support the penguins, they form a Performing Penguin troupe and take their birds on tour. A delightful chapter book for kids aged 5–9.

On the Wing: Bird Poems and Paintings

Douglas Florian; Harcourt Brace, 1996

A clever collection of 21 poems featuring a wide variety of birds, among them the hummingbird, the hawk, the vulture, the roadrunner, and the emperor penguin. Each poem is paired with a humorous color illustration of a bird. The pictured roadrunner has wheels; the hawk perches on a branch, prepared to search for prey with a set of binoculars. For readers aged 4–8.

Owl Moon

Jane Yolen; Philomel Books, 1987

A little girl goes on a night walk in the woods with her father, looking for owls. An enchanting picture book with lovely moonlit illustrations. For readers aged 4–8.

Owls in the Family

Farley Mowat; Dell, 1996

An autobiographical account of growing up on the plains in Canada with a pair of adopted owls, Wol and Weeps. Humorous, touching, and delightful.

Peter and the Pigeons

Charlotte Zolotow; Greenwillow, 1993

Little Peter is a pigeon watcher and he loves everything about pigeons. One day his father takes him on a trip to the zoo, where Peter sees many wonderful new animals—but you can guess what he likes best. For bird lovers aged 3–6.

9 13 *Seabird*

Holling C. Holling; Houghton Mifflin, 1978

Ezra, a young sailor, carves an ivory gull modeled on a bird he saw soaring through an ocean storm, and the little carving is passed down through four generations, from whaling ship to clipper ship to steamship and, finally, to airplane. For readers aged 9–13.

5 9 *The Tale of the Mandarin Ducks*

Katherine Paterson; Puffin, 1995

A beautifully illustrated Japanese tale in which a greedy and cruel lord imprisons a mandarin duck so that he can admire its gorgeous plumage. The captive duck miserably pines for his mate until a pair of kindhearted servants take pity on him and set him free. The lord angrily sentences them to death, but the grateful duck comes to their rescue. For readers aged 4–9.

9 13 *That Quail, Robert*

Margaret Stanger; HarperPerennial, 1992

The true story of an adopted quail who answers the telephone, eats at the dining room table, and sleeps in the Christmas tree.

8 11 *The Trumpet of the Swan*

E. B. White; HarperTrophy, 1973

Louis the trumpeter swan is born without a voice; to make up for it, he learns to play the trumpet. A wonderful story by the author of *Charlotte's Web* and *Stuart Little,* for readers aged 8–11.

7 10 *When Birds Could Talk and Bats Could Sing: The Adventures of Bruh Sparrow, Sis Wren and Their Friends*

Virginia Hamilton; Scholastic, 1996

A lovely collection of African-American bird tales for kids aged 7–10, illustrated with colorful bird paintings. Included are the adventures of Brown Wren, who flew too high after boasting that she could touch the sky; of Ugly Bat, who was once a beautiful bird; and of Blue Jay and Swallow, who bravely stole fire from the Old Firekeeper to heal a sick child.

COLORING AND PAPER-CRAFTS BOOKS

8 12 *Audubon's Birds of America*

George Glenn; Running Press

A coloring book in the *Start Exploring* series with 60 reproductions of Audubon's bird paintings to color plus, on facing pages, a kid-friendly informational text.

$8.95 from bookstores or
Running Press Book Publishers
125 South 22nd St.
Philadelphia, PA 19103
(215) 567-5080 or (800) 345-5359/fax (800) 453-2884

6 + *Audubon's Birds of America Coloring Book*

Features 46 of Audubon's famous bird paintings, transformed into black-line drawings for coloring. The originals, in color, are reproduced on the front and back covers.

$2.95
Dover Publications, Inc.
31 E. Second St.
Mineola, NY 11501

6 + *Audubon Bird Stickers in Full Color*

Contains 53 full-color stickers based on Audubon's bird paintings in an eight-page booklet.

$3.50
Dover Publications, Inc.
31 E. Second St.
Mineola, NY 11501

8 + *Birds in Origami*

John Montroll; Dover Publications

Simple instructions for making a dozen favorite birds, including the swan, flamingo, duck, and stork. Also see *Fun With Bird Origami,* which includes an additional 15 projects plus 24 sheets of origami paper.

$4.95
Dover Publications, Inc.
31 E. Second St.
Mineola, NY 11501

Fifty Favorite Birds Coloring Book

Lisa Bonforte; Dover Publications

An informational coloring book with detailed black-line drawings of familiar birds, with descriptive captions. Also see the *Birds of Prey Coloring Book* and the *Tropical Birds Coloring Book*.

$2.95 apiece
Dover Publications, Inc.
31 E. Second St.
Mineola, NY 11501

Paper Birds That Fly

Norman Schmidt; Sterling Publications, 1996

The book describes how a bird flies, using wings, tail, and feathers, and includes instructions and patterns for building 15 paper birds that really fly.

HANDS-ON ACTIVITIES

Backyard Birds Field Identification Cards

Forty plastic-coated cards, each with a full-color photograph of a common backyard bird on one side, with species description, habitat, and range on the other. These cards are meant to be toted about in the field as quick identification aids; they also lend themselves beautifully to homemade bird games. Our kids, presented with them, invented an elaborate board game in which players—birders—move around an illustrated playing path attempting to add birds (cards) to their "Life Lists," while dealing with bears, swamps, "No Trespassing" areas, landslides, lightning strikes, aggressive hordes of mosquitoes, and a UFO.

$6.50
Carolina Biological Supply Co.
2700 York Rd.
Burlington, NC 27215
(800) 334-5551

Beastly Abodes: Homes for Birds, Bats, Butterflies & Other Backyard Wildlife

Bobbe Needham; Lark Books, 1996

This book, illustrated with lovely color photographs, includes detailed instructions for building three dozen wildlife houses, including a rustic bat house, three kinds of butterfly houses, grapevine nest baskets, nest boxes and shelves, gourd houses, and roosts for birds, squirrel boxes, bee houses, and even— a particularly nice project for small kids—a toad house. (It's a painted clay flowerpot, set on its side and partially buried.) The book also includes information about potential house dwellers.

Beastly Abodes is also sold as a "Beastly Abodes Book and Kit," which includes precut cedar pieces for making a butterfly house (Sterling Publishing).

The Bird Book & Feeder

Neil Dawe; Workman, 1988

A kid-size guide to 24 common backyard birds plus a small plastic feeder, suitable for stuffing with seeds and hanging from a tree or attaching to a windowsill.

Birds Expedition Kit

The kit, one of the Scientific Explorer Expedition series (see page 223), is intended for young out-in-the-field birders. The kit contains activity booklets, with suggestions for many bird-related experiments and instructions for building a simple bird-luring feeder, bird identification charts, a birdcall, a songbird census form, and packets of seeds for planting a bird lover's garden.

$15.95
Scientific Explorer, Inc.
2802 E. Madison, Suite 114
Seattle, WA 98112
(206) 322-7611 or (800) 900-1182/fax (206) 322-7610
e-mail: sciex@scientificexplorer.com
Web site: www.scientificexplorer.com

Bluebird House

A build-your-own birdhouse kit from Curiosity Kits. Included are all necessary materials—precut cedar pieces, hardware, a screwdriver, and a sheet of sandpaper—for making a 12 × 4″ house, especially designed to appeal to bluebirds.

$18 from toy and craft stores; for a local source contact Curiosity Kits

Box 811

Cockeysville, MD 21030

(410) 584-2605 or (800) 584-KITS/fax (410) 584-1247

e-mail: Ckitsinc@aol.com

Christmas Bird Count

ALL The Christmas Bird Count, sponsored annually by the National Audubon Society, first took place in 1900, which makes it one of the oldest cooperative research projects in the United States. All volunteers are welcome to participate in the count, which entails keeping records of the number of birds of each species seen within a 15-mile-diameter area on a single day within two weeks of Christmas. The collected data are used to study population trends in individual bird species. To participate, contact:

American Birds

National Audubon Society

950 Third Ave.

New York, NY 10022

Feed the Birds

Helen and Dick Witty; Workman, 1991

Instructions for what to feed which birds, and a large collection of easy-to-make bird-food recipes. The book comes with a little red mesh suet bag.

The Great Bird Detective

John Elcome; Chronicle Books, 1995

A "Detective's Notebook" for bird-watchers aged 4–8, filled with information about birds, fill-in-the-blank record sheets, and a foldout "detective path" page to which kids stick colorful stickers to record bird-watching trips and adventures.

John James Audubon: Wildlife Art

An ornithological art activity unit from KidsArt. This 16-page booklet covers the life and work of Audubon, and the work of other wildlife artists, from prehistoric cave painters to participants in the annual U.S. Duck Stamp Contest. Among the many suggested activities are making bird drawings, a mallard mobile, model decoys, and feather prints.

$3

KidsArt

Box 274

Mt. Shasta, CA 96067

(916) 926-5076

Owl Pellet Kit

Owls, like sharks, gulp down their dinner whole. The usable parts of the meal are digested; the inedible bits—fur, bones, and teeth—are packaged in the gizzard into tidy little rolls called *pellets*, which the owl coughs up and spits out on the ground. Dissected, these owl discards give a clear picture of just what the owl ate.

Owl pellets are available from scientific supply companies. Most kits include three pellets (fumigated to eliminate clothes moth larvae and wrapped in foil), a set of forceps, a magnifying glass, and an informational booklet, which includes dissection instructions and identification aids. (Our owl ate shrews.)

Kits, about $15; additional single pellets, about $2.50

Edmund Scientific Co.

101 E. Gloucester Pike

Barrington, NJ 08007-1380

(800) 728-6999

Web site: www.edsci.com

or

Carolina Biological Supply Co.

2700 York Rd.

Burlington, NC 27215

(800) 334-5551

or

Insect Lore Products

Box 1535

Shafter, CA 93263

(800) LIVE-BUG

Web site: www.insectlore.com

or

ETA

620 Lakeview Pkwy.

Vernon Hills, IL 60061

(708) 816-5050 or (800) 445-5985

Web site: www.etauniverse.com

There's also an entire company devoted to the business of owl pellets:

Pellets, Inc.

3004 Pinewood

Bellingham, WA 98225

(206) 733-3012

Games

The Hummingbird Game

A card game for hummingbird lovers in which players attempt to match 16 North American hummingbirds with their proper flowers, insects, and geographical ranges. The game includes a deck of 60 cards, beautifully illustrated with color paintings of birds, insects, and flowers. For two to six players, aged 8 and up.

> $15.95 from game stores or
> Ampersand Press
> 750 Lake St.
> Port Townsend, WA 98368
> (800) 624-4263

The Orchard Game

A simple cooperative board game for players aged 3 and up. Kids attempt to fill tiny baskets with little wooden fruits—apples, plums, pears, and cherries—gathered from the trees on the playing board before the hungry raven in the middle gobbles them all up. Who eats (or picks) what is determined by the roll of a bird-and-fruit-patterned die. Bird lovers, the instructions explain sympathetically, can choose to leave a few pieces of fruit on the trees for the bird.

> $28
> Animal Town
> Box 757
> Greenland, NH 03840
> (800) 445-8642/fax (603) 430-0334

Audiovisual Ornithology

Bird Walk by Habitat Series

Learn to identify birds by their calls. Titles in the series, available on CD or audiocassette, include "Backyard Birdwalk" and "Marshland Birdwalk." Each tape or CD features 24 birds. A narrated segment describes and identifies each bird before listeners hear a recording of its song; a nonnarrated segment contains the birdsong recordings only for practice purposes.

> Audiocassettes, $12.95; CDs, $16.95.
> NorthSound
> NorthWood Press, Inc.

> Box 1360
> Minocqua, WI 54548
> (800) 336-6398

Common Bird Songs

Donald J. Borror; Dover Publications

An audiocassette with an accompanying explanatory manual. "Common Bird Songs" is a cacophonous collection of squawks, croaks, and outright yells that the boys found hilarious. ("What's *that?*") Also see *Songs of Eastern Birds* and *Songs of Western Birds*.

> $8.95 each
> Dover Publications, Inc.
> 31 E. Second St.
> Mineola, NY 11501

Know Your Bird Sounds Series

The series includes two volumes of recorded bird calls and songs: "Yard, Garden, and City Birds" (Volume I), which features 35 common backyard birds of eastern and central North America (including the warbling vireo and the eastern screech owl); and "Birds of the Countryside," which features 35 birds inhabiting meadows, woodlands, marshes, and seashores, among them the hairy woodpecker, the hermit thrush, and the indigo bunting. Each tape comes with an informational booklet on birdsong.

> Audiocassettes, $12.95; CDs, $16.95
> NorthSound
> NorthWord Press, Inc.
> Box 1360
> Minocqua, WI 54548
> (800) 336-6398
> e-mail: nwpinc@newnorth.net

Computer Software

Birds of North America

All about birds on CD-ROM. Included are nearly 3,000 color photographs, over 100 video clips, 1,200 recordings of birdsongs and -calls, and detailed information about the habits of hundred of North American birds. There are also on-line quizzes for birders of all ages and links to bird-related Internet sites. For Windows.

$65

Thayer Birding Software

Box 43243

Cincinnati, OH 45243

(800) 865-2473

Web site: www.birding.com

ORNITHOLOGY ON-LINE

Birdlines

Users can search for information about birds by individual name, family, country, or continent. The site also includes general information about bird-watching and links to many other bird-related sites.

www.phys.rng/nl/mk/people/wpv/birdlink.html

The Nutty Hatch

A color photo gallery of birds, each with background information and information on the basics of bird-watching, including a wild bird food chart, nest-box specifications, and bird identification tips, listed by color.

www.geocities.com/Yosemite/7727

ZOOLOGY

Zoology, officially, is the study of animals—with many subdivisions denoting the study of specific animals, as in entomology, the study of insects (see page 226), ichthyology, the study of fish (see page 317), ornithology, the study of birds (see page 329), and the like. In our zoological studies, we studied many animals or animal families—among them frogs, snakes, wolves, elephants, whales, bats, and bears—in each case, inspired by interest on the part of one or all of the boys. These studies usually took the form of multidisciplinary projects. An investigation of elephants, for example, involved reading assorted nonfiction and fiction books about elephants, visiting the zoo to see live elephants and a museum to see fossil mammoth teeth, making an elephant family tree, learning about the ivory trade, locating elephant territories on the world map, making bar graphs comparing average elephant weight and life span to that of other animals, and putting on an elephant play, based on the Indian legend of Ganesh, the elephant-headed god.

The boys also studied animal classification systems or taxonomy—once at the early elementary level, using assorted reference books, Millicent Selsam's *Benny's Animals and How He Put Them in Order* (see page 339), and a lot of animal pictures; again, in more detail, at an upper-elementary/middle school level.

From my homeschool journal:

◆ **March 28, 1990. Josh is eight; Ethan, seven; Caleb, five.**

The project for today was frogs. We began by reading the fairy tale "The Frog Prince," after which the boys drew pictures of what they thought an enchanted frog should turn into instead of a handsome prince: Josh opted for a poodle, Ethan for a cat, and Caleb for a mink. (He wasn't sure what a mink looked like, so we looked it up.) We then defined and discussed amphibians, drew diagrams of the frog life cycle, and defined metamorphosis. *Josh: "That's what happens when a caterpillar turns into a butterfly, too." We read about how frogs drink and breathe (through their skins) and studied a picture of a frog skeleton, attempting to identify what frogs are missing (bonewise) that humans have. Ethan got it: "Frogs have no ribs!"*

We looked at lots of frog pictures in various reference books and discussed the many kinds of frogs and their wide range of sizes. The boys made simple bar graphs, comparing the sizes of the little grass frog, the bullfrog, and the Goliath frog. We talked about frogmen and their equipment, and the boys drew pictures of themselves in selected underwater gear. We calculated how far each boy should be able to jump if he were a frog (20 times body length) and measured how long a jump each kid could actually make (about one times body length) and I told an abbreviated version of Mark Twain's "The Celebrated Jumping Frog of Calaveras County," which the boys thought hilarious.

We read about frog ears and eyes and learned how to tell a male frog from a female frog. The kids studied all the frog pictures in Joanna Cole's A Frog's Body *(lots of terrific color photographs) and Douglas Florian's* Discovering Frogs *(all stylized drawings, which were less helpful, but some interesting information). The boys then each dissected a frog, which was a great hit—and, though* it's a finicky process, they all did excellent jobs. Using the key from William Berman's How to Dissect (see page 276), they managed to identify the sex of their frogs (all female), checked out the attachment of the tongue ("In front!"), and identified the esophagus, stomach, intestines, liver, heart, lung, oviducts, cloaca, and kidneys. They discussed frog skin color and camouflage. Josh: "Do frogs usually have spots?" All identified the frog's transparent third eyelid, and Ethan carefully dissected out the lens of the eye. Ethan: "How does this work?"

They then put on swim goggles and hopped off to play a game of Giant Alien Frogs.

Books

Aardvarks to Zebras
Melissa S. Tulin; Citadel Press, 1995

A fat and fascinating collection of animal science, history, folklore, and anecdotes—plus attention-grabbing facts in boxes (Napoléon was scared of cats; the giant panda's closest relative looks like a raccoon) and animal quizzes. The book covers all the families in the animal kingdom, as well as mythical animals, animals in religion, and animals in the popular culture. A fun resource for families.

Animal Alphabet Series
Jerry Pallotta; Charlesbridge Publishing

A series of attractive alphabet books, each featuring a different kind of animal. Titles include The Frog Alphabet Book, The Furry Alphabet Book, and The Yucky Reptile Alphabet Book. The Frog Alphabet Book, for example, includes color paintings and a bit of interesting information about 26 different frogs (and friends), from Amazon horned frog to Zigzag salamander.

The Beginner's Guide to Animal Autopsy: A Hands-In Approach to Zoology
Steve Parker; Copper Beech Books, 1997

A highly helpful guide for dissection projects, illustrated with cartoonlike drawings showing a range of animals and their internal organs.

See **Dissecting Kits** (page 275).

Benny's Animals and How He Put Them in Order
Millicent Selsam; HarperCollins, 1966

An introduction to taxonomy for kids aged 5–8. Benny, who likes to classify things, struggles to sort his many pictures of animals into proper categories. He finally succeeds with the help of a museum expert.

Chickens Aren't the Only Ones
Ruth Heller; Price Stern Sloan, 1993

Chickens Aren't the Only Ones is an enchantingly illustrated picture book with a brief rhyming text all about egg layers—not only chickens, but snakes, lizards, crocodiles, turtles, dinosaurs, frogs, fish, octopi, spiders, snails, insects, and two peculiar mammals: the spiny anteater and the duck-billed platypus. The equally beautiful follow-up, *Animals Born Alive and Well* (1993), covers the many different kinds of mammals. Read both and your youngest zoologists will never forget the meanings of *oviparous* and *viviparous*.

The Children's Animal Atlas: How Animals Have Evolved, Where They Live Today, Why So Many Are in Danger
David Lambert; Millbrook Press, 1992

Zoogeography for kids aged 9–12. The book includes maps showing the locations of various animals, an interesting text explaining how animals have evolved to fill various ecological niches on the planet, and information on environmental dangers to animals.

Extremely Weird Series
Sarah Lovett; John Muir Publications

A series of 48-page books illustrated with full-page color photographs. Each photograph is paired with scientific illustrations and an interesting explanatory text. Each book covers a single group of "extremely weird" animals or animal behaviors. Titles include *Extremely Weird Reptiles*, *Extremely Weird Mammals*, *Extremely Weird Primates*, and *Extremely Weird Disguises*.

Extremely Weird Bats, for example, includes 21 strange-looking bats, among them the fisherman bat, the frog-eating bat, Townsend's big-eared bat (which has ears like a rabbit), the Gothic bat (which has a nose shaped like a sword), and the not-so-weird little brown bat. For all ages.

From bookstores or
John Muir Publications
Box 613
Santa Fe, NM 87504
(505) 982-4078 or (800) 888-7504

Eyewitness Series: Zoology
Alfred A. Knopf

A large series of 64-page groups on a range of themes, each lushly illustrated with color photographs, diagrams, and drawings, all with detailed explanatory captions. Zoology-related titles in the series include *Amphibian, Bird, Cat, Dog, Elephant, Fish, Horse, Mammal,* and *Reptile.*

How Nature Works
David Burnie; Reader's Digest, 1990

"100 Ways Parents and Kids Can Share the Secrets of Nature" in 192 pages. The book begins with the basic chemistry of life and the simplest organisms, and continues through fungi and flowering plants, trees, fish, insects, birds, reptiles, and mammals, each with associated projects, activities, and experiments. Each activity includes precise step-by-step instructions, illustrated with wonderful color photographs. Sample projects include taking transect and quadrant plant surveys, measuring the height of a tree, building a moth trap, dissecting owl pellets, and experimenting with a model lung.

See **How Things Work Series** (page 235).

Of Kinkajous, Capybaras, Horned Beetles, Seladangs, and the Oddest and Most Wonderful Mammals, Insects, Birds, and Plants of Our World
Jeanne K. Hanson and Deane Morrison; HarperPerennial, 1992

Contains 277 short—some very short—vignettes on animal and plant life, filled with fascinating tidbits of information. Titles include "The Real Sea Monsters," "Tadpole Meringue," "Are Sloths Slothful?," "Why Do Some Beetles Have Horns?," "Poison-Packing Amphibians," "The Most Artistic Animal," "The Irritated Oyster," "Insect Thermometers," and "How Dangerous Are Vampire Bats?" Great for reading aloud bit by bit, in odd moments.

The Robot Zoo: A Mechanical Guide to the Way Animals Work
John Kelly; Turner Publishing, 1994

Terrific cutaway robotic diagrams explain the functions of biological systems in a number of different animals.

What's Hatching Out of That Egg?
Patricia Lauber; Crown, 1991

A superb collection of black-and-white photographs of just-hatching eggs and newly hatched infants, in fascinating detail. Included are newborn ostriches, crocodiles, spiders, bullfrogs, octopi, penguins, salmon, green turtles, monarch butterflies, snakes, and even an infant duck-billed platypus.
Also see **Chickens Aren't the Only Ones** (page 339).

Why Is a Frog Not a Toad?
Q. L. Pearce; Lowell House, 1992

A 32-page picture book about pairs of animal species that look alike but aren't. Pearce explains the differences between such deceptive duos as frogs and toads, crocodiles and alligators, butterflies and moths, bees and wasps, wolves and coyotes, and jaguars and leopards.

Zoobooks Series
A large collection of short (17 pages) illustrated booklets, each concentrating on an individual animal or animal group. The text is short and interesting, illustrated with color photographs, paintings, and diagrams. Each issue also includes hands-on activities and puzzles. There are 59 booklets in the series, from "Alligators & Crocodiles" and "Animal Babies" through "Wolves" and "Zebras."

Can be purchased individually or obtained by subscription (one book a month for an annual fee of $20.95)
Zoobooks
Wildlife Education Ltd.
9820 Willow Creek Rd., Suite 300
San Diego, CA 92131
(800) 477-5034/fax (619) 678-9658

Biographies of Zoologists

Batman: Exploring the World of Bats
Laurence Pringle; Macmillan, 1991

Laurence Pringle has written several short books on the life and work of modern-day zoologists, each illustrated with color photographs. The books also include information about the animals each scientist studies. *Batman,* for example, is the story of Merlin Tuttle, founder of Bat Conservation International, and his bats. *Elephant Woman* (Atheneum, 1997) is an account of the work of Cynthia Moss, whose research on elephants has helped protect them from poachers. Also see *Dolphin Man* (1995), *Jackal Woman* (1993), and *Scorpion Man* (1994).

Carl Linnaeus: Father of Classification
Margaret Jean Anderson; Enslow Publishing, 1997

A 128-page biography of Linnaeus, the 18th-century Swedish botanist who devised the system of binomial nomenclature used to classify living things today. For readers aged 10–13.

Dian Fossey: Befriending the Gorillas
Suzanne Freedman; Raintree/Steck Vaughn, 1997

A 112-page biography of the life and accomplishments of Dian Fossey, the zoologist famed for her work with mountain gorillas in central Africa, for readers aged 9–12.

For teenagers, see Fossey's own account of her landmark gorilla research in *Gorillas in the Mist* (Dian Fossey; Houghton Mifflin, 1988). Also see the video of the same name, starring Sigourney Weaver as Fossey.

Earthkeepers: Observers and Protectors of Nature
Ann T. Keene; Oxford University Press, 1992

A collection of short biographies of over 100 naturalists, among them Carl Linnaeus, Rachel Carson, Jane Goodall, John and William Bartram, and John Muir. The book is arranged chronologically; included are color and black-and-white illustrations, fact sidebars, and informational appendices. For readers aged 12 and up.

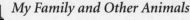

My Family and Other Animals
Gerald Durrell; Peter Smith Publishing, 1983

Gerald Durrell—naturalist, zoo collector, and humorist—describes his animal-filled childhood on the Greek island of Corfu. The book is a mix of zoology, anecdote, and autobiography, centering around a 10-year-old's adventures with butterfly net, jam jar, and an island full of toads, scorpions, geckos, and octopi.

Durrell has written many other books about his life with animals; all are delightful. For kids aged 9 and up. Fun for all ages.

My Life With the Chimpanzees
Jane Goodall; Minstrel Books, 1996

An autobiography written for readers aged 9–12 in which naturalist Jane Goodall describes her life and work with African animals, particularly with the chimpanzees of the Gombe Stream Reserve in Tanzania.

For teenagers, see a more complete account of Goodall's chimpanzee research in *In the Shadow of Man* (Houghton Mifflin, 1988).

The Tarantula in My Purse and 172 Other Wild Pets
Jean Craighead George; HarperTrophy, 1997

The author of *Julie of the Wolves* (see page 110) tells the stories of the many wild creatures that lived with her family while her children were growing up, among them a screech owl who liked television and toy trains, a bat who frequented the refrigerator, and 170 other creatures, from raccoons to ferrets to boa constrictors. For kids aged 9 and up.

Literature Links to Zoology: for Adults

The Bat-Poet
Randall Jarrell; HarperTrophy, 1996

The bat—"a little light brown bat, the color of coffee with cream in it"—stays awake in the daytime, discovers all the wonders of the sunlit world, meets an admiring chipmunk and an overly sensitive mockingbird, and invents magical poems about all he sees. His last and favorite poem, though, just before he falls asleep with the other bats for the long winter, is about the nighttime life of bats.

Of Bugs and Beasts: Fact, Folklore, and Activities

Lauren J. Livo, Glenn McGlathery, and Norma J. Livo; Teacher Ideas Press, 1995

Chapters cover a wide range of animals, among them bats, snakes, coyotes, skunks, and toads. For each is included associated folktales and legends, scientific background information, and suggestions for projects and activities. For kids of all ages.

$23.50
Libraries Unlimited
Box 6633
Englewood, CO 80155-6633
(303) 770-1220 or (800) 237-6124/fax (303) 220-8843
e-mail: lu-books@lu.com
Web site: www.lu.com

Consider the Lemming

Jeanne Steig; Farrar, Straus & Giroux, 1988

A delightful collection of humorous animal poems about such creatures as the penguin, the parrot, the elephant, and the weasel. And, of course, the lemming.

Exploring the World of Animals: Linking Fiction to Non-fiction

Phyllis J. Perry; Teacher Ideas Press, 1997

Fiction and nonfiction books about animals, listed under four categories: animals as pets, farm animals, animals in the woods, and animals in the wild. Included are plot summaries of the books, discussion questions, and suggestions for student projects. For kids in grades K–5.

$24.50
Libraries Unlimited
Box 6633
Englewood, CO 80155-6633
(303) 770-1220 or (800) 237-6124/fax (303) 220-8843
e-mail: lu-books@lu.com
Web site: www.lu.com

The Jungle Book

Rudyard Kipling; Children's Classics, 1989

The classic tale of Mowgli, raised in the jungle by wolves, educated in its ways by Baloo the bear and Bagheera the panther, and threatened by Shere Khan, the great tiger. This version also includes several of Kipling's other animal tales, among them "Rikki-Tikki-Tavi," the story of the gallant mongoose who protects his people from Nag and Nagina, the cobras.

The Just-So Stories

Rudyard Kipling; Children's Classics, 1987

A wonderful collection of animal stories, including "How the Camel Got His Hump," "How the Rhinoceros Got His Skin," "The Cat That Walked By Himself," and—our boys' favorite—"The Elephant's Child."

Stellaluna

Janell Cannon; Harcourt Brace, 1993

Stellaluna, a very young bat, crashes into a bird nest and is raised by the birds until she finally finds her own mother again. It's a nicer version of the "Ugly Duckling" story—little Stellaluna clearly isn't a bird; she hangs upside-down and wakes up at night—but her differences are special, not sneered at. After she returns to the bats, she and her bird family stay friends.

The Wainscott Weasel

Tor Seidler; HarperTrophy, 1996

The enchanting illustrated story of the animals who live in Wainscott Wood on the shore of Long Island. The young weasel, Bagley Brown Jr., struggles to save his beloved Bridget, a fish, from a predatory osprey. A chapter book for kids aged 8–11.

Watership Down

Richard Adams; Scribner, 1996

A rich and exciting tale of very real rabbits and their complex society, complete with language, legends, religious beliefs, and social hierarchy. Developers are moving in and the rabbits must move away from their home. A tale of adventure, trial, tragedy, and triumph, as Hazel and friends set out for new territory, departing "fu Inle," which means—in rabbit—"after moonrise." For readers aged 12 and up.

The Wind in the Willows

Kenneth Grahame; Viking, 1983

The classic tale of the Mole, the Water Rat, the wise Badger, and the obstreperous Mr. Toad (and his motorcar). For all ages.

Zoo

Ogden Nash; Stewart, Tabori & Chang, 1987

A collection of short poems about animals, among them the clam, the ant, the armadillo, the kangaroo, and the panther. ("If called by a panther/Don't anther.")

ACTIVITY BOOKS

Animals and Birds

Florence Temko; Millbrook Press, 1996

A paper-crafts book including step-by-step instructions for making many creative paper animals, among them a jumping frog, a butterfly ornament, and a shiny aluminum foil swan. For kids aged 9–12.

The Curiosity Club Kids' Nature Activity Book

Allene Roberts; John Wiley & Sons, 1992

Puzzles, projects, experiments, stories, games, and a lot of scientific information, for kids aged 6–12. The book is divided into seven major sections: "Trees," "Green Plants," "Soil," "Animals," "Birds," "Insects and Spiders," and "Weather." Readers invent their own plants in "The Adaptation Game," solve a mysterious "track story," and make leaf rubbings, a model honeycomb, and a wind sock.

The Kids' Nature Book: 365 Indoor/Outdoor Activities and Experiences

Susan Milord; Williamson, 1996

Nature activities for every day of the year, for kids aged 8–12. Users monitor meteor showers, catch fireflies, hatch frog eggs, measure trees and keep tree diaries, and stuff a pillow with cattail fluff.

Zoology: 49 Science Fair Projects

H. Steven Dashefsky; McGraw-Hill, 1994

A fascinating selection of science projects for serious student researchers aged 12 and up. The author provides detailed instructions for each project, emphasizes accurate methods of data collection and analysis, and includes thought-provoking follow-up questions. Sample projects involve determining respiration rates in goldfish and identifying antigens in human blood.

COLORING AND STICKER BOOKS

The Ultimate Animal Sticker Book

Dorling Kindersley, 1994

Sixty stickers, each terrific color photographs of such animals as lions, tigers, and bears. Kids peel and place them within the proper outlined shape in the text. Includes brief, interesting information.

Wild Animals Coloring Book

John Green; Dover Publications

A zoology coloring book with over 40 black-line drawings of such animals as snow leopards, giant pandas, and kangaroos, accompanied by a brief informational text. Other related titles include *African Plains Coloring Book, North American Desert Life Coloring Book, Reptiles and Amphibians Coloring Book,* and *Monkeys and Apes Coloring Book.*

$2.95

Dover Publications, Inc.

31 E. Second St.

Mineola, NY 11501

The Zoology Coloring Book

Lawrence M. Elson; Barnes & Noble, 1982

A 200+-page collection of detailed black-and-white scientific drawings and diagrams, with a very thorough high school– to college-level text. The book covers the basics of animal development and includes inner details of many kinds of animals, from the sea anemone, the clam, and the earthworm to the grasshopper, the frog, and the fetal pig. A good accompaniment for dissection projects. For definitely advanced colorers. Also see *The Biology Coloring Book* (Robert D. Griffin; Barnes & Noble, 1986).

GAMES AND HANDS-ON ACTIVITIES

SCIENCE

[8][+] *Alpha Animals*

A nature-based board game in which players proceed around the (mostly green) A-to-Z alphabetical playing board one step at a time, attempting to name an animal that begins with the landed-upon letter. The roll of a die on each turn determines which type of animal must be named: mammal, reptile, bird, fish, insect, or amphibian (or free choice). Periodically players land on an "Alpha Space" and must draw an Alpha Card and attempt to answer a question about zoology or natural history.

An accompanying instruction book includes long, alphabetized lists of animal names for those who simply can't think of a fish beginning with *K*.

$25
Aristoplay
450 S. Wagner Rd.
Ann Arbor, MI 48107
(800) 634-7738 or (888) GR8-GAME
fax (734) 995-4611
Web site: www.aristoplay.com

[8][+] *Alpha Nature*

A nature-based board game similar in format to "Alpha Animals" (see above). Players move, space by space, around an alphabetical playing path, rolling an eight-sided die on each turn to determine the category of play. Depending on the outcome, they must then name either a tree, edible plant, space object (comet, asteroid, planet), animal, body of water (lake, sea, river), flower, or land mass (continent or country) beginning with the space's letter. Occasionally players land on an "Alpha Card" space, and must draw an Alpha Card and answer a question on science and nature. There are two questions on each card, one "Easier" for younger players, one "Harder" for more advanced kids.

Each game includes an instruction booklet with long, alphabetized lists of helpful hints for those who get stumped for a a tree starting with *U* or a space object starting with *W*. Recommended for two to four players aged 8 and up.

$25 from toy and game stores or
Old Game Store
Route 11/30
Manchester Center, VT 05255
(802) 362-2756 or (800) 818-GAME
Web site: www.vtweb.com/oldgame

[4][7] *Animal Families*

A card game that teaches kids the names of male, female, and baby animals. Cards cover 13 animal families; each is illustrated with a labeled color picture. For kids aged 4–7.

$8
Aristoplay
450 S. Wagner Rd.
Ann Arbor, MI 48107
(800) 634-7738 or (888) GR8-GAME
fax (734) 995-4611
Web site: www.aristoplay.com

[ALL] *AnimalTalk Cards*

A pack of attractive magenta-printed cards intended as conversation starters for talkers of all ages. Each card briefly describes an interesting or unusual animal fact, then poses a question for further discussion, speculation, and imaginative invention. Examples:

The earliest ancestors of kangaroos lived in trees. Today there are eight different kinds of tree kangaroos. They live in the rain forest and only come down from the trees to drink water.

If you lived in a tree, what would your home look like? In what kind of tree would you build it?

Over 7,000 years ago, the cheetah was a symbol of power for the Egyptians. The eagle is a symbol of power for the United States. The bears on the Missouri state flag stand for bravery.

If you could choose any animal to describe you, which animal would you choose? How is it like you?

$5.95
TableTalk
Six Country Life Acres
St. Louis, MO 63131-1403

(314) 997-5676 or (800) 997-5676/fax (314) 997-3602

Web site: www.tbltalk.com

See **Tabletalk** (page 67).

Aqua Scope

ALL For a nondisruptive look at pond life, try the Aqua Scope, a sturdy upside-down periscope for underwater viewing. Users dunk the bottom end in the pond and look through the clear plastic window in the top.

One version is available from

ETA

620 Lakeview Pkwy.

Vernon Hills, IL 60061-99231

(847) 816-5050 or (800) 445-5985/fax (800) ETA-9326

e-mail: info@etauniverse.com

Web site: www.etauniverse.com

Another model, the "Inflatable Underwater Viewer," is available from

Edmund Scientific Co.

101 E. Gloucester Pike

Barrington, NJ 08007-1380

(800) 728-6999

e-mail: scientifics@edsci.com

Web site: www.edsci.com

The Bat Book and See-Through Model

Luann Colombo; Andrews & McMeel, 1995

The kit includes a 48-page informational book on bats, filled with "amazing bat facts," and a snap-together model bat. The bat, complete, hangs upside-down on a plastic stand. Wings are bat brown, but the rest of the bat is clear plastic so that observers can study the bat's internal organs.

$14.95 from bookstores

Frog Hatchery Kit

ALL Frog hatchery kits, available from most science supply stores and catalogs, generally include a plastic aquarium, a pack of tadpole chow, and—sometimes— some underwater landscaping items, such as aquarium gravel and a plant. Also included is a coupon for frog embryos.

Depending on hatchery size, $15 to $30

ETA

620 Lakeview Pkwy.

Vernon Hills, IL 60061

(847) 816-5050 or (800) 445-5985/fax (800) ETA-9326

e-mail: info@etauniverse.com

Web site: www.etauniverse.com

or

Edmund Scientific Co.

101 E. Gloucester Pike

Barrington, NJ 08008-1380

(800) 728-6999

e-mail: scientifics@edsci.com

Web site: www.edsci.com

or

Delta Education

Box 3000

Nashua, NH 03061-3000

(800) 442-5444/fax (800) 282-9560

Web site: www.delta-ed.com

Living Wonders Habitat

ALL The habitat is a clear plastic aquarium with an "escape-proof" lid; it comes with colored gravel, a scenic plastic plant, a water dish, food, and animal-raising instructions. Owners may populate their habitats with any of six animals: land hermit crabs, painted lady butterflies, African frog tadpoles (not available to Californians), dwarf aquarium frogs, fantail goldfish, or American chameleons. Each habitat comes with two animals (of the same kind). Replacement animals and food are available separately. We raised hermit crabs in our habitat; the boys were fascinated.

Habitat, plus two resident animals, about $20

Carolina Biological Supply Co.

2700 York Rd.

Burlington, NC 27215

(800) 334-5551/fax (800) 222-7112

or

Delta Education

Box 3000

Nashua, NH 03061-3000

(800) 442-5444/fax (800) 282-9560

Web site: www.delta-ed.com

or

ETA

620 Lakeview Pkwy.

Vernon Hills, IL 60061

(847) 816-5050 or (800) 445-5985/fax (800) ETA-9326

e-mail: info@etauniverse.com

Web site: www.etauniverse.com

The Nature of Cats

A science kit for pet owners containing a detailed instructions book and materials—among them a catnip mouse—for a series of friendly experiments involving the household cat. Kids test their pets' senses of taste, smell, and hearing, investigate pet memory, and learn how animals really see the world. Also see *The Nature of Dogs* for an equivalent set of experiments featuring the family dog.

$19.95

Scientific Explorer, Inc.

2802 E. Madison, Suite 114

Seattle, WA 98112

(800) 900-1182

Web site: www.scientificexplorer.com/

The Pond Book and Tadpole Tank

The tank has a handle, for gripping while dunking in pond water, and a built-in strainer and magnifying lens in the lid. The accompanying book, by Karen Dawe, is a field and activity guide, with descriptions of over 40 kinds of pond life (that "slither or swim").

$14.95 from bookstores or

Workman Publishing Co.

708 Broadway

New York, NY 10003-9555

(212) 254-5900 or (800) 722-7202/fax (212) 254-8098

Web site: www.workmanweb.com

AUDIOVISUAL ZOOLOGY

All Creatures Great and Small

Based on the book by James Herriot, this delightful video follows the life and adventures of a young veterinarian in a little English village. Humorous and heartwarming for all animal lovers.

$19.99

Movies Unlimited

3015 Darnell Rd.

Philadelphia, PA 19154

(215) 637-4444 or (800) 4-MOVIES

e-mail: movies@moviesunlimited.com

Web site: www.moviesunlimited.com

Eyewitness Video Series: Zoology

Video versions of the books (see page 340), with superb photography and interesting narration, for kids of all ages. Zoology titles in the series include *Fish, Amphibians, Reptiles, Birds, Cats, Dogs, Horses, Elephants, Apes, Shells, Sharks, Insects, Butterflies and Moths*, and *Mammals*. Each video runs about 30 minutes.

$12.95 apiece

Dorling Kindersley Publishing

1224 Heil Quaker Blvd.

LaVergne, TN 37086

(888) DIALDKP

Web site: www.dk.com

Frog Heaven

An hour of frog croaks, honks, squawks, creaks, peeps, and bellows recorded from frogs all over the world. Included are frogs from the Florida Everglades, California, Georgia, Washington state, and Sri Lanka. An impressive performance by the frogs and an education for those who thought frogs only go "Ribbet."

$9.95

World Disc Music

NorthWord Press, Inc.

Box 1360

Minocqua, WI 54548

(800) 336-6398

Lyrical Life Science Volume 2: Mammals, Ecology, and Biomes

Sixteen science songs, each set to a well-known popular tune, covering the major orders of mammals, general ecology, and biomes. Included are such ditties as "Ungulates: The Hoofed Mammals" to the tune of "Home on the Range" and "Bats," to the tune of "Take Me Out to the Ball Game." The information is accurate; the songs are simply priceless.

The set includes an audiocassette and a 112-page illustrated text with detailed scientific background information, all the song lyrics, and sheet music. There's also an optional student workbook.

Tape and text, $20; with workbook, $25

Lyrical Learning

8008 Cardwell Hill

Corvallis, OR 97330

(541) 754-3579

National Geographic Video

Many excellent titles on animals.

National Geographic Home Video

Box 5073

Clifton, NJ 07015

(800) 627-5162

Web site: www.nationalgeographic.com

The Trials of Life Series

David Attenborough's acclaimed BBC series on the struggles animals go through to survive and raise their families. Titles in the series include "Arriving," "Growing Up," "Finding Food," "Hunting and Escaping," "Home-making," "Living Together," "Fighting," "Friends and Rivals," "Finding the Way," "Talking to Strangers," "Courting," and "Continuing the Line." Attenborough, with fascinating narration and wonderful film footage, covers everything from the care of orphaned babies by elephants to the elaborate nests of weaver birds to whale song. Each video runs about 60 minutes.

Series, $249.95

Movies Unlimited

3015 Darnell Rd.

Philadelphia, PA 19154

(215) 637-4444 or (800) 4-MOVIES

e-mail: movies@moviesunlimited.com

Web site: www.moviesunlimited.com

ZOOLOGY ON-LINE

Amazing Animal Facts

"A Collection of Totally Useless Animal Information," all of it fascinating. Users click on an animal icon to discover an array of interesting and unusual facts, illustrated with color photographs. Discover, for example, the name and weight of the world's biggest chicken and the identity and location of the world's deadliest snake.

zebu.cum.msu.edu/~dawsonbn

Animal Omnibus

Links to many animal sites on the web, categorized by family (amphibians, fishes, arthropods, mammals,

birds, mollusks, dinosaurs, and reptiles). Also included are links to sites featuring animal sounds.

www.birminghamzoo.com/ao

The Electronic Zoo

A wealth of animal information on all kinds of animals, listed by category from amphibians, birds, and cats to reptiles, rodents, and small ruminants. The site also includes information on wildlife in general, zoo animals, and fictional animals.

netvet.wustl.edu/ssi.htm

Interactive Frog Dissection

An on-line program initially designed for high school students but equally interesting for younger biologists. Kids can dissect a frog—precise instructions show you the right way to go about it—and identify its internal organs.

curry.edschool.virginia.edu/~insttech/frog

Searching the Animal Diversity Web

Users select an animal and access information about its scientific classification, physical traits and behaviors, and habitat, complete with color photographs and audio clips.

www.oit.itd.umich.edu/bio/biogate-p.cgi/bio/
bio-index

The Tree of Life

Everything for students of animal classification. The site includes detailed diagrams of the family trees of living things, supplemented with an explanatory text and color photographs. Users can search the tree by family or name of a specific organism (frog). A site for investigating phylogeny and biodiversity.

128.196.42.70/tree/phylogeny.html

CHEMISTRY

Chemistry, in the typical school science curriculum, is a late arrival on the scene. Kids generally do not study chemistry in any depth until eighth or ninth grade, when they cover atomic theory, the periodic table of elements, and compounds and mixtures, as part of a general physical sciences class. Chemistry as a full-year course is usually taught in eleventh grade. It's a shame that chemistry does not figure more prominently in elementary-level science programs, since chemistry has tremendous appeal for most kids. It's fascinating, fun, and messy; and enormous amounts of scientific information can be absorbed in the enthralling process of concocting gunks and goos, creating phenomenal fizz, or turning things surprising colors

Stocking a home-style chemistry lab is not difficult. A stock phrase in elementary-level chemistry books is "uses only ordinary household items," which means that most of the described experiments can be handled with spoons, soda straws, paper cups, measuring cups, and other items gleaned from the kitchen cupboards. For older kids interested in a more substantive approach to chemistry, most science supply companies carry such basics as laboratory glassware, test tubes and racks, pipettes, spatulas, plastic tubing, alcohol lamps, and safety goggles.

A solid background in basic chemistry through the high school level can, with a little effort, be acquired at home. That, however, is as far as it goes: advanced chemistry is poisonous, flammable, and involves expensive equipment. If you've got a serious teenaged chemistry student, consider looking into course offerings at a local community college or comparable institution.

From my homeschool journal:

◆ **July 17, 1991. Josh is ten; Ethan, eight; Caleb, six.**

Five kids (aged seven to ten) came over today to share an afternoon of chemistry lessons with the boys. We began by covering the basics of atoms, elements, and compounds; then made aluminum-foil "sugar boats" and cooked sugar in the oven, turning it into a blackened mess of carbon, thus demonstrating that sugar is a carbon-containing compound.

Then explained the principles and uses of chromatography, and the kids all experimented with paper chromatography, separating out the colors in Magic Marker inks.

Defined electrolyte *and identified assorted electrolytes using homemade galvanometers (made by wrapping plastic compasses with bell wire).*

Defined acid, base, *and* pH; *made pH indicator from red-cabbage juice; and tested assorted substances, classifying them as acid, base, or neutral. The kids then tested everything with litmus and hydrion pH paper, which last gives accurate pH readings.*

Discussed solutions and saturated solutions; and each kid started a batch of rock candy. "If we put the sugar solution in the refrigerator, would the crystals form faster?" (We're trying it.)

Everybody got a test tube rack and a handful of test tubes to take home: the boys and Randy made the racks this past weekend out of wood strips and dowels.

The kids all had a great time: they never stopped asking questions. "In chromatography, what if a little molecule travels so fast that it runs right off the end of the paper?" "What does the P in pH stand for?" "What's the pH of sulfuric acid?" "What's the pH of blood?"

MAGAZINES

Chem Matters

A quarterly publication of the American Chemical Society for high school–aged chemistry students. Each 16-page issue includes four illustrated articles on truly interesting chemical topics, plus hands-on activities and a chemistry puzzle. An accompanying four-page "Classroom Guide" includes supplementary information (with references), notes, suggestions, and additional instructions on the lab activities, and lists of questions on each article. Titles of past articles have included "Making Ice Cream: Cool Chemistry," "BuckyBalls," "Peanut Brittle," "Survival at Sea," and "The Making of a Mummy."

Annual subscription (4 issues), published October, December, February, and April, $3.75 (plus $4 postage/handling). Back issues also available
Chem Matters
American Chemical Society
Dept. L-0011
Columbus, OH 43268-0011
(800) 333-9511

WonderScience

A magazine of "Fun Physical Science Activities for Children and Adults to Do Together" intended for elementary school–aged kids and published by the American Chemical Society. Each issue centers around a single topic; back issues, for example, have covered "The Science of Soda," "Rubber," "Playground Physics," "Plant Science," "Toys in Space," "Physics of Music," "The Chemistry of Art," "Static Electricity," and "Surface Tension." Each colorfully illustrated eight-page issue includes short informational articles and clear, simple instructions for several related hands-on science activities, plus a teacher's guide and student worksheets.

Annual subscription (8 issues), $12 (plus $3.50 postage/handling). Back issues, available as annual sets, $7.50 (plus $1.50 postage/handling)

American Chemical Society

Education Division

Room 810

1155 16th St., NW

Washington, DC 20077-5768

(800) 333-9511

Also see **General Science Magazines** (see page 218).

EQUIPMENT AND SUPPLIES

Most scientific supply companies (see page 221) sell laboratory glassware, equipment, and chemicals. Obtaining the latter, unfortunately, can be a problem for homeschoolers: many companies do not sell chemicals to private individuals. Sources that do include:

Aves Science Kit Company

Box 220

Peru, ME 04290

(207) 562-7032

The Wild Goose Company

375 Whitney Ave.

Salt Lake City, UT 84115

(801) 466-1172 or (800) 373-1498

Web site: www.wildgoosescience.com/

BOOKS: CHEMISTRY

Braving the Elements

Harry B. Gray, John D. Simon, and William C. Trogler; University Science Books, 1995

A "nonmathematical" overview of modern chemistry, filled with understandable scientific informa-

tion, historical background, and interesting stories. Sample chapter titles include "The Periodic Table," "Newsworthy Molecules" (medicinal chemicals from aspirin to antibiotics, chemical dependencies, and chemical weapons), "Wall Street Chemistry" (commodity chemicals and petrochemicals), "Biochemistry," and "Atmospheric Chemistry." Readers learn what acid-base reactions have to do with the treatment of ulcers, what the inside of a nuclear reactor looks like, how sunblock works, and the chemical composition of fiberglass. For teenagers and curriculum-designing adults.

Chemically Active!

Vicki Cobb; J. B. Lippincott, 1985

A 154-page introduction to chemistry for middle school–aged kids in which clear and entertaining explanations of fundamental chemical principles are paired with better-than-average hands-on experiments.

In many hands-on children's science books, the scientific principles behind the fun-to-do activities are barely touched upon, leaving kids at a loss when it comes to assembling this new information into a coherent scientific framework. Not here. In *Chemically Active!* each chapter covers a separate chemical topic—matter and its analysis, chemical reactions, electrolytes—alternating a chattily informative text with intriguing experiments designed to illustrate the principles discussed. Matter, for example, explains Cobb in "What's the Matter With Matter?," is complicated stuff, "so the first order of the business of chemistry is to simplify matter: to break down materials into their basic components." Kids then learn several basic methods for doing so and the reasons behind each, experimenting sequentially with filtration, distillation, and crystallization.

Experiments are challenging, which makes them doubly interesting, especially since they all work. Kids "split water" by electrolysis and test the collected gases, make a galvanometer and assess the conductivity of solutions, electroplate a nickel, demonstrate the chemical basis of fireworks, and separate the pigments in spinach leaves using paper chromatography.

Also see **The Secret Life of . . . Series** (page 351).

Chemistry

Ann Newmark; Dorling Kindersley, 1993

One of the silver-covered Eyewitness Science series (see page 226). Each double-page spread concentrates on a different chemical topic, through superb color photographs, drawings, and diagrams, all with detailed captions. Examples include "The first chemists," "Atoms and molecules" (with a photograph of John Dalton's wooden atom models and an electron micrograph of uranium atoms), "The elements," "Investigating compounds," "The periodic table," "Chemical reactions," "Acids and bases," and "The story of chemical analysis."

Chemistry Made Simple

Fred C. Hess; Doubleday, 1984

All the basic information, all in one place. This self-study guide for high school or early college students contains 27 chapters, concisely covering such topics as "The Structure of Matter," "Gases," "Liquids and Solids," and "Electrochemistry." Included are tables, diagrams, and instructions for 30 experiments. A list of practice problems appears at the end of each chapter, with answers at the back of the book.

The Chemy Called Al

Wendy Isdell; Free Spirit Publishing, 1996

Julie falls asleep with her chemistry book under her head and is magically transported to the "Land of Science," where she meets Al, the Chemy-lion, explores the "States of Matter," learns about the elements of the periodic table, and overcomes dangers by using her knowledge of chemistry and math. For readers aged 13 and up.

Also available is a teacher's guide, *Using The Chemy Called Al in the Classroom* (Free Spirit Publishing, 1996).

Book, $5.95; teacher's guide, $6.95

Free Spirit Publishing

400 First Ave. N, Suite 616

Minneapolis, MN 55401-1724

(612) 338-2068 or (800) 735-7323/fax (612) 337-5050

e-mail: help4kids@freespirit.com

Exploring Chemical Elements and Their Compounds

David L. Heiserman; TAB Books, 1992

An element-by-element tour of the periodic table, from hydrogen (1) up to the as-yet-unnamed super-heavy elements. For each element, there's a table of basic physical properties, some chatty historical information, a detailed discussion of chemical behavior and isolation or production methods, and lists of important compounds and known isotopes. A useful and interesting reference for chemists aged 12 and up.

We referred to it in devising a homemade "Guess-the-Element" trivia game, dredging up facts to fit such clues as:

This element was discovered when a farmer's cows refused to drink water from a well in Epsom, England.

This element was discovered when a French chemist added a lot of sulfuric acid to a liquid made from burned seaweed.

The famous World War II German gun, Big Bertha, contained this special metal.

Answers: magnesium, iodine, and molybdenum.

First Books: Chemistry

Franklin Watts

Each 64-page book in this series covers the story of a single element, from its discovery through its present-day uses. *The Story of Carbon* (Mark D. Uehling; 1995), for example, covers the chemistry of carbon and its role in organic chemistry, radiocarbon dating procedures, fossil fuels, and the greenhouse effect; *The Story of Gold* (Hal Hellman; 1996) discusses the place of gold in history and modern technology; and *The Story of Hydrogen* (Mark D. Uehling; 1996) covers hydrogen balloons, the *Hindenburg* disaster, hydrogen fusion, and the hydrogen bomb. Also see *The Story of Iron* (1997), *The Story of Nitrogen* (1997), and *The Story of Oxygen* (1996), all by Karen Fitzgerald.

The Magic School Bus Gets Baked in a Cake: A Book About Kitchen Chemistry

Joanna Cole; Scholastic, 1995

The Magic School Bus, class and all, gets baked in a cake for Ms. Frizzle's birthday. A simple introduction to mixtures and chemical reactions for kids aged 4–8.

See the **Magic School Bus Series** (page 227).

The Periodic Kingdom

P. W. Atkins; Basic Books, 1995

A "geographic" tour of the periodic table, from the vast western desert of metals to the shimmering lakes of mercury and bromine in the east, the strange southern island of the lanthanides and actinides, and, in the north, "like Iceland off the northwestern edge of Europe," the isolated island of hydrogen. The book covers the history and characteristics of the elements and explains their place in the ordered periodic table. For high school–aged readers and older. The book is intended for a general audience. No chemistry background necessary.

The Same and Not the Same

Roald Hoffman; Columbia University Press, 1995

A wonderful overview of modern chemistry by Nobel Prize winner Roald Hoffman, covering the science, history, art, and poetry of this versatile discipline. Hoffman discusses in absorbing detail such purely chemical topics as mirror-image molecules, molecular structure, and chemical synthesis; he also considers the social implications of chemistry and chemistry's often negative public image. The book is illustrated with many color photographs and black-and-white diagrams. For teenagers and up.

The Secret Life of . . . Series

Vicki Cobb

Each book covers the history and chemistry of everyday items, with instructions for associated hands-on experiments and activities. *The Secret Life of Cosmetics*, for example, covers the chemistry of soap, toothpaste, perfume, nail polish, and permanent waves; *The Secret Life of Hardware* explains the chemistry of paint, glue, and batteries; *The Secret Life of School Supplies* covers ink, rubber, paste, and paper. A thoroughly interesting approach to chemistry for kids aged 10 and up.

The Visual Dictionary of Chemistry

Jack Challoner; Dorling Kindersley, 1996

A 64-page volume in the Eyewitness Visual Dictionary series, covering all the fundamentals of chem-

istry through precisely labeled full-color photographs and diagrams. Topics covered include the elements of the periodic table, chemical bonding, chemical reactions, organic chemistry, and biochemistry.

See **Eyewitness Visual Dictionary Series** (page 132).

BOOKS: HISTORY OF CHEMISTRY

Antoine Lavoisier: Founder of Modern Chemistry

Lisa Yount; Enslow Publishing, 1997

A 128-page biography of the 18th-century "Father of Chemistry," famed for the discovery of oxygen.

From Caveman to Chemist

Hugh W. Salzberg; American Chemical Society, 1991

A 294-page history of chemistry, from ancient times to the early 20th century. Chapter titles include "Hellenic Chemical Science," "Medieval and Renaissance Alchemists and Natural Philosophers," and "Lavoisier and the Chemical Revolution."

Marie Curie

Leonard Everett Fisher; Atheneum, 1994

A biography of Marie Curie, the Polish-born scientist who won two Nobel Prizes for her work in chemistry and physics. Dramatic black-and-white illustrations, a map, and a biographical timeline. For readers aged 7–11.

Marie Curie

Ibi Lepscky; Barron's Juveniles, 1993

A very simple picture-book biography of the discoverer of radium, concentrating on her childhood, for kids aged 4–8.

ACTIVITY BOOKS

Adventures With Atoms and Molecules: Chemistry Experiments for Young People

Robert C. Mebane and Thomas R. Rybolt; Enslow Publishing, 1995

Thirty chemistry experiments, tackling—in methodically scientific form—such questions as "Can freezing temperatures harm plants?" For each, the authors include detailed instructions, background information, and suggestions for further projects. For kids aged 11 and up.

Chemical Curiosities: Spectacular Experiments and Inspired Quotes

H. W. Roesky, K. Mockel, and Roald Hoffman; John Wiley & Sons, 1996

Splashy and educational chemistry experiments, coupled with apt literary quotations. Experiments include "Fireworks from Ice," "Volcano," "Barking Dog," and "Eruptions with Zinc and Sulfur."

GEMS Handbooks: Chemistry

The Great Explorations in Math and Science series of teachers' guides from the Lawrence Hall of Science (see page 235) includes many study units involving chemistry for kids of all ages. Sample titles include *Bubble-ology, Chemical Reactions, Discovering Density, Involving Dissolving, Of Cabbages and Chemistry,* and *Solids, Liquids, and Gases.*

University of California
Lawrence Hall of Science Store
Lawrence Hall of Science, #5200
Berkeley, CA 94720-5200
(510) 642-1016/fax (510) 642-1055
Web site: www.lhs.berkeley.edu

How to Make a Chemical Volcano and Other Mysterious Experiments

Alan Kramer; Franklin Watts, 1991

Author Alan Kramer—a.k.a. "Captain Chemical"—is a 13-year-old chemist with an unerring eye for what kids find irresistible. The book is a collection of 30 surefire chemical hits. Each experiment is preceded by a friendly short-story-like introduction, culminating in a brief explanation of the science involved in the experiment. Experiments include making a chemical peacock, an eerie floating eye, lemon gumdrops, invisible ink, and a "Mystical Mothball Tree," as well as a chemical volcano, which is guaranteed to enthrall your kids for hours, if not days or weeks.

Icky Sticky Foamy Slimy Ooey Gooey Chemistry Set

Kristine Petterson, Scholastic, 1997

Twenty-five notably yucky experiments for kids aged 8–12. Readers learn about density gradients, polymer chemistry, and pH through Festering Foam, the Lava Jar, and others of the same ilk.

Science Experiments You Can Eat

Vicki Cobb; HarperCrest, 1994

Cobb turns the family kitchen into a chemistry lab. *Science Experiments You Can Eat* covers eight major scientific topics: "Solutions," "Suspensions, Colloids, and Emulsions," "Carbohydrates and Fats," "Proteins," "Kitchen Chemistry," "Plants We Eat," "Microbes," and "Enzymes." Under each, kids use ordinary items to demonstrate hefty scientific concepts, all clearly and comfortably explained, with friendly little diagrams and illustrations. Young chemists, for example, learn about the phases of solutions while making rock candy, demonstrate the Tyndall effect with a glass of cider, bake a batch of hygroscopic cookies, test fruit juices for iron (with tea), study yeast activity by making bread and pretzels, and observe enzyme activity with junket. And you can eat all the results. Also see, by the same author, *More Experiments You Can Eat* (1994).

Science for Kids: 39 Easy Chemistry Experiments

Robert W. Wood; McGraw-Hill, 1991

A collection of experiments for kids aged 9 and up, each with background information and detailed instructions. Examples include "How to Remove Iodine from Water" and "Soap That Eats an Egg."

Snowflakes, Sugar, and Salt: Crystals Up Close

Chu Maki; Lerner, 1993

All about crystals for kids aged 5–9. The book covers such common crystals as ice, snow, sugar, and salt, and includes instructions for crystal-making experiments. Illustrated with photographs.

Teaching Chemistry With Toys

Jerry L. Sarquis, Mickey Sarquis, and John P. Williams; Learning Triangle Press, 1995

Chemistry activities and experiments for kids in grades K–9, all based on common toys, such as balloons, paint-with-water books, fortune-telling fish, weather bunnies, lightsticks, Silly Putty, drinking birds, and all kinds of things that glow in the dark. Experiments are categorized by appropriate age group (for grades K–3, 4–6, or 7–9).

CHEMISTRY KITS

Nearly all scientific supply companies (see page 221) sell chemistry experiment kits in various sizes, styles, and complexities.

Aves Science Kit Company

Small packaged science kits targeted at kids in independent or home study programs.

> Aves Science Kit Co.
> Box 229
> Peru, ME 04290

Carolina Biological Supply Company

Chemistry equipment, supplies, and many chemistry kits, large and small. Among these is a series of kits for advanced placement high school chemistry programs. These include chemicals, a teacher's manual, and student worksheets; you come up with your own laboratory glassware and supplies. Many of the chemistry kits are available only in classroom sizes, containing enough materials for 30 students; some are also available as student or "demonstration" kits, suitable for one to three kids.

> Carolina Biological Supply Co.
> 2700 York Rd.
> Burlington, NC 27215
> (800) 334-5551/fax (800) 222-7112
> e-mail: carolina@carolina.com

Edmund Scientific Company

A good source for chemistry kits and lab demonstrations. Samples from the catalog include chemical lightsticks (in six different colors), a "Make Your Own

Chewing Gum Kit," a superball molding kit, and a large selection of interesting chemical quickies. Among these are the "Chemistry Tub Kits," which include all the materials for several related experiments packaged in a neat little plastic tub. Titles include the "Patriotic Colors Chemistry Experiment Kit," with which kids can turn three colorless solutions, respectively, red, white, and blue; and the "Goofy Glowing Gel Kit," with which kids can make several oozy polymers, including one that glows in the dark.

> Edmund Scientific Co.
> 101 E. Gloucester Pike
> Barrington, NJ 08007-1380
> (800) 728-6999/fax (609) 547-3292
> e-mail: scientifics@edsci.com

Lab-Aids

Lab-Aids approaches chemistry seriously: no glitz and no zany illustrations. Available is a large assortment of thematic chemistry kits for elementary and upper-level students. Titles for younger students include the "Identification of Chemical Reactions Kit," with which kids learn to identify four kinds of chemical reactions with seven different solutions; titles for older students include the "Introduction to Oxidation-Reduction Kit," "Flame Tests and Emission Spectroscopy Experiment," and "Qualitative Analysis Chromatography Kit."

Most Lab-Aids kits are intended for classroom-size groups and include materials for 12 to 15 pairs of students; despite this, however, some are reasonably priced, and home learners can always (1) use the extra stuff, or (2) share.

> Lab-Aids, Inc.
> 17 Colt Ct.
> Ronkonkoma, NY 11779
> (516) 737-1133/fax (516) 737-1286

Wild Goose Company

The kits are available as "MegaLabs," which include materials for 10 or so related experiments, or as "ChemShorts," which contain materials for a particularly appealing experiment. Chemistry Megalabs include "Slime Chemistry," a gooey introduction to colloids and polymers; "Crash & Burn Chemistry," which centers around comparisons of chemical and physical reactions; "Oooh Aaah Chemistry," which features pH indicators, a touch of rocket engine design, and a truly spectacular smokescreen; "Kitchen Table Chemistry," which shows kids how basic chemical principles can be demonstrated with ordinary kitchen materials; and "Microcrystal Chemistry," with which kids produce an array of colorful and very fast-growing crystals. All include thorough and kid-friendly instruction books, attention-grabbing experiments, and hilarious illustrations. Variously recommended for kids in grades K–6.

"MegaLabs," 29.95; "ChemShorts," $5 to $6

Wild Goose Co.

375 Whitney Ave.

Salt Lake City, UT 84115

(801) 466-1172 or (800) 373-1498/fax (801) 466-1186

HANDS-ON ACTIVITIES

Friendly Chemistry

A terrific book-and-game set for beginning chemists. "This book," begins the introduction, "was written to serve as a general chemistry guide to be used by any student, of any age, who is curious about chemistry." The book is a fat (250+ pages) yellow wire-bound manual, stuffed with illustrations, charts, diagrams, and capsule biographies of famous chemists, as well as a lot of substantive information presented, as promised, in very friendly fashion. The book is designed to be written in—there are tables to complete, exercises, problems, and spaces for notes—but a little judicious copying allows multiple kids to share. Sample chapter titles include "Delving Into the Atom," "The Arrangement of Electrons, Protons, and Neutrons," "Applying Quantum Mechanics," "Relating Electron Configuration to Reactivity," "Ion Formation," and "Chemical Reactions and Equations." Also included are a glossary of chemical terms, an appendix of sample practice problems, and the rules of all the games.

The "Friendly Chemistry" set includes the materials and instructions for nine games (each with assorted variations), variously intended to teach kids the orbital arrangements of electrons, the names and chemical symbols of the elements of the periodic table, element families, ion symbols and charges, and the formulae, weights, and compositions of chemical compounds. Electron arrangement, for example, is taught with the "Doo-Wop Board," in which labeled rows of little plastic cups set in heavy cardboard represent electron orbits and a handful of fuzzy pom-poms, in red or white, represent electrons (the different colors indicate clockwise or counterclockwise spins). Users, referring to their periodic tables, fill the cups with the proper numbers of pom-poms (Doo-Wops) for each element and then translate the results into written orbital notation. Chemical symbols are taught with a game of "Element Bingo": the game leader draws an Element Flashcard and reads the name of the listed element; players attempt to locate the element's symbol on their playing cards. If it is present, they mark it with a colored playing chip. The first chemist to get five symbols in a row yells "Bingo!" and—if all symbols are correct—wins the game.

The "Friendly Chemistry" set, including the book, two sets of flashcards (elements and ions), three sets of game cards, game boards, Doo-Wop board and Doo-Wops, playing chips, and score cards, $120. Set components can also be purchased separately.

Hideaway Ventures

HC 68 Box 20

Westerville, NE 68881

(308) 935-1264 or (800) 774-3447

e-mail: hideaway@juno.com

Molecular Model Kits

ALL Molecular model kits are assortments of colored balls, in plastic, wood, or Styrofoam, plus connecting struts, with which kids can assemble models of atoms or inorganic or organic molecules.

Kits, generally about $10 to $30

Lab-Aids, Inc.

17 Colt Ct.

Ronkonkoma, NY 11779

(516) 737-1133

or

Schoolmasters Science

745 State Circle

Box 1941

Ann Arbor, MI 48106

(800) 521-2832/fax (313) 761-8711

Web site: www.school-tech.com

or

Edmund Scientific Co.

101 E. Gloucester Pike

Barrington, NJ 08007-1380

(800) 728-6999

e-mail: scientifics@edsci.com

Web site: www.edsci.com

or

Carolina Biological Supply Co.

2700 York Rd.

Burlington, NC 27215

(800) 334-5551/fax (800) 222-7112

TOPS Chemistry Modules

TOPS Learning Systems publishes several modules of chemistry topics aimed at kids in grades 7–12. Each is a collection of open-ended "Task Cards" listing an experimental objective, instructions, and questions to answer based on experimental results. Answers, explanations, and detailed teachers' notes are included. Sample modules for chemists include "Analysis" (16 lessons), in which kids study quantitative and qualitative analysis and experiment with titration; "Oxidation" (16 lessons), in which they experiment with burning, breathing, and rusting, and calculate the percentage of oxygen in room air; "Solutions" (28 lessons), in which they study dilute, concentrated, and saturated solutions, make colloidal suspensions, and experiment with distillation and crystallization; and "Cohesion/Adhesion" (24 lessons), in which they learn about surface tension and capillary action, perform ink-spot chromatography, and investigate the chemical action of soaps. All TOPS modules use very simple materials in very creative ways.

$8 to $13

TOPS Learning Systems

10970 S. Mulino Rd.

Canby, OR 97013

(888) 773-9755/fax (503) 266-5200

Web site: www.topscience.com

See **TOPS** (page 224).

GAMES

Chem Cubes

The "Chem Cubes" look like colored dice and are available in two sets, "Elements" and "Ions." Each set contains six cubes. "Elements" cubes, which have a different chemical symbol on each face, are used to teach names and chemical symbols of common metallic and nonmetallic elements, use of the periodic table, and the writing of simple chemical equations. "Ions" cubes show the chemical symbol and valence of common ions. Instructions are included for nine games in which players learn about ions, radicals, binary compounds, and replacement equations. For two to six players, aged 12 and up.

Each game, $13.95

Carolina Biological Supply Co.

2700 York Rd.

Burlington, NC 27215

(800) 334-5551

ElementO

This is a Monopoly-style board game for young chemists, based on the periodic table of elements. There's a bright-colored periodic table in the center of the board, surrounded by a playing path on which each square represents a different element. Each element on the path is identified by both chemical symbol and name, which is useful for those who either don't know or can't remember that *Nb* stands for *niobium*. The cash, which looks just like Monopoly money, in the same Necco-wafer colors, comes in the form of "proton" and "neutron" certificates. Players start the game with an allotted stash of each and collect 50 additional neutrons every time they work their way around the board and pass Start.

The object of the game is to collect as many protons as possible, while jockeying your opponents into protonless chemical bankruptcy. This is done by laying claim to elements and element groups. Players who manage to corner a whole group of elements are in a formidable position; anybody who lands on any one of the group must pay the owner the entire group's worth in protons. This can be horrifically expensive, and is the "ElementO" equivalent of slapping a hotel on Boardwalk.

The inert gases (He, Ne, Ar, Kr, Rn, and Xe) cannot be purchased; players who land on one of these must draw one of the 30 "ElementO Cards." The cards add human interest to the game: each lists some object or function with which a given element is associated. Examples include: "BATTERY SALE! *Lithium* required for rechargeable batteries. Each player gives you 3 protons." "RUST! You left Dad's tools outside. Give allowance to *Iron* works. Pay 6 protons." "LIGHT BULBS! *Tungsten* required for filament. 74 protons."

The game has a couple of shortcomings. First, no explanatory background information on the periodic table is included, which may leave absolute beginners and those nonchemist adults who haven't laid a finger on a test tube since high school at loose ends. Before tackling "ElementO," you might consider priming your players with a book or two, such as Vicki Cobb's *Chemically Active!* (see page 349).

Second, the periodic table as pictured on the "ElementO" game board lists no atomic weights, which means that players have no opportunity to see where all those mysterious numbers of neutrons are coming from. A quick explanation of atomic number and atomic weight would add a lot to the basic premise of the game. And finally, there aren't enough of those interesting "ElementO Cards."

These quibbles aside, "ElementO" is attractive, fast paced, and fun; and players, after a few rounds, do learn all the elements of the periodic table by name, number, and chemical symbol, which is no small feat. The game is recommended for two to six players, aged 10 and up.

$31.95 (plus $3.95 shipping/handling)
ElementO
Lewis Educational Games
Box 727
Goddard, KS 67052
(316) 794-8239 or (800) 557-8777

9 Elements

The board is the periodic table; the playing pieces are colored chips representing the elements. The game—which takes only 15 minutes or so to play—is designed to teach kids the names of the elements, their chemical symbols, and their positions on the periodic table. Recommended for two to six players in grade 7 and up.

$22.95
Carolina Biological Supply Co.
2700 York Rd.
Burlington, NC 27215
(800) 334-5551/fax (800) 222-7112

AUDIOVISUAL CHEMISTRY

13 Chemistry

A high school chemistry class on videotape, emphasizing the mathematical aspects of chemistry. The series includes thirty 30-minute lessons, covering such fundamental chemical concepts as density, stoichiometry, molarity, chemical equilibrium, and pH. The basic information is there; the teacher, however—despite multiple awards for "Outstanding Chemistry Teaching"—is uninspiring and dull. For kids already interested in chemistry who want some mathematical help. The course includes four videotapes and a workbook.

$99.95
The Teaching Co.
7405 Alban Station Ct., Suite A-107
Springfield, VA 22150-2318
(800) 832-2412

COMPUTER SOFTWARE

10 Hungry Frog Chemistry

Kids learn basic chemistry through a series of games based on frogs eating large and bizarre bugs. There are five games in the series. "Chemistry I," for kids in grades 5–12, teaches charges and formulas of common ions; "Chemistry II," for grades 10–12, teaches qualitative analysis; "Chemistry III," for grades 5–12, introduces kids to the periodic table and teaches element names and symbols; "Chemistry IV" and "Chemistry V," for kids in grades 7–12, deal with balancing chemical equations. For Mac or Windows.

Individual games, $23.95; the set of five, $39.95
Science Educational Software, Inc.
Box 60790
Palo Alto, CA 94306
Web site: www.hungryfrog.com

Lift Off!

Students solve real-world chemistry problems, using basic background knowledge and mathematical calculations. Succeed and your spacecraft achieves lift-off, accompanied by impressive NASA film footage. On CD-ROM for Mac or Windows.

$34.95

Sci Tech International

2525 N. Elston Ave.

Chicago, IL 60647

(773) 486-9191 or (800) 622-3345

Web site: info@scitechint.com

CHEMISTRY ON-LINE

The Catalyst

A site for high school chemistry teachers, with many links to general and specific chemistry sites, on-line laboratory experiments, chemistry magazines, and software.

home.fuse.net/thecatalyst

Chem4Kids

A great site for young chemists, covering such fundamentals as matter, atoms, elements, chemical reactions, and math through a clear, friendly text and colorful graphics. Also includes profiles of famous chemists and chemistry quizzes.

www.chem4kids.com

ChemiCool Periodic Table

Users enter the name or chemical symbol of an element or click on its image on a big, multicolored periodic table to access detailed chemical information, arranged in tables.

wild-turkey.mit/edu/Chemicool

Chemistry Tutor

Introduces students to the many different branches of chemistry, explains the major kinds of chemical reactions, and lists information about the common ions and elements. Users can also access a periodic table or ask questions through "ChemTalk!," a helpful question-and-answer page.

tqd.advanced.org/2923/html/index1.html

ChemTeam

Detailed information on a wide range of chemistry topics for high school students. Included is a selection of classic papers in chemistry, a photo gallery of famous chemists, a list of suggested student projects, and instructions for hands-on activities.

dbhs.wvusd.k12.ca.us/ChemTeam

CHEMystery

A virtual chemistry book for high school students covering a wide range of chemistry topics, among them atoms and moles, states of matter, chemical reactions, the periodic table, thermodynamics, acids and bases, and organic chemistry.

tqd.advanced.org/3659

Lawrence Hall of Science

Activities for kids, teacher resources, and tours of exhibits, among them "ChemMystery," in which kids solve a crime using chemistry techniques. The site includes links to the GEMS (Great Explorations in Math and Science) science activity guides (see pages 235, 352).

www.lhs.berkeley.edu

Microworlds

Current research in materials sciences from the Berkeley Labs Advanced Light Source. The sight includes a tour of the Advanced Light Source, an explanation of how it is used to study the structure of materials, and instructions for related student projects, including making model crystals and molecules, studying diffusion, and demonstrating hydrogen bonding.

www.lbl.gov/MicroWorlds

pH Factor

On-line interactive experiments demonstrating the concept of pH. Kids choose an icon from a table of everyday substances, among them lemon juice, Liquid-Plumr, and aspirin, and are shown a pH reading and told whether the substance is an acid or a base. The site includes instructions for pH-related hands-on activities, lesson plans, and teaching suggestions.

www.miami.org/pH

The T.W.I.N.K.I.E.S. Project

Chemistry with a sense of humor. T.W.I.N.K.I.E.S. stands for "Tests With Inorganic Noxious Kakes In Extreme Situations." The site includes instructions for chemistry and physics experiments involving Twinkies, complete with color photographs.

www.owlnet/rice/edu/~gouge/twinkies.html

EARTH SCIENCE: Geology, Meteorology, and Paleontology

GEOLOGY

In our homeschool program, we studied geology as we did the majority of other academic subjects, through a series of multidisciplinary study units, interweaving scientific information and activities with literature, history, geography, math, and the arts. This sounds elegant, but it frequently wasn't.

From my homeschool journal:

◆ **February 22, 1989. Josh is seven; Ethan, six; Caleb, four.**

We started the morning reading books about volcanoes, variously covering famous volcanic eruptions, the different types of volcanoes, how volcanoes form, plate tectonics, and the definitions of magma and lava. The boys and I then mixed up a batch of instant papier-mâché and the kids made elaborate volcano models, complete with cones, parasitic cones, craters, and calderas.

◆ **February 23, 1989**

The boys painted their model volcanoes; then erupted them—repeatedly—using a mix of baking soda and vinegar, plus lots of red food coloring and sprinkles of glitter to simulate sparks.

◆ **February 14, 1992. Josh is ten; Ethan, nine; and Caleb, seven.**

We've been studying New Hampshire in an ongoing series of United States geography units. Today we discussed state nicknames, among them New Hampshire's: "The Granite State." Looked at samples of granite from our rock collection; read about granite in a couple of reference books, identifying it as an igneous rock composed of mica, feldspar, and quartz. Reviewed the definitions of igneous, sedimentary, and metamorphic rock, illustrating each with rock collection samples.

"How hard is granite? Which is harder, granite or steel?"

Explained Mohs' scale of hardness and tested assorted rock specimens.

"So if diamond is the hardest thing there is, how does anybody ever cut a diamond?"

The boys then designed an assortment of spectacular granite tombstones, located the White Mountains on the map of New Hampshire, and made a bar graph comparing the height of Mount Washington to other mountains worldwide.

CATALOGS

Creative Dimensions

A small catalog of rock and mineral collections, fossils, and hands-on earth science kits for kids. Included are seismogram kits (elementary and secondary level), which include reproductions of the seismograms recorded during the 48-hour period of the 1964 Alaskan earthquake and aftershocks; a plate tectonics kit, with which kids can reconstruct the separation of the continents from ancient Gondwanaland; a sand activity kit, with which kids compare characteristics of sand samples from seven beaches; and a Mount St. Helens activity kit, which includes a detailed teacher's guide with suggested activities and reproducible worksheets, a full-color map of Mount St. Helens and the surrounding area, and samples of ash from the 1980 eruption.

Creative Dimensions

Box 1393

Bellingham, WA 98227

(360) 733-5024/fax (360) 733-4321

D. J. Minerals

ALL Earth science supplies, including geologists' tools, field guides, posters and charts, and an enormous inventory of minerals, rocks, and fossils, available individually (in multiple sizes) or packaged as collections.

> D. J. Minerals
> Box 761
> Butte, Montana 59703-0761
> (406) 782-7339

Forestry Suppliers

ALL A catalog of educational materials for "Life, Earth & Environmental Sciences." Included are geologists' tools, field guides, water and soil test kits, weather instruments, and compasses and materials for orienteering programs.

> Forestry Suppliers, Inc.
> Box 8397
> Jackson, MS 39284-8397
> (800) 647-5368/fax (800) 543-4203

MAGAZINES

Earth

12+ A bimonthly magazine on "The Science of Our Planet." Each issue includes a collection of interesting and very well written articles on topics in the earth sciences: geology, paleontology, and meteorology. Regular columns cover earth sciences resources, computer software and book reviews, the latest research news, and "Elements," a column all about them. An advertising section, "The Rock Shop," lists sources for rocks, gems, minerals, fossils, and related products, scheduled events for interested collectors, and field expedition opportunities.

> Annual subscription (6 issues), $20
> *Earth*
> Box 738
> Waukesha, WI 53187-0738
> (800) 533-6644
> Web site: www.earthmag.com

Rock and Gem

12+ A monthly magazine for dedicated rock hounds. Each issue includes informational articles on collecting, digging, and geology in general. The magazine also lists many (often inexpensive) sources for unusual geological specimens, such as Australian opals, gold nuggets, meteorites, and fossils.

> *Rock and Gem*
> Box 6925
> Ventura, CA 93006-9878
> (805) 644-3824

BOOKS

4 8 *The Big Rock*

Bruce Hiscock; Atheneum, 1988

A picture-book history of a very big rock. Hiscock tells the life story of a granite boulder in the Adirondacks. For kids aged 4–8.

12+ *The Crust of Our Earth*

Chet Raymo; Prentice-Hall, 1983

Sixty short illustrated chapters on the closely related fascinations of geology and geography. Chapter titles include "The San Francisco Quake," "Meteor Impact!," "Yellowstone Hot Spot," "The Making of the Great Lakes," "The Making of Cape Cod," "White Cliffs of Dover," "Last Days of Pompeii," "The Great Rift," and "Ancient Life." Readers learn a great deal of basic earth science, as well as the true identity of Atlantis, the site of America's worst recorded earthquake, the origin of New Hampshire's famous granite "Old Man of the Mountains," and the exciting history of the Rock of Gibraltar. A useful and highly interesting resource.

9+ *Discover Nature in the Rocks*

Rebecca Lawton, Diana Lawton, and Susan Panttaja; Stackpole Books, 1997

Interesting and comprehensive information, illustrations, and many related hands-on activities covering all areas of geology. The book, in 216 packed pages, covers minerals, rocks, volcanoes, fossils, erosion, continental drift, earthquakes, and even rocks in space. Each chapter is followed by lists of supplementary books and videos. Activities include making models of sedimentary layers, cooking up a batch of "conglomerate," making a geologic timeline, and making a cardboard Pangaea puzzle. An excellent resource for kids aged 9 and up.

Everybody Needs a Rock
Byrd Baylor; Aladdin, 1987

Everybody needs a special rock—one you find yourself and treasure forever. Baylor includes rules for finding and choosing a very personal rock. For readers aged 4–8.

Eyewitness Series: Geology
Alfred A. Knopf

Geology-related volumes in the Eyewitness series include *Crystal and Gem* (R. F. Symes and R. R. Harding; 1991), *Rocks and Minerals* (R. F. Symes and the staff of the Natural History Museum, London, 1988), and *Volcano and Earthquake* (Susanna Van Rose; 1992). Each is beautifully illustrated with color photographs, drawings, and diagrams. The books are divided into a series of double-page spreads, each covering a single topic. *Rocks and Minerals,* for example, covers "How rocks are formed," "Igneous rocks," "Sedimentary rocks," "Limestone caves," "Metamorphic rocks," "The story of coal," "Rocks from space," "Gemstones," and "Ore minerals and metals." *Volcanoes and Earthquakes* topics include "The world on a plate," "Hot spots," "The great eruption of Vesuvius," "Volcanoes on other planets," and "Measuring earthquake waves."

How to Dig a Hole to the Other Side of the World
Faith McNulty; HarperTrophy, 1990

What's inside the earth? A curious small boy prepares to find out by digging a hole to the other side of the world. He starts out small, in the backyard with a shovel; eventually, equipped with a space-capsule-like power drill, he digs his way through the earth's crust, mantle, and core, pops out in the Indian Ocean, and makes his way back home by submarine. For readers aged 5–9.

How the Earth Works
John Farndon; Reader's Digest, 1992

"100 Ways Parents and Kids Can Share the Secrets of the Earth." This book, targeted at 8–14-year-olds, covers the earth's structure, rocks and soils, the ocean, and the atmosphere. Projects, some of which are ambitious, include making a continental jigsaw, demonstrating mountain formation with clay layers, building a Stevenson screen (a white box with louvered sides, used by weather stations for thermometers) and a wind vane, and testing the fluidity of several different kinds of "lava." Illustrated throughout with color photographs.

See **How Things Work Series** (page 235).

Let's-Read-and-Find-Out Science Series: Geology
HarperTrophy

This series of short, colorfully illustrated science books for readers aged 4–9 includes several geology titles. In *Let's Go Rock Collecting* (Roma Gans; 1997), for example, kids learn about the three major kinds of rocks and how they are formed; in *How Mountains Are Made* (Kathleen Weidner Zoehfeld; 1995), they learn about the layers of the lithosphere, tectonic plates, and volcanoes and discover why there are fossil seashells on top of Mount Everest. *Follow the Water From Brook to Dam* (Arthur Dorros; 1991) traces the path of water from brook to stream to river, over waterfall, through canyon and over manmade dam, until it finally reaches the ocean. The book explains the many ways in which moving water changes the shape of the earth. Also see *Earthquakes* (1990) and *Volcanoes* (1985), both by Franklyn M. Branley.

See **Let's-Read-and-Find-Out Science Series** (page 227).

The Magic School Bus Inside the Earth
Joanna Cole; Scholastic, 1987

Ms. Frizzle's class boards the Magic School Bus for a rock-collecting expedition and ends up burrowing into the depths of the earth. The real geological info is presented at the edge of each page, in the form of short, student-written reports ("How Rock Layers Were Formed" by Molly) printed on three-hole notebook paper. At the end of the trip, the bus is blasted back above ground in a volcanic explosion and floats back to the school parking lot on a rainbow-colored parachute.

See **Magic School Bus Series** (page 227).

On My Beach There Are Many Pebbles
Leo Lionni; Mulberry, 1995

This picture book inspires kids to focus on their surroundings, studying and appreciating the beauty and uniqueness of quite ordinary things—such as pebbles.

See **The Private Eye** (page 239).

 The Pebble in My Pocket: A History of Our Earth

Meredith Hooper; Viking, 1996

A little girl finds a pebble and asks, "Where did you come from, pebble?" The answer begins 480 million years ago, with erupting volcanoes, and continues through the ages, telling of changes in the earth's surface, the rise and fall of seas, the appearance of dinosaurs, the first mammals, and early human beings, and the rise of modern civilization. The pebble is trod upon by dinosaurs, dragged by glaciers, grabbed by cavepeople. Finally, in the 20th century, it is discovered by a curious little girl. The book is illustrated with marvelous color paintings and includes a timeline. For readers aged 9–12.

Roadside Geology Series

A great resource for family field trips. Each 300+-page volume in the series covers the roadside geology of a different state. Included are descriptions of the rocks and landforms found along the state's major highways, general information about the geology of the state, and geologic overviews of selected special areas. *The Roadside Geology of North Dakota,* for example, includes geologic tours of the Black Hills, Mount Rushmore, Wind Cave National Park, and Jewel Cave National Monument. Illustrated with maps and photographs.

Mountain Press Publishing Co.

Box 2399

Missoula, MT 59806

(406) 728-1900 or (800) 234-5308/fax (406) 728-1635

e-mail: mtnpress@montana.com

The Rock

Daniel A. Birchmore; Cucumber Island Storytellers, 1997

The story of a rock's journey through time, thrust up by mountains, worn by the sea, serving as a shelter for animals and a playground for children. The rock remains cheerful and steadfast throughout. A delightful geological tale for readers aged 4–8, illustrated with brilliant crayon drawings.

Seymour Simon's Geology

Seymour Simon; William Morrow

These short books are characterized by beautiful photographs and a concise, clear, and informative text. Titles include *Earthquakes* (1991), *Icebergs and Glaciers* (1987), *Mountains* (1994), and *Volcanoes* (1988). For readers aged 4 and up.

By the author of **Seymour Simon's Astronomy Series** (see page 254).

LITERATURE LINKS TO GEOLOGY

Hill of Fire

Thomas P. Lewis; HarperTrophy, 1985

The story of the sudden appearance of a volcano in a cornfield near a little Mexican village. For readers aged 4–8.

Iktomi and the Boulder: A Plains Indian Story

Paul Gobel; Orchard Press, 1991

The wily trickster Iktomi is trapped by an angry boulder; his efforts to get out from under it explain why today there are boulders scattered about the Great Plains (and, incidentally, why bats have flat faces). Lovely colorful illustrations. For readers aged 5–8.

 The Lucky Stone

Lucille Clifton; Yearling, 1986

A young black girl is given a special stone by her great-grandmother, who tells her its story: it has been passed down through their family since the days of slavery, and has brought good luck to its owners. For readers aged 9–12.

 Sylvester and the Magic Pebble

William Steig; Simon & Schuster, 1988

Sylvester, an endearing little donkey, finds a shiny bright red wishing pebble. He is thrilled with his luck—until he panics at the appearance of a hungry lion and turns himself into a rock. For readers aged 5–9.

Who's That Stepping on Plymouth Rock?

Jean Fritz; Putnam, 1975

A delightful geological trip through history that tells the story of the famous rock that the Mayflower Pilgrims—or "First Comers"—certainly didn't land upon. Their descendants, however, climbed upon it, built a wharf around it, broke it in half, and built a monument over it. Funny, informational, and a great read. For kids aged 8–12.

ACTIVITY BOOKS

Earth Science Learning Activity Packets

Zephyr Press

Spiral-bound learning activity packets, each containing approximately 50 project and activity suggestions presented at two levels, for kids in grades K–3 and 4–8. Titles include *Earth Science, Geology, Rocks and Minerals,* and *Volcanology.* In *Volcanology,* for example, younger kids identify famous volcanoes worldwide, make a volcano diagram and label all its parts, compare the formation of normal mountains and volcanoes, read and illustrate a volcano legend, and make volcano flip books; older kids make maps of the "Pacific Ring of Fire" and timelines showing the dates of famous volcanic eruptions, compare geothermal energy to other types of energy, and invent a volcano game.

$22 each

Zephyr Press

Box 66006

Tucson, AZ 85728-6006

(800) 232-2187/fax (520) 323-9402

e-mail: neways2learn@zephyrpress.com

Web site: www.zephyrpress.com

Earthquake Games

Matthys Levy and Mario Salvadori; Margaret K. McElderry, 1997

A collection of games and experiments that demonstrate the workings of earthquakes and volcanoes for kids aged 9–12.

Geology Crafts for Kids: 50 Nifty Projects to Explore the Marvels of Planet Earth

Alan Anderson, Gwen Diehn, and Terry Frautwurst; Sterling Publications, 1996

A terrific collection of geological information and truly nifty projects for kids aged 8 and up. The book covers a wide range of topics, among them plate tectonics, volcanic eruptions, earthquakes, mountain formation, erosion, fossils, rocks and minerals, and crystals. Kids make paper crystal models, earth crayons, rock jewelry, a seismograph, and a landform pop-up book. Illustrated with wonderful color photographs. The book also includes a geologic "Big Time Line."

Geology Projects for Young Scientists

Bruce Smith and David McKay; Franklin Watts, 1992

Experiments covering such topics as the age of the earth, plate tectonics, earthquakes, and hydrogeology. For kids aged 9–12.

COLORING AND STICKER BOOKS

Rocks and Minerals Coloring Book

T. D. Burns; Dover Publications

There are 36 black-line illustrations of rocks and minerals, with descriptive captions. Artistic geologists can color tourmaline, crazy lace agate, emerald, amethyst, malachite, smoky quartz, and fool's gold.

$2.95

Dover Publications, Inc.

31 E. Second St.

Mineola, NY 11501

The Ultimate Rocks & Minerals Sticker Book

Dorling Kindersley, 1995

The book contains 60 big color-photo stickers, to be peeled and paired to their proper outlines and captions in the text. The stickers are irresistibly attractive: there's a bug in amber, diamonds in kimberlite, rainbow-colored opals, and a wealth of other gemstones, birthstones (all of them labeled by month), crystals, precious metals, and fossils.

$6.95 from bookstores or

Dorling Kindersley Publishing

SCIENCE

1224 Heil Quaker Blvd.
LaVergne, TN 37086
(888) DIALDKP
Web site: www.dk.com

KITS AND SUPPLIES

Common geological kits and supplies for children include crystal kits and dig-your-own-rocks kits. Both are widely available from science supply catalogs and toy and game stores. Crystal kits are fun to set up and end results range (usually) from the interesting to the gorgeous, though the requisite waiting period in between can be hard on the very young and impatient. While most of the fun of rock collecting, for kids of all ages, is the opportunity to get out there with pick, shovel, or bent kitchen spoon to unearth your own, dig-your-own-rock kits are excellent substitutes for those whose digging circumstances are limited (or seasonal).

Crystal Magic Kits

There are four different kinds of "Crystal Magic" kits from Edmund Scientific in which four kinds of truly unusual crystals are grown in glass tubes of silica gel. Titles, which have to do with artistic effect rather than scientific truth, include "Saucer Invasion," "Ocean Bloom," "Stardust," and "Aurora Borealis."

For fans of the Starship *Enterprise,* the company also sells a "Star Trek Space Age Crystal Growing Kit," with which kids can produce 14 kinds of colored crystals, including the famous "dilithium."

Edmund Scientific Co.
101 E. Gloucester Pike
Barrington, NJ 08007-1380
(800) 728-6999
e-mail: scientifics@edsci.com
Web site: www.edsci.com

The Gem Hunter's Kit

Eight rocks and minerals, including copper, fluorite, hematite, obsidian, and ulexite ("television rock"), embedded in a slab of clay. Kids soak the slab in water, then excavate the specimens using a wooden spatula. Included is an illustrated 64-page manual (*The Gem Hunter's Handbook* by Tim Lutz) of general information about gems and specifics on how to identify those included in the kit. A more expensive version of the kit contains a supplementary CD-ROM.

Basic kit, $18.95; CD-ROM version, $29.95
Running Press Book Publishers
125 South 22nd St.
Philadelphia, PA 19103
(215) 567-5080 or (800) 345-5359/fax (800) 453-2884

GeoCore

This kit contains two simulated (made in the laboratory) geological cores: a marine core, containing sample shells, echinoderms, and coral, and a terrestrial core, containing bones, seeds, and fossils (about 40 specimens, total). The accompanying guide helps kids identify their finds. Also included: probes, paintbrushes, and scrapers, specimen bottles and labels.

$9.50
Aves Science Kit Co.
Box 229
Peru, ME 04290

Geologic Time Illustrated

An attractive and information-crammed 23 × 32-inch illustrated chart. A series of world maps aligned horizontally across the top shows the progress of continental drift over time. Vertical columns list the time scales of the major geologic periods; maps and legends link these time periods to geologic and evolutionary events in North America. An illustrated central panel shows a large assortment of representative animals and plants correlated to their place in geologic time, from simple single-celled organisms at the chart bottom through ascending layers of trilobites, crinoids, cycads, dinosaurs, giant sloths, and woolly mammoths.

$7
D. J. Minerals
Box 761
Butte, MT 59703-0761
(406) 782-7339

Gold Panning Kit

Your own gold pan, a packet of gold-containing sand, and an instruction booklet.

Creative Dimensions

Box 1393

Bellingham, WA 98227

(206) 733-5024

Or you can buy a bag of "Mine Rough," soil containing fool's gold and gem fragments and provide your own pan.

Edmund Scientific Co.

101 E. Gloucester Pike

Barrington, NJ 08007-1380

(800) 728-6999

e-mail: scientifics@edsci.com

Web site: www.edsci.com

Introduction to Mineral Crystal Kits

Lab Aids produces kits with a scientifically serious approach to crystals. With the "Introduction to Mineral Crystals Kit," kids build (fold-up cardboard) models of the four basic crystal forms (cubic, tetragonal, orthorhombic, and hexagonal) and compare these to the crystal structures of real minerals. The kit contains enough material to build 60 models (15 of each). The "Geometry of Crystals Kit" is more complex: users build models of six basic crystal shapes using transparent die cuts, insert plastic axes at the indicated center points, and analyze the crystals by measuring axes, angles, and crystal faces. Materials are included for 60 models (10 of each).

With the "Mineral Structure—Cleavage and Fracture Experiment Kit," kids study nine kinds of mineral specimens, showing different cleavage patterns and fracture properties, and learn how these characteristics relate to the commercial uses of each mineral. The "Diamond Crystal Molecular Model" and "Graphite Crystal Molecular Model" kits allow users to build elaborate three-dimensional models of the stuff, respectively, of engagement rings and pencils. "Diamonds" includes 168 plastic carbon atoms and 283 covalent bond linkages; "Graphite" contains 200 carbon atoms, 260 covalent bonds, and 60 (flexible) van der Waal's forces. Each kit includes a detailed instruction manual.

Lab-Aids, Inc.

17 Colt Ct.

Ronkonkoma, NY 11779

(516) 737-1133/fax (516) 737-1286

Make Your Own Geode Kit

The kit includes molds and crystal-growing chemicals for producing two amethyst-colored "geodes," each six inches in diameter.

ETA

620 Lakeview Pkwy.

Vernon Hills, IL 60061

(847) 816-5050 or (800) 445-5985/fax (800) ETA-9326

e-mail: info@etauniverse.com

Web site: www.etauniverse.com

Microcrystal Chemistry Kit

Wild Goose's "Microcrystal Chemistry" kit includes instructions and materials for experiments in which crystals "grow, change color, change shape, and appear instantly in front of your eyes"—these are *small* crystals, but young scientists will still be impressed. The company also sells an "Eggshell Geode" kit with which kids can make an imitation geode by growing copper sulfate crystals in an empty eggshell; the kit also includes a real geode, for comparison purposes.

Wild Goose Co.

375 Whitney Ave.

Salt Lake City, UT 84115

(801) 466-1172 or (800) 373-1498/fax (801) 466-1186

Web site: www.wildgoosescience.com

Microslides for Earth Sciences

Sets of photomicro- and macrographs, for use with the Microslide Viewer (see page 272). Each Microslide set includes a strip of eight photographs and an informational text folder. Geology-related titles include "Rocks and Rock-Forming Minerals," "The Elements," "Minerals and Crystal Systems," "Natural Resources," "Mineral Characteristics and Identification," "Earth History," "Plate Tectonics," and "Minerals and Life."

"Rocks and Rock-Forming Minerals," for example, includes photomicrographs of thin sections of sedimentary, igneous, and metamorphic rocks; the accompanying folder identifies and describes each specimen and explains the rock cycle. "Plate Tectonics" includes eight geologic, biologic, and oceanographic specimens, which support the theory of continental drift; the text folder explains plate tectonics and defines such useful terms as *paleomagnetism* and *geosyncline*.

Microslide sets, $7 apiece
National Teaching Aids, Inc.
1845 Highland Ave.
New Hyde Park, NY 11040
(516) 326-2555/fax (516) 326-2560

Mineral Exploration Kit

Twelve common minerals in gravel: kids pick them out with forceps and identify them using the included streak plate, magnifying glass, and identification booklet.

$17.95
Delta Education
Box 3000
Nashua, NH 03061-3000
(800) 442-5444/fax (800) 282-9560
Web site: www.delta-ed.com

Popcorn Rocks

"Popcorn Rocks" dunked in vinegar sprout puffy crystalline clusters of calcium carbonate. The company is a good source for several other small, inexpensive crystal-growing kits and packs of break-your-own real geodes. Most of these are about the size of Ping-Pong balls. Put them in a sock, whack them with a hammer, and admire the crystalline innards. All from:

American Science & Surplus
3605 Howard St.
Skokie, IL 60076
(847) 982-0870/fax (800) 934-0722
Web site: www.sciplus.com

Prospector's Mystery Rock

Three fossils, four gemstones, and four rocks are embedded in a hunk of clay; kids dig them out, using the included scraper and cleaning tool, and identify them with the accompanying manual.

$24.95
Educational Insights
16941 Keegan Ave.
Carson, CA 90746
(800) 933-3277/fax (310) 605-5048 or (800) 995-0506
Web site: www.edin.com

Rock and Mineral Hunt Kit

Contains 25 specimens, concealingly scrambled in loose gravel. The kit includes cleaning brushes, specimen bags, labels, and an informational guide.

$21.95
ETA
620 Lakeview Pkwy.
Vernon Hills, IL 60061
(847) 816-5050 or (800) 445-5985/fax (800) ETA-9326
e-mail: info@etauniverse.com
Web site: www.etauniverse.com

Rock Tumblers

Rock tumblers polish rocks, turning dull, rough-cut little pebbles into gleaming jewelry-quality stones. They're easy to operate, if you don't mind listening to a small machine growling away day after day on the kitchen counter. (The noise didn't bother our children, but after the third or fourth batch of rocks, I banished the tumbler to the basement where it could grind annoyingly all by itself.) To polish, you place rocks and abrasive polishing grit in the tumbler barrel, attach the barrel to the machine proper, turn on the motor, and let the barrel revolve. It usually takes four (or five) rounds of grinding to get rough rocks to the sleekly polished stage, using four (or five) grades of grit in sequence, from coarse to fine. A single-barrel tumbler is plenty for most families; small models can generally handle about three pounds of little rocks.

Rock tumblers are available through most science supply catalogs. Student models often come with an assortment of rough semiprecious stones, four grades of grits and polish, an instruction manual, and jewelry findings for making wearable ornaments out of the finished products.

Edmund Scientific Co.
101 E. Gloucester Pike
Barrington, NJ 08007-1380
(800) 728-6999
e-mail: scientifics@edsci.com
Web site: www.edsci.com
or
ETA
620 Lakeview Pkwy.
Vernon Hills, IL 60061
(847) 816-5050 or (800) 445-5985/fax (800) ETA-9326
e-mail: info@etauniverse.com
Web site: www.etauniverse.com
or
Schoolmasters Science

745 State Circle

Box 1941

Ann Arbor, MI 48106

(800) 521-2832/fax (313) 761-8711

Web site: www.school-tech.com

Volcano Kit

The kit includes materials for making your very own small erupting volcano: instant clay, a plastic vial (you embed it in the volcano's cone), and an instruction booklet. Just add baking soda and vinegar (and a spot of food coloring) for a spectacular eruption. Available from most scientific supply companies.

$11.95

Edmund Scientific Co.

101 E. Gloucester Pike

Barrington, NJ 08007-1380

(800) 728-6999

e-mail: scientifics@edsci.com

Web site: www.edsci.com

Volcanoes, Dinosaurs and Fossils

A multifaceted activity kit designed to introduce kids in grades K–6 to the basics of geology. Included are assorted rock and fossil samples, instructions and chemicals for constructing an erupting volcano, materials for making plaster fossil casts, and more, as well as an informational, but hilarious, instruction manual.

$29.99

Wild Goose Co.

375 Whitney Ave.

Salt Lake City, UT 84115

(801) 466-1172 or (800) 373-1498/fax (801) 466-1186

Web site: www.wildgoosescience.com

ROCK AND MINERAL SPECIMENS

For those whose personal collections are a bit on the bland side—say, eight pieces of shale, a lump of quartz, and a chunk of playground asphalt—most scientific supply companies sell nice rocks. Preassembled rock collections cost on the average somewhere between $12 and $50.

Carolina Biological Supply Company

Offers a large number of rock and mineral collections and individual specimens, along with mixed "Gemstone Buckets" from which kids, by washing in a screen shaker, can pick out rough gems and minerals; and a "Geologic Oddities" set, which includes lodestone (magnetite), ulexite ("TV rock"), uncut geodes, and tektites.

Carolina Biological Supply Co.

2700 York Rd.

Burlington, NC 27215

(800) 334-5551/fax (800) 222-7112

e-mail: carolina@carolina.com

D. J. Minerals

Standard mineral, rock, and combination collections, variously containing 16, 30, 54, or 77 specimens, in 1×1-inch or 2×2-inch sizes.

$6 to $65

D. J. Minerals

Box 761

Butte, Montana 59703-0761

(406) 782-7339

Edmund Scientific Company

Rock and mineral collections of various sizes, including—for a truly impressive geological experience—assortments of fluorescent mineral rocks. The "Fluorescent Mineral Set," for example, includes 15 labeled specimens ($29.95); a three-pound mixed bag of fluorescent mineral rocks costs $15.95. Put either set under a shortwave/longwave UV lamp and the rocks glow spectacularly in a range of brilliant colors. The lamps cost $85.

Edmund Scientific Co.

101 E. Gloucester Pike

Barrington, NJ 08007-1380

(800) 728-6999

e-mail: scientifics@edsci.com

Web site: www.edsci.com

ETA

Assorted rock and mineral kits, among them the popular "Washington School Collection," which includes 40 specimens (20 minerals and ores and 20 igneous, metamorphic, and sedimentary rocks) for $34. These come packed in a compartmentalized box, like chocolates, with keyed descriptions printed in the box lid. It's more economical, but considerably trickier, to identify the rocks on your own: 40 specimens unlabeled (the "Student Set") cost a mere $6.

ETA
620 Lakeview Pkwy.
Vernon Hills, IL 60061
(847) 816-5050 or (800) 445-5985/fax (800) ETA-9326
e-mail: info@etauniverse.com
Web site: www.etauniverse.com

GAMES AND HANDS-ON ACTIVITIES

Cinnabar

A card game of rocks and minerals. Each card is illustrated with a color painting of a rock or mineral. Instructions are included for five games, among them a rummy-type card game in which players attempt to collect four-card sets, grouped by chemical family.

$7.95
Carolina Biological Supply Co.
2700 York Rd.
Burlington, NC 27215
(800) 334-5551

Earth Science Contracts

A collection of activities for four one- to two-week units on earth science–based topics for kids in grades 5–9. Activities include written, oral, visual, kinesthetic, musical, and art projects, though all focus on the earth sciences. A sample, from the "Rock and Minerals" unit, centers around birthstones: "Is there more than one for each month? What is yours? Select five family members and five friends and find out what their birth dates and birthstones are. Bring in sample stones if you can and give a brief talk about them to the class." From "Fossils and Dinosaurs": "Find or draw pictures of five or more fossils. Glue them onto heavy paper and make a jigsaw puzzle." From "Earth Resources": "Research and then graph the rate of oil consumption in this country over the last 10 to 15 years."

$34
Interact
1825 Gillespie Way, #101
El Cajon, CA 92020-1095
(619) 448-1474 or (800) 359-0961/fax (619) 448-6722
or (800) 700-5093
Web site: www.interact-simulations.com

The Game of EARTH

There are four variations on "The Game of EARTH" described in the accompanying instruction pamphlet. In all, players attempt to acquire *E, A, R, T,* and *H* cards to allow them to spell the word *EARTH.* They win cards by correctly answering questions in each of the five letter-coded categories. *E* cards carry questions about the environment; *A* cards, the atmosphere; *R* cards, rocks; *T* cards, tectonics; and *H* cards, the hydrosphere. Each card includes questions at four levels of difficulty. Beginners, for example, are asked "What organic rock formed from dead plants buried in ancient swamps?" Advanced players get "What large volcanic conduit located in the state of Wyoming displays splendid columnar jointing?" Nobody in our house so far claims to be advanced. Recommended for two to eight players, aged 10 and up.

$9.95
Other Worlds Educational Enterprises
Box 6193
Woodland Park, CO 80866-6193
(719) 687-3840

Gem and Mineral Rummy

A card game from the Smithsonian, illustrated with 32 color photographs from the museum's collection, including samples of gold, copper, and silver, star rubies and sapphires, and the Hope Diamond. Players compete to collect four-card sets of gems and minerals. For players aged 6 and up.

$5.95
ETA
620 Lakeview Pkwy.
Vernon Hills, IL 60061
(847) 816-5050 or (800) 445-5985/fax (800) ETA-9326
e-mail: info@etauniverse.com
Web site: www.etauniverse.com

9 Mountaineering

A cooperative board game for active or would-be mountain climbers. The board is an impressive and towering color photograph of snowy mountain peaks: players struggle to scale the mountain (Mount Robson in British Columbia), from base camp to summit and back again, dealing with such dangers as crevices, ice, blizzards, avalanches, and snow blindness. The climbers must share equipment—such as pitons, hooks, crampons, links, wedges, goggles, and first-aid supplies—and must help each other out to survive. To win the game, the whole team has to make it safely home.

> $22
> Animal Town
> Box 757
> Greenland, NH 03840
> (800) 445-8642/fax (603) 430-0334

6 Rocky Bingo

The 35 game cards each include a color photograph of a rock or mineral, plus geological information, interesting facts, and a proper pronounciation guide. Playing boards also include color photographs of (24) rocks and minerals. The game is played just like number bingo, with a geological twist. Also included: four genuine rock and mineral samples. Recommended for kids aged 6 and up.

> $14.95
> Carolina Biological Supply Co.
> 2700 York Rd.
> Burlington, NC 27215
> (800) 334-5551/fax (800) 222-7112

AUDIOVISUAL GEOLOGY

8 Blue Planet

We first saw this impressive film at the IMAX Theatre at the Smithsonian Institution in Washington, D.C. It's glorious. *Blue Planet* was photographed from the space shuttle; it's hard to believe, in these days of special effects, that those views are real. The film deals with the natural (and not-so-natural) forces that affect the face of our planet: storms, volcanoes, earthquakes, and a growing population of people.

> $29.95
> Movies Unlimited
> 3015 Darnell Rd.
> Philadelphia, PA 19154
> (215) 637-4444 or (800) 4-MOVIES
> e-mail: movies@moviesunlimited.com
> Web site: www.moviesunlimited.com

8 Killer Quake

A 60-minute video from NOVA, the award-winning science television series, with interesting narration and exciting photography. Other geology-related NOVA productions include "Hawaii: Born of Fire" and "Buried in Ash."

> $19.98
> Delta Education
> Box 3000
> Nashua, NH 03061-3000
> (800) 442-5444/fax (800) 282-9560
> Web site: www.delta-ed.com
> or
> Movies Unlimited
> 3015 Darnell Rd.
> Philadelphia, PA 19154
> (215) 637-4444 or (800) 4-MOVIES
> e-mail: movies@moviesunlimited.com
> Web site: www.moviesunlimited.com

8 Volcano!

A 60-minute National Geographic video about an erupting volcano and the volcanologists studying it.

> $19.98
> National Geographic Home Video
> Box 5073
> Clifton, NJ 07015
> (800) 627-5162
> Web site: www.nationalgeographic.com
> or
> Movies Unlimited
> 3015 Darnell Rd.
> Philadelphia, PA 19154
> (215) 637-4444 or (800) 4-MOVIES
> e-mail: movies@moviesunlimited.com
> Web site: www.moviesunlimited.com

GEOLOGY ON-LINE

Earth Science Explorer

A varied site for kids and educators, covering earth systems topics (plate tectonics, geologic time, biomes and biodiversity) and dinosaurs, including an analysis of extinction theories. All with a kid-friendly text, colorful graphics, and a bespectacled dinosaur guide.

www.cotf.edu/ete/modules.msese/explorer.html

Earthquake Information

The latest information on recent earthquakes, earthquake safety tips, general information on earthquakes, including earthquake history, frequently asked questions, an explanation of earthquake research, and suggestions for earthquake-related science fair projects.

quake.wr.usgs.gov

Smithsonian Gem and Mineral Collection

Color pictures and descriptions of gems and minerals from the Smithsonian.

galaxy.einet.net/images/gems/gems-icons.html

Understanding the Planet Through Chemistry

A detailed account of how geologists and chemists use the techniques of analytical chemistry to study the age of the earth, volcanic eruptions, atmsopheric changes over time, past asteroid collisions, and other topics. Includes an illustrated text.

helios.cr.usgs.gov/gips/aii-home.htm

U.S. Geological Survey

A rich source of information on the earth sciences. The site includes information on earthquakes, volcanoes, plate tectonics, fossils and fossil collecting, rocks and minerals, and prospecting, and a "Learning Web" of educational resources for kids in grades K–12.

www.usgs.gov

Virtual Cave

A virtual tour of a spectacular cave. Explorers can click on a list of features for close-up looks at such for-mations as bathtubs, death coral, pearls, popcorn, and soda straws.

www.goodearth.com/virtcave.html

Volcano World

All about volcanoes, including impressive color photographs, slide shows, movies, detailed information, and world maps showing locations.

volcano.und.nodak.edu/vw.html

METEOROLOGY

The study of weather—meteorology—is a wonderful home-study project. All the research materials are readily available—the weather, after all, is always right there outside the windows, doing something. Add a back-porch thermometer, a refrigerator-posted record chart or two, and daily sessions with a televised weather report, and you've got the makings of an ongoing weather project.

We began studying meteorology with assorted introductory books, plus a trio of temperature charts taped to the wall next to the back door: the boys recorded and graphed daily temperature fluctuations. Later we rigged an amateur weather station on the back porch, complete with rain gauge, thermometer, and wind vane, for more detailed observations and record keeping. We visited a local (professional) weather station. We built an anemometer and a hygrometer.

Then the boys meshed meteorology with an interest in photography, which resulted in an immense photo album crammed with cloud pictures, all labeled and categorized by date, location, and cloud type. I remember during this period continually pulling off the road during car trips at the agonized behest of photographers in the back seat who had spotted a particularly photogenic bank of clouds.

CATALOGS

Weather Affects

A catalog of weather instruments, books, videos, calendars, and diaries for weather watchers.

Weather Affects

440 Middlesex Rd.

Tyngsboro, MA 01879

(800) 317-3666

Wind and Weather

ALL A catalog of instruments, resources, and supplies for meteorologists of all ages.

Wind and Weather

Box 2320-WW

Mendocino, CA 95460

(707) 964-1284

MAGAZINES

Earth

A terrific bimonthly magazine on "The Science of Our Planet," featuring articles on meteorology, geology, and paleontology.

Annual subscription, $20

Earth

Box 738

Waukesha, WI 53187-0738

(800) 533-6644

Web site: www.earthmag.com

Also see **Geology** (page 358).

Weatherwise

A bimonthly magazine for dedicated weather enthusiasts. Contents include articles on the science and history of weather, weather forecasting, and unusual weather events, reviews of books and resources for amateur meteorologists, an almanac of weather records and anomalies, and many color photographs.

Annual subscription (6 issues), $29

Weatherwise

Haldref Publications

1319 18th St. N.W.

Washington, DC 20036

(800) 365-9753

BOOKS

Can It Really Rain Frogs? The World's Strangest Weather Events

Spencer Christian; John Wiley & Sons, 1997

A 128-page collection of fun facts, general weather information, maps, photographs, and diagrams. Read-

ers learn about rains of frogs, singing caves, and auroras, as well as weather instruments and their functions, weather forecasting, and weather lore.

The Cloud Book

Tomie de Paola; Holiday House, 1985

A picture-book introduction to clouds for the very young, with enchanting illustrations. De Paola describes the different kind of clouds, including cirrocumulus clouds (that look like sheep) and cirrostratus clouds (that look like bedsheets), cloud legends, cloud superstitions, and—at the very end—a very silly cloud story.

How Artists See the Weather: Sun, Wind, Snow, Rain

Colleen Carroll; Abbeville Press, 1996

Color reproductions of paintings featuring weather by artists from a range of different time periods and countries, with a short explanatory text.

How the Weather Works

Michael Allaby; Reader's Digest, 1995

Detailed and interesting information and over 100 hands-on experiments for kids in grades 3–9, beautifully illustrated with color photographs.

See **How Things Work Series** (page 235).

How Weather Works

Rob DeMillo; Ziff Davis Press, 1994

A wonderful account of how weather works, illustrated with gorgeous full-color diagrams. Section headings include "A Blanket of Air," "The Source of Power," "Mild Weather: Earth and Its Seasons," "Tantrums: Violent Weather," "Microclimates and Unusual Natural Phenomena," "The Atmosphere of Our Neighbors," and "Human Activity and the Atmosphere." Includes clear scientific descriptions (and worth-a-thousand-words pictures) of cloud formation, the six major air circulation cells, the jet stream, the causes of ice ages, the life cycle of a thunderstorm, the dynamics of hurricanes, and the atmospheres of the other planets in the solar systems.

It's Raining Cats and Dogs: All Kinds of Weather and Why We Have It

Franklyn M. Branley; Houghton Mifflin, 1987

A catchy 112-page explanation of how weather works, filled with humorous illustrations, hands-on activities, and fascinating facts. Readers learn about rains of frogs, pink snow, ball lightning, the shapes of clouds, hurricanes, dust devils, and the meaning of the "horse latitudes." They also find out how to calculate the number of snowflakes in a snowstorm, how to make rain in a coffeepot and generate a (very small) bolt of lightning, and how to build a wind direction indicator.

Let's-Read-and-Find-Out Science Books: Weather

Franklyn M. Branley; HarperTrophy

This series of short science picture books for readers aged 4–9 (see page 227) includes several weather-related titles. *Flash, Crash, Rumble, and Roll* (1985) contains a simple explanation of the science of thunderstorms, plus storm safety hints; *Sunshine Makes the Seasons* (1986) explains what causes the changing seasons of the year and includes instructions for a hands-on demonstration in which readers simulate the position of the earth at different seasons with an orange, a pencil, and a flashlight. Also see *Hurricane Watch* (1987), *Snow Is Falling* (1986), and *Tornado Alert* (1990).

The Magic School Bus Inside a Hurricane

Joanna Cole; Scholastic, 1996

The Magic School Bus books (see page 227) are a series of humorous scientific adventures in which the zany teacher, Ms. Frizzle, takes her class on fantastic field trips, each a mix of science, silliness, magic, and surprise. In *The Magic School Bus Inside a Hurricane,* the class visits a weather station; en route their bus turns into a hot-air balloon and whisks them into the center of a hurricane. Also see *The Magic School Bus at the Waterworks,* in which the class ends up participating in the water cycle, shrinking to the size of raindrops and falling from the clouds to enter the town's water system. Each book includes a lot of weather facts and general information, presented in the form of short, hand-printed school reports posted on each page.

Seymour Simon's Meteorology

Seymour Simon; William Morrow

A simple, fact-filled scientific text paired with spectacular full-page color photographs, for readers aged 5 and up. Titles include *Storms* (1989), *Weather* (1993), and *Lightning* (1997).

Snow Crystals

W. A. Bentley and W. J. Humphreys; Dover Publications, 1985

Over 200 pages of fascinating photomicrographs of snowflakes, the work of W. A. ("Snowflake") Bentley of Jericho, Vermont, originally published in 1931. A brief introduction covers the science of snow.

Pair this one with *Snowflake Bentley* by Gloria May Stoddard (New England Press, 1985), a short biography of the first—and surely the most devoted—snowflake photographer.

Weather

Brian Cosgrove; Alfred A. Knopf, 1991

A volume in the Eyewitness series heavily illustrated with color photographs, drawings, and diagrams. Most of the information is contained in the picture captions. Topics covered include "A sunny day," "Frost and ice," "Water in the air," "The birth of a cloud," "Fronts and lows," "Thunder and lightning," "Wind," and "Colors in the sky."

The Weather Companion

Gary Lockhart; John Wiley & Sons, 1988

A compendium of meteorological history, science, legend, and folklore, filled with information, quotations, quirky facts, and black-and-white drawings and diagrams. Chapter titles include "Weather Past," "Weather Tools," "Weather Phenomena," "Weather and Wildlife," and "Botanical Weather." For teenagers.

The Weather Factor

David M. Ludlum; Houghton Mifflin, 1984

The weather in American history. Ludlum covers colonial weather events, the weather of the Revolutionary War, the War of 1812, and the Civil War, Election and Inauguration Day weather, weather and sports events, and weather in the history of aviation. An interesting and unusual reference.

The Weather Sky
Bruce McMillan; Farrar, Straus & Giroux, 1996

The book covers all the basics of weather, including moving air masses, highs and lows, fronts, and cloud formations; and presents an overview of changing weather patterns through the seasons. Each page of the book features a gorgeous color photograph of the sky, a corresponding weather map, and a chart showing cloud heights. For readers aged 9–12.

Weather Words and What They Mean
Gail Gibbons; Holiday House, 1990

Big bright pictures and simple definitions of such "weather words" as *temperature*, *air pressure*, and *moisture*. For kids aged 5–8.

ACTIVITY BOOKS

Making and Using Scientific Equipment
David E. Newton; Franklin Watts, 1993

Includes directions for building your own thermometer, barometer, anemometer, hair hygrometer, and rain gauge, with background information on each instrument and suggestions for related science activities. For kids aged 12 and up.

Meteorology
Zephyr Press

A spiral-bound learning activities packet containing 50 meteorology-related activities for kids at two levels, grades K–3 and 4–8. Project suggestions connect weather to math, music, and literature.

$22

Zephyr Press

Box 66006

Tucson, AZ 85728-6006

(800) 232-2187/fax (520) 333-9402

e-mail: neways2learn@zephyrpress.com

Web site: www.zephyrpress.com

Puddle Jumpers
Jennifer Story Gillis; Storey Communications, 1996

A collection of simple weather-related projects for early elementary-level students.

Snow and Ice
Stephen Krensky; Scholastic, 1994

An illustrated account of snow and ice (and blizzards and igloos and icebergs) for readers aged 5–9, with many suggestions for simple hands-on activities and experiments. You need snow for a couple of these; most of the activities, however, can be done in Florida, provided you have access to a refrigerator freezer.

Weatherwatch
Valerie Wyatt; Addison-Wesley, 1990

Over 90 pages of weather information, hands-on projects, quizzes, puzzles, and humorous illustrations for creative young meteorologists. Kids make a pair of Inuit-style sunglasses, generate a cloud in a bottle, learn how to measure raindrops, make (and dissect) a hailstone, build a barometer, and learn to read a weather map.

LITERATURE LINKS TO METEOROLOGY: FOR ADULTS

Rainy, Windy, Snowy, Sunny Days: Linking Fiction to Nonfiction
Phyllis J. Perry; Teacher Ideas Press, 1996

The book is divided into four parts (Rainy, Windy, Snowy, and Sunny Days). Under each are listed 12 fiction and 12 nonfiction books, related to rain, wind, snow, or sun. There's a short description of each book and an accompanying list of suggested discussion starters or topics for further investigation. Some simple hands-on activities, but the majority of the suggestions involve writing assignments or class reports. The listed books are appropriate for kids in grades K–5.

$22

Libraries Unlimited

Box 6633

Englewood, CO 80155-6633

(303) 770-1220 or (800) 237-6124/fax (303) 220-8843

e-mail: lu-books@lu.com

Web site: www.lu.com

The World's Regions and Weather:

Linking Fiction to Nonfiction

Phyllis J. Perry; Teacher Ideas Press, 1996

The book is divided into four major sections: "Snow, Hail, and Ice," "Drought, Dust, and Dunes," "Clouds, Rain, and Floods," and "Winds: Hurricanes, Tornadoes, and Typhoons." Under each is included a list of related fiction and nonfiction books, with detailed plot descriptions and lists of suggestions for discussion starters, multidisciplinary activities (largely written reports or library research projects), and topics for further investigations. The listed books are appropriate for kids in grades 5–9.

$22

Libraries Unlimited

Box 6633

Englewood, CO 80155-6633

(303) 770-1220 or (800) 237-6124/fax (303) 220-8843

e-mail: lu-books@lu.com

Web site: www.lu.com

LITERATURE LINKS TO METEOROLOGY: FOR KIDS

Bartholomew and the Oobleck

Dr. Seuss; Random House, 1949

King Derwent is sick of ordinary weather, so he demands that the royal wizards invent something new to fall from the sky. The wizards produce a dreadful green glop called oobleck. For readers aged 4–8.

Bringing the Rain to Kapiti Plain

Verna Aardema; Dial, 1992

An African tale, told with a catchy rhyming refrain, about Ki-Pat, who shot an arrow into the clouds and brought down the rain, ending a drought. For readers aged 3–6.

Brr!

James Stevenson; Greenwillow, 1991

Maryann and Louie's wonderful storytelling grandpa tells of a snowstorm when he was a little boy that was so deep it buried the entire town and so cold that even sneezes froze. For readers aged 4–8.

Cloudy With a Chance of Meatballs

Judi Barrett; Aladdin, 1982

In the land of Chewandswallow, meals fall from the sky: breakfast brings clouds of scrambled eggs and showers of orange juice; blizzards of mashed potatoes roll in at dinnertime. Also see *Pickles to Pittsburgh: The Sequel to Cloudy With a Chance of Meatballs* (Atheneum, 1997).

Earthmaker's Tales

Gretchen Will Mayo; Walker & Company, 1991

A collection of native American legends about "Earth happenings." Each legend is preceded by an introductory paragraph about its tribal source. Legends variously cover the origins of thunder and lightning, snow, fog, the rainbow, mountains, volcanoes, and earthquakes. For kids aged 8–12. Also see, by the same author, *More Earthmaker's Tales* (Walker, 1991).

It's Snowing! It's Snowing!

Jack Prelutsky; Greenwillow, 1984

Seventeen short poems about snow for kids aged 4–8.

Katy and the Big Snow

Virginia Lee Burton; Houghton Mifflin, 1973

Katy, the indomitable snowplow, clears the roads of town after a giant snowstorm. Illustrations include wonderful little maps of Katy's plowed roads. For readers aged 4–8.

Night of the Twisters

Ivy Ruckman; HarperTrophy, 1986

Dan, his best friend, Arthur, and his little brother, Ryan, are alone in the house when tornadoes strike their Nebraska town. An exciting survival story for readers aged 9–12.

Thunder Cake

Patricia Polacco; Paper Star, 1997

What do you do when you're afraid of a thunderstorm? You bake a thundercake. A lovely picture book about a little girl and her Russian grandmother, for readers aged 4–7.

4 **8** *We Hate Rain!*
James Stevenson; Greenwillow, 1988

Maryann and Louie's grandpa tells the story of a monumental rain, when he was a small boy, that filled the whole town with water. Fish swam through the parlor, and the family had to move to the rooftop. For readers aged 4–8.

5 **9** *Weather: Poems for All Seasons*
Lee Bennett Hopkins; HarperTrophy, 1995

A 64-page illustrated book of poems all dealing with different aspects of weather, by such poets as Ogden Nash and Langston Hughes. For kids aged 5–9.

HANDS-ON ACTIVITIES AND SUPPLIES

Rainstick Kit

7 **+** All the materials to make your own Chilean rain stick, used by native South American tribes in rain-bringing ceremonies. The kit includes a hollow cactus stalk, pebbles, cactus thorns, decorative yarn, and instructions.

> $14.95
> American Science & Surplus
> 3605 Howard St.
> Skokie, IL 60076
> (847) 982-0870/fax (800) 934-0722
> Web site: www.sciplus.com
> or
> Weather Affects
> 440 Middlesex Rd.
> Tyngsboro, MA 01879
> (800) 317-3666

Sunprint Paper

ALL Photosensitive paper that undergoes a chemical change when exposed to sunlight. Kids simply place an object—a leaf, for example—on the sunprint paper and expose the pair to sunlight for five minutes. Rinse with water and they'll have a permanent white outline

print of their leaf on a blue background. Fun for artists and students of sunshine.

> $12.95 for 30 sheets, plus instructions
> Available from most scientific supply companies or
> Edmund Scientific Co.
> 101 E. Gloucester Pike
> Barrington, NJ 08007-1380
> (800) 728-6999
> e-mail: scientifics@edsci.com
> Web site: www.edsci.com

Tornado Tube

ALL A cheap but enthralling little plastic device with which kids can transform a pair of 2-liter plastic soda bottles into a nice demonstration of tornado action. Water swirls from the top bottle to the bottom in a spiraling replica of a tornado vortex. Add a drop or two of food coloring and you can make red, green, and blue tornadoes. Our boys found this almost endlessly fascinating.

> Tubes, $4 for a package of two
> Available through most science supply stores and catalogs or
> Delta Education
> Box 3000
> Nashua, NH 03061-3000
> (800) 442-5444/fax (800) 282-9560
> Web site: www.delta-ed.com
> or
> ETA
> 620 Lakeview Pkwy.
> Vernon Hills, IL 60061
> (847) 816-5050 or (800) 445-5985/fax (800) ETA-9326
> e-mail: info@etauniverse.com
> Web site: www.etauniverse.com
> or
> Edmund Scientific Co.
> 101 E. Gloucester Pike
> Barrington, NJ 08007-1380
> (800) 728-6999
> e-mail: scientifics@edsci.com
> Web site: www.edsci.com

For an enhanced tornado tube experience, see Steve Spangler's *Taming the Tornado Tube,* a 112-page collection of 50 tube-related hands-on activities.

Weather Instruments

ALL High-quality meteorological instruments are expensive, but most—thermometers, barometers, anemometers, wind meters, wind vanes, rain gauges, psychrometers, and hygrometers—are available in affordable student models from most scientific supply companies.

> Student thermometers with both Fahrenheit and Centigrade scales, about $2; hand-held wind meters, about $16; mountable plastic rain gauges, $10.95; and sling psychrometer/humidity detectors, $2.95.
> Delta Education
> Box 3000
> Nashua, NH 03061-3000
> (800) 442-5444/fax (800) 282-9560
> Web site: www.delta-ed.com

Also see *Making and Using Scientific Equipment* (page 372).

The Weather Tracker's Kit

Our kids were given this kit as a Christmas gift. At the time, no one was in a meteorological phase; interest in the weather was confined to a three-second daily assessment of the presence (or absence) of adequate snow for cross-country skiing. I figured the kit was destined for the back of the closet, gathering dust. The boys, however, who never quite behave as anticipated, were delighted with it. They posted the poster-size cloud chart on the refrigerator and attached the weather station to the back-porch railing. The kit's weather station is a little plastic device equipped with a wind speed and direction indicator, a rain gauge, and a thermometer. It's easy to mount (two screws), reasonably tough, and easy to read. Around here, somebody (or everybody) read it daily and kept records. I was impressed.

> The kit, including an 80-page illustrated book, *The Weather Tracker's Handbook* by Gregory C. Aaron, $18.95; with an accompanying CD-ROM (Mac or PC), $29.95
> Available through science supply and bookstores or
> Running Press Book Publishers
> 125 South 22nd St.
> Philadelphia, PA 19103
> (215) 567-5080 or (800) 345-5359/fax (800) 453-2884

GAMES

Snowstorm

A cooperative board game in which players work to keep the roads of Little City free of snow so that all the inhabitants can move from place to place and get their errands done. Playing pieces picture snowplows, sand trucks, cars, a skating rink, and snow-covered houses; the board is illustrated with a charming little snowy village. For kids aged 5–8.

> $18.50
> Animal Town
> Box 757
> Greenland, NH 03840
> (800) 445-8642/fax (603) 430-0334

Weatherslam

A card game for the weather conscious, played with a primary deck of 52 illustrated cards representing the seasons of the year. ("Spring" cards are green; "Summer" cards yellow; "Autumn," orange; and "Winter," black.) Certain seasonal cards are assigned a point value depending on the weather condition depicted: "Balmy Weather" cards, for example, are worth 25 points apiece; "Tornadoes," 15 points; "Clouds," "Frost," or "Snow Flurries," 5 points. The object of the game is to reach game score by accumulating "fronts" or "tricks." An instruction booklet includes directions for several variations on the game. Recommended for two to six players, aged 8 and up.

> U.S. Games Systems, Inc.
> 179 Ludlow St.
> Stamford, CT 06902
> (203) 353-8400 or (800) 544-2637

AUDIOVISUAL METEOROLOGY

NOVA: Weather

Weather-related episodes from the science television program *NOVA* include "Lightning!," "Hurricane!," "Tornado!," and "Flood!" All include fascinating scientific information, clear explanations, and spectacular film footage. Each video runs about 60 minutes.

$19.98

Delta Education

Box 3000

Nashua, NH 03061-3000

(800) 442-5444

or

Movies Unlimited

3015 Darnell Rd.

Philadelphia, PA 19154

(215) 637-4444 or (800) 4-MOVIES

e-mail: movies@moviesunlimited.com

Web site: www.moviesunlimited.com

Skywatching

Purple Crayons Productions

A *Video Guide to the Daytime Sky,* covering the science, history, and lore of the wild blue yonder. The video pairs narrative with wonderful film footage of rainbows, clouds, glorious sunsets, and sizzling lightning bolts. Viewers learn why the sky is blue, what makes rainbows, what causes wind, why there are many kinds of clouds, and what warning signs signal a tornado.

$19.95

Edmund Scientific Co.

101 E. Gloucester Pike

Barrington, NJ 08007-1380

(800) 728-6999

e-mail: scientifics@edsci.com

Web site: www.edsci.com

Weather Dude: A Musical Guide to the Atmosphere

Nick Walter; Small Gate Media

Ten weather-related songs for elementary-aged kids, with an accompanying songbook.

$14.95 on audiocassette

Small Gate Media

Box 9536

Seattle, WA 98109-0535

METEOROLOGY ON-LINE

About Rainbows

A very detailed explanation of what rainbows are and how they form, with color diagrams.

www.unidata.ucar.edu/staff/blynds/rnbw.html

Dan's Wild Weather Page

A terrific site for young weather watchers. Kids can access information on a wide range of weather topics, among them clouds, temperature, wind, forecasting, satellites, and hurricanes, or they can ask Dan, the resident weatherman, a question of their own. The site includes lots of great graphics and kid-friendly explanations, plus hands-on activities and lesson plans.

www.whnt19.com/kidwx

K–12 Weather Curriculum

A large collections of lesson plans, hands-on activities, and weather resources for kids of all ages.

groundhog.spr1.umich.edu/curriculum

Kids' Lightning Information and Safety

All about lightning, how to tell how far away a thunderstorm is, kids' lightning pictures, and a spectacular lightning photograph.

www.azstarnet.com/anubis/zaphome.htm

Weather Here and There

A multidisciplinary weather unit for kids in grades 4–6.

www.ncsa.uius.edu/Edu/RSE/RSEred/weatherHome .html

The Weather Unit

Complete weather study units for kids in grades 2–4.

faldo.atmos.uiuc/WEATHER/weather.html

PALEONTOLOGY

Josh collects fossils; Caleb builds dinosaur models; and Ethan loved the movie *Jurassic Park* because (he said) of the superb computer graphics. Such were our jumping-off points into the study of paleontology.

Given the average five-year-old's passion for dinosaurs, however, this is a topic that can hardly miss.

Magazines

Dinosaurus

If your kids are temporarily or permanently fascinated by dinosaurs, this may be the magazine for you. *Dinosaurus*, the "Magazine of the Mesozoic," is 46 oversize glossy pages long, colorfully illustrated, featuring a mix of dino-science and dino-fantasy. My sample issue includes articles on theropods, archaeopteryx, primitive nondinosaurian reptiles, and the relationship between dinosaurs and present-day birds, plus an episode in an ongoing serial about Albert, a dinosaur being raised by young Jimmy Harkin's scientist father on the family farm, and an interview with James Gurney, author of *Dinotopia*. Also included are puzzles, quizzes, and a section of kids' drawings and letters to the editor.

Annual subscription (9 issues), $18.95

Dinosaurus

505 Eighth Ave.

New York, NY 10018

(212) 563-0918

Earth

An excellent bimonthly magazine featuring articles on paleontology, geology, and meteorology, with terrific color illustrations. It's targeted at adults but is a valuable addition to any earth sciences study program.

Annual subscription, $20

Earth

Box 738

Waukesha, WI 53187-0738

(800) 533-6644

Web site: www.earthmag.com

Books

See **World History: Prehistoric Peoples** (page 606).

An Alphabet of Dinosaurs

Peter Dodson; Byron Press, 1995

The right-hand pages are full-color paintings of dinosaurs, 26 of them, in alphabetical order from ankylosaurus to zephyrosaurus. Left-hand pages includes a couple of short, descriptive sentences about the dinosaur, plus a drawing of a sample skull, skeleton, or fossil.

Before the Dinosaurs

Miriam Schlein; Scholastic, 1996

A richly illustrated introduction to life on earth before the evolution of the dinosaurs, covering trilobites, crinoids, sharks, and early reptiles. For readers aged 5–8.

Dinosaur Dig

Kathryn Lasky; William Morrow, 1990

Every kid's dream. Two children participate in a real-life dinosaur dig, learning about both the work of paleontologists and the dinosaurs they dig up. The book, 64 pages long, is illustrated throughout with color photographs.

Dinosaurs All Around: An Artist's View of the Prehistoric World

Caroline Arnold; Clarion, 1997

A detailed account of the work of sculptor Stephen Czerkas, who makes life-size models of dinosaurs. The book follows the entire process, from clay model to museum exhibit. Illustrated with color photographs.

Dinosaurs Walked Here and Other Stories Fossils Tell

Patricia Lauber; Aladdin, 1992

An explanation of what fossils are and what they tell us about the prehistoric world and the plants and animals that lived in it. For readers aged 9–12.

Eyewitness Series: Paleontology

Alfred A. Knopf

Volumes with paleontological themes in the Eyewitness series include *Dinosaur* (David Norman and Angela Milner; 1989), *Fossil* (Paul D. Taylor; 1990), and *Prehistoric Life* (William Lindsay; 1994). All are heavily illustrated with terrific color photographs and drawings. *Dinosaurs* covers such topics as dinosaur teeth, feet, eggs, and theories of extinction; *Fossils* traces the fossil record from the stony remains of bacteria and algae to birds and mammals; and *Prehistoric Life* covers the evolution of life on earth, from its earliest beginnings in the ocean through the appearance of humankind.

How Dinosaurs Came to Be
Patricia Lauber; Simon & Schuster, 1996

The evolution of dinosaurs, from their distant amphibian ancestors who lived in the Permian era, nearly 300 million years ago. The book includes a dinosaur family tree. For readers aged 9–12.

If You Are a Hunter of Fossils
Byrd Baylor; Aladdin, 1984

A fossil hunter in the Texas mountains poetically describes what the land was like millions of years ago. For readers aged 8–11.

In My Own Backyard
Judi Kurjian; Charlesbridge Publishing, 1993

A child looks out a bedroom window and sees the backyard as it would have looked in distant geologic periods, complete with dinosaurs and gigantic ferns. For readers aged 4–8.

Let's-Read-and-Find-Out Science Series: Paleontology
HarperTrophy

This series of short science picture books includes several on paleontological topics for kids aged 4–9. *Dinosaurs Are Different* (Aliki; 1985), though clearly written for the very young, provides more detailed scientific information that the usual beginner's dino book. The dinosaur "differences" are anatomical and taxonomic. Aliki explains the dinosaur family tree and shows the differences between the two orders of dinosaurs: the "lizard-hipped" saurischians and the "bird-hipped" ornithischians. Pictures, with big color-coded hip bones, teach kids how to tell one from the other. The book then discusses (and classifies) individual dinosaurs, explaining the further division of the two main orders into suborders. Illustrations include lots of little kids in bright-colored T-shirts and overalls, exchanging dinosaur information in conversational cartoon balloons. ("Plant-eaters are herbivores." "If you're two-legged, you're a biped!") There's also a nice comic book–style page in which a very well informed little boy in green pants explains the differences between dinosaurs and modern reptiles. The kid even knows the definition of "diapsid skull." Also see *Dinosaur Bones* (Aliki; 1990), *Digging Up Dinosaurs* (Aliki; 1988), *Fossils Tell of Long Ago* (Aliki; 1990), *My Visit to the Dinosaurs* (Aliki; 1985), and *What Happened to the Dinosaurs?* (Franklyn M. Branley; 1991).

See **Let's-Read-and-Find-Out Science Series** (page 227).

The Magic School Bus in the Time of the Dinosaurs
Joanna Cole; Scholastic, 1994

Ms. Frizzle's class, aboard the marvelous Magic School Bus, takes a trip far back in time to the days of the dinosaurs. The kids learn a great deal about ancient reptiles and life in the Jurassic and Triassic eras. Scientific information is presented in short, kid-written reports tacked in the margins: "Dinosaurs Were Reptiles" by Carlos, "Cold Blood/Warm Blood" by Tim, "Triassic Plants" by John, "What Were Sauropods?" by Amanda Jane. With humorous illustrations by Bruce Degen. Ms. Frizzle's wardrobe, as always, is hilarious.

See the **Magic School Bus Series** (page 227).

The Science of Jurassic Park and the Lost World or, How to Build a Dinosaur
Rob De Salle and David Lindley; Basic Books, 1997

An adult popular science book that explains, in clear and pleasant fashion, the preservative properties of amber, the processes of DNA sequencing and cloning, the production (doubtful) of baby dinosaurs, and the problems inherent in introducing them to a new 20th-century environment. Thoroughly interesting for teenagers and a good reference source for the parents of young *Jurassic Park/Lost World* fans who have more questions than they know what to do with.

Traces of Life: The Origins of Humankind
Kathryn Lasky; William Morrow, 1990

An introduction to paleoanthropology—the study of hominid fossils—for middle-grade and older readers.

The Visual Dictionary of Dinosaurs
David Lambert; Dorling Kindersley, 1993

The 64-page book is organized chronologically in double-page spreads, stretching from the Triassic to the

Cretaceous era. Each page includes superb color photographs, detailed anatomical models, and drawings, all precisely labeled. The book also covers dinosaur relatives and dinosaur classification.

See **Eyewitness Visual Dictionary Series** (page 132).

Where to Look for a Dinosaur

Bernard Most; Voyager Books, 1997

A geographical tour for dinosaur lovers showing where different dinosaurs once lived all over the world. For readers aged 4–8.

Why Did the Dinosaurs Disappear? The Great Dinosaur Mystery

Melvin Berger; Ideals Children's Books, 1995

An overview of dinosaur extinction theories, for readers aged 5–9.

Wild and Woolly Mammoths

Aliki; HarperCollins, 1998

The life and times of the woolly mammoths, including general scientific information, a chart listing the many types of mammoths, and appealing illustrations, for readers aged 4–8.

FAMOUS PALEONTOLOGISTS

American Dinosaur Hunters

Nathan Aaseng; Enslow Publishing, 1996

A collection of ten biographies of well-known American paleontologists, among them Edward Hitchcock, Joseph Leidy, Roy Chapman Andrews, and Jack Horner.

Dinosaur Hunters

John R. Jones and Kate H. McMullan; Random House, 1989

A story of paleontologists, their methods, and their discoveries, for readers aged 5–8.

The Dragon in the Cliff

Sheila Cole; Lothrop, Lee & Shepard, 1991

A novel based on the life of early 19th-century fossil hunter Mary Anning who collected fossils from the cliffs near her seaside home in England. Anning discovered the first ichthyosaur skeleton when she was 13 years old.

Dragon in the Rocks: A Story Based on the Childhood of the Early Paleontologist, Mary Anning

Marie Day; Owl Communications, 1995

A 32-page illustrated biography of Mary Anning, the 19th-century fossil hunter, for kids aged 4–8.

Fossil Feud: The Rivalry of the First American Dinosaur Hunters

Thom Holmes; Julian Messner, 1997

The fossil feud was waged in the 19th century between Othniel C. March of Yale's Peabody Museum and Edward Drinker Cope of the the Philadelphia Academy of Natural Sciences, each racing to grab the biggest and the best of the West's newly discovered dinosaur bones. Holmes's book details the excitement (and danger) of the early dinosaur-hunting expeditions—Cope, for example, was searching for fossils in Montana just after Custer clashed with the Sioux at the Battle of the Little Bighorn—and describes both the paleontological significance of the discoveries and the very human aspects of science. (It was Marsh, incidentally, who was responsible for what Holmes calls the biggest dinosaur blooper of all time: a matter of mixed-up skulls.)

Also see *The Bone Wars* (Kathryn Lasky; William Morrow, 1988).

Reading Between the Bones: The Pioneers of Dinosaur Paleontology

Susan Clinton; Franklin Watts, 1997

A 128-page overview of the work of eight paleontologists, filled with science, excitement, and human interest. Illustrated with black-and-white photographs. For kids aged 12 and up.

The Riddle of the Dinosaur

John Noble Wilford; Vintage, 1987

A detailed history of dinosaur discoveries and theories, through the stories of foremost paleontologists in the field, from the early 1800s to the present day. Chapter titles include "First Bones," "Measuring Time," "Early Bird," "Hot Times Over Warm Blood," and "The

Great Dying." An interesting and informational reader for high school students.

LITERATURE LINKS TO PALEONTOLOGY

A Bone From a Dry Sea
Peter Dickinson; Laurel Leaf, 1995

The discovery of fossils in Africa paves the way for the tale of a tribe of primitive hominids and the changes in their way of life brought about by a brilliant young female called Li. The book alternates between Li's story in ancient times and the story of Vinny, daughter of a modern-day anthropologist who—four million years later—is searching for fossils in the area where Li once lived. For high school students.

Bone Poems
Jeffrey Moss; Workman, 1997

A delightful collection of dinosaur poems, including a verse to a dinosaur egg, a dinosaur math quiz, "A (Mostly) Dinosaur Alphabet," and a poem about how paleontologists measured the intelligence of early hominids (by filling the skulls with rice).

Danny and the Dinosaur
Syd Hoff; HarperCrest, 1993

Originally published in the 1950s, this is the classic picture-book tale of a little boy who makes friends with one of the dinosaurs in the museum. The dinosaur follows him home and the two have a wonderful time together. Gentle fun for kids aged 4–7.

Sequels include *Danny and the Dinosaur Go to Camp* (HarperCollins, 1996) and *Happy Birthday, Danny and the Dinosaur!* (HarperTrophy, 1997).

Dinotopia

James Gurney; Turner Publishing, 1994

Dinotopia is a utopian civilization on a mysterious island, stumbled upon in 1862 by a shipwrecked biologist and his young son. Here people and dinosaurs have lived together for centuries, building a peaceful, complex, and marvelous civilization. The book is illustrated with beautiful detailed paintings. There are at least two adult sequels to the original novel, and several short Dinotopia books for young readers. *Dinotopia* itself, however, is a classic for all ages.

The Enormous Egg
Oliver Butterworth; Little, Brown, 1993

One of the chickens on Nate's family farm lays a perfectly enormous egg that hatches a triceratops. Funny, exciting, and fun for kids aged 8–11.

Jacob Two-Two and the Dinosaur
Mordecai Richler; McClelland & Stewart, 1995

Jacob is the youngest in his family; he's nicknamed "Two-Two" because he always has to say everything twice before anybody pays attention to him. In this short chapter book, Jacob's pet lizard turns out to be a massive but friendly diplodocus dinosaur (named Dippy, who loves pizza). When the government attempts to imprison Dippy, Jacob helps his pet escape to the wilds of British Columbia. For readers aged 8–11.

Prehistoric Pinkerton

Steven Kellogg; Dial, 1991

Pinkerton, the rambunctious and gigantic puppy, attends Dinosaur Day at the local museum, where he gets into trouble with some enormous and valuable bones. For readers aged 4–8.

Tyrannosaurus Was a Beast: Dinosaur Poems
Jack Prelutsky; Mulberry, 1992

Fourteen funny illustrated poems about dinosaurs for kids aged 4–8.

What Happened to Patrick's Dinosaurs?
Carol Carrick; Clarion, 1988

A little boy's lovely fantasy about what really happened to the dinosaurs, with a happy ending. For readers aged 4–8.

Activity Books

The Big Beast Book: Dinosaurs and How They Got That Way

Jerry Booth; Little, Brown, 1988

A delight for young paleontologists, filled with interesting information and out-of-the-ordinary hands-on projects. Instructions are included, for example, for making a truly dinosaur-size geologic timeline—you'll need 100 yards of playground, open field, or city block, plus cardboard for signs—for making an "edible geology" layered desert from flavored gelatin, and for calculating dinosaur top running speed based on measurements of their femurs. There's also a list of good vacation spot for dinosaur lovers.

Crafts for Kids Who Are Wild About Dinosaurs

Kathy Ross; Millbrook Press, 1997

Instructions for 20 dinosaur-related craft projects, including a dinosaur ringtoss game, a dinosaur puppet, and a dinosaur window decoration.

Discover Dinosaurs: Become a Dinosaur Detective

Chris McGowan; Addison-Wesley, 1993

Interesting information and hands-on activities showing kids just how paleontologists learn about dinosaurs.

Draw 50 Dinosaurs and Other Prehistoric Animals

Lee J. Ames; Main Street Books, 1985

Step-by-step instructions for drawing a wide range of dinosaurs and relatives, including *Tyrannosaurus rex,* stegosaurus, and triceratops.

The Fossil Factory: A Kid's Guide to Digging Up Dinosaurs, Exploring Evolution, and Finding Fossils

Niles Gregory and Douglas Eldredge; Addison-Wesley, 1989

Lots of activities on finding and analyzing fossils, information on the geological history of the earth, and a guide to prime fossil-finding sites.

Make Your Own Dinosaur Out of Chicken Bones: Foolproof Instructions for Budding Paleontologists

Chris McGowan; HarperCollins, 1997

This book, in 176 illustrated pages, shows readers how to transform ordinary chicken bones into an "incredibly realistic" apatosaurus skeleton. This is a definitely challenging project, but you'll learn a lot doing it. It takes three whole chickens. (Included are recipes for the leftovers.) A fun read.

Paleontology

Zephyr Press

A spiral-bound learning activities packet containing 50 multidisciplinary activities at two levels, for kids in grades K–3 and 4–8.

$22
Zephyr Press
Box 66006
Tucson, AZ 85728-6006
(800) 232-2187/fax (520) 323-9402
e-mail: neways2learn@zephyrpress.com
Web site: www.zephyrpress.com

Coloring and Paper-Crafts Books

Cut and Make Dinosaur Skeleton

A. G. Smith

The book includes instructions and pieces for making a 20-inch-long 3-D brontosaurus.

$3.95
Dover Publications, Inc.
31 E. Second St.
Mineola, NY 11501

The Dinosaur Bones Sticker Book

Snapshot; Dorling Kindersley, 1994

A 16-page activity book in which kids match 60 beautifully colored dinosaur stickers to the appropriate captioned outline shape.

$3.95 from bookstores

The Dinosaur Coloring Book

Anthony Rao; Dover Publications

Black-line pictures and a brief informational text for colorers of all ages. *The Dinosaur Coloring Book* includes 45 drawings of dinosaurs and their companions, among them tyrannosaurus, stegosaurus, and archaeopteryx. Also see *The Days of the Dinosaur Coloring Book, The Dinosaur ABC Coloring Book,* and *Prehistoric Mammals Coloring Book. Prehistoric Mammals,* for example, includes 41 black-and-white line drawings of long-gone mammals, among them the saber-toothed tiger and the woolly mammoth. Dover is a lush source of inexpensive dinosaur materials; the catalog also carries dinosaur stencils, stickers, connect-the-dots books, cut-and-assemble panoramas, and paper dinosaur masks.

$2.95

Dover Publications, Inc.

31 E. Second St.

Mineola, NY 11501

Dinosaurs: The Big Book of Mobiles

Nicholas Harris; Time-Life, 1997

A 24-page dinosaur activity book including all the pieces for making two brightly colored dinosaur mobiles.

$12.95 from bookstores

Prehistoric Origami

John Montrell; Dover Publications

Detailed instructions for making 20 prehistoric paper creatures, including tyrannosaurus, stegosaurus, and tricerotops.

$9.95

Dover Publications, Inc.

31 E. Second St.

Mineola, NY 11501

HANDS-ON ACTIVITIES AND KITS

Build Your Own Dinosaurs: Book and Rubber Stamp Set

Dennis Schatz; Andrews & McMeel, 1994

Information on seven dinosaurs, plus 24 labeled rubber stamps of dinosaur bones with which kids can stamp out accurate skeletons of each.

$14.95 from bookstores

Dino Traces

A set of model fossil forms—including pelvises, leg bones, rib cages and vertebrae—with which kids can make rubbings on paper in the shape of dinosaur bones. The rubbings can then be cut out and reassembled to form complete skeletons measuring up to 19 inches long. Each kit includes six plaster fossil forms, black crayons for making rubbings, and a 24-page lesson plan, with suggestions for using "Dino Traces" at three levels of difficulty.

Three Dino Traces kits are available, including "Velociraptor," "Tricerotops," and "Tyrannosaurus rex."

$39.95 each (plus shipping/handling)

Skullduggery, Inc.

624 South B St.

Tustin, CA 92680

(800) 336-7745/fax (714) 832-1215

Dinosaur Kits

There are several kits in this series, in which kids dig a small-size replica of a dinosaur skeleton out of a chunk of clay. The skeleton is sunk in a flat slab of rock, which has been broken into a couple of large-size pieces. Young paleontologists uncover and clean these, piece them together, and glue. It's not precisely field-grade paleontology, but it's fun, and the end results look nice displayed on mantelpiece, bookcase, or bureau.

Kits include "Apatosaurus," "Stegosaurus," "Tyrannosaurus," "Tyrannosaurus Skull," "Triceratops," "Teranodon," and—especially for fans of *Jurassic Park*—"Velociraptor."

$18 each; available from many science supply companies or

Schoolmasters Science

745 State Circle

Box 1941

Ann Arbor, MI 48106

(800) 521-2832/fax (313) 761-8711

Web site: www.school-tech.com

The Dinosaur Hunter's Kit

The kit contains a clay slab in which is embedded a much-reduced replica of an apatosaurus skeleton. Kids soak the slab in water, then uncover the fossil with a scraper and paintbrush. The kit also includes an informational 64-page book, *The Dinosaur Hunter's Hand-*

book by Ted Daeschler, which describes the work of paleontologists in the field.

A more expensive version of the kit includes "The Dinosaur Hunter" CD-ROM (Mac or PC), which allows kids to "visit" famous digs and learn about specific dinosaurs.

Kit, $18.95; with CD-ROM, $29.95

Running Press Book Publishers

125 South 22nd St.

Philadelphia, PA 19103

(215) 567-5080 or (800) 345-5359/fax (800) 453-2884

Dinosaur Models

Given a little imagination—which is what kids have a lot of—you can make a dinosaur out of practically anything, from shoe boxes to modeling clay to Lego blocks. If you're looking for something a bit more professional, however, Woodkrafter Kits produces a series of wooden dinosaur model kits. Kids punch out the slotted wooden pieces and fit them together—no glue necessary—to turn out skeletons of stegosaurus, apatosaurus, tyrannosaurus, plesiosaurus, and the like. (There's also a woolly mammoth kit.) The kits range in size from about 10 inches long (the mammoth) to a tail-dragging 39 inches (apatosaurus).

Most kits, about $7

Edmund Scientific Co.

101 E. Gloucester Pike

Barrington, NJ 08007-1380

(800) 728-6999

e-mail: scientifics@edsci.com

Web site: www.edsci.com

or

Schoolmasters Science

745 State Circle

Box 1941

Ann Arbor, MI 48106

(800) 521-2832/fax (313) 761-8711

Web site: www.school-tech.com

Fossil Activity Kit

 This kit is terrific. It contains 15 genuine fossils, ranging in age from two billion (bacteria) to one million (mollusk shell) years old. Included are samples of amber, dinosaur bone, agatized coral, and petrified wood, and a trilobite, a brachiopod, a crinoid, and a

shark tooth. And more. For each fossil, there's a double-sided 8½ × 11″ illustrated card of background information and suggestions for activities. Recommended for kids in grades 4–12.

$26

Creative Dimensions

Box 1393

Bellingham, WA 98227

(360) 733-5024/fax (360) 733-4321

Fossil Hunt

This is a big box of volcanic sand from which kids, armed with teaspoons, fingers, and cleaning brushes, can extract over 20 absolutely genuine fossils, among them a bit of dinosaur bone and a small-size trilobite. Also included is a magnifying lens, specimen bags, labels, and a color-illustrated fossil guide.

$19.95

Schoolmasters Science

745 State Circle

Box 1941

Ann Arbor, MI 48106

(800) 521-2832

or

Carolina Biological Supply Co.

2700 York Rd.

Burlington, NC 27215

(800) 334-5551

or

ETA

620 Lakeview Pkwy.

Vernon Hills, IL 60061

(847) 816-5050 or (800) 445-5985/fax (800) ETA-9326

e-mail: info@etauniverse.com

Web site: www.etauniverse.com

I Dig Dinosaurs

Kids chip into the "Dinostone" block to uncover a realistic three-dimensional dinosaur skull. Each kit includes a Dinostone base with enclosed skull, and a chisel, hammer, and brush. The skull is in three parts; once unearthed and cleaned, it can be easily assembled with glue. Five kits are available: "Velociraptor," "Triceratops," "Tyrannosaurus rex," and "Pachycephalosaurus" skulls, and a "Fossil Kit," which contains tyrannosaur teeth and claws cast from actual fossils. Recommended for paleontologists in grade 4 and up.

$28.95

Earth Lore Natural History Products

315 William Ave.

Winnipeg, Manitoba R3A 0H6, Canada

(204) 947-1983/fax (204) 947-2081

e-mail: earthlor@wpg.ramp.net

or

ETA

620 Lakeview Pkwy.

Vernon Hills, IL 60061

(847) 816-5050 or (800) 445-5985/fax (800) ETA-9326

e-mail: info@etauniverse.com

Web site: www.etauniverse.com

Introduction to Radioactivity and Half-Life Experiment Kit

Much safer than it sounds. Kids study radioactivity and the concept of radioactive half-life using a collection of plastic "radioactive atoms." With these and the included activity sheets, they collect and graph data, thus calculating the amount of carbon-14 present in an insect embedded in amber 18,000 years ago and a piece of charcoal burned 28,000 years ago, and determining the age of a pollen sample from its carbon-14 content. An interesting introduction to radiocarbon dating. The kit contains enough materials for 15 lab groups of two students each.

$49.95

Lab-Aids, Inc.

17 Colt Ct.

Ronkonkoma, NY 11779

(516) 737-1133/fax (516) 737-1286

Neanderthal Book and Skeleton

Stephen Cumbaa and Barbara Hehner; Workman, 1997

An illustrated book filled with information about Neanderthal man, with related activity suggestions, and a 25-piece, foot-tall model of a Neanderthal skeleton, with display stand. Complete instructions for assembly are included.

$16.95 from bookstores or

Workman Publishing Co.

708 Broadway

New York, NY 10003

(212) 254-5900 or (800) 722-7202/fax (212) 254-8098

Web site: www.workmanweb.com

Science in a Nutshell: Fossil Formations

Actually science in a green plastic box, containing enough materials for one to three elementary-level science students. "Fossil Formations" includes an assortment of real fossils, materials for molding and casting your own (plaster) fossils, a detailed activity guide with suggestions for many hands-on projects, and (one) student journal. (Additional journals, in packets of five, are available separately.)

$29.95

Delta Education

Box 3000

Nashua, NH 03061-3000

(800) 442-5444/fax (800) 282-9560

Web site: www.delta-ed.com

Volcanoes, Dinosaurs, and Fossils MegaLab

The emphasized word on the cover of this kit is *dinosaurs*, which appears in giant letters: the kit itself, however, has a more general emphasis, covering basic concepts in geology and paleontology. The kit includes materials for about 10 experiments (with room for repeats): users erupt a chemical volcano, for example, study fumaroles, and make their own plaster "fossils." The kit also contains a small collection of volcanic rocks and (real) fossils. Recommended for kids aged 8 and up.

$29.99

Wild Goose Co.

375 Whitney Ave.

Salt Lake City, UT 84115

(801) 466-1172 or (800) 373-1498/fax (801) 466-1186

Web site: www.wildgoosescience.com

Walking Tyrannosaurus Rex

A model kit with which kids can produce a wooden dinosaur that walks on its hind legs, while its forearms and head move back and forth. The kit includes precut wooden parts for a very basic dinosaur, a preassembled gearbox with electric motor, a forward/reverse switch, and a battery box. (To walk, *T. Rex* requires two AA batteries.)

$19.95

Edmund Scientific Co.

101 E. Gloucester Pike

Barrington, NJ 08007

(800) 728-6999/fax (609) 547-3292

e-mail: scientifics@edsci.com

Web site: www.edsci.com

FOSSIL SPECIMENS

Fossil specimens, for those who don't have enough (or any) of their own, are available through many general science supply companies (see page 221). Sources include:

Creative Dimensions

Fossil kits and individual specimens, among them samples of amber, nautiloids, trilobites, ammonites, and water beetles from the La Brea tar pits.

Creative Dimensions

Box 1393

Bellingham, WA 98227

(206) 733-5024

D. J. Minerals

An excellent source for fossils of all kinds, including brachiopods, trilobites, crinoid stems, dinosaur bones, fossil fish, and fossil ferns. Also available is an "Introductory Fossil Kit" containing 16 numbered specimens from the main fossil groups, plus a master key and a hand lens; and an "Advanced Fossil Kit," which includes 33 numbered specimens.

D. J. Minerals

Box 761

Butte, MT 59703-0761

(406) 782-7339

ETA

Assorted fossil kits, among them a 15-specimen "Fossil Collection," which comes with a geologic time chart.

$15.95

ETA

620 Lakeview Pkwy.

Vernon Hills, IL 60061

(708) 816-5050 or (800) 445-5985

GAMES

Dino Math Tracks

A mathematical board game for kids aged 6 and up, in which players attempt to move their herds of dinosaurs from the waterfall to the rainbow using a variety of simple math skills.

$19.95 from toy and game stores

See **Mathematics** (page 188).

Dinosaurs and Things

A dinosaur board game playable at multiple levels for a range of ages. Players move their playing pieces along a colorful pathway, while answering challenging questions about dinosaurs. Players must also match dinosaur puzzle pieces to the correct dinosaur skeletons, set around the edge of the playing board.

$24.95

Aristoplay

450 S. Wagner Rd.

Ann Arbor, MI 48107

(800) 634-7738 or (888) GR8-GAME

fax (734) 995-4611

Web site: www.aristoplay.com

Survival or Extinction: The Dinosaur Game

A board game for dinosaur fans. Players play the parts of dinosaurs, moving through an ancient landscape and dealing with volcanic eruptions, predators, and famines in an attempt to escape extinction. Questions cards teach players the characteristics of specific dinosaurs.

$24.95 from toy and game stores

AUDIOVISUAL PALEONTOLOGY

The Dinosaurs

A four-part PBS series on the lives and times of dinosaurs and the paleontologists who study them, from the early dinosaur discoveries in the 1820s through modern-day theories of dinosaur extinction. Four hours on four videotapes.

$39.98

PBS Home Video

1320 Braddock Pl.

Alexandria, VA 22314-1698

(800) 345-4PBS

Dinosaur Hunt

A three-tape collection from *NOVA*. "Curse of *T. rex*" tells the tale of the discovery of Sue, the superb Tyrannosaurus skeleton that touched off a massive political battle; "Case of the Flying Dinosaur" discusses the controversy over the relationship between ancient dinosaurs and modern birds; and "*T. rex* Exposed" details the mythology and reality of this most famous dinosaur. Three hours on three videotapes.

$39.95

PBS Home Video

1320 Braddock Pl.

Alexandria, VA 22314-1698

(800) 345-4PBS

Dinosaurs of the Gobi

From *NOVA*, a 60-minute video about the discovery of dinosaur fossils in China's Gobi Desert.

$19.95

Movies Unlimited

3015 Darnell Rd.

Philadelphia, PA 19154

(215) 637-4444 or (800) 4-MOVIES

e-mail: movies@moviesunlimited.com

Web site: www.moviesunlimited.com

Jurassic Park

The dinosaurs are incredible, the story is gripping, and any little problems with the science can be cleared up with *The Science of Jurassic Park and the Lost World* (see Books, page 378). Parents of kids under nine should screen this one first; it's scary for the very young.

$14.99

Movies Unlimited

3015 Darnell Rd.

Philadelphia, PA 19154

(215) 637-4444 or (800) 4-MOVIES

e-mail: movies@moviesunlimited.com

Web site: www.moviesunlimited.com

Wee Sing Dinosaurs

Price Stern Sloan Publishing, 1994

An audiocassette and songbook filled with catchy dinosaur songs for kids aged 4–8.

See **Wee Sing Series** (page 756).

PALEONTOLOGY ON-LINE

Dinosaur Hall of the National Museum of Natural History

Dinosaur information and exhibit tours from the Smithsonian Institution.

photo2.si.edu/dino.html

Dinosaur Society

Visit a dinosaur dig, tour an exhibit on the dinosaurs of Jurassic Park, view dinosaur art, and share in a pen pal net for dinosaur fans.

www.dinosociety.org

The Dinosauria

An informational hypertext on dinosaurs, graphics, and exhibits.

www.ucmp.berkeley.edu/diapsids/dinosaur.html

Yogi's Behemoth: Geologic Time Line

A detailed and complete geologic timeline.

icecube.acf-lab.alaska.edu/~fsklb/geo-time.html

PHYSICS

In the public school science curriculum, simple physical principles are introduced in early elementary school. Kids in first through third grades learn about simple machines, magnets, electricity, and energy and its sources. Upper-elementary and middle school kids study light and optics, nuclear energy and radioactivity, electricity and magnetism in more detail, and are introduced to Newton's laws of motion. Ninth-grade general science usually involves studies of light, energy, simple and complex machines, and atomic structure; and kids who pursue an intensive science program usually study physics as a full-year course in twelfth grade. We studied it when our kids were interested, which was almost immediately.

Physics, of all the sciences, is perhaps the most multiheaded, encompassing mechanics, magnetism and electricity, light and optics, sound, matter and energy, nuclear physics—everything, in other words, from the distortions of fun-fair mirrors to the growth of snow crystals to *Star Trek*'s hypothetical warp drive. The wealth of possibilities makes physics both easy and difficult to study/teach. Almost anything can be used to introduce basic physics principles—marbles, magnets, mirrors, Erector sets, soap bubbles—plus toy stores and science supply companies sell assorted inexpensive classic physics toys. Collision or balance balls, for example, are favorites for demonstrating Newton's third law of motion ("Every action has an equal and opposite reaction"). These usually consist of a row of steel balls suspended from a frame: pull one ball back and let it swing, banging into the rest of the row, and one balanced ball will swing out from the opposite end. Pull back *two* balls and two balls at the opposite end will respond. Gyroscopes demonstrate principles of rotation, center of gravity, and centrifugal force; radiometers demonstrate the effects of solar energy; prisms show how white light can be split into the colors of the visible spectrum.

Our early experiments with physics were based on just such a collection of intriguing toys: the boys threw rainbows on the wall with a prism, burned their initials in blocks of wood by focusing the sun's rays through a magnifying glass, painted pictures with pendulums, built kites and model airplanes, raced marbles down an inclined plane, and rigged up a series of devices that allowed them to drop an egg out of a second-story bedroom window and hit the ground without breaking. (There were also a number of devices in which the eggs smashed into smithereens; good scientists, however, learn as much from their mistakes as from their successes.) All this, while attention holding and fun, was definitely disorganized: Bernoulli's principle one day, the definition of friction the next, a comparison of concave and convex lenses the day after that. This didn't seem to bother the boys—if there's anything kids are good at, it's assimilating disparate bits of information and building them into a pattern of their own—but as

they grew older, we felt they would benefit from a more coherent and in-depth curriculum.

This, it turned out, was easier said than done. Physics materials abound, but there aren't any readymade in-depth physics programs out there for interested eleven-year-olds—at least none that interested *our* eleven-year-old, who optimistically wanted particle physics, wave mechanics, and the equation for calculating rocket escape velocities. We tackled these demands with experimental kits, activity books, computer programs, high school and college textbooks, and by acquiring, through a friend of a friend, a kindhearted and helpful e-mail pen pal from the physics department at Cornell.

From my homeschool journal:

◆ **November 2, 1995. Josh is fourteen; Ethan, twelve; Caleb, eleven.**

We started a new science study unit today, creatively titled "Measuring Waves," using homemade workbooks and assorted references. Today we defined wave, *compared transverse and longitudinal waves, demonstrating both, and defined* frequency *and* wavelength. *Made charts of wavelengths of light in the visible spectrum; in each case, converted nanometers to meters in scientific notation. Made illustrated diagrams of the electromagnetic spectrum, from radio waves (very long) to cosmic rays (very short), discussing each class of electromagnetic waves. Thus we ran through radio waves, television waves, radar, microwaves, infrared, visible light, ultraviolet, X rays, gamma rays, and cosmic rays, all with relevant bits of history and science. Josh's diagram is particularly hilarious: he titled it "A Cartoon Guide to the Electromagnetic Spectrum."*

We then built a color-filter box using red and green cellophane and used it to study the effects of one-color light on objects of various colors. Discussed why things look colored.

Defined refraction *and demonstrated it experimentally: compared light bending between a spoon in plain water and a spoon in a saturated sugar solution. The kids all understood why. Defined* incident ray, reflected ray, refracted ray, *and* index of refraction, *using diagrams; then learned to calculate index of refraction and did a number of sample problems.*

Ethan: "What if light went through a piece of glass and then through a sugar solution and then back through a piece of glass—would it bend back and forth like a zigzag?"

Caleb: "Why is it dark at the bottom of the ocean? What actually happens to the light energy? Does it just get absorbed by water molecules until it's all gone?"

Ethan: "What happens when light goes through different thicknesses of glass? How far can a laser travel through glass?"

Josh: "What about a stained-glass window? That must get really complicated—some wavelengths of light are reflected, so that the different panes look different colors, and the waves that go through get refracted. Do different wavelengths get refracted differently?"

Ethan: "Yes! Remember the book we read about why the sky is blue? Blue light bends more. Think of a prism."

As the refraction experiment cooled down, the sugar began to come out of solution and accumulate on the bottom of the glass. We discussed the reason for this, and defined solution, suspension, *and* saturated solution. Caleb decided to make rock candy with the refraction experiment leftovers.

MAGAZINES

Quantum

A bimonthly magazine for high school–aged physics and math students. Each issue includes several feature articles on physics and math topics, math puzzles and challenges, and suggestions for hands-on activities and projects. This magazine, unlike some, does not adapt well to younger students; most of the articles assume an understanding of advanced math. An excellent resource for teenagers.

Annual subscription, $25

Quantum

National Science Teachers Association

1840 Wilson Blvd.

Arlington, VA 22201-3000

(800) 722-NSTA

Web site: www.nsta.org

Also see **General Science: Magazines** (page 218).

BOOKS

Balloon Science
Etta Kaner; Addison-Wesley, 1990

You wouldn't believe how much physical science you can do with a bag of balloons. This book describes 54 balloon-based experiments for elementary school–aged kids. Users study air pressure, jet propulsion, and static electricity, make a Cartesian diver, a model hovercraft, a balloon-powered boat, and a "magical" merry-go-round, and find out how to blow up a balloon with a bottle of soda pop. Also included are a lot of balloon riddles, balloon games and challenges, and unusual balloon facts.

The Berenstain Bears' Science Fair
Stan and Jan Berenstain; Random House, 1984

An introduction to physics for absolute beginners, in rhyme with colorful cartoonish illustrations. The Bear family—including Brother and Sister Bear, Mama Bear, and the inept (but confident) Papa Bear—are in search of projects for the upcoming science fair. On the way, with the help of the knowledgeable "Actual Factual Bear," they learn about simple machines, the three states of matter, and the different sources of energy.

The Best of Rube Goldberg
Rube Goldberg; Prentice-Hall, 1979

Cartoonist Reuben Goldberg was possibly the world's most innovative user of the simple machine. Goldberg is famed for his convoluted and hilarious devices for performing simple tasks, each using not only levers, pulleys, wedges, inclined planes, and wheels, but also squirting seltzer bottles, cuckoo clocks, porcupines, bumblebees, bowling balls, fishing poles, and canaries. Your kids will pore over this one endlessly, figuring out how each sequence of interconnecting "machines" works.

Cars and How They Go
Joanna Cole; HarperTrophy, 1986

A picture book intended for kids aged 5–9, with charming, bright-colored illustrations by Gail Gibbons. The book, in simple straightforward language, delivers a lot of detailed information, explaining the parts of the car and their functions, one by one. Each part, labeled, is shown in place in a picture of a transparent car. Supplementary diagrams show the workings of pistons, spark plugs, and exhaust system, cooling system, oil pump and lines, and brakes.

The Cartoon Guide to Physics

Larry Gonick and Art Huffman; HarperPerennial, 1991

Real physics, complete with equations, but all is presented so clearly, through many clever and creative little pictures, that even the stickiest concepts become reader-friendly. The *Guide* is about 200 pages long, divided into two main sections, "Mechanics" and "Electricity and Magnetism." "Mechanics" covers Newton's laws of motion, gravity, satellite motion, momentum and impulse, energy, collions, and rotations; "Electricity and Magnetism," charge, electrical fields, currents, magnetic fields, faraday induction, Maxwell's equations and light, and quantum electrodynamics.

See **Computer Software:** *The Cartoon Guide to Physics* (page 401).

Developing Critical Thinking Through Science

Critical Thinking Press

In two volumes. Book One (June Main and Paul Eggen, 1991) is aimed at students in grades 1–4; Book Two (Paul Eggen and June Main, 1990) at students in grades 4–6. Both are collections of reproducible hands-on science activities that require only very simple materials. The activities are designed for "the 'non-science' teacher who needs to teach science" and are thus described in foolproof detail. Most of the activities take about 20 minutes. The book introduces each by listing the experimental goal, necessary materials, and instructions for any necessary preparations. This is followed by a "Procedure and Questioning Strategy," which lists, in proper sequence, the questions the teacher should ask in the course of the activity, plus, highlighted, the correct student response. Each activity concludes with a "Practical Application" section in which the kids are asked to relate what they have just learned to some real-world event.

Book One includes 41 activities in 7 physical-science categories: "Observing," "Water," "Buoyancy and Surface Tension," "Air," "Moving Air—Air Pressure," "Force," and "Space, Light, and Shadows."

Book Two includes 80 activities, variously grouped under "Process Skills," "Force, Movement, Work, Systems, and Weight," "States of Matter," "Mass, Volume, and Density," "Air Pressure," "Heat, Expansion, and the Movement of Molecules," "The Transfer of Heat," "Flight and Aerodynamics," "The Speed of Falling Bodies," "Graphing, the Flight of Helicopters, and Controlling Variables," "The Flight of Rockets and Action-Reaction," "Inertia and the Flight of Satellites," "Surface Tension," "Bubbles," "Sound," "Light," and "Magnetism and Electricity."

Critical Thinking Press & Software

Box 448

Pacific Grove, CA 93950-0448

(800) 458-4849/fax (408) 372-3230

Einstein for Beginners

Joseph Schwartz and Michael McGuinness; Pantheon Books, 1990

A creative 173-page history of Einstein and his ideas, heavily illustrated with cartoons, prints, photographs, quotations in boxes, conversations in balloons, and clever little charts, tables, and diagrams.

Eyewitness Science: Physics

Dorling Kindersley

Several volumes in the Eyewitness Science series feature physical science themes, among them *Electricity* (Steve Parker; 1992), *Energy* (Jack Challoner; 1993), *Force and Motion* (Peter Lafferty; 1992), *Light* (David Burnie; 1992), *Matter* (Christopher Cooper; 1992), *Electronics* (Roger Bridgman; 1993), and *Technology* (Roger Bridgman; 1995). All are 64 pages long and elaborately illustrated with color photographs, prints, and diagrams. In these books, each double-page spread concentrates on a different subject-related topic. Topics covered in *Force and Motion,* for example, include "Ramps and wedges" (with diorama of pyramid builders), "Wheels and axles," "Floating and sinking,"

"Levers," "The science of the cannonball," "Getting into gear," "Newton's Laws in action," "Weight and mass," "Friction," "Pressure and flow," "Making waves," and "The ultimate speed limit" (with photos of speeding rockets and a stationary Albert Einstein). Illustrations include everything from oxcarts to quasars, plus, in between, an 18th-century clockwork model of the universe, a Roman balance scale, a wineglass shattering in response to a sound wave, and a World War II gyrocompass.

The Flying Circus of Physics
Jearl Walker; John Wiley & Sons, 1988

A large collection of intriguing, puzzling, and just plain quirky physics-based questions. Samples include "Monster movies always have a howling wind as a background sound to the sinister deeds of the monster. How does wind howl?" "Why are most clouds white? Why aren't they blue like the sky?" Answers are in the back of the book. For each question and answer, Walker also includes a list of related scientific references, though unfortunately many of these—*The Journal of Fluid Mechanics,* for example—aren't easy to find in the average small-town library.

Flying Tinsel
Grant Mellor; Cuisenaire Company, 1993

An introduction to electricity, using very simple materials—try tinsel—and with activities that recreate the research of early 17th- to 19th-century scientists. The book includes over 30 hands-on experiments, recommended for kids in grades 5–8. Users, for example, make a milk-jug Leyden jar, an electrophorus, a juice-can speaker, and a Tesla coil.

Gravity Is a Mystery
Franklyn M. Branley; HarperTrophy, 1986

This is a short picture-book explanation of gravity for readers aged 4–9. Included is an account of just what would happen if you fell through a hole stretching all the way through the earth and a chart showing what a 60-pound kid would weigh on all the planets in the solar system, plus the moon and the sun (16,740 pounds).

How Things Work: The Physics of Everyday Life
Louis A. Bloomfield; John Wiley & Sons, 1997

A creative and fascinating physics textbook—yes, you heard me—intended for use in introductory college courses but appropriate for bright high school–aged kids. The book specializes in a "backward" approach to physics, first explaining how everyday items function, then explaining the physics behind them. Each chapter begins with "Questions to Think About" and simple, illustrative "Experiments to Do" to help the thinking process along. The book covers all the fundamentals of physics in 19 detailed chapters, from Newton's laws of motion and simple machines through optics, material science, and nuclear physics—and all by means of seesaws, Frisbees, woodstoves, violins, audio amplifiers, and the like. Each chapter concludes with review questions, exercises, and problems; some of the answers are in the book.

Illustrated with many black-and-white diagrams, drawings, and photographs. A terrific, but challenging, text.

Light Action! Amazing Experiments with Optics
Vicki Cobb and Josh Cobb; HarperCollins, 1993

Vicki Cobb is a science teacher with a talent for explaining heavy-duty scientific concepts to kids; Josh Cobb is an optical engineer. It's a winning combination for an introduction to optics. Topics covered include "Blocking Light," "Bending Light," "Bouncing Light," "Color," "Making Waves," and "Polarized Light" (and more). Readers learn, for example, how scientists first measured the speed of light, that early eyeglasses were called "glass lentils," why a diamond sparkles and how fiber-optic cables work, what feathers and CDs have to do with diffraction gratings, and how a hologram is made. Included are dozens of truly interesting experiments. Recommended for kids aged 11 and up.

The Magic School Bus and the Electric Field Trip
Joanna Cole; Scholastic, 1997

The amazing Ms. Frizzle takes her elementary school class on a magical field trip that teaches them all about electricity, from the atomic basis of electrical current through the workings of common electrically powered household machines. Much of the information is delivered in "School Reports" shown at the margins of the pages: samples include "Traveling Electrons *Are* Electricity" by Michael, "What is Lightning?" by Phoebe, and "How to Make an Electromagnet" by Tim. See the **Magic School Bus Series** (page 227).

Physics: An Incremental Development

John H. Saxon Jr.; Saxon Publishers, 1993

Those familiar with the Saxon math texts (see page 177) will know what to expect from Saxon's *Physics*. The text is massive (796 pages), thorough, serious, and dry. It covers, in 100 in-depth lessons, the basic material generally taught in the first two semesters of a university physics course; it is also appropriate for advanced-placement high school physics students. The "incremental development" indicates that the lessons build upon each other in an interlocking sequence, with plenty of repetition and practice intended to "emblazon the fundamental concepts of physics in the long-term memory of the student." Dedicated users may learn a lot of physics, but they won't learn to love it.

Physics Begins With an M . . . Mysteries, Magic, and Myth

John W. Jewett Jr.; Allyn & Bacon, 1994

Each chapter in this fat (about 400 pages) illustrated book begins with a collection of "Mysteries," "Magic," and "Myths." The Mysteries are "questions about everyday life that can be understood by means of applications of the principles of physics." Examples include "Why do golf balls have dimples?," "How do astronauts 'weigh' themselves?," "Why do people talk funny after they have breathed helium?," "Why do you sometimes appear in photographs with red eyes?," "Why doesn't dry ice melt?," and "Why is the ocean blue?" The Magic is a series of demonstrations with unexpected and surprising results that can be performed in (or out of) classrooms; most are fast, simple, and impressive. The Myths are common misconceptions and mistakes that can be debunked by persons with a knowledge of physics. Try "Stars twinkle," "All lenses have curved surfaces," and "Heat rises." Each Mystery, Magic trick, and Myth is followed by a detailed physical explanation, with text, diagrams, mathematical equations, and references.

The three Ms are grouped by topic into chapters, which are arranged in the standard order found in most introductory physics texts. The book thus begins with "Vectors, Measurement and Other Mathematical Preliminaries" and proceeds through 29 chapters, including "Newton's Laws," "Circular Motion," "Temperature," "Harmonic Motion," "Waves," "Sound," "Electrical Fields and Forces," and "Reflection and Refraction."

Physics Begins With an M is intended for high school or university students or for "informed laypersons." It's challenging, thorough, interesting, and fun. Also see the sequel, *Physics Begins With Another M . . . Mysteries, Magic, Myth* (Allyn & Bacon, 1996).

The Physics of Everyday Phenomena

Jearl Walker, ed.; W. H. Freeman & Company, 1979

A collection of physics-related articles from *Scientific American*, explaining the complex science behind such everyday phenomena as the formation of snow crystals, the shape of raindrops, thunder, ocean waves, and fog.

Physics in the Hardware Store

Robert Friedhoffer; Franklin Watts, 1996

In this entertaining book, kids learn about basic physical principles through everyday objects found in the hardware store, studying friction, work, force, and simple machines with such common items as sandpaper, wheelbarrows, window shades, and crowbars. Also see, by the same author, *Physics in the Housewares Store* in which kids study the principles of pressure, centripetal force, permeability, density, and heat transmission with toilet plungers, frying pans, eggbeaters, and coffee percolators.

Physics for Kids Series

Robert Wood; TAB Books

There are several books in this hands-on series, intended for kids in grades 5–8. Titles include *49 Easy*

Experiments with Mechanics, 49 Easy Experiments with Heat, 49 Easy Experiments with Acoustics, and *49 Easy Experiments with Optics.* The experiments use inexpensive and easy-to-find materials; each can be completed in about 30 minutes.

Physics in the Real World

Keith Lockett; Cambridge University Press, 1990

The book alternates informational readings on such topics as weightlessness, plastic bullets, the space shuttle, risks from radiation, firewalking, helicopters, lightning strikes, ocean waves, and nuclear winter, with pages of creative related problems. A catchy and challenging approach to physics. The problems require a good deal of background scientific and mathematical knowledge. The answers, with brief explanations, are all in the back. Appropriate for high school–aged and older students.

The Physics of Star Trek

Lawrence M. Krauss; Basic Books, 1995

Physics for fans of James T. Kirk, Jean-Luc Picard, and the peripatetic Starship *Enterprise.* The book discusses the real-life physics behind (or not behind) such *Star Trek* staples as warp speed, transporter beams, matter-antimatter engines, and the holodeck. The science is well presented and interesting; the book is an excellent springboard for teenage Trekkies with a little science background. A warning for hopeful galactic explorers: Krauss finds major problems with the technology underlying the United Federation of Planets.

Roller Coaster Science: 50 Wet, Wacky, Wild, Dizzy Experiments About Things Kids Like Best

Jim Wiese; John Wiley & Sons, 1994

This 113-page book introduces basic physics principles with pizzazz, through popular rides at the playground and amusement park. Kids study kinetic and potential energy on the slides, the oscillations of pendulums on the swings, the physics of collisions in the bumper cars, and centripetal force on the merry-go-round, and learn about clothoid loops on the roller coaster. Readers also experiment with soap bubbles, baseballs, Frisbees, popcorn, and cotton candy.

Switch On, Switch Off

Melvin Berger; HarperTrophy, 1989

An explanation of electricity and electrical circuits for scientists aged 4–8. Berger discusses electricity in general, the workings of electrical generators and how they supply electricity to houses, and what really happens when you flick the electrical switch on and off. The book includes nice colorful diagrams, cute pictures of kids and cats, and instructions for making and testing an electromagnet.

Teaching Physical Science Through Children's Literature

Susan E. Gertz, Dwight J. Portman, and Mickey Sarquis; Learning Triangle Press, 1995

Twenty lessons for teaching physical science to kids in grades K–6 using popular fiction and nonfiction books. Included are instructions for hands-on activities and reproducible student worksheets.

Teaching Physics With Toys

Jerry L. Sarquis, Mickey Sarquis, and John P. Williams; Learning Triangle Press, 1996

A large collection of hands-on experiments designed to teach physical principles using everyday toys, such as Slinkys, yo-yos, Play-Doh, wind-up toys, rubber balls, beanbags, and rubber band–powered airplanes. The activities are categorized by age group, as appropriate for students in grades K–3, 4–6, or 7–9.

Thinking Physics: Practical Lessons in Critical Thinking

Lewis Carroll Epstein; Insight Press, 1994

The book, a fat paperback crammed with cartoons and diagrams, is divided into eight sections: "Mechanics," "Fluids," "Heat," "Vibrations," "Light," "Electricity and Magnetism," "Relativity," and "Quanta." Each section is a collection of questions, with a list of multiple-choice answers. At this point, suggests the author, readers should *stop,* close the book, and think about it for a while. "The most important problem in physics," writes Epstein, "is *perception,* how to conjure mental images, how to separate the non-essentials from the essentials and get to the heart of the problem." Once you've reached a conclusion, you can flip the book open and compare your choice to the correct answer, with accompanying crystal-clear explanation. Epstein's examples are generally close to home and down to earth. For example: "You throw a stone into some nice soft and gushy mud. It penetrates one inch. If you want the stone to penetrate four inches, you would have to throw it into the mud (a) twice as fast, (b) three times as fast, (c) four times as fast, (d) eight times as fast, (e) sixteen times as fast."

It's fun; it's interesting; and it definitely makes you think. We spent one entire dinner arguing over an Epstein problem involving a giant magnet attached to the front end of a railroad car.

The Thomas Edison Book of Easy and Incredible Experiments

The Thomas Alva Edison Foundation; John Wiley & Sons, 1988

Dozens of challenging experiments based on Edison's original research. The book covers "Simple Experiments in Electricity, Electrochemistry, and Basic Chemistry," "Simple Experiments in Magnetism and Electricity," "Selected Experiments from Edison's Phonograph to his Motion-Picture Camera," "Useful Science Projects: Electric Pens to a Simple Radio," "Energy for the Future," "Alternative Energy Sources," and "Nuclear Experiments." Students, for example, make an electric battery, an electroscope, a burglar alarm, an electric motor, a radio, and a cigar-box microphone, build a model steam engine and a solar-powered hot water heater, and convert wind energy into electricity. Some of these projects are intended for older students and require considerable building expertise, plus some out-of-the-ordinary components; others are appropriate for younger children, with some adult help. Also see *The Ben Franklin Book of Easy and Incredible Experiments* (Lisa Jo Rudy, ed.; John Wiley & Sons, 1995), a collection of experiments on weather, electricity, music, light, and sound.

A Tour of the Subatomic Zoo: A Guide to Particle Physics

Cindy Schwarz; American Institute of Physics, 1992

A 112-page interactive text designed to teach beginning high school– or college-level physics stu-

dents about elementary particle physics—that is, about the subatomic particles and forces that make up the ultimate building blocks of matter. The book is divided into eight major sections: "Matter in the Early 20th Century," "Forces and Interactions," "A Glimpse at the Particle Zoo," "More Particles and Conservation Rules," "Quarks," "The Standard Model," "Particle Accelerators," and "Particle Detectors." Under each, there are several subsections containing a short, clear text illustrated with charts and diagrams. At the end of each chapter, there's a "Self Test" (followed by the answers) and a "Summary," listing the important points covered.

The Way Things Work

David MacAulay; Houghton Mifflin, 1988

An enormous and marvelously illustrated volume on the way *everything* works, from the grand piano and the parking meter to the rocket engine and the nuclear reactor. This is the reference for those curious about how the space telescope operates—or the smoke detector, the photocopier, the microscope, the submarine, the windmill, the thermostat, or the hot-air balloon. Our middle son—the mechanical one—got *The Way Things Work* for his ninth birthday. For months he carried it with him everywhere—all 384 pages of it—and he still keeps it on his bedside table.

The book is divided into four major parts: "The Mechanics of Movement," "Harnessing the Elements," "Working With Waves," and "Electricity and Automation." Basic background information in each section is presented through a series of hilarious drawings centering around a population of endearing woolly mammoths. The principle of levers, for example, is illustrated with a log (lever) balanced on a boulder (fulcrum); at one end balances a puzzled-looking woolly mammoth; on the other a cluster of people. (In a subsequent sketch, all the people but one leap suddenly to the ground, the mammoth thuds to earth, and the unlucky last person catapults into the air.) Illustrated accounts of individual machines follow these general explanations, with detailed drawings showing insides, outsides, and operating procedures. All the parts are labeled, and text and captions are helpfully clear. This book is addictive. And the illustrations are irresistible.

Also see **Computer Software:** *The Way Things Work* (page 402).

Why Toast Lands Jelly-side Down
Robert Ehrlich; Princeton University Press, 1997

This book uses very simple equipment and crystal-clear demonstrations to illustrate complex physics principles. The demos use such low-tech materials as pennies, balloons, coffee filters, toilet paper, ballpoint pens, a soda can with a hole poked in the side, and toast and jelly. The everyday qualities of the materials, however, doesn't mean that the physics lessons are comparably simpleminded. Chapter titles include "Newton's Laws," "Orbital Motion and Angular Momentum," "Conservation of Momentum and Energy," "Fluids," "Thermodynamics," and "Mechanical Oscillations and Waves." All is beautifully explained, but to handle the equations, students will need a background in algebra and trigonometry. Interested young physicists, however, will find it absolutely fascinating. It's had all of us experimentally shoving toast (with blackberry jam) off the kitchen counter. The stuff does always land jam-side down, and we now have the equation to explain it.

The World of Atoms and Quarks
Albert Stwertka; Henry Holt, 1995

This "Scientific American Sourcebook" is an illustrated 96-page account of nuclear physics for kids, covering the history and science of the atom from the hypotheses of the ancient Greeks to the complexities of the present-day "standard model." The book is divided into nine short, understandable chapters. It also includes a list of suggested further readings, a color-coded chart of the periodic table, a "Particle Guide," and a glossary.

HANDS-ON ACTIVITIES AND KITS

AC/DC

A card game of electric circuits. The game includes 84 cards, 80 representing elements of electric circuits—wires, fuses, batteries, bulbs, and switches—plus four unpleasant surprise cards (SHOCKs and SHORTs). The object is to lay down the cards in the form of a workable circuit, including—at the very least—an energy source, a switch, an energy user, and enough wire connectors to string them all together. Players accumulate points according to the number of cards used and the complexity of the circuit. Each card in a completed series circuit is worth one point, for example; each card in a series/parallel circuit is worth two. The first player to reach an agreed-upon number of points wins the game.

$9.95 from game stores or
Ampersand Press
750 Lake St.
Port Townsend, WA 98368
(800) 624-4263
Web site: www.ampersandpress.com

Camera Obscura Kit

Users fold and assemble the cardboard camera and load it with black-and-white photopaper. After making the exposure, the picture simply develops, Polaroid-style, before the viewer's eyes. An accompanying "Dark Room Kit," with chemicals, a red bulb for illuminating the darkroom, and photographic paper, is available for those interested in making prints from their developed originals.

"Camera Obscura Kit," $11.50; "Dark Room Kit," $25.95
American Science & Surplus
3605 Howard St.
Skokie, IL 60076
(847) 982-0870/fax (800) 934-0722
Web site: www.sciplus.com
or
Edmund Scientific Co.
101 E. Gloucester Pike
Barrington, NJ 08007-1380
(800) 728-6999
e-mail: scientifics@edsci.com
Web site: www.edsci.com

See also **Fun With Photography** (page 397) and *Pinhole Photography* (page 399).

SCIENCE

Capsela Kits

The Capsela Science Discovery system is a series of interlocking and interchangeable parts—including motors, gears, and switches, encased in clear plastic capsules—with which kids can make an increasingly complex series of machines. They can see for themselves just how each machine works, since all gears and wheels are visible. There is a range of kits in the series, from the "#175 Introductory Set"—29 parts and instructions for five working projects—to the "#1000 Expert Set"—108 parts, including chain links, a blinking light source, variable speed control, water pump, and vacuum device—with which kids can build 100 different land and water models. Using the kits and the included science booklet, "See How It Works!" by physicist Clifford Swartz (father of six), kids variously study scientific concepts of force, work, energy, and momentum, the principles behind the operation of simple machines, and the ins and outs of electrical circuitry, the law of buoyancy, and Newton's third law of motion. They have fun too.

Capsela also packages a "Hand Generator Kit" with which kids can watch mechanical energy being converted to electrical energy as they turn the hand crank and light up a small bulb, and assorted "voice command" robot kits with which advanced builders can turn out versatile flashing, beeping contraptions that scuttle about the floor in response to verbal commands or manual remote control.

Kits, about $20 to $100 in toy and science supply
stores, or
Creative Learning Systems (Transtech Catalog)
16510 Via Esprillo
San Diego, CA 92127
(800) 458-2880/fax (619) 675-7707
Web site: www.clsinc.com

Discovery Kits
Running Press

Creative and educational kits for young physicists. The "Build Your Own Flashlight Kit" includes everything needed to build a functioning flashlight in a snazzy multicolored cardboard case (bulb, socket, switch, battery holder, reflector, and lens). The illustrated handbook, *The Flashlight Book,* by Jim Becker and Andy Mayer, includes instructions, an explanation of how flashlights work, and a number of activities demonstrating scientific concepts of light, shadow, and color.

With the "Build Your Own Walkie-Talkies Kit," kids turn out a pair of working walkie-talkies (in lightning-bolt-patterned cardboard cases) and learn about radio waves and communications; the "Build Your Own Radio Kit" produces a working AM radio, in a turquoise cardboard case with tuner and volume adjustment dials. The accompanying handbook, *The Radio Book,* explains in detail the workings of all the radio components.

Kits, $12.95 to $19.95; available from game or book
stores or
Running Press Book Publishers
125 South 22nd St.
Philadelphia, PA 19149
(215) 567-5050 or (800) 345-5359/fax (800) 453-2884

Easy-to-Make Periscope
A. G. Smith; Dover Publications

The completed periscope is 18 inches high, in camouflage-patterned cardboard; mirrors are made from an included Mylar sheet.

$4.95
Dover Publications, Inc.
31 E. Second St.
Mineola, NY 11501

Edible Optics Kit

An optical lens-making project kit for elementary-level students and—at the same time—a highly creative use for Jell-O. Kids cast converging and diverging Jell-O lenses (in petri dishes, using watch glasses) and study their properties. Three colors of Jell-O are included, for color-mixing experiments, along with a spherometer for measuring curvature of the lenses, and an informational instruction manual.

$39.95
Edmund Scientific Co.
101 E. Gloucester Pike

Barrington, NJ 08007-1380

(800) 728-6999

e-mail: scientifics@edsci.com

Web site: www.edsci.com

or

ETA

620 Lakeview Pkwy.

Vernon Hills, IL 60061

(847) 816-5050 or (800) 445-5985/fax (800) ETA-9326

e-mail: info@etauniverse.com

Web site: www.etauniverse.com

Electronics Kits

Electronics kits, at various levels of difficulty (and price), are available through most science supply catalogs.

American Science & Surplus

3605 Howard St.

Skokie, IL 60076

(847) 982-0870/fax (800) 934-0722

Web site: www.sciplus.com

or

ETA

620 Lakeview Pkwy.

Vernon Hills, IL 60061

(847) 816-5050 or (800) 445-5985/fax (800) ETA-9326

e-mail: info@etauniverse.com

Web site: www.etauniverse.com

or

Edmund Scientific Co.

101 E. Gloucester Pike

Barrington, NJ 08007-1380

(800) 728-6999

e-mail: scientifics@edsci.com

Web site: www.edsci.com

Electronic Project Lab Kits

Available in various sizes with which users can complete 30 to 200 projects. The kits consist of a "bread board" upon which all the basic electronic parts necessary for the projects are built in and clearly labeled: batteries, diodes, switches, transistors, resistors, capacitors, LEDs, radio circuits, and the like. Each component is connected to spring terminals. Kids sim-

ply connect wires—the kits include lots, in different colors—from spring terminal to spring terminal, in the proper order, to produce everything from an "Electronic Woodpecker" and an "Electronic Cat" to a light dimmer, an LED strobe light, a musical tempo generator, a two-transistor radio, and a variable R-C oscillator. The accompanying instruction book includes explanations of the science behind each project, a description of expected results, and precise wiring sequence directions.

From Radio Shack stores or

Carolina Biological Supply Co.

2700 York Rd.

Burlington, NC 27215

(800) 334-5551/fax (800) 222-7112

Exploring Electronics Kit

A simple kit with which kids can build an electronic burglar alarm suitable for attaching annoyingly to bedroom or closet door: all components are included, plus an informational instruction book.

Scientific Explorer, Inc.

2802 E. Madison, Suite 114

Seattle, WA 98112

(800) 900-1182/fax (206) 322-7610

e-mail: sciex@scientificexplorer.com

Web site: www.scientificexplorer.com

Fischertechnik Kits

A series of superb model-building kits for young physicists and engineers. Among these are: The "Universal Kit," a good bet for beginners: it includes building components and instructions for making 24 working models, among them a balance scale, a garage door, a sewing machine, and an automobile transmission. "I'm Walking—Bionic Biology in Technology," for builders aged 9 and up, includes a battery-powered motor and 380+ pieces for building six animal-like models that variously crawl, creep, hop, or walk. "CarTech," for kids aged 10 and up, includes materials for a series of motorized models demonstrating such automotive features as differential gears, floating axles, manual transmissions, and four-wheel drive. And many more.

$35 to $130 from toy and game stores or
Timberdoodle Co.

E. 1510 Spencer Lake Rd.

Shelton, WA 98584

(360) 426-0672

e-mail: mailbag@timberdoodle.com

Web site: www.timberdoodle.com

Fun With Photography

The kit includes materials for making a pinhole camera and a slide projector, sunprint paper, and supplies for assembling a photo album and a newspaper. An instruction book explains how a camera works and gives complete instructions for all activities.

$19.95

Creativity for Kids

1802 Central Ave.

Cleveland, OH 44115

(800) 642-2288

Web site: www.creativityforkids.com

How to Fly

A *NOVA* "Curiosity Kit" with which kids can build and test a dozen flying machines, including a boomerang, a collection of paper airplanes, a kite, a paper helicopter, and a jet propulsion machine. The kit comes with an informational instruction booklet, the *Aviation Explorer's Log*. All materials are included, and everything works.

$19.95 from toy and game stores

For a local source contact:

Curiosity Kits

Box 811

Cockeysville, MD 21030

(410) 584-2605 or (800) 584-KITS

e-mail: CKitsinc@aol.com

K'NEX Kits

The kits contain assorted color-coded snap-together rods, connectors, pulleys, tires, and rubber bands organized so that kids can build a large number of creative structures using not only straight lines and angles but also curves, slopes, and circles. The "Basic Set" contains 325 pieces, with instructions for 20 models; the "Intermediate Set," 770 pieces, with instructions for 35 models; and the "Giant Set," 1,800 pieces, with instructions for 50 models.

The "K'NEX Education Primer Set" contains 730 pieces, plus instructions for 40 models. There's a color-illustrated teacher's guide to go with it, which costs almost as much as the set itself, with instructions for over 250 K'NEX-based activities involving math and science for kids in grades K–8.

The "Racing Energy Set"—600 pieces—teaches kids about potential and kinetic energy and energy conversion with the design and testing of several racing car models; a teacher's guide is included. The cars are rubber-band- or spring-motor-powered.

The "Roller Coaster Physics Set" is a spectacular learning experience for kids in grade 6 and up: the kit includes 2,600 pieces, plus instructions for building two different (but equally impressive) models. The roller coaster, for example, is over eight feet long and three feet high, with 25 feet of track. Building the model is an education in itself, introducing students to structural and engineering concepts. Once the model is completed, kids, using coaster cars and balls, experiment with loops and inclined planes, learn about centripetal force, and measure and graph speeds at different points on the roller-coaster track. An accompanying teacher's guide supplies physics curriculum support.

With the "Big Ball Factory Set"—3,100 pieces—kids study force and motion by constructing a hand-crank-operated five-foot-tall maze tower, through which balls plummet down a vertical chute, roll down an inclined plane, negotiate pivot arms and a helical spiral, and bump down a ladder.

$35 (the "Basic Set") to $120 (the "Giant Set," "Roller Coaster," or "Big Ball Factory"); at toy and game stores or

Edmund Scientific Co.

101 E. Gloucester Pike

Barrington, NJ 08007-1380

(800) 728-6999

e-mail: scientifics@edsci.com

Web site: www.edsci.com

or

Creative Learning Systems
16510 Via Esprillo
San Diego, CA 92127
(800) 458-2880/fax (619) 675-7707
Web site: www.clsinc.com

or

Delta Education
Box 3000
Nashua, NH 03061-3000
(800) 442-5444/fax (800) 282-9560
Web site: www.delta-ed.com

Lego Dacta/Lego Technic Kits

Lego Dacta is the educational division of Lego Systems, Inc., the company that makes all those wonderful sets of interlocking little plastic blocks with which our kids over the years have built starships, castles, pirate ships, fortresses, and anything else they could think of. The Lego Technic kits, continuing in this praiseworthy tradition, are excellent vehicles for introducing kids to physics.

The "Lego Technic I" kit ("Simple Machines") includes 179 pieces, among them gears, pulleys, wheels, axles, and belts, plus 20 creative Activity Cards. Each of the Activity Cards shows a photograph of a real-life machine—such as a windmill or crane—followed by step-by-step instructions for building a working Lego Technic equivalent. "Technic II" ("Transmissions Systems") moves up a step in complexity. It contains 278 pieces, including motor and battery box, plus 20 Activity Cards with instructions for building motorized models. Teachers' guides are available for each, with lesson plans and suggestions for additional activities.

For younger physicists, aged 6–9, the "Early Simple Machines" kit includes 71 bigger Duplo-block-size pieces, among them wheels, axles, pulleys, levers, and gears, plus eight Activity Cards; an additional "Early Simple Machines Activity Pack" is available separately, with 11 more Activity Cards and a teacher's guide.

A smaller "Mechanical Toy Shop Set," with 32 Duplo-size pieces, teaches kids how handles turn to make things move: the two Activity Cards picture a jack-in-the-box, a drummer machine, and an amusement park boat ride.

The "Pneumatic Set" introduces kids to machines that operate via compressed-air pumps: the kit includes a pneumatic pump, two pneumatic cylinders, two pneumatic switches, tubes, connectors, and five Activity Cards. The cards picture such pneumatic devices as dentists' chairs, vertical presses, and sliding doors, followed by step-by-step building instructions.

The "Manufacturing Systems Set" brings "real-life systems into your technology classroom," with 282 components, including a 9-volt motor, battery box, gears, differential, cams, pulleys, wheels, tires, and axles, and a crane hook, plus 16 Activity Cards; the "Simple Control Building Set" introduces kids to programmable control without a computer. Builders create and run simple programs to control a number of motorized models, including a rotating stage, an elevator, a robot plotter, and a walking dinosaur. The kit contains 220 pieces, including sound elements with connecting leads, and four Activity Cards.

About $20 to $85

Lego Dacta
555 Taylor Rd.
Box 1600
Enfield, CT 06083-1600
(203) 749-2291 or (800) 527-8339/fax (203) 763-2466

or

Delta Education
Box 3000
Nashua, NH 03061-3000
(800) 442-5444/fax (800) 282-9560
Web site: www.delta-ed.com

or

Creative Learning Systems
16510 Via Esprillo
San Diego, CA 92127
(800) 458-2880/fax (619) 675-7707
Web site: www.clsinc.com

Levitron

This is an "antigravity top" and a truly amazing little toy, though getting it to function properly is much trickier than it looks. The antigravity effect—the top spins entrancingly in midair—is produced by opposed permanent magnets. The kit includes a wooden base (with embedded magnet), a plastic lifting tray, and a magnetic top. Also included is an assortment of colored washers in different weights and materials that are added to the top for weight adjustment: if the top is too light, it will flip off the base sideways; if too heavy, it will never lift off the ground. Ideally, when it is properly adjusted, you start the top spinning on the plastic tray and base, boost it gently to its "floating height" by lifting the plastic tray, and finally scoot the tray out from underneath the top, leaving it to spin magically in the air over its wooden base. It's marvelous to watch, but finicky to operate and set up. A challenge for older kids.

$49 from toy and game stores

The Magic Mirror: An Antique Optical Toy
McLoughlin Bros.; Dover Publications, 1979

A reproduction of a 19th-century children's book containing 24 anamorphic images—distorted pictures that make sense only when seen reflected in a tubular mirror. The book includes the mirror, which is a sheet of flexible silver Mylar. Roll this into a cylinder and position it on the circle marked beneath each picture and the colorful smears on the pages, viewed in the mirror, resolve themselves into a ballet dancer, an elephant, a squirrel eating a nut, or a French policeman on a bicycle.

Dover Publications, Inc.
31 E. Second St.
Mineola, NY 11501

Movit Robot Kits
Caleb, our 12-year-old, includes these hopefully on every birthday and Christmas list. The Movit series is a collection of computerized battery-powered robot kits, each with preassembled PC boards, hardware, and mechanical drive systems, appropriate for builders aged 10 and up, armed with a handful of simple tools. The finished products are elegant. The "Line Tracker," for example, is a gray-and-turquoise robot with an elephant-trunk-like extension in front that operates as a photo interrupter, projecting and receiving infrared

rays. Black absorbs the rays; white reflects them, which difference allows the robot to follow a black line drawn on white paper. The "Medusa," which looks like a transparent jellyfish on legs, walks and stops upon preset command; the "Manta" reverses itself when it senses a loud noise, such as a yelp or a hand clap; and the "Soccer Robot," a red box on six legs, runs forward and backward, turns right, left, or all the way around in a circle, and kicks a paper soccer ball. The Movit series is made by OWI, Inc., which also produces a line of "easy" kits for younger builders, including an air-propelled jet racer, a scooter, and an electromagnetic train.

$30 to $80
OWI, Inc.
1160 Mahalo Pl.
Compton, CA 90220-5443
(310) 638-4732/fax (310) 638-8347
or
Edmund Scientific Co.
101 E. Gloucester Pike
Barrington, NJ 08007-1380
(800) 728-6999
e-mail: scientifics@edsci.com
Web site: www.edsci.com
or
Creative Learning Systems
16510 Via Esprillo
San Diego, CA 92127
(800) 458-2880/fax (619) 675-7707
Web site: www.clsinc.com

Pinhole Photography Kit
The "Pinhole Photography Kit" (John Adams Toys) includes everything needed for kids to make a pinhole camera and then develop and print their own photographs. Users assemble the camera from precut black cardboard, poke a precise pinhole, and load a sheet of photographic paper. This is slow-speed paper, rather than the high-speed film used in regular cameras, which means that it takes at least 30 seconds of exposure to take a picture (on a bright sunny day). (Active pets and moving vehicles, advises the instruction booklet, make poor pinhole subjects.) The exposed film is then developed, in the dark,

using the included chemicals (developer and fixer) and rinsing trays. To make a print, kids place the developed negative facedown on a new piece of photographic paper and expose the two to white light; the print is then processed in developer and fixer. The end result, if all goes well, should be a nice, clear black-and-white photograph—taken with a cardboard box. The kit includes 25 sheets of 3 × 3-inch photographic paper, enough for 12 negatives, 12 prints, and one mistake.

> $32.95
> Young Explorers
> 825 S.W. Frontage Rd.
> Ft. Collins, CO 80522
> (800) 239-7577 or (800) 777-8817/fax (970) 484-8067

Sir Isaac Newton Scientific Explorer Kit

A "History of Science" kit based on the work of one of the greatest physicists—perhaps *the* greatest physicist—of all time. Kids build a spectroscope and a color viewing box, launch a rocket, and re-create Newtonian experiments demonstrating the laws of motion and gravity. The kit includes an informational booklet that contains instructions for activities and a brief account of Newton's life and work.

> $23.95
> Scientific Explorer, Inc.
> 2802 E. Madison, Suite 114
> Seattle, WA 98112
> (206) 322-7611 or (800) 900-1182/fax (206) 322-7610
> e-mail: sciex@scientificexplorer.com
> Web site: www.scientificexplorer.com

STEREOSCOPE KITS

The stereoscope is a device that, through the wonders of binocular vision, transforms flat, two-dimensional images into 3-D. Invented in 1838 by an optical researcher named Charles Wheatstone, it was a popular parlor toy of the 19th century. Versions are available from many science supply companies or you can make your own. With the "American Stereoscope Kit" (Van Cort Instruments), kids can make a replica of a 19th-century scope, in heavy-duty cardboard, with a wooden handle and leather viewing hood. Materials (cards and color prints) are included to make six of stereoscopic pictures for 3-D viewing. Also included is a camera adaptor, so that you can take stereoscopic photographs of your own.

> $26 from toy and game stores

Whitewings

The world's best paper airplanes. Several kits are available in the Whitewings series: some for all-paper planes; some for paper-and-balsa-wood gliders. Some kits include precut parts—kids punch out the pieces and glue them together; in others, the pieces are printed on heavy-stock paper and must be cut out. The Whitewings planes were designed by master paper pilot Yasuaki Ninomiya—grand-prize winner in the First Great International Airplane Contest—and have set many paper flight records. The planes, once launched, are said to stay airborne for up to 10 minutes. Kits include rubber bands and catapult launchers.

> Kits, about $16 apiece
> AG Industries, Inc.
> 15335 N.E. 95th St.
> Redmond, WA 98052
> (206) 885-4599
> or
> Creative Learning Systems
> 16510 Via Esprillo
> San Diego, CA 92127
> (800) 458-2880/fax (619) 675-7707
> Web site: www.clsinc.com
> or
> Edmund Scientific Co.
> 101 E. Gloucester Pike
> Barrington, NJ 08007-1380
> (800) 728-6999
> e-mail: scientifics@edsci.com
> Web site: www.edsci.com
> or
> Carolina Biological Supply Co.
> 2700 York Rd.
> Burlington, NC 27215
> (800) 334-5551/fax (800) 222-7112

Wild Goose Physics Kits

The Wild Goose Company packages creative (and funny) science kits, among them several for young physicists. "Dit Dah Dit" is an electrical experiment kit, filled with gadgets for building electric circuits: copper wire, bell wire, batteries and battery clips, lightbulbs and sockets, a knife switch, and a buzzer, plus associated wood supports and hardware. Kids build series and parallel circuits, evaluate conductors and insulators, and build a nerve tester, an electromagnet, and a working telegraph. The illustrated instruction booklet includes a Morse code chart, for enthusiastic telegraphers.

With "Newton's Puzzle Box," kids learn about Newton's laws of motion and experiment with centers of gravity; with "Magnet Mania," they study magnets and static electricity; and with "Out to Launch," they perform over 30 experiments having to do with air pressure, Bernoulli's law, and aerodynamics. Recommended for kids in grades K–6.

> $29.95 each
> Wild Goose Co.
> 375 Whitney Ave.
> Salt Lake City, UT 84115
> (801) 466-1172 or (800) 373-1498/fax (801) 466-1186
> Web site: www.wildgoosescience.com

You're a Special Effects Movie Artist Kit

A *NOVA* "Curiosity Kit" based on movie illusions. The kit includes all the equipment for making a thaumatrope, a zoetrope, and a stereoscope, along with an informational activity booklet. Optics, with an interesting twist.

> About $20 from toy and game stores
> For a local source contact:
> Curiosity Kits
> Box 811
> Cockeysville, MD 21030
> (410) 584-2605 or (800) 584-KITS/fax (410) 584-1247
> e-mail: Ckitsinc@aol.com

COMPUTER SOFTWARE

The Cartoon Guide to Physics

Based on the book of the same name by Larry Gonick (see page 389), this program introduces kids to physics through clever animations, narrations, and text. Users have a choice of entering "Lucy's World," where they are treated to a series of explanations and demonstrations of physics concepts, choosing from a menu of 11 major topics (among them "Motion," "Projectiles," "Rotations"); or heading for "The Workshop," where they participate in physics experiments. In "Rollercoaster," for example, by adjusting initial potential energy, they attempt to shoot a ball through a roller-coaster-shaped tube; in "Projectiles," by choosing the mass of a cannonball and setting the angle of a fat little cannon, they attempt to hit an octopus. Also included is a glossary of physics terms and a timeline of philosophers and physicists from Plato to Niels Bohr, with brief biographies of each.

The animations are terrific, but despite the attractive packaging, the information sounds and/or reads like a classroom lecture. Our middle son, intent on learning physics, liked it; the other two, after an initial run through the cartoons, dropped it. On CD-ROM for Mac and Windows

> HarperCollins Interactive
> 10 E. 53rd St.
> New York, New York 10022
> (800) HCI-6234
> Web site: www.harpercollins.com/interactive/hcinteractive.html

The Incredible Machine 3

Some years ago we stumbled upon an earlier incarnation of this program: "The Even More Incredible Machine," a collection of marvelous puzzles in which kids assemble Rube Goldberg–style mechanical contraptions to perform specific functions, each set in motion upon completion at the touch of a button. For each puzzle, a few parts have been placed in the proper order already; it's up to the player to fill in the blanks. Available parts include not only such traditional engineering standbys as light switches and conveyor belts but also trampolines, bowling balls, vacuum cleaners, windmills, rockets, and balloons, which variously roll, bounce, blow, tilt, smash, drop, or explode. All goes according to the laws of physics, which means that there's a definite scientific logic to each puzzle solution. And they're funny too.

"The Incredible Machine 3" provides more, and just as enthralling, of the same: 150 puzzles, all to be set in working order with the gadgets from Professor Tim's Parts Bin. On CD-ROM for Mac or Windows.

$19.95

Sierra Online

7100 W. Center Rd., Suite 301

Omaha, NB 68106

(800) 757-7707

The Way Things Work

Based on the book of the same name by David MacAulay (see page 393), this is an absorbing multimedia demonstration of the way anything you can possibly think of works. Users can observe demonstrations of basic "Principles of Science," choosing from among 22 topics (among them "Pulleys," "Wheels," "Sound," "Heat," "Flying," and "Computers"). Principles are explained through text, narration, and hilarious "Mammoth Movies," animated science demos in which woolly mammoths are the key players. Under "Pressure," for example, a water-filled mammoth is used to demonstrate the workings of a piston: squashed from behind by a giant piston, the mammoth compresses and squirts a stream of water from its trunk, thus putting out a fire. "Machines" accesses an enormous alphabetical encyclopedia of machines: click on any one and users see a working diagram, with explanation. "History" includes a timeline of inventions—click on any one for more information and an up-close look—and "Inventors" is a listing of short, illustrated biographies of famous scientists and inventors. (Click on the picture of the invention for more information about it.) Our kids have spent hours lost in this one. On CD-ROM for Mac or Windows.

$39.95

Dorling Kindersley Publishing

1224 Heil Quaker Blvd.

LaVergne, TN 37086

(888) DIALDKP

Web site: www.dk.com

PHYSICS ON-LINE

Ask the Physics Guy

The site includes a "Who's Who in Physics," with biographies and information about famous physicists,

basic physics information with text and graphics, a list of fundamental constants, physics cartoons, physics puzzlers, and a place to ask questions of a friendly physicist.

www.gwi.net/~eiko/physicsguy.htm

Contemporary Physics Education Project

The site includes an interactive tour of the atom and a tutorial on nuclear fusion.

www-pdg.lbl.gov/cpep.html

Fermilab

A tour of Fermilab, lesson plans and projects for kids of all ages, and access to "Quark Quest," an on-line newspaper about particle physics for middle-grade kids.

www-ed.fnal.gov

How Things Work

Physical explanations of how things work, grouped into categories such as "Falling Balls" and "Electric and Magnetic Forces." The site is maintained by physicist Louis Bloomfield, author of *How Things Work: The Physics of Everyday Life* (see page 390).

www.phys.virginia.edu/Education/Teaching/
HowThingsWork

Interactive Physics Problems

Physics problems, categorized in 15 chapters. Kids can try their hands at solving them; then view detailed step-by-step solutions and interactive demonstrations.

info.itp.berkeley.edu/Vol1/Contents.html

Internet Plasma Physics
Education Experience

Interactive pages on matter, electricity, magnetism, energy, and fusion, a virtual tour of a fusion reactor and examples of real data from fusion experiments to analyze, and an "Ask a Scientist" page for student questions.

ippex.pppl.gov/ippex

Learn Physics Today!

An interactive on-line tutorial in basic physics. Clear and understandable text, many examples, and quizzes.

library.advanced.org/10796

Playground Physics

Complete lesson plans for physics at the playground for kids in grades 4–7. Plans include "jungle-gym drop," a study of gravity and its effect on falling objects; "see-saw physics," a study of levers; and "swing-set physics," a study of pendulums.

lyra.colorado.edu/sbo/mary/play

Unit Conversion

How do you get from miles/hour to meters/second? From degrees Fahrenheit to degrees Centigrade? From grams to pounds? This site explains one of the major student sticking points in physics problems: unit conversion. Users can access units of distance, area, volume, mass, speed, power, and many more for lists of equivalents and helpful hints.

www.soton.ac.uk/~scp93ch/refer/convfact.htm

GEOGRAPHY

Our country is the world—our countrymen
are all mankind.

WILLIAM LLOYD GARRISON

Geography, roughly, is divided into three parts. "Physical geography," closely linked to earth science and geology, covers the scientific lay of the land, as in "How did the Grand Canyon form?," "What is the Pacific Ring of Fire?," and "What makes mountains?" It also encompasses such topics as climatology, ecology, and topography. "Cultural geography" covers world cultures and ways of life; "political geography" covers man-made aspects of territory, such as national boundaries and their impact on society, capital cities, and population demographics.

While we covered all of these, more or less, in the course of our homeschool curriculum, geography in our hands was best learned in an integrated cross-curricular fashion—that is, it was most readily absorbed in the process of studying something else altogether. One of our foremost geography program successes—I hate to admit this—involved a prolonged investigation of international tragedies, catastrophes, and disasters. Our sons, who collectively displayed a monumental lack of interest in learning the capital of Myanmar or the principal products of Paraguay, positively fell over each other to locate the sites of horrendous volcanic eruptions, devastating earthquakes, horrific explosions, bloody battles, and tragically sunken ships. All three boys, without visible effort, quickly learned to pinpoint the ex-island of Krakatoa, the ex-city of Pompeii, the onetime location of Carthage (blitzed by the Romans at the end of the Third Punic War), Siberia's Tunguska Forest (exploding asteroid), and the fatal spot in the North Atlantic where the *Titanic* went down. There were no commercial resources that meshed with this morbid taste, so we ended up writing interactive workbooks of our own, complete with disaster descriptions, outline maps, mind-expanding geographical background information, and suggested projects. The boys, inspired, learned a lot about lava, Apollo objects, icebergs, geologic faults, and Hannibal's elephants. They also learned how to use an atlas, and today they seem to know their way around the world map. After all, there have been an awful lot of disasters.

Homemade theme-oriented activity books, tailored to the boys' interests—word processed, printed, and stapled together—have always been a mainstay of our geography program. After reading a collection of stories about Paul Bunyan, for example, we began our "Geography with Paul Bunyan" series, in which the boys traveled the United States in the footsteps of the tall-tale hero, starting out in the state of Maine, and ending up in the state of Washington where Paul, in pursuit of the Giant Moose, ran north to Alaska and back again. En route, they drew and colored state maps, popped a batch of popcorn to commemorate Paul's famous popcorn blizzard, cooked a messy (but large) breakfast of flapjacks, designed elaborate pens that never ran out of ink, just like Johnny Inkslinger's,

read books about moose, geysers, and the formation of the Grand Canyon, and—using logs pulled from the family woodpile—studied tree rings, with a brief academic side trip into the biology of trees.

In another thematic workbook series, the boys—who had become interested in spelunking—toured the country with caves, starting with Mammoth Cave in Kentucky. In another, they traveled from state to state after gold and jewels, starting with the diamond mines of Arkansas. This proved so popular that we tried a gem-studded world geography tour, covering, for example, Burmese rubies, Colombian emeralds, Japanese pearls, and South African diamonds. Another series featured monsters, starting with Washington Irving's Headless Horseman of the Hudson River Valley; and another, birds, starting—all at once—with the seven states whose official feathered friend is the cardinal.

From my homeschool journal:

◆ **January 29, 1991. Josh is nine; Ethan, eight; and Caleb, six.**

We began the morning with our latest geography project, "Geography With Caves," using homemade workbooks. The boys each decorated a big cardboard box (their "Exploration Vehicles") and a cover for a spiral-bound notebook ("Exploration Logbooks"); and each adopted an explorer's name. Josh, for geographical purposes, is now "Mr. Mystic"; Ethan, "Jack Sea"; and Caleb, "Captain Explorer Searcher." We concentrated on Kentucky this morning, site of Mammoth Cave. The boys first located, labeled, and colored Kentucky on outline maps of the United States; and we pinpointed the location of Mammoth Cave, using the road atlas. We then read about limestone caves in Caves *by Jenny Wood, discussed chemical composition of limestone, dug a chunk of limestone out of our rock collection, and tested it: add vinegar to limestone and you get bubbles of carbon dioxide. Everybody took turns making bubbles. We looked at photographs of cave systems and of Mammoth Cave, after which the boys, each equipped with a flashlight and their logbooks, crawled under our bed (a cave) and drew their own cave system maps.*

We looked up the cardinal, the state bird of Kentucky, in the Peterson's field guide and the boys drew cardinal pictures (male) in their logbooks. We read a book about horses and discussed Kentucky bluegrass—Josh: "Is it really blue?"—after which they all went outside, collected a few (dead) grass samples, colored them blue with magic markers, taped them in their logbooks, and labeled them "blue grass."

During lunch, we talked about the early settlement of Kentucky and read a short biography of Kentucky settler Daniel Boone, (Daniel Boone, Frontier Adventurer, by Keith Brandt). Josh and Ethan then decamped to build stick models—using real sticks—of Fort Boone at Boonesboro; Caleb stayed behind to build a fort of his own out of Lincoln logs.

◆ January 30, 1991

Geography: concentrated on Missouri today, which has lots of caves, notably Meramec Caverns, which the boys remember visiting. I found photographs taken in the caverns for each boy to paste in his Exploration Logbook. Located Missouri on the United States map; colored and labeled it on outline maps. Josh: "How come Missouri is written as MO?" The boys made illustrated lists of spelunking equipment; we read a biography of Mark Twain, born and raised in Missouri, (Mark Twain? What Kind of a Name Is That? by Robert Quackenbush) (see page 87), and the story of Tom Sawyer's adventures in the cave. We read about crinoids—the Missouri state fossil—in A Field Guide to Fossils; studied the crinoid specimens in our rock collection; and the boys drew and labeled crinoid pictures in their logbooks. Reminisced about our past caving expeditions: the boys' favorite was a tour of Fisher Cave in Missouri, a "wild" cave in which we all had to carry our own lanterns and where we saw a colony of bats.

◆ February 1, 1991

Carlsbad Caverns, New Mexico. We located New Mexico on the map (also Old Mexico); labeled/colored New Mexico on outline maps. The boys discussed—and enthusiastically imitated—the New Mexico state bird, the roadrunner, and drew pictures of roadrunner tracks, which are shaped like the letter X, in their logbooks. Looked up and discussed different kinds of bird tracks.

We read an advertisement for Pony Express riders, which included the ominous phrase "Orphans preferred." Caleb: "What's an orphan?" Read a short book about the Pony Express, traced the route the express riders probably took, from Missouri through New Mexico to California. We checked out pictures of the Carlsbad Caverns, with and without bats, and the boys drew and labeled pictures of stalactites and stalagmites. We read about how stalactites/stalagmites form, and about the tallest cave pillar in the world—it's 128 feet tall, in China. Ethan: "How tall is that?" We then set up an experiment to make stalactites and stalagmites of our own, using two jars of sodium carbonate solutions with a yarn wick running between them, as described in Jenny Wood's Caves. Unfortunately, this does not seem to be working as claimed; the boys have several suggestions explaining the failure and ideas for remedying it. We're trying them.

◆ February 5, 1991

We've moved on to South Dakota. The boys located South Dakota on the United States map; colored/labeled South Dakota on their own outline maps. We then read about the carving of Mount Rushmore and discussed the four presidents on it; and the boys drew their own versions of Mount Rushmore, none of which featured a presidential portrait. (Joshua's was a huge stone wizard.) Read a biography of Teddy Roosevelt—Don't You Dare Shoot That Bear! A Story of Teddy Roosevelt by Robert Quackenbush—who not only appears on Mount Rushmore but also owned a ranch in South Dakota. We then read about Wind Cave in the Black Hills, and the boys all made spooky wind cave noises by blowing across the tops of bottles. Looked up the South Dakota state bird, the ring-necked pheasant, in the field guide, and the boys drew pictures of pheasants in their logbooks.

◆ February 6, 1991

North to Alaska. Caleb: "On the map, why does Alaska always look like it's floating?" Located Alaska (floating) on the United States map, and (anchored in position) on the world map and the globe. Discussed our past studies of Alaska: the boys recalled a surprising amount of information about igloos, seals, Eskimos, kayaks, Denali, and Kodiak bears.

Located Kodiak Island on the map, and the boys drew dramatic pictures of evil-looking Kodiak bears in their logbooks. Studied gorgeous pictures of Alaskan ice caves in National Geographic's Geo-Whiz! Read Icebergs by Roma Gans, and the boys drew descriptive iceberg pictures: Caleb drew icebergs forming from glaciers; Josh and Ethan drew diagrams of icebergs above and below water. We discussed differences between icebergs from the North Pole (pointy tops) and the South Pole (flat tops)—Ethan: "So the iceberg that sank the Titanic must have been pointed!"—and the boys devised a number of creative ways to use icebergs to provide drinking water for water-deprived California.

◆ February 8, 1991

California, which has lava caves. The boys located California on the U.S. map; labeled/colored it on their outline maps. We discussed California trees: redwoods, sequoias, and bristlecone pines, respectively the tallest, biggest, and oldest trees in the world, which led to a brief excursion into comparative math. We found pictures of all three trees; and the boys made scale drawings of a person standing next to a redwood tree, which meant calculating how many people four feet tall would have to stand on top of each other to get to the top of a redwood. Ethan: "How tall is the second tallest tree in the world?" Caleb: "How long would it take for a squirrel to climb all the way to the top of a redwood tree?" Josh: "Were some of those bristlecone pine trees alive when there were cave people?"

Discussed the California state nickname, "The Golden State", and Josh told us all about a book he read at the library last month about the Gold Rush and the forty-niners. Looked up banana slugs, the California state mollusk, and the boys drew life-size pictures in their logbooks. Played a tape of environmental kids' songs by the Banana Slug String Band (see page 301).

◆ February 11, 1991

More lava caves. Looked at photographs of lava caves. Caleb: "It would be really dark inside a black cave!" Read a book about volcanoes, and the boys drew and labeled volcano diagrams in their logbooks. We found pieces of lava in our rock collection—several sent to us by friends visiting Hawaii, which we located on the globe. The rock collection also contains a piece of pumice, which the boys dropped in water and watched float. Caleb: "What makes a rock float?" Ethan: "This one floats because it's full of little air bubbles."

The boys spent the rest of the morning making model volcanoes from instant papier-mâché, painting the volcanoes, and then erupting the volcanoes, repeatedly, with a mix of baking soda and vinegar. We discussed the chemistry of this reaction, but I suspect the technical details got lost in the excitement.

◆ February 12, 1991

Howe Caverns in New York. We located New York on the U.S. map; the boys labeled and colored it on their outline maps. Located New York City and looked up its population, which the boys recorded in their logbooks. Ethan: "What number comes after a million? What comes after a billion? How high can you go?" Read a biography of Peter Stuyvesant—Old Silver Leg Takes Over, by Robert Quackenbush (see page 471)—and a book about the building of the Statue of Liberty, which fascinated Ethan, who likes to know how everything is put together inside. Located Niagara Falls on the map; read about the legend of Sam Patch, who tried to jump over it. Compared the heights of Niagara Falls and Angel Falls in Venezuela, the world's highest waterfall, by making a bar graph. The boys invented their own devices for safely going over Niagara Falls. No barrels; Ethan's is a sort of padded submarine, with rocket boosters.

Briefly reviewed the states located so far: Kentucky, Missouri, New Mexico, South Dakota, Alaska, California, and New York. Next we're going to continue U.S. geography with gold and jewels.

When the boys were younger, a major success of our geography program was a homemade map trivia game. We started out with a world map, tacked to the dining room wall at kid level, and a pack of index cards, each with a handprinted question (and answer). Eventually this expanded to two packs of index cards.

Later we added a United States map and a third pack of index cards. The premise of the game is simple: a reader draws a card and reads the question; the player answers the question and identifies the location on the map. Our game started out with such questions as: "What country did Paddington Bear come from?" "Where did Pippi Longstocking live?" "Where would you go to see the highest waterfall in the world?" Later questions became more sophisticated—"Where did Stanley find Dr. Livingstone?" "In what country was Marie Curie born?"—and soon the boys began adding cards of their own, reflecting special interests: "Find Krakatoa." "Find the island that might have been Atlantis." "Where was the ancient city of Troy?" Commercial geography games, despite stunningly superior illustration and packaging, have never quite matched our homemade game in appeal, and the price—especially if you pick up your world map for a quarter at the library used-book sale—is hard to beat.

Making maps was also a popular activity. The boys started out drawing "story maps" based on such favorites as *The Wizard of Oz, The Hobbit,* and "Little Red Riding-Hood" (showing, as I recall, Little Red's house, complete with garden and doghouse, Grandma's house, the path through the woods, the hunter's camp, and a truly spectacular lair for the Wolf). Later they advanced to "memory maps:" maps of all the houses and areas where we've lived, with notable sites labeled ("Our treehouse," "The place where Caleb fell off his bike," "Blackberry bushes," "Our piano teacher's house").

In yet another (never quite completed) project, we set out to read our way across the United States and around the world, choosing books based in different states or countries, and adding stickers to our maps as we covered each location. (We tried pins at first, like professional map markers, but the cat kept pulling them out and dropping them down the radiator.) We read, for example, many volumes in Lucy Fitch Perkins's Twins series, short chapter books each featuring a pair of international twins: titles include *The Japanese Twins, The Scottish Twins, The Mexican Twins,* and many more. These are all long out of print—they were published by Houghton Mifflin in the 1920s—but can be found at libraries and used-book stores. They're somewhat inaccurate culturally and definitely deficient in political correctness, but, for what it's worth, the boys enjoyed most of them, plus learned the meaning of the term "negative stereotype." We also read multicultural folk- and fairy tales (see pages 658, 664, 671, and 685), such as Mordicai Gerstein's *The Mountains of Tibet,* Katherine Paterson's *The Tale of the Mandarin Ducks,* and John Steptoe's *Mufaro's Beautiful Daughters,* and books with distinctive geographical settings, such as Jean Craighead George's *Julie of the Wolves* (Alaska), Thomas Lewis's *Hill of Fire* (Mexico), and Farley Mowat's *Owls in the Family* (Canada).

ATLASES FOR KIDS

Atlas of the Earth
4 8 Gallimard Jeunesse and Jean-Pierre Verdet, eds.; Scholastic, 1997

A 24-page illustrated atlas for 4–8-year-olds, emphasizing the impressive features of planet Earth, from the depths of the Pacific Mariana Trench to the heights of Mount Everest.

Children's Atlas of the World
9 12 Rand McNally, 1992

Political and thematic maps and a fact-filled text for kids aged 9–12.

Circling the Globe: A Young
ALL People's Guide to Countries and Cultures of the World
Sue Grabham, ed.; Kingfisher Books, 1995

Contains 640 pages of attractively presented information on all the countries of the world. Maps of each continent are followed by individual country maps, supplemented with photographs and drawings, and an explanatory text on the history, geography, and economy of the featured region. For each country, there's also a "Facts and Figures" box listing area, population, capital city, major cities, highest point, official language, main religion, currency, main exports, type of government, and per capita GNP. For many, there's also a box for language buffs, teaching readers a few words in the native language.

The DK Geography of the World
David Green; Dorling Kindersley, 1996

An impressive 304-page atlas for kids of all ages, including hundreds of beautiful maps, 1,000 color photographs, 500 illustrations, charts, and diagrams, and an explanatory text. The book covers all the countries of the world, including information on physical features, climate, national flags, agriculture and industry, ethnic groups, everyday life, and recent history. An excellent reference.

The Eyewitness Atlas of the World
Dorling Kindersley, 1994

A 160-page collection of detailed worldwide maps, grouped by continent, with lots of accompanying color photographs and illustrations. The map of France, for example, is surrounded by captioned photos of the Eiffel Tower, a bottle of champagne, a bustling sidewalk cafe, historical chateaus, a wheel of cheese, a plate of snails, and a craggy view of the island of Corsica.

The Facts on File Children's Atlas
David and Jill Wright; Facts on File, 1997

The book begins with general world geographical information: "Our Planet Earth," with relevant facts and figures; "Mountains, Plains and Seas," with a green-and-yellow physical world map; "Countries of the World," with a multicolored political world map; "People of the World," with a map indicating population distribution; "Hot and Cold Lands," with world maps indicating June and December temperatures; and "Wet and Dry Lands," with maps indicating rainfall and vegetation type. Maps of each continent follow, with maps of individual countries or groups of countries. Maps are accompanied by color photographs, interesting and ususual facts about each country, and occasional puzzles ("Can you spot eight famous London landmarks on this stamp?") Under "Central America," for example, are photographs of Guatemalan coffee beans, the temples of Chichen Itza, and ships on the Panama Canal, plus an inset map of the canal and a recipe for Mexican tortillas. The atlas is creatively organized, but countries tend to be lumped together in bunches so that there's not all that much information about each one. Includes 48 detailed maps and 240 illustrations, diagrams, and photographs.

Kids' U.S. Road Atlas
Rand McNally, 1992

Take this one along in the car. An 80-page 8½ × 11-inch softcover road atlas for younger travelers, it includes road maps of all 50 states (in alphabetical order), plus color illustrations of each state's flower, bird, and tree, and a "spotter" map showing the state's position in the greater U.S. For bored travelers, there's also a puzzle or activity on each page: mazes, color-by-number pictures, crosswords, "backseat bingo," connect-the-dots, riddles, scrambled words, and secret codes. The kids' road maps are simplified versions of the adult maps. The major roads are all there, but little fine detail. Unfortunately this leaves some states—our own Vermont among them—practically empty. Don't expect your kids to be able to follow along if you do a lot of driving off the beaten track.

The Student World Atlas
Julia Gorton; Lodestar Books, 1994

The maps in this 48-page atlas are all crammed with colorful little people and objects, each illustrating some important feature of the country, Spain, for example, is speckled with a tiny olive tree, a pile of oranges, a bottle of port wine, a roll of cork bark, flamenco dancers, a plate of paella, and portraits of the Tower of Belem, El Escorial, and the Alhambra. "Fact-Finder" boxes list interesting and unusual information about each country or world region—for example, "When the volcano on the Greek island of Santorini erupted over 3000 years ago, it caused the GREATEST EXPLOSION anyone has ever heard."

MAPS

Hammond, Inc.
Atlases, maps, and charts for geographers of all ages. The company publishes both a general catalog and an education catalog.
Hammond, Inc.
515 Valley St.
Maplewood, NJ 07040
(201) 763-6000 or (800) 526-4953/fax (201) 763-7658

Maps My Way—U.S.A.

A collection of three-hole-punched teacher and student outline maps on glossy paper. Included are maps of the entire United States and of all 50 states. Major rivers and bodies of water are marked; each map page also has numbered and lettered coordinates, a title space, lines at the bottom for filling in additional information, and a small "spotter" map showing the position of the featured state on a map of the country. Student maps are blank. Teacher maps are completely labeled with names of states, capital cities, and major cities; state capital, population, nickname, flower, and bird are listed at the bottom of the page. There's also a list of instructions for using *Maps My Way* (the publisher recommends colored pencils) and suggestions for lesson topics and projects.

$21.98 (plus $3.50 shipping/handling)
AlmaNiche Publisher Services
300 S. 20th St., Suite R-4
Hattiesburg, MS 39401
(601) 584-8932

National Cartographic Information Center

"The single best source for information on maps produced or distributed by the federal government" according to *The Map Catalog* (see page 417). Write for their free pamphlet, "Popular Publications of the USGS."

National Cartographic Information Center
507 National Center
12202 Sunrise Valley Dr.
Reston, VA 22092
(703) 860-6045

National Geographic Society

Maps of all kinds, plus atlases, reference books, games, multicultural craft kits, and videos. The society publishes both general and education catalogs.

General catalog:
National Geographic Society
Box 10543
Des Moines, IA 50340
(888) 225-5647
Educational Services Catalog (schools and libraries):
National Geographic Educational Services

Box 10597
Des Moines, IA 50340
(800) 368-2728

Rand McNally

Maps, atlases, charts, and travel guides.
Rand McNally
Box 7600
Chicago, IL 60680
(312) 673-9100

U.S. Geological Survey

The USGS publishes free state-by-state indexes of topographic, geologic, and general maps and nationwide indexes of maps by category. Indexes of available maps, informational pamphlets, price lists, and order forms are available upon request. An excellent resource for geographers of all ages.

U.S. Geological Survey
Map Distribution
Federal Center, Building 41
Box 25286
Denver, CO 80225
(303) 236-7477
Web site: www.usgs.gov

U.S. Government Printing Office

Over 100 free subject indexes are available, listing available publications by category, among them "Maps and Atlases."

Superintendent of Documents
U.S. Government Printing Office
Washington, DC 20402
(202) 783-3238

GEOGRAPHY RESOURCES

CATALOGS

National Geographic Society
See left.

Social Studies School Service:
Geography Catalog

An excellent source for educational geographical resources for kids of all ages, stuffed with books, activity books, videos, computer software, games, kits, posters, charts, maps, and globes. Various catalog sections include "World Geography," "U.S. Geography," "Economic Geography," "Physical Geography," "The Environment," "Global Education," and "Cross-Cultural Studies."

Social Studies School Service

10200 Jefferson Blvd.

Box 802

Culver City, CA 90232-0802

(310) 839-2249 or (800) 421-4246

Web site: SocialStudies.com

MAGAZINES

Book Links

Book Links (see Reading, page 69), a bimonthly publication of the American Library Association, includes many feature articles linking children's books by theme. Many of these involve geographic or multicultural topics.

The September 1994 issue of *Book Links,* for example, includes an article titled "Read Across America" that describes over 50 books for kids of all ages "with a strong sense of place." Among the selections are such old favorites as Marguerite Henry's *Brighty of the Grand Canyon* (Arizona) and Barbara Cooney's *Island Boy* (Maine). Other sample geography-related articles have featured Russia, Japan, India, Hawaii, and Mexico, each with long and detailed book lists.

Back issues are usually available at libraries or

Book Links

434 W. Downer

Aurora, IL 60506

(630) 892-7465 or (800) 545-2433, ext. 5715

Web site: www.ala.org/BookLinks

Faces

A magazine of world cultures for kids in grades 4–9. Each issue is centered around a main topic featuring a single country or ethnic group (back issues have included "Asante World," "Australia," "Indonesia," and "The Philippines") or a world view of a common theme (courtship, hats, money, music, and pottery). Each illustrated issue includes both nonfiction articles and fictional stories or folktales, directions for projects and activities, and a suggested reading list.

The March 1990 issue, titled "Maps," includes several nonfiction articles on the different kinds of present-day maps and historical maps and their uses, a Portuguese folktale titled "The Maker of Maps," mapmaking instructions for kids who want to tackle their own, and a map-reading game based on the Washington Metro.

Annual subscription (9 issues), $23.95; back issues, $4.50

Cobblestone Publishing, Inc.

30 Grove St.

Peterborough, NH 03458-1454

(603) 924-7209 or (800) 821-0115/fax (603) 924-7380

e-mail: custsvc@cobblestone.mv.com

Web site: www.cobblestonepub.com

Kids Discover

Targeted at kids aged 6 and up, each issue of *Kids Discover* is devoted to a single geographical, historical, or scientific topic. Past issues have included "Pyramids," "North and South Poles," "Australia," and "Trees." Each is 20 pages long, with lots of colorful illustrations and glossy photographs, a simple text, and suggestions for projects and activities.

Annual subscription (10 issues), $19.95

Kids Discover

Box 54205

Boulder, CO 80322

(800) 284-8276

Mercator's World

Subtitled the "Magazine of Maps, Atlases, Globes, and Charts," this is a wonderful find for map lovers: 80+ pages of superbly illustrated articles on all aspects of maps. Included are articles on map history, mapmaking (past and present), unusual types of maps, and map collecting, plus many color reproductions of maps old and new.

Annual subscription (6 issues), $39.95

Mercator's World

Aster Publishing Corp.

Box 10603

Eugene, OR 97440-9940

(541) 345-3800 or (800) 840-3810

e-mail: circulation@mercatormag.com

Web site: www.mercatormag.com

National Geographic

Our oldest son has been a member of the National Geographic Society for years and is thus a subscriber to the chunky yellow *National Geographic* magazine, which arrives every month, crammed with interesting international articles, stunning color photographs, and—five times a year or so—a detailed full-color map. Latest issues have included articles on pythons, Siberian tigers, Peruvian mummies, Neantherthals, Icelandic volcanoes, Sri Lanka, Sir Joseph Banks, and the city of Jerusalem; there's something here for everybody. A thoroughly valuable resource. The Society also publishes a catalog of books, games, maps, videos, computer software, and multicultural craft kits.

Annual membership in the National Geographic Society, including 12 issues of *National Geographic* magazine, $27

National Geographic Magazine

Box 60001

Tampa, FL 33660

(800) 647-5463

Web site: www.nationalgeographic.com

For younger readers, see *National Geographic World* (below).

National Geographic World

Younger geographers can become junior members of the National Geographic Society, with an accompanying subscription to *National Geographic World*, a monthly collection of brilliantly illustrated articles on science, nature, and life around the world, plus games, puzzles, contests, and activity suggestions.

A junior Society membership, including 12 issues of *National Geographic World*, $17.95

National Geographic World

Box 60001

Tampa, FL 33660

(800) 647-5463

Web site: www.nationalgeographic.com

Skipping Stones

A multicultural children's magazine that includes stories, articles, poems, drawings, photographs, maps, and even an occasional recipe, from all over the world. Many literary entries appear in two languages, that of the original writer and an English translation. The "News Quarterly" column lists the dates of upcoming international holidays and the highlights of worldwide news; "Bookshelf" includes reviews of books on international or multicultural themes; and "A Guide for Parents and Teachers" includes suggestions for activities and discussion questions to accompany articles in the current issue. There's also an extensive list of international pen pals. *Skipping Stones* is published bimonthly during the school year.

Annual subscription (5 issues), $25

Skipping Stones

Box 3939

Eugene, OR 97403

(541) 342-4956

BOOKS: NONFICTION

All Over the Map: An Extraordinary Atlas of the United States Featuring Towns That Actually Exist!

David Jouris; Ten Speed Press, 1996

The exclamation point is because these towns have truly outlandish names. (Ever hear of Boring, Oregon?) The book is a collection of 33 "thematic maps," each of which pinpoints towns with related, but strange, names. There's a map showing the locations of American towns named after animals, for example. A sequel, *All Over the Map Again: Another Extraordinary Atlas of the United States Featuring Towns That Actually Exist!*, has another 33 thematic maps, variously including such geographic gems as Chili Bar, California; Vesuvius, Ohio; and Bland, Missouri.

America the Beautiful Series
Enchantment of the World Series
From Sea to Shining Sea Series

Children's Press

Informational geography books for upper elementary and middle school students.

The *America the Beautiful Series* includes 52 books, one on each of the 50 states, plus Puerto Rico and Washington D.C. Each is about 144 pages long, illustrated with color photographs, plus maps, and are targeted at readers in grades 5–8.

The *From Sea to Shining Sea Series* is the same thing on a younger scale: 52 books, covering the 50 states as well as Puerto Rico and Washington D.C., each 64 pages long, illustrated with color photographs, plus maps, brief biographies of famous state persons, and a timeline of state history.

The *Enchantment of the World Series* includes 97 books, each on a different country of the world, from *Afghanistan* and *Algeria* to *Zambia* and *Zimbabwe*. The books, which cover geography, history, economics, and culture, are about 150 pages long, illustrated with color photographs, and intended for kids in grades 6–9. Useful if you're writing a school report, but not inherently fascinating reading.

American History Through Maps
Hammond, Inc., 1993

A 48-page collection of colorful historical maps from "Migrations to the New World" to "The Middle East 1945 to the Present." The maps are big, clear, and simplified—in some cases, too simplified. In "Exploration of the United States," for example, the routes taken by historic explorers—among them Samuel de Champlain, Ponce de León, Coronado, and Lewis and Clark—are marked in distinctive different colors on a bright yellow map of North America. The background map, however, is essentially featureless, so, while readers get the general idea, it's impossible to tell just exactly where each expedition went. For each map, there's a page of explanatory text and a list of suggestions for associated exercises and activities.

Hammond, Inc.
515 Valley St.
Maplewood, NJ 07040
(201) 763-6000

Anno's U.S.A.
Mitsumasa Anno; Paper Star, 1998

An exquisite wordless picture book in which a traveler on horseback crosses the United States from west to east. The detailed pictures are filled with information about aspects of American geography, history, and culture. The more you look, the more you see. Also see *Anno's Britain* (Philomel Books, 1982) and *Anno's Italy* (Philomel Books, 1978).

Annual Editions: Geography
Dushkin Publishing Group/Brown & Benchmark; 1996–97

Continually updated, this volume is a wonderful resource for high school students. Each book in the Annual Editions series is a collection of articles gleaned from a wide range of contemporary magazines, newspapers, and professional journals. The *Geography* volume includes articles on geographical discoveries, theories, issues, and controversies, assembled from such publications as *Earth, The Atlantic Monthly, The Journal of Geography, Scientific American,* and *World Watch.*

From bookstores or
Social Studies School Service
10200 Jefferson Blvd.
Box 802
Culver City, CA 90232-0802
(310) 839-2249 or (800) 421-4246
Web site: SocialStudies.com

As the Crow Flies: A First Book of Maps
Gail Hartman; Aladdin, 1993

A geography book for beginners, in which kids view the world not only as the crow flies but also as the rabbit hops, the horse trots, and the seagull glides. In a sequel, *As the Roadrunner Runs: A First Book of Maps,* readers trace the paths traveled by a scampering roadrunner, a lizard, a jackrabbit, a mule, and a deer across a landscape of the southwest.

The Book of Where, or How to Be Naturally Geographic
Neill Bell; Little, Brown, 1982

This is one of the innovative Brown Paper School Book series, created by a group of California teachers, writers, and artists for kids in approximately grades 4–8. If you don't know your way around the world, this book begins, "You might guess that the Andes are a giant fish or a bar located on the top floor of a skyscraper—instead of a towering mountain range in

South America." Chapter titles, designed to lure kids into geographical literacy, begin at home and branch out: "Starting at Home," "The Streets Where You Live," "All Around the Town," "The Great State of . . . ," "Getting the Lay of the Land," "The Global Grapefruit," "Superislands," and "The Big Puddles." The book covers everything from the layout of city streets to tectonic plates, with a clever combination of text, illustrations, maps, puzzles, jokes, quizzes, and projects.

Children from Australia to Zimbabwe: A Photographic Journey Around the World

Anna Rhesa Versola and Maya K. Ajmera; Charlesbridge Publishing, 1997

The book covers 26 countries, ABC-style, including for each color photograph of kids in typical settings, a greeting in the native language, a map, a short fact sheet, and a brief text with interesting snippets of geographical and cultural information. Recommended for readers aged 9–12.

See *Children Just Like Us* (below).

Children Just Like Us

Barnabas and Anabel Kindersley; Dorling Kindersley, 1995

This book, developed in association with UNICEF, visits kids from 30 world countries and documents each visit with wonderful color photographs. On each double-page spread, there's a photograph of the featured child in native dress, along with pictures of his/her family, home, school, pets, food, clothing, and scenes from daily life. Readers will be enthralled to find that so many children from places far away are indeed "just like me." The book includes a subscription form for the "Children Just Like Me Penpal Club," designed to link kids from all over the world.

Also see *Children from Australia to Zimbabwe: A Photographic Journey Around the World* (above).

Colors of the World Series

Carolrhoda, 1997

A series of 24-page picture books for 4–8-year-olds in which different colors are related to interesting facts about each country's geography, history, and culture. Titles in the series to date include *Colors of Australia* (Lynn Ainsworth Olawsky), *Colors of Germany* (Holly Littlefield), *Colors of Japan* (Holly Littlefield), *Colors of Mexico* (Lynn Ainsworth Olawsky), and *Colors of the Navajo* (Emily Abbink).

See the **Count Your Way Series** (below).

Count Your Way Series

Jim Haskins; Carolrhoda

There are now 16 books in this ever-growing series of picture books: *Count Your Way Through Africa, Brazil, Canada, China, France, Germany, Greece, India, Ireland, Israel, Italy, Japan, Korea, Mexico, Russia,* and *The Arab World.* Each teaches kids to count to 10 in the language of the country. There is one number per illustrated double-page spread; each number is related to a number of objects representing the culture, history, or geography of the featured country. In *Count Your Way Through Russia,* for example, 1 (the Cyrillic name and pronunciation are included) stands for one Kremlin; 2 for two snowshoes, needed for walking in the long Russian winters; 3 is for troika, a sleigh drawn by three horses. A short explanatory text and big bright pictures.

See the **Colors of the World Series** (above).

Don't Know Much About Geography

Kenneth C. Davis; Avon Books, 1995

Nearly 400 pages of fascinating and factual information; whoever the title applies to, it's not the author. Chapter titles include "The World Is a Pear," "What's So Bad About the Badlands?," "If People Were Dolphins, the Planet Would Be Called Ocean," "Elephants in the Alps," "Paradise Lost?: Geography, Weather, and the Environment," and "Lost in Space?" Under each, information is presented in short and addictively readable chunks. Sample subtitles include "Why Is the Orient Called 'the Orient?,'" "What Does the Continental Divide Divide?," "Why Did Hannibal Take Elephants Across the Alps and Did Napoleon Know How Far It Was to Moscow?," and "What's So Hot About the Equator?" Each chapter also includes a timeline of "Geographical Milestones." For high school–aged and older readers, but a delightful reference work for all teachers/students of geography.

8 12 Earthsearch: A Kids' Geography Museum in a Book

John Cassidy; Klutz Press, 1994

Earthsearch is a terrific collection of photographs, catchy information, activities, demonstrations, and projects, all having to do with the life and times of planet Earth. The cover is a solid sheet of shiny aluminum, whose history, from bauxite to royal cutlery to airplane wing to Russian Coke can, is described in the text. Also inside is a "population clock"—a 10-second plastic timer that reads "Every ten seconds 45 people are born on planet Earth"—a lot of innovative information about mapmaking, including a pop-out-and-tape-together Tennis Ball Earth (you supply the tennis ball), instructions for making a contour map of the back of your hand, a plastic overlay map of the United States, and an assortment of real coins from all over the world. There's a wonderful activity, for which you'll need only an apple and a paring knife, designed to demonstrate the composition of the planet: by the time you get down to the minuscule scrap of peel that represents the Earth's total farmable land, your kids will be impressed. There's a sobering demonstration, using spinner wheels and M&M's, of the unequal distribution of the world's food and energy supplies; there's a People Color Wheel, capable of creating all possible human skin tones; and there's an intriguing explanation of how you, at this very moment, are sharing some of Caesar's last breath. Young geographers will love it.

9 13 Everyday Geography: A Concise, Entertaining Review of Essential Information About the World We Live In

Kevin McKinney; Contemporary Books, 1994

A continent-by-continent and country-by-country compilation of geographical information, with lots of labeled black-line maps. Each chapter ends with a 20+ question quiz. It's not, unfortunately, all that entertaining, but it is stuffed with useful facts.

12 + Everything is Somewhere: The Geography Quiz Book

Jack McClintock and David Helgren; William Morrow, 1994

A collection of 30 quizzes on world geography, variously covering the "Earth," "The Human Imprint,"

"World Regions," "North America," and "Geography of the Mind." These aren't your ordinary "What are the principal products of Portugal?" types of quizzes. Try these questions: "Where is the Sphinx's beard?" "Where are the best Panama hats made?" "Where do the oldest trees on earth grow?" Persevere and you'll also learn what makes waves, what sound a dog makes in Chinese, and where the world's largest spider comes from. Answers and explanations immediately follow the quizzes. Recommended for kids in grade 9 and up.

Also see, by the same authors, *Everything is Somewhere in the U.S.A.: The New Geography Quiz Book* (1994), which contains 31 creative quizzes on U.S. geography, plus map challenges. Sample questions include "What is Nebraska marble?," "Where is the world's biggest mushroom farm?," and "Where was Washington going when he crossed the Delaware?" Answers and explanations are all thoughtfully included.

9 13 Everything You Need to Know About Geography Homework

Anne Zeman and Kate Kelly; Scholastic, 1997

A desk reference for kids in grades 5–9, covering all the basics of middle school geography, with attractive and colorful illustrations, charts, and diagrams.

5 9 Geography From A–Z: A Picture Glossary

Jack Knowlton; HarperTrophy, 1997

Geography terms simply and clearly described, from *A* (archipelago, atoll) and *B* (badland, bay, beach, and butte) to *Z* (zone). Each definition is accompanied by an attractive and brightly colored illustration.

7 10 Hopscotch Around the World

Mary D. Lankford; Beech Tree Books, 1996

Practically everyone, everywhere, plays some version of hopscotch. This 49-page picture book includes histories, rules, and diagrams for 19 international games of hopscotch. Kids in Bolivia play La Thunkuna; kids in El Salvador play Peregrina—using a mango seed as a marker. Read the book, find a sidewalk and a piece of chalk, and hop your way around the world. Also see, by the same author, *Dominoes Around the World* (William Morrow, 1998) and *Jacks Around the World* (William Morrow, 1996).

How to Read a Map

9 12 Scott E. Morris. ed.; Chelsea House, 1995

A 47-page explanation of the basics of map reading and the various uses of maps, for 9–12-year-olds.

How We Learned the Earth Is Round

5 9 Patricia Lauber; HarperCollins, 1992

"Today nearly everybody knows that the earth is round," the book begins, "But long ago, people were sure that the earth was flat. They thought it was flat because it looked flat. It still does." Then follows a clear and simple explanation of how the Greeks figured out that the world is round—with instructions for a supporting experiment you can do yourself, using a flashlight, a paper plate, and a ball—plus descriptions of voyages of world exploration, including the round-the-world voyage of Magellan. The book ends with a photograph of our definitely round planet as seen from space.

International Biographies Series

10 + Center for Learning, 1992–93

Try traveling around the world while learning about famous people. Each book in this series contains 14 multidisciplinary lessons centering around famous persons from different parts of the world. Titles include *Africa and Middle East* (with such famous persons as Cleopatra, Lawrence of Arabia, Nelson Mandela, Nefertiti, and Anwar Sadat), *Asia, Australia, and Oceania* (Corazon Aquino, Buddha, Indira Gandhi, Mao Tsetung), *Europe, Central and Southern* (Bismarck, Charles de Gaulle, Joan of Arc, Martin Luther), *Europe, Eastern* (Alexander the Great, Attila the Hun, Marie Curie, Mikhail Gorbachev), *Europe, Northern and Western; Latin America,* and *North America, U.S. and Canada.* Each lesson includes an illustrated minibiography with enough information to get kids started, teaching plans, activity suggestions, and reproducible student handouts. Recommended for students in grades 5–12.

$19.95 each

Social Studies School Service (Geography Catalog)
10200 Jefferson Blvd.
Box 802
Culver City, CA 90232-0802
(310) 839-2436 or (800) 421-4246/fax (310) 839-2249
or (800) 944-5432
Web site: SocialStudies.com

Kids Learn America

8 12 Patricia Gordon and Reed C. Snow; Williamson, 1992

An illustrated state-by-state tour of the U.S.A. with maps, quizzes, puzzles, projects, quotations, historical facts, and interesting anecdotes. Creative features include "Map Talk," which gives general information about maps and globes; "The Curious W's," a who/what/where/why quiz on persons, places, and events for each state; "Pack Your Bags," which lists interesting things to see or do in each state; and "How's Your Latitude Attitude?," which makes worldwide latitude connections. (Example: Did you know that Little Rock, Arkansas, and Algeria, Africa, are on the same approximate latitude?) For each state, there are also a couple of catchy memory exercises: "Picture This" helps kids remember the shape of the state map by comparing it to some familiar object (Minnesota, given a little imagination, looks like a ski boot; West Virginia like a leaping frog); while "Lights, Camera, Action!" prods kids to memorize the names of state capitals through creative visualizations. To remember Tallahassee, Florida, for example, kids are told to imagine *Lassie* mopping the floor with a *towel: towel-Lassie* = Tallahassee.

Sample projects include building a papier-mâché car (Michigan), baking Navajo bread (New Mexico), making a Lincoln-style log cabin using brown paper rolled "logs" (Illinois), and carving potato prints (Idaho). Kids are also encouraged to make collages for each state and to play homemade state games.

Let's Investigate Marvelously Meaningful Maps

6 10

Madelyn Wood Carlisle; Barron's Juveniles, 1992

A 32-page introduction to many different kinds of maps, including weather, road, topographic, and undersea maps, plus simple explanations of such basic map concepts as scale, symbol, latitude, and longitude.

The Librarian Who Measured the Earth

7 11 Kathryn Lasky; Little, Brown, 1994

An attractive and interesting picture-book biography of Eratosthenes, chief librarian of the famous library at Alexandria in Egypt, and a detailed account of his clever method for measuring the circumference of the earth. He used the sun, shadows, and geometry—kids may need a little extra explanation to understand the principles involved—and his answer was pretty close. An excellent link between geography and math.

Longitude

Dava Sobel; Walker & Company, 1995

The absorbing tale of navigation's "longitude problem" and its solution by 18th-century clock maker John Harrison. Fascinating reading for teenagers and adults.

The Map Catalog

Joel Makower and Laura Bergheim, eds.; Vintage Books, 1992

"Every Kind of Map and Chart on Earth and Even Some Above It" reads the subtitle. Maps, in this 250+-page book, are grouped into three general categories: Land Maps, Sky Maps, and Water Maps. The largest of these, Land Maps, includes some 33 kinds of maps, in alphabetical order from Aerial Photographs and Agricultural Maps to Wildlife Maps and World Maps. (In between: Bicycle Route Maps, Geologic Maps, Historical Site Maps, Railroad Maps, and Treasure Maps.) For each map type, there is an informational text explaining the map and its uses, information on sources for ordering maps, and assorted map illustrations in both color and black and white. For older readers, but an excellent resource for all map lovers.

Mapping the Changing World

Yvette de la Pierre; Thomassen-Grant and Lickle, 1997

An 80-page history of mapmaking for middle school readers and up, filled with wonderful illustrations. The book covers maps from their very beginnings—Marshall Island sticks-and-stones maps, Chinese silk maps, painted Aboriginal maps, and Inuit sealskin maps—through "The Golden Age of Mapping," "Mapping America," and "Mapping Earth from Space." Included is a section on the science of mapping a round world flat on paper.

Maps: Getting From Here to There

Harvey Weiss; Houghton Mifflin, 1995

A 64-page illustrated introduction to maps and their uses. The 10 chapters cover direction, scale distances, map symbols, elevation and contour lines, latitude and longitude, globes, marine charts, specialty maps, and historical maps, and include directions for mapping your own local area using a compass, protractor, and self-made scale. Recommended for kids in grades 3–6, but leaning toward older readers.

Maps and Globes

Jack Knowlton; HarperTrophy, 1986

A useful 42-page picture-book explanation of the different kinds and uses of maps and globes for kids aged 7–10. It covers all the basics, including direction, scale, latitude and longitude, elevation and depth, and physical, political, and local maps. The no-frills text is clear and straightforward; the illustrations by Harriett Barton are big, bright, informational, and appealing and save the book from blahness.

Maps and Mazes: A First Guide to Mapmaking

Gillian Chapman and Pam Robson; Millbrook Press, 1993

An explanation of the fundamental components of maps, including symbols, scale, direction, and latitude and longitude, plus assorted early mapmaking activities, from finding a path through a maze to designing a map of your own neighborhood. Recommended for mapmakers aged 7–10.

Material World: A Global Family Portrait

Peter Menzel, Charles C. Mann, and Paul Kennedy; Sierra Club Books, 1995

A 255-page photo essay on families from 30 countries worldwide. Statistics on each country, listing area, population, literacy rate, household size, life expectancy, and the like, are graphically brought home by an impressive series of creative photographs, each showing an average family with all their material possessions posed outside their home. The text is for older readers and adults, but the pictures will fascinate all.

New True Books: Geography

Children's Press

The New True Book series of 48-page easy-to-read informational books are beautifully illustrated with color photographs and targeted at kids in grades 2–4.

Among these are 13 books on individual countries (examples include *Argentina, Canada,* and *The Russian Federation*), 22 books on geography (including *Africa, Antarctica, Deserts, Jungles, Mountains, Oceans, Continents,* and *Tropical Rain Forests*), and 12 books on individual national parks (including *Carlsbad Caverns, Grand Canyon,* and *Yellowstone*).

North, South, East, and West
Allan Fowler; Children's Press, 1993

A "Rookie Read-About Science Book" for kids aged 4–8, explaining the four principal directions of the compass and how to use the sun to determine direction.

Off the Map: The Curious Histories of Place Names
Derek Nelson; Kodansha International, 1997

A thoroughly fascinating history of how places get their names. The practice of geographic naming, explains the author, is an exercise in imagination, history, propaganda, wishful thinking, and sheer wrongheadedness—and occasionally outright nastiness, as in the case of the Adirondack Mountains, which gets its name from a Mohawk insult aimed at the resident Algonquians. The book is for teenagers and adults; it is also a wonderful source of unusual geographic facts for geography curriculum designers.

People
Peter Spier; Doubleday, 1988

A delightfully illustrated picture-book introduction to peoples and cultures worldwide for readers of all ages. One double-page spread pictures 25 colorful little scenes of different kinds of homes; another— "Not nearly all the world's people can read and write, yet there are almost one hundred different ways of doing it"—shows examples of 40 alphabets, from Cyrillic, Armenian, and Tibetan to Arabic, Cherokee, and Korean. Friendly and fascinating.

Puzzle Maps
Nancy L. Clouse; Henry Holt, 1994

A collection of colorful picture puzzles (turtles, clowns, puppy dogs) assembled using state map shapes.

Readers are challenged to identify the component states in each picture. If your kids find this fun, try taking the puzzles a step further: color a blank U.S. map, cut it up, and design a few puzzle pictures of your own.

Strange Science: Planet Earth
Bernard Mascher; Tor Books, 1993

The weird side of physical geography: Did you know that mirages can be photographed? That only 20 percent of the Sahara Desert is sand? About 60 illustrated pages of odd and unexpected information, plus sidebars, minibiographies, and suggestions for experiments.

Talking Walls
Margy Burns Knight; Tilbury House, 1995

An award-winning picture-book tour of 14 walls worldwide, from the Great Wall of China to the Lascaux caves in France, the Wailing Wall in Jerusalem, the walls of Great Zimbabwe and Machu Picchu in Peru, the Vietnam Veterans' Memorial Wall, and the now-vanished Berlin Wall.

An accompanying 100+-page teacher's guide contains detailed descriptions of multidisciplinary projects, activities, and discussion topics related to each "talking wall." Included are wall-by-wall suggestions for activities in language arts, social studies, science, and mathematics, instructions for arts and crafts projects, recipes, lists of Internet and community resources, and a lengthy bibliography. For Wall 11, for example, "Northern Ireland: Peace Line in a War Zone," the guide lists selections of Irish folk music, gives contact addresses for Irish pen pals, provides sources for study units on Irish culture and British/Irish history, and suggests a science project on growing potatoes and a mathematical exercise using Irish population statistics. Also see *Talking Walls: The Stories Continue* (1997), which tells the stories of 17 more walls, among them Hadrian's Wall in Britain, the mural-painted Maya walls of Mexico, and the Dog Wall of Tokyo, Japan.

USA From Space
Anne-Catherine Fallen; Firefly Books, 1997

Maps from space. The book is a collection of wonderful full-color satellite images, picturing such geographical landmarks as the city of Chicago, the Grand Canyon, the Mississippi River, and the Great Salt Lake. The book includes an explanation of how satellite images are made and the many ways in which they can be used.

Where Do I Live?

Neil Chesanov; Barron's Juveniles, 1995

A lovely picture-book answer to a small child's first geography question. The book takes the reader from bedroom to house, neighborhood, town, state, country, planet, solar system, Milky Way Galaxy, and back again.

Where in the World Are You?
A Guide to Looking at the World

Kay Cooper; Walker & Company, 1990

A 95-page survey of the basics of geography, including how it enables you to pinpoint where you are and to figure out how to get where you want to go.

Where on Earth: A Geografunny Guide to the Globe

Paul Rosenthal; Alfred A. Knopf, 1992

This looks like a comic book, but it's actually a clever and funny introduction to geography and its powerful influence on life on earth. Included are maps of all the continents, with the countries labeled.

Where to Look for a Dinosaur

Bernard Most; Voyager Books, 1997

Dinosaurs, once upon a time, were found practically everywhere, which is why geography and dinosaurs make such a good pair. Fun for dino lovers aged 4–8.

Why Do They Call It Topeka?:
How Places Got Their Names

John W. Pursell; Citadel Press, 1995

Over 200 pages of place names in alphabetical order, with a couple of lines about the origins of each.

Why Do You Speak As You Do?
A Guide to World Languages

Kay Cooper; Walker & Company, 1992

Covers the origins of language and the many different languages and dialects spoken in the world today, with in-depth discussions of a few. Chapter titles include "What is English?" and "Can You Climb a Language Family Tree?" For readers in grades 4–8.

See **Foreign Languages,** page 696.

Yo, Sacramento! (And All Those Other State Capitals You Don't Know: Memorize Them All Forever in 20 Minutes—Without Trying!)

Will Cleveland and Mark Alvarez; Goodwood Press, 1994

Silly story-style mnemonics and cartoon illustrations help kids memorize all the state capitals, with reinforcing quizzes every few pages just for practice.

See *Yo, Millard Fillmore!* (page 583), which helps kids memorize all the presidents in order.

LITERATURE LINKS TO GEOGRAPHY FOR ADULTS

Against Borders: Promoting Books for a Multicultural World

Hazel Rochman; American Library Association, 1993

The author discusses how to use books to promote multicultural awareness, to demonstrate cross-cultural similarities, and to combat racial prejudice, and includes annotated lists of books categorized by ethnic group.

Building Bridges With Multicultural Picture Books

Janice J. Beaty; Merrill Publishing Company, 1996

Lists of picture books and related activities for developing a multicultural curriculum for kids aged 3–5.

Our Family, Our Friends, Our World: An Annotated Guide to Multicultural Books for Children and Teenagers

Lyn Miller-Lachmann; R. R. Bowker, 1992

Detailed reviews of over a thousand books, both fiction and nonfiction. Books are categorized by reading level ("Preschool–Grade 3," "Grades 4–6," "Grades

7–9," and "Grades 10–12") and are divided among 18 ethnic and geographical categories. Also included is a list of multicultural series books and a bibliography of professional resources for parents and teachers. A valuable reference for geography programs.

Read Across America
5/10 Gloria Rothstein; Scholastic, 1995

Lists of popular children's books related to seven geographical regions of the United States, generally targeted at kids in grades 1–4. Selections include Barbara Cooney's *Miss Rumphius* (Viking, 1982) from Maine, Cynthia Rylant's *When I Was Young in the Mountains* (Penguin, 1982) from West Virginia, and Patricia Polacco's *Thunder Cake* (Scholastic, 1990) from Michigan. For each of the 23 books listed, there are associated projects and activities, plus reproducible student pages.

LITERATURE LINKS TO GEOGRAPHY FOR KIDS

America in Literature Series
12/+ Charles Scribner's Sons, 1979

Six anthologies of short stories, essays, journal excerpts, and poems each centering around a different region of the United States. Titles in the series include *The Northeast* (James Lape, ed.), *The West* (Peter Monahan, ed.), *The South* (Sara Marshall, ed.), *The Midwest* (Ronald Szymanski, ed.), *The Small Town* (Flory Jones Schultheiss, ed.), and *The City* (Adele Stern, ed.). Selections from *The Northeast,* for example, include "The Blueberry Picking" by Donald Hall, "Going to Shrewsbury" by Sarah Orne Jewett, "The Lightning-Rod Man" by Herman Melville, "Walden" by E. B. White, and works by Emily Dickinson, Robert Frost, Henry David Thoreau, John Greenleaf Whittier, and John Cheever. An excellent geography tie-in for secondary students.

The Armadillo from Amarillo
5/9 Lynne Cherry; Gulliver Books, 1994

An armadillo trekking through Texas not only learns about Texas geography but also discovers his relative place in the country, on the continent, and on the planet. He covers ground first on foot, then in the air with a friendly eagle, and finally on board the space shuttle. The book is an excellent starting point for activities closer to home: pick a favorite animal and travel through your own home state, plotting the route on the map.

Around the World in Eighty Days
10/+ Jules Verne; Morrow Junior Books, 1989

Jules Verne's rapid-travel classic, first published in 1873, tells the exciting tale of Phileas Fogg who—on a bet—sets out with his French valet, Passepartout, to circumnavigate the globe in a mere 80 days. (He wins, by the skin of his teeth.)

Ben's Dream
6/10 Chris Van Allsburg; Houghton Mifflin, 1997

Ben falls asleep and dreams that he and his house are sailing past the world's greatest monuments, all half underwater. (It's raining outside and he's been studying for a geography test.) Softly eerie black-and-white illustrations.

Blast Off to Earth! A Look at Geography
5/9 Loreen Leedy; Holiday House, 1992

Geography for sci-fi fans aged 5–9. A group of aliens blast off to earth and swoop from continent to continent, learning about the unique features of each.

Favorite Folktales From Around the World
ALL Jane Yolen, ed.; Pantheon, 1988

The book, divided into chapters by theme, includes 160 folktales from 40 cultures in a massive 498 pages. A good reference work for those planning to read their way around the world.

See **World History** (page 658), **Tales Alive!** (page 421), **World Folklore Series** (page 422), and **Tales to Tell** (page 436).

How to Make an Apple Pie and See the World

5/9 Marjorie Priceman; Dragonfly, 1996

A picture-book journey around the world in search of the ingredients to make a perfect apple pie: semolina wheat for flour from Italy, eggs from France, bark from the kurundu tree (cinnamon) from Sri Lanka, milk from England, sugarcane from Jamaica, and apples from Vermont. Included is a recipe for your own international apple pie.

Jamaica Sandwich (It Could Be Verse)
Brian P. Cleary; Lerner, 1996

A rhyming picture book of geographical puns, all on the order of "Jamaica sandwich?" There are illustrations to accompany each, which include excerpts from maps so that giggling readers can identify the geographical butt of the joke. A geography quiz appears at the end, which—be warned—gives kids a chance to invent their own awful puns.

Kate Heads West
Pat Brisson; Simon & Schuster, 1990

Kate, who has a discerning eye for geography, describes her trip through Oklahoma, Texas, New Mexico, and Arizona in a series of letters to family and friends back home. (She also visits the Grand Canyon and attends the World Watermelon Seed-Spitting Contest.) Recommended for readers in grades 1–4. Try following Kate's travels on the map. Also see *Your Best Friend, Kate,* in which Kate tours the mid-Atlantic states, and *Kate on the Coast,* in which she visits the Pacific Coast states, Alaska, and Hawaii.

Let's Go Traveling
Robin Rector Krupp; Morrow Junior Books, 1992

Rachel tours the world, visiting six famous ancient monuments: the prehistoric painted caves of France, the pyramids of Egypt, the Uxmal Maya temples of Mexico, Machu Picchu in Peru, Stonehenge, and the Great Wall of China. Each stop is illustrated with a fascinating collage of pictures and text, including photographs, excerpts from Rachel's travel diary, picture postcards, and lists of foreign words learned. By the same author, see *Let's Go Traveling in Mexico* (1996).

Paddle-to-the-Sea
Holling C. Holling; Houghton Mifflin, 1980

"Put me back in water. I am Paddle-to-the-Sea." A young boy carves a wooden Indian in a canoe and launches him, accompanied by this message, into the water of the Great Lakes. The little Indian thus embarks on a long and adventurous journey that eventually leads up the St. Lawrence River and into the Atlantic Ocean. The book, with wonderful illustrations and many detailed maps, follows the Indian throughout his travels.

Somewhere in the World Right Now
Stacey Schuett; Alfred A. Knopf, 1995

As a child goes to bed—at 8 P.M.—in Boston, many other things are happening all over the world at exactly the same time: a London baker is making bread for British breakfasts, African elephants are sleeping, dawn is breaking in India, and koala bears in Australia are sheltering from the midday sun. A picture-book trip through 24 time zones.

Stringbean's Trip to the Shining Sea
Vera B. Williams and Jennifer Williams; Scholastic, 1991

Stringbean heads west to the Pacific with his older brother, sending descriptive postcards home along the way. The illustrations are terrific: all the postcards are there, complete with pictures, messages, and canceled stamps.

Tales Alive! Ten Multicultural Folktales with Activities
Susan Milord; Williamson, 1995

Ten short illustrated tales from around the world, with activities suitable for elementary-aged children. Also see *Tales of the Shimmering Sky: Ten Global Folktales with Activities* (page 256).

Three Days on a River in a Red Canoe
Vera B. Williams; Greenwillow, 1984

This was our middle child's favorite book for years. It's the story of two cousins and their mothers who buy a red canoe and set off on an exciting three-day river trip. The story of the trip is illustrated with many creative and colorful little maps.

Wish You Were Here: Emily's Guide to the Fifty States
Kathleen Krull; Doubleday, 1997

Young Emily is traveling through all 50 states with her grandmother. Emily describes each state as they visit it, in a double-page illustrated spread covering basic state facts and features, lots of interesting extras, plus a map.

World Folklore Series
Teacher Ideas Press

Each volume in this series features a different world culture or ethnic group. The books include background information on the culture, geographical region, and history of the featured people, 30 to 40 representative folktales and legends, and suggested extension projects and activities. Titles include *The Corn Woman: Stories and Legends of the Hispanic Southwest* (Angel Vigil; 1994), *Why Ostriches Don't Fly and Other Tales from the African Bush* (I. Murphy Lewis; 1997), *From the Mango Tree and Other Folktales from Nepal* (Kavita Ram Shrestha and Sarah Lamstein; 1997), and *The Magic Egg and Other Tales from the Ukraine* (Barbara J. Suwyn; 1997). Illustrated with color photographs and drawings.

Libraries Unlimited
Box 6633
Englewood, CO 80155-6633
(303) 770-1220 or (800) 237-6124/fax (303) 220-8843
e-mail: lu-book@lu.com
Web site: www.lu.com

ACTIVITY BOOKS

Activity Atlas
Sally Hewitt; Barron's, 1995

The *Activity Atlas* is an oversize book of big, shiny labeled contour maps, in earthy greens and browns, with accompanying packets of over 250 reusable stickers of national flags, animals, architectural monuments, and natural features, to be stuck to the maps in the proper geographical locations. Also included with the maps are packs of "Postcards," illustrated with color photographs, each with geographical quiz questions; a "Passport," in which Atlas users can keep records of their geographical progress; and an informational "Activity Fact Wheel" built into the book's front cover.

Around the World With Phineas Frog: A Geographical Puzzle
Paul Adshead; Child's Play International, 1996

Phineas Frog and daughter travel the world; as they arrive in each country, readers are challenged to figure out where they are, using landmarks, city names, money, costumes, and souvenirs as clues.

Art From Many Hands
Jo Miles Schuman; Davis Publications, 1984

A terrific assortment of multicultural art projects for kids of all ages. Each chapter features projects from a different geographical area, including the Middle East, Central America, Asia, West Africa, Europe, the Caribbean Islands, the United States, and Canada. See **The Arts** (page 731). Also see *The Kids' Multicultural Art Book* (page 424).

Celebrations Around the World: A Multicultural Handbook
Carole S. Angell; Fulcrum, 1996

A 200+-page month-by-month listing of holidays celebrated all over the world. For each holiday, the author includes historical background information, a brief account of how the holiday is celebrated today, and a list of multidisciplinary activities and projects related to the holiday. January, for example, features the Independence Days of Australia, Cameroon, Haiti, Sudan, and Western Samoa, Junkanoo in the Bahamas, St. Knut's Day in Sweden, Tet in Vietnam, the Lantern Festival in China, the Winter Festival in India, and Emancipation Day and Martin Luther King Jr. Day in the United States.

Appendixes include lists of multicultural folktales, recipes, musical selections, and a bibliography.

Crafts of Many Cultures: 30 Authentic Craft Projects from Around the World
Scholastic, 1996

A step-by-step guide to 30 multicultural craft projects for elementary-level students, with background information and supplementary activity suggestions.

The Geography Coloring Book
Wynn Kapit; Addison-Wesley, 1992

Very detailed black-and-white maps for very advanced colorers, plus an encyclopedic amount of geographic information in small, dense print. Maps are grouped into nine categories: Continents, North America, South America, Europe, Asia, Oceania, Africa, Polar

Regions, and World Thematic Maps. Under each are included whole-continent political and physical maps, and smaller and more detailed subset maps showing details of individual countries or groups of countries. The "World Thematic Maps" section includes specialty maps illustrating world climatic regions, rainfall and temperature, winds and ocean currents, vegetation, population distribution, and official languages and religions. Precise instructions are provided for coloring—this isn't your ordinary grab-a-crayon-and-scribble coloring book. The author recommends fine-point felt-tipped pens or colored pencils; users will need at least 12 colors, including a basic medium gray. A challenging hands-on learning experience. Read the text first.

Geography Wizardry for Kids

Margaret Kenda and Phyllis S. Williams; Barron's Juveniles, 1997

Over 200 creative geography projects and activities for kids aged 9–12. Users, for example, try their hands at different kinds of mapmaking, invent their own postage stamp, travel the ancient Silk Road by caravan, and design a Roman villa.

See *Cooking Wizardry for Kids* (page 818), *Gardening Wizardry for Kids* (page 826), *Math Wizardry for Kids* (page 185), *Science Wizardry for Kids* (page 238).

$14.95 from bookstores or
Barron's Education Series, Inc.
250 Wireless Blvd.
Hauppauge, NY 11788
(800) 645-3476/fax (516) 434-3217

Gumshoe Geography

Richard S. Jones; Zephyr Press, 1996

A huge collection of "detective" projects for map readers in a fat 320-page spiral-bound book. The book begins with a short "Student Training Manual," which explains the basics of map reading: direction, latitude, longitude, grids, scales, and distances. Upon completion of the Training Manual, readers are told that they have been selected for service "in the elite information-gathering corps of an ultra-secret committee known only as The Committee." And off they go, armed with a (reproducible) Data Report Form, to complete mission assignments in locations all over the globe.

Assignments fall into 11 categories: "One Country," in which kids track down sites within single countries; "World Regions," "United States Regions," and "Continental Topics," which spread the to-be-located sites over larger areas; "Urban Topics," in which kids locate assorted cities (for example, "Forbidden Cities," "Top 10 Large Cities," and "Summer Olympic Games Cities"), "Rural Cultures," "World Climatic Regions," "Specific Physical Georgraphy" (including "Islands of the World," "Historic Volcanoes," and "Waterfalls"), "Human-Made Geography," "Historical Periods and Events," and "World Exploration." It's more complicated than it sounds: young gumshoes are simply given an assignment and a set of latitudinal and longitudinal coordinates (10 to 12 sets per assignment); then they're on their own to track down all necessary maps and research materials.

One sample assignment: "Your job is to visit the following sacred mountains and find out about the geography of the peak and the region around each site. Be prepared to tell us what makes the mountain in question different from the other mountains in the area or from the surrounding terrain. Follow all orders and good luck."

Answers are all in the back. Also included is a 40-page collection of reproducible black-line maps (no labels, no grids).

$39
Zephyr Press
3316 N. Chapel Ave.
Box 66006-C
Tucson, AZ 85728-6006
(520) 322-5090/fax (520) 323-9402

Hands Around the World: 356 Creative Ways to Build Cultural Awareness & Global Respect

Susan Milord; Williamson, 1992

Many multicultural activities for kids in grades K–6. Included are arts and crafts projects, creative writing and storytelling activities, songs and dances, and recipes. Kids learn, for example, how different cultures say hello and good-bye, how to brew Japanese tea, and how to recite the letters of the alphabet in sign language.

How to Draw Maps and Charts

Pam Beasant and Alastair Smith; EDC Publishing, 1993

A 32-page activity book with definitions and explanations of essential map features, plus instructions for drawing many kinds of maps, including town maps, treasure maps, and wildlife maps. For mapmakers aged 9–14.

Janice Van Cleave's Geography for Every Kid: Easy Activities That Make Learning Geography Fun

Janice Van Cleave; John Wiley & Sons, 1993

Inexpensive activities for kids in grades 3–7 (leaning more toward 3) that teach the nuts and bolts of geography. Users learn to read maps—there are activities based on map scales, map legends, latitude, and longitude—and to make their own, constructing, for example, a compass rose and a topographical map made from clay. Each lesson is clearly organized, with brief background information, a recipe-style materials list, precise instructions, a description of the desired results, and an after-action explanation. Unfortunately the effort to make the activities simple often makes them unexciting.

The Kids' Multicultural Art Book: Art and Craft Experiences from Around the World

Alexandra M. Terzian; Williamson, 1993

A host of creative international projects for kids aged 3–9. Kids make, for example, Chippewa dream catchers, Mexican tin roosters, Egyptian paper beads, African calabashes, and Chinese good luck dragons. And much more.

Also see *Art From Many Hands* (page 422).

The Kids' Multicultural Cookbook: Food and Fun Around the World

Deanna F. Cook; Williamson, 1995

Illustrations, "fun facts," and many international recipes for cooks aged 4 and up. The recipes are grouped by geographical region: Asia, Europe, Africa and the Middle East, the Americas, and the South Pacific. Among the included goodies are Indian chapatis and Sherpa popcorn, *apfelpfannekuchen* (apple cakes) from Germany, Ghanan peanut butter, Mexican quesadillas, and kiwi-in-a-cup from New Zealand.

See *How to Make an Apple Pie and See the World* (page 420) and multicultural listings in **Cooking** (page 815).

The Map Corner

Arnold B. Cheyney and Donald L. Capone; Good Year Books, 1991

A map-related activity book for kids in grades 4–8, including project and activity suggestions, historical and scientific background information, and an appendix of 50 reproducible black-line maps from all areas of the globe. Lesson plans include learning to read road maps, tracking thunderstorms and hurricanes on maps, following bird and butterfly migrations, and tracing the routes of 10 famous explorers, among them Marco Polo, Ferdinand Magellan, Meriwether Lewis and William Clark, and Amelia Earhart. There are also 23 "Map Activity Quizzes" based on the lesson plans, which reinforce basic map skills.

MayaQuest

Kids can follow a team of scientists and archaeologists biking through Central America. An accompanying teacher's guide and newsletter provide materials for a multidisciplinary study unit based on the trip, covering the biology and ecology of the rain forest, the ancient Mayan civilization, and the geography and culture of the area today. Past MayaQuest expeditions are available on CD-ROM (see page 435).

MayaQuest
529 South 7th St., Suite 320
Minneapolis, MN 55415
(612) 349-6584 or (800) 919-MAYA
e-mail: earthtreks@usinternet.com

Multicultural Math: Hands-On Math Activities from Around the World

Claudia Zaslavsky, Marti Shohet, and Mona Mark; Scholastic, 1996

Circle the globe with the math. The book contains hands-on math projects and activities from cultures around the world; chapters include "Numbers and Numerations," "Using Numbers in Real Life," "Space, Shape, and Size," and "Fun and Games." The book includes background information on each culture and reproducible student worksheets. Also see *Math Around the World* (Beverly Braxton, Philip Gonsalves, Linda Lipner, and Jacqueline Barber; University of California, 1996).

My World & Globe: An Interactive First Book of Geography

Ira Wolfman; Workman, 1991

An attractive 64-page informational book, in black, white, and robin's-egg blue, plus an 18-inch inflatable globe and a collection of 100 illustrated stickers and labels. Following instructions in the book, kids paste stickers on the globe pinpointing North and South Poles, glaciers and volcanoes, moving tectonic plates, the reversed seasons in northern and southern hemispheres, animal habitats, capital cities, and man-made landmarks. Lots of information, attractively presented, and the stickers are cute.

$13.95 from bookstores or
Workman Publishing Co.
708 Broadway
New York, New York 10003-9555
(212) 254-8098 or (800) 722-7202/fax (212) 254-8098
Web site: www.workmanpub.com

NetAmerica: Travel the 50 States on the Information Highway

Gary M. Garfield and Suzanne McDonough; Good Apple, 1996

An activity book for kids in grades 4–8 that centers around the use of the Internet for the study of U.S. geography. The book lists four Internet sites for each of the 50 states, along with suggestions for related activities.

Science Around the World

Shar Levine and Leslie Johnstone; John Wiley & Sons, 1996

A collection of projects and experiments related to 10 countries. Under Egypt, for example, kids learn about the building of the pyramids and experiment with inclined planes, friction, and mechanical advantage; under China, they make paper, build a sand clock, and learn about the invention of the seismograph. Each chapter begins with a map.

Science for Kids: 39 Easy Geography Activities

Robert W. Wood; TAB Books, 1991

A more challenging assortment of experiments than the Van Cleave projects (see page 424), with detailed scientific explanations, for kids aged 8–13.

A Trip Around the World

Barbara Schaff; Teacher Created Materials, 1993

A multidisciplinary activity book for kids in grades 4–8 centered around world geography. The book tours six continents and 15 countries through hands-on activities: users, for example, translate Egyptian hieroglyphics, invent Japanese haikus, learn to count in Swahili, and "visit" the Curie Institute in Paris for a physics lesson. Included in the book are world and country maps, lists of foreign words and phrases with their English translations, reproducible passports and travel journal pages, and supplementary reading suggestions.

Windows to the World

Nancy Everix; Good Apple, 1984

A multicultural activity book for kids in grades 2–8. The book covers seven countries—China, Mexico, Australia, Brazil, Canada (British Columbia), West Germany, and Egypt. Under China, for example, kids make a Chinese paper lantern, a set of paper tangrams, and a "fortune fan" based on the 12 animals of the Chinese zodiac, write a story using Chinese calligraphic characters, draw a picture of a Chinese junk, read about giant pandas, and bake fortune cookies. Also see, by the same author, *More Windows to the World*.

GAMES AND HANDS-ON ACTIVITIES

Amigos

A simulation for students in grades 5–9, in which teams race from El Paso, Texas, to Tierra del Fuego. The simulation takes place in three parts: in Round 1, kids travel through Mexico and Central America; in Round 2, they tour the West Indies; and in Round 3, they race through South America. Prior to each race, kids research their routes and prepare fact sheets on the countries they will be passing through; during the race they proceed by using their accumulated knowledge to answer questions on the included Information, Land/Resource, and Government/Economics Cards. "Give two reasons why the Orinoco and Amazon Rivers would be unsafe for you to swim in." "A group of islands off Ecuador's coast has a strange species of animals. Name the islands and animals." "What is this country's type of government and what is its official money?" The race ends at the tip of South America with—if you're up to it—a riotous fiesta.

$34

Interact

1825 Gillespie Way, #101

El Cajon, CA 92020-1095

(619) 448-1474 or (800) 359-0961/fax (619) 448-6722

Web site: www.interact-simulations.com

See **Caravans** (right), **Heritage** (page 428), and **Pacific Rim** (page 430).

Atlas-in-a-Box

An offshoot of the popular game of "Take Off!" (page 431). "Atlas-in-a-Box" contains (nearly) 200 individual country cards and a colorful folding world map. The country cards, great little learning aids, are two-sided: one side includes a color picture of the country's national flag and the name of its capital city, two "country clues," and a list of national statistics (area, population, life expectancy, literacy rate, and per capita (GNP). Kids are challenged to identify, for example, "The nation whose splendid Alhambra Palace is a testament to its nearly 800 years of Moorish rule" or "The former home of the deposed dictator and one-time self-proclaimed President-for-Life Idi Amin Dada." The flip side of each card shows a highlighted map of the featured country; bordering countries, in lighter colors, are helpfully labeled. Also included is a list of basic political and geographical information: date of independence, official language, ethnic groups, religions, currency, climate, and major landforms. Each card is numbered: if you simply can't figure out what the country is, there's a number-coded "Country Index" printed on the enclosed world map. Instructions are included for four different games, suitable for kids aged 8 and up.

$11.95 (plus $3 shipping/handling)

Resource Games, Inc.

Box 151

Redmond, WA 98052

(206) 883-3143 or (800) 275-8818/fax (206) 883-3136

The Book of Classic Board Games

Klutz Press, 1990

A spiral-bound collection of 15 international games, with colorful heavy-duty game boards and an attached mesh sack of playing pieces. Games include checkers, "Dalmation Pirates and the Volga Bulgars" (traditionally known as "Fox and Geese" and a favorite of Queen Victoria's), "Hasami Shogi" from Japan, "Go" from China, "Mancala" from Africa, and backgammon, "a game that's been on the best-seller lists for 2,000 years."

Available at bookstores or

Klutz Flying Apparatus Catalogue

2121 Staunton Ct.

Palo Alto, CA 94306

(415) 424-0739

Caravans

A world geography adventure simulation in which kids, grouped in teams or "caravans," tour the world searching for specific museum artifacts—among them a picture of Humphrey Bogart from Casablanca, Morocco, a yurt from Ulan Bator, Mongolia, and a dog sled from Whitehorse, Canada. Caravans move from place to place by means of "travel dots," earned by completing geography challenges and activities. For every five cities visited, caravan members gain new abilities and advantages, graduating from their initial rank as "Travelers," poky beginners with a tendency to get lost, to "Voyagers," "Discoverers," and finally "World Class Explorers," savvy experts able to deal with quicksand, pirates, headhunters, and dangerous mountain passes. Daily "Fate Cards" (such as "Killer Bees") affect the progress of each caravan.

Materials include 35 twelve-page student handbooks, a poster-size map, 72 Fate Cards, and a teacher's guide. The simulation is targeted at 20 to 35 students in grades 5–9 but can be adapted to much smaller groups.

$53

Interact

GEOGRAPHY

1825 Gillespie Way, #101

El Cajon, CA 92020-1095

(619) 448-1474 or (800) 359-0961/fax (619) 448-6722

Web site: www.interact-simulations.com

See **Heritage** (page 428), **Amigos** (page 425), and **Pacific Rim** (page 430).

Flying High: Around the World in 80 Plays

A geography board game in which players, piloting little plastic planes, travel from the City of Departure to the Winner's Circle/Home, attempting to win Travel Dollars and answer quiz questions as they go. To complete a world tour, each player must land on each of the board's seven cities and, while there, correctly answer a question from a "Geo-Quiz" or "Mystery Quiz" card. The multiple-choice or fill-in-the-blank questions—1,100 in all—test both geographic and general knowledge. Level 1 questions are intended for 7–10-year-olds; Level 2 questions for 11-year-olds and up. Sample Level 1 Mystery Questions—to my mind a bit challenging for the average 7-year-old—include "Plants have what two principal types of roots?" and "The invention of the modern detective story is credited to . . . Edgar Allan Poe, John Steinbeck, or Hermann Hesse?" Sample Level 1 Geo-Quiz questions include "The official language of Guadeloupe is . . . Spanish or French?" and "Mameys are tropical . . . spiders, fruits, or flowers?"

The game also includes "Adventure Cards" ("Beware! The suspicious-looking person on your left may be a spy!"), "Problem Cards" ("Your cat was checked in on another flight. Go back to the last city or pay $300 to have him sent."), and "Fun Island Cards," with which players can challenge their opponents to tennis, golf, or soccer matches, or have a try at winning the lottery. For three to six players aged 7 and up.

$22 (plus shipping/handling)

Viv Familee Games International

9651 Odlin Rd.

Richmond, BC V6X 1E1, Canada

(604) 273-5683

Web site: www.intergate.bc.ca/business/vfgi

GeoChallenge

Arnold Cheyney; Good Year Books, 1996

Contains 180 geography challenges, one for each day of the public school year. Challenges are listed one per page in an illustrated spiral-bound book designed to stand up on end like a desk calendar. *GeoChallenge* is available at three levels of difficulty: Level 1, for kids aged 8–10; Level 2, for ages 9–11; and Level 3, for ages 10 and up. Sample level 3 challenges: "The international boundary between the U.S. and Canada runs between the two waterfalls at Niagara Falls. How much water runs over the two falls every second? What is the name of the boat that takes sightseers up to see the falls?" "The second-smallest state in the United States is Delaware. Where does your state or province rank in size among the other states or provinces?" "The long narrow country running down the west coast of South America is Chile. How long is Chile?" There's an answer key in the back of the book.

$9.95 from bookstores

Geo/Derby

A board game aimed at kids aged 8 and up. The playing board is a racetrack; the playing pieces little colored plastic horses. (Hence the "Derby.") Players race to the finish line by answering questions about U.S. geography, referring, if need be, to the included folding map of the United States.

On each turn, a player picks a question card from the stack in the middle of the playing board. The question cards are colored to match the states on the map; Vermont and its card, for example, are both a flashy bubblegum pink. Each card lists eight questions (with answers) about its featured state; which of these is answered is determined by the roll of an eight-sided die. Experts who manage to answer the question without hints from the map move their horse forward three spaces; persons who need to peek before answering are allowed to move only two. Also included is an assortment of "Scrambler" cards, with a mix of questions all based on different states. If you're playing with children of different ages, you may have to tailor the questions a bit to match ability levels: questions can get quite sticky and specific. My geographical knowledge, which dwindles rapidly outside New England, proved unequal to "The Salton Sea is in which state?" and "What river crosses northern Alabama?" The game moves fast, and map lovers should like it.

$19.95 (plus shipping/handling)

Talicor, Inc.

8845 Steven Chase Ct.

Las Vegas, NV 89129

(800) 433-4263/fax (702) 655-4366

Web site: www.talicor.com

GeoSafari

An electronic learning game for kids in grade 3 and up. The "GeoSafari" machine is a foot-tall plastic console with a numbered keyboard set in the base. Color-illustrated question-and-answer lesson cards are slid into place on the console; players type in answer numbers on the keyboard and the machine responds with a bevy of flashing red lights and—depending—cheerful beeps or depressed buzzes. A basic set of map lesson cards comes with the machine, designed to teach kids the names of continents and major bodies of water, countries and major cities of the world, and states and capital cities of the United States. Each lesson card pictures a large colorful map with 26 numbered sites; correct names of the sites, to be matched to the proper number by the player, are listed down the sides of the cards. Since its initial introduction as a geography game, "GeoSafari" has become increasingly versatile: there are now many different lesson card packs available, covering not only geography but also such topics as "U.S. History," "World History," "Science," "Wonders of the Smithsonian," "Learn Basic Spanish," "Learn Basic French," "Earth's Ecosystems," and "Animals of the World."

A younger version of the game, "GeoSafari Jr.," is available for kids in preschool through grade 2: lesson card sets include early reading games, phonics, basic science concepts, and puzzles.

Machines, $99.95; lesson card packs (10 two-sided cards each), $14.95

Educational Insights

16941 Keegan Ave.

Carson, CA 90746

(800) 933-3277/fax (310) 605-5048 or (800) 995-0506

Web site: www.edin.com

Heritage

A simulation for upper-elementary to middle school geographers, in which students travel from San Diego, California, to Bangor, Maine, visiting 15 histor-ical sites along the way. Associated activities include keeping travel diaries and logs and researching the historical significance of the visited sites.

$34

Interact

1825 Gillespie Way, #101

El Cajon, CA 92020-1095

(619) 448-1474 or (800) 359-0961/fax (619) 448-6722

Web site: www.interact-simulations.com

See **Amigos** (page 425), **Caravans** (page 426), and **Pacific Rim** (page 430).

Highlights Best Board Games from Around the World

Robert Dugan; Essential Learning Products, 1993

A tour of the world in 16 board games, all assembled in an oversize book with colorful game boards printed on heavy cardboard pages and punch-out cardboard playing pieces. The boards are beautifully illustrated, and each is accompanied by a brief history of the game, plus playing instructions. Games include "Jumpers and Stumpers," an ancient Arab game brought to Spain by the conquering Moors (they called it "Albuquerque"); "Poindexter," invented by a frustrated Frenchman imprisoned in the Bastille; "Wari" from Africa, in which the playing pieces represent seeds and the game board squares, fields; and "Nine Man's Morris," a version of an ancient game whose playing board has been found carved in the roof of a 3,000-year-old Egyptian temple, on the deck of a Viking ship, and on the cloister seats of Westminster Abbey.

Available at bookstores or

Highlights for Children, Inc.

2300 W. Fifth Ave.

Box 269

Columbus, OH 43216-0269

Also see *The Book of Classic Board Games* (page 426).

Mad Dash

"Mad Dash!", subtitled "Three Minutes Across America," is a map-based geography game for players aged 8 and up. The game consists of four folding United States maps, a pack of 50 playing cards, each bearing the name of a state, and a timer. Players each

GEOGRAPHY

get a map and half the (shuffled) pack of state cards: the object is to line up as many of your cards as possible, forming a chain of bordering states that stretches across the country, all in three minutes. Each state is assigned a point value, depending on the number of states with which it shares borders. Total state points are added up at the end to determine the winner, which makes for some quick math practice; there's also a bonus for getting all the way across the country. It's fast and fun. The drawback, at least in our more-than-two-kids household, is that the game—which *everybody* wants to play—is for two people. We solved this by making a duplicate state card deck out of index cards, thus neatly boosting it to a four-person game, which is how many maps you have, anyway.

$13.95 from toy or game stores or
ITOS Enterprises
395 Windsor Rd.
York, PA 17402
(717) 757-9666 or (800) 827-5725

Mapping the World by Heart
David Smith; Tom Snyder Productions, 1992

An innovative geography program in which students learn to draw a detailed world map from memory. "Mapping the World by Heart" includes lesson plans, reproducible student maps and handouts, and a list of geography resource addresses in a loose-leaf binder, plus a short instructional video. For kids in grade 5 and up.

$59.95
Zenger Media
10200 Jefferson Blvd.
Box 802
Culver City, CA 90232-0802
(310) 839-2436 or (800) 421-4246/fax (310) 839-2249
or (800) 944-5432
e-mail: access@ZengerMedia.com
Web site: ZengerMedia.com/zenger

Maptitude
The main focus of the game is a pack of 192 beautifully illustrated "Country Cards," each encyclopedically packed with information, including a map of the featured country (color-coded by continent) with capital city and bordering neighbors labeled, a list of essential statistics, a full-color picture of the national flag, a bar graph showing area, population, and average life expectancies, and a couple of interesting extras. Example: "The diamond- and coffee-producing country that lies at the geographic center of Africa." These little tidbits aren't used for anything in the official "Maptitude" game but make for a nice little geography quiz if you take the Country Cards along on car trips.

The game itself concentrates not only on country identification, but on global relationships. Players, by sequentially drawing and discarding Country Cards, attempt to collect cards whose countries touch one another on the world map ("Border Matches") and to assemble sequences of cards representing countries from each of the six continents (a "Continent Sweep"). For two to four players, aged 10 and up.

$15
Resource Games, Inc.
Box 151
Redmond, WA 98052
(425) 883-3143 or (800) 275-8818/fax (425) 883-3136

My World Quilt
A kit with which kids can make their own geographical quilt. The kit contains nine preprinted quilt squares, which can be illustrated and colored with fabric markers. Squares are variously titled "This is My Home," "This is My Town," "This is My State," "This is My Country," and "This is My Earth." All materials are included for the assembly of a completed quilt, as well as a 60-page atlas of state maps, flowers, flags, and mottoes.

$19.95 from toy and arts and crafts stores; for a local source, contact
Curiosity Kits
Box 811
Cockeysville, MD 21030
(410) 584-2605 or (800) 584-KITS/fax (410) 584-1247
e-mail: CKitsinc@aol.com
See **American History, Quilts** (page 515).

Name That Country
This easy-to-play board game from Educational Insights teach kids the names, capital cities, and interesting facts about the countries of the world. On the game board, the playing path circles a map of the world. Players move around the path by twirling a spinner,

identifying on the map the country on which the arrow lands, and then—if they answered correctly—moving the number of spaces designated by the spinner. Often the move will land a playing piece on a "Postcard" square: the player then draws a card from the included pack which, postcard-style, has a friendly greeting in a foreign language, an interesting fact about the country of the postcard writer, and a quiz question.

"Name That State" is essentially the same game, homestyle. The playing path circles a map of the United States; players must locate the state designated by the spinner. "Postcards" here arrive from all over the country, each with an interesting fact and a quiz question about one of the 50 states. The games are fast-moving and fun, for two to four players in grades 3 and up.

> Each game, $19.95
> Educational Insights
> 16941 Keegan Ave.
> Carson, CA 90746
> (800) 933-3272/fax (310) 605-5048 or (800) 995-0506
> Web site: www.edin.com

Odyssey Atlasphere

The "Odyssey Atlasphere" combines a colorful globe (though the oceans are white instead of blue) with an encyclopedic computer to generate interactive, addictive, and multifaceted geography lessons. The base of the globe is fitted with a touch pad and special stylus. Users select a labeled key on the touch pad control panel and then touch a location on the globe with the stylus: a pleasant male voice responds with the name of the country and—if desired—a wealth of other information, including population statistics, political status, major religions, languages, land area, type of currency, and average rainfall. Hit the "Sounds" key and you get samples of regional music; "Time" announces current time anywhere in the world; "Distance" estimates the distance between two points—how far is it from Lima, Peru, to Tokyo, Japan?—or calculates the length of a line traced by the stylus, thus allowing users to determine the length of the Chinese border or the Nile River. "Comparisons" allows kids to compare any two countries or regions by population, area, wealth, and energy consumption. If you're totally lost—where *is* Belize, anyway?—you can spell out the name of the mystery region on the letter panel on the

side of the globe, and the Atlasphere will respond with helpful locational hints: continent, latitude and longitude, nearest neighbors.

The globe is equipped with removable cartridges, which are a source of geography games or additional information.

More game/information cartridges are in preparation, as well as assorted Atlasphere overlays, which will allow users to transform the globe into a 3-D game board, map of the constellations, map of the ocean floor, or map of the historical world. It's a marvelous machine; our 12-year-old, who has never cared all that much for raw geography, has spent hours hunkered over it, intrepidly exploring. *He* can find Belize.

> "The Odyssey Atlasphere," with AC power adaptor and two game cartridges, $399
> Explore Technologies, Inc.
> 2880 Lakeside Dr., Suite 130
> Santa Clara, CA 95054
> (408) 654-9600 or (888) 456-2343
> Web site: www.globeheads.com

Pacific Rim

A simulation in which kids race by ship from Japan to New Zealand, receiving visas in their passports for each Pacific Rim country they pass through. They earn points that allow them to travel by answering questions about the geography, economy, government, and culture of each country. Recommended for kids in grades 5–9.

> $34
> Interact
> 1825 Gillespie Way, #101
> El Cajon, CA 92020-1095
> (619) 448-1474 or (800) 359-0961/fax (619) 448-6722
> Web site: www.interact-simulations.com

See **Amigos** (page 425), **Caravans** (page 426), and **Heritage** (page 428).

Post It Home

Players travel across a colorful map of the world, attempting to mail postcards home from six cities: Cape Town, London, New York, Rio de Janeiro, Sydney, and Tokyo. As they travel—by air, sea, or rail—they must answer general "Journey Questions" ("What is a Volkswagon Beetle?" "Where would you find a pore?") or geography-related "Postbox Questions" ("Is Africa a hot continent or a cold continent?" "What is the name of the longest river in the world?") Once players have reached a city and correctly answered a question, they are allowed to mail postcards home, addressing each card, stamping it with the included cancellation stamp, and dropping it in the included postbox. The postbox, assembled from folded cardboard, is bright red; "Post It Home" is published in Great Britain. A delightful geography game for 7–12-year-olds.

$37 from game stores or

Old Game Store

Route 11/30

Manchester Center, VT 05255

(802) 362-2756 or (800) 818-GAME

Web site: www.vtweb.com/oldgame

Souvenirs

A board game of world geography. The playing path is printed with colorful little outline maps of six continents (no Antarctica). On each turn, players roll a die, advance their piece, draw a question card, and attempt to answer the question pertaining to the continent their piece has landed upon. Land on a map of Asia, for example, and you may get "The world's most photographed mountain is this country's Mount Fuji"; land on Europe, and you may be challenged with "The Brandenburg Gate is this German capital's landmark." The correct answer to a question wins the player a "souvenir token"; the first person to collect a souvenir from each continent and return back home wins the game. For two to four players in grades 4 and up.

$19.95 from game stores or

Social Studies School Service

10200 Jefferson Blvd., Room 64

Box 802

Culver City, CA 90232-0802

(310) 839-2436 or (800) 421-4246/fax (310) 839-2249

or (800) 944-5432

Web site: SocialStudies.com

Take Off!

The playing board is a laminated map of the world bordered with color pictures of world flags; the playing pieces are fleets of plastic jet planes; and the object of the game is to be the first to move an entire fleet of planes around the world, from Hawaii (east) to Hawaii

(west), following the colored lines indicating air routes. Moves are determined by the roll of a pair of eight-sided multicolored dice. Occasionally the dice turn up a "Take off!" sign, at which point the player draws one of the 200 Take off! cards, and reads the name of the capital city printed above the national flag. He/she then identifies the country—by matching the flag on the card to the flag (labeled with the country name) on the game board—and sends a jet to that capital city. (Depending on direction, this can be an advantage; often, however, it isn't.)

In a more advanced version of the game, players, upon drawing a Take off! card, take a "Challenge Quiz," attempting to name the featured country from the clues on the card: "The country where the White Nile begins its journey north from Lake Victoria. It's a home to the mountain gorilla and the white rhinoceros." "The ancient birthplace of democracy and of the Olympic Games. Its landmarks include the Acropolis, the site of the Parthenon temple ruins." For two to six players, aged 6 and up.

$24.95 (plus $5 shipping/handling)

Resource Games, Inc.

Box 151

Redmond, WA 98052

(425) 883-3143 or (800) 275-8818/fax (425) 883-3136

TravelTalk

A collection of geography-oriented conversation cards from TableTalk. Each card in the series presents an interesting fact, followed by an open-ended, discussion-provoking question. The cards are intended to promote family or classroom conversations. The publisher proposes that they be used at the family dinner table, as a creative alternative to bedtime stories, on walks, or during trips in the car.

A sample from the TravelTalk deck reads "China's Yellow River earned its name because of the golden silt that gives the 3000-mile waterway its color. Ireland is known as the Emerald Isle because of its rich, green countryside. The Red Sea gets its sometimes rosy hue from red algae that grow in it. What is the most colorful place you have ever been? If you could give that place a new name based on its hue, what would you call it?"

$5.95

TableTalk

Box 31703

St. Louis, MO 63131

(314) 997-5676 or (800) 997-5676

Web site: http://www.tbltalk.com

See **TableTalk** (page 67).

6 *Uncle Happy's Train Game*

The game boxtop pictures a bug-eyed locomotive and a goony cartoon engineer in striped overalls. I glanced at it once and decided, unfairly, that Uncle Happy wasn't worth a second look. Get that top off, however, and "Uncle Happy's Train Game" is a delightful geography game for kids aged 6 and up. The playing board is a large plastic-coated map of the United States, Players work their way across it from coast to coast, drawing imaginary railroads in erasable crayon, learning state names, shapes, and locations as they go.

The game includes a pack of 51 state cards (the extra is the District of Columbia) and 50 "product chips," each with a picture representing the principal product of a state. Uncle Happy's products are of more interest to kids than the average: along with the Hawaiian pineapples, Maine lobsters, and Alabama peanuts, there are Vermont teddy bears, Ohio crayons, and Alaskan sleds. At the beginning of the game, each player draws three state cards. Then, in turn, each player draws a railroad, connecting their three states with others to form a transcontinental chain. (Alaska, for Uncle Happy's purposes, is said to border Washington; Hawaii, to border California.)

$14.95

Mayfair Games, Inc.

5211 W. 65th St.

Bedford Park, IL 60638

(800) 432-4376/fax (708) 458-3931

Web site: www.coolgames.com

10 *Voyagers*

A geographical trivia game, described as a "Multicultural Expedition" for persons aged 10 to adult. The expedition consists of a fat pack of question-and-answer cards covering five cultural regions of the globe: North America, South America, Africa/Oceania, Asia, and Europe. There are 80 cards per region, each listing questions in three categories: People, Places, and Things. From a sample North America card:

PEOPLE: This child of slaves discovered 300 uses for the peanut, which increased demand for this important southern crop.

PLACES: The largest remaining unspoiled tropical rain forest in North America can be found in . . . Costa Rica, Cuba, or Nicaragua?

THINGS: China invented this, America's favorite dessert, over 4000 years ago.

An occasional nongeographical question is thrown in, such as "Have you ever been left 'in the lurch'? What is a lurch?" You flip the card over for the answer, expecting an interesting tidbit of multicultural linguistic history; instead you get "This leaves us in the lurch! Any answer okay." Our kids found this approach annoying. There are also a number of geographical misspellings.

If your older kids like trivia-type games, however, it's probably challenging and interesting enough to hold their attention. And it can be played in the car.

$19.95

Voyagers, Inc.

Box 87

Essex, CT 06426

(860) 767-3317 or (800) 767-3317

Also see **Voyagers: The Lure of the Sea** (page 324).

9 *Where in the World?*

This is a truly gorgeous-looking geography game, complete with 186 question cards, topped with color pictures of national flags, and six two-sided, lushly colored game boards, illustrated with detailed maps of North America, South America, Oceania, Asia, Africa, and Europe. Instructions are included for six different games, in the course of which young players learn crucial information about 194 countries: capital city, population, major imports and exports, languages, religions, and monetary units. The game is continually updated to keep pace with ever-changing world geography; the latest edition, for example, includes the 15 new countries of the reshuffled Soviet Union. "Where in the World?" is a perennial best-seller, according to the publisher, and educators have lavished it with praise.

Our children, however, who showed no interest in memorizing the population of Bolivia, the major languages of Bhutan, or the literacy rate of Zimbabwe, pronounced it dull and callously likened it to learning the multiplication tables. We eventually used the game boards, which are terrific, for other, livelier games of our own invention, which is doubtless why none of our children to this day can name the principal products of Portugal.

$32

Aristoplay

450 S. Wagner Rd.

Ann Arbor, MI 48107

(800) 634-7738 or (888) GR8-GAME/

fax (734) 995-4611

Web site: www.aristoplay.com

Where in the U.S.A. is Carmen Sandiego?
Where in the World is Carmen Sandiego?

These are board game versions of the popular computer games from Broderbund (see page 435), in which players pursue the V.I.L.E. henchpersons of master villain Carmen Sandiego across the map, attempting to intercept the criminals and retrieve a stolen national or international monument, landmark, or treasure. (Carmen's people steal big; they've been known to make off with the Grand Canyon, Niagara Falls, and Mexico City's Chapultepec Park.) A successful pursuit and capture involves solving clues and answering questions about locations nation- or world-wide. Each game includes a colorful map playing board, 220 geography question cards, and a generous supply of entertaining mysteries.

Each game, about $25, from toy or game stores

World Geo Puzzle

An award-winning National Geographic Curiosity kit in which kids color printed continent stickers with felt-tipped markers, then peel them apart and stick the squares onto the sides of twelve 1¾-inch-square wooden blocks. The result is six world "geo puzzles," one for each continent—provided you can get the blocks back in the proper order again. The kit also includes a to-be-colored world map poster.

$16 from toy and game stores; for a local source,

contact

Curiosity Kits

Box 811

Cockeysville, MD 21030

(410) 584-2605 or (800) 584-KITS

e-mail: CKitsinc@aol.com

AUDIO GEOGRAPHY

Geography Songs

"You never forget what you sing!" state the publishers of *Geography Songs*. We all know this is true: witness how quickly we forget the rules of trigonometry but remember all six verses to the "Camp Wendy Goodnight Song." *Geography Songs* thus combines the memory-boosting advantages of music with to-be-memorized academic information: here, the names of the countries of the world. The kit includes a 72-page workbook containing all the song lyrics, related blackline maps, a fill-in-the-blanks "Geography Songs Test" and a world geography crossword puzzle, plus 23 insidiously catchy songs on audiocassette. Words and music to these songs are no great shakes—our kids compared them cruelly to television commercials—but they learned every single one of them, without visible effort. So did I.

$19.95

Audio Memory Publishing

501 Cliff Dr.

Newport Beach, CA 92663

(800) 365-SING

See *States & Capitals Songs* (page 434).

Rhythm, Rhyme, and Read:
States and Capitals

A 40-minute audiocassette of patriotic songs designed to teach state names and capitals. Optional accompaniments include a 24-page student "Lyric Activity Book" and a teacher's reproducible activity book, with song lyrics, games, maps, graphs, project suggestions, and creative writing activities, suitable for kids aged 7–12.

Tape and teacher's book set, $14.95

Twin Sisters Productions

1340 Home Ave., Suite D

Akron, OH 44310

(800) 248-TWIN/fax (216) 633-8988

Also see *Yo, Sacramento!* (page 419).

7 12 *States & Capitals Songs*

States & Capitals Songs comes as a kit, including an audiocassette of songs teaching the names of all 50 states and their capital cities, a 25 × 36" map of the United States to color, and the song lyrics.

$9.95
Audio Memory Publishing
501 Cliff Dr.
Newport Beach, CA 92663
(800) 356-SING

See *Geography Songs* (page 433).

VIDEO GEOGRAPHY

4 8 *Big Bird in China*

Sesame's lovable Big Bird and dog friend take a trip to China in search of the magical Phoenix. While there, they visit historical sites and geographical landmarks, learn about the native culture and traditions, and even learn a few words and phrases in Chinese, including "I love you." A delightful geographical experience for 4–8-year-olds. Also see *Big Bird in Japan*.

$14.95
Movies Unlimited
3015 Darnell Rd.
Philadelphia, PA 19154
(215) 637-4444 or (800) 4-MOVIES
e-mail: movies@moviesunlimited.com
Web site: www.moviesunlimited.com

See **World History, Asia** (page 661).

National Geographic Video

ALL The National Geographic Society is famed for an extensive line of terrific films in the fields of physical and cultural geography, anthropology, and natural history. ("National Geographic special," in our house, is a phrase with influence.) Sample video titles include *African Wildlife*, *Australia's Improbable Animals*, *Land of the Tiger*, *Yukon Passage*, *Hawaii: Strangers in Paradise*, *Volcano!*, *The Great Indian Railway*, *Cyclone!*, and *Jewels of the Caribbean Sea*. Available from most video rental stores, or it can be purchased from:

National Geographic Home Video
Box 5073

Clifton, NJ 07015
(800) 627-5162
Web site: www.nationalgeographic.com

10 + *The Silk Road*

A six-part geographic and cultural journey across Asia, along the ancient Silk Road in the footsteps of Marco Polo.

$149.95
PBS Home Video
1320 Braddock Pl.
Alexandria, VA 22314-1698
(800) 645-4PBS

See **World History, Asia** (page 661).

COMPUTER SOFTWARE

10 + *AfricaTrek*

Kids travel along with a team of bicyclists trekking across Africa from Tunisia to South Africa. On their journey, they learn about the geography, ecology, history, and culture of Africa through maps, photographs, graphics, and games. On CD-ROM for Mac or Windows.

$49.95
The Learning Company
6160 Summit Dr. N
Minneapolis, MN 55430-4003
(800) 622-3390/fax (612) 589-1151
Web site: www.learningco.com

9 + *Amazon Trail II*

An update of the original *Amazon Trail* in which players travel through the Amazon rain forest in search of cinchona bark to cure an Inca king of malaria. En route they learn about the geography, history, and ecology of the Amazon region while contending with piranhas, headhunters, poisonous snakes, whirlpools, accidents, and lost supplies. *Amazon Trail II* expands upon the original experience: players choose among 17 dangerous assignments, interact with a large cast of characters, among them scientists, naturalists, explorers, conquistadors, and Amazon natives, and meet over 100 different Amazon animals. The game can be played at

GEOGRAPHY

three levels, for kids of different ages and abilities, and includes color photographs, video and audio clips, graphics, and maps. On CD-ROM for Mac or Windows.

$29.99

The Learning Company

6160 Summit Dr. N

Minneapolis, MN 55430-4003

(800) 622-3390/fax (612) 589-1151

Web site: www.learningco.com

Cartopedia

Modestly subtitled "The Ultimate World Reference Atlas," this CD-ROM is an immense compilation of beautifully presented and readily usable information. There are over 600 detailed maps, from which one can zoom out for continental or world overviews or in for close-ups; 7,000 pop-up windows dispensing geographical, political, and cultural information; hundreds of color photographs and video sequences (kids can, for example, view each country's flag and listen to a rendition of its national anthem); and a gazetteer of 25,000 place-names. Recommended for kids in grade 3 and up. On CD-ROM for Mac or Windows.

$53.95

Dorling Kindersley Publishing

1224 Heil Quaker Blvd.

LaVergne, TN 37086

(888) DIALDKP

Web site: www.dk.com

GeoSafari

CD-ROM versions of the electronic game (see page 428). Like the "Geosafari" learning machine, the software programs function like a quiz game, allowing kids to tackle questions in a range of subject areas. The programs include color photographs, illustrations, animations, and video clips. Players click on the answer; the computer keeps score. Titles include *Geosafari Geography, History, Science,* and *Animals.* On CD-ROM for Mac or Windows.

$24.95 each

Educational Insights

16941 Keegan Ave.

Carson, CA 90746

(800) 933-3297/fax (310) 605-5048 or (800) 995-0506

Web site: www.edin.com

MayaQuest

Based on a real-life bicycle trip through Central America in search of the ancient Mayan civilization. In this reenactment, kids travel through the Yucatán peninsula, learning about the culture, geography, and ecology of the area, visiting archaeological digs, and interacting with people they meet along the way. Included are photographs from the original trip, video and audio clips, maps, and an informational text. On CD-ROM for Mac or Windows.

$9.99

The Learning Company

6160 Summit Dr. N

Minneapolis, MN 55430-4003

(800) 622-3390/fax (612) 589-1151

Web site: www.learningco.com

Also see *MayaQuest* (page 424) and **World History** (page 593).

Where in the U.S.A. is Carmen Sandiego?
Where in the World is Carmen Sandiego?

In these clever and highly popular geography games, student players, as budding detectives, attempt to track down the peripatetic members of archvillain Carmen Sandiego's criminal gang and to recover some stolen national or international monument, landmark, or treasure. (The crooks even pinch the *Mona Lisa*'s smile.) "Where in the World" features marvelous National Geographic color photos from 45 countries, plus maps and clever animations; it's definitely a learning experience, as well as tremendous fun. A "Junior Detective Version" is available for kids aged 5–8, with visual, rather than text-based, clues.

"Where in the U.S.A." follows the same format, featuring full-color digitalized photos, topographical maps of each state, and hilarious animations and sound effects.

$34.95

Broderbund

Box 6125

Novato, CA 94948-6125

(800) 521-6263

Web site: www.broderbund.com or www.carmensandiego.com

GEOGRAPHY ON-LINE

Earth Viewer
What Earth looks like, right at this very minute, from outer space. Once it's in view, kids can move in closer, zeroing in on any spot on the planet's surface. Ditto the Moon.

> www.fourmilab.ch/earthview/vplanet.html

Finding Your Way with Map and Compass
Learn to read topographic maps on-screen, with the help of the U.S. Geological Survey.

> info.er.usgs.gov/fact~sheets/finding-your-way/finding-your-way.html

Flags of the World
A site devoted to vexillology, the study of flags. There are over 1,500 color images of flags, accessible by keyword or by clicking on a world map. A brief description accompanies each flag.

> fotw.digibel.be/flags

Geography Lesson Plans
A series of detailed lesson plans with reproducible maps and activity sheets for kids of upper-elementary age through junior high from the master mappers at the U.S. Geological Survey.

> internet.er.usgs.gov/education/teacher/what-do-maps-show/oindex.html

Geography USA: A Virtual Textbook
An entire introductory college geography text on-line, with useful links to other sites. You can download and print the chapters if you don't want to read the book on the computer screen.

> www.nau.edu/~alew/ustxtwlc.html

Heritage Map Museum
The museum includes a large viewing gallery of beautiful 15th- to 19th-century antique maps.

> www/carto.com

Map Viewer
An interactive world or United States map; users can zoom in and out, and add or delete features such as political borders, rivers, and mountains.

> pubweb.parc.xerox.com/map

Mapmaker, Mapmaker, Make Me a Map
"How does Peter Pan get to Never Never land?," this site begins. A terrific step-by-step tour of map-making for kids from the Cartographic Services Laboratory at the University of Tennessee.

> loki.ur.utk.edu/ut2kids/maps/map.html

The Multicultural Pavilion
Information and discussion on multicultural education, a "Teacher's Corner," with links to student activities and lesson plans, reading lists, and on-line multicultural resources for kids, and links to many related sites.

> curry.edschool.Virginia.EDU/go/multicultural

National Geographic Society
On-line versions of the society's magazines, *National Geographic* (see page 412) and *National Geographic World* (see page 412), an on-line store, links to all kinds of maps and map sites, geography education resources, including lesson plans and activity suggestions for kids in grades K–12, and an excellent kids' site, with geography quizzes and games, a pen pal network, digital field trips, and questions from the annual National Geography Bee.

> www.nationalgeographic.com

PCL Map Collection
Over 200,000 maps of all conceivable kinds: city, state, region, country, continent, political, topographical, thematic, outline, and practically anything else you can imagine.

> www.lib.utexas.edu/Libs/PCL/Map_collection

Tales to Tell
Illustrated multicultural stories for kids from all over the world, including rhymes, fables, adventure stories, legends, and folk- and fairy tales.

> www.thekids.com

U.S. Geological Survey
Geography straight from the horse's mouth; lots of information, plus links to many geography-related other sources.

> www.usgs.gov

GEOGRAPHY

The Virtual Quilt

🌐 **ALL** A "patchwork panorama of communities from around the world." Kids create a patch representing their own town or region of the country and submit it, with a written description, to the Virtual Quilt site.

Users can view all current patches and click on each for a close-up and descriptive text. For elementary and middle school students.

www.sunsite.unc.edu/~ephesus/quilt.html

HISTORY
GENERAL, AMERICAN, AND WORLD

History is more or less bunk.

HENRY FORD

Histories make men wise.

FRANCIS BACON

W hy," asked Ethan, our second and very future-oriented son, "do we have to study history? I hate history. It's not good for anything. It doesn't have anything to do with the things I'm interested in—and if I ever *really* need to know something about it, I can always look it up in the encyclopedia."

This is-it-good-for-anything argument, which at various points in our homeschool program has been applied by one child or another to everything from the multiplication tables to Shakespeare, is not trivial—and it indeed poses particular difficulties in the field of history. Even professional historians are sometimes hard-pressed to explain precisely what their field is good for or why and how it should be presented to schoolchildren. History proponents commonly argue that a knowledge of the past is essential for an understanding of the present; that the study of history is the means by which children learn good citizenship practices; that history provides children with a sense of their place in the long story of humanity; and that history serves as a basis for the study of many other academic disciplines, among them philosophy, literature, the arts, religion, law, and government. This multiplicity of arguments has contributed to the wild fluctuations in the public school history curricula, which over the years have ranged in content from the specialized and utilitarian to the sweepingly comprehensive.

The utilitarian approach to history emphasizes present-day relevance: kids concentrate on current social issues, civics, and geography. Students, for example, debate environmental and gender-equity issues, study the principal products of Portugal, and learn the function of the electoral college, the makeup of the Senate and the House of Representatives, and the responsibilities of the justices of the Supreme Court. This undeniably useful information, however—devoid of historical context—is undeniably dull. A lecture on the duties of the secretary of state is flavorless stuff compared to a discussion of the treasures of Tutankhamen's tomb, the Trojan War, the Viking raiders, the Crusades, the Salem witch trials, or Custer's Last Stand. Good history, at heart, is good stories.

"It seems to me," says Joshua, rising to Ethan's antihistory bait, "that one of the most important things about history is that it connects to everything else. Anything new that you learn about, whether it's Beethoven or Picasso or DNA or Socrates, all fits into a place in history."

This argument is the prime defense for a comprehensive traditional history curriculum. History, states the Bradley Commission on History in Schools, is *the* central humanistic discipline, the structural framework on which all other learning can be hung. It's in this role—as a connector, a central organizer—that history is featured so prominently in our homeschool program. From a central historical trunk, investigative topics branch and rebranch: a study of ancient Greece, for example, leads to the mathematics of the Pythagorean theorem, the science behind Archimedes' principle, the use of the letters of the Greek alphabet to indicate the brightness of stars in the constellations, the enthralling tales of the *Iliad* and *Odyssey,* the biochemistry of winemaking, and the fascinating pros and cons of the famous trial of Socrates. A discussion of Ben Franklin's role in the Revolutionary War leads to studies of electricity, explanations of how kites fly, why lightning strikes, and how lightning rods work, and investigations into the behavior of lenses and the invention of the rocking chair.

The public-school elementary history curriculum in past years has been dominated by the belief that small children relate well only to the present time and to their own familiar and personal surroundings. Hence the curriculum of "expanding horizons," in which students, year by year, study increasingly larger chunks of their local environments. Kindergarteners begin at dead center, studying themselves; first-graders study families; second-graders, neighborhoods; third-graders, local communities; and so on. A more recent take on beginning history studies, however, argues that children love great stories, in which history abounds. Historical enrichment, this approach insists, should begin as soon as possible, with folktales from other cultures, myths, stories of heroes and heroines, historical adventure stories, and biographies of interesting and influential persons. This, for us, was clearly the way to go: our boys, at very young ages, were entranced by historical and multicultural stories: Japanese folktales, Greek myths, tales of knights and castles, Indian legends, stories of children who lived during the Revolutionary War or headed west on the wagon trains. Even Ethan, our historical devil's advocate, loved these.

None of this answers the inevitable question "What is history good for?" Our conclusion—which we periodically preach to our children—is that history has both integrative and analytical functions. History provides an underlying structure that facilitates other forms of learning. All of us, as best we can, struggle to form a picture of how the world works: history, to this end, serves as an organizing principle. As a supporting structure, however, history is not fixed and static; it is continually being reinterpreted in the light of new discoveries, new ideas, new social situations. Studied in this light, history becomes an active experience in the pursuit of truth, a mind-broadening exercise in creative and analytical thinking.

"What good is it for?" is not a frivolous question, and the answer is central to any educational program. Why are we learning this stuff? What is education good for? Is its fundamental purpose job training? Molding responsible citizens? Creating cooperative team players? Inculcating multicultural values? Developing social expertise?

While such educational goals are nothing to scoff at—certainly we want our kids to find rewarding jobs, participate in the democratic process, get along socially, and behave in a morally upright fashion—none of this, to my mind, explains what education is really for. Education is not solely for absorbing a battery of marketable skills. Education is for the expansion of the intellect, the growth of the spirit, and the glory of the human mind.

GENERAL HISTORY RESOURCES

HISTORY CURRICULA

The typical school history curriculum begins, in early elementary school, with studies of families, both close to home and around the world, worldwide holidays and festivals, and the functions of local communities. Upper-elementary kids study American history and world cultures. Seventh-graders may study world history, from prehistory through the birth of ancient civilizations to the Industrial Age; or alternatively may concentrate on state and local history. Eighth-graders commonly study American history through the post–Civil War era; ninth-graders, multicultural, feminist, and environmental issues and the foundations of American government. Tenth grade is usually devoted to an intensive course in world history; eleventh, to American history; and twelfth, to American government.

Our homeschool history program has been organized somewhat differently. We've tended to study American and world history simultaneously as two concurrent courses—which could mean that on any given day the boys investigated the American Revolution in the morning and learned about the Crusades in the afternoon. We've always progressed along both historical tracks unevenly, spending prolonged amounts of time on subjects that the boys found interesting and zipping over topics that they didn't. This worked fine; the boys managed to package newly acquired historical information into a coherent whole, and all—generally—stayed curious and interested. Even Ethan was won over by histories of inventions and machines: he studied ancient Egypt with the inclined plane; ancient Greece with the Archimedean screw; medieval Europe with catapult and crossbow; and colonial America with the innards of the flintlock gun.

America Revised: History Schoolbooks in the Twentieth Century
Frances Fitzgerald; Vintage Books, 1980

A history of school history textbooks, showing how different political attitudes and social agendas have shaped and reshaped the way history is taught in the public schools.

Historical Literacy: The Case for History in American Education
Paul Gagnon and the Bradley Commission on History in the Schools, eds.; Houghton Mifflin, 1991

A stirring defense of the central importance of history in education, plus descriptions of the various ways in which history programs are organized and recommendations for a revised and improved national history curriculum.

What Do Our 17-Year-Olds Know?: A Report on the First National Assessment of History and Literature
Diane Ravitch and Chester E. Finn Jr.; Harper & Row, 1987

A summary of an exhaustive study on the historical and literary competency of American high school seniors. The book compares what kids ought to know with what they actually do.

TIMELINES

Timelines help kids of all ages put historical events in perspective. "Timeline books" have been a notably useful resource in our history program. Each boy has one of his own. Our Timeline Books are homemade, in lined spiral-bound notebooks, with a span of years—say, "A.D. 1400–A.D. 1450"—printed at the top of each page. Our books run from 10,000 B.C. to the present, first in 1,000-year jumps (10,000 to 2000 B.C.), then in 100-year jumps (to A.D. 1400), and finally in 50-year jumps (to A.D. 2000).

The boys maintain their Timeline Books almost daily, entering persons and events from all academic subjects. Famous mathematicians, scientists, authors, poets, artists, and musicians all have their places in the books, as do landmark scientific discoveries and inventions and important political occurrences. The books, while having some common ground, reflect the boys' individual interests. Caleb's book, for example, is filled with archaeological events: the building of the Great Pyramid, the burial of Pompeii by the eruption of Mount Vesuvius, the unearthing of the Rosetta stone, the discovery of Troy by Heinrich Schliemann. Josh's is stuffed with literary figures; Ethan's with physicists and their discoveries.

An alternative or supplement to a homemade timeline or timeline book is a commercial model, of which there are many available.

American History Timeline

ALL A series of ten 17 × 22-inch colorfully illustrated posters, documenting events in American history from 1490 to the present. Each poster covers five decades; under each, crucial happenings are listed in vertical columns. The set comes with an accompanying guidebook.

$38.95
Knowledge Unlimited
Box 52
Madison, WI 53701-0052
(608) 836-6660 or (800) 356-2303
Web site: www.ku.com

Ancient Civilizations Map and Timeline

ALL A 21 × 33-inch poster map, showing the locations of nine major civilizations of the ancient world: Sumer, Egypt, India, China, Greece, Rome, the Incas, the Aztecs, and the Maya. A timeline at the bottom of the map shows when each of these civilizations flourished.

$11.95
Knowledge Unlimited
Box 52
Madison, WI 53701-0052
(608) 836-6660 or (800) 356-2303
Web site: www.ku.com

A Graphic History of Mankind

ALL The history of people, from the beginnings of civilization to the present, all on one 50 × 19-inch wall chart. Each nation/ethnic group is represented by a vertical colored stripe, dotted with dates of important events and names of key historical persons. Users can follow the chart vertically to trace the history of a particular civilization or group, or horizontally to compare developments and events throughout the world at a particular period.

$8
Michael Olaf's Essential Montessori
Box 1162
Arcata, CA 95518
(707) 826-1557/fax (707) 826-2243
or
Social Studies School Service
10200 Jefferson Blvd.
Culver City, CA 90232-0802
(310) 839-2436 or (800) 421-4246/fax (310) 839-2249
or (800) 944-5432
Web site: SocialStudies.com

Timeline: 3500 B.C.–A.D. 2000

ALL Pictorial Charts Education Trust

You can wrap this chart halfway around the living room; assembled, it's seven inches wide and over 13 feet long, in full color on shiny coated paper. (For those who don't have 13 feet of uninterrupted wall space, the

Timeline actually comes in four separate sequential strips, which means that users can either skip intervening doors and windows or can post the strips vertically one beneath the other. The *Timeline* is illustrated with photographs and illustrations of historical artifacts, artworks, and geographic locations—among them photos of a Sumerian clay tablet, the Egyptian pyramids, the Greek statue *The Discus Thrower,* and a British helmet from the age of King Arthur.

$10.95

Social Studies School Service

10200 Jefferson Blvd.

Box 802

Culver City, CA 90232-0802

(310) 839-2436 or (800) 421-4246/fax (310) 839-2249 or (800) 944-5432

Web site: SocialStudies.com

Timelines Series
Franklin Watts

Each volume in this series of 48-page illustrated books is devoted to a single theme or topic, which is followed timeline-style from its earliest origins to the present day. Titles include *Crime & Punishment: Law & Order* (Fiona Macdonald; 1995), *Entertainment: Screen, Stage & Stars* (Jacqueline Morley; 1994), *Explorers: Expeditions & Pioneers* (Fiona Macdonald; 1994), *Food: Feasts, Cooks & Kitchens* (Richard Tames; 1994), *Houses: Habitats & Home Life* (Fiona Macdonald; 1994), *Inventions: Inventors & Ingenious Ideas* (Peter Turvey; 1992), *Kings & Queens: Rulers & Despots* (Fiona Macdonald; 1995), *Cities: Citizens & Civilizations* (Fiona Macdonald; 1992), *Flight: Fliers and Flying Machines* (David Jefferis; 1991), *Ships: Sailors and the Sea* (Richard Humble; 1991), and *Transport: On Land, Road and Rail* (Eryl Davies; 1992). Each book includes an illustrated timeline.

Timescale: An Atlas of the Fourth Dimension
Nigel Calder; Viking, 1983

The book is divided into three major sections: "Overview," which includes a history of how people such as astronomers, archaeologists, geologists, and molecular biologists measure time; "Maps," a wonderful full-color series illustrating changes in landforms and populations over the last 560 million years; and "Narrative and Timescale," an illustrated 100-page history of time from the big bang to the present. The timeline runs steadily along the bottom of the narrative pages, which begin by explaining the earliest postbang events: the formation of subatomic particles and the consolidation of atoms, then the formation of galaxies, stars, and planets, the appearance of life on earth, and eventually developmental events in the history of mankind. Included is a large annotated reference index.

The Timetables of American History
Laurence Urdang, ed.; Touchstone Books, 1996

A 470-page annotated timeline of American history, from A.D. 1000. Years are listed in a vertical column in the left-hand margin of each double-page spread; events in four historical categories are listed horizontally across the page. Categories are "History and Politics," "The Arts," "Science and Technology," and "Miscellaneous." Under each are included events occurring in America and those occurring "Elsewhere." Lots of information, illustrated with black-and-white engravings and photographs.

The Timetables of History
Bernard Grun; Touchstone Books, 1991

A 700+-page annotated timeline covering over 30,000 events from 7,000 years of history. Years, from 5000 B.C. to the present, are listed vertically in red along the left-hand margin of each double-page spread, first in multiyear chunks, then—from A.D. 501 on—one year at a time. Happenings worldwide for each time period or year are listed in seven horizontal categories: "History and Politics," "Literature and Theatre," "Religion, Philosophy, and Learning," "Visual Arts," "Music," "Science, Technology, and Growth," and "Daily Life." There's lots of information in small print. A horizontal skim of 1840, for example, shows that in this year Queen Victoria married Prince Albert; James Fenimore Cooper's *The Pathfinder* was a best-seller; Monet, Renoir, Rodin, and Tchaikovsky all were born; naturalist Louis Agassiz wrote a famous book on the movements of glaciers; ninepins was the most popular game in America; and Great Britain introduced penny postage stamps.

A Visual Timeline of the Twentieth Century
Simon Adams; Dorling Kindersley, 1996

A 48-page chronological overview of the 20th century, with yearly entries listing important happenings in the arts, science and technology, everyday life, and world events. Each entry includes a brief snippet of text, and most are accompanied by a photograph, drawing, or other visual supplement. For readers aged 12 and up.

TIMELINE GAMES

Chronology

In "Chronology," the "Card Game For All Time," players attempt to construct ordered timelines, which may extend from the completion of the pyramids (circa 2500 B.C.) through the launching of the space shuttle *Columbia* in 1981. The game includes a fat box of 480 cards, each bearing the description of a historical event and its date. To begin a game, each player draws a card from the pack, reads it aloud, and places it faceup in front of him/her. This is the first card of each about-to-be-assembled timeline. As the play proceeds, each player in turn draws a card and reads the description of the listed event aloud without revealing the crucial date. Listeners, in turn, then guess where the card belongs on their timeline. First player to build a timeline of 10 ordered cards wins the round.

The game is trickier than it sounds. Most of us can figure out that fiber optics were invented after the Trojan War, or that the first nuclear-powered submarine was launched after the burning of Rome, but the time scale can narrow fast. Which came first, for example: diet Pepsi or the Hula Hoop? Nylon stockings or fluorescent lights? The Battle of the Little Bighorn or the founding of Yellowstone National Park?

"Chronology" is recommended for two to eight players aged 12 and up; a simpler version, "Chronology Jr.," is available for younger players.

$29.95 from toy and game stores or
Turn Off the TV
Box 4162
Bellevue, WA 98009
(800) 949-8688/fax (425) 558-7564
Web site: www.turnoffthetv.com

Perspective

A terrific board game—one of our family favorites—in which players order historical persons or events on a four-part timeline. The board pictures four parallel timelines in four colors: "Ancient," in blue, covers "time begins" to A.D. 476; "Middle," in red, covers 477–1588; "Modern," yellow, 1589–1900; and "Twentieth Century," green, 1901 to the present. The game includes 200 color-coded timeline cards, each listing an historical event on one side, the date on the back. Cards can be divided into two sets, for play with a range of age groups and historical competencies: the 100 "Basic" cards are easier; the 100 "Master" cards, more difficult.

At the beginning of the game, players are each dealt six timeline cards, faceup. They then in turn attempt to place their cards in order on the four timelines. If you feel that one of your opponents has ordered his/her cards incorrectly, you challenge, then check the date on the back of the card. Whoever made the wrong guess gets penalized. Winner is the first person to unload all of his/her cards.

Sample cards include: "Cleopatra, Queen of Egypt, dies"; "Cave Paintings Drawn in Lascaux, France"; "Inca Empire Conquered by Spaniards"; "Isaac Newton Establishes Laws of Gravity"; "Taj Mahal Begun in Agra, India"; "Shakespeare Writes 'Hamlet'"; and "Marie Curie Wins Nobel Prize in Chemistry."

$29.95 from toy and game stores or
Old Game Store
Rt. 11/30
Manchester Ctr., VT 05255
(802) 362-2756 or (800) 818-GAME
Web site: www.vtweb.com/oldgame

When? The Game of Cultural History

Over 200 preprinted event cards, each with an historical event, a cultural landmark, or an invention listed on one side, the date on the other. Players must arrange the cards in chronological order, determining which came first, neon signs or electric stoves? Or the completion of Mount Rushmore? Items variously cover 19th- and 20th-century American and world history. The cards arrive in a booklet, in sheets, which must be cut apart; also included are three blank sheets (of 18 cards each) for the addition of your own selected events. Recommended for players in grade 4 and up.

$12

Social Studies School Service

10200 Jefferson Blvd.

Box 802

Culver City, CA 90232-0802

(310) 839-2436 or (800) 421-4246/fax (310) 839-2249

or (800) 944-5432

Web site: SocialStudies.com

8 *Where in Time Is Carmen Sandiego?*

A board version of the popular Broderbund computer game (see below), in which players track Carmen Sandiego's thieving henchpersons through time, following historical clues to apprehend the criminal and recover the stolen goods. For two or more players aged 8 and up.

$21.95 from toy and game stores or

Worldwide Games

Box 517

Colchester, CT 06415-0517

(800) 888-0987/fax (800) 566-6678

e-mail: service@snswwide.com

Web site: www.snswwide.com

TIMELINE COMPUTER SOFTWARE

9 *Where in Time Is Carmen Sandiego?*

It's the rare kid these days who has not had an encounter with archvillain Carmen Sandiego and her gang of criminal underlings. Carmen initially figured in a terrific software geography game, "Where in the World is Carmen Sandiego?" (see Geography, page 436), and has since been popularized in a PBS children's television show, a cartoon series, and assorted books and board and card games. In this version, players, as employees of the Acme Detective Agency, move back and forth through time following a trail of historical clues, attempting to recover a stolen historical artifact and arrest the evil culprit. Carmen's villains are truly creative thieves, pinching such valuables as the Parthenon, the Washington Monument, and the *Mona Lisa*'s smile. On CD-ROM for Mac or Windows.

Broderbund

Box 6125

Novato, CA 94948-6125

(800) 521-6263/fax (415) 382-4419

Web site: broderbund.com or

www.carmensandiego.com

CATALOGS

10 **Avalon Hill Game Company**

A large selection of strategy games, both board games and computer software, many based on world or American history events or periods. Game titles include "Civilization," "Age of the Renaissance," "Hannibal: Rome vs. Carthage," "Napoleon's Battles," and "Gettysburg."

Avalon Hill Game Co.

4517 Harford Rd.

Baltimore, MD 21214

(410) 254-9200 or (800) 999-3222/fax (410) 254-0991

e-mail: AH GAMES@aol.com

Web site: www.avalonhill.com

Bellerophon Books

Unusual, inexpensive, and highly informational coloring books for hands-on historians of all ages. Detailed black-and-white (to-be-colored) illustrations are accompanied by an explanatory text. A long list of titles is available, covering a wide range of historical periods and topics. Examples include *Ancient China, Ancient Egypt, The Middle Ages, The American Revolution,* and *Great Explorers.*

Bellerophon also carries assorted paper-crafts activity books: for example, famous fighter planes to cut out and fly, castles and totem poles to color and cut out, an Etruscan chariot to assemble, and impressive Renaissance helmets to make (in flashy golds and silvers).

Bellerophon Books

36 Ancapa St.

Santa Barbara, CA 93101

(800) 253-9943/fax (800) 965-8286

Dover Publications

An excellent and inexpensive source of world or American history-oriented paper-crafts activity books and educational coloring and sticker books on a wide range of topics. Activity books, for example, include an easy-to-make Plains Indians tepee village, a southwestern pueblo village, a medieval knight in armor, an Egyptian mummy case, and a not-quite-so-easy paper model of the *Mayflower,* which, should you manage to complete it, will result in a 17-inch replica of the original under full sail. Dover also sells historical paper dolls, including costumed American families of the colonial, pioneer, and Civil War eras, 13 presidential families from the Washingtons to the Clintons, "Great Empresses and Queens," "Annie Oakley and Buffalo Bill," and "Medieval Costumes."

Also available from Dover: a immense selection of classic books in affordable softcover editions, many of them replicas of rare out-of-print volumes.

Dover Publications, Inc.

31 E. Second St.

Mineola, NY 11501

Interact

Interact designs "participatory units" covering a wide range of academic disciplines for learners of all ages. Participatory units—especially those with a historical orientation—generally take the form of group games or simulations involving role-play and hands-on activities. For each age group (elementary, middle school, or high school), historical units cover all historical periods, from the prehistoric to the present day.

Kids, for example, reenact 19th-century schoolhouse life, a westward journey by wagon train, or life among the Vikings; dramatize the "Middle Passage" of captured slaves from Africa to the American colonies; or simulate the cultures of ancient Greece, Rome, or China. Interact simulations are generally designed with classrooms (10 to 35 students) in mind, but most adapt readily to smaller groups.

Most simulations, between $10 and $50

Interact

1825 Gillespie Way, #101

El Cajon, CA 92020-1095

(800) 359-0961/fax (619) 448-6722

Web site: www.interact-simulations.com

Jackdaw Publications

Portfolios of information and primary source material on a wide and varied range of American and world history topics. There are over 50 portfolios, each a generous collection of reproductions of actual documents, letters, diary entries, photographs, and newspaper articles from the past, intended to give young readers an experience of real history. Each contains some eight to 18 reproduction source materials, assorted illustrated "Broadsheet" essays, which give historical background information on the topic under study, a sheet of annotated notes on the source materials, a supplementary reading list, and a "Jackdaw Study Guide," which includes reproducible student worksheets, suggestions for research projects and cross-curricular activities, discussion questions, and reading lists. Sample portfolio titles include "Columbus & the Age of Explorers," "The American Revolution," "The Civil War," "Salem Village and the Witch Hysteria," "California Gold Rush: 1849," "Slavery in the United States," "Shakespeare's Theatre," "Tutankhamun and the Discovery of the Tomb," "The Conquest of Mexico," "The World of Islam," and "Pasteur and the Germ Theory."

$37 each

Jackdaw Publications

Box 503

Amawalk, NY 10501-0503

(914) 962-6911 or (800) 789-0022/fax (800) 962-9101

Knowledge Unlimited

Videos, filmstrips, CD-ROMs, resource books, games, and many creative and informational posters for kids of all ages. The catalog carries resources for a range of academic subjects, but the emphasis is on social studies. Categories covered include "U.S. Government," "Early American History," "American West," "Civil War," "Twentieth Century," "Civil Rights," "African American Studies," "Asian/Latino Studies," "Native Americans," "Social Issues," "Ancient Civilizations," "World History," "World Cultures," and "Geography." Prices range from tooth-gratingly expensive to very reasonable.

Knowledge Unlimited

Box 52

Madison, WI 53701-0052

(608) 831-1570 or (800) 618-1570/fax (608) 831-1570 or (800) 831-1570

e-mail: ku-mail@ku.com

Web site: www.ku.com

Social Studies School Service

ALL Despite its dampingly dull title, this superb and enormous (450+ pages) catalog contains practically anything one could possibly need or want for the teaching/learning of American or world history. Resources include books (fiction and nonfiction), activity books, workbooks, teachers' guides, games, manipulatives, videos, audiocassettes, CD-ROMs, maps, charts, posters, primary source reproductions, and photograph collections. There are several specialized catalogs available; ask for a complete list.

Social Studies School Service

10200 Jefferson Blvd.

Box 802

Culver City, CA 90232-0802

(310) 839-2436 or (800) 421-4246/fax (310) 839-2249 or (800) 944-5432

e-mail: access@SocialStudies.com

Web site: SocialStudies.com

Also see **American History Catalogs** (pages 447–449) and **World History Catalogs** (page 596).

ON-LINE RESOURCES

Biography

9+ Over 20,000 entries of notable people from all times and places. Users can enter a name or search an alphabetized index for biographical information.

www.biography.com

The History Highway:
A Guide to Internet Resources

Dennis A. Trinkle, Dorothy Auchter, Scott A. Merriman, and Todd E. Larson; M. E. Sharpe, Inc., 1997

An annotated list of Internet sites for historians, variously grouped under "General History," "Ancient History," "Medieval and Renaissance History," "World History" (by region; "American History" sites are listed under North America), "History of Science and Technology," "Military History," and "Religious History."

Also listed are links to genealogical and state historical societies, maps, electronic texts, on-line journals, libraries, and discussion groups.

The History Net

10+ Articles and information on a wide range of world and American history topics.

www.TheHistoryNet.com

History Online

10+ Many resources for world and American history, from ancient civilizations through the American Revolution.

www.jacksonesd.k12.or.us/k12projects/jimperry/history.html

AMERICAN HISTORY

From my homeschool journal:

◆ **May 28, 1991. Josh is ten; Ethan, eight; Caleb, six.**

We started studying the American Revolution today, using homemade interactive workbooks ("Yankees and Redcoats I"). Covered the French and Indian War, discussed the expense of wars and reason for postwar tax increases. Defined tax *and* national debt; *made bar graphs illustrating the size of the British national debt before and after the French and Indian War and after the American Revolution.*

Discussed the Revenue Act of 1764 and the Stamp Act; and the boys designed and colored their own stamps.

Then we discussed molasses—one of the items taxed under the Revenue Act—where it came from, how it was made, the part it played in the triangular (New England–Africa–West Indies) slave trade. Drew the routes taken by the traders on a world map. Reviewed fermentation, the process by which molasses is converted into rum.

Read "The Boston Tidal Wave" in More of Paul Harvey's The Rest of the Story *(see page 455), about a*

19th-century molasses disaster. This simply fascinated the boys and triggered lots of speculation as to how all that molasses was cleaned up. "Does molasses freeze? If it froze, could you skate on it? Can you swim in molasses? Is there some kind of mask you can wear so that you could breathe in molasses?"

Defined viscosity, explained the molecular basis for viscosity, and the boys ranked six liquids—molasses, maple syrup, water, olive oil, vinegar, and corn syrup—in order, from high to low viscosity. Discussed how scientists test viscosity. The boys had lots of ideas of their own. ("What about a drip test?") I started to explain the scientific technique: "You drop a small bead into a measured sample . . ." and Ethan promptly chimed in, "I see! And you time how long it takes the bead to get to the bottom!"

The boys then measured samples of their six liquids into test tubes, dropped in pellets, and (roughly) timed how long it took the pellets to sink to the bottom.

◆ May 29, 1991

American Revolution continues. Covered the practice of tar and feathering this morning, with the boys drawing their own tax collectors, then dabbing them with glue and topping them with paper feathers. Josh: "Why did the colonists have to be so mean? Couldn't they understand that the tax collectors were just doing their jobs?"

Read about the Sons of Liberty and did a short matching quiz on Paul Revere, John Hancock, and Sam Adams. Read about/discussed the Boston Massacre; looked at a reproduction of Paul Revere's engraving of the massacre; defined massacre and propaganda. Read about the Boston Tea Party, and the boys invented and drew their own tea party disguises. Caleb chose an elaborate Indian ensemble; Josh decided on a bag over his head, with holes cut for the eyes; Ethan designed an enormous pencil costume.

Covered King George's reaction to the Boston Tea Party, the closing of the port of Boston, and General Thomas Gage. Told story of the Boston boys protesting to General Gage about British soldiers wrecking their snow forts. The kids then designed their own snow forts, with built-in protection against destructive British soldiers. Caleb's surrounded by a series of tiger-pit-like traps; Ethan's armed with a catapult.

AMERICAN HISTORY RESOURCES

CATALOGS

Bluestocking Press

ALL If you had to obtain all your children's American history materials from a single source, Jane Williams's Bluestocking Press would be it. The catalog itself—60+ packed pages of newsprint—is organized as an overview of American history, from the arrival of Columbus to the present day. Selections are chronologically grouped into categories by historical period, from "Columbus" and "Pilgrims–1620" through "American Revolution," "Westward Expansion," and "World War II." Under each is offered a creative collection of informational texts, fiction and nonfiction books for readers of a wide range of ages, hands-on crafts kits and activity books, study guides, audiocassettes of period music, and reproductions of historical documents. Suggestions for students of the American Revolution, for example, include a replica of the original Declaration of Independence, letters and diaries of young people who lived during the Revolutionary War, reprints of historical newspapers, reproduction colonial banknotes, quill pens and ink powder, fictional books set in the Revolutionary War period, and Revolutionary era music.

Bluestocking materials encourage a critical and multisided approach to history, promoting discussion, debate, and thoughtful reassessment.

Catalog, $3
Bluestocking Press
Box 2030
Shingle Springs, CA 95682-2030
(916) 622-8586 or (800) 959-8586/fax (916) 642-9222

Chatham Hill Games

A creative catalog of historical games, maps, and prints. Chatham Hill publishes the "American Adventure Games," a series of inexpensive "cut-and-fold" board games with paper boards and pieces, many developed in cooperation with museums or historical institutions. Game titles include "The Voyage of the

Mayflower," "The Battle of Bunker Hill," "The Underground Railroad," and "The Wright Brothers."

> Chatham Hill Games, Inc.
> Box 253
> Chatham, NY 12037
> (518) 392-5022 or (800) 554-3039/fax (518) 392-3121
> e-mail: CHGames@taconic.net
> Web site: www.ocdc.com/Chatham_Hill_games

Educational Materials Associates

EMA publishes a series of detailed and inexpensive history and geography games, designed to help students learn basic facts about major historical events and their geographical locations. The playing boards—on heavy coated paper—are number-coded maps; informational playing cards match map sites to key historical happenings. History titles in the series include "American Revolution," "Presidents," "Civil War," "North American Indians," "Discovery and Exploration," "Expansion of the U.S.," "War of 1812," "World War I," and "World War II."

> Most games, around $10
> Educational Materials Associates, Inc.
> Box 7385
> Charlottesville, VA 22906
> (804) 293-GAME/fax (804) 293-5322

LibertyTree

A catalog of historical, economic, political, revolutionary, creatively independent—and occasionally ornery—books and audiotapes, covering issues of liberty from the philosophical debates of the Founding Fathers through the social controversies of the present day. Included are many adult publications on the present (and future) state of American education, and a selection of historical and political books, both fiction and nonfiction, for children.

> LibertyTree
> 134 98th Ave.
> Oakland, CA 94603
> (800) 927-8733/fax (510) 568-6040

National Women's History Project Catalog

The National Women's History Project is a California-based nonprofit organization that works to promote "gender equity through public recognition of women's diverse lives and accomplishments." Their catalog includes books, videos, posters, teaching guides, and resources on women's history themes. Among these are women's history coloring books and paper doll kits, biographies of prominent women for young readers, resource lists and curriculum units on the women's suffrage movement in American history, women's history activity place mats to color, and the award-winning CD-ROM "Her Heritage: A Biographical Encyclopedia of Famous American Women" (see page 569).

Also available: a play by Laura Burges, *American Women Making History*, appropriate for actors in grade 4 and up, which covers 300 years of women's history in 30 minutes (cast size can vary from a handful of key players to large numbers).

> National Women's History Project
> 7738 Bell Rd.
> Windsor, CA 95492
> (707) 838-6000
> Web site: www.nwhp.org

Pleasant Company

In 1985 Pleasant Company launched its resoundingly successful "American Girl" collection based on the lives and adventures of five girls from different historical periods in America's past: Felicity, growing up in Williamsburg, Virginia, in 1774; Kirsten, whose family immigrated from Sweden to the Minnesota frontier in 1854; Addy, a black girl whose family escaped from slavery to live in Philadelphia in the days of the Civil War; Samantha, an orphan living with her wealthy Victorian grandmother in 1904; and Molly, helping her family on the home front in 1944, while her father is away at war. There are now six short (about 70 pages) historical fiction books available about each girl: *Meet Felicity, Felicity Learns a Lesson, Felicity's Surprise, Happy Birthday, Felicity!, Felicity Saves the Day*, and *Changes for Felicity*. (Titles are the same for the other American girls; just substitute proper names.)

For "American Girl" lovers, Pleasant Company sells dolls representing each girl, complete with elaborate and authentic costumes (right down to the underwear), accessories, toys, furniture, and dishes. Also available for each girl: crafts kits and books (for example, learn to hook a rug with Addy, weave a sash with

Kirsten, knit a cap with Molly, or embroider a sampler with Felicity), doll dress patterns, paper dolls, cookbooks, theater kits, and the "American Girls Collection" on CD-ROM (see page 777).

Pleasant Company
8400 Fairway Pl.
Box 620190
Middleton, WI 53562-0190
(800) 845-0005/fax (608) 836-0761

MAGAZINES

American Heritage

A top-of-the-line 100+-page magazine covering all aspects of American history from the pre-Columbian period to the present day. Extensively researched articles, largely written by professional historians and journalists, are beautifully illustrated with color photographs, prints, and art reproductions. There are usually five major articles per issue, plus a number of short regular columns, among them "The Business of America," which profiles an American business or businessperson; "History Happened Here," which features a historically important American place; "My Brush With History," a collection of personal descriptions of historical encounters (readers are encouraged to submit accounts of their own experiences); and "The Time Machine," which briefly describes interesting historical happenings of 300, 200, 100, 75, 50, and 25 years ago (or so).

For high school–aged readers and up; an excellent reference for all American history programs.

Annual subscription (8 issues), $20
American Heritage
Subscription Dept.
Box 5023
Harlan, IA 51593-2521
(800) 777-1222

Cobblestone

A 48-page monthly American history magazine targeted at kids in grades 4–9. Each issue is devoted to a single American history topic. Examples include "American Immigration," "Westward Expansion," "Alexander Hamilton," "Old-Time Schools," "Presiden-

tial Elections," and "The Industrial Revolution." Each issue includes an assortment of fiction and nonfiction articles on the featured topic, plus maps, timelines, games, puzzles, and instructions for hands-on projects. A superb resource for young historians. Back issues of *Cobblestone* are continually available.

Annual subscription (9 issues), $24.95
Cobblestone Publishing, Inc.
30 Grove St.
Peterborough, NH 03458-1454
(603) 924-7209 or (800) 821-0115/fax (603) 924-7380
Web site: www.cobblestonepub.com

Historic Traveler

A great find for both traveling history buffs and curious homebodies. Each issue includes feature articles on five or six historic sites, plus assorted shorter pieces on historical travel topics. The articles, illustrated with many color photographs, discuss the historical significance of each site, and include maps, directions, information on hours, admission, and tours, a list of suggested restaurants and places to stay, and a description of other things to see in the area. Sample sites covered in the past have included Valley Forge, Monticello, the Alamo, Gettysburg, and the Carlsbad Caverns. Also included: a schedule of historic festivals and exhibits nationwide.

Annual subscription (6 issues), $16.95
Historic Traveler
Box 720
Mount Morris, IL 61054-9898
(800) 435-9610

Time Machine

An American history magazine for kids, published in partnership with the Smithsonian's National Museum of American History. "History is stories," write the editors. "Great stories. Stories where you really want to know what happens." *Time Machine* is 32 glossy pages long, packed with colorful illustrations, historical and contemporary photographs, catchy quizzes and games, and interesting text. Each issue centers around a single historical topic. The summer 1996 issue, for example, featured the Olympic Games, including a timeline of the Olympics (from ancient Greece to the present day), articles on the histories of bathing suits and ice skates, biographical pieces on Jim Thorpe, Jesse Owens, and Sonja Henie, and a series of short first-person stories by present-day athletes.

> Annual subscription (8 issues), about $18
>
> *Time Machine*
>
> Box 2879
>
> Clifton, NJ 07015-9611
>
> (800) 742-5401

BOOKS

Amzerica: Ready-to-Use Interdisciplinary Lessons and Activities for Grades 5–12 (Volume 1)
Dwila Bloom; Center for Applied Research in Education, 1997

Over 350 illustrated pages of American history information and activities, including recipes, quizzes, arts and crafts projects, games, music, maps, vocabulary lists, journal and creative writing exercises, and supplementary reading suggestions. The book is divided into three major study units: "The Thirteen Colonies," "An Expanding Nation" (including the Midwest, the Great Plains, and the Mississippi Valley), and "The Beckoning West" (including the Southwest, the Northwest, and the far West).

American Diaries Series
Kathleen Duey; Aladdin

American history as told through the diaries of a series of young girls. The books cover a wide range of times and geographical locations. *Emma Eileen Grove: Mississippi, 1865,* for example, describes the experiences of 12-year-old Emma and her younger brother and sister, orphaned in the Civil War; *Mary Alice Peale: Philadelphia, 1777,* tells the story of the Revolution through the eyes of 12-year-old Mary, whose father is a Tory and whose brother has joined the Continental Army; *Ellen Elizabeth Hawkins: Mobeetie, Texas, 1886,* describes the life of a girl growing up on a ranch in Texas. Each book is about 140 pages long. Enjoyable reading for kids aged 9–12.

Also see the **Dear America Series** (page 452).

American Lives
Willard Sterne Randall and Nancy Nahra; Addison-Wesley, 1997

A two-volume collection of short biographies of famous (and not quite so famous) American historical figures. Volume I covers the years up to 1876 (20 biographies); Volume II, 1877 to the present (24 biographies). Each biography is about 15 pages long, illustrated with a black-and-white portrait, and followed by a list of discussion questions and a short bibliography of further suggested readings. "It is impossible to write or to study history without considering the lives of people," state Randall and Nahra. "Perhaps nowhere is this more true than in studying the history of America, where diversity has encouraged individualism. Even great social, economic, intellectual, and political forces took shape in the minds of individual Americans. The record of their lives documents their personal actions."

Volume I begins with Christopher Columbus; followed by religious rebel Anne Hutchinson; American Indians Teedyuscung and Tom Quick; and Benjamin Franklin and his Tory son, William; Thomas Jefferson; Abigail Adams; Sam Houston; Harriet Beecher Stowe; and Robert E. Lee.

Volume II starts out with Mark Twain and Sitting Bull and proceeds through Andrew Carnegie, W. E. B. Du Bois, Eugene V. Debs, Theda Bara, Margaret Sanger, Eleanor Roosevelt, Harry Truman, Cesar Chavez, and Sandra Day O'Connor. And many more. An excellent resource for teenagers and their parents/teachers.

American War Series
Enslow Publishing, 1994

This series of illustrated books for high school–aged students covers American history through its major wars, from the American Revolution to the Gulf War. Books include maps, photographs, chronologies, and descriptions of major events, battles, and military figures. There are eight titles in the series, among them *The American Revolution: "Give Me Liberty, or Give Me Death!"* (Deborah Kent), *The Civil War: "A House Divided"* (Zachary Kent), *World War I: "The War to End Wars"* (Zachary Kent), *World War II in the Pacific: "Remember Pearl Harbor!"* (R. Conrad Stein), and *The Vietnam War: "What Are We Fighting For?"* (Deborah Kent).

Annual Editions: American History

Robert James Maddox, ed.; Dushkin Publishing Group/Brown & Benchmark Publishers, 1997

Each volume in the Annual Editions series is a collection of current articles on a specific topic or theme, gathered from a wide selection of magazines, newspapers, and professional journals. The articles in the *American History* volumes are arranged in chronological order: Volume I articles cover the precolonial period through Reconstruction; Volume II, Reconstruction through the present day. Articles are gleaned from such publications as *Archaeology, History Today, Early American Life, American Heritage, Civilization, The Wilson Quarterly, U.S. News and World Report*, and *Scientific American*, and all are fascinating. Among the 30 titles in Volume I, for example, are "Columbus: Hero or Villain?," "Entertaining Satan," "Editing the Declaration," "The Lives of Slave Women," and "Christmas in 19th-Century America." Titles in Volume II include "A New View of Custer's Last Battle," "Why Suffrage for American Women Was Not Enough," "The Biggest Decision: Why We Had to Drop the Atomic Bomb," and "Trumpet of Conscience: A Portrait of Martin Luther King, Jr."

A terrific and varied alternative to history as packaged in textbooks, for secondary-level readers.

A Book of Americans

Rosemary and Stephen Vincent Benet; Henry Holt, 1987

American history through poetry. This is a collection of 55 poems, covering famous American persons and events from before the arrival of Columbus through Woodrow Wilson. Individuals immortalized in verse include—among many others—Peregrine White and Virginia Dare, Pocahontas, Captain Kidd, Abigail Adams, Benjamin Franklin, Thomas Jefferson, Johnny Appleseed, Dolly Madison, Andrew Jackson, Nancy Hanks, Sam Houston, Stonewall Jackson, Abraham Lincoln, Clara Barton, P. T. Barnum, and the Wright brothers. For all ages.

Also see *Hand in Hand: An American History Through Poetry* (Lee Bennett Hopkins; Simon & Schuster, 1994) and *Singing America: Poems That Define a Nation* (Neil Philip, ed.; Viking, 1995).

The Cartoon History of the United States

Larry Gonick; HarperPerennial, 1991

The Cartoon History, says its author/illustrator, is a work of "graphic nonfiction," which means lots of clever little black-and-white drawings plus an informationally accurate (but often humorously tongue-in-cheek) text. The book covers American history from the crossing of the Asia-to-Alaska land bridge some 15,000 years ago to the 1990 Gulf War. There are 29 creative chapters, including "Mighty Beefs From Little Beavers Grow," "In Which Happiness is Pursued, Gun in Hand," "Railroads, Over- and Underground," and "War and Peace and Warren Harding." The style is breezy and highly readable; funny pictures are visual memory aids. An especially good bet for history-resistant teenagers.

Childhood of Famous Americans Series

Aladdin

This series of short large-print chapter books first appeared in the 1940s; the originals, in hardcover, can often be found in used-book stores and occasionally at library discard sales. The books are also currently available: many have been reissued in modern orange-and-blue-covered paperback editions ($4.95 each), and the series has been updated to include latterday famous Americans, such as John F. Kennedy and Martin Luther King Jr. Other subjects include Daniel Boone, Davy Crockett, Henry Ford, Benjamin Franklin, Molly Pitcher, Paul Revere, Betsy Ross, Abigail Adams, Crispus Attucks, George Washington, Martha Washington, Clara Barton, Susan B. Anthony, and the Wright brothers. The books are written as stories about the great and famous as kids; adult accomplishments of each are rapidly summed up in a couple of pages at the very end. The books are recommended for readers aged 8–12, but as read-alouds they appeal to younger listeners.

Cornerstones of Freedom Series

Children's Press

The Cornerstones of Freedom series has recently been updated and reformatted: each 32-page book now includes more photographs (many in color) and historical engravings; and the covers are white, decked out with a blue stripe and an eagle. There are 65 titles now available in the new format, each dealing with an important event in American history, targeted at kids in grades 4–6. Examples include *The Boston Tea Party* (R. Conrad Stein; 1996), *The California Gold Rush* (R. Conrad Stein; 1995), *The Constitution* (Marilyn Prolman; 1995), *The Gettysburg Address* (Kenneth G. Richards; 1992), *The Great Depression* (R. Conrad Stein; 1993), *The Montgomery Bus Boycott* (R. Conrad Stein; 1993), *The Pony Express* (Peter Anderson; 1996), *The Star-Spangled Banner* (Deborah Kent; 1995), and *The Transcontinental Railroad* (Peter Anderson; 1996). Many older titles are also slated for reissue in the new format.

The books are a useful resource but vary in quality; some are markedly more interesting and readable than others. Keep an eye out for these books at used-book stores; the older versions are not difficult to find and are usually inexpensive.

Children's Press
Box 1331
Danbury, CT 06813
(800) 621-1115/fax (203) 797-3657

Critical Thinking in United States History Series

Kevin O'Reilly; Critical Thinking Press & Software, 1991

This series of four lesson books, intended for kids in grades 8–12, presents readers with opposing views of historical events, then teaches students to apply critical-thinking skills to their readings, analyzing the presented historical evidence by defined criteria. These criteria are identified by the acronym PROP:

P: Is the information from a *primary* or secondary source?
R: Does the author have a *reason* to lie or exaggerate?
O: Is there *other* evidence to verify this statement or viewpoint?
P: Is this a *public* or private statement?

Kids are also taught to evaluate comparisons, spot generalizations, pinpoint assumptions, and otherwise view historical statements and interpretations with a discerning eye. Titles in the series include *Colonies to Constitution, New Republic to Civil War, Reconstruction to Progressivism,* and *Spanish-American War to Viet-*

nam War. Sample topics covered include "What Caused the Salem Witch Hysteria?," "Was the Stamp Act Justified or Were the Colonists Justified in Not Paying It?," "What Arguments Were Made For and Against Women's Rights?," and "Should the United States Restrict Immigration?"

Critical Thinking Press & Software
Box 448
Pacific Grove, CA 93950
(800) 458-4849/fax (408) 372-3230

Dear America Series

Scholastic

History as recorded by a 12- or 13-year-old girl in the pages of her diary. Various volumes in the series describe the lives and times of young girls voyaging to the New World with the Pilgrims, in the Revolutionary War, working in the Lowell textile factories, in the Civil War, or on the Oregon Trail. Titles include *A Journey to the New World: The Diary of Remember Patience Whipple* (Kathryn Lasky; 1996); *A Picture of Freedom: The Diary of Clotee, a Slave Girl* (Patricia C. McKissack; 1997); and *Across the Wide and Lonesome Prairie: The Oregon Trail Diary of Hattie Campbell* (Kristiana Gregory; 1997).

Also see the **American Diaries Series** (page 450).

From Sea to Shining Sea: A Treasury of American Folklore and Folk Songs

Amy L. Cohn; Scholastic, 1993

A 400-page tour of American history through folktales and songs, gloriously illustrated in color by 11 Caldecott Award winners, among them Anita Lobel, Molly Bang, Barbara Cooney, and Chris Van Allsburg. The tour begins "In the Beginning," with traditional Indian legends and songs; then moves to "Coming To America," which includes tales of "The First Thanksgiving" and "The Shot Heard 'Round the World," the texts of "Paul Revere's Ride" by Henry Wadsworth Longfellow and "Concord Hymn" by Ralph Waldo Emerson, and words and music to such period favorites as "Yankee Doodle" and "Johnny Has Gone for a Soldier." The book moves on, section by section, through time: "Let My People Go" includes the story of Harriet Tubman, the black folktale "The People Could Fly," and words and music to "Swing Low, Sweet Chariot" and "Follow the Drinkin' Gourd"; "I've Been Working on the Railroad" tells the tales of John Henry and Casey Jones and includes Paul Goble's retelling of the Indian legend "The Death of the Iron Horse"; and "In Our Time" concludes with words and music to "Blowin' in the Wind" and "This Land is Your Land" and the text of Martin Luther King's "I Have a Dream" speech. A beautiful book.

Great Lives Series
Charles Scribner's Sons

Each book in the series is a collection of short illustrated biographies of 25 or so famous persons, grouped by area of accomplishment. Titles include *American Government* (Doris and Harold Faber; 1988), *Exploration* (Milton Lomask; 1988), *Human Rights* (William Jay Jacobs; 1990), *World Government* (William Jay Jacobs; 1992), *Nature and the Environment* (Doris and Harold Faber; 1991), *Science and Technology* (Milton Lomask; 1992), *Medicine* (Robert H. Curtis; 1992), *Sports* (George Sullivan; 1988), and *Painting* (Shirley Glubok; 1994).

Her Story Series
Dorothy Hoobler and Thomas Hoobler; Silver Burdett

A series of historical fiction books for kids aged 8–12, each featuring a young girl. Titles include *Priscilla Foster: The Story of a Salem Girl* (1997), *The Sign Painter's Secret: The Story of a Revolutionary Girl* (1994), *Sally Bradford: The Story of a Rebel Girl* (1997), *Julia Meyer: The Story of a Wagon Train Girl* (1997), and *Florence Robinson: The Story of a World War I Girl* (1997).

Historic Communities Series
Bobbie Kalman; Crabtree Publishing

Each volume in this series of 32-page books concentrates on a single aspect of American life in the 18th or 19th century. The books are heavily illustrated with black-and-white and color photographs and drawings; many of the photographs are of living history reenactors in period costumes, involved in traditional chores, crafts, and activities. Sample titles include *Colonial Life, Colonial Crafts, A One-Room School, Fort Life, Visiting a Village, Tools and Gadgets, Life on a Plantation,* and *Pioneer Projects.*

A History of US Series
Joy Hakim; Oxford University Press

This 10-book series is our pick of history texts for young people. The term *text* here, though nicely describing the solid scholastic worth of the series, fails to convey the fascinating—if not positively gripping—character of the volumes. "History is full of stories," writes author Joy Hakim in the introduction, "true stories—the best ever. Those stories have real heroes and real villains. When you read history, you are reading real-life adventures." This is precisely what "A History of US" delivers: great stories, well researched and woven into an absorbing trip through time. The books are heavily illustrated in black-and-white, with photographs, engravings, maps, sketches, and political cartoons, plus catchy quotations and interesting asides in highlighted boxes.

Each book is about 150 to 200 pages long; chapters are generally short, suitable for (in our case) reading aloud at the lunch table. Collectively, the books cover American history from the arrival of the Stone Age nomads from Asia to the end of the cold war. Titles include *The First Americans; Making Thirteen Colonies; From Colonies to Country; The New Nation; Liberty for All?; War, Terrible War; Reconstruction and Reform; An Age of Extremes; War, Peace, and All That Jazz;* and *All the People.*

The series is recommended for kids aged 8–13, but the content is so interesting that I'd expand this to "for all ages."

Available individually or as a complete set from bookstores or

Oxford University Press
2001 Evans Rd.
Cary, NC 27513
information (800) 445-9714; orders (800) 451-7556

If You . . . Series
Scholastic

Each of these short (64- to 80-page) books is written in a chatty question-and-answer format and is fun to read aloud, since listeners then get a chance to answer the questions first—"What were the dangers on the frontier?"—before hearing the author's answer. Lots of reader-friendly information about everyday life in different times and places. Titles include *If You Lived*

With the Sioux Indians (Ann McGovern), *If You Lived in Colonial Times* (Ann McGovern), *If You Traveled West in a Covered Wagon* (Ellen Levine), *If You Lived at the Time of the Civil War* (Kay Moore), and *If Your Name Was Changed at Ellis Island* (Ellen Levine).

The books are recommended for kids aged 7–10.

Scholastic, Inc.

2931 E. McCarty St.

Jefferson City, MO 65101

(800) 724-6527/fax (573) 635-5881

Web site: www.scholastic.com

It Happened in America
Lila Perl; Henry Holt, 1996

Fifty-one "true stories from the fifty states" (plus one from the District of Columbia). The book is arranged in alphabetical order by state, from Alabama to Wyoming. Each state is introduced by a page or so of general information, always including the origin of the state name and nicknames (*Minnesota* comes from a Sioux Indian phrase meaning "sky-tinted water"), an account of the state's early settlement, and a brief description of major events in state history. The meat of the book, however, is its wonderful stories from each state's past. These cover a wide range of historical periods, from early colonial to modern times, with one quick trip back 140 million years in the account of paleontologist Earl Douglass's discovery of what became Dinosaur National Monument in northeastern Utah. In "James Black and the Arkansas Toothpick," readers learn the true story behind the famous Bowie knife; in "Yours Till Niagara Falls," they learn some surprising history about New York's famous waterfall, including the story of Sam Patch, who dived off it twice and survived; and in "Brave as the Blue Hen's Chickens," they learn how Captain Caldwell's feisty blue hen became the mascot of Delaware's Revolutionary War militia. The extra, fifty-first story—from the District of Columbia—tells how Dolley Madison saved George Washington's portrait before the burning of the White House by the British in the War of 1812.

Kids' America
Steven Caney; Workman, 1978

A big red-white-and-blue book filled with information, activities, projects, puzzles, recipes, and games based on American history from colonial days to the present. Chapters include "American Heritage," in which kids construct a family tree and design a family crest; "American Know-How," in which they make butter, soap, and a punched-tin lantern; "American Homes," in which they learn how nails are made, build a tree house and a five-pole tepee, and try their hands at stenciling; "American Backyards and Gardens," in which they plant peanuts, make a scarecrow and a bird feeder, and throw a jumping frog contest; "Eating in America," in which they get a chance to whip up many all-American recipes, including dried apple rings, popcorn (in a homemade corn popper), Philadelphia pretzels, and molasses taffy; "American School Days," in which they make ink and quill pens and practice writing like John Hancock; and "Made in America," in which they try whittling, gravestone rubbing, scrimshaw, and silhouettes. All this and much more in 414 illustrated pages.

My Fellow Americans: A Family Album
Alice Provensen; Browndeer Press, 1995

A colorful and oversize picture-book collection of many of the unique individuals who have contributed to the history and heritage of America, presented family-photo-album-style in single or group portraits. Particularly outstanding persons rate a page all to themselves: Thoreau, for example, poses alone, surrounded by quotations, with his Walden Pond cabin in the background; similarly singular are Clarence Darrow, Thomas Edison, the Wright brothers (with airplane), Martin Luther King Jr., and R. Buckminster Fuller. Others appear in small to large groups, including "Pilgrims and Puritans," "Warriors and Patriots," "Radical Reformers and Humanitarians," "Mega-millionaires and Financiers," and "Abolitionists and Suffragists." Included is a whole page of American writers, each holding his/her best-known books, a page of poets (ditto), artists (with their paintings), "Composers, Classy Tunesmiths and All That Jazz" (with their instruments), and "Scoundrels and Thieves," which groups Benedict Arnold, Frank and Jesse James, Belle Starr, and Butch Cassidy. A book for all ages.

New True Books: Social Studies
Children's Press

A large collection of short (48 pages), simple books, illustrated with full-color photographs and artwork, on

a range of nonfiction topics. The series includes 32 books on American Indians and nine on U.S. History/ Government: *The Constitution, The Declaration of Independence, Explorers, The Flag of the United States, Pioneers, Presidents, Voting and Elections, The Thirteen Colonies,* and *The Bill of Rights.* All have a straightforward large-print text that provides basic information to young readers. The books are recommended for kids in grades 2–4, reading independently. Read out loud, they're suitable for much younger children.

Available through bookstores or

Children's Press

Box 1331

Danbury, CT 06813-1331

(800) 621-1115/fax (203) 797-3657

Opposing Viewpoints Series

David L. Bender and Bruno Leone, eds.; Greenhaven Press

The purpose of this challenging series, explain the editors, is to present balanced opposing points of view of complex and controversial issues. The cited opposing viewpoints are obtained from a wide range of sources— historical documents, magazines, journals, newspapers, and books—by an equally varied range of persons, among them historians, political commentators, and historical eyewitnesses. Each book considers a number of issues related to a single central theme. *Christopher Columbus and His Legacy,* for example, includes diametrically opposed opinions of European explorers and their actions in the New World. Article titles include, for example: "The Conquistadors' Motives Were Pure," "The Conquistadors Were Murderers," "Modern Attacks on Columbus Are Unwarranted," and "History Should Acknowledge Columbus as a Ruthless Exploiter." A brief biography of the author of the opinion and a list of questions to consider while reading accompany each article. The books are about 300 pages long. Titles in the series include *The Creation of the Constitution, The Bill of Rights, Immigration, The Civil War, Reconstruction, The Great Depression, The Cold War, Racism in America, Social Justice,* and many more. For teenagers.

Paul Harvey's The Rest of the Story

Paul Aurandt; Bantam Books, 1985

Paul Harvey's history stories, once upon a time, were heard on the radio, which is why they read so beautifully aloud: each is short, attention grabbing, and dramatic, and each has a surprising twist at the end. Titles don't give the show away, so reading parents should peek ahead to the end to make sure they'll have a hit. (The necessity for this becomes clear the first time you hit a generational gap. "And that man was . . ." you read impressively, "the *Lone Ranger!*," only to have your audience stare at you blankly.) Most of the 81 stories, however, still pack a punch. There are unexpected tales about Mark Twain, Patrick Henry, Sherlock Holmes, potato chips, John Paul Jones, football, Ulysses S. Grant, "Yankee Doodle," Charles Lindbergh, George Washington, and Alexander Graham Bell. Fun for all. (The desired audience response is a gasp, followed by a "Wow!") Also see *More of Paul Harvey's The Rest of the Story* (Paul Aurandt; Bantam Books, 1986).

Perspectives on History Series

Discovery Enterprises

The series includes over 50 titles intended to provide background material for studies of specific periods or episodes in American history for kids in grades 5–12. Each 60 (or so)-page book is a "concise anthology of primary and secondary source materials," including journal excerpts and letters, essays, poems and songs, newspaper reports, maps, photographs, and cartoons, plus a bibliography and list of suggestions for further reading.

The Lowell Mill Girls: Life in the Factory, for example, includes excerpts from the *Lowell Offering,* quotes from a mill girl's diary, an illustrated historical fiction story about the Lowell mills, words to period songs, and essays about the Industrial Revolution by modern historians; *The Shot Heard Round the World: The Beginnings of the American Revolution* includes excerpts from Paul Revere's *Reminiscences,* military reports filed by British soldiers, quotes from letters and journals of Revolutionary War participants and onlookers, an account of the origin of "Yankee Doodle," and the poem "Paul Revere's Ride" by Henry Wadsworth Longfellow.

The company also publishes American History plays, generally suitable for kids in grades 5–9. All are designed for classroom production, which means large casts of characters, but most, with a little creative fiddling, can be adapted to smaller groups. Titles include

The First Voyage of Christopher Columbus (which has two suggested endings, one from the point of view of the Spaniards, the other from the point of view of the Indians; kids are encouraged to write their own versions of the narrator's final speech).

Single copies of "Perspectives on History" titles, $5.95; individual plays (reproducible for 30 copies), $10

Discovery Enterprises, Ltd.

31 Laurelwood Dr.

Carlisle, MA 01741

information (508) 287-5401; orders (508) 287-5403 or (800) 729-1720/fax (508) 287-5402

Social Studies Through Children's Literature: An Integrated Approach

Anthony D. Fredericks; Teacher Ideas Press, 1991

Social studies as presented through 32 popular children's picture books for elementary-level students. A descriptive plot summary of each of the chosen books is followed by lists of discussion questions and supplementary readings, and a large number of multidisciplinary activities, variously based on history, geography, math, science, art, music, and creative writing. Featured books include *A Picture Book of Abraham Lincoln, Once There Were Giants,* and *Jambo Means Hello.* See also *U.S. History Through Children's Literature* (at right).

The Story in History: Writing Your Way into the American Experience

Margot Fortunato Galt; Teachers & Writers Collaborative, 1992

American history through creative writing projects, for students in upper-elementary school to adults. Kids, for example, write poems based on family histories and short prose pieces about family names, nicknames, and name origins; compose dramatic monologues delivered by historical heroes or heroines (or villains); write essays based on historical maps and odes based on American flora and fauna; invent pioneer diaries and Civil War ballads; write radio plays; and compose two-voice poems, in which each speaker comes from a different historical era. Project starters and examples include excerpts from Henry David Thoreau's *Walden* and John Steinbeck's *Cannery Row,*

poems by Pablo Neruda, Langston Hughes, N. Scott Momaday, and Gwendolyn Brooks, an Oglala Sioux "Winter Count," Walt Whitman's descriptions of the Civil War, 16th-century maps, and ads from 1940s issues of *Life* magazine. The creative literary possibilities, derived from the entire span of American history, are wonderful.

U.S. History Through Children's Literature

Wanda J. Miller; Teacher Ideas Press, 1997

Historical fiction and nonfiction books categorized under various events or periods in American History. Among the category headings are the American Revolution, Pioneer Life and Westward Movement, the Civil War, Immigration, and World Wars I and II. Each book listing is accompanied by a plot summary, discussion questions, and suggestions for projects and activities. Featured titles include *The Courage of Sarah Noble, The Sign of the Beaver, Sarah, Plain and Tall, Number the Stars,* and *Rosie the Riveter.*

Also see *Social Studies Through Children's Literature* (at left).

USKids History Series

Howard Egger-Bovet and Marlene Smith-Baranzini; Little, Brown, 1996

Engaging and interesting books in which history is presented through a series of dramatic stories (based on original sources), interspersed with reader-friendly informational essays, illustrations, maps, quotations, and many suggestions for supplementary hands-on activities, cooking and creative writing projects, and games. Titles include *Book of the American Indian, Book of the American Colonies, Book of the American Revolution,* and *Book of the New American Nation.* For readers aged 9–13.

The World Series

Genevieve Foster; Beautiful Feet Books

There are four of these books, originally written in the 1940s and 1950s, and recently reissued. Titles include *The World of Captain John Smith* (see page 472), *George Washington's World, Abraham Lincoln's World,* and *Augustus Caesar's World* (see page 620).

Older versions can often be obtained through libraries or used-book stores. Tracking them down is worth the effort; Foster's series provides young readers with an interesting horizontal slant on history.

Each book is between 300 and 400 pages long and is divided into sections based on periods in the life of the title character. Each section includes nine or 10 storybooklike accounts both of incidents in the life of the title character and of historical events happening at that time in different parts of the world. *The World of John Smith,* for example, covers events occurring when Smith was a boy, a young soldier, a leader at Jamestown, and an older man in retirement, writing history. When Smith was a boy, Foster explains, Sir Francis Drake had just returned to England a hero, the first Englishman to sail around the world; Queen Elizabeth I defeated the Spanish Armada; Sir Walter Raleigh's colony in Roanoke, Virginia, vanished mysteriously; young William Shakespeare arrived in London to become an actor; and El Greco was painting portraits of saints in Spain.

History, viewed horizontally, can be a revelation, and our boys found it fascinating: "You mean *Pocahontas* was at the same time as *Galileo?*"

The Young Reader's Companion to American History

John A. Garraty, ed.; Houghton Mifflin, 1994

A very large (964 pages) and reader-friendly encyclopedia of American history, aimed at readers aged 10 and up. The book contains articles on the basics of political history—entries include, for example, "Erie Canal," "Marshall Plan," and "Monroe Doctrine"—as well as biographies of famous Americans from all walks of life and articles on social and cultural topics. Flip through *The Young Reader's Companion* and you'll come across biographies of Rachel Carson, Louis Armstrong, Elvis Presley, Malcolm X, Crazy Horse, and Patrick Henry; articles on comic strips, cowboys, jazz, libraries, race riots, tobacco, the feminist movement, and welfare; and many illustrations, including maps, charts, tables, cartoons, reproductions of advertisements and artworks, and black-and-white and color photographs. Also includes cross-references and suggested supplementary readings. An excellent reference.

GAMES

American Adventure Games

A series of "cut-and-fold" board games with heavy paper boards and playing pieces, each based on a landmark event in American history. Each game is illustrated with period artwork or photographs and includes both detailed historical background information and playing instructions. There are many titles in the series, among them "The Voyage of the Mayflower" (see page 476), in which players attempt to sail their ships safely across the stormy Atlantic to Massachusetts before supplies run out; "The Redcoats Are Coming!" (see pages 488, 495), in which players race to warn the colonists of the approaching British, while attempting to save Sam Adams and John Hancock from capture; "The Underground Railroad" (see page 540), in which—as runaway slaves—players travel north along a perilous path to freedom; and "The Monitor and the Merrimack" (see page 549), in which players re-enact the famous Civil War sea battle.

$6.95 each

Chatham Hill Games, Inc.

Box 253

Chatham, NY 12037

(518) 392-5022 or (800) 554-3039/fax (518) 392-3121

e-mail: CHGames@taconic.net

Web site: www.ocdc.com/Chatham_Hill_games

Brain Quest: American History

Workman, 1995

A thousand questions and answers for kids in grades 4–6 in a format suitable for playing practically everywhere. Questions, printed on two colorful packs of skinny seven-inch-long two-sided cards, are arranged in seven categories: "Colonial Days," "Birth of a Nation," "New Frontiers," "Civil War Period," "Modern Times," "America's Best," and the catch-all "Mixed Bag." Rules are included for competitive play, but the game is more comfortable—at least in our hands—when played by single kids ("Solitaire") or as a cooperative group.

$10.95 from bookstores or

Workman Publishing Co.

708 Broadway

New York, NY 10003-9555

(212) 254-5900 or (800) 722-7202/fax (212) 254-8098

Web site: www.workmanweb.com

Discover America

A board game of American history, geography, and culture (plus a bit of spelling). Spaces on the circular playing path, colored a patriotic red, white, and blue, are labeled with the names of the 50 states. Players start on "Hawaii" and move around the board counter-clockwise, finishing up in "Washington, D.C." On each move, players can decide either to name a state capital or answer a history question from one of 200 "Quiz Cards." There are six questions on each card: a Who, What, Where, When, and Which question, plus a word definition or spelling challenge. (Answers appear on the card back.) Sample questions include:

Who was the second President of the United States?
What is the nickname of the state of Alaska?
Where is the geographic center of the continental United States?
When did the Civil War start?
Which state has the most U.S. national parks?
Spell Massachusetts.

Players earn money for each space moved (plus receive occasional financial windfalls from "Lucky" cards); first person to reach Washington, D.C., with the most cash wins the game. Recommended for two to four players aged 9 and up.

$29.99

Second Avenue Creations

108 S. Fourth Ave.

Box 472

St. Nazianz, WI 54232

(414) 773-3053 or (800) 713-1105

COMPUTER SOFTWARE

American Girls Collection

A CD-ROM featuring five American girls—Felicity, Kirsten, Addie, Samantha, and Molly—each growing up in a different historical period, from the Revolutionary War era to World War II. Using this pro-

gram, kids can enact their own historical stories, complete with accurate costumes, stage sets, props, period music, and dialogue. Also included are printable scripts and tutorials. On CD-ROM for Mac or Windows.

$34.99

The Learning Company

6160 Summit Dr. N

Minneapolis, MN 55430-4003

(800) 622-3390/fax (612) 589-1151

Web site: www.learningco.com

Also see **Pleasant Company** (page 448).

American Journey

A CD-ROM series of historical primary source materials. These wide-ranging collections include letters, journal excerpts, newspaper articles, famous speeches, maps, photographs, and period songs and poems, as well as timelines, explanatory picture captions, historical essays, and supplementary resource suggestions. The materials are categorized by theme or time period. Titles include "The African-American Experience from the 1400's–the Civil War," "The American Revolution," "The Civil War," "The Westward Expansion," "The Immigrant Experience," "Women in America," and "The Depression and the New Deal."

$149 each

Primary Source Media

12 Lunar Dr.

Woodbridge, CT 06525

(800) 444-0799

Web site: www.thomson.com/psmedia

History of the United States for Young People: American Heritage

Kids pop into a time-travel capsule to tour American history from prehistoric times to the present. Included are an interactive timeline, biographies of all the American presidents, histories of the arts and entertainment media, and 3-D "virtual-reality walk-throughs" of typical American homes from the 17th century to modern times. Creative graphics, film footage, maps, and a searchable library. The box claims that this is "the only software your kids will ever need for American history." On CD-ROM for Mac or Windows.

$34.95

Social Studies School Service

10200 Jefferson Blvd.

Box 802

Culver City, CA 90232-0802

(310) 839-2436 or (800) 421-4246/fax (310) 839-2249

or (800) 944-5432

Web site: www.SocialStudies.com

Skytrip America

A tour of American history in the flying machine of your choice, from the 18th-century balloon to the ultramodern hovercraft. The program centers around a "Pony Express" game that challenges players to deliver letters to specific historical persons or places. The game covers 12 geographical regions of the United States and includes background historical information, photographs, videos, and audio clips. History is approached from a range of cultural perspectives: visitors to the Old West, for example, learn the points of view of American Indians, Spaniards, and American homesteaders. On CD-ROM for Mac or Windows.

$19.95

Discovery Channel Multimedia

Box 1089

Florence, KY 41022

(800) 678-3343

Web site: www.discovery.com

AUDIO VISUAL RESOURCES

American Heroes and Legends Series
Rabbit Ears Video

This series of half-hour videos for elementary-aged viewers is a collection of historical stories, folktales, and legends, told through animated illustrations. Each is narrated, storybook-style, by an award-winning actor. Titles include "Annie Oakley," "Davy Crockett," "Follow the Drinking Gourd: A Story of the Underground Railroad," "John Henry" (narrated by Denzel Washington, with music by B. B. King), "Rip Van Winkle," "Johnny Appleseed," "Paul Bunyan," "The Song of Sacajawea," and "Squanto and the First Thanksgiving." Great stories, beautifully done.

Each video, $9.95

Movies Unlimited

3015 Darnell Road

Philadelphia, PA 19154

(215) 637-4444 or (800) 4-MOVIES

e-mail: movies@moviesunlimited.com

Web site: www.moviesunlimited.com

or

Social Studies School Service

10200 Jefferson Blvd.

Box 802

Culver City, CA 90232-0802

(310) 839-2436 or (800) 421-4246/fax (310) 839-2249

or (800) 944-5432

Web site: SocialStudies.com

Early American History: Native Americans Through the Forty-Niners

The Teaching Company specializes in tracking down talented college and high school teachers and videotaping their courses, thus making them available to the general public. *Early American History,* a high school–level course by teacher Lin Thompson of Bellflower High School in Los Angeles, is presented as a series of 30 half-hour lessons. In each, Thompson takes on the persona of a historical personage, complete with accent and elaborate costume, so that listeners get not only the historical facts and figures but also a taste for a first-person perspective on historical events. Thompson, for example, teaches "Pre-Columbian America" in the character of a Viking explorer, Bjorn Herjulfson, "Pilgrims and Puritans" as John Winthrop, "The Declaration of Independence" as Miliatiaman Thompson, "The Era of Jefferson" as Aaron Burr, and "Texas" as Jim Bowie. Don't expect PBS: Thompson is an enthusiastic teacher and a talented speaker, but these are history lectures, as delivered in a classroom.

The series (30 lessons on 4 videotapes), $199.95

The Teaching Co.

7405 Alban Station Ct., Suite A-107

Springfield, VA 22150-2318

(800) 832-2412

Great American Speeches
Alexandra Hanson-Harding; Scholastic

A book-and-audiocassette set. The cassette features recordings of 20 famous American speeches; the book contains corresponding background information and suggested activities for each. Included are selections by Eleanor Roosevelt, Chief Joseph, Sojourner Truth, Ronald Reagan, Patrick Henry, Martin Luther King Jr., Abraham Lincoln, Thomas Jefferson, and Frederick Douglass.

6 10 *This is America, Charlie Brown! Series*

A collection of seven videotapes covering American history from the arrival of the Pilgrims through the twentieth century. These are witty, informational, and charming: in each, the Peanuts characters travel back in time and take part in historical events. Included in each episode, along with the cartoon sequences, are historic photographs and film clips and period background music. Titles include "The Mayflower Voyagers," "The Building of the Transcontinental Railroad," "The Great Inventors," "The Wright Brothers at Kitty Hawk," "The Birth of the Constitution," "The Smithsonian and the Presidency," and "The Music and Heroes of America." Each episode is about 30 minutes long. For kids aged 6–10.

> Individual tapes, $14.95; the seven-tape set, $99
> Social Studies School Service
> 10200 Jefferson Blvd.
> Box 802
> Culver City, CA 90232-0802
> (310) 839-2436 or (800) 421-4246/fax (310) 839-2249
> or (800) 944-5432
> Web site: SocialStudies.com
> or
> Movies Unlimited
> 3015 Darnell Rd.
> Philadelphia, PA 19154
> (215) 637-4444 or (800) 4-MOVIES
> e-mail: movies@moviesunlimited.com
> Web site: www.moviesunlimited. com

13 *The United States At War*

The history of the United States through its many wars on 24 audiocassettes, narrated by George C. Scott. The series covers America's wars from the Revolution through Vietnam. Each episode covers the reasons behind the war, the historical context, varying viewpoints of the conflict, and major events. Titles include "The American Revolution," "The War of 1812," "The Mexican-American War," "The Civil War," "The Spanish-American War," "World War I," "World War II," and "The Korean War/The Vietnam War." Each title consists of a two-cassette pack.

> $17.95 each
> Knowledge Products
> 722 Rundle Ave., Suite A-12
> Box 305151
> Nashville, TN 37230
> (800) 876-4332

AMERICAN HISTORY ON-LINE

12 *American Historical Documents*

The text—just the text, no frills—of American historical documents, including the Mayflower Compact, the Declaration of Independence, the Constitution, the Emancipation Proclamation, and a host of lesser items.

> gopher://wiretap.spies.com/11/Gov/US-History

9 *American Memory*

A massive multimedia collection from the Library of Congress. Users can view some of the earliest movies ever made—including several by Thomas Edison and a view of Buffalo Bill in full western regalia in a New York City parade, as well as thousands of photographs, and hundreds of oral histories, collected from interviews with people all over the country and compiled by members of the Federal Writers' Project during the Depression.

> rs6.loc.gov/amtitle.html

9 *Biography*

Includes an immense database of over 20,000 names, past and present. Click on a letter for an alphabetized list or enter a name for a short biography, some with illustrations and video clips.

> www.biography.com

9 *Explorers of the World*

Explorers are categorized under "Land," "Sky," "Ideas," and "Art." Click on a name for a brief biography. Also included is "The Biography Maker," a series of lessons on how to write good biographies.

> www.bham.wednet.edu/explore.htm

From Revolution to Reconstruction

 American history from the colonial period through modern times in hypertext format, with links to illustrations, primary sources, historical essays, and biographies of important historical figures.

grid.let.rug.nl/~welling/usa/revolution.html

Historical Maps of the US

Over 100 maps tracing the growth of America and its territories, plus historical, regional, and city maps.

www.lib.utexas.edu/Libs/PCL/MapCollection/histus.html

The History Net

Many articles on a wide range of topics in American and world history, eyewitness accounts of historical events, personality profiles, and much more.

www.thehistorynet.com

Links to the Past

Information on historical and archaeological sites in national parks.

www.cr.nps.gov

Today in History

What happened on this very day in history. Includes a brief illustrated description with links to related sites. Users can also access "Yesterday in History" and a large archive of previous days.

lcweb2.loc.gov/ammem/today/today.html

EARLY AMERICAN HISTORY

PRE-COLUMBIAN AMERICA

Also see **World History: Prehistoric Peoples** (pages 606–610) and **American History: American Indians** (pages 501–511).

BOOKS

The Ancient Cliff Dwellers of Mesa Verde

 Caroline Arnold; Clarion, 1992

The civilization of the Cliff Dwellers of Mesa Verde, Colorado, vanished nearly 200 years before Columbus arrived in America. The book describes this ancient culture for readers in grades 2–5. Illustrated with photographs of archaeological sites and artifacts.

Before You Came This Way

Byrd Baylor; E. P. Dutton, 1969

A picture-book story of the southwest before the arrival of the Europeans. The illustrations are based on prehistoric rock drawings.

See *If Rocks Could Talk* (page 463) and *Native American Rock Art* (page 462).

Cities in the Sand: The Ancient Civilizations of the Southwest

 Scott Warren; Chronicle Books, 1992

An informative study of three prehistoric cultures: the Anasazi, the Hohokam, and the Mogollon. Illustrated with full-color photographs. For readers in grades 4–7.

The Culture of Pre-Columbian North America

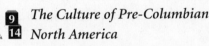 *Cobblestone;* April 1993

This issue of *Cobblestone* magazine covers the native cultures of America before the arrival of the Columbus, including information on the Cahokia mound builders, hands-on activities, and a supplementary reading list for readers aged 9–14.

Available from most libraries or $4.50 from

Cobblestone Publishing, Inc.

30 Grove St.

Peterborough, NH 03458-1454

(603) 924-7209 or (800) 821-0115

Web site: www.cobblestonepub.com

See *Cobblestone* (page 449).

First Came the Indians

 M. J. Wheeler; Macmillan, 1983

A short chapter book on early North American Indian cultures: featured tribes are the Iroquois, Creek,

Ojibwa, Makah, Sioux, and Hopi. The book discusses their probable route to the North American continent and subsequent settlement. For readers in grades 2–5.

If You Lived in the Days of the Wild Mammoth Hunters
Mary Elting and Franklin Folsom; Scholastic, 1968

What life was like 11,000 years ago, explained in conversational question-and-answer format. "Who were the mammoth hunters?" "What was a mammoth hunt like?" "How do archaeologists find mammoth hunters' camps?" "Were mammoth hunters the first Americans?" See *If You . . . Series* (pages 453–454).

Morning Girl
Michael Dorris; Hyperion, 1994

The book, in alternating voices, describes the lives of Morning Girl and Star Boy, growing up on a Caribbean island in pre-Columbian America. The children describe their love for the world about them, the struggles of growing up, and the events, large and small, of their island society. The book ends, ominously, with the arrival of strange visitors from across the sea: the epilogue, from a very different perspective, is an excerpt from the diary of Christopher Columbus. For readers aged 9–12.

Native American Rock Art: Messages from the Past
Yvette La Pierre; Lickle Publishing, 1994

The history and technique of ancient North American rock art. The author describes the processes of creating rock art, explains the difference between *petroglyph* and *pictograph,* and includes photographs and drawings of early artworks. The text describes the life and culture of ancient Americans. For readers aged 9–13.
Also see *Before You Came This Way* (page 461) and *If Rocks Could Talk* (page 463).

One Small Blue Bead
Byrd Baylor; Charles Scribner's Sons, 1992

The picture-book tale of a young boy from the ancient Southwest whose small blue bead is discovered by a child in the present day. For readers in grades 2–4.

People of the Breaking Day

Marcia Sewall; Aladdin, 1997

The picture-book story of the everyday life of the Wampanoag Indians of Massachusetts in the days before the arrival of the European colonists.

San Rafael: A Central American City through the Ages
Xavier Hernandez; Houghton Mifflin, 1992

The book traces the Central American city through time, from 1000 B.C. to the present day. Illustrated with very detailed pen-and-ink drawings.

Village of Blue Stone
Stephen Trimble; Macmillan, 1990

An account of the everyday life of the Anasazi, who vanished from history in the early 14th century, leaving behind pueblo villages and cities in the American Southwest. For readers in grades 3–7.

Wild and Woolly Mammoths
Aliki; HarperCollins, 1998.

A charmingly illustrated picture book about mammoths and the Stone Age people who hunted them. (The mammoth of North America, young readers learn, is sometimes called the Jeffersonian Mammoth, after Thomas Jefferson, who was the president of the United States when the remains of one were discovered.)

MYTHS AND LEGENDS

Also see **World History: The Americas, Folktales and Legends** (page 658).

All of You Was Singing
Richard Lewis; Atheneum, 1991

A picture-book version of an Aztec creation myth that explains the beginnings of music. For readers aged 4–9.

The Hummingbird King: A Guatemalan Legend
Argentina Palacios; Troll Associates, 1993

A traditional Central American legend about a young chief, beloved by a hummingbird, who is killed by his wicked uncle and then magically transformed into a beautiful quetzal. Also in this series see *When Sun Ruled the Land: A Story from Cuba* and *Why Owl Comes Out at Night: A Story from Haiti* (Janet Palazzo-Craig, 1997).

Journey of the Nightly Jaguar
Burton Albert; Atheneum, 1996

The ancient Maya of Central America, the author explains, believed that their gods could take the form of animals. In this picture-book tale, the jaguar prowls the jungle by night and then rises into the sky in the morning as the sun. For readers aged 4–8.

People of the Corn: A Mayan Story
Mary-Joan Gerson; Little, Brown, 1995

A creation myth explaining how the first people were made from corn. Illustrated with colorful paintings based on Mayan symbols and patterns. For readers aged 4–8.

Pre-Columbian Stories
Robert Hull and Vanessa Cleall; Thomson Learning, 1994

A collection of seven traditional tales from the pre-Columbian Indian tribes of South and Central America for readers aged 9–12.

Quetzal: Sacred Bird of the Cloud Forest
Dorothy Hinshaw Patent; William Morrow, 1996

A short chapter book about the gorgeously feathered quetzal. Included are an account of the bird's natural history, behavior, and modern environment, and a detailed discussion of its part in Central American art, myth, and legend. It once appeared as the great Aztec god Quetzalcoatl, the Plumed Serpent. For readers aged 8–11.

HANDS-ON ACTIVITIES

If Rocks Could Talk
Jane Bush; Dale Seymour Publications, 1993

A "multimedia kit," consisting of a 20-minute video showing photographs of ancient southwestern petroglyphs with explanatory background narration, a

student text on early American Indian cultures as studied through rock art, a teacher's guide, and two posters illustrating major American Indian art styles. Included are maps, charts, lists of supplementary readings, and many activity suggestions. Recommended for kids in grades 4–8.

$34.95
Cuisenaire/Dale Seymour Publications
Box 5026
White Plains, NY 10602-5026
(800) 872-1100 or (800) 237-0338/
fax (914) 328-5487 or (800) 551-ROOS
Web site: www.aw.com/dsp/

Also see *Before You Came This Way* (page 461) and *Native American Rock Art* (page 462).

Indian Life in Pre-Columbian North America Coloring Book
John Green; Dover Publications, 1994

Black-line drawings of pre-1492 everyday life among the North American Indian tribes, with a short explanatory text.

$2.95
Dover Publications, Inc.
31 E. Second St.
Mineola, NY 11501

Rock Art Painting Kit
Make your own pre-Columbian rock paintings. The kit includes four packets of natural pigments, a pair of twig tools, and an informational instruction booklet. Painters must supply their own rocks.

$14.50
Ancient Graffiti
52 Seymour St.
Middlebury, VT 05753
(802) 388-2919 or (888) 725-6632
e-mail: ancientg@sovernet.com

PRE-COLUMBIAN HISTORY ON-LINE

Chaco Canyon
This site provides information on the archaeology of Chaco Canyon, New Mexico, and the Anasazi cul-

ture, including a link to a 3-D model of the Chetro Ketl Great Kiva.

www.chaco.com/park

Ice, Mammoths, and Hunters

A short informational text plus a picture of mammoths.

rbcm1.rcbm.gov.bc.ca/notes/mammoth.html

Native American History and Archaeology Resources

Links to American Indian archaeological and anthropological sites.

hanksville.phast.umass.edu/misc/NAhistory.html

COLUMBUS AND OTHER EXPLORERS

BOOKS: NONFICTION

1492: The Year of the New World

Piero Ventura; Putnam, 1992

The book discusses international happenings in the landmark year 1492, both in the Old World and in the New, including events among the Taino, Aztec, Inca, Maya, Hopi, Buffalo Hunger, and Lake and Forest Tribes peoples. Illustrated with detailed and colorful little pictures and maps.

Christopher Columbus and His Legacy

David L. Bender, Bruno Leone, and Mary Ellen Jones, eds.; Greenhaven Press, 1992

A volume in the Opposing Viewpoints Series (see page 455), which includes articles pro and con evaluating the actions of Columbus, the policies of the Spanish in the New World, the takeover of Indian lands, and the cultural clashes between new arrivals and natives. About 300 pages long, for high school–aged readers.

The Columbian Encounter

A lesson unit for students in grades 5–9, including a 102-page teacher's guidebook with background information and suggestions for student activities.

Included, for example, are maps, excerpts from Columbus's log, and writings by Bartolmé de las Casas. The guidebook is packaged with two issues of *Cobblestone* magazine (see page 449), *The Legacy of Columbus* and *The Cultures of Pre-Columbian America,* and two issues of *Faces* magazine (see page 411), *Ancient Mexico* and *First Americans, First Encounters.* The illustrated magazines include nonfiction and fiction features, games, recipes, maps, and timelines.

$28.95

Cobblestone Publishing, Inc.

30 Grove St.

Peterborough, NH 03458-1454

(603) 924-7209 or (800) 821-0115/fax (603) 924-7380

e-mail: custsvc@cobblestone.mv.com

Web site: www.cobblestonepub.com

Columbus

Ingri and Edgar Parin D'Aulaire; Doubleday, 1955

The classic Columbus legend, in 58 oversize color-illustrated pages. "Once, when Christopher held an orange in his hand, he saw the tips of a butterfly's wings peeping up from behind it. He thought that just like this did the sails of a ship, far away, rise slowly over the horizon. It must be true that the world was round!"

The Discovery of the Americas

Betsy and Giulio Maestro; Mulberry, 1991

The Discovery of the Americas is a chronological account of the multiple "discoveries" of the Americas from the crossing of the Asia-to-Alaska land bridge during the last Ice Age to the circumnavigation of the globe by Magellan. The short text is somewhat dry and schoolbookish, but there are lots of big, brightly colored illustrations and maps, on which the paths taken by various explorers are clearly marked.

The accompanying *The Discovery of the Americas Activity Book* (Lothrop, Lee & Shepard, 1992) describes 43 activities, games, and projects based on the original book. Suggestions include putting on a puppet show based on famous explorers, writing newspaper articles based on famous voyages of discovery, making an alphabet book or quilt based on the discovery of the New World, inventing a board game based on Magellan's trip around the world, building a model pre-

HISTORY

Columbian city, and making an illustrated timeline/ mural of the discovery of the Americas.

A sequel in similar format, *Exploration and Conquest: The Americas After Columbus 1500–1620* (Lothrop, Lee & Shepard, 1994) covers explorers who followed Columbus to the New World, among them Cortés, Pizarro, De Soto, Champlain, and Hudson, and describes the early settlements at Roanoke and Jamestown.

First Americans, First Encounters
Faces; January 1992

This issue of the magazine includes articles on pre-Columbian art, ancient civilizations of the Andes and their modern descendants, the Taino Indians encountered by Columbus, the Aztecs, and the first American languages, plus instructions for making (Taino-style) cornhusk dolls.

Available from most libraries or $4.50 from
Cobblestone Publishing, Inc.
30 Grove St.
Peterborough, NH 03458-1454
(603) 924-7209 or (800) 821-0115/fax (603) 924-7380
e-mail: custsvc@cobblestone.mv.com
Web site: www.cobblestonepub.com
See *Faces* (page 411).

Follow the Dream
Peter Sis; Dragonfly, 1996

A simple history of Columbus's first and most famous voyage to the New World, exquisitely illustrated with paintings reminiscent of medieval maps. For readers aged 4–8.

Forgotten Voyager: the Story of Amerigo Vespucci
Ann Fitzpatrick Alper; Carolrhoda, 1991

The often neglected story of Amerigo Vespucci's life and accomplishments, illustrated with black-and-white photographs, prints, and maps.

If You Were There in 1492
Barbara Brenner; Simon & Schuster, 1991

The theme of Brenner's book is "What else besides the voyage of Columbus was going on in 1492?" A great deal, it appears: the book covers everyday life in the late 15th century, including information on food, clothes, housing, health, entertainment, and education, and gives readers a glimpse at the lives of the rich and famous. Included is a photograph of Queen Isabella's favorite castle and a description of her court clothes (green velvet, russet brocade, and seed pearls). Historical happenings in 1492: Michelangelo was 17; Leonardo da Vinci was 40 (and designing a flying machine); Torquemada was directing the Spanish Inquisition; and Martin Behaim of Germany was constructing a globe of the world. A fascinating book.

In 1492
Jean Marzollo; Scholastic, 1991

A very simple version of Columbus's voyage for very young readers, written in short rhyming couplets, with bright humorous illustrations. "In fourteen hundred ninety-two / Columbus sailed the ocean blue. / He had three ships and left from Spain / He sailed through sunshine, wind, and rain."

The Legacy of Columbus
Cobblestone; January 1992

This issue of the magazine includes articles on Columbus's voyages and initial encounters with American natives, and subsequent cultural exchanges between New and Old Worlds, along with suggestions for activities and a supplementary reading list.

Available from most libraries or $4.50 from
Cobblestone Publishing, Inc.
30 Grove St.
Peterborough, NH 03458-1454
(603) 924-7209 or (800) 821-0115/fax (603) 924-7380
e-mail: custsvc@cobblestone.mv.com
Web site: www.cobblestonepub.com
See *Cobblestone* (page 449).

Our Own Spanish Conquest
Cobblestone; March 1981

This issue of the popular history magazine for upper-elementary and middle-grade kids (see *Cobblestone,* page 449) covers early Spanish exploration and settlement in North America through fiction and nonfiction articles, illustrations, maps, and activities. Also see *Saint Augustine: America's Oldest City* (*Cobblestone*; November 1995).

Available from most libraries or $4.50

Cobblestone Publishing, Inc.

30 Grove St.

Peterborough, NH 03458

(603) 924-7209 or (800) 821-0115/fax (603) 924-7380

e-mail: custsvc@cobblestone.mv.com

Web site: www.cobblestonepub.com

Where Do You Think You're Going, Christopher Columbus?

Jean Fritz; Paper Star, 1997

A delightful 80-page biography of Columbus, stuffed with all the entrancing details that textbooks so often and so shortsightedly leave out. Readers learn what Columbus took along to eat on board the *Santa María* (sea biscuits, salt meat, cheese, raisins, beans, honey, rice, almonds, sardines, and anchovies), what he brought back home with him after his first landmark voyage (six Caribbean Islanders, a lot of parrots, and a belt embroidered with red and white fishbones), and what he used to say when he was upset ("By San Fernando!"). Plus all the basics, with colorful illustrations by Margot Tomes.

The World in 1492

Jean Fritz, Katherine Paterson, Patricia and Frederick McKissack, Margaret Mahy, and Jamake Highwater; Henry Holt, 1992

The authors jointly cover the state of the world at the time of Columbus's famous voyage. Each section of the book concentrates on a different continent: Europe, Asia, Africa, Oceania, the Americas. Included under each is an overview of the region's history, descriptions of native life and culture, and accounts of important historical events and influential people. The book is 160 pages long, illustrated with drawings, photographs, and maps. For readers aged 11–14.

BOOKS: FICTION

Encounter

Jane Yolen; Harcourt Brace, 1992

The story of the arrival of the Europeans as told by a young Taino boy. Young readers get a feel for what it must have been like to experience the arrival of the Europeans from the other side. The book is simple, moving, and sad, illustrated with full-color paintings. Also see *Morning Girl* (page 462).

I Discover Columbus

Robert Lawson; Little, Brown, 1991

Subtitled "A True Chronicle of the Great Admiral & his Finding of the New World, narrated by the Venerable Parrot Aurelio, who Shared in the Glorious Venture." This, says the author, is the *real* story of the famous voyage, seen through the eyes of a canny Central American parrot who not only was there but who engineered the whole thing. A humorous and delightful chapter book for readers aged 8–11, by the author of *Ben and Me* (see page 491).

I Sailed With Columbus

Miriam Schlein; HarperCollins, 1991

A description of the famous voyage for readers aged 8–12, based on the (fictional) diary of a 12-year-old cabin boy, Julio de la Vega Medina, on board the *Santa María*. The book, heavy in historical detail, covers 15th-century shipboard life and the first encounters with the New World Indians.

COLORING BOOKS

The Exploration of North America Coloring Book

Peter Copeland; Dover Publications

The Exploration of North America Coloring Book contains 36 illustrations depicting a range of early discoverers, from the Vikings arriving in Vinland, through Columbus, Cabot, and Ponce de León.

Also see the *Columbus Discovers America Coloring Book,* which includes 41 detailed drawings of Columbus's expedition, from his meeting with Ferdinand and Isabella of Spain through his arrival in the New World.

$2.95 each

Dover Publications, Inc.

31 E. Second St.

Mineola, NY 11501

HISTORY

6 + *My First Voyage: Christopher Columbus*
An illustrated account of the famous 1492 voyage in Columbus's own words, with text in both English and Spanish.

$2.95

Bellerophon Books

36 Ancapa St.

Santa Barbara, CA 93101

(800) 253-9943/fax (800) 965-8286

GAMES AND HANDS-ON ACTIVITIES

13 + *Columbus & the Age of Explorers*
A portfolio of primary source documents and historical essays on the early voyages of American discovery and their subsequent impact on New and Old Worlds. The portfolio includes 14 facsimiles of historical documents, including reproductions of world maps from the 16th to the early 18th centuries, a 1512 portrait of Columbus, a page from a 13th-century Icelandic manuscript, and a full-color copy of Samuel de Champlain's chart of the Gulf of Maine. The portfolio also contains four illustrated "Broadsheet Essays" providing historical background information: "Columbus's World and Enterprise," "Contacts, Encounters, Relationships," "Encounters Before Columbus," and "Naming America." Also included are detailed notes on each document, a reading list, and a student study guide.

$37

Jackdaw Publications

Box 503

Amawalk, NY 10501

(800) 789-0022/fax (800) 962-9101

See **Jackdaw Publications** (page 445).

6 + *Columbus Panorama*
The "Easy-to-Make Columbus Discovers America Panorama" is attractively printed in color on thin cardboard. Kids cut out and assemble the pieces. It really is easy to make; the pieces are big, with simple outlines. The finished product includes assorted Spaniards and Caribbean natives, canoes, Columbus's three ships, and a nice backdrop of an island scattered with huts and palm trees. For kids aged 6 and up.

$2.95

Dover Publications, Inc.

31 E. Second St.

Mineola, NY 11501

8 12 *Explorations*
Nicola Baxter; Franklin Watts, 1994

This is one of the "Craft Topics" series (see World History, page 603), a collection of 32-page books recommended for kids in grades 4–6, each of which combines historical background information with instructions for related crafts projects. Color illustrations include photographs of museum artifacts. The *Explorations* volume features an overview of the "Age of Exploration," concentrating on the voyages of Christopher Columbus and Hernán Cortés. Instructions are included for making simple navigational instruments and Aztec ornaments and masks.

7 12 *Explorers: Cooperative Learning Activities*
Mary Strohl and Susan Schneck; Scholastic, 1993

A 112-page collection of hands-on activities for kids in grades 3–6 based on eight famous explorers and the peoples they encountered in the Americas. Explorers covered include Columbus, Cortés, De Soto, Coronado, Cartier, Hudson, Champlain, and Marquette and Joliet. As kids read about the accomplishments of each and about the native cultures each expedition encountered, they experiment with recipes, art projects, timelines, mapmaking, and creative writing activities. Included are reproducible worksheets and game materials.

$15.95

Scholastic, Inc.

2931 E. McCarty St.

Jefferson City, MO 65101

(800) 724-6527

Web site: www.Scholastic.com

8 + *Land Ho! Tierra! Tierra!*
A bilingual (English and Spanish) and beautifully illustrated board game in which players set sail for the New World on the *Niña,* the *Pinta,* or the *Santa María.* First ship to make it safely to America is the winner. Safely crossing the Atlantic, however, in the face of nasty weather, sea monsters, and enemy vessels, is a challenging business. Included are listings from Columbus's

original daily ships' logs and a pack of historical fact cards. The game is recommended for two or three players, aged 8 and up.

$22

Aristoplay

450 S. Wagner Rd.

Ann Arbor, MI 48107

(800) 634-7738 or (888) GR8-GAME/

fax (734) 995-4611

Web site: www.aristoplay.com

Who Really Discovered America?

A simulated "panel show" in which kids act the parts of seven explorers, all claiming to be the "true discoverer of America": Hoei-Shin, a fifth-century Buddhist monk; Brendan the Bold, an Irish priest; Bjarni Herulfsson, an Icelander; Leif Eriksson, founder of Vinland; Prince Madoc, a 12th century Welsh noble; Christopher Columbus, of *Santa María* fame; and Howling Wolf, chief of the Crow Indian tribe.

Materials include a detailed teacher's guide, reproducible student handouts, role descriptions and scripts, and a list of suggested essay topics. The simulation, recommended for students in grades 5–8, takes one to two hours.

$22

Interact

1825 Gillespie Way, #101

El Cajon, CA 92020-1095

(619) 448-1474 or (800) 359-0961/fax (619) 448-6722 or (800) 700-5093

Web site: www.interact-simulations.com

COLUMBUS AND OTHER EXPLORERS ON-LINE

1492 Exhibit

A six-part exhibit from the Library of Congress with detailed information on pre-Columbian Caribbean island societies, the Mediterranean world at the time of Columbus, the life of Columbus himself, and the story of the early European voyagers to America. Includes color illustrations and an informational text.

sunsite.unc.edu/expo/1492.exhibit

Christopher Columbus/Stereotypes

Views of Columbus from a number of different perspectives, most of them negative.

www.indians.org/welker/columbus1.htm

Columbus and the Age of Discovery

A large and comprehensive database on Columbus and his time.

marauder.millersv.edu/~columbus

Discoverers Web Homepage

A multifaceted and comprehensive site including information on notable voyages of discovery, a timeline of exploration, biographies of famous explorers (indexed alphabetically or by world region), a gallery of pictures and photographs, and maps.

www.win.tue.nl/cs/fm/engles/discovery/index.html

Explorers of the World

Biographies and information about a wide range of explorers, among them Columbus, Eric the Red, and Pizarro.

www.bham.wednet.edu/explorer.htm

Also see **Vikings** (**World History**, pages 626–630) and **Age of Exploration** (**World History**, pages 652–657).

THE COLONIAL PERIOD

From my homeschool journal:

◆ **January 3, 1991. Josh is nine; Ethan, eight; Caleb, six.**

We're starting a new history unit on the early European settlement of America, using a set of four homemade workbooks, variously covering Dutch, French, Spanish, and English colonization. Today we started "The Dutch in America: Wooden Shoes, Tulips, and a Headless Horseman." First we read a chapter on Henry Hudson and the Dutch fur traders in Roger Duvoisin's And There Was America, *and the boys designed and colored flags for Hudson's ship, the* Half Moon. *We located*

New York on the United States map; and found the Hudson River, Manhattan Island, and several other landmarks on the map of New York State.

Caleb: "Why is that city [Albany] marked with a little star?"

Discussed the Dutch purchase of Manhattan from the resident Indian tribe for $24 worth of trinkets, read how the island's estimated worth today is over 30 billion dollars, and the boys, impressed, practiced writing numbers in the billions.

Looked at pictures of modern Manhattan in the Children's Picture Atlas *and discussed the age, functions, and relative heights of the Empire State Building, the Statue of Liberty, and the United Nations Building. The boys designed and drew pictures of their own skyscrapers. We compared pictures of modern and 19th-century skyscrapers.*

Then read about Henry Hudson, his voyage on the Discovery, *and the mutiny that resulted in Henry's being marooned and thus vanishing from history. The boys discussed the pros and cons of the mutineers' act and argued over what they would have done if they had been Henry Hudson (conclusion: sneak back aboard the* Discovery *and stow away). Drew samples of the kind of house Hudson should have built to live in on Hudson Bay. Located Hudson Bay on the world map; the boys located a possible Northwest Passage. Discussed why it wasn't practical.*

◆ January 4, 1991

Reviewed Henry Hudson and his explorations; then read Old Silver Leg Takes Over! A Story of Peter Stuyvesant *by Robert Quackenbush (see page 471). This so fascinated the boys that they spent the rest of the morning fashioning wooden legs for themselves and playing at being irascible Dutch captains battling the invading British.*

◆ January 7, 1991

Historical digression: we've been reading The Indian in the Cupboard *by Lynne Reid Banks (see page 105) as a bedtime book. The boys wanted to continue reading it this morning—then were curious about longhouses. "How long were they? What did they look like?*

Did they have pointed roofs?" We looked up longhouses (and tepees, hogans, etc.) in American Indian Habitats, *which included both information and pictures. The boys then went outside and collected a box of twigs, bark, and sticks and began building their own model longhouses. By the time they'd finished building, we had also finished the book.*

◆ January 9, 1991

Back to the Dutch colonists: we reread Old Silver Leg Takes Over *(popular demand) and the boys drew and colored portraits of Peter Stuyvesant. Located the Netherlands on the world map; discussed the use of dikes and the meaning of "sea level."*

A fight at this point did in the rest of the history lesson.

After resolution of the fight, the boys had cocoa and we read Dr. Seuss's The King's Stilts, *suggested by Ethan because it takes place in an imaginary country surrounded by dikes, just like the Netherlands.*

◆ January 10, 1991

The boys looked at a series of paintings and photographs of windmills; then drew diagrams showing their guesses of what a windmill looks like inside. We then looked up windmills in David MacAulay's The Way Things Work *(see page 393) and compared their guesses to the real thing.*

Read a short biography of Rembrandt by Mike Venezia (see Getting to Know the World's Greatest Artists Series, *page 722); looked through our art postcard collection to find works by Rembrandt and other Dutch painters.*

Read The First Tulips in Holland *by Phyllis Krasilovsky; made tulips out of construction paper and taped them in the kitchen windows.*

Planted three pots of tulip bulbs.

◆ January 11, 1991

The boys learned about Dutch wooden shoes— klompen—and took turns trying on my clogs (our closest equivalent) and clomping about the house in them. Drew pictures of people wearing wooden shoes (Josh and

Caleb) and designed a machine for making wooden shoes (Ethan).

Discussed the English invasion of New Amsterdam and what the boys would have done in Peter Stuyvesant's place (fight).

Read about Dutch words that have been incorporated into English; everybody who didn't know how already learned how to spell cookie.

Defined pseudonym, *as in Washington Irving's pen name "Dr. Dietrich Knickerbocker," and the boys chose pseudonyms of their own.*

Read picture-book versions of Rip Van Winkle *and* The Legend of Sleepy Hollow.

The boys watched a version of "The Legend of Sleepy Hollow" on videotape.

Books: Nonfiction

A Break With Charity: A Story About the Salem Witch Trials

Ann Rinaldi; Harcourt Brace, 1992

Fourteen-year-old Susanna craves the friendship of the girls who gather around old Tituba at the parsonage, but she changes her mind when the girls' malicious behavior plunges the town into the horror of the Salem witch trials. Susanna, aware of the girls' deceptions, finally helps end the witch-hunt. Recommended for readers aged 12 and up.

The Crucible: A Play in Four Acts

Arthur Miller; Penguin, 1995

Arthur Miller's gripping play about the Salem witch trials, in which the hysteria sweeping the colonial town of Salem is linked to the 20th-century Communist "witch-hunt" spearheaded by Senator Joe McCarthy.

The Double Life of Pocahontas

Jean Fritz; Viking, 1987

The strange, sad story of the 11-year-old Indian girl who saved the life of Jamestown's Captain John Smith and grew up to marry an Englishman. This is history, not Disney. Recommended for readers aged 9–14.

Eating the Plates: A Pilgrim Book of Food and Manners

Lucille Recht Penner; Aladdin, 1997

A short, interesting history of Pilgrim food and table manners for readers aged 9–12. The book describes their many encounters with new foods, from the sea biscuits on board the *Mayflower* to Squanto's Indian corn, and includes 10 simple Pilgrim-style recipes. (It was fine to eat the plates; they were made of bread.)

The First Thanksgiving Feast

Joan Anderson; Clarion, 1989

A dramatized account of life in the Plymouth colony and of the first Thanksgiving feast in 1621, illustrated with wonderful black-and-white photographs taken at the Plimouth Plantation living-history museum.

Jamestown

Cobblestone; April 1994

This issue of the magazine includes articles on Pocahontas, John Smith, and the history of tobacco, plus a recipe for roasted pumpkin seeds and a supplementary reading list. For readers in grades 5–9.

Available from most libraries or $4.50

Cobblestone Publishing, Inc.

30 Grove St.

Peterborough, NH 03458-1454

(603) 924-7209 or (800) 821-0115

Web site: www.cobblestonepub.com

For general information on *Cobblestone,* see page 449.

Margaret Pumphrey's Pilgrim Stories

Revised by Elvajean Hall; Rand McNally, 1991

A collection of 17 stories about the Pilgrims, based on historical records. Included are tales of the Brewster family's near-capture by the king's officers, of the Pilgrims' escape to Holland, of young Francis Billington, who nearly blew up the *Mayflower* by playing with gunpowder, and of the surprising first meeting with the English-speaking Squanto. A final chapter lists all the children on the *Mayflower* by name and (probable) age.

N. C. Wyeth's Pilgrims

Robert San Souci; Chronicle Books, 1996

A picture-book account of Pilgrim settlement and experiences in the New World, with impressive color illustrations from artist N. C. Wyeth's 14-panel mural of the 1940s.

The New Americans: Colonial Times 1620–1689

Betsy Maestro; Lothrop, Lee & Shepard, 1998

A picture-book history of colonial times from the establishment of the first trading posts to the late 17th century. Maestro covers the arrival of the Pilgrims, the Dutch of New Amsterdam, the settlers of New Sweden, and the French voyageurs, all with large colorful paintings and a thorough, though somewhat dry, text. The book includes information on colonial relations with the American Indians and the early Indian wars.

Old Silver Leg Takes Over! A Story of Peter Stuyvesant

Robert Quackenbush; Prentice-Hall, 1986

The story of hot-tempered Peter Stuyvesant (who had a silver-trimmed wooden leg) and the early Dutch colony of New Amsterdam (later New York), with snappy asides from a pair of feisty little cartoon pigs. More appealing than Quackenbush's biographies of Washington (page 494) and Jefferson (page 496).

Pilgrims to a New World

Cobblestone; November 1989

This issue of Cobblestone magazine includes Pilgrim history, an account of the writing of the Mayflower Compact, the story of Squanto, and a description of the first Thanksgiving, with illustrations, activities, and a supplementary reading list. For kids in grades 5–9.

Available from most libraries or $4.50

Cobblestone Publishing, Inc.

30 Grove St.

Peterborough, NH 03458-1454

(603) 924-7209 or (800) 821-0115

Web site: www.cobblestonepub.com

See Cobblestone (page 449).

The Plymouth Thanksgiving

Leonard Weisgard; Doubleday, 1967

An attractively illustrated history of the Pilgrims and account of their famous first Thanksgiving. The text, based largely on William Bradford's original diary entries, provides both basic information and a lot of interesting detail.

Pocahontas

Ingri and Edgar Parin d'Aulaire; Doubleday, 1985

The classic legend of Pocahontas, which charmingly smooths over the cruel realities of her history. Beautifully illustrated.

The Powhatan Indians

Melissa McDaniel; Chelsea House, 1995

An 80-page history of the Powhatan Indians, describing the consolidation of the tribes under the rule of Pocahontas's father, Powhatan, and their rocky relationship with the English colonists at Jamestown.

The Story of William Penn

Aliki; Simon & Schuster, 1994

A picture-book biography of the Quaker founder of Pennsylvania, charmingly illustrated, for young readers.

The Thirteen Colonies Series

Dennis Brindell Fradin; Children's Press

A series of 13 books, one about each of the original 13 colonies. Titles include The Connecticut Colony, The Massachusetts Colony, and The Virginia Colony. Each covers the early history of the colony, from the first settlements through the days leading up to the Revolutionary War. The books are 144 to 190 pages long, illustrated with prints and black-and-white photographs. For readers aged 9 and up.

Tituba of Salem Village

Ann Petry; HarperCollins, 1991

The story of the Salem witch hysteria, centering around the black slave woman Tituba, whose spooky stories told to a group of teenaged girls set the stage for the ensuing trials and executions. For readers in grades 6–9.

Turkeys, Pilgrims, and Indian Corn: The Story of Thanksgiving Symbols

Edna Barth; Houghton Mifflin, 1981

A history of the Pilgrims and the first Thanksgiving. Chapter titles include "The Pilgrim Fathers," "The Pilgrim Mothers," "Pilgrim Children," "Pilgrim Clothes," "Pilgrim Houses," and "Indian Neighbors," plus assorted chapters on the history and lore of traditional Thanksgiving foods, such as pumpkins, turkey, and cranberries.

Witch Hunt: It Happened in Salem Village

Stephen Krensky; Random House, 1989

A Step Into Reading book for kids in grades 2–4, describing in six short illustrated chapters the events leading to the Salem witch trials of the 1690s and their aftermath.

Witchcraft

Cobblestone; October 1986

This issue of *Cobblestone* magazine centers around the Salem witchcraft trials, through a mix of fiction and nonfiction articles, activities, and supplementary reading suggestions. For readers in grades 5–9.

Available at most libraries or $4.50

Cobblestone Publishing, Inc.

30 Grove St.

Peterborough, NH 03458-1454

(603) 924-7209 or (800) 821-0115

Web site: www.cobblestonepub.com

See *Cobblestone* (page 449).

Who's That Stepping On Plymouth Rock?

Jean Fritz; Putnam, 1975

The hilarious (and totally true) tale of the famous rock, upon which the "First Comers" probably didn't step, from before the arrival of the *Mayflower* to the present day. Our boys were so entranced by this story that we ended up taking a trip to Plymouth, Massachusetts, where we gazed upon the actual rock (and commented disappointedly on its smallness), toured the replica of the *Mayflower* moored in Plymouth Harbor (ditto), and spent much of one afternoon quizzing the Pilgrim reenactors at nearby Plimouth Plantation about rock stepping.

The World of Captain John Smith

Genevieve Foster; Charles Scribner's Sons, 1959

A "horizontal" view of history, describing what was happening elsewhere in the world when John Smith was a young boy, a soldier, a leader of the Jamestown Colony, and an old man. Black-and-white illustrations and an interesting story-style text.

See the **World Series** (page 456).

BOOKS: FICTION

Amos Fortune, Free Man

Elizabeth Yates; Puffin, 1989

Amos Fortune, born a prince in Africa, was kidnapped as a teenager and sold into slavery in America in the 1720s. The book details Amos's long struggle to free himself and his loved ones, and describes his life in colonial New Hampshire through the years of the Revolutionary War until his death in 1801. Based on a true story.

The Courage of Sarah Noble

Alice Dalgliesh; Aladdin, 1991

Eight-year-old Sarah Noble accompanies her father to the family's new home in the Connecticut wilderness in 1707. When her father returns to Massachusetts to fetch the rest of the family, Sarah stays behind and lives with the neighboring Indians. A short chapter book for readers aged 7–10.

The House on Stink Alley

F. N. Monjo; Yearling, 1991

The story of eight-year-old Love-of-God Brewster, Pilgrim, whose family fled from England to Holland to escape religious persecution. Now the Brewsters prepare to embark on a more challenging journey: to leave for the New World on board the *Mayflower*. For readers aged 7–11.

A Journey to the New World: The Diary of Remember Patience Whipple

Kathryn Lasky; Scholastic, 1996

The story of the voyage to the New World on board the *Mayflower* through the diary of a young Pilgrim girl.

Patience records her experiences in the early days of the Plymouth colony—including her first meeting with American Indians and the tragic death of her mother. The book is based on actual Pilgrim diaries and letters; it includes a short illustrated appendix of historical background information. For readers in grades 5–9.

See the *Dear America Series* (page 452).

A Lion to Guard Us
Clyde Robert Bulla; HarperTrophy, 1989

A trio of 17th-century English children set out on their own to join their father in Jamestown after their mother dies; they finally make it, after being ship-wrecked in the Caribbean. The lion—their good-luck talisman—is an iron door knocker in the shape of a lion's head, which accompanies them through thick and thin. A short chapter book for readers aged 7–10.

On the Mayflower: Voyage of the Ship's Apprentice and a Passenger Girl
Kate Waters; Scholastic, 1996

A picture-book account of the voyage of the *Mayflower* from the point of view of Will Small, ship's apprentice, who, in the course of the long dangerous journey, makes friends with Ellen Moore, a Pilgrim girl. The book is illustrated throughout with wonderful color photographs of the *Mayflower II* and of Pilgrim reenactors from the Plimouth Plantation living-history museum.

Puritan Adventure
Lois Lenski; J. B. Lippincott, 1944

An absorbing historical novel for readers aged 8–11. *Puritan Adventure* is a story of life in the Massachusetts Bay Colony as experienced by the Partridge family: mother, father, and children Seaborn and Comfort. The colony is disrupted when the children's pretty Aunt Charity arrives from England with a wardrobe of bright-colored clothes, a sense of fun, and a love of English games and festivals. Charity charms the children, makes friends with the local Indians, and—by virtue of her kindness and bravery—proves herself an asset to the new colony, in spite of the efforts of the nasty Goody Lumpkin (who ends up on the dunking stool). Look for it at the library.

Sarah Anne Hartford: Massachusetts, 1651
Kathleen Duey; Aladdin, 1996

One of the American Diaries Series (see page 450) for readers aged 9–12. Puritan life in colonial Massachusetts through the diary of a 12-year-old girl. Sarah and her best friend, Elizabeth, are caught breaking the Sabbath—they go sliding on an icy hill—and end up in the pillory. The story centers around Sarah's struggle with her conscience and her belief in the values of her community.

Sarah Morton's Day: A Day in the Life of a Pilgrim Girl
Kate Waters; Scholastic, 1993

Sarah Morton describes the events of her day—"Come thee with me. Let me show thee how my days are"—from getting up in the morning, dressing, eating breakfast, feeding the chickens, milking the family goat, polishing the brass, studying her lessons, helping to prepare supper, and finally saying her prayers and going to bed, where she tells the events of the day to her "poppet" before she falls asleep. Illustrated with superb color photographs of Pilgrim reenactors at the Plimouth Plantation living-history museum.

In the same format: *Samuel Eaton's Day: A Day in the Life of a Pilgrim Boy* (Scholastic, 1996) and *Tapenum's Day: A Day in the Life of a Wampanoag Boy* (Scholastic, 1996).

The Sign of the Beaver
Elizabeth George Speare; Yearling, 1994

In the 1760s, 12-year-old Matt is left alone at the new family cabin in Maine while his father returns to Massachusetts for the rest of the family. His father is gone much longer than expected, and Matt survives with the help of Attean, a Penobscot boy of his own age and a member of the Beaver clan.

A video version, $29.95
Social Studies School Service
10200 Jefferson Blvd.
Box 802
Culver City, CA 90232-0802
(310) 839-2436 or (800) 421-4246
Web site: www.SocialStudies.com

Stranded at Plimouth Plantation: 1626
Gary Bowen; HarperCollins, 1994

Pilgrim life described through the journal of 13-year-old Christopher Sears, stranded at Plimouth Plantation after a shipwreck and awaiting passage south to Jamestown. Illustrated with beautiful wood-cuts. Recommended for readers aged 8–12.

Three Young Pilgrims
Cheryl Harness; Aladdin, 1995

The three young Pilgrims are the Allerton children—Mary, Remember, and Bartholomew—and this is the picture-book tale of their adventures, from the sailing of the *Mayflower* in 1620 through the first Thanksgiving in 1621. The children's story, which begins as they stand on the deck of the ship, watching for mermaids, whales, and pirates, is told against a detailed historical background. Included are colorful maps, timelines, a complete list of *Mayflower* passengers, and an account of events happening elsewhere in the world in 1620.

The Witch of Blackbird Pond
Elizabeth George Speare; Yearling, 1972

Seventeen-year-old Kit is sent from Barbados to live with her Puritan uncle's family in New England. Kit wasn't cut out to be a Puritan; her lively sense of humor and independent spirit are frowned upon by her strict new relations. She finds comfort with a new friend, Hannah, a gentle and kindly Quaker woman who, ostracized by the community, is known as the "Witch of Blackbird Pond." A wonderful read for kids aged 10–14.

COLORING AND PAPER-CRAFTS BOOKS

13 Colonies
A historical coloring book from Bellerophon, based on sphragistics, the study of seals. Included are black-and-white line drawings of the seals of the original colonies and settlements (New Amsterdam's features a chipper-looking beaver); accompanying each is a page of informational text.

$3.95

Bellerophon Books
36 Ancapa St.
Santa Barbara, CA 93101
(800) 253-9943/fax (800) 965-8286

American Family of the Pilgrim Period Paperdolls
Eight dolls, of assorted ages and sexes, and 28 different costumes, historically accurate down to the last jerkin and shift.

$3.95

Dover Publications, Inc.
31 E. Second St.
Mineola, NY 11501

Cut and Assemble the Mayflower
This kit, in booklet form, claims simple instructions and easy-to-follow diagrams; in practice, this version of the *Mayflower* has over 350 pieces, some so teeny that they have to be snipped out with manicure scissors and manipulated with tweezers. Definitely not a project for beginning model builders. Advanced builders, given enough time and determination, should end up with a 17-inch-long replica of the Pilgrims' ship, under full sail. We, unfortunately, didn't.

$6.95

Dover Publications, Inc.
31 E. Second St.
Mineola, NY 11501

Pocahontas Coloring Book
Forty-eight detailed black-line scenes from the life of Pocahontas, from her saving the life of Captain John Smith to her presentation at the British court as "Lady Rebecca."

$2.95

Dover Publications, Inc.
31 E. Second St.
Mineola, NY 11501

GAMES AND HANDS-ON ACTIVITIES

Discovery 3
A simulation of early American colonization. Participants, in small cooperative groups, take on the roles

HISTORY

of would-be colonists, practicing mapping skills in plotting overseas routes to destinations in the New World. Upon arrival, each group establishes its own separate colony, making daily political, economic, and military decisions that affect the colony's well-being, and recording their experiences in diaries. "Fate Cards," detailing sickness, food shortages, hostile Indians, or unwise leadership practices, and interactions among colonies—which may include trade competition or reciprocity, or military alliance or enmity—determine each colony's degree of success. There's a "winner" in this simulation: at the completion of the exercise, the wealthiest colony wins.

Simulation materials include 35 24-page student guides, a detailed teacher's guide, lesson plans, and reproducible student handouts. The simulation is recommended for kids in grades 5–8 and is estimated to take 15 to 23 hours, total. Though Interact simulations are designed for classroom use, they work well in smaller groups.

$51

Interact

1825 Gillespie Way, #101

El Cajon, CA 92020-1095

(800) 359-0961/fax (619) 448-6722

Web site: www.interact-simulations.com

Immigration in Colonial Times

A portfolio of primary source materials, including 10 historical documents pertaining to 17th- and early 18th-century immigration to the New World, five illustrated historical background essays, and a study guide. Essay titles include "Reason for Immigration," "English Immigrants," "Non-English Immigrants," and "The Perilous Crossing." Documents include the *Mayflower* passenger list, a 1680 gravestone rubbing, a period map, and a page of prayers to be used at sea, dating to 1636.

$37

Jackdaw Publications

Box 503

Amawalk, NJ 10501

(914) 962-6911 or (800) 789-0022/fax (800) 962-9101

The Mayflower & the Pilgrim Fathers

A portfolio of nine historical primary source documents, five illustrated historical background essays

("The First Colony," "The England They Left," "From England to Leyden," "The Mayflower," and "Of Plymouth Plantation"), explanatory notes on the documents, and a study guide. Among the historical document facsimiles are the record of the Pilgrims' original request to settle in Leyden, Holland, a copy of the first map of New England to be printed in the New World, the Plymouth Patent granted to the Pilgrims by King James I, a list of provisions that prospective settlers were advised to bring with them from England, and pages from William Bradford's *A History of Plimouth Plantation*.

$37

Jackdaw Publications

Box 503

Amawalk, NY 10501

(914) 962-6911 or (800) 789-0022/fax (800) 962-9101

Pilgrims

A cooperative simulation in which kids reenact the first year at the Plymouth Colony. Participants first group themselves into colonial teams, board the *Mayflower* (outlined on the floor), and cross the Atlantic. Then, in the New World, they collaborate in "Survival Activities" typical of early colonial life: finding food, building houses, planting crops, interacting with the Indians, and paying off their debt to their financial backers in England. Each student Pilgrim keeps a daily diary: reproducible preprinted student "Pilgrim Logs," each with an assigned writing activity, are included. The simulation culminates, if you're up to it, with a re-creation of the first Thanksgiving feast.

"Pilgrims" is recommended for four to 35 kids in grades 2–4; the unit takes an estimated 9 to 35 hours to complete.

$43

Interact

1825 Gillespie Way, #101

El Cajon, CA 92020-1095

(619) 448-1474 or (800) 359-0961/fax (619) 448-6722

Web site: www.interact-simulations.com

Salem Village and the Witch Hysteria

A portfolio of 11 historical source documents, six illustrated historical essays (among them "European Background," "Salem Village," and "The Witch Hysteria

Begins"), notes on the documents, and a detailed study guide with reproducible worksheets and suggestions for activities. Historical document reproductions include a map of Salem Village in 1692, four pages from the Salem Village Church Record Book during the trial period (with transcript), a confession from an accused witch, a jailer's bill, and a list of persons who were executed as witches.

$37

Jackdaw Publications

Box 503

Amawalk, NY 10501

(914) 962-6911 or (800) 789-0022/fax (914) 962-9101

The Voyage of the Mayflower

An "American Adventure Game" from Chatham Hill Games (see pages 447–448). We discovered this line of historical games some years ago, during a lucky visit to a museum gift shop. There are 15 games available in the series, and more in the works. All are attractive, thoroughly researched, solidly historical, inexpensive, and—best of all—fun. The games are printed on heavy paper in earthy antique colors and packaged in oversize envelopes. Each includes a paper playing board and assorted cut-and-assemble playing pieces and game spinners.

In "Voyage of the Mayflower," players attempt to sail their Pilgrim-laden ship safely across the Atlantic before their supplies run out, battling storms, contrary winds, pirates, and the horse latitudes. The game is designed for two players, one taking the part of Sailing Master, the other acting as Navigator. In an alternative version of the game, "The Race Across the Ocean," players, as Merchant Adventurers, race a pair of ships across the Atlantic from London; winner is the first to reach Massachusetts with supplies for the new Plymouth colony. The accompanying information sheet includes a historical account of the *Mayflower* voyage, a copy of the *Mayflower* passenger list, a cutaway view of the ship (showing the 102 Pilgrims crowded below deck), and suggestions for related activities. "The Voyage of the Mayflower" is also available in sturdier form as a classic board game, with a heavy-duty folding game board, cardboard playing pieces in colored plastic holders, and a professional four-color spinner.

Basic game, $6.95

Chatham Hill Games, Inc.

Box 253

Chatham, NY 12037

(518) 392-5022 or (800) 554-3039/fax (518) 392-3121

e-mail: CHGames@taconic.net

Web site: www.ocdc.com/Chatham_Hill_games

VIDEOS

The Crucible

The 1996 film version of the Arthur Miller play about the Salem witchcraft hysteria (see page 470), starring Daniel Day-Lewis and Winona Ryder as John Proctor, whose wife Elizabeth is among the accused, and Abigail Williams, one of her accusors.

Available as a rental from most video stores or $99.95

Zenger Media

10200 Jefferson Blvd.

Box 802

Culver City, CA 90232-0802

(310) 839-2436 or (800) 421-4246/fax (310) 839-2249 or (800) 944-5432

e-mail: access@ZengerMedia.com

Web site: ZengerMedia.com/Zenger

The Mayflower Voyagers

One of the This is America, Charlie Brown! Series (see page 460). There are eight episodes in this animated historical series, each about 25 minutes long. In "The Mayflower Voyagers," the Peanuts kids (and dog) participate in the founding of the Plymouth colony and attend the first Thanksgiving celebration.

$12.99

Movies Unlimited

3015 Darnell Rd.

Philadelphia, PA 19154

(215) 637-4444 or (800) 4-MOVIES

e-mail: movies@moviesunlimited.com

Web site:www.moviesunlimited.com

Plymouth Adventure

Spencer Tracy plays Christopher Jones, the crusty sea captain who transports the Pilgrims to America on the *Mayflower*. The *Adventure* takes place in black and white and lasts 105 minutes.

$14.95

Movies Unlimited

3015 Darnell Rd.

Philadelphia, PA 19154

(215) 637-4444 or (800) 4-MOVIES

e-mail: movies@moviesunlimited.com

Web site:www.moviesunlimited.com

Pocahontas

The 1995 politically correct Disney cartoon version, starring a very grown-up Pocahontas. It's not history, but it does include a terrific talking raccoon.

Available as a rental from most video stores

or $26.95 from

Movies Unlimited

3015 Darnell Rd.

Philadelphia, PA 19154

(215) 637-4444 or (800) 4-MOVIES

e-mail: movies@moviesunlimited.com

Web site: www.moviesunlimited.com

Squanto and the First Thanksgiving

Rabbit Ears Video

This 30-minute video is presented in "dissolve animation" form, which makes it seem as if viewers were participating, page by colorful page, in the reading of a storybook. The video tells the tale of Squanto's life, from his kidnapping as a young boy, through his years as a slave in Spain, his return to America, and his help to the Pilgrims as they struggled to survive their first winter at Plymouth. Narrated by Graham Greene.

$12.99

Movies Unlimited

3015 Darnell Rd.

Philadelphia, PA 19154

(215) 637-4444 or (800) 4-MOVIES

e-mail: movies@moviesunlimited.com

Web site:www.moviesunlimited.com

Three Sovereigns for Sarah

A three-part PBS miniseries starring Vanessa Redgrave and Phyllis Thaxter, in which a woman goes to court to clear the names of her two sisters, hanged for

witchcraft in Salem in 1692. A series of flashbacks tells the tale of the Salem witchcraft trials. On three cassettes, each about one hour long.

$59.95

Movies Unlimited

3015 Darnell Rd.

Philadelphia, PA 19154

(215) 637-4444 or (800) 4-MOVIES

e-mail: movies@moviesunlimited.com

Web site: www.moviesunlimited.com

THE COLONIAL PERIOD ON-LINE

13 Originals

Brief descriptions of the original 13 colonies in chronological order by date of settlement, plus extensive lists of links relating to each. Among these are connections to general history resources, genealogical sites, maps, photographs, archives and libraries, and military history listings.

www.seanet.com/users/pamur/13colony.html

America's Homepage: Plymouth, MA

A multifaceted site on the Pilgrims, including a virtual tour of Plimouth Plantation (the living-history museum in Plymouth, Massachusetts); color photographs of Pilgrim reenactors; the true story of the first Thanksgiving; biographies of famous Pilgrims and associated American Indians; the *Mayflower* passenger list; and the text of the Mayflower Compact.

www.media3.net/plymouth

Biography of William Penn

A detailed biography of the founder of the Pennsylvania colony.

www.quaker.org/wmpenn.html

Colonial American History Social Studies Resources

Information and virtual tours of many colonial history sites, stories of important colonial people, historical documents, information on colonial life and religion, and period maps.

www.bham.wednet.edu/colonial.htm

Jamestown Colony Timeline

A timeline of historical events in and around the Jamestown Colony from 1607 to 1620, with colorful kid-drawn illustrations and an informational text.

look.net/gunstonelem/GunstonElemF/Jamestown.html

Jamestown Rediscovery Project

Details of the excavation of James Fort, the first permanent English settlement in America, built in 1607. The Web site includes photographs and descriptions of artifacts, a history of Jamestown, a timeline, and maps.

www.widomaker.com/~apva

Jamestown Society

An illustrated history of Jamestown in hypertext format, information on the original settlers, and an ancestor search.

www.jamestowne.org

The Mayflower Web Pages

Includes the *Mayflower* passenger list with general and genealogical information about each Pilgrim on board, an illustrated history of the *Mayflower* itself, full texts of various Pilgrim writings, and a wealth of information about Pilgrim life and culture, including religious beliefs, clothing, weapons, and food. The site also includes a biography of Squanto.

members.aol.com/calebj/mayflower.html

Salem Witch Museum

A brief history of the Salem witchcraft hysteria, frequently asked questions about the trials, information about Roger Conant and the founding of the Salem colony, and a virtual tour of "1692 sites."

www.salemwitchmuseum.com

Salem Witch Trials Chronology

A detailed chronology of the Salem witch trials, interspersed with quotes from the accused.

www.Salemweb.com/memorial

The Spanish Missions of California

History of the early Spanish missions, a virtual tour of a mission, descriptions of typical days of the different people who lived in and near the missions

(padres, soldiers, native inhabitants), and suggestions for class projects.

tqd.advanced.org/3615

The Thirteen Colonies

List of all 13 colonies with information on many aspects of colonial life and history, including arts and crafts, education, food, houses, medicine, family life, and crime and punishment. The site includes a series of color illustrations by fifth-graders.

pen.k12.va.us/Anthology/Div/Albemarle/Schools/
Yancey/Colonies/COLONIES.HTML

A Walking Tour of Plimouth Plantation

A virtual tour of the Plimouth Plantation living-history museum in Plymouth, Massachusetts. Users can tour both the Pilgrim settlement and the nearby village of the Wampanoag Indians. Almost like being there.

spirit.lib.uconn.edu/ArchNet/Topical/Historic/
Plimoth/Plimoth.html

FRENCH AND INDIAN WAR

BOOKS

Calico Captive

Elizabeth George Speare; Yearling, 1973

In the days of the French and Indian War, young Miriam Willard is captured in an Indian raid and taken from her home in New Hampshire to Montreal, where she is sold to the French. An enthralling story, based on a true narrative of captivity published in 1807. For readers aged 10 and up.

The Fall of Quebec and the French and Indian War

George Ochoa; Silver Burdett, 1991

A 64-page history of the French and Indian War for readers aged 9–12.

Indian Captive: The Story of Mary Jemison

Lois Lenski; HarperTrophy, 1995

The book is based on the true story of a young girl captured by the Seneca Indians during the days of the

French and Indian War. Renamed Corn Tassel because of her yellow hair, Mary gradually adjusts to the Seneca culture and—with the help of her friend Little Turtle and his wise grandfather—learns to love the Seneca people.

The Last of the Mohicans
James Fenimore Cooper; Atheneum, 1986

James Fenimore Cooper's exciting and dramatic tale about Natty Bumppo (a.k.a. Hawkeye, wilderness scout), his noble Mohican companion Uncas, and their struggle to save two beautiful young maidens from the enemy Iroquois and deliver them safely to their father, commander of the British Fort William Henry, in the days of the French and Indian War. This edition includes wonderful color illustrations by N. C. Wyeth.

Several shorter versions of the book are available for younger readers, among them a 32-page volume in the Living Classics Series from Barron's Juveniles (1997).

The Matchlock Gun
Walter D. Edmonds; Troll Associates, 1990

A short chapter book set in a Dutch settlement in upstate New York during the French and Indian War. With his father off fighting with the militia, 10-year-old Edward must protect the family from Indian attack with his great-grandfather's enormous and unwieldy matchlock gun. Based on a true story. For readers aged 7–10.

VIDEOS

The Last of the Mohicans
The 1996 film version of the book (see above), starring Daniel Day-Lewis as Hawkeye. Spectacular scenery. It's rated R (for violence); parents should preview.

$19.98
Zenger Media
10200 Jefferson Blvd.
Box 802
Culver City, CA 90232-0802
(310) 839-2436 or (800) 421-4246/fax (310) 839-2249
or (800) 944-5432
e-mail: access@ZengerMedia.com
Web site: ZengerMedia.com/Zenger
or

Movies Unlimited
3015 Darnell Rd.
Philadelphia, PA 19154
(215) 637-4444 or (800) 4-MOVIES
e-mail: movies@moviesunlimited.com
Web site: www.moviesunlimited.com

The Light in the Forest
A treaty at the conclusion of the French and Indian War requires the Delaware Indians to return all white captives to their families. Among these is a young boy captured as a very small child and raised by the Indians. The movie chronicles his reluctance to return to the white world and his difficulties in adjusting to life with his original family. Based on the novel of the same name by Conrad Richter. It's a Disney movie, appropriate for kids aged 9 and up.

Available at most video rental stores or $19.99 from
Zenger Media
10200 Jefferson Blvd.
Box 802
Culver City, CA 90232-0802
(310) 839-2436 or (800) 421-4246/fax (310) 839-2249
or (800) 944-5432
e-mail: access@ZengerMedia.com
Web site: ZengerMedia.com/Zenger
or
Movies Unlimited
3015 Darnell Rd.
Philadelphia, PA 19154
(215) 637-4444 or (800) 4-MOVIES
e-mail: movies@moviesunlimited.com
Web site: www.moviesunlimited.com

FRENCH AND INDIAN WAR ON-LINE

1755: The French and Indian War Homepage
A general history of the war, lists of participating soldiers, period documents, and a book list.
web.syr.edu/~laroux

Montcalm and Wolfe
An attractive site including a general history of the French and Indian War, accounts of major battles,

information on French and British forts, and a bibliography.

www.kiva.net/~gorham/wolfe.html

EARLY AMERICAN LIFE

CATALOGS

HearthSong

ALL The catalog carries a number of colonial-style craft kits for children. Among these are simple wooden lap and tabletop looms for beginning weavers, a small quilt-making kit, beeswax candle-dipping and -rolling kits, a soap-casting kit, and a pine needle basket kit.

HearthSong

6519 N. Galena Rd.

Box 1773

Peoria, IL 61656-1773

(800) 325-2502/fax (309) 689-3857

Lark Books

9 + A catalog of craft books, kits, and supplies. A number of the kits make excellent supplements for an early American history program. The "Punch Tin Kit," for example, includes a pair of (blank) 10¾-inch-tall tin candle scones, a set of three wooden-handled punching tools, and an assortment of tin-punch patterns. The "Natural Dyeing Kit" includes six skeins of white yarn and four (premeasured) packs of colonial-style natural dyes: cochineal (scarlet), logwood (bluish purple), madder root (soft red), and osage orange (bright yellow), plus a detailed instruction book. The "Drop Spinning Video Kit" includes a hardwood drop spindle, a package of carded wool fiber, and an instructional video that shows you how to spin your own yarn. There are also kits for potential candle makers, soap makers, and weavers.

"Punch Tin Kit," $56.50; "Natural Dying Kit," $16.90; "Drop Spinning Video Kit," 29.95

Lark Books

50 College St.

Asheville, NC 28801

(800) 284-3388/fax (704) 253-0467

BOOKS

ABC Book of Early Americana

ALL Eric Sloane; Henry Holt, 1990

An alphabet book of early American tools and inventions, beautifully illustrated with detailed pen-and-ink drawings. Each illustration is accompanied by a sentence or two of interesting explanatory text. *C,* for example, is for Covered Bridge, Conestoga Wagon, Cigar-Store Indian, Coal Pan, Cornhusk Doll, Candy, and George Washington's Coffee Grinder; *P* is for Paddle Boat, Post Axe, Popcorn, Piggy Churn, Pie Peel, and Plumping Mill. (*Z* is for Zax, which is an axe for cutting roof slates.)

Child Life in Colonial Days

13 + Alice Morse Earle; Berkshire House, 1993

Earle's books, filled with quotations, anecdotes, fascinating information, and lots of human interest, are intended for adult readers, but there's much here to interest historians of all ages. *Child Life in Colonial Days* covers, for example, children's dress, school life and schoolbooks, diaries, storybooks, discipline, manners, games, and toys. Readers can learn about young Joseph Sewall who, on November 6, 1692, threw a "knop of Brass" at his sister and was soundly spanked by his father. Also by Earle: *Curious Punishments of Bygone Days* (Applewood Books, 1995), which includes such chapters as "The Stocks," "The Ducking Stool," and "The Scarlet Letter"; *Customs and Fashions in Old New England* (Berkshire House, 1990); and *Home Life in Colonial Days* (Berkshire House, 1993).

Colonial American Craftsmen Series

9 12 Leonard Everett Fisher; David R. Godine

This series of short (48 pages) paperbacks includes *The Doctors, The Papermakers, The Schoolmasters, The Tanners, The Cabinetmakers, The Printers, The Shipbuilders,* and *The Silversmiths.* Each book presents historical background, general information on the early practice of the title profession, and accounts of historical practitioners. Useful, but heavier on facts than human interest. Also see *Colonial Craftsmen* (*Cobblestone;* June 1990).

The Diary of an Early American Boy
Eric Sloane; Ballantine, 1974

The diary was kept in a little leather-bound book by a Connecticut farm boy named Noah Blake in 1805, the year Noah was fifteen. Sloane alternates original diary entries with pages of supplementary information—the tale of a year in Noah's life, told in story form—and with many detailed pen-and-ink drawings of early American tools, utensils, and buildings. Our sons were fascinated by Noah and the mechanics of his everyday life.

Everyday Life in Early America
David Freeman Hawke; HarperCollins, 1989

A 195-page history of colonial American life, including basic information and historical anecdotes. Chapter titles include "O Strange New World," "The Farm," "The House," "Health," "Manners and Morals," "Red, White, and Black"—which discusses Indians, indentured servants, and slaves—and "Wonders of the Invisible World," which covers colonial superstitions and Salem witchcraft. For teenagers.

A Gathering of Days
Joan Blos; Aladdin, 1990

Life on an early 19th-century New Hampshire farm as seen through the eyes of 13-year-old Catherine Hall, who records in her diary the death of her best friend, the remarriage of her father, and her decision to help a runaway slave. A Newbery Medal winner, for readers in grades 3–7.

In Small Things Forgotten: The Archaeology of Early American Life
James Deetz; Anchor Books, 1996

An explanation of how archaeologists learn about everyday colonial life from "small things forgotten," among them broken china, gravestones, cellar holes, garbage piles, and estate inventories. Deetz discusses both what archaeologists find and how their discoveries enable them to form a picture of early American Society.

Ox-Cart Man
Donald Hall; Viking, 1983

An early 19th-century farmer packs up the produce from his fields and all the surplus goods he and his family have made over the past year and sets off in his oxcart to trade in town. Beautiful illustrations and a simple text for kids aged 4–8.

Ox-Cart Man has been featured on the popular children's television show *Reading Rainbow.*

ACTIVITY BOOKS

Colonial Days: Discover the Past with Fun Projects, Games, Activities, and Recipes
David C. King; John Wiley & Sons, 1997

An illustrated account of the everyday life of the Mayhew family (Sarah, Nathan, Benjamin, and Anne) in the Massachusetts colony in 1732, with instructions for many colonial activities and projects, among them making candles, churning butter, dyeing wool, constructing a colonial sundial, making potpourri, and playing a native American stick toss game.

Colonial Kids: An Activity Guide to Life in the New World
Laurie Carlson; Chicago Review Press, 1997

The illustrated book includes a timeline of colonial settlement, historical background information, and instructions for many creative projects, crafts, and activities related to the colonial period. These are organized into several thematic chapters: under "Sailing and Settling," for example, kids tie knots, make a compass and a flag, and build a model ship; under "Dinnertime!," they churn butter, make trenchers, and bake a pumpkin pie; and under "Everyday Life," they make soap and cough syrup, piece a quilt, compose an almanac, and try their hands at target practice. For kids aged 5–12.

Kids' America
Steven Caney; Workman, 1978

A hands-on approach to American history, filled with information and project suggestions. Many of the activities are related to the colonial era: for example, kids make black-walnut ink, quill pens, colonial-style hats, and dried apple rings. And much more.

See listing on page 454.

10 Silhouettes: How to Cut for Fun and Money
Ann and Deirdre Woodward; Profile Press, 1987

The history and how-tos of the popular colonial art of cutting silhouettes. The book is also available as a kit, which comes with all necessary materials for silhouette making, including silhouette paper and backing.

Profile Press
3004 S. Grant St.
Arlington, VA 22202

9 Slumps, Grunts, and Snickerdoodles: What Colonial America Ate and Why

Lila Perl; Clarion, 1979

Recipes and historical information for colonial-style cooks. The book includes 13 colonial recipes, among them recipes for the title slumps, grunts, and snickerdoodles, as well as spoonbread and succotash.

COLORING BOOKS

6 Early American Crafts and Occupations Coloring Book

Peter Copeland; Dover Publications

The *Early American Crafts and Occupations Coloring Book* includes 40 detailed drawings of colonial Americans at work, among them sawyers, potters, dyers, and furniture makers: Also see the *Early American Trades Coloring Book,* which contains 44 illustrations of colonial craftspersons, including shoemakers, hatters, and glassblowers; and the *Everyday Dress of the American Colonial Period Coloring Book,* which pictures just what these workers and their customers wore. The 46 illustrations show the ordinary dress of men, women, and children, including peddlers, farmers, sailors, and many more.

$2.95 each
Dover Publications, Inc.
31 E. Second St.
Mineola, NY 11501

GAMES AND HANDS-ON ACTIVITIES

8 Made for Trade
A beautifully illustrated board game of colonial life in which players—as colonists—travel around town, attempting to acquire the items on their "Inventory Lists" from the potter, the blacksmith, the tinsmith, the silversmith, the glass shop, the music shop, the cabinetmaker, and the general store. As they move along the playing path, they cope with tithes and taxes, pay customs duties, lose turns loitering in the local tavern or languishing in "gaol," and respond to "Event Cards," which describe contemporary historical happenings, large and small. Examples: "With the first successful inoculations for smallpox in 1721, American doctors have outdone their European counterparts. Take another turn to represent this advance." "The Quartering Act of 1774 says civilians can be ordered to house British soldiers. Three soldiers have arrived at your house. Pay expenses of 2 s." The *s* stands for shilling: the game includes 60 plastic replicas of 1652 shillings, 8 colonial character playing pieces, 48 "Object Cards," each with an accurate black-and-white drawing of an early American artifact, and 60 "Event Cards." The game is recommended for two to six players, aged 8 and up.

$24
Aristoplay
450 S. Wagner Rd.
Ann Arbor, MI 48107
(800) 634-7738 or (888) GR8-GAME/
fax (734) 995-4611
Web site: www.aristoplay.com

EARLY AMERICAN LIFE ON-LINE

Candlemaking
Complete instruction for candle making plus many unusual candle-making projects.
homepage.interaccess.com/~bmolo/basics.html

HISTORY

Colonial Homes

🌐 **ALL** A color photo gallery of colonial houses, with information about their histories and original inhabitants.

www.microweb.com/harle/colonial.html

Colonial Williamsburg

🌐 **ALL** The site includes a colonial timeline, a virtual tour of the town, and detailed information on all aspects of colonial life, including food, gardens, family, holidays, tools, and trades (listed alphabetically, from "apothecary" to "wigmaker").

www.history.org

THE REVOLUTION AND THE NEW NATION

THE REVOLUTIONARY WAR

From my homeschool journal:

◆ **May 28, 1991. Josh is ten; Ethan, eight; Caleb, six.**

We're still studying the Revolutionary War era. This morning we read Longfellow's poem "Paul Revere's Ride," and followed it up with a short biography of Paul Revere. The boys were interested, since they asked a lot of questions: "How would hanging a light in the Old North Church work? The British could see it too!" "What's a yardarm?" "How did silversmiths stamp the things they made? Wouldn't a stamp just fall off?" "How hard is it to ring a huge bell? How do you stop the bell from ringing once it's swinging?" "How do you make a bell?" "What kind of silver did Paul Revere make?"

They then made colonial-style punched-tin lanterns, using hammers, nails, and giant-size juice cans. We put a candle in each and lit them, but the effect wasn't very impressive in the middle of the day; we'll try it again tonight.

BOOKS: NONFICTION

8 / 12 *Can't You Make Them Behave, King George?*
Jean Fritz; Paper Star, 1996

This is one of a series of clever, entertaining, and thoroughly researched biographies covering the main characters and events of the Revolutionary War. Many children's biographies purport to bring history to life; these really do. Irresistibly interesting. Other titles in the series include *And Then What Happened, Paul Revere?*, *What's the Big Idea, Ben Franklin?*, *Where Was Patrick Henry on the 29th of May?*, *Why Don't You Get a Horse, Sam Adams?*, and *Will You Sign Here, John Hancock?* Recommended for kids in grades 3–6; enjoyable for practically everybody.

9 / 14 *Cobblestone: American Revolution*
The September 1983 issue of *Cobblestone* magazine, *Patriotic Tales of the American Revolution*, concentrates on not-quite-so-famous people and events of the American Revolution. Included are the stories of Luther Blanchard, who played the fife at the Battle of Concord; John Honeyman, a spy for General Washington; young Sybil Ludington, who took a wild ride on horseback to warn the citizens of Danbury, Connecticut, that the British were coming; and financial wizard Haym Salomon, who helped the colonists pay for the Revolution. Also see *Boston Massacre* (March 1980), *Alexander Hamilton* (March 1987), *Loyalists of the Revolution* (August 1987), *The Adams Family* (November 1993), *Benjamin Franklin* (September 1992), *Thomas Jefferson* (September 1989), and *George Washington* (April 1992).

Available at most public libraries or $4.50 each from

Cobblestone Publishing, Inc.

30 Grove St.

Peterborough, NH 03458-1454

(603) 924-7209 or (800) 821-0115/fax (603) 924-7380

Web site: www.cobblestonepub.com

See *Cobblestone* (page 449).

David Bushnell and His Turtle: The Story of America's First Submarine

June Swanson; Atheneum, 1991

The book that convinced our history-avoiding middle child that the 18th century had its interesting bits. This is the story of the four-foot-long egg-shaped wooden submarine with which inventor David Bushnell tried to sink the British navy during the early days of the Revolution. Also see *Submarines in American History* (*Cobblestone;* January 1982).

 The Declaration of Independence

Dennis B. Fradin; Children's Press, 1994

A simple history of the writing of the Declaration of Independence, illustrated with prints, paintings, and photographs, for readers in grades 2–4.

 Fireworks, Picnics, and Flags: The Story of the Fourth of July Symbols

James Cross Giblin; Houghton Mifflin, 1983

A historical overview of the Revolutionary War, with detailed explanations of the importance of such national symbols as the Liberty Bell and the American flag and plenty of attention-catching anecdotes. Readers learn that Uncle Sam was a real person and that Ben Franklin's pick for America's national bird was the turkey.

The Fourth of July Story

Alice Dalgliesh; Aladdin, 1995

The picture-book story of the Declaration of Independence and the glorious Fourth of July for readers aged 5–9.

If You Were There in 1776

Barbara Brenner; Simon & Schuster, 1994

An account of everyday life at the time of the Revolutionary War. Brenner discusses food, clothes, work, and play as they appeared on a small New England farm, a southern plantation (either for a child in the slave quarters or in the big house), or the frontier (for a young pioneer or an American Indian). Interesting information, maps, and a bibliography of supplementary readings. For readers aged 9–12.

 King George's Head Was Made of Lead

F. N. Monjo; Coward, McCann, 1974

A short and delightful chapter book about the events leading up to the American Revolution, from the Stamp Tax through the Boston Tea Party to the Declaration of Independence, all narrated by the cantankerous statue of King George III that once stood on New York City's Bowling Green. For readers aged 7–10.

 The Secret Soldier: The Story of Deborah Sampson

Ann McGovern; Scholastic, 1990

The biography of feisty Deborah Sampson, who disguised herself as a man and fought gallantly in the American Revolution. For readers aged 8–12. Also see *Deborah Sampson Goes to War* (Bryna Stevens; Dell, 1991).

Songs and Stories from the American Revolution

Jerry Silverman; Millbrook Press, 1994

An illustrated collection of 10 ballads from the Revolutionary War era, with lyrics, guitar and piano arrangements, and historical background information about each song. Song titles include "Yankee Doodle," "The Riflemen of Bennington," and "In the Days of Seventy-Six." Illustrations include period paintings and prints.

Young John Quincy

Cheryl Harness; Simon & Schuster, 1994

An overview of the early days of the Revolutionary War through the eyes of eight-year-old John Quincy Adams, who describes the Battles of Lexington and Concord and Bunker Hill, the meeting of the Continental Congress, and the signing of Declaration of Independence.

BOOKS: FICTION

Aaron and the Green Mountain Boys

Patricia Lee Gauch; Shoe Tree Press, 1988

A picture-book tale of a young boy who aids Ethan Allen and his Green Mountain Boys in their surprise attack on the British Fort Ticonderoga. For readers aged 5–8.

The Boston Coffee Party

5 8 Doreen Rappapoort; HarperTrophy, 1990

Nobody drinks tea anymore in Boston during the Revolutionary War, so a greedy merchant decides to make a fortune by overcharging his customers for coffee and sugar. A pair of clever young sisters teaches him a lesson. An I Can Read book for beginners.

Buttons for General Washington

6 9 Peter and Connie Roop; Carolrhoda, 1987

Fourteen-year-old John smuggles messages concealed in his coat buttons out of British-occupied Philadelphia and delivers them to George Washington. Based on a true story. A simple large-print book for readers aged 6–9.

Carry On, Mr. Bowditch

12 + Jean Lee Latham; Scholastic, 1983

In the last years of the Revolutionary War, young Nat Bowditch, to his great dismay, is about to be apprenticed for nine long years to a ship chandler. This fictionalized biography follows Nat into adulthood as he masters the mathematical art of navigation, writes *The American Practical Navigator,* the famous "Sailor's Bible," and captains his own ship. Recommended for readers aged 12 and up.

Early Thunder

10 + Jean Fritz; Viking, 1987

In Salem, Massachusetts, in the days just prior to the Revolution, 14-year-old Daniel struggles with his loyalties to the king and his growing sympathy for the patriot cause. Recommended for readers aged 10 and up.

The Fifth of March: A Story of the Boston Massacre

12 + Ann Rinaldi; Gulliver Books, 1994

Fourteen-year-old Rachel, a nursemaid in the household of John and Abigail Adams, becomes friends with Matthew Kilroy, a young British soldier. When Matthew is arrested for his part in the Boston Massacre, Rachel—despite her employers' protests—visits him in prison. John Adams is instrumental in defending the accused British, who are eventually cleared. Matthew is sent back to Britain; Rachel, dismissed from her post with the Adams family, goes to Philadelphia to work for a Quaker family. A thought-provoking book that deals with multiple views of political issues and the importance of independent thinking. For readers aged 12 and up.

The Fighting Ground

11 14 Avi; HarperTrophy, 1987

Thirteen-year-old Jonathan rushes to join in the fighting in the Revolutionary War and is captured by Hessian soldiers. He discovers that war is tragic and dreadful, rather than the glorious undertaking he had imagined. A powerful historical novel for readers aged 11–14.

George the Drummer Boy

7 9 Nathaniel Benchley; HarperTrophy, 1987

The Battle of Lexington and Concord from the point of view of a young British drummer boy. A short picture book for readers in grades 2–4.

Also see *Sam the Minuteman* (page 486).

Guns for General Washington

9 13 Seymour Reit; Harcourt Brace, 1992

A fictionalized account of the heroic winter journey of Henry Knox, the bookseller who managed to transport the great guns of Fort Ticonderoga to General Washington's troops in Boston. For readers aged 9–13.

Johnny Tremain

10 + Esther Forbes; Houghton Mifflin, 1992

The gripping story of Johnny Tremain, silversmith's apprentice, who, after his hand is crippled in an accident, is swept up in the events of the Revolutionary War. A Newbery Medal winner. For readers aged 10 and up.

Also available on video (see page 490).

Katie's Trunk
5 9 Ann Turner; Aladdin, 1997

Katie and her family are Tories in Revolutionary War–era New England; when angry rebels attack the house, the frightened children hide in a big leather trunk. The kindness of a rebel leader, however, helps Katie begin to adjust to changing times. A picture book for readers aged 5–9.

Little Maid Series
9 12 Alice Turner Curtis; Applewood Books

This series of Revolutionary War–era historical fiction books features young girls caught up in the turmoil of the times. There are many titles in the series, among them *A Little Maid of Ticonderoga*, *A Little Maid of Old Philadelphia*, *A Little Maid of Old New York*, *A Little Maid of Maryland*, and *A Little Maid of Massachusetts Colony*. Enjoyable and exciting chapter books for readers aged 9–12.

Mary Alice Peale: Philadelphia, 1777
9 12 Kathleen Duey; Aladdin, 1996

Twelve-year-old Mary Alice, whose parents are wealthy loyalists, tries to help her older brother, a soldier in General Washington's army, who has been wounded in battle. The book is a volume in the American Diaries series (see pag 450), for readers aged 9–12.

My Brother Sam is Dead
10 14 James Lincoln Collier and Christopher Collier; Scholastic, 1989

Sam, a young Minuteman, is captured and executed by the British; his death devastates his family, especially his younger brother. A Newbery Award winner about conflicting loyalties during the Revolution, for readers in grades 5–9.

Phoebe the Spy
8 11 Judith Berry Griffin; Scholastic, 1991

In 1776, Phoebe Fraunces—a 13-year-old free black girl—lives in New York City, where her father is the owner of the popular Queen's Head Tavern. When her father asks for her help in protecting George Washington from a plot against his life, Phoebe rises heroically to the occasion and helps capture a poisoner. Based on a true story. For readers aged 8–11.

The Printer's Apprentice
9 12 Stephen Krensky; Bantam Doubleday Dell, 1995

Ten-year-old Gus Croft is a printer's apprentice in New York City in 1734, during the trial of John Peter Zenger. Zenger is jailed for printing articles critical of the government of the colony and of New York's Royal Governor. Gus is concerned that his master, John Bradford, refuses to get involved or to defend Zenger. Gus takes matters into his own hands, carrying a crucial letter to lawyer Andrew Hamilton, who wins Zenger a not guilty verdict. A short chapter book for readers aged 9–12.

Rabbits and Redcoats
9 12 Robert Newton Peck; Walker & Company, 1976

Young Interest Wheelock and Chapter Harrow (who wants to be a journalist like Boston's Sam Adams), armed with rabbit guns, set off to accompany Ethan Allen and his Green Mountain Boys in their famous attack on Fort Ticonderoga. For readers aged 9–12.

The Riddle of Penncroft Farm
10 + Dorothea Jensen; Harcourt Brace, 1991

Lars Olafson and his family move to a farm near Valley Forge, Pennsylvania, where Lars meets the ghost of young Geordie Hargreaves, listens to his tales of the days of the Revolutionary War, and solves a modern mystery. For readers aged 10 and up.

Sam the Minuteman
7 9 Nathaniel Benchley; HarperTrophy, 1987

Young Sam Brown, who lives on a farm in Massachusetts, participates in the Battle of Lexington and Concord. An illustrated I Can Read book, recommended for kids in grades 2–4.
Also see *George the Drummer Boy* (page 485).

Sarah Bishop
11 14 Scott O'Dell; Houghton Mifflin, 1980

Sarah's Tory father has been tarred and feathered by the rebels; her brother has been killed fighting with the Continental Army. Sarah, torn by conflicting loyalties, runs away from home. After many difficult times—she is accused of witchcraft and brought to trial—she forges a new life for herself, with the help of a Quaker. A thought-provoking book for readers aged 11–14.

Toliver's Secret

9–12 Esther Brady; Random House, 1993

Shy 10-year-old Ellen Toliver smuggles a message hidden in a loaf of bread out of British-occupied New York to George Washington's forces in neighboring New Jersey. An exciting chapter book for readers aged 9–12.

The Winter of the Red Snow: The Revolutionary War Diary of Abigail Jane Stewart

10–14 Kristiana Gregory; Scholastic, 1996

Eleven-year-old Abigail's diary details the dreadful winter of 1777 in Valley Forge, Pennsylvania. The book is based on actual diaries of the period; included is an appendix of historical resources. One of the Dear America series (see page 452), recommended for readers in grades 5–9.

Yankee Doodle: A Revolutionary Tail

5–9 Gary Chalk; Dorling Kindersley, 1993

Yankee Doodle, in this historical account, is a patriotic 18th-century mouse who relates the story of the war from the Boston Tea Party through the British surrender at Yorktown. The gist of the story is told in rhyme—"The Redcoats were surprised to find/Us Yankees set on winning./At Lexington a shot rang out,/It was the war's beginning"—with supplementary historical facts and notes in prose. All the characters are animals—mice, cats, pigs, rabbits, and frogs—and the book begins with a double-page spread of the music and words (16 verses' worth) to "Yankee Doodle."

COLORING AND PAPER-CRAFTS BOOKS

Heroes of the American Revolution

6+ This historical coloring book includes black-line portraits of prominent Revolutionary War–era figures, coloring hints, and an informational text that tells their exciting stories. Also see *A Coloring Book of the American Revolution, Flags of the American Revolution, New England Soldiers of the American Revolution, Southern Soldiers of the American Revolution,* and *Ships of the American Revolution.*

$3.95 each
Bellerophon Books
36 Ancapa St.
Santa Barbara, CA 93101
(800) 253-9943

Paper Soldiers of the American Revolution

6+ *Paper Soldiers of the American Revolution* is a collection of free-standing military men (and artillery), to be colored, cut out, and used in stirring battle reenactments. For those who prefer to play the parts of soldiers themselves, see *Caps & Helmets of the American Revolution,* which contains three sets of "splendid" paper headgear in golds and silvers to cut out, assemble, and wear.

$3.95 each
Bellerophon Books
36 Ancapa St.
Santa Barbara, CA 93101
(800) 253-9943/fax (800) 965-8286

The Story of the Revolution Coloring Book

6+ Peter F. Copeland; Dover Publications

The Story of the Revolutionary War Coloring Book includes 40 scenes of the Revolutionary War, among them the Boston Massacre, Paul Revere's ride, the Battle of Lexington and Concord, the execution of Nathan Hale, and Washington's camp at Valley Forge. Also see *Uniforms of the American Revolution Coloring Book,* which includes 31 detailed drawings of soldiers in military garb, with instructions for accurate coloring.

$2.95 each
Dover Publications, Inc.
31 E. Second St.
Mineola, NY 11501

GAMES AND HANDS-ON ACTIVITIES

The American Revolution

13+ A portfolio of primary source materials from the Revolutionary War period, containing 18 historical documents, five historical background essays ("Tea, Tax, and Trouble," "Gentleman Johnny," "The Old Fox," "The World Turned Upside Down," and "The Big Country"), and a study guide. Included among the historical document facsimiles are a letter from a colonist to the East India Company in London about the Boston Tea Party, a map of Boston and Bunker Hill, a proclamation from George III, a copy of the original Declaration of Independence (with notes and amendments), a commission in the Continental Army, American paper money, a letter written by General George Washington, and a map of Revolutionary War battlefields.

Also see "Women in the American Revolution," which includes 10 historical documents, among them an "Ode to General Washington" by poet Phillis Wheatley, and *The Treaty of Paris,* an educational packet designed by the Smithsonian Institution, which contains a 44-page teacher's guide detailing the history of the treaty, a timeline of events leading up to the treaty, games and puzzles, suggestions for student activities, and a reading list. Historical documents include a full-color map of North America in 1784, a 17 × 23-inch full-color poster titled "The Treaty of Paris 1783," portraits of John Jay, Benjamin Franklin, John Adams, and Henry Laurens, and a copy of the "Definitive Treaty."

"The American Revolution" and "Women in the American Revolution," $37 each; "The Treaty of Paris," $12.95.

Jackdaw Publications
Box 503
Amawalk, NY 10501
(914) 962-6911 or (800) 789-0022/
fax (914) 962-9101

The Battle of Bunker Hill

A simple, fast-paced strategy game for two players based on the old-fashioned "Fox and Geese," in which players attack or defend the redoubt on Breed's (not Bunker) Hill during the famous battle of June 17, 1775. The game includes historical background information and a map.

$6.95
Chatham Hill Games, Inc.
Box 253
Chatham, NY 12037
(518) 392-5022 or (800) 554-3039/fax (518) 392-3121
Web site: www.ocdc.com/Chatham_Hill_games

Flames Across the Valley

A board game based on a Revolutionary War encounter of October 1780, when Sir John Johnston's British soldiers and Indian allies attacked New York's Schoharie Valley. Invading loyalists, advancing across a paper playing board picturing a map of the valley, must contend with three American forts plus assorted stubborn settlers. The reverse side of the game board includes a historical account of the battle.

$6.95
Chatham Hill Games, Inc.
Box 253
Chatham, NY 12037
(518) 392-5022 or (800) 554-3039/fax (518) 392-3121
Web site: www.ocdc.com/Chatham_Hill_Games

Independence 2

A simulation of the years and issues leading up to the American Revolution. Participants take on the identities of either loyalists, patriots, or "neutralists," each earning "Power Points" by completing research challenges and projects, and by debating their various points of view in the Stamp Act Congress and the First and Second Continental Congresses. The unit ends with the signing of the Declaration of Independence.

Materials for the simulation include a detailed teacher's guide, a time chart, assorted historical bulletins, descriptions of student "identities," loyalist and patriot arguments to be presented in debates, "Fate Cards," and 35 eight-page student guides. The simulation is intended for 20 to 35 kids in grades 5–9, but it adapts well to smaller numbers.

$34
Interact
1825 Gillespie Way, #101
El Cajon, CA 92020-1095
(800) 359-0961
Web site: www.interact-simulations.com

The Redcoats Are Coming!

A board game based on Paul Revere's near-legendary ride. Paul Revere and William Dawes race the advancing British from Boston to Lexington and Concord, attempting to evade capture by roving patrols. To win the game, they must not only outrun the British but also save John Hancock and Sam Adams and protect the colonists' stockpiled military supplies.

$6.95
Chatham Hill Games, Inc.

Box 253

Chatham, NY 12037

(518) 392-5022 or (800) 554-3039/fax (518) 392-3121

Web site: www.ocdc.com/Chatham_Hill_Games

10 *The Revolution Game*

A board game of the Revolutionary War. The playing board is a historical map of the eastern United States, with an insert of a partial map of Europe. A pack of 50 two-sided playing cards lists the name of a historical event ("Siege of Boston," "Battle of Yorktown") or geographical location ("Pennsylvania," "France") on one side (side A) and a number on the other (side B)—which corresponds to a numbered site on the map. Side B also includes a short list of hints (Card no. 31: "American Victory; Turning Point of the War; Eastern New York; 19 Sept and 7 Oct 1777"). In the "Side A" version of the game, players draw a card from the pack and identify the event/location listed on side A by stating its number on the playing board. In the "Side B" version, players are given the number on the card and must identify the historical event or name the geographical location of the matching number of the map. In more advanced versions of play, players—as well as identifying events and locations by name and number—must provide additional information about each, such as battle outcomes, dates, and descriptions.

The game includes *The Revolution Study Guide*, which contains detailed data sheets, a Revolutionary War chronology, and a balance sheet listing relative military advantages of the opposing sides.

$10.95

Educational Materials Associates, Inc.

Box 7385

Charlottesville, VA 22906

(804) 293-GAME/fax (804) 293-5322

11 *We the People*

A challenging strategy game in which players, as Americans or British, fight the Revolution, from the shot heard around the world at Lexington and Concord to the final surrender (maybe) of Cornwallis at Yorktown. Players must use political and historical events as well as military maneuvers; strategy cards representing, for example, the Declaration of Independence or the execution of Nathan Hale, can affect the

final outcome. The game includes 96 strategy cards, 64 battle cards, and 100 color-coded playing pieces. The playing board is a map of the colonies.

Extra strategy cards are available for an expanded version of the game, bringing into play such events as the cruel winter at Valley Forge and David Bushnell's invention of the submarine, the *Turtle*.

Game; $39.95; expansion cards, $5

Avalon Hill Game Co.

4517 Harford Rd.

Baltimore, MD 21214

(410) 254-9200 or (800) 999-3222/fax (410) 254-0991

e-mail: AH GAMES@aol.com

Web site: www.avalonhill.com

VIDEOS

1776

A musical version of the argumentative meetings of the Continental Congress in the summer of 1776, ending with the landmark signing of the Declaration of Independence. Entertaining and historically informative.

$19.95

Zenger Media

10200 Jefferson Blvd.

Box 802

Culver City, CA 90232-0802

(310) 839-2436 or (800) 421-4246/fax (310) 839-2249

or (800) 944-5432

Web site: SocialStudies.com

or

Bluestocking Press

Box 2030

Shingle Springs, CA 95682-2030

(916) 621-1123 or (800) 959-8586/fax (916) 642-9222

10 *The American Revolution*

A six-part series on the American Revolution from A&E, tracing the conflict from the events immediately preceding the war to the surrender of Cornwallis at Yorktown and the early days of the new American republic. Titles in the series include "The Conflict Ignites," "1776," "Washington and Arnold," "The World at War," "England's Last Chance," and

"Birth of the Republic." Episodes contain commentary by professional historians, still photographs of historical art prints and documents, and many battle reenactments, heavy on musket fire. It's interesting and our boys enjoyed it, but if you're expecting the quality of Ken Burns's *The Civil War,* you'll be disappointed.

$79.95

Zenger Media

10200 Jefferson Blvd.

Box 802

Culver City, CA 90232-0802

(310) 839-2436 or (800) 421-4246/fax (310) 839-2249 or (800) 944-5432

8 Johnny Tremain

A video version of the book by Esther Forbes (see page 485) in which the title character, a silversmith's apprentice, becomes involved with the Sons of Liberty and eventually joins the fight against the British. A Disney film, recommended for kids in grades 4–12.

$19.99

Movies Unlimited

3015 Darnell Rd.

Philadelphia, PA 19154

(215) 637-4444 or (800) 4-MOVIES

e-mail: movies@moviesunlimited.com

Web site: www.moviesunlimited.com

12 Liberty!

A wonderful six-hour production covering American history from the end of the French and Indian War through the forging of the new American nation. The series includes readings from letters and diaries, commentary by historians, period prints and paintings, live-action reenactments, and the haunting fiddle music of Mark O'Connor. Episode titles include "The Reluctant Revolutionaries," "The Times That Try Men's Souls," and "Are We to Be a Nation?"

$59.98

PBS Home Video

1320 Braddock Pl.

Alexandria, VA 22314-1698

(800) 645-4PBS

7 11 Schoolhouse Rock: America Rock

A flashy musical rock and roll overview of American history, spotted with cartoon sequences. Songs on this 30-minute videotape include "Fireworks," "No More Kings," "The Great American Melting Pot," and "I'm Just a Bill." If your young listeners are rock and roll fans, the musical information will stick nicely in their memories. (It also sticks if they're not, but they'll make fun of the singers.)

$14.99

Movies Unlimited

3015 Darnell Rd.

Philadelphia, PA 19154

(215) 637-4444 or (800) 4-MOVIES

e-mail: movies@moviesunlimited.com

Web site: www.moviesunlimited.com

THE REVOLUTION ON-LINE

10 American Revolution On-Line

A wealth of information, including historical background on each of the 13 original colonies, descriptions of events leading to the Revolution, biographies of prominent people, military information, document texts, and information on period culture, including clothing, music, literature, and art.

users.southeast.net/~dixe/amrev/index.htm

12 The American Revolution and the Struggle for Independence

Pictures, a historical text, and links to other historical sources. This site includes an overview of American history from the colonial period through World War I.

grid.let.rug.nl/-welling/usa/revolution.html

12 Archiving Early America

Presents the text of important American documents, including the Declaration of Independence, the Constitution, and the Bill of Rights, historical maps, early American newspaper articles, a portrait gallery, biographies of prominent early Americans (including the entire text of *The Autobiography of Benjamin Franklin*), and information on "Early American Firsts!," among them the nation's first newspaper, copper penny, and political cartoon. There's also an early American crossword puzzle.

earlyamerica.com

Betsy Ross Homepage

 Includes a history of the flag, a flag timeline, an American flags picture gallery, a biography of Ross, and a virtual tour of the Betsy Ross House in Philadelphia. Visitors to the site can also learn how to cut a five-pointed star in one snip.

libertynet.org/iha/betsy

The Early America Review

An on-line "Journal of Fact and Opinion on the People, Issues and Events of 18th Century America." The site includes illustration articles on American history, a "Town Crier" page where visitors can post their own historical questions, and a puzzle.

earlyamerica.com/review

Historic Philadelphia

A virtual tour of historic Philadelphia, including Independence Hall, the Betsy Ross House, and the Liberty Bell.

libertynet.org/iha/virtual.html

IMPORTANT PEOPLE OF THE REVOLUTIONARY WAR PERIOD

BENEDICT ARNOLD

Finishing Becca: A Story About Peggy Shippen and Benedict Arnold

Ann Rinaldi; Gulliver Books, 1994

In Revolutionary War–era Philadelphia, 14-year-old Becca is a lady's maid to the wealthy Shippens' youngest daughter, the beautiful and spoiled Peggy. Becca's family has lost their money, and Becca has been told to "finish herself" by learning social skills in the Shippen household. Becca, whose brother is in George Washington's Continental Army, is appalled by the Shippens' loyalist sympathies. The British are eventually forced to leave the city, and Becca watches as Peggy meets, charms, and marries the brilliant American general Benedict Arnold—and subsequently persuades him to abandon the American cause. Enjoyable historical fiction for readers aged 12 and up.

Traitor: The Case of Benedict Arnold

Jean Fritz; Paper Star, 1997

An excellent biography for readers aged 10 and up about a complex and controversial man. "When Benedict Arnold was a teenager," Fritz begins, "some people in his hometown of Norwich, Connecticut, predicted that he'd grow up to be a success. Others said, No. Benedict Arnold would turn out badly. As it happened, everyone was right."

BENJAMIN FRANKLIN

BOOKS

The Autobiography of Benjamin Franklin

Benjamin Franklin; Macmillan, 1997

A fascinating and friendly book by a talented, articulate, and delightful man. ("By my rambling Digressions," Franklin writes ruefully, "I perceive myself to be grown old.") An engaging picture of Franklin and his times. For teenagers. Who should all read it.

Ben and Me

Robert Lawson; Little, Brown, 1988

A perennial favorite in our family. *Ben and Me,* the "Astonishing Life of Benjamin Franklin as written by his Good Mouse Amos," begins "Since the recent death of my lamented friend and patron Ben Franklin, many so-called historians have attempted to write accounts of his life and his achievements. Most of these are wrong in so many respects that I feel the time has now come for me to take pen in paw and set things right." Then follows, in 15 short, funny, and endearing chapters, a mouse's-eye view of Franklin's life, in which Amos, Ben's pet, corrects the proofs of *Poor Richard's Almanack,* flies aloft with the famous kite, and rallies the downtrodden French mice of Versailles to fight for their liberty. For readers aged 7–11.

By the same author: *Mr. Revere and I* (Little, Brown, 1988), the story of Paul Revere as told by his horse (see page 495); and *Captain Kidd's Cat* (Little, Brown, 1984), the tale of the famous pirate as told by his ship's cat, McDermot, who wears a ruby earring in one ear.

Ben Franklin's Glass Armonica
Bryna Stevens; Carolrhoda, 1992

Ben Franklin knew how to play the harp, the guitar, and the violin, and he even invented a new musical instrument: the glass armonica. Read this picture book; then fill some kitchen glasses with different amounts of water and let the kids compose their own tunes on the "musical glasses." For readers aged 5–9.

Ben Franklin's Poor Richard's Almanack for Kids
Benjamin Franklin; New Hope Press, 1994

A shortened version of Franklin's famous epigram-filled *Almanack* for readers aged 9–12.

Benjamin Franklin
Ingri and Edgar Parin d'Aulaire; Doubleday, 1987

A 48-page traditional biography of Franklin with beautiful color illustrations. For readers aged 7–10.

Benjamin Franklin
Cobblestone; September 1992

This issue of the history magazine (see *Cobblestone,* page 449) covers Franklin's family, life, and many accomplishments, with activity suggestions and a supplementary reading list. For kids in grades 5–9.

Available from most libraries or $4.50 from
Cobblestone Publishing, Inc.
30 Grove St.
Peterborough, NH 03458-1454
(603) 924-7209 or (800) 821-0115
Web site: www.cobblestonepub.com

The Many Lives of Benjamin Franklin
Aliki; Simon & Schuster, 1988

A charmingly illustrated picture-book biography of Ben Franklin. "Benjamin Franklin was born with just one life," the book begins, "But as he grew, his curiosity, his sense of humor, and his brilliant mind, turned him into a man with many lives." Ben's many lives—as a printer, a writer, a scientist, an inventor, a diplomat, and a politician—are described through a combination of simple text and captioned pictures.

Poor Richard in France
F. N. Monjo; Holt, Rinehart, and Winston, 1973

A short chapter biography of Benjamin Franklin as told by his seven-year-old grandson, Benny, who accompanied his famous grandpa on his Revolutionary War–era diplomatic mission to France. For readers aged 7–10.

What's the Big Idea, Ben Franklin?
Jean Fritz; Paper Star, 1996

A 48-page illustrated biography of Franklin, fascinatingly packed with unusual details. (He was born on Milk Street in Boston; he once wrote a poem about Blackbeard the pirate; he spent six cents to see the first lion ever brought to America.) For readers aged 8–12.

HANDS-ON ACTIVITIES

The Ben Franklin Book of Easy & Incredible Experiments
Lisa Jo Rudy, ed.; John Wiley & Sons, 1995

An 144-page activity book from Philadelphia's Franklin Institute Science Museum. Includes instructions for many Ben Franklin–related science projects, among them building a printing press, a weather station, and an optical toy shop. For kids aged 9–12.

Kites for Everyone
Margaret Greger; 1984

A terrific how-to book for young kite makers, containing precise instructions for 50 different kites. Most are very simple to make—there are sled and delta kites, for example, made from plastic trash bags—and all really fly. An excellent resource for beginners.

$13.95 from bookstores or
Into the Wind
1408 Pearl St.
Boulder, CO 80302-5307

(800) 541-0314/fax (303) 449-7315

e-mail: kites@intothewind.com

Web site: www.intothewind.com

VIDEOS

Ben and Me

6 | 10

A 25-minute animated Disney version of the book (see page 491). Cute, but the book is better.

$12.99

Movies Unlimited

3015 Darnell Rd.

Philadelphia, PA 19154

(215) 637-4444 or (800) 4-MOVIES

e-mail: movies@moviesunlimited.com

Web site: www.moviesunlimited.com

BENJAMIN FRANKLIN ON-LINE

The World of Benjamin Franklin

10 | +

A multimedia view of Franklin's life and work—political, philosophical, and scientific—through a large collection of pictures, documents, and video clips.

sln.fi.edu/franklin/rotten.html

GEORGE WASHINGTON

BOOKS

The Adventures of George Washington

8 | 12

Margaret Davidson; Scholastic, 1989

A short chapter book that recounts, in nicely readable storytelling style, the many "adventures" of George Washington, from his participation in the French and Indian War to his death in 1799. For readers aged 8–12.

George Washington

9 | 14

Cobblestone; April 1992

This issue of the magazine (see *Cobblestone,* page 449), for kids in grades 5–9, covers George Washington's life, family, and accomplishments, with activity suggestions and a supplementary reading list.

Available from most libraries or $4.50 from

Cobblestone Publishing, Inc.

30 Grove St.

Peterborough, NH 03458-1454

(603) 924-7209 or (800) 821-0115

Web site: www.cobblestonepub.com

George Washington

7 | 10

Ingri and Edgar Parin d'Aulaire; Doubleday, 1987

An oversize beautifully illustrated 60-page biography of Washington, from boyhood through his years as the first president of the new United States. The text smoothly tells the classic Washington legend. He never tells a lie, everyone loves him, and in all the pictures, he's riding a white horse.

George Washington: A Picture Book Biography

5 | 8

James Cross Giblin; Scholastic, 1998

A short simple biography illustrated with colorful paintings. The book begins with the very young George on a swing ("George Washington grew up in a big family"), and then follows George's career through the French and Indian War, the Revolution, his terms as president, and his life in retirement at Mount Vernon. Detailed appendixes include a list of important dates in Washington's life, a version of the famous cherry tree story, "George Washington's Rules of Good Behavior," a list of monuments to Washington, and information about Mount Vernon.

George Washington's Breakfast

7 | 10

Jean Fritz; Paper Star, 1998

Young George Allen, born on George Washington's birthday and named for George, wants to know what George Washington ate for breakfast. In the course of finding out—which isn't easy—he learns something about the process of historical research and a great many interesting facts about Washington. For readers aged 7–10.

George Washington's Cows

4 | 8

David Small; Farrar, Straus & Giroux, 1997

The rhyming story of George Washington's very elegant and persnickety cows, whose demands for

HISTORY

satins, perfumes, and their own special bedrooms upstairs at Mount Vernon finally drove the general into politics. For readers aged 4–8.

George Washington's Expense Account

General George Washington and Marvin Kitman; HarperCollins, 1988

A less than reverent slant on Washington. Upon taking command of the Continental Army, he refused a salary but did ask that the Congress pay his "expences." The book includes a reproduction of Washington's original expense account, as kept from 1775 to 1783, followed by a transcription of the account with funny, factual, and fascinating annotations by author Marvin Kitman. For high school–aged readers.

I Did It With My Hatchet:
A Story of George Washington

Robert Quackenbush; Pippin Press, 1989

An informational 36-page illustrated biography of Washington. Comic relief is provided by a cartoon trio of Revolutionary War soldiers, who appear at the foot of alternate pages, cracking jokes. For readers aged 8–11.

If You Grew Up With George
Washington

Ruth Belov Gross; Scholastic, 1993

Everyday life in Washington's time, presented through a conversational question-and-answer format. "What kind of a house did George Washington live in when he was a little boy?" "What did children do to have fun?" "What kind of school did George Washington go to?"

See If You . . . Series (pages 453–454).

GAMES AND HANDS-ON ACTIVITIES

ConFigure

This unusual game of mosaic pattern formation is played on a board that pictures the floor plan of either Washington's boyhood home, Little Hunting Creek Plantation, or the larger, expanded version of the house, now known as Mount Vernon. Players use a collection of attractive marbleized two-color tiles, in squares and triangles, to cover each room of the floor plan in one- or two-color patterns. A brief history of George Washington's homes, an explanation of mathematical means for calculating area, and instructions for four different games are included with each "ConFigure" set. History, with a mathematical twist.

"George Washington's Boyhood Home" set, $29.95; the "Mount Vernon" set, $44.95. Available from game stores or
Learning Passport Co.
7104 Loch Lomond Dr.
Bethesda, MD 20817
(301) 229-9630 or (800) U-LEARN-2
fax (301) 229-5940
Web site: www.learningpassport.com

George Washington and His
Family Paper Dolls

George and Martha Washington, and Martha's two children, Jacky and Patsy Custis, plus period costumes.
$3.95
Dover Publications, Inc.
31 E. Second St.
Mineola, NY 11501

VIDEOS

George Washington

This five-part PBS miniseries, first aired in 1984 and 1986, covers Washington's life from his Virginia boyhood through his participation in the French and Indian War, his command of the Continental Army during the Revolution, his attendance at the Constitutional Convention, and his presidency. With Barry Bostwick as George and Patty Duke Astin as Martha.
$79.95
Movies Unlimited
3015 Darnell Rd.
Philadelphia, PA 19154
(215) 637-4444 or (800) 4-MOVIES
e-mail: movies@moviesunlimited.com
Web site: www.moviesunlimited.com

GEORGE WASHINGTON ON-LINE

Biography of George Washington
The life and accomplishments of Washington, including myths and legends (the cherry tree), anecdotes, and excerpts from his personal journal.

www.mountvernon.org/image/george.html

Historic Mount Vernon
A virtual tour of George Washington's plantation, information on archaeological projects at Mount Vernon, a picture gallery, an on-line quiz, and assorted educational resources.

www.mountvernon.org

PAUL REVERE AND OTHER REVOLUTIONARY RIDERS

BOOKS

Jack Jouett's Ride
Gail Haley; Viking, 1976

Thomas Jefferson owed his life to Jack Jouett, who took a wild ride through the Virginia countryside to warn Jefferson, Patrick Henry, and other Virginia patriots that the British were marching toward Charlottesville. A 32-page picture book, illustrated with watercolor-tinted woodcuts.

Mr. Revere and I
Robert Lawson; Little, Brown, 1953

The story of Paul Revere as told by his horse, Scheherazade—once the pride of His Royal Majesty's 14th Regiment of Foot, now a dedicated rebel. A humorous and delightful account of the early days of the Revolution for readers aged 9–12.

By the same author, see *Ben and Me* (page 491).

Paul Revere's Ride
Henry Wadsworth Longfellow; Greenwillow, 1985

"Listen, my children, and you shall hear/Of the midnight ride of Paul Revere. . . ." Longfellow's famous poem, beautifully illustrated by Nancy Winslow Parker.

Sybil Rides for Independence
Drollene P. Brown; Albert Whitman, 1985

An account of the dangerous ride of 16-year-old Sybil Ludington, warning the minutemen of a British attack on the town of Danbury, Connecticut. For readers aged 7–10.

This Time, Tempe Wick?
Patricia Lee Gauch; Putnam, 1992

Tempe—short for Temperance—Wick of Morristown, New Jersey, helps the soldiers who camp on her family's farm until they decide to mutiny and one of them tries to steal her beloved horse. Cleverly she hides it in her bedroom. For readers aged 7–10. A longer account of the same story for readers aged 12 and up is *A Ride Into Morning: The Story of Tempe Wick* (Ann Rinaldi; Gulliver Books, 1995).

GAMES

The Redcoats Are Coming!
A board game based on Paul Revere's famous ride. Revere and corider William Dawes race from Boston to Lexington, attempting to outrun the advancing British, to save John Hancock and Sam Adams from capture, and to protect the colonists' military stores. The game includes historical background information and a map.

$6.95

Chatham Hill Games, Inc.

Box 253

Chatham, NY 12037

(518) 392-5022 or (800) 554-3039/fax (518) 392-3121

Web site: www.ocdc.com/Chatham_Hill_Games

THOMAS JEFFERSON

BOOKS

Grand Papa and Ellen Aroon
F. N. Monjo; Holt, Rinehart, and Winston; 1974

Jefferson's life as told by his youngest and favorite granddaughter, Ellen Randolph. Nine-year-old Ellen quotes letters from her famous grandpa, mentions Jefferson's pet mockingbird, Dick, describes Jefferson's "whirligig chair," counts the different kinds of peas in Jefferson's garden, lists the names of Jefferson's mules, and looks forward to the arrival of a live prairie dog sent to Monticello by the Lewis and Clark Expedition.

Pass the Quill, I'll Write a Draft

8 12 Robert Quackenbush; Pippin Press, 1989

A solidly informational but somewhat dry 36-page biography of Jefferson, which gives readers the nuts and bolts of the election of 1800, the repeal of the Alien and Sedition Acts, and the Louisiana Purchase. Brief interesting asides about Jefferson's life, interests, and inventions are mentioned in cartoon conversation balloons, by a pair of busy kids playing with building blocks.

A Picture Book of Thomas Jefferson

4 8 David A. Adler; Holiday House, 1991

A short, simple biography for your youngest Jeffersonians, with color illustrations.

Thomas Jefferson

9 14 *Cobblestone;* September 1989

This issue of *Cobblestone* magazine (see page 449) is devoted to Thomas Jefferson. Various short articles cover Jefferson's childhood, his writing of the Declaration of Independence, his inventions, his years as president, his scientific interests, and his gardens. Also included: a puzzle based on major events in Jefferson's life, a Jeffersonian timeline, and a play based on Jefferson's early years in the Virginia House of Burgesses.

Available from most libraries or $4.50 from
Cobblestone Publishing, Inc.
30 Grove St.
Peterborough, NH 03458-1454
(603) 924-7209 or (800) 821-0115
Web site: www.cobblestonepub.com

Thomas Jefferson: Man on a Mountain

Natalie Bober; Aladdin, 1997

A thoroughly researched 300+-page account of Jefferson's life and times for readers aged 12 and up.

Thomas Jefferson: Man with a Vision

9 12 Ruth Crisman; Scholastic, 1992

A solid 152-page biography of Jefferson, illustrated with black-and-white prints. It's recommended for kids in grades 3–6, but my guess is that it's a little much for the average third-grader.

HANDS-ON ACTIVITIES

Colonial Writing Supplies

For a hands-on Jeffersonian experience, try writing your own Declaration of Independence with a quill pen and a packet of Bolton's ink powder ("A convenient portable powder for the instant making of ink"; just add water).

Pens, $1.50 each; ink powder, $4.25
Bluestocking Press
Box 2030
Shingle Springs, CA 95682-2030
(916) 621-1123 or (800) 959-8586/fax (916) 642-9222

A Delightful Recreation: The Music of Thomas Jefferson

The Colonial Williamsburg Foundation, 1993

Jefferson considered music "a delightful recreation." Some of his favorites are performed here by the Governor's Musick of Colonial Williamsburg, on violin, harpsichord, and German flute. Included are pieces by Vivaldi, Corelli, Handel, and Purcell.

$10.95 on audiocassette; $16.95 on CD. From music stores or
Audiovisual Distribution
Box 1776
Williamsburg, VA 23187-1776

Great Buildings Model Kit

Julian Bicknell and Steve Chapman; Clarkson N. Potter, 1995

Includes materials and instructions for building scale card-stock models of four famous buildings, among them Thomas Jefferson's Monticello. An accompanying informational booklet contains color photographs of Monticello and historical background.

HISTORY

Monticello Resource Packets

The Education Department of the Thomas Jefferson Memorial Foundation publishes a series of resource packets for interested students of Jefferson. Each includes a teacher's guidebook, assorted student lesson plans, and reproducible facsimiles of primary source materials. Titles include "Thomas Jefferson's Family Life" (four lessons, grades 3–6), "Monticello Architecture" (three lessons, grades 3–6), "Jefferson and Travel," "Monticello: A Working Plantation," "Thomas Jefferson: Architect," "Digging Monticello: Archaeology at Monticello Today," and "Finding Isaac Jefferson."

> $10 to $30
> Education Dept. of the Thomas Jefferson Memorial
> Foundation
> Box 316
> Charlottesville, VA 22902

VIDEOS

Jefferson in Paris

A 1994 film with Nick Nolte in the title role. A beautiful production, but our sons—two of whom really *like* history—found it slow and dull. Parents should preview it if they think their children might be interested; there's a lush scene or two with Sally Hemings.

> Movies Unlimited
> 3015 Darnell Rd.
> Philadelphia, PA 19154
> (215) 637-4444 or (800) 4-MOVIES
> e-mail: access@ZengerMedia.com
> Web site: www.moviesunlimited.com

Thomas Jefferson

The life of Thomas Jefferson on two videocassettes by master filmmaker Ken Burns. Part One covers Jefferson's early life and marriage, his writing of the Declaration of Independence, and his years in Paris, as U.S. Minister to France. Part Two covers his vice presidency under John Adams, his struggles with the Federalists, highlights of his own presidency, including the Louisiana Purchase, and his later years at Monticello. An interesting three hours about a brilliant and controversial man.

> $29.98
> PBS Home Video
> Box 4030
> Santa Monica, CA 90411
> (800) 645-4PBS
> Web site: www.pbs.org
> or
> Zenger Media
> 10200 Jefferson Blvd.
> Box 802
> Culver City, CA 90232-0802
> (310) 839-2436 or (800) 421-4246/fax (310) 839-2249
> or (800) 944-5432
> e-mail: access@ZengerMedia.com
> Web site: ZengerMedia.com/Zenger

Thomas Jefferson: A View From the Mountain

A two-cassette biography of Jefferson, concentrating on Jefferson's attitudes toward slavery. Attractive film footage, but otherwise a politically correct attempt to evaluate an 18th-century man by 20th-century standards.

> $29.98
> PBS Home Video
> Box 4030
> Santa Monica, CA 90411
> (800) 645-4PBS
> Web site: www.pbs.org
> or
> Zenger Media
> 10200 Jefferson Blvd.
> Box 802
> Culver City, CA 90232-0802
> (310) 839-2436 or (800) 421-4246/fax (310) 839-2249
> or (800) 944-5432
> e-mail: access@ZengerMedia.com
> Web site: ZengerMedia.com/Zenger

THOMAS JEFFERSON ON-LINE

Thomas Jefferson

A multimedia presentation of the life and works of Thomas Jefferson, with links to other web sites.

> grid.let.rug.nl/-welling/usa/jefferson.html

THE CONSTITUTION

Books

Cobblestone: Starting a New Nation
Several issues of *Cobblestone*, the history magazine for kids in grades 5–9 (see page 449), center around the Constitution and the establishment of the new American nation. These include *The Constitutional Convention* (September 1987), *The Meaning of the Constitution* (September 1982), *Our Bill of Rights* (September 1991), and *Starting a Nation: 1780–1790* (September 1984).

> Available from most libraries or $4.50 each from
> Cobblestone Publishing, Inc.
> 30 Grove St.
> Peterborough, NH 03458-1454
> (603) 924-7209 or (800) 821-0115
> Web site: www.cobblestonepub.com

The Constitution
Warren Colman; Children's Press, 1987

The Constitution, in six very short, large-print chapters, covers the history and content of our nation's most important document, with lots of colorful illustrations. Also see, by the same author, *The Bill of Rights*, in the same format, which clearly explains the first 10 amendments to young readers. For kids in grades 2–4.

The Great Little Madison
Jean Fritz; Paper Star, 1998

An absorbing 160-page biography of James Madison, our fourth (and shortest) president, which covers in detail Madison's role in the writing and ratification of the Constitution.

If You Were There When They Signed the Constitution
Elizabeth Levy; Scholastic, 1992

The story of the Constitutional Convention of 1787, told in question-and-answer format. "What rules did the thirteen states have before the Constitution?" "What were the delegates like?" "What was the first big argument?" "What was the 'Great Compromise'?" "How did the delegates invent a President?" "What is an amendment?"

See *If You . . . Series* (pages 453–454).

A More Perfect Union: The Story of Our Constitution
Betsy and Giulio Maestro; Mulberry, 1990

An attractive 48-page picture-book story of the writing of the Constitution, with a short no-nonsense text. An appendix of "Additional Information" at the back briefly summarizes the articles of the original Constitution and its subsequent amendments, lists the signers of the Constitution by state, and lists (in order) the date of each state's ratification of the Constitution.

Shh! We're Writing the Constitution
Jean Fritz; Paper Star, 1998

A fascinating account of the debates surrounding the writing of the Constitution, plus some interesting asides on the personalities and activities of the delegates. (George Washington wrote home worrying about his carrots; Oliver Ellsworth of Connecticut took time off from the Constitutional Convention to go see an Egyptian mummy; Elbridge Gerry of Massachusetts fussed about everything so much that the other delegates called him "Grumbletonian.") For readers aged 8–12.

The U.S. Constitution for Everyone
Mort Gerberg; Perigee Books, 1991

The annotated Constitution and amendments, in 64 clearly documented pages. An introductory chapter gives a brief but interesting history of the writing of the Constitution; the remainder of the book consists of the text of the Constitution and its 26 amendments, printed on the left-hand pages, and, on the facing right-hand pages, explanatory notes and additional information. If you or your older kids have never sat down and read the Constitution all the way through, this is the way to do it.

We the People: The Constitution of the United States of America
Peter Spier; Doubleday, 1991

The book opens with an account of the Constitutional Convention and ratification; then follows a wonderful visual presentation—in many colorful little pictures—of the points in the Constitution's preamble. "We the People of the United States," for example, is followed by pictures of people from all walks of life, in both colonial and modern periods: farm families and city dwellers, blacksmiths, preachers, schoolchildren, and factory workers. "In Order to form a more Perfect Union" is accompanied by pictures showing various aspects of the democratic process: debates between candidate, voting booths, campaign posters, the floor of the Senate, a panorama of Washington, D.C., at night. The complete text of the Constitution is included.

ACTIVITY BOOKS

The Making of the Constitution

A portfolio of primary source documents on the writing and ratification of the Constitution. Included are nine facsimiles of historical documents, five detailed historical background essays, and a study guide. Among the historical documents are a map of the United States from the year 1784, a chronology of the making of the Constitution, a list of the delegates' names, copies of Edmund Randolph's "Virginia Plan" and George Mason's speech on slavery, a collection of portraits of key convention participants, and a broadside version of the Constitution itself.

> $37
> Jackdaw Publications
> Box 503
> Amawalk, NY 10501
> (914) 962-6911 or (800) 789-0022/fax (914) 962-9101

The Story of the Constitution

A study unit on the Constitution for students aged 11–13. The portfolio contains a resource book, a "Jackdaw Times" historical newspaper, and a collection of 10 period documents. The resource book includes a history of the Constitution, entertaining biographies of key persons in its composition, a timeline of events, and assorted puzzles, problems, and activity suggestions. Documents include a copy of the Constitution itself, a period map, the U.S. census of 1790, James Madison's will, and an engraving of George Washington's inauguration.

> $37
> Jackdaw Publications
> Box 503
> Amawalk, NY 10501
> (914) 962-6911 or (800) 789-0022
> fax (800) 962-9101

VIDEOS

This is America, Charlie Brown; Volume 6: The Birth of the Constitution

Charlie Brown and company travel to the Constitutional Convention in Philadelphia, 1787, where they learn a good deal about the principles upon which our government was founded.

> $12.99
> Movies Unlimited
> 3015 Darnell Rd.
> Philadelphia, PA 19154
> (215) 637-4444 or (800) 4-MOVIES
> e-mail: movies@moviesunlimited.com
> Web site: www.moviesunlimited.com
> or
> Zenger Media
> 10200 Jefferson Blvd.
> Box 802
> Culver City, CA 90232-0802
> (310) 839-2436 or (800) 421-4246/fax (310) 839-2249
> or (800) 944-5432
> Web site: ZengerMedia.com/Zenger

THE CONSTITUTION ON-LINE

The Constitution On-line

The entire text of our nation's most important document.

> www.house.gov/Constitution/Constitution.html

THE LEWIS AND CLARK EXPEDITION

BOOKS

The Incredible Journey of Lewis & Clark

Rhoda Blumberg; Beech Tree Books, 1995

A terrific 144-page account of the Lewis and Clark Expedition, heavily illustrated with maps, portraits, photographs, art reproductions, and sketches from William Clark's journal. The detailed text is filled with historical information, anecdotes, fascinating facts, and original journal quotes.

 9 13 *Lewis and Clark*
Cobblestone, September 1980

This issue of the magazine (see *Cobblestone*, page 449) includes biographical information about Meriwether Lewis, William Clark, and Sacagawea, plus information on the expedition, a map of its route, and a supplementary reading list.

> Available from most libraries or $4.50 from
> Cobblestone Publishing, Inc.
> 30 Grove St.
> Peterborough, NH 03458-1454
> (603) 924-7209 or (800) 821-0115
> Web site: www.cobblestonepub.com

HANDS-ON ACTIVITIES

13 + *Lewis and Clark Expedition: 1804–1806*
A portfolio of primary source documents, maps, and charts. Also included are five historical background essays ("The Louisiana Purchase." "Preparing for the Journey," "The Voyage of Discovery," "The Legacy of the Expedition," and "Contemporary Expeditions"), a timeline of expedition events, and a detailed study guide with reproducible worksheets. Among the historical documents are a map of the Louisiana Territory from 1757, a copy of President Jefferson's instructions to the expedition, maps and sketches from Clark's journals, and a copy of an 1806 newspaper article on the return of Lewis and Clark.

> $37
> Jackdaw Publications
> Box 503
> Amawalk, NY 10501
> (914) 962-6911 or (800) 789-0022/fax (800) 962-9101

6 + *Lewis and Clark Expedition*
Coloring Book

> Peter F. Copeland; Dover Publications

Illustrations picture the expedition's departure from Missouri, travels by land and river, encounters with the Indians, and all the members of the party, including, of course, Sacagawea. With explanatory captions.

> $2.95
> Dover Publications, Inc.
> 31 E. Second St.
> Mineola, NY 11501

VIDEOS

10 + *Lewis & Clark: The Journey*
of the Corps of Discovery

A superb history of the Lewis and Clark Expedition as documented by master filmmaker Ken Burns. The program covers the lives and experiences of the members of the expedition and traces their journey from coast to coast, using period artwork, journal excerpts, commentary by historians, and beautiful landscape photography. Four hours on two videocassettes.

> $29.98
> PBS Home Video
> 1320 Braddock Pl.
> Alexandria, VA 22314-1698
> (800) 645-4PBS
> Web site: www.pbs.org

4 9 *The Song of Sacajawea*
The story of the young Indian woman who accompanied Lewis and Clark on their expedition to the Pacific Ocean in the early 19th century. The story is presented in "dissolve animation" sequence, which gives the viewers the effect of reading a picture book. Narrated by Laura Dern. The video is about 30 minutes long.

> $14.99
> Movies Unlimited
> 5015 Darnell Rd.
> Philadelphia, PA 19154
> (215) 637-4444 or (800) 4-MOVIES
> e-mail: movies@moviesunlimited.com
> Web site: www.moviesunlimited.com

LEWIS AND CLARK ON-LINE

6 + *Lewis and Clark*
The site, based on the Ken Burns film (see above), includes a map of the expedition's journey, a timeline,

journal excerpts, biographical information about expedition members, a copy of the expedition's equipment list, general historical background, and lesson plans and activity sheets for middle school students, with suggestions for extensions and adaptations for high school– and elementary-level kids.

www.pbs.org/lewisandclark

AMERICAN INDIANS

Also see **Pre-Columbian America** (pages 461–464).

From my homeschool journal:

◆ **January 22, 1990. Josh is eight; Ethan, seven; Caleb, five.**

The boys all took a class on "Navajo Lifeways" this past weekend at the Colorado History Museum. They enjoyed it thoroughly—all three talked about it a mile a minute all the way home in the car. They played Navajo games, sampled Navajo food, made sandpaintings, were taken on a tour of the museum's Navajo exhibits, tried carding and spinning wool, saw a display of Navajo textiles, and met a real Navajo Indian (named David) and his daughter, who told Navajo folktales. All three boys received Navajo names: Josh's was Askinez, which means "Tall Boy"; Caleb's was Nahte, which means "Leader"; and Ethan lost his name tag.

Navajo enthusiasm was still running so high today that we continued Navajo projects this morning in homeschool. We read a couple of picture books on the Navajo and an assortment of Navajo legends, located Navajo territory on a map of the United States, and the boys designed and colored Navajo blankets and turquoise squash-blossom necklaces. We then made belt looms out of craft sticks; when the glue dries, the boys plan to weave Navajo headbands.

CATALOGS

Ancient Graffiti

A collection of high-quality American Indian arts-and-crafts kits. Among these are the Southwest Amer-

ican Indian Pottery Making Kit, which contains two pounds of clay, a handmade twig brush and scraper, four natural pigments for decoration, and a booklet of historical information; and the "Southwest Fetish Carving Kit," which includes soapstone, turquoise, beads, feathers, and imitation "sinew," plus an instruction booklet. (Carving can be done with a kitchen knife; you'll need to supply your own.) The company also makes totem pole kits, an Indian dart game kit (see page 508), jewelry-making kits, and rock art kits.

Ancient Graffiti
52 Seymour St.
Middlebury, VT 05753
(802) 388-2919 or (888) 725-6632
e-mail: ancientg@sovernet.com

Curiosity Kits

There are several Curiosity Kits available for kids interested in traditional Indian crafts. These include a "Wooden Bead Loom" kit, with which users build and string a 10½ × 6½-inch loom and use it to weave three different bead projects; an "American Indian Pottery" kit, with which kids made a coiled red-clay painted pot; a "Southwest Jewelry" kit, containing silver feathers, liquid silver tubes, silver and turquoise beads, and mother-of-pearl fetishes, with instructions for making Indian-style necklaces and earrings; a "Native American Kachina" kit, with which kids paint and decorate a ceramic kachina doll; and—our favorite—an "American Indian Moccasins" kit, with which users design, stitch, and decorate a pair of beaded moccasins. (They're felt, not deerskin, but kids get the idea.) The kits, include *all* necessary materials.

Available at toy and crafts stores
or for a local source, contact
Curiosity Kits
Box 811
Cockeysville, MD 21030
(410) 584-2605 or (800) 584-KITS/fax (410) 584-1247
e-mail: CKitsinc@aol.com

HearthSong

The catalog carries a number of Indian crafts kits for kids of all ages. Examples include moccasin kits, turquoise jewelry–making kits, bead looms, mask-making kits, and soapstone-carving kits.

HearthSong
6519 N. Galena Rd.
Box 1773
Peoria, IL 61656-1773
(800) 325-2502/fax (309) 689-3857

Roots and Wings

This creative catalog of multicultural and educational materials carries an excellent collection of American Indian resources. Included are teaching guides, crafts and activity books, maps, nonfiction accounts of Indian histories, cultures, and modern Indian life, and collections of Indian legends.

Roots and Wings
Box 19678
Boulder, CO 80308-2678
(800) 833-1787/fax (303) 776-6090
Web site: www.rootsandwingscatalog.com

BOOKS: NONFICTION

Ahyoka and the Talking Leaves
Peter and Connie Roop; Beech Tree Books, 1994

A fictionalized 60-page biography of the Cherokee scholar Sequoya, who devised the Cherokee alphabet and written language, as told through the eyes of his little daughter, Ahyoka. The Cherokee syllabary is included at the front of the book.

Buffalo
Emilie U. Lepthien; Children's Press, 1989

The story of the buffalo, past and present, in large print, illustrated with great color photographs. The book, in short simple text, covers the natural history of the buffalo, Indian buffalo hunts, the importance of the buffalo to the Indian way of life, the 19th-century slaughter of the buffalo, and the buffalo today.

Buffalo Hunt
Russell Freedman; Holiday House, 1995

The story of the buffalo hunt and the central importance of the buffalo in Plains Indian life, with over 30 reproductions of paintings by such Western artists as George Catlin and Karl Bodmer. For readers aged 9–13.

Bury My Heart At Wounded Knee: An Indian History of the American West
Dee Brown; Henry Holt, 1991

A painful account of the 19th-century Indian Wars and the extermination of the Plains Indian tribes. The book, originally published in 1971, was one of the first attempts to present American history from an Indian point of view. For high school students.

Cobblestone: American Indians

Cobblestone publishes several excellent educational magazines for children, including *Faces* (see page 411) and *Cobblestone* (see page 449). Several issues of *Faces* magazine concentrate on American Indian tribes and cultures. Among these are *Around the Arctic* (November 1989), which includes nonfiction articles on Arctic Indian tribes, an Eskimo legend "The Old Man and the Volcano," and instructions for making paper snowflakes; *The Iroquois* (September 1990), which contains nonfiction accounts of the Iroquois League, an article on the Iroquois language, Iroquois folktales, instructions for playing "The Sacred Bowl Game," and a recipe for succotash; and *Plains Indians* (October 1992), which includes nonfiction articles about Plains Indians, historical and modern, a Pawnee folktale, "Lone Boy and the Old Dun Horse," and instructions for making corncob darts and pemmican patties.

Cobblestone magazine issues featuring American Indian themes include *The Cherokee Indians* (February 1984), *Dine: The People of the Navajo Nation* (July 1989), *The Eskimos of Alaska* (November 1985), *Indians of the Northeast* (November 1994), *Indians of the Northwest* (November 1992), *Joseph, a Chief of the Nez Perce* (September 1990), and *The Sioux* (June 1992). Each includes both fiction and nonfiction articles, activities and puzzles, and a supplementary reading list.

Back issues of *Faces* and *Cobblestone* are available from most libraries or $4.50 from
Cobblestone Publishing, Inc.
30 Grove St.
Peterborough, NH 03458-1454
(603) 924-7209 or (800) 821-0115/fax (603) 924-7380
Web site: www.cobblestonepub.com

HISTORY

Corn Is Maize: The Gift of the Indians
5
9
Aliki; HarperTrophy, 1986

A delightfully illustrated picture-book account of the science and history of corn, with information about the ancient peoples who first grew it. Included are simple instructions for making a corn-husk wreath, the only really tricky part of which is bending a coat hanger into a perfect circle.

Also see *The Popcorn Book* (page 504) and *People of the Corn* (page 463).

First Books: Indians of the Americas
8
12
Franklin Watts

This series of books covers the cultures, histories, and traditions of individual North and South American tribes. Each volume, recommended for readers in grades 4–6, is 64 pages and illustrated with color photographs. Titles in the series include *The Abenaki* (Elaine Landau; 1996), *The Algonquians* (Patricia Ryon Quiri; 1992), *The Apaches and Navajos* (Katherine M. and Craig A. Doherty; 1989), *The Aztecs* (Donna Walsh Shepherd; 1992), *The Cherokees* (Elaine Landau; 1992), *The Chilula* (Elaine Landau; 1994), *The Chippewa* (Jacqueline D. Greene; 1993), *The Comanches* (Judith Alter; 1994), *The Creek* (Shirlee P. Newman; 1996), *The Hopi* (Elaine Landau; 1994), *The Incas* (Shirlee P. Newman; 1992), *The Inuits* (Shirlee P. Newman; 1993), *The Iroquois* (Katherine M. and Craig A. Doherty; 1989), *The Maya* (Jacqueline D. Greene; 1992), *The Nez Perce* (Madelyn Klein Anderson; 1994), *The Ottawa* (Elaine Landau; 1996), *The Pawnee* (Arthur Myers; 1993), *The Penobscot* (Katherine M. and Craig A. Doherty; 1995), *The Pomo* (Elaine Landau; 1994), *The Pueblos* (Suzanne Powell; 1993), *The Seminoles* (Martin Lee; 1989), *The Shawnee* (Elaine Landau; 1996), *The Shoshoni* (Alden R. Carter; 1989), *The Sioux* (Elaine Landau; 1989), *The Wampanoag* (Katherine M. and Craig A. Doherty; 1995) and *The Zunis* (Katherine M. and Craig A. Doherty; 1993).

Teachers' guides are available to accompany the books: *Teachers Guide for First Books—Indians of the Americas: Volume One* and *Volume Two* (Sharon Spencer; 1995). Each includes individual lesson plans for 10 of the books, plus reproducible maps and worksheets.

Indian Chiefs
9
12
Russell Freedman; Holiday House, 1992

Biographies of six prominent Indian chiefs, illustrated with wonderful historical photographs. Subjects include Red Cloud, Santana, Quanah Parker, Washakie, Chief Joseph, and Sitting Bull.

Indian Signals and Sign Language
6
+
George Fronval and Daniel Dubois; Wings Books, 1994

The how-tos of sign language, each sign or signal illustrated with a color photograph of a signing American Indian in native costume. Included are signs for familiar objects, names of family members, animals, events of daily life, happenings "on the trail," and feelings or emotions.

Native American Resource Library
5
13
Dana Newmann; Center for Applied Research in Education

A series of illustrated 200-page sourcebooks packed with historical and cultural information, biographies, myths and legends, arts and crafts, games, and activities for kids in grades K–8. Each book centers around the tribes of a different geographical region. Titles include *Ready-to-Use Activities and Materials on Desert Indians* (1995), *. . . on Plains Indians* (1995), *. . . on Coastal Indians* (1996), and *. . . on Woodlands Indians* (1997).

New True Books: American Indians
7
9
Children's Press

A series of informational 48-page large-print books for kids in grades 2–4, heavily illustrated with historical engravings, art reproductions, maps, and color photographs. The series includes 32 books on individual American Indian tribes. Each covers, in a few very short, simple chapters, the history of the tribe and characteristic features of its culture.

Titles include *The Anasazi, The Apache, The Aztec, The Cayuga, The Cherokee, The Cheyenne, The Chippewa, The Choctaw, The Chumash, The Crow, The Delaware, The Eskimo: Inuit and Yupik People, The Hopi, The Inca, The Mandans, The Maya, The Menominee, The Mohawk, Native Americans, The Navajo, The Nez Perce, The Oneida, The Onondaga, The Pawnee, The*

Penobscot, The Pomo, The Seminole, The Seneca, The Shoshoni, The Sioux, The Tlingit, and *The Tuscarora.*

North American Indian Sign Language

Karen Liptak; Franklin Watts, 1992

A brief illustrated history of Indian sign language and instructions for how to speak it, arranged dictionary-style, with easy-to-imitate little diagrams of moving hands. Readers can learn how to say "How old are you?," "I want to eat now," and "We hunt buffalo on the prairie." By the same author: *North American Indian Ceremonies* (1992), *North American Indian Medicine People* (1990), *North American Indian Survival Skills* (1990), and *North American Indian Tribal Chiefs* (1992).

Also see *Indian Signals and Sign Language* (page 503).

North American Indians

David Murdoch; Alfred A. Knopf, 1995

A volume in the Eyewitness series, heavily illustrated with superb color photographs and drawings. Each double-page spread covers a different geographical region/Indian territory or aspect of Indian life. Most of the text is in the picture captions.

Only the Names Remain: The Cherokees and the Trail of Tears

Alex W. Bealer; Little, Brown, 1996

A history of the Cherokee nation, focusing on the tragic Trail of Tears in the years 1837 to 1839, when, in accordance with the Indian Removal Act of 1830, the federal government forced the Cherokees to leave their ancestral lands in Georgia and relocate to Arkansas. For readers aged 9–12.

The Popcorn Book

Tomie de Paola; Holiday House, 1989

A picture-book story of popcorn, including history, science, and legend. Our boys always loved the American Indian tale of the furious little man inside each kernel of corn who finally, irritated beyond belief, simply explodes. Includes two popcorn recipes. For readers aged 4–8.

Also see *Corn Is Maize* (page 503) and *People of the Corn* (page 463).

The Story of America's Buffalo

Cobblestone, August 1981

This issue of *Cobblestone* magazine (see page 449) concentrates on the buffalo, past and present. Included are nonfiction accounts of the Indians' close relationship with the buffalo, a map showing the original range of the buffalo, a Plains Indian legend ("Small Deer and the Buffalo Jump"), a short biography of Buffalo Bill, Carl Sandburg's poem "Buffalo Dusk," an article on Scotty and Sarah Philip and their efforts in the late 1800s to save the buffalo from extinction, and step-by-step instructions for drawing a buffalo.

Available from most libraries or $4.50 from
Cobblestone Publishing, Inc.
30 Grove St.
Peterborough, NH 03458-1454
(603) 924-7209 or (800) 821-0115
Web site: www.cobblestonepub.com

Tomatoes, Potatoes, Corn, and Beans: How the Foods of the Americas Changed Eating Around the World

Sylvia A. Johnson; Atheneum, 1997

An explanation of how six foods—tomatoes, potatoes, corn, beans, peanuts, and peppers—were first used by the American Indians and subsequently spread throughout the world. For readers aged 11 and up.

BOOKS: FICTION

The Courage of Sarah Noble

Alice Dalgliesh; Aladdin, 1991

This short chapter book tells the story of eight-year-old Sarah Noble, who travels with her father to make a new home in the Connecticut wilderness in 1707. When Sarah's father returns to Massachusetts for the rest of the family, Sarah stays behind and lives with the Indians.

Indian Captive

Lois Lenski; HarperTrophy, 1995

Based on the true story of Mary Jemison, captured as a child by the Seneca Indians of New York. The book begins with Mary's life on the farm before the Indian raid and follows her as she adjusts—sometimes painfully—to the new and strange ways of an Indian village. Renamed Corn Tassel, she learns to love her new home and eventually, when given the choice, decides to stay with the Indians rather than return to white society. For readers aged 8–12.

The Indian in the Cupboard
Lynne Reid Banks; Camelot, 1991

Young Omri gets a magical cupboard for his birthday: plastic toys placed inside it come alive. Omri's toy Indian figure becomes Little Bear, a very real (but miniature) Iroquois from the time of the French and Indian War. For readers aged 8–12. Sequels include *The Return of the Indian* (1990), *The Secret of the Indian* (1990), and *The Mystery of the Cupboard* (1996). Also available on video (see page 510) and audiocassette (Listening Library, 1996).

The Ledgerbook of Thomas Blue Eagle
Jewel H. Gruman and Gay Matthaei; Thomassen-Grant, 1994

This unusual book looks like an old-fashioned blue ledger; inside, the pages are lined and the text is in (extremely neat) cursive longhand. The book purports to be the autobiography of young Thomas Blue Eagle, illustrated by himself with wonderful colored hand drawings. "I was born in the Moon When Ponies Shed Their Shaggy Hair," begins young Thomas, and goes on to tell the story of his childhood and his experiences at the Carlisle Indian School, where his teachers did their best to wipe out his Indian heritage. Thomas is fictional, but the Carlisle Indian School was real, in operation from 1879 to 1918.

Remember My Name
Sara Harrel Banks; Roberts Rinehart Publishers, 1993

Young Annie Rising Fawn Stuart is sent to live with her Cherokee uncle, a plantation owner in Georgia, where she makes friends with a slave girl. When the government orders the Cherokees to leave their land in 1830, the girls and Annie's uncle flee to the mountains. For readers aged 9–13.

The Sign of the Beaver
Elizabeth George Speare; Yearling, 1994

Twelve-year-old Matt is left alone at the new family cabin in Maine while his father returns to Massachusetts to fetch the rest of the family. His father is gone much longer than expected, and Matt survives with the help of Attean of the beaver clan, an Indian boy of his own age, and Saknis, Attean's wise grandfather.

Sing Down the Moon
Scott O'Dell; Laurel Leaf, 1998

The story of Bright Morning, a Navajo girl first kidnapped by the Spaniards and sold into slavery, then forced off her ancestral lands by the United States government. For readers aged 9–13.

Songs of Our Ancestors: Poems About Native Americans
Mark Turcotte; Children's Press, 1995

A 48-page illustrated collection of poems about North American Indians and their history.

Tapenum's Day: A Wampanoag Indian Boy in Pilgrim Times
Kate Waters; Scholastic, 1996

The story of a single day in the life of Tapenum, a young Indian boy living in the vicinity of Plimouth Plantation in the early 1600s. Illustrated with wonderful photographs from the Plimouth Plantation living-history museum.

Where the Buffaloes Begin
Olaf Baker; Viking, 1985

Ten-year-old Little Wolf journeys to the great lake where the buffalo begin and saves his people from an attack by their enemies. Illustrated with lovely soft-pencil drawings.

MYTHS AND LEGENDS

Arrow to the Sun: A Pueblo Indian Tale
Gerald McDermott; Viking, 1977

A brilliantly illustrated picture-book account of how the spirit of the Sun came to Earth, for readers aged 4–8. By the same author: *Coyote: A Trickster Tale from the Southwest* (Harcourt Brace, 1994) and *Raven: A Trickster Tale from the Pacific Northwest* (Harcourt Brace, 1993).

Buffalo Woman
Paul Goble; Aladdin, 1987

The picture-book version of a Plains Indian legend in which a young man marries a buffalo who has been magically transformed into a beautiful girl. Colorful stylized illustrations. For readers aged 7–10.

Earthmaker's Tales: North American Indian Stories About Earth Happenings
Gretchen Will Mayo; Walker & Company, 1989

Sixteen tales of mountains, volcanoes, earthquakes, blizzards, thunderstorms, rainbows, and eclipses. Each tale begins with a brief description of its tribe of origin. Also see *More Earthmaker's Tales* (1991) and *Star Tales* (page 507).

The First Strawberries: A Cherokee Story
Joseph Bruchac; Dial, 1993

A picture-book version of a Cherokee legend about the origin of strawberries. In the early days of creation, the first man and the first woman have an argument; the strawberries are a present from the Sun, to remind people to be kind to each other. Other single-legend picture books by Joseph Bruchac include *Fox Song* (Philomel Books, 1993) and *The Great Ball Game: A Muskogee Story* (Dial, 1994).

Flying With the Eagle, Racing the Great Bear: Stories from Native North America
Joseph Bruchac; Troll Associates, 1995

Tales from 16 tribal cultures about boys attaining manhood. Tribes represented include the Cherokee, Osage, Lakota, Tlingit, Navajo, and Wampanoag.

Four Ancestors
Joseph Bruchac; BridgeWater Books, 1996

The four ancestors are fire, earth, water, and air. For each, there is a collection of legends and poems, with illustrations by an American Indian artist.

The Girl Who Loved Wild Horses
Paul Goble; Aladdin, 1993

A Plains Indian legend, with colorful illustrations reminiscent of traditional American Indian artwork. For readers aged 4–9.

Paul Goble has written and illustrated many picture-book versions of traditional Indian legends and stories, among them *Death of the Iron Horse* (Aladdin, 1993) and *Iktomi and the Ducks: A Plains Indian Story* (Orchard Books, 1994).

The Girl Who Married the Moon: Tales from Native North America
Joseph Bruchac and Gayle Ross; Troll Associates, 1996

Sixteen legends, each from a different Indian tribe, featuring the adventures of young women.

The Legend of the Indian Paintbrush
Tomie de Paola; Paper Star, 1996

The enchantingly illustrated Plains Indian tale of Little Gopher, who paints a marvelous picture of the sunset and brings the flower known as "Indian paintbrush" to earth.

This book was featured on the *Reading Rainbow* television series, in which host LeVar Burton travels to the Taos Pueblo in New Mexico to visit Pueblo artists.

By the same author: *The Legend of the Bluebonnet* (Paper Star, 1996).

Mud Pony
Caron Lee Cohen; Scholastic, 1992

A picture-book retelling of a Pawnee tale about a young boy and a magical horse made from clay.

Native American Legends Series
Terri Cohlene; Watermill Press, 1991

A series of beautifully illustrated picture books, each retelling a single Indian legend centering around a young boy or girl. Titles in the series include *Clamshell Boy: A Makala Legend, Dancing Drum: A Cherokee Legend, Ka-ha-si and the Loon: An Eskimo Legend, Little Firefly: An Algonquian Legend, Quillworker: A Cheyenne Legend,* and *Turquoise Boy: A Navajo Legend*. In each, the legend is followed by several pages of information about the featured Indian tribe, illustrated with colorful maps, drawings, and photographs. The Navajo legend, *Turquoise Boy,* for example, includes a cross-sectional diagram showing the construction of a Navajo hogan, a photograph of a real-life hogan with inhabitants, a map of the southwestern United States showing the territories of the native Indian tribes, photographs of Navajo ceremonial masks, a color reproduction of a Navajo sandpainting, a photograph of a Navajo weaver and a completed blanket, and a timeline of important dates in Navajo history.

The Star Maiden: An Ojibway Tale
Barbara Juster Esbensen; Little, Brown, 1991

The story of a star who longs to come to earth and live among the people. Eventually she is transformed into a beautiful water lily.

Star Tales: North American Indian Stories About the Stars
Gretchen Will Mayo; Walker & Company, 1991

A collection of 14 legends from several Indian tribes about the stars and constellations. Also see *More Star Tales* (1991) and *Earthmaker's Tales* (page 506).

The Story of Jumping Mouse: A Native American Legend
John Steptoe; Mulberry, 1989

A picture-book version of a traditional legend in which a brave young mouse sets off on a perilous journey to the Far-Off Land and is finally transformed into a great eagle.

Thirteen Moons on Turtle's Back: A Native American Year of Moons
Joseph Bruchac and Jonathan London; Paper Star, 1997

Thirteen poems based on the legends of several American Indian tribes, among them Lakota, Cherokee, Abenaki, and Cree. The book includes a poem for each moon (lunar month) of the year—among them the Moon of Popping Trees, the Baby Bear Moon, the Frog Moon, and the Strawberry Moon. Beautifully illustrated.

ACTIVITY BOOKS

Earthmaker's Lodge: Native American Folklore, Activities, and Food
E. Barrie Kavasch; Cobblestone Publishing, 1994

An illustrated collection of stories, legends, and poems, with related crafts projects. The book is categorized by region, from the Arctic to Mexico. For kids in grade 5 and up.

Keepers of the Earth: Native American Stories and Environmental Activities for Children
Michael J. Caduto and Joseph Bruchac; Fulcrum, 1997

A 200+-page collection of Indian legends from many different tribes, each with associated discussion questions and hands-on scientific activities. After reading "Gluscabi and the Wind Eagle," for example, an Abenaki tale about a mischievous boy who captures the great eagle that makes the winds blow, kids hear a scientific explanation of the causes of winds, study clouds and wind-borne seeds, build toy sailboats, launch balloon rockets, assemble a wind sock, learn about weather maps, and research air pollution. The book is targeted at kids aged 5 through 12, but the scientific discussions and more challenging activities will hold the interest of older children.

Sequels, in similar format, include *Keepers of the Animals: Native American Stories and Wildlife Activities for Children* (Fulcrum, 1997), *Keepers of the Night* (Fulcrum, 1994), and *Keepers of Life* (Fulcrum, 1997).

More Than Moccasins: A Kid's Activity Guide to Traditional North American Indian Life
Laurie Carlson; Chicago Review Press, 1996

Over 100 projects, activities, games, songs, dances, and recipes for kids aged 3–9. Included are instructions for making turtle-shell and whale rattles, corncob and kachina dolls, parfleches and birchbark boxes, masks, and warbonnets; and recipes for fried squash blossoms and maple sugar candy.

Native American Gardening: Stories, Projects and Recipes for Families
Michael J. Caduto and Joseph Bruchac; Fulcrum, 1996

Detailed instructions for planting an American Indian garden. Included are plant-related Indian legends, American Indian recipes, and directions for crop-related crafts projects, such as making gourd rattles and corn-husk dolls.

COLORING AND PAPER-CRAFTS BOOKS

Chocolate, Chipmunks, and Canoes: An American Indian Words Coloring Book

Juan S. Alvarez; Red Crane Books, 1992

A coloring book of commonly used English words derived from American Indian languages.

Easy-to-Make Plains Indians Teepee Village

A. G. Smith; Dover Publications

The *Easy-to-Make Plains Indians Teepee Village* includes five cut-and-fold decorated tepees, assorted Indians, on and off horseback, and a buffalo herd. All the pieces are colorful cardstock; they're attractive and easy to put together. Also see the *Easy-to-Make Pueblo Village,* which includes an assortment of cut-and-fold adobe dwellings, plus ladders and inhabitants; and the *Northwest Coast Punch-Out Indian Village,* which contains all the pieces for a village of shingled houses, totem poles, Indians, and a decorated dugout canoe.

Dover also publishes paper-crafts books of Indian masks, totem poles, and kachina dolls to cut and assemble, and assorted coloring books.

$2.95 to $3.95

Dover Publications, Inc.

31 E. Second St.

Mineola, NY 11501

Folktales of Native Americans Coloring Book

A 128-page "Start Exploring" coloring book pairs American Indian legends with black-line pictures for coloring.

$8.95 from bookstores or

Running Press Book Publishers

125 S. 22nd St.

Philadelphia, PA 19103-4399

(215) 567-5080 or (800) 345-5359/fax (800) 453-2884

Indian Tribes of North America Coloring Book

Dover Publications

Black-line drawings of hunts, ceremonial dances, battles, and everyday life among the North American Indians, each picture accompanied by a brief informational text.

Also see *Great Native Americans,* which includes portraits of Chief Joseph, Sitting Bull, and Geronimo; *North American Indian Crafts,* which depicts weavers, potters, totem-pole carvers, and canoe makers; *North American Indian Dances and Rituals; Woodlands Indians Coloring Book; Southeast Indians Coloring Book; Southwest Indians Coloring Book; Plains Indians Coloring Book;* and *Northwest Coast Indians Coloring Book.*

$2.95 each

Dover Publications, Inc.

31 E. Second St.

Mineola, NY 11501

GAMES AND HANDS-ON ACTIVITIES

American Indian Dart Game Kit

Users make their own replica of an ancient Indian game, played with stick-and-feather darts and a painted target. Enough materials—sticks, feathers, canvas, natural pigments, and a twig brush and scraper—are included for making three darts, plus a target. An accompanying informational booklet gives instructions and a brief history of the game. For kids aged 8 and up.

$21.95

Ancient Graffiti

52 Seymour St.

Middlebury, VT 05753

(802) 388-2919 or (888) 725-6632

e-mail: ancientg@sovernet.com

The American Indians Treasure Chest

A creative kit on the culture of the Plains Indians, packaged in a sturdy 8 × 8 × 3-inch cardboard treasure chest, complete with tiny lock and key. The kit includes an illustrated informational book on the Plains Indians, plus materials to make a beaded headband (with an assemble-it-yourself bead loom), build a model tipi, and play an Indian-style string game.

$19.95 from book or game stores or

Running Press Book Publishers

125 S. 22nd St.

Philadelphia, PA 19103-4399

(215) 567-5080 or (800) 345-5359/fax (800) 453-2884

Beaver Tooth

A game played by the "First People of the Pacific Northwest." The game includes a basket, a set of four carved (reproduction) beaver teeth, and a bundle of (reproduction) counting bones. Depending on the fall of the carved teeth, players win various numbers of counting bones; player with the most at the end of the game wins. An accompanying illustrated booklet contains an Indian legend about the origin of the beaver, information about the Indian tribes of the Northwest, a supplementary reading list, and a brief history of the Beaver Tooth game. Simple, fast-paced, and fun.

$19.95

Skookum Jump Rope Co.

Box 1159

Port Townsend, WA 98368

(800) 255-9526/fax (360) 379-9049

Geronimo

A strategy game based on the Indian Wars of 1850–1890. The gameboard is a colorful map of the West; players variously represent the western Indian tribes or the U.S. cavalry. The game includes 32 "tribal cards" representing the famous tribes of the West, among them the Blackfoot, Apache, and Shoshone; and 40 "shaman cards," describing historical, political, and physical events which influence the outcome of the action, among them winter storms, the arrival of buffalo hunters, the building of railroads, and political corruption in Washington.

$39

Avalon Hill Game Co.

4517 Harford Rd.

Baltimore, MD 21214

(410) 254-9200 or (800) 999-3222

e-mail: AH GAMES@aol.com

Web site: www.avalonhill.com

Green Thumbs: Corn and Beans

The science of those classic American Indian foods, corn and beans. "Green Thumbs: Corn and Beans" is a precisely organized unit of activities for budding botanists. Included are extremely detailed directions and notes for parents/teachers, and a thick swatch of reproducible illustrated activity sheets for students. The unit contains a month's worth of hands-on corn-and-bean activities. Kids make seed trays, sprout corn and bean seeds, make balances for weighing their developing seeds and pole planters for measuring the growth of seedlings, dissect corn and bean seeds, and make leaf rubbings, all while maintaining a daily journal of observations and discoveries. All necessary materials are cheap and readily available. The "Corn and Beans" unit can be done at any season of the year (provided the seeds are kept in a reasonably warm room); you do, however, need to plan an uninterrupted month for the projects, since the experiments are tightly scheduled. Recommended for kids in grades 3–10.

$14.95

TOPS Learning Systems

10970 S. Mulino Rd.

Canby, OR 97013

Honor

A simulation of an American Indian coming-of-age in the time "before the horse." Participants read three Indian legends, demonstrating the virtues of industry, truth, and courage, and then set off on a "one-moon stray," during which each must complete three challenges: "The Naming Story," "Tool Acquisition," and "Shelter Construction." Action is traced on an included map of tribal lands; experiences are dictated by "Fate Cards." (Example: "Fate Card at Cliff Lake: Suddenly you spot a bald eagle's nest in a dead tree high above the lake. A bald eagle's tail feather is a sign of courage in your tribe. The tall tree has grown over a dangerous rock outcropping. If you fall while climbing, the fall could be fatal. Write your decision in picture language.") Each student keeps a "Stray Log" written in his/her own invented picture language.

The simulation is recommended for kids in grades 4–8 and takes an estimated 10 to 15 hours to complete. Materials include 35 eight-page student guides, a 79-page teacher's guide, maps, and reproducible student handouts.

$34

Interact

1825 Gillespie Way, #101

El Cajon, CA 92020-1095

(619) 448-1474 or (800) 359-0961/fax (619) 448-6722

Web site: www.interact-simulations.com

Indian Resistance: The Patriot Chiefs

A portfolio of primary source documents, historical background essays, and a study guide. Essay titles include "King Philip's War," "Tecumseh and Expansion Across the Plains," and "American Expansion on the Plains." Historical documents include a Paul Revere drawing of King Philip, a map of Indian tribal territories by George Catlin, a letter in the Nez Perce language, and Frederic Remington's painting of the Ghost Dance of the Oglala Sioux.

$37
Jackdaw Publications
Box 503
Amawalk, NY 10501
(914) 962-6911 or (800) 789-0022/fax (800) 962-9101

Indians of North America

A portfolio of primary source documents and an informational study guide, with reproducible student worksheets. Included are a collection of Indian myths and legends, a map showing the distribution of prominent Indian tribes, portraits of famous Indian chiefs, instructions for making ceremonial masks, and a copy of an 1894 Hopi petition to the federal government.

$37
Jackdaw Publications
Box 503
Amawalk, NY 10501
(914) 962-6911 or (800) 789-0022/fax (800) 962-9101

Native American Indians of the Southwest Discovery Kit

The kit includes an illustrated 64-page book on the Pueblo Indian cultures of the Southwest, plus—embedded in a chunk of clay—the replica of an ancient Anasazi bowl, in archaeologically realistic fragments. Tools and instructions are included for unearthing and assembling the artifact, and for decorating it in traditional patterns.

$17.95 from book or game stores or
Running Press Book Publishers
125 S. 22nd St.
Philadelphia, PA 19103-4399
(215) 567-5080 or (800) 345-5359/fax (800) 453-2884

A Time for Native Americans

A biographical card game for two to four players, aged 8 and up. The game consists of 49 full-color heavy-duty cards, each carrying the portrait and short biography of a well-known American Indian. Flip the cards over and they form a giant puzzle map of North America; areas where each of the biographical subjects lived are labeled.

Instructions are included for four different games: kids can assemble the map puzzle, order the cards on a timeline (two game variations), or play "Who's Who?" in which players attempt to guess the identity of a subject from biographical details.

$10
Aristoplay
450 S. Wagner Rd.
Box 7529
Ann Arbor, MI 48107
(800) 634-7738 or (888) GR8-GAME
fax (734) 995-4611
Web site: www.aristoplay.com

VIDEOS

Dances With Wolves

Wonderful footage of Indian life, plus a dramatic story, directed by (and starring) Kevin Costner. Costner plays an army officer sent to the Dakota Territory in the 1860s, where he learns to love and respect the local tribe of Sioux Indians. Rated PG-13.

$14.99
Movies Unlimited
3015 Darnell Rd.
Philadelphia, PA 19154
(215) 637-4444 or (800) 4-MOVIES
Web site: www.moviesunlimited.com
e-mail: movies@moviesunlimited.com

The Indian in the Cupboard

Based on Lynn Reid Banks's book (see page 505), this is the story of Omri, who receives for his birthday a magical cupboard that has the power to bring tiny toy figures to life. Omri first uses the cupboard on Little Bear, a miniature (but very real) Indian; then on a toy

Texas cowboy named Boone. Facts, fantasy, and lessons about life.

$19.99

Movies Unlimited

3015 Darnell Rd.

Philadelphia, PA 19154

(215) 637-4444 or (800) 4-MOVIES

e-mail: movies@moviesunlimited.com

Web site: www.moviesunlimited.com

The Native Americans

A six-part PBS miniseries on American Indian history and culture, past and present. Titles in the series include "The Tribes of the Southeast: Persistent Cultures of Resilient People," "The Tribal People of the Northwest: Living in Harmony with the Land," "The Nations of the Northeast: The Strength and Wisdom of the Confederacies," "The People of the Great Plains (Part One): Buffalo People and Dog Days," "The People of the Great Plains (Part Two): The Coming of the Horse, the White Man, and the Rifle," and "The Natives of the Southwest: Artists, Innovators, and Rebels."

$59.98

PBS Home Video

1320 Braddock Pl.

Alexandria, VA 22314-1698

(800) 645-4PBS

Web site: www.pbs.org

The Song of Sacajawea

The true story of the young Indian woman who helped guide the Lewis and Clark Expedition in their trek to the Pacific Ocean in the early 19th century. In "dissolve animation" storybook form from Rabbit Ears Video, narrated by Laura Dern. The videotape is about 30 minutes long.

$14.99

Movies Unlimited

3015 Darnell Rd.

Philadelphia, PA 19154

(215) 637-4444 or (800) 4-MOVIES

e-mail: movies@moviesunlimited.com

Web site: www.moviesunlimited.com

See **Lewis and Clark Expedition** (pages 499–501).

AMERICAN INDIANS ON-LINE

Index of Native American Resources on the Internet

A comprehensive list of links, grouped under such categories as language, museums, archaeology, culture, history, art, and educational resources.

hanksville.phast.umass.edu/misc/NAresources.html

Native American Indian Resources

A very detailed site, including native maps, stories, and recipes, information on Indian art, astronomy, herbal medicine, and food, links to official tribal sites, and an assortment of games for kids.

indy4.fdl.cc.mn.us/~isk/mainmenu.html

National Museum of the American Indian

A tour of museum exhibits, with color photographs of artifacts, educational resources, and links to many related sites.

www.si.edu/nmai

THE WAR OF 1812

BOOKS

Abigail's Drum

John A. Minahan; Pippin Press, 1995

The daughters of a Massachusetts lighthouse keeper fool the British into thinking that the American army is near by playing "Yankee Doodle" on the fife and drum.

An American Army of Two

Janet Greeson; Carolrhoda, 1992

During the War of 1812, young Rebecca and Abigail Bates save the town from the British by playing "Yankee Doodle" on the fife and drum. The British troops, thinking that the American army is approaching, retreat. For readers aged 5–9.

By Dawn's Early Light: The Story of the Star-Spangled Banner

Steven Kroll; Scholastic, 1994

A dramatically illustrated picture-book account of the War of 1812, centering around the story of Francis Scott Key, sent as an envoy to free an American prisoner on a British ship, who watches the British attack on Baltimore's Fort McHenry and subsequently writes "The Star-Spangled Banner." The full text of the anthem is included, with music. There's also a map of the Battle of Baltimore and a supplementary reading list. For readers aged 7–12.

An Introduction to the War of 1812

Cobblestone; January 1988

The January 1988 issue of *Cobblestone* magazine (see page 449) concentrates on the War of 1812. Included are nonfiction articles on "Old Ironsides," Oliver Hazard Perry ("We have met the enemy, and they are ours") and the Battle of Lake Erie, 12-year-old midshipman David Farragut on board the *Essex,* the burning of Washington by the British, the birth of "The Star-Spangled Banner," and Andrew Jackson and the Battle of New Orleans; biographies of the Shawnee chief Tecumseh and the pirate Jean Lafitte; a War of 1812 timeline; and War of 1812 word games and puzzles.

Available from most libraries or for $4.50 from

Cobblestone Publishing, Inc.

30 Grove St.

Peterborough, NH 03458-1454

(603) 924-7209 or (800) 821-0115

Web site: www.cobblestonepub.com

Old Ironsides: Americans Build a Fighting Ship

David Weitzman; Houghton Mifflin, 1997

The building of "Old Ironsides" as seen through the eyes of young John Aylwin, son of a Boston ship's carpenter. John watches the building process from the first drawing of the plans (in chalk on the wooden floor of the mold loft) through the launch of the finished ship. An epilogue describes the famous battle with the *Guerriere,* in which young John participates as the sailing master. The book is illustrated with marvelously detailed drawings and cross-sectional diagrams.

 The Star-Spangled Banner

Peter Spier; Yearling, 1992

A beautifully illustrated history of the War of 1812, including the story of the writing of our national anthem, with a reproduction of Francis Scott Key's original manuscript. For readers aged 5–10.

The Story of Old Ironsides

Norman Richards; Children's Press, 1967

One of the Cornerstones of Freedom series (see page 451), this 32-page book tells the story of the U.S.S. *Constitution,* from its construction (to scare off the Barbary pirates) in post–Revolutionary War Boston, through the famous battle in the War of 1812 when she earned her famous nickname, to the sad day in the 19th century when the navy ordered the old ship destroyed. She was saved at the last minute by a poem, written by a Boston college student named Oliver Wendell Holmes, and by half a million dollars in pennies, collected by schoolchildren.

Washington City is Burning!

Harriette Gillem Robinet; Atheneum, 1996

Virginia, a 12-year-old slave girl, is sent to the White House to serve First Lady Dolley Madison. There she becomes involved in a plan to help escaping slaves, gets an intimate look at presidential life, and witnesses the burning of "Washington City" by the British in 1814.

The White House

Leonard Everett Fisher; Holiday House, 1989

The history of the White House, from its design during George Washington's term in office through its completion, its destruction by the British during the War of 1812, its later rebuilding and changes in modern times. For readers aged 8–12. Also see *The Story of the White House* by Kate Walers (Scholastic, 1992).

GAMES AND HANDS-ON ACTIVITIES

Don't Give Up the Ship!

A board game based on the Battle of Lake Erie on September 10, 1813, in which—historically—the American commodore Oliver Hazard Perry defeated

HISTORY

the British fleet under Captain Robert Barclay. Players, as either British or American commanders, deploy their ships (paper playing pieces, to be cut out and folded) on a blue paper playing board representing the open water of Lake Erie where the famous battle took place. Opponents must deal with adverse winds, enemy fire, boarding, loss of crew members, and deaths of their captains; the winner is the first to put the majority of the enemy ships out of commission. It doesn't always work out as predicted.

The reverse side of the game board includes a brief account of the War of 1812 and a more detailed description of the Battle of Lake Erie, a list of the ships involved in the battle, and an 1812 map of Lake Erie and the surrounding area.

$6.95

Chatham Hill Games, Inc.

Box 253

Chatham, NY 12037

(518) 392-5022 or (800) 554-3039/fax (518) 392-3121

Web site: www.ocdc.com/Chatham_Hill_Games

Frigates!

There are seven different versions of this board game, in which the U.S.S. *Constitution* ("Old Ironsides") and/or its sister ship, the U.S.S. *Constellation,* battle a combination of enemy British and French ships. The paper game board is a crosshatch-patterned chunk of blue ocean; ships (paper playing pieces, to be cut out and folded) are subject to favorable or unfavorable winds, proper or improper firing positions, firing damage, sinking, explosion, broken masts, and loss of crew or captain. All disasters suffered are recorded on the reproducible score sheet as "damage points." The ship with the most victories (sinkings or captures) at the end of the game wins.

$6.95

Chatham Hill Games, Inc.

Box 253

Chatham, NY 12037

(518) 392-5022 or (800) 554-3039

Web site: www.ocdc.com/Chatham_Hill_Games

The War of 1812

A board game designed to teach kids basic historical events and geographical locations associated with

the War of 1812. The board pictures a map of the United States with crucial battle sites numbered.

$10.95

Educational Materials Associates, Inc.

Box 7385

Charlottesville, VA 22906

(804) 293-GAME/fax (804) 293-5322

THE NINETEENTH CENTURY

WHALING DAYS

BOOKS

Hunting Neptune's Giants: True Stories of American Whaling

Catherine Gourley; Millbrook Press, 1995

A fascinating history of whaling written in association with Mystic Seaport Museum. The book includes many first-person accounts, excerpts from journals and diaries, and period prints and photographs. For readers aged 10 and up.

John Tabor's Ride

Edward C. Day; Random House, 1992

A tall tale of whaling in the 1840s in which harpooner John Tabor is taken on the ride of his life by a sperm whale. For readers aged 5–9.

Moby Dick

Herman Melville; Troll Associates, 1988

There are many adaptations of this classic book for young readers. This version, retold by Bernice Selden, is 48 pages long, for kids aged 8–12. A dramatic plot woven around whales, whaling, and 19th-century life at sea.

New England Whaler

Robert F. Baldwin; Lerner, 1996

A 48-page history of whaling, covering ships, life at sea, the whale hunt, and the different kinds of whales. For readers aged 8–12.

Seabird

9 +

Holling Clancy Holling; Houghton Mifflin, 1975

Ezra, ship's boy on a 19th-century whaling ship, is warned away from an iceberg by a seagull. He carves a little gull out of walrus tusk, and the "seabird" becomes a family heirloom, eventually traveling on board a whaler, a clipper ship, a steamboat, and an airplane. Life on board the whaling ship is described in detail, illustrated with color paintings and labeled pen-and-ink diagrams. For readers aged 9 and up.

Whaling

9 14

Cobblestone; April 1984

This issue of the magazine (see *Cobblestone,* page 449) includes a history of whaling, from the Indians to the present day, general information on whales, instructions for making a paper whale, and a supplementary reading list. For kids in grades 5–9.

Available from most libraries or for $4.50 from
Cobblestone Publishing, Inc.
30 Grove St.
Peterborough, NH 03458-1454
(603) 924-7209 or (800) 821-0115
Web site: www.cobblestonepub.com

Whaling Days

9 12

Carol Carrick; Clarion, 1996

A short history of whales and whaling, a detailed description of a 19th-century whale hunt, and a brief account of whaling in modern times, beautifully illustrated with woodcuts. A glossary and bibliography are included. For readers aged 9–12.

COLORING BOOKS

The Story of Whaling Coloring Book

6 +

Peter F. Copeland; Dover Publications

From sighting to chase to oil barrels in 45 black-line drawings. Included are pictures of breaching whales, whaling ships, shipboard life, and harpooners in action.

$2.95
Dover Publications, Inc.

31 E. 2nd St.
Mineola, NY 11501

Whales and Dolphins Coloring Book

6 +

John Green; Dover Publications

Over 40 black-line drawings of whales, among them sperm whales, blue whales, right whales, and orcas.

$2.95
Dover Publications, Inc.
31 E. 2nd St.
Mineola, NY 11501

GAMES

Save the Whales

8 +

Twentieth-century players cooperate to save the whales from whalers in this beautifully illustrated board game. There are eight species of great whales under attack—each represented by a cast-metal playing piece—which must be moved around the board to the safety of the open ocean. Game cards variously provide help, bring trouble, or offer interesting information about whales.

$39
Animal Town
Box 757
Greenland, NH 03840
(800) 445-8642/fax (603) 403-0334

Thar She Blows!

8 +

It's July 1823, and the crews of the whaling ships *Essex* and *Emelia* are cruising the North Atlantic in search of whales. The object of the game is to chase and capture a whale, while trying to avoid fog, icebergs, damaged whaleboats, badly aimed harpoons, and Nantucket sleigh rides. Player with the most whale oil at the end of the game wins. The game is played on a paper mapboard with cut-and-fold pieces.

$6.95
Chatham Hill Games, Inc.
Box 253
Chatham, NY 12037
(518) 392-5022 or (800) 544-3039/fax (518) 392-3121
Web site: www.ocdc.com/Chatham_Hill_Games

HISTORY

VIDEO

8 *The Great Whales*

A National Geographic documentary about the world's largest animals, now threatened with extinction. Interesting information and spectacular film footage.

$19.99

Movies Unlimited

3015 Darnell Rd.

Philadelphia, PA 19154

(215) 637-4444 or (800) 4-MOVIES

e-mail: movies@moviesunlimited.com

Web site: www.moviesunlimited.com

or

National Geographic Home Video

Box 5073

Clifton, NJ 07015

(800) 627-5162

Web site: www.nationalgeographic.com

10 *Moby Dick*

The classic and exciting tale of Captain Ahab of the whaling ship *Pequod* and his obsessive quest for Moby Dick, the Great White Whale. This 1956 version, with Gregory Peck as Ahab, has terrific scenes of life on the high seas in the 19th century.

$19.98

Zenger Media

10200 Jefferson Blvd.

Box 802

Culver City, CA 90232-0802

(310) 839-2436 or (800) 421-4246/fax (310) 839-2249 or (800) 944-5432

e-mail: access@ZengerMedia.com

Web site: ZengerMedia.com/Zenger

QUILTS

Quilts—those handmade patchwork coverlets that the pioneers once slept under—have found a place in the modern educational curriculum. A quilt can be a joint art project, a needlework lesson, or a creative bridge into history, genealogy, geography, or mathematics.

BOOKS

5 *Eight Hands Round: A Patchwork Alphabet*

Ann W. Paul; HarperTrophy, 1996

The book pictures 26 quilt patterns in colorful order from *A* to *Z*, with historical notes on how each pattern may have originated.

5 9 *The Josefina Quilt Story*

Eleanor Coerr; HarperTrophy, 1989

As Faith and her pet hen, Josefina, travel west to California in 1850, Faith stitches a quilt that tells the story of their adventures on the trail.

5 9 *The Keeping Quilt*

Patricia Polacco; Simon & Schuster, 1994

Great-Gramma Anna makes a memory quilt, stitched from clothes that came with the family from Russia—including her own cherished babushka. The quilt serves as a Sabbath tablecloth, a picnic blanket, a wedding canopy—for three generations of brides—and a baby blanket. A lovely story of family history.

4 8 *The Quilt Story*

Tony Johnston; Paper Star, 1996

A homemade quilt, stitched with patterns of falling stars, comforts two generations of little girls moving to a new home, one traveling west in a wagon train, one moving in modern times. Charming folk-art illustrations by Tomie de Paola.

5 9 *Sam Johnson and the Blue Ribbon Quilt*

Lisa Campbell Ernst; Mulberry, 1992

Sam Johnson, rejected by the Rosedale Women's Quilting Club, decides to form a rival "men only" quilting club of his own.

9 12 *Stitching Stars: The Story Quilts of Harriet Powers*

Mary E. Lyons; Aladdin, 1997

A biography of folk artist Harriet Powers, born a slave in 1837, who began making appliquéd quilts in 1886. (Each is a work of art, picturing traditional folktales and Bible stories.) The book is illustrated with color photographs.

Sweet Clara and the Freedom Quilt

Deborah Hopkinson; Random House, 1995

Clara, a young slave girl, stitches a patchwork quilt showing escape routes. When she finally flees north to freedom, she leaves her quilt behind to serve as a map so that others may follow.

HANDS-ON ACTIVITIES

My World Quilt

A personal quilt kit for kids aged 6 and up. The quilt consists of 12 preprinted squares, to be illustrated and colored with fabric markers by the quilt maker. Squares are titled "This Is Me," "This Is My Family," "This Is My Room," "This Is My Home," "This Is My Street," "This Is My Town," "This Is My State Flower," "This Is My State," "This Is My Flag," "This Is My Country," "This Is My Earth," and "This Is My Universe." The completed quilt is then assembled and quilted. All materials are included, along with a 60-page atlas picturing state flowers, flags, mottoes, and maps.

$19.95 from toy and game stores or for a local source, contact

Curiosity Kits

Box 811

Cockeysville, MD 21030

(410) 584-2605 or (800) 584-KITS/fax (410) 584-1247

e-mail:

Quilting Tiles

A collection 300 red and blue plastic squares and (right) triangles for making patchwork patterns, a skill which, according to mathematics educators, helps children develop spatial abilities. Accompanying one-inch-square graph paper is available for laying out tile patterns.

Tiles, $13.95; graph paper, $14.95

Cuisenaire/Dale Seymour Publications

Box 5026

White Plains, NY 10602-5026

(800) 872-1100 or (800) 237-0338/fax (914) 328-5487

or (800) 551-RODS

Web site: www.cuisenaire.com or www.awl.com/dsp

Quilt Design Masters

Luane Seymour Cohen; Dale Seymour Publications

Reproductions of 300 traditional quilt patch designs, with reproducible grids on which students can design and color their own patterns.

$14.95

Cuisenaire/Dale Seymour Publications

Box 5026

White Plains, NY 10602-5026

(800) 872-1100 or (800) 237-0338/fax (914) 328-5487

or (800) 551-RODS

Web site: www.cuisenaire.com or www.awl.com/dsp

Quilt Making: A Traditional Woman's Art Form

Mary Ruthsdotter; National Women's History Project

A quilt-pattern project kit for kids in grades 1–6. The kit includes 12 eight-inch-square colored quilt block reproductions, a sample fabric quilt block, and instructions for an art-and-math-based quilting activity.

$16.95

National Women's History Project

7738 Bell Rd.

Windsor, CA 95492-8518

(707) 838-6000

Also see *A Quilt-Block History of Pioneer Days* (page 531).

THE ERIE CANAL

BOOKS

The Amazing Impossible Erie Canal

Cheryl Harness; Simon & Schuster, 1995

A delightfully told account of the building of the famous canal from Albany to Buffalo and the Great Lakes, with wonderful detailed illustrations, maps, and diagrams. Readers find out why the canal was built, discover how locks operate, and learn about the 10-day celebration that marked the canal's opening in 1825.

The Erie Canal

Cobblestone; October 1982

All about the Erie Canal: the building of the canal, life on the canal, and the impact of the canal on west-

HISTORY

ern settlement. The illustrated magazine also includes activities and a supplementary reading list. For readers in grades 5–9.

Available from most libraries or for $4.50 from
Cobblestone Publishing, Inc.
30 Grove St.
Peterborough, NH 03458-1454
(603) 924-7209 or (800) 821-0115
Web site: www.cobblestonepub.com
See *Cobblestone* (page 449).

GAMES

The Erie Canal

A board game in which players load their canal boats with cargo and move them along the playing board, a beautifully drawn map of the Erie Canal (1839). As the boats—the westbound *Oneida Chief* and eastbound *Van Rensselaer*—proceed, they pass through the canal's locks, pay tolls and fines on overweight cargo, deal with broken towlines, tired horses, floating logs, and collisions, and make extra money by picking up passengers. At the end of the line, in Albany or Buffalo, they sell their cargo at auction; the player with the most profit wins the game.

A "Game and Music Set" version of "The Erie Canal" is also available, which includes a 30-minute cassette tape of Erie Canal songs.

Game only, $6.95; "Game and Music Set," $14.95
Chatham Hill Games, Inc.
Box 253
Chatham, NY 12037
(518) 392-5022 or (800) 554-3039/fax (518) 392-3121
Web site: www.ocdc.com/Chatham_Hill_Games

THE RAILROADS

BOOKS

The Death of the Iron Horse

Paul Goble; Aladdin, 1993

A band of young Cheyenne warriors ride off to battle the fearsome Iron Horse that breathes smoke and has a voice like thunder. Based on a true story, in which the Cheyennes derailed a Union Pacific freight train on August 7, 1867. Beautifully illustrated.

Full Steam Ahead: The Race to Build a Transcontinental Railroad

Rhoda Blumberg; National Geographic Society, 1996

A 159-page history of the transcontinental railroad, from conception through Golden Spike, covering politicians, financiers, engineers, and ordinary workmen. Interestingly written and illustrated with period photographs, prints, and maps. For readers aged 12 and up.

Iron Horses Across America: The Transcontinental Railroad

Discovery Enterprises

One of the Perspectives on History Series (see page 455) for kids ages 11 and up, this is a 60+-page anthology of primary and secondary source materials on the building of the transcontinental railroad and its effect on American society. Included are maps, photographs, period newspaper articles, letters, and journal excerpts.
$5.95
Discovery Enterprises, Ltd.
31 Laurelwood Dr.
Carlisle, MA 01741
(800) 729-1720

Kate Shelley and the Midnight Express

Margaret K. Wetterer; Carolrhoda, 1991

In July 1881, the railroad bridge breaks, causing a train to crash into the waters of Honey Creek. Fifteen-year-old Kate Shelley must fetch help—and must stop the *Midnight Express* from trying to cross the broken bridge. For 5–9-year-olds, based on a true story.

This book was featured on *Reading Rainbow;* in this episode, host LeVar Burton travels along the California coastline on the Amtrak *Starlight.* Viewers get a personal tour of the engineer's cab and an overview of train history.

Also see *Kate Shelley: Bound for Legend,* a version of the same story by Max Ginsberg (Dial, 1995), with illustrations by Robert San Souci.

Look Inside Cross-Sections: Trains

ALL Michael Johnstone; Dorling Kindersley, 1995

Trains from every possible angle: above, below, and sliced through the center, so that young readers can see how they work.

The Railroaders

13+ Time-Life; 1975

One of the volumes in The Old West Series (see page 526): 240 pages of interesting and informational text, heavily illustrated with photographs, prints, maps, and art reproductions. The text is for older and adult readers; the pictures, which are superb, tell the story by themselves and will fascinate all.

Tales from Gold Mountain: Stories of the Chinese in the New World

9 13 Paul Yee; Macmillan, 1989

A collection of stories told by Chinese immigrants who arrived in the 19th century to work in the gold-fields and on the railways; stories include "Spirits of the Railway." For readers aged 9–13.

Train

4 8 Gail Gibbons; Holiday House, 1988

A simple and brightly illustrated tour of trains for young engineers. The book covers trains historic and modern, with labeled illustrations of steam, diesel, and electric engines, plus pictures of boxcars, tank cars, passenger cars, refrigerator cars, and everybody's favorite, the caboose.

The Transcontinental Railroad

8 12 Peter Anderson; Children's Press, 1996

One of the Cornerstones of Freedom series (see page 451) for kids in grades 4–6. This is 32-page account of the building and operation of the great cross-country railroad, illustrated with photographs.

The Transcontinental Railroad

9 14 Cobblestone; May 1980

This issue of *Cobblestone* magazine (see page 449) covers the history of the transcontinental railroad, with information about the Golden Spike ceremony, the Indian response to the railroad, and Chinese railroad workers. For readers in grades 5–9.

Available from most libraries or for $4.50 from Cobblestone Publishing, Inc.
30 Grove St.
Peterborough, NH 03458-1454
(603) 924-7209 or (800) 821-0115
Web site: www.cobblestonepub.com

GAMES AND HANDS-ON ACTIVITIES

1830: The Game of Railroads and Robber Barons

12+ A dramatic game of transcontinental railroad-building in which players attempt to lay track, buy trains and stations, and manipulate stocks, thus beating out opponents in the race to control the railroad industry. (The game reflects the robber baron attitude of the times; we're out to build railroads here, not character.) Avalon Hill, the game's publisher, is noted for complex camps of military strategy. These are generally rated by level of difficulty on a scale of 1 to 10. "1830" rates a 4, which means that it is recommended for knowledgeable players who have had some previous experience with strategy games.

$30
Avalon Hill Game Co.
4517 Harford Rd.
Baltimore, MD 21214
(410) 254-9200 or (800) 999-3222
e-mail: AHGAMES@aol.com
Web site: www.avalonhill.com

Antique Locomotives Coloring Book

6+ Tre Tryckare Co.; Dover Publications

Detailed drawings of 19th-century American and European locomotives, with descriptive picture captions.

$2.95
Dover Publications, Inc.
31 E. Second St.
Mineola, NY 11501

Great Trains to Cut Out and Assemble

6+ Four famous trains to cut, fold, and piece together.
$3.95
Bellerophon Books

36 Ancapa St.

Santa Barbara, CA 93101

(800) 253-9943

James Watt and Steam Power

A portfolio of primary source materials, supplementary essays, and explanatory notes covering the development of steam power from its earliest known application (by the ancient Greeks) to James Watt's economically feasible engine. Included among the nine facsimile historical documents in the packet are an engraved portrait of James Watt, photographs and diagrams of Watt's engines, a letter from Robert Fulton requesting an engine for his steamboat, illustrations of the first steamship, steam locomotive and steam-powered coach, and a pictorial chart showing the many uses of steam power.

$37

Jackdaw Publications

Box 503

Amawalk, NY 10501

(800) 789-0022/fax (800) 962-9101

Jensen Dry Fuel Steam Engine

This wonderful device is a working replica of a single-action, oscillating cylinder steam engine of the 1700s. The all-metal engine comes in pieces and must be assembled using basic tools (hammer, screwdriver, and pliers); completed, it's just over eight inches tall, equipped with nickel-plated boiler, throttle valve, water gauge, whistle, safety valve, and a power takeoff pulley to drive accessories. (Accessories, available separately, include an AC generator and brass light set.) The engine runs on dry fuel pellets, which are safe and simple to use, and—no matter how many times you fire it up—it's a thrill.

$99.95 and up

Edmund Scientific Co.

101 E. Gloucester Pike

Barrington, NJ 08007-1380

(609) 547-8880 or (800) 728-6999/fax (609) 573-6295

e-mail: scientifics@edsci.com

Web site: www.edsci.com

Transcontinental

A simulation of the building of the Transcontinental Railroad, in which teams of students research the history of transportation while racing to reach Promontory Point and drive the Golden Spike. The simulation takes about 15 hours total. For students in grades 4–8.

$37

Interact

1825 Gillespie Way, #101

El Cajon, CA 92020-1095

(619) 448-1474 or (800) 359-0961/fax (619) 448-6722 or (800) 700-5093

Web site: www.interact-simulations.com

Videos

Iron Road: The Story of America's First Transcontinental Railroad

The story of the famous railroad, with period photographs, live-action film footage, music, maps, and a lot of good human interest stories.

$19.95

Zenger Media

10200 Jefferson Blvd.

Box 802

Culver City, CA 90232-0802

(310) 839-2436 or (800) 421-4246/fax (310) 839-2249 or (800) 944-5432

e-mail: access@ZengerMedia.com

Web site: ZengerMedia.com/Zenger

This is America, Charlie Brown; Volume 3: The Building of the Transcontinental Railroad

The Peanuts kids and dog participate in the building of the transcontinental railroad and are present at the driving of the famous Golden Spike at Promontory Point, Utah, when Atlantic and Pacific lines finally meet. Twenty-four minutes long.

$12.99

Movies Unlimited

3015 Darnell Rd.

Philadelphia, PA 19154

(215) 637-4444 or (800) 4-MOVIES

e-mail: movies@moviesunlimited.com

Web site: www.moviesunlimited.com

TEXAS AND THE ALAMO

BOOKS

Make Way for Sam Houston
Jean Fritz; Coward, McCann, 1986

An interesting chapter biography of flamboyant Texas leader Sam Houston for readers aged 9–13.

Remember the Alamo!
Cobblestone; March 1982

This issue of the history magazine for readers in grades 5–9 (see page 449) includes the history of the Alamo, the story of the famous Battle of the Alamo, information about Davy Crockett, Jim Bowie, and Susanna Dickinson, and an Alamo diagram.

Available from most libraries or for $4.50 from
Cobblestone Publishing, Inc.
30 Grove St.
Peterborough, NH 03458-1454
(603) 924-7209 or (800) 821-0115
Web site: www.cobblestonepub.com

Susanna of the Alamo: A True Story
John Jakes; Harcourt Brace, 1986

The picture-book story of Susanna Dickinson, the Texas woman who, with her little daughter, survived the Battle of the Alamo, and carried the news of its fall to Sam Houston.

HANDS-ON ACTIVITIES

The Mexican-American War
A portfolio of primary source documents, six historical background essays, and a study guide with reproducible student worksheets. Documents include a timeline, a map of the Mexican-American War (1845–1848), and a collection of period newspaper articles. Essay titles include "Heading West," "Manifest Destiny," "Inside Mexico," and "Our Country, Right or Wrong?"

$37
Jackdaw Publications
Box 503
Amawalk, NY 10501
(914) 962-6911 or (800) 789-0022/fax (800) 962-9101

Southwest
A six-part "participatory notebook program" in which kids, through a variety of activities and projects, study the geography, native peoples, explorers, missions, Mexican historical period, and American statehoods of regions in the Southwest, finishing up with a Mexican-American fiesta. Students cover the histories of California, Arizona, New Mexico, and Texas.

$46
Interact
1825 Gillespie Way, #101
El Cajon, CA 92020-1095
(800) 359-0961/fax (800) 700-5093
Web site: www.interact-simulations.com

Texas: A Lone Star History
A portfolio containing six illustrated essays, a timeline of Texas history (1519–1990), 15 historical documents and primary source materials, and a detailed study guide. Essay titles include "Native Americans, Explorers, and the Land," "Spain and Mexico: 1718–1835," "The Republic, the Union, and the Confederacy: 1836–1865," and "Texas in the Twentieth Century." Primary source materials include historical maps, letters, diary excerpts, and posters—among them a letter from Santa Anna to Sam Houston (1836).

$37
Jackdaw Publications
Box 503
Amawalk, NY 10501
(914) 962-6911 or (800) 789-0022/fax (800) 962-9101

VIDEOS

The Alamo
From American Heritage and the History Channel, a historical overview of the events leading up to the confrontation at the Alamo, detailed coverage of the capture of San Antonio, the 13-day siege, and the devastating nine-minute battle, as well as an account of Santa Anna's final defeat and Texas liberation. 110 minutes on 2 videocassettes.

HISTORY

$29.95

Zenger Media

10200 Jefferson Blvd.

Box 802

Culver City, CA 90232-0802

(310) 839-2436 or (800) 421-4246/fax (310) 839-2249

or (800) 944-5427

Web site: ZengerMedia/Zenger

e-mail: access@ZengerMedia.com

Texas

Based on the James Michener novel of the same title, this is the history of the 19th-century Texan struggle for freedom from Spain. The action opens in 1821, with Mexico's General Santa Anna firmly in power, and continues through the incendiary Battle of the Alamo and Texas's eventual attainment of independence. With Stacy Keach as Sam Houston, Patrick Duffy as Stephen Austin, John Schneider as Davy Crockett, and David Keith as Jim Bowie.

$19.99

Movies Unlimited

3015 Darnell Rd.

Philadelphia, PA 19154

(215) 637-4444 or (800) 4-MOVIES

e-mail: movies@moviesunlimited.com

Web site: www.moviesunlimited.com

THE GOLD RUSH

BOOKS: NONFICTION

The Fortyniners

William Weber Johnson; Time-Life, 1974

A 240-page history of the gold rush, heavily illustrated with photographs, prints, diagrams, maps, drawings, and art reproductions. Chapter titles include "Gold, Gold, Gold in California!," "Sailing for El Doraldo," "The Rough Realities of Grubbing for Gold," "The Sprouting Shantytowns," "Boomtown on the Bay," and "Wondrous End of a Wild Quest." The text is for high school–aged or older readers, but the (captioned) pictures—a history by themselves—will interest a wide range of ages.

Gold Fever!

Catherine McMorrow; Random House, 1996

A simple but catchy picture-book history of the California gold rush for kids in grades 2–5.

The Gold Rush

Liza Ketchum; Little, Brown, 1996

One of a three-volume series intended to accompany Stephen Ives's PBS miniseries, *The West* (see page 536). This 136-page history, lushly illustrated with period photographs, is an entertaining account of an exciting era, filled with fascinating anecdotes and many stories of real people who were there.

The Glory of Gold

Faces; December 1989

This issue of *Faces* magazine for readers in grades 4–9 includes nonfiction articles on the chemistry of gold and the practice of gold mining, goldsmithing, the golden treasures of ancient cultures, and alchemy; as well as an Indian legend, "The Golden Stag"; a recipe for "Gold Cake"; and instructions for making medieval-style gold-illuminated manuscripts and gold face ornaments based on designs from ancient Peru.

Available from most libraries or for $4.50 from

Cobblestone Publishing, Inc.

30 Grove St.

Peterborough, NH 03458-1454

(603) 924-7209 or (800) 821-0115

Web site: www.cobblestonepub.com

For general information on *Faces* magazine, see page 411.

Gold and Silver, Silver and Gold: Tales of Hidden Treasure

Alvin Schwartz; Sunburst, 1993

Ten chapters of tales about hidden treasure (mostly still lost, but occasionally found) from all over the world, some complete with maps, secret messages, and ciphers. Also included are some how-to hints for amateur treasure hunters. For readers aged 9–13.

Gold: The True Story of Why People Search for It, Mine It, Trade It, Steal It, Mint It, Hoard It, Shape It, Wear It, Fight and Kill for It

Milton Meltzer; HarperCollins, 1994

The title says it all. Alexander the Great, readers learn, was one of the greatest gold hunters of all time;

the first recorded "gold rush" took place in Brazil in 1695; and the first genuine gold rush in the United States occurred in 1828, when gold was discovered in Georgia, on Cherokee land. Fascinating reading for kids aged 8–12.

The Great American Gold Rush
Rhoda Blumberg; Bradbury Press, 1989

A detailed account of the California gold rush from 1848 to 1852, illustrated with historical prints, art reproductions, and photographs, with many quotes from contemporary sources. Factual and fascinating.

Striking It Rich: The Story of the California Gold Rush
Stephen Krensky; Aladdin, 1996

A humorous take on the Gold Rush for young readers, beginning with the building of a sawmill near the sleepy little town of San Francisco and the discovery of a gold nugget by a carpenter named James Marshall. California was soon inundated by gold seekers, arriving by land and sea, panning and digging for gold, outfitting themselves in Levi Strauss's brand-new blue jeans, and settling down in towns named Bedbug and Grizzly Flats. A fun and interesting read.

Tales and Treasure of the California Gold Rush
Randall A. Reinstedt; Ghost Town Publications, 1994

A collection of enthralling tales of the Gold Rush days and people; chapters include "How the Prospectors Came to California," "How Mining Camps Got Their Names," "Women in the Gold Rush," and "Hidden Treasures and Lost Outlaw Loot."

An accompanying activity book, *Hands-On History: Projects and Activities for Tales and Treasures of the California Gold Rush,* includes a range of multidisciplinary projects: kids, for example, use maps to conduct a treasure hunt, solve Gold Rush math problems, write their own stories about gold town names, and reenact a miners' court.

Book, $10.95; activity book, $8.95
Bluestocking Press
Box 2030
Shingle Springs, CA 95682-2030
(916) 622-8586 or (800) 959-8586/fax (916) 642-9222

True-Life Treasure Hunts
Judy Donnelly; Random House, 1993

A Step-Up Book for kids who have outgrown beginning readers (but still like large print). The book covers, in five appealing chapters, buried pirate gold, sunken Spanish treasure ships, the discovery of the treasure-filled Sacred Well in the ancient Mayan city of Chichén Itzá, the discovery of Tutankhamen's tomb, and hidden treasure worldwide. The endpapers of the book show (very general) locations of lost treasure on a map of the United States; this used to fascinate our boys when they were younger, and inspired considerable optimistic interest in the study of geography.

The Yukon Gold Rush
Cobblestone; August 1980

This issue of the historical magazine for kids in grades 5–9 (see page 449) covers the history of the Klondike gold rush; also included is a map of the Yukon, a supplementary reading list, and a sourdough recipe.

Available from most libraries or for $4.50 from
Cobblestone Publishing, Inc.
30 Grove St.
Peterborough, NH 03458-1454
(603) 924-7209 or (800) 821-0115
Web site: www.cobblestonepub.com/

BOOKS: FICTION

By the Great Horn Spoon!
Sid Fleischman; Little, Brown, 1988

The family finances are in dire straits, so young Jack Flagg, along with Praiseworthy, his Aunt Arabella's unflappable butler, stow away on a paddlewheeler en route to the California goldfields. The action begins as Praiseworthy, in bowler hat and umbrella, emerges elegantly from his hiding place in a potato barrel and continues through adventures with outlaws, claim jumpers, grizzly bears, and obstreperous burros. They make (and lose) a fortune in gold, but all ultimately live happily ever after.

Chang's Paper Pony
Eleanor Coerr; HarperTrophy, 1993

Little Chang—who dreams of owing a pony—and his grandfather, Chinese immigrants, struggle to make a living in a California gold-mining town. For readers aged 4–8.

A Small Tall Tale From the Far Far North
5 10

Peter Sis; Alfred A. Knopf, 1993

A story of the explorer Jan Welzel who travels to the vast icy spaces of the Arctic. There he discovers a mountain of gold, falls, and is saved from freezing to death by Eskimo hunters. He lives with the Eskimos, learning their legends, customs, and crafts, but he becomes worried that his friends will suffer at the hands of the prospectors arriving to search for gold. Finally he decides to lead the prospectors away from the Eskimos, to the gold mountain. The illustrations are exquisite and convey even more information than the text.

GAMES AND HANDS-ON ACTIVITIES

California Gold Rush 1849
13 +

A portfolio of primary source documents, historical background essays, and a study guide. Included are two historical maps, a gold rush "Bill of Fare," posters titled "The Miner's Ten Commandments" and "Mining Methods," copies of *Harper's Weekly* (October 3, 1857), *The Placer Times* (April 28, 1849), and *The New York Herald* (February 16, 1849), a page from President James K. Polk's diary, the sheet music for Stephen Foster's "Oh! Susanna" (1848), and a "panoramic daguerrotype" of gold rush–era San Francisco Harbor. Essay titles include "Discovery," "Forty-Niners," "To California by Sea," "To California by Land," and "San Francisco."

$37

Jackdaw Publications

Box 503

Amawalk, NY 10501

(800) 789-0022/fax (800) 962-9101

Gold . . . And How to Find It!
9 +

A gold-panning activity kit, recommended for kids in grades 5–12. The kit includes a container of gold-bearing sand ("placer gold"), a gold pan, and an illus-trated guidebook including historical background, instructions, and suggestions for additional activities.

$26

Creative Dimensions

Box 1393

Bellingham, WA 98227

(206) 733-5024/fax (206) 733-4321

Gold Rush
8 13

A cooperative simulation in which participating kids from mining companies travel to the goldfields of "Golden Gulch," stake claims and mine for gold, dealing as they proceed with food shortages, nasty weather, and claim jumpers. Included are instructions for an end-of-unit "Mining Camp Saturday Night" celebration.

Materials for the simulation, which is aimed at classroom-size groups, include 35 student guidebooks, a teacher's guide, and assorted reproducible handout sheets. "Gold Rush" is recommended for kids in grades 4–8; the entire simulation takes somewhere between 10 and 13 hours. Interact simulations work well—even better—with smaller numbers of kids and are excellent projects for cooperative groups of home learners.

$51

Interact

1825 Gillespie Way, #101

El Cajon, CA 92020-1095

(619) 448-1474 or (800) 359-0961/fax (619) 448-6722

Web site: www.interact-simulations.com

Gold Rush: The Young Prospector's Guide to Striking It Rich
8 12

James Klein; Tricycle Press, 1998

A 96-page how-to book for young prospectors, which combines information about treasure hunting with historical information, including the story of the California Gold Rush of 1849, profiles of wacky Gold Rush personalities, and tales of great treasure finds.

The Story of the California Gold Rush Coloring Book
6 +

Peter F. Copeland; Dover Publications

Forty scenes from the California gold rush, from the discovery of gold at Sutter's Mill through the arrival of the prospectors and the building of the mining camps. Explanatory historical information is included in the picture captions.

$2.95
Dover Publications, Inc.
31 E. Second St.
Mineola, NY 11501

VIDEOS

Gold Rush

A PBS video on the history of the gold rush, including period photographs, diary and journal excerpts, and commentary by historians. About one hour long; narrated by John Lithgow.

$19.95
PBS Home Video
1320 Braddock Pl.
Alexandria, VA 22314-1698
(800) 645-4PBS
Web site: www.pbs.org

COMPUTER SOFTWARE

The Yukon Trail

A computer software adventure from the makers of the popular *Oregon Trail* (see page 536). Players head north to Alaska in the Klondike gold rush of 1897. Travelers must deal with all the perils of the trail—dangerous rapids, robbers, vicious weather, disease, and hunger—on their way to the goldfields, where they may (or may not) strike it rich. The program features excellent 3-D graphics, plus period photographs and topographical maps. Travelers have the option of obtaining information and helpful advice from people that they meet en route, including both famous historical figures and ordinary citizens. They can also explore the towns, villages, and camps that they encounter, entering various buildings—included assorted gambling halls where, if they feel lucky, they can participate in a risky game of poker. On CD-ROM for Mac or Windows.

$39.95
The Learning Company
6160 Summit Dr. N
Minneapolis, MN 55430-4003

(800) 662-3390/fax (612) 589-1151
Web site: www.learningco.com

THE GOLD RUSH ON-LINE

The Gold Rush

A comprehensive site about the California Gold Rush, including historical information, fun facts, a timeline, test questions, activity suggestions, and related links.
www.isn.edu/~trinmich/home.html

THOREAU AND THE TRANSCENDENTALISTS

Henry David Thoreau: American Naturalist

Peter Anderson; Franklin Watts, 1996

A 64-page chapter biography of Thoreau, illustrated with black-and-white prints and photographs, and beautiful full-color photographs of Walden Pond at different seasons of the year. This is one of the American Conservationist Series of biographies; others by Anderson include the life stories of John James Audubon, Aldo Leopold, John Muir, and Gifford Pinchot.

Into the Deep Forest with Henry David Thoreau

Jim Murphy; Clarion, 1995

Descriptions of three of Thoreau's trips into the deep forests of Maine, with excerpts from Thoreau's journals. The book is illustrated with paintings of forest scenes and wildlife drawings. Included is a brief biography of Thoreau. For readers aged 7–12.

A Man Named Thoreau

Robert Burleigh; Atheneum, 1985

A picture-book biography of Thoreau illustrated with soft black-and-white pencil drawings. Included are many quotes from Thoreau's writings.

The Night Thoreau Spent in Jail

Jerome Lawrence and Robert E. Lee; Bantam Books, 1983

An inspiring and thought-provoking play, based on the night Thoreau spent in jail in 1846 for refusing to pay taxes to support the Mexican War. Through flashbacks and conversations with his cellmate and visiting friends (among them Ralph Waldo Emerson and his wife, Lydian), the play covers—wonderfully—Thoreau's life and philosophy.

The Transcendentalists
Cobblestone; June 1987

This issue of *Cobblestone* magazine (see page 449) includes an overview of the Transcendentalist movement, profiles of such Transcendentalists as Ralph Waldo Emerson, Henry David Thoreau, and Bronson Alcott, and a reading list. For readers in grades 5–9.

Available from most libraries or for $4.50 from

Cobblestone Publishing, Inc.

30 Grove St.

Peterborough, NH 03458-1454

(603) 924-7209 or (800) 821-0115

Web site: www.cobblestonepub.com

Walden, or Life in the Woods
Henry David Thoreau; Penguin, 1986

Walden, now an American classic, is Thoreau's account of his two years spent in a little cabin on the banks of Walden Pond, an enviable experiment in living a simple life close to the wonders of nature that never ceases to inspire. This edition also contains *On the Duty of Civil Disobedience,* Thoreau's famous essay on liberty, explaining that individuals have an obligation to use their own moral judgments to make independent decisions, regardless of government policy. The language is both dense and rich; the book is most appropriate for advanced readers, who should certainly read it.

THE WESTWARD MOVEMENT

BOOKS: NONFICTION

The American West
Dee Brown; Touchstone Books, 1995

A sweeping history of the West, told in part through the tales of prominent Westerners. *The Ameri-can West,* along with accounts of the social and political events of frontier history, tells the stories of Red Cloud, Billy the Kid, Wyatt Earp (and brothers), and Chief Joseph. Also see *The Westerners* (Galahad Books, 1974), which covers Western history from the arrival of the Spanish conquistadors to the end of the 19th century, featuring such notables as Lewis and Clark, George Catlin, Brigham Young, Charles Goodnight, and Teddy Roosevelt. Illustrated with maps, black-and-white photographs, and color art reproductions. For teenagers. See *Bury My Heart at Wounded Knee* (page 502).

Buffalo Bill and the Pony Express
Eleanor Coerr; HarperCollins, 1995

The story of young Bill Cody, whose letters home give readers an exciting picture of life in the Wild West, complete with galloping horses, bandits, and Indian attacks. For readers in grades 2–4.

Children of the Wild West
Russell Freedman; Clarion, 1990

An account of the lives of pioneer and native American children in the West from 1840 to the turn of the century, illustrated with period black-and-white photographs. For readers aged 8–12.

Cobblestone: The West

Several issues of *Cobblestone,* the history magazine for kids in grades 5–9 (see page 449), have Western history themes. *The Oregon Trail* (December 1981) includes a map of the trail, nonfiction articles on wagon trail life, covered wagons, Independence Rock in Wyoming (the "Great Register of the Desert" on which the pioneers paused to carve their names), the Whitman mission, and Red Cloud, chief of the Oglala Sioux, as well as short stories, poems, and word puzzles. *Annie Oakley* (January 1991) includes information about Oakley's life and times, her career (real and legendary) as a sharpshooter, and her starring role in Buffalo Bill's Wild West show; *Daniel Boone* (June 1988) contains articles about Boone's life, family, and accomplishments, along with a recipe for frontier-style fritters. *The North American Beaver Trade* (June 1982) includes articles on the 18th- and 19th-century fur trade, the natural history of the beaver, and the Rocky Mountain trappers, as well as a Pacific Northwest Indian legend about the beaver ("The Legend of Wishpoosh") and step-by-step instructions for drawing a beaver.

Available from most libraries or for $4.50 from

Cobblestone Publishing, Inc.

30 Grove St.

Peterborough, NH 03458-1454

(603) 924-7209 or (800) 821-0115

Web site: www.cobblestonepub.com

Daniel Boone
Laurie Lawlor; Albert Whitman, 1988

A detailed biography of the famous frontiersman who led his family Westward through the Cumberland Gap to settle in Kentucky. It's historically accurate but is so full of hair-raising escapades that it reads like fiction. Recommended for readers aged 10–14.

Growing Up in America: 1830–1860
Evelyn Toynton; Millbrook Press, 1995

The book traces the everyday lives and activities of children in early 19th-century America, comparing kids from a New England farm family, a southern slave family, an urban family, a Sioux family, and a pioneer family on the western frontier. For readers aged 8–13.

If You Traveled West in a Covered Wagon
Ellen Levine; Scholastic, 1992

Everyday life on the Oregon Trail, presented in friendly question-and-answer format. "What was the best time of year to start the trip?" "How would you cross rivers when there were no bridges?" "Where would you sleep?" "How would you build a fire if you didn't have any wood?" "Without road signs, how would you know where you are?"
See *If You . . . Series* (pages 453–454).

The Old West Series
Time-Life

The series includes many titles, among them *The Trailblazers* (Bill Gilbert), *The Indians* (Benjamin Capps), *The Fortyniners* (William Weber Johnson), *The Railroaders* (Keith Wheeler), *The Texans* (David Nevin), *The Soldiers* (David Nevin), *The Cowboys* (William H. Forbis), and *The Great Chiefs* (Benjamin Capps). All are

about 240 pages long, bound in fancy embossed cowboy boot–style fake leather, and heavily illustrated with photographs, art reproductions, prints, drawings, and maps. The text is targeted at adult readers, but the pictures are for almost all ages. Parents should preview some volumes first for the very young: some photographs from the period of the Indian Wars are brutally graphic.

The Oregon Trail
Leonard Everett Fisher; Holiday House, 1990

A 64-page history of the Oregon Trail, illustrated with dramatic graphics, for readers aged 8–13.

Pony Express!
Steven Kroll; Scholastic, 1996

The story of the Pony Express from its official beginnings in April, 1860, illustrated with maps, photographs, and drawings. For readers aged 6–9.

Quit Pulling My Leg! A Story of Davy Crockett
Robert Quackenbush; Simon & Schuster, 1987

A cleverly illustrated biography of the now legendary western hero for 7–11-year-olds. The text sticks to the facts, which are gaudy enough by themselves; a pair of cartoon-style raccoons at the bottom of alternate pages exchanges Crockett tall-tale anecdotes.

They're Off! The Story of the Pony Express
Cheryl Harness; Simon & Schuster, 1996

Our boys always loved stories of the Pony Express, with its ominous advertisements for riders ("Orphans preferred"). This is a beautifully illustrated history of the fastest mail carriers in the business from 1860 until 1861, when they were replaced by the even faster telegraph. Included are accounts of background events—Lincoln's election, westward expansion, and the impending Civil War—and interesting fact boxes (the last Pony Express rider died in 1955). For readers aged 7–10.

The West: An Illustrated History for Children
Dayton Duncan; Little, Brown, 1996

A three-volume series written to accompany Stephen Ives's PBS miniseries, *The West* (see page 536). The first volume in the series, *The West,* is a fascinating

136-page historical overview of western history, heavily illustrated with black-and-white period photographs, and peppered with quotations, interesting anecdotes, and personal stories.

Other titles in the series include *The Gold Rush* (Liza Ketchum) and *The People of the West* (Dayton Duncan).

Books: Fiction

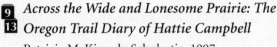

Across the Wide and Lonesome Prairie: The Oregon Trail Diary of Hattie Campbell
Patricia McKissack; Scholastic, 1997

Thirteen-year-old Hattie sets out with her family in 1847 on a six-month journey by covered wagon from Missouri to Oregon. Her diary records the hardships encountered along the way: harsh weather, accidents, disease, and fear of Indian attacks.

One of the Dear America series (see page 452) for readers in grades 5–9. An appendix of historical information and resources is included.

Araminta's Paintbox
Karen Ackerman; Atheneum, 1991

A charming picture book in which Araminta, traveling west by wagon train with her family in 1847, loses her treasured paint box. The box is found by a Mennonite family, then is passed on to a doctor's wife en route to join her husband at a fort in Colorado, a family of Mormons on their way to Utah, and a gold prospector, before finally returning to Araminta, now settled in California.

Caddie Woodlawn
Carol Ryrie Brink; Aladdin, 1990

Tomboy Caddie Woodlawn, growing up with her sister and brothers on the 19th-century Wisconsin frontier, copes with the ups, downs, and adventures of pioneer life. In a mysterious subplot, Caddie's father turns out to be the heir to an aristocratic British estate, and the family must decide whether to return to England or stay in America. Our boys liked Caddie; her unsinkable personality and trouble-prone pizzazz are reminiscent of the even more popular Anne of Green Gables.

A beautifully done video version of the book is available from the popular PBS *Wonderworks* series.

Wonderworks: Caddie Woodlawn, $29.99
Movies Unlimited
3015 Darnell Rd.
Philadelphia, PA 19154
(215) 637-4444 or (800) 4-MOVIES
e-mail: movies@moviesunlimited.com
Web site: www.moviesunlimited.com

Dakota Dugout
Ann Turner; Aladdin, 1989

A picture-book account of life on a Dakota homestead in the late 19th century, simply written in free verse.

Ellen Elizabeth Hawkins: Mobeetie, Texas, 1886
Kathleen Duey; Aladdin, 1997

Twelve-year-old Ellen lives on a ranch in Texas and wants to be a cattle rancher—a job that her family feels is impossible for a girl. When disaster strikes, however, Ellen saves the day and a thirsty herd of cows. One of the American Diaries series (see page 450) for readers aged 9–12.

Grasshopper Summer
Ann Turner; Troll Associates, 1991

Young Sam and his family settle in the Dakota Territory in the late 19th century and struggle against harsh conditions and a plague of invading grasshoppers. For readers aged 8–12.

Home on the Range: Cowboy Poetry
Paul B. Janeczko; Dial, 1997

Twenty illustrated poems about cowboy life for readers aged 8–11.

Little House in the Big Woods
Laura Ingalls Wilder; HarperTrophy, 1971

This, the first in an eight-book series based on the life of the author, is the story of young Laura Ingalls, growing up in a cabin in the "big woods" of Wisconsin in the late 19th century. A gentle and appealing account of everyday life long ago. Sequels, featuring an increasingly older Laura, are *Little House on the Prairie, On the Banks of Plum Creek, By the Shores of Silver Lake, The Long Winter, Little Town on the Prairie, These Happy Golden Years,* and *The First Four Years.* The related *Farmer Boy* tells the childhood story of Almanzo Wilder, who grows up to become Laura's husband.

For lovers of the popular Little House books, many supplementary educational materials are available. Among these are sets of Ingalls Wilder postcards, illustrated with photographs of persons and places from the books, biographies of Laura and the members of her family, the *Laura Ingalls Wilder Songbook* (see page 534) and cassette tapes of Little House songs (as played on Pa's fiddle), and Little House cookbooks, maps, timelines, and paper dolls (all the members of the family, plus Jack the bulldog, along with an inside/outside backdrop of the Little House itself).

An excellent source for Little House materials
Bluestocking Press
Box 2030
Shingle Springs, CA 95682-2030
(916) 622-8586 or (800) 959-8586/fax (916) 642-9222
Also see *Laura Ingalls Wilder, Growing Up on the Prairie* (Cobblestone; February 1986).
Available from most libraries or for $4.50 from
Cobblestone Publishing, Inc.
30 Grove St.
Peterborough, NH 03458-1454
(603) 924-7209 or (800) 821-0115
Web site: www.cobblestonepub.com

The Orphan Train Series
Joan Lowery Nixon; Bantam Books, 1996

This series of six books is based on a true historical incident, in which, between 1854 and 1880, 100,000 children from the slums of New York City were sent west under the auspices of the Children's Aid Society on the "orphan trains." The first book in the series, *A Family Apart,* opens in New York in the 1850s, where Mrs. Kelly, a poor widow, is unable to support her large family. When she discovers that Mike, her eldest son, has become a pickpocket to help feed his hungry brothers and sisters, she decides to send the children west on the "Orphan Train," to be adopted by frontier families who will provide them with a better life. Subsequent books trace the adventures of each child with his or her new family, while providing readers with historical background information about 19th-century pioneer life. Titles in the series are *A Family Apart, Caught in the Act, In the Face of Danger, A Place to Belong, A Dangerous Promise,* and *Keeping Secrets.*

Sarah, Plain and Tall
Patricia MacLachlan; HarperTrophy, 1987

Sarah, who describes herself as "plain and tall," comes to the western prairies as a mail-order bride for Anna and Caleb's widowed father and makes a great difference in all of their lives. A sequel, detailing further events in the life of Anna and Caleb, is *Skylark* (HarperTrophy, 1997).

Excellent Hallmark Hall of Fame adaptations of the books are available on video, starring Glenn Close and Christopher Walken.

$14.99 each
Movies Unlimited
3015 Darnell Rd.
Philadelphia, PA 19154
(215) 637-444 or (800) 4-MOVIES
e-mail: movies@moviesunlimited.com
Web site: www.moviesunlimited.com

Tree in the Trail
Holling C. Holling; Houghton Mifflin, 1990

The tree is an aged cottonwood and the trail is the Santa Fe Trail. Holling's book traces the history of the tree, from its discovery by a Kansan Indian boy in the early 17th century until it was brought down by lightning in 1834. The tree comes to symbolize the history of the West: Indian arrowheads are embedded in its trunk, along with the blade of a Spanish dagger and a bullet from a French trapper's gun. It witnesses buffalo hunts, Indian councils, and encampments of mountain men; it serves as a post office to western travelers, who tuck notes in its hollows. Finally, fashioned into an ox yoke by a pair of traders, it heads southwest with a wagon train and comes to rest in Santa Fe. Illustrated with color paintings, maps, and detailed pencil drawings and diagrams.

Wagon Train: A Family Goes West in 1865
Courtni C. Wright; Holiday House, 1995

The picture-book story of a black family traveling west from Virginia to California, battling rattlesnakes, hunger, broken wagon wheels, racial prejudice, and a long long walk, before they finally reach their new home.

Wagon Wheels
Barbara Brenner; HarperTrophy, 1993

Based on a true story, this tells of a black family with three young sons that travels west to homestead in Kansas in the 1870s. An I Can Read book for kids in grades 2–4.

Willow Chase: Kansas Territory, 1847
Kathleen Duey; Aladdin, 1997

Young Willow Chase, traveling west by wagon train, is swept overboard and lost when her family fords the Platte River. She survives, with the help of friendly Indians, and manages to rejoin her family. One of the American Diaries series (see page 450) for readers aged 9–12.

TALL TALES AND LEGENDS

American Tall Tales
Mary Pope Osborne; Alfred A. Knopf, 1991

A collection of tall-tale classics, starring such folk characters as Stormalong, John Henry, and Paul Bunyan, beautifully illustrated with woodblock prints. For readers aged 7–10.

John Henry: An American Legend
Ezra Jack Keats; Alfred A. Knopf, 1987

The picture-book tale of the famous "steel-driving man" who single-handedly saves a riverboat after its paddlewheel breaks and becomes a legend working on the railroad. For readers aged 4–8.

Johnny Appleseed
Steven Kellogg; Mulberry, 1996

A mix of Johnny Appleseed history and legend, with colorful illustrations, for readers aged 5–9.

Mike Fink
Steven Kellogg; Mulberry, 1998

The picture-book tale of the legendary frontiersman who ran away from home when he was two days

old and grew up to wrestle alligators and become king of the river keelboatmen.

The Narrow Escapes of Davy Crockett
Ariane Dewey; Mulberry, 1993

A picture-book account of Davy's most dangerous and outlandish escapes from a bear, a boa constrictor, a hoop snake, an elk, an owl, eagles, rattlesnakes, wildcats, trees, and tornadoes. There's also an account of the time he rode an alligator up Niagara Falls. For readers aged 4–8.

Paul Bunyan
Steven Kellogg; Mulberry, 1994

A delightful tale of the larger-than-life lumberjack who grew from gigantic babyhood to tour the country with his crew, living on skating rink–size flapjacks and carving out such geographical landmarks as the Great Lakes, the Grand Canyon, and the St. Lawrence River.

Pecos Bill
Steven Kellogg; Mulberry, 1992

The picture-book tall tale of the larger-than-life cowboy who was raised by coyotes, invented the lariat, and tamed all the wild horses of Texas.

Sally Ann Thunder Ann Whirlwind Crockett
Steven Kellogg; William Morrow, 1995

Sally Ann could "out-talk, out-grin, out-scream, out-swim, and out-run any baby in Kentucky." She tackles a grizzly bear, makes a lasso out of rattlesnakes, battles alligators, wears skunk perfume, and grows up to marry the equally legendary Davy Crockett.

Also see the book of the same name by Caron Lee Cohen (Greenwillow, 1985) in which Davy bets Mike Fink, King of the Keelboatmen, that Mike won't be able to scare Crockett's wife, Sally Ann. Mike thinks it's not much of a challenge until he meets the spectacular Mrs. Crockett.

Shooting Star: Annie Oakley, the Legend
Debbie Dadey; Walker & Company, 1997

A picture-book biography of Annie Oakley that mixes historical information and tall tale: Annie could spit bullets as a baby; as an adult, she shot the points off a star and blasted three new craters on the moon; when she died, she became a shooting star. For readers aged 5–8.

The Story of Johnny Appleseed
Aliki; Aladdin, 1987

The picture-book tale of gentle Johnny Appleseed, his life in the wilderness, and his gift of apple trees. For readers aged 4–8.

A Telling of the Tales: Five Stories
William J. Brooke; HarperCollins, 1990

Five classic tales with new twists, including the stories of Paul Bunyan, Johnny Appleseed, and John Henry. In "The Growin' of Paul Bunyan," the world's greatest tree planter—Johnny Appleseed—meets the world's greatest lumberjack, old Paul himself. For readers aged 9–13.

COLORING AND PAPER-CRAFTS BOOKS

American Pioneer Family Paper Dolls
Parents, children, and 46 costumes, including calico dresses, gingham pinafores, and some nice sets of frontier buckskins.

$4.95
Dover Publications, Inc.
31 E. Second St.
Mineola, NY 11501

The American West
An interesting 128-page coloring book with a friendly and fact-filled historical text and 60 black-line pictures to color.

$8.95 from bookstores or
Running Press Book Publishers
125 S. 22nd St.
Philadelphia, PA 19103-4399
(215) 567-5080 or (800) 345-5359/fax (800) 453-2884

Annie Oakley and Buffalo Bill Paper Dolls
Four dolls (Annie, Bill, Frank Butler, and Sitting Bull) and 27 full-color period costumes, 15 of them for Annie.

$4.95
Dover Publications, Inc.
31 E. Second St.
Mineola, NY 11501

Cowboys
A historical coloring book of the Wild West, from the early Spanish vaqueros to Buffalo Bill and Roy Rogers. Also see *Cowgirls, The Black Cowboy, Missions of the Southwest,* and *The Story of California* (3 volumes).

$3.95
Bellerophon Books
36 Ancapa St.
Santa Barbara, CA 93101
(800) 253-9943/fax (800) 965-8286

My Horse Coloring Book
John Green; Dover Publications

A coloring book for horse lovers, including pictures of horse training, grooming, and care, with explanatory picture captions. Also see *Horses of the World Coloring Book.*

$2.95 each
Dover Publications, Inc.
31 E. Second St.
Mineola, NY 11501

Western Pioneers Coloring Book
Peter F. Copeland; Dover Publications

The pictures, with explanatory captions, are scenes from the lives of the pioneers, among them images of wagon trains, keelboats, stagecoaches, and outlaws. There's also a picture showing the resuce of the ill-fated Donner Party.

Also see *Cowboys of the Old West Coloring Book* and *Legendary Outlaws and Lawmen of the Old West Coloring Book.*

$2.95
Dover Publications, Inc.
31 E. 2nd St.
Mineola, NY 11501

ACTIVITY BOOKS

The Amazing Apple Book
Paulette Bourgeois; Addison-Wesley, 1990

Link this book to a study of John Chapman, better known as Johnny Appleseed. Apple science, history, lore, and hands-on activities, for kids aged 6–10. Included are the stories of such apple heroes as Johnny Appleseed, William Tell, and Isaac Newton, a scientific description of the development of an apple from pollination to picking, an explanation of grafting, instructions for sprouting your own apple seeds, directions for making apple prints and apple dolls, and recipes for dried apples, apple yogurt, and candy apples.

Galloping Along the Old West Trails
Gary M. Garfield and Suzanne McDonough; Teacher Ideas Press, 1996

An integrated social studies unit for kids in grades 4–8 in which students follow the travels of "The Cowboy" and his horse, Kaper King, across the West in the 1850s. They trace the Cowboy's route, from St. Louis to Oregon on the map and receive letters from the Cowboy and other Old West characters he meets along the trail, among them a railroad engineer, a stagecoach driver, a frontier schoolteacher, a pioneer child, an Indian woman, western politicians, a trail cook, and a cattle rancher. Instructions for hands-on activities and projects accompany each letter. For example, kids calculate horse sizes and feeding costs and design a stable, build a model covered wagon and log cabin, learn Morse code, make horehound candy and griddle cakes, hold a political forum on western issues, write cowboy poetry, sing cowboy songs, produce a small-town western newspaper, play an Indian stick game, and make a topographical map of the wilderness.

The 180+-page book—there's a photograph of the authors in the back, in 19th-century western garb—includes a companion disk (Mac or IBM compatibles) with the texts of all 33 letters in the book, so that copies can be printed out for each participating kid.

$25

Libraries Unlimited

Box 6633

Englewood, CO 80155-6633

(303) 770-1220 or (800) 237-6124/fax (303) 220-8843

e-mail: lu-books@lu.com

Web site: www.lu.com

Hunter's Stew and Hangtown Fry: What Pioneer America Ate and Why
Lila Perl; Houghton Mifflin, 1979

Background historical information on pioneer-era food and a variety of easy-to-make pioneer recipes.

Pioneer Crafts
Barbara Greenwood; Kids Can Press, 1997

A 40-page collection of pioneer crafts for kids aged 8–12, each with background historical information and complete instructions. For example, kids make a punched-tin lantern, a pair of felt moccasins, and a rag doll.

Pioneer Days: Discover the Past with Fun Projects, Games, Activities, and Recipes
David C. King; John Wiley & Sons, 1997

Readers learn about the everyday life of Sam and Liz Butler, two children who live on the western frontier in 1843. The book includes instructions for 40 different projects and activities based on pioneer life. Many terrific illustrations. For kids aged 9–12.

A Pioneer Sampler: The Daily Life of a Pioneer Family in 1840
Barbara Greenwood; Ticknor & Fields, 1995

A year in the life of the Robertson family—Ma, Pa, Granny, Meg, George, Sarah, Willy, Lizzie, and the baby—on a frontier farm in 1840. The book includes a wealth of information about pioneer life, with wonderful illustrations and labeled diagrams, along with instructions for related projects, crafts, and activities. Readers make butter, cheese, onion dye, and ink, try finger spinning and candle dipping, construct a fiddle, and make a toy jumping jack.

A Quilt-Block History of Pioneer Days
Mary Cobb; Millbrook Press, 1995

A history-and-project book centered around the theme of early American quilts. The text traces the settlement of America, covering westward expansion—one double-page spread shows a map of the United States with prominent pioneer trails marked in color—and everyday life on the frontier. Each stage in the historical journey is illustrated with characteristic quilt block patterns, beginning with the "album quilt," in which a patch was made by each friend and family member and the quilt given to departing pioneers as a memento of loved ones left behind. Other quilt patterns represent travels on the wagon trails west (Rocky Road to Kansas, Trail of the Covered Wagons, Broken Dishes), pioneer family life (Rail Fence, Log Cabin, Sugar Cone, Churn Dash), and frontier experiences (Indian Hatchet, Bear's Paw, Fox and Geese, Weather Vane, Corn and Beans).

Accompanying projects are designed as paper crafts—simpler for younger quilt-block makers—but can easily be translated into sewing projects for enthusiastic young quilters. Readers design a classic nine-patch collage and make quilt-block-patterned bookmarks, puzzles, treasure boxes, greeting cards, recipe folders, and weather diaries. Templates and instructions are included. Also see **Quilts** (pages 515–516).

Westward Ho! An Activity Guide to the Wild West

Laurie Carlson; Chicago Review Press, 1996

A collection of projects, games, crafts, recipes, and activites for kids aged 5–12, all centering around the American West. Included are recipes for dried apples, sourdough bread, and root beer, directions for making a "possibles" bag, a gold-weighing balance, a sunbonnet, and a trapper's journal, and instructions on dowsing for water, panning for gold, and playing a cattle-drive board game.

The World of the Little House

Carolyn Strom Collins; HarperCollins, 1996

Historical background information and creative hands-on activities for each of Laura Ingalls Wilder's *Little House* books (see page 527). The book includes a biography of Laura herself, an Ingalls family tree, and a map showing the locations of the Ingallses' frontier homes, followed by individual chapters on each of the nine *Little House* books. For each is included a map of the family

property, a detailed floor plan of the house (complete right down to the patchwork quilts on the beds), historical background information, and assorted arts and crafts projects and recipes. For *By the Shores of Silver Lake*, for example, there are instructions for how to dance the polka and the waltz, directions for making Mary's beaded bracelet and Laura's autograph book, and recipes for popcorn balls and "Almanzo's Buckwheat Pancakes."

GAMES AND HANDS-ON ACTIVITIES

The American West Cards

ALL An attractive pack of 40 picture cards, each with a full-color reproduction of an artwork representing the history of the American West. Text on the back gives the historical background on each pictured subject.

$7
Aristoplay
450 S. Wagner Rd.
Ann Arbor, MI 48107
(800) 634-7738 or (888) GR8-GAME
fax (734) 995-4611
Web site: www.aristoplay.com

Dam Builders

A beautifully illustrated board game in which players—all beavers—cooperate to build a dam and lodge and to amass a supply of food for the winter. To do this, they proceed around the playing board collecting (real) little sticks and avoiding such beaver challenges as forest fires, flash floods, traps, wolves, and the depredations of the "Corps," represented by an ominously advancing bulldozer. Included is a detailed illustrated booklet with game rules and a lot of general information about beavers.

$26
Animal Town
Box 757
Greenland, NH 03840
(800) 445-8642/fax (603) 430-0334

Herd Your Horses!

A Wild West board game in which players—as horses—escape from the corral and head across country toward the hidden Green River Valley. Along the way they land on "Adventure Card" spaces, which signal perils on the trail: predatory mountain lions, rattlesnakes, poisonous water, or horse-capturing human "mustangers." In alternate versions of the game, players—now ranchers—attempt to round up horses with matching brands, colors, or markings. The game, which received the blessings of the National 4-H Council, the American Quarter Horse Association, and the U.S. Pony Club, includes 55 color-illustrated horse cards describing 32 breeds of horses. For two to four players, aged 8 and up.

$24

Aristoplay

450 S. Wagner Rd.

Ann Arbor, MI 48107

(800) 634-7738 or (888) GR8-GAME

fax (734) 995-4611

Web site: www.aristoplay.com

The Oregon Trail

A portfolio of illustrated essays, primary source materials, a timeline, and an integrated study guide on 19th-century journeys west over the Oregon Trail. There are five historical essays, among them "Who Traveled West and Why?," "Packing Up," and "Daily Life Along the Trail"; and 16 primary source materials, including a diagram of a covered wagon, period maps, pioneer letters and diary excerpts, photographs, and a poster showing modern landmarks and markers along the still existing trail.

Other Jackdaw portfolios with Western history themes include *Mountain Men and the Fur Trade, The Oklahoma Land Rush, Custer's Last Stand,* and *The Santa Fe Trail.*

$37 each

Jackdaw Publications

Box 503

Amawalk, NY 10501

(914) 962-6911 or (800) 789-0022/fax (800) 962-9101

Pioneers

A cooperative simulation for students in grades 5–9 in which kids join a wagon train headed westward to Oregon in 1846. Each participant gets a pioneer identity, helps choose supplies for the trip, and keeps a trail diary. As the simulation proceeds, the kids track their progress on a detailed trail map, make a variety of choices and decisions en route, and cope with the vagaries of "Fate Cards," which deal out hostile Indians, bad weather, broken wagon wheels, and rattlesnakes. Like all Interact simulations, the unit is intended for classroom use: the materials packet includes one teacher's guide and 35 24-page student guides. These work beautifully, however, with smaller groups and are ideal for groups of homeschoolers interested in cooperative learning activities.

Also see "Homestead," in which students take on the identity of a pioneer homesteader and help establish a farm and frontier town; and "Skins," in which kids form fur-trading companies and set out on trapping expeditions.

Shorter simulations ("Early American History Activators") include "Mountain Men Rendezvous," in which kids act the parts of fur trappers and traders, first competing in a "wilderness obstacle run" in which they deal with hostile Indians, grizzly bears, blizzards, snakes, and flooding rivers, and then sit down around the campfire to tell tall tales, based on the included "Yarn Cards"; and "Cattle Drive," a very active "Activator" in which kids as cowboys attempt to drive herds of cattle (paper balls) with brooms through teams of threatening cattle rustlers armed with Frisbees.

"Homestead," $55; "Skins," $37; History Activators, $11

Interact

1825 Gillespie Way, #101

El Cajon, CA 92020-1095

(619) 448-1474 or (800) 359-0961/fax (619) 448-6722

Web site: www.interact-simulations.com

Make Your Own Rag Doll Kit

Alicia Merret; Running Press, 1995

An illustrated instruction book plus all the materials you need to make a traditional rag doll of the sort played with by small-size pioneers. The finished doll is 15½ inches tall, with yarn hair, an old-fashioned red calico dress, and a miniature matching doll baby of her own.

$19.95 from book, game, or craft stores or

Running Press Book Publishers

125 S. 22nd St.

Philadelphia, PA 19103-4399

(215) 567-5080 or (800) 345-5359/fax (800) 453-2884

The Old West from A to Z

A set of 36 picture cards—one for each letter of the alphabet, plus 10 portraits of famous Old West characters—based on items in the Buffalo Bill Historical Center in Cody, Wyoming. A brief explanatory text is included on the back of each card.

$7

Aristoplay

450 S. Wagner Rd.

Ann Arbor, MI 48107

(800) 634-7738 or (888) GR8-GAME

fax (734) 995-4611

Web site: www.aristoplay.com

WAGON TRAINS

For the truly dedicated, wagon trains still roll today. Flint Hills Overland Wagon Trips offers weekend wagon journeys through the Flint Hills of Kansas; Oregon Trail Wagon Train organizes one- to six-day treks across the Nebraska prairie, with accompanying historically appropriate activities.

Flint Hills Overland Wagon Trips

Box 1076

El Dorado, KS 67042

or

Oregon Trail Wagon Train

Route 2, Box 502

Bayard, NE 69334

(308) 586-1850

AUDIO RESOURCES

Country & Blues Harmonica for the Musically Hopeless

Jon Gindick; Klutz Press, 1984

This musical kit includes an illustrated instruction book, a cassette tape of harmonica music, and a Hohner "Pocket Pal" harmonica in a blue case. Instructions cover the general principles of harmonica playing and show beginners how to play such traditional western songs as "Red River Valley," "Clementine," "Wabash Cannonball," "On Top of Old Smokey," and "Home on the Range."

Guitars for Kids

Small-size acoustic guitars with either nylon or steel strings. The ½-size guitar ($48.95), suitable for players aged 3–5, is 29 inches long; the ⅝-size guitar ($73.95), for ages 6–10, is 34 inches long; and the ¾-size guitar ($88.95), for kids aged 7–15, is 36 inches long.

Music for Little People

4320 Marine Ave.

Box 1720

Lawndale, CA 90260

(800) 346-4445/fax (800) 722-9505

For instruction books, see **Homespun Tapes** (page 749).

The Laura Ingalls Wilder Songbook

HarperCollins; 1992

Words and music to the songs mentioned in the *Little House* books (see page 527), with appropriate citations from the books.

Songs of the Wild West

Alan Axelrod; Simon & Schuster, 1991

A collection of 45 traditional songs of the Old West, illustrated with paintings from the Metropolitan Museum of Art and the Buffalo Bill Historical Center in Cody, Wyoming.

Westward Ho!

A "History Alive! Through Music" book and cassette tape set. The tape features 14 well-known (and not quite so well known) songs from the Old West, among them "Home on the Range," "Little Old Sod Shanty," "Sweet Betsy from Pike," "Boll Weevil," and "The San Juan Pig War." The accompanying book includes lyrics and music for each song, plus historical background material.

$19.95

Hear & Learn Publications

603 S.E. Morrison Rd.

Vancouver, WA 98664

(206) 694-0034

VIDEOS

Davy Crockett

Rabbit Ears Video

This 30-minute version of the Crockett pioneer legend is presented in "dissolve animation," which gives viewers the impression of reading a storybook on screen. Davy Crockett's voice is done by Nicolas Cage.

$14.99
Movies Unlimited
3015 Darnell Rd.
Philadelphia, PA 19154
(215) 637-4444 or (800) 4-MOVIES
e-mail: movies@moviesunlimited.com
Web site: www.moviesunlimited.com

Davy Crockett, King of the Wild Frontier

The full-length Disney version of Crockett's life, beginning on a mountaintop in Tennessee and ending at the Alamo. Fess Parker plays the title role as the man in the coonskin cap.

$19.99
Movies Unlimited
3015 Darnell Rd.
Philadelphia, PA 19154
(215) 637-4444 or (800) 4-MOVIES
e-mail: movies@moviesunlimited.com
Web site: www.moviesunlimited.com

Jeremiah Johnson

Robert Redford plays a mountain man who learns to survive life in the wilderness and deal with the cruelties on both sides in the ongoing Indian wars, finally becoming a lasting legend. Breathtaking scenery. Rated PG.

$14.99
Movies Unlimited
3015 Darnell Rd.
Philadelphia, PA 19154
(215) 637-4444 or (800) 4-MOVIES
e-mail: movies@moviesunlimited.com
Web site: www.moviesunlimited.com

Johnny Appleseed

Rabbit Ears Video

The tale of the strange and gentle man who planted apples throughout the Ohio Valley in the early 1800s, presented in "dissolve animation" storybook format and narrated by the wonderful voice of Garrison Keillor. About 30 minutes long.

$14.99
Movies Unlimited

3015 Darnell Rd.
Philadelphia, PA 19154
(215) 637-4444 or (800) 4-MOVIES
e-mail: movies@moviesunlimited.com
Web site: www.moviesunlimited.com

Johnny Appleseed

This humorous hour-long version of the legend of the pioneer tree planter is part of the *Tall Tales and Legends* series in Shelley Duvall's popular *Faerie Tale Theatre*. Real actors portray the characters: here, Martin Short plays Johnny Appleseed, with Rob Reiner and Molly Ringwald in supporting roles.

$12.99
Movies Unlimited
3015 Darnell Rd.
Philadelphia, PA 19154
(215) 637-4444 or (800) 4-MOVIES
e-mail: movies@moviesunlimited.com
Web site: www.moviesunlimited.com

Rocky Mountain Beaver Pond

A close-up look at the animal whose pelt was so valued by the 19th-century mountain men. This 44-minute color video from *National Geographic* covers the daily and very busy life of the beaver.

$24.95
National Geographic Home Video
Box 5073
Clifton, NJ 07015
(800) 627-5162
Web site: www.nationalgeographic.com

Seven Alone

The Sager family heads west to Oregon from Missouri in the winter of 1843; when their parents die, the seven children determinedly finish the journey on their own. Based on a true story.

$19.99
Movies Unlimited
3015 Darnell Rd.
Philadelphia, PA 19154
(215) 637-4444 or (800) 4-MOVIES
e-mail: movies@moviesunlimited.com
Web site: www.moviesunlimited.com

The West

10 + This eight-part PBS series, directed by Stephen Ives and written by Geoffrey C. Ward and Dayton Duncan, is an overview of the history of the West from the days before the arrival of the white settlers through the late 19th century. Titles in the series include "The People," "Empires on the Trail," "Speck of the Future," "Death Runs Riot," "The Greatest Empire Under God," "Fight No More Forever," "Geography of Hope," and "One Sky Above Us." Each runs about two hours and is packed with photographs, film clips, literary quotations, first-person narratives, and commentary by modern historians.

> $149.95
> PBS Home Video
> 1320 Braddock Pl.
> Alexandria, VA 22314-1698
> (800) 645-4PBS

COMPUTER SOFTWARE

Oregon Trail II

9 + The wagon train on computer. This is a much-improved update of the popular historical simulation, complete with maps, over 5,000 photographs, 3-D graphics, and video and computer-generated animations. Players, preparing to head west, take on the persona of a historical character—picking from among 25 occupations—and select supplies for the trail, assemble a wagon train, decide upon a departure date, and choose among three possible trails: the Oregon Trail, the California Trail, or the Mormon Trail. Once they embark on the long trek west, players must cope with endless challenges and make continual decisions along the way: they tackle raging rivers, intimidating mountains, snakebite, hunger, broken axles, and disease; they meet and converse with tradespeople, historical figures, soldiers, Indians, and fellow pioneers; they visit forts, Indian villages, and towns. A detailed guidebook provides information, historical background, and useful advice. On CD-ROM for Mac or Windows.

> $39.95
> The Learning Company
> 6160 Summit Dr. N
> Minneapolis, MN 55430-4003

(800) 662-3390/fax (612) 589-1151
Web site: www.learningco.com
See **The Yukon Trail** (page 524).

THE WEST ON-LINE

The Oregon Trail

9 + A comprehensive site on the Oregon Trail, including maps of the route, general descriptions of the journey, information about discovery and exploration, native inhabitants, wildlife, lists of unusual facts, and historic sites along the trail.

> ww.isu.edu/~trinmich/Oregontrail.html

The Spanish Missions of California

9 + A history of the Spanish in California, a virtual tour of a typical mission, and information about the people who lived in the missions, among them Spanish monks, American Indians, and soldiers. Includes suggestions for educational activities.

> tqd.advanced.org/3615

WestWeb

9 + Western history resources on-line, including information on cowboys, African American migration, life on the frontier, Spanish exploration and settlement, military history, ancient peoples, and settlers. An extensive site with many related links.

> www.library.csi.cuny.edu/westweb

SLAVERY AND THE UNDERGROUND RAILROAD

BOOKS: NONFICTION

The Amistad Slave Revolt and American Abolition

13 Karen Zeinert; Linnet Books, 1997

In 1839 a group of African slaves seized control of the ship that was transporting them to slavery in Cuba. They attempted to return to Africa but ended up in New York, where all were brought to trial, and defended by John Quincy Adams. The book explains the legal complexities of the revolt and the varying viewpoints of abolitionists, lawyers, politicians, and slaveholders. For readers aged 9–13.

The Anti-Slavery Movement
Cobblestone; February 1993

This issue of *Cobblestone* magazine (see page 449) includes a history of the abolitionist movement, the story of the slave ship *Amistad,* and a play about the Underground Railroad. For kids in grades 5–9. Also see *Frederick Douglass: Fighter for Freedom (Cobblestone;* February 1989) and *Harriet Tubman: The Woman Called Moses (Cobblestone;* February 1981).

Available from most libraries or for $4.50 from
Cobblestone Publishing, Inc.
30 Grove St.
Peterborough, NH 03458-1454
(603) 924-7209 or (800) 821-0115
Web site: www.cobblestonepub.com

Dear Benjamin Banneker
Andrea Davis Pinkney; Harcourt Brace, 1994

A biography of Benjamin Banneker, a free black in 18th-century Maryland, famed as a gifted astronomer and mathematician. The book describes both the letter he wrote to Thomas Jefferson, asking how a man who so strongly defended freedom could continue to own slaves, and Jefferson's (weak) reply. For readers aged 7–10.

Escape From Slavery: The Boyhood of Frederick Douglass in His Own Words
Michael McCurdy, ed.; Alfred A. Knopf, 1994

This is a shortened version of the first of Douglass's three autobiographies—*Narrative of the Life of Frederick Douglass, An American Slave, Written by Himself,* originally published in 1845—presented in nine short chapters. Each chapter is introduced with an explanatory paragraph of background biographical information. Illustrated with woodcuts by Michael McCurdy.

Freedom Train: The Story of Harriet Tubman
Dorothy Sterling; Scholastic, 1991

An 191-page fictionalized biography of Harriet Tubman, who escaped from slavery and then returned south to lead over 300 people to freedom. Exciting, interesting, and the basic facts are accurate.

Harriet and the Promised Land
Jacob Lawrence; Aladdin, 1997

A biography of Harriet Tubman in short, simple rhymes, spectacularly illustrated with paintings by artist Jacob Lawrence.

Harriet Beecher Stowe and the Beecher Preachers
Jean Fritz; Putnam, 1994

A fascinating biography of Harriet Beecher Stowe, author of the best-selling *Uncle Tom's Cabin,* and her outspoken family (her seven brothers all became preachers). The book covers both the details of Harriet's life and the history of her times, all in interest-grabbing fashion. Author Jean Fritz has a talent for making history human.

If You Traveled on the Underground Railroad
Ellen Levine; Scholastic, 1993

Lots of interesting information, presented as questions and answers. "How did the Underground Railroad get its name?" "How did owners try to catch the fugitives?" "Did you use special signals and codes on the Underground Railroad?" "How would you trick the slave hunters?" "What happened if you were caught?" See the *If You . . . Series* (pages 453–454).

John Brown: One Man Against Slavery
Gwen Everett; Rizzoli International Publications, 1993

The story of John Brown's attack on Harper's Ferry from the point of view of his teenage daughter Annie. The book is illustrated with 16 beautiful paintings by African-American artist Jacob Lawrence. For readers aged 7–12.

Many Thousand Gone: African Americans from Slavery to Freedom
Virginia Hamilton; Alfred A. Knopf, 1995

A history of slavery through the individual stories of the persons who lived through it. Included are the stories of Ukawsaw Gronniosaw, born a prince in

Nigeria and sold into slavery as a child for two yards of checkered cloth; of Crispus Attucks, killed in the Boston Massacre; of Gabriel Prosser and Nat Turner, who led slave rebellions; of Isabella Baumfree, who took the name Sojourner Truth; and of Henry "Box" Brown, who mailed himself north to freedom. A wonderful book. Also by Virginia Hamilton: *The People Could Fly: American Black Folktales* (Alfred A. Knopf, 1993).

Minty: A Story of Young Harriet Tubman

6
10 Alan Schroeder; Dial, 1996

A 40-page illustrated story of Harriet Tubman's childhood as a slave on a Maryland plantation in the 1820s. For readers aged 6–10.

A Picture Book of Frederick Douglass

4
8 David A. Adler; Holiday House, 1993

A short, simple, and colorfully illustrated biography of Frederick Douglass for readers aged 4–8. Also see *A Picture Book of Harriet Tubman* (1992).

Rebels Against Slavery: American Slave Revolts

9
13 Patricia C. McKissack and Fredrick L. McKissack; Scholastic, 1996

Profiles of slaves who fought against slavery from colonial times to the Emancipation Proclamation. Included are biographies of Nat Turner, Harriet Tubman, Toussaint L'Ouverture, Gabriel Prosser, Osceola, and Denmark Vesey. For readers aged 9–13.

Sojourner Truth: Ain't I a Woman?

10
+ Patricia C. McKissack and Fredrick L. McKissack; Scholastic, 1992

A detailed biography of Sojourner Truth, born a slave, who spent her life fighting slavery and defending the rights of blacks and women. For readers aged 10 and up.

To Be a Slave

10
+ Julius Lester; Dial, 1993

A powerful collection of short first-person narratives, based on the stories of 19th-century slaves (largely recorded by white abolitionists) and interviews with ex-slaves conducted in the 1930s by participants in the Federal Writers' Project. The slaves' stories are interspersed with background information or additional explanation (in italics). It's easy to see why this book won multiple awards. This is history brought painfully close, through the still living words of real people. "I was here in slavery times. I was here." By the same author: *Long Journey Home: Stories From Black History* (Dial, 1993).

The Underground Railroad

8
12 Raymond Bial; Houghton Mifflin, 1995

A 48-page account of the operation of the Underground Railroad, with descriptions of routes and stories of escapes. The book is illustrated with lovely color photographs, some that simply provide atmosphere—lighted oil lamps in windows, sunset over swamps—others of real houses on the Railroad and their hiding places for fugitives, among them concealed rooms under the eaves and a secret tunnel under a Wisconsin inn.

"Wanted Dead or Alive": The True Story of Harriet Tubman

7
10 Ann McGovern; Scholastic, 1991

A clearly and interestingly written biography of Harriet Tubman, from her childhood as a slave in Maryland through her frightening escape north, her years as "Moses," the daring conductor on the Underground Railroad, her work as a spy for the Union Army during the Civil War, and her later years in Auburn, New York. (She died at the age of 90, in 1913.)

BOOKS: FICTION

Aunt Harriet's Underground Railroad in the Sky

4
8 Faith Ringgold; Crown, 1995

In this marvelously illustrated and poetic picture-book tale, Cassie and her little brother, Be Be, are transported to a magical locomotive in the sky, emblazoned with the message "Go free north or die." There they meet Harriet Tubman and learn the story of the Underground Railroad. For readers aged 4–8.

The Drinking Gourd

4
8 F. N. Monjo; HarperTrophy, 1993

An I Can Read book about young Tommy Fuller, who helps his father smuggle a family of escaping slaves northward toward Canada. The book includes the text of the song, "The Drinking Gourd." Also see *Follow the Drinking Gourd* by Jeannette Winter (Alfred A. Knopf, 1992) and *Follow the Drinking Gourd* by Bernardine Connelly (Simon & Schuster, 1997).

The House of Dies Drear

Virginia Hamilton; Aladdin, 1984

Thomas Small and his family move into an old house in Ohio that was once a station on the Underground Railroad. There, over a hundred years ago, the owner, Dies Drear, and two escaping slaves were murdered. A local legend holds that the ghosts of Dies Drear and the slaves still haunt the house. As Thomas experiences more and more strange happenings, he eventually participates in solving a modern mystery and learns the real secret of Dies Drear. Also see the sequel, *The Mystery of Drear House* (Scholastic, 1997). See the video version of the book (page 541).

Nettie's Trip South

Ann Turner; Aladdin, 1995

Just before the outbreak of the Civil War, young Nettie makes a visit to Richmond, Virginia. While there, she writes letters to her friend Addie back home in Albany, describing slavery as she sees it all around her. The slaves, Nettie observes with horror, are counted as "three-quarters of a person," have no last names, sleep in huts, and can be sold away from their families. The book is based on a diary kept by the author's great-grandmother. Recommended for readers aged 5 and up.

Nightjohn

Gary Paulsen; Laurel Leaf, 1995

A first-person narrative by a 12-year-old slave girl, Sarny, who tells the courageous story of Nightjohn, who risks death and torture to teach slaves how to read. A brutal and painful but indomitable book. For readers aged 12 and up.

A Picture of Freedom: The Diary of Clotee, A Slave Girl

Barry Denenberg; Scholastic, 1997

Twelve-year-old Clotee has learned—secretly—to read and write, while fanning the master's son, William, during his school lessons. She records her experiences living on a Virginia plantation in 1859—including, when William's tutor becomes a conductor on the Underground Railroad, her struggle to decide whether to stay with her slave "family" or escape north to freedom. One of the Dear America series (see page 452) for readers in grades 5–9; includes an appendix of historical information and resources.

The Slave Dancer

Paula Fox; Laurel Leaf, 1996

"Ship: *The Moonlight*," begins Fox's heart-wrenching book. "Cargo: 98 slaves whose true names were remembered only by their families, except for the young boy, Ras. Shipwrecked in the Gulf of Mexico, June 3, 1840. Survivors: 2." This is the story of young Jessie Bollier, press-ganged into service aboard a slave ship, where one of his duties is to play the flute while the chained slaves are exercised on deck. An unforgettable but painful story.

Sweet Clara and the Freedom Quilt

Deborah Hopkinson; Random House, 1995

A picture book about Clara, a 12-year-old slave girl who stitches a patchwork quilt showing escape routes to the north. When she herself escapes—and is reunited at last with her mother—she leaves the quilt behind to help others gain their freedom. For readers aged 5–10.

Thee, Hannah!

Marguerite DeAngeli; Doubleday, 1989

The story of Hannah, a young Quaker girl who helps a fugitive slave mother and child. A chapter book for readers aged 7–12.

GAMES AND HANDS-ON ACTIVITIES

Harriet Tubman Game and Study Set

The game includes a 20×26-inch black-line playing board, suitable for coloring and laminating, illustrated with a winding playing path that stretches from the cotton fields of the slave-owning South to freedom in Canada. Each step on the path represents risks and adventures encountered by escaping slaves on the Underground Railroad. The game comes with a short biography of Harriet Tubman, assorted activity suggestions and discussion questions, a bibliography of related readings, a song sheet, a package of felt-tipped markers, and a die. Recommended for players in grades 2–6.

Game and study set, $7.95

National Women's History Project

7738 Bell Rd.

Windsor, CA 95492-8518

(707) 838-6000/fax (707) 838-0478

The Slave Trade and Its Abolition

A portfolio of eight primary source documents, six illustrated historical background essays, and a study guide, with reproducible worksheets. Essay titles include "Slavery," "The Middle Passage," and "The Plantations"; documents include a diagram of a slave ship, a bill advertising a slave auction, and a collection of prints of "scenes from slave life."

$37

Jackdaw Publications

Box 503

Amawalk, NY 10501

(800) 789-0022/fax (800) 962-9101

Slavery in the United States

A portfolio of nine primary source documents, six illustrated historical essays, and a study guide with reproducible student worksheets. Essay titles include "Slavery Comes to the Colonies," "Slavery in the Nineteenth Century," and "Lincoln and the Emancipation Proclamation." Documents include reproductions of period newspapers, a slave bill of sale, and a copy of the Emancipation Proclamation.

$37

Jackdaw Publications

Box 503

Amawalk, NY 10501

(800) 789-0022/fax (800) 962-9101

The Underground Railroad

A board game in which players, as runaway slaves, travel north through slave and free states, finally crossing the Canadian border to freedom. The paper game board is a crosshatched map, divided into "Slave States" and "Free States." Players, starting in the "Slave Quarters" next to an engraved illustration of a plantation Big House, move their pieces north, dealing with swamps, rivers, forests, and slave catchers, and encountering both safe Underground Railroad stations and unfriendly proslavery houses. Text on the reverse side of the game board tells the story of the Underground Railroad and includes a list of suggested supplementary educational activities.

The game is available alone or as a "Game and Music Set," with an accompanying cassette tape of Underground Railroad songs, including "No More Auction Block for Me," "Follow the Drinking Gourd," "Go Down Moses," and "One More River to Cross."

Game alone, $6.95; with cassette tape, $14.95

Chatham Hill Games, Inc.

Box 253

Chatham, NY 12037

(518) 392-5022 or (800) 554-3039/fax (518) 392-3121

Web site: www.ocdc.com/Chatham_Hill_Games

See *American Adventure Games* (page 457).

VIDEOS

The Autobiography of Miss Jane Pittman

Jane Pittman, 110 years old, tells the story of her long life, from her childhood as a slave through her participation in the Civil Rights movement of the 1960s. Starring Cicely Tyson.

$39.95

Zenger Media

10200 Jefferson Blvd.

Culver City, CA 90232-0802

(310) 839-2436 or (800) 421-4246/fax (310) 839-2249

or (800) 944-5432

Web site: ZengerMedia.com/Zenger

Follow the Drinking Gourd

A tale of the Underground Railroad based on the folk song "Follow the Drinking Gourd." The story is narrated by Morgan Freeman and presented in a "dissolve animation" format that gives viewers the effect of reading a picture book. About 30 minutes long.

$14.99

Movies Unlimited

3015 Darnell Rd.

Philadelphia, PA 19154

(215) 637-4444 or (800) 4-MOVIES

e-mail: movies@moviesunlimited.com

Web site: www.moviesunlimited.com

12 *Frederick Douglass: When the Lion Wrote History*

The life story of Frederick Douglass, born a slave in 1818, who became a journalist, diplomat, and a powerful force in the struggle for black emancipation and civil rights. This 90-minute PBS special includes archival photographs, interviews with modern historians, and film footage taken at historical locations.

$19.98

PBS Home Video

1320 Braddock Pl.

Alexandria, VA 22314-1698

(800) 645-4PBS

Web site: www.pbs.org

10 *Roots*

A six-part video series based on Alex Haley's Pulitzer Prize–winning family history. The story begins in Gambia, West Africa, in 1767, where young Kunta Kinte is kidnapped by slavers, and continues through three more generations, ending (almost) with Kunta Kinte's indomitable grandson, Chicken George, leading his family to a new home in Tennessee after the Civil War.

Episode 1 covers Kunta Kinte's early life in Africa, his capture, and his terrible sea voyage to America; Episode 2 describes Kunta Kinte's sale at a slave auction in Annapolis and his defiant early days of plantation life. In Episode 3, Kunta Kinte escapes and is captured and viciously maimed by slave catchers; he marries and has a daughter, whom he names Kizzy, which, in his native language, means "stay put." Episode 4 follows the life of Kizzy, sold at the age of 16 to a new master, to whom she bears a son, who grows up to become Chicken George. In Episode 5, Chicken George is sent to England as payment for his master's gambling debts; there he earns his freedom, and returns home, 14 years later, to fight on the Union side in the Civil War. In Episode 6, Chicken George's family is being terrorized by white raiders in the aftermath of

the war; Chicken George returns home, and the family departs for a new life in Tennessee. Throughout the story runs the proud heritage of Kunta Kinte. As the family heads west toward their new home, Chicken George begins to tell his tale to his little grandson.

The story is powerful and painful, defiant and brave. Many scenes are cruel and frightening, too much so for very young viewers. To our boys, it was horrifying, fascinating, and a valuable revelation.

$149.99

Movies Unlimited

3015 Darnell Rd.

Philadelphia, PA 19154

(215) 637-4444 or (800) 4-MOVIES

e-mail: movies@moviesunlimited.com

Web site: www.moviesunlimited.com

9 *Wonderworks: The House of Dies Drear*

Based on Virginia Hamilton's gripping novel (see page 539), this excellent video adaptation tells the story of a modern family that moves into a house haunted by the ghost of Dies Drear, an abolitionist and conductor on the Underground Railroad, mysteriously murdered in the days before the Civil War; it's 116 minutes long.

$29.99

Movies Unlimited

3015 Darnell Rd.

Philadelphia, PA 19154

(215) 637-4444 or (800) 4-MOVIES

e-mail: movies@moviesunlimited.com

Web site: www.moviesunlimited.com

THE CIVIL WAR AND RECONSTRUCTION

From my homeschool diary:

◆ **February 20, 1991. Josh is nine; Ethan, eight; Caleb, six.**

We've just begun a study of the Civil War, using a series of home-written workbooks. The boys began by drawing detailed maps of a southern cotton plantation, complete with big house, slave cabins, workshops, barns, well, gardens, pastures, and cotton fields. ("What kind of plant does cotton grow on?" "How do you pick it?") We then defined abolitionist, discussed the process of bringing new states into the Union and the controversy that developed in the pre–Civil War years over whether new states should be slave or free. Josh: "Why couldn't the new states just vote and choose for themselves?" Which led nicely into a discussion of the Missouri Compromise, the Kansas-Nebraska Act, and "bleeding Kansas."

We read "Wanted Dead or Alive": The Story of Harriet Tubman by Ann McGovern (see page 538) and The Drinking Gourd by F. N. Monjo, (see page 538) and the boys invented—on paper—their own methods for escaping from slavery: Josh thought slaves should have joined traveling circus acts, pretending to be part of the circus until they reached the safety of the North; Ethan devised a secret boat made from an upside-down floating bathtub in which slaves could paddle to freedom. Discussed the Fugitive Slave Law, and Harriet Beecher Stowe and Uncle Tom's Cabin, using illustrations from a number of reference books. The boys designed their own book covers for copies of the famous book. (Joshua's featured some truly dramatic bloodhounds.)

◆ February 21, 1991

Began the school morning—after three bowls of strawberry oatmeal and a stack of Berenstain Bear books—with the escaping slaves' guidepost, the Drinking Gourd. We first read The Big Dipper and You (E. C. Krupp) (see page 252), which was a gem—lots of Dipper information, all interesting. We spent a lot of time figuring out how many miles we've all traveled through space, at the rate of 583 million miles per year, which fascinated the boys—and me, for a slightly different reason; rarely is there so much spontaneous enthusiasm for arithmetic. The boys then drew diagrams of the Big Dipper (in one color) and added the stars of Ursa Major (in another)—which led to an explanation of the difference between constellations and asterisms, and a lot of comments on the fact that the Great Bear looks absolutely nothing like a bear. Then identified Big and Little Dippers on a map of the night sky, and the boys learned how to find the North Star.

On outline maps of the United States, the boys colored all the states in the Confederacy; we defined seces-

sion, and discussed the relative differences between northern and southern populations, political opinions, and economies. The kids then looked at a series of pictures of Civil War uniforms, picked their favorites, and designed versions of their own.

We all went out after dark and located the Big and Little Dippers, the "pointer stars," the North Star, and Mizar and Alcor, the double-star pair in the Big Dipper's handle, which all the kids can see, and their parents can't. We noted the relative position of the Big Dipper in the sky (the handle is hanging down; it's winter), and pointed out Orion, Cassiopeia, and Betelgeuse. Caleb found a satellite, zipping across the sky way up— that child has eyes like an eagle. The boys peppered us with questions: "What's the name of the biggest crater on the moon?" "Why do planets orbit—why don't they just hang there in space?" "What's outer space made of—is it just totally empty?" "How fast do satellites go?" "How big is a black hole?" By that time we were all freezing, so we went in and read books about astronomy.

◆ February 22, 1991

Discussed Generals McClellan, Grant, and Lee this morning, looking at photographs of all three, reading short biographies of Grant and Lee, and poems about Grant, Lee, Lincoln, and Nancy Hanks in A Book of Americans by Stephen Vincent Benet (see page 451). The boys then designed swords (for Grant) and battle flags (for Lee)—the genuine Confederate flag, they all felt, was a trifle unimaginative.

They then went to their weekly music class (a singing group for homeschooled kids; there are usually about 15 or 20 participants, aged from 4 to 12) where they told the music teacher about their Civil War studies and asked if they could learn some Civil War songs. The teacher, never at a loss, taught them "Goober Peas."

◆ February 25, 1991

Began the morning with a stack of picture books, ending with Gettysburg: Tad Lincoln's Story by F. N. Monjo, an account of the Civil War and the crucial Battle of Gettysburg through the eyes of Abraham Lincoln's young son Tad. The book generated a lot of questions: "What's a cipher?" "What did a Rebel yell sound like?"

HISTORY

What kind of guns did they have in the Civil War?" "Was General Grant at the Battle of Gettysburg?" Located Pennsylvania and Gettysburg on the U.S. map. Josh, thoroughly interested, then drew his own detailed map of the battlefield, showing what he would have done if he had been General Pickett, rather than charging right smack across an open field.

Read John Greenleaf Whittier's poem "Barbara Frietchie," with illustrations by James Thurber, all of which the boys, perversely, found hilarious, breaking into hysterical giggles at the phrase "'Shoot if you must this old gray head/But spare your country's flag,' she said." Josh, much taken with Frietchie, wrote a poem of his own on the same theme, with a much more exciting but less positive ending.

◆ February 26, 1991

Read If You Grew Up With Abraham Lincoln (see page 545) and True Stories About Abraham Lincoln (see page 545), both by Ruth Belov Gross, and looked at photographs of Lincoln and family in Russell Freedman's Lincoln: A Photobiography (see page 545) and the Time-Life American History series. On the U.S. map, located the states where Lincoln lived. We then measured 6 feet 4 inches (up) to see how tall Lincoln really was, added a foot for his stovepipe hat, and determined that he wouldn't have been able to fit through our kitchen door without stooping. The boys then drew and colored Lincoln portraits, a flashy array that we posted on the refrigerator: Josh's Lincoln has purple boots, Ethan's sports long pink hair, and Caleb's is practically all hat. Defined and discussed the Emancipation Proclamation. ("Shouldn't the war just have been over then?")

Discussed Ford's Theater and John Wilkes Booth—the boys came up with several excellent schemes that would have prevented the assassination. "Who becomes president if the president dies?" "Where is Lincoln buried?" "What happened to John Wilkes Booth?" Then—backtracking—we read and discussed the Gettysburg Address. Josh: "How much is a score?"

Built models of Lincolnesque log cabins using logs made from rolls of brown paper and modeling clay for chimney stones. They came out pretty well, though Caleb was horrified to realize, right at the end, that his cabin had no hole for a door.

◆ February 27, 1991

Read a short story about Civil War spies, which included an account of women smuggling messages under their hoop skirts. This stirred up some interest: "What's a hoop skirt?" And, when explained, "How do you sit down in one?" We spent some time flipping through various books, looking up Civil War–era clothing; the boys then made labeled drawings of their own methods for smuggling secret messages. Josh planned to disguise himself as a Mexican musician, hiding the message in the hatband of his sombrero; Ethan briefly considered hoop pants, but decided instead to conceal the message inside his bicycle, after screwing off the bicycle seat. Caleb planned to fold the message several times and then slide it inside a cut hot dog, which he would then wrap and carry in a lunch bag.

Read about the Lincoln penny, and the boys made penny rubbings. "Who's on a nickel?" "Who's on a dime?" "What about a quarter?" "What's the very biggest coin?" So we found out.

◆ February 28, 1991

Read a book about the Monitor, the Merrimac, and their famous battle. This particularly appealed to Ethan; he spent much of the rest of the morning inventing his own versions of both ships, with much improved equipment. (He may be a little vague on the causes of the Civil War, but he will never forget that the Monitor had the first revolving gun turret.) Discussed the blockade and blockade runners—the boys all had some creative ideas for blockade running—then the final days of the war and the surrender at Appomatox Courthouse.

Played a homemade game of Civil War trivia—questions on index cards—just to see how much the boys are retaining of all this stuff: a lot, apparently.

As a bedtime book, we've started reading Susan's Secret by Hildreth Winston, a chapter book about a little girl in Vermont who discovers that her parents are conductors on the Underground Railroad.

◆ March 1, 1991

The Civil War with maps. Using outline maps of the United States, the boys colored the northern and southern states in two different colors, counted the numbers of states on each side, and located the Mason-Dixon line. We then located and discussed some important Civil War sites: Washington, D.C., Richmond, Fort Sumter, Gettysburg, Hampton Roads, Appomatox Courthouse. Lots more questions: "What happened to General Lee after the war?" "What happened to his horse?" "What happened to the plantations now that there weren't any slaves to work on them anymore?" "What happened to the Monitor and the Merrimac?"

Josh is writing—with a little prodding—a report on the Battle of Gettysburg, from the point of view of General Meade. It begins, "Hi. I'm General Meade. I'm an expert on Gettysburg. I reckon that's because I was there."

◆ **March 4, 1991**

We made an illustrated American history timeline marked off in 100-year segments—one foot per hundred years; the boys measured and marked on a roll of brown wrapping paper. Included: the arrival of Columbus in the New World, Pocahontas and Jamestown, the arrival of the Pilgrims, the Revolutionary War, the Civil War, the Wright brothers' flight at Kitty Hawk, World Wars I and II, the first moon landing, and the present day. The boys took turns drawing small pictures to illustrate each event, which they cut out and pasted onto the timeline in the proper places.

Me: "There's an easy little rhyme that helps you remember when Columbus first came to America: 'In fourteen hundred ninety-two/Columbus sailed the ocean blue.' There ought to be something like that for the Civil War."

Josh: "How about: 'In eighteen hundred sixty-one/The Civil War had just begun'?"

Played another round of Civil War trivia, discussing the answers to the questions as we went. The boys renamed Robert E. Lee's horse, Traveller having been deemed a dull name. In the running: Thunderstorm, Night Runner, Ghost. ("What was the name of General Grant's horse?")

BOOKS: NONFICTION

Abe Lincoln Goes to Washington: 1837–1865
Cheryl Harness; National Geographic Society, 1996–97

Harness has written a pair of delightful picture-book biographies of Lincoln for kids aged 6–10, each with many information-crammed illustrations. The first, *Young Abe Lincoln: The Frontier Days* (1996), covers Lincoln's log-cabin frontier childhood, his early job experiences (as a boatman, postmaster, storekeeper, and surveyor), and his education as a lawyer. *Abe Lincoln Goes to Washington* begins with Lincoln's arrival in Springfield, Illinois, and covers his marriage to Mary Todd, the births of his children, his entry into politics, his presidency and the Civil War, and the assassination.

Abe Lincoln's Hat
Martha Brenner; Random House, 1994

A short cheerful biography of Lincoln for readers aged 5–8. The book begins with Lincoln, a young lawyer, buying a tall black stovepipe hat, in which he later stores his papers. Interesting anecdotes.

Behind Rebel Lines: The Incredible Story of Emma Edmonds, Civil War Spy
Seymour Reit; Harcourt Brace, 1991

Emma Edmonds, eager to do her part in the Civil War, cut off her hair, put on a pair of trousers, and joined the Union Army. As a spy, she crossed the Rebel lines time and again, cleverly disguised as everything from a slave to a washerwoman to an itinerant peddler, collecting information to help the Union cause. An exciting read for kids aged 12 and up.

The Boys' War: Confederate and Union Soldiers Talk About the Civil War
Jim Murphy; Clarion, 1993

Army life during the Civil War, largely based on the firsthand accounts of young soldiers under 16. Illustrated with 50 period photographs. For readers aged 10 and up.

Cobblestone: Civil War and Reconstruction
Cobblestone magazine (see page 449), the history magazine for kids in grades 5–9, has devoted many issues to Civil War themes and famous persons. Each includes illustrated nonfiction and fictionalized articles, suggestions for activities, reading lists, maps, and timelines. Titles include *Abraham Lincoln* (May 1994), *Aftermath of the Civil War: Reconstruction* (May 1987), *The Battle of Gettysburg* (July 1988), *Civil War High-*

lights (April 1981), *Robert E. Lee* (September 1993), and *Ulysses S. Grant* (October 1995).

Available from most libraries or for $4.50 from Cobblestone Publishing, Inc.

30 Grove St.

Peterborough, NH 03458-1454

(603) 924-7209 or (800) 821-0115

Web site: www.cobblestonepub.com

Don't Know Much About the Civil War
Kenneth G. Davis; William Morrow, 1996

This is an adult book, but the reader-friendly format makes it appropriate for a wide range of ages. The book is arranged chronologically, covering the early days of slavery, the events leading up to the Civil War, the war itself, and its aftermath. Each chapter answers a series of questions, such as "Who brought slavery to America?," "Where did the Underground Railroad run?," and "What happened at Antietam?" Interspersed with the answers are "Civil War Voices": related quotations and first-person accounts. An accessible reference for all.

If You Grew Up With Abraham Lincoln
Ann McGovern; Scholastic, 1992

Everyday life in the first half of the 19th century, as experienced by Abraham Lincoln. The book is written in question-and-answer format: If you grew up with Abraham Lincoln . . . "What kind of house would you live in?" "What kind of school did you go to?" "What books did children read?" "What were the biggest dangers on the frontier?" "What was Springfield like?"
See *If You . . . Series* (pages 453–454).

The Illustrated Gettysburg Address
Sam Fink; Random House; 1994

The words of the Gettysburg Address, one phrase per page, are paired with pen-and-ink portraits of Lincoln and excerpts from Lincoln's writings or quotes about him.

Just a Few Words, Mr. Lincoln: The Story of the Gettysburg Address
Jean Fritz; Price Stern Sloan, 1993

Anything by Jean Fritz is good. This illustrated story of the famous address, targeted at kids in grades 2–4, also includes facts about Lincoln's life and the Civil War, with memorable notes about the speech itself ("It took longer to boil an egg").

Lincoln: A Photobiography
Russell Freedman; Clarion, 1989

A superb biography of Lincoln, covering his life from backwoods childhood to tragic assassination, illustrated with period photographs. A Newbery Medal winner. For readers aged 12 and up.

Me and Willie and Pa: The Story of Abraham Lincoln and His Son Tad
F. N. Monjo; Simon & Schuster, 1973

"When I look back, thinking about our time in Washington," the book begins, in Tad's voice, "most everything I remember is sad." The book covers the years 1860 to 1865, from Lincoln's election through the Civil War years to his assassination by John Wilkes Booth. Not always sad, but always interesting. Also by Monjo: *Gettysburg: Tad Lincoln's Story* and *The Vicksburg Veteran*.

Mr. Lincoln's Whiskers
Karen Winnick; Boyd's Mills Press, 1996

The picture-book story of an 11-year-old girl named Grace who wrote Lincoln a letter advising him to grow a beard. He did and was pleased with the result. Based on a true story. For readers aged 5–9.

Stonewall
Jean Fritz; Paper Star, 1997

An excellent chapter biography of General Thomas "Stonewall" Jackson, who earned his famous nickname at the Battle of Bull Run. He rode a horse named Sorrel, liked to suck lemons, refused to mail letters on Sundays, and was such a great soldier that Robert E. Lee once said that he would be willing to follow him into battle blindfolded. The book also covers the history of the Civil War era and Jackson's place within it. Fritz has a talent for making history come fascinatingly alive.

True Stories About Abraham Lincoln
Ruth Belov Gross; Scholastic, 1991

Delightful (and true) tales of Abraham Lincoln, from his birth on February 12, 1809, in a cabin in Ken-

HISTORY

y

tucky, to his death, from an assassin's bullet in 1865. Each of the 23 true stories is just one page long; all are printed in red and illustrated with woodcuts. For readers aged 6–10.

Where Lincoln Walked
Raymond Bial; Walker & Company, 1998

A brief biography of Lincoln, stunningly illustrated with full-color photographs showing the many places where Lincoln lived and walked. For kids aged 8–12.

Books: Fiction

Across Five Aprils
Irene Hunt; Berkley Publishing Group, 1991

The first April is April 1861, and Jethro Creighton, planting potatoes on his family's farm in Illinois, is just nine years old. Over the next four Aprils, through the terrible years of the Civil War, Jethro struggles to understand the beliefs of his father and brothers— pulled in different directions by the war—and to cope with danger and loss. A rich family story, a wise and understanding account of a boy's coming of age, and an unforgettable slice of American history. For readers aged 12 and up. A video version of the book, retitled *Civil War Diary,* is also available.

$19.95
Zenger Media
10200 Jefferson Blvd.
Box 802
Culver City, CA 90232-0802
(310) 839-2436 or (800) 421-4246/fax (310) 839-2249
or (800) 944-5432
Web site: ZengerMedia.com/Zenger

Brady
Jean Fritz; Viking, 1987

A novel of torn loyalties: Brady's mother is a southerner, but his father is an abolitionist and a conductor on the Underground Railroad. For readers aged 11 and up.

Bull Run
Paul Fleischman; HarperTrophy, 1995

A gripping tale of the Civil War, told in a series of short vignettes by 16 very different people, eight from the North, eight from the South. The speakers include a Mississippi slave woman, a free black man fighting in the Union army, a plantation owner's wife, a fifer boy, a Minnesota farm girl, and a coachman, hired to drive the townspeople of Washington, D.C., to a hill above the Bull Run battleground, where they planned to nibble picnic lunches, sip champagne, and watch the fight. A creative and very real look at Civil War history. For readers aged 10 and up.

The Killer Angels
Michael Shaara; Ballantine, 1996

The perennially popular historical novel about the Battle of Gettysburg. The history is accurate; the personal portraits are vivid and unforgettable. An enthralling read for teenagers.

Meet Addy
Connie Porter; Pleasant Company, 1993

Addy is one of the young girls featured in the American Girls series (see page 448), a black girl born a slave in North Carolina. The first book details her life on the plantation, the sale of her father and brother, and her escape north with her mother, which ends with their safe arrival in Philadelphia. The series continues through five other books, telling about Addy's new life in the north in the days of the Civil War and the Reconstruction. An accompanying teacher's guide, *Addy 1864: Teacher's Guide to Six Book About Civil War America* (Pleasant Co., 1996) includes plot summaries of all six Addy books, historical background information, multidisciplinary project and activity suggestions, reproducible student worksheets, and a map.

Also see *Addy's Cookbook: A Peek at Dining in the Past With Meals You Can Cook Today* (1994), *Addy's Craft Book: A Look at Crafts from the Past With Projects You Can Make Today* (1994), and *Addy's Paper Doll* (1994).

Pink and Say
Patricia Polacco; Philomel Books, 1994

A wonderful story, but a tearjerker. Say and Pink, both Union soldiers, meet on the battlefield. Say has been wounded and left for dead; Pink, a black soldier, saves his life and takes him home to his mother for nursing. Pink's mother is killed by marauders; Say and Pink are captured by Confederate soldiers and sent to Andersonville prison. Pink is hanged in prison, but Say lives to tell their tale. It's a simple book, intended for 4–8-year-olds, but parents should preview it first; the material may be too upsetting for the very young. Based on a true story.

The Red Badge of Courage
Stephen Crane; Washington Square Press, 1996

The Civil War classic about a young soldier coming to terms—not only physically, but also psychologically—with the realities of battle. Originally published in 1895, this book has been touted as one of the most realistic war novels ever written. For teenagers.

Also see the video version of the book (page 551).

Thunder at Gettysburg
Patricia Lee Gauch; Yearling, 1990

A short chapter book about a young girl's experience of the Battle of Gettysburg, illustrated with black-and-white drawings. For readers aged 6–8.

When Will This Cruel War Be Over?: The Civil War Diary of Emma Simpson
Barry Denenberg; Scholastic, 1996

The Civil War as seen through the diary kept by a young Confederate girl in Gordonsville, Virginia, in 1864. The book includes an appendix of historical resources.

One of the Dear America series (see page 452); recommended for readers in grades 5–9.

COLORING AND PAPER-CRAFTS BOOKS

American Family of the Civil War Era Paper Dolls

The *Civil War Era* family includes parents, three children, and multiple period costumes in full color for each, among them the father's blue Union Army uniform. Other titles include *American Family of the Confederacy Paper Dolls* (parents and three kids, the father

uniformed in gray) and *Southern Belles Paper Dolls,* which includes an entire spectacularly outfitted wedding party. Also see the *Ulysses S. Grant Family Paper Dolls,* which consists of 16 dolls and 17 costumes, including Grant's military uniform and inaugural frock coat; *Abraham Lincoln and His Family Paper Dolls* (Abe, Mary Todd, three children, and everything from a stovepipe hat to longjohns); and *Robert E. Lee and His Family Paper Dolls.*

$4.95 each
Dover Publications, Inc.
31 E. Second St.
Mineola, NY 11501

Civil War Postcards
A pack of 24 cards with black-and-white period photographs by Civil War photographer Matthew Brady.

$4.95
Dover Publications, Inc.
31 E. Second St.
Mineola, NY 11501

A Coloring Book of the Civil War
An array of Civil War uniforms and battles, all with a brief explanatory text.

Other educational coloring book titles include *Billy Yank: The Union Soldier in the Civil War, Johnny Reb: The Confederate Soldier in the Civil War, Black Soldiers of the Civil War, Civil War Heroes, Civil War Heroines,* and *Civil War Flags.*

$3.95
Bellerophon Books
36 Ancapa St.
Santa Barbara, CA 93101
(800) 253-9943

The Story of the Civil War Coloring Book
Over 40 black-line drawings of Civil War scenes from Fort Sumter to Appomattox, plus a brief historical text. Also see the *Abraham Lincoln Coloring Book, Civil War Uniforms Coloring Book,* and *Naval Battles of the Civil War Coloring Book.*

$2.95
Dover Publications, Inc.

31 E. Second St.

Mineola, NY 11501

Union Army Paper Soldiers

Contains 24 free-standing examples, in full color. For battle reenactment purposes, also see *Confederate Army Paper Soldiers*.

$3.95

Dover Publications, Inc.

31 E. Second St.

Mineola, NY 11501

GAMES AND HANDS-ON ACTIVITIES

Across Five Aprils

A collection of five strategy board games, variously simulating the battles of Bull Run, Pea Ridge, Shiloh, Gettysburg, and Bentonville. All are played according to the same short, basic rules. For players aged 10 and up.

$30

Avalon Hill Game Co.

4517 Harford Rd.

Baltimore, MD 21214

(410) 254-9200 or (800) 999-3222

e-mail: AH GAMES@aol.com

Web site: www.avalonhill.com

The Civil War

A portfolio of nine historical documents with accompanying notes, five informational "Broadsheet Essays" by historians, a list of suggested reading materials and discussion questions for students, and a detailed study guide. Essay titles include "Billy Yank and Johnny Reb," "The Two Presidents," and "Grant and Lee." Historical documents include copies of soldiers' letters, Union and Confederate recruiting posters, a copy of the Emancipation Proclamation, pages from period newspapers, and a collection of Civil War photographs.

$37

Jackdaw Publications

Box 503

Amawalk, NY 10501

(914) 962-6911 or (800) 962-0022/fax (800) 962-9101

Civil War

A simulation of civilian and military life during the American Civil War. This is a five-part unit in which students, divided into Yankee and Rebel camps, move through the five years of the war, keeping diaries, fighting historical battles (the outcomes determined by "Combat Cards"), tracing their forces' progress on a map, reenacting crucial events from the war years, and writing letters to loved ones at home. Enough materials and lesson plans are provided for six weeks' worth of Civil War activities. Examples include holding interviews with soldiers, learning to play "Rounders" (the original baseball), competing for the "Best Lincoln" award in a Gettysburg Speech Contest, studying Civil War music, poetry, painting, and photography, reenacting the surrender at Appomatox Courthouse and the assassination of Lincoln at Ford's Theater, and holding debates on pivotal Civil War questions, with each participant taking the role of a prominent Civil War personality (included: Mary Todd Lincoln and Frederick Douglass).

Simulation materials include a 199-page teacher's manual (in a looseleaf binder), 35 24-page student guides, "Character" and "Combat" cards, and maps. The unit is recommended for 20 to 35 students in grades 5–11, though it is also appropriate for smaller groups of home learners.

$64

Interact

1825 Gillespie Way, #101

El Cajon, CA 92020

(619) 448-1474 or (800) 359-0961/fax (619) 448-6722

Web site: www.interact-simulations.com

The Civil War: Literature Units, Projects, and Activities

Janet Cassidy; Scholastic, 1995

A collection of discussion questions and activity suggestions for students in grades 4–8 based on Civil War books such as *Across Five Aprils* (page 546), *Lincoln: A Photobiography* (page 545), and *The Boys' War* (see page 544).

The Civil War Game

An inexpensive educational board game consisting of a number-coded Civil War map and a packet of informational playing cards. The game can be played at a number of levels of expertise; basically players attempt to match numbered sites on the map to the historical events listed on the cards.

$10.95

Educational Materials Associates, Inc.

Box 7385

Charlottesville, VA 22906

(804) 293-GAME/fax (804) 293-5322

13 For the People

A sweeping Civil War strategy game, covering the entire war from the opening shots at Fort Sumter to the surrender at Appomatox Courthouse. Players, as either Abraham Lincoln or Jefferson Davis, command armies, conduct amphibious assaults and cavalry raids, indulge in political intrigue, promote or dismiss generals, and contend with trouble and unrest on the homefront. The Confederacy, for example, can build ironclad ships, lay naval mines, purchase supplies from abroad, and negotiate for foreign aid; the Union can establish a naval blockade of the southern coast and issue the Emancipation Proclamation. The game can be played as a full-scale war, which takes eight hours, or as a series of distinct scenarios, which take 2 to 3 hours each. The board consists of two detailed maps of the United States in the 1860s; the game includes 96 strategy cards listing historical and military events and hundreds of color-coded pieces representing the opposing forces. A complex challenge for teenagers.

Avalon Hill Game Co.

4517 Harford Rd.

Baltimore, MD 21214

(410) 254-9200 or (800) 999-3222

e-mail: AH GAMES@aol.com

Web site: www.avalonhill.com

10 Gettysburg

A board game based on the famous Civil War battle, published by Avalon Hill in conjunction with the Smithsonian Institution. The board is a detailed map of the battlefield; players act as either General Lee or Meade, directing the movements of their forces over the four historic days of the battle. The game is recommended for two players, aged 10 and up.

$20

Avalon Hill Game Co.

4517 Harford Rd.

Baltimore, MD 21214

(410) 254-9200 or (800) 999-3222

e-mail: AH GAMES@aol.com

Web site: www.avalonhill.com

12 Great Campaigns of the Civil War Games

A series of strategy board games based on Civil War battles. Titles include "Stonewall Jackson's Way" (the Second Bull Run campaign), "Here Come the Rebels!" (Lee's invasion of Maryland, culminating in the Battle of Antietam), "Roads to Gettysburg," and "Stonewall Jackson in the Valley" (the Shenandoah campaign). The publisher, which rates games on a scale of 1 to 10 in order of difficulty, assigns these games a 5, a moderate level of sophistication and complexity, assuming that players have previous experience of strategy games. Games rated at levels 1 to 3 are appropriate for beginners; "Gettysburg," for example (see left), is rated at level 2.

Avalon Hill Game Co.

4517 Harford Rd.

Baltimore, MD 21214

(410) 254-9200 or (800) 999-3222

e-mail: AH GAMES@aol.com

Web site: www.avalonhill.com

8 The Monitor and the Merrimack

A board game in which players reenact the famous Civil War "Battle of the Ironclads." The paper game board is a map of the area at the mouth of Virginia's James River known as Hampton Roads; playing pieces (to be cut out and assembled) include six Union warships, among them the famous *Monitor,* and three Confederate warships, including the *Merrimack.* Play mimics the two-day course of the original battle, with each player attempting to sink or disable his/her opponent's ships.

$6.95

Chatham Hill Games, Inc.

Box 253

Chatham, NY 12037

(518) 392-5022 or (800) 554-3039/fax (518) 392-3121

Web site: www.ocdc.com/Chatham_Hill_Games

Reconstruction

A portfolio of 10 historical documents, five historical background essays, and a study guide. Essay titles include "No More Driver's Lash for Me," "Forty Acres and a Mule," and "From Sheriff to Senator"; historical documents include a timeline of Reconstruction, a collection of Thomas Nast cartoons, and extracts from the Reconstruction Constitution.

> $37
> Jackdaw Publications
> Box 503
> Amawalk, NY 10501
> (914) 962-6911 or (800) 789-0022/fax (800) 962-9101

VIDEOS

The Civil War

Ken Burns's superb nine-part documentary on the Civil War is essential—and enthralling—viewing for all students of American history. Episode titles include "1861 The Cause: At the Crossroads of Our Being," "1862 A Very Bloody Affair: From the Peninsular Campaign to Shiloh," "1862 Forever Free: Emancipation: The War Ennobled," "1863 Simply Murder: Fredericksburg and Chancellorsville," "1863 The Universe of Battle: From Gettysburg to Lookout Mountain," "1864 Valley of the Shadow of Death: The Wilderness to Atlanta," "1864 Most Hallowed Ground: From the Crater to Shenandoah," "1865 War is All Hell: The Final Offensives," and "1865 The Better Angels of Our Nature: Victory, Assassination, Rebirth." Each includes 70 to 100 minutes of photographs, film clips, quotations from historical figures, and commentary by modern historians. The result is absorbing, heart-wrenching, and breathtaking. Recommended viewing age is difficult to gauge. Our two older boys, who first watched it at ages 10 and 11, were glued to the screen; but it didn't, at the time, hold the interest of our youngest, then aged 7.

> The series (9 videocassettes, boxed), $149.98
> PBS Home Video
> 1320 Braddock Pl.
> Alexandria, VA 22314-1698
> (800) 645-4PBS
> Web site: www.pbs.org

Gettysburg

Based on Michael Shaara's fictionalized account of the battle, *The Killer Angels* (see page 546), Ted Turner's spectacular 1993 movie covers the three dramatic days of the Battle of Gettysburg, doubtless the most famous battle of the Civil War. Gripping battle sequences and an impressive cast, including Tom Berenger, Martin Sheen, Jeff Daniels, Stephen Lang, and Richard Jordan. Rated PG.

> $24.95
> Movies Unlimited
> 3015 Darnell Rd.
> Philadelphia, PA 19154
> (215) 637-4444 or (800) 4-MOVIES
> e-mail: movies@moviesunlimited.com
> Web site: www.moviesunlimited.com

Gone With the Wind

The spectacular 1939 four-hour film version of Margaret Michener's classic Civil War–era novel, with Vivien Leigh as the unsinkable Scarlett O'Hara, Olivia de Havilland as the saintly but saccharine Melanie, and Clark Gable as the dashing Rhett Butler. Our boys were particularly fond of the burning of Atlanta and the legendary line "Frankly, my dear, I don't give a damn."

> Available for rent at most video stores or $89.99
> Movies Unlimited
> 3015 Darnell Rd.
> Philadelphia, PA 19154
> (215) 637-4444 or (800) 4-MOVIES
> e-mail: movies@moviesunlimited.com
> Web site: www.moviesunlimited.com

Lincoln

A four-part PBS miniseries, much of it in Lincoln's own words, drawn from letters, speeches, and diaries. Titles of the hour-long episodes, which cover Lincoln's life from log cabin to assassination, are "The Making of a President: 1860–1862," "The Pivotal Year: 1863," "'I Want to Finish This Job': 1864," and "'Now He Belongs to the Ages': 1865." The voice of Lincoln is read by Jason Robards; also with Glenn Close and James Earl Jones.

> $49.98
> PBS Home Video
> 1320 Braddock Pl.

Alexandria, VA 22314-1698

(800) 645-4PBS

Web site: www.pbs.org

The Red Badge of Courage

This film version of the classic book (see page 547) was made back in 1951, with Audie Murphy playing the part of Henry Fleming, the young recruit who comes of age fighting with the Union Army in the Civil War. Seventy minutes long in black and white.

$24.99

Movies Unlimited

3015 Darnell Rd.

Philadelphia, PA 19154

(215) 637-4444 or (800) 4-MOVIES

e-mail: movies@moviesunlimited.com

Web site: www.moviesunlimited.com

Songs of the Civil War

A companion to Ken Burns's PBS series *The Civil War* (see page 550), this 60-minute video features 24 songs of the Civil War era, sung by prominent performers, among them Kathy Mattea, Richie Havens, Waylon Jennings, and Judy Collins. Songs, along with Jay Ungar and Molly Mason's haunting fiddle tune "Ashokan Farewell," include "No More Auction Block for Me," "Lincoln and Liberty," "Rebel Soldier," "Battle Hymn of the Republic," "When Johnny Comes Marching Home," "Lorena," and "Hard Times Come Again No More."

$19.99

Movies Unlimited

3015 Darnell Rd.

Philadelphia, PA 19154

(215) 637-4444 or (800) 4-MOVIES

e-mail: movies@moviesunlimited.com

Web site: www.moviesunlimited.com

Also available on CD or audiocassette (Columbia Records) from music stores

Wonderworks: Booker

The story of Booker T. Washington's childhood at the end of the Civil War, as he deals with emancipation and all the challenges it brings. Desperate to learn to read, he convinces a black Union soldier from Ohio to become the schoolteacher for his West Virginia community. Fifty-eight minutes long.

$14.95

Movies Unlimited

3015 Darnell Rd.

Philadelphia, PA 19154

(215) 637-4444 or (800) 4-MOVIES

e-mail: movies@moviesunlimited.com

Web site: www.moviesunlimited.com

THE CIVIL WAR ON-LINE

The American Civil War Homepage

Much information, including graphic images, letters and diaries, timelines, regimental histories, battle accounts, and general background.

sunsite.utk.edu/civil-war

American Civil War Maps and Exhibits

A timeline of Civil War history, battle maps (listed by state), historical background information, biographies of prominent people, and photographs.

www.californiacentralcoast.com/commun/map/civil/civil.html

The Civil War Home Page

A multifaceted site with connections to Civil War battles and documents, a Civil War timeline, a photo gallery, biographies of famous Civil War people, and many related links.

www.civil-war.net

Civil War Page

The site covers a large number of interesting Civil War topics, including information about army life, Civil War flags, art and poetry, uniforms, medicine, and women in the Civil War. There are also audio recordings of Civil War bugle calls, a photo gallery, and links to Civil War museums.

homepages.dsu.edu/jankcj/civilwar/civilwar.htm

Civil War World Wide Web Information Archive

Links to a wealth of information about the Civil War, including photo archives, letters, documents, and diaries, and all manner of related Web sites.

www.access.digex.net/~bdboyle/cw.html

The Gettysburg Address

The famous speech, with images of various handwritten drafts, and transcripts.

lcweb.loc.gov/exhibits/G.Address/gadrft.html

Harriet Tubman

An account of Harriet Tubman's life and times.

www.acusd.edu/~jdesmet/tubman.html

Lincoln On-line

Biographical information, photographs, speeches, and links to other Lincoln-related Web sites.

www.netins.net/showcase/creative/lincoln.html

IMMIGRATION

BOOKS

The American Family Album Series

Dorothy Hoobler and Thomas Hoobler; Oxford University Press

This series of books traces the experiences of various immigrant groups in America, using a mix of archival photographs, diaries, letters, interviews, and profiles of well-known people belonging to the featured ethnic group. Titles include *The Irish Family Album, The Mexican Family Album,* and *The Chinese Family Album.* Other ethnic groups covered in the series include the Germans, Italians, Scandinavians, Jews, Japanese, and Cubans. Each book is 127 pages long. For readers of all ages.

American Origins Series

John Muir Publications

A series of 46-page illustrated books on the immigration experience of various ethnic groups. Each book discusses life in the immigrants' homeland, reasons for coming to America, the process of assimilation, and the contributions the group has made to modern American life. Titles in the series include *Tracing Our English Roots* (Sharon Moscinski; 1995), *Tracing Our German Roots* (Leda Silver; 1994), *Tracing Our Irish Roots* (Sharon Moscinski; 1993), *Tracing Our Italian Roots* (Kathleen Lee; 1993), *Tracing Our Japanese*

Roots (Gary Kawaguchi; 1994), and *Tracing Our Jewish Roots* (Miriam Sagan; 1993). For readers aged 9–12.

Cobblestone: Immigration

Several issues of *Cobblestone,* the history magazine for students in grades 5–9 (see page 449), center around immigration and the establishment of various ethnic groups in America. Each issue includes nonfiction articles, fictionalized stories, hands-on activities, and suggestions for supplementary readings. Issues on immigration in general include *America's Immigrants: Part I* (December 1982) and *America's Immigrants: Part II* (January 1983).

Issues on specific subsets of the immigrant experience include *Chinese Americans* (March 1991), *Greek Americans* (December 1996), *Hispanic Americans* (April 1989), *Irish Americans* (March 1994), *Italian Americans* (December 1992), *Japanese Americans* (April 1996), *Jewish Americans* (November 1991), and *Polish Americans* (May 1995).

Available from most libraries or for $4.50 from

Cobblestone Publishing, Inc.

30 Grove St.

Peterborough, NH 03458-1454

(603) 924-7209 or (800) 821-0115

Web site: www.cobblestonepub.com/

Coming to America: The Story of Immigration

Betsy Maestro; Scholastic, 1996

A picture-book account of the history of American immigration, from the first travelers over the Asia-to-Alaska land bridge to the present day. Information is clearly and pleasantly presented; included in an appendix is a timeline of crucial dates and a list of "Other Interesting Facts About Immigration." For readers aged 7–11.

How Many Days to America?: A Thanksgiving Story

Eve Bunting; Clarion, 1990

A family makes a dangerous escape to freedom, traveling by boat across the Caribbean and finally arriving safely in the United States. For readers aged 6–10.

HISTORY

6 + *I Was Dreaming to Come to America:*
Memories from the Ellis Island
Oral History Project

Veronica Lawlor; Puffin, 1995

Short quotes about the immigrant experience from the people who lived it, paired with colorful collage illustrations. The featured immigrants came from all over the world, among them Golda Meir, who arrived in America from Russia in 1906, when she was eight years old. Brief biographies of each immigrant are included in an appendix. For readers aged 6 and up.

7 10 *If Your Name Was Changed*
at Ellis Island

Ellen Levine; Scholastic, 1994

An account of what it was like to be an immigrant, written in a friendly question-and-answer format. "Why did people leave their homelands?" "Would everyone in your family come together?" "Where would you eat and sleep on the ship?" "Was the ocean voyage dangerous?" "What did Americans think about the new immigrants?" Recommended for 7–10-year-olds. See the *If You . . . Series* (pages 453–454).

10 + *Immigrant Kids*

Russell Freedman; Puffin, 1995

A 72-page collection of first-person stories illustrated with wonderful period photographs that give readers a real feel for what it was like to be a 19th-century immigrant child. The book is divided into five sections: "Coming Over," "At Home," "At School," "At Work," and "At Play."

5 9 *Immigrants*

Gare Thompson; Children's Press, 1997

A 32-page picture-book history of immigration from the very first arrivals in America to the present day. An attractively designed book, illustrated with prints and photographs, plus "Did You Know?" fact boxes. For readers aged 5–9.

5 8 *The Long Way to a New Land*

Joan Sandin; HarperTrophy, 1986

An I Can Read book about a young Swedish boy and his family coming to America in the 19th century.

For readers aged 5–8. A sequel, in which the family travels west and settles in Minnesota, is titled *The Long Way Westward* (HarperCollins, 1992).

5 9 *Molly's Pilgrim*

Barbara Cohen; Yearling, 1990

Molly, whose family came to the United States from Russia, is teased by her third-grade classmates because of her accent, customs, and strange clothes. Then, as a Thanksgiving project, each child is asked to make a doll—and Molly's is different from all the rest, a Russian-Jewish doll. Through Molly's pilgrim, the children learn a lasting lesson about religious freedom.

7 10 *The Story of the Statue of Liberty*

Betsy and Giulio Maestro; Mulberry, 1989

The story of the famous statue, from French sculptor Frédéric Bartholdi's clay models through the building of the statue, its packing and shipment—in 214 monstrous crates—to America, its erection on Bedloe's Island, and its dedication in 1886 by Grover Cleveland. Colorful and impressive illustrations show the statue in pieces and assembled, inside and out.

5 9 *Watch the Stars Come Out*

Riki Levinson; Puffin, 1995

"Every Friday night, after the dishes were put away," this beautifully illustrated book begins, "Grandma's Mama would come to her room and tell her a special story." The special story is about how Grandma's Mama—the narrator's great-grandmother—and her brother came to America from Europe long ago by ship. The book tells what the voyage, crowded with immigrants, was like, ending at last with the sight of the Statue of Liberty, a long wait at Ellis Island, and finally a reunion with their mother and father.

"Watch the Stars Come Out" was featured on the PBS *Reading Rainbow* program. In this episode, host LeVar Burton visits Ellis Island and takes viewers on a tour of the Statue of Liberty.

6 10 *Who Belongs Here? An American Story*

Margy Burns Knight; Tilbury House, 1996

The experiences of Nary, a young Cambodian, newly arrived in America, are used to discuss the histories of the many other immigrants to the United States and to answer the question "Who belongs here?" (Everybody.) For readers aged 6–10.

HANDS-ON ACTIVITIES

Ellis Island: The Immigrants' Experience
ALL A photo collection containing 12 poster-size photographs of immigrants and their possessions, and of today's Ellis Island Museum. Included with the collection is a background "Broadsheet Essay" on immigration and the history of Ellis Island, a timeline of U.S. immigration, and a study guide.

> $19.95
> Jackdaw Publications
> Box 503
> Amawalk, NY 10501
> (914) 962-6911 or (800) 789-0022/fax (800) 962-9101

Gateway
10+ A simulation in which kids in grades 5–11 take on the characters of turn-of-the-century Greeks, Italians, Russians, Scandinavians, Germans, or Poles arriving at Ellis Island. Participants study immigration from 1600 to the present; then pass through the stations of the immigration hall at Ellis Island, striving for admission to the United States. (Successful candidates end the simulation by taking the Loyalty Oath; failures get deported.)

> $37
> Interact
> 1825 Gillespie Way, #101
> El Cajon, CA 92020-1095
> (619) 448-1474 or (800) 359-0961/fax (619) 448-6722
> or (800) 700-5093
> Web site: www.interact-simulations.com

Immigration: 1870–1930
13+ A portfolio of primary source documents, historical background essays, a timeline, and a detailed study guide, with reproducible student worksheets. *Immigration: 1870–1930* includes seven illustrated background essays, among them "Immigration in the Industrial Age," "Asians: The Chinese," and "Jewish Immigration." Also included are 14 documents, among them an Ellis Island photo poster, a U.S. Census questionnaire, and a

"What Every Immigrant Should Know" booklet, published in 1922.

Also see *Modern Immigration: 1930–1995,* which includes six essays and 15 documents, among them assorted newspaper articles, a collection of foreign recipes, a Guatemalan "Family Scrapbook," and a naturalization application.

> $37
> Jackdaw Publications
> Box 503
> Amawalk, NY 10501
> (914) 962-6911 or (800) 789-0022/fax (800) 962-9101

Statue of Liberty and Ellis Island Coloring Book
6+ A. G. Smith; Dover Publications, 1985

Black-line ready-to-color illustrations of the building of the Statue of Liberty, the arrival of the 19th-century immigrants, and their experiences on Ellis Island.

> $2.95
> Dover Publications, Inc.
> 31 E. Second St.
> Mineola, NY 11501

IMMIGRATION ON-LINE

Immigration, Ellis Island
9+ Information on Ellis Island and the immigrant experience, an aerial view of the island, and a gallery of historical black-and-white photographs.

> cmp1.vcr.edu/exhibitions/immigration_id.html

INVENTORS AND INVENTIONS

BOOKS: TIMELINES

The Picture History of Great Inventors
9+ Gillian Clements; Alfred A. Knopf, 1994

A decade-by-decade list of the world's great inventors, with historical information and interesting anecdotes about each. An illustrated timeline of events runs along the bottom of each page.

The Smithsonian Visual Timeline of Inventions

Richard Platt; Dorling Kindersley, 1994

A 64-page history of invention from the Stone Age on, in four parallel illustrated timelines: travel/conquest, agriculture/industry, daily life/health, and counting/communication. The pictures—this is a Dorling Kindersley book—are wonderful full-color photographs; captions include inventors' names, dates, and historical information.

The Timetables of Technology: A Chronology of the Most Important People and Events in the History of Technology

Brian Bunch and Alexander Hellemans; Simon & Schuster, 1993

A fascinating and detailed 490-page collection of timetables dealing with inventions in the categories of architecture, communications, transportation, agriculture, energy, and medicine, from the Stone Age to the present day. Sidebars provide extra details on particularly interesting events and developments.

Books

Accidents May Happen: Fifty Inventions Discovered by Mistake

Charlotte Foltz Jones; Delacorte Press, 1996

The illustrated stories of cornflakes, ice-cream sodas, daguerreotypes, fingerprinting, the yo-yo, and many more, all surprising and interesting.

By the same author: *Mistakes That Worked* (Doubleday, 1991), which contains 40 more stories, including those of penicillin, Coca-Cola, Popsicles, vulcanized rubber, Velcro, and blue jeans.

African-American Inventors

Patricia McKissack and Fredrick McKissack; Millbrook Press, 1994

A 96-page overview of black inventors. The book covers the history of the patent laws and the work of many notable black inventors, among them Thomas L.

Jennings, James Forten, Jan Ernst Matzeliger, and Elijah McCoy. By the same authors: *African-American Scientists* (Millbrook Press, 1994).

Cobblestone: Inventors and Inventions

Issues of *Cobblestone* magazine (see page 449) that feature inventions or inventors include *African American Inventors* (February 1992), *Women Inventors* (June 1994), *Convenience Hits the Road: The Automobile in History* (July 1987), *Thomas Edison* (February 1980), *America At Work: The Industrial Revolution* (September 1991), *The Magic of Radio* (October 1988), *Tuning In To Television* (October 1989), and *The Wright Brothers and the Story of Aviation* (December 1984). Each magazine contains fiction and nonfiction articles, timelines, puzzles, activity suggestions, and supplementary reading lists. For students in grades 5–9.

Available from most libraries or for $4.50 from
Cobblestone Publishing, Inc.
7 School St.
Peterborough, NH 03458-1454
(603) 924-7209 or (800) 821-0115
Web site: www.cobblestonepub.com

Dear Benjamin Banneker

Andrea Davis Pinkney; Harcourt Brace, 1994

When Thomas Jefferson was president of the United States, the brilliant and articulate Banneker wrote him a letter, criticizing Jefferson for owning slaves; Jefferson, whose moral position was weak, nonetheless replied. His letter, beginning "Dear Benjamin Banneker," is a centerpiece of the book, which also describes Banneker's life, inventions, and many other accomplishments.

Elijah McCoy, Inventor

Garnet Nelson Jackson; Modern Curriculum Press, 1992

A simple picture-book biography about the 19th-century black inventor who engineered an automatic oil cap for use on trains. For readers aged 4–8.

From Indian Corn to Outer Space: Women Invent in America

Ellen H. Showell and Fred M. B. Amram; Cobblestone Publishing, 1995

A 160-page history of women and their inventions, from precolonial times to the present day. For students aged 10 and up.

Great Lives: Invention and Technology
Milton Lomask; Atheneum, 1992

A collection of 27 short biographies of famous inventors, illustrated with photographs and prints. Subjects include Alexander Graham Bell, Carl Benz, George Washington Carver, George Eastman, Thomas Alva Edison, Philo Taylor Farnsworth, Robert Fulton, Robert H. Goddard, Cyrus Hall McCormick, Eli Whitney, and Wilbur and Orville Wright.

Invention
Lionel Bender; Alfred A. Knopf, 1991

One of the volumes in the well-known Eyewitness series. There's not much in the way of text; these books are basically collections of superb color photographs. *Inventions,* in 64 high-quality pages, covers creative innovations from the stone ax and the wheel to the silicon chip. Various double-page spreads picture histories of the steam engine, batteries, photography, the telephone, recording, the internal combustion engine, the radio, the cathode-ray tube, and flight.

Outward Dreams: Black Inventors and their Inventions
Jim Haskins; Walker & Company, 1991

A history of black inventors and their inventions, including biographies of Benjamin Banneker, George Washington Carver, and Madam C. J. Walker. For readers aged 10 and up.

A Pocketful of Goobers: A Story About George Washington Carver
Barbara Mitchell; Carolrhoda, 1989

An interesting five-chapter biography of George Washington Carver, illustrated with pencil sketches, for readers aged 8–12.

The Real McCoy: The Life of an African American Inventor
Wendy Towle; Scholastic, 1995

The 32-page picture-book biography of the inventive engineer who gave his name to the admiring expression "the real McCoy." For readers aged 5–9.

They All Laughed: From Light Bulbs to Lasers—The Fascinating Stories Behind the Great Inventions That Have Changed Our Lives
Ira Flatow; HarperPerennial, 1993

Historical and scientific information and a lot of great stories about inventors and their inventions—many of which the public didn't think much of in their early stages. Flatow covers 24 famous inventions, including—along with the lightbulb and the laser—the microwave oven, the fax machine, Velcro, Teflon, Silly Putty, television, and the typewriter.

A Weed is a Flower: The Life of George Washington Carver
Aliki; Aladdin, 1988

A simple picture-book biography of George Washington Carver, from his childhood as a slave through his adult work in agriculture. For readers aged 5–8.

What Are You Figuring Now? A Story About Benjamin Banneker
Jeri Ferris; First Avenue Editions, 1990

A short chapter book detailing the remarkable life of Benjamin Banneker, astronomer, surveyor, author, printer, and abolitionist. He also contributed to the design of the city of Washington, D.C.

What's Inside? Great Inventions
Dorling Kindersley, 1993

Terrific color photographs of such landmark inventions as the telephone, the radio, and the flush toilet, with cutaway diagrams and detailed captions explaining how each works. For readers aged 5–9.

Women Invent!

Susan Casey; Chicago Review Press, 1997

A seven-chapter history of invention and women inventors, illustrated with black-and-white photographs. The book discusses, for example, Martha Coston, who invented the "telegraphic night signals" used during the Civil War; Rebecca Schroeder, aged six, the world's youngest patent holder; and Andrea Tier-

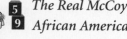

ney, inventor of the live bug house. Included is a resource guide for readers interesting in inventing something of their own. For kids aged 10 and up.

Also see **The Airplane** (pages 559–560), **The Automobile** (pages 561–562), **Thomas Edison and Electricity** (pages 563–564), and **The Telegraph and the Telephone** (pages 565–566).

ACTIVITY BOOKS

Girls and Young Women Inventing

Frances A. Karnes and Suzanne M. Bean; Free Spirit Publishing, 1995

The book is divided into three parts: Part I is a collection of first-person stories by successful young female inventors; Part II includes instructions for would-be inventors; and Part III contains information about inventors' organizations, a timeline of women inventors, and a list of recommended readings. For kids aged 11 and up.

Inventors and Inventions

Lorraine Hopping Egan; Scholastic, 1997

An activity and lesson plan book for students in grades 4–8, filled with games, puzzles, projects, quizzes, reading lists, and cross-curricular connections. The book is divided into three main sections: "What's an Invention?," "Inventions: Past, Present, and Future," and "Inventive Thinking and Creating." Kids, for example, make "Inventor Trading Cards," take a poll to determine the world's ten greatest inventions, make a timeline of inventions, and devise a Rube Goldberg–type automated pizza delivery machine. Also included in the book is the "Great All-Time Inventions Game," with a pull-out board and a collection of illustrated cut-out cards to be ordered on a timeline. Inventions described on the cards include the thermometer, the ratio, the steam engine, chocolate, coins, concrete, the robotic submarine, and the mechanical clock.

The Kids' Invention Book

Arlene Erlbach; Lerner, 1997

The book begins with the story of 15-year-old Chester Greenwood of Maine, who invented earmuffs in 1873; then profiles a series of modern chil-

dren who are successful inventors; and ends with how-to information and suggestions for developing and patenting an invention of one's own. For readers aged 9–12.

Steven Caney's Invention Book

Steven Caney; Workman, 1985

The book is both an instruction manual for would-be young inventors, with discussions of projects, tools, record keeping, product naming, and the ins and outs of the U.S. Patent Office, and a collection of histories of famous inventions, among them the Jeep, the Ferris wheel, the drinking straw, Scotch tape, sneakers, Eskimo pies, the ballpoint pen, and roller skates. Creatively illustrated.

HANDS-ON ACTIVITIES

Grow a Nut-Bush

Emulate inventor George Washington Carver. As a science kit, there's not much to this one: it includes a Spanish peanut seed and a starter cup. The peanut, however, is "guaranteed to sprout in 2 days," and, if carefully cultivated and transplanted, will eventually flower, dive underground, and develop more peanuts. Our peanuts sprouted, but never progressed as far as the flower-and-new-peanut stage; perhaps, however, this had something to do with the indignity of transporting a southern plant to Vermont.

A package of three peanut kits, $4.95

Edmund Scientific Co.

101 E. Gloucester Pike

Barrington, NJ 08007-1380

(609) 547-8880 or (800) 728-6999

fax (609) 573-6295

e-mail: scientifics@edsci.com

Web site: www.edsci.com

Invent

A multifaceted simulation from Interact in which kids research a famous inventor and his/her invention(s) and compile the results in a group "Invention Book," devise an original invention that would help a familiar character in literature, and develop the invention, completing the patent process, and then advertising and marketing the final product. The simulation is topped off with a "Thomas Edison Day," in which kids display the results of their work.

"Invent" is intended for 20 to 35 students (though it can be adapted for smaller groups) in grades 4–8. Simulation materials include 35 eight-page student guides, a teacher guide, and assorted reproducible handouts.

$34
Interact
1825 Gillespie Way, #101
El Cajon, CA 92020-1095
(619) 448-1474 or (800) 359-0961/fax (619) 448-6722
Web site: www.interact-simulations.com

The Inventor's Workshop

A creative kit with which kids—with a little inventive creativity—can construct a self-propelled car, a flying machine, a clock, and more. All parts are included, among them a collection of gears, a propeller, belts and rubber bands, and a small electric motor. An accompanying *Inventor's Handbook* provides historical information, suggestions, and instructions.

$18.95 from bookstores or
Running Press Book Publishers
125 South 22nd St.
Philadelphia, PA 19103
(215) 567-5080 or (800) 345-5359/fax (800) 453-2884

Young Inventors and Creators Program

A contest for creative kids (or groups of up to three kids) in nine categories: Inventions, Computer Programs, Dramatic Work/Video, Music Composition, Painting/Graphics, Photography, Poetry, Sculpture, and Short Story.

National Inventive Thinking Association
Box 836202
Richardson, TX 75083
(603) 271-3769

VIDEOS

Freedom Man

A 60-minute "docudrama" on videotape about the life of Benjamin Banneker, "First Black Man of Science," which includes both biographical facts and a rousing subplot about Banneker's aid to two fugitive slaves pursued by bounty hunters.

$29.99
Movies Unlimited
3015 Darnell Rd.
Philadelphia, PA 19154
(215) 637-4444 or (800) 4-MOVIES
e-mail: movies@moviesunlimited.com
Web site: www.moviesunlimited.com

Invention

A 14-part series on three videocassettes from the Smithsonian Institution, originally aired on the Discovery Channel. The series, through an attention-grabbing combination of clever animation, historical film footage, and interviews with inventors, covers the history of invention, from Leonardo da Vinci's flying machine to the latest innovations of modern times. Among the many inventions featured are the espresso machine, the elevator brake, a car that runs on vegetable oil, high-definition television, Kevlar, champagne, and radiocarbon dating.

$59.95
Zenger Media
10200 Jefferson Blvd.
Box 802
Culver City, CA 90232-0802
(310) 839-2436 or (800) 421-4246/fax (310) 839-2249
or (800) 944-5432
Web site: ZengerMedia.com/Zenger

This Is America, Charlie Brown; Volume 1: The Great Inventors

A delightful 24-minute animation in which the Peanuts kids and dog tour American history, visiting famous inventors and learning about their inventions. Among the visited are Thomas Edison, Alexander Graham Bell, and Henry Ford.

$12.99
Movies Unlimited
3015 Darnell Rd.
Philadelphia, PA 19154
(215) 637-4444 or (800) 4-MOVIES
e-mail: movies@moviesunlimited.com
Web site: www.moviesunlimited.com

Computer Software

Invention Studio

A research laboratory, production facility, and patent office for young inventors in which kids, under the guidance of the brilliant but wacky Doc Howard (whose ears stick out), design, build, and test a wide range of creative and incredible machines. On CD-ROM for Mac or Windows.

$19.95

Discovery Channel Multimedia

Box 1089

Florence, KY 41022

(800) 678-3343

Web site: www.discovery.com

InventorLabs

InventorLabs: Teachnology is an interactive overview of the inventions of Alexander Graham Bell, Thomas Edison, and James Watt; kids learn about the history behind the inventors and their inventions, reenact the original experiments, and create their own working inventions. *InventorLabs: Transportation,* in similar format, covers the inventions of Wilbur and Orville Wright, Gottlieb Daimler (the first motorcycle), and George Stephenson (the steam locomotive). On CD-ROM for Mac or Windows.

$24.95 each

The Edutainment Catalog

Box 21210

Boulder, CO 80308

(800) 338-3844/fax (800) 226-1942

Web site: www.edutainco.com

Also see **The Way Things Work** (page 393).

Inventors On-Line

Invention Dimension

A searchable database of inventors and inventions in alphabetical order, plus a featured inventor of the week and lists of invention-related resources and links.

web.mit.edu/afs/athena.mit.edu/org/i/invent/www/archive.html

Inventure Place

Subtitled the "National Inventors Hall of Fame," the site includes information on competitions and awards for inventors of all ages, links to hands-on museums and exhibits, historical and scientific information about inventions and inventors, and "creativity" sites for kids.

www.invent.org

Online Histories of Inventors

Illustrated biographies of the Wright brothers, Thomas Edison, and Henry Ford, a history of the Ford Motor Company, and exhibits from the Henry Ford Museum and Greenfield Village.

www.hfmgv.org/histories/projects.html

The Tech Museum of Innovation

Interviews with modern-day inventors and a changing array of hands-on exhibits. Visitors to the site can build, launch, and operate their own satellite.

www.thetech.org

THE AIRPLANE

Books

Charles A. Lindbergh: A Human Hero

James Cross Giblin; Clarion, 1997

A detailed biography of Lindbergh for readers aged 11 and up, covering his early love of flying, the famous solo flight that made him the first modern media celebrity, the tragic kidnapping and murder of his son, and his unpopular pro-Nazi political views during World War II.

Clear the Cow Pasture, I'm Coming in for a Landing! A Story of Amelia Earhart

Robert Quackenbush; Simon & Schuster, 1990

A biography of Amelia Earhart, the first woman to make a solo flight across the Atlantic Ocean. For readers aged 8–11.

First Flight: The Story of Tom Tate and the Wright Brothers

George Shea; HarperCollins, 1997

The story of young Tom Tate, the second person to fly in the Wright brothers' famous airplane. For readers aged 6–9.

Flight: The Journey of Charles Lindbergh

Robert Burleigh; Paper Star, 1997

The story of Lindbergh's famous solo flight across the Atlantic Ocean in 1927, beautifully illustrated with double-page paintings. For readers aged 6–9.

Nobody Owns the Sky: The Story of "Brave Bessie" Colman

Reeve Lindbergh; Candlewick, 1996

A beautifully illustrated picture-book biography of Bessie Colman, who became the world's first licensed black aviator. For readers aged 4–8.

Take Me Out to the Airfield: How the Wright Brothers Invented the Airplane

Robert Quackenbush; Parents' Magazine Press, 1976

The delightfully illustrated story of the Wright brothers and their famous airplane, introduced by a song, to be sung, the author explains, to the tune of "Take Me Out to the Ball Game." It begins: "Take me out to the airfield!/Tell me all about planes!" Included are instructions for building your own model Wright Flyer, using Styrofoam egg-carton tops and toothpicks (we tried it; it works about as well as the original) and an appendix explaining how an airplane flies.

Vanished! The Mysterious Disappearance of Amelia Earhart

Monica Kulling; Random House, 1996

A short chapter book on Amelia Earhart's life and final famous flight, illustrated with photographs, drawings, and colorful maps. For readers in grades 2–4.

The Wright Brothers and the Story of Aviation

Cobblestone; December 1984

This issue of Cobblestone (see page 449) covers the history of the airplane and the lives and accomplishments of Wilbur and Orville Wright, and includes

instructions for making assorted flying toys. For readers in grades 5–9.

Available from most libraries or for $4.50 from Cobblestone Publishing, Inc.
30 Grove St.
Peterborough, NH 03458-1454
(603) 924-7209 or (800) 821-0115
Web site: www.cobblestonepub.com

The Wright Brothers: How They Invented the Airplane

Russell Freedman; Holiday House, 1994

An excellent 132-page biography of the famous brothers, illustrated throughout with fascinating original photographs. Recommended for readers in grades 4–8.

GAMES AND HANDS-ON ACTIVITIES

History of Flight Coloring Book

A. G. Smith; Dover Publications

From the 18th-century balloon to the Wright brothers' *Flyer,* the *Concorde,* and the space shuttle, with explanatory picture captions. Also see *Antique Airplanes Coloring Book* (Peter Copeland).

$2.95 each
Dover Publications, Inc.
31 E. Second St.
Mineola, NY 11501

The Wright Brothers

 A board game based on the early days of flight in which players move their playing pieces (representing Orville and Wilbur, on bicycles) along a labeled playing path tracing the history of the invention of the airplane. The play passes from historical experiments with gliders (Otto Lilienthal, 1891) through the Wright brothers' many models and tests, culminating at Kitty Hawk on December 17, 1903. Winner is the first player to fly the Wright brothers' airplane through the four squares required for a "successful flight." Included is a tiny 3-D paper model of the airplane (finicky to assemble) for the Kitty Hawk flight and historical background information on the Wright brothers and their famous invention, printed on the reverse side of the playing board.

$6.95

Chatham Hill Games, Inc.

Box 253

Chatham, NY 12037

(518) 392-5022 or (800) 554-3039/fax (518) 392-3121

Web site: www.ocdc.com/Chatham_Hill_Games

Wright Flyer Model

A Monogram plastic model of the *Flyer,* the plane that made the first successful powered flight at Kitty Hawk. This version has a 12-inch wingspan and doesn't fly at all but is said to make an excellent desk or table display.

$8 from game and hobby stores or

America's National Parks Catalog

1100 E. Hector St., Suite 105

Conshohocken, PA 19428

(800) 821-2903

VIDEOS

Smithsonian Dreams of Flight

A three-part series on the history of aviation from the Smithsonian's Air and Space Museum. The series is a chronology of flight from its beginnings, through the Wright brothers, Charles Lindbergh's transatlantic crossing, Chuck Yeager's conquest of the sound barrier, space flight, and the launching of the space shuttle. Titles on three videocassettes, are "In the Beginning," "The Golden Age and Beyond," and "Higher . . . Faster . . . Farther."

A sequel, *Dreams of Flight 2,* covers the moon missions and space exploration. Titles, on two videocassettes, are "To the Moon" and "Beyond the Moon."

Dreams of Flight, $69.95; *Dreams of Flight 2,* $44.95

Smithsonian Institution

Box 700

Holmes, PA 19043

(800) 927-7377

This Is America, Charlie Brown; Volume 2: The Wright Brothers at Kitty Hawk

In this 24-minute animation, Snoopy and his feathered friend, Woodstock, visit the Wright brothers, learn a great deal about the invention of the airplane, and participate in the famous flight at Kitty Hawk in 1903.

$12.99

Movies Unlimited

3015 Darnell Rd.

Philadelphia, PA 19154

(215) 637-4444 or (800) 4-MOVIES

e-mail: movies@moviesunlimited.com

Web site: www.moviesunlimited.com

To Fly

This marvelous history of flight from the balloon to the Blue Angels was originally filmed in giant-screen IMAX format; viewers feel as though they're really in the air.

$29.95

Smithsonian Institution

Box 700

Holmes, PA 19043

(800) 927-7377

THE AUTOMOBILE

BOOKS

Along Came the Model T! How Henry Ford Put the World on Wheels

Robert Quackenbush; Parents' Magazine Press, 1978

An illustrated biography of Henry Ford, with catchy supplementary facts presented at the bottom of alternate pages by a knowledgeable gas station attendant talking to a pair of curious kids. The book includes a detailed double-page description of how a car works, with a helpful diagram; and instructions for building your own Tin Lizzie out of Styrofoam egg cartons and toothpicks. (You're supposed to spray-paint the end result a shiny black.)

Cars and How They Go

Joanna Cole; HarperTrophy, 1986

An absolutely clear explanation of how cars go, with many colorful diagrams showing what they look like inside, for readers aged 4 and up.

9 14 *Convenience Hits the Road: The Automobile in History*

Cobblestone; July 1987

This issue of *Cobblestone* magazine (see page 449) covers the history of the automobile and the life and accomplishments of Henry Ford, with illustrations, activities, and a supplementary reading list.

Available from most libraries or for $4.50 from

Cobblestone Publishing, Inc.

30 Grove St.

Peterborough, NH 03458-1454

(603) 924-7209 or (800) 821-0115

Web site: www.cobblestonepub.com

7 + *Tin Lizzie*

Peter Spier; Doubleday, 1990

The Tin Lizzie featured in the book—officially a "Model T Ford Touring Car"—is first purchased by George Barnhart (father of three) in 1909. Then, over the years, it passes from hand to hand, until finally—over half a century later—it is discovered, covered in weeds behind a barn, by an appreciative mechanic and lovingly restored. Spier's detail-crammed drawings on every page are a timeline of urban and rural 20th-century life, from the horse-drawn carriages, sleighs, and newfangled velocipedes of the first decade of the century to the superhighways of modern times. The back endpapers include a double-page labeled schematic diagram of the Tin Lizzie, inside and out. The text is interesting, but it's great fun just to look at.

8 12 *We'll Race You, Henry: A Story About Henry Ford*

Barbara Mitchell; Carolrhoda, 1988

A short (five chapters) biography for middle-grade readers, starting with Henry's childhood on the farm—"Henry loved mechanical things: springs and cogs and wheels, things that clicked and ticked and turned"—through the Tin Lizzies pouring out of the Ford Motor Company factories in the early 20th century.

HANDS-ON ACTIVITIES

12 + *Ford Assembly Line*

A simulation in which kids role-play factory workers and supervisors at the Ford manufacturing facility in 1922. Challenge: to turn out 50 to 100 Fords in a set time limit. For 10 to 35 students (though adapts to smaller groups) in grades 6–12. The simulation takes anywhere from 30 minutes to 2 hours.

$11

Interact

1825 Gillespie Way, #101

El Cajon, CA 92020-1095

(800) 359-0961

Web site: www.interact-simulations.com

8 + *Henry Ford's River Rouge*

A cut-and-fold (that is, you assemble the pieces) board game based on Henry Ford's assembly line and the brand-new Model A.

$6.95

Chatham Hill Games, Inc.

Box 253

Chatham, NY 12037

(518) 392-5022 or (800) 554-3039/fax (518) 392-3121

Web site: www.ocdc.com/Chatham_Hill_Games

6 + *History of the American Automobile Coloring Book*

A. G. Smith and Randy Mason; Dover Publications.

Over 40 black-line drawings of historic automobiles, among them the famous Ford Model T. Picture captions include historical information. Also see *Antique Automobiles* (Clarence Hornung).

$2.95 each

Dover Publications, Inc.

31 E. Second St.

Mineola, NY 11501

9 + *Truly Gorgeous Old Cars to Cut Out and Put Together*

A paper-crafts book from Bellerophon; users get a lush assortment of full-color antique cars to cut and assemble, plus a descriptive text about each.

$3.95

Bellerophon Books

36 Ancapa St.

Santa Barbara, CA 93101

(800) 253-9943/fax (800) 965-8286

Visible V-8 Combustion Engine Kit

The completed model is a quarter-size scale model of a real V-8 engine. The engine is operated by a hand crank (no batteries required) which, when turned, causes all the parts to move "just like the real thing": the crankshaft rotates, valves open and close, rods and pistons move up and down. This is not a model for beginners.

Kit, $50

Edmund Scientific Co.

101 E. Gloucester Pike

Barrington, NJ 08007-1380

(609) 547-8880 or (800) 728-6999/fax (609) 573-6295

or

e-mail: Scientifics@edsci.com

Web site: www.edsci.com

VIDEOS

Merrily We Roll Along

A delightful hourlong NBC video documentary on the history of the automobile, with archival photographs, film clips, and commentary by Groucho Marx ("a Stutz Bearcat man"). The program shows how the automobile—first scathingly denigrated as a "stinkwagon"—rapidly changed the character of American society.

$19.99

Movies Unlimited

3015 Darnell Rd.

Philadelphia, PA 19154

(215) 637-4444 or (800) 4-MOVIES

e-mail: movies@moviesunlimited.com

Web site: www.moviesunlimited.com

THOMAS EDISON AND ELECTRICITY

BOOKS

The Story of Thomas Alva Edison, Inventor: The Wizard of Menlo Park

Margaret Davidson; Scholastic, 1992

A straightforward chapter biography of Edison, with black-and-white illustrations, for readers aged 9–12.

Thomas Alva Edison, Great Inventor

David A. Adler; Holiday House, 1990

A short chapter biography illustrated with pencil drawings for readers aged 7–10.

Thomas Alva Edison: Inventing the Electric Age

Gene Adair; Oxford University Press, 1997

A biography of Thomas Edison, concentrating on his research and accomplishments. The book discusses, for example, his work on the telegraph, the phonograph, the early movie projector, and the famous electric lightbulb. Illustrated with photographs and Edison's own sketches and patent drawings. For readers aged 13 and up.

Thomas Edison

Cobblestone; February 1980

This issue of Cobblestone magazine (see page 449) includes information on the life and accomplishments of Thomas Edison, instructions for making a telegraph sender and receiver, and a supplementary reading list. For students in grades 5–9.

Available from most libraries or for $4.50 from

Cobblestone Publishing, Inc.

30 Grove St.

Peterborough, NH 03458-1454

(603) 924-7209 or (800) 821-0115

Web site: www.cobblestonepub.com

Thomas Edison and Electricity

Steve Parker; Chelsea House, 1995

This 32-page biography not only gives an account of Edison's life but also discusses the science behind his inventions. The book is illustrated with photographs, portraits, art reproductions, and diagrams, and includes a timeline of "The World in Edison's Time," showing major happenings in science, western expansion and exploration, politics, and the arts.

What Has Wild Tom Done Now?: A Story of Thomas Alva Edison

Robert Quackenbush; Prentice-Hall, 1981

A short, humorously illustrated biography of Edison—whose youthful experiments occasionally went disastrously wrong—for readers aged 8–11.

The Wizard of Sound: A Story about Thomas Edison

Barbara Mitchell; Carolrhoda, 1992

A catchy 64-page biography of Edison that covers his life from boyhood through his invention of the phonograph (completed in 1889). For readers aged 9–12.

Games and Hands-On Activities

The Invention Factory: Thomas Edison's Laboratories

This is a "Teaching With Historic Places" lesson plan developed in association with the National Register of Historic Places. The packet centers around Edison's West Orange, New Jersey, research complex. Included is a historical overview of Edison's life and work, illustrated with maps and photographs, assorted reproductions of primary source materials, a list of suggestions for student reading and activities, and directions to, and information about, the historical site.

$8

Jackdaw Publications

Box 503

Amawalk, NY 10501

(914) 962-6911 or (800) 789-0022/fax (800) 962-9101

The Wizard of Menlo Park

A cut-and-fold (you assemble the pieces) board game produced in cooperation with the Henry Ford Museum and Greenfield Village. Players act as assistants in Edison's Menlo Park laboratory, racing to assemble a successful incandescent lightbulb before Edison's assigned deadline: New Year's Eve.

$6.95

Chatham Hill Games, Inc.

Box 253

Chatham, NY 12037

(518) 392-5022 or (800) 544-3039/fax (518) 392-3121

e-mail: CHGames@taconic.net

Web site: www.ocdc.com/Chatham_Hill_Games

Videos

The Edison Effect

A three-part video documentary from the A&E Network on the life and work of Thomas Edison, and the impact his inventions have had on life in America. The three videotapes in the series are titled "A Dozen Years," "Three Inventions," and "A Whole New World."

$39.95

PBS Home Video

1320 Braddock Pl.

Alexandria, VA 22314-1698

(800) 645-4PBS

Web site: www.pbs.org

Computer Software

The Genius of Edison

The life, times, and inventions of master inventor Thomas Edison. Kids can investigate 13 of Edison's best-known inventions (among them the lightbulb) through a creative combination of animation, color graphics, historical film footage, photographs, period music, and more. Included is an interactive period newspaper, filled with advertisements, interviews, and news stories, a timeline, games, and quizzes. There's also a database of information about historical events and famous people of Edison's day, such as Amelia Earhart, George Gershwin, and Vincent van Gogh. On CD-ROM for Mac or Windows.

$44.95

The Learning Company

6160 Summit Dr. N

Minneapolis, MN 55430-4003

(800) 622-3390/fax (612) 589-1151

Web site: www.learningco.com

EDISON ON-LINE

Edison National Historic Site Home Page

Biographical information on Edison, a timeline of inventions, historical photographs, and samples of early sound recordings. Included is a "Kids' Corner" on Edison and his work.

www.nps.gov/edis/ed000000.htm

THE TELEGRAPH AND THE TELEPHONE

BOOKS

Ahoy! Ahoy! Are You There?: A Story of Alexander Graham Bell

Robert Quackenbush; Prentice-Hall, 1981

A 36-page biography of inventor Alexander Graham Bell (he picked his middle name himself, when he was 11), with clever, cartoonish illustrations. Bell proposed a cheerful "Ahoy!" as the standard answer to a ringing telephone; early telephone users, however, preferred "Hello." For readers aged 8–11.

Alexander Graham Bell and the Telephone

Steve Parker; Chelsea House, 1995

A 32-page biography of Bell, concentrating on the science behind his most famous invention. Illustrated with color photographs and diagrams. For readers aged 9–12.

Quick, Annie, Give Me a Catchy Line!: A Story of Samuel F. B. Morse

Robert Quackenbush; Prentice-Hall, 1983

A 36-page humorously illustrated biography of Samuel F. B. Morse, the inventor of the telegraph (who really wanted to be a painter). Annie was Morse's wife; the catchy line turned out to be "What hath God wrought?" The International Morse Code is included on the inside back cover.

Samuel F. B. Morse

Jean Lee Latham; Chelsea House, 1991

An 80-page biography of Samuel Morse, famed for his inventions of Morse code and the telegraph. (But he really wanted to be a painter.) For readers aged 9–12.

HANDS-ON ACTIVITIES

Build Your Own Telephone Kit

Jim Becker and Andy Mayer; Running Press, 1997

The kit includes the 64-page *Telephone Handbook*, which explains just how the telephone works, plus all the materials needed to make your own working telephone (with red cord in a brightly striped cardboard case). Plug it in when you're finished and say "Ahoy!" to your grandmother in Indiana.

$19.95 from bookstores or

Running Press Book Publishers

125 S. 22nd St.

Philadelphia, PA 19103

(215) 567-5080 or (800) 345-5359/fax (800) 453-2884

VIDEOS

The Story of Alexander Graham Bell

The story of the invention of the telephone, told with flair and a love interest. The film, made in 1939, is in black and white and stars Don Ameche (as Alexander) and Loretta Young.

$19.95

Movies Unlimited

3015 Darnell Rd.

Philadelphia, PA 19154

(215) 637-4444 or (800) 4-MOVIES

e-mail: movies@moviesunlimited.com

Web site: www.moviesunlimited.com

The Telephone

From the PBS *The American Experience* series, this hourlong program, narrated by Morley Safer, details the history of the telephone—"the invention that forever changed the way the world interacts"—from its invention by Alexander Graham Bell to the first coast-to-coast telephone call in 1915 to the wired world we live in today.

$19.98
PBS Home Video
1320 Braddock Pl.
Alexandria, VA 22314-1698
(800) 645-4PBS
Web site: www.pbs.org

REFORM AND REFORMERS

Cheap Raw Material
Milton Meltzer; Viking, 1994

The history of child labor from ancient times to the 20th century, documenting such abuses as the lives of young chimney sweeps, the plight of children in 19th-century mines and mills, and the factory "sweatshops" of the 19th and 20th centuries. (Children in the mills worked 80 hours a week under dangerous conditions for a wage of a few pennies.) The book includes quotations, journal excerpts, and accounts by the children themselves and describes the long battle among employers, activists, and government officials to protect children's rights. Illustrated with photographs.

Child Labor: The Shame of the Nation
A collection of 12 poster-size black-and-white photographs by Lewis W. Hine of children at work in the late 19th/early 20th century, showing pictures of kids at work in the fields, mines, and factories, children making cigars at home, young chimney sweeps, and wiped-out young workers asleep at school. The pictures are accompanied by a historical background essay, a timeline, and reproducible student activity sheets.

$19.95
Jackdaw Publications
Box 503
Amawalk, NY 10501
(914) 962-6911 or (800) 789-0022/fax (800) 962-9101

Cobblestone: Reform
Several issues of *Cobblestone* magazine (see page 449) center around reformers and reform. Titles include *The History of Labor* (October 1992), *Prohibition* (October 1993), *Public Works* (August, 1983), and *Mary McLeod Bethune* (February 1996). Each contains fiction and nonfiction articles, timelines, puzzles and activity suggestions, and supplementary reading lists. For students in grades 5–9.

Available from most libraries or for $4.50 from Cobblestone Publishing, Inc.
30 Grove St.
Peterborough, NH 03458-1454
(603) 924-7209 or (800) 821-0115
Web site: www.cobblestonepub.com

Fire at the Triangle Factory
Holly Littlefield; First Avenue Editions, 1996

A fictionalized account of two young girls working at the infamous Triangle Shirtwaist Factory, which suffered a disastrous fire in 1911, thus bringing national attention to the plight of workers in the garment industry. For readers in grades K–3.

Great Lives: Human Rights
William Jay Jacobs; Atheneum, 1990

Biographies of 30 Americans who have been instrumental in defending human rights, among them Thomas Paine, Cesar Chavez, Sojourner Truth, Susan B. Anthony, and Martin Luther King Jr. For readers aged 10 and up.

Kids At Work: Lewis Hine and the Crusade Against Child Labor
Russell Freedman; Clarion, 1998

A history of the campaign to end child labor, illustrated with over 60 of Lewis Hine's impressive early 20th-century photographs, taken when he worked as an investigator for the National Child Labor Committee. Kids are shown at work in mines, mills, fields, and factories.

Lyddie

Katherine Paterson; Puffin, 1994

Thirteen-year-old Lyddie's family has lost their farm, and Lyddie goes to work in a Massachusetts mill. The book describes the harsh conditions of mid-19th-century factories and Lyddie's battle to earn enough money to buy back the farm and reunite her family. For readers aged 10 and up.

Mother Jones: One Woman's Fight for Labor

Betsy Harvey Kraft; Clarion, 1995

A 116-page biography of Mary Harris ("Mother") Jones, the feisty Irish immigrant whose outrage over unfair working conditions fueled the American labor movement, leading to the organization of unions and the passing of legislation to protect workers' rights. Illustrated with photographs.

Peace and Bread: The Story of Jane Addams

Stephanie Sammartino McPherson; Carolrhoda, 1993

A short chapter biography of social worker Jane Addams and her work at Hull House. For readers aged 9–12.

She's Wearing a Dead Bird on Her Head!

Kathryn Lasky; Hyperion, 1995

The story of Harriet Hemenway and Minna Hall, the two women who founded the Massachusetts Audubon Society, and their fight to save birds from the women's hat trade. They begin by persuading society ladies to give up their outrageous feather-laden hats; then they convince schoolchildren and sportsmen to join their campaign. Amusingly told and illustrated.

So Far From Home: The Diary of Mary Driscoll, an Irish Mill Girl

Barry Denenberg; Scholastic, 1997

The diary of a young Irish immigrant working in the mills of Lowell, Massachusetts, in 1847. The diary chronicles the hard work and miserable working conditions in the mills, and Mary's disappointments in America. For readers aged 9–12.

A volume in the **Dear America Series** (see page 452).

Strike!

Penny Colman; Millbrook Press, 1995

A chronological overview of the dreadful struggles of American labor from the 17th century to the present, beginning with the first strike in 1677 (which resulted in a wholesale firing of the Boston carters) and ending with the recent baseball strikes. The book is illustrated with black-and-white photographs and includes a timeline of labor history and a supplementary reading list.

We Shall Not Be Moved: The Women's Factory Strike of 1909

Joan Dash; Scholastic, 1998

A account of the landmark strike by the New York shirtwaist workers who, together with support from the wealthy "mink brigade," began to improve working conditions for women in American factories. Includes quotations, period photographs, and descriptions of life among the immigrants of New York's Lower East Side. For readers aged 10 and up.

WOMEN'S RIGHTS

BOOKS

The Ballot Box Battle

Emily Arnold McCully; Alfred A. Knopf, 1996

"No votes for pea-brained females!" shouts Cordelia's brother, but Cordelia has other opinions. Cordelia's next-door neighbor is the redoubtable Elizabeth Cady Stanton, from whom Cordelia learns a great deal—including, triumphantly, how to jump a four-foot fence on horseback. For readers aged 5–9.

Bloomers!

Rhoda Blumberg; Atheneum, 1993

A clever picture book about Amelia Bloomer, whose invention of an outrageous new fashion—pants for women—contributed to the fight for women's rights. For readers aged 5–9.

Forward Into Light: The Struggle for Women's Suffrage

Discovery Enterprises

A collection of primary source materials on the women's suffrage movement, from Sojourner Truth through Carrie Chapman Catt. Included are journal excerpts, archival photographs, poems, songs, historical essays, political cartoons, and clips from period newspapers.

$5.95

Discovery Enterprises, Ltd.

31 Laurelwood Dr.

Carlisle, MA 01741

(508) 287-5403 or (800) 729-1720

Herstory: Women Who Changed the World

Ruth Ashby and Deborah Gore Ohrn, eds.; Viking, 1995

A collection of short biographies of 120 prominent women. The book is divided into three main sections: "The Dawn: Prehistory to 1750," "From Revolution to Revolution: 1750 to 1850," and "The Global Community: 1890 to the Present." Entries include Queen Hatshepsut, Anna Pavlova, "Mother" Jones, Elizabeth Cady Stanton, Susan B. Anthony, Sacajawea, and Eleanor Roosevelt. Fascinating information, conversationally presented.

A Long Way to Go: A Story of Women's Right to Vote

Zibby Oneal; Puffin, 1992

In 1917, eight-year-old Lila learns about women's rights from her feisty grandmother, who is involved in the women's suffrage movement. For readers aged 9–12.

The Road to Seneca Falls: A Story About Elizabeth Cady Stanton

Gwenyth Swain; Lerner, 1996.

A short chapter biography of the prominent women's rights crusader for readers aged 9–12.

Susan B. Anthony and the Women's Movement

Cobblestone; March 1985

This issue of Cobblestone (see page 449) includes a history of the women's suffrage movement, information on the lives of such women as Susan B. Anthony and Elizabeth Cady Stanton, a play, Working Woman, and a reading list. For students in grades 5–9.

Available from most libraries or for $4.50 from Cobblestone Publishing, Inc.

30 Grove St.

Peterborough, NH 03458-1454

(603) 924-7209 or (800) 821-0115

Web site: www.cobblestonepub.com

The Timetables of Women's History

Karen Greenspan; Touchstone Books, 1996

Thousands of entries covering women's history from 4000 B.C. to the present day. Events are listed under 10 categories, among them "Daily Life," "Humanities/Fine Arts," "Reform," and "Science/Technology." Also included are capsule biographies of prominent individuals, short historical essays on such topics as witchcraft, female Renaissance artists, and women warriors, and over 100 black-and-white photographs.

You Want Women to Vote, Lizzie Stanton?

Jean Fritz; Putnam, 1995

An 88-page biography of Elizabeth Cady Stanton, in eight short, conversational chapters. Historical information is accompanied by fascinating dollops of personal anecdote: Ms. Stanton, readers learn, was a whiz at chess; she loathed the color red and hated embroidery; she had seven children; and her husband called her "Lizzie Lee."

GAMES AND HANDS-ON ACTIVITIES

Great Women Biographical Card Games

There are five card games in this series. Each card carries a photograph or portrait of a famous woman, plus brief biographical facts. Sets are "Foremothers," featuring such political leaders as Susan B. Anthony, Lucretia Mott, Elizabeth Cady Stanton, and Sojourner Truth; "Founders and Firsts," including Clara Barton, Elizabeth Blackwell, Nellie Bly, Amelia Earhart, and Mary Lyon; "Poets and Writers," including Louisa May Alcott, Emily Dickinson, Phillis Wheatley, and Harriet Beecher Stowe; "Composers," including Barbara Kolb, Clara Schumann, Dame Ethel Smyth, and Fanny Mendelssohn; and "Athletes," including Nadia Comaneci, Babe Didrikson Zaharias, Sonja Henie, and Billie Jean King.

$7.95

Aristoplay

450 S. Wagner Rd.

Ann Arbor, MI 48107

(800) 634-7738 or (888) GR8-GAME

HISTORY

fax (734) 995-4611

Web site: www.aristoplay.com

6 Great Women Paper Dolls

Some of the featured "Great Women"—such as Cleopatra, Sappho, and Joan of Arc—have nothing to do with the women's suffrage movement; also included, however, are Susan B. Anthony and Elizabeth Cady Stanton. All in all, 22 women, with costumes to color and cut out, plus an appropriate short speech for each woman's chosen cause.

$3.95

Bellerophon Books

36 Ancapa St.

Santa Barbara, CA 93101

(800) 253-9943/fax (800) 965-8286

13 Votes for Women:
The Fight for Suffrage

A portfolio of 14 primary source reproductions, five historical background essays, a list of suggested student readings and discussion questions, and a study guide. Essay titles include "The Beginning of Suffrage Agitation," "Women Organize," and "The Antisuffrage Movement." Primary source documents include facsimiles of *The Revolution* by Susan B. Anthony, "Votes for Women" postcards (in color), handbills from the Congressional Union for Woman Suffrage, collections of antisuffrage publications, and the sheet music to a prosuffrage song of 1916, "Be Good to California, Mr. Wilson."

$37

Jackdaw Publications

Box 503

Amawalk, NY 10501

(914) 962-6911 or (800) 789-0022/fax (800) 962-9101

COMPUTER SOFTWARE

10 Her Heritage

A biographical encyclopedia of over a thousand famous women, complete with historical information, photographs, illustrations, and video clips. On CD-ROM for Mac or Windows.

$42.95

National Women's History Project

7738 Bell Rd.

Windsor, CA 95492-8518

(707) 838-6000

e-mail: nwhp@aol.com

WOMEN'S HISTORY ON-LINE

10 75th Anniversary of a Woman's Right to Vote

A history of the women's suffrage movement, a timeline, short biographies of prominent participants, the text of the 19th Amendment, and links to historic sites and other related women's history resources.

www.cc.rochester.edu:80/SBA/95-75

8 Distinguished Women of Past and Present

Biographies of prominent women. Users can search the site by name, by alphabetical index, or by field of activity.

www.netsrq.com/~dbois/index.html

8 Votes for Women

Portraits and biographies of important individuals in the women's suffrage movement, historical background information, a timeline of events, and a collection of historical photographs from 1850 to 1920.

lcweb2.loc.gov/ammem/vfwhtml/vfwhome.html

THE TWENTIETH CENTURY

HISTORICAL OVERVIEWS AND TIMELINES

12 American Letters

An innovative history/creative writing program in which students, as various historical characters, exchange letters detailing their lives and experiences. Each unit in the program covers a 13- to 15-year period of 20th-century history (1900–1913, 1914–1929, 1930–1945, 1946–1960, and 1961–1975). The units consist of 15 "seed" projects, each of which provides background information on an historical event, describes two persons who are somehow involved in the event, and lists suggestions for an exchange of letters between the two. In the period 1914–1929, for example, roles in one "seed" are that of a young soldier fighting in France during World War I and his girlfriend back home. Other "seeds" from this unit cover the Russian Revolution, the League of Nations, immigration, the 19th Amendment, the Scopes Trial, and the stock market crash that ushered in the Great Depression.

$37 each

Interact

1825 Gillespie Way, #101

El Cajon, CA 92020-1095

(619) 448-1474 or (800) 359-0961/fax (619) 448-6722 or (800) 700-5093

Web site: www.interact-simulations.com

The Glory and the Dream: A Narrative History of America 1932–1972

William Manchester; Bantam Doubleday Dell, 1990

Fascinating, fact filled, and fat—nearly 1,400 pages long. This is a detailed and notably well-written history of the mid-20th century. For family reference or for very motivated teenagers.

Great 20th Century Expeditions Series

Dillon Press

A collection of short informational books on landmark 20th-century expeditions, each illustrated with photographs. Titles include *Amelia Earhart Flies Around the World* (Kath Davis; 1994), *Armstrong Lands on the Moon* (Gordon Charleston; 1994), *Hillary and Tenzing Climb Mount Everest* (Bob Davidson; 1993), *Perry Reaches the North Pole* (Gordon Charleston; 1993), *Robert Scott in the Antarctic* (Philip Arthur Sauvain; 1993), and *Thor Heyerdahl and the Kon-Tiki Voyage* (Philip Steele; 1993). Each book not only covers the details of the featured expedition but places it in the context of its times.

The United States in the 20th Century

David Rubel; Scholastic, 1995

An attractive and interesting timeline history of the century, divided into 10 sections, running from the "New Century" and the "Progressive Era" through the "Nineties." Each page traces historical and cultural happenings in four parallel horizontal timelines: "Politics," "Everyday Life," "Arts and Entertainment," and "Science and Technology." Major events are noted in each field, along with capsule biographies of prominent people, photographs, color illustrations, and fun fact boxes.

A Visual Timeline of the Twentieth Century

Simon Adams; Dorling Kindersley, 1996

A 48-page timeline of world and American history, covering the fields of the arts, science and technology, everyday life, and world events. Heavily illustrated with color photographs and drawings.

WORLD WAR I

Also see **World History: Modern Times** (pages 677–680)

BOOKS

America in World War I

Edward F. Dolan; Millbrook Press, 1996

A comprehensive 96-page history for kids aged 10–13, covering the causes of the war, major events of the war, and prominent World War I personalities. Many photographs and interesting facts in sidebars.

Casey Over There

Staton Rabin; Harcourt Brace, 1994

When three months pass by without a word from Aubrey's older brother Casey, fighting in Europe during World War I, Aubrey writes a letter to the "Honorable Uncle Sam" and receives a reply from President Woodrow Wilson. For readers aged 7 and up.

The U.S. in World War I

Cobblestone; June 1986

This issue of *Cobblestone* (see page 449) includes an overview of America in World War I, including articles about World War I airplanes, nurses, trench warfare, and the gallant Pigeon Service.

Available from most libraries or for $4.50 from

Cobblestone Publishing, Inc.

30 Grove St.

Peterborough, NH 03458-1454

(603) 924-7209 or (800) 821-0115

Web site: www.cobblestonepub.com

 World War I

Tom McGowen; Franklin Watts, 1993

A basic 64-page history of the war for readers aged 9–12, illustrated with maps and photographs.

The Year of the Perfect Christmas Tree:
An Appalachian Story

Gloria Houston; Puffin, 1996

The year is 1918, and it is the turn of Ruthie's family to choose the perfect Christmas tree for the church in their little mountain community in North Carolina. They choose the tree, and then Ruthie's father leaves for World War I. With beautiful illustrations by Barbara Cooney.

GAMES AND HANDS-ON ACTIVITIES

Airplanes of World War I Coloring Book

Carlo Demand; Dover Publications

Over 40 detailed black-line drawings of World War I fighter planes, bombers, and transports, with explanatory picture captions.

$2.95

Dover Publications, Inc.

31 E. Second St.

Mineola, NY 11501

Doughboy Boot Camp

A historical simulation in which kids role-play "doughboys" in training, before shipping out to France in 1917. Participants variously act out the parts of trainees and drill sergeants, medical personnel, French language instructors, song leaders, and officers. For 10 to 35 students in grades 6–12 (though can be adapted to smaller groups).

$11

Interact

1825 Gillespie Way, #101

El Cajon, CA 92020-1095

(800) 359-0961

Web site: www.interact-simulations.com

World War I Game

A map-based board game that teaches players the major events of World War I and their locations. Numbered event cards are paired to numbered sites on a world map.

$10.95

Educational Materials Associates

Box 7385

Charlottesville, VA 22906

(804) 293-GAME

THE GREAT DEPRESSION AND THE NEW DEAL

BOOKS: NONFICTION

 Brother, Can You Spare a Dime?
The Great Depression, 1929–1933

Milton Meltzer; Facts on File, 1991

A 144-page history of the Great Depression and Franklin Delano Roosevelt's New Deal, using many firsthand accounts, for readers aged 12 and up. Illustrated with period photographs.

Eleanor

Barbara Cooney; Viking, 1996

A simple, beautifully illustrated picture-book biography of young Eleanor Roosevelt from babyhood through her school years, when her future philosophies were greatly influenced by a beloved schoolmistress, Mlle Marie Souvestre. For readers aged 6–9.

Franklin Roosevelt: A Life of Discovery

Russell Freedman; Clarion, 1990

A detailed, interesting, and well-written biography, heavily illustrated with photographs, for readers aged 11 and up. By the same author, also see *Eleanor Roosevelt: A Life of Discovery* (Houghton Mifflin, 1997).

 The Great Depression

Cobblestone; March 1984

This issue of *Cobblestone* (page 449) includes a history of the Great Depression of the 1930s, stories of everyday life in the depression, an account of a Civilian Conservation Corps camp, activities, and a supplementary reading list. For students in grades 5–9.

Available from most libraries or for $4.50 from Cobblestone Publishing, Inc.

30 Grove St.

Peterborough, NH 03458-1454

(603) 924-7209 or (800) 821-0115

Web site: www.cobblestonepub.com

 12 + *Hard Times: An Oral History of the Great Depression*

Studs Terkel; Pantheon, 1986

A 400+-page collection of firsthand accounts of the depression era. The stories, anecdotes, and reminiscences, by a wide range of people, are variously funny, sad, courageous, and fascinating. Personalized history for all ages.

 7 10 *The Story of the Great Depression*

R. Conrad Stein; Children's Press, 1985

A simple 32-page explanation of the causes and effects of the Great Depression, for readers aged 7–10, illustrated with photographs.

BOOKS: FICTION

9 12 *Blue Willow*

Doris Gates; Puffin, 1971

A classic novel about migrant workers during the Great Depression, as seen through the eyes of young Janey Larkin. Janey cherishes a blue willow–patterned plate picturing the house and stream she wishes her family had. For readers aged 9–12.

8 12 *Ida Early Comes Over the Mountain*

Robert Burch; Puffin, 1990

The setting is rural Georgia in the penny-pinching days of the Great Depression; and Ida Early comes over the mountain, looking for a job. She is hired as housekeeper by Mr. Sutton, whose wife has recently died. The book tells the story of Ida's developing relationship with the four Sutton children, who learn to treasure her

warmth, wisdom, and irrepressible eccentricity. Sequel: *Christmas With Ida Early* (Puffin, 1985).

 6 9 *In Coal Country*

Judith Hendershot; Alfred A. Knopf, 1992

A picture-book story of everyday family life, love, and hardship during the Great Depression in the coal country of Ohio, as seen by a young miner's daughter. For readers aged 5–10.

 5 8 *Potato: A Tale from the Great Depression*

Kate Lied; National Geographic, 1997

A picture-book tale of the Great Depression years, based on a true family story. Clarence, Agnes, and their small daughter, Dorothy, pack up and head to Idaho, hoping to find work digging potatoes. There they live in tents, work all day, and finally—the job over—head home to Iowa with a car loaded with potatoes.

 9 12 *Roll of Thunder, Hear My Cry*

Mildred D. Taylor; Viking, 1997

A Newbery Medal winner about the struggles of the Logan family, black landowners in the rural South at the height of the Great Depression.

8 11 *Soup*

Robert Newton Peck; Alfred A. Knopf, 1976

Heartwarming, funny, and fun-to-read tales of the author's childhood in rural Vermont of the 1920s and the escapades he shared with his best friend, Luther Wesley Vinson, otherwise known as Soup. We loved it. Luckily there are lots of sequels, including *Soup and Me, Soup for President, Soup in the Saddle, Soup on Wheels, Soup's Drum, Soup on Fire, Soup on Ice, Soup's Goat,* and *Soup's Uncle.*

12 + *A Time of Troubles*

Pieter Van Raven; Charles Scribners' Sons, 1990

Fourteen-year-old Roy Purdy and his father, broke and homeless in the days of the Great Depression, ride the rails, heading west across the Oklahoma dust bowl toward California, where they hope to find work as fruit pickers. They arrive in the midst of a labor dispute, and Roy and his father find themselves taking opposite sides. For readers aged 12 and up.

H I S T O R Y

HANDS-ON ACTIVITIES

Build Your Own Radio Kit
Build your own radio, suitable for listening to the exciting serials of the 1930s. The kit includes an informational *Radio Book* by Jim Becker and Andy Mayer, which explains just how a radio works, plus all the components for making your own working AM radio using "simple twist-and-tape connections." The end product is a nice solid little radio, in a turquoise cardboard case, which does really work. It's a great project.

> $19.95 from book or game stores or
> Running Press Book Publishers
> 125 S. 22nd Street
> Philadelphia, PA 19103-4399
> (800) 345-5359/fax (800) 453-2884

See *Radio Shows* (right).

The Depression
A portfolio of 12 primary source documents, five illustrated historical background essays ("The Crash," "Depression in Urban America," "Depression in Rural America," "Protest and Discontent," and "Impact of the Depression"), a list of reading materials and discussion questions for students, and a detailed study guide. Included among the historical document facsimiles are collections of depression era photographs and posters, a broadside from the "Veterans March to Washington" in 1932, sample daily newspaper pages, and a sign: "Unemployed—Buy apples 5 each."

Also see *The Depression Hits Home*, a photo collection that includes a historical background booklet, a timeline, and 12 poster-size black-and-white photographs of depression era subjects, showing pictures of Wall Street on the fatal Black Tuesday, October 29, 1929, families in the dust bowl, an urban soup kitchen, and (photo no. 12) "Trying to Pull Out: Woman teaching kids at home."

> "The Depression" portfolio, $37; the photo collection, $19.95
> Jackdaw Publications
> Box 503
> Amawalk, NY 10501
> (914) 962-6911 or (800) 789-0022/fax (800) 962-9101

Eleanor Roosevelt: First Lady of the World
A portfolio of primary source materials, illustrated historical essays, timelines, and a study guide. Essay titles include "Early Life," "Democrat with a Capital 'D,'" "The War Years," and "The United Nations and Human Rights." There are 14 primary source materials and documents, among them samples of Eleanor's newspaper columns from the 1930s, letters, and a poster picturing the contents of Eleanor's wallet at the time of her death.

> $37
> Jackdaw Publications
> Box 503
> Amawalk, NY 10501
> (800) 789-0022/fax (800) 962-9101

The New Deal
A portfolio of 11 historical documents, six illustrated historical background essays, and a study guide. Essay titles include "The Depression and Franklin Roosevelt" and "The New Deal in Action"; documents include a copy of FDR's Inaugural Address, the script of a 1933 fireside chat, period newspaper pages, a map of the Tennessee Valley Authority, and two anti-Roosevelt political cartoons.

> $37
> Jackdaw Publications
> Box 503
> Amawalk, NY 10501
> (914) 962-6911 or (800) 789-0022/fax (800) 962-9101

Radio Shows
Among the few pleasures of the depression years, state the writers of the Interact catalog, were the newly invented game of "Monopoly" and radio shows. In this simulation, "Radio Shows" participants write and produce their own short radio scripts, complete with clever sound effects, based on popular serials of the depression era, such as *The Lone Ranger, The Shadow, Fibber McGee and Molly,* and *Jack Armstrong, the All-American Boy.* The simulation is recommended for kids in grades 6–12.

> $11
> Interact
> 1825 Gillespie Way, #101

El Cajon, CA 92020-1095

(619) 448-1474 or (800) 359-0961/fax (619) 448-6722

Web site: www.interact-simulations.com

THE DEPRESSION ERA ON-LINE

 The New Deal Network

Information on the lives and accomplishments of Franklin and Eleanor Roosevelt, highlights of the New Deal proposals, and their successes and failures.

newdeal.feri.org

WORLD WAR II

See **World History: Modern Times** (page 677).

BOOKS: NONFICTION

Cobblestone: World War II

Several issues of *Cobblestone* magazine (see page 449) feature World War II themes. Among these are *World War II: Americans in Europe* (January 1993), *World War II: Americans in the Pacific* (January 1994), and *The Home Front* (December 1995). Each issue includes fiction and nonfiction articles, maps, timelines, activities, and a supplementary reading list. For students in grades 5–9.

Available from most libraries or for $4.50 from

Cobblestone Publishing, Inc.

30 Grove St.

Peterborough, NH 03458-1454

(603) 924-7209 or (800) 821-0115

Web site: www.cobblestonepub.com

Don't You Know There's a War On?

James Stevenson; Greenwillow, 1997

A picture-book recollection of life on the home-front during World War II. Stevenson, who was in elementary school during the early 1940s, gives readers a child's view of the war, telling of gas and food rationing, blackouts, worries about a father and an older brother in the armed forces, and the exciting search for neighborhood spies. For readers aged 5–9.

 Rosie the Riveter: Women Working on the Home Front in World War II

Penny Colman; Crown, 1998

A 120-page account of how 18 million women on the home front entered the work force during World War II, illustrated with many black-and-white photographs. Includes a World War II chronology and a lot of interesting facts and figures.

Uncle Sam Wants You! Military Men and Women of World War II

Sylvia Whitman; Lerner, 1993

The experiences of World War II military personnel, told through stories, anecdotes, and interviews. The book covers the beginnings of the draft, boot camp and barracks life, training, combat, and—finally—discharge. Readers also learn about the popular culture of the 1940s. Illustrated with photographs.

V Is for Victory: America Remembers World War II

Kathleen Krull; Random House, 1995

An appealingly designed book crammed with photographs, postcards, recruiting posters, newspaper headlines, and personal letters home—as well as basic historical information covering World War II from Pearl Harbor to the dropping of the atomic bomb. Krull also discusses, in highly readable fashion, life on the home front, with its Victory gardens and ration cards, and covers such wartime personalities as Franklin Roosevelt, Adolf Hitler, and Tokyo Rose.

World War II

Tom McGowen; Franklin Watts, 1996

A short illustrated overview of the war for readers aged 9–12.

Also see McGowen's **World War I** (page 571).

World War II 50th Anniversary Series

Wallace B. Black; Silver Burdett, 1991

A series of 20 short (48 pages) illustrated books covering World War II history for readers aged 9–12. Titles include *America Prepares for War*, *Pearl Harbor!*, *D-Day, Guadalcanal, Iwo Jima and Okinawa*, and *Hiroshima and the Atomic Bomb*.

HISTORY

World War II Series

John Devaney; Walker & Company

A year-by-year anecdotal approach to World War II history, based on primary source material, with many stories, quotations, and accounts of personal events. Titles in the series include *America Goes to War: 1941*, *America Fights the Tide: 1942*, *America on the Attack: 1943*, *America Storms the Beaches: 1944*, and *America Triumphs: 1945*. Each volume includes maps, photographs, a timeline, and capsule biographies of key individuals. The books are about 200 pages long, for readers aged 12 and up.

Books: Fiction

Aloha Means Come Back

Dorothy and Thomas Hoobler; Silver Burdett, 1994

One of the Her Story Series (see page 453), in which young Laura and her mother travel to Hawaii to join Laura's father in 1941, just before the Japanese attack on Pearl Harbor.

The Human Comedy

William Saroyan; Harcourt Brace, 1991

The main characters in *The Human Comedy* are young Homer and Ulysses Macauley, growing up in the days of World War II. Their older brother, Marcus, a soldier, is away at the front; Homer, 14, has a part-time job as a telegraph messenger, which brings him into daily contact with the joys and sorrows of the people around him. The book is the story of everyday life in a small town in the shadow of a great war; it's also the story of life on a grander scale—of the loves, fears, questions, and truths that make us human. Glad, sad, and beautiful.

Journey to Topaz

Yoshiko Uchida; Creative Arts Book Company, 1988

The story of an 11-year-old Japanese American girl, Yuki Sakane, who is sent with her family to an internment camp in California after the bombing of Pearl Harbor. For readers aged 11 and up.

Meet Molly

Valerie Tripp; Pleasant Company, 1986

Molly, featured in the popular American Girl Collection from Pleasant Company (see page 448), is a feisty third-grader dealing with life on the home front in 1944, while her father is away at war and her mother works for the Red Cross. Sequels include *Molly Learns a Lesson; Molly's Surprise; Happy Birthday, Molly!*, in which Emily, a young English refugee, comes to stay with Molly's family; *Molly Saves the Day*; and *Changes for Molly*. For readers aged 7–11.

Pearl Harbor Is Burning! A Story of World War II

Kathleen V. Kudlinski; Puffin, 1993

Two fifth-grade boys—Frank and his friend Kenji, a Japanese American—watch the bombing of Pearl Harbor in 1941. The book deals with conflicting racial prejudices in the Hawaiian islands of the 1940s—and ends with Frank asking Kenji how to say "friend" in Japanese.

The Summer of My German Soldier

Bette Greene; Dell, 1981

A coming-of-age story in which Patty, a Jewish storekeeper's daughter living in Arkansas in the days of World War II, befriends Anton, an escaped German prisoner-of-war.

Under the Blood-Red Sun

Graham Salisbury; Bantam Doubleday Dell, 1995

December 7, 1941, is the beginning of two wars for young Tomikazu Nakaji. After the attack on Pearl Harbor, Tomi's father and grandfather are sent to an internment camp, leaving the rest of the family to struggle with bigotry, loneliness, and financial disaster. A tale of war, courage, and friendship; winner of the Scott O'Dell Award for Historical Fiction.

"Who Was That Masked Man, Anyway?"

Avi; Camelot, 1994

Set in the last year of World War II, the book features 12-year-old Frankie Wattleston (also known as "Chet Barker, Master Spy"), whose love of radio melodrama plummets him and his best friend into a series of hilarious adventures. Modeling themselves on the Green Hornet, the Lone Ranger, and the mysterious Shadow, the boys set out to right the wrongs of the world—and, incidentally, to rid themselves of the Wattleston family boarder and to link Tom,

Frankie's shell-shocked soldier brother, with the sixth-grade schoolteacher, who looks like Veronica Lake.

GAMES AND HANDS-ON ACTIVITIES

Atomic Bomb

A portfolio of primary source materials covering the history of World War II in the Pacific theater, the development of the atomic bomb, the decision to use the bomb against Japan, and the postwar debate about the decision. The portfolio includes five illustrated historical background essays ("War in the Pacific," "The Manhattan Project," "The Diplomatic Scene in 1945," "Destruction of Hiroshima and Nagasaki," and "Postwar Debate"), a timeline of events (1931–1945), and reproductions of 13 historical documents, including a petition from scientists urging Truman not to use the bomb, newspaper articles from 1945 on the bombing of Japan, and a copy of the 1958 Resolution of Hiroshima. Also includes a study guide with reproducible student worksheets.

$37
Jackdaw Publications
Box 503
Amawalk, NY 10501
(800) 789-0022/fax (800) 962-9101

Third Reich

A strategy board game of World War II in Europe, covering the military action from 1939 through the end of the war. The game, which is played on a detailed map of Europe, includes three different versions or scenarios: "Blitzkrieg (Fall 1939–Summer 1942)," "Turning Point (Spring 1942–Winter 1944)," or "Fuhrer Bunker (Spring 1944–Winter 1946)." Players meet in battle, participate in diplomatic negotiations, form alliances, and struggle to acquire strategically valuable territory. A complex game for teenagers and up.

Also see "Empire of the Rising Sun," a strategy board game of World War II in the Pacific. The game is played on a map board of the Pacific Ocean; playing counters represent famous American or Japanese ships. The game involves political, economic, and technological strategies as well as battle maneuvers; the winner of the race to develop the atomic bomb, for example, has significant history-changing potential.

"Third Reich," $30; "Empire of the Rising Sun," $50
Avalon Hill Game Co.
4517 Harford Rd.
Baltimore, MD 21214
(410) 254-9200 or (800) 999-3222
e-mail: AH GAMES@aol.com
Web site: www.avalonhill.com

World War II Game

A map-based board game in which players learn the crucial events of World War II and their geographical locations, by pairing a series of numbered event cards to their corresponding numbers on the world map.

$10.95
Educational Materials Association, Inc.
Box 7385
Charlottesville, VA 22906
(804) 293-GAME

WORLD WAR II ON-LINE

A Guide to the Good War: Resources on World War II

A comprehensive site including maps, diaries and letters, interviews, visual and sound archives, and a photograph collection.

www.wisc.edu/shs-archives/ww2guide/index.html

Hiroshima Archive

Includes a map of Japan, photographs of artifacts from the Hiroshima Peace Memorial Museum, and pictures of the *Enola Gay,* the plane that dropped the first atomic bomb.

www.lclark.edu/~history/HIROSHIMA

THE COLD WAR, THE KOREAN WAR, AND VIETNAM

BOOKS

Cobblestone: Post–World War II

Several issues of *Cobblestone* magazine (see page 449) center around post–World War II events. Titles include *The Cold War* (May 1991), *The U.S. and the U.S.S.R.* (February 1985), *The Voyage to the Moon* (July 1981), and *Television* (October 1989). Each includes fiction and nonfiction articles, activity suggestions, and a supplementary reading list. For students in grades 5–9.

> Available from most libraries or for $4.50 from
> Cobblestone Publishing, Inc.
> 30 Grove St.
> Peterborough, NH 03458-1454
> (603) 924-7209 or (800) 821-0115
> Web site: www.cobblestonepub.com

The Cold War: Opposing Viewpoints

William Dudley; Greenhaven, 1992

Nothing is simple. The book explores conflicting opinions of the Soviet threat to democracy. For readers aged 12 and up.

The Korean War: "The Forgotten War"

R. Conrad Stein; Enslow Publishing, 1994

One of the American War series (see page 450). The book, 128 pages long and illustrated with maps, photographs, and timelines, covers the historical background of the war, the major events of the conflict, and the final (stalemate) outcome. Stein includes assorted anecdotes about the so-called Forgotten War: when one Chicago Marine returned home from combat in Korea, a puzzled neighbor asked if he had been out of town.

Also see *The Korean War* (Carter Smith; Silver Burdett, 1991).

The Vietnam War

John Devaney; Franklin Watts, 1992

An overview of the Vietnam war from the French involvement and the Battle of Dien Bien Phu through the fall of Saigon in 1975. For readers aged 10–13.

The Wall

Eve Bunting; Houghton Mifflin, 1992

The Wall is the famous memorial to the veterans of the Vietnam war; in this beautiful and touching picture book, a small boy and his father visit the Wall to find his grandfather's name.

Also see *A Wall of Names: The Story of the Vietnam Veterans Memorial* (Judy Donnelly; Random House, 1991) for readers aged 4–8.

HANDS-ON ACTIVITIES

The Cold War

A portfolio of 15 primary source documents, five historical background essays, a timeline, and a study guide. Essay titles include "Origins of the Cold War," "Cuban Missile Crisis," "McCarthyism," "The Forgotten War: Korea," and "The Berlin Wall, End of Communism and the Cold War." Documents include a copy of a letter from Khrushchev to Kennedy about the Cuban missiles, period newspaper articles, and the text of the 1950 anti-Communist McCarran Act.

> $37
> Jackdaw Publications
> Box 503
> Amawalk, NY 10501
> (800) 789-0022/fax (800) 962-9101

The Vietnam War

A portfolio containing five illustrated historical essays ("Beginnings to the Gulf of Tonkin," "Gulf of Tonkin and the Tet Offensive," "The Anti-War Movement," "Vietnamization and the Paris Peace Accords," and "The Fall of Saigon and the Aftermath"), a timeline of events (1941–1982), and copies of 16 historical documents, among them newspaper stories, a draft document poster, and a Vietcong after-action report.

> $37
> Jackdaw Publications
> Box 503

Amawalk, NY 10501

(914) 962-6911 or (800) 789-0022/fax (800) 962-9101

THE CIVIL RIGHTS MOVEMENT

BOOKS

The African-American Experience Series
Franklin Watts

A series of 128-page books on key events and experiences in the history of black Americans, targeted at middle-grade readers. Titles in the series include *Between Two Fires: Black Soldiers in the Civil War* (Joyce Hansen; 1994), *No Easy Victories: Black Americans and the Vote* (Clarence Lusane; 1996), *The Black Press and the Struggle for Civil Rights* (Carl Senna; 1994), and *The Negro Leagues: The Story of Black Baseball* (Jacob Margolies; 1993).

Cobblestone: Civil Rights Movement
Several issues of *Cobblestone* magazine (see page 449) feature Civil Rights themes. Titles include *Black History Month: The Struggle for Rights* (February 1983), and *Martin Luther King, Jr., and the Civil Rights Movement* (February 1994). Each issue includes fiction and nonfiction articles, timelines, activities, and supplementary reading lists. For students in grades 5–9. Also see *Harlem Renaissance* (February 1991), *Jazz* (October 1983), *Louis Armstrong* (October 1994), and *African-American Inventors* (February 1992).

Available from most libraries or for $4.50 from
Cobblestone Publishing, Inc.
30 Grove St.
Peterborough, NH 03458-1454
(603) 924-7209 or (800) 821-0115
Web site: www.cobblestonepub.com

I Have a Dream: The Life and Words of Martin Luther King, Jr.
Jim Haskins; Millbrook Press, 1994

A 112-page biography of Martin Luther King Jr., with an introduction by Rosa Parks. Boxes in the margins include quotations and excerpts from King's speeches in writings. For younger readers, see *I Have a Dream: The Story of Martin Luther King* (Margaret Davidson; Scholastic, 1986).

If You Lived at the Time of Martin Luther King
Ellen Levine; Scholastic, 1994

The story of the Civil Rights movement of the 1950s and 1960s, written in an appealing question-and-answer format. Kids learn what it was like to participate in the Montgomery Bus Boycott, to join in a lunch counter sit-in, and to march on Washington with Martin Luther King.

See the *If You . . . Series* (pages 453–454).

Milestones in Black History Series
Chelsea House

A series of illustrated books for high school–aged students covering American black history from the beginnings of the slave trade through the present. Titles in the series include *The Birth of Black America: The Age of Discovery and the Slave Trade* (Andrew Frank; 1996), *Days of Sorrow, Years of Glory 1813–1850: From the Nat Turner Revolt to the Fugitive Slave Law* (Timothy J. Paulsen; 1994), *Great Ambitions: From the "Separate But Equal" Doctrine to the Birth of the NAACP 1896–1909* (Pierre Hauser and Martin Luther King; 1995), and *Struggle and Love: From the Gary Convention to the Aftermath of the Million Man March* (Mary Hull; 1996). *Struggle and Love,* for example, covers the first national black political convention in 1972, desegregation, affirmative action, Jesse Jackson's presidential campaigns, and black influence on modern American culture.

One More River to Cross: The Stories of Twelve Black Americans
Jim Haskins; Scholastic, 1994

A collection of brief, interesting biographies, including the stories of Crispus Attucks, Malcolm X, Madam C. J. Walker (the first woman millionaire), Eddie Robinson ("the winningest football coach ever"), Marian Anderson, Ralph Bunche, and Charles Drew.

A Picture Book of Martin Luther King, Jr.

David A. Adler; Holiday House, 1991

A simple brightly illustrated introductory biography for kids aged 5–8. By the same author, also see *A Picture Book of Rosa Parks* (1995).

The Story of Booker T. Washington

Patricia and Frederick McKissack; Children's Press, 1991

A volume in the Cornerstones of Freedom series (see page 451), this biography, illustrated with prints and photographs, covers the events of Washington's life and his role in the fight for black rights.

Timetables of African-American History

Sharon Harley; Touchstone Books, 1996

A chronology of significant events in black history from 1492 to the present. Events are listed under ten categories, among them "Education," "Laws and Legal Actions," "Arts," "Science, Technology, and Medicine," and "Sports."

GAMES AND HANDS-ON ACTIVITIES

Black Heritage Brain Quest

This double packet of hinged cards includes 850 questions (and answers) covering 5,000 years of African American culture and history for kids aged 9 and up. "Where did Martin Luther King deliver his 'I Have a Dream' speech?" "Who wrote *The Invisible Man?*" Questions categories include "Eminent Leaders," "Scientists, Educators, and Entrepreneurs," "The African Continent," "Art and Literature," "Black History," and "This and That."

Available from bookstores or
Workman Publishing Co.
708 Broadway
New York, NY 10003
(212) 254-5900 or (800) 722-7202/fax (212) 254-8098
Web site: www.workmanweb.com

Black History Playing Cards

An illustrated deck of 52 playing cards, each picturing a famous person in the arts, science, industry, or the human rights movement. A booklet of (very short) biographies is included in the box. The cards can be used for any number of imaginative historical activities, plus all the standard card games.

$8
Aristoplay
450 S. Wagner Rd.
Ann Arbor, MI 48107
(800) 634-7738 or (888) GR8-GAME/
fax (734) 995-4611
Web site: www.aristoplay.com

Black Voting Rights

A portfolio of materials on the long fight for black voting rights. Included are four illustrated background essays covering the movement from the post–Civil War years through the 20th century ("Reconstruction," "Disenfranchisement," "Blacks Organize," and "We Shall Overcome"), a study guide, and 19 reproductions of primary source documents, among them a collection of political cartoons (three from the 1860s by Thomas Nast), newspaper articles, and NAACP handbills and pamphlets.

$37
Jackdaw Publications
Box 503
Amawalk, NY 10501
(800) 789-0022/fax (800) 962-9101

VIDEOS

Eyes on the Prize: 1954–1985

A powerful award-winning documentary on the history of the Civil Rights movement, using photographs, film clips, and interviews. The series covers such events as the *Brown v. the Board of Education* Supreme Court decision, public school integration in Little Rock, Arkansas, the Montgomery bus boycott, and the March on Washington led by Martin Luther King Jr. About 14 hours on 7 videocassettes.

$149.98
PBS Home Video
1320 Braddock Pl.
Alexandria, VA 22314-1698

The Long Walk Home

A dramatization of the 1955 Montgomery bus boycott, starring Whoopi Goldberg and Sissy Spacek.

$14.98

Zenger Media

10200 Jefferson Blvd.

Box 802

Culver City, CA 90232-0802

(310) 839-2436 or (800) 421-4246/fax (310) 839-2249 or (800) 944-5432

e-mail: access@ZengerMedia.com

Web site: ZengerMedia.com/Zenger

To Kill a Mockingbird

Based on the Pulitzer Prize–winning book by Harper Lee, this wonderful movie adaptation stars Gregory Peck as lawyer Atticus Finch, who defends a black man unjustly accused of rape, thereby teaching his children and his small Alabama town a powerful lesson about the evils of prejudice. The trial and its aftermath are seen through the eyes of the Finch children, Jem and Scout.

$19.95

Movies Unlimited

3015 Darnell Rd.

Philadelphia, PA 19154

(215) 637-4444 or (800) 4-MOVIES

e-mail: movies@moviesunlimited.com

Web site: www.moviesunlimited.com

Wonderworks: And the Children Shall Lead

In Mississippi in the 1960s, a 12-year-old black girl and some white friends bravely set out to defuse rising racial tensions. With Danny Glover, LeVar Burton, and Pam Potillo. The video is 58 minutes long.

$14.95

Movies Unlimited

3015 Darnell Rd.

Philadelphia, PA 19154

(215) 637-4444 or (800) 4-MOVIES

e-mail: movies@moviesunlimited.com

Web site: www.moviesunlimited.com

BLACK HISTORY ON-LINE

African American History

A comprehensive site with many links to the events and people in black history, as well as journal and magazine articles, genealogies, museums, famous speeches, and resources for teachers.

www.msstate.edu/Archives/History/USA/Afro-Amer

The African-American Mosaic

Black history and culture resources from the Library of Congress, including ex-slave narratives from the WPA Federal Writers' Project.

www.loc.gov/exhibits/african/intro.html

Black History Activities

Activities for kids based on the history of slavery, prominent African American leaders, oral histories, poetry and literature, and landmark Civil Rights events. Kids can also participate in an Internet-based black history treasure hunt.

www.kn.pacbell.com/wired/BHM/AfroAm.html

National Civil Rights Museum

A virtual tour of the history of the Civil Rights movement.

www.mecca.org/~crights/cyber.html

POLITICS, PRESIDENTS, AND FIRST LADIES

BOOKS

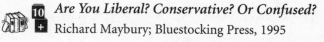

Are You Liberal? Conservative? Or Confused?

Richard Maybury; Bluestocking Press, 1995

An explanation of the political scene, written as a series of letters from the perspicacious Uncle Eric to his young niece or nephew, Chris. Chris, in letter one, is definitely confused and has written her/his uncle asking for definitions of "all the political labels—

liberal, conservative, left, right, democrat, republican, moderate, socialist, communist, fascist, libertarian, centrist, populist." Uncle Eric (himself a "juris naturalist") leaps to the rescue, firing off 26 thoroughly fascinating letters on political positions and philosophies, past, present, and future. The book is recommended for readers aged 14 and up, but—as a group read-aloud—I'd crank it down a few years. Uncle Eric is as clear as a bell.

$9.95

Bluestocking Press

Box 2030

Shingle Springs, CA 95682-2030

(916) 621-1123 or (800) 959-8586/fax (916) 642-9222

Arthur Meets the President

Marc Brown; Little, Brown, 1992

Arthur, star of Marc Brown's ongoing series for 6–8-year-olds, writes a prizewinning essay ("How I Can Make America Great") and is chosen to read it for the president of the United States. Arthur, his classmates, and his pesty little sister take a tour of Washington, D.C., and Arthur—though it looks iffy for a while—manages to meet the president.

The Buck Stops Here

Alice Provensen; Harcourt Brace, 1997

A page (or at least half a page) per president, from George Washington through George Bush. The text consists of silly (but insidiously memorable) couplets: "First and foremost, Washington/Our beloved President One"; "Thomas Jefferson, number Three/Rigged the Sale of the Century." The illustrations are marvelous: colorfully detailed spreads with a portrait of each president, plus labeled pictures representing important occurrences or accomplishments during his term(s) in office. Teddy Roosevelt, for example, shown with pince-nez and grin, is accompanied by pictures of the Wright brothers aloft at Kitty Hawk, a group portrait of his six children with a teddy bear, an Oklahoma state flag ("Oklahoma admitted as the 46th state, 1907"), a picture of immigrants with the Statue of Liberty in the background, a cluster of flaming buildings ("San Francisco Earthquake, 1906"), and a western panorama of mountains and forests ("U.S. Reclamation Act, 1902"). Details of each picture are explained in an appendix in the back, just in case you missed anything.

Cobblestone: The Political System

Several issues of *Cobblestone* magazine (see page 449) cover political or presidential topics. Titles include *The Presidential Elections* (October 1980), *The Two-Party System* (November 1988), *First Ladies* (March 1992), and *A Historical Look at Washington, D.C.* (January 1996). Each issue contains fiction and nonfiction articles about the featured topic, plus activities and a supplementary reading list. For students in grades 5–9.

Available from most libraries or for $4.50 from

Cobblestone Publishing, Inc.

30 Grove St.

Peterborough, NH 03458-1454

(603) 924-7209 or (800) 821-0115

Web site: www.cobblestonepub.com

Encyclopedia of Presidents Series

Children's Press

Not all American presidents have been equally blessed with biographers, but Children's Press has covered them all in the Encyclopedia of Presidents series. The Encyclopedia currently includes 41 illustrated biographies, each 100 pages long, targeted at kids in grades 5–8. You'll find all the presidents here, from Washington to Clinton, even including such biographical hard cases as Millard Fillmore and Franklin Pierce. The books cover all the basics and are illustrated with prints and photographs.

From bookstores or

Children's Press

Sherman Turnpike

Box 1331

Danbury, CT 06813

(800) 621-1115

First Children: Growing Up in the White House

Katherine Leiner; Tambourine Books, 1996

The stories of kids from 17 First Families, from George Washington's 14-year-old stepdaughter, Nellie Custis, through Tad Lincoln, Teddy Roosevelt's rambunctious "White House Gang," Caroline Kennedy, and Chelsea Clinton. An afterword tells what became of the First Children after they grew up and lists statistics on presidential families.

Fun and Facts About the Presidents
George Sullivan; Scholastic, 1994

Trivial and not-so-trivial information about each president. Included are the heights of each president, from tallest (Lincoln) to shortest (Madison), numbers and names of presidential children, presidential birthdays, favorite foods of selected presidents, anecdotes about presidential pets, and a list of presidential nicknames. Readers learn that the first words ever spoken by a president over the telephone were "Please speak more slowly" (Rutherford B. Hayes), that John Quincy Adams used to swim naked in the Potomac River, and that Andrew Jackson's favorite food was turkey hash.

Ghosts of the White House
Cheryl Harness; Simon & Schuster, 1998

Sara, on a class tour of the White House, is suddenly pulled into a painting by a portrait of George Washington and taken to meet an interesting assortment of presidential ghosts. The book is appealingly designed and stuffed with information, including capsule biographies of all the presidents, a timeline of American history, and a lot of unusual and fascinating facts. For readers aged 7–11.

The Last Known Cow on the White House Lawn and Other Little Known Facts About the Presidency
Barbara Seuling; Doubleday, 1978

Fascinating presidential anecdotes, including the scoop on who kept the very last White House cow.

The Look-It-Up Book of Presidents
Wayne Blassingame; Random House, 1996

Brief biographies and vital statistics on each president, from George Washington to Bill Clinton. For readers aged 9 and up.

Mr. President: A Book of U.S. Presidents
George Sullivan; Scholastic, 1997

All the basics on each president, in chronological order. Included are a portrait or photograph of each, a list of vital statistics (dates of birth, death, and term of office, birthplace, previous experience, and political party), several short biographical paragraphs, and a highlighted list of important events that took place during each presidency.

The President's Cabinet and How It Grew
Nancy Winslow Parker; HarperCollins; 1991

Charming picture-book illustrations along with a thoroughly informational text covering the history of the developing cabinet, from Washington's four secretaries to the present-day 15. Included are explanations of the function of each cabinet position and a big multicolored bar graph showing how much money we spend on each cabinet department. Pictures are cleverly mnemonic: the secretary of education is shown with a stack of alphabet blocks and a red apple, the secretary of labor with a pile of hard hats, the secretary of agriculture with a sheep, a cheerful-looking duck, and a shock of wheat.

The Smithsonian Book of the First Ladies: Their Lives, Times, and Issues
Edith P. Mayo, ed.; Henry Holt, 1996

A 302-page collection of short biographies of First Ladies from Martha Washington to Hilary Rodham Clinton. The biographies are divided into four historical sections: "The New Nation 1775–1830," "Growing Pains, Slavery, and the Civil War 1830–1865," "The Post–Civil War Era, the Age of Reform, and World War I 1865–1920," and "Modern Times 1920 to the Present." The biographies, each illustrated with photographs and period prints, are interspersed with historical essays explaining crucial issues of the times: "Did the American Revolution Change Things for Women?" "What Role Did Women Play in the Temperance Movement?"

The Story of the White House
Katie Waters; Scholastic, 1992

A short, informational history, packed with maps, drawings, photographs, reproductions of old engravings, and interesting facts. Includes a section on other government buildings and departments and a collection of (tiny) presidential portraits.

Voting and Elections
Dennis B. Fradin; Children's Press, 1986

An explanation of the political process in simple text with many colorful illustrations, including art reproductions and photographs. This book covers the history and practice of voting, from ancient times to the present, plus a brief discussion of the importance of free elections and a description of the voting process. For kids aged 6–9.

The White House

Leonard Everett Fisher; Holiday House, 1989

A history of the White House, from original design and construction through its burning by the British during the War of 1812, rebuilding, and subsequent modifications through the Reagan years. The book includes intriguing anecdotes and some wonderful photographs, among them a shot of the Wright brothers landing their airplane on the South Lawn. For readers aged 8–12.

The White House Kids

Rose Blue and Corinne J. Naden; Millbrook Press, 1995

Stories of the children who have lived in the White House, from John Adams's little granddaughter (a toddler who threw temper tantrums) to Chelsea Clinton. The book is illustrated with prints, portraits, and photographs, and filled with appealing accounts of kids rollerskating down the halls, stargazing from the roof, and smuggling a pony upstairs in the elevator. For readers aged 9–12.

Wooden Teeth and Jelly Beans: The Tupperman Files

Ray Nelson, ed.; Beyond Words Publishing, 1995

Strange and fascinating facts about the presidents, each of whom is pictured in a big, brightly colored caricature. A humorous and enjoyable take on presidential history for kids aged 9–12. (The wooden teeth belonged to George Washington.)

Yo, Millard Fillmore! And All Those Other Presidents You Don't Know

Will Cleveland and Mark Alvarez; Millbrook Press, 1997

Memorize all the presidents, from Washington to Bush, in a mere 20 minutes. Readers do this through a series of mnemonic cartoons, linked together in order by a memory-jogging silly story. Cartoon no. 1 shows a gigantic *washing* machine—big enough to wash a *ton* of laundry—parked on the White House lawn. *Washington + ton* = George Washington. In cartoon no. 2, the lid of the washing machine has been opened to reveal a lot of enormous *atoms* swirling around in the soap bubbles. *atoms* = John Adams. Next, a *chef's son* in a towering white hat has fished the atoms out of the washing machine and is frying them on a griddle. *Chef's son* = Thomas Jefferson. Foolish as this sounds, it really does work: vivid mental imagery and the invention of bizarre stories are time-honored techniques for locking information in memory. Just to make sure you're absorbing it all, there are periodic quizzes.

COLORING AND PAPER-CRAFTS BOOKS

American Presidents Paperdolls

Each paper doll collection features a presidential family (in full color) plus an assortment of period costumes. Included are George Washington, Abraham Lincoln, Ulysses S. Grant, Theodore Roosevelt, Franklin D. Roosevelt, Dwight Eisenhower, John F. Kennedy, Lyndon Johnson, Richard Nixon, Gerald Ford, Jimmy Carter, George Bush, and Bill Clinton.

$4.95 per set
Dover Publications, Inc.
31 E. Second St.
Mineola, NY 11501

America's First Ladies Coloring Book

Leslie Franz; Dover Publications

All the First Ladies from Martha Washington to Hillary Rodham Clinton, with brief historical picture captions.

$2.95
Dover Publications, Inc.
31 E. Second St.
Mineola, NY 11501

A Coloring Book of Our Presidents

Black-line portraits of each president to color, with an accompanying brief informational text.

$3.95
Bellerophon Books
36 Ancapa St.

Games and Hands-On Activities

Hail to the Chief

A board game of presidential elections for budding politicians aged 10 and up. Players begin their candidacies by traveling a playing path illustrated with presidential portraits that runs around the border of the red, white, and blue board, answering questions about the Constitution and past presidents as they proceed. They then set off on the campaign trail, moving from state capital to state capital across a map of the United States, answering questions about American history and geography. Questions are written at four levels of difficulty.

$25

Aristoplay

450 S. Wagner Rd.

Ann Arbor, MI 48107

(800) 634-7738 or (888) GR8-GAME

fax (734) 995-4611

Web site: www.aristoplay.com

The Presidency

A portfolio of 11 historical primary source reproductions illustrating the functions of the presidency, plus six illustrated historical background essays, a list of suggested student readings and discussion questions, and a detailed study guide. Essay titles include "The Constitution Basics for the Presidency," "Chief Executive," and "Legislative and Judicial Powers and Duties." Primary source documents include facsimiles of pages on the presidency from the Constitution, a chart of the executive branch of the government, a presidential veto (by Grover Cleveland), a ticket for Andrew Johnson's impeachment hearings, letters by Abraham Lincoln and Franklin Roosevelt, and a ticket to John F. Kennedy's Inaugural Ball.

$37

Jackdaw Publications

Box 503

Presidents Cards

A pack of high-quality colorful cards, each with a portrait of a president, from George Washington to Bill Clinton. Names and dates appear on the backs of the cards, along with a short paragraph of biographical information. These can be used in any number of imaginative ways: order the cards on timelines, use them as starting points for historical anecdotes or writing projects, invent an accompanying board game.

$7.50

Aristoplay

450 S. Wagner Rd.

Ann Arbor, MI 48107

(800) 634-7738 or (888) GR8-GAME

fax (734) 995-4611

Web site: www.aristoplay.com

The Presidents Game

A board game of presidents. The playing board carries numbered black-and-white portraits of all the presidents in order, from George Washington to Bill Clinton. Playing cards list the name of a president on one side; his corresponding number, political party, state, and dates in office on the other. The game can be played on several levels; in its simplest permutation, players attempt to match numbered portraits to names. Also included are a few reproducible student activities, among them word games and puzzles, and a three-page "Presidential Report" to be filled out for each president. (At the end, students can evaluate each, on a scale of "Great" to "Failure.")

$10.95

Educational Materials Associates, Inc.

Box 7385

Charlottesville, VA 22906

(804) 293-GAME/fax (804) 293-5322

Teaching With Historic Places/Presidents

This series of lesson plan packets from Jackdaw Publications was developed with the National Register of Historic Places, each centering around a famous American historical site. Several feature sites important in the lives of presidents/First Ladies or the events of presidential administrations, among them "Camp Hoover: A Presidential Retreat" (Shenandoah National Park, Virginia), "Woodrow Wilson: Prophet of Peace" (Washington, D.C.), "Growing into Public Service: William Howard Taft's Boyhood Home" (Cincinnati, Ohio), "First Lady of the World: Eleanor Roosevelt at Val-Kill" (Hyde Park, N.Y.), and "Birthplace of John F. Kennedy: Home of the Boy Who Would Be President (Brookline, Mass.). Each includes historical background information, reproductions of primary source documents and materials, maps and photographs, reading lists and suggested student activities, and directions to the featured historical site.

$7 each
Jackdaw Publications
Box 503
Amawalk, NY 10501
(914) 962-6911 or (800) 789-0022/fax (800) 962-9101

VIDEOS

The American President
A political romance in which Michael Douglas plays the president and Annette Bening plays an extremely articulate environmental lobbyist. A look at the ins and outs of politics and at everyday life in the White House, plus a rousing speech at the end that would have won my vote. Also with Martin Sheen and Michael J. Fox. It's rated PG-13.

$14.95
Movies Unlimited
3015 Darnell Rd.
Philadelphia, PA 19154
(215) 637-4444 or (800) 4-MOVIES
e-mail: movies@moviesunlimited.com
Web site: www.moviesunlimited.com

The Candidate
Robert Redford plays the idealistic and upstanding candidate running for the Senate against a savvy old-timer; as the race proceeds, he learns a great deal about the unpleasant realities of modern campaign practices.

$19.99
Movies Unlimited

3015 Darnell Rd.
Philadelphia, PA 19154
(215) 637-4444 or (800) 4-MOVIES
e-mail: movies@moviesunlimited.com
Web site: www.moviesunlimited.com

Congress: The History and Promise of Representative Government
A documentary by Ken Burns on the history and function of the United States Congress. The program features archival photographs, film clips, interviews with journalists and historians, and quotations from journals, letters, and famous speeches of Congressional leaders. It is divided into three 30-minute segments: "The Builders and the Debaters," "The Bosses and the Progressives," and "The Managers and the Hill."

$14.95
Zenger Media
10200 Jefferson Blvd.
Box 802
Culver City, CA 90232-0802
(310) 839-2436 or (800) 421-4246/fax (310) 839-2249
or (800) 944-5432
Web site: ZengerMedia.com/Zenger

Mr. Smith Goes to Washington
Frank Capra's wonderful classic in which Jimmy Stewart plays Mr. Smith, the young and idealistic senator who successfully takes on the Washington establishment. (Watch this one and you'll never forget what "filibuster" means.) Also starring Jean Arthur, who starts out cynical but comes around.

$19.95
Movies Unlimited
3015 Darnell Rd.
Philadelphia, PA 19154
(215) 637-4444 or (800) 4-MOVIES
e-mail: movies@moviesunlimited.com
Web site: www.moviesunlimited.com

This Is America, Charlie Brown: The Smithsonian and the Presidency
Charlie Brown and friends take a trip to the Smithsonian, where they travel back in time to meet Abraham Lincoln at Gettysburg, to camp with Teddy

Roosevelt in Yosemite, and to attend the depression-era inauguration of Franklin Delano Roosevelt.

$14.95

Movies Unlimited

3015 Darnell Rd.

Philadelphia, PA 19154

(215) 637-4444 or (800) 4-MOVIES

e-mail: movies@moviesunlimited.com

Web site: www.moviesunlimited.com

POLITICS, PRESIDENTS, AND FIRST LADIES ON-LINE

The First Ladies

Biographies and portraits of each.

www.whitehouse.gov/WH/glimpse/firstladies

The Presidents of the United States

Click on the president's name for a portrait, biography, and text of his inaugural address.

www.whitehouse.gov/WH/glimpse/presidents

Presidents of the United States

Basic information about each president, plus election results, names of cabinet members, highlights of the presidency, historical documents, and links to related resources.

www.ipl.org/POTUS

Project Vote Smart

Described as "a complete source of U.S. political information," this site provides general information on the workings of the government, biographies and voting records of all the members of Congress and information on how to contact each, and links to many other related political sites.

www.vote-smart.org

The White House for Kids

A virtual tour of the White House, conducted by Socks, the Clinton family cat, plus information on the presidents, White House kids and pets, photographs, and a place to write the president.

www.whitehouse.gov/WH/kids

THE LAW

CATALOGS

Government & Law: Social Studies School Service

The Social Studies School Service publishes a separate catalog of materials for government/law education, including books, activity books, games, audiocassettes, videos, computer software, posters, and simulations.

Social Studies School Service

10200 Jefferson Blvd.

Box 802

Culver City, CA 90232-0802

(310) 839-2436 or (800) 421-4246/fax (310) 839-2249

or (800) 944-5432

Web site: SocialStudies.com

BOOKS

Cobblestone: Law

Several issues of Cobblestone magazine (see page 449) have law-related themes. Titles include Important Supreme Court Cases (March 1989) and Great Debates (January 1987). Each issue contains informational articles, activity suggestions, and a supplementary reading list. For students in grades 5–9.

Available from most libraries or for $4.50 from

Cobblestone Publishing, Inc.

30 Grove St.

Peterborough, NH 03458-1454

(603) 924-7209 or (800) 821-0115

Web site: www.cobblestonepub.com

The Day They Came to Arrest the Book

Nat Hentoff; Bantam Doubleday Dell, 1983

The book is Mark Twain's *The Adventures of Huckleberry Finn*, which the students of George Mason High School have been assigned to read by their American history teacher. When a group of students and parents demand the withdrawal of the book from the school curriculum on grounds of racist, sexist, and immoral conduct, Barney Roth, editor of the school paper, spearheads an anticensorship protest movement. The book is not only a good story but is also a thought-provoking debate over First Amendment rights and the nature of individual freedoms—and, incidentally, the real meaning of *Huckleberry Finn*. For students aged 12 and up.

Great Trials in History
Betty Lou Kratoville; High Noon Books, 1990

The 12 trials described in Kratoville's book can hardly help to provoke interest, inquiry, and debate: included are the trials of Socrates, Joan of Arc, Galileo, Peter Zenger, Lizzie Borden, Alfred Dreyfuss, Edith Cavell, Sacco and Vanzetti, and John Scopes, the Salem witchcraft trials, the impeachment trial of Andrew Johnson, and the post–World War II Nuremberg trials. Unfortunately in this treatment, the accounts of trials and legal issues are truncated and the accompanying student exercises are pointless, consisting largely of fill-in-the-blank tests and lists of vocabulary words. Can be used as a starting point.

Bluestocking Press
Box 2030
Shingle Springs, CA 95682-2030
(916) 622-8586 or (800) 959-8586/fax (916) 642-9222

It's The Law!
Faces; October 1990

This issue of *Faces* magazine (see page 411) includes a multicultural overview of the law, with non-fiction articles on the evolution of law from ancient times, the practice of law in medieval Iceland, a history of lawyers, slave trials, and law among the Asante of West Africa, plus a West African folktale, "Guinea Fowl and Rabbit Get Justice," a law-related word puzzle, and—for no particular reason—a recipe for apple crisp. For readers in grades 4–9.

Available from most libraries or for $4.50 from
Cobblestone Publishing, Inc.
30 Grove St.
Peterborough, NH 03458-1454
(603) 924-7209 or (800) 821-0115
Web site: www.cobblestonepub.com

Whatever Happened to Justice?
Richard J. Maybury; Bluestocking Press, 1993

This book, I'm firmly convinced, is one of the most important our family has ever read. It has inspired hours of discussion and debate, has altered and clarified our individual political philosophies, and has given the boys an invaluable lesson in the art of independent thinking. Written as a collection of letters from Uncle Eric—Maybury's alter ego—to a young niece or nephew, Chris, *Whatever Happened to Justice?* deals with the history of law, its evolution in America, and its effect on our economic system. There are two fundamental scientific laws, according to Maybury: "Do all you have agreed to do" and "Do not encroach on other persons or their property." Everything else is political meddling.

Uncle Eric is concise, clear, and fascinating; this is a thought-provoking and thoroughly worthwhile read, whether you agree with his conclusions or not. Included is a list of movies to elicit discussions about the nature of law and a supplementary reading list. *Whatever Happened to Justice?* is recommended for readers aged 14 and up, but—as an adult-supported read-aloud—it should interest kids as young as 10.

Bluestocking Press
Box 2030
Shingle Springs, CA 95682-2030
(916) 622-8586 or (800) 959-8586/fax (916) 642-9222

You Be the Jury Series
Marvin Miller; Scholastic

Ten courtroom mysteries. For each, there's a short description of the case and evidence, in the form of three illustrated exhibits. Readers must reach a conclusion based on the presented information and render a verdict: guilty or not guilty. The proper verdict is explained (upside down, which makes it harder to peek) at the end of each mystery. Mystery titles include "The Case of the Dangerous Golf Ball," "The Case of the Squashed Scooter," and "The Case of the Crazy Parrot." There are several sequels.

You Can't Eat Peanuts in Church and Other Little-Known Laws
Barbara Seuling; Doubleday, 1975

A collection of strange and sidesplitting (but absolutely genuine) laws. It's against the law to sing out of tune in North Carolina, to put tomatoes in clam chowder in Massachusetts, to "worry a squirrel" in Topeka, Kansas, or to hitch a crocodile to a fire hydrant in Michigan. And many more of the same. By the same author: *It's Illegal to Quack Like a Duck & Other Freaky Laws* (Lodestar).

🎲 12 ➕ You Decide! Applying the Bill of Rights to Real Cases

George Bundy Smith and Alene L. Smith; Critical Thinking Press & Software, 1992

Students review and discuss actual Supreme Court cases related to each of the 10 amendments in the Bill of Rights. Several cases are listed for each amendment; background information is included, plus a clear description of the case under debate, suggested student activities, and an explanation of the final court decision. Both student book and teacher's manual are available.

Critical Thinking Press & Software

Box 448

Pacific Grove, CA 93950-0448

(800) 458-4849/fax (408) 372-3230

GAMES AND HANDS-ON ACTIVITIES

✋ 13 ➕ American History Re-Creations: Trials

A series of "participatory mini-units" targeted at students in grades 7–12. In each, students reenact famous trials of the past, prosecuting or defending, for example, religious freedom in the trial of Anne Hutchinson (1637), vigilante abolitionism in the trial of John Brown (1859), the "high crimes and misdemeanors" of Andrew Johnson (1868), the teaching of evolution in the Scopes trial (1925), or the Vietnam war crimes of Lt. William Calley (1970). Each unit involves an introductory historical background session, a role-playing re-creation of the featured trial, and a posttrial discussion session.

The units are designed for classroom-size numbers of students but can be adapted for smaller groups. Materials include 35 eight-page student guides, a detailed teacher's guide, and assorted reproducible student handouts.

$34 to $39

Interact

1825 Gillespie Way, #101

El Cajon, CA 92020-1095

(619) 448-1474 or (800) 359-0961/fax (619) 448-6722

Web site: www.interact-simulations.com

♟ 11 ➕ Blind Justice

A board game of lawsuits, based on actual civil trials described on the included decks of "District Court" and "Superior Court Case Cards." Players hop their pieces through the judicial system; winner is the first to arrive at the Supreme Court with three million dollars in his/her pocket, acquired by obtaining favorable verdicts and settlements from juries en route.

Players alternately act as either attorneys or jurors. When a player lands on a "Jury" square on the playing path, for example, he/she becomes an attorney, drawing a "Court Case Card" and reading the description of the case aloud. The other players, as jurors, render a verdict. Here's a sample: "A customer brought in 4 cans of paint to be returned. When the employee discovered that the cans were filled with water, he bopped the customer on the head with a wooden mallet. A mild concussion resulted from the assault. The defendant claimed it should not be held responsible for such unforseeable conduct of an employee." Included is a "Verdict Book" that lists the real-life court decisions and settlements in each case. (In "Water Colors," the case quoted above, the court awarded the bopped customer $200,000.) Fast-paced and fun; for three or more players, aged 11 and up.

$25

Avalon Hill Game Co.

4517 Harford Rd.

Baltimore, MD 21214

(410) 254-9200 or (800) 999-3222

e-mail: AHGAMES@aol.com

Web site: www.avalonhill.com

🎧 13 ➕ May It Please the Court

A collection of live recordings of the Supreme Court in session from the National Archives in Washington, D.C. The six audiocassettes include the arguments made in 23 landmark cases of the 20th century, among them *Miranda v. Arizona, Gideon v. Wainwright, Nixon v. United States,* and *Roe v. Wade.* With voice-over narration explaining the issues and identifying the speakers. An accompanying 376-page book includes historical background information and transcriptions of the arguments. For advanced students.

$35

Zenger Media

10200 Jefferson Blvd.

Box 802

Culver City, CA 90232-0802

(310) 839-2436 or (800) 421-4246/fax (310) 839-2249

or (800) 944-5432

Web site: ZengerMedia.com/Zenger

VIDEOS

Inherit the Wind

Spencer Tracy as Clarence Darrow confronts Fredric March as William Jennings Bryan in a gripping reenactment of the Scopes "Monkey Trial" of 1925. Tracy defends a young teacher jailed for teaching Darwin's theory of evolution.

$19.95

Movies Unlimited

3015 Darnell Rd.

Philadelphia, PA 19154

(215) 637-4444 or (800) 4-MOVIES

e-mail: movies@moviesunlimited.com

Web site: www.moviesunlimited.com

Judgment at Nuremberg

A 1961 dramatization of the post–World War II Nazi war crimes trials, starring Spencer Tracy, Burt Lancaster, Maximilian Schell, Richard Widmark, and Marlene Dietrich.

$29.99

Movies Unlimited

3015 Darnell Rd.

Philadelphia, PA 19154

(215) 637-4444 or (800) 4-MOVIES

e-mail: movies@moviesunlimited.com

Web site: www.moviesunlimited.com

To Kill a Mockingbird

Gregory Peck plays Atticus Finch, a small-town southern lawyer in the 1930s who, in the teeth of public opinion, defends a young black man unjustly accused of rape. The story is told from the point of view of Atticus's precocious six-year-old daughter. A wonderful movie; the book, by Harper Lee, is even better.

$19.95

Movies Unlimited

3015 Darnell Rd.

Philadelphia, PA 19154

(215) 637-4444 or (800) 4-MOVIES

e-mail: movies@moviesunlimited.com

Web site: www.moviesunlimited.com

Twelve Angry Men

An inside look at the jury process, as 12 jurors, among them Henry Fonda, Lee J. Cobb, and E. G. Marshall, debate their decisions on the verdict in a murder trial. It's in black and white, all the action takes place in one room, and it will keep you on the edge of your seat.

$14.95

Movies Unlimited

3015 Darnell Rd.

Philadelphia, PA 19154

(215) 637-4444 or (800) 4-MOVIES

e-mail: movies@moviesunlimited.com

Web site: www.moviesunlimited.com

Witness for the Prosecution

Based on a mystery by Agatha Christie, this superb 1957 courtroom drama—with a definitely unexpected twist ending—centers around the trial of a man accused of murdering a wealthy widow. Starring Charles Laughton, Elsa Lanchester, Marlene Dietrich, and Tyrone Power.

$19.95

Movies Unlimited

3015 Darnell Rd.

Philadelphia, PA 19154

(215) 637-4444 or (800) 4-MOVIES

e-mail: movies@moviesunlimited.com

Web site: www.moviesunlimited.com

HISTORY

THE LAW ON-LINE

The Federal Judiciary Homepage
12 + Includes a hypertext overview of the judicial branch of the federal government, with links to related sites.

www.uscourts.gov

Justice for Kids and Youth
ALL A wealth of information on law, the courts, and criminal investigation for kids (grades K–5) and youth (grades 6–12) from the U.S. Department of Justice. The site includes a history of Civil Rights legislation, summaries of famous FBI cases (among them "Bonnie and Clyde" and the Lindbergh kidnapping), explanations of scientific crime detection techniques (from polygraphs to DNA testing), and "Inside the Courtroom," which covers courtroom officials and procedures.

www.usdoj.gov/kidspage

Oyez Oyez Oyez
ALL A virtual tour of the Supreme Court Building, biographies and portraits of famous justices, abstracts of key court cases, some with associated audio clips of court debate, and a history of the word "Oyez!"

court.it-services.nwu.edu/oyez

FAMILY TREES AND LOCAL HISTORY

BOOKS

Ancestors
9 13 *Faces;* April 1992

This issue of *Faces* magazine (see page 411), titled *Ancestors,* concentrates on family history. Included are nonfiction articles on family trees and genealogical research, accounts of ancestor memory in other cultures, the story of a modern Japanese family reunion, an article on family recipes and a historical recipe for gingerbread, and directions for making a family tree on a window shade. For readers in grades 4–9.

Available from most libraries or for $4.50 from Cobblestone Publishing, Inc.
30 Grove St.
Peterborough, NH 03458-1454
(603) 924-7209 or (800) 821-0115
Web site: www.cobblestonepub.com
Also see **Genealogy: A Personal History** (*Cobblestone*; November 1980).

Do People Grow on Family Trees?
8 12 *Genealogy for Kids and Other Beginners*
Ira Wolfman; Workman, 1991

An interesting illustrated overview of genealogy for kids and their parents, with information on how to trace their family history and complete a family tree.

Genealogy On-line
12 + Elizabeth Powell Crowe; McGraw-Hill, 1998

A fat collection of resources on the Web for would-be genealogists, plus instructions for making the most of them.

The Great Ancestor Hunt: The Fun
9 12 *of Finding Out Who You Are*
Lila Perl; Houghton Mifflin, 1991

How to research and create a family history chart, with lots of examples of family history stories, including tales of immigrant ships, Ellis Island examinations, and westward wagon train journeys. Illustrated with period black-and-white photographs. For readers aged 9–12.

How to Tape Instant Oral Biographies
9 + Bill Zimmerman; Bantam Books, 1992

An excellent and easy-to-follow how-to book for persons interested in recording family histories. The book includes suggestions for audio- and videotaping, a long list of reminiscence-inducing sample questions to ask, and pages of reproducible fill-in-the-blank "Family History Sheets."

Know Your Hometown History:
9 13 *Projects and Activities*
Abigail Jungreis; Franklin Watts, 1992

A collection of projects on local and state history for kids in the middle grades. The book includes instructions for making a contour map and model of your town, a "patchwork quilt" of local history, a family tree, and a local history picture archive. An appendix lists locations of historical archives in all 50 states.

Me and My Family Tree
Paul Showers; Thomas Y. Crowell, 1978

One of the Let's-Read-and-Find-Out Science series (see page 227), this is a simple 33-page introduction to family trees for young readers. Included is a clear explanation of what a family tree is, with illustrated diagram, plus information on Gregor Mendel and the scientific study of heredity.

My Backyard History Book
David Weitzman; Little, Brown, 1975

"Open this book," reads the blurb on the cover, "and you'll find projects that have to do with grandparents, old-time music, making time capsules, and other fun activities that you won't find in your normal history class." Included are directions for making a personal timeline, a family history wall, a family map, and several kinds of family trees, including an anthropological kinship chart, and suggestions for assembling a family archive and recording a family oral history. Lots of information for historians aged 9–12.

What's Your Name? From Ariel to Zoe
Eve Sanders; Holiday House, 1995

The book is a collection of 26 large color photographs of children, in alphabetical order by first name. A brief paragraph under each portrait tells something about the meaning or history of each first name in the child's own words: Ariel's name means "lion" in Hebrew; Diego, whose name means "James" in English, was named after the Mexican painter Diego Rivera; Eva was named after her great-grandmother; Kossi's name, which is West African, means "a boy born on Sunday"; Shandin means "sunshine" in Navajo; Whitney was named after California's Mount Whitney; and Zoe means "life" in Greek.

Who Put the Cannon in the Courthouse Square?
Kay Cooper; Walker & Company, 1985

How-to hints for hometown historians, with many suggestions for local research projects. Kids are encouraged to discover how their hometown and its landmarks got their names, to identify its original settlers, to learn about its oldest industries, houses, and cemeteries, and to track down the stories behind interesting local lore. Included are lists of potential sources, suggestions for oral history interviews, and ideas for compiling historical information.

BOOKS: FAMILY HISTORIES

Homeplace
Anne Shelby; Orchard Books, 1995

A charming picture-book story told by a grandmother to her small granddaughter about the seven generations of their family who have lived on the "homeplace" and the changes they and the house have seen over time. The story begins 200 years ago, in the time of the little girl's four-times-great-grandparents, who first cleared the land, planted corn, and built a cabin, and ends in the present day, with the little girl sitting in her grandma's lap—and being rocked in the old wicker rocker that was ordered long ago from a catalog by three-times-great-grandpa when he built the new porch. For readers aged 5–9.

The Hundred Penny Box
Sharon Bell Mathis; Puffin, 1986

Michael's great-great-aunt Dew has a precious box of 100 pennies, one from each year of her long life. As Michael counts out the pennies and listens, she tells stories of long ago, based on the dates on the pennies, starting with the penny from 1874, the year that she was born. For readers aged 6–10.

The Lucky Stone
Lucille Clifton; Bantam Doubleday Dell, 1986

Tee's great-grandmother tells her the story of a special lucky stone, passed down from generation to generation in their family since the days of slavery. For readers aged 8–11.

The Remembering Box

Eth Clifford; William Morrow, 1992

Joshua always spends the Sabbath with his grandmother; after dinner, they look through Grandma's remembering box, filled with treasured pictures and mementos, each of which inspires a story of her past life. Finally, as a special gift, Joshua is given a remembering box of his own.

They Were Strong and Good
Robert Lawson; Viking, 1972

"This is the story of my mother and my father and of their fathers and mothers," begins this simple family history, illustrated with pen-and-ink drawings. Mother's father was a Scottish sea captain; Father's father was an Englishman who lived in Alabama and fought in the Civil War, joining the Confederate army when he was 14. For readers aged 5–9.

When I Was Nine
James Stevenson; Greenwillow, 1986

A lovely picture-book reminiscence about growing up in the late 1930s. Stevenson explains what small-town life was like: kids climbed trees, listened to radio serials, played baseball, and skated on the frozen town pond. In 1939, the summer he was nine years old, Stevenson recalls, he and his family took a vacation, traveling by car through the West, where they visited a cave in Missouri, saw the Northern Lights, and rode horses on a ranch in New Mexico. For readers aged 5–9.

When I Was Young in the Mountains
Cynthia Rylant; E. P. Dutton, 1982

A dreamy, gentle book about the author's childhood in the mountains of West Virginia, where her grandfather came home black with coal dust, children splashed in the swimming hole on hot summer days, and families sat on porch swings in the evenings and talked softly under the stars. For readers aged 5–9.

HANDS-ON ACTIVITIES

Climb Your Family Tree!
A Genealogy Detective's Kit
Anne Depue; Hyperion, 1996

The kit includes an instructional guidebook for young genealogical researchers, a "Genealogy Detec-

tive's Notebook" for recording research results, a fill-in-the-blank family tree poster, and a treasure box for storing heirlooms and mementos (provided they're fairly small and flat).

Family Fill-In Book: Discovering Your Roots
Dian Dincin Buchman; Scholastic, 1994

A fill-in-the-blank family tree book, with space for basic information, names, dates, anecdotes, notes, and family stories. The book is divided into four sections: "Me," "My Mom and Her Side of the Family," "My Dad and His Side of the Family," and "My Grandparents."

Make Your Own Time Capsule Kit
Steven Caney; Workman, 1991

The kit includes a 64-page idea book, assorted identification tags, "historic object containment envelopes," a sealing label, and a sturdy bullet-shaped time capsule in steel-colored plastic. A fun project for families.

$14.95 from bookstores or
Workman Publishing Co.
708 Broadway
New York, NY 10003
(212) 254-5900 or (800) 722-7202/fax (212) 254-8098
Web site: www.workmanweb.com

My Family Tree Workbook:
Genealogy for Beginners
Rosemary Chorzempa; Dover Publications

A 55-page consumable workbook to be filled in by the user. The book includes pages for photographs and information about each member of the immediate family (through great-grandparents), a fill-in-the-leaves family tree, pages for autographs and favorite family stories, and pages for information about ancestors' homelands. There are, for example, places for maps of immigrant ancestors' countries, for pictures of ethnic dress, for word lists in your ancestors' native languages, and for descriptions of ethnic foods and customs.

$2.95
Dover Publications, Inc.
31 E. Second St.
Mineola, NY 11501

HISTORY

VIDEOS

10 *Ancestors*

Subtitled "A Beginner's Video Guide to Family History Research," this PBS miniseries covers the excitements, complications, and challenges of genealogical research, through the stories of real people using many different methods to trace their ancestors. About five hours on two videocassettes.

$59.95
PBS Home Video
1320 Braddock Pl.
Alexandria, VA 22314-1628
(800) 645-4PBS
Web site: www.pbs.org

WORLD HISTORY

World history is a challenge. Students and would-be curriculum designers quickly realize that the subject is so immense that a thorough coverage of its varied topics would take years—more time, certainly, than the average school program has to devote to it. Typically world history is a high school–level class, taught in a single year in grade 10.

An overview of available world history resources quickly reveals a drop in materials' variety and appeal starting somewhere around the late eighteenth century. The assumption seems to be that world history—a subject for teenagers—will be learned primarily from a comprehensive textbook, rather than through an eclectic collection of supplements and hands-on activities. Books for young adults on individual world history topics—say, the Jacobite Rebellion, the Boer War, or the politics of Otto von Bismarck—tend to be nononsense presentations of facts, resources for the writing of assigned school reports. Often the sense of history as an exciting story, populated by unique and interesting human beings, is absent.

With this nervously in mind, we set out to design a homeschool world history program of our own. We began by making a massive master list, based on assorted textbooks and history timelines, which cate-gorized by historical period all the topics we felt should conceivably be covered in a world history course. It's six pages long, single-spaced, and looks intimidating. We are now working through it, in somewhat jerky fashion, depending on the availability of resources and the level of the boys' interest.

When the boys were of elementary-school age we studied world history at an introductory level, from prehistory through the Renaissance (and bits beyond), using a multidisciplinary approach, with many tie-ins to science, art, music, geography, literature, and math. For each segment of the curriculum, the kids played games, concocted recipes, tried science experiments, made crafts projects, read stacks of related fiction and nonfiction books, and kept track of new topics on a homemade timeline. There is a wealth of materials available for this age group on such irresistible subjects as the mummies of ancient Egypt, the gods and goddesses of ancient Rome, and the knights and castles of medieval Europe.

For teenagers, there's less fun stuff. The educational literature is more detailed and informative; it's also—often—more boring. This is, in part, the inevitable result of time constraints. If you're trying to cram a lot of information into a limited time frame, you're forced to cut all the trimmings—the human interest stories, the anecdotes, the unusual viewpoints, the related folktales and fiction books—in order to get to the end of the twentieth century by June. It's these discarded trimmings, however—Peter the Great kept a personal army of seven-foot-tall giants; the Atlantis legend may have originated with a gigantic volcanic eruption; medieval physicians believed that walnuts would cure diseases of the brain—that inspire true enthusiasm for history.

Our approach to history thus puts quality ahead of quantity: better to study fewer topics with real interest than many topics without. We use texts to provide a chronological framework for our program; the boys do not, however, study solely—even primarily—from basic texts. For each world history topic, they use a mix of journal and magazine articles, fiction books, and selections from varied adult history books, many of which are beautifully written. Even the chronological framework sometimes goes by the board; we often skip, skim, and study things out of place. If the list calls for the Elizabethan Age, while Caleb—just finishing Art

Spiegelman's *Maus* (see page 680)—convinces his brothers that all should investigate World War II, we leap to World War II.

Does this work? That depends, of course, on your definition of educational success. I don't think any of our boys could name, in order, the kings and queens of England or produce an accurate date for the fall of Constantinople or the First Crusade. All three of them, on the other hand—even Ethan, with his less-than-desirable attitude toward history—can spend dinnertime and beyond discussing the philosophies of Confucius, the trial of Socrates, the Russian Revolution, and the pros and cons of Harry Truman's decision to drop the atom bomb.

From my homeschool journal:

◆ March 28, 1994. Josh is twelve; Ethan, eleven; Caleb, nine.

World history: the boys are learning about ancient civilizations. We spent much of this morning on ancient Greece, using a series of home-written workbooks. We began with geography. Located and labeled Greece on outline maps of Europe, plus assorted associated areas: the Mediterranean, Aegean, Ionian, Adriatic, and Black Seas, Turkey, Crete, the Peloponnesus, Athens, Sparta, Mount Olympus. (Caleb, startled: "You mean Mount Olympus is real?") We then made a timeline, indicating the periods when various ancient civilizations (Sumerians, Babylonians, Egyptians, Greeks, Romans, Maya, Aztecs) were in power. Practiced writing the Greek alphabet, including translating everybody's name into Greek; discussed the Greek pantheon and various favorite myths, which we took turns retelling. Read—together, out loud—the story of archaeologist Arthur Evans and his excavation of the Minoan city of Knossos on Crete, with ill-advised (but nice-looking) restorations of the Minoan wall paintings.

Played a game of "By Jove!" (see page 90) based on Greek/Roman mythology.

Each boy has a list of suggested Greek readings to tackle on his own. Caleb's list includes several Greek myths, The Trojan Horse: How the Greeks Won the War *by Emily Little (see page 90) and* The Spartan Twins *by Lucy Fitch Perkins (this last warily; Lucy wrote her Twins series sometime around World War I, and his-*

torical accuracy is not her strong suit). Josh is reading prose versions of The Odyssey *and* The Iliad. *For Ethan, who doesn't want to read anything Greek,* The Tales of Pan *by Mordecai Richler, which may appeal because it's very clever and the illustrations are funny.*

Caleb and Josh collaborated on a cartoon-style mural picturing the Greek gods and goddesses. It's hilarious: Zeus is shown dropping a lightning bolt on his foot; Athena has immense thick glasses; Poseidon has a snorkel and flippers.

◆ March 29, 1994

Read an article on the history of wine making, with particular attention to the ancient Greeks; looked at pictures of Greek amphorae. "How did those stand up? They have pointed bottoms."

Discussed the chemistry of fermentation, during which we covered chemical symbols, located oxygen, hydrogen, and carbon on the periodic table and drew atomic diagrams, reviewed definitions of atom, *mole-*cule, element, *and* compound. *Explained chemical formulas and compared formulas for water, carbon dioxide, sugar, and alcohol. Ethan: "Is all alcohol the same?" Which led to a discussion of classes of compounds, kinds of alcohols, kinds of sugars. Learned the chemical equation for fermentation; explained meanings of* anaerobic *and* aerobic. *"So why are those exercises called aerobics?"*

Then designed and set up a yeast-growing experiment. Yeast in warm and cold water, with and without sugar—and the boys added a number of interesting twists, including yeast in boiling water, yeast with ice cubes, yeast in milk, yeast in orange juice, yeast with a dash of rubbing alcohol, yeast on a sunny windowsill, yeast in a dark closet. They observed their yeast at five-minute intervals and noticed the amount of bubbling. "How does the carbon dioxide get in soda?" "Why does soda *really fizz when you pour it over ice cubes?" "Why does soda explode when you shake up the bottle?" "How come champagne is fizzy and plain wine isn't?" We took samples from various yeast containers and studied them under the microscope. (Verdict: okay, but not nearly as interesting as pond water.)*

The boys then made wine—that is, they squashed bowls full of red or green grapes, tasted the juice, added water and yeast, covered the bowls with plastic wrap, and left the result for nature to take its course. They plan to observe it every day: when it stops bubbling, we'll strain it and they can taste the horrible stuff. They also collaborated on making two loaves of bread, with accompanying discussion of why—chemically—yeast makes bread rise.

Played several rounds of Greek Myths and Legends card game (see page 91).

Josh read The Olympians, *a collection of stories about the Greek gods and goddesses.*

◆ March 30, 1994

Covered everyday life in ancient Greece, Greek city-states, and the Greek wars with Persia, which have lots of good battle stories: the Battle of Thermopylae, the Battle of Marathon, the Battle of Salamis. ("Where was Persia?") The boys devised alternative scenarios for various battles—they were particularly disgusted with the outcome at Thermopylae. "If I had been at Thermopylae," said Josh tersely, "I would have retreated."

The boys then tried a small-size archaeological excavation, using a Greek vase kit. The vase was in pieces, embedded in a hunk of clay: the kids soaked the clay in water, dug out all the pieces, cleaned them up, and glued them together. It's plain red clay—kit users are supposed to paint it—but none of the boys wanted to paint. Instead we looked at pictures of Greek pottery and discussed redware versus blackware pots. Ethan: "It's like photographs and photograph negatives."

◆ March 31, 1994

Greek math. Read biography of Pythagoras in Mathematicians Are People Too (see page 203) and Triangles in the "Young Math" series (see page 181). Defined right angle and right triangle. The boys got presents of nice new protractors; I showed the kids how to use them, explaining angles and degrees. The boys practiced, measuring many different angles and drawing sample right triangles. Also covered obtuse and acute angles, and isosceles and equilateral triangles.

Explained the famous Pythagorean theorem, which included defining square numbers and hypotenuse; solved several Pythagorean problems, using calculators.

Each boy then got a copy of Easy-to-Make 3D Shapes (see page 189), with which they made—and learned the names of—collections of big, bright-colored Pythagorean solids. Most popular: the icosahedron.

Caleb painted our Greek pot.

◆ April 5, 1994

More Greek math. We read two short biographies of Archimedes, which caught Ethan's attention: at last, an inventor. Followed this up with two books on various kinds of simple machines: levers, wedges, inclined planes, screws, pulleys. The boys then attempted to figure out how Archimedes' inventions worked—our books weren't too forthcoming. They all drew diagrams demonstrating how Archimedes could have used mirrors and lenses to set distant ships on fire, pulleys to yank a huge ship up out of the water, and (Josh) a lever to move the world.

Defined radius, diameter, *and* circumference *of a circle; measured an assortment of circular objects (cereal bowls, coffee cups, plates, a Frisbee) with a piece of string and a ruler. Demonstrated the formula for calculating circumference; defined* pi. *Tried a few circumference problems, drawing circles of specified diameters with compasses. Kitchen table now poked full of holes.*

The boys strained, bottled, and tasted their wines, which were perfectly awful.

◆ April 6, 1994

The Peloponnesian Wars. We started the morning reviewing Greek geography, locating crucial sites—the Peloponnesus, Athens, Sparta, Corinth, Mycenae, the Aegean Sea—on the map. Discussed the cultural and political differences between Athens and Sparta and made pairs of illustrated posters comparing the two. The boys all felt strongly that they would prefer to be Athenian.

We then read, jointly, "The Melian Dialogue" by Thucydides in Introduction to the Great Books (see page 76)—it was a challenge for the younger boys, but we took it slowly, explaining as we read. Then went through all the suggested discussion questions, which elicited lots of passionate argument. The Athenians no longer look quite so good.

◆ April 7, 1994

We spent this morning on Greek architecture. Looked at lots of pictures; drew and labeled diagrams of the three kinds of classical columns: Doric, Ionic, and Corinthian. (Unanimous favorite: Ionic.) Using Mark Wahl's A Mathematical Mystery Tour *(see page 186), defined the* golden ratio *and completed a golden ratio puzzle/ demonstration, which involved measuring and comparing various parts of a Greek statue. Each boy then made a "Golden Rectangle" puzzle.*

Drew diagrams of a Greek temple, identifying and labeling the various parts, and each kid designed a temple frieze. Looked a pictures of actual friezes: Josh identified Bacchus in one. ("You can tell because of the grapes and leopards.")

Made a model of the Parthenon out of clay—not exactly accurate, but the boys had fun and got the general architectural idea. This took a while, since the columns kept falling over.

Had Greek olives with lunch.

Josh wrote a short story narrated by a resentful caryatid.

◆ April 8, 1994

Began the morning with a game of "By Jove!"—it's one of our more successful games; the boys love it.

Began working our way through the Greek alphabet, using enriching excerpts from Alpha to Omega: The Life and Times of the Greek Alphabet *(see page 620) by Alexander and Nicholas Humez. Under Alpha, read about the origin of the alphabet, discussed what it means to be an alpha wolf, and read a short book about wolves and their behavior. Beta: defined* boustrophedon, *an early form of Greek writing that ran forward, then backward, across the page, "as the ox plows." The boys tried it. To Ethan, it comes naturally; I've been trying to break him of boustrophedon for years. Gamma, as in gamma rays: the boys made illustrated diagrams of the electromagnetic spectrum. Reviewed/discussed wavelength and energy. Delta: symbol for heat in chemistry, delta-wing planes and kites, and river deltas. Located the Mississippi River and its delta on the map; discussed why deltas form. "How long is the Mississippi River?" "Where does it start?" "How solid is a delta? Can you walk on it?"*

By then the kids were ready to move on to something else; tomorrow we'll tackle epsilon, zeta, eta, and theta.

And coming up next: The trial of Socrates.

WORLD HISTORY RESOURCES

CATALOGS

Also see listings under **General History Resources: Catalogs** (pages 444–446).

Social Studies School Service

ALL An excellent source of world history materials for students in grades K–12. Materials include activity and project books, posters, games, fiction and nonfiction books, simulations, computer software, and videos for all historical periods. The company publishes many catalogs; particularly useful for world history studies are the *World History* catalog and, for those with younger children, the *Social Studies Grades K–6* catalog, which includes a large "World History" section.

Catalogs are free from
Social Studies School Service
10200 Jefferson Blvd.
Box 802
Culver City, CA 90232-0802
(310) 839-2436 or (800) 421-4246/fax (310) 839-2249
or (800) 944-5432
e-mail: access@SocialStudies.com
Web site: SocialStudies.com

MAGAZINES

Archaeology

Caleb, our youngest, who presently plans to be an archaeologist, is devoted to this magazine, which is a bimonthly publication of the Archaeological Institute of America. Each issue includes four or five feature articles on archaeological discoveries and sites worldwide, plus assorted shorter pieces. *Archaeology* is an adult magazine, but motivated kids will find it interesting. And it's got great pictures.

Annual subscription (6 issues), about $20

Archaeology

Subscription Service

Box 420423

Palm Coast, FL 32142-0423

(800) 829-5122

e-mail: subscription@archaeology.org

Web site: www.archaeology.org

📖 10 14 Calliope

The magazine of "World History for Young People," targeted at kids in grades 5–8. Each issue centers around a single historical topic or theme and includes nonfiction articles, folktales, myths, or short stories, puzzles and crafts projects, a timeline, and a bibliography of additional topic-related books and articles. Back issues of the magazine are also available; ask for a list of titles.

Annual subscription (5 issues), $17.95

Calliope

Cobblestone Publishing, Inc.

30 Grove St.

Peterborough, NH 03458

(603) 924-7209 or (800) 821-0115

Web site: www.cobblestonepub.com

📖 6 10 Kids Discover

Each 20-page issue concentrates on a single historical, geographical, or scientific topic: examples include *Pyramids, Columbus, Knights & Castles, Airplanes,* and *North & South Poles.* In each, a simple informational largish-print text is accompanied by many color illustrations, photographs, and creative graphics. Also included are games, puzzles, and craft activities, and a short suggested reading list.

Annual subscription (10 issues), $16.95; back issues are available

Kids Discover

170 Fifth Ave.

New York, NY 10010

(212) 242-5133/fax (212) 242-5628

📖 13 Old News

A 12-page tabloid-size newspaper of really old news, appropriate for readers in grade 7 and up. Each black-and-white issue includes several detailed jour-

nalistic reports on important worldwide events over a wide range of historical periods, illustrated with historical prints and photographs. "Crewman Describes Wreck of the *Titanic!*" trumpets the headlines, or "Gold Found in Klondike Hills!" or "Bonaparte in Love!" Each article is followed by a short list of historical sources.

Annual subscription (9 issues), $15

Old News

400 Stackstown Rd.

Marietta, PA 17547-9300

(717) 426-2212

Books

12 + The 100: A Ranking of the Most Influential Persons in History

Michael H. Hart; Citadel, 1993

A 500+-page collection of short biographies, in order, of the 100 most influential persons in the history of the world. Not the *greatest,* the author hastens to explain in the introduction, but the most *influential,* in terms of their personal impact on the course of human history and on the everyday lives of other human beings. Thus Adolf Hitler (no. 39) and Joseph Stalin (no. 66) both make the list, while Mohandas Gandhi doesn't, though he gets an Honorable Mention. The biographies of the chosen 100 are interesting; the explanations of why each person was assigned his/her rank in line—whether you agree with the author or not—is equally so. Included is a timeline of the crucial 100, plus important world events, and an appendix listing another 100 who might have made the top list but didn't. Number 1, incidentally, is Muhammad.

13 + Annual Editions: World History: Volumes I and II

David McComb, ed.; Dushkin Publishing Group/ Brown & Benchmark Publishers, 1996

The volumes in the Annual Editions series are collections of newspaper, magazine, and journal articles discussing important topics and new research and theories in a given field. In *World History Volume I: Prehistory to 1500,* articles, arranged in chronological order, range from "The Cosmic Calendar" by Carl Sagan and

"The Evolution of Life on Earth" by Stephen Jay Gould through "Reconsidering Columbus" by Robert P. Hay. The volume includes 48 articles in all, drawn from such publications as *Discover* magazine, *Scientific American, The New York Times, History Today, U.S. News & World Report,* and *American History Illustrated.* Article topics include the discovery of the 5,000-year-old "Iceman" in the Alps, the history of writing, the art of ancient Nubia, the role of sports in history, the quest for the historical Jesus, the philosophy of Confucius, the horses of Genghis Khan, and the making of the Magna Carta. *Volume II: 1500 to the Present* includes 41 articles, on such topics as Martin Luther, Adam Smith, the scientific importance of Napoléon's Egyptian campaign, the impact of New World food crops on the Old World, the opium trade, the atomic bomb, the Berlin Wall, world population projections, and AIDS. A fascinating overview of world history as its practitioners see it. Volumes are continually updated to keep abreast of new discoveries and viewpoints.

The Ascent of Man
J. Bronowski; Little, Brown, 1976

An intellectual and cultural history of humankind from our earliest beginnings to the present day. This is the story of the growth of human ideas, from cave paintings to agriculture, architecture, metallurgy, mathematics and astronomy, to the harnessing of power, the elucidation of atomic structure, the study of genetics, and the invention of the computer. Smoothly and fascinatingly written; appropriate for high school–aged readers and an excellent reference for all.

The Cambridge Introduction to World History Series
Trevor Cairns; Cambridge University Press

A world history program for secondary students that consists of four "Course Books" (*The Coming of Civilization, The Romans and Their Empire, The Middle Ages, Renaissance and Reformation*), each a 96-page basic text, and 16 shorter "Topic Books," each centering around a specific topic, intended for supplementary enrichment. The course books provide a chronological overview of world history from the development of civilization through the mid-17th century, illustrated with paintings, drawings, photographs, and maps. Topic book titles, which cover world history through the 19th century, include *Life in the Old Stone Age, The Parthenon, Julius Caesar, Iron & the Industrial Revolution, The Viking Ships,* and *Life in a Medieval Village.*

> Course books, $18.95 apiece; topic books, $11.95 apiece; the entire set (20 books), $255. From bookstores or
> Social Studies School Service
> 10200 Jefferson Blvd.
> Box 802
> Culver City, CA 90232-0802
> (310) 839-2436 or (800) 421-4246

The Cartoon History of the Universe
Larry Gonick; Doubleday, 1990

This wonderfully witty book covers the history of the universe "From the Big Bang to Alexander the Great." Sample sections are titled "The Evolution of Everything," "Sticks and Stones," "River Realms," "Brains and Brawns," and "Who Are These Athenians?" The sequel, *The Cartoon History of the Universe II: From the Springtime of China to the Fall of Rome* (Doubleday, 1994), includes "Is Everything Sacred?", "Jaded Princes," "Republicans," and "Render Unto Caesar." In each book, universal history is told through hundreds of clever, memorable, and hilarious little captioned pictures. The facts are all there, too, plus an occasional helpful map. A great resource for teenagers discouraged by textbooks, but younger kids will also enjoy Gonick's unique and imaginative take on history. Our boys were hooked by the age of 10.

The Cartoon History of the Universe is also available on CD-ROM (see page 605).

Connections
James Burke; Little, Brown, 1995

In *Connections,* James Burke traces the historical innovations that led to such world-changing inventions as the computer, the airplane, telecommunications, and the atom bomb. The road that led to the computer, for example, began with the Roman grain mill and wandered through the medieval fair, the printing press,

HISTORY

Renaissance fountains, the Jacquard loom, and Herman Hollerith's punched card "tabulator."

Also see, by the same author, *The Day the Universe Changed* (Little, Brown, 1995), which similarly traces connections, discussing major changes in world history, society, and thought that are attributable to such intellectual breakthroughs as the scientific method, the Industrial Revolution, and the theory of evolution. An interesting slant on world history for science-minded teenagers.

Also see *Connections* on video (page 604).

Eyewitness Series: World History
Alfred A. Knopf

The ever-growing Eyewitness series is a collection of 64-page hardcover picture books, exquisitely illustrated with color photographs. Titles cover a range of disciplines, many related to world history. Examples include *Ancient Egypt* (George Hart; 1990), *Ancient Rome* (Simon James; 1990), *Castle* (Christopher Gravett; 1994), and *Knight* (Christopher Gravett; 1993). Each double-page spread in the books is devoted to a single topic. *Ancient Rome,* for example, includes 28 such short "chapters," among them "The Emperors," "The Legionary," "The Women of Rome," "Builders and Engineers," and "The Bloody Arena." There's a thin trickle of text, most of it in the picture captions.

Footprints in Time Series
Children's Press

A "gentle introduction" to world history and cultures for kids in grades 2–3. Each colorfully illustrated 24-page book includes a simple history of the featured culture, plus detailed instructions for related hands-on activities, projects, and crafts. Titles in the series include *The Aztecs* (Sally Hewitt; 1996), *The Egyptians* (Ruth Thomson; 1995), *The Greeks* (Sally Hewitt; 1995), *The Rainforest Indians* (Ruth Thomson; 1996), *The Romans* (Sally Hewitt; 1995), and *The Vikings* (Ruth Thomson; 1995). Young readers, for example, variously make a cardboard Aztec headdress, an Egyptian clay scarab and paper "jeweled" collar, a Roman paper bracelet, and a cardboard Viking longship.

Heroes: Great Men Through the Ages
Rebecca Hazell; Abbeville Press, 1997

An illustrated collection of 12 thoroughly interesting biographies of famous persons, in chronological order, from different times and countries. *Great Men* includes the stories of Socrates, Mansa Musa, Sequoya, Mozart, Leonardo da Vinci, Mohandas Gandhi, William Shakespeare, and Martin Luther King Jr. Also see, by the same author, *Heroines: Great Women Through the Ages* (1996), which includes profiles of Lady Murasaki Shikibu, Eleanor of Aquitaine, Joan of Arc, Sacagawea, Harriet Tubman, Marie Curie, and Amelia Earhart. Each book also contains maps and a bibliography.

History of the World
Plantagenet Somerset Fry; Dorling Kindersley, 1994

A lavishly illustrated 384-page history of the world, stuffed with 1,500 color photographs, maps, and artworks. The book is divided into 20 chronological chapters, each introduced by a timeline charting historical happenings on each continent and a world map pinpointing the locations of important events of the period. An excellent reference, interesting to read, and wonderful to look at.

History of the World Series
Raintree/Steck Vaughn

A large series of illustrated 72-page books on world history topics. Titles include *Africa and the Origins of Humans, Civilizations of the Middle East, Europe at the Time of Greece and Rome, The Early Middle Ages, China from the 7th to 19th Century,* and *The Americas in the Colonial Era.* And many more. For readers aged 9–12.

How Would You Survive? Series
Franklin Watts

A collection of illustrated 48-page books aimed at kids in grades 5–8. Each book covers various aspects of life during a different historical period. What did you do all day? What did you eat? Where did you live? What happened when you, an ancient Egyptian, had a toothache? What happened if you, an ancient Greek athlete, tried to cheat at the Olympic Games? Why did you, an American Indian, use sign language? Each book ends with a "Survival Quiz," which allows readers to see how well they would have functioned in times gone by. Titles in the series include *How Would You Survive . . . As an Ancient Egyptian* (Jacqueline Morley; 1995), *. . . As an Ancient Greek* (Fiona Macdonald; 1995), *. . . As an Ancient Roman* (Anita Ganeri; 1995), *. . . As an Aztec* (Fiona Macdonald; 1995), *. . . As a Viking* (Jacqueline Morley; 1995), *. . . As an American Indian* (Scott Steedman; 1996), *. . . In the American West* (Jacqueline Morle; 1996), and *. . . In the Middle Ages* (Fiona Macdonald; 1995). See **How Would You Survive?** on CD-ROM (page 612).

The Illustrated History of the World Series
Facts on File, 1993

This series of eight attractively designed and illustrated books covers world history from the appearance of the Stone Age hunting tribes to the technological advances of the present day. Titles in the series are *The Earliest Civilizations* (Margaret Oliphant), *Rome and the Ancient World* (Mike Corbishley), *The Dark Ages* (Tony Gregory), *The Middle Ages* (Fiona Macdonald), *The Age of Discovery* (Hazel Mary Martell), *Conflict and Change* (Fiona Reynoldson), *The Nineteenth Century* (Michael Pollard), and *The Modern World* (Stephen Hoare). For students aged 12 and up.

The Kingfisher Illustrated History of the World
Charlotte Evans and Jack Zevin, eds.; Kingfisher Books, 1993

Nearly 800 pages of creatively presented information, stuffed with colorful maps, drawings, photographs, and art reproductions covering the history of the world from 40,000 B.C. to the present. The book is divided into 10 major sections: "The Ancient World," "The Classical World," "The Early Middle Ages," "The Middle Ages," "The Renaissance," "Trade and Empire," "Revolution and Independence," "Unification and Colonization," "The World at War," and "The Modern World." At the beginning of each section, an illustrated world map pinpoints the locations of important events, and a comprehensive set of timelines ("The Years at a Glance") summarizes major his-

torical happenings by continent. There are six of these abbreviated timelines—for the Americas, Europe, Africa, the Near East, Asia and the Far East, and Australasia and the Pacific—which run vertically, so that readers can easily make chronological and geographical comparisons.

A much more detailed (gold-colored) timeline runs down the sides of the pages throughout the book, listing historical happenings worldwide in year-by-year chronological order; key events in the arts and sciences and major battles are highlighted by identifying symbols. The nicely readable text correlates (pretty much) to this timeline and is interspersed with highlighted boxes containing additional factual information or brief biographies of prominent people.

The massive size of the book is at first glance intimidating—this is the sort of tome we tuck under our five-year-olds so they can reach the Thanksgiving dinner table—but its contents are readily accessible, masterfully organized, and appealing. And there's a *lot* of information here. An excellent resource for history students.

Also see **The Kingfisher Book of the Ancient World: From the Ice Age to the Fall of Rome** (page 610).

Metropolis: Ten Cities/Ten Centuries
Albert Lorenz; Harry N. Abrams, 1996

Contains 42 pages of wonderfully detailed illustrations of cities, from 11th-century Jerusalem to very modern-day Manhattan. Included are aerial views, interiors, cross-sections, famous monuments, and lots of inhabitants.

The One Hundred Series
Bluewood Books

Each title in the series begins with "100." There are at least 10 of these, including *100 Events That Shaped World History* (Bill Yenne; 1993), *100 Inventions That Shaped World History* (Bill Yenne; 1993), *100 Wars That Shaped World History* (Samuel Willard Crompton; 1997), and *100 Women Who Shaped World History* (Gail Meyer Rolka and Bill Rolka; 1994). In each, subjects are arranged chronologically, one per page. The books are illustrated with black-and-white prints, photographs, and maps. For readers aged 12 and up.

Past Imperfect: History According to the Movies

Mark C. Carnes, ed., Henry Holt, 1995

We frequently use movies as supplements to our boys' history programs. In fact, in the case of the middle boy, who vociferously dislikes history, movies have succeeded in arousing interest where any amount of appealing literature has wretchedly failed. History by Hollywood, however, is a tricky proposition. Such painstakingly researched documentaries as Ken Burns's *The Civil War* are clearly historically reliable, but what about *Gone With the Wind? Mutiny on the Bounty? Spartacus?*

Past Imperfect is a critical survey of nearly 100 historical films, analyzed by knowledgeable historians. For each film or group of films (two on Christopher Columbus, for example, three on Joan of Arc, and five on World War I), the author discusses the known history of the featured subject and points out where the film stuck virtuously to historical truth and where it missed the mark. "If Santa Anna had as much artillery as this film suggests," writes Marshall De Bruhl of *The Alamo* (1960), in which John Wayne played a very gallant Davy Crockett, "the Alamo would have been reduced to rubble in a matter of minutes." Illustrations include period prints and photographs contrasted with scenes from the modern movies. A useful and interesting resource, and a valuable warning that you shouldn't believe everything that you see on-screen.

Profiles in World History Series

Joyce Moss, ed.; U*X*L, 1995

A series of eight books covering events from the beginning of civilization through modern times. Each chapter concentrates on a key historical event, followed by short biographies of prominent people who were involved. Titles include *Beginnings of Civilization to Expansion of World Powers, Crusades to Building Empires in the Americas, Beginnings of the Age of Discovery to the Industrial Revolution,* and *Reshaping Nations*

to Cold War. The books are heavily illustrated with photographs, prints, and maps. For readers aged 11 and up.

Reading Through the Ages

Linda Thornhill and Sally Barnard; Trisms, 1997

A 62-page list of biographies and historical fiction books covering world history from 3000 B.C. to the present day. Books are grouped by historical period. A reading level recommendation, from *E* for "easy reader" (ages 6–9) to *A* (adult), accompanies each selection. Each entry also includes title, author, number of pages, and a few (very brief) words of description.

$15

Trisms

3710 E. 63rd Pl.

Tulsa, OK 74136

(918) 491-6826

Web site: www.trisms.com

The Story of Mankind

Hendrik Willem Van Loon; Liveright, 1994

An updated version of the original classic history ("of all ages, for all ages"), first published in 1921, when it promptly won the first Newbery Medal. The expanded book now covers the history of mankind from prehistory through the 1990s, in 76 charmingly readable chapters illustrated with pen-and-ink sketches. *The Story of Mankind,* true to its name, reads much like a (long) fireside story. Chapter titles include "The Egyptians Invent the Art of Writing and the Record of History Begins," "The Greeks Were the First People to Try the Difficult Experiment of Self-Government," "The Strange Double Loyalty of the People of the Middle Ages and How It Led to Endless Quarrels Between the Popes and the Holy Roman Emperors," and "The Extraordinary Rise of a Little State in a Dreary Part of Northern Germany, Called Prussia." Informational, chatty, and enjoyable.

Time Traveller Books

Usborne Books/EDC Publishing

There are four 32-page books in this series: *Pharaohs and Pyramids* (Tony Allan and Philippa

Wingate; 1998), *Rome and Romans* (Heather Amery and Patricia Vanags; 1997), *Viking Raiders* (Anne Civardi, J. Graham-Campbell, and Philippa Wingate; 1998), and *Knights and Castles* (Judy Hindley; 1977). All are written in the same format: each double-page spread covers a different aspect of life in ancient times, with an appealingly interesting text and many bright-colored little pictures. Text and illustrations combine to deliver a large amount of information in a purely enjoyable fashion.

> EDC Publishing
> 10302 E. 55th Pl.
> Tulsa, OK 74146
> (800) 475-4522
> Web site: www.edcpub.com

World History Library Series
Facts on File

An information-stuffed series for high school students. Each book in the series is about 150 pages long, the text supplemented with interesting facts in boxes, capsule biographies, and illustrations. There are many titles in the series, among them *Africa: The Struggle for Independence* (Denise Wepman), *The Italian Renaissance* (Paul Robert Walker), *The Mechanical Age: The Industrial Revolution in England* (Celia Bland), and *"Peace, Land, Bread!": A History of the Russian Revolution* (John J. Vail).

The World in the Time of . . . Series
Fiona Macdonald; Dillon Press

What else was going on in the world in the time of . . . Alexander the Great, Leonardo da Vinci, Marco Polo, Marie Antoinette, Charlemagne, Tutankhamen? What was happening in Asia when Leonardo da Vinci was painting the *Mona Lisa?* What was happening in Africa when Marie Antoinette was queen of France? This series of books sets the world stage during the lifetimes of various famous historical figures, describing events is seven different regions around the globe. Each is illustrated with maps, paintings, and photographs of museum artifacts. Titles include *The World in the Time of Alexander the Great* (1997), . . . *Leonardo da Vinci* (1998), . . . *Marco Polo* (1997), . . . *Marie Antoinette* (1998), . . . *Tutankhamen* (1997), and . . . *Charlemagne* (1998).

GAMES AND HANDS-ON ACTIVITIES

Civilization

A board game covering the history of civilization from 8000 B.C. to the founding of Rome (around 250 B.C.). Players guide their budding civilizations from the Stone Age through the building of cities, the development of trade, and the growth of complex culture. The game, played on a four-panel map of the Mediterranean region, includes decks of civilization cards, which allow players to acquire cultural and technological advances (Pottery, Metalworking, Navigation, Drama and Poetry, Democracy), trade cards (papyrus, bronze, gold, salt), and calamity cards, which subject civilizations to such catastrophes as floods, volcanoes, pirates, and plague. The game accommodates two to seven players, and takes 4 to 5 hours to complete. Also available on CD-ROM for IBM/PC.

> Game, $40; CD-ROM version, $45
> Avalon Hill Game Co.
> 4517 Harford Rd.
> Baltimore, MD 21214
> (410) 254-9200 or (800) 999-3222
> e-mail: AH GAMES@aol.com
> Web site: www.avalonhill.com

Cooking Up World History
Patricia C. Marden and Suzanne I. Barchers; Teacher Ideas Press, 1994

Recipes from over 20 countries commonly studied in the elementary and/or middle grades. (There are several recipes for each country, enough to assemble a complete multicultural meal.) Also included: background information, suggestions for research projects linking foods to world history, and supplementary reading lists. For kids aged 5–12.

Costumes for Coloring: Kings and Queens Around the World
Jenny Williams, illustrations; Laura Driscoll, text; Grosset & Dunlap, 1996

A collection of detailed black-line portraits of kings and queens throughout history and from all parts of the world. Names, dates, and a short paragraph of bio-

graphical and historical information appear on the back of each picture. Featured monarchs, all in elaborate regalia, include Elizabeth I of England, Nicholas II and Alexandra of Russia, Shah Jahan of India, and Tutankhamen and Ankhsenamen of ancient Egypt.

Craft Topics Series
Franklin Watts

A collection of short (32 pages) illustrated history-and-crafts books for kids in grades 4–6. Each book in the series combines historical background information with related crafts. *Castles* (Rachel Wright, 1992), for example, contains instructions for making a model castle, a tapestry, and a catapult; *Vikings* (Rachel Wright, 1993) includes instructions for making a longboat, a brooch, a helmet, and a shield. There are 16 titles in the series, among them *Aztecs* (Ruth Thomsen, 1993), *Egyptians* (Rachel Wright, 1993), *Greeks* (Rachel Wright, 1993), and *Romans* (Nicola Baxter, 1992).

Historic Happenings
Joyce Stulgis Blalock; Dandy Lion, 1996

A 64-page collection of history projects for kids in grades 5–8, designed to integrate history and language arts. Projects fall into nine categories, among them "Ancient Civilizations," "Middle Ages and Renaissance," "Discovery and Settlement of the New World," "Important People and Their Contributions," and "General Assignments," this last applicable to a range of historical periods and places. Sample projects include making illustrated posters about ancient civilizations, writing an ancient Greek-style myth, publishing a medieval manor "newspaper," writing a biography of an important Renaissance figure, designing descriptive travel posters to lure settlers to the new American colonies, and performing a live news broadcast on an event from the Revolutionary War.

$8.95
Dandy Lion Publications
3563 Sueldo, Suite L
San Luis Obispo, CA 93401
(800) 776-8032/fax (805) 544-2823

History of the World

A board game of world history from the time of ancient Sumeria to World War I. The game is played on a detailed world map, on which each player controls seven empires, each fated to rise and fall with the passage of time. As the game proceeds, players may build monuments in Egypt, breech the Great Wall of China, conquer enemy cities, and contend with barbarians, earthquakes, and political treachery. The game includes 40 empire cards, each representing one of the world's great civilizations, among them Rome, China, and Egypt; and a deck of event cards, variously dealing out technological advances, powerful leaders, peasant revolts, natural disasters, and holy wars. The game is also available on CD-ROM for Windows.

Game, $35; CD-ROM version, $45
Avalon Hill Game Co.
4517 Harford Rd.
Baltimore, MD 21214
(410) 254-9200 or (800) 999-3222
e-mail: AH GAMES@aol.com
Web site: www.avalonhill.com

Kings & Queens of England

Forty cards with full-color portraits of all the monarchs of England from William the Conqueror, who appropriated the throne in 1066, to the present-day Queen Elizabeth II. The reverse side of each card lists name(s), dates, and historical highlights of each monarch's reign. These cards can be put to a number of creative uses: order them on a timeline, use them as historical story starters, invent a royal board game.

$7
Aristoplay
450 S. Wagner Rd.
Ann Arbor, MI 48107
(800) 634-7738 or (888) GR8-GAME
fax (734) 995-4611
Web site: www.aristoplay.com

Pyramids to Pueblos: 15 Pop-Up Models for Students to Make
Helen H. Moore and Carmen R. Sorvillo; Scholastic, 1995

Most kids adore pop-ups, and this innovative project book manages to combine irresistible pop-up paper crafts with world history and architecture. The book includes reproducible patterns for 15 famous historical structures from around the world, among them a southwestern pueblo, the Great Pyramid, the Taj Mahal, and a medieval castle. Included is historical background information on each architectural structure, plus suggestions for additional activities and curriculum connections.

$9.95

Scholastic, Inc.

2931 E. McCarty St.

Jefferson City, MO 65101

(800) 724-6527/fax (573) 635-5881

Web site: www.scholastic.com

Zephyr Learning Packets

Each learning packet is a "self-directed learning unit" on a different historical period or topic, containing project suggestions and reproducible worksheets for about 50 activities. Packets are in the form of 8½ × 11-inch comb-bound booklets; all include two levels of suggested activities, one set appropriate for kids in grades K–3, the other more appropriate for kids in grades 4–8. Titles in the series include *Early People: What do Anthropologists Study?; The Americas: Cultures in the Time Before Written History; Ancient Civilizations: In the Fertile Crescent, Ancient Egypt, Ancient Greece and Rome; Early Japan; The Jade Garden: Ancient to Modern China; Old Russia; Middle Ages; The Renaissance;* and *The Columbus Encounter: A Multicultural View.*

The books are collections of assignments, challenges, and suggestions only, which means they contain next to nothing in the way of background information or project directions. Each does contain a wide-ranging list of *what* to do; for how to do it, you're on your own.

Each packet, $18

Zephyr Press

3316 N. Chapel Ave.

Box 66006

Tucson, AZ 85728-6006

(800) 232-2187/fax (520) 323-9402

e-mail: neways2learn@zephyrpress.com

Web site: www.zephyrpress.com

VIDEOS

Civilisation

Spelled with an *s* because it comes to us from the BBC. This now classic series, narrated by historian (Lord) Kenneth Clark, traces the growth of human civilization over 16 centuries, from the fall of Rome to the present day. Titles in the series include "The Skin of Our Teeth," "The Great Thaw," "Romance and Reality," "Man—The Measure of All Things," "The Hero As Artist," "Protest and Communication," "The Pursuit of Happiness," "The Smile of Reason," "The Worship of Nature," and "Heroic Materialism." The series is a masterful overview of western arts: art, architecture, philosophy, literature, and music; college history and art history courses have used it as a supplement or component of the core curriculum. It is beautiful to look at; reviewers have dubbed it the "hallmark series against which all other cultural programs are measured." It is not, however, particularly accessible to younger viewers, which is a shame. For teenagers. Thirteen 50-minute programs on seven videocassettes.

$119.95

Zenger Media

10200 Jefferson Blvd.

Box 802

Culver City, CA 90232-0802

(310) 839-2436 or (800) 421-4246/fax (310) 839-2249

or (800) 944-5432

Web site: ZengerMedia.com/Zenger

Connections

This is a marvelous mix of science and history, as James Burke, a narrator who simply bubbles with enthusiasm, traces through the centuries the (often seemingly insignificant) happenings that eventually led to inventions that radically changed all our lives. Titles in the 10-cassette series include "The Trigger Effect," "Death in the Morning," "Distant Voices," "Faith in Numbers," "Wheel of Fortune," "Thunder in the Skies," "The Long Chain," "Eat, Drink and Be Merry," "Countdown," and "Yesterday, Tomorrow, and You." Watchers learn, for example, how the ancient Chinese loom led to the modern-day computer, and how Napoléon's hungry soldiers influenced the space program. Each episode is about an hour long; all are terrific.

A sequel, *Connections 2,* includes another 20 episodes in the series. These continue interesting—who can resist, for example, discovering a link between the medieval Buddhist tea ceremony and modern radio static?—but *Connections 2* is not as good as the original. Each episode in the sequel is only 30 minutes long; the pace is too rapid-fire for comfort.

$129.95

Discovery Channel Multimedia

Box 1089

Florence, KY 41022

(800) 678-3343

Web site: www.discovery.com

Also see the book of the same title (page 598).

Testament

A superb seven-part series on the Bible as history, narrated by British archaeologist John Romer. Episodes include "As It Was in the Beginning," the story of the nomadic peoples of the ancient Middle East and the beginnings of monotheism; "Chronicles and Kings," the story of the rise and fall of ancient Israel; "Mightier Than the Sword," on the historical context into which Jesus was born; "Gospel Truth," which explains the historical origins of the Christian Bible; "Thine is the Kingdom," the story of the Christian conversion of the Roman Empire through the reign of the Emperor Constantine; "The Power and the Glory," the history of the Dark Ages and the restablishment of reading and writing under Charlemagne; and "Paradise Lost," the history of the Bible from the Martin Luther and the Protestant Reformation to biblical research in the present day. A fascinating and balanced view of the Bible; the emphasis is on archaeology and history.

$179.95

Films for the Humanities & Sciences, Inc.

Box 2053

Princeton, NJ 08543-2053

(800) 257-5126

Web site: www.films.com

World History: The Fertile Crescent to the American Revolution

A high school class on video, featuring Lin Thompson of Bellflower High School in Los Angeles, who teaches his classes in costume and in the character of famous and not so famous historical characters. The *World History* series includes 30 half-hour lessons, each narrated by a different Thompson persona, from Lesson 1: "Civilizations of the Fertile Crescent," with "Mr. History"; "Ancient Greece" (Olympian Thompson);

"Ancient Rome" (Senator Linus Thompsoneus); "The Rise of Islam" (Abu Bakr); "The Crusades" (Sir Thomas); "The Old World vs. the New" (Potato Thompson); "The Protestant Reformation" (Martin Luther); "The Growth of Democracy" (Father Time); and finally "The American Revolution" (Patrick Henry). Mr. Thompson is a pleasant and enthusiastic speaker, and the costumes are fun: the lectures, however, are clearly classroom oriented—this is a teacher rapidly cramming essential information into students—and the real possibilities of the video format are almost entirely ignored. It would help student understanding greatly if—every once in a while—Thompson had directed the camera toward an illustration, a timeline, or a map. Thirty 30-minute lessons on 4 VHS videotapes:

$199.95

The Teaching Co.

7405 Alban Station Ct., Suite A-107

Springfield, VA 22150-2318

(800) 832-2412/fax (703) 912-7756

Also see *Early American History: Native Americans Through the Forty-Niners* (page 459).

COMPUTER SOFTWARE

Advanced Civilization

Players attempt to lead their burgeoning societies from 8000 B.C. to 250 B.C. through a combination of cultural, economic, political, and military advances and maneuvers. The game features multiple maps, superb graphics and animations, dramatic sound effects, and a lot of intellectual challenge. On CD-ROM for IBM or compatibles. Recommended for players aged 12 and up.

$45

Avalon Hill Game Co.

4517 Harford Rd.

Baltimore, MD 21214

(410) 254-9200 or (800) 999-3222

e-mail: AH GAMES@aol.com

Web site: www.avalonhill.com

Also see **Civilization** (page 602).

The Cartoon History of the Universe

An interactive time-travel adventure game based on the book of the same name by Larry Gonick (see page 598). Players progress, volume by volume, through a colorful animation of the book's 13 billion years of history. Along the way they enter the Minotaur's maze and battle the monster, explore the mysterious inner chambers of the Great Pyramid of Cheops, solve a series of Egyptian puzzles, rebuild the Acropolis, and captain a trireme in an Athenian sea battle. The book's text appears on-screen with the pictures and animations, read aloud by a wild-haired character called "The Professor," whose squeaky little voice fast becomes dreadfully annoying; luckily you can turn him off. Includes links to related Internet sites. On CD-ROM for Mac/Windows.

$24.95
Human Code
319 Congress, Suite 100
Austin, TX 78701
(512) 477-5455
Web site: www.humancode.com

Eyewitness History of the World

A lush source of beautifully presented information based on *History of the World* by Plantagenet Somerset Fry (see page 599). From the main screen, users can plunge into 10 different time periods, each crammed with illustrations, text, animations, and video footage. Kids can watch a medieval archer in action with the longbow or view the fall of the Berlin Wall, access biographies of historical figures, discover—by clicking on pictured objects—the facts about historical artifacts, and test their general history knowledge with the multiple-choice "Quizmaster." On CD-ROM for Mac or Windows.

$39.95
Dorling Kindersley Publishing
1224 Heil Quaker Blvd.
LaVergne, TN 37086
(888) DIALDKP
Web site: www.dk.com

Where in Time Is Carmen Sandiego?

As in the other programs in the popular Carmen Sandiego series (see page 435), students act as detectives, tracking down the villainous members of Carmen Sandiego's thieving gang—this time through 1,500 years of world history. Kids hop through 12 countries

and four major time periods, zeroing in on the crooks through clues based on historical events, famous historical figures, and scientific inventions. Recommended for kids aged 9 and up. On CD-ROM for Mac or Windows.

$34.95
Broderbund
Box 6125
Novato, CA 94948-6125
(800) 521-6263/fax (415) 382-4419
Web site: www.broderbund.com or www.carmen-sandiego.com

PREHISTORIC PEOPLES

BOOKS

All About Arrowheads and Spear Points
Howard E. Smith Jr.; Henry Holt, 1989

This 56-page pleasantly readable book includes a couple of short chapters on how to start an arrowhead collection; the bulk of the text, however, is a history of prehistoric peoples and their weapons, illustrated with precise pencil drawings. Sample chapter titles include "The First Spear Points," "The First Bows and Arrows," "Inuit Ivory Points," and "The Deer Hunters." Each chapter includes a map, showing where each type of arrowhead or spear point is found.

The book is interesting on its own but is even better paired with a museum trip or an up-close hands-on encounter. Our boys, fascinated, spent several postbook hours pawing through their father's arrowhead collection, happily identifying bird points, ax heads, polished stone points, and northeastern flint arrowheads.

Ancestors: In Search of Human Origins
Donald Johanson, Lenora Johanson, and Blake Edgar; Villard Books, 1994

The stories of the four-million-year course of human evolution and of the investigators whose fossil discoveries have contributed to present theories of human origins. Chapter titles include "The Ape That Stood Up: *Australopithecus afarensis*," "Scavenger Hunt: *Homo habilis*," "The Nutcracker People: *Australopithecus robustus*," "Big Bodies, Big Brains: *Homo erectus*,"

"Neandertal Enigma: *Homo neanderthalensis,*" and "The Human Revolution: *Homo sapiens.*" A good resource for high school–aged readers and adults. Illustrated with many black-and-white and color photographs.

Also see the video of the same title (page 609) and the **"Explore Our Human Origins" Curiosity Kit** (at right).

Archaeology

Dennis B. Fradin; Children's Press, 1983

Nine very short chapters in large print cover the history and practice of archaeology and discuss famous archaeological discoveries. One chapter, "Discoveries by Children," describes the finding of the Altamira cave paintings by a nine-year-old Spanish girl and of the Dead Sea Scrolls by a pair of young Palestinian shepherd boys. Illustrated with color photographs. For readers in grades 2–4.

Cobblestone: Anthropology and Archaeology

Archaeology: Finding the Past, the March 1991 issue of *Faces,* the multicultural magazine for kids (see page 411), includes nonfiction articles on the history of archaeology, the excavation of Pompeii, an archaeological project in the Venezuelan Andes, the discovery of a lost Spanish mission, a scientific explanation of the techniques archaeologists use for determining the age of artifacts, a fictionalized account of the discovery of the Lascaux cave paintings by four young French boys in 1940, a Pompeiian puzzle, and a board game for diggers.

Also see *Bones: What They Tell Us* (*Faces;* November 1994), *Fieldwork: Anthropologists at Work* (*Faces;* October 1993), and *Archaeology: Digging Up History* (*Cobblestone;* June 1983).

> Available from most libraries or for $4.50 from
> Cobblestone Publishing, Inc.
> 30 Grove St.
> Peterborough, NH 03458-1454
> (603) 924-7209 or (800) 821-0115/fax (603) 924-7380
> Web site: www.cobblestonepub.com
> See *Cobblestone* (page 449).

Early Humans

Nick Merriman; Alfred A. Knopf, 1989

This volume in the Eyewitness series covers prehistoric people from the first hominids through the early days of civilization. Titles of double-page spreads, illustrated with prints, drawings, and color photographs of museum artifacts, include "The Toolmakers," "Life in the Ice Age," "The First Artists," "The Beauties of Bronze," and "Men of Iron." Most of the information appears in the picture captions.

Prehistoric People

Ovid K. Wong; Children's Press, 1988

Seven very short, simple chapters in big print, titled "What Are Humans?," "How Scientists Study Prehistoric People," "*Homo habilis,*" "*Homo erectus,*" "*Homo sapiens,*" "How the Species Were Related," and "Learning from Prehistoric People." The book, for readers in grades 2–4, is illustrated with color photographs, maps, and art reproductions.

HANDS-ON ACTIVITIES

Bones & Stones

A simulation of Stone Age life for kids in grades 4–8. Participants learn about tool- and weapon-making, compete in a Stone Age "hunt," invent a prehistoric language, experiment with cave painting, interview a typical Stone Age family, and cooperate to build a scale replica of Stonehenge. The simulation includes background information, teaching instructions, and suggestions for many interdisciplinary activities.

> $46
> Interact
> 1826 Gillespie Way, #101
> El Cajon, CA 92020
> (800) 359-0961/fax (800) 700-5093
> Web site: www.interact-simulations.com

Explore Our Human Origins

From Curiosity Kits in conjunction with *NOVA,* this hands-on activity kit was inspired by the film *In Search of Human Origins* (see page 609). The kit contains everything a young anthropologist or paleontologist needs for his/her first experiments: a foldout poster illustrating the development of life on earth since the pre-Cambrian period, an assortment of eight (or more) plant and animal fossils in sand, to be sifted out, identified, and labeled on the included "Fossil Card," plaster for making a hand- or footprint cast, and a stone slab and paints for making a "cave painting." Also included is an *Anthropologist's Field Guide,* with instructions and background information.

> $20 from toy and game stores; for a local source, contact
> Curiosity Kits
> Box 811
> Cockeysville, MD 21030
> (410) 584-2605 or (800) 584-KITS
> e-mail: ckitsinc@aol.com

The Neanderthal Book and Skeleton

Stephen Cumbaa and Barbara Hehner; Workman, 1997

A 64-page illustrated book on the Neanderthals plus a foot-tall 25-piece model of a Neanderthal skeleton, and replicas of a bone flute and stone spearpoint.

> $16.95 from bookstores or
> Workman Publishing Co.
> 708 Broadway
> New York, NY 10003
> (212) 254-5900 or (800) 722-7202/fax (212) 254-8098
> Web site: www.workmanweb.com

Prehistoric Cave Painting Kit

Ancient Graffiti specializes in arts and crafts kits based on "the lives and art of indigenous and ancient peoples around the world." The kits are beautifully designed and packaged; most are appropriate for kids aged 8 and up. The "Prehistoric Cave Painting Kit" includes a foot-square stone tile for painting upon, a stone palette, a grinding stone, a handmade twig brush and stick pointer/scraper, and four packets of natural pigments: users grind and mix the colors themselves. The kit includes an illustrated booklet which gives complete instructions and a brief history of cave painting.

A smaller version of the cave painting kit, the "Rock Art Painting Kit," includes four pigments, a pair of handmade twig tools, and a detailed history-and-instruction booklet; users supply their own rocks.

The "Grotte Chauvet Cave Painting Kit" contains a (reusable) 6-inch-square painting tile, a pair of handmade stick tools, four pigment packets, and an instruction booklet including an account of the recently discovered Grotte Chauvet cave paintings in France. The Grotte Chauvet cave paintings and American Indian rock art paintings are also available as coloring pages: each booklet, the *Grotte Chauvet Coloring Pages* or *Amer-*

ican Indian Rock Art Coloring Pages, includes 12 pages of black-line art images for coloring with watercolors, crayons, or colored pencils, instructions and historical background information, and blank pages for experimenting with your own versions of ancient designs.

> Ancient Graffiti
> 52 Seymour St.
> Middlebury, VT 05753
> (802) 388-2919 or (888) 725-6632/fax (802) 388-7104
> e-mail: ancientg@sovernet.com

Prehistoric Man Explorer's Kit

The kit contains an illustrated 64-page book, *The First Humans: A Prehistoric Guide,* by anthropologist Alan E. Mann, plus an ancient hominid fossil embedded in a hunk of clay. Excavation tools and instructions are included.

> $18.95 from book or game stores or
> Running Press Book Publishers
> 125 S. 22nd St.
> Philadelphia, PA 19103-4399
> (215) 567-5080 or (800) 345-5359/fax (800) 453-2884

ARCHAEOLOGY FIELD WORK

Some archaeological digs and projects welcome student volunteers. Some sources include:

Archaeological Fieldwork Opportunities Bulletin

For young archaeologists eager for hands-on experience, the Archaeological Institute of America publishes the *Archaeological Fieldwork Opportunities Bulletin (AFOB),* a comprehensive listing of ongoing digs, field schools, and special programs with openings for volunteers and students. Each entry includes a description of the project, cost, required age/experience, and a contact name and address.

> *AFOB,* $9 (AIA members) or $11 (nonmembers) (plus $4 shipping/handling)
> Kendall/Hunt Publishing Co.
> 4050 Westmark Dr.
> Order Department
> Dubuque, IA 52002
> (319) 589-1000 or (800) 228-0810

Archaeological Fieldwork Opportunities: On-Line

An updated list of openings for volunteers, students, and paid workers, and information on archaeological field schools.

durendal.cit.cornell.edu

Passport in Time

A program of the USDA Forest Service that accepts volunteers of all ages (kids must be accompanied by adults) to participate in archaeological digs at Forest Service–sponsored sites. The program publishes a detailed newsletter listing current projects.

Passport in Time
PIT Clearinghouse
Box 31315
Tucson, AZ 85751-1315
(520) 722-2716 or (800) 281-9176
e-mail: SRIArc@aol.com

VIDEOS

NOVA: In Search of Human Origins

This three-part video series is hosted by anthropologist Donald Johansen, discoverer of the ancient hominid skeleton known as Lucy, possibly the world's most famous fossil. Titles in the series, which covers Johansen's landmark find and other discoveries contributing to modern theories of human evolution, include "In Search of Lucy," "Surviving in Africa," and "The Creative Revolution." Each videotape is about an hour long.

The 3-tape set, $59.99
Movies Unlimited
3015 Darnell Rd.
Philadelphia, PA 19154
(215) 637-4444 or (800) 4-MOVIES
e-mail: movies@moviesunlimited.com
Web site: www.moviesunlimited.com

COMPUTER SOFTWARE

Introduction to Archaeology

An interactive CD-ROM centering around the discovery of a skeleton at an archaeological dig. Students learn basic archaeological techniques as they analyze their find, attempting to determine sex, age, year and cause of death, cultural practices, and religious beliefs. Includes video clips, color graphics, a dictionary, an "archaeologist's manual," and student games. For Mac or Windows.

$59.95
Zenger Media
10200 Jefferson Blvd.
Box 802
Culver City, CA 90232-0802
(310) 839-2436 or (800) 421-4246/fax (310) 839-2249
or (800) 944-5432
e-mail: access@ZengerMedia.com
Web site:ZengerMedia.com/Zenger

Origins of Mankind

An interactive CD-ROM covering some 70 million years of human evolution. Kids can explore a range of evolutionary periods, study theories of evolution, view famous paleontological discoveries, and play an archaeological expedition game. Includes a multiple-choice quiz. For Mac or Windows.

$29.95
Zenger Media
10200 Jefferson Blvd.
Box 802
Culver City, CA 90232-0802
(310) 839-2436 or (800) 421-4246/fax (310) 839-2249
or (800) 944-5432
e-mail: access@ZengerMedia.com
Web site: ZengerMedia.com/Zenger

PREHISTORIC PEOPLES ON-LINE

Flints and Stones

A virtual tour of the Ice Age from the British Museum of Antiquities. Users find out what life was like as a hunter-gatherer.

www.ncl.ac.uk/~nantiq

Fossil Hominids

Short descriptions of the various species and subspecies of early man, plus a timeline and links to related sites.

earth.isc.uci.edu: 8080/faqs/fossil-hominids.html

9 + *Paleolithic Cave Paintings*

An account of the discovery of the underground network of caves in southern France, decorated with elaborate paintings from 17,000 to 20,000 years ago. Text and visuals, plus links to other prehistoric wall painting sites.

www.culture.fr/culture/gvpda-en.htm

ANCIENT CIVILIZATIONS

BOOKS

8 12 *Baboons Waited on Tables in Ancient Egypt! Weird Facts About Ancient Civilizations*

Melvin Berger and Gilda Berger; Scholastic, 1997

Strange but absolutely true information about ancient history for readers aged 8–12.

9 14 *Calliope: Ancient Civilizations*

Issues of *Calliope*, Cobblestone's "World History" magazine (see page 597), with ancient civilization themes include *Athens vs. Sparta* (November 1994), *Carthage* (September 1992), *Cities of the Past* (May 1996), *Epic Heroes I* (January 1991), *Epic Heroes II* (January 1994), *Heroes and Heroines of Early Rome* (September 1995), *Lost Cities* (May 1991), *Mesopotamia* (September 1993), *Pharaohs of Egypt* (September 1994), *Queens of Egypt* (November 1991), and *Vanished Civilizations* (May 1992). All contain fiction and nonfiction articles, quizzes and puzzles, maps, timelines, and supplementary reading lists. For kids in grades 5–9.

Available from most libraries or for $4.50 from

Cobblestone Publishing, Inc.

30 Grove St.

Peterborough, NH 03458-1454

(603) 924-7209 or (800) 821-0115

Web site: www.cobblestonepub.com

9 12 *Eyewitness Series: Ancient History*

Alfred A. Knopf

Several titles in the eye-catching Eyewitness books series are excellent resources for students of ancient history. Titles include *Archaeology, Ancient Egypt, Ancient Greece, Ancient Rome, Bible Lands, Mummy,* and *Pyramid.* All are light on text—most of the information is found in the picture captions—but heavy in stunning illustrations: sophisticated color photographs of artworks and archaeological artifacts. "A mini-museum in a book," writes one reviewer.

8 12 *First Books: Ancient Biographies*

Robert Green; Franklin Watts, 1996

This series of illustrated 64-page biographies of prominent people in the ancient world is recommended for readers in grades 4–6. Titles include *Alexander the Great, Cleopatra, Hannibal, Herod the Great, Julius Caesar,* and *Tutankhamun.*

ALL *The Kingfisher Book of the Ancient World: From the Ice Age to the Fall of Rome*

Hazel Mary Martell; Kingfisher Books, 1997

A heavily illustrated chronological history of the ancient world from prehistoric times to the decline and fall of the Roman Empire. The book covers events in all parts of the world: the Middle East, Asia, Europe, Africa, the Americas, and Oceania. Included are maps, drawings of artifacts, wonderful color paintings, interesting fact boxes, detailed timelines, and a glossary.

10 13 *Outrageous Women of Ancient Times*

Vicki Leon; John Wiley & Sons, 1997

Collective biographies of feisty, opinionated, and sometimes thoroughly outrageous women who made their marks in ancient society. *Outrageous Women,* targeted at readers aged 10–13, covers 15 women from across the world, including Greece, Rome, Egypt, and the Far East, among them the female pharaoh Hatshepsut and the poet Sappho. Also see, by the same author, *Uppity Women of Ancient Times* (Conari Press, 1995), a longer and more freewheeling coverage of the same subject for older readers (aged 13+) profiling 150 women. All, if not precisely admirable, are definitely interesting.

12 + *Then & Now*

Stefania Perring and Dominic Perring; Macmillan, 1991

The authors use a creative series of plastic overlays to show re-creations of ancient sites as they were (then)

in their heyday, and photographs of the sites as they appear today. (The authors call this "an exercise in considered imagination.") Included among the book's 20 sites are the Acropolis and the Agora in Athens, the Forum and the Colosseum in Rome, and, also in Italy, Hadrian's Villa and Pompeii. The text, in small, dense print, is for older readers, but the pictures are for everybody. A colored timeline in the front of the book locates each archaeological site in time.

In the same format, also see *Battlefields Then and Now* (John Man and Timothy Newark; Macmillan, 1997).

The Visual Dictionary of Ancient Civilizations

Dorling Kindersley, 1994

One of the volumes in the increasingly large Eyewitness Visual Dictionaries Series, which convey information through color photographs, each elaborately and precisely labeled. If, for example, you want to know the names of all the parts of a Greek vase or Roman temple, *The Visual Dictionary of Ancient Civilizations* is an ideal reference. It covers, in glorious pictures, some 16 ancient civilizations, among them the Mesopotamians, the Egyptians, the Babylonians, the Persians, the Celts, the Minoans, the Greeks, the Romans, the Maya, the Incas, and the Chinese.
See *Eyewitness Visual Dictionary Series* (page 132).

GAMES AND HANDS-ON ACTIVITIES

Building Stonehenge

A *NOVA* Curiosity Kit with which kids make a baked-clay model of Britain's famous Stonehenge, attach the model to a display board, and use it to predict the sun's position. Also included: a solar tracker, a make-it-yourself sundial, and a detailed instruction booklet with historical background information. Recommended for kids aged 8 and up.

> $20 from toy and game stores; for a local source,
> contact
> Curiosity Kits
> Box 811
> Cockeysville, MD 21030

(410) 584-2605 or (800) 584-KITS/fax (410) 584-1247
e-mail: CKitsinc@aol.com

Expedition! Archaeology Around the World

A multipurpose kit with which young archaeologists/paleontologists can unearth their own fossils and artifacts. The kit contains an informational instruction booklet, tools, and six blocks of clay, each containing a find from a different archaeological "expedition." Diggers variously visit ancient Europe, ancient Egypt, the dinosaur bone fields of Montana, and the Central American rainforest, as they uncover bones, stones, and a relief from Tutankhamen's tomb.

> $32.95
> Young Explorers
> 825 S.W. Frontage Rd.
> Ft. Collins, CO 80524
> (800) 239-7577 or (800) 777-8817/fax (970) 484-8067
> Web site: www.youngexplorers.summitlearning.com

The Holy Land Treasure Chest

Study the history of the ancient Middle East with this activity-packed kit. The "Treasure Chest" includes an illustrated 32-page book; a scroll map of the Holy Land; a set of replica Crusader coins; "knuckle bones" and instructions for an ancient Roman game; a set of ancient Hebrew letter stamps; a build-it-yourself model of the Temple of Jerusalem; a map of the Holy Land to be illustrated with stickers of important people, places, and events; a decoder wheel for translating ancient Hebrew words into modern English; and pictures to color illustrating episodes from the Old Testament and the Koran. Recommended for kids aged 8–13.

> $19.95 from book or game stores or
> Running Press Book Publishers
> 125 S. 22nd St.
> Philadelphia, PA 19103-4399
> (800) 345-5359/fax (800) 453-2884

COMPUTER SOFTWARE

Ancient Lands

All about ancient Egypt, Greece, and Rome through an attractive mix of text, illustrations, film clips, and animations. Kids can approach ancient history through one of three topics ("Monuments & Mysteries," "People & Politics," or "Work & Play") or they can take a historical tour led by a selected contemporary "Guide"—among them Homer, an Egyptian embalmer's daughter, and the Emperor Nero's right-hand man. Lots of interesting and unusual information, nicely presented. The program also includes maps, timelines, excerpts from primary sources, puzzles, and games. On CD-ROM for Mac or Windows.

$35.95

Zenger Media

10200 Jefferson Blvd.

Box 802

Culver City, CA 90232-0802

(310) 839-2436 or (800) 421-4246/fax (310) 839-2249 or (800) 944-5432

e-mail: access@ZengerMedia.com

Web site: ZengerMedia.com/Zenger

How Would You Survive?

An interactive CD-ROM in which kids explore the worlds of the ancient Egyptians, the Vikings, or the Aztecs of ancient Mexico. The program covers the daily life, food, homes, clothing, languages, and religion of each culture through an appealing combination of animations and graphics, maps, timelines, and text. At the end of each episode, kids can test their newly acquired knowledge with a "Have You Survived?" quiz. For Mac or Windows.

$31.95

Zenger Media

10200 Jefferson Blvd.

Box 802

Culver City, CA 90232-0802

(310) 839-2436 or (800) 421-4246/fax (310) 839-2249 or (800) 944-5432

e-mail: access@ZengerMedia.com

Web site: ZengerMedia.com/Zenger

ANCIENT CIVILIZATIONS ON-LINE

Ancient Civilizations

A exciting on-line game in which players—in character, as a princess, a merchant, or a scholar—travel back in time to ancient Greece. Success depends on the player's ability to make choices based on his/her knowledge of ancient times.

tqd.advanced.org/2840/index.html

Ancient Sites

Virtual tours of Rome, Athens, and ancient Egypt, plus on-line action games, variously set in Greece, Rome, or "Nieuw Amsterdam" in 1642. In this last, you've just set off for the New World with only 16 guilders in your pocket, and a ship full of drunken sailors.

www.ancientsites.com

Exploring Ancient World Cultures

A gem; this is a survey of great ancient cultures of the world, including Egypt, Greece, Rome, the Arab world, and China. Wonderful photographs, virtual tours, a chronology, an informative text, and links to many other related sites.

eawc.evansville.edu:80/index.htm

History for Kids

Lesson plans on many historical topics, activities, and links to a wide range of interesting Internet sets. Sample topics include Roman palaces, ancient Greek ships, the Mayan empire, the Vikings, medieval castles, and the Seven Wonders of the Ancient World.

www.bottco.com/HISTORY.html

Mr. Donn's Ancient History Page

A large collection of study units, lesson plans, and activities on ancient civilizations, including Greece, Egypt, Rome, China, India, Africa, the Maya, and the Incas.

members.aol.com/DonnandLee/index.html

EGYPT

BOOKS: NONFICTION

Cleopatra

Diane Stanley and Peter Vennema; William Morrow, 1994

A lushly illustrated biography of the famous queen, for readers in grades 4–8. The cover pictures Cleopatra in Roman mosaic; the text describes her affairs—political and personal—with Julius Caesar

HISTORY

and Marc Antony, her awesome court at Alexandria, and her final defeat at the Battle of Actium.

The Egyptian News
9 12 Scott Steedman; Candlewick, 1997

This clever oversize book purports to be a "daily newspaper" of ancient Egypt, complete with national and international news, profiles of famous people, classified ads, political cartoons, fashion updates, recipes, and information on sports events and the state of the economy. Headlines include "Egypt Reunited, Hyksos Hammered!" and "Boy King Dies!" A lot of historical and cultural information in a humorous and unusual format. Fun for kids aged 9–12.

Gods and Pharaohs
9 13 Elizabeth Payne; Random House, 1964

A chronological history of ancient Egypt for young readers, interestingly written and illustrated with black-and-white photographs. The book opens with the "rediscovery of ancient Egypt" by Napoléon's soldiers; it then surveys Egyptian history, from the earliest settlers in the Nile valley through Cheops and the Great Pyramid; Queen Hatshepsut, who wore a ceremonial beard and ruled Egypt as a man; the religious upheavals under Pharaoh Akhenaton and his wife, Nefertiti; the warmongering Ramses the Great; and the arrival of Alexander the Great, who came, conquered, and built Alexandria.

How to Make a Mummy Talk
9 13 James M. Deem; Bantam Books, 1997

Not *talk* literally; instead the book explains how scientists study and analyze mummies, using them to learn about life in the ancient world. The book covers the processes of making mummies, discusses the various ways in which ancient cultures dealt with death, and describes research on assorted famous mummies, among them Egyptian mummies, Chinese mummies, and the 5,000-year-old "Iceman" recently discovered in the Alps. Humor, science, and ancient history in 194 pages for readers aged 9–13.

Learning About Mummies
6 10 Laura Alden; Children's Press, 1988

An illustrated 46-page account of mummies, including a simple explanation of the Egyptian mummy-making process, an Egyptian mummy tale called "The Dead Prince," and the story of the famous discovery of Tutankhamen's tomb (and mummy), plus short accounts of unusual mummies from other parts of the world, among them the green "Copper Man" from Chile, the ancient Chinese "Lady of Hunan," and even the American naval hero John Paul Jones. For readers aged 6–10.

"Mumab: The Making of a Modern Mummy"
13 + Nancy Touchette; *Chem Matters;* February 1996

This issue of *Chem Matters* (see page 348) a quarterly magazine aimed at high school–aged chemistry students, includes an article on the making of a modern mummy using ancient Egyptian techniques. The illustrated article contains a brief history of mummy making, a step-by-step account of the process used and problems encountered by the modern researchers, and an explanation of the chemistry of natron, the salt mixture used by the ancient Egyptians for drying the body.

Back issues from
American Chemical Society
Dept. L-0011
Columbus, OH 43268-0011
(800) 333-9511

Mummies Made in Egypt
7 10 Aliki; HarperTrophy, 1985

A picture-book account of Egyptian religion and burial rites, covering the making of a mummy, the preparation of the coffin, the funeral, and the structure of Egyptian tombs and pyramids (with intriguing cross-sectional sketches). Many of the detailed and colorful little illustrations are based on Egyptian tomb paintings. For readers aged 7–10. *Mummies Made in Egypt* was selected for *Reading Rainbow,* the popular PBS television series.

Mummies, Tombs, and Treasure: Secrets of Ancient Egypt
9 + Lila Perl; Clarion, 1990

The Egyptian cult of death, the process of mummification, the building of the pyramids, and tales of Egyptian gods and goddesses, pharaohs, tomb robbers, and archaeologists. There's also a chart of Egyptian dynasties and a floor map of King Tut's tomb. Illustrated with drawings and photographs. Recommended for readers in grade 4 and up.

Pyramid

ALL David MacAulay; Houghton Mifflin, 1982

A fascinating account of the construction of a great pyramid on the west bank of the Nile in the years 2470 to 2439 B.C., illustrated with exquisitely detailed pen-and-ink drawings. For all ages.

See the video of the same name (page 618) and *Pyramid* (James Putnam; Alfred A. Knopf, 1994) in the Eyewitness Series (page 599).

Ramses II and Egypt

9 12 Oliver Tiano; Henry Holt, 1995

A clever and creatively designed history of ancient Egypt, centering around the rule of pharaoh Ramses II. The book is filled with interesting and unusual information, great graphics, maps, photographs, paintings, and a detailed timeline of ancient Egyptian history in the form of a brightly striped cobra. Included are a page of Egyptian dream interpretations (it's good to dream of diving into a river), a Ramses II paper doll with multiple costumes, an explanation of hieroglyphics paired with a photograph of the Rosetta Stone, and a page about ancient Egyptian religion, "So Many Gods, So Little Time."

The Riddle of the Rosetta Stone

9 13 James Cross Giblin; HarperTrophy, 1993

The story of the Rosetta Stone, which provided the crucial clues that allowed archaeologists to translate ancient Egyptian hieroglyphics. The stone, discovered in 1799 by Napoléon's soldiers, was carved with the same message in three languages: Greek, hieroglyphic, and demotic. The work of decoding the message makes an interesting detective story. The book includes photographs of the stone and an appendix of information about ancient writing systems. For readers aged 9–13.

Tales Mummies Tell

7 10 Patricia Lauber; Thomas Y. Crowell, 1985

Egyptian mummies, Peruvian mummies, Scythian mummies—there's even the story of a woolly mammoth mummy.

Tut's Mummy . . . Lost and Found

6 8 Judy Donnelly; Random House, 1988

A Step Into Reading book for kids in grades 2–3, with color illustrations, plus a few black-and-white and color photographs. Five short chapters in large print tell the story of Tutankhamen's burial and of the discovery of his tomb over 3,000 years later by Howard Carter and Lord Carnarvon.

BOOKS: FICTION

Bill and Pete Go Down the Nile

4 8 Tomie De Paola; Paper Star, 1996

Bill and his pal Pete (crocodiles) take a class trip down the Nile to visit the pyramids. Humorous and informational, with De Paola's wonderful illustrations. For kids aged 4–8.

The Egypt Game

9 14 Zilpha Keatley Snyder; Yearling, 1986

April and her friend Melanie begin the "Egypt Game," inventing a world based on ancient Egypt with the help of artifacts found in the storage yard of a neighborhood antique shop. The game grows steadily, becoming richer and more complex. April and Melanie are joined by Melanie's little brother, Marshall (a boy pharaoh), then by an imaginative Chinese-American girl named Elizabeth, and finally by a pair of sixth-grade boys who stumble upon Egypt one Halloween and, fascinated, decide to stay. For readers aged 9–14.

The Egyptian Cinderella

5 9 Shirley Climo; HarperCollins, 1992

The picture-book tale of the Greek slave girl Rhodopis, whose tiny rose red sandal is stolen by a falcon. The falcon drops it at the feet of the young pharaoh who just happens to be looking for a wife. Illustrated by Ruth Heller. For readers aged 5–9.

Gift of the Nile: An Ancient Egyptian Legend

5 9 Jan M. Mike; Troll Associates, 1992

The tale of a young slave girl, Mutemwia, who befriends the pharaoh and wins her freedom on a magical journey down the Nile. A brightly illustrated picture book for readers aged 5–9. This is one of the Legends of the World series from Troll, a large collection of illustrated multicultural legends for young readers.

His Majesty, Queen Hatshepsut

Dorothy S. Carter; Lippincott-Raven, 1987

A historical novel based on the dramatic life of Hatshepsut, the daring young princess who appropriated the throne of Egypt from her brother, declared herself pharaoh, and ruled the kingdom as a man. The book opens when Hatshepsut is 13; it includes historical notes and a bibliography. For readers aged 12 and up.

I Am the Mummy Heb-Nefert

Eve Bunting; Harcourt Brace, 1997

An ancient Egyptian mummy, now in a museum case, tells the story of her life. A 32-page picture book for readers aged 6–10.

Zekmet, the Stone Carver:
A Tale of Ancient Egypt

Mary Stolz; Harcourt Brace, 1988

A stone carver, given the task of carving a memorial for the pharaoh, creates the Sphinx. For readers aged 5–8.

COLORING AND PAPER-CRAFTS BOOKS

Ancient Egypt

Peter Der Manuelian; Running Press

A volume in the Start Exploring fact-filled coloring books series. Each is 128 pages long and includes a detailed kid-friendly informational text paired with 60 black-line illustrations. Kids learn about ancient life along the Nile, famous pharaohs, pyramids and temples, mummies, and hieroglyphic writing.

$8.95 from book or game stores or
Running Press Book Publishers
125 S. 22nd St.
Philadelphia, PA 19103-4399
(215) 567-5080 or (800) 345-5359/fax (800) 453-2884

Ancient Egyptian Costumes Paper Dolls

Two dolls and 16 colorful costumes from all walks of Egyptian life.

$3.95
Dover Publications, Inc.
31 E. Second St.
Mineola, NY 11501

A Coloring Book of Ancient Egypt

A coloring book of ancient Egyptian art, picturing gods and goddesses, kings and queens, dancers, hunters, and scenes of daily life. Other coloring books with ancient Egyptian themes include *A Coloring Book of Cleopatra, A Coloring Book of Queen Nefertiti, A Coloring Book of Tutankhamen,* and *Ramses the Great.*

$2.95
Bellerophon Books
36 Ancapa St.
Santa Barbara, CA 93101
(800) 253-9943/fax (800) 965-8286

Egyptian Punch-Out Mummy Case

Kids can make an Egyptian sarcophagus, in full color, with removable lid and mummy. Also see *Cut and Make Egyptian Masks,* with which kids can make five colorful masks, including a falcon, a crocodile, and a replica of Tutankhamen's famous gold funeral mask.

Punch-Out Mummy Case, $3.95; *Masks,* $6.95
Dover Publications, Inc.
31 E. Second St.
Mineola, NY 11501

The Ultimate Ancient Egypt Sticker Book

Dorling Kindersley, 1994

Kids match 60 truly beautiful full-color stickers—all photographs of ancient Egyptian artworks and museum artifacts—to their proper outline and descriptive caption.

$6.95 from bookstores or Dorling Kindersley
Publishing
1224 Heil Quaker Blvd.
LaVergne, TN 37086
(888) DIALDKP
Web site: www.dk.com

GAMES AND HANDS-ON ACTIVITIES

Ancient Egypt Explorer's Kit
The kit includes *Life in Ancient Egypt,* a 64-page illustrated book of historical information and activity suggestions, and a block of clay from which young Egyptologists can unearth replicas of a scarab, an *udjat*-eye amulet, and a *ushabti* figure.

$18.95 from book or game stores or
Running Press Book Publishers
125 S. 22nd St.
Philadelphia, PA 19103-4399
(215) 567-5080 or (800) 345-5359/fax (800) 453-2884

Ancient Egypt Treasure Chest
This kit, in the form of a colorful cardboard treasure chest (with tiny metal lock and key), contains a packet of facsimile ancient Egyptian beads with which to make a necklace, a set of hieroglyphic stamps, an ink pad and a sheet of papyrus, a pair of Egyptian board games, a map of ancient Egypt with attachable stickers, charts of Egyptian gods and pharaohs, and *Life in Ancient Egypt,* an informational booklet illustrated with color photographs of museum artifacts.

$19.95 from book or game stores or
Running Press Book Publishers
125 S. 22nd St.
Philadelphia, PA 19103-4399
(215) 567-5080 or (800) 345-5359/fax (800) 453-2884

Egypt
A simulation of ancient Egyptian civilization for kids in grades 5–10. Students, as members of a "nome" (agricultural/political district), participate in a series of multidisciplinary activities, competing to see who will travel the greatest distance along the Nile to be crowned Ra (pharaoh of Egypt). The simulation is divided into six "cataracts," based on the six series of waterfalls and rapids on the Nile River. Kids create a 3-D map of the Nile, learn about Egyptian hieroglyphs and numbers, study Egyptian religion and myths, design a tomb painting and a mask, learn about pyramid-building methods, research a famous ancient Egyptian, and play ancient Egyptian games. And much more.

$46
Interact
1826 Gillespie Way, #101
El Cajon, CA 92020
(800) 359-0961/fax (800) 700-5093
Web site: www.interact-simulations.com

Fun With Beads: Ancient Egypt
Janet Coles; Metropolitan Museum of Art/Viking

This high-quality kit includes 3,500 ancient Egyptian–style ceramic and metal beads, plus all the accessories necessary for making jewelry: gold wire, needle and thread, earring wires, and fasteners. A 96-page instruction booklet gives directions for making jewelry designs based on ancient Egyptian ornaments and includes historical information about ancient Egyptian jewelry.

$25
Metropolitan Museum of Art
255 Gracie Station
New York, NY 10028-9998
(800) 468-7386

Fun With Hieroglyphics
Catharine Roehrig; Metropolitan Museum of Art/Viking, 1990

This kit, encased in a nice heavy folding box with a magnetic snap closure, includes a hieroglyph alphabet chart, 24 hieroglyphic stamps, an ink pad, and an informational booklet on the history, meanings, and uses of hieroglyphic symbols.

$25
Metropolitan Museum of Art
255 Gracie Station
New York, NY 10028-9998
(800) 468-7386

In the Land of Egypt
A collection of eight card and dice games centering around the culture and customs of ancient Egypt. The games variously involve creative storytelling, sequencing and visual identification skills, memory, strategy, and just plain luck.

In "The Last Pyramid," for example, players are challenged to put 30 lushly illustrated "Pyramid Cards" in the proper order so as to tell a coherent story about the building of a great pyramid by Queen Misis. Each "Pyramid

Card" has a colorful picture on one side, a few lines of descriptive text on the other. The first card in the story, for example, reads "Queen Misis has ordered you to build the finest pyramid for all time. So you study the finest pyramids of past times. The Step Pyramid of King Zoser is the oldest. Zoser's 'staircase to heaven' has four steps." Players then use these clues to track down the next card in the series, finding a picture of King Zoser's Step Pyramid. The game includes 75 illustrated cards, a pair of "Egyptian" dice patterned with hieroglyphic symbols, and a detailed instruction booklet. For players aged 8–12.

$14.95
Aristoplay
450 S. Wagner Rd.
Ann Arbor, MI 48103
800 (634) 7738 or (888) GR8-GAME
fax (734) 995-4611
Web site: www.aristoplay.com

Mummy's Message

A simulation in which kids, as "archaeologists," move through the passages and chambers of a pyramid collecting pieces of a mysterious "Hieroglyphic Tablet" and attempting to put it together to read the "Mummy's Message." Players progress by answering "Question Cards" about life in ancient Egypt; correct answers earn "Hieroglyphic Cards," which include hieroglyphic symbols and translations necessary for solving the "Mummy's Message." Progress is not trouble-free; participants also encounter and must deal with "Problem Cards," each describing actual problems and perils suffered by real-life archaeological teams.

There's an option for a longer version of the simulation, involving additional library research and hands-on projects. Materials are also provided for participants at two levels (upper elementary/middle school and high school). The simulation is designed for 12 to 35 kids in grades 5–10, but it adapts well to smaller groups. Simulation materials include a 55-page teacher's guide.

$53
Interact
1825 Gillespie Way, #101
El Cajon, CA 92020-1095
(619) 448-1474 or (800) 359-0961/fax (619) 448-6722
or (800) 700-5093
Web site: www.interact-simulations.com

Pyramid Action Pack
Dorling Kindersley, 1994

An interactive activity pack that teaches kids about the pyramids and ancient Egyptian culture. The pack includes an illustrated informational booklet, a cardboard pyramid model, a colorful map of ancient Egypt, an Egyptian game, a hieroglyphics decoder, and a letter (written in hieroglyphics) to decode.

$17.95 from book and game stores or
Dorling Kindersley Publishing
1224 Heil Quaker Blvd.
LaVergne, TN 37086
(888) DIALDKP
Web site: www.dk.com

Pyramids: 50 Hands-On Activities to Experience Ancient Egypt
Avery Hart and Paul Mantell; Williamson, 1997

A 96-page collection of activities and projects centering around ancient Egyptian culture. Included are recipes, games, and arts and crafts projects for kids aged 4–9.

$12.95 from bookstores or
Williamson Publishing Co.
Box 185
Church Hill Rd.
Charlotte, VT 05445
(802) 425-2102 or (800) 234-8791/
fax (802) 425-2199
or (800) 304-7224

Senet

One of our boys' favorites. This fast-paced strategy game was played by the Egyptian pharaohs; a playing board was found in King Tutankhamen's tomb. Players move their pawns along the hieroglyphic-patterned path on the playing board; winner is the first to get all of his/her pieces off the board. It's trickier than it sounds. Our version includes both conventional dice and Egyptian throwing sticks, which are much more fun. For two players aged 8 and up.

$27.50 from game stores or
Animal Town
Box 757
Greenland, NH 03840
(800) 445-8642/fax (603) 430-0334

Take An Egyptian Adventure

A *NOVA* Curiosity Kit based on the film *This Old Pyramid* (see page 619). The kit includes a foldout poster (to be colored) on the building of the pyramids, a 78-block wooden model pyramid, template and paints for carving and painting a hieroglyphic message, and an informational instruction booklet, the *Egyptologist's Field Guide.* Recommended for kids aged 10 and up.

$25 from game stores or for a local source, contact

Curiosity Kits

Box 811

Cockeysville, MD 21030

(410) 584-2605 or (800) 584-KITS/

fax (410) 584-1247

e-mail: Ckitsinc@aol.com

Tutankhamun and Ancient Egypt Action Pack

Dorling Kindersley, 1996

The kit includes a guidebook of historical background information and instructions, a color poster of the art treasures found in Tutankhamen's tomb, a fold-out freize of traditional Egyptian wall paintings, and the materials for several hands-on craft projects and activities. Kids can make cardboard models of Tutankhamen's three caskets and his gold funeral mask, a replica of an Egyptian jeweled collar, and a scarab bookmark. Also included are a set of hieroglyph stencils, a pack of mix-and-match Egyptian god cards, and a paper board and playing pieces for the ancient Egyptian game of "Duat."

$17.95 from bookstores or toy and game stores or

Dorling Kindersley Publishing

1224 Heil Quaker Blvd.

LaVergne, TN 37086

(888) DIALDKP

Web site: www.dk.com

Tutankhamun & the Discovery of the Tomb

A portfolio of primary source documents and historical background essays centering around the discovery of Tutankhamun's tomb by archaeologist Howard Carter and Lord Carnarvon. The portfolio contains 10 "historical documents," among them color prints of Tutankhamun's throne, a wall painting from the burial chamber, and a page from the papyrus of

Ani detailing Egyptian religious beliefs, a page from the *News of the World,* April 8, 1923, announcing the death of Lord Carnarvon, samples of Carter's original notes and drawings, and a paper model (in metallic colors) of the tomb's outer shrine. Also included are four historical background essays, comprehensive notes on each document, lists of suggested student readings and discussion questions, and a study guide.

$37

Jackdaw Publications

Box 503

Amawalk, NY 10501

(914) 962-6911 or (800) 789-0022/fax (914) 962-0034

Wadjet

A truly beautiful board game of archaeological discovery set in Egypt in 1923. Players, as competing archaeologists, travel around an exquisite Egyptian-patterned playing board attempting to find the stolen treasures of the pharaoh. This is a hazardous business; the archaeologists run into many troubles, from inadequate overseas funding to the angry cobra goddess (Wadjet) who guards the pharaoh's tomb. The game, which is based in part on actual historical events, includes a map and an expedition log. For two to four players, aged 10 and up.

$59.95 from game stores or

Timbuk II Inc.

Box 4495

Burlington, VT 05406-4495

(800) 863-9053/fax (802) 863-4097

VIDEOS

Pyramid

Based on David MacAulay's book of the same title (page 614). The video, through an appealing mix of cartoon animation, real-life sequences of archaeological sites, and narration, details the construction of an ancient Egyptian pyramid. About one hour. Available as a four-cassette set, with *Roman City, Castle,* and *Cathedral.*

Set of 4, $79.98

PBS Home Video

1320 Braddock Pl.

Alexandria, VA 22314-1698

(800) 645-4PBS

Web site: www.pbs.org

or

Pyramid, $19.98

Zenger Media

10200 Jefferson Blvd.

Box 802

Culver City, CA 90232-0802

(310) 839-2436 or (800) 421-4246/fax (310) 839-2249

or (800) 944-5432

e-mail: access@ZengerMedia.com

Web site: ZengerMedia.com/Zenger

This Old Pyramid

Archaeological theory meets hands-on practice in this fascinating 90-minute *NOVA* video. This episode covers the history and structure of the ancient Egyptian pyramids and follows the work of a team of American and Egyptian stonemasons as they build a pyramid of their own, using ancient tools and 200 two-ton stone blocks.

$19.95

Movies Unlimited

3015 Darnell Rd.

Philadelphia, PA 19154

(215) 637-4444 or (800) 4-MOVIES

e-mail: movies@moviesunlimited.com

Web site: www.moviesunlimited.com

COMPUTER SOFTWARE

Pyramid: Challenge of the Pharaoh's Dream

An interactive CD-ROM in which players, as the pharaoh's master builder, must design and construct a (grave-robber-proof) pyramid, foil a plot to overthrow the pharaoh, and finally oversee the preparation of the pharaoh's mummy and its placement in the tomb. Filled with colorful and clever graphics and information about the culture, technology, and religion of ancient Egypt. For Windows.

$38.95

Zenger Media

10200 Jefferson Blvd.

Box 802

Culver City, CA 90232-0802

(310) 839-2436 or (800) 421-4246/fax (310) 839-2249

or (800) 944-5432

e-mail: access@ZengerMedia.com

Web site: ZengerMedia.com/Zenger

The Road to Ancient Egypt

A tutorial on the history and culture of ancient Egypt from the first settlements along the Nile to the New Kingdom. The program contains color photographs and graphics, an informational text, a glossary, a timeline, quizzes, puzzles, games, and project suggestions.

$49.95

Zenger Media

10200 Jefferson Blvd.

Box 802

Culver City, CA 90232-0802

(310) 839-2436 or (800) 421-4246/fax (310) 839-2249

or (800) 944-5432

e-mail: access@ZengerMedia.com

Web site: ZengerMedia.com/Zenger

or

The Edutainment Catalog

Box 21210

Boulder, CO 80308

(800) 338-3844/fax (800) 226-1942

e-mail: teccat@tecdirectinc.com

Web site: www.edutainco.com

EGYPT ON-LINE

Ancient Egypt

An immense collection of resources on ancient Egypt, including information on Egyptian history, art, everyday life, medicine, and religion. For example, users can see their names written in hieroglyphics, view an image of the pyramids (as seen from the space shuttle), and participate in a study of the Great Pyramid.

PersonalWebs.myriad.net/steveb/egypt.html

Institute of Egyptian Art and Archaeology

The institute is located in Memphis, Tennessee; on-line visitors have access to a virtual tour of ancient Egyptian sites, including the pyramids, and a photo gallery of the institute's collection of Egyptian artifacts.

www.memst.edu/egypt/main.html

5 *Little Horus Web Site*

An excellent site on ancient Egypt just for kids, hosted by Little Horus, a bright blue cartoon-style bird. The site covers 7,000 years of Egyptian history in easy-to-read format; there's also a colorful map of Egypt, a description of Egyptian life today, and links to related sites.

www.horus.ics.org.eg

10 *Reeder's Egypt Page*

History, art, and archaeology of Egypt, plus links to many other Egypt-related Web sites. Users can explore the Tomb of Niankhkhnum and Khnumhotep (both Overseers of the Manicurists in the Palace of the King), learn the secret of the "enigmatic tekenu," access the on-line version of *KMT: A Modern Journal of Ancient Egypt,* and view a gallery of ancient Egyptian art.

www.egyptology.com/reeder

GREECE AND ROME

BOOKS: NONFICTION

13 *Alpha to Omega: The Life & Times of the Greek Alphabet*

Alexander and Nicholas Humez; David R. Godine, 1983

Alpha to Omega includes an essay for each letter of the Greek alphabet, from alpha, beta, and gamma to chi, psi, and omega, each covering Greek history, culture, and mythology, as well as the history of the Greek alphabet and language. Open it anywhere and you'll find something to grab your attention. *M* (mu), for example, stands for myth, Minoan, and Mycenean: the chapter discusses Homer, perhaps the greatest myth-maker of all time, Heinrich Schliemann and his search for Homer's Troy, the ancient Minoans and their two confusing pictographic scripts, and the Myceneans of mainland Greece, who built walled cities with stones so huge that legends claimed they were built by giants. For high school–aged to adult readers; a valuable reference for all ancient history programs.

See, by the same authors, *ABC Et Cetera: The Life and Times of the Roman Alphabet* (1985) which, in similar format, contains an essay for each letter of the

Roman alphabet, each discussing Roman history, culture, and mythology, as well as the evolution of the Roman alphabet and the Latin language.

9 *Ancient Greek and Roman Resource Series*

Golden Owl Publishing

A series of resource books targeted at kids in grades 4–12. Each includes reproducible worksheets and pages, lesson plans, activity suggestions, detailed background information, and a bibliography. There are ten titles in the series, among them *Inventions and Inventors,* which covers everything from the lyre, the chariot, and the sundial to the Corinthian column, the Archimedean screw, and the Greek version of the computer; *Ancient Athletic Games: Heracles and the Olympics; Inspirational Women: Muses & Women in Antiquity;* and *The Twelve Olympians: Their Stories.* Also included in the series is the *Critical Bibliography for Teaching the Ancient World,* an annotated list of books, videos, computer software, and Internet sites on ancient history topics, each with grade level recommendations.

$24.95 each

Jackdaw Publications

Box 503

Amawalk, NY 10501

(800) 789-0022/fax (800) 962-9101

12 *Ancient Rome: How It Affects You Today*

Richard J. Maybury; Bluestocking Press, 1995

An answer for those who demand "Why study history?" Because history repeats, states author Maybury's alter ego, Uncle Eric, in a series of thought-provoking letters to his young nephew, Chris. The Roman model—the idea that nations should be ruled by powerful central governments that can tax and control everything—has had ominous implications for much of future history. We read this book months ago and still haven't stopped arguing about it.

9 *Augustus Caesar's World*

12 Genevieve Foster; Charles Scribner's Sons, 1947

Pleasantly readable world history from the time of Augustus Caesar (44 B.C. to A.D. 14). The book describes, in story-style prose, what was happening in Augustus

HISTORY

Caesar's Rome and what was happening simultaneously in other parts of the world. The history is divided into five sections: "When Augustus Was the Schoolboy Octavius" (Julius Caesar was murdered, the Roman calendar established); "When Octavius Was the Young General Octavian" (Antony fell in love with Cleopatra, Herod was made King of the Jews); "When Octavian Was Given the Title of Augustus" (the Druids were a power in Gaul, Virgil wrote the *Aeneid*); "When Augustus Was Worshipped as a God" (the Maya flourished in Central America, the caste system began in India); and "When Augustus Was Honored as the Father of his Country" (Jesus was a boy, the Germans rebelled against Rome).

See *The World Series* (page 456).

City: A Story of Roman Planning and Construction

David MacAulay; Houghton Mifflin, 1983

In 26 B.C., a disastrous spring flood wipes out the villages (and an important bridge) along the banks of the Po River. The Emperor Augustus dispatches a crew of 45 military engineers to rebuild the bridge and to construct new roads and a new city. The engineers faithfully carry out the emperor's orders; what follows is a detailed and wonderfully illustrated account of the building of bridge, roads, and city, from the drawing of the master plan and the quarrying of the limestone through the completion of the public baths, the amphitheater, and the temple of Jupiter.

Gladiator

Richard Ross Watkins; Houghton Mifflin, 1997

The story of the Roman gladiators: their history, training, equipment, amphitheaters, and spectacularly bloody combats. Illustrated with black-and-white drawings. For readers aged 10 and up.

The Greek News

Anton Powell and Philip Steele, eds.; Candlewick, 1996

If the ancient Greeks had published daily newspapers, complete with marvelous color illustrations, they might just possibly have looked like this. This 32-page creative oversize book is a fascinating collection of national and international news stories, political cartoons, trade and sporting news, advertisements, fash-

ion hints, recipes, and health and political advice. The news covers a wide range of time: headline stories include "Greece in Peril," an account of the Battle of Marathon in which the Greeks defeated the Persians in 480 B.C., "Sparta Attacks!" (431 B.C.), and "Alexander Wins!" (334 B.C.).

A lot of historical information in a clever and delightful format. Kids will love the advertisements. ("TUTOR FOR SALE: Well-educated Greek teacher, 28 years old, to instruct your children at home. Only 800 sestertii. Box No. 8294.") For readers aged 9–12. Also see *The Roman News* (Andrew Langley and Philip De Souza, eds; Candlewick Press, 1996).

I Wonder Why Romans Wore Togas and Other Questions About Ancient Rome

Fiona Macdonald; Kingfisher Books, 1997

An illustrated introduction to ancient Roman culture in conversational question-and-answer format for kids aged 5–9.

Pompeii . . . Buried Alive!

Edith Kunhardt; Random House, 1987

A Step Into Reading book for kids in grades 2–3 about the fatal eruption of Mount Vesuvius that buried the Roman city of Pompeii.

BOOKS: FICTION

Also see **Classical Mythology** (pages 89–92).

Black Ships Before Troy: The Story of the Iliad

Rosemary Sutcliff; Delacorte Press, 1993

A wonderful recounting of Homer's classic epic, filled with drama, disaster, heroism, tragedy, triumph, and gore. The book begins with the fatal Apple of Discord (inscribed "to the fairest") and continues through the abduction of Helen, the pursuit by the Greeks, the long years of the Trojan War (with attendant meddling by the gods and goddesses), the clever ploy of the Trojan Horse, and the final defeat. Illustrated with color paintings.

Also see the sequel, *The Wanderings of Odysseus: The Story of the Odyssey* (1996).

Dateline: Troy

11 **+** Paul Fleischman; Candlewick, 1996

Retellings of episodes from Homer's *Iliad* are juxtaposed with collages of modern-day newspaper clippings, drawings, photographs, and diagrams, drawing attention to (depressing) historical parallels. For readers aged 11 and up.

Detectives in Togas

9 **12** Henry Winterfeld; Harcourt Brace, 1990

The book features a group of Roman schoolboys who, with the help of their wise Greek teacher, Xantippus, solve mysteries. The author explains that the inspiration for the books was an inscription, discovered in 1936, scrawled in a child's hand on a wall in Pompeii. It read *"Caius asinius est,"* politely translated in the books as "Caius is a dumbbell." Also see the sequel, *Mystery of the Roman Ransom.*

Inside the Walls of Troy

10 **+** Clemence McLaren; Atheneum, 1996

The story of the Trojan War, alternately told by the beautiful Helen (who loved horses, played the flute, and bit her nails) and the young Cassandra, whose frightening dreams come true. For readers aged 10 and up.

The Lion in the Gateway

10 **13** Mary Renault; Harper & Row, 1964

An exciting fictionalized account of the battles between the Greeks and the Persians at Marathon, Salamis, and Thermopylae. For readers aged 10–13.

Running Out of Time

9 **12** Elizabeth Levy; Alfred A. Knopf, 1980

Three friends, Nina, Francie, and Bill, running through a fog, suddenly emerge on the Appian Way in Rome, in the year 73 B.C. There they are taken to the gladiatorial arena where they meet Spartacus, leader of the famous slave revolt. For readers aged 9–12.

We Were There With Caesar's Legions

9 **12** Robert N. Webb; Grosset & Dunlap, 1960

The story of two young Britons, Una and Orlex, in the days when Julius Caesar's legions first invaded the British Isles. For readers aged 9–12.

COLORING AND PAPER-CRAFTS BOOKS

A Coloring Book of Ancient Greece

6 **+** Greek art to color from the work of "the finest ancient vase painters," including portraits of gods and goddesses, dancers and musicians, warriors, chariot races, and scenes of daily life. Other coloring books with ancient Greek or Roman themes include *Alexander the Great, A Coloring Book of the Olympics, A Coloring Book of Rome,* and *The Trojan War.*

> $2.95 each
> Bellerophon Books
> 36 Ancapa St.
> Santa Barbara, CA 93101
> (800) 253-9943/fax (800) 965-8286

Etruscan Chariot

6 **+** The Etruscan civilization occupied the Italian peninsula before the Romans. With this book, kids can cut out and assemble an Etruscan chariot. All pieces on card stock in full color.

> $6.95
> Bellerophon Books
> 36 Ancapa St.
> Santa Barbara, CA 93101
> (800) 253-9943/fax (800) 965-8286

Life in Ancient Greece Coloring Book

6 **+** Scenes from the Olympic Games, the building of the Parthenon, the trial of Socrates, and everyday life in ancient Greece. Each picture is accompanied by a brief informational text.

> $2.95
> Dover Publications, Inc.
> 31 E. Second St.
> Mineola, NY 11501

The Ultimate Greece & Rome Sticker Book

6 **+** Dorling Kindersley; 1994

Kids make their very own picture books, matching over 60 full-color stickers—all wonderful photographs of museum artifacts and artworks—with their proper outlines and captions. (It's okay if you goof; you can peel the stickers off and try again.)

$6.95 from bookstores or
Dorling Kindersley Publishing
1224 Heil Quaker Blvd.
LaVergne, TN 37086
(888) DIALDKP
Web site: www.dk.com

GAMES AND HANDS-ON ACTIVITIES

Ancient Greece Scientific Explorer Kit

This high-quality kit allows young users to re-create ancient experiments and discoveries that contributed to the development of modern science. With the "Ancient Greece" kit, kids study the foundations of geometry, building a glass-tile mosaic in a terra-cotta frame, constructing Platonic solids, and learning about the Pythagorean theorem and the Archimedean spiral. Also see the *Ancient Rome Scientific Explorer Kit,* with which users build and calibrate a wonderful terra-cotta-framed water clock and design a lunar calendar. Each kit includes a detailed instruction booklet, with historical background information and suggestions for additional experiments and projects.

Each kit, $23.95
Scientific Explorer, Inc.
2802 E. Madison, Suite 114
Seattle, WA 98112
(800) 900-1182/fax (206) 322-7610
e-mail: sciex@scientificexplorer.com
Web site: www.scientificexplorer.com

Archiblocks

These are high-quality architectural block sets. The blocks are made of maple, beautifully shaped and finished; each kit contains 50 to 75 blocks. The blocks are grouped in period sets, complete with assorted columns, pediments, lintels, and arches in the proper styles and proportions. Available sets include "Greek" and "Roman," as well as "Islamic," "Gothic," "Renaissance," "Santa Fe," and "Post-Modern."

Sets, about $60 apiece, from toy and game stores or
Zephyr Press
3316 N. Chapel Ave.
Box 66006

Tucson, AZ 85728-6006
(800) 232-2187/fax (520) 323-9402
e-mail: neways2learn@zephyrpress.com
Web site: www.zephyrpress.com

Circus Maximus

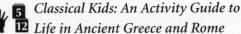

A board game set in the Circus Maximus of ancient Rome, in which players, using a number of strategies, compete to win the chariot race. (Among the options: players can arm their chariots, bribe their opponents' drivers, and place bets.) The game can be played at three skill levels.

$15
Avalon Hill Game Co.
4517 Harford Rd.
Baltimore, MD 21214
(410) 254-9200 or (800) 999-3222
e-mail: AH GAMES@aol.com
Web site: www.avalonhill.com

Classical Kids: An Activity Guide to Life in Ancient Greece and Rome

Laurie Carlson; Chicago Review Press, 1998
A wealth of creative activities for kids aged 5–12.

Greeks
Romans

Historical/cultural simulations for kids in grades 6–10. In "Greeks," students variously take on an ancient Greek persona and receive a Greek "education" (learning, among other things, the Greek alphabet), debate Greek political issues, build a Greek temple, enact short Greek plays, compete in a version of the Greek Olympic Games, hold a symposium in which each participant represents a famous ancient Greek, and wind the unit up with a festival and "Panhellenic Quiz Bowl."

In "Romans," kids acquire Roman names, build Roman houses, read Roman myths, and learn Roman history; they also map Roman roads, make model aqueducts, play a chariot-race board game, put on a play about the fall of Rome, and bring a "famous Roman" (in full-size cardboard cutout form) to an end-of-unit banquet.

$43 each
Interact
1825 Gillespie Way, #101

El Cajon, CA 92020-1095

(619) 448-1474 or (800) 359-0961/fax (619) 448-6722

or (800) 700-5093

Web site: www.interact-simulations.com

Republic of Rome

A strategy board game based on Roman history during the period of the Republic, from the time of the Punic Wars through the assassination of Julius Caesar and the beginning of the Roman Empire. The game is played on a detailed mapboard of ancient Rome; players compete to control the Roman Senate. The outcome of the game is influenced by the illustrated historical event cards, which compel players to deal with barbarian invasions, political intrigue, the rise of powerful popular leaders, gladiator revolts, assassinations, and natural catastrophes.

$40

Avalon Hill Game Co.

4517 Harford Rd.

Baltimore, MD 21214

(410) 524-9200 or (800) 999-3222

e-mail: AH GAMES@aol.com

Web site: www.avalonhill.com

Roman Arch Blocks

The Roman Arch (which was probably invented by the ancient Babylonians) was an impressive architectural invention, and it's just as impressive in miniature. With this kit, builders construct the arch on a temporary support; then, triumphantly, they insert the keystone block, remove the support, and watch the arch stand solidly on its own. The kit includes 76 hardwood blocks, six arch supports, and an instruction book containing historical background information.

$30.00 from toy and game stores or

Michael Olaf's Essential Montessori

Box 1162

Arcata, CA 95518

(707) 826-1557/fax (707) 826-2243

Rome Action Pack

Dorling Kindersley, 1995

The kit includes an informational guidebook, assorted facsimiles of ancient Roman documents, a full-color cross-sectional poster of the Roman Coliseum, and all the materials for several hands-on craft projects

and activities. Users can make a three-dimensional model of a Roman town house, minimodels of a Roman temple, aqueduct, and triumphal arch, a diorama picturing some of the many different people in Roman society, a paper mosaic, and a chariot-race board game.

$16.95 from bookstores or toy and game stores or

Dorling Kindersley Publishing

1224 Heil Quaker Blvd.

LaVergne, TN 37086

(888) DIALDKP

Web site: www.dk.com

Spend the Day in Ancient Greece

Linda Honan; John Wiley & Sons, 1998

Kids follow an ancient Greek family through a very full day, experiencing daily life through a series of hands-on projects and activities. In "Helen's Peplos," for example, they make their own ancient Greek costumes; in "Alexander's Lessons," they learn the ancient Greek alphabet; and in "Athena's Feast," they try some ancient Greek recipes. The illustrated text includes lots of interesting historical facts in sidebars and boxes. For kids aged 8–12.

VIDEOS

Ben-Hur

Set in the days of the Roman Empire, this is the epic tale of Judah Ben-Hur and his erstwhile friend Marcellus, who become bitter enemies over differences of politics and religion. Dramatic sea battles, a spectacular chariot race, and a miraculous ending. With Charlton Heston in the title role.

$24.95

Movies Unlimited

3015 Darnell Rd.

Philadelphia, PA 19154

(215) 637-4444 or (800) 4-MOVIES

e-mail: movies@moviesunlimited.com

Web site: www.moviesunlimited.com

In the Shadow of Vesuvius

An hourlong National Geographic documentary on the ancient Roman cities of Pompeii and Herculaneum, buried in A.D. 79 when the volcano Vesuvius erupted. Includes fascinating on-site film footage.

$19.95
Movies Unlimited
3015 Darnell Rd.
Philadelphia, PA 19154
(215) 637-4444 or (800) 4-MOVIES
e-mail: movies@moviesunlimited.com
Web site: www.moviesunlimited.com
or
National Geographic Home Video
Box 5073
Clifton, NJ 07015
(800) 627-5162
Web site: www.nationalgeographic.com

Roman City

Based on David MacAulay's book *City* (see page 621). The video uses a creative combination of narration, animated sequences, and real-life scenes filmed on location at archaeological sites to trace the building of a Roman city. About one hour. Available as a four-cassette set, with *Pyramid*, *Castle*, and *Cathedral*.

Set of 4, $79.98
PBS Home Video
1320 Braddock Pl.
Alexandria, VA 22314-1698
(800)-645-4PBS
Web site: www.pbs.org
or individually, $19.98
Zenger Media
10200 Jefferson Blvd.
Box 802
Culver City, CA 90232-0802
(310) 839-2436 or (800) 421-4246/fax (310) 839-2249
or (800) 944-5432
e-mail: access@ZengerMedia.com
Web site: ZengerMedia.com/Zenger

Spartacus

The stirring tale of the slave rebellion led by the gladiator Spartacus in the days of republican Rome. Exciting scenes of gladiatorial combat and battle, but the film also conveys the greater thought-provoking issues: Is a stable political order worth the price of tyranny and slavery? Spartacus doesn't win. Kirk Douglas plays the ill-fated slave leader; the movie also stars Sir Laurence Olivier, Jean Simmons, Charles Laughton, and Peter Ustinov.

$19.98
Zenger Media
10200 Jefferson Blvd.
Box 802
Culver City, CA 90232-0802
(310) 839-2436 or (800) 421-4246/fax (310) 839-2249
or (800) 944-5432
e-mail: access@ZengerMedia.com
Web site: ZengerMedia.com/Zenger

COMPUTER SOFTWARE

See *Ancient Lands* (page 611).

Recess in Greece

Morgan, a befuddled chimpanzee, is transported back to ancient Greece, where everyone thinks he is Odysseus and he must win the Trojan War in order to get himself back home. He's not completely on his own here: he can expect some input from the Greek gods, all of whom appear in modern guise, beginning with Zeus, a strutting sheriff ornamented with two badges, a star, and a lightning bolt. Clicking on individual items and characters on the screen calls up information on ancient Greek culture, religion, arts, history, and geography; and the "Recess in Greece" feature challenges kids with a series of quizzes in which they must answer multiple-choice questions, learn the letters of the Greek alphabet, identify Greek roots in modern English words, and solve the mathematical problems in the "Magic Squares." On CD-ROM for Mac or Windows.

$24.95
Zenger Media
10200 Jefferson Blvd.
Box 802
Culver City, CA 90232-0802
(310) 839-2436 or (800) 421-4246/fax (310) 839-2249
or (800) 944-5432
e-mail: access@ZengerMedia.com
Web site: ZengerMedia.com/Zenger

The Road to Ancient Greece

A tutorial on CD-ROM on ancient Greek history and culture, from the Minoan Age through the Hellenistic Age, covering the Persian and Peloponnesian

Wars, the rise of the city-states, the beginnings of democracy, and the rise of Greek drama, philosophy, and art. Included are many color photographs and graphics, an informational text, a timeline, quizzes, puzzles, and games, and student project suggestions.

Also see *The Road to Ancient Rome* which, in similar format, covers the history and culture of Rome, from its beginnings through the Roman Republic, the emperors, and the decline and fall.

$49.95 each

Zenger Media

10200 Jefferson Blvd.

Box 802

Culver City, CA 90232-0802

(310) 839-2436 or (800) 421-4246/fax (310) 839-2249

or (800) 944-5432

e-mail: access@ZengerMedia.com

Web site: ZengerMedia.com/Zenger

or

The Edutainment Catalog

Box 21210

Boulder, CO 80308

(800) 338-3844/fax (800) 226-1942

e-mail: teccat@tecdirectinc.com

Web site: www.edutainco.com

GREECE AND ROME ON-LINE

The Ancient City of Athens

A photographic archive of archaeological sites in Athens. Students can take a virtual tour of major excavations and prominent monuments.

www.indiana.edu/~kglowack/Athens/Athens.html

Pompeii On-Line

Maps, pictures, and text on the unfortunate (for everyone but archaeologists) Roman city of Pompeii.

www.tulane.edu/pompeii/text/pompeii.html or
jefferson.village.virginia.edu/pompeii/page-1.html

ROMARCH (Roman Art and Archaeology)

Resources on the art and archaeology of ancient Rome.

www.personal.umich.edu/~pfoss/ROMARCH.html

VIKINGS

From my homeschool journal:

◆ October 18, 1990. Josh is nine; Ethan, seven; Caleb, six.

We started studying the Vikings this morning, using a trio of homemade workbooks. Located the Viking home countries on the world map; defined and found fjords, a word Caleb found simply hilarious. Read about ship burials, drew pictures of Viking ships, and made a paper model of a dragon ship from a kit, which didn't come out badly except that the sail kept falling over. During lunch, we read Norse myths from D'Aulaire's Norse Gods and Giants *(see page 629); the boys then drew and labeled pictures of Odin and Thor and decorated elaborate Viking brooches (cardboard circles with safety pins taped on the back) with gold and silver Magic Markers. We used a couple of reference books to get a look at real Viking brooches and to find out how Vikings wore them; the boys then dressed up in capes and brooches and set off to reenact stories of Viking battles, Valkyries, and Valhalla.*

Started The Story of Leif Ericson *(William O. Steele), a chapter book, as a bedtime book. Josh: "How do they know about what happened when Leif Ericson was a little boy?"*

◆ October 19, 1990

Read about daily life in Viking times, using a combination of reference and picture books, among them Robin Place's The Vikings: Fact and Fiction, *which included color photographs of Viking artifacts from archaeological digs and* The Story of the Vikings Coloring Book *(see page 629). Studied the runic alphabet, and the boys learned how to write their names in runes. Discussed Viking surnames. Josh: "So if I were a Viking, my name would be Joshua Randallson. What about girls' names?"*

Josh was so taken with the runic alphabet that he sat down and wrote a letter entirely in runes to a friend in California. ("It's like a secret code.") He thoughtfully included a key so that Lisa will be able to translate it.

Began a very messy art project, making three Viking helmets out of papier-mâché. At the moment, we have a

HISTORY

lot of paste-drenched newspaper plastered on balloons drying in a corner of the kitchen. I can't think what we're going to do for horns; everything we've tried so far makes the helmets look like alien space gear.

Continued reading The Story of Leif Ericson.

◆ October 22, 1990

Discussed the origins of the names of the days of the week—many of them Norse. Read more Norse myths in D'Aulaire's Norse Gods and Giants. *Made weeklong calendars on which each day has a label and a more or less appropriate historical illustration. Ethan's "Sunday" includes a lot of doomed rocket ships plunging into the sun; Josh's entire calendar is labeled using the runic alphabet.*

We finished the Viking helmets, which (1) don't fit very well, and (2) have paper cones for horns, which aren't very satisfactory because they don't curve. Over the weekend, however, Randy helped the boys make and paint wooden Viking swords, which look wonderful and compensated for the helmet failure.

Also finished The Story of Leif Ericson.

◆ October 23, 1990

Identified Viking countries (Norway, Sweden, Denmark, Iceland, Greenland) on the world map; colored and/or labeled them on an outline map. Traced the routes of the voyages of Eric the Red and Leif Ericson on the maps, adding illustrations of dragon boats and sea monsters. Discussed the deceptiveness of the name Greenland *and why Eric the Red came up with it. Josh: "Who owns Greenland now? Does anybody live there?"*

Made a timeline showing the period when the Vikings lived and marking Leif Ericson's discovery of Vinland.

Discussed Viking skalds and sagas, and Josh wrote a short, but action-packed saga of his own, which he and his brothers plan to act out (with recitation and sword fights) this evening when their father gets home.

Started Clyde Bulla's Viking Adventure *(see page 628).*

◆ October 24, 1990

The boys collaborated on making and playing a Viking board game, marked out in squares on a piece of poster board and illustrated with felt-tipped markers. Players, all Viking warriors, hop their pieces from a Viking village in Norway to a new settlement in Greenland, with a stop-off in the middle at Iceland. En route they encounter numerous disasters (storms, sharks, pirates, blizzards, fog, ice) that cause them to move back spaces; whoever lands on a space with a pictured sword has a battle with another player; and if you land on the fatal Your Ship Sinks space, you go back to the beginning and start all over again.

Finished Viking Adventure.

BOOKS

10
13
Braving the North Atlantic: The Vikings, the Cabots, and Jacques Cartier Voyage to America
Delno C. West and Jean M. West; Atheneum, 1996

A history of North Atlantic crossings from the sixth to the 17th century, covering the voyages of such explorers as Saint Brendan, Leif Eriksson, John Cabot and his son, Sebastian, Jacques Cartier, Martin Frobisher, and Henry Hudson. Illustrated with maps, paintings, prints, reproductions of manuscripts, and photographs of archaeological sites and artifacts. For readers aged 10–13.

6
10
Eric the Red and Leif the Lucky
Barbara Schiller; Troll Associates, 1979

A 48-page biography of the famous father and son, from Eric's discovery of Greenland to Leif's early 11th-century voyage to Vinland. For readers aged 6–10.

9
+
Harald the Ruthless: The Saga of the Last Viking Warrior
Andrea Hopkins; Henry Holt, 1996

Harald the Ruthless was a real person who lived from A.D. 1015–1066; his exploits were first recorded by Snorri Sturluson of Iceland around 1230. The book gives readers the broad outlines of the original saga, illustrated in black and white, with liberal spatters of blood red. This looks like a picture book, but the activities of Harald, who really was ruthless, are too violent for very young readers.

How We Know About the Vikings
9 12 Louise James; Peter Bedrick Books, 1997

An overview of Viking life and customs, showing how our picture of the Viking past has been pieced together using evidence from archaeological excavations. For readers aged 9–12.

How Would You Survive as a Viking?
9 13 Jacqueline Morley; Franklin Watts, 1996

Readers travel back in time to A.D. 1000 in the days of the Vikings. The text, heavily illustrated with many captioned drawings and diagrams, tells all about Viking life. A quiz at the end of the book gives kids a chance to find out how well they would have survived in Viking times. For readers aged 9–13.

See *How Would You Survive? Series* (page 599).

Leif's Saga
5 9 Jonathan Hunt; Simon & Schuster, 1996

An appealing (and informational) picture book in which a boat-building Norse father tells his redheaded little daughter the story of explorer Leif Eriksson and his trip to North America. Colorful illustrations show many details of Viking life. For readers aged 5–9.

Viking
9 12 Susan M. Margeson; Alfred A. Knopf, 1994

This volume in the Eyewitness series presents an overview of Viking history and culture through a superb series of photographs of museum artifacts and reproductions. Each double-page spread concentrates on a different aspect of Viking life. Titles include, for example, "A Viking Warship," "Viking Warriors," "A Viking Fort," "Discovering New Lands," "Women and Children," "In the Workshop," "Gods and Legends," "Runes and Picture Stones," and "Viking Burials."

The Vikings
9 14 *Calliope;* November/December 1992

This issue of *Calliope,* Cobblestone's "World History" magazine (see page 597), centers around the Vikings. Included are nonfiction articles on Viking history and culture, a Viking legend, instructions for making a Viking board game, and stories about archaeological techniques used at Viking sites, plus timelines, maps, and word puzzles.

Available from libraries or for $4.50 from
Cobblestone Publishing, Inc.
30 Grove St.
Peterborough, NH 03458-1454
(603) 924-7209 or (800) 821-0115/fax (603) 924-7380
e-mail: custsvc@cobblestone.mv.com
Web site: www.cobblestonepub.com

The Vikings
6 8 Ruth Thomson; Children's Press, 1995

One of the Footprints in Time series (see page 599), this colorfully illustrated 24-page book, recommended for kids in grades 2–3, includes a brief history of the Vikings and their culture, along with detailed instructions for related hands-on crafts and projects. For example, readers can make a model Viking longship, a decorated Viking brooch, and a cardboard Viking helmet.

Viking Adventure
7 10 Clyde Robert Bulla; Thomas Y. Crowell, 1963

Young Sigurd, excited by his father's tales of Leif Eriksson, goes on a dangerous journey to Wineland in North America. A 117-page chapter book in biggish print for intermediate readers.

Who Came to America Before Columbus?
9 14 *Cobblestone;* October 1984

This issue of *Cobblestone* magazine includes articles on early voyages of discovery that preceded Columbus, by the Chinese, the Irish, the Vikings, and the Welsh. For readers in grades 5–9.

Available from most libraries or for $4.50 from
Cobblestone Publishing, Inc.
30 Grove St.
Peterborough, NH 03459-1454
(603) 924-7209 or (800) 821-0115/fax (603) 924-7380
e-mail: custsvc@cobblestone.mv.com
Web site: www.cobblestonepub.com
For general information on *Cobblestone,* see page 449.

Who Discovered America?: Mysteries and Puzzles of the New World
7 11 Patricia Lauber; HarperCollins, 1992

Who did discover America? Early Irish monks, Chinese sailors, Viking explorers, Christopher Columbus,

HISTORY

or Stone Age hunters from Asia? An overview of the possibilities in several short chapters, for readers 7–11.

MYTHS AND LEGENDS

D'Aulaire's Norse Gods and Giants
ALL Ingri and Edgar Parin D'Aulaire; Delacorte Press, 1986

An illustrated collection of tales of the Norse gods, goddesses, and giants, from the creation of the world through Ragnarok (which ends with the last of the gods playing chess in a green meadow). Stories include "Freya's Wonderful Necklace," "The Theft of Thor's Hammer," and "The Death of Balder."

Favorite Norse Myths
9 12 Mary Pope Osborne; Scholastic, 1996

Straightforward retellings of classic Norse myths, with historical information about the myths and their sources, the sixth-century *Poetic* and *Prose Eddas*. The book is illustrated with beautiful full-color paintings. For kids aged 9–12.

Odin's Family: Myths of the Vikings
9 12 Neil Philip; Orchard Books, 1996

Stories from Norse mythology, including the tales of Odin, Loki, Thor, Frigg, and the fierce giants of Jotunheim, illustrated with colorful oil paintings.

Stolen Thunder: A Norse Myth
7 11 Shirley Climo; Clarion, 1994

A picture-book version of the traditional tale in which the Frost King steals Thor's magic hammer and refuses to return it until Freya, the beautiful goddess of love, consents to be his bride. Loki, the clever trickster god, persuades Thor to disguise himself as Freya and attend the wedding feast. For readers aged 7–11.

COLORING AND PAPER-CRAFTS BOOKS

Myths and Legends of the Vikings
6 + Black-line drawings of Viking heroes based on Old Norse art with a descriptive text.

$3.95
Bellerophon Books

36 Ancapa St.
Santa Barbara, CA 93101
(800) 253-9943

The Story of the Vikings Coloring Book
6 + Thirty-eight detailed drawings of Viking life, including everyday scenes in a Viking village, Viking ships and weapons, Erik the Red en route to Greenland, and the first meeting of the Vikings with the North American Indians, all with a brief accompanying text.

$2.95
Dover Publications, Inc.
31 E. Second St.
Mineola, NY 11501

Viking Ships
8 + A collection of full-color cardboard Viking ships to cut out and assemble, with instructions and accompanying explanatory text.

$5.95
Bellerophon Books
36 Ancapa St.
Santa Barbara, CA 93101
(800) 253-9943/fax (800) 965-8286

GAMES AND HANDS-ON ACTIVITIES

The Viking Game
8 + The "Viking Game" is a 1,500-year-old Scandinavian precursor of chess in which 37 black or white playing pieces, molded to look like the original game's miniature carved warriors, attack, evade, and/or defeat each other on a grid-patterned playing cloth. An included booklet gives historical background information about the game, which is beautifully made and strategically challenging. For two players aged 8 and up.

$60 from game stores or
Old Game Store
Rt. 11/30
Manchester Center, VT 05225
(802) 362-2756 or (800) 818-GAME
Web site: www.vtweb.com/oldgame

Vikings

A cooperative simulation in which kids, acting the parts of Viking characters (boys variously become Erik Bloodaxe, Canute the Fearless, or Sax the Manslayer; girls, Thorfina, Rurika, or Raghild), participate in a series of hands-on projects designed to teach Viking history and culture. They learn Viking runes, do a map project that delineates the Viking trade network, build a model dragon ship and decorate a Viking brooch, simulate the trials of lawbreakers before a meeting of the Althing, act out an Old Norse saga, and complete the unit in grand style by throwing a feast for a dead warrior at which the mourners recite their own skaldic poetry.

Simulation materials, packaged in a loose-leaf notebook, include daily lesson plans, maps, descriptions of Viking role identities for the players, reproducible student handouts, and a saga script. The simulation occupies a total of four to seven hours, is appropriate for kids in grades 6–10, and can incorporate 20 to 36 students, though it also adapts nicely to smaller groups.

$43

Interact

1825 Gillespie Way, #101

El Cajon, CA 92020-1095

(619) 448-1474 or (800) 359-0961/fax (619) 448-6722

or (800) 700-5093

Web site: www.interact-simulations.com

VIDEO

The Vikings

Glorious adventure set in ninth-century Norway and Britain, starring Ernest Borgnine as Ragnar, the Viking chieftain, Kirk Douglas as Einar, his son, Tony Curtis as Erik, the slave, and Janet Leigh as a British princess. The historical detail is precise and impressive: there are wonderful scenes of Viking village life, rowdy feasts, and sailing longships, and the movie ends with a spectacular Viking funeral in which a blazing dragon ship carries the body of a chieftain out to sea. There's no really graphic gore, but there are raids, brawls, battles, and lots of clashing swords. Tony Curtis gets his hand chopped off and Ernest Borgnine leaps into a wolf pit; viewers don't actually *see* anything but it's clear what's going on. The movie is recommended for "all ages," but parents of younger Viking watchers might want to preview this one first.

Available as a rental from most video stores or $19.98

Zenger Media

10200 Jefferson Blvd.

Box 802

Culver City, CA 90232-0802

(310) 839-2436 or (800) 421-4246/fax (310) 839-2249

or (800) 944-5432

e-mail: access@ZengerMedia.com

Web site: ZengerMedia.com/Zenger

or

Movies Unlimited

3015 Darnell Rd.

Philadelphia, PA 19154

(215) 637-4444 or (800) 4-MOVIES

e-mail: movies@moviesunlimited.com

Web site: www.moviesunlimited.com

THE VIKINGS ON-LINE

The Viking Network Web

All about the Vikings, with lots of text, a few pictures, and a video clip of a Viking sword fight.

odin.nls.no/viking/vnethome.htm

Viking Voyage 1000

The site centers around a modern-day attempt to replicate a Viking voyage that took place in A.D. 1000. The site includes photographs of the ship, a map of the voyage, and numerous activities for kids, including a game in which players become honorary Viking captains, a mapping activity, and a writing project in which kids write a Viking saga using the included Viking vocabulary list.

www.viking1000.org

The World of Vikings

A wealth of information about Viking life, including color photos of Viking reenactors, pages on the runic alphabet, Viking ships, and Viking sagas, links to museums with Viking exhibits, and more.

www.pastforward.co.uk/vikings/index.html

HISTORY

THE MIDDLE AGES

BOOKS: NONFICTION

Anno's Medieval World
Mitsumasa Anno; Philomel Books, 1990

Wonderfully detailed illustrations show many faces of medieval life, from the castle to the village to the shipyard, each surrounded by an elaborate illuminated border. The accompanying text discusses the beliefs common in the Middle Ages, and the slow and gradual discovery that the world is round, rotates on its axis, and revolves around the sun. A picture book for all ages.

Armor
Charlotte Yue and David Yue; Houghton Mifflin, 1994

A history of armor from the fall of the Roman Empire through the 16th century, covering the different types of armor and how they were made, how a knight got dressed, and how armor functioned to protect its wearer in battle. The book also answers such crucial questions as how a knight managed to pee once his armor was on. (Our kids all asked.) For readers aged 8–12.

Bibles and Bestiaries: A Guide to Illuminated Manuscripts
Elizabeth B. Wilson; Farrar, Straus & Giroux, 1994

A 64-page introduction to medieval bookmaking for readers in grade 4 and up, illustrated with marvelous full-color photographs of illuminated manuscripts from the Pierpont Morgan Library collection. See **Testament** video series (page 605).

Castle
David MacAulay; Houghton Mifflin, 1982

An enthralling tale of medieval architecture. King Edward I of England, in March, 1283, sends Lord Kevin le Strange to build a castle and town in northeastern Wales. The great building project, from initial plan to final completion, is precisely detailed through a combination of interesting text and wonderful pen-and-ink drawings and diagrams. Also see Macauley's *Cathedral* (1973) which follows the building of a French cathedral, starting in 1252.

Video versions of the books are also available (see page 644).

Cobblestone: The Middle Ages
Calliope, the world history magazine for students in grades 5–9 (see page 597), has several issues with medieval themes, among them *The First Crusades* (January 1995), *Defenders of France* (March 1992), and *Early Christianity* (March 1996). Each includes illustrated fiction and nonfiction articles, maps, timelines, activities, and reading lists. Also see *Faces* magazine (page 411), *Castles and Palaces* (March 1995) for readers in grades 4–8.

Available from most libraries or for $4.50 from
Cobblestone Publishing, Inc.
30 Grove St.
Peterborough, NH 03458-1454
(603) 924-7209 or (800) 821-0115
Web site: www.cobblestonepub.com

The Duke and the Peasant: Life in the Middle Ages
Sister Wendy Beckett; International Book Import Service, 1997

Medieval art, history, and daily life. The book centers around 12 paintings—one for each month of the year—from the medieval *Book of Hours* of Jean, Duc de Berry. Full-page color reproductions of the paintings are paired with a chatty text explaining the pictured activities and stressing the differences between the lives of the peasants and the nobles. For readers aged 8–12.

Eyewitness Series: Middle Ages
Alfred A. Knopf

Volumes in the Eyewitness series that deal with medieval topics include *Arms and Armor*, *Castle*, *Knight*, and *Medieval Life*. Each book is 64 pages long, crammed with full-color illustrations and photographs of museum artifacts and historical reenactors in period costumes. The pictures are terrific; most of the text is in the picture captions.

I Wonder Why Castles Had Moats and Other Questions About Long Ago

Philip Steele; Kingfisher Books, 1997

An illustrated introduction to medieval life for kids aged 5–9, written in a friendly question-and-answer format.

Illuminations

Jonathan Hunt; Bradbury Press, 1993

An illuminated alphabet book of the Middle Ages. Letters, based on a 12th-century alphabet, introduce 26 words related to medieval culture and history, from alchemist to zither. (*B* is for Black Death.)

Nexus: The Lion in Winter and the Middle Ages

The Fall 1995 issue of *Nexus,* the magazine that connects learning to a common literary core (see page 78), features James Goldman's *The Lion in Winter,* a play based on the jockeyings of Eleanor and Henry's sons to inherit the throne of England. The magazine connects the play to a range of other topics, including articles on Gothic architecture, the Crusades, feudalism, the Magna Carta, troubadors and Gregorian chants, falconry, courtly love and the medieval love poets, holy relics, medieval medicine, Arab astronomy, and the physics of the crossbow.

Back issues, $6

Nexus

5017 Archmere Ave.

Cleveland, OH 44144

Also see *The Lion in Winter* video (page 644).

Outrageous Women of the Middle Ages

Vicki Leon; John Wiley & Sons, 1998

Medieval history with a feminist twist. The book profiles independent-minded, unusual, and outrageous women of the Middle Ages from all around the world: Europe, the Middle East, Africa, and Asia. Featured are 14 feisty women, among them Aud the Deep-Minded of Norway, who led her people on a dangerous sea journey from Ireland to Iceland; Eleanor of Aquitaine, who accompanied her first husband to the Crusades; and Lady Murasaki of Japan, author of *The Tale of Genji,* the world's first novel.

By the same author, also see *Uppity Women of Medieval Times* (Conari Press, 1997). *Outrageous Women* is targeted at readers aged 10 and up; *Uppity Women* is more appropriate for older readers aged 13 and up.

See *Outrageous Women of Ancient Times* and *Uppity Women of Ancient Times* (page 610).

Stephen Biesty's Cross-Sections: Castle

Richard Platt; Dorling Kindersley, 1994

The anatomy of a 14th-century castle, with Stephen Biesty's exquisitely detailed illustrations. The castle is shown in slices, allowing readers a fascinating view of the way medieval buildings work. For all ages.

See **Castle Explorer** software (page 645).

The Story of a Castle

John S. Goodall; McElderry/Macmillan, 1986

A wordless picture book that traces 800 years in the life of a castle, from its construction as a Norman fortress to the present day. Also by Goodall in similar format: *The Story of an English Village* (McElderry/Macmillan, 1979), which wordlessly traces changes in an English village from medieval times to the present; and *Above and Below the Stairs* (McElderry/Macmillan, 1983), which contrasts the everyday lives of upper (above the stairs) and lower (below the stairs) classes from the Middle Ages to modern times.

The Truth About Castles

Gillian Clements; Carolrhoda, 1990

An information-packed picture book all about castles, with many cleverly captioned, comical little drawings. Readers learn the distinctions among motte and bailey castles, stone keeps, and concentric castles, find out how castles were built, and learn about daily life in and around castles. For readers aged 5–9.

When Plague Strikes: The Black Death, Smallpox, and AIDS

James Cross Giblin; HarperCollins, 1995

The book covers three of history's deadliest epidemics: bubonic plague, which—known as the "Black Death"—killed a third of the population of Europe in the mid-1300s; smallpox, finally brought under control in the 19th century by Edward Jenner's lifesaving vaccine; and AIDS, the lethal and rapidly spreading disease of the 20th century. In each case, Giblin covers the causes, treatments, and social repercussions of the disease. For readers aged 11–14.

The World in the Time of Marco Polo
Fiona Macdonald; Dillon Press, 1997

What was going on in the world when Marco Polo set out on his 13th-century journey to distant Cathay? The English and French had just embarked upon the Hundred Years' War, the Anasazi were abandoning the pueblo cities of the American Southwest, the Byzantine Empire was at the height of its power, Mansa Musa ruled Mali, and the Mongols were conquering China. Macdonald describes Marco Polo's landmark journey and its historical context and explains concurrent happenings in seven other regions of the world. Heavily illustrated with maps, paintings, and photographs of artifacts. For readers aged 9–13.

See *Marco Polo: His Notebook* (page 654).

Books: Fiction

Adam of the Road
Elizabeth Janet Gray; Puffin, 1988

Eleven-year-old Adam is a minstrel, traveling the roads of 13th-century England with his father and his red spaniel, Nick. Then disaster strikes: Nick is stolen; Adam and his father are separated; and Adam is left to make his own way in the world. His adventures give a rich and fascinating picture of medieval life. There's also a happy ending. Recommended for readers aged 8–12.

The Black Arrow
Robert Louis Stevenson; Atheneum, 1987

High adventure in the 15th century, in the days of the War of the Roses. Young Dick Shelton, betrayed by his evil guardian, joins forces with John Amend-All, leader of the secret Fellowship of the Black Arrow. By the book's end, he has survived a shipwreck, fought in a great battle on behalf of Dick Crookback—soon to be King Richard III of England—and won the hand of a fair lady. For readers aged 12 and up.

The Canterbury Tales
Adapted by Geraldine McCaughrean; Oxford University Press, 1995

A retelling of Geoffrey Chaucer's famous *Canterbury Tales,* written in the late 14th century. The stories, abbreviated and rewritten in a language accessible to young readers, still retain the flavor of the originals. Included are 13 tales, among them versions of "The Knight's Tale," "The Nun's Priest's Tale," "The Wife of Bath's Tale," and "The Pardoner's Tale." With color illustrations.

Catherine, Called Birdy
Karen Cushman; Houghton Mifflin, 1994

The year is 1290; Catherine, aged 14, is due to be married, and her father's choices please her not at all. The story is told in Catherine's own words, in the form of a diary; readers learn not only about Catherine herself but also much about daily life in the Middle Ages. "12th Day of September," Catherine crossly begins. "I am commanded to write an account of my days: I am bit by fleas and plagued by my family." Recommended for readers aged 12 and up. By the same author set in the same era: *The Midwife's Apprentice* (HarperTrophy, 1996).

The Door in the Wall
Marguerite De Angeli; Yearling, 1990

Young Robin, the son of a nobleman in 14th-century London in the days of the great plague, is crippled. He knows, with his useless legs, that he will never be a knight like his father, who is presently away in Scotland, fighting with the king's army. Robin is taken in by the monks of St. Mark's and comes under the tutelage of the wise Brother Luke, who tells him, "Thou hast only to follow the wall far enough and there will be a door in it." Robin comes to understand what Brother Luke means as he finds, at last, his own door—and, in finding it, becomes a hero.

Harold the Herald: A Book About Heraldry
Dana Fradon; Dutton Children's Books, 1990

A talking suit of armor (once the property of Sir Dana of Domania) tells the story of Harold, born in London in the year 1342. Harold grows up, becomes a page, and eventually attains his goal of becoming a herald to Prince Lionel. Readers, along with Harold, learn the language and symbols of heraldry—there are colorful diagrams of all the basic symbols used on coats of arms—and pick up a lot of information about everyday life in a medieval castle.

The King's Fool: A Book About Medieval and Renaissance Fools
8–12

Dana Fradon; E. P. Dutton, 1993

A statue of a Renaissance court fool hops down from a glass museum case to tell a class of visiting kids about the history of court jesters. The book includes general historical information about the life and times of the kings' fools and many stories about famous jesters—among them Will Sommers, fool to Queen Elizabeth I. The book is illustrated with many colorful and humorous drawings, plus comic asides and historical footnotes. For readers aged 8–12.

Knight's Castle
8–12

Edward Eager; Harcourt Brace, 1989

Four children find themselves magically transported to the days of Ivanhoe, where they take part in the siege of the castle of Torquilstone and considerably improve the ending of Sir Walter Scott's famous story. This humorous and exciting tale inspired our oldest son to read the original *Ivanhoe*.
See the video version of **Ivanhoe** (page 644).

A Medieval Feast
5–9

Aliki; HarperTrophy, 1986

The king is coming to visit, and the lord of Camdenton Manor and his servants must make elaborate preparations for a feast. A lot of historical information in storybook form, with colorful and detailed medieval-style illustrations (including one of blackbirds flying out of a pie). For readers aged 5–9.

Medieval Monk
9–12

Giovanni Caselli; Peter Bedrick Books, 1986

The life and times of the medieval monasteries, through the story of a young boy's first months as a member of a 12th-century Benedictine order. For readers aged 9–12.

Merry Ever After: The Story of Two Medieval Weddings
5–9

Joe Lasker; Puffin, 1976

A delightful picture of medieval life told through the contrasting celebrations of two weddings, one in the castle, the other in the peasant village. For readers aged 5–9.

A Proud Taste for Scarlet and Miniver
9–13

E. L. Konigsburg; Yearling, 1985

The fictionalized story of Queen Eleanor of Aquitaine, first married to Louis VI of France, with whom she traveled to Constantinople on the Second Crusade, and then to Henry II of England. (With Henry, she had seven children, including Richard the Lionhearted and John Lackland, who reputedly gave Robin Hood so much trouble.) The action begins with Eleanor in heaven, impatiently waiting to see whether Henry, after 800 years in hell, is finally going to make it Up. A clever and fascinating tale for readers aged 9–13.

Puck of Pook's Hill
10+

Rudyard Kipling; Puffin, 1987

The enchanting British classic in which young Dan and Una, acting out *A Midsummer Night's Dream* in a Sussex meadow, summon up Puck himself, the Oldest of the Old. Through Puck, the children meet and hear the tales of people from old English history: Sir Richard, whose father came to England in the train of William the Conqueror; Parnesius, a centurion of the Thirtieth Legion, sent to guard Hadrian's Wall; and the Renaissance craftsman Hal o' the Draft. For readers aged 10 and up.

The Ramsay Scallop
12+

Frances Temple; HarperTrophy, 1995

The year is 1299, and 14-year-old Elenor's betrothed, Thomas, is on his way home from a crusade to the Holy Land. Elenor has no wish to marry; neither, it turns out, does Thomas, not yet recovered from the horrors and disillusionments of war. The wise old village priest, Father Gregory, sends the pair on a pilgrimage to Spain, in the course of which the two young people find healing, understanding, and love. They also learn much from the other members of their pilgrim band who tell their stories as they travel—a fascinating and varied collection of people, among them a Muslim and an Albigensian heretic. For readers aged 12 and up.

The Reluctant Dragon
ALL Kenneth Grahame; Holiday House, 1989

Our favorite version of the Saint George story will always be Kenneth Grahame's gentle version, which features an intelligent and poetic dragon, an understanding and tolerant saint, and a wholly bloodless battle. A classic for all ages.

Also see *Saint George and the Dragon* (below).

Roland the Minstrel Pig
4 8 William Steig; Simon & Schuster, 1988

A talented lute-playing pig sets off for the king's castle to make his fortune. On the way, he runs into trouble with a musically appreciative (but very hungry) fox. For readers aged 4–8.

Saint George and the Dragon
5 9 Margaret Hodges; Little, Brown, 1990

The tale of George's legendary battle with the dragon, based on Spenser's *Faerie Queen*. The illustrations resemble those in illuminated medieval manuscripts. For readers aged 5–9.

See *The Reluctant Dragon* (above).

Sir Dana: A Knight, As Told
8 12 by his Trusty Armor

Dana Fradon; E. P. Dutton, 1988

Miss Quincy's class, visiting the medieval room of the museum, encounters a 600-year-old talking suit of armor who tells about the life of its former owner, Sir Dana of Domania. The armor answers questions from the kids: "What's a squire?" "What is chivalry?" "Could a girl be a knight? Was Joan of Arc a knight?" "Tell us something about castles." "What did Sir Dana eat?" "Did Sir Dana ever kill a dragon?" Lots of information about life as a medieval knight, with delightful cartoon-style illustrations, which isn't surprising since the author is a cartoonist for *The New Yorker*.

A String in the Harp
10 13 Nancy Bond; Aladdin, 1996

Young Peter Morgan finds an ancient tuning key to a harp on the beach; the key transports him back to sixth-century Wales, where he becomes caught up in the life of the bard Taliesin. For readers aged 10–13.

A Tournament of Knights
7 10 Joe Lasker; HarperCollins, 1989

Justin, a young knight, is about to enter his first tournament, where he hopes to save the family fortunes. Lots of information about medieval tournaments, wonderful pictures, and a triumphant conclusion. For readers aged 7–10.

TALES OF KING ARTHUR

BOOKS

Camelot
9 12 Jane Yolen, ed.; Philomel Books, 1995

A collection of 11 strange and fantastic Arthurian stories by 11 master storytellers. In one of them, Uther Pendragon's heir turns out to be a daughter. For readers aged 9–12.

The Crystal Cave
13 + Mary Stewart; Ballantine, 1996

Set in fifth-century Britain, the spellbinding tale of Merlin, from his childhood through his role in the begetting of the baby who would be King Arthur. Sequels, which continue the King Arthur legend, include *The Hollow Hills*, *The Last Enchantment*, and *This Wicked Day*. For teenagers.

The Dark Is Rising Series
10 + Susan Cooper; Aladdin, 1993

There are five books in this superb series based on the King Arthur mythos. Titles are *Over Sea, Under Stone; Greenwitch; The Dark Is Rising; The Grey King;* and *Silver on the Tree*. In the first, *Over Sea, Under Stone*, the three Drew children, Barney, Jane, and Simon, discover an ancient map in the attic of an old house in Cornwall that provides clues to the whereabouts of King

Arthur's long-lost Grail. The story continues in subsequent volumes: in each the theme is the battle between the forces of good and evil, carried on through time.

King Arthur and the Knights of the Round Table

Marcia Williams; Candlewick, 1996

The legend of King Arthur told comic-strip fashion, with voice balloons, text captions, and delightful little illustrations. Each double-page spread is a minichapter. Titles include "Excalibur," "Morgan Le Fay," "Lancelot and Elaine," and "Merlin." For kids aged 6–10.

The Kitchen Knight: A Tale of Arthur

Margaret Hodges; Holiday House, 1993

The picture-book tale of young Gareth, who begins his career as a scullery boy in the castle kitchen, is given permission to go on a quest (to free a damsel in distress), succeeds gloriously, and becomes one of King Arthur's greatest knights. For readers aged 6–9.

Knights of the Kitchen Table

Jon Scieszka; Puffin, 1994

The giggle-provoking tale of the Time Warp Trio, three inventive kids who—by means of a magical book—end up in the time of King Arthur, where they defeat an ominous Black Knight and a giant, and unwisely lob a baseball through Merlin's tower window. For readers aged 8–11.

Light Beyond the Forest: The Quest for the Holy Grail

Rosemary Sutcliff; Puffin, 1994

A trilogy based on the King Arthur legend by Rosemary Sutcliff, who writes a terrific and very authentic historical novel. The first volume, *Light Beyond the Forest*, tells of the quest for the Holy Grail. *Sword and the Circle: King Arthur and the Knights of the Round Table* includes the legends of Sir Gawain and the Green Knight, Lancelot and Elaine, Tristan and Iseult, and Sir Percival; *The Road to Camlann: The Death of King Arthur* tells the tales of Launcelot and Guinevere,

Arthur's son Mordred, the last battle, and the magical land of Avalon. For readers aged 11 and up.

The Once and Future King

T. H. White; Ace Books, 1996

A glorious version of the King Arthur legend, told in four parts: "The Sword in the Stone," "The Queen of Air and Darkness," "The Ill-Made Knight," and "A Candle in the Wind." The first part of the book, "The Sword in the Stone," the tale of Arthur's childhood in the household of Sir Ector, his meeting with Merlin, and his strange and wonderful (and thought-provoking) education, ending with his coronation, is most accessible to young readers and is available separately. "The Sword in the Stone" has also been made into an animated Disney film, which, unlike the book, is cute and silly. *The Once and Future King* in its entirety is complex, powerful, dramatic, funny, tragic, and heartrending. For mature readers.

GAMES AND HANDS-ON ACTIVITIES

Origami in King Arthur's Court

Lew Rozelle; St. Martin's Press, 1997

Detailed instructions for making a terrific origami castle, complete with drawbridge and towers, the king and his court, Merlin's dragon, knights and horses, and assorted royal furniture, including a banquet table and a throne.

Quests of the Round Table

An "adventure card game" based on the King Arthur legend. Players, using three packs of beautifully illustrated cards, set out on an assigned quest (for example, "Slay the Dragon" or "Rescue the Fair Maiden"). Picks from the packs variously provide assistance or threaten disaster. The "Sir Lancelot," "Merlin," and "Excalibur" cards, for example, help you on your way; "Thieves," "Saxons," or "Robber Knight" may block your quest. Successful questers attain knighthood and a seat at Arthur's Round Table. Recommended for two to four players, aged 10 and up.

$24.95 from toy and game stores or

Worldwide Games

Box 517

Colchester, CT 06415-0517

(800) 888-0987/fax (800) 566-6678

e-mail: service@snswwide.com

Web site: www.worldwidegames.com

AUDIOVISUAL RESOURCES

Camelot

9 + A video version of the Lerner and Loewe musical, with lots of medieval panoply, starring Richard Harris and Vanessa Redgrave.

$29.95

Movies Unlimited

3015 Darnell Rd.

Philadelphia, PA 19154

(215) 637-4444 or (800) 4-MOVIES

e-mail: movies@moviesunlimited.com

Web site: www.moviesunlimited.com

King Arthur and His Knights

ALL Legends of King Arthur on audiocassette or CD, beautifully told by our favorite storyteller, Jim Weiss. Stories include "The Sword in the Stone," "King Arthur," "Guinevere," "Sir Percival Meets a Lady," "The Round Table," "Sir Lancelot's Journey," "A Queen," "Sir Bedivere," and "Merlin's Magic." For listeners of all ages.

Cassette, $9.95; CD, $14.95

Greathall Productions

Box 5061

Charlottesville, VA 22905-5061

(800) 477-6234

Knights of the Round Table

9 + The tale of Arthur from the founding of the Round Table to the last tragic battle. A 1953 movie production in grand style, with Mel Ferrer and Ava Gardner.

$19.98

Movies Unlimited

3015 Darnell Rd.

Philadelphia, PA 19154

(215) 637-4444 or (800) 4-MOVIES

e-mail: movies@moviesunlimited.com

Web site: www.moviesunlimited.com

KING ARTHUR ON-LINE

Avalon

12 + The site is devoted to the historical and mythical king, with links to related resources, among them the script of the Monty Python's Arthurian spoof, *Monty Python and the Search for the Holy Grail.*

Reality.sgi.com/employees/chris_manchester /guide.html

The Camelot Project

12 + Information about each of the major characters in the King Arthur legends (listed in alphabetical order), the symbols and motifs of the legends (including the Holy Grail and Excalibur), and the major locations mentioned, as well as texts of the legends and a gallery of King Arthur illustrations by various artists.

rodent.lib.rochester.edu/camelot

TALES OF ROBIN HOOD

BOOKS

The Outlaws of Sherwood

12 + Robin McKinley; Greenwillow, 1988

A rich and detailed retelling of the Robin Hood legend, from young Robin's early days in Sherwood Forest through his father's death, the assembly of his outlaw band of companions, and his battles with the Sheriff of Nottingham. Finally there's the happy ending, with the return of King Richard the Lionhearted and Robin's marriage to Maid Marian. For readers aged 12 and up.

Robin Hood

7 12 Sarah Hayes; Henry Holt, 1989

An adventurous collection of Robin Hood tales, beginning with Robin's rescue from Prince John's men by Will Scarlet, his joining of the outlaw band in Sherwood Forest, his meetings with Little John, Friar Tuck, and minstrel Alan A'Dale, and his defeat of the wretched Sheriff of Nottingham. Recommended for readers aged 7–12.

Audiovisual Resources

The Adventures of Robin Hood

For older viewers, several versions of the Robin Hood story are available on video. Our favorite continues to be *The Adventures of Robin Hood* (1938), in which Robin is played by the swashbuckling Errol Flynn and Maid Marian by Olivia de Haviland. It sticks nicely to the traditional story, complete with sword fights, flaming arrows, a villainous Sheriff, and a dramatic happy ending.

$19.99

Movies Unlimited

3015 Darnell Rd.

Philadelphia, PA 19154

(215) 637-4444 or (800) 4-MOVIES

e-mail: movies@moviesunlimited.com

Web site: www.moviesunlimited.com

Robin Hood

For youngest viewers, Disney has produced as animated cartoon version of Robin Hood in which all of the characters are animals. Alan A'Dale, who introduces the film, is a singing chicken, Robin and Marian are foxes, Little John, a bear, and Prince John, a whining lion. It's attractively done and most kids love it.

$24.99

Movies Unlimited

3015 Darnell Rd.

Philadelphia, PA 19154

(215) 637-4444 or (800) 4-MOVIES

e-mail: movies@moviesunlimited.com

Web site: www.moviesunlimited.com

The Three Musketeers and Robin Hood

A delightful collection of traditional tales on audiocassette or CD by master storyteller Jim Weiss. Story titles include "The Queen's Diamonds," "Robin and Little John," and "Lady Marion." Wiess's presentation captures all of the excitement and interest of the stories without the violence.

Cassette, $9.95; CD, $14.95

Greathall Productions

Box 5061

Charlottesville, VA 22905-5061

(800) 477-6234

Robin Hood On-Line

Robin Hood: Bold Outlaw of Sherwood

A history of Robin Hood and his legend, a picture gallery of Robin Hood images, interviews with Robin Hood scholars, authors, and actors, a collection of Robin Hood stories and songs, and a discussion forum.

geocities.com/Athens/Acropolis/4198/rhood.html

Robin Hood on the Web

Information about the historical Robin Hood and his times, his Merry Men, Sherwood Forest and its surroundings, and folktales and ballads about Robin Hood. Visitors to the site also have an opportunity to write their own Robin Hood legends.

www.benturner.com/robinhood

Coloring and Paper-Crafts Books

Castles to Cut Out & Put Together

A paper project book with which kids can construct the Tower of London and Richard the Lionhearted's Chateau Gaillard.

$5.95

Bellerophon Books

36 Ancapa St.

Santa Barbara, CA 93101

(800) 253-9943/fax (800) 965-8286

A Coloring Book of the Middle Ages

Detailed black-line portraits of such key medieval figures as King Arthur, Sir Lancelot, Charlemagne, William the Conqueror, and Richard the Lionhearted, each with a brief explanatory text. Also see the *Chaucer Coloring Book,* which includes scenes from *The Canterbury Tales,* and *A Medieval Alphabet to Illuminate,* which contains reproductions of elaborately decorated letters from medieval manuscripts, from *A* to *Z,* simplified for coloring.

$2.95

Bellerophon Books

36 Ancapa St.

Santa Barbara, CA 93101

(800) 253-9943/fax (800) 965-8286

Costumes to Color: Knights and Ladies

Jenny Williams and Martha Bushko; Grossett & Dunlap, 1996

Detailed black-line drawings of knights and ladies to color, with one to two short paragraphs of text on the reverse side of each page, explaining the pictured scene and giving interesting details about medieval history.

Cut & Assemble a Medieval Castle

Make a card-stock replica of Caernavon Castle in Wales. The book includes all the pieces and instructions for cutting, folding, and assembling.

$6.95

Dover Publications, Inc.

31 E. Second St.

Mineola, NY 11503

Cut and Make a Knight in Armor

Kids can construct a 13½-inch tall suit of armor, complete with lance and helmet. Also see *Cut and Make a Knight's Helmet,* with which kids can build a full-size steel-colored cardboard replica of a closed-visor 15th-century helmet.

Knight in Armor, $4.95; *Knight's Helmet,* $3.95

Dover Publications, Inc.

31 E. Second St.

Mineola, NY 11503

Knights in Armor Paper Dolls

Knights in Armor Paper Dolls includes two (flat) knights and eight historically accurate sets of armor. Also see *Medieval Knights Paper Soldiers* with 22 full-color figures to cut and assemble (once completed, they stand up) and *Medieval Costumes Paper Dolls,* which includes two dolls and 16 elaborate 13th-century costumes.

$4.95

Dover Publications, Inc.

31 E. Second St.

Mineola, NY 11503

Life in a Medieval Castle and Village Coloring Book

Over 40 scenes of medieval life, among them battles, hunts, tournaments, sieges, and images of peasants and craftspersons at work. Other coloring books with medieval themes include *Knights and Armor Coloring Book* and *Castles of the World Coloring Book*

$2.95

Dover Publications, Inc.

31 E. Second St.

Mineola, NY 11503

Paper Soldiers of the Middle Ages: The Crusades

A collection of freestanding armored knights to color and assemble. Also see *Paper Soldiers of the Middle Ages: The Hundred Years War.*

$4.95

Bellerophon Books

36 Ancapa St.

Santa Barbara, CA 93101

(800) 253-9943/fax (800) 965-8286

Stained-Glass Coloring Books

A medieval stained-glass experience through coloring books, in which the designs are printed on translucent paper such that, when colored and hung in a window, they acquire a stained-glass-like look. It's not quite as effective as the real thing, but it's cheaper. Books with medieval themes include the *Mythical Beasts Stained Glass Coloring Book* (Peter F. Copeland), *Cathedral Stained Glass Coloring Book* (Ed Sibbett Jr.), and the *Stained Glass Windows Coloring Book* (Paul Kennedy).

$3.95 apiece

Dover Publications, Inc.

31 E. Second St.

Mineola, NY 11501

The Ultimate Arms and Armor Sticker Book

Dorling Kindersley, 1994

Sixty reusable stickers—all marvelous full-color photographs of museum artifacts—to be matched to the proper outline and picture caption in the 8-page 8½ × 11-inch book.

$6.95 from bookstores or

Dorling Kindersley Publishing
1224 Heil Quaker Blvd.
LaVergne, TN 37086
(888) DIALDKP
Web site: www.dk.com

ACTIVITY BOOKS

Days of Knights and Damsels
Laurie Carlson; Chicago Review Press, 1998

An illustrated and information-filled activity book on the Middle Ages for kids aged 5–12. The book is divided into eight main sections: "Let's Dress Up," "Time to Eat," "Heraldry," "Fun & Games," "Write It Down," "Arts & Crafts," "Everyday Life," and "A House Is a Home." Included are over 100 suggestions for projects, activities, and games. Kids can make a suit of armor out of plastic milk cartons, bake raisin custard tarts or "4 & 20 Blackbird Pie," design a coat-of-arms, experiment with calligraphy, construct a sand glass, make a falcon puppet and a cardboard castle, and play a game of medieval-style draughts.

The Middle Ages
A self-directed learning unit containing activity and research project suggestions on medieval topics for students in either grades K–3 or 4–8. Sample activities include "Find out about the Magna Carta OR Marco Polo OR St. Francis of Assisi OR Attila the Hun OR Genghis Khan. Present 5 facts in a booklet, picture, or report"; "Find out about how young boys became knights. Pretend you are a young boy about to begin learning to be a knight. Keep a journal of your training from page to knight"; "Create a stained glass window, medieval banner, knight in armor, castle, or unicorn tapestry: your choice."

$18
Zephyr Press
3316 N. Chapel Ave.
Box 66006
Tucson, AZ 85732-6006
(800) 232-2187/fax (520) 323-9402
e-mail: neways2learn@zephyrpress.com
Web site: www.zephyrpress.com

Picture the Middle Ages
Linda Honan; Golden Owl/Higgins Armory Museum, 1994

An interactive curriculum for upper elementary and middle school–aged kids, crammed with illustrations, photographs, maps, diagrams, patterns (for costumes, helmets, breastplates, and shields), worksheets, games, musical scores, stories and poems, instructions for projects and activities, and a historical text. Included are a timeline of the medieval period and a pull-out poster (kids color it) picturing the four major medieval centers of population: the town, the castle, the monastery, and the manor.

The 142-page book provides all the information you need for an engrossing study unit on the Middle Ages. Chapter titles include "The Middle Ages: Historic View," "The Town: Craftsmen & Guilds," "The Castle: Lords & Ladies, Knights & Chivalry," "Heraldry & Coats of Arms," "The Monastery: Monks & Nuns," "The Manor: Farming, Food, & Feasting," "Making Costumes & Armor," "Music & Dance," "Artists & Art," and "Literature."

$24.95
Jackdaw Publications
Box 503
Amawalk, NY 10501
(914) 962-6911 or (800) 789-0022/fax (800) 962-9101

GAMES AND HANDS-ON ACTIVITIES

1066
A Jackdaw portfolio of primary source documents and supplementary materials (historical background essays, notes, reading lists, and study guides) centering around the Norman Conquest of England in 1066. Included in the historical materials are art prints taken from the Bayeux Tapestry, a copy of the first known painting of the Battle of Hastings, pictures comparing Saxon and Norman architecture, and pages on the crucial year 1066 from the *Anglo-Saxon Chronicle*.

Other portfolios with medieval themes include *Alfred the Great*, an overview of the ninth-century Anglo-Saxon king, who successfully defended England

HISTORY

from the invading Danes; the portfolio includes 14 facsimile historical documents, among them a map of Anglo-Saxon England, a picture sheet of Anglo-Saxon coins, pages from the *Lindisfarne Gospels* and the *Anglo-Saxon Chronicle,* and paper models of an Anglo-Saxon warship and the ninth-century church of St. Laurence.

Magna Carta centers around the landmark document signed so unwillingly by King John at Runnymede in 1215; the portfolio contains nine historical documents, including a facsimile of the original Magna Carta, pages from a 12th-century Bestiary, and photographs of King John's tomb.

The Black Death—a gruesome but educational portfolio—covers the devastating outbreak of bubonic plague that decimated Europe in the mid-1300s and its subsequent political and economic effects; the portfolio contains nine historical documents, among them an engraving titled *Dance of Death* and a plague banner.

The equally gruesome *Spanish Inquisition* details the activities of the powerful courts first established by the pope in the 13th century to stamp out heresy; included are eight historical documents, including an engraving of an auto-da-fé and an English ballad sheet titled "The Loyal Martyrs."

Portfolios, $37 each
Jackdaw Publications
Box 503
Amawalk, NY 10501
(914) 962-6911 or (800) 789-0022/fax (800) 962-9101

Cathedral

Subtitled "The Game of the Medieval City," this is an attractive strategy game in which the playing board represents a walled city of the Middle Ages. Players attempt to place their playing pieces—architecturally shaped hardwood blocks designed to resemble castles and cathedrals—in positions that allow them to capture increasing amounts of territory.

$64.95 from toy and game stores or
Family Games, Inc.
Box 97
Snowdon
Montreal, Quebec H3X 3T3 Canada
or

Turn Off the TV
Box 4162
Bellevue, WA 98009
(800) 949-8688/fax (425) 558-7564
Web site: www.turnoffthetv.com

Cathedrals, Abbeys & Minsters

A deck of 40 picture cards, each with a color photograph of a famous cathedral, abbey, or minster on the front; historical and architectural information about each structure is printed on the back.

$7
Aristoplay
450 S. Wagner Rd.
Ann Arbor, MI 48107
(800) 634-7738 or (888) GR8-GAME
fax (734) 995-4611
Web site: www.aristoplay.com

Christendom

A simulation of medieval history for kids in grades 6–10. Participants take on the role of a medieval character—lord, lady, knight, monk, serf, craftsperson, or Crusader—and then proceed through the eight phases of the simulation: "Feudalism," "Manorialism," "Knighthood," "Monastery," "Crusades," "Guilds," "Tapestry," and "Banquet." (There's an option for a test at the very end, called "Torture Chamber.") In "Feudalism," kids learn about castles and negotiate a feudal contract; in "Manorialism," they map a medieval fief and manor and build manor dwellings. In "Knighthood," they learn the rules of chivalry, set out on a quest, design a coat of arms, and compete in a tournament. "Monastery" involves a study of medieval religion; "Crusades," an expedition to the Holy Land. In "Guilds," kids become craftspersons; in "Tapestry," they produce their own medieval tapestries, on paper or canvas; and finally, in "Banquet," they throw a medieval feast, recite medieval poetry, and hear cases at the "Lord's Court." The unit is designed for 20 to 35 students, but it adapts well to smaller groups.

$43
Interact
1825 Gillespie Way, #101
El Cajon, CA 92020-1095

(619) 448-1474 or (800) 359-0961/fax (619) 448-6722
or (800) 700-5093

Web site: www.interactsimulations.com

Color Calligraphy Projects Workstation

Manda Hanson; Design Eye Holdings Ltd./Price Stern
Sloan, 1993

The kit includes a 48-page color-illustrated book
on the art of decorative calligraphy, two alphabets for
decorating, 16 pages of colored paper, stencils, templates, a calligraphy pen (with two nibs), a paintbrush,
4 tubes of watercolor paint, and a cake of shiny gold
paint. Introduces kids aged 8 and up to the techniques
used in making the illuminated manuscripts of the
Middle Ages and Renaissance.

$21.95 from bookstores

See **Calligraphy** resources (pages 115–116).

Eagle Kingdoms

This unusual and gorgeous game is based on a
medieval "bird shooting festival" and played on a gold-
and-purple felt banner illustrated with a very royal double eagle. The game includes 45 colored figures of
medieval characters on plastic stands (kings, queens,
duchesses, dukes, knights, minstrels, merchants, jesters,
tradespeople, and children) and 46 "eagle" puzzle pieces.
On each turn, players attempt to add pieces to the puzzle and to take possession of a medieval character. The
player with the most "captured" figures at the end of the
game wins, and is awarded the title "Bird Queen" or
"Bird King." For two to six players, aged 8 and up.

$24.95 from toy and game stores or

Turn Off the TV

Box 4162

Bellevue, WA 98009

(800) 949-8688/fax (425) 558-7564

Web site: www.turnoffthetv.com

Fun With Stained Glass

Mary B. Shepard and Fifi Weinert; Metropolitan
Museum of Art/Viking

This kit includes all the materials necessary for
making eight "stained-glass windows" based on
medieval and modern designs from objects in the collections of the Metropolitan Museum of Art. The
"windows" are sheets of acetate printed with black-line

pictures, to be painted with the included "special"
translucent paints. Stick the finished paintings in a
window, and when the light shines through them,
you'll get the effect of genuine stained glass. The kit
contains a 64-page detailed instruction book that
includes a history of stained glass.

$19.95

Metropolitan Museum of Art

255 Gracie Station

New York, NY 10028-9998

(800) 468-7386

Gargoyles

A kit with which users can produce their own
medieval-style gargoyles. Each kit contains materials
and tools for carving and painting two 7- to 9-inch-tall
foam-and-cardboard gargoyles. The foam is a stone-
colored and -textured polymer and looks pretty much
like the real thing. A great project for kids aged 8 and up.

$19.95 from toy and game stores; for a local source,
contact

Creativity for Kids

1802 Central Ave.

Cleveland, OH 44115-2325

(216) 589-4800 or (800) 642-2288

Knights and Castles

A board game for young aspiring knights. Players,
represented by brightly colored plastic knights, set off
on the castle-patterned "Questing Trail" as pages, rising
to the rank of squire and knight by correctly answering
questions about the medieval period from the 48
included "Chivalry Cards" and by winning jousts with
their opponents. For two to four players, aged 6 and up.

$25

Aristoplay

450 S. Wagner Rd.

Ann Arbor, MI 48107

(800) 634-7738 or (888) GR8-GAME

fax (734) 995-4611

Web site: www.aristoplay.com

Knights Treasure Chest

A high-quality activity kit for young medievalists,
packaged in a lockable treasure chest–shaped box.
The kit includes a 32-page book of instructions and

historical background information, a cardboard castle model, a build-it-yourself working catapult, framed "stained-glass" Gothic windows to color, a full-color map of medieval Europe, a poster of knights in armor, an impressive "royal proclamation," games to assemble and play, and a heraldic signet ring, plus sealing clay.

> $19.95 from book or game stores or
> Running Press Book Publishers
> 125 S. 22nd St.
> Philadelphia, PA 19103-4399
> (215) 567-5080 or (800) 345-5359/fax (800) 453-2884

A Medieval Fairy Tale Adventure Kit

This attractively packaged craft kit includes an oversize fairy-tale story-and-coloring book, plus all the materials and instructions necessary to make a pointed hennin hat (with floating veil), an amulet necklace, a musical wind wand, a potpourri pouch, and a felt flag bearing the maker's own heraldic device.

> $14.95 from toy and game stores; for a local source, contact
> Curiosity Kits
> Box 811
> 243 Cockeysville Rd.
> Cockeysville, MD 21030
> (410) 584-2605 or (800) 584-KITS/fax (410) 584-1247
> e-mail: CKitsinc@aol.com

Princess

A charming cooperative board game for the very young, in which players pass through green forests, blue mountains, yellow fields, and villages of little thatched cottages, collecting magical objects with which to free the captive princess in the castle in the middle of the board. Recommended for two to four players, aged 4–7.

> $15.95
> Turn Off the TV
> Box 4162
> Bellevue, WA 98009
> (800) 949-8688/fax (206) 889-8194
> Web site: www.turnoffthetv.com
> or
> PlayFair Toys
> Box 18210

Boulder, CO 80308
(800) 824-7255

Stained Glass Kit

With this kit, kids can try their hands at the medieval art of stained glass, making "stained-glass" panels using sheets of colorful acrylic "glass" and self-stick copper stripping. Each kit includes patterns and materials for making either one 4 × 6-inch and one $3\frac{1}{2} \times 4\frac{1}{2}$-inch panel or three $3\frac{1}{2} \times 4\frac{1}{2}$-inch panels. An included informational booklet discusses the history of stained glass.

> $16.95 from toy and game stores; for a local source, contact
> Curiosity Kits
> Box 811
> Cockeysville, MD 21030
> (410) 584-2605 or (800) 584-KITS/fax (410) 584-1247
> e-mail: CKitsinc@aol.com

VIDEOS

Becket

An impressive historical drama starring Richard Burton as the Thomas à Becket and Peter O'Toole as King Henry II. The king appoints Becket, his best friend, Archbishop of Canterbury in hopes of bringing the powerful church under the control of the crown; the friendship shatters and ultimately ends in murder when Becket's conscience clashes with the king's political policy. Our boys said it was wonderful, but too sad to watch twice. Not for very young viewers.

> Available as a rental from most video stores or for
> $59.95 from
> Movies Unlimited
> 3015 Darnell Rd.
> Philadelphia, PA 19154
> (215) 637-4444 or (800) 4-MOVIES
> e-mail: movies@moviesunlimited.com
> Web site: www.moviesunlimited.com

Brother Cadfael

Brother Cadfael—ex-Crusader, now a Benedictine monk at the Abbey of St. Peter and St. Paul in the 12th-

643

century town of Shrewsbury—is also a talented detective. The video series, starring Derek Jacobi as Brother Cadfael, is based on the medieval mysteries of Ellis Peters.

> *Brother Cadfael I* (four mysteries), $79.95; *Brother Cadfael II* (three mysteries), $59.95
> PBS Home Video
> 1320 Braddock Pl.
> Alexandria, VA 22314-1698
> (800) 645-4PBS
> Web site: www.pbs.org

Castle

Based on the book of the same name by David MacAulay (see page 631). The video combines narration, animation, and live-action footage to demonstrate—fascinatingly—the construction of a 13th-century Welsh castle. Also see *Cathedral,* in the same format, which follows the building of a French cathedral. Each video is 60 minutes long.

> $79.98 as part of a four-cassette set (with *Pyramid* and *Roman City*)
> PBS Home Video
> 1320 Braddock Pl.
> Alexandria, VA 22314-1698
> (800) 645-4PBS
> Web site: www.pbs.org
> or
> $19.98 each
> Zenger Media
> 10200 Jefferson Blvd.
> Box 802
> Culver City, CA 90232-0802
> (310) 839-2436 or (800) 421-4246/fax (310) 839-2249
> or (800) 944-5432
> e-mail: access@ZengerMedia.com
> Web site: ZengerMedia.com/Zenger

The Crusades

Hosted by medievalist Terry Jones of Monty Python fame, this terrific four-cassette series traces the 200-year history of the Crusades and their attendant social and economic consequences, using a clever combination of reenactments, computer animations, films on location, works of art that come to life, and "creative anachronisms." The entire series is about 200 minutes long.

> $59.95
> Zenger Media
> 10200 Jefferson Blvd.
> Box 802
> Culver City, CA 90232-0802
> (310) 839-2436 or (800) 421-4246/fax (310) 839-2249
> or (800) 944-5432
> e-mail: access@ZengerMedia.com
> Web site: ZengerMedia.com/Zenger

El Cid

A spectacular re-creation of the medieval legend (based on a real person), starring Charlton Heston, Sophia Loren, and a 5,000-person Spanish army.

> $29.99
> Movies Unlimited
> 3015 Darnell Rd.
> Philadelphia, PA 19154
> (215) 637-4444 or (800) 4-MOVIES
> e-mail: movies@moviesunlimited.com
> Web site: www.moviesunlimited.com

Ivanhoe

A PBS miniseries based on Sir Walter Scott's dramatic and romantic tale, in which Sir Wilfred of Ivanhoe, noble Saxon knight, contends with the henchmen of evil Prince John, younger brother of Richard the Lionhearted, and falls in love, to find himself torn between the Saxon Rowena and the Jewish Rebecca. (In my opinion, he makes the wrong choice.) Battle, adventure, and glorious costumes and scenes of medieval life. There's even a meeting with Robin Hood. Our boys loved it. Five hours on six videocassettes.

> $99.95
> PBS Home Video
> 1320 Braddock Pl.
> Alexandria, VA 22314-1698
> (800) 645-4PBS
> Web site: www.pbs.org

The Lion in Winter

The tale of Queen Eleanor of Aquitaine and King Henry II of England in their later years. Henry has clapped Eleanor into prison; their sons are grown and are bickering over the succession to the throne. An all-star cast, with Katharine Hepburn as an acerbic

HISTORY

Eleanor and Peter O'Toole as Henry. A wonderful movie for older viewers. Available for rental from most video stores.

See *Nexus: The Lion in Winter and the Middle Ages* (page 632).

COMPUTER SOFTWARE

Castle Explorer

Players, in the character of a page, a knight, or a serving maid, explore a 14th-century castle searching for evidence—information on medieval life—that will lead to the whereabouts of the evil Baron Mortimer. The CD-ROM includes Stephen Biesty's wonderful cutaway drawings and diagrams (see *Stephen Biesty's Cross-Sections: Castle,* page 632), live-action video clips and narration, and over 30,000 words of text. The CD-ROM is packaged with a cardboard castle model and a jousting diorama. For players aged 11 and up. On CD-ROM for Mac or Windows.

$29.95

Dorling Kindersley Publishing

1224 Heil Quaker Blvd.

LaVergne, TN 37086

(888) DIALDKP

Web site: www.dk.com

THE MIDDLE AGES ON-LINE

Castles

Explore the process of building a castle, view different types of castles, and learn about life in a castle and about medieval kings and knights through hypertext with color illustrations and photographs.

www.emg.com/castles

Castles for Kids

An extensive picture library of castles, a glossary of castle terms, and a kid-made page on medieval life.

fox.nstn.ca/~tmonk/castle/castkids.html

The European Middle Ages

The site, in adult-oriented text, includes detailed information about feudalism, the medieval church, and medieval peoples (Celts, Anglo-Saxons, Norse,

Normans). Also included are maps, a timeline, and a glossary.

www.wsu.edu/~dee/MA/MA.HTM

Medieval/Renaissance Subjects

Articles on the medieval period and the Renaissance, with links to maps, pictures, and related Web sites.

www.honors.indiana.edu/~atrium/script/articles.html

The Middle Ages

Castles, medieval art and architecture, cathedrals, monasteries, a history of knighthood, and much more.

pw2.netcom.com/~giardina/medieval.html

Middle Ages Resources

Information on a wide range of topics, among them castles, everyday medieval life, knighthood and chivalry, arms and armor, heraldry, medieval art, and the history of the medieval period.

topcat.bridgew.edu/~kschrock/ED560/thaxter/res.htm

THE RENAISSANCE THROUGH THE SEVENTEENTH CENTURY

BOOKS: NONFICTION

Fine Print: A Story about Johann Gutenberg

Joann Johansen Burch; Carolrhoda, 1992

A 64-page biography of the inventor of movable type for readers aged 8–11.

Good Queen Bess: The Story of Queen Elizabeth I of England

Diane Stanley; Four Winds, 1990

A picture-book biography of Queen Elizabeth I, with full-page color illustrations and a nicely readable text. The book begins with young Bess's father, King Henry VIII, and the break with the Catholic Church that allowed him to marry Anne Boleyn. It then covers the birth of the little redheaded princess, the king's other (mostly ill-fated) wives and children, the reigns of Elizabeth's brother, Edward, and sister, "Bloody Mary," and finally Elizabeth's ascent of the throne and long—and mostly happy—rule. Recommended for readers in grades 3–6.

Gutenberg
Leonard Everett Fisher; Macmillan, 1993

An impressively illustrated biography of the 15th-century German printer who revolutionized the world with his invention of movable type. For readers aged 8–12.

Gutenberg's Gift: A Book Lover's Pop-Up Book
Nancy Willard; Harcourt/Wild Honey, 1995

A clever rhyming account of the invention of movable type, with pop-up illustrations, among them an entire printing press. For readers aged 5–9.

Introduction to the Renaissance
Calliope; May 1994

This issue of *Calliope* magazine (see page 597) includes nonfiction articles about the Renaissance, a short play starring Niccolò Machiavelli and four members of the de Medici family (as talking statues), Renaissance recipes, an art project (in which kids "Become An Apprentice" and copy the *Mona Lisa*), a Renaissance timeline, a map of Renaissance Italy, and a supplementary reading list. For readers in grades 5–9.

Available from most libraries or for $4.50 from

Cobblestone Publishing, Inc.

30 Grove St.

Peterborough, NH 03458-1454

(603) 924-7209 or (800) 821-0115

Web site: www.cobblestonepub.com

The King's Day: Louis XIV of France
Aliki; HarperCollins, 1991

A beautifully illustrated picture-book account of a day in the life of the fabulous Sun King. Included are labeled double-page spreads of the king's palace at Versailles, portraits of the king's entire family (including two mistresses and eight illegitimate children), and three pages of pictures of all the attendants who participated in getting the king out of bed in the morning.

Leonardo da Vinci
Diane Stanley; William Morrow, 1996

A marvelous 32-page biography of Leonardo for kids in grades 3–8, illustrated with Renaissance-style paintings and reproductions of Leonardo's own work, and filled with accounts of his many marvelous inventions, among them a submarine, a telescope, and a flying machine. The back of the dust jacket is printed backwards in mirror writing, just like the script Leonardo used in his notebooks.

Leonardo da Vinci: The Artist, Inventor, Scientist in Three-Dimensional Movable Pictures
Alice and Martin Provensen; Kestrel Press, 1989

Leonardo would have loved it. A cleverly engineered pop-up book of Leonardo's projects, including a three-dimensional flying machine and astrolabe.

Michelangelo and His Times
Veronique Milande; Henry Holt, 1996

An innovative overview of the Renaissance, centering around the life and works of the artist Michelangelo. The book uses a clever combination of drawings, cartoons, maps, and fictionalized interviews to cover Renaissance life and history, including the ups and downs of the Italian political scene, Renaissance inventions and scientific advances, and the outrageous Medici family.

See *Victoria and Her Times* (page 674), *Ramses II and Egypt* (page 614), and *Montezuma and the Aztecs* (page 657), all in the same creative format.

Nexus: Romeo and Juliet and the Renaissance

This issue of *Nexus* (see page 78), the literature-centered multidisciplinary magazine for secondary students, features articles related to Shakespeare's play *Romeo and Juliet*. Topics covered include Shakespeare's theater, Renaissance fashion and art, Leonardo da Vinci, Italian family feuds, Renaissance music, and Galileo's studies of astronomy. An accompanying four-page "Teachers' Guidelines" booklet includes suggestions for supplementary activities.

$6

Nexus

5017 Archmere Ave.

Cleveland, OH 44144

The Tower of London

Leonard Everett Fisher; Macmillan, 1987

A history of England from 1066—the year of the Norman Conquest—to 1666, centering around events taking place at the Tower of London. There, for example, Henry VIII and Anne Boleyn held their wedding feast; there Anne Boleyn was beheaded; there Anne's daughter, Elizabeth, was imprisoned by her older sister, Mary.

BOOKS: FICTION

Alberic the Wise

Norton Juster; Simon & Schuster, 1992

A wonderful fable set in the days of the Renaissance. Alberic, a farmer, sets out to see the world and to learn new skills. He masters many crafts, one after the other, though is never truly talented in any—until his vast accumulation of knowledge over the years causes people to deem him "wise." Alberic tries to convince them that their judgment is false. Failing, he sets out on his journeys once more, saying, "It is much better to look for what I may never find than to find what I do not really want." A thought-provoking book for readers aged 10 and up.

Antonio's Apprenticeship: Painting a Fresco in Renaissance Italy

Taylor Morrison; Holiday House, 1996

Antonio is an apprentice in his uncle Charbone's artist's studio in 15th-century Florence, where he grinds paint pigments, makes charcoal sticks, and mixes plaster. Eventually he takes his first steps toward becoming an artist in his own right, sharing in the creation of a series of 22 frescoes for the Chapel of San Francesco. The beautifully illustrated book introduces readers to life in the Renaissance and describes in detail the process of fresco painting. For readers aged 7–12.

See *Neptune Fountain: The Apprenticeship of a Renaissance Sculptor* (below).

The Children of Green Knowe

L. M. Boston; Harcourt Brace, 1989

The eerily enchanting story of young Tolly, who comes to live with his great-grandmother at the ancient stone house Green Knowe. There he meets the ghosts of three 17th-century children who once lived in the house—Toby, Alexander, and little Linnet—and learns about life in their time, solves a mystery, and defeats a great evil. Sequels include *The Treasure of Green Knowe, The River at Green Knowe, A Stranger at Green Knowe,* and *An Enemy at Green Knowe.*

The Ghost of Thomas Kempe

Penelope Lively; Puffin, 1995

James Harrison and his family move into an English cottage that turns out to be haunted by the ghost of Thomas Kempe, an early 17th-century sorcerer who claims James as his new apprentice. For readers aged 9–12.

Neptune Fountain: The Apprenticeship of a Renaissance Sculptor

Taylor Morrison; Holiday House, 1997

The book follows the career of 15-year-old Marco, apprentice to the great Roman sculptor Luigi Borghini. Marco begins his apprenticeship drawing cadavers and painstakingly copying works of art; then he learns to make wax and clay models; eventually he is sent to the famous Carrara marble quarries for a block of white marble for Borghini's latest commission, the *Neptune Fountain.* At last, Marco begins to carve in stone, sharing in the making of the finished masterpiece. A picture book for readers aged 7–12.

The Second Mrs. Giaconda

E. L. Konigsberg; Aladdin, 1998

A fictionalized story of Leonardo da Vinci and the *Mona Lisa,* as told by Leonardo's rascally young apprentice, Salai. For readers aged 11 and up.

COLORING AND PAPER-CRAFTS BOOKS

6+ *A Coloring Book of the Renaissance*
Scenes from all walks of Renaissance life and black-line portraits of such prominent persons as Cesare and Lucretia Borgia. The book contains a brief historical text. Also see *Renaissance Women*.

$3.95
Bellerophon Books
36 Ancapa St
Santa Barbara, CA 93101
(800) 253-9943/fax (800) 965-8286

6+ *Elizabethan Costumes Paper Dolls*
Two dolls and 16 historically accurate costumes, all in color.

$3.95
Dover Publications, Inc.
31 E. Second St.
Mineola, NY 11501

6+ *Queen Elizabeth I Paper Dolls*
Queen Elizabeth I Paper Dolls features the queen and an assortment of Elizabethan gowns copied from original portraits, and Sir Walter Raleigh, plus armor, all to color yourself. Also see *Henry VIII and His Wives Paper Dolls,* which includes Henry and all six wives, with gowns, armor, robes, and jewelry.

$3.95
Bellerophon Books
36 Ancapa St.
Santa Barbara, CA 93101 (800) 253-9943/fax (800) 965-8286

ACTIVITY BOOKS

9 13 *Picture the Renaissance*
Robert M. Wilhelm; Golden Owl Publishing, 1998

An activity and resource book for upper elementary and middle school students. Chapter titles include "The Passion for Exploration," "Music and Dance," "Architecture of the Renaissance," "Art of the Renaissance," "Science and Inventions," and "The Reformation and Response of the Catholic Church." The book includes all necessary historical background information, maps, timelines, architectural plans, instructions for arts and crafts activities, music, recipes, and costume designs.

$24.95
Jackdaw Publications
Box 503
Amawalk, NY 10503
(914) 962-6911 or (800) 789-0022/fax (800) 962-9101

5 13 *The Renaissance A.D. 1300–1600*
A "learning packet" in the form of a spiral-bound book filled with suggestions for activities in the fields of art, history, philosophy, literature, and architecture. Activities are divided into two sections by appropriate grade level: grades K–3 and 4–8. Younger students, for example, invent and play Renaissance games, draw maps, work on assorted art projects (such as "Invent a guild emblem for a trade of your choice"), and keep diaries of voyages of discovery. Projects for older kids generally involve more detailed research: for example, there are lists of suggested report topics. The packet includes lots of brief ideas and suggestions, but no instructions and not much in the way of background information: all that must be supplied by the users. Be prepared to do some running to the library.

$18
Zephyr Press
3316 N. Chapel Ave.
Box 66006
Tucson, AZ 85732-6006
(800) 232-2187/fax (520) 323-9402
e-mail: neways2learn@zephyrpress.com
Web site: www.zephyrpress.com

GAMES AND HANDS-ON ACTIVITIES

12+ *Age of the Renaissance*
A strategy board game of economic and intellectual development, played across a colorful map of Europe. Players compete to develop their Renaissance civilizations through trade and territorial conquest, and through advances in such fields as science, reli-

gion, communications, and exploration. The winner is the first player to acquire 26 Renaissance discoveries or achievements (among them gunpowder and the printing press). Outcome of the game is influenced by event cards, which list historical or political happenings (pirate raids, Mongol invasions, the Black Death, the Crusades, enlightened rulers, famines), key personalities (Galileo, Isaac Newton, Johann Gutenberg, Erasmus, Charlemagne, Marco Polo, Prince Henry the Navigator), and desirable trade goods (wine, cloth, fur, grain, silk, spices). The game, which can be played at three levels of difficulty, is recommended for three to six players, aged 12 and up.

$54.95

Avalon Hill Game Co.

4517 Harford Rd.

Baltimore, MD 21214

(410) 254-9200 or (800) 999-3222

e-mail: AH GAMES@aol.com

Web site: www.avalonhill.com

Elizabeth I

A portfolio of primary source documents and historical essays related to the reign of Elizabeth I, England's Good Queen Bess. "Elizabeth I" includes six illustrated historical essays, covering Elizabeth's life and reign from "Childhood" through "Old Age," and 11 replicas of historical documents and materials, among them facsimiles of letters written by Elizabeth, assorted portraits of the queen, a 1570 inventory of her jewels, a warrant for the execution of the Earl of Essex, and a ballad written at the time of the queen's death.

Also see "The Armada" portfolio, which centers around the famous battle of 1588, in which Queen Elizabeth's smaller, nippier fleet of English ships defeated the vast and "invincible" armada of King Philip II of Spain. The portfolio contains seven illustrated historical background essays (among them "The Quarrel and the Men," "Singeing the King of Spain's Beard," "Did Drake Drum Them Up the Channel?," and "The End of the Armada") and seven replicas of historical documents and materials, including engravings of the armada ships, a map showing the English defenses on the Thames River, and portraits of Charles Howard (commander of the English fleet), Sir Francis Drake, and Queen Elizabeth I.

Each portfolio also includes explanatory notes on the documents and a detailed study guide, with reproducible worksheets and suggestions for student activities.

$37 each

Jackdaw Publications

Box 503

Amawalk, NY 10501

(914) 962-6911 or (800) 789-0022/fax (800) 962-9101

Kingmaker

A strategy game based on the War of Roses, the object of the game is to acquire an heir to the throne, crown him king, and then, in fine medieval style, execute all opposing heirs. The game is played on a beautifully illustrated map of England, complete with forests, winding roads, towns, cathedrals, and castles. Includes a large cast of characters and a deck of event cards, which enhance or detract from the action (powerful nobles are abruptly dispatched to the Scottish border; heirs are lost in storms at sea).

$30

Avalon Hill Game Co.

4517 Harford Rd.

Baltimore, MD 21214

(410) 254-9200 or (800) 999-3222

e-mail: AH GAMES@aol.com

Web site: www.avalonhill.com

Machiavelli

A strategy game set in Renaissance Italy. Players compete to take control of the Italian peninsula, through a Machiavellian combination of secret plots, negotiations, alliances, and military force. Event cards add to the action, providing players with options for sieges, bribes, and assassinations of rivals, or landing then with plagues and famines. The game is played on a mapboard of Italy.

$35

Avalon Hill Game Co.

4517 Harford Rd.

Baltimore, MD 21214

(410) 254-9200 or (800) 999-3222

e-mail: AH GAMES@aol.com

Web site: www.avalonhill.com

Martin Luther

A portfolio of essays and primary source materials on Martin Luther and the Protestant Reformation. Included are six illustrated historical essays, including "Luther's World," "The Diet of Worms," and "The Reformation Spreads," and nine documents, including a copy of Luther's "Ninety-five Theses" (with translation), a portrait of Martin Luther, and a page from a 16th-century Lutheran hymnal. The portfolio also contains a study guide with reproducible student worksheets.

$37
Jackdaw Publications
Box 503
Amawalk, NY 10503
(914) 962-6911 or (800) 789-0022/fax (800) 962-9101

Renaissance

A simulation in which kids become "chrononauts," traveling back in time to rescue artistic and scientific treasures of the Renaissance—such as Leonardo da Vinci's *Mona Lisa*—which have been caught in a modern-day time warp and whisked back to their place and time of origin. Participants take on a Renaissance name and identity, study the daily life and customs of the time they are heading for, and then move along the playing path on a Renaissance game board, dealing with "Blunder," "Stump," "Interview," and "Treasure" cards. (Among the challenges: decipher Leonardo's secret handwriting.) They also accumulate gold and silver florins by completing supplementary Renaissance-related activities in geography, science, math, art, and literature. The simulation is recommended for 20 to 35 students in grades 7–12, though it adapts readily to smaller groups.

$43
Interact
1825 Gillespie Way, #101
El Cajon, CA 92020-1095
(619) 448-1474 or (800) 359-0961/fax (619) 448-6722
or (800) 700-5093
Web site: www.interactsimulations.com

VIDEOS

Elizabeth R

This six-part miniseries first played on *Masterpiece Theatre* in 1971, with Glenda Jackson as the redheaded princess who became Queen Elizabeth I. The series covers Elizabeth's life from her imprisonment and near execution by her sister, Queen Mary, through her coronation and the 45 eventful years of her reign. 9 hours on six videocassettes.

$149.98
PBS Home Video
1320 Braddock Pl.
Alexandria, VA 22314-1698
(800) 645-4PBS
Web site: www.pbs.org
or
Zenger Media
10200 Jefferson Blvd.
Box 802
Culver City, CA 90232-0802
(310) 839-2436 or (800) 421-4246/fax (310) 839-2249
or (800) 944-5432
e-mail: access@ZengerMedia.com
Web site: ZengerMedia.com/Zenger

The Life of Leonardo da Vinci

A five-part miniseries on the life and times of Leonardo, the quintessential Renaissance man, from his childhood through the spectacular artistic and scientific achievements of his adulthood. Beautifully acted; filmed on location in Italy. About 4 hours and 30 minutes on 3 videocassettes.

$59.95
Public Television Videofinders Collection
National Fulfillment Center
Box 27054
Glendale, CA 91225
(800) 799-1199

A Man for All Seasons

The church and state are in conflict in Tudor England as Henry VIII, desperate for a male heir, seeks to divorce Queen Catherine of Aragon in order to marry Anne Boleyn. Thomas More, Henry's Lord Chancellor, opposes the divorce and chooses to go to the block rather than compromise his beliefs. This Academy Award winner from 1966 stars Paul Scofield, Wendy Hiller, Robert Shaw, and Orson Welles.

$19.99
Movies Unlimited

3015 Darnell Rd.

Philadelphia, PA 19154

(215) 637-4444 or (800) 4-movies

e-mail: movies@moviesunlimited.com

Web site: www.moviesunlimited.com

(800) 4-MOVIES

The Man in the Iron Mask

The man in the iron mask is Philippe, King Louis XIV's identical (and just slightly older) twin brother. An exciting story, a daring plot, gorgeous costumes and scenery, and the better man wins. The 1976 version stars Richard Chamberlain as both brothers, along with Jenny Agutter, Louis Jourdain, Sir Ralph Richardson, and Patrick McGoohan. It's terrific. The 1998 version, with Leonardo diCaprio as Louis/Philippe, isn't.

$19.99

Movies Unlimited

3015 Darnell Rd.

Philadelphia, PA 19154

(215) 637-4444 or (800) 4-MOVIES

e-mail: movies@moviesunlimited.com

Web site: www.moviesunlimited.com

Also see *The Count of Monte Christo* and *The Three Musketeers.*

The Six Wives of Henry VIII

A marvelous six-part miniseries originally shown on *Masterpiece Theatre,* with Keith Michell as the increasingly irascible king. Each dramatic 90-minute episode tells the story of one of the six wives: Catherine of Aragon, Anne Boleyn, Jane Seymour, Anne of Cleves, Catherine Howard, and Catherine Parr.

$99.95

Public Television Videofinders Collection

National Fulfillment Center

Box 27054

Glendale, CA 91225

(800) 799-1199

COMPUTER SOFTWARE

Leonardo the Inventor

A multimedia exploration of the life and inventions of Leonardo da Vinci. Kids can investigate Leonardo's inventions in the fields of Flight (click on Flight and a little blue plane buzzes over Mona Lisa's head; she ducks), Water, Music, Civil Engineering, and Warfare; read Leonardo's biography (in 19 chapters); view some of his paintings; and play some of his instruments. There's also a da Vinci timeline—the column of dates on the left lists events in Leonardo's life; the column on the right lists events occurring elsewhere in the world. Kids can also play three interactive games, in which they variously soar over a Renaissance world on Icarus-style wings, dive to the bottom of the sea after sunken treasure, and attempt to escape from Leonardo's mazelike fortress. Recommended for kids aged 9 and up. On CD-ROM for Mac or Windows.

$39.95

Zenger Media

10200 Jefferson Blvd.

Box 802

Culver City, CA 90232-0802

(310) 839-2436 or (800) 421-4246/fax (310) 839-2249

or (800) 944-5432

e-mail: access@ZengerMedia.com

Web site: ZengerMedia.com/Zenger

Louis Cat Orze: The Mystery of the Queen's Necklace

Players find themselves at the court of Louis XIV at the Palace of Versailles in 1697 where—horrors!—the queen's necklace has been stolen. Guided by a friendly palace pet, Louis Cat Orze, kids become official investigators, collecting clues, tracking down the crook, and recovering the jewels. To do so, they need money—which they win by playing the "Palace Games," multiple-choice quizzes of French history and culture. In general, however, crime solving involves prowls through the lushly detailed palace, from banquet hall to orangerie to queen's bedchamber, chance encounters with famous persons, and descriptions and demonstrations of 17th-century customs and historical happenings, all to a background of period music. On CD-ROM for Mac or Windows.

$41.95

Zenger Media

10200 Jefferson Blvd.

Box 802

Culver City, CA 90232-0802

(310) 839-2436 or (800) 421-4246/fax (310) 839-2249
or (800) 944-5432

e-mail: access@ZengerMedia.com

Web site: ZengerMedia.com/Zenger

THE RENAISSANCE ON-LINE

European Renaissance

A large and varied collection of Renaissance links. Included are lesson plans on the Renaissance and Reformation, maps, and information on Renaissance literature, food, medicine, art, architecture, science, and politics. Included are many links to prominent Renaissance figures, among them Shakespeare, Galileo, Dante, Leonardo da Vinci, Michelangelo, the Medicis, and Henry VIII.

www.execpc.com/~dboals/rena.html

The Renaissance

Visitors to the site can embark on a virtual 15th-century sea voyage, view a gallery of Leonardo da Vinci drawings, listen to Renaissance music, and learn about Renaissance art and science, medicine, dance, history, and much more.

www.hist.unt.edu/09w-ed0d.htm

Virtual Renaissance

A terrific site for young historians. Kids can access a clickable "map of the Renaissance," visiting many Renaissance sites and conversing with people from different places, time periods, and walks of life. They learn about Renaissance religion from Father John at the Cathedral of Santa María; see a demonstration of glassblowing by Pritchard, glassmaker in the town marketplace; hear about Shakespeare's life from Richard Burbage at the Globe Theatre; and take a tour of the Tower of London with Henry the Helpless. (They also meet the ghost of Anne Boleyn, who shares information about British royalty.) The site also includes a chronology of the Renaissance and links to related sites.

www.district125.k12.il.us/Renaissance/GeneralFiles/
Introduction.html

AGE OF EXPLORATION

From my homeschool journal:

◆ **November 6, 1990. Josh is nine; Ethan, eight; Caleb, six.**

Spent most of our time this morning reading and discussing the book Marco Polo *by Gian Paolo Ceserani, with lots of questions form the boys: about Venice ("How did the water get in the canals? Do gondolas ever have motors?"), silkworms ("Are they like gypsy moths? Does it kill the worm when you unwind its cocoon?"), sedan chairs ("What's inside them?"), the Khan's hunting eagles ("How big were they? Could they really pick up a wolf?"), and deathbeds ("What's a* deathbed*?"). All interesting.*

◆ **November 7, 1990**

More Marco Polo, using homemade workbooks. The boys colored maps of Italy, locating Venice and Genoa; read about and drew pictures of gondolas (Josh wrote an accompanying gondolier song); designed a Venetian merchant's warehouse (heavily furnished with wine barrels and elaborate Persian carpets); invented a mirage, such as might have been seen by the Polos in the Gobi Desert; designed a device other than the Great Wall that might have kept the Mongols out of China; and drew spectacular palaces for Kublai Khan. They also practiced tracing the routes Marco Polo took, going to and from China, on the world map.

◆ **November 8, 1990**

Started the morning with watercolor painting, by popular demand—then finished our Marco Polo workbooks. The boys designed sedan chairs of the sort Marco Polo probably rode in as emissary of the Khan. Read about and made booklets of the Chinese inventions that most impressed Marco Polo: fireworks, asbestos, spectacles, coal, paper money, the compass, silk, and paper. Experimented with compasses ("Why does the earth have a North Pole? Does the moon have poles? What about Mars?") Drew a series of Chinese junks with much refer-

HISTORY

ence to various pictures; traced Marco Polo's return route on the world map; designed a cover for Marco Polo's book. Looked through the book The Travels of Marco Polo *by Mike Rosen.*

◆ November 9, 1990

Explorer of the day: Vasco da Gama. The boys designed a da Gama family crest; located Portugal, Spain, Africa, Mozambique, Madagascar, the Indian Ocean, and India on the world map; and traced the route of da Gama's famous voyage to India. Drew pictures of the stone pillars da Gama was supposed to have set up to mark his landings (Ethan designed an elaborate Corinthian column; Josh produced a cartoon of annoyed natives chopping down the stone pillars); looked up Hottentots (da Gama met them) in the encyclopedia and drew pictures. Read a short history of calico; the boys designed and colored their own calico patterns. Identified samples of real spices: cinnamon sticks, whole cloves, whole nutmegs, peppercorns, and (unfortunately, ground) ginger. Drew portraits of Vasco da Gama as Admiral of the Ocean Sea of India, complete with plumes and gold lace.

Made a long list of African animals, played an African animal charades game, and looked at African animal photographs in National Geographic's Safari.

◆ November 13, 1990

Began a study of Magellan using homemade workbooks titled "Around the World in 1,083 Days." The boys began the morning with a mapmaking exercise, drawing maps of the dining room and their bedroom. Then drew portraits of Magellan and Duke (later King) Manuel; designed a figurehead for Magellan's ship Trinidad; *and located the Philippine Islands on the world map. Discussed the Treaty of Tordesillas and drew a line through the Atlantic Ocean, showing the way the world was divided between Spain and Portugal. (The boys felt this was unjustified and unprincipled.) Designed tombstones for Magellan.*

Traced Magellan's route on the world map, with particular attention to the Strait of Magellan. Also located Argentina, Patagonia, the Spice Islands, Spain, and Por-

tugal. Colored one-third of a pie graph to demonstrate the portion of the world occupied by the Pacific Ocean.

Read a short biography of Magellan.

Designed covers for Antonio Pigafetta's diary. Pigafetta, the chronicler of Magellan's world voyage, I told the boys, came from Venice. Caleb: "That's the city with the streets full of water!" Josh: "That's the city Marco Polo came from!"

Verdict: Magellan preferable to Columbus (who was mean) or Vasco da Gama (who was selfish).

See **American History: Columbus and Other Explorers** (pages 464–468) and **World History: Vikings** (pages 626–630).

Books

7
12
Around the World in a Hundred Years From Prince Henry the Navigator to Magellan
Jean Fritz; Putnam, 1994

A 128-page illustrated account of 10 explorers and their accomplishments, good and bad: Prince Henry the Navigator, Bartholomeu Diaz, Christopher Columbus, Vasco da Gama, Pedro Alvares Cabral, John Cabot, Amerigo Vespucci, Juan Ponce de León, Vasco Núñez de Balboa, and Ferdinand Magellan. For readers in grades 2–6.

9
13
The Children's Atlas of Exploration: Follow in the Footsteps of the Great Explorers
Antony Mason; Millbrook Press, 1993

A beautifully designed atlas of exploration through history, from prehistoric times to the space age. Photographs, many maps, drawings, and an informative text. For readers aged 9–13.

9
14
Cobblestone: Explorers
Issues of *Calliope* magazine (see page 597) featuring explorers include *Great Explorers to the East* (September 1990) and *Great Explorers to the West* (January 1991). Both include several illustrated nonfiction articles, maps and timelines, games and puzzles, and a supplementary reading list. *Great Explorers to the East*, for example, covers ancient Egyptian explorers, the travels of Alexander the Great and Marco Polo, the Portuguese voyages to India, and the legend of Prester John. For readers in grades 5–9.

Available from most libraries or for $4.50 from
Cobblestone Publishing, Inc.
30 Grove St.
Peterborough, NH 03458-1454
(603) 924-7209 or (800) 821-0115
Web site: www.cobblestonepub.com

Explorer

Rupert Matthews and Jim Stevenson; Alfred A. Knopf, 1991

One of the Eyewitness series, heavily illustrated with wonderful color photographs, *Explorer* covers exploration from the voyages of the ancient Phoenicians to the modern space program. Included are pictures of Roman merchant ships, Viking longboats, Polynesian canoes, and Arab dhows; a map of the Silk Road; and photos of a sailor's sea chest and a cat-o'-nine-tails, Captain Cook's chronometer and Charles Darwin's microscope, and an astronaut in full space gear.

Explorers Who Got Lost

Diane Sansevere Dreher; Tor Books, 1994

A 135-page account of eight famous explorers who either weren't sure where they were going in the first place or who ended up in places they never intended but still managed to make landmark discoveries. Confused characters covered include Bartolomeu Dias, Vasco da Gama, Christopher Columbus, John Cabot, Ferdinand Magellan, Giovanni da Verrazano, Jacques Cartier, and Henry Hudson. Included is a cartoon-style foldout map (impossible to read), a chronology of exploratory events from the establishment of the first school of navigation in Portugal by Prince Henry the Navigator in 1419 to the mutiny of Henry Hudson's men in 1610 (which ended with Hudson's being set adrift in a rowboat and vanishing forever from history). For readers aged 10–13.

Exploring the World

Fiona Macdonald; Peter Bedrick Books, 1996

A 48-page overview of the expeditions of several famous world explorers, among them Columbus, Vasco da Gama, Sir Francis Drake, and Captain Cook, with colorful illustrations and maps. For readers aged 9–12.

First Books: Explorers

William Jay Jacobs; Franklin Watts, 1994

Volumes in a series of 64-page illustrated biographies intended for readers in grades 4–6. Titles on explorers include *Champlain: A Life of Courage; Coronado: Dreamer in Golden Armor; Cortés: Conqueror of Mexico; La Salle: A Life of Boundless Adventure; Magellan: Voyager with a Dream;* and *Pizarro: Conqueror of Peru.*

The History News: Explorers

Michael Johnstone; Candlewick, 1997

In eye-catching newspaper format, *The History News* is an overview of the history of exploration from 1500 B.C. to the present day. The book covers the exploits of the ancient Phoenecians, ancient Chinese, and Vikings; the landmark expeditions of such explorers as Columbus, Magellan, Captain Cook, and David Livingstone; the European explorations of Mexico, South America, North America, Africa, and Australia; expeditions to the North and South Poles; and explorations beneath the oceans. The book is stuffed with maps, timelines, capsule biographies, colorful fact boxes, clever letters to the editor, and humorous advertisements ("Why Sleep on Deck . . . when you can snooze in a hammock?").

Marco Polo: His Notebook

Susan L. Roth; Doubleday, 1990

A fictionalized account of Marco Polo's famous 13th-century journey to Cathay, written in journal form, and heavily illustrated with prints, photographs, and historical maps. The book is based on Marco Polo's own account of his experiences, *The Travels of Marco Polo,* written after his return home to Italy.

See *The World in the Time of Marco Polo* (page 633).

Prince Henry the Navigator

Leonard Everett Fisher; Macmillan, 1990

The picture-book story of the 15th-century Portuguese prince whose school of navigation supported and inspired a century of world exploration. Recommended for readers in grades 4–7.

HISTORY

The Remarkable Voyages of Captain Cook
Rhoda Blumberg; Bradbury Press, 1991

An excellent and interesting account of Cook's three major voyages of discovery, including visits to Tahiti, New Zealand, Australia, Antarctica, Easter Island, and—finally and fatally—Hawaii. The book is filled with maps, prints, excerpts from expedition notebooks, and reproductions of portraits and paintings, plus an informational and detailed text.

Ship
David Macauley; Houghton Mifflin, 1993

Illustrated with Macauley's wonderful detailed pen-and-ink drawings, *Ship* is the story of the recovery of a sunken 15th-century Spanish caravel by marine archaeologists in the Caribbean. The archaeologists also discover a journal detailing the construction of the caravel; included are descriptions of these ships and their uses in 15th-century voyages of exploration and discovery.

Sir Frances Drake, His Daring Deeds
Roy Gerrard; Farrar, Straus & Giroux, 1988

A colorful picture book with a catchy rhyming text for readers aged 4–8.

World Explorer Series
Chelsea House

Each volume in this series features a famous explorer or group of explorers. Books are between 110 and 130 pages long, illustrated with prints, paintings, and maps; each includes a timeline and a bibliography. Titles are *Captain James Cook: And the Explorers of the Pacific* (David Haney; 1992); *Christopher Columbus and the First Voyages to the New World* (Stephen C. Dodge; 1991); *Ferdinand Magellan and the Discovery of the World Ocean* (Rebecca Stefoff; 1990); *From Coronado to Escalante: The Explorers of the Spanish Southwest* (John Miller Morris; 1992); *Henry Stanley and the European Explorers of Africa* (Steven Sherman; 1993); *Jacques Cartier, Samuel de Champlain, and the Explorers of Canada* (Tony Coulter; 1993); *La Salle and the Explorers of the Mississippi* (Tony Coulter; 1991); *Marco Polo and the Medieval Explorers* (Rebecca Stefoff; 1992); *Sir Francis Drake and the Struggle for an*

Ocean Empire (Alice Smith Duncan; 1993); and *Vasco da Gama and the Portuguese Explorers* (Rebecca Stefoff; 1993). For high school–aged readers.

GAMES AND HANDS-ON ACTIVITIES

A Coloring Book of Great Explorers
Black-line portraits of famous explorers—among them Columbus, Balboa, Cortés, and John Cabot—with an accompanying historical text.

$3.95

Bellerophon Books

36 Ancapa St.

Santa Barbara, CA 93101

(800) 253-9943/fax (800) 965-8286

Columbus and the Age of Exploration
A portfolio of illustrated historical essays and primary source materials. Essays include "Columbus's World and Enterprise," "Encounters Before Columbus," and "Naming America." Source materials include reproductions of early world maps, a portrait of Christopher Columbus, a page from the 13th-century *Icelandic Saga*, and Samuel de Champlain's chart of the Gulf of Maine. The portfolio also contains a study guide with reproducible student worksheets.

$37

Jackdaw Publications

Box 503

Amawalk, NY 10503

(914) 962-6911 or (800) 789-0022/fax (800) 962-9101

Discovery and Exploration Game
The game is played on a number-coded map; players match numbered cards, each with the name of a famous explorer and description of the expedition, to the map sites. The game can be played at three levels of difficulty, for increasingly skillful players.

$10.95

Educational Materials Associates, Inc.

Box 7385

Charlottesville, VA 22906

(804) 293-GAME/fax (804) 293-5322

6 *Explorers Card Game*

This pack of color-illustrated cards includes four each of 13 famous explorers (or pairs of explorers): Leif Eriksson, Marco Polo, Alexander the Great, Christopher Columbus, Ferdinand Magellan, Vasco da Gama, Sir Francis Drake, Samuel de Champlain, La Salle, Captain Cook, Lewis and Clark, Stanley and Livingstone, and Robert Perry. The cards can be used for games of rummy, in which players collect sets of all four explorers; or can be ordered on timelines or used for writing or storytelling activities.

$6
Aristoplay
450 S. Wagner Rd.
Ann Arbor, MI 48107
(800) 634-7738 or (888) GR8-GAME
fax (734) 995-4611
Web site: www.aristoplay.com

12 *New World*

A strategy board game set in the Age of Exploration. The game is played on a detailed mapboard of the Americas; players, each representing a different European nation, compete to explore, conquer, and colonize the New World. Colonization requires a combination of diplomacy, military might, good management, and luck. Each region of the New World comes with a distinctive set of natural resources, native inhabitants, climatic conditions, and wealth (gold), all of which influence the outcome of the game. Players must also cope with event cards, which may inflict them with storms at sea, pirates, or disease.

$25
Avalon Hill Game Co.
4517 Harford Rd.
Baltimore, MD 21214
(410) 524-9200 or (800) 999-3222
e-mail: AH GAMES@aol.com
Web site: www.avalonhill.com
Also see *Land Ho! Tierra! Tierra!* (page 467).

COMPUTER SOFTWARE

9 *Explorers of the New World*

A wealth of information on explorers and their accomplishments. The program features Columbus,

Cortés, and Magellan, covering the details and historical importance of their landmark voyages through a combination of video reenactments, animations, text, puzzles, and quizzes. Also included are maps, a timeline of exploration, and information on 60 other explorers of the time period. On CD-ROM for Mac or Windows.

$39.95
Zenger Media
10200 Jefferson Blvd.
Box 802
Culver City, CA 90232-0802
(310) 839-2436 or (800) 421-4246/fax (310) 839-2249
or (800) 944-5432
e-mail: access@ZengerMedia.com
Web site: ZengerMedia.com/Zenger

9 *Stowaway!*

A marvelous tour of an 18th-century ship, with animations, audio clips, information, and fascinatingly detailed cross-sectional illustrations by artist Stephen Biesty. Kids can explore the entire ship, meet the crew, and read descriptive journals describing shipboard life. On CD-ROM for Mac.

$29.95
Dorling Kindersley Publishing
1224 Heil Quaker Blvd.
LaVergne, TN 37086
(888) DIALDKP
Web site: www.dk.com

EXPLORERS ON-LINE

9 *Age of Exploration Curriculum Guide*

A complete course on the Age of Exploration from the Mariners Museum in Newport News, Virginia. The guide covers the history of exploration from ancient times through the 18th century, including information on famous explorers, the evolution of ships, maps, and navigation, and accounts of everyday life on board. Included are photographs and illustrations, a timeline, activity suggestions, and a bibliography.

www.mariner.org/age/index.html

Discoverers Web

Information on a large number of explorers (in alphabetical order), a picture gallery, a page on explorers who died on their voyages, biographies of such prominent figures as Prince Henry the Navigator, the Cabots, Cartier, and Coronado, and many links to related sites.

www.win.tne.nl/cs/fm/engels/discovery

THE AMERICAS

Also see *Pre-Columbian America* (pages 461–464).

BOOKS

The Amazing Potato: A Story in Which the Incas, Conquistadors, Marie Antoinette, Thomas Jefferson, Wars, Famines, Immigrants, and French Fries All Play a Part
Milton Meltzer; HarperCollins, 1992

The title pretty much sums it up. A fascinating history of the (American) potato in several short chapters. Readers learn that the Incas of Peru cultivated potatoes, that Queen Marie Antoinette wore potato blossoms in her hair, that Thomas Jefferson introduced "French fries" to America, and all about the disastrous Irish potato famine. For readers aged 9–12.

The Aztec News
Philip Steele, Penny Bateman, and Norman Rosso; Candlewick, 1997

The daily news from Tenochtitlán, island city of Montezuma, reflecting the latest in politics, religion, fashion, farming, sports, and medicine, plus updates on the newly arrived European invaders.

Aztec, Inca, & Maya
Elizabeth Baquedano; Alfred A. Knopf, 1993

A 64-page volume in the Eyewitness series, light on text but heavily illustrated with terrific color photographs, drawings, and diagrams. Each double-page spread covers a different subtopic.

Cobblestone: The Americas/World History

Issues of *Faces* magazine (see page 411) concentrating on Central and South American history topics include *Ancient Mexico* (June 1990), *The Maya Civilization* (November 1985), and *The Incas* (November 1986). Each contains nonfiction and fiction articles, activity suggestions, and a reading list. *Ancient Mexico,* for example, includes articles on the Olmecs, the Aztecs, ancient Mexican religions, and the mysterious Aztec city of Teotihuacán, a Mexican folktale about popcorn, a recipe for quesadillas, directions for making a "Tree of Life" clay candleholder, and a playing board and instructions for the ancient Mexican game of "Patolli." Also see *Spanish South America* (*Calliope;* May 1993), which concentrates on South American independence movements; included are brief biographies of José de San Martín and Simón Bolívar. For readers in grades 4–9.

Available at most libraries or for $4.50 from
Cobblestone Publishing, Inc.
30 Grove St.
Peterborough, NH 03458
(603) 924-7209 or (800) 821-0115
Web site: www.cobblestonepub.com
See *Calliope* magazine (page 597).

Montezuma and the Aztecs
Mathilde Helly and Remy Courgeon; Henry Holt, 1997

An innovative approach to the history of Aztec civilization, filled with fascinating facts, creative graphics, and intriguing presentations of historical information. Included are a page of Aztec fortunes, a biography of Montezuma, portraits of famous Spanish explorers, maps, a timeline, an account of Aztec religion titled "The Gods Are Like Germs: They Are Countless, Invincible, and Hyperactive," and an illustrated page comparing things that "Did Not Exist in Spain" (jaguars, turkeys, tomatoes, artichokes, hummingbirds) to things that "Did Not Exist in Mexico" (horses, pigs, wool, sailing ships).

In the same series, see *Michelangelo and His Times* (page 646), *Ramses II and Egypt* (page 614), and *Victoria and Her Times* (page 674).

A Picture Book of Simón Bolívar
David A. Adler; Holiday House, 1992

A simple picture-book biography of the "Liberator" who led the 19th-century South American revolt against Spain. For readers aged 5–8.

Pyramid of the Sun, Pyramid of the Moon
Leonard Everett Fisher; Macmillan, 1988

The story of two ancient Central American pyramids, used by the Toltec and Aztec peoples. The text is straightforwardly informational; the subject includes bloody religious rituals and human sacrifice. There's a timeline at the front of the book. For readers aged 8–12.

FOLKTALES AND LEGENDS

All of You Was Singing
Richard Lewis; Atheneum, 1991

An illustrated version of an Aztec creation myth that explains the origins of music. For readers aged 5–9.

Feathers Like the Rainbow: An Amazon Indian Tale
Flora; HarperCollins, 1989

An Indian myth explaining why all the Amazonian birds are gorgeously colored except for the gray-winged trumpeter. For readers aged 5–9.

The Hummingbird King: A Guatemalan Legend
Argentina Palacios; Troll Associates, 1993

A young Indian chief, protected by a hummingbird, is killed by his wicked uncle and then magically transformed into a beautiful quetzal. For readers aged 5–9.

The Llama's Secret: A Peruvian Legend
Argentina Palacios; Troll Associates, 1993

In this Peruvian version of the Great Flood story, a llama warns the people to seek shelter on a mountaintop to avoid the rising sea. For readers aged 5–9.

The Rain Forest Storybook: Traditional Stories from the Original Forest Peoples of South America, Africa, and Southeast Asia
Rosalind Kerven; Cambridge University Press, 1994

Folktales grouped by geographical location; each is introduced by information about the lives and culture of the people of origin. For all ages.

Rain Player
David Wisniewski; Clarion, 1991

A young Mayan ballplayer challenges the rain god to a game to save his people from a terrible drought. For readers aged 5–9.

A Ring of Tricksters: Animal Tales from America, the West Indies, and Africa
Virginia Hamilton; Scholastic, 1997

A wonderful illustrated collection of folktales featuring such cunning characters as Bruh Rabbit, Anansi the Spider, and a very clever turtle, from the Americas and Africa. Included is historical information about trickster tales. For all ages.

The Sea Serpent's Daughter: A Brazilian Legend
Margaret H. Lippert; Troll Associates, 1993

The Sea Serpent makes a gift of darkness, which brings night to the people of the rain forest. For readers aged 5–9.

COLORING BOOKS

A Coloring Book of Incas, Aztecs, & Mayas
Black-line reproductions of artworks by pre-Columbian artists, including portraits of gods and goddesses, calendars and counting devices, warriors, kings, and ballplayers. Also see *The Story of Mexico*, which covers Mexican history from the days of Montezuma to modern times, with a historical text in both Spanish and English.

$3.95 each

Bellerophon Books

36 Ancapa St.

Santa Barbara, CA 93101

(800) 253-9943/fax (800) 965-8286

Life in Ancient Mexico Coloring Book

Drawings of Mexican cities and monuments, religious ceremonies, warriors, and craftspeople and artisans at work.

$2.95

Dover Publications, Inc.

31 E. Second St.

Mineola, NY 11501

GAMES AND HANDS-ON ACTIVITIES

Ancient Aztecs Treasure Chest

An activity-packed kit containing a 32-page illustrated booklet of instructions and historical information, plus materials to make an Aztec feather headdress, a replica pottery flute, and a model of the Great Temple; a labeled map of ancient Central America; and a paper board and playing pieces for the ancient Mexican game of "Patolli."

$19.95 from book or game stores or

Running Press Book Publishers

125 S. 22nd St.

Philadelphia, PA 19103-4399

(215) 567-5080 or (800) 345-5359/fax (800) 453-2884

Lost Civilizations Explorer's Kit

The kit contains a 64-page illustrated book of historical background information, plus a block of clay from which kids can excavate and reconstruct a model of the Temple of the Giant Jaguar at Tikal, an ancient Mayan city in Guatemala.

A CD-ROM version of the kit is also available: all of the above plus an interactive CD-ROM with which kids can visit famous archaeological digs or travel back in time to experience life in ancient cultures.

Kit, $18.95; CD-ROM version, $29.95; from book or game stores or

Running Press Book Publishers

125 S. 22nd St.

Philadelphia, PA 19103-4399

(215) 567-5080 or (800) 345-5359/fax (800) 453-2884

Maya

A simulation in which kids, as sixth-century Maya Indians, participate in the building of Mayan civilization. Each participant or group of participants represents a different Mayan city-state. Kids learn about Mayan religion, culture, technology, history, and geography, while completing art and research projects. For students aged 10 and up.

$37

Interact

1825 Gillespie Way, #101

El Cajon, CA 92020

(800) 359-0961/fax (800) 700-5093

Web site: www.interact-simulations.com

Mexican Artdeck

A beautiful pack of 52 playing cards, illustrated with color reproductions of works by 13 20th-century Mexican artists.

$10

Aristoplay

450 S. Wagner Rd.

Ann Arbor, MI 48107

(800) 634-7738 or (888) GR8-GAME

fax (734) 995-4611

Web site: www.aristoplay.com

Peruvian Ocarina Whistle

A craft kit for kids aged 7 and up. Users paint a terra-cotta ocarina patterned with a stylized face based on ancient South American artifacts; then they decorate it and attach a bone-beaded leather cord. All necessary materials are included, plus playing instructions.

$11 from toy and game stores; for a local source, contact

Curiosity Kits

Box 811

Cockeysville, MD 21030

(410) 584-2605 or (800) 584-KITS/fax (410) 584-1247

e-mail: CKitsinc@aol.com

VIDEOS

The Incas

This one-hour PBS special combines an overview of the history of Inca civilization with spectacular film footage of sites of their South American empire.

$19.95
PBS Home Video
1320 Braddock Pl.
Alexandria, VA 22314-1698
(800) 645-4PBS
Web site: www.pbs.org

Lost Cities of the Mayas

From National Geographic, a tour of Mayan civilization, with visits to present-day archaeological sites and re-creations of scenes from ancient Mayan life. Narrated by Susan Sarandon.

$19.95
National Geographic Home Video
Box 5073
Clifton, NJ 07015
(800) 627-5162
Web site: www.nationalgeographic.com

COMPUTER SOFTWARE

Amazon Trail

A rain forest adventure from the makers of the popular "Oregon Trail" (see page 536). Players embark on a back-in-time mission to find some cinchona—the bark is the source of malaria-curing quinine—and deliver it to the ailing Inca king. As kids paddle along the Amazon in canoes, they tangle with piranhas and hostile natives and risk capsizing and running out of supplies. Traveling the trail is a dangerous business. It's also informative; kids pick up a lot of information along the way on the history, geography, and biology of the Amazon region. With photographs, colorful graphics, South American music, and maps. On CD-ROM for Mac or Windows.

Also see "Amazon Trail II," another expedition along the Amazon and through time, in which travelers view over 100 Amazon animals and meet 50 historical characters, among them Teddy Roosevelt and a Spanish conquistador.

$39.95
The Learning Company
6160 Summit Dr. N
Minneapolis, MN 55430-4003
(800) 622-3390/fax (612) 589-1151
Web site: www.learningco.com

MayaQuest

Players follow in the treads of bicyclist Dan Buettner, whose 1994 trip through Central America in search of ancient Mayan civilization provided hosts of schoolchildren with a geographical/archaeological experience via the Internet. In this creative reenactment, kids set out on an expedition through the Yucatán Peninsula. They visit rain forests, archaeological digs, and modern sites, and converse with the people they encounter along the way, all the while attempting to determine the reason for the collapse and disappearance of the Mayan civilization. The program includes over a thousand photographs from the original Buettner trip, plus film clips and audio recordings, maps, an informational text, and creative graphics. On CD-ROM disk for Mac or Windows.

$49.95
The Learning Company
6160 Summit Dr. N
Minneapolis, MN 55430-4003
(800) 622-3390/fax (612) 589-1151
Web site: www.learningco.com

Also see *MayaQuest* (page 424).

THE AMERICAS ON-LINE

The Ancient Maya Civilization

Information about Mayan life and history, a map of the Mayan empire, pictures of artifacts, Mayan recipes and handicrafts, and links to archaeological sites.

pacific.st.vsm.edu/~tpparker/maya.html

The Incas

The history of the Inca empire, maps, a timeline of events from 22,000 B.C. to A.D. 1535, and color photographs of Inca artworks and buildings.

www.colourprep.com/jorge/Incas/Incas.htm

Lords of the Earth

Archaeological and anthropological information on the Maya, Aztec, Inca, Mextec, and North American Indian civilizations.

www.realtime.net/maya

Rabbit in the Moon

An attractive and interesting site on Mayan civilization, filled with information, illustrations, photographs, games, a map of the Mayan empire, and a search function. Included are pages on Mayan hieroglyphic writing, calendars, languages, culture, and architecture. Users can view virtual reality scale models of Mayan buildings.

www.halfmoon.com

Telecom Amazon Adventure Page

A virtual trip along the Amazon River through Brazil and Peru, with information about people, places, animals, the environment, and history. The page includes maps of South American countries and many color photographs. Under Incas, for example, the site includes information on Inca life, religion, history and conquest, language, archaeological sites, and modern-day descendants.

vif27.icair.iac.org.nz/index.htm

ASIA

CATALOGS

Asia for Kids

A catalog of Asian resources for children, including books, videos, audiocassettes, language texts, cookbooks, CD-ROMs, posters, and arts and crafts resources. Included are materials about the cultures, histories, and languages of China, Korea, Japan, and Vietnam.

Asia for Kids
Box 9096
Cincinnati, OH 45209
(513) 563-3100 or (800) 765-5885
Web site: www.afk.com

BOOKS: NONFICTION

A to Zen: A Book of Japanese Culture

Ruth Wells; Picture Book Studio, 1992

This beautiful alphabet book, like a Japanese book, reads back to front. Each word, from *Aikido* to *Zen*, is shown in both Roman letters and Japanese characters, illustrated with a full-color painting, and accompanied by a paragraph of explanation. Words are chosen that represent important aspects of Japanese culture: *E* is for Eto, the Japanese zodiac; *I* for Ichinisan or "counting" (readers are taught Japanese words and characters for the numbers 1 to 10), *K* is for Kimono, *O* for Origami, and *Y* for Yen.

Ancient China

Arthur Cotterell, Alan Hills, and Geoff Brightling; Alfred A. Knopf, 1994

A 64-page volume in the Eyewitness series, light on text but lavishly illustrated with terrific color photographs—many of museum artifacts—and drawings.

China's Long March: 6000 Miles of Danger

Jean Fritz; Putnam, 1988

A 124-page account of the 6,000-mile "Long March" across China made by Mao Zedong's Communist Army in 1934–1935 during the conflict with the forces of Chiang Kai-shek. The book is based in part on interviews with survivors of the march. History made human for readers aged 10 and up.

Cobblestone: Asian History

Issues of *Calliope* magazine (see page 597) with Asian themes include *The Ming Dynasty* (May/June 1995), *The Mongols* (November/December 1993), and *Shoguns and Samurai of Japan* (January/February 1993). Each includes several illustrated nonfiction articles, a map and a timeline, games and puzzles, and a supplementary reading list. *The Mongols*, for example, contains articles on Genghis (Chinggis) and Kublai Khan, medieval travelers to the East, an account of life in the time of the Mongols, an update on modern Mongolia, an interview with an archaeologist working in Mongolia, and an ancient Mongolian folktale.

Issues of *Faces* magazine (see page 411) with Asian themes include *Japan* (April 1990) and *Dragons* (April,

1985). *Japan* contains nonfiction articles on modern and ancient Japan, among them "The Samurai," a Japanese folktale and song, a recipe for teriyaki, and an article on ikebana, with instructions for making your own traditional Japanese flower arrangement. *Dragons* contains a nonfiction account of the dragon in Asian culture and history, two Chinese dragon folktales, a connect-the-dots dragon puzzle, and a Chinese paper cutout dragon project.

> Available from most libraries or for $4.50 from
> Cobblestone Publishing, Inc.
> 30 Grove St.
> Peterborough, NH 03458
> (603) 924-7209 or (800) 821-0115
> Web site: www.cobblestonepub.com

Commodore Perry in the Land of the Shogun
Rhoda Blumberg; Lothrop, Lee & Shepard, 1985

A fascinating 144-page account of Commodore Matthew Perry and the "opening" of isolated Japan to interaction with the West in 1853. "If monsters had descended upon Japan the effect could not have been more terrifying," the book begins. "People in the fishing village of Shimoda were the first to spot four huge hulks, two streaming smoke, on the ocean's surface approaching shore. 'Giant dragons puffing smoke,' cried some. 'Alien ships of fire,' cried others. According to a folktale, smoke above water was made by the breath of clams." That last line alone was enough to hook our kids. Illustrated with period prints and drawings, many by Japanese artists.

Gandhi
Leonard Everett Fisher; Atheneum, 1995

A biography of Gandhi, dramatically illustrated in black and white, describing his role in the protest against South African apartheid and in the struggle to free India from British colonial rule through a policy of peaceful resistance. For readers aged 9–13.

The Great Wall of China
Leonard Everett Fisher; Aladdin, 1995

A picture-book account of the building of the Great Wall some 2,500 years ago to keep the invading Mongols out of the country. A phrase in red Chinese calligraphy appears on each page (with translations at the end of the book).

In the Land of the Taj Mahal: The World of the Fabled Mughals
Ed Rothfarb; Henry Holt, 1998

An overview of the fabulous world of Mughal India from the 16th to the 18th century for readers aged 9–12.

Inside Story: A Samurai Castle
Fiona Macdonald and David Antram; Peter Bedrick Books, 1995

The book takes readers inside a samurai castle for a look at the lives and times of the Japanese samurai warriors. For readers aged 9–12.

Red Scarf Girl: A Memoir of the Cultural Revolution
Ji-Li Jiang; HarperCollins, 1997

Jiang was a teenager in the 1960s at the time of Chairman Mao's Cultural Revolution. Her book is a chilling memoir of the political and cultural witch-hunt in Communist China, a policy that shattered Chinese society and resulted in the literal destruction of Chinese history. Students, organized in the Red Guard, forcibly rooted out the "Four Olds": old ideas, old culture, old customs, and old habits. For readers aged 12 and up.

BOOKS: FICTION

Between the Dragon and the Eagle
Mical Schneider; Lerner, 1996

The story of a bolt of sky blue silk, traveling the ancient Silk Road from China to Rome in A.D. 100. The silk's journey is narrated first by a Chinese caravan leader, then a Turkmenistan merchant and his son, an Arab camel guide, a family of Egyptian women, and finally—at the receiving end—citizens of Rome. For readers aged 9–13.

The Boy and the Samurai

Erik Christian Haugaard; Houghton Mifflin, 1991

Set in 16th-century Japan in the days of civil war, this story tells how young Saru, an orphan, helps a samurai warrior to rescue his wife, who has been imprisoned by a wicked warlord. For readers aged 11 and up.

The Cat Who Went to Heaven

Elizabeth Coatsworth; Aladdin, 1990

The classic tale of a poor Japanese artist, his much-loved white cat, Good Fortune, a very special painting commission, and a Buddhist miracle. For readers aged 8–11.

Grass Sandals: The Travels of Basho

Dawnine Spivak; Atheneum, 1997

A picture book about the 17th-century Japanese poet Basho. Each double-page spread contains a section of the ongoing story of Basho's travels across Japan, a haiku written by Basho, and a Japanese word shown in kanji characters and in English translation. Beautifully illustrated with Japanese-style paintings. For readers aged 6–10.

Kim

Rudyard Kipling; Bantam, 1983

Kim, an Irish orphan, lives on his own in Lahore, India, in the days of the British Raj. He becomes a chela—disciple and guide—to a Tibetan lama on a quest and travels through 19th-century India, eventually becoming entangled in the intrigue and excitement of the "Great Game." For readers aged 12 and up.

The Master Puppeteer

Katherine Paterson; HarperTrophy, 1989

A historical novel set in 18th-century Japan in which Jiro, the son of a puppet maker, runs away from home and apprentices himself to the Hanaza puppet theater in Osaka. Other historical novels of Japan by Paterson include *Of Nightingales That Weep* (1989), and *The Sign of the Chrysanthemum* (1988). See *Rebels of the Heavenly Kingdom* (right).

Ming Lo Moves the Mountain

Arnold Lobel; Mulberry, 1993

Ming Lo and his wife are miserable living in the dreary shadow of the great neighboring mountain, until the very clever village wise man comes up with a way to make the mountain move. For readers aged 4–9.

Rebels of the Heavenly Kingdom

Katherine Paterson; Puffin, 1995

A story set in mid-19th-century China. Young Wang Lee, son of a poverty-stricken peasant family, is kidnapped by bandits during the Taiping Rebellion. He is saved by Mai Lin, a member of the Taiping Tienkuo, a secret society dedicated to the overthrow of the ruling Manchu government. For readers aged 12 and up.

Rikki-Tikki-Tavi

Rudyard Kipling; Candlewick, 1997

Rikki-Tikki-Tavi is a mongoose, adopted by a English family living in India. Rikki manages to thwart the plans of the dangerous cobras, Nag and Nagina, who want to kill the humans and raise their family in the deserted bungalow. An exciting tale for readers aged 6–11.

The Tale of the Mandarin Ducks

Katherine Paterson; Puffin, 1995

In ancient Japan, a cruel overload captures a beautiful wild duck and imprisons it on his estate. The duck, with the help of the lord's chief steward, Shozo, escapes, and, together with his mate, helps Shozo and the little kitchen maid whom he loves escape in turn to live happily ever after in the forest. Illustrated with beautifully colored Japanese-style paintings. For readers aged 5–9.

Tikki Tikki Tembo

Arlene Mosel; Henry Holt, 1989

Once upon a time firstborn Chinese children were given long names—until the fateful day when Tikki Tikki Tembo No Sa Rembo Chari Bari Ruchi Pip Peri Pembo fell down the well. A perennial favorite. For readers aged 4–8.

FOLKTALES AND LEGENDS

The Empress and the Silkworm
Lily Toy Hong; Albert Whitman, 1995

The fairy-tale version of the origin of silk. The wife of the Yellow Emperor is having tea and mooncakes in the garden when a silkworm's cocoon falls from an overhanging mulberry bush into her teacup. The wet cocoon unwinds into a long shimmering thread that the Empress, a clever woman, realizes could be woven into a marvelous cloth. For readers aged 5–9.

The Gifts of Wali Dad:
A Tale of India and Pakistan
Aaron Shepard; Atheneum, 1995

Wali Dad, a grass cutter, sends a gold bracelet to the princess who is the "noblest lady" in the land. Grateful, she sends him a rich gift—which Wali Dad sends to the prince. The prince reciprocates, and Wali Dad again passes the present on. Eventually the prince and princess are brought together to live happily ever after and Wali Dad is happy to be a presentless grass cutter once again. For readers aged 4–8.

The Girl Who Loved Caterpillars
Jean Merrill; Paper Star, 1997

A picture-book tale of independent-minded young Izumi, who prefers worms, toads, and caterpillars to the amusements of the ladies at the emperor's court. Based on a 12th-century folktale. For readers aged 5–9.

The Golden Goose King:
A Tale Told by the Buddha
Judith Ernst; Parvardigar Press, 1995

A traditional Jakata tale—one of some 500 Buddhist parables—about a hunter who seeks a golden goose for the king. He captures a pair of geese, whose love, courage, and fidelity so impress the king and queen that they are allowed to go free. Beautifully illustrated with Indian-style paintings. For readers aged 6–10.

Jojofu
Michael Waite; Lothrop, Lee & Shepard, 1996

Jojofu is the bravest and smartest hunting dog in all the land, who saves his master, Takumi, from dan-

ger after danger. Based on a folktale taken from medieval Japanese scrolls.

Lon Po Po: A Red Riding Hood
Story from China
Ed Young; Paper Star, 1996

Three clever sisters defeat a big bad Chinese wolf by trapping him in the gingko tree. For readers aged 4–8.

The Mountains of Tibet
Mordicai Gerstein; HarperTrophy, 1989

Based on the Tibetan *Book of the Dead,* this is the life story of a Tibetan woodcutter who, at the end of his life, must make a decision whether to become a part of heaven or to be reborn to live another life. Beautiful and thought provoking. For readers aged 6–10.

The Rainbow People

Laurence Yep; HarperCollins, 1992

A collection of 20 Chinese folktales in five categories: "Tricksters," "Fools," "Virtues and Vices," "In Chinese America," and "Love."

Rama and the Demon King:
An Ancient Tale from India
Jessica Souhami; Little, Brown, 1997

A picture-book version of a Hindu tale from the *Ramayana.* The book tells the story of good prince Rama, exiled by his jealous stepmother to a forest of demons where he must live for 14 years. Rama is accompanied into exile by his wife, Sita, who is stolen by Ravana, the 10-headed Demon King. Rama and his brother, with the aid of Hanuman the Monkey King and his army, manage to defeat the demons and save Sita. They then return to India, where Rama becomes king and rules wisely and well. For readers aged 5–9.

The Samurai's Daughter
Stephen T. Johnson; Dial, 1992

A picture book based on a medieval Japanese legend about the brave Tokoyo, whose father has raised her with all the virtues and principles of the samurai. When Tokoyo's father is unfairly exiled, Tokoyo sets out to join him, tackling bandits, ghosts, and a sea monster en route. Finally she manages to remove a terrible curse, returning her father to the emperor's favor. For readers aged 6–10.

 ### Savitri: A Tale of Ancient India
Aaron Shepard; Albert Whitman, 1992

A picture-book version of a tale from the *Mahabharata* about the beautiful Princess Savitri who, insisting on choosing a husband for herself, marries the poor son of a conquered king—in spite of a dreadful prophecy that the prince is to die in just one year. When Death appears to claim her husband, clever Savitri outwits him and does it so well that she not only saves his life but restores his kingdom. For readers aged 6–10.

The Stonecutter: A Japanese Folktale
Gerald McDermott; Viking, 1978

A picture-book version of a Japanese folktale about a stonecutter, granted wishes to take on forms increasingly great and powerful, until he finally discovers that being himself, a stonecutter, is the best of all. For readers aged 5–9.

Tales of a Chinese Grandmother
Frances Carpenter; Charles E. Tuttle, 1994

Thirty Chinese folktales told by Grandmother Lao Lao to her two grandchildren, all with wonderful titles: "The Poet and the Peony Princess," "The First Emperor's Magic Whip," "The Mandarin and the Butterflies."

 ### Yeh-Shen
Ai-Ling Louie; Paper Star, 1996

The Chinese version of Cinderella, in which the downtrodden daughter wishes on the bones of a magical fish and receives a glorious kingfisher feather cloak and a pair of tiny golden sandals. For readers aged 5–9.

COLORING AND PAPER-CRAFTS BOOKS

Ancient China
Bellerophon publishes several coloring books on Asian culture and civilizations. *Ancient China* contains black-line illustrations of Chinese artworks and paintings and portraits of emperors and empresses. Also see *A Coloring Book of Japan,* a history of Japanese arts from ancient to modern times. Each book includes an informational text.

$3.95

Bellerophon Books

36 Ancapa St.

Santa Barbara, CA 93101

(800) 253-9943/fax (800) 965-8286

A Coloring Book of Ancient India
Black-line illustrations covering the period from the arrival of Alexander to Great to the 12th century, with many scenes from Hindu legends. (There's also a marvelous white elephant on the cover.) The book contains a brief informational text.

$3.95

Bellerophon Books

36 Ancapa St.

Santa Barbara, CA 93101

(800) 253-9943/fax (800) 965-8286

Easy Origami
John Montroll; Dover Publications

For kids interested in the Oriental art of origami, Dover publishes a wide selection of instruction books for paper folders of all skill levels. Many are packaged with packs of 7 × 7-inch multicolored origami paper. *Easy Origami* contains instructions for 32 simple projects, among them a hat, a swan, and a frog. Also for beginners see *Fun With Easy Origami* (32 projects and 24 sheets of paper) and *Fun With Origami* (17 projects, plus paper). A number of origami theme books are also available, specializing in patterns for origami birds, sea life, airplanes, African animals, insects, and dinosaurs.

Dover Publications, Inc.

31 E. Second St.

Mineola, NY 11501

Japanese Kimono Paper Dolls
Japanese paper dolls in full color with two dolls and 26 kimonos. Also see *Kabuki Costumes,* which includes two dolls and 16 costumes.

$4.95

Dover Publications, Inc.

31 E. Second St.

Mineola, NY 11501

The Usborne Book of Origami
Kate Needham; Usborne Publishing, 1992

This is an excellent instruction book for novices—even I, a perfect dunce at origami, can manage it. The book is targeted at absolute beginners (it even shows you how to fold a sheet of paper in half), and the instructions are detailed, clear, and easy to follow. There's none of this business so common to more advanced origami instruction books where suddenly, between steps 5 and 6, the instructions make an incomprehensible leap from little square into jointed cricket. The book describes about 15 projects, some with variations, and many have added attractions: they fly, snap, inflate, explode, or make banging noises. Included are a fluttering butterfly, an inflatable bunny rabbit, a jumping frog, and a whole set of finger puppets.

EDC Publishing

10302 E. 55th Pl.

Tulsa, OK 74146

(800) 475-4522

Web site: www.edcpub.com

ACTIVITY BOOKS

Long is a Dragon: Chinese Writing for Children
Peggy Goldstein; Scholastic, 1991

A delightful Chinese red 30-page paperback that teaches kids the history of Chinese pictographs with simple instructions, complete with numbered strokes and directional arrows for making them. Stick it out until page 26 and you'll learn how to write "a giant general-purpose transistorized digital computer" in Chinese. Also by Goldstein: *Hu Is a Tiger: An Introduction to Chinese Writing*.

Teaching East Asia
Over 40 lesson plans, outlines, and activity suggestions for middle school students. The plans are thematically and geographically categorized and cover the culture, governments, geography, and economic policies of East Asian countries.

$10

East Asian Studies Center

Memorial Hall West 207

Indiana University

Bloomington, IN 47405

(800) 441-3272

GAMES AND HANDS-ON ACTIVITIES

Ancient China Scientific Explorer Kit

A "History of Science" kit from Scientific Explorer (see pages 223–224) with which kids can build a magnetic compass based on a Chinese model from 300 B.C., make a printing stamp and learn about the world's oldest written language, and construct a model of an ancient Chinese kite and use it to study aerodynamics. The kit includes a detailed booklet of instructions and historical background information.

$23.95

Scientific Explorer, Inc.

2802 E. Madison, Suite 114

Seattle, WA 98112

(206) 322-7611 or (800) 900-1182/fax (206) 322-7610

e-mail: sciex@scientificexplorer.com

Web site: www.scientificexplorer.com

Ancient China Treasure Chest
A beautifully illustrated treasure chest–shaped box with a locking clasp, stuffed with activities and information about life in ancient China in the period 1523 B.C. to A.D. 906. The box includes a three-dimensional color model of the Great Wall, complete with cardboard soldiers, a Chinese brush and ink block for practicing calligraphy, a set of I-Ching fortune-telling coins, and materials for making a folding Chinese fan, plus posters, maps, and a 32-page book of instructions and historical background information by Chao-Hui Jenny Liu.

$19.95 from book or game stores or

Running Press Book Publishers

125 S. 22nd St.

Philadelphia, PA 19103-4399

(215) 567-5080 or (800) 345-5359/fax (800) 453-2884

The Arabs

A portfolio of historical essays and primary source materials. "The Arabs" includes essays on the cultural heritage of the Arabs, the development of the modern Arab states, and the political influence of the Arab countries in the world today. Supplementary source materials include a timeline of Arab history from 3000 B.C. to the present, an illustrated introduction to the Arab language, biographies of prominent Arabs, and a document titled "Palestine: The Search for a Just Solution."

Also see "The World of Islam" (see Religion, page 805), which contains essays on Islamic religion, art, science, and history. Supplementary materials include a color reproduction of a page from the Qur'an (Koran), historical maps charting the spread of Islam, biographies of famous Muslim rulers, and a survey of famous Islamic cities.

$37

Jackdaw Publications

Box 503

Amawalk, NY 10503

(914) 962-6911 or (800) 789-0022/fax (800) 962-9101

China: A Cultural Heritage

A portfolio of essays and primary source materials illustrating the long, rich history of Chinese culture from ancient to modern times. The portfolio contains four illustrated historical background essays ("Artists, Craftsmen, Techniques, Materials," "Chinese Society, Dress and Behavior," "Literature in Poetry and Prose," and "Search for Harmony and Tranquillity: Religion in China") and nine facsimiles of historical documents or materials, including a six-foot-long "Great Wall Chart" with a timeline of Chinese history, copies of handscroll paintings, a color photograph of the jade burial suite of Princess Tou Wan, a copy of the *Analects* of Confucius, a chart illustrating Chinese technological achievements, instructions for making an octagon kite, and a copy of a Cultural Revolution propaganda poster. Also included are notes on the historical documents and materials, and a detailed study guide.

$37

Jackdaw Publications

Box 503

Amawalk, NY 10501

(914) 962-6911 or (800) 789-0022/fax (800) 962-9101

Chinese Brush Painting Workstation

Hsu I-Ching; Design Eye Holdings, Ltd./Price Stern Sloan, 1993

This attractive kit contains a color-illustrated book, *Chinese Brush Painting*, by Hsu I-Ching, 32 pages of Chinese paper, and all the supplies needed for beginning Chinese-style painters: ink stick and inkstone, two bamboo brushes, colored paints, and a blue-and-white porcelain mixing dish. The book includes step-by-step instructions and many models for copying, among them "traditional subjects" such as roosters, fish, bamboo, and butterflies, landscapes, and Chinese calligraphy.

$21.95 from bookstores

Honor of the Samurai

In this creative card game, each player—a samurai warrior—competes to become the bravest and most honorable in the land. Color-illustrated cards add to the adventure, conferring advantage or threatening danger or disgrace. Included are four Oriental-patterned dice. For three to six players aged 10 and up.

$23.95 from game stores or

Turn Off the TV

Box 4162

Bellevue, WA 98009

(800) 949-8688/fax (425) 558-7564

Web site: www.turnoffthetv.com

Maharaja

A strategy game covering 3,000 years of Indian history, from the invasion of the Aryans of Central Asia through the arrival of the Portuguese in the 15th century to the establishment of the British Raj in 1849. Each player controls several nationalities, all competing to establish a leader as "Great King" of India. The game is played on a detailed mapboard of the Indian subcontinent.

$30

Avalon Hill Game Co.

4517 Harford Rd.

Baltimore, MD 21214

(410) 254-9200 or (800) 999-3222

e-mail: AH GAMES@aol.com

Web site: www.avalonhill.com

Video

Big Bird in China

In *Big Bird in China, Sesame Street*'s Big Bird and his floppy friend Barkley travel to China in search of the legendary Phoenix. There they see many famous historical sights, including the impressive Great Wall, meet the magical Monkey King, and learn a few useful Chinese phrases, among them "Hello" and "I love you."

Also see *Big Bird in Japan,* which takes the Bird to Japan, where he visits historical sites and landmarks, makes friends with a Japanese family, learns about Japanese culture, and picks up a few words in Japanese. For kids aged 4–9.

$14.95
Movies Unlimited
3015 Darnell Rd.
Philadelphia, PA 19154
(215) 637-4444 or (800) 4-MOVIES
e-mail: movies@moviesunlimited.com
Web site: www.moviesunlimited.com

Gandhi

A stirring and spectacularly photographed biography of Mahatma Gandhi, with Ben Kingsley in the title role. The film, which won an Academy Award, covers Gandhi's life from his struggles with apartheid in South Africa through his efforts to free India from British colonial rule to his tragic death. 200 minutes on two videocassettes.

$29.99
Movies Unlimited
3015 Darnell Rd.
Philadelphia, PA 19154
(215) 637-4444 or (800) 4-MOVIES
e-mail: movies@moviesunlimited.com
Web site: www.moviesunlimited.com

The Silk Road

A photographic journey along the fabulous Silk Road, the same path traveled by Marco Polo en route to Cathay. Viewers begin in Xi'an (the world's largest city circa A.D. 600), home of the famous Clay Army, and proceed through a tour of famous Asian historical sites, including the Ma-gao Caves of the Gobi Desert, a vast underground network of caves and tunnels filled with over 3,000 painted murals and statues. The six-part series includes "A Thousand Kilometers Beyond the Yellow River," "Across the Taklamacan Desert," "The Art Gallery in the Desert," "In Search of the Kingdom of Lou-Lan," "Glories of Ancient Chang-An," and "The Dark Castle." On six videocassettes.

$149.95
PBS Home Video
1320 Braddock Pl.
Alexandria, VA 22314-1698
(800) 645-4PBS
Web site: www.pbs.org

Computer Software

The First Emperor of China

The first emperor of China was Qin Shi Huang Di, whose tomb—guarded by an army of 7,000 life-size terra-cotta soldiers—was discovered in 1974. This CD-ROM includes a timeline, multiple interactive maps, historical background on the emperor and his reign, over 2,000 illustrations, live film footage of the excavations at his tomb, and an aerial tour of the Great Wall of China (which the emperor completed). On CD-ROM for Mac or Windows.

$38.95
Learn Technologies Interactive
Box 2284
S. Burlington, VT 05417
(888) 292-5584
Web site: voyager.learntech.com/cdrom
or
Zenger Media
10200 Jefferson Blvd.
Box 802
Culver City, CA 90232-0802
(310) 839-2436 or (800) 421-4246/fax (310) 839-2249
or (800) 944-5432
e-mail: access@ZengerMedia.com

The Silk Road

An interactive journey along the fabulous Silk Road which stretches from Xian, China, to the Indian Ocean. The program is filled with wonderful color photographs, audio clips, maps, games, and quizzes centering around the history, geography, and many cultures found along the road. On CD-ROM for Mac or Windows.

$39.95

Zenger Media

10200 Jefferson Blvd.

Box 802

Culver City, CA 90232-0802

(310) 839-2436 or (800) 421-4246/fax (310) 839-2249 or (800) 944-5432

e-mail: access@ZengerMedia.com

Web site: ZengerMedia.com/Zenger

ASIA ON-LINE

Empires Beyond the Great Wall: The Heritage of Genghis Khan

A biography of Genghis Khan plus a virtual tour of an exhibit of Genghis Khan–era artifacts, including clothing, armor, and pottery.

www.com/khan

Encyclopaedia of the Orient

A lot of information arranged alphabetically: look up Pharaoh, for example, and you get a definition, a discussion of Egyptian rulers, and a timeline of Egyptian dynasties. By "Orient," the site means north Africa and the Middle East.

i-cias.com/e.o/index.htm

Oriental Institute Archaeology

The site provides information on current digs and archaeological projects by the Oriental Institute at the University of Chicago, with links to related sites.

www-oi.uchicago.edu/OI/PROJ/OI_Archaeology.html

The Silk Road

A detailed history of the Silk Road that linked Europe and the Orient in ancient times, with assorted illustrations.

www.atm.ch.cam.ac.uk/~oliver/silk.html

South Asia Before 1947

Historical background information, a photo gallery, sound clips of Mahatma Gandhi, and on-line tours of archaeological sites. Included is a slide tour of ancient Indian civilization titled "Around the Indus in 90 Slides."

www.harappa.com

AFRICA

BOOKS

Africa

Yvonne Ayo, Geoff Dann, and Ray Moller; Alfred A. Knopf, 1995

A volume in the Eyewitness series, covering the world of precolonial Africa through a fascinating collection of color photographs and drawings. Most of the text is in the picture legends.

African Beginnings

Jim Haskins, Kathleen Benson, and Floyd Cooper; Lothrop, Lee & Shepard, 1998

A beautifully designed chronological history of 11 ancient African civilizations, covering the period from 3800 B.C. to A.D. 1665. The book is 48 pages long, illustrated with color paintings, plus maps, a timeline, and an extensive bibliography. For readers aged 9–12.

African Kingdoms of the Past Series

Kenny Mann; Dillon Press, 1996

An attractive six-volume series on ancient African history, written in an engaging, reader-friendly style, and richly illustrated with maps, drawings, engravings, and photographs of archaeological sites and artifacts— including textiles, pottery, and jewelry. The books cover the history of each civilization, the customs and everyday life of the people, profiles of famous individuals, and indigenous myths and legends. Titles include *Egypt, Kush, Aksum: Northeast Africa; Ghana, Mali, Songhay: The Western Sudan; Kongo Ndongo: West Central Africa; Monomotapa, Zulu, Basuto: Southern Africa; Oyo, Benin, Ashanti: The Guinea Coast;* and *Zenj, Buganda: East Africa.* Each is over 100+ pages long; for readers aged 10 and up.

Ashanti to Zulu: African Traditions

Margaret Musgrove; Dial, 1992

A richly illustrated alphabet book of African cultures, from Ashanti, Baule, and Chagga to Xhosa, Yoruba, and Zulu. For each, there's a short paragraph of catchy information.

The Day Gogo Went to Vote

Elinor Batezat Sisulu; Little, Brown, 1996

April 1994 in South Africa: the date on which black South Africans were allowed to vote for the first time in a national election. This picture-book account of a landmark political event is told through the eyes of Thembi, whose great-grandmother, Gogo, is so old that she hasn't left the house in many years. She insists, however, on going to cast her vote for Nelson Mandela in the election, and Thembi goes with her.

From Afar to Zulu: A Dictionary of African Cultures

Jim Haskins; Walker & Company, 1995

A 212-page introduction to African culture. Haskins describes the history, traditions, social and political structure, and everyday life of 30 African ethnic groups. Illustrated with photographs and maps.

Jambo Means Hello: A Swahili Alphabet Book

Muriel Feelings; Dial, 1985

An illustrated introduction to everyday life in East Africa, from *A* to *Z* in Swahili, the national language of Kenya, Tanzania, and Uganda. By the same author: *Moja Means One: A Swahili Counting Book* (1992)

Mandela: From the Life of the South African Statesman

Floyd Cooper; Philomel Books, 1996

A picture-book biography of Nelson Mandela, from his childhood as a chieftain's son through his struggles with apartheid in South Africa, his activities as a member of the African National Congress, his imprisonment, and his election as the first president of the new South Africa. A few more biographical details (such as Mandela's award of the Nobel Peace Prize in 1993) are mentioned in a note in the back. Illustrated with color paintings. For readers aged 7–10.

The Kingdoms of Africa Series

Philip Koslow; Chelsea House

A series of 60+-page books on the religious, social, and political histories of the kingdoms of ancient Africa. Titles include *Ancient Ghana: The Land of Gold* (1995); *Asante: The Gold Coast* (1996); *Benin: Lords of the River* (1996); *Building a New World: Africans in America 1500–1900* (1997); *Dahomey: The Warrior Kings* (1996); *Hausaland: The Fortress Kingdoms* (1995); *Kanem-Borno: 1000 Years of Splendor* (1995); *Lords of the Savanna: The Bambara, Fulani, Igbo, Mossi and Nupe* (1997); *Mali: Crossroads of Africa* (1995); *Senegambia: Land of the Lion* (1996); *Songhay: The Empire Builders* (1995); and *Yorubaland: The Flowering of Genius* (1996). For readers aged 12 and up.

The Royal Kingdoms of Ghana, Mali and Songhay: Life in Medieval Africa

Patricia McKissack and Fredrick McKissack; Henry Holt, 1995

A history of the flourishing medieval civilizations of western Africa, with their talented metalsmiths, their gold and salt mines, and their near-legendary leaders, such as Sundiata and Mansa Kankan Musa. The text isn't all that catchy but includes a lot of information not ordinarily found in world history texts. For readers aged 12 and up.

Shaka King of the Zulus

Diane Stanley and Peter Vennema; Mulberry, 1994

Shaka ruled the Zulus for 12 years in the early part of the 19th century; he was a powerful military and political leader who became, at the end of his life, viciously insane. This storybook-style account of his life is illustrated with Zulu art and artifacts. It looks like a picture book for little kids but is more appropriate for middle-grade readers.

Sundiata: Lion King of Mali

David Wisniewski; Clarion, 1992

The tale of the crippled young king whose kindness eventually allows him to triumph. Terrific cut-paper illustrations. For readers aged 5–9.

HISTORY

Folktales and Legends

Anansi the Spider
Gerald McDermott; Henry Holt, 1987

An Ashanti trickster tale about Anansi and his six sons, which tells how the moon came to be placed in the sky. Also by McDermott: *Zomo the Rabbit: A Trickster Tale from West Africa* (Harcourt Brace, 1992).

Bringing the Rain to Kapiti Plain
Verna Aardema; Dial, 1992

A magical arrow shot brings the rain to Kapiti Plain. A young-child-pleasing repetitive text and colorful stylized illustrations.

How Many Spots Does a Leopard Have? And Other Tales
Julius Lester; Scholastic, 1994

An illustrated collection of 12 folktales—10 from Africa—variously explaining why monkeys live in trees, why the sun and moon live in the sky, and why nobody knows how many spots a leopard has. For all ages.

The Leopard's Drum: An Asante Tale from West Africa
Jessica Souhami; Little, Brown, 1996

Nyame, the sky god, offers a reward to whoever can bring him Osebo the leopard's fine, huge, and magnificent drum. The little tortoise, Achi-cheri, succeeds, cleverly tricking the leopard, and wins a protective shell as a reward. For readers aged 6–10.

Marriage of the Rain Goddess: A South African Myth
Margaret Olivia Wolfson; Shooting Star Press, 1996

A picture-book version of a Zulu myth in which the rain goddess Mbaba Mwana Waresa searches for true love and finds it in the person of a simple cattle herder from a little village. Brief notes describe Zulu culture and customs. Illustrated with colorful paintings. For readers aged 6–11.

Misoso: Once Upon a Time Tales from Africa
Verna Aardema; Alfred A. Knopf, 1994

A brilliantly illustrated collection of 12 African folktales, among them "Kindai and the Ape," an African version of the "Androcles and the Lion" legend, a Temne tale about how crying came to the world, and an Anansi the Spider tale from Liberia. A note on the culture and history of the people that originated the story follows each tale, and a colorful map shows each story's place of origin. For readers aged 4–10.

Mufaro's Beautiful Daughters
John Steptoe; Lothrop, Lee & Shepard, 1987

A Zimbabwean Cinderella tale of Mufaro's two beautiful daughters, Manyara, who is selfish and mean, and Nyasha, who is kind and good.

The River That Went to the Sky: Twelve Tales by African Storytellers
Mary Medlicott, ed.; Kingfisher Books, 1995

Twelve illustrated stories from different regions of Africa, all by contemporary writers. Nine of of the stories are based on traditional folktales.

The Village of Round and Square Houses
Ann Grifalconi; Little, Brown, 1985

A tale from Cameroon, which explains why, in the little village of Tos, men live in square-shaped houses, while women and children live in round houses.

Why Mosquitoes Buzz in People's Ears: A West African Tale
Verna Aardema; Dial, 1992

Mosquito tells a dreadful lie that results in the sun's not rising; when the other animals figure out what happened, Mosquito is punished. With Aardema's wonderful illustrations of lavender pythons, green iguanas, blue crows, and orange owls.

Aardema has written many other picture-book versions of African folktales for young readers, among them *How the Ostrich Got Its Long Neck: A Tale from the Akamba of Kenya* (Scholastic, 1995), *The Lonely Lioness and the Ostrich Chicks: A Masai Tale* (Alfred A. Knopf, 1996), and *Rabbit Makes a Monkey Out of Lion: A Swahili Tale* (Puffin, 1993).

See *A Ring of Tricksters* (page 658) and *The Rain Forest Storybook* (page 658).

Coloring Books

A Coloring Book of Ancient Africa

Black-line reproductions of artworks from Benin. Also see *Ancient Africa Volume 2: The Art of Ife,* artworks from the 11th- to 15th-century kingdom of Ife.

$2.95 each
Bellerophon Books
36 Ancapa St.
Santa Barbara, CA 93101
(800) 253-9943/fax (800) 965-8286

The Story of Africa and Her Flags to Color

An alphabetical country-by-country overview of African history, from Algeria to Zimbabwe. For each country, there's a black-line drawing of the national flag to color (with description, so you can't go wrong), plus a brief history.

$3.95
Bellerophon Books
36 Ancapa St.
Santa Barbara, CA 93101
(800) 253-9943/fax (800) 965-8286

Games and Hands-On Activities

Africa 1880: The Game of Exploration and Exploitation

A strategy game of colonization in which the European nations race to control the "Dark Continent." The board is a colorful map of Africa; playing pieces are resin-cast stone huts. Players must annex territory, negotiate alliances, and declare war on their colonial neighbors to come out on top. For two to four players aged 14 and up.

From game stores or Clash of Arms Games
The Byne Building, #205
Lincoln and Morgan Sts.
Phoenixville, PA 19460
(610) 935-7622
Web site: www.clashofarms.com

African Artdeck

A pack of color-illustrated playing cards picturing 52 African artifacts from a 200-year span of African culture. Included are statues, carvings, headdresses, and masks.

$10
Aristoplay
450 S. Wagner Rd.
Ann Arbor, MI 48107
(800) 634-7738 or (888) GR8-GAME
fax (734) 995-4611
Web site: www.aristoplay.com

African Mask

The kit includes a precut 14-inch cardboard mask; kids color the mask and decorate it with multicolored strands of raffia (to be knotted through prepunched holes). The result is showily impressive and can be used for storytelling, game playing, or just plain hanging on the wall. For kids aged 6 and up.

$12 from toy and game stores; for a local source, contact
Curiosity Kits
Box 811
Cockeysville, MD 21030
(410) 584-2605 or (800) 584-KITS/fax (410) 584-1247
e-mail: Ckitsinc@aol.com

Big Bag Dashiki

Large white paper bags, with a couple of scissor cuts, sponge printing, and Magic Marker work, turn into a terrific traditional African dashiki. Available in packs of 36, for a whole class of kids or a party, including brushes, sponges, paint, and Magic Markers. The bags measure $17\frac{1}{2} \times 24\frac{1}{2}$ inches and fit most elementary school–aged (and –sized) kids. If you're already supplied with sponges, paint, brushes, and markers, white bags are available alone, still in a 36-pack.

Complete kit, $21.99; bags alone, $9.99
S & S Arts & Crafts
Box 513
Colchester, CT 06415-0513
(800) 243-9232/fax (800) 566-6678
Web site: www.snswwide.com

7 The Games of Africa

Jennifer Prior; HarperFestival, 1994

Five respresentative African games, bound in a book, which somehow manages to include a plastic "Mancala" playing board and 48 red and yellow playing pieces. Games include "Mancala," "Achi" (an African version of tic-tac-toe), "Yote" (checkers with a twist), "Sey," and a "Guinean String Puzzle." Everything is included, plus information about the history of each game and its country or region of origin.

8 Mancala

This ancient African game has been played for thousands of years; a version of a "Mancala" board was found carved in the stone of the Great Pyramid of Cheops. In its simplest incarnation, the game was played on homemade "boards" scooped out in the ground, and an equivalently homemade modern version can be made with a cardboard egg carton. The "Mancala" board has six shallow cups or compartments on each side, plus a larger reservoir at either end to hold captured pieces. Many small objects make good playing pieces: beans, polished stones, ceramic beads, pennies. "Mancala" is a strategy game. The rules are simple: basically players take turns scooping pieces out of individual compartments and distributing them one by one around the board; the aim is to drop your last piece so as to capture pieces in the compartments on your opponent's side of the board. It's fun, fast-paced, suitable for a wide range of ages, and trickier than it sounds. Many incarnations of the game are on the market. Ours, on the lower end of the scale, has a pine board and a lot of smooth little playing pebbles; before that, we used an egg carton and kidney beans.

$12 to $45 from toy and game stores or
$24
Animal Town
Box 757
Greenland, NH 03840
(800) 445-8642/fax (603) 430-0334

7 Thumb Piano

Make your own 6½ × 5-inch painted African mbira, using precut wood pieces and bamboo sticks.

Playing instructions and some beginner's sheet music are included.

$13.50 from toy and game stores; for a local source, contact
Curiosity Kits
Box 811
Cockeysville, MD 21030
(410) 584-2605 or (800) 584-KITS/fax (410) 584-1247
e-mail: CKitsinc@aol.com

COMPUTER SOFTWARE

10 AfricaTrail

In "AfricaTrail," indomitable Dan Buettner, who bicycled through Central America in "MayaQuest" (page 660), pedals from Tunisia to South Africa. On-screen, kids can travel along, learning as they go about the geography, history, and culture of Africa—and juggling the requirements of a cross-continental bike trip, managing the budget, buying supplies, selecting routes, and obtaining visas and changing money at each border crossing. Includes maps, illustrations, photographs, and games. Recommended for players aged 10–16. On CD-ROM for Mac or Windows.

$49.95
The Learning Company
6160 Summit Dr. N
Minneapolis, MN 55430-4003
(800) 622-3390/fax (612) 589-1151
Web site: www.learningco.com

AFRICA ON-LINE

9 Africa Odyssey Interactive

Resources for teaching about the arts and cultures of Africa. Included are historical information about the ancient empires of Africa, maps, and a history of the mapping of Africa.

artsedge.kennedy_center.org/odyssey.html

9 African Studies:
Country-Specific Information

Statistics, language information, a color picture of the national flag, a map, and a list of related links for all the countries of Africa, listed in alphabetical order from Algeria to Zimbabwe.

www.sas.upenn.edu/African_Studies/k-12/menu_EduKNTR.html

K–12 Africa Guide
ALL Many Internet resources for teachers on a wide range of African topics.

www.sas.upenn.edu/African_Studies/Home_Page/AFR_GIDE.html

THE EIGHTEENTH AND NINETEENTH CENTURIES

BOOKS: NONFICTION

Daily Life in a Victorian House
Laura Wilson; Preservation Press, 1993

What was everyday life like in the 19th century? The book tells all about the lives of a Victorian-era family and their servants, with many color photographs and drawings. For readers aged 9–12.

A History of France Through Art
Jillian Powell; Thomson Learning, 1996

An overview of French history, as shown through famous paintings. For readers aged 9–12.

Victoria and Her Times
Jean-Loup Chiflet and Alain Beaulet; Henry Holt, 1996

An unusual, graphically creative, and thoroughly interesting account of the life and times of Queen Victoria, illustrated with photographs, Victorian pictures, drawings, cartoons, and maps. Included are fictionalized interviews and journal entries, Albert Saxe-Coburg-Gotha's "résumé" (he liked ice-skating, beekeeping, and early bedtimes), accounts of notable Victorian-era inventions, the stories of such Victorian luminaries as Disraeli, Jack the Ripper, and Sir Arthur Conan Doyle, and labeled royal family por-

traits and family trees. A fun, fascinating, and enlightening read.

Victorian Family Celebrations
ALL Sarah Ban Breathnach; Simon & Schuster, 1990

A month-by-month account of 19th-century family life, traditions, and holidays, with many poems, stories, and quotations, illustrated with wonderful period photographs and color and black-and-white prints. For each month, there are suggestions for family-oriented activities, recipes, and Victorian-style crafts. August, for example, includes suggestions for making a scrapbook memory garden, "putting on a neighborhood circus, inventing Victorian theatricals, camping in the backyard while cooking 'Doughboys' over an open fire, and making 'flower dollies.'"

What Jane Austen Ate and Charles Dickens Knew: From Fox Hunting to Whist/The Facts of Daily Life in 19th-Century England
Daniel Pool; Touchstone Books, 1994

The book is 416 pages long, counting the index and the enormous glossary, which defines such essential Victorianisms as *muffin man*, *Newgate prison*, and *loo*. The text is divided into six major sections: "The Basics," "The Public World," "Transition," "The Country," "The Private World," and "The Grim World." (This last discusses the awful realities of orphanages, workhouses, consumption, and chimney sweeping.) The information is presented in short and delightfully readable chunks—there are lots of subtitles. Flip it open anywhere and read a two-page account of some interesting aspect of 19th-century life: schools, debtors' prisons, coaches, the army, women's clothing, or Christmas pudding. There's also a nice explanation of *entail*, which is why it was so important for the five Bennett sisters in Jane Austen's *Pride and Prejudice* to find husbands.

BOOKS: FICTION

The Court of Stone Children
Eleanor Cameron; Puffin, 1992

At the French Museum in San Francisco, Nina discovers reconstructed rooms from a Burgundy château dating to the time of the French Revolution. There she meets Dominique, a girl of her own age—who is a visitor from the past. Dominique's father was shot as a traitor for speaking out against the emperor Napoléon, but Dominique knows that he was innocent of wrong. Together—and with the help of the museum curator, who is writing his biography—the girls, real and ghost, manage to set the record straight. For readers aged 10 and up.

Jeremy Visick

David Wiseman; Houghton Mifflin, 1990

Twelve-year-old Matthew insists that history is "rubbish" until he finds an old tombstone in the graveyard and becomes involved in a mystery involving Jeremy Visick—just his age—who died in a Cornish mine tragedy in 1852.

Meet Samantha

Susan S. Adler; Pleasant Company, 1986

Samantha, of Pleasant Company's American Girls series (see page 448), is not quite a "Victorian beauty" as the company describes her, since the *Samantha* books are set in 1904. Still Samantha, an orphan, lives with her definitely Victorian-era grandmother, and the flavor of daily life is close.

Stand Up, Mr. Dickens!

Edward Blishen; Houghton Mifflin, 1996

Illustrated excerpts from many of Dickens's most famous works, suitable for reading aloud at Dickens-style public lectures, accompanied by information about Dickens's life and work. Interested kids can do their own dramatic readings of scenes from *The Pickwick Papers, David Copperfield, Great Expectations,* and *A Christmas Carol.* For readers aged 12 and up.

A Tale of Two Cities

Charles Dickens; Puffin, 1996

Charles Dickens's classic novel of love, adventure, tragedy, and nobility during the French Revolution, featuring the unforgettable Madame Defarge, who knits beside the guillotine as the aristocratic heads fall; Charles Darnay and his beloved Lucie; and their friend Sydney Carton, who goes to the guillotine in Darnay's stead, declaiming "It is a far, far better thing I do than

I have ever done." Kids are of two minds about this one: in our house, Josh liked it; Ethan, after one look at the first paragraph, refused to touch it; and Caleb remains cautiously undecided. Worth a try. For teenagers.

Tom's Midnight Garden

Philippa Pearce; HarperCollins, 1992

Young Tom wakes up in the middle of the night to find that a mysterious garden has appeared that carries him back to share the lives of children in Victorian times. For readers aged 9–12.

COLORING AND PAPER-CRAFTS BOOKS

Fashions of the Regency Period Paper Dolls

Two dolls and 15 period costumes in full color. Also see *Great Fashion Designs of the Victorian Era Paper Dolls* and *Victorian Bride and Her Trousseau Paper Doll.*

$4.95

Dover Publications, Inc.

31 E. Second St.

Mineola, NY 11501

The French Revolution

A collection of paper dolls and period costumes to color and cut out. Dolls include Louis XVI, Marie Antoinette, and family, plus leading revolutionary figures. (No guillotines.) The accompanying text is in both French and English.

$5.95

Bellerophon Books

36 Ancapa St.

Santa Barbara, CA 93101

(800) 253-9943/fax (800) 965-8286

GAMES AND HANDS-ON ACTIVITIES

The French Revolution

A portfolio of historical background essays and primary source materials, with an accompanying study guide.

"The French Revolution" includes essays on the events leading up to the revolution, the storming of the Bastille, the debates over the form the new French government should take, and the frightening Reign of Terror. Supplementary source materials include pages from the Declaration of the Rights of Man (in French, with translation), a signed voting list on the death of Louis XVI, and a poster published in England in 1793 titled "Massacre of the French King."

Also see "The Rise of Napoleon," which contains seven illustrated essays covering Napoleon's life and career, a timeline of events from 1769 to 1804, and 11 historical documents, among them a portrait of Napoleon, period newspaper articles, and a ("stern") letter from Napoleon to the French royal family.

$37

Jackdaw Publications

Box 503

Amawalk, NY 10501

(914) 962-6911 or (800) 789-0022/fax (800) 962-9101

Liberté

A simulation of the French Revolution for kids in grades 7–9. Kids represent five socioeconomic groups in 1789 France: royalty, aristocrats, clergy, bourgeoisie, and peasants. Each earns (or loses) "RIPs" (Revolutionary Influence Points) by acquiring historical background information on his/her assigned identities and by dealing with historical bulletins that affect financial, social, and political status. (Rich merchants who are awarded titles, for example, lose "RIPs.") As the simulation progresses, participants debate the fate of King Louis XVI, deal with Robespierre and his Reign of Terror, and bring him to trial. The simulation is designed for 20 to 35 students, but adapts to smaller groups.

$22

Interact

1825 Gillespie Way, #101

El Cajon, CA 92020-1095

(619) 448-1474 or (800) 359-0961/fax (619) 448-6722
or (800) 700-5093

Web site: www.interactsimulations.com

Victorian Jewelry Box

Queen Victoria herself is said to have practiced decoupage as a schoolgirl; this Curiosity Kit provides kids with all the materials for their own 19th-century craft project. Users sand, paint, and line a hinged 4 × 7-inch wooden box, then decorate it with Victorian-style "paper scraps" and layer it with varnish. The result: a finished Victorian jewelry or treasure box.

$20 from toy and game stores; for a local source,

contact

Curiosity Kits

Box 811

Cockeysville, MD 21030

(410) 584-2605 or (800) 584-KITS/fax (410) 584-1247

e-mail: CKitsinc@aol.com

VIDEOS

David Copperfield

Runner-up to the Queen herself as spokesperson for the Victorian Age is probably Charles Dickens, many of whose novels of life (and hard times) in 19th-century England have been issued on film. Among these is the 1970 British production of *David Copperfield*, which follows young David through his dreadful days at boarding school into adult life—and chronicles his meetings with such memorable characters as the insolvent Mr. Micawber and the 'umble Uriah Heep. Also available: *Oliver Twist, The Old Curiosity Shop, Nicholas Nickleby, Great Expectations, Little Dorrit,* and *Bleak House.*

$19.99

Movies Unlimited

3015 Darnell Rd.

Philadelphia, PA 19154

(215) 637-4444 or (800) 4-MOVIES

e-mail: movies@moviesunlimited.com

Web site: www.moviesunlimited.com

Pride and Prejudice

A recent burst of popularity for Jane Austen has resulted in a spate of wonderful movies based on her novels: now available on video are *Emma, Persuasian, Mansfield Park, Northanger Abbey,* and *Sense and Sensibility,* along with at least three versions of *Pride and Prejudice.* Our pick of these is the 1985 BBC *Pride and Prejudice* production starring Elizabeth Garvie and David Rintoul: it's beautiful to look at, an always appealing story, and a fascinating slice of early 19th-century life. The scatterbrained Mrs. Bennett is marvelous. On two videocassettes.

$29.99
Movies Unlimited
3015 Darnell Rd.
Philadelphia, PA 19154
(215) 637-4444 or (800) 4-MOVIES
e-mail: movies@moviesunlimited.com
Web site: www.moviesunlimited.com

The Scarlet Pimpernel

Sir Percy Blakeney, a foolishly foppish British aristocrat, is really the daring Scarlet Pimpernel, risking his life to rescue doomed French aristocrats from the guillotine in the days of the French Revolution. There's a terrific 1982 production starring Anthony Andrews, Jane Seymour, and Ian McKellen. For an extra $4.95 you also get a paperback copy of the book by Baroness Orczy.

$19.98
Zenger Media
10200 Jefferson Blvd.
Box 802
Culver City, CA 90232-0802
(310) 839-2436 or (800) 421-4246/fax (310) 839-2249
or (800) 944-5432
e-mail: access@ZengerMedia.com
Web site: ZengerMedia.com

A Tale of Two Cities

An exciting tale of the French Revolution—the two cities are Paris and London—with a sad but noble ending as Sydney Carton gallantly goes to his far, far better rest. There have been several movie versions, among them a 1935 MGM production starring Ronald Colman, Edna May Oliver, and Basil Rathbone; and a 1958 British production with Dirk Bogarde and Dorothy Tutin. Both are in black and white. For an additional $3.95 you get a paperback copy of the book by Charles Dickens.

$19.98
Zenger Media
10200 Jefferson Blvd.
Box 802
Culver City, CA 90232-0802

(310) 839-2436 or (800) 421-4246/fax (310) 839-2249
or (800) 944-5432
e-mail: access@ZengerMedia.com
Web site: ZengerMedia.com

MODERN TIMES

Also see **American History: Twentieth Century** (pages 569–578).

Books

The Children's Atlas of the Twentieth Century: Chart the Century from World War I to the Gulf War and from Teddy Roosevelt to Nelson Mandela

Sarah Howarth; Millbrook Press, 1995

A geographical, social, and political atlas of the changing 20th-century world, with an informative text covering such modern milestones as African independence, the crisis in the Balkans, and the rise of the automobile, the airplane, and the personal computer.

Chronicle of the 20th Century

Dorling Kindersley, 1995

A massive (1,456 pages) reference book covering—in chronological order and fascinating detail—the history of the 20th century. The book includes month-by-month accounts of the events of each year through short news reports liberally illustrated with black-and-white and color photographs and drawings. It's all here: politics, science and technology, the arts, sports, military affairs, and natural disasters. For readers aged 13 and up.

For younger readers, see the abbreviated (336 pages) *Junior Chronicle of the 20th Century,* which is of similar design and content but written at a fourth-grade reading level.

WORLD WAR I

Also see **World War I** (pages 570–571).

Books

First World War
John D. Clare, ed.; Harcourt Brace, 1994

This is a Living History Book, a 64-page informational text illustrated with period photographs and with color photographs of reenactments of World War I scenes. Readers see, for example, views of life in the trenches in France, on the eastern front, on the home front in England, and onboard a German U-boat.

In Flanders Fields
Linda Granfield; Doubleday, 1995

I happen to know John McCrae's poem "In Flanders Fields" by heart, having had to memorize it in sixth grade. This poem of World War I, which begins "In Flander Fields the poppies blow/Between the crosses, row on row . . . ," inspired the annual wearing of poppies on November 15 ("Poppy Day") in honor of veterans of the Great War. Granfield's picture book includes a short and simple history of World War I, an account of John McCrae's part in it (he died in France in 1918), descriptions of a soldier's life at the front, and the complete text of the famous poem, a line or two per page, with dramatic color illustrations. The book's end pages show the map of Europe in 1915, with the sites of major battles labeled.

World War I
Tom McGowen; Franklin Watts, 1993

A 64-page illustrated chronological overview of World War I for students in grades 4–6. Included is information on the events leading up to the war, accounts of major battles and battle strategies, and profiles of prominent people.

Coloring and Paper-Crafts Books

Aces & Airplanes of World War I Coloring Book
Historical airplanes to color, plus an informational text.
$3.95
Bellerophon Books

36 Ancapa St.
Santa Barbara, CA 93101
(800) 253-9943

Airplanes of World War I Coloring Book
Famous airplanes of World War I to color, among them the Fokker Triplane and the Sopwith Camel.
$2.95
Dover Publications, Inc.
31 E. Second St.
Mineola, NY 11501

World War I Uniforms Coloring Book
Black-line representations of soldiers, sailors, and pilots from both sides of the conflict, among them a German flying ace, a British infantryman, and an American Marine.
$2.95
Dover Publications, Inc.
31 E. Second St.
Mineola, NY 11501

Games and Hands-On Activities

World War I: 1914–1918
A portfolio of illustrated historical essays and primary source materials, plus a study guide with reproducible student worksheets. Essay titles include "War Clouds Over Europe," "The Beginning of Modern Warfare," "America Enters the War," and "The Legacy of World War I." Supplementary materials include period maps and photographs and documents from the U.S. Signal Corps, the National Archives, and the Library of Congress.
$37
Jackdaw Publications
Box 503
Amawalk, NY 10503
(914) 962-6911 or (800) 789-0022/fax (800) 962-9101

World War I Game
A board game of World War I history and geography. The board is a number-coded map of Europe; cor-

respondingly numbered playing cards list names, dates, and descriptions of battles and historical events. Players attempt to match sites on the map to the proper card. The game can be played at different levels: beginners, for example, simply match names to numbered map sites; more advanced players must add dates and descriptions.

$10.95

Educational Materials Associates, Inc.

Box 7385

Charlottesville, VA 22906

(804) 293-GAME/fax (804) 293-5322

VIDEOS

All Quiet on the Western Front

The story of a group of young German soldiers in the final days of World War I, based on the classic Erich Maria Remarque novel. The 1979 version stars Richard Thomas as a young German recruit and Ernest Borgnine as his war-hardened sergeant.

$12.99

Movies Unlimited

3015 Darnell Rd.

Philadelphia, PA 19154

(215) 637-4444 or (800) 4-MOVIES

e-mail: movies@moviesunlimited.com

Web site: www.moviesunlimited.com

The Blue Max

The story of a German combat pilot in World War I who is eager to win the prestigious combat medal the Blue Max. Made in 1966, the movie stars George Peppard, Ursula Andress, and James Mason. Impressive aerial combat sequences.

$19.99

Movies Unlimited

3015 Darnell Rd.

Philadelphia, PA 19154

(215) 637-4444 or (800) 4-MOVIES

e-mail: movies@moviesunlimited.com

Web site: www.moviesunlimited.com

The Great War and the Shaping of the 20th Century

A miniseries from PBS covering the history of World War I and its aftermath through period film footage, eyewitness accounts, and narration. Titles in the eight-part series on four videocassettes are "Explosion & Stalemate," "Total War & Slaughter," "Hatred and Hunger & War Without End," and "Mutiny & Collapse."

$99.98

PBS Home Video

1320 Braddock Pl.

Alexandria, VA 22314-1698

(800) 645-4PBS

Web site: www.pbs.org

The Last Voyage of the Lusitania

In this National Geographic documentary, Dr. Robert Ballard, of *Titanic* fame, investigates the sinking of the *Lusitania* on May 7, 1915, by a German U-Boat.

$19.99

Movies Unlimited

3015 Darnell Rd.

Philadelphia, PA 19154

(215) 637-4444 or (800) 4-MOVIES

e-mail: movies@moviesunlimited.com

Web site: www.moviesunlimited.com

or

National Geographic Home Video

Box 5073

Clifton, NJ 07015

(800) 627-5162

Web site: www.nationalgeographic.com

Sergeant York

Gary Cooper won an Academy Award in 1941 for his portrayal of Alvin York, the pacifistic Tennessee farmer who became a hero in World War I. With Walter Brennan, Ward Bond, and Joan Leslie.

$19.99

Movies Unlimited

3015 Darnell Rd.

Philadelphia, PA 19154

(215) 637-4444 or (800) 4-MOVIES

e-mail: movies@moviesunlimited.com

Web site: www.moviesunlimited.com

WORLD WAR I ON-LINE

World War I: Trenches on the Web

The site is an "Internet History of the Great War," including information on battles, weapons, airplanes, important people, and life on the home front.

www.worldwar1.com

WORLD WAR II AND THE HOLOCAUST

Also see **World War II** (pages 574–576).

BOOKS: NONFICTION

Anne Frank: The Diary of a Young Girl Hiding From the Nazis

Anne Frank; Bantam Books, 1993

The now world-famous diary of 13-year-old Anne, hiding in a "Secret Annex" in the attic during the Nazi occupation of Holland. Anne's reflections on the trials of growing up are timeless and these, against the terrifying circumstances of her daily life, make for a powerful and heartrending book. For readers aged 12 and up.

Atom Bomb

Tom Seddon; W. H. Freeman & Company, 1995

A 48-page overview of early atomic research, the development of nuclear weapons, the Manhattan Project, and the dropping of the first atom bombs on Hiroshima and Nagasaki. Illustrated with photographs. For readers aged 12 and up.

Hiroshima

John Hersey; Vintage Books, 1989

A powerful account of the bombing of Hiroshima through the reports of eyewitnesses. Hersey tells what was happening in the lives of six ordinary people—a filing clerk, a seamstress, a physician at a private hospital, a young surgeon, a Methodist minister, and a Catholic priest—at 8:15 on the morning of August 6, 1945, and follows them through the dreadful hours afterward. For teenagers.

Learning About the Holocaust: Literature and Other Resources for Young People

Elaine C. Stephens, Jean E. Brown, and Janet E. Rubin; Library Professional Publications, 1995

An annotated bibliography of Holocaust materials, listed by grade level (primary, elementary, junior high/middle school, and secondary). Materials include nonfiction and historical fiction books, personal narratives and memoirs, biographies, photo essays, plays, poems, and videos. The book also contains addresses of organizations and institutions that provide Holocaust information.

The Little Ships: The Heroic Rescue at Dunkirk in World War II

Louise Borden; Margaret K. McElderry, 1997

A picture-book account of the heroic rescue of the stranded Allied army from the beaches of France in 1940, in which hundreds of small civilian boats joined the British navy to transport over 300,000 soldiers back to England. The story is told by a young girl who sailed on her father's fishing boat, the *Lucy*, as part of the rescue fleet. A dramatic, brave, and wonderful tale.

Maus: A Survivor's Tale

Art Speigelman; Pantheon, 1991.

A tragically serious comic book, described by reviewers as "a new kind of literature." *Maus* and its sequel are memoirs, relating the story of Speigelman's father, Vladek, a survivor of the Holocaust. The books move back and forth in time, between present-day New York, where the author struggles to forge a relationship with his father, and Hitler's Germany. *Maus* covers Vladek Speigelman's life through the early war years up to his incarceration at Auschwitz; *Maus II: And Here My Troubles Began* (1991) covers the concentration camp years to the present. The book titles are derived from their main characters: the Jews, in Speigelman's opus, are mice; the Germans, cats.

Never to Forget: The Jews of the Holocaust

Milton Meltzer; HarperCollins, 1991

A collection of first-person accounts of the Holocaust, illustrated with photographs. For readers aged

HISTORY

12 and up. A companion book, *The Rescue: The Story of How Gentiles Saved the Jews in the Holocaust* (Harper-Collins, 1991), uses primary sources to tell the stories of the many people who attempted to save the Jews from the Nazi exterminators.

A Picture Book of Anne Frank
David A. Adler; Holiday House, 1993

A simple picture-book biography for young readers, illustrated in both color and photograph-style black and white, that tells the story of Anne, her family, and their concealed "Secret Annex," their eventual discovery by the Nazis, and Anne's death in a concentration camp. For readers aged 5–9.

Remember Not to Forget:
A Memory of the Holocaust
Norman H. Finkelstein; William Morrow, 1993

A short (31 pages) survey of Jewish history for young readers, including an explanation of anti-Semitism, the story of the Holocaust, and the celebration of Tom Hashoa, Holocaust Remembrance Day, in memory of six million dead. For readers aged 9–12.

Sadako and the Thousand Paper Cranes
Eleanor Coerr; Putnam, 1990

Sadako Sasaki was two when the atomic bomb was dropped on Hiroshima; at 12, she died of radiation-induced leukemia. The story tells how Sadako folded hundreds of origami paper cranes after hearing an old Japanese legend that whoever folds one thousand paper cranes will be granted a wish and made well again. Today children leave paper cranes at Sadako's memorial in the Hiroshima Peace Park. For readers aged 7–12.

World War II
Tom McGowen; Franklin Watts, 1993

An illustrated 64-page overview of World War II for readers in grades 4–6, covering the reasons for the war, major events of the war, and profiles of World War II leaders, among them Adolf Hitler, Benito Mussolini, Winston Churchill, and Franklin Roosevelt.

BOOKS: FICTION

Behind the Bedroom Wall
Laura E. Williams; Milkweed Editions, 1996

Thirteen-year-old Korinna Rehme, a member of Hitler Youth, is completely devoted to the Nazi party—until she discovers that her parents are hiding a Jewish family in a secret room behind her bedroom wall. Korinna at first is horrified; then her principles and loyalties begin to change. Finally she helps defend her family from a Gestapo raid. For readers aged 9–13.

The Devil's Arithmetic
Jane Yolen; Puffin, 1990

"I'm tired of remembering," 12-year-old Hannah tells her mother on the way to her grandparents' house to celebrate the Passover Seder. She learns to understand her family's link to the past, however, when she is suddenly transported back in time to a Polish village of the 1940s. There, with the rest of the villagers, she is sent by the Nazis to a concentration camp.

Hiroshima
Laurence Yep; Apple, 1996

A 64-page fictionalized account of the atomic bomb attack on Hiroshima in 1945. The book describes events on board the *Enola Gay,* the plane that dropped the bomb, and the experiences of schoolchildren in a Hiroshima classroom, explains the science behind the bomb, and discusses the aftermath of the bombing. The book centers around a 12-year-old girl named Sachi who, suffering from the effects of radiation, eventually comes to the United States for medical treatment. For readers aged 9–12.

Hiroshima No Pika
Toshi Maruki; William Morrow, 1982

The title—which translates as "The Flash of Hiroshima"—refers to the blinding explosion of the first atomic bomb on August 6, 1945. The book is the story of that fatal day in the life of a small Japanese girl, starting peacefully in the morning at the family breakfast table, through a journey across a shattered city in the afternoon with her mother and wounded father.

The story is told in part through full-page paintings, but—though this is a picture book—it is not for the very young.

9 + *I Never Saw Another Butterfly:*
Children's Drawings and Poems
from Terezin Concentration Camp
   Hana Volavkova, ed.; Schocken Books, 1994

Fifteen thousand children under the age of 15 passed through Terezin Concentration Camp from 1942 to 1944; of these, only 100 survived. This book is a small collection of the paintings, drawings, and poems that they left behind. The poems are heartbreaking for those of us who know the rest of the story; the children themselves, however, write with optimism, hope, and courage, as well as sadness and fear. An appendix at the back tells what little is known about the young authors and artists.

9 12 *Number the Stars*
   Lois Lowry; Yearling, 1990

This Newbery Medal–winning novel is set in Denmark in 1943, where young Annemarie Johansen and her family unite to save Annemarie's best friend, Ellen, a Jewish girl, from the invading Nazis, by pretending that Ellen is Annemarie's sister. For readers aged 9–12.

7 11 *Snow Treasure*
   Marie McSwigan; Scholastic, 1997

Based on a true story, this is the tale of a group of Norwegian schoolchildren who managed to save nine million dollars in gold from the invading German army. For readers aged 7–11. A Disney film of the same title, based on the book, is available on video.

7 12 *Twenty and Ten*
   Claire Huchet Bishop; Puffin, 1991

Based on a true story, the book tells how 20 French schoolchildren successfully hid 10 Jewish children during the Nazi occupation of France. Recommended for readers aged 7–12.

Also see the video version of the book, *Wonderworks: Miracle at Moreaux* (page 684).

10 + *When Hitler Stole Pink Rabbit*
   Judith Kerr; Paper Star, 1997

The story of a Jewish family in Germany in the 1930s. Anna, her mother, and brother flee to Switzerland when Hitler comes to power, where they join Anna's journalist father; from there, they begin a long journey as refugees from the Nazis, traveling through several countries across Europe during the days of World War II. For readers aged 10 and up.

COLORING AND PAPER-CRAFTS BOOKS

6 + *Airplanes of the Second*
World War Coloring Book
   46 accurate drawings of fighters, bombers, transport planes, and more.
   $2.95
   Dover Publications, Inc.
   31 E. Second St.
   Mineola, NY 11501

9 + *Famous Fighters to Color, Cut Out, & Fly*
   A very accurate collection of historical paper planes to color and assemble, including such World War II superstars as the Spitfire, the Zero, and the Messerschmitt 109.
   $3.95
   Bellerophon Books
   36 Ancapa St.
   Santa Barbara, CA 93101
   (800) 253-9943/fax (800) 965-8286

6 + *Paper Soldiers of Our Fighting*
Men & Women
   Dress-uniform- and battlegear-garbed soldiers, sailors, Marines, and Air Force pilots, all to be colored and cut out.
   $2.50
   Bellerophon Books
   36 Ancapa St.
   Santa Barbara, CA 93101
   (800) 253-9943/fax (800) 965-8286

HISTORY

GAMES AND HANDS-ON ACTIVITIES

Afrika Corps

The Avalon Hill Game Company publishes a number of strategic and tactical games based on famous battles of World War II. Games are rated on a scale of 1 to 10, depending on level of difficulty; ratings of 1 to 3 denote games appropriate for beginners. Among these are "Afrika Corps," a board game in which players reenact the North African conflict between Generals Montgomery and Rommel (Level 2); "Naval War," a card game for three to six players based on World War II naval combat (Level 1); and "Victory in the Pacific," a board game in which players, deploying forces on land, on the sea, and in the air, attempt to gain control of the World War II Pacific (Level 3).

"Afrika Corps," $25; "Naval War," $13; "Victory in the Pacific," $25

Avalon Hill Game Co.

4517 Harford Rd.

Baltimore, MD 21214

(410) 254-9200 or (800) 999-3222

e-mail: AH GAMES@aol.com

Web site: www.avalonhill.com

American History Series: World War II Strategy Games

The Avalon Hill Game Company, in collaboration with the Smithsonian Institution, publishes a series of five strategy board games based on famous World War II battles, playable at both an introductory and a more advanced level, for players aged 12 and up. Titles include "D-Day" (a "chess-like" strategy game; rules can be learned in 10 minutes); "Guadalcanal," "Battle of the Bulge," "Mustangs," and "Midway."

$25 to $35

Avalon Hill Game Co.

4517 Harford Rd.

Baltimore, MD 21214

(410) 254-9200 or (800) 999-3222

e-mail: AH GAMES@aol.com

Web site: www.avalonhill.com

The Coming of War: 1939

A portfolio of historical essays and primary source materials on the roots of World War II. The portfolio contains 11 varied historical document replicas, including maps, newspapers, letters, timelines, and photographs, a list of reading suggestions and discussion questions, and a detailed study guide. Essay titles include "Hitler's Rise to Power" and "The Road to Munich."

Related portfolios featuring World War II topics include "The Atomic Bomb," "The Holocaust," "Japanese-American Internment: The Bill of Rights in Crisis," and "Winston Churchill."

"The Atomic Bomb," for example, includes five illustrated historical essays, among them "The Manhattan Project," "Destruction of Hiroshima and Nagasaki," and "Postwar Debate," a timeline of atomic research covering the years 1931 to 1945, and 13 supplementary source documents, including a letter from Albert Einstein to President Franklin Roosevelt, a Truman diary entry on the use of the bomb, and period newspaper articles on the dropping of the bomb.

$37

Jackdaw Publications

Box 503

Amawalk, NY 10501-0503

(914) 962-6911 or (800) 789-0022/fax (914) 962-0034

World War II Game

A map-based board game of World War II, with accompanying historical playing cards. Players must pair battles or important World War II events to numbered sites on the map. The game can be played at multiple levels; more advanced players must come up with names, dates, and information about each site or event.

$10.95

Educational Materials Associates, Inc.

Box 7385

Charlottesville, VA 22906

(804) 293-GAME

VIDEOS

The Diary of Anne Frank

Based on the diary kept by young Anne during the two years that she, her family, and friends hid in a secret attic room in an attempt to escape capture by the Nazis. The story, with its tragic and heartrending conclusion, is emotionally difficult; be prepared to discuss tyranny, human rights, morality, and civil disobedience. The Twentieth Century Fox production, in black and white, stars Millie Perkins and Shelley Winters. An accompanying copy of the book in paperback is available for $4.99.

Two videocassettes, $24.98
Zenger Media
10200 Jefferson Blvd.
Box 802
Culver City, CA 90232-0802
(310) 839-2436 or (800) 421-4246/fax (310) 839-2249
or (800) 944-5432
e-mail: access@ZengerMedia.com
Web site: ZengerMedia.com/Zenger

Judgment at Nuremberg

A dramatization of the postwar trials of Nazi war criminals, with Spencer Tracy, Judy Garland, Burt Lancaster, Maximilian Schell, and Montgomery Clift. A thought-provoking film that deals with issues of personal responsibility and the meaning of universal human rights. In black-and-white.

Two videocassettes, $24.98
Zenger Media
10200 Jefferson Blvd.
Box 802
Culver City, CA 90232-0802
(310) 839-2436 or (800) 421-4246/fax (310) 839-2249
or (800) 944-5432
e-mail: access@ZengerMedia.com
Web site: ZengerMedia.com/Zenger

Wonderworks: Miracle at Moreaux

An inspiring story based on the book *Twenty and Ten* by Claire Huchet Bishop (see page 682). In December 1943, during the Nazi occupation of France, three Jewish children are sheltered by Sister Gabrielle (Loretta Swit) at the Catholic school in the town of Moreaux. The children at the school—at first resentful and frightened by the presence of the young refugees—soon become sympathetic to their tragic plight and devise a daring plot to smuggle them across the border to safety. A wonderful film.

$14.95
Movies Unlimited
3015 Darnell Rd.
Philadelphia, PA 19154
(215) 637-4444 or (800) 4-MOVIES
e-mail: movies@moviesunlimited.com
Web site: www.moviesunlimited.com

World War II

A 15-part history of World War II from the rise of the Nazi party in Germany to the final Allied victory in 1945, narrated by master journalists Walter Cronkite and Charles Kuralt.

Eight videocassettes, $139.98
PBS Home Video
1320 Braddock Pl.
Alexandria, VA 22314-1698
(800) 645-4PBS
Web site: www.pbs.org

WORLD WAR II ON-LINE

Anne Frank Online

The life and times of Anne Frank, a virtual tour of the "Secret Annex," a photo scrapbook of Anne's life and family, and a history of the Holocaust.
www.annefrank.com

Cranes for Peace

A site devoted to Sadako Sasaki, a toddler at the time of the Hiroshima bombing, who died of radiation-induced leukemia 10 years later. Sadako's story is told in the book *Sadako and the Thousand Paper Cranes* (see page 681); the site includes a teacher's guide for the book and a Sadako resource list.
www.hc.net/~sparker/cranes.html

A Guide to the Good War: Resources on World War II

An information-packed site, including photographs, historical articles, maps, visual and sound archives, letters and diaries, interviews, and memoirs.
www.wisc.edu/shs-archives/ww2guide

HISTORY

Hiroshima Archive

Information about the bombing of Hiroshima, including a map of Japan, a picture of the *Enola Gay*, photographs of the city after the bombing, and artifacts from the Hiroshima Peace Memorial Museum.

www.lclark.edu/~history/HIROSHIMA

U.S. Holocaust Memorial Museum

A brief history of the Holocaust, information about children and the Holocaust, on-line museum exhibits, and detailed guidelines for teachers. The site also includes a list of Holocaust videos that have been used effectively in classrooms.

www.ushmm.org

RUSSIA/U.S.S.R.

Books

The Breakup of the Soviet Union

Bernard Harbor; New Discovery, 1993

A 48-page account of the dissolution of the U.S.S.R., the breakdown of Soviet communism, and the establishment of a democratic government. For readers aged 9–12.

Carl Fabergé

Geza Von Habsburg; Harry N. Abrams, 1994

A beautifully illustrated biography of Carl Fabergé, jeweler and goldsmith to the Russian czars, containing 36 color photographs of his fabulous works. For readers aged 12 and up.

The Cold War

Cobblestone; May 1991

This issue of *Cobblestone* magazine (see page 449) covers the origins of the cold war, the Berlin Wall, Korea and Vietnam, and the Cuban Missile Crisis. Included is a "war or peace" board game and a supplementary reading list. For kids in grades 5–9.

Available from most libraries or for $4.50 from Cobblestone Publishing, Inc.
30 Grove St.

Peterborough, NH 03458-1454
(603) 924-7209 or (800) 821-0115
Web site: www.cobblestonepub.com

"Peace, Land, Bread!": A History of the Russian Revolution

John J. Vail; Facts on File, 1996

A volume in the World History Library Series (see page 602) for readers aged 12 and up.

Russia Under the Czars

James I. Clark; Raintree/Steck Vaughn, 1990

A 48-page overview of czarist Russia, from the mid-800s to the assassination of the last Romanov ruler, Czar Nicholas II, in the days of the Russian Revolution. For readers aged 9–12.

Russian Girl: Life in an Old Russian Town

Russ Kendall; Scholastic, 1994

A short photo-essay about nine-year-old Olga, who lives in Suzdal, a small town about 150 miles from Moscow. The books details the economic difficulties of life in post-Soviet Russia against a background of a normal childhood: Olga goes to school, does her chores, plays, and puts a lost tooth under her pillow for the Tooth Mouse to find. Also included are a couple of Russian recipes and a copy of the Cyrillic alphabet. For readers aged 7–10.

Folktales and Legends

Baba Yaga: A Russian Folktale

Katya Arnold; North South Books, 1996

The story of the scary witch Baba Yaga who lives in a house on chicken legs. The witch kidnaps a little boy to cook and eat, but the clever child outwits her and escapes. The book is illustrated with hand-colored woodcuts. For readers aged 4–8.

Bearhead: A Russian Folktale

Eric A. Kimmel; Holiday House, 1997

Bearhead—who has a man's body, but the head of a furry bear—becomes the servant of a witch and infuriates his mistress by taking her every order literally.

(Asked to clear the table, he throws the whole thing out the window.) Finally she tries to get rid of him by sending him to a froglike goblin. Bearhead overcomes all and lives happily ever after with great wealth. For readers aged 4–8.

The Little Humpbacked Horse: A Russian Tale

Elizabeth Winthrop; Clarion, 1997

Ivan, the youngest of three sons, captures a mare who has been stealing hay from the family haystack. He lets her go free and in exchange receives three colts, two who become magnificent stallions, and one of whom is the homely (but very wise) little humpbacked horse. The "Tsar," impressed by the beauty of the horses, makes Ivan his "Master of the Stables"; Ivan, with the help of the little humpbacked horse, makes the most of the situation, completing three impossible tasks and winning the hand of the "Tsaritsa." For readers aged 7–11.

The Little Snowgirl: An Old Russian Tale

Carolyn Croll; Paper Star, 1996

A Russian couple who want a child more than anything in the world find a daughter in the little snowgirl—a child made of snow who magically comes to life. For readers aged 4–8.

The Magic Gold Fish: A Russian Folktale

Aleksandr Sergeyevich Pushkin; Henry Holt, 1995

An old fisherman catches a magical talking fish, which he sets free—but the fisherman's wife keeps sending him back to the fish to ask for rewards in the form of more and more magic wishes. For readers aged 4–8.

The Sea King's Daughter: A Russian Legend

Aaron Shepard; Atheneum, 1997

A lovely and romantic tale in which a poor musician, asked to play in the Sea King's wonderful undersea palace, is asked to stay and marry one of the Sea King's daughters. For readers aged 5–10.

The Tale of Tsar Sultan

Aleksandr Sergeyevich Pushkin; Dial, 1996

A Russian fairy tale in which the "Tsarina" and her baby son are marooned on a desert island by the "Tsarina's" jealous older sisters. There the boy grows up and, with the help of a magic swan, reveals the sisters' wicked plot to his father and reunites his parents. (The swan is really a bewitched and beautiful princess). For readers aged 7–10.

The Wolfhound

Kristine L. Franklin; Lothrop, Lee & Shepard, 1996

Pavel, a peasant boy in czarist Russia, rescues a wolfhound from a snowstorm. Wolfhounds are royal dogs—only the czar is permitted to keep them—but Pavel and his dog, by virtue of their love for each other, manage to overcome all. For readers aged 4–8.

HANDS-ON ACTIVITIES

The Cold War

A portfolio of illustrated historical essays and primary source materials, plus a timeline and study guide. Essay titles include "Origins of the Cold War," "Cuban Missile Crisis," "McCarthyism," "The Forgotten War: Korea," and "The Berlin Wall, End of Communism and the Cold War." Supplementary source materials include period newspaper articles and letters, among them a letter from Nikita Khrushchev to John F. Kennedy on the deterrent nature of the Cuban missiles.

$37

Jackdaw Publications

Box 503

Amawalk, NY 10503

(914) 962-6911 or (800) 789-0022/fax (800) 962-9101

Russian Imperial Costume Paper Dolls

Two dolls and 28 magnificent costumes, based on clothing designed for 11 czars and czarinas.

$4.95

Dover Publications, Inc.

31 E. Second St.

Mineola, NY 11501

The Russian Revolution

A portfolio of historical essays and primary source materials, with an accompanying study guide. Included are six illustrated essays, among them "The February Revolution," "The Bolshevik Revolution," and "Russia Since the Revolution," and 11 supplementary source materials, among them a picture chart showing the events leading up to the revolution, period newspaper pages, and a copy of Stalin's police file.

$37
Jackdaw Publications
Box 503
Amawalk, NY 10503
(914) 962-6911 or (800) 789-0022/fax (800) 962-9101

VIDEOS

Nicholas and Alexandra

The last years of the Romanovs, showing the lush life of the royal family, their relationship with Rasputin, the 1905 war with Japan, World War I, the Bolshevik uprisings, and the assassination of the czar, czarina, and their children. Interesting and lovely to look at, but don't expect a happy ending.

Two videocassettes, $29.98
Zenger Media
10200 Jefferson Blvd.
Box 802
Culver City, CA 90232-0802
(310) 839-2436 or (800) 421-4246/fax (310) 839-2249
or (800) 944-5432
e-mail: access@ZengerMedia.com
Web site: ZengerMedia.com/Zenger

Red Empire

A seven-part video series covering the history of Russia from the last years of Czar Nicholas II through the revolution, the rise of Lenin, civil war, the Stalinist era, the cold war, and the reforms of Mikhail Gorbachev. Each episode is about one hour long; titles are "Revolutionaries," "Winners and Losers," "Class Warriors," "Enemies of the People," "Patriots," "Survivors," and "Prisoners of the Past."

$99.98
Zenger Media
10200 Jefferson Blvd.
Box 802
Culver City, CA 90232-0802
(310) 839-2436 or (800) 421-4246/fax (310) 839-2249
or (800) 944-5432
e-mail: access@ZengerMedia.com
Web site: ZengerMedia.com/Zenger

RUSSIA ON-LINE

Russian History

A hypertext account of Russian history from founding of the Russian state in the 800s to the present day.
www.bucknell.edu/departments/russian/history.html

The Russian Revolution

Maps, photographs, quotations, and historical information on the Russian Revolution.
www.barnsdle.demon.co.uk/russ/rusrev.html

POST–WORLD WAR II

Also see American History (pages 577–578).

BOOKS

Black Stars in Orbit: NASA's African-American Astronauts

Khephra Burns and William Miles; Gulliver Books, 1995

A history of black astronauts, from the days of the first black pilots during World War II through the space program. Includes quotations from black astronauts and many photographs. For readers aged 9–12.

Floating in Space

Franklyn M. Branley; HarperCollins, 1998

A book in the Let's-Read-and-Find-Out Science Series (see page 227) on space exploration, centering around life in orbit on board the space shuttle. The book describes how astronauts live and what they do,

HISTORY

and explains such concepts as "zero gravity" for readers aged 4–9.

The Korean War
Tom McGowen; Franklin Watts, 1992

A 64-page illustrated overview of the war for readers in grades 4–6. The book explains the causes of the war, covers the major events of the three-year conflict, and discusses the controversial actions of General Douglas MacArthur.

Neil Armstrong, Young Flyer
Montrew Dunham; Aladdin, 1996

A biography of Neil Armstrong for young readers in the Childhood of Famous Americans Series (see page 451), emphasizing his childhood years. Adult accomplishments—notably the spectacular "one small step for a man"—are summarized in the final chapter. For readers aged 5–9.

Space Exploration
Carole Stott; Alfred A. Knopf, 1997

A volume in the Eyewitness series, tracing the history of space exploration from the first satellite launches in the 1950s to the present day, filled with wonderful color photographs, diagrams, and drawings. Readers view a lunar lander, the Hubble space telescope, space station Mir, astronauts in full gear, and much more. With a brief explanatory text, primarily in the picture captions.

U.S. Space Camp Book of Astronauts
Anne Baird; William Morrow, 1996

Biographical profiles of 14 astronauts, among them Neil Armstrong and Sally Ride, and a brief history of the space program, illustrated with color photographs. For readers aged 9–12.

The Vietnam War
John Devaney; Franklin Watts, 1992

A 64-page illustrated history of the war for readers in grades 4–6. The book covers the Vietnam conflict from the French defeat at the Battle of Dien Bien Phu to the fall of Saigon in 1975.

GAMES AND HANDS-ON ACTIVITIES

Computers

A portfolio of historical essays and supplementary source materials on the history and social impact of computers, plus a study guide with reproducible student worksheets. The portfolio includes five illustrated essays, among them "From Pebbles to Gears," "Babbage's Calculating Engines," "Modern Computers," and "Computer Intelligence." Supplementary source materials include a picture of Stonehenge (a prehistoric computer), an engraving of the first slide rule, an explanation of the binary alphabet, and a printout of a conversation between a computer and its programmer.

$37
Jackdaw Publications
Box 503
Amawalk, NY 10503
(914) 962-6911 or (800) 789-0022/fax (800) 962-9101

History of Space Exploration Coloring Book

Contains 44 illustrations tracing the history of space exploration, with a brief explanatory text.

$2.95
Dover Publications, Inc.
31 E. Second St.
Mineola, NY 11501

Moonshot

A board game based on the history of American space exploration, from the establishment of the National Aeronautics and Space Administration (NASA) and the launching of the Bell X-1 missions, through Projects Mercury, Gemini, and Apollo. Players proceed around the illustrated game board attempting to launch their spacecraft, complete their missions, earn colorful mission patches, and land on the moon. The game includes 180 playing cards illustrated with wonderful NASA photographs; each lists detailed information about each pictured spacecraft.

$30 from game stores; for a local source, contact
The Galactic Attic
Box 25396

Chattanooga, TN 37422-5396

(888) 240-4415

Web site: www.galacticattic.com

The Story of Space Exploration
ALL *Wall Chart*

Penguin, 1994

An 11-foot-long full-color chart picturing the planets and moons of the solar system and the space probes that have visited them.

$14.95 from bookstores

The Vietnam War

A portfolio of illustrated historical essays and primary source materials, plus a study guide and timeline covering the years 1941 to 1982. Essay titles include "Beginnings to the Gulf of Tonkin," "Gulf of Tonkin and the Tet Offensive," "The Anti-War Movement," "Vietnamization and the Paris Peace Accords," and "The Fall of Saigon and the Aftermath." Supplementary materials include period newspaper articles, combat reports, a copy of the Vietcong policy toward POWs, and a "Joint Peace Treaty" between American students and Vietnam.

$37

Jackdaw Publications

Box 503

Amawalk, NY 10503

(914) 962-6911 or (800) 789-0022/fax (800) 962-9101

VIDEOS

Spaceflight

A PBS series tracing the history of spaceflight from Chuck Yeager's breaking of the sound barrier through the launching of Sputnik, the flight of Yuri Gagarin, the Apollo missions, and the first moon landing. Titles in the series are "Thunder in the Skies," "The Wings of Mercury," "One Giant Leap," and "The Territory Ahead." Four hours on four videocassettes.

$59.98

PBS Home Video

1620 Braddock Pl.

Alexandria, VA 22314-1698

(800) 645-4PBS

Vietnam: A Television History

A seven-part history of the Vietnam conflict, from the Vietnamese Communist revolution and the defeat of French colonialism through the years of American involvement and the final peace settlements. Thirteen hours on seven videocassettes.

$99.95

PBS Home Video

1320 Braddock Pl.

Alexandria, VA 22314-1698

(800) 645-4PBS

Web site: www.pbs.org

FOREIGN LANGUAGES

Away with him! Away with him! He speaks
Latin.

WILLIAM SHAKESPEARE

The ideal way to learn a foreign language is to have your parents speak it to you, fluently, from infancy on. We have enviable friends whose children are growing up painlessly trilingual: the mother is French, the father is Greek, both speak English, and their two kids speak all of the above. We, unfortunately, had no such linguistic gifts to offer our boys. My husband and I, singly and jointly, speak only English, and thus our kids were doomed to acquire foreign languages the hard way, by deliberate study. In retrospect, I realize that we put this off much too long.

Our initial attempts to introduce a foreign language (on cassette tapes) were stymied for some time by the boys' inability to agree on which language to learn. We could provide materials for *one* foreign language, not three, I had announced arbitrarily, feeling that I couldn't possibly manage to juggle three kids and three languages at the same time. Worse, not one of the boys was interested in learning either of the languages in which I had at least some background (French and Spanish), but instead were variously demanding German, Japanese, Russian, and Latin. I found this prospect so intimidating that for an entire year after the initial discussion we did nothing.

Eventually—after a last-ditch pitch for French—I came around. Ethan and Caleb tackled Japanese; Josh plunged into Latin. Caleb experimented briefly with

Russian—a niece, taking Russian classes at college, generously sent a sample cassette tape, a vocabulary list, and a copy of the Cyrillic alphabet. We provided audiotapes, programmed texts, workbooks, supplementary background materials, and encouragement. We also began to look for tutors.

The ideal way to learn a language is by "immersion," in which beginners simply surround themselves with the language—preferably as spoken by native speakers—and learn in context. Kids spending a few months as exchange students in a foreign country or as visitors in the home of a foreign-language-fluent friend or relative, for example, learn a second language naturally, in the same manner in which they learned their first. If none of these is a viable option, second best is a formal program that provides plenty of exposure to the spoken language. (Nobody ever became fluent by conjugating verbs in a workbook.) Many programs targeted at small children include song tapes, which are excellent: kids practice speaking/singing and listening, with the added extras of melody and rhythm as memory aids.

How to Find a Tutor

1. Trade. Homeschool support groups, neighborhoods, and towns are filled with persons of many skills and talents. Often families looking for a language tutor—or for assistance in math, chemistry, or modern dance—can negotiate an academic trade. Most of us have something to offer. Piano lessons for chemistry experiments; French for algebra; babysitting for art history.

2. Advertise. Post a note on a public bulletin board—try the public library—or take out an advertisement in the local paper asking for a tutor. State your children's ages and your preferences in times and pay rates. (If they're negotiable, say so.) Often retirees, college students, and others are interested in part-time employment.

3. Recruit. If there is a college in your area, call the foreign-language department and ask if there are any students interested in part-time tutoring. Try foreign-language teachers at local private or public schools; often their connections include potential tutors.

4. Join a class. If none of the above works out satisfactorily, there's the option of enrolling in a formal language class. For homeschoolers, some public schools allow kids to attend selected classes. Community colleges offer language programs. Occasionally after-school enrichment programs are available for younger children.

GENERAL FOREIGN-LANGUAGE RESOURCES

CATALOGS

Audio-Forum

ALL The Audio-Forum catalog carries an immense assortment of foreign-language self-instruction programs, in 97 languages, from French, Spanish, Japanese, German, and Italian to Cherokee, Finnish, Gaelic, Sanskrit, Swahili, Xhosa, Tlingit, and Tagalog.

Programs are available for learners of all ages. Examples for younger students include the *Storybridges* series (see page 695) and the *Phrase-A-Day* series (see page 695).

For older learners and adults, Audio-Forum carries a large number of *Foreign Service Institute Language Courses*, originally developed for use by State Department employees assigned overseas. The courses are based on a process of listening to, then repeating, phrases as spoken by native speakers—over and over until a level of fluency is attained. "The process is very similar to the way you learned English," the catalog explains, "which you probably spoke fluently long before you could read or understand rules of grammar." Each course is roughly equivalent to one semester of college-level foreign-language instruction, and includes 10 to 12 cassette tapes, plus an approximately 200-page text.

The Audio-Forum catalog also includes foreign-language games, flash cards, songs and stories on tape, dictionaries, ethnic music selections, and foreign-language videos. A source for French crossword puzzles, Spanish Monopoly and Scrabble, German fairy tales, and *The Iliad* in the original Greek. And much more.

Audio-Forum

96 Broad St.

Guilford, CT 06437

(203) 453-9794 or (800) 243-1234/fax (203) 453-9774

e-mail: 74537.550@Compuserve.com

Web site: agoralang.com/audioforum.html

Dover Publications

Dover publishes a number of inexpensive resources for young language learners, including coloring books in French, Spanish, German, and Hebrew; sticker books in Japanese, Italian, French, and Spanish; easy French and Spanish crossword puzzles; and foreign-language versions of children's books. Among these are Beatrix Potter's *Tale of Peter Rabbit* in Spanish and Italian, and Lewis Carroll's *Alice in Wonderland* in Spanish, French, German, and Russian.

Dover Publications, Inc.

31 E. Second St.

Mineola, NY 11501

Educational Record Center

A source for multicultural music, foreign-language songbooks, tapes, and CDs, and *Spanish* read-along book-and-tape sets. The *Read-Alongs* (*Los Audi-Cuentos*) are Spanish versions of many popular children's picture books, among them *Alexander and the Terrible, Horrible, No Good, Very Bad Day; Corduroy; Good Night, Moon; Stone Soup; The Story of Ferdinand;* and *Sylvester and the Magic Pebble.*

Educational Record Center, Inc.

3233 Burnt Mill Dr., Suite 100

Wilmington, NC 28403-2698

(800) 438-1637/fax (888) 438-1637

e-mail: erc-inc@worldnet.att.net

Web site: www.erc-inc

Multilingual Books and Tapes

A source for multilingual books, foreign-language learning programs, computer software, audiocassettes, and CD-ROMS.

Multilingual Books and Tapes

1205 E. Pike

Seattle, WA 98122

(206) 328-7922 or (800) 21-TAPES/fax (206) 328-7445

e-mail: esl@esl.net

Web site: www.esl.net/mbt

National Textbook Company

The National Textbook Company's "Foreign Languages" catalog is crammed with resources for students of all ages. Included are texts, readers, workbooks, books on foreign cultures, foreign folklore collections, games and puzzles, coloring books, music, dictionaries, audiocassettes, videotapes, and computer software. The materials are categorized under six major language headings—Spanish, French, German, Italian, Russian, and Japanese—plus "Other Languages," which cover Latin, Greek, Hebrew, Chinese, Korean, Indonesian, Polish, Swedish, Scandinavian, Portuguese, and Turkish.

Programs for kids include Catherine Bruzzone's book/audio children's language programs, *Spanish, French, German,* and *Italian for Children* (Passport Books). Each program includes two 60-minute audiocassettes containing 20 songs and 10 lesson units dealing with the basics of language: greetings, likes and dislikes, talking about family and friends, counting, telling time, and describing people and objects. A color-illustrated book contains lesson-related stories about Super Cat (Gato, Katze, Chat, Gatto), plus activities, games, language challenges, and puzzles.

National Textbook Co.

4255 W. Touhy Ave.

Lincolnwood, IL 60646-1975

(708) 679-5500 or (800) 323-4900/fax (708) 679-2494

Penton Overseas, Inc.

Penton Overseas carries several language-learning

FOREIGN LANGUAGES

resources and programs for young beginners. Among these are the "LinguaFun!" Language Learning Card Games. The games include an instructional audiocassette and a deck of 54 red, white, and blue cards, each bearing a foreign-language word or phrase, and illustrated with conversational parrots. Players aged 7 and up use these to play familiar games like rummy, "concentration," and "go fish" with a linguistic twist, arranging cards to form foreign-language sentences. About $12.95; available in Spanish or French.

The *Lyric Language* series introduces kids to foreign languages through catchy bilingual songs performed by the pudgily endearing characters of the *Family Circus* comic strip by Bill Keane. The series is available in French, German, Italian, Japanese, Spanish, and Swedish on audiocassette; some languages are also available on videotape or CD-ROM.

> Penton Overseas, Inc.
> 2470 Impala Dr.
> Carlsbad, CA 92008
> (619) 431-0060 or (800) 748-5804/fax (619) 431-8110
> e-mail: pentonosea@aol.com
> Web site: www.pentonoverseas.com

World of Reading

Foreign-language software programs, books, audiocassettes, and videos for kids of all ages and adults. Materials cover over 30 different languages.

> World of Reading
> Box 13092
> Atlanta, GA 30324-0092
> (404) 233-4042 or (800) 729-3703/fax (404) 237-5511
> e-mail: polyglot@wor.com
> Web site: www.wor.com

FOREIGN-LANGUAGE MAGAZINES

Aduléscens

 A magazine in Latin for elementary-level students, filled with games, puzzles, comic strips, and short articles about life in ancient Rome.

Also see *Iúvenis,* in similar format, for intermediate-level Latin students.

> An annual subscription (7 issues), $19.95
> MEP School Division

915 Foster St.
Evanston, IL 60201
(847) 866-6289/fax (847) 866-6290 or (800) 380-8919
Web site: www.mep-eli.com

Mary Glasgow Magazines

A series of foreign-language magazines for secondary school students, available in French, Spanish, or German, from Scholastic. Each magazine includes interviews with popular public figures, feature articles on foreign cultures, and word games, quizzes, and conversation exercises. Magazines are available at four levels of language expertise. French magazines include *Allons-Y!* (Level 1), *Bonjour* (Level 2), *Ça Va?* (Level 3), and *Chez Nous* (Level 4); Spanish magazines include *Que Tal?* (Level 1), *Ahora* (Level 2), and *El Sol* (Level 3); German magazines, *Das Rad* (Level 1), *Schuss* (Level 2), and *Aktuell* (Level 3). For Level 1 and 2 magazines, an optional accompanying activity book is available.

> Subscriptions (6 monthly issues), $6.95; subscriptions with accompanying activity books, $7.95
> Scholastic, Inc.
> Box 7502
> Jefferson City, MO 65102
> (800) 631-1586
> Web site: www.scholastic.com

Skipping Stones

A multicultural children's magazine in which many of the literary entries appear in two languages, that of the original writer and in English translation.

> Annual subscription (5 issues), about $25
> *Skipping Stones Magazine*
> Box 3939
> Eugene, OR 97403
> (541) 342-4956

FOREIGN-LANGUAGE PROGRAMS AND COURSES

Early Advantage

A BBC video language course for children, starring Muzzy, who is big, furry, and blue. The videos feature the adventures of the King, the Queen, the beautiful princess, the humble gardener who loves her, the evil prime minister, and Muzzy—all in English, plus your choice of French, Spanish, Italian, or German. The videos are designed to introduce kids to a second language in the same manner in which they learned their first: by listening, watching, and imitating. The course is designed for very young language learners (from birth, the accompanying brochure explains) through age 12. The complete course includes four animated story videos (two in English, two in the chosen foreign language) which contain six simple stories, two audio-cassettes, and an interactive CD-ROM (for Windows 3.1 or 95). With this last, kids can listen to a story, practice their comprehension and speaking skills, and play assorted foreign-vocabulary-based games. Also included is a video vocabulary builder, in which the Muzzy characters teach such language basics as numbers, shapes, colors, parts of the body, greetings, and names of family members. A video script book includes the texts of all the stories for parents or for older kids who like to read along.

Each language course, $169
Early Advantage
Box 320368
Fairfield, CT 06432
(888) 327-5923
Web site: www.early-advantage.com

Learn the Fun and Easy Way Series
Barron's Educational Series, Inc.

A series of 250+-page books or book-and-cassette sets available in French, German, Italian, Spanish, and Japanese. The books, crammed with color illustrations, maps, puzzles, quizzes, and a set of to be cut out vocabulary cards, are divided into 15-minute lessons, each concentrating on the language as used in everyday situations: meeting people, telling time, traveling, eating in restaurants, shopping, camping, talking on the telephone. Also included: basic rules of grammar, information about foreign currency, and general vocabulary. All foreign-languages words and phrases are accompanied by their English translations and a phonetic pronounciation guide. Featured words and phrases and their meanings are highlighted.

In book-and-cassette versions, the conversations in the book are included on four 90-minute audiocas-

sette tapes. First, listeners hear a short dialogue by native speakers; then selected phrases are repeated, with pauses for students to practice their speaking skills. The conversations are conducted at the speed of normal speech, which—to a novice—sounds intimidatingly rapid; we had to listen to each many times before finally catching on.

The books are intended for traveling adults, but the attractive and friendly format makes them fun for all.

Barron's Educational Series, Inc.
250 Wireless Blvd.
Hauppauge, NY 11788
(518) 434-3311 or (800) 645-3476/fax (516) 434-3723
Web site: barronseduc.com

The Learnables
The International Linguistics Corporation publishes *The Learnables,* a series of foreign-language programs designed for home education. Learnables begin at Step 1 with "Listening," a picture book and five-cassette set with which kids simply look at the numbered pictures and listen to the words. (The instructions recommend one lesson of 100 pictures at a time, which takes about 20 minutes.) There are periodic short picture tests, for review purposes. "Listening" is followed by "Reading," or "Basic Structures," a book and four-cassette set, which adds new vocabulary and introduces simple sentences and the rudiments of grammar. The book pairs each phrase or sentence to a numbered picture.

The program proceeds through five graded steps, each consisting of "Learnables/Listening" and "Basic Structures/Reading" book-and-tape sets. "Learnables" sets are available for Spanish, French, German, Russian, Chinese, Hebrew, Czech, and Japanese. Many users have found these programs pleasantly paced and easy for children as young as 6 or 7. The downside: For a program so dependent on pictures, the black-and-white illustrations are unattractive; and our boys found the endless one-word repetitions—"car car car apple apple apple bread bread bread"—grindingly monotonous.

International Linguistics Corporation
3505 E. Red Bridge
Kansas City, MO 64137
(800) 237-1830/fax (816) 765-2855
Web site: www.learnables.com

Living Language Children's Courses
Random House

Available as *Children's Living French* and *Children's Living Spanish*. Each set includes 40 language lessons on two audiocassettes, an illustrated lesson book, and a picture dictionary. No introductory vocabulary drill here: the tapes, from lesson one, plunge listeners into short conversations. The first lesson, for example, is a family conversation about a little girl who has slept late saying good morning to the members of her family, followed by a "Good morning" song. The accompanying lesson book includes the text of each dialogue in French or Spanish, an English translation, and a word study section or short quiz highlighting important concepts from each lesson. The taped conversation, by native speakers, are slow and clear; our boys were soon able to follow them easily.

$29.95 from bookstores or

Audio-Forum

96 Broad St.

Guilford, CT 06437

(203) 453-9794 or (800) 243-1234/fax (203) 453-9774

e-mail: 74537.550.compuserve.com

Web site: agoralang.com/audio-forum.html

Phrase-A-Day Series
An audiocassette-and-coloring/workbook program for kids aged 5–11 keyed to the four seasons of the year. Kids learn basic vocabulary words and everyday phrases by listening to native speakers and coloring related pictures. Programs are available in French and Spanish. Each consists of two audiocassettes and a coloring/workbook; additional books may be purchased separately.

$24.95 from bookstores or

Audio-Forum

96 Broad St.

Guilford, CT 06437

(203) 453-9794 or (800) 243-1234/fax (203) 453-9774

e-mail: 74537.550@compuserve.com

Web site: agoralang.com/audioforum.html

Power-glide Language Courses
An exciting series of language lessons on audiocassettes. Robert Blair, designer of the *Power-glide Language Courses,* compares the learning of a second language to a military invasion. A frontal assault on the formidable obstacles of foreign vocabulary, explains Blair, is often punishingly difficult. Instead, learners do better interacting frequently and creatively with native speakers in a variety of interesting contexts. *Power-glide* courses attempt to provide just this, introducing students to a new language through a series of interactive stories and problem-solving games.

The programs start out with a bang. It is just before dawn; you and your companion are intelligence officers assigned to parachute onto a tiny island in the Caribbean. The island has been seized by invaders from outer space. "Your mission is to discover why this tiny island was singled out for capture. What is there there that is of such value? A submarine will pick you up in ten days at midnight at the north point of the island." You're a beginner, so you don't have much in the way of language skills. The program supplies you with a few basic phrases and you're off.

The *Power-glide* courses take learners through a second-year college level of competency in reading, writing, and speaking a foreign language. Each course includes six 90-minute audiocassettes and a 140-page illustrated workbook. Courses are available in Spanish, French, Russian, Japanese, and German.

$89.95 each

Power-glide Language Courses

988 Cedar Ave.

Provo, UT 84604

(800) 596-0910

Web site: www.power-glide.com

Storybridges Series
Jeffrey Norton Publishers

A bilingual storytelling program for kids aged 4–8, available in French, Spanish, or German. The program consists of six familiar stories—among them "Goldilocks and the Three Bears" and "Little Red Riding Hood"—on three audiocassettes, each narrated partly in English, partly in the featured foreign language. Kids join in the tale by repeating foreign words and phrases where appropriate. The cassettes are accompanied by an activity workbook.

$8.95 from bookstores or

Audio-Forum

96 Broad St.

Guilford, CT 06437

(203) 453-9794 or (800) 243-1234/fax (203) 453-9774

e-mail: 74537.550@compuserve.com

Web site: agoralang.com/audioforum.html

Teach Me Tapes

2
12 A cheerful musical approach to foreign-language learning for kids aged 2–12. Each *Teach Me* set consists of a 45-minute audiocassette of phrases, simple conversations, and songs, and an accompanying coloring book, which includes foreign-language text and song lyrics, English translations, and cute pictures. The *Teach Me* series is a "musical journey through the day," introducing young learners to numbers, the alphabet, the days of the week, greetings, and everyday phrases in Chinese, English, French, German, Hebrew, Italian, Japanese, Russian, and Spanish. In the continuing *Teach Me More* series, kids accompany their foreign counterparts on a trip to the zoo, a visit to a farm, a picnic at the beach, a birthday party, and a holiday celebration; and in the *Teach Me Even More* series, available in French and Spanish, pen pals exchange information about their lives, share 21 songs, and learn to make friendship bracelets. The songs are short, catchy, and based on tunes already familiar to most kids: "The More We Get Together," "Day-O," "Going to the Zoo," "Silent Night," and "If You're Happy and You Know It." French and Spanish programs are also available on CD.

Also available: French and Spanish coloring posters, based on either the letters of the alphabet or the seasons of the year, teaching guides, and songbooks.

Book-and-tape sets, $12.95

Teach Me Tapes, Inc.

9900 Bren Rd. E

B-1 Opus Center, Suite 100

Minnetonka, MN 55343-9664

(800) 456-4656

Web site: www.wavetech.net/~teachme

Twin Sisters: Listen and Learn a Language

4
+ Musical language learning for kids aged 4 and up. Each *Listen and Learn a Language* set includes a 60-minute audiocassette, which introduces kids to Span- ish, French, German, or Italian, first through the spoken words, then by incorporating newly learned words and phrases in a simple memory-sticking song. (The Twin Sisters specialize in light rock, jazz, and swing.) Each tape covers about 100 words, including the alphabet, numbers, colors, foods, animals, greetings, the days of the week, and weather words. Side one is aimed at English-speaking students learning a foreign language; side two at foreign-language speakers learning English. An accompanying 24-page illustrated learning guide includes all the song lyrics.

$10

Twin Sisters Productions

1340 Home Ave., Suite D

Akron, OH 44310

(800) 248-TWIN/fax (330) 633-8988

Web site: www.twinsisters.com

BOOKS: HISTORY OF LANGUAGES

The Beginning of Language

9
12 Clarice Swisher; Greenhaven Press, 1989

History, philosophy, and science surrounding the mysterious origins of human language.

King Nimrod's Tower

5
9 Leon Garfield and Michael Bragg; Lothrop, Lee & Shepard, 1982

A picture-book tale of the origin of human languages. *King Nimrod's Tower* is a version of the biblical story of the Tower of Babel, in which the vain and boastful King Nimrod decides to build a tower as high as heaven. God, angry at the King's presumption, stops the work by causing each workman to speak a different language, thus preventing them from communicating with each other.

What Is Your Language?

3
6 Debra Leventhal; Puffin, 1998

A simple picture book in which a small boy travels around the world, learning the names of the languages spoken in different countries and how to say "yes" and "no" in each. Ten languages are represented, among them French, Russian, Arabic, Swahili, Japanese, Spanish, and Inuktitut.

Who Talks Funny: A Book About Language for Kids

Brenda S. Cox; Linnet Books, 1997

All about the history and basic structure of languages, with many unusual facts. Included, for example, is a list of names of the days of the week in 27 languages.

Why Do You Speak as You Do?: A Guide to World Languages

Kay Cooper; Walker & Company, 1992

A 66-page book for kids in grades 4–8, covering the origins of human languages and language families, with more detailed discussions of such languages as French, Japanese, and Hebrew. Chapter titles include "What is Language?," "What Is English?," "How Do You Know How to Talk?," and "Can You Climb a Language Family Tree?"

BOOKS: MULTIPLE FOREIGN LANGUAGES

Alphabet Times Four: An International ABC

Ruth Brown; E. P. Dutton, 1991

An alphabet book in four languages—English, Spanish, French, and German—with phonetic pronunciations. (Y is for "yeti," which is the same in all four.)

Cock-A-Doodle Doo!: What Does It Sound Like to You?

Marc Robinson; Stewart, Tabori & Chang, 1993

A picture-book description of how sounds are heard in other languages, including the English, Spanish, Chinese, and Hebrew versions of a rooster's crow, a dog's bark, and a train's whistle.

Count Your Way Series

Jim Haskins; Carolrhoda

A series of 24-page picture books in which kids learn to count from 1 to 10 in a foreign language. Each number is illustrated with some feature of the culture, history, or geography of the title country or countries and accompanied by a brief, informative text. Titles include *Count Your Way Through Brazil* (1996), *. . . Through France* (1996), *. . . Through Greece* (1996), *. . . Through Ireland* (1996), *. . . Through Africa* (1989), *. . . Through Canada* (1989), *. . . Through China* (1987), *. . . Through Germany* (1992), *. . . Through India* (1989), *. . . Through Israel* (1990), *. . . Through Italy* (1990), *. . . Through Japan* (1987), *. . . Through Korea* (1989), *. . . Through Mexico* (1989), *. . . Through Russia* (1987), and *. . . Through the Arab World* (1987).

The First Thousand Words Series

Usborne's First Thousand Words series is a collection of heavily illustrated oversize picture books illustrating a thousand common words in English, French, Spanish, German, Italian, Hebrew, Russian, and Japanese. The books feature a series of busily humorous double-page spreads of families in action: in the kitchen, in the garden, at the farm, in the city, at the beach, at school, and in the supermarket. Individual items from the big pictures surround the borders of the pages, each labeled with its name in a foreign language. Readers also learn shapes, colors, and numbers, and the names of family members, parts of the body, and articles of clothing. Illustrations, by Stephen Cartwright, are clever, colorful, and appealing, and—for an extra bit of fun—there's a fat yellow duck hidden on each page, for young language learners to find. A complete index and pronunciation guide is found in the back of the book.

For even younger readers, the First 100 Word Series, also illustrated by Cartwright, is available in English, French, Spanish, and German; the English, French, and Spanish books are also available in "Sticker Book" versions, each with 100 reusable stickers to further reinforce newly learned word names.

Usborne also publishes a number of other early language–learning series and bilingual readers for beginners.

EDC Publishing
Box 470663
Tulsa, OK 74147-0663
(800) 331-4418

How to Learn a Foreign Language
Arthur H. Charles Jr.; Franklin Watts, 1994

This is one of the Speak Out, Write On! series, a collection of practical how-to books for kids in grades 7–12. Helpful hints, suggestions, and approaches for foreign-language students.

If I Had a Paka: Poems in Eleven Languages
Charlotte Pomerantz; Greenwillow, 1993

Twelve poems using words and phrases from 11 languages, among them Serbo-Croatian, Swahili, Yiddish, Indonesian, Dutch, Vietnamese, and Samoan. Accompanying color illustrations make their meanings absolutely clear.

Surf's Up! Series
Jeffrey Norton Publishers

A series of 220-page interactive "Website Workbooks" for beginning to intermediate foreign language learners. The books are available for French, German, or Spanish students; each contains 50 student assignments based on explorations of the World Wide Web. The projects involve both practice in language skills and investigations of the culture of native speakers. For each is included detailed instructions and an organized list of related Web sites. The books also contain annotated lists of hundreds of useful foreign-language Web addresses.

From bookstores or for $14.95 from
Audio-Forum
96 Broad St.
Guilford, CT 06437
(203) 453-9794 or (800) 243-1234/fax (203) 453-9774
e-mail: 94537-550.compuserve.com
Web site: agoralang.com/audioforum.html

COMPUTER SOFTWARE

Language Now! Series
Don't panic, the program cautions, when you see a screen full of foreign words: *Language Now!* is an "immersion approach" to language learning, and it works. The programs center around a "Title" text in the featured language: as students read through the sentences on the screen, words and phrases are simultaneously translated, and grammar concepts are explained. Games, which involve filling in blanks, unscrambling words, and completing crossword puzzles, are based on the "Title" texts. A "Listen and Speak" function gives dictation—kids type in the dictated word—or allows users to practice pronunciation of words and sentences; a "Reference" function gives students access to a long list of grammar and vocabulary aids.

For each of the available languages in the series—Spanish, French, German, Italian, Russian, Latin, and English—there are assorted "Add-On Titles" for additional practice. (Each requires the original *Language Now!* program to run.) These include mysteries, short stories, travel accounts, and histories—and, for Latin students, Caesar's *Gallic Wars,* Virgil's *Aeneid,* and Ovid's version of classic myths. The series is recommended for kids aged 12 and up. For Mac or Windows.

Diskettes, $99; CD-ROM, $129
Transparent Language
22 Proctor Hill Rd.
Box 575
Hollis, NH 03049-0575
(603) 465-2230 or (800) 752-1767
Web site: www.transparent.com

Learn to Speak Series
The *Learn to Speak* series is a collection of interactive language programs for students in grades 7–12, available in French, Spanish, or German. Each includes 30 lessons centering around videos of native speakers, accompanied by illustrations, vocabulary word lists, and grammar notes. Kids hear the spoken phrases and see the text in both English and the featured language. Each lesson involves vocabulary acquisition, reading comprehension, pronunciation practice, and writing. Each program is paired with a 400-page text/workbook. On CD-ROM for Mac or Windows.

$89.95
The Learning Company
6160 Summit Dr. N
Minneapolis, MN 55430-4003
(800) 685-6322
Web site: www.learningco.com

TriplePlay Plus! Series

An excellent program of interactive games and conversations for language learners aged 8–adult. A speech recognition and playback function allows users to perfect their pronunciations, while learning over 1,000 foreign words and phrases. New vocabulary is presented in six topic categories (food, people, places, numbers, home, and office), each at three increasingly complex skill levels. Kids can also perfect their language skills by listening to native speakers in a series of humorous talking comic strips (listeners can slow the conversational speed or request instant repeats as desired.) Programs are available in Spanish, German, Italian, French, English, Hebrew, and Japanese.

$99

Syracuse Language Systems
5790 Widewaters Pkwy.
Syracuse, NY 13214
(800) 797-5264

Who Is Oscar Lake?

Language learning by way of an adventurous mystery. Oscar Lake is a notorious international jewel thief who has just pinched a priceless blue diamond known as "The Light" and absconded with it, leaving you holding the bag. You end up in a foreign city where you must track down the thief and recover the loot, solving the mystery in the language of the country. Players continually interact with native foreign-language speakers (there's an on-line dictionary and an instant translation function, in case you need extra help)—and, depending on your language expertise, a number of possible outcomes to the story.

Available in Spanish, French, German, Italian, and English. On CD-ROM for Mac or PC.

$60

Audio-Forum
96 Broad St.
Guilford, CT 06437
(203) 453-9794 or (800) 243-1234/fax (203) 453-9794
e-mail: 94537.550.compuserve.com
Web site: agoralang.com/audioforum.html

WordAce!

A detailed dictionary, translator, verb conjugator, spell checker, and pronunciation guide (with audio clips of native speakers), all in one handy program. Also included are two vocabulary-building matching games: the "Verb Game," which allows players to practice verb conjugations, and the "Synonym Game," which enhances vocabulary skills. *WordAce!* is available in Spanish, French, German, Italian, and Russian (with native speaker sound); and in Portuguese, Swedish, Dutch, Finnish, Danish, and Norwegian (without sound).

$99

Transparent Language
22 Proctor Hill Rd.
Box 575
Hollis, NH 03049-0575
(603) 465-2230 or (800) 752-1767/fax (603) 465-2779
Web site: www.transparent.com

FOREIGN LANGUAGES ON-LINE

All the Scripts of the World

General facts and figures about the world's 6,000 languages, with lists and examples of many kinds of world scripts, among them Indian, Asian, Greek, Semitic, Chinese, Japanese, and Korean.

idris.com/scripts/Scripts.html

The Big List of Languages

An extensive alphabetical list of languages, each linked to a large number of related language resources.

www.tesarta.com/www/resources/languages.html

Digital Librarian: Languages

A librarian's choice of the best foreign-language sites on the Web. The large list includes teacher resources, French poetry, dictionaries and grammars, foreign scripts and fonts, and on-line foreign-language texts.

www.servtech.com/~mvail/languages.html

Foreign-Language Resources for Teachers and Students

Many varied links to foreign-language-related sites, German, French, and Spanish newspapers and magazines, homework helps, suggestions for classroom language projects, and a Spanish chat line for students.

www.geocities.com/~lagringa

Greetings in Many Languages

"Merry Christmas" and "Happy New Year" in many many languages; also "Hello," "Good-bye," "Thank you," "I love you," and "Happy birthday."

members/aol.com/wscaswell/message.htm

Greetings to the Universe in 55 Different Languages

Text and audio greetings in 55 languages from the Voyager Interstellar Outreach Program.

vraptor.jpl.nasa.gov/voyager/lang.html

Hi There!

How to say "Hi!" in over 50 languages.

www.angelfire.com/ok/matilda/hej.html

The Human Languages Page

This site is a comprehensive catalog of language resources on the Internet. Included are over 1,000 links to foreign-language materials, listed alphabetically by language, beginning with the Aboriginal Languages of Australia. For each language, links are included to related sites, tutorials, alphabets, dictionaries, native stories and texts, and general information.

www.june29.com/HLP

Intercultural E-Mail Classroom Connections

The IECC program helps teachers and classes find penpals in other countries and cultures via e-mail. Interested persons can subscribe on-line.

www.stolaf.edu/network/iecc

Just Cows

How to say "cow" in many languages. The name of the language, the phonetic pronounciation of the foreign word for "cow," and the region of the world where the language is spoken are listed for each entry.

www.arrakis.es/~eledu/justcows.htm

Language Dictionaries and Translators

A large assortment of links to foreign-language dictionaries, on-line language courses (for 50 languages), free on-line translations, and foreign-language chat sites.

rivendel.com/~ric/resources/dictionary.html

Language Resources on the WWW

A large list of resources ordered by language or by general category, among them "Language and Culture," "Teacher Resources," "Linguistics," and "News and Media."

www.georgetown.edu/centers/LLT/web.html

Ñandutí: Early Foreign Language Learning

The site title—Ñandutí—means "spiderweb" in Guarani, the language of the natives of Paraguay. The site itself is a collection of resources and information about teaching foreign languages to kids in grades K–8.

www.cal.org/earlylang

Newspapers and Magazines in Foreign Languages

Links to newspapers, magazines, literature, and translators in many languages from around the globe. Users can search by country or by language.

lausd.k12.ca.us/~mvanbaal/language.htm

Numbers from 1 to 10 in Over 2000 Languages

Click on a region of the world map or the name of a foreign language for a simple counting lesson.

www.tezcat.com/~markrose/numbers.shtml

Schumann's Foreign Language Tests

Test your knowledge of German, Spanish, French, Italian, Dutch, and Indonesian with many multiple-choice, fill-in-the-blank vocabulary tests.

ourworld.compuserve.com/homepages/joschu/index.htm

Sounds of the World's Animals

What sound does a duck make in Dutch? The sounds made by 29 animals, from the bee to the wolf, in 23 languages. Click on the animal name to access a color photograph of the animal, plus a multilingual list of its appropriate sounds.

www.georgetown.edu/cball/animals/animals.html

StudyOnline!

Flash card vocabulary quizzes on-line for foreign-language students.

www.studyonline.com

Timo's Hypertext Puzzle on European Languages

Can you recognize which foreign language is which? A multiple-choice on-line quiz in which students read a phrase in a foreign language, then identify the language.

www.cis.hut.fi/~tho/puzzle

Voice Map

Hear spoken phrases in many languages by native speakers from around the world. Voices, which include Tokyo Voice, Greek Voice, African-Zulu Voice, and Turkey Voice, each say three short simple phrases; the words appear in the foreign language and in English translation.

www.threeweb.ad.jp/~nakanisi/voicemap.html

WWW Foreign Language Resources

Many interesting Web sites for foreign language learners, in alphabetical order by language, from Arabic to Yiddish.

www.itp.berkeley.edu/~thorne/HumanResources.html

CHINESE

CATALOGS

China Guide

A supplier of CD-ROMs on all things Chinese, including arts and crafts, food and cooking, traditional medicine, and the written and spoken Chinese language. Each CD-ROM is described and reviewed on-line.

Of particular interest to beginning Chinese students is *ABC Interactive Chinese*, a comprehensive series of language lessons involving speech recognition, character writing, interactive games, a Chinese-English dictionary, Chinese history and literature, and conversational practice. Suggested for younger children is *Bo Po Mo Zoo*, in which a small donkey teaches kids 37 Chinese phonetic symbols through interactive games.

ABC Interactive Chinese (basic edition, 20 lessons), $29.95; the deluxe edition (145 lessons), $149.95. Available for Windows. *Bo Po Mo Zoo*, available for Mac/PC, $24.95. Contact

China Guide Company
642 Leonard St.
Brooklyn, NY 11222
(718) 389-4876/fax (718) 383-6515
www.china-guide.com

Also see **Foreign Language Catalogs** (pages 691–693).

BOOKS

Count Your Way Through China

Jim Haskins; Carolrhoda, 1988

Chinese characters and pronunciations for the numbers 1 to 10, each illustrated with a feature from Chinese history, geography, or culture.

See *Count Your Way Series* (page 697).

Long is a Dragon: Chinese Writing for Children

Peggy Goldstein; Scholastic, 1991

A simple history of Chinese writing for kids, dramatically illustrated in red and black. By the time kids reach the end of the book, they can manage to read and write a whole Chinese sentence: "The ox and the sheep ride the train." Also see, by the same author, *Hu is a Tiger: An Introduction to Chinese Writing.*

COMPUTER SOFTWARE

Power Chinese

An interactive language program for beginners, covering pronunciation, grammar, vocabulary, conversation, and writing. Readers are introduced to the Chinese language through an informative text that explains crucial differences between English and Chinese ("In English, forming a question usually involves a change in word order; not so in Chinese"), through many practice exercises, video and audio clips of native speakers, and humorous animations. The equivalent of a one-year introductory college course. On CD-ROM for Windows.

$159

Transparent Language

22 Proctor Hill Rd.

Box 575

Hollis, NH 03049-0575

(603) 465-2230 or (800) 752-1767/fax (603) 465-2779

Web site: www.transparent.com

CHINESE ON-LINE

Chinese Language-Related Information Page

A long list of Chinese language resources accessible on the Internet.

www.webcom.com/~bamboo/chinese/chinese.html

Speaking Chinese

Elementary Chinese language lessons on-line, with text and audio.

redgum.bendigo.latrobe.edu.au/~zhang/speaking.htm

Also see **The Learnables** (page 694) and **Teach Me Tapes** (pages 696).

FRENCH

Also see **Foreign Language Catalogs** (page 691).

VIDEOS

French in Action

French in Action, developed by Pierre Capretz at Yale University, is a "planned immersion" language course on videotape in which learners follow the lives and adventures of Robert, an American student in France, and Mireille, a young Frenchwoman. The videos were filmed at many locations in France—Robert and Mireille, for example, tour Paris and visit Burgundy, Brittany, Chartres, the Sorbonne, and the Luxembourg Gardens—and include thousands of clips of French television, movies, cartoons, and advertisements. Viewers listen to—and increasingly understand—real-life French conversations. *French in Action* is available in

two parts. Part I includes 26 half-hour programs on 7 videotapes, a 300+-page text (covers both Parts I and II), a student workbook, a study guide, and a set of practice audiocassettes; Part II includes another 26 programs, plus workbook, study guide, and audiocassettes.

Part I, about $300; Part II, about $260

Annenberg/CPB Project

1111 16th St. NW

Washington, DC 20036

(800) LEARNER

Web site: www.learner.org

For an equivalent program in spanish, see *Destinos* (page 710).

FRENCH ON-LINE

French Lessons from Everywhere

An immense list of French lessons for students of all levels available on-line.

globegate.utm.edu/french/globegate_mirror/frlesson.html

Resources for Learning French

Detailed reviews of French language programs and learning resources.

www.fourmilab.ch/francais/lfrench.html

STP Call: French

French lessons on-line. Lessons consist of a short text in French with many highlighted vocabulary words; click on each for a translation.

stp.ling.uu.se/Call/french

Surfez Le Net: French Web Sites

An annotated list of French Web sites arranged by category, among these language, news, tourism, arts and culture, entertainment, and hobbies. Includes sources for French pen pals.

www.learner.org/collections/multimedia/languages/fiseries/frweb

Also see **Early Advantage** (page 693), **The Learnables** (page 694), **Learn the Fun and Easy Way Series** (page 694), **Living Language Children's Courses** (page 695), **Power-glide Language Courses** (page 695), **Phrase-A-Day Series** (page 695), **Storybridges** (page 695), **Teach Me Tapes** (page 696), **Twin**

Sisters Listen and Learn a Language (page 696), **The First Thousand Word Series** (page 697), **Surf's Up! Series** (page 698), **Language** *Now!* (page 698), **Learn to Speak Series** (page 698), **TriplePlay Plus! Series** (page 699), and **Who Is Oscar Lake?** (page 699).

GERMAN

See **Foreign Language Catalogs** (pages 691–693), **Early Advantage** (page 693), **The Learnables** (page 694), **Learn the Fun and Easy Way Series** (page 694), **Power-glide Language Courses** (page 695), **Storybridges** (page 695), **Teach Me Tapes** (page 696), **Twin Sisters: Listen and Learn a Language** (page 696), **Count Your Way Series** (page 697), **Mary Glasgow Magazines** (page 693), **The First Thousand Words Series** (page 697), **Surf's Up! Series** (page 698), **Language** *Now!* (page 698), **Learn to Speak Series** (page 698), **TriplePlay Plus! Series** (page 699), and **Who Is Oscar Lake?** (page 699).

GREEK AND LATIN

See **Classical Mythology** (pages 89–92) and **World History: Greece and Rome** (pages 620–626).

CATALOGS

American Classical League

ALL The American Classical League, a nonprofit organization dedicated to promoting the study of classical languages and cultures, publishes a catalog of teaching materials for Latin, Greek, and the classical humanities. Included are books, activity books, and workbooks for teachers and students of Latin, books and pamphlets on word etymology and grammar, hands-on project kits, nonfiction books and novels on classical history, books in Latin, including Latin versions of Cinderella and Rumpelstiltskin, posters, maps, charts, audiocassettes, videotapes, games, and a large selection of Latin computer software. Also included: O, Loca Tu Ibis! (Theodore S. Geisel/Leone Roselle), a Latin reader and activity book based on Dr. Seuss's Oh, The Places You'll Go!; the Appella Me series, a collection of inter-

If you're in the market for a Latin program but are still nervously undecided, the National Committee for Latin and Greek (NCLG), a committee of the American Classical League, has assembled a pair of "Information Packets for Exemplary Latin Programs," one for elementary and one for middle schools. Each describes and compares six to eight Latin programs and text series.

Packets cost $7 apiece from the American Classical League.

views with children's storybook and nursery rhyme characters on cassette tape, half in Latin and half in English; and The Mythology Songbook, the stories of 28 myths set to well-known popular tunes.

American Classical League
Miami University
Oxford, OH 45056
(513) 529-7741/fax (513) 529-7742
e-mail: AmericanClassicalLeague@MUOhio.edu

Bolchazy-Carducci Publishers

A comprehensive catalog of materials for Latin and Greek students of all ages. Included are books, activity books, language programs, dictionaries and grammars, classical texts, and audiocassettes. Everything from the *Aeneid* to collections of popular songs in Latin.

Bolchazy-Carducci Publishers, Inc.
1000 Brown St., Unit 101
Wauconda, IL 60084
(847) 526-4344/fax (847) 526-2807
e-mail: orders@bolchazy.com
Web site: www.bolchazy.com
See *Artes Latinae* (below).

PROGRAMS AND COURSES

Artes Latinae

Artes Latinae, states the brochure, "is like having a Latin teacher in your home." The two-level program was developed by University of Michigan classics professor Waldo E. Sweet. Each level includes two hefty programmed texts, 12 to 15 text-coordinated audiocassette tapes, test booklets, reference notebooks, teachers' manuals, and graded readers, each containing Latin poems, prose, and proverbs at increasing levels of difficulty. The program is designed for self-instruction, which makes it particular useful for Latinless homeschooling parents, and is appropriate for students over a wide range of ages. Strictly speaking, *Artes Latinae* Level I covers high school (or college) first-year Latin; Level II, second-year Latin. The programmed texts, however, which allow students to work alone and to pace themselves, can be used with kids as young as 8 or 9.

The company also publishes the *Home Schoolers' Latin Network* newsletter for homeschooled Latin students, which includes information on Latin education, listings of Latin pen pals ("Amicus Stylo"), and the Latin Network, a long list of names, addresses, and telephone numbers of persons willing to answer questions about the program and to provide help for struggling students.

> The complete program at Level I or Level II, about $300; individual program phases, of which there are four per level, can be purchased separately. *Artes Latinae* is also now available on CD-ROM (Mac or Windows); each level, including manual, reference notebook, test booklet and guide, and graded readers, about $270
>
> Bolchazy-Carducci Publishers, Inc.
> 1000 Brown St., Unit 101
> Wauconda, IL 60084
> (708) 526-4344/fax (708) 526-2867
> e-mail: orders@bolchazy.com
> Web site: www.bolchazy.com

Athenaze Series

Maurice Balme and Gilbert Lawall; Oxford University Press, 1990, 1991

Athanaze: An Introduction to Ancient Greek is a course on the reading of ancient Greek, intended for secondary- and college-level students. The books center around the fictional adventures of an Athenian farmer named Dicaeopolis and his family, set against a real historical background in the fifth century B.C. Students are taught the alphabet and some introductory grammar, and then plunged immediately into transla-

tion. Each Greek reading is preceded by a new vocabulary list and some helpful hints, which enable the reader, with a little effort, to puzzle it out. The selections start out short and simple: Dicaeopolis tends his oxen, yells at his slave, and moves rocks around in his beautiful fields. As student skill increases, selections become longer and more complex, involving quotations from ancient Greek historians, philosophers, and political figures, recountings of mythological tales, and accounts of Dicaeopolis' experiences in the Peloponnesian Wars. The books also include black-and-white illustrations, maps, historical background information, and student exercises.

The series includes *Athenaze: Books I* and *II,* with accompanying *Teachers' Handbooks,* which are essential, since they contain all the translations, explanations, and answers to the exercises.

Greek 'n' Stuff

A series of workbooks and readers for young Greek and Latin students, preschool to upper-elementary age. The beginning Greek reader, *Hey, Andrew! Teach Me Some Greek!,* teaches kids the letters of the Greek alphabet; the accompanying workbook (Level 1) reinforces the lessons with puzzles and quizzes. Subsequent workbooks (Levels 2–4) cover simple vocabulary, sentences, and grammar. The series has a Christian slant; the books include Bible verses.

The Latin series, *Latin's Not So Tough!,* includes Level 1 and 2 workbooks, appropriate for kids of early elementary age and up.

> $9.95 to $18.95
> Greek 'n' Stuff
> Box 882
> Moline, IL 61266-0882
> e-mail: timohs@earthlink.net
> Web site: home.earthlink.net/~tomohs

Oxford Latin Course

Michael Balme and James Morwood; Oxford University Press

This series has been recently redesigned and reissued (1996, 1997) in a new four-volume set, lushly illustrated with full-color cartoons, drawings, photographs, and maps. The readings, based on the life of

Horace in the first century B.C., are both historically accurate and eventually—once you pick up a bit of a vocabulary—entertaining. Book I, for example, begins with simple accounts of Horace's everyday life; then, as Horace enters school, proceeds to retellings of famous stories based on the *Iliad* and the *Aeneid*. Each chapter begins with a series of cartoon-style panel illustrations, captioned with simple Latin sentences, introducing the topic to be studied. These are followed by a new vocabulary list, Latin passages to be read and translated, practice exercises, and an illustrated essay on Roman history and culture. A section at the back of the book, "Grammar and Exercises," explains the relevant rules of grammar for each chapter and includes a series of practice exercises.

The books—*Oxford Latin Course Parts I, II, III, and IV*—are each accompanied by a *Teacher's Book*, with explanatory notes, translations, and answers to all the practice exercises.

Oxford University Press
198 Madison Ave.
New York, NY 10016
(800) 230-3242/fax (919) 677-1303
Web site: www.oup-usa.org/orbs

Trivium Pursuit

A source for classical language programs and materials. Trivium Pursuit is a small, home-based company founded by a Christian homeschooling family. Catalog listings include *A Greek Alphabetarion Workbook*, a 60-page book designed to teach, one by one, the letters of the Greek alphabet and their pronunciations. (A short section "History of Languages" at the back explains that all modern languages date to the Tower of Babel and are based on the racial divisions of the three sons of Noah, a notion not shared by most professional linguists.) Accompanying Greek alphabet materials include Greek alphabet flash cards and a game—"Athens vs. Sparta"—intended to teach the names and order of the Greek letters to kids aged 10 and up. Once the alphabet has been mastered, kids can move on to *Homeschool Greek,* an interactive programmed text for students aged 12 and up.

Trivium Pursuit
139 Colorado St., Suite 168
Muscatine, IA 52761

BOOKS

ABC Et Cetera: The Life and Times of the Roman Alphabet

Alexander and Nicholas Humez; David R. Godine, 1985

A tour of the Roman alphabet, from *A* to *X,Y,Z*. There's a chapter for each letter, filled with interesting information about Roman history, everyday life in ancient Rome, and the ins and outs of the Latin language. It's an adult book, but advanced readers may enjoy it on their own. An excellent supplement to a Latin course.

See *Alpha to Omega: The Life and Times of the Greek Alphabet* (below) and *Latina pro Populo* (below).

Alpha to Omega: The Life and Times of the Greek Alphabet

Alexander and Nicholas Humez; David R. Godine, 1983

Learn the Greek alphabet, along with a great deal of Greek history, mythology, and etymology. The book covers the Greek alphabet from alpha to omega, in just over 200 information-packed pages.

See *Latina pro Populo* (below) and *ABC Et Cetera: The Life and Times of the Roman Alphabet* (above).

Amo, Amas, Amat and More: How to Use Latin to Your Own Advantage and to the Astonishment of Others

Eugene Ehrlich; HarperCollins, 1993

An enormous alphabetical collection of Latin phrases with pronounciation guide and explanation, among them the ever-useful *Excelsior!* Also see, by the same author, *Veni, Vidi, Vici: Conquer Your Enemies, Impress Your Friends With Everyday Latin* (Harper-Collins, 1995).

Gardener's Latin

Bill Neal; Algonquin Books, 1992

Over 2,500 entries explaining the Latin tags used to describe and differentiate among plants, with color illustrations, related background information, and lore.

Latina pro Populo/Latin for People

Alexander and Nicholas Humez; Little, Brown, 1978

The basics of Latin for beginners, with a sense of humor.

See *ABC Et Cetera: The Life and Times of the Roman Alphabet* (page 705) and *Alpha to Omega: The Life and Times of the Greek Alphabet* (page 705).

 Learning Latin Through Mythology

Jayne L. Hanlin and Beverly E. Lichtenstein; Cambridge University Press, 1991

An illustrated retelling of familiar Roman myths in simple Latin, with English translations. The book includes related activities and exercises for beginners.

 Roman Numerals I to M: Numerabilia Romanana Uno Ad Duo Mila

Arthur Geisert; Houghton Mifflin, 1996

A marvelously illustrated picture-book introduction to Roman numerals with many pigs (and a little bit of Latin).

Winnie Ille Pu: A Latin Version of A. A. Milne's Winnie-the-Pooh

A. A. Milne and Alexander Lenard; E. P. Dutton, 1991

The adventures of Pu, Porcellus, Lepus, Ior, and Christophorum Robinus.

GREEK AND LATIN ON-LINE

Greek 'n' Stuff

Learn a Greek letter, a Greek word, and a Latin word; there's also a "Bible Nugget of the Month."

home.earthlink.net/~tomohs

Hellenic Electronic Center

Greek lessons on-line, starting at the very beginning, with the alphabet. Users have an option to hear Greek vocabulary words spoken; also included are written texts with phonetic pronunciations and English translations, and drills and quizzes.

www.greece.org/gr-lessons

 The Perseus Project

A digital library of resources for studying the ancient world, including texts in Greek and Latin with their English translations.

www.perseus.tufts.edu

Resources for Latin Teachers

 A searchable database stuffed with information on texts, dictionaries, history, mythology, art and archaeology, specific classical authors, and much more.

www.uky.edu/ArtsSciences/Classics/schools.html

Also see *Aduléscens* (page 693) and **Language Now! Series** (page 698).

HEBREW

Also see **Foreign Language Catalogs** (pages 691–693).

BOOKS

Alef-Bet: A Hebrew Alphabet Book

Michelle Edwards; Lothrop, Lee & Shepard, 1992

A picture-book introduction to the Hebrew language through the everyday life of an Israeli family.

Alef-Bet Fun

Lillian S. Abramson and Jessie Robinson; Bloch Publishing, 1997

A workbook of exercises and games for learning the names, sounds, and sequence of the characters in the Hebrew alphabet.

Count Your Way Through Israel

Jim Haskins; Carolrhoda, 1990

A simple picture book in which kids learn to count from 1 to 10 in Hebrew while finding out about the culture, history, and geography of Israel.

See the *Count Your Way Series* (page 697).

HEBREW ON-LINE

 Hebrew: A Living Language

An excellent site for beginners, including a tutorial that teaches the Hebrew alphabet, basic grammar lessons, a hypertextual story, a Hebrew "Phrase of the Week," and a Hebrew-English dictionary.

hebrew.macom.co.il

FOREIGN LANGUAGES

Also see **The Learnables** (page 694), **Teach Me Tapes** (page 696), **The First Thousand Words Series** (page 697), and **TriplePlay Plus! Series** (page 699).

ITALIAN

See **Foreign Language Catalogs** (pages 691–693), **Early Advantage** (page 693), **Learn the Fun and Easy Way Series** (page 694), **Teach Me Tapes** (pages 696), **Twin Sisters: Listen and Learn a Language** (page 696), **Count Your Way Series** (page 697), **The First Thousand Words Series** (page 697), **Language *Now!*** (page 698), and **TriplePlay Plus! Series** (page 699).

JAPANESE

Also see **Foreign Language Catalogs** (pages 691–693).

BOOKS

Count Your Way Through Japan
Jim Haskins; Carolrhoda, 1987

Japanese characters and pronunciations for numbers 1 through 10, in 24 picture-book pages. Each number word is illustrated with a Japanese landmark or cultural feature, with a brief explanation. One, for example, is for the one and only Mount Fuji.

See **Count Your Way Series** (page 697).

Hiragana Gambatte!
Deleece Batt; Kodansha International, 1993

A workbook for kids, narrated cartoon-style by Gamba, the mischievous Japanese monkey. Users work their way through the 46-character hiragana alphabet, learning Japanese vocabulary words and information about Japanese history, geography, and culture. The book includes games, quizzes, puzzles, and humorous black-and-white illustrations.

Japanese for Children
Yoshiaki Kobo, Reiko Mori, and George Okuhara; Passport Books

A straightforward approach to written and spoken Japanese for kids in elementary through junior high school. The program contains 17 lessons on one 60-minute audiocassette, a student workbook of Japanese and English versions of the words and phrases on the tape, exercises in the writing of the hiragana and katakana alphabets, and a teacher's guide.

National Textbook Co.
4255 W. Touhy Ave.
Lincolnwood, IL 60646-1975
(708) 679-5500 or (800) 323-4900/fax (708) 679-2494

Let's Learn Hiragana: First Book of Basic Japanese Writing
Yasuko Kosaka Mitamura; Kodansha International, 1985

Demonstrations and practice exercises teach the characters of the hiragana and katakana alphabets. Users learn to write individual characters, syllables, and words, along with a good deal of Japanese vocabulary. Also see, by the same author, *Let's Learn Katakana: Second Book of Basic Japanese Writing.*

COMPUTER SOFTWARE

Power Japanese
An interactive language program for beginners on CD-ROM, featuring color graphics, humorous animations, audio and video clips of native speakers, a 10,000-word dictionary, many practice drills, games, and a record function with which students can assess their Japanese pronounciation skills. The program includes an introduction of the hiragana and katakana syllabaries, as well as basic Japanese grammar, vocabulary, and conversation. For Windows.

$159
Transparent Language
22 Proctor Hill Rd.
Box 575
Hollis, NH 03049-0575
(603) 465-2230 or (800) 725-1767/fax (603) 465-2779
Web site: www.transparent.com

Also see **TriplePlay Plus! Series** (page 699).

JAPANESE ON-LINE

Asian Language Terminology
General information about Chinese and Japanese writing, plus Japanese hiragana and katakana character charts.

www.aproposinc.com/pages/asianterm.htm

7 *Japan Window*

+ The site, along with many links to Japanese resources, features a Kid's Window, which includes instruction in hiragana, katakana, and kanji writing, language lessons, a picture dictionary, and assorted stories.

jw/nttam.com:80/KIDS/kids_home.html

Also see **The Learnables** (page 694), **Learn the Fun and Easy Way Series** (page 694), **Power-glide Language Courses** (page 695), **Teach Me Tapes** (page 696), and **The First Thousand Words Series** (pages 697).

RUSSIAN

See **Foreign Language Catalogs** (pages 691–693), **The Learnables** (page 694), **Power-glide Language Courses** (page 695), **Teach Me Tapes** (page 695), **Count Your Way Series** (page 697), **The First Thousand Words Series** (page 697), and **Language *Now!* Series** (page 698).

SIGN LANGUAGE

BOOKS

3
9 *The Handmade Alphabet*
Laura Rankin; Puffin, 1996

A beautifully illustrated sign language alphabet book in which the hand symbol for each letter is paired with an object beginning with that letter. The *I* hand, for example, is accompanied by glittering icicles; the *O* hand dangles a Christmas ornament.

3
9 *Handsigns: A Sign Language Alphabet*
Kathleen Fain; Chronicle Books, 1995

A colorful animal alphabet book in which an inset picture of a human hand teaches the sign for the beginning letter of each animal name.

4
9 *Handtalk: An ABC of Finger Spelling and Sign Language*
Remy Charlip and Mary Beth Miller; Simon & Schuster, 1984

A beginner's introduction to signing, demonstrating both letter-by-letter finger spelling and signs representing whole words or concepts.

4
9 *Handtalk Zoo*
George Ancona and Mary Beth Miller; Aladdin, 1996

Mary Beth and a group of excited kids visit the zoo, where the children learn signs and finger spellings for the names of the animals they see there (and a bit about telling time). Illustrated with color photographs. Also see *Handtalk School* (Simon & Schuster, 1991), *Handtalk Birthday* (Simon & Schuster, 1987), and *Handtalk: An ABC of Finger Spelling and Sign Language* (left).

10
+ *The Joy of Signing: The Illustrated Guide for Mastering Sign Language and the Manual Alphabet*
Lottie L. Riekehof; Gospel Publishing House, 1987

A 300+-page guide to sign language for motivated learners, divided into 25 very comprehensive vocabulary categories. Also see *Signing Illustrated: The Complete Learning Guide* (Mickey Flodin; Perigee, 1994).

3
8 *My Signing Book of Numbers*
Patricia B. Gillen; Kendall Green, 1987

How to count in sign language. Users learn the numbers 0 to 20 by ones, 30 to 100 by tens, and the signs for 1,000 and 1 million.

4
8 *Sign Language ABC With Linda Bove*
Linda Bove; Random House, 1985

Deaf actress Linda Bove of *Sesame Street* and the Muppets teach the manual alphabet and a scattering of signs for alphabetical words. Under *A*, for example, kids learn the signs for airplane, alligator, and apple. See *Sign Language Fun With Linda Bove* (below).

4
8 *Sign Language Fun With Linda Bove*
Linda Bove; Random House, 1980

A sign language picture book with which kids can learn the signs for many everyday words and phrases. Categories include "The Family," "School Days," "Colors," "On the Farm," "Things That Are Opposite," "Action Words," "Seasons," "In the Jungle," and "The

Way You Feel." Big double-page illustrations give readers a chance to practice: "How many things is this picture can you 'sign'?"

See *Sign Language ABC With Linda Bove* (page 708).

Signed English Series

Harry Bornstein and Karen L. Saulnier; Kendall Green

A series of children's picture books with accompanying diagrams showing each word of the text in sign language. Titles include *Little Red Riding Hood: Told in Signed English* (1991), *Nursery Rhymes from Mother Goose: Told in Signed English* (1992), and *Goldilocks and the Three Bears: Told in Signed English* (1996).

A Show of Hands: Say It in Sign Language

Mary Beth Sullivan and Linda Bourke; HarperCollins, 1988

Sign language for beginners, presented through cartoon-style illustrations.

Signing Is Fun: A Child's Introduction to the Basics of Sign Language

Mickey Flodin; Perigee, 1995

A 95-page illustrated introduction to the sign language alphabet and basic everyday phrases.

Signing for Kids

Mickey Flodin; Perigee, 1991

A 142-page introduction to signing for kids aged 8–14. The book is arranged by general subject area: kids learn the manual alphabet, and words and phrases about pets, people, food, sports, school, money, numbers, and travel.

You Don't Need Words: A Book About Ways People Talk Without Words

Ruth Belov Gross; Scholastic, 1991

A short introduction to sign language and other ways in which people communicate without spoken words, including facial expressions, pantomime, picture-writing, and gestures. (In Swaziland, a finger drawn across the throat means "I love you.")

VIDEOS

Say It By Signing

A 60-minute series of dramatized sign language lessons from Living Language, beginning with the manual alphabet, followed by greetings, names of family members, days of the week, sports terms, food and drink, clothing, colors, numbers, and money. Presentations are straightforward and informational, targeted at older learners and adults. An animated signing scene, without subtitles, begins each lesson, representing an everyday interaction such as meeting an old friend in the park or a shopping expedition. Viewers are then taught individual signs for words and concepts, and some aspects of signing grammar; the scene is replayed, with captions, so that viewers can follow along.

Random House
400 Hahn Rd.
Westminster, MD 21157
(800) 733-3000

SIGN LANGUAGE ON-LINE

ASL Spelling Study: The Alphabet

Users can learn the American Sign Language alphabet, then test themselves on their new knowledge.

www.sirius.com/~dub/CALL/asl.html

A Basic Guide to ASL

A searchable dictionary that includes both text definitions and animated hand signs. Separate entries teach the signs for the numbers 1 to 10 and the letters of the alphabet.

home.earthlink.net/~mastertech/ASLDict.html

Interactive ASL and Braille Guide

An introduction to American Sign Language with an interactive finger spelling guide, general information about Braille, and an interactive guide to the Braille alphabet.

www.disserv.stu.umn.edu/Altform

SPANISH

CATALOGS

Also see **Foreign Language Catalogs** (pages 691–693).

Bueno

"Friendly Foreign Language Learning" for persons of all ages. Many language-learning resources are available, but the bulk of the materials are Spanish. Included are Spanish/English bilingual folktales, children's stories, and coloring books, songs and games, and even Spanish versions of Charlie Brown ("Carlitos") and Garfield ("*el rey de los gatos*") cartoons. The 16-page catalog is published four times yearly.

Bueno
In One Ear Publications
29481 Manzanita Dr.
Campo, CA 91906-1128
e-mail: buenobks@aol.com

VIDEOS

Destinos

Destinos is a "planned immersion" approach to language learning on videotape. Here, listeners follow the soap opera–like adventures of an L.A. lawyer, Raquel Rodriguez, who travels through Mexico, Spain, Argentina, and Puerto Rico attempting to solve a mystery. The program is available in two parts, each including 26 half-hour programs on seven videotapes, plus text, workbook, study guide, and audiocassettes.

Annenberg/CPB Project
1111 Sixteenth Ave. NW
Washington, DC 20036
(800) LEARNER
Web site: www.learner.org

See **French in Action** (page 702).

SPANISH ON-LINE

Basic Spanish for the Virtual Student

Spanish lessons on-line, including pronunciation guides, grammar instruction, vocabulary lists, and bilingual stories.

www.umr.edu/~amigos/Virtual

Cuentos para los Niños

Poems, stories, and songs for children, all in Spanish.

pw2.netcom/~dylanjab/cuentos.html

Elementary Spanish Curriculum

How and what to teach in Spanish language programs, from grades K–8. The site includes a list of appropriate goals for each grade level, with suggested activities and vocabulary lists.

www.veen.com/Veen/Leslie/Curriculum/index.html

Learn Spanish

Many vocabulary lists, including "Almost all the things you can find in a house" and "List of clothes," verb form charts, links to related Spanish language sites, and an on-line bookstore.

www.lingolex.com/spanish.html

Spanish Vocabulary Builder

Select a category (foods, transportation, sports, animals, verbs, weather, occupations, holidays, time) and click on a picture to hear the Spanish word.

home.earthlink.net/~mikcav

Tecla

An on-line magazine for students and teachers, with articles and related activities, all in Spanish.

www.bbk.ac.uk/Departments/Spanish/
TeclaHome.html

Web Spanish Lessons

The lessons teach basic vocabulary and grammar, with audio recordings of spoken Spanish.

www.willamette.edu/~tjones/Spanish/lesson.html

Also see **Early Advantage** (page 693), **The Learnables** (page 694), **Learn the Fun and Easy Way Series** (page 694), **Living Language Children's Courses** (page 695), **Phrase-A-Day Series** (page 695), **Power-glide Language Courses** (page 695), **Storybridges** (page 695), **Teach Me Tapes** (page 696), **Twin Sisters: Listen and Learn a Language** (page 696), **The First Thousand Words Series** (page 697), **Surf's Up! Series** (page 698), **Language *Now!* Series** (page 698), **Learn to Speak Series** (page 698), **TriplePlay Plus! Series** (page 699), and **Who Is Oscar Lake?** (page 699).

SWAHILI

Also see **Foreign Language Catalogs** (pages 691–693).

BOOKS

Jambo Means Hello: Swahili Alphabet Book
Muriel Feelings; Dial, 1992

An alphabet book of East African culture through words beginning with the 24 (no *Q* or *X*) sounds of the Swahili alphabet.

Moja Means One: Swahili Counting Book
Muriel Feelings; Dial, 1992

A beautifully illustrated counting book of East African culture.

SWAHILI ON-LINE

The Kamusi Project: The Internet Living Swahili Dictionary

Lists of African and Swahili language resources, Swahili song lyrics, Swahili-English and English-Swahili on-line dictionaries, a simple introductory word list of beginners, a brief history of the language, and beginning Swahili language lessons.

www.cis.yale.edu/swahili

Kiswahili Home Page

General information about the language, introductory lessons covering the alphabet, numbers, time, and days of the week, beginning vocabulary, and verb tenses, an English-Swahili/Swahili-English dictionary, and links to related language sites.

conn.me.queensu.ca/kassim/documents/kiswa/
swahili.com

FOREIGN-LANGUAGE PEN PALS

KIDLINK

 Foreign languages for kids. The site includes foreign-language newsletters for kids in Portuguese, Japanese, French, Spanish, Dutch, Norwegian, Danish, and Russian, and is a source for foreign-language e-mail pals.

kids.ccit.duq.edu

Penpals Corner

ALL Pen pals from all over the world for people of all ages. Register (free) to add your name to an international list.

www.wp.com/andre

Rigby Heinemann Keypals

A site for teachers and kids looking for pen pals around the world, categorized by grade (K–8 or 9–12). Choose from a long list of posted international messages.

reedbooks.com.au/heinemann/global/keypals.html

Skipping Stones

 ALL This children's magazine (see page 693) includes an extensive list of international pen pals for kids of all ages.

World Pen Pals

For an application form, send a stamped, self-addressed envelope to the address below. The organization links persons aged 12–20 to pen pals from all over the world.

Acquiring a single pen pal costs $4.50; two, $8.50; and three, $12

World Pen Pals
1694 Como Ave.
St. Paul, MN 55108

THE ARTS

It's clever, but is it Art?

RUDYARD KIPLING

Art, for most homeschool families, is—compared to, say, algebra—a piece of cake. Most kids love it, in some form or another. Most parents are comfortable with it, since art instruction—at least in its early stages—is usually a simple matter of providing basic supplies (paint, paper, pencils, crayons, paste, clay, colored chalk) and letting creativity flourish, which it does. There's the matter of post-art cleanup, of course, but even that, with a little forethought—*no India ink on the carpet*—is manageable.

As children grow older, however, the process of designing arts programs becomes more challenging. Interests expand into the fields of art and music history and appreciation; soon parents and teachers are fielding questions about flying buttresses, chamber music, the stories behind the great operas, and Shakespearean plays. In our homeschool program, we have generally approached the arts, in all their many permutations, through cross-curricular studies, incorporating art, music, drama, architecture, and dance into all academic disciplines. A unit on medieval history, for example, included viewing the works of period painters, learning about the design and building of cathedrals, experimenting with stained glass, and writing, staging, and performing a play based on the story of St. George and the dragon. A unit on the science of sound involved building and playing simple wind and string instruments. A study of Ireland inspired great interest in Celtic music and dance, reinforced by awed viewings of Michael Flatley's *Riverdance,* an Irish dance spectacular available on video (see page 794).

The ability to experience, appreciate, or participate in the arts may be the most valuable gift we give our kids. The arts, singly and collectively, are a lifelong source of intellectual and emotional sustenance and enduring joy. Most kids, as they enter adulthood, begin to specialize, tailoring academic input to personal interests and future careers. Most, in this process, inevitably leave a lot behind: engineers drop sonnets; historians forget physics; poets chuck calculus. How many of us—depending on current lifestyles and occupations—can still, for example, conjugate Latin verbs, produce the proof for a geometric theorem, label a map of Africa? We pick and choose from an educational smorgasbord. Not so with art and music. These are with us forever, unbroken threads.

The universal appeal of the arts is generally reflected in the community. Most of us are within reach of an art or craft center, a music teacher, a potter or weaver willing to give lessons. Museums—even small ones—often provide excellent art programs. Our boys have taken art classes of various kinds every year, beginning with a preschool class held in the kindergarten room of the local public elementary school, where they made handprint murals, construction-paper butterflies, and cardboard box castles. Most recently, they took pottery classes at the craft center up the road, where they all learned to use a potter's wheel and turned out a wonderful collection of pots, bowls, plates, vases, and (one) green coffee mug. In between, they've learned to knit, weave, and make latchhook rugs; they've experimented with acrylic and watercolor paints, pastels, colored pencils, and sidewalk chalk; they've made murals, mobiles, collages, dioramas, and linoleum block prints. They've tried their hands at wood and stone carving, papermaking, and bookbinding. They've taken museum classes in colonial crafts, Indian crafts, medieval crafts. They've tried origami, photography, fabric painting. They've made Halloween costumes and very creative jack-o'-lanterns, Ukrainian pysanky eggs, Christmas ornaments (heavy in glitter), and a lot of perfectly beautiful walking sticks.

As the boys have grown older, their interests—inevitably—have diverged. Ethan's passion for computer technology, Josh's love for English literature, and Caleb's absorption in ancient history—"Did you know that Alexander the Great named a city after his *horse?"*—are all their own. The arts, however, remain common ground. Tastes, of course, aren't quite the same.

On a trip this past summer to a local art festival, the boys each zeroed in on a favorite artwork. Caleb favored a dreamy impressionistic oil of a snowy hillside. Ethan chose a crisply realistic painting of an island sunset. Josh fell for a gigantic glass-and-metal sculpture titled *Insecticycle.*

From my homeschool journal:

◆ October 24, 1991. Josh is ten; Ethan, eight; Caleb, seven.

We are still studying events surrounding Columbus's landmark voyage of 1492. Today covered Michelangelo, who was alive and well in Italy at the time. Read about Michelangelo in 1492: Year of Columbus *by Genevieve Foster and* The World of Michelangelo *by Piero Ventura. Michelangelo, we discovered, lived to be 89 years old and died of stone disease. The boys: "What's stone disease?" "Do people still get it today?" "How do you cure it?" "In black lung disease, do your lungs really turn black?"*

We then looked at many pictures of paintings and sculptures by Michelangelo and discussed the process of stone carving and stone carvers' tools. "How did he get the stone so smooth?"

In lieu of stone, the boys then made soap carvings (two bears and a spaceship).

◆ **January 28, 1992. Josh is ten; Ethan, nine; Caleb, seven.**

We're reading Seabird *by Holling C. Holling (see page 514), and the boys are carving their own seabirds out of balsa wood. In the course of deciding how to paint their birds, they looked up seagulls in assorted bird books and compared various species. Then this afternoon we saw seagulls in the grocery store parking lot. The boys, thrilled, promptly identified them as herring gulls. ("Look! Seagulls! What color feet do they have?")*

◆ **May 11, 1992. Josh is eleven; Ethan, nine; Caleb, seven.**

We started the morning with a homemade art appreciation game. Each kid made himself a series of index card with symbols drawn on them, each representing a personal response or general description of a work of art. A star, for example, meant "I really love this one!"; a black X meant "I don't like it"; a sun indicated a cheerful painting; a tree indicated a landscape painting; and so on. Once the boys had amassed a collection of these symbol cards, we went through a big stack of our art postcards and prints, choosing symbols for each picture and discussing our choices. We variously covered paintings by Rembrandt, Cézanne, Kandinsky, van Gogh, Millet, Grandma Moses, Winslow Homer, Matisse, and Magritte.

Then the kids—who liked the game—drew and critiqued a series of their own pictures.

◆ **September 10, 1994. Josh is thirteen; Ethan, eleven; Caleb, nine.**

Today is the anniversary of the first Mickey Mouse cartoon (which hit the theaters in 1928), so we celebrated using home-written workbooks covering the art, science, and history of Mickey. The boys made illustrated timelines, showing the birth of Walt Disney, the first appearance of Mickey Mouse in Steamboat Willie, the invention of the*

motion-picture projector, and assorted other landmarks. We read the essay "A Biological Homage to Mickey Mouse" in Stephen Jay Gould's The Panda's Thumb, *which discussed the appeal of juvenile features in mammals and the "evolution" of Mickey Mouse (from tall and ratlike to short, round, and cute); the boys then made scale drawings on graph paper showing Mickey's changing facial proportions.*

We then built a zoetrope—a hand-held "motion-picture machine"—and the boys made a series of drawing strips that, when positioned on the zoetrope and spun, became animated. Animations included a knight being chased by a dragon, a galloping dinosaur, a rocket launch, and an exploding colored firework.

In conjunction with this, we reviewed the workings of the human eye; and Josh reminisced about a past field trip to the Cartoon Museum of Art (in Rye, New York).

The boys, inspired by Mickey, spent much of the rest of the day jointly writing and drawing a comic book of their own: a science-fiction adventure, drawn in black ink and elaborately colored with felt-tipped pens, with dialogue in balloons and text in boxes.

Among all the positive art experiences, however, was the occasional negative.

From my homeschool journal:

◆ **February 11, 1992. Josh is ten; Ethan, nine; Caleb, seven.**

To the art center this afternoon for the boys' classes. These unfortunately aren't turning out very well. Ethan and Caleb are both taking "Painting and Drawing," with a teacher who has about as much personality as a wet sock. As of the third class, the kids are still doing geometric paintings, with assigned shapes and colors, which they find restrictive. Ethan today cracked. "This time," he told me, "I mixed my own colors when she wasn't looking."

Josh, I thought, had been enjoying his drama class, but things apparently didn't go well today. The teacher, said Josh, wanted him to talk like a loud showman, and he didn't like that.

"Drama class," said Josh ominously, "is like the unicorn trials."

"The what?" I said.

"When a baby unicorn gets old enough," Josh said, "his mother takes him into a frightening forest and leaves *him there under a tree until he learns to conquer his fear. That's what this class is like."*

Well. We'll see how it goes next week.

ART

CATALOGS

Creativity for Kids

The company designs and packages many terrific boxed arts and crafts kits for kids. Examples include "Mixed Media Mosaics," with which kids decorate a 5-inch-square mirror and a 7½-inch framed "glass window" with miniature ceramic tiles and colored glass nuggets; "Lampscape," with which they make their own bedside lamp, with decorated base and painted lampshade; and "Sculpture," a collection of wood scraps, plaster, clay, wire, paper, and cloth for making 10 or more varied projects, including soft sculptures, mobiles, and carvings. Also available: many jewelry-making kits ("wearable art"), a selection of Native American craft kits, and a Preschool series, which includes kits for making collages, puppets, clay models, and pictures (painted or printed), for kids aged 3 and up.

> Available through toy and game stores or
> Creativity for Kids
> 1802 Central Ave.
> Cleveland, OH 44115
> (216) 589-4800 or (800) 642-2288/fax (216) 589-4803
> Web site: www.creativityforkids.com

Crizmac

The company publishes a catalog of creative resources for art education with a multicultural slant. Included are comprehensive programs on Australian, African, Haitian, and Mexican art, books, games, posters, and art prints. Books include how-to project books, art histories, and collections of multicultural folktales and legends. Games, designed to enhance observation and art appreciation skills, include "Artery" (see page 737), "Philosophy & Art" (see page 739), and "Token Response" (see page 740).

> Crizmac
> Box 65928
> Tucson, AZ 85728-5928
> (800) 913-8555/fax (520) 323-6194
> Web site: www.crizmac.com

Crystal Productions

Crystal Productions publishes a catalog of art education resources for students of all ages, including books, curriculum guides, videos, posters, prints, slides, games, and computer software. Videos include instructional programs on everything from watercolor to stained-glass windows, pottery, and bookbinding; art history programs; and biographies of famous artists. Books include how-to manuals, art appreciation books, kids' activity books, biographies, and art histories. An excellent source for multicultural art resources.

> Crystal Productions
> Box 2159
> Glenview, IL 60025-6159
> (800) 255-8629
> e-mail: crystal@interaccess.com

Curiosity Kits

A varied assortment of excellent boxed arts and crafts kits for kids of all ages. The kits are fully equipped, which means that they contain absolutely everything needed to complete the projects, right down to the glue, scissors, and little pieces of sandpaper. Each kit also contains an illustrated instruction booklet, with cultural, historical, or scientific background. Titles include "Stone Sculpture" ("stone mix," molding materials, and tools), "Self-Portrait" (oil pastels, a canvas, instructions, and a wooden frame to assemble and paint), "Stained Glass" (colored acrylic "glass" pieces, self-stick copper stripping, patterns, and suction cups), "Blockprinting Natural Notepaper" (10 sheets of colorful handmade paper, envelopes, printing blocks, and inks), "World Jewelry" (materials for making African earrings, a Chinese cloisonné bracelet, a Peruvian necklace, Venetian glass bead earrings, and an Egyptian scarab pin), and "African Mask" (a precut mask to color and decorate with multicolored raffia).

> From arts and crafts stores. For a local source, contact
> Curiosity Kits

Box 811

Cockeysville, MD 21030

(410) 584-2605 or (800) 584-KITS

e-mail: ckitsin@aol.com

Far Out Explorations

A catalog of over 350 art books for kids, parents, teachers, and other art-loving adults. The catalog collection is a multidisciplinary and multifaceted approach to art. Included are biographies of famous artists and musicians, art appreciation books, architecture books, art-based activity books for kids of all ages, art coloring books, art ABC books, and art postcard collections. There are also art-and-poetry books, such as the exquisite *Talking to the Sun* (Kenneth Koch and Kate Farrell, eds.; see page 151), an anthology of poems for young people illustrated with paintings and sculptures from the Metropolitan Museum of Art, and a selection of books that creatively combine art, science, and math.

Far Out Explorations

Box 308

Milford, CT 06460

(203) 877-2962 or (800) 510-ARTS/fax (203) 874-9099

Flax Art & Design

The Flax catalog is an eclectic collection of gifts and out-of-the-ordinary knickknacks, as well as art supplies, books, puzzles, and markedly creative kits for artistic kids.

Flax Art & Design

240 Valley Dr.

Brisbane, CA 94005-1206

(800) 547-7778/fax (800) FLAX-123

e-mail: catalog@flaxart.com

Web site: www.flaxart.com

KidsArt

Books, art supplies, and kits for kids in grades K–8. KidsArt also publishes the KidsArt units, a series of 16-page illustrated booklets, packed with activities, background information, and art history. Each unit is centered around a single topic: a specific art technique or medium, a famous artist, a period in art history, or the art of a particular culture. Titles of basic art units include, for example, "Color," "Draw People," "Clay,"

"Collage," "Printmaking," "Fiber Arts," and "Chalk and Charcoal." Units on great artists include "Leonardo," "Rembrandt," "The Impressionists," "Winslow Homer," and "Audubon and Wildlife Art"; art history and multicultural unit titles include "Ancient Egypt," "Ancient Rome," "Oriental Art," "World Folk Art," "Traditional Arts of Africa," and "Northwest Coast Native Art."

Units, $3 apiece. Some are available in packs of 10 (assorted), as the "KidsArt Art Skills Set" and the "KidsArt Art History Set"; sets, $20

KidsArt

Box 274

Mt. Shasta, CA 96067

(916) 926-5076

Web site: www.kidsart.com

Knowledge Unlimited, Inc.

A source for art posters, prints, videos, and activity books, many with a strong multicultural component.

Knowledge Unlimited, Inc.

Box 52

Madison, WI 53701-0052

(608) 836-6660 or (800) 356-2303/fax (608) 831-1570 or (800) 618-1570

Web site: www.ku.com

Lakeshore Learning Materials

The catalog includes a large selection of arts and crafts supplies specifically intended for young children. Included are fingerpaints, tempera paints, beginners' paintbrushes (with nice fat handles), crayons (in "First," "Jumbo," "Large," and "Standard" sizes), playground chalks, rubber and sponge print stamps, and stencils. Among our favorites: the "Lakeshore Wood Scraps" set, which contains 25 pounds of interesting wood scraps (balls, sticks, arcs, screws, squiggles, squares, cylinders, rings, and triangles) for young sculptors; and the "Classroom Collage Box," which includes a marvelous and enormous assortment of buttons, sequins, pom-poms, colored macaroni, craft rocks, yarn, crinkle sticks, feathers, doilies, stickers, "rainbow sticks," and foam shapes, plus four jars of glitter and 30 collage trays. For older kids, see the *Lakeshore 1-2-3* and *Lakeshore Basics & Beyond* catalogs.

Lakeshore Learning Materials
2695 E. Dominguez St.
Box 6261
Carson, CA 90749
(310) 537-8600 or (800) 421-5354/fax (310) 537-5403
Web site: www.lakeshorelearning.com

Nasco Arts & Crafts

ALL A comprehensive catalog of arts and crafts supplies for students in kindergarten through college, including materials of drawing, painting, printmaking, leather and wood crafts, ceramics, weaving, and stained glass.

Nasco
Fort Atkinson
901 Janesville Ave.
Box 901
Fort Atkinson, WI 53538-0901
fax (920) 563-8296
or
Nasco-Modesto
4825 Stoddard Rd.
Box 3837
Modesto, CA 95352-3837
(800) 558-9595/fax (209) 545-1669
Web site: www.nascofa.com

RB Walter Art and Craft Materials

ALL A fat catalog of resources for artists of all ages, including arts and crafts supplies, activity books, art history and appreciation materials, art prints, games, and videos.

RB Walter Art and Craft Materials
Box 6231
Arlington, TX 76005
(800) 447-8787

S & S Arts & Crafts

ALL A good source for arts and crafts supplies, activity and instruction books, and kids' project kits. The 200+-page catalog includes sand art supplies, clays and modeling media, jewelry-making materials, fabric paints and canvas projects, stained glass and "baking crystals," craft sticks, paints, brushes, crayons, and markers, papers of all kinds, collage materials, candle-making supplies, lacing and weaving projects, fabric craft kits, looms, latch-hook, cross-stitch, and macramé kits, basket-weaving supplies, ceramic tiles and projects, and wood project kits.

Many of the project kits are sold as "group packs," which is highly cost-effective if you're willing to make 10 to 20 of something. A make-your-own kaleidoscope kit, for example, costs $18 for a package of 25; an African Mask project, $12 for a pack of nine (includes precut masks, raffia, elastic cord, markers, and patterns); blank draw-your-own jigsaw puzzles, $8 for a pack of 24.

S & S also sells plain white cigar-box-style "Treasure Boxes" with fliptop lids, suitable for creative decorating. These cost $2 apiece. We've used them for years for the kids' pencil (etc.) boxes; decorating a new pencil box has become a family first-day-of-school tradition.

S & S Arts & Crafts
Box 513
Colchester, CT 06415-0513
(800) 243-9232/fax (800) 566-6678
e-mail: service@snswwide.com
Web site: www.snswwide.com

Sax Arts & Crafts

ALL A 500+-page catalog of art supplies, equipment, books, kits, videos, computer software, games, and art prints for students of all ages, from crayons, blunt-tipped scissors, and fingerpaint to potter's wheels, silkscreen printing kits, calligraphy supplies, and stone-carving tools.

Among our favorites: scented construction paper, the "Sax Small Collage Box," a not-so-small collection of lick-and-stick shapes, foil strips, doilies, neon-colored papers, and tissue, plus 10 recycled paper trays for collage bases, the "Create-a-Crayon" recycling kit, with which users can melt down all those squashed, broken, and too short remainders and mold them into new usable crayons, and the "Fine Art Rubber Stamp Art Museum Set," with which kids can stamp out reproductions of Leonardo da Vinci's *Mona Lisa*, Vincent van Gogh's *Starry Night*, Grant Wood's *American Gothic*, and Edvard Munch's *The Scream*.

The catalog is free to schools or institutions; for everybody else, $5 (refundable with your first order)
Sax Arts & Crafts
Box 510710
New Berlin, WI 53151

orders (800) 558-6696; customer service (800) 522-4278/fax (414) 784-1176

Young and Creative
ALL Varied kits and crafts supplies for kids of all ages.
Young & Creative
4315 Walney Rd.
Chantilly, VA 22021-2103
(800) 609-8697/fax (703) 263-3303

ART MUSEUM CATALOGS

Many art museums publish catalogs that include affordable art prints and postcards, and art-related kits, toys, books, puzzles, and computer software for kids. Among these are:

The Art Institute of Chicago
The Museum Shop
111 S. Michigan Ave.
Chicago, IL 60603
orders (800) 621-9337; customer service (800) 637-9110/fax (847) 299-8286

Metropolitan Museum of Art
Special Service Office
Middle Village, NY 11381-0001
(800) 468-7386
Web site: www.metmuseum.org

Museum of Fine Arts, Boston
Box 244
Avon, MA 02332-0244
(800) 225-5592/fax (508) 588-9678
Web site: www.mfa.org

Museum of Modern Art, New York
11 W. 53rd St.
New York, NY 10019
(212) 708-9400
Web site: www.moma.org

National Gallery of Art
Constitution Ave. NW
Washington, DC 20565
(202) 737-4215 or (800) 697-9350
Web site: www.nga.gov

MAGAZINES

Arts & Activities
ALL A magazine of activities, resources, lesson plans, techniques, information, and product reviews for art educators. Past issues have included articles on student art projects centered around geodesic domes, artifacts from the imperial tombs of China, bridges, bugs, African masks, and junk. Each issue also includes a foldout full-color "Clip and Save Art Print," with information and student activity suggestions on the back. The magazine is published monthly (except in July and August).

Annual subscription (10 issues), $25
Arts & Activities
591 Camino de la Reina, Suite 200
San Diego, CA 92108
(619) 297-8032

Book Links
5 13 A publication of the American Library Association (see pages 48–49, 69, 75), dedicated to connecting books, kids, classrooms, and libraries in innovative ways. Many feature articles deal with illustrations and illustrators, illustrative techniques, book design, and other visual aspects of books.

Annual subscription (6 issues), $24.95
Book Links
434 W. Downer
Aurora, IL 60506
(630) 892-7465 or (800) 545-2433, ext. 5715
Web site: www.ala.org/BookLinks

ART APPRECIATION AND HISTORY

Annotated Art
12 + Robert Cumming; Dorling Kindersley, 1995

The book includes 45 color reproductions of famous paintings, from Botticelli's *The Birth of Venus* to Picasso's *Guernica,* each heavily annotated: that is, many little lines connect various features in the paintings to many explanatory notes. Readers thus absorb information while examining the details of the paintings. The very design of the book plunges kids into art appreciation; the process of linking text to picture ensures that readers will see more in each painting that you ever thought possible.

The Annotated Mona Lisa:
A Crash Course in Art History
from Prehistoric to Post-Modern
Carol Strickland and John Boswell; Andrews & McMeel, 1992

A 198-page tour through the history of art, written for persons with no previous art history background. The book is creatively designed, filled with page-length essays, informational sidebars and boxes, and 300 illustrations, in both black and white and color. Chapter titles include "Greece: They Invented a Lot More Than the Olympics," "African Art: The First Cubists," and "Impressionism: Let There Be Color and Light."

The Art Pack
Christopher Frayling, Helen Frayling, and Ron Van Der Meer; Alfred A. Knopf, 1993

"A Unique, Three-Dimensional Tour Through the Creation of Art over the Centuries," reads the subtitle, "What Artists Do, How They Do It, and the Masterpieces." All this, and more, is packaged into this stunningly creative interactive book on the history and practice of art, filled with pop-ups—including a wonderful pop-up Parthenon, pullouts, inserts, demonstrations, and manipulatives. An audiocassette tucked in the back cover includes descriptions of the world's 20 greatest masterpieces.

> $45 from bookstores or
> Sax Arts & Crafts
> Box 510710
> New Berlin, WI 53151
> orders (800) 558-6696; customer service (800) 522-4278

See *The Architecture Pack* (page 781) and *The Music Pack* (page 753).

Art Smart!
Susan Rodriguez; Prentice-Hall, 1988

An art history and art appreciation course for kids in grades 3–9. The *Art Smart!* book, which contains background information, teaching suggestions, and 94 creative hands-on activities, is accompanied by 40 full-color slides of works by famous artists in a wide range of styles and periods.

The Child's Book of Play in Art
Lucy Micklethwait; Dorling Kindersley, 1996

A series of simple challenges gets kids to examine famous paintings. Readers are asked, for example, to find the hoop rollers in a Japanese print and in an oil painting by Pieter Brueghel, both called *Children's Games*. A delightful exploration of art for kids aged 4–9, with over 70 color reproductions of famous works of art.
See the **I Spy Series** (page 721).

Color
Ruth Heller; Grosset & Dunlap, 1995

A beautifully illustrated account of how artwork is transferred from the artist's original to the printed page of a picture book. A four-page acetate printer's proof is bound right into the book.

Come Look With Me: Discovering
Photographs With Children
Jean S. Tucker; Lickle Publishing, 1994

Twelve full-page color or black-and-white photographs by such artists as Diane Arbus, Ansel Adams, and Matthew Brady, accompanied by a text that, by posing questions, encourages kids to study and explore each work.

Come Look With Me Series
Gladys S. Blizzard; Lickle Publishing

Each 32-page book includes reproductions of 12 famous paintings, each sharing a specific theme, with descriptive information, biographical facts about the artist, and questions intended to stimulate discussions. Titles: *Come Look With Me: Animals in Art* (1992), including Albrecht Dürer's famous rabbit; *Come Look With Me: Enjoying Art With Children* (1991); *Come Look With Me: Exploring Landscape Art With Children* (1992); and *Come Look With Me: World of Play* (1993). Also see *Come Look With Me: Exploring Native American Art With Children* (Stephanie Salomon; 1998).

A Drawing in the Sand: The Story of African American Art

Jerry Butler; Zino Press, 1998

A color-illustrated 64-page history of African American art, combining history, art, and personal memoir. Included are descriptions of the lives and work of such black artists as Edward Bannister, Augusta Savage, and Jacob Lawrence.

See *Be a Friend: The Story of African American Music* (page 751).

Eyewitness Art Series

Dorling Kindersley

A series of marvelously illustrated books on art history, art techniques, and famous artists, filled with color reproductions and photographs. Titles include *Color* (Alison Cole; 1993), *Composition* (Sarah Kent, 1995), *Perspective* (Alison Cole; 1993), *Impressionism* (Jude Welton; 1993), and *Post-Impressionism* (Colin Wiggins; 1993).

The Great Art Adventure

Bob Knox; Rizzoli International Publications, 1993

Two children visit the magical Museum of World Art, where all the artworks and paintings, including an Egyptian mural, a Roman mosaic, a Tibetan scroll, an ancient Greek vase painting, a Russian icon, and an American Indian buffalo skin painting, come informatively to life.

Great Painters

Piero Ventura; Putnam, 1984

An exquisitely illustrated 160-page history of art, from the 13th-century frescoes of Giotto to the 20th-century cubists. Reproductions of 140 works of art are shown against elaborately detailed background scenes of colorful little people and places. The paintings are all reproduced to scale, so that huge works are clearly huge, and small works small. Many are shown in place: reproductions of Andrea Mantegna's Bridal Chamber frescoes, for example, overlay the walls of a stylized palace, complete with little paint pots stacked about on the floors and a passing couple in Renaissance garb. An appendix gives biographical information on all the artists discussed in the text.

History of Art for Young People

H. W. Janson and Anthony F. Janson; Harry N. Abrams, 1997

This is a pared-down version of the massive text used in college art history courses; even truncated, however, it's 632 pages long. The book is detailed, thorough, and encyclopedic. It's a reference text rather than an enjoyable read. All the names, dates, and definitions are here, from the earliest examples of prehistoric art to the present day. The book covers painting, sculpture, architecture, and photography. Over 600 illustrations, 252 of them in color.

How Artists See Series

Colleen Carroll; Abbeville Press, 1996

This series of 48-page illustrated books introduces kids aged 8 and up to great art through common everyday experiences. The author, in friendly conversational style, encourages young readers to take a close look at famous paintings. "What other animals are in the picture?" she asks of Goya's *Portrait of Don Manuel Osorio de Zúñiga,* the famous picture of the little boy in red, holding a pet magpie on a string. "How many can you find? Look carefully and count twice, because there's a surprise lurking somewhere in the painting."

Titles in the series include *How Artists See Animals: Mammal, Fish, Bird, Reptile; How Artists See People: Boy, Girl, Man, Woman; How Artists See the Weather: Sun, Wind, Snow, Rain;* and *How Artists See the Elements: Earth, Air, Fire, Water.*

How to Use Child-Size Masterpieces for Art Appreciation

Aline D. Wolf; Parent Child Press, 1996

This is a revised version of *Mommy, It's a Renoir!* (1984), which had a much nicer title. The essence of the books, however, is the same; both present a comprehensive program for teaching art appreciation to kids aged 3–12, using postcard-size reproductions of famous paintings. The program proceeds through eight steps. Kids first match pairs of identical paintings; then pair two similar paintings by the same artist; then group four paintings by each of three artists. They then proceed to learning the names of famous artists and the titles of famous paintings; next, they learn the characteristics of different schools of art and begin to sort and group postcards by school. Finally, they practice ordering paintings on timelines.

The book is accompanied by a series of *Child-Size Masterpieces* postcard books appropriate for various steps in the program. Each contains 32 to 44 postcards or postcard pairs, which must be cut out by the user (or the user's parents) and stored in pocket folders or envelopes.

We never quite followed the formal program directions for use of our Child-Size Masterpieces, but simply playing with the postcards can be an art appreciation education in itself. ("Isn't this by Picasso too? It looks a lot like . . .") We keep our ever-growing postcard collection in a blue shoebox; the boys, over the years, have sorted them, played with them, copied them, tacked them to their bedroom walls, and taped them to the refrigerator. Somehow, in the process, they picked up a good deal of information about art, artists, and famous paintings.

> Manual and postcard books, $10.95 apiece; package discounts available. A "Starter Package," for example, including *How to Use Child-Size Masterpieces* and the first three postcard volumes, $39.95
> Parent Child Press
> Box 675
> Hollidaysburg, PA 16648-0675
> (814) 696-7512/fax (814) 696-7510

4 8 I Spy Series
Lucy Micklethwait; Greenwillow

A series of innovative and artistic picture books, based on the traditional rhyming game "I Spy" ("with my little eye"). In *I Spy: An Alphabet in Art,* readers identify objects beginning with the letters from *A* to *Z* in a series of 26 famous paintings by such artists as Matisse, Botticelli, Chagall, Rousseau, and Picasso. *A,* for example, is for Apple, as seen in Magritte's *Son of Man,* a painting of a gentleman in a bowler hat with a gigantic green apple hiding his face. Other titles by Micklethwait include *I Spy Two Eyes: Numbers in Art* (1993), *I Spy a Lion: Animals in Art* (1994), and *I Spy a Freight Train: Transportation in Art* (1996).
See ***The Child's Book of Play in Art*** (page 719).

9 12 Looking at Painting Series
Peggy Roalf; Hyperion, 1992–93

Each book in the series includes 18 to 20 paintings, covering a span of over 1,000 years, grouped around a central theme and arranged in chronological order. A color reproduction of the painting appears on each right-hand page; artist, title, and a discussion of the historical context in which the work was painted on the facing page. *Landscapes,* for example, includes historically and stylistically varied paintings of mountains, fields, lakes, and rivers, by such artists as Pissarro, Hiroshige, and O'Keeffe. Other titles in the series include *Cats, Children, Circus, Dancers, Dogs, Families, Flowers, Horses, Musicians, Seascapes,* and *Self-Portraits.*

5 9 The Nine-Ton Cat Behind the Scenes at an Art Museum
Peggy Thomson, Barbara Moore, and Carol Eron; Houghton Mifflin, 1997

An account of what goes on behind the scenes at the National Gallery of Art. Readers learn what curators, exhibit designers, and restorers do, and get a tour of workshops, offices, and laboratories. Illustrated with color photographs.

4 8 The Pottery Place
Gail Gibbons; Harcourt Brace Jovanovich, 1987

A description of a potter's work, from clay to fired finished product, with big, bright illustrations. Included is a brief history of pottery and a labeled diagram showing the parts of a potter's wheel.

9 13 A Short Walk Around the Pyramids & Through the World of Art
Philip M. Isaacson; Alfred A. Knopf, 1993

A creative tour of art history and art in the world around us, illustrated with wonderful color photographs and reproductions. Chapters include "A Simple Form," "Sculpture," "Color," "Images," "Photographs," "Useful Things," and "Towns and Cities." The tour moves dramatically through time and space, beginning in the sun-drenched Egyptian desert with photographs of the pyramids, then leaping to the dazzling glass pyramid designed by American architect I. M. Pei for the courtyard of the Louvre in Paris.

The Story of Painting: The Essential Guide to the History of Western Art

Sister Wendy Beckett; Dorling Kindersley, 1994

From cave paintings to modern art, gloriously illustrated with over 400 color reproductions of artworks and over 200 color photographs, maps, and drawings. The book, by Sister Wendy Beckett of the acclaimed PBS art history series, covers the lives and times of the painters, as well as the technical aspects of their paintings. Includes informational sideboxes and timelines. Sister Wendy's love for her subject is contagious. Also see *Sister Wendy's Grand Tour: Discovering Europe's Great Art* (Stewart, Tabori & Chang, 1996) and the video *Sister Wendy's Story of Painting* (page 741).

The Usborne Story of Painting: Cave Painting to Modern Art

Anthea Peppin; Usborne Publishing, 1980

The history of art from cave painting to Roy Lichtenstein, in 30 pages, crammed with information and colorful little drawings.

A Visit to the Art Galaxy

Annie Reiner; Green Tiger Press, 1991

A visit to the art museum turns into a fantastic fictional flight to the "Land of Modern Art" and an introduction to the works of Henri Matisse, Pablo Picasso, Mark Rothko, Franz Klein, Alberto Giacometti, and Chris Burden.

Visiting the Art Museum

Laurene Krasny Brown and Marc Brown; E. P. Dutton, 1992

Two parents and three kids, one of them an obstreperous baby, take a hilarious tour of the Metropolitan Museum of Art. Illustrations include color reproductions of artworks from the museum, with detailed explanations in an appendix in the back.

What Makes a . . . Series

Richard Muhlberger; Metropolitan Museum of Art/ Viking.

A series of 10 books that show readers how to identify a particular artist's distinctive style, through his/her use of color, line, shape, composition, brush-work, and subject matter. The books, each 48 pages long, are illustrated with close-up details from each artist's works which illustrate the author's points. Titles in the series include *What Makes a Raphael a Raphael?,* . . . *a Brueghel?,* . . . *a Monet?,* . . . *a van Gogh?,* . . . *a Degas?,* . . . *a Rembrandt?,* . . . *a Goya?,* . . . *a Picasso?,* . . . *a Cassatt?,* and . . . *a Leonardo?* For artists aged 10 and up.

BIOGRAPHIES OF ARTISTS: GENERAL

Art for Children Series

Ernest Raboff; HarperTrophy, 1988

A series of biographical art appreciation books, each featuring the work of a single famous artist. The books include about 15 full-color reproductions of the featured artist's work, plus numerous smaller drawings, each carefully described and explained in the accompanying hand-lettered and multicolored text.

Titles in the series include *Renoir, Da Vinci, Rembrandt, Picasso, Van Gogh, Michelangelo, Raphael, Chagall, Gauguin, Velásquez, Klee, Rousseau, Matisse, Remington, Dürer,* and *Toulouse-Lautrec.*

Getting to Know the World's Greatest Artists Series

Mike Venezia; Children's Press

A terrific series of artist's biographies; the publisher deems them suitable for kids in grades 3–4, but they're so delightful that both younger and older children will enjoy them. Each book is 32 pages long, with a short, simple text illustrated with full-color reproductions of the featured artist's paintings and/or sculptures and with Mike Venezia's zany and colorful cartoons.

Titles in the series include *Botticelli* (1991), *Da Vinci* (1989), *Diego Rivera* (1994), *Edward Hopper* (1990), *El Greco* (1997), *Francisco Goya* (1991), *Georgia O'Keeffe* (1993), *Grant Wood* (1995), *Henri Matisse* (1997), *Henri de Toulouse-Lautrec* (1995), *Jackson Pollock* (1994), *Andy Warhol* (1996), *Mary Cassatt* (1990), *Michelangelo* (1991), *Monet* (1990), *Paul Gauguin* (1992), *Paul Klee* (1991), *Picasso* (1988), *Pierre-Auguste Renoir* (1996), *Pieter Brueghel* (1992), *Rembrandt* (1988), *Salvador Dalí* (1993), and *Van Gogh* (1988).

Great Lives: Painting

Shirley Glubok; Charles Scribner's Sons, 1994

A collection of brief biographies of 23 famous European and American artists, illustrated with black-and-white photographs.

Lives of the Artists: Masterpieces, Messes (and What the Neighbors Thought)

Kathleen Krull; Harcourt Brace, 1995

A collection of short, intriguing biographies of 16 artists, among them Leonardo da Vinci, Michelangelo, Pieter Brueghel, Katsushika Hokusai, Henri Matisse, Marc Chagall, Georgia O'Keeffe, William H. Johnson, Salvador Dalí, Diego Rivera, and Andy Warhol. Each biography is accompanied by a full-page portrait of the artist by Kathryn Hewitt. A list of fascinating facts—"Artworks"—follows each biography: readers learn the Matisse worried that the bright colors in his paintings would frighten viewers and that the idea for the three melting watches in Salvador Dalí's most famous painting, *The Persistence of Memory,* came as the artist stared at a melting Camembert cheese.

Talking With Artists

Pat Cummings; Bradbury Press, 1992

Interviews with 14 well-known illustrators, among them Steven Kellogg, Amy Schwartz, and Chris Van Allsburg, who, in kid-friendly fashion, tell about their lives and work. Also see *Talking With Artists: Volume II* (Macmillan, 1995), interviews with 13 well-known children's picture-book illustrators, including Julie Downing, William Joyce, Brian Pinckney, and Vera B. Williams.

A Weekend With the Artist Series

Rizzoli International Publications

Each 64-page book in this beautifully done series centers around a weekend visit with a famous artist, including biographical information, photographs, and reproductions of artworks.

Titles include *A Weekend With Picasso* (Florian Rodian; 1991), *A Weekend With Van Gogh* (Rosabianca Skira-Venturi; 1994), *A Weekend with Renoir* (Rosabianca Skira-Venturi; 1990), *A Weekend With Degas* (Rosabianca Skira-Venturi; 1992), *A Weekend With*

Leonardo da Vinci (Rosabianca Skira-Venturi; 1994), *A Weekend With Rousseau* (Gilles Plazy; 1993), *A Weekend With Velázquez* (Florian Rodari; 1993), *A Weekend With Winslow Homer* (Ann Keay Beneduce; 1993), *A Weekend With Matisse* (Florian Rodari; 1994), *A Weekend With Rembrandt* (Pascal Bonafoux; 1994), and *A Weekend With Diego Rivera* (Barbara Braun; 1994).

BOOKS ABOUT ARTISTS: INDIVIDUAL

Alexander Calder and His Magical Mobiles

Joan Lipman and Margaret Aspinwall; Hudson Hills Press, 1981

A 96-page introduction to the life and art of Alexander Calder, with photographs of his works and a guide to his sculptures and mobiles in museums.

Artist in Overalls

John Duggleby; Chronicle Books, 1996

A short chapter biography of artist Grant Wood, the shy Iowa farm boy who became a great artist. Included are full-page color reproductions of many of Wood's works, including his famous *American Gothic.*

Benjamin West and His Cat Grimalkin

Marguerite Henry; Checkerboard Press, 1987

Young Benjamin West's Quaker family thought painting sinful, so Benjamin secretly mixed his own paints from colored clay and made brushes from the fur of his cat's tail. Eventually his outstanding artistic talent convinced his parents to support his decision to become a painter. A delightful biography for middle-grade readers.

A Blue Butterfly: A Story About Claude Monet

Bijou le Tord; Doubleday, 1995

A simple picture-book story about Claude Monet and his paintings, beautifully illustrated in soft watercolors.

Bosch, Hieronymus

See *Pish, Posh, Said Hieronymus Bosch* (page 727).

The Boy Who Drew Sheep
5 / 9
Anne Rockwell; Atheneum, 1973

A picture-book biography of Giotto, the famous 13th-century fresco painter, beginning with his childhood as a shepherd boy, when he drew wonderful sheep on the rocks of the pasture.

Brueghel, Pieter
See *Getting to Know the World's Greatest Artists Series* (page 722), *Pieter Brueghel's The Fair* (page 727), and *What Makes a . . . Series* (page 722).

Calder, Alexander
See *Alexander Calder and His Magical Mobiles* (page 723) and *Roarr: Calder's Circus* (page 727).

Camille and the Sunflowers
4 / 8
Laurence Anholt; Barron's, 1994

Young Camille walks home from school every day through a great field of sunflowers ("Where Camille lived, the sunflowers grew so high they looked like real suns") and meets the sunflower-painting artist Vincent van Gogh. The books includes color reproductions of several of van Gogh's paintings.

Cassatt, Mary
See *Getting to Know the World's Greatest Artists Series* (page 722) and *What Makes a . . . Series* (page 722).

Chagall, Marc
See *Art for Children Series* (page 722), *Chagall From A to Z* (below), and *Chagall: My Sad and Joyous Village* (below).

Chagall: My Sad and Joyous Village
9 / 12
Jacqueline Loumaye; Chelsea House, 1994

An introduction to Chagall's life and art for kids aged 9–12, combining biographical information, a child-told story, reproductions of the artist's work, photographs, and drawings.

Chagall From A to Z
6 / 10
Marie Sellier; Peter Bedrick Books, 1996

Short scenes from the life and work of painter Marc Chagall, arranged in alphabetical order under an A-to-Z sequence of French words. By the same author: *Matisse From A to Z* (1995).

The Country Artist: A Story About Beatrix Potter
9 / 12
David R. Collins; Carolrhoda, 1989

A short chapter biography of Beatrix Potter, whose first animal pictures were of creatures smuggled into the house by the family butler.

Leonardo da Vinci
See *Art for Children Series* (page 722), *Getting to Know the World's Greatest Artists Series* (page 722), *Leonardo da Vinci* (page 725), *Leonardo da Vinci: The Artist, Inventor, Scientist in Three-Dimensional Movable Pictures* (see page 725), *Mona Lisa: The Secret of the Smile* (page 726), *The Second Mrs. Giaconda* (page 647), *What Makes a . . . Series* (page 722), *Leonardo the Inventor* (page 742), *The Life of Leonardo da Vinci* video (page 650), *Bio: Leonardo da Vinci* (page 744), *The Da Vinci Project* (page 744), and *Exploring Leonardo* (page 744).

Da Vinci: The Painter Who Spoke With Birds
9 / 12
Jacqueline Loumaye; Chelsea House, 1994

An introduction to Leonardo through a mix of biographical information, a child-narrated story, and reproductions of paintings and drawings.

Degas, Edgar
See *A Weekend With the Artist Series* (page 723) and *What Makes a . . . Series* (page 722), *Degas: The Painted Gesture* (below), and *Degas and the Little Dancer* (below).

Degas: The Painted Gesture
9 / 12
Jacqueline Loumaye; Chelsea House, 1994

The life and works of Degas for 9–12-year-olds through a mix of biographical information, a child-told story, and reproductions of Degas's paintings, drawings, and sculptures.

Degas and the Little Dancer: A Story About Edgar Degas
6 / 10
Laurence Anholt; Barron's Juveniles, 1996

The fictionalized tale of the little dancer who modeled for Degas's famous sculpture *The Little Dancer*. Marie wants badly to be a ballerina, but her family is too poor to pay her dancing school fees. Marie begins modeling at the school for an artist—Edgar Degas—and, when his statue is completed, becomes a famous ballerina for all time. The book is illustrated with lovely watercolors and reproductions of Degas's paintings.

6 10 Diego
Jonah Winter; Alfred A. Knopf, 1994

A brilliantly colored picture-book biography of Mexican muralist Diego Rivera, in both Spanish and English. A "Reading Rainbow" selection.

5 10 Dinner at Magritte's
Michael Garland; Dutton Children's Books, 1995

Pierre is invited to dinner at the unusual house next door, where he meets the painter René Magritte and family, and friend Salvador Dalí, and takes a surprising tour through—right through—Magritte's surrealistic paintings.

Escher, M. C.
See *The M. C. Escher Coloring Book* (page 736), *M.C. Escher Kaleidocycles* (page 736), *The M.C. Escher Sticker Book* (page 736), *The Pop-Up Book of M.C. Escher* (page 727). *Escher Interactive* (page 742), *Tessellations Project* (page 746), *World of Escher* (page 746), and *The Worlds of M. C. Escher* (page 746).

Gauguin, Paul
See *Art for Children Series* (page 722) and *Getting to Know the World's Greatest Artists Series* (page 722).

Giotto
See *The Boy Who Drew Sheep* (page 724) and *Giotto and Medieval Art* (below).

9 13 Giotto and Medieval Art
Lucia Corrain and Sergio Riciardi; Publishing Group West, 1995

A 64-page introduction to the life and world of Giotto, with a discussion of his innovative art techniques and his impact on art history. Included are color reproductions of his works.

Goya, Francisco
See *Getting to Know the World's Greatest Artists Series* (page 722) and *What Makes a . . . Series* (page 722).

El Greco
See *Getting to Know the World's Greatest Artists Series* (page 722).

Homer, Winslow
See *A Weekend With the Artist Series* (page 723) and *Winslow Homer and the Sea* (page 728).

Hopper, Edward
See *Getting to Know the World's Greatest Artists Series* (page 722).

12 + I, Juan de Pareja
Elizabeth de Trevino; Farrar, Straus & Giroux, 1965

The Newberry Medal–winning story of painter Diego Velázquez, as told through the eyes of his black slave.

Johnson, William
See *Li'l Sis and Uncle Willie* (below).

Klee, Paul
See *Art for Children Series* (page 722) and *Getting to Know the World's Greatest Artists Series* (page 722).

8 13 Leonardo da Vinci
Diane Stanley; Morrow Junior Books, 1996

An excellent picture-book biography of Leonardo da Vinci, illustrated with Renaissance-style paintings and color reproductions of Leonardo's artworks. For kids in grades 3–8.

5 9 Leonardo da Vinci: The Artist, Inventor, Scientist in Three-Dimensional Movable Pictures
Alice and Martin Provensen; Viking, 1984

A cleverly engineered pop-up book of Leonardo's projects, including a three-dimensional flying machine and a pop-up portrait of the *Mona Lisa*.

8 12 Li'l Sis and Uncle Willie: A Story Based on the Life and Paintings of William H. Johnson
Gwen Everett; Hyperion, 1994

A short fictionalized biography illustrated with Johnson's own paintings.

Linnea in Monet's Garden

Christina Bjork; Farrar, Straus & Giroux, 1987

Linnea, a charming little girl in broad-brimmed hat and pinafore, visits Claude Monet's beautiful flower garden and learns about the painter's life and work. Illustrations include photographs of Monet and color reproductions of his paintings.

A video version of the book is also available (see page 741). Also see **Gardening** (pages 824–830).

Magritte, René

See *Dinner at Magritte's* (page 725).

Matisse, Henri

See *Art for Children Series* (page 722), *Getting to Know the World's Greatest Artists Series* (page 722), *Matisse from A to Z* (see *Chagall from A to Z*, page 724), and *A Weekend with the Artist Series* (page 723).

Michelangelo

See *Art for Children Series* (page 722), *From the Mixed-Up Files of Mrs. Basil E. Frankweiler* (page 729), *Getting to Know the World's Greatest Artists Series* (page 722), *Michelangelo and His Times* (page 646), and *The Hideaways* (page 741).

Miró: Earth and Sky

Jacqueline Loumaye; Chelsea House, 1994

An introduction to the life and work of Miró for readers aged 9–12, through a combination of biographical information, a child-told story, reproductions of the artist's works, and photographs.

Mona Lisa: The Secret of the Smile

Letizia Galli; Doubleday, 1996

A beautifully illustrated picture-book biography of Leonardo da Vinci (who, the author tells us, loved secrets) and his painting the Mona Lisa.

Monet, Claude

See *A Blue Butterfly* (page 723), *Getting to Know the World's Greatest Artists Series* (page 722), *Linnea in Monet's Garden* (above), *Monet Art Activity Pack* (page 731), *My Monet Art Museum* (page 736), *Once Upon a Lily Pad* (right), *What Makes a . . . Series* (page 722), and *The Monet Gallery* (page 745).

O'Keeffe, Georgia

See *Georgia O'Keeffe* (below) and *Getting to Know the World's Greatest Artists Series* (page 722).

Georgia O'Keeffe

Robyn Montana Turner; Little, Brown, 1993

A short account of O'Keeffe's life and work, illustrated with photographs and reproductions of paintings. The book emphasizes O'Keeffe's close link with nature, in her paintings of monstrous flowers, desert scenes, and cityscapes.

Once Upon a Lily Pad

Joan Sweeney; Chronicle Books, 1996

An enchanting picture book about two frogs—Hector and Henriette—who live in the water-lily pond in painter Claude Monet's garden. Sometimes they watch the painter, an old man in a battered straw hat, at work at his easel. Included is a foldout page of a Monet water-lily painting.

Painting the Wind

Michelle Dionetti; Little, Brown, 1996

Van Gogh's years in Arles, as seen through the eyes of his housekeeper's little daughter, Claudine. Though many of the townspeople are frightened of the strange artist (whom they call "Fou Roux," the Redheaded Fool), Claudine learns to admire him and to love his glorious paintings.

Pablo Picasso

Ibi Lepscky; Barron's, 1993

A simple beginner's biography of the artist, emphasizing his childhood, for readers aged 4–7.

Picasso, Pablo

See *Pablo Picasso* (above), *Getting to Know the World's Greatest Artists Series* (page 722), *Art for Children Series* (page 722), *Picasso: A Day in His Studio* (below), *A Weekend With the Artist Series* (page 723), and *What Makes a . . . Series* (page 722).

Picasso: A Day in His Studio

Jacqueline Loumaye; Chelsea House, 1994

An introduction to Picasso for readers aged 9–12, through biography, a child-narrated story, and color reproductions of the artist's works.

Pieter Brueghel's The Fair

Ruth Craft; J. B. Lippincott, 1975

The medieval festival pictured in Brueghel's painting *The Fair* is described and explained in the accompanying rhyming text.

Pish, Posh, Said Hieronymus Bosch

Nancy Willard; Harcourt Brace, 1991

A marvelously illustrated picture book in rhyme, based on the bizarre 15th-century art of Hieronymus Bosch. Bosch's imaginary creatures bedevil his house-keeper.

The Pop-Up Book of M. C. Escher

M. C. Escher/Michael Solomon Sachs; Pomegranate Books, 1992

Nine Escher prints gone fascinatingly three-dimensional, including *Ascending and Descending*, *Drawing Hands*, and *Hand With Reflecting Sphere*.

Potter, Beatrix

See *The Country Artist* (page 724).

The Princess and the Painter

Jane Johnson; Farrar, Straus & Giroux, 1994

A picture book in which a 5-year-old Spanish princess, the Infanta Margarita, waits for the unveiling of painter Diego Velázquez's new painting, *Las Meninas*—and finds it filled with family, friends, and even a picture of herself.

Rembrandt

See *Art for Children Series* (page 722), *A Weekend With the Artist Series* (page 723), *Rembrandt's Beret* (below), and *Museum of Art: Rembrandt* (page 745).

Rembrandt's Beret: Or the Painter's Crown

Johnny Alcorn; Tambourine Books, 1991

Portraits and self-portraits of the Old Masters come to life before the surprised eyes of Tiberius, a young boy who is accidentally locked in the Uffizi art gallery one afternoon. Rembrandt himself paints the boy's portrait and allows him to keep his beret as a memento.

Renoir, Pierre-Auguste

See *Art for Children Series* (page 722), *Getting to Know the World's Greatest Artists Series* (page 722), *The Girl with the Watering Can* (page 729), and *A Weekend With the Artist Series* (page 723).

Rivera, Diego

See *Diego* (page 725), *Getting to Know the World's Greatest Artists Series* (page 722), *A Weekend With the Artist Series* (page 723), and *Diego Rivera Web Museum* (page 744).

Roarr: Calder's Circus

Maira Kalman; Delacorte Press, 1993

An artistic picture book in which Alexander Calder's wonderful circus animal sculptures come to life and parade through town.

Rousseau, Henri

See *Art for Children Series* (page 722) and *A Weekend With the Artist Series* (page 723).

The Second Mrs. Giaconda

E. L. Konigsberg; Atheneum, 1975

The story of Leonardo da Vinci, as told by his impish young assistant, Salai, for readers aged 9–12.

Van Gogh, Vincent

See *Art for Children Series* (page 722), *Camille and the Sunflowers* (page 724), *Getting to Know the World's Greatest Artists Series* (page 722), *My Van Gogh Art Museum* (page 736), *Painting the Wind* (page 726), *Van Gogh Activity Pack* (page 731), *Van Gogh: A Touch of Yellow* (below), *A Weekend With the Artist Series* (page 723), *What Makes a . . . Series* (page 722), and *The Vincent Van Gogh Information Gallery* (page 746).

Van Gogh: A Touch of Yellow

Jacqueline Loumaye; Chelsea House, 1994

A 57-page introduction to van Gogh for readers aged 9–12, including biographical information, a child-told story, and reproductions of the artist's works.

Velázquez, Diego

See *Art for Children Series* (page 722), *I, Juan de Pareja* (page 725), *The Princess and the Painter* (left), and *A Weekend With the Artist Series* (page 723).

West, Benjamin

See *Benjamin West and His Cat Grimalkin* (page 723).

 9 13 *Winslow Homer and the Sea*
Carl Little; Pomegranate Books, 1995

An 80-page biography of Winslow Homer, including 33 full-page reproductions of his paintings.

Wood, Grant

See *Artist in Overalls* (page 723) and *Getting to Know the World's Greatest Artists Series* (page 722).

Yani, Wang

See *A Young Painter* (below).

9 + *A Young Painter: The Life and Paintings of Wang Yani—China's Extraordinary Young Artist*
Zheng Zhensun and Alice Low; Scholastic, 1991

The story of Wang Yani, who began painting wonderful pictures of monkeys and cats at the age of three and, as a teenager, became the youngest artist to have a show at the Smithsonian Institution. Illustrated with photographs and reproductions of the artist's work.

LITERATURE LINKS FOR PARENTS AND TEACHERS

5 12 *Art Through Children's Literature*
Debi Englebaugh; Teacher Ideas Press, 1994

Projects and activities emphasizing such basic artistic principles as color, shape, texture, and line. Lessons are based on the illustrations in 57 Caldecott Books, among them *Owl Moon, Ox-Cart Man, Why Mosquitoes Buzz in Peoples's Ears,* and *Where the Wild Things Are.*

$22.50

Libraries Unlimited

Box 6633

Englewood, CO 80155-6633

(303) 770-1220 or (800) 237-6124/fax (303) 220-8843

e-mail: lu-books@lu.com

Web site: www.lu.com

LITERATURE LINKS FOR KIDS

5 9 *All I See*
Cynthia Rylant; Orchard Books, 1994

A little boy, Charles, spends his summer watching an artist painting a seascape on his outdoor easel. The artist paints whales, even though there are no whales in sight. Charles learns about the technical aspects of painting and also about painting from the imagination. For readers aged 5–9.

9 13 *The Apprentice*
Pilar Molina Llorente; Sunburst, 1994

A story of Renaissance Florence, in which 13-year-old Arduino, a wealthy tailor's son, apprentices himself to an artist. The apprenticeship is miserable; the master painter starves his young apprentices and even keeps one young boy, an exceptionally talented artist named Donato, in chains. Arduino befriends Donato and eventually helps him triumph when the master becomes too ill to work in the middle of a major commission. For readers aged 9–13.

4 8 *Art Dog*
Thatcher Hurd; HarperCollins, 1996

When the *Mona Woofa* is stolen from the Dogopolis Museum of Art, it's a job for Art Dog, a mild-mannered museum guard by day, a mysterious masked painter/superhero when trouble calls. The book includes dog versions of many famous paintings, beginning with the *Mona Lisa*. For readers aged 4–8.

4 8 *The Art Lesson*
Tomie de Paola; Paper Star, 1997

Young Tommy wants to be an artist when he grows up, but his first art lesson at school is upsetting when he discovers that he has to use school crayons with only eight colors and copy a picture of a pilgrim off the blackboard. For readers aged 5–8.

5 8 *The Artist's Model*
Allison Barrows; Carolrhoda, 1996

A little girl's father, an artist, asks her to pose for a painting; during the process, the new model learns how a painting is created. For readers aged 5–8.

Benjamin's Portrait

Alan Baker; Lothrop, Lee & Shepard, 1987

A hamster struggles to paint a self-portrait; illustrations detail every step along the way. For painters aged 4–8.

Bonjour, Mr. Satie

Tomie de Paola; Putnam, 1991

Mr. Satie (a cat) has many famous friends in the Paris art world of the 1920s (among them Pablo, who once painted his portrait in blue). In this story, Mr. Satie helps end a feud between rival painters. For readers aged 4–8.

The Boy Who Drew Cats

Arthur A. Levine; Dial, 1994

A Japanese legend about a young boy who is expelled from the monastery because he spends all his time drawing. His talents, however, allow him save the monastery from disaster by defeating a powerful demon rat. For readers aged 6–11.

The Cat Who Went to Heaven

Elizabeth Coatsworth; Aladdin, 1990

A lovely short novel set in ancient Japan about a starving artist and his faithful white cat, a marvelous painting, and a Buddhist miracle. For readers aged 9–12.

The Dreamer

Cynthia Rylant; Scholastic, 1993

A lovely picture book in which the Creator himself is shown as an artist, carefully clipping out the stars with scissors and imagining the marvelous shapes of animals.

The Etcher's Studio

Arthur Geisert; Houghton Mifflin, 1997

A beautifully illustrated picture book in which the young narrator helps his grandfather prepare etchings for a sale. The entire process is detailed, as the two print and hand-color the etchings. For readers aged 5–7.

The Fantastic Drawings of Danielle

Barbara McClintock; Houghton Mifflin, 1996

A picture book set in turn-of-the-century France. Young Danielle, who wants to be an artist, makes delightfully imaginative paintings, but her father, a photographer, doesn't approve of them. When her father gets sick, Danielle bravely sets off to earn their living as a photographer. While setting up the camera, she meets a successful artist, a woman who paints imaginary scenes and landscapes. The artist, a kindred spirit, hires Danielle to work in her studio, and Danielle is soon supporting the family by doing art in her own way. For readers aged 4–9.

From the Mixed-Up Files of Mrs. Basil E. Frankweiler

E. L. Konigsberg; Atheneum, 1967

Claudia and Jamie run away from home to live, very imaginatively, in the Metropolitan Museum of Art. There, with the help of the rich and elderly Mrs. Basil E. Frankweiler, they solve a mystery about a statue of an angel that just might have been carved by Michelangelo. Funny, fascinating, and delightful.

See the video version of the book *The Hideaways* (page 741).

The Gentleman and the Kitchen Maid

Diane Stanley; Dial, 1994

An art student, working in the museum, realizes that two portraits hanging across from each other are in love, and the student finds a way to bring the two— the gentleman and the kitchen maid—together. For readers aged 6–11.

The Girl with the Watering Can

Eva Zadrzynska; Chameleon Books, 1990

The little blue-clad girl in Renoir's painting, *The Girl with the Watering Can*, steps out of the picture frame and visits 10 other famous paintings in Washington's National Gallery of Art. For readers aged 5–9.

Hattie and the Wild Waves

Barbara Cooney; Viking, 1990

Hattie, growing up in Brooklyn, New York, is the daughter of an immigrant family. She wants to be an artist and spends her summers at the beach, painting and listening to the wild waves. Based on the life of the author's mother.

I, Juan de Pareja

9 13 Elizabeth de Trevino; Farrar, Straus & Giroux, 1965

Juan de Pareja is a black slave, inherited by the Spanish painter Diego Velázquez. The story of their lives and developing relationship is beautifully told in this historical novel for readers aged 9–13.

The Incredible Painting of Felix Clousseau

5 9 Jon Agee; Farrar, Sunburst, 1990

The paintings of Felix Clousseau—an owlish little French painter, with a beard and a beret—are incredible because they come to life. For readers aged 5–9.

Liang and the Magic Paintbrush

5 9 Demi; Henry Holt, 1988

Liang is given a magic paintbrush; whatever he paints with it comes to life. He uses his magic gift to defeat the evil emperor. For readers aged 5–9. For another version of the same tale, see *Tye May and the Magic Brush* (Molly Bang; Mulberry, 1992).

Linnea in Monet's Garden

6 11 Christina Bjork; R & S Books, 1985

A charming story about a little girl who visits Claude Monet's flower garden and learns about the painter's life and art.
See page 741.

Lion

5 10 William Pène Du Bois; Penguin, 1983

Artist Foreman, a designer in the celestial Animal Factory, is doing his best to paint and create a lion. The first draft is a spectacular multicolored creature with feathers that goes "peep peep," but eventually—after some critical advice—the painting becomes the perfect lion. For readers aged 5–10.

The Little Painter of Sabana Grande

4 8 Patricia Mahoney Markun; Simon & Schuster, 1993

Fernando, who lives in a little village in Panama, wants to be an artist but worries about being able to paint during the school vacation. His teacher has shown him how to make his own paints, from berries, charcoal, and colored clay, but he has no paper. Then he sees the blank white wall of the family house—which he decorates with wonderful vines, flowers, and animals.

Matthew's Dream

5 8 Leo Lionni; Random House, 1995

Matthew, an artistic mouse, dreams of becoming a famous painter after a visit to the art museum. For readers aged 5–8.

Mouse Paint

4 8 Ellen Stoll Walsh; Voyager, 1995

Three chubby white mice fall into pots of red, blue, and yellow paint and then patter about in the puddles, demonstrating all the principles of color mixing. For readers aged 4–8.

Norman the Doorman

5 9 Don Freeman; Viking, 1981

Norman, the talented mouse who guards a hole in the art museum, makes himself a studio in a knight's helmet. There he creates a wonderful wire sculpture (made from pieces of mousetraps) that wins first prize in the museum art contest. For readers aged 5–9.

The Painter and the Wild Swans

5 9 Claude Clement; Penguin, 1993

A Japanese painter is enchanted by the beauty of a flock of wild swans. A picture-book tale based on the life of Japanese photographer Teiji Saga. For readers aged 5–9.

The Painter's Cat

5 9 Sharon Wooding; Putnam, 1994

Micio, a cat, lives in Venice, Italy, during the Renaissance with an artist named Lorenzo. Feeling neglected because Lorenzo spends all his time painting, Micio leaves home but soon returns, homesick, to find that he has played a most important role in his friend's art. The book is based on the life of artist Lorenzo Lotto and is colorfully illustrated with Renaissance-style paintings. For readers aged 5–9.

A Rat's Tale

8 12 Tor Seidler; Farrar, Straus & Giroux, 1990

Montague, an artistic young rat who paints pictures on seashells, tries to win the heart of the aristo-

THE ARTS

cratic Isabel Moberly Rat and to save the rat community from extermination, with the help of an eccentric and artistic uncle. For readers aged 8–12.

 5 8 *The Wonderful Towers of Watts*
Patricia Zelver; Mulberry, 1996

An Italian sculptor and a young boy build three marvelous towers with found objects—glass bottles, seashells, steel pipes, and broken tiles—in the poor Watts neighborhood of Los Angeles.

See the video *Daniel and the Towers* (page 740).

6 10 *The Young Artist*
Thomas Locker; Puffin, 1993

Adrian, a young artist, has been commissioned to paint portraits of the royal courtiers, who want to be painted as they wish they looked rather than as they really are.

FOLK ART BOOKS

ALL *A Fish That's a Box: Folk Art from the National Museum of American Art*
M. M. Esterman; Great Ocean Publishing, 1991

Photographs of 35 wonderful works of folk art from the Smithsonian Institution's National Museum of American Art, with an explanatory text.

4 9 *The Folk Art Counting Book*
Amy Watson; Harry N. Abrams, 1992

A counting book from 1 to 20, each number illustrated with a work of American folk art from the Abby Aldrich Rockefeller Folk Art Center in Williamsburg, Virginia. Included are whirligigs, paintings, and quilts. For the number 20, for example, kids are told to count the eagles in a 19th-century woven coverlet.

5 12 *Folk Art Tells a Story: An Activity Guide*
Susan Conklin Thompson; Teacher Ideas Press, 1998

A multicultural view of art for kids in grades K–6. The book is divided into three sections: traditional art activities, which include making birdhouses, weather vanes, and scarecrows; projects using natural materials (clay masks, decorated gourds); and projects using fabric (batik, tie-dye). Each lesson includes related songs, stories, and recipes, a book list, historical background information, and photographs of works by a folk artist.

$23.50
Libraries Unlimited
Box 6633
Englewood, CO 80155-6633
(303) 770-1220 or (800) 237-6124/fax (303) 220-8843
e-mail: lu-books@lu.com
Web site: www.lu.com

ACTIVITY BOOKS

8 13 *Adventures in Art: Art and Craft Experiences for 8- to 13-Year-Olds*
Susan Milord; Williamson, 1997

A large assortment of out-of-the-ordinary art projects for older kids, among them sand-cast candles, Japanese books, topiary animals, batik, and shadow puppets.

6 11 *Art & Activities for Kids Series*
Kim Solga; North Light Books

There are several big bright-colored volumes in this series. Each is 48 pages long, illustrated with color photographs and filled with art activities for kids aged 6–11. Titles include "Draw!," "Paint!," "Make Prints!," "Make Gifts!," "Make Cards!," "Make Crafts!," and "Make Sculptures!" "Paint!," for example, includes recipes for pudding paint, sawdust paint, salt paint, and egg tempera, instructions for glass-painting, marble-rolling, and pointillism projects, suggestions for experimenting with unusual brushes, face-painting patterns, and instructions for watercolor batik.

North Light Books
1507 Dana Ave.
Cincinnati, OH 45207
(800) 289-0963

6 10 *Art Activity Packs*
Mila Boutan; Chronicle Books, 1996

The *Art Activity Packs,* designed in collaboration with the Musee d'Orsay in Paris, are shiny cardboard folders, each containing an informational book about the featured artist and his art, an activity book with

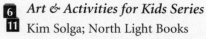

project suggestions and blank pages for kids to complete themselves, and a large-size poster to color. Each pack features a different artist.

Titles currently available include "Cézanne," "Monet," "Van Gogh," and "Matisse." The emphasis is on style and technique: kids are encouraged to look closely at specific aspects of each artist's works. The "Matisse Art Activity Pack" includes stencils and colored paper for making Matisse-style cut-paper collages.

Art From Many Hands
Jo Miles Schuman; Davis Publications, 1984

An excellent collection of multicultural art projects. Each chapter concentrates on a different segment of the globe: the Middle East, Central America, Asia, West Africa, Europe, the Caribbean Islands, the United States, and Canada. Projects include Egyptian hieroglyphic tablets, West African tapestry weavings, Swedish cookie stamps, Woodland Indian quillwork (if you can't find a porcupine, Schuman suggests dyed toothpicks), Caribbean maracas, Mexican tin sculpture, Japanese woodcuts, and Italian marionettes. The book contains very clear instructions, historical background information, and photographic illustrations of both genuine ethnic art and kid-made reproductions. The projects are intended for kids in kindergarten through early high school. Many, however, are too complex for very small kids without a lot of adult participation.

Art Projects Made Easy: Recipes for Fun
Linda J. Arons; Teacher Ideas Press, 1995

Art Projects Made Easy is organized like a cookbook—"Appetizers," "Salads and Vegetables," "Main Dishes," and so on. "Salads and Vegetables," it turns out, is a series of collage projects. For each of the book's activities a recipe-style list of ingredients and directions are included, plus suggestions for additional related projects ("What Shall We Cook Up Tomorrow?"), and ideas for relating the activity to other academic disciplines ("Stirring in the Curriculum"). Under a "Junk Sculpture" project, for example, the author suggests a science tie-in (study trash recycling) and an art history tie-in (learn about famous sculptors like Henry Moore and Alexander Calder).

$16
Libraries Unlimited
Box 6633
Englewood, CO 80155-6633
(800) 237-6124/fax (303) 220-8843
e-mail: lu-books@lu.com
Web site: www.lu.com

The Art and Science Connection: Hands-On Activities for Primary Students
Kimberly Tolley; Addison-Wesley, 1993

Thirty art-and-science lessons for elementary-level kids, categorized under "Structure," "Interactions," and "Energy." Sample lesson titles include "Exploring the Structure of Earthworms," "Using Chemistry to Bake a Sculpture," and "Investigating Light and Shadow." Young scientists and artists study leaf structure with leaf prints, investigate gravity with spatter paintings, design recycling posters and ecosystem murals, and make shadow drawings.

Artists: Exploring Art through the Study of Five Great Lives
Chris Brewer; Zephyr Press

Short biographies of Leonardo da Vinci, Vincent van Gogh, Winslow Homer, Rembrandt, and M. C. Escher are accompanied by related art activities in a variety of different media.

$25
Zephyr Press
3316 N. Chapel Ave.
Box 66006
Tucson, AZ 85732-6006
(800) 232-2187/fax (520) 323-9402
e-mail: neways2learn@zephyrpress.com
Web site: www.zephyrpress.com

Bottlecaps to Brushes: Art Activities for Kids
Lynn-Steven Engelke; Smithsonian Institution, 1995

Kids take a tour of the National Museum of American Art under the guidance of a knowledgeable cartoon giraffe. An introduction to famous artists and their works, with related art projects using everyday materials.

Drawing on the Right Side of the Brain: A Course in Enhancing Creativity and Artistic Confidence

Betty Edwards; J. P. Tarcher, 1989

This was our first family experience with a how-to-draw book, and it was a revelation. *Drawing on the Right Side of the Brain* is described as "a course enhancing creativity and artistic confidence"; it's also a fascinating perspective on the process of learning to draw. Inept artists, of the sort whose pictures of houses look like melted marshmallows, are, Edwards argues, drawing on the left side of the brain, recording preconceived shapes from (faulty) memory rather than accurately reproducing what they see in front of them. In lieu of this, Edwards attempts to teach would-be artists to visualize objects with the right side of the brain, using purely spatial skills. The book is filled with exercises intended to demonstrate and encourage right-brained drawing, among them the technique of "inverted drawing," which means copying something upside down. Edwards has her students try this with a Picasso line drawing, *Portrait of Igor Stravinsky.* In the case of two of our children, the contrast between Igor right side up (drawn under the influence of the verbal left side of the brain) and Igor upside down (drawn with the nonverbal right) was astounding. (Ethan, who is left-handed, turned out to be totally right-brained, which meant that upending Igor made no difference. But that's another story.)

Drawing With Children

Mona Brookes; J. P. Tarcher, 1996

Mona Brookes's "Monart" method was originally developed, the author explains, to teach kids the basics of drawings "prior to the critical stage they reach when they conclude, 'I can't.'" Many of us have seen this happen with one kid or another: a cheerfully scribbling 4-year-old becomes a frustrated 8-year-old who refuses to pick up a pencil. The Monart method—first implemented with preschoolers—gives kids the tools for getting what they see down on paper, by translating their subjects into an "alphabet" of five basic elements of shape. Taught to observe and draw in this manner, young children turn out impressive works of art; the book is filled with examples, by artists aged 4–11.

Drawing With Children begins with a series of exercises in which kids reproduce an assortment of blackline patterns and designs of increasing complexity. This helps parents or teachers determine the student's lesson starting level. (Most 4-year-olds are ready for Level 1 lessons; 6–8-year-olds, Level 2; and 8–13-year-olds, Level 3.) The book then proceeds through a varied series of projects that teach kids the essential five elements of shape and how to apply these to drawing. All are challenging and fun, and even the most reluctant artists quickly become delighted with their newly revealed talents.

Also see *Drawing for Older Children & Teens* (J. P. Tarcher, 1991), which applies the Monart method on a more sophisticated level for older beginners. Both books are also recommended for hopeful adult artists (the subtitle reads "A Creative Method for Adult Beginners, Too"); this program is terrific for family groups.

Dribble Drabble: Art Experiences for Young Children

Deya Brashears; DMC Publications, 1986

A little comb-bound paperback stuffed with simple art projects for preschoolers, variously involving crayons, paint, collage, simple sculpture, clay and dough, chalk, and printmaking. Projects include bubble-blowing painting, balloon spatter painting, pretzel sculpture, and instructions for making place mats. Also included: recipes for play dough, goop, moon craters mix, peanut butter dough, and soap dough.

EcoArt: Earth-Friendly Art and Craft Experiences for 3- to 9-Year-Olds

Laurie Carlson; Williamson, 1992

Dozens of activities for kids aged 3–9. Carlson first shows independent and earth-friendly families how to make their own arts and crafts supplies: there are recipes for paste, glue, clays, and dyes, plus instructions for making your own yarn and quill pens. Individual activities all use natural or recycled items. For example, kids make vine baskets, twig animals, spiderweb prints, rose petal beads, dried flowers, and an ant ranch; and there are 11 projects involving discarded plastic jugs, among them making a doorstop, a flowerpot, a dollhouse, and a watering can.

Ed Emberley Drawing Book Series
Little, Brown

Artist Ed Emberley has written a large number of step-by-step how-to-draw books for kids, among them *The Big Green Drawing Book* (1979), *The Big Orange Drawing Book* (1980), *The Big Purple Drawing Book* (1981), and *The Big Red Drawing Book* (1988). In each, using a simple add-one-line-at-a-time technique, Emberley demonstrates how to draw anything from a fish and a fire engine to a dragon, a space alien, and a three-masted pirate ship. It's not great art, but it's cute, and the process is excellent for developing fine-motor skills.

Our boys also enjoyed Emberley's *The Great Thumbprint Drawing Book* (1977), which shows kids how—with a few added lines—to turn ink prints of their own thumbs into a wide range of animals and objects, including dog, cats, birds, pigs, and caterpillars. See **Art on Video:** *Squiggles, Dots, and Lines* (page 741).

Encouraging the Artist in Your Child (Even If You Can't Draw)
Sally Warner; St. Martin's Press, 1989

Contains 101 "failure-proof, home-tested" projects for kids aged 2–10, with detailed instructions, suggestions for art concepts to introduce in the course of the project, and general information about art and child development. The book is divided into two parts, by age: Part I covers kids aged 2–5; Part II, ages 6–10. Under each are listed activities in drawing, painting, collage, yarn art, and sculpture.

Glues, Brews, and Goos: Recipes and Formulas for Almost Any Classroom Project
Diana F. Marks; Teacher Ideas Press, 1996

Recipes for practically everything, from paint and (recycled) paper to bubble soap, candles, salt map mix, and (edible) cheese.

Libraries Unlimited
Box 6633
Englewood, CO 80155-6633
(303) 770-1220 or (800) 237-6124/fax (303) 220-8843
e-mail: lu-books@lu.com
Web site: www.lu.com

See *Kids' Crazy Concoctions* (right) and *Recipes for Art and Craft Materials* (page 735).

Good Earth Art: Environmental Art for Kids
Mary Ann F. Kohl and Cindy Gainer; Bright Ring, 1991

Over 200 creative art activities for kids using earth-friendly recycled materials. Each activity is categorized: simple icons on each page indicate appropriate age, use of natural materials, use of recycled materials, good group project, edible project, homemade (that is, a substitute for a commercial item) project, good gift, supervision required, or caution necessary (usually those projects that require the use of sharp tools). Projects include making cattail baskets, natural dyes, earth paints, newspaper sculptures, branch weavings, log totem poles, eggshell crayons, cereal box buildings, seed necklaces, and bracket fungi paintings.

The Incredible Clay Book
Sherri Haab and Laura Torres; Klutz Press, 1994

A colorfully illustrated, spiral-bound book with basic modeling information and instructions for over 150 hands-on modeling projects, among them beads, bug tacks, and finger puppets. The book comes with eight 1-ounce blocks of polymer clay in different colors for readers who can't wait to get started.

Kids' Crazy Concoctions
Jill Frankel Hauser; Williamson, 1994

Fifty mysterious and artistic mixtures for kids aged 4 and up: readers, for example, turn out watercolor paint cakes, soap-on-a-rope, and custom-made stickers.

See *Glues, Brews, and Goos* (left) and *Recipes for Art and Craft Materials* (page 735).

Kids Create! Art and Craft Experiences for 3- to 9-Year-Olds
Laurie Carlson; Williamson, 1990

Over a hundred projects for small artists, variously listed under "Paper and Paste," "Clay and Dough," "Printmaking," "Sculpture," and "Seasonal Projects." Users make crayon cookies, snow globes, butterfly puppets, fingerprint dinosaurs, toothpick sculptures, pinwheels, eggshell mosaics, apple dolls, rubber stamps, and a creative collection of cactuses (the spines are short sticks of uncooked spaghetti).

The Kids' Multicultural Art Book

3 **9** Alexandra M. Terzian; Williamson, 1993

"Art and Craft Experiences From Around the World" for 3–9-year-olds. Among the projects are a Lakota-Sioux charm bag, a Chippewa dream catcher, a Mexican tin rooster, an African calabash and a Chinese good-luck dragon.

The Little Hands Art Book

2 **6** Judy Press; Williamson, 1994

The Little Hands Art Book contains over 70 art projects for 2–6-year-olds, among them making a paper-bag picnic basket, muffin-cup birds, Popsicle-stick flower gardens, and a milk carton caboose.

Also see, by the same author, *The Little Hands Big Fun Craft Book* (1995) includes 80 projects for very young craftspersons, including making a paper friendship quilt, aluminum pie-tin wind chimes, and a handprint family tree.

Mudworks: Creative Clay, Dough, and Modeling Experiences

4 **10** MaryAnn Kohl; Bright Ring, 1989

If Play-Doh is popular at your house, you might try these variations on the dough theme: Kohl's *Mudworks* includes over 100 innovative recipes for doughs, pastes, clays, glops, and goos—all modeling media—plus suggestions for what to do with them. Kids, for example, try leaf- or sand-casting, map modeling, and soapstone carving, build indoor snowmen, a sand castle, and a gingerbread house, and make bread clay, stained-glass dough, toothpaste putty, and their own doggie biscuits. Also see *Scribble Cookies and Other Independent Creative Art Experiences for Children* (MaryAnn F. Kohl; Bright Ring, 1986).

My Journey Through Art

7 **+** Kathryn Cave and Melvin Bramich; Barron's, 1993

Instructions for creating kids' artworks based on the paintings in the National Gallery of Art in Washington, D.C. Kids are given reproductions of a piece of a famous painting and encouraged to complete the picture on their own.

Also see *All My Own Work!* (Carole Armstrong and Anthea Pippin; Barron's, 1993), a painting-and-coloring book in which kids complete famous artworks from the National Gallery, London.

Recipes for Art and Craft Materials

6 **+** Helen Roney Sattler; Beech Tree Books, 1994

Do-it-yourself recipes for all the basics—paste, paint, ink, modeling compounds, and papier-mâché—plus a few unusual mixes, such as crystal-garden compound, suitable for cultivating a homemade garden of Magic Rocks.

COLORING AND PAPER-CRAFTS BOOKS

Anti-Coloring Books

6 **+** Susan Striker; Henry Holt

A series of creative noncoloring books for kids in which young artists, rather than coloring somebody else's pictures, invent and color their own. There are six numbered books in the series, from the original *Anti-Coloring Book* (with Edward Kimmel) through *The Sixth Anti-Coloring Book,* along with such specialty volumes as *The Anti-Coloring Book of Exploring Space on Earth, The Anti-Coloring Book of Red-Letter Days, The Anti-Coloring Book of Celebrations,* and *The Newspaper Anti-Coloring Book.* Each page in the books includes an art starter: a piece of a picture, a frame, a blank poster, an empty window, a deserted landscape. From these jumping-off points, kids are encouraged to use their imaginations, inventing, for example, an underwater city, a wonderful tree house, a strange animal, a space alien, a magical garden, or a fabulous new machine.

Young artists may especially enjoy *The Anti-Coloring Book of Masterpieces,* in which the art starters are segments of famous paintings, museum artifacts, and sculptures, some shown in color, others in black and white. Users, for example, complete an illuminated medieval manuscript page ("A raging storm at sea illustrated this manuscript page from a prayer book"), design a stage set for Degas ballerinas, provide pets for Goya's little boy in red (*Don Manuel Osorio de Zúñiga*), add an exciting background to Rousseau's sleeping gypsy, and give Picasso's *Girl Before a Mirror* a reflection. An appendix in the back of the book includes black-and-white photographs of the (complete) masterpieces, titles, descriptions, and biographical information about the artists.

Color Your Own Modern Art Masterpieces

Muncie Hendler; Dover Publications

Ready-to-color black-line drawings of 30 modern artworks, among them Picasso's *Three Musicians* and Mondrian's *Broadway Boogie-Woogie.* Each drawing is accompanied by a brief explanatory text.

Also from Dover, see the *Japanese Prints Coloring Book* (Ed Sibbet Jr.), 38 drawings based on the prints of famous Japanese artists, the *Ancient Egyptian Design Coloring Book* (Ed Sibbett Jr.), *Celtic Design Coloring Book* (Ed Sibbett Jr.), *Pennsylvania Dutch Designs for Hand Coloring* (J. Rettich), *Geometrical Design Coloring Book* (Spyros Horemis), *Prismatic Design Coloring Book* (Peter Von Thenen), and *Op Art Coloring Book* (Jean Larcher).

> $2.95 each
> Dover Publications, Inc.
> 31 E. Second St.
> Mineola, NY 11501

The M. C. Escher Coloring Book

Harry N. Abrams, 1995

Contains 24 images from Escher artworks to color, including a removable foldout poster. Also see *The M. C. Escher Sticker Book* (1995), with 79 full-color stickers of Escher works.

M. C. Escher Kaleidocycles

Doris Schattschneider and Wallace Walker; Pomegranate Artbooks, 1977

A *kaleidocycle,* explains the instruction manual, is a three-dimensional ring made from a chain of tetrahedrons. Making one is not as impossible as it sounds. The kit includes colorful preprinted patterns based on the ingenious interlocking graphic artwork of M. C. Escher, to be punched out and folded into three-dimensional models. Materials are included for 17 models, gorgeously patterned with butterflies, starfish and shells, lizards, fish, flowers, and birds.

> $20
> Sax Arts & Crafts

> Box 510710
> New Berlin, WI 53151
> orders (800) 559-6696
> customer service (800) 522-4278

Make Your Own Museum

Andrea Bellioli; Houghton Mifflin, 1994

The kit, published in conjunction with the J. Paul Getty Museum, includes three 3-D museum galleries, which kids can decorate with reusable stickers picturing over 70 works of art and populate with punch-out figures of museum guides and visitors. Artworks include paintings, statuary, and antique furniture, plus assorted geometric shapes for creating abstract art. An accompanying illustrated guidebook covers the history and workings of museums.

Masterpieces

Mary Martin and Steven Zorn; Running Press

A "fact-filled" coloring book in Running Press's educational Start Exploring series. In *Masterpieces,* 60 famous paintings have been redrawn in simplified black-line form for coloring. Facing pages include the painting's title, artist's name and dates, and related interesting information. *Masterpieces* includes such works as Henri Rousseau's *Sleeping Gypsy,* Vincent van Gogh's *Starry Night,* Thomas Gainsborough's *Blue Boy,* and Paul Cézanne's *Still Life with Apples.* Also see *Masterpieces of American Art* (Alan Gartenhaus), which includes Winslow Homer's *Bear Hunting, Prospect Rock,* Georgia O'Keeffe's *Yellow Calla,* Edward Hopper's *Cape Cod Morning,* and Claes Oldenburg's *Flying Pizza.*

> $8.95 from bookstores or
> Running Press Book Publishers
> 125 South 22nd St.
> Philadelphia, PA 19103
> (215) 567-5080 or (800) 345-5359/fax (800) 453-2884

My Art Museum: A Sticker Book of Paintings

Carole Armstrong; Philomel Books, 1994

A do-it-yourself art museum in a book. The museum's picture frames are empty; each is accompanied by the title of a famous painting and a helpful description. Kids fill the frames with the correct painting, using peel-off stickers picturing full-color reproductions of famous artworks. The book measures 9 ×

12 inches, is 16 pages long, and includes 25 reusable stickers and an answer key.

By the same author: *My Monet Art Museum* (1995) and *My Van Gogh Art Museum* (1996). Each includes 25 sticker reproductions of the featured artist's paintings, titles, descriptions/clues, and biographical information about the artist.

GAMES AND HANDS-ON ACTIVITIES

Artery

The "Artistic Literacy Game" for kids in grades 4–12. *Artery* teaches the fundamentals of art—principles of design, media and techniques, subject matter, and expression—and encourages critical examination and evaluation of artworks. Players examine and analyze a series of artworks in a range of different styles. The game includes fifty-four 5 × 8-inch color reproductions of artworks (both western and nonwestern), a pack of 162 bilingual playing cards, divided into five color-coded categories, and 204 color-coded playing tokens. Card categories are "Subject" (landscape, cityscape, seascape, portrait, still-life), "Sensory" (line, color, shape, texture), "Formal Structure" (balance, unity, pattern, center of interest), "Technical" (paint, pencil, print, mosaic, collage, sculpture), and "Expressive" (meaning, mood, theme). The game can be played at beginning and advanced levels. A teacher's guide and reproducible student worksheets are included.

$59
Crizmac
Box 65928
Tucson, AZ 85728-5928
(800) 913-8555/fax (520) 323-6194
Web site: www.crizmac.com

Art History Timeline

The "Art History Timeline" covers 40 centuries of Western art, from prehistoric carvings to pop art, in nine 27 × 13-inch laminated card-stock panels. Each panel spans about 500 years of art, except the first, an overview of prehistory and the beginnings of civilization. The panels are designed to interconnect—a dated timeline, indicating important world events, runs along the top of each—but can also be displayed separately, for those who lack 20 feet of uninterrupted wall space. Each panel shows several large color or black-and-white photographs of period art works, including paintings, prints, sculptures, tapestries, mosaics, and stained-glass windows. A descriptive text beneath each illustration provides historical background information.

Also see the "Art Concepts Timeline," a set of ten 26 × 19-inch posters with over 200 captioned illustrations, shows how 15 art concepts—for example, shape, texture, proportion, light and shadow, and linear perspective—have evolved from 3200 B.C. to the present day. Concepts are traced horizontally, in rainbow-colored stripes.

"Art History Timeline," $47; "Art Concepts Timeline," $40
Sax Arts & Crafts
Box 510710
New Berlin, WI 53151
(800) 558-6696
or
Crystal Productions
Box 2159
Glenview, IL 60025-6159
(800) 255-8629

Art Lotto

Lotto boards and cards are beautifully illustrated with color reproductions of masterpieces from the National Gallery of Art in Washington, D.C. The game includes five playing boards, each with nine pictures, and 45 small playing cards. Players draw cards from the deck and attempt to make matches with the pictures shown on their boards. Each art reproduction is accompanied by a title, artist, and date.

$12 from toy and game stores or
Sax Arts & Crafts
Box 510710
New Berlin, WI 53151
(800) 558-6696

Art Memo Game

An artistic version of "Concentration," in which players turn over two cards at a time, attempting to make matches. The game includes 72 cards and full-color reproductions of 36 paintings by artists from Leonardo da Vinci to Andy Warhol. An included information booklet lists each work by artist, title, and museum.

In the similar "Impressionist Memo Game," players attempt to match 36 pairs of color reproductions of paintings by famous Impressionists.

$23 from toy and game stores or
Sax Arts & Crafts
Box 510710
New Berlin, WI 53151
(800) 558-6696

Artdeck Game

The original "Artdeck" game is a double pack of playing cards, illustrated with color reproductions of 52 works by 13 famous artists: Monet, Degas, Renoir, Seurat, Gauguin, van Gogh, Cézanne, Braque, Picasso, Kirchner, Kandinsky, Klee, and Miró. A second deck of Artist cards includes information about each of the featured artists. The game is played like double rummy: players pair Art and Artist cards and earn extra points by answering art questions. For two to six players, aged 10 and up.

Additional Artdecks are also available: "The Game of Modern European Masters" is a single deck of 52 cards, with four paintings by each of 13 European artists; "The Game of Modern Mexican Masters" includes four works each by such artists as Rivera, Kahlo, Orozco, Siquieros, and Murillo; and "The Game of African Artifacts" features color photographs and reproductions of artifacts from over 200 years of African culture, including carvings, headdresses, and masks.

"Artdeck" game, $15; single "Artdecks," $10
Aristoplay, Ltd.
450 S. Wagner Rd.
Ann Arbor, MI 48107
(800) 634-7738 or (888) GR8-GAME/
fax (734) 795-4611
Web site: www.aristoplay.com

Artists Stamp Sets

Portraits of famous artists on rubber stamps. Six different sets are available, each containing six artist stamps.

Also see *Museum Stamps*, rubber-stamp versions of famous paintings. Among these are van Gogh's *Starry*

Night, Leonardo da Vinci's *Mona Lisa,* Picasso's *Three Musicians,* and Grant Wood's *American Gothic.*

Artists Stamp Sets, $6.95; *Museum Stamps,* $6.49 each
United Art and Education Supply Co.
Box 9219
Fort Wayne, IN 46899
(219) 478-1121 or (800) 322-3247/fax (219) 478-2249

Clay

There's no such thing as just plain clay; art supply catalogs include page after page of natural clays, polymer clays, sculpting compounds, and modeling media. *Potters' clays* generally can be hardened only by kiln-firing; they air-dry to a brittle "greenware" that smashes if you tip it over. Some specialty potter's-type clays will "self-harden" in the air or can be hardened by baking in an ordinary oven; these look good but aren't waterproof, so if your kids want to make flowerpots, you'll have to treat the finished products with a sealant before using.

Modeling clays are usually plastic-based compounds, available in many colors and permutations, some nonhardening, some air-hardening, and some that must be hardened by baking. Among the latter are the popular FIMO clay, available in sets or in individual packets, in every color under the sun; Sculpey clay, which is similar, but generally less expensive; and Friendly Clay, which is available in single-colored packets or "millefiori" canes. The canes are multicolored prepatterned cylinders of clay, with embedded designs of flowers, stars, mosaics, or tiny people's faces. These can be sliced, shaped, or rolled into beads.

Assorted tools are also available for clay workers of all ages, including cutters, rollers, and "extruders," which squeeze clay into flat noodlelike strips or skinny spaghetti-style worms.

Clays, modeling compounds, instruction books, and tools are available from art supply stores and catalogs.

See **Catalogs** (page 715–718), *Dribble Drabble* (page 733), *The Incredible Clay Book* (page 734), *Mudworks* (page 735), *Recipes for Art and Craft Materials* (page 735), and **Suse's Play Dough** (page 738).

3 *Colorforms*

These have been around since 1951—I played with them as a tot, and our boys loved them. The basic "Colorforms" set consists of 213 geometric shapes in bright-colored vinyl—circles, triangles, squares, rectangles, and strips in blue, yellow, green, red, and white—and a laminated play board upon which the pieces can be stuck (and restuck) to create imaginative patterns and pictures. (A wonderful art project for the car; see how long it takes before your kids figure out that the shapes also stick to the windows.) Recommended for kids aged 3 and up.

Colorforms sets, $15 to $30
Available from toy and game stores

6 *In the Picture*

An art-based board game for kids aged 6 and up, in which the illustrated board represents the galleries of a museum. Players hop their pieces from room to room, collecting "clue" cards, each representing a segment of a larger painting. Clue cards are acquired by correctly answering questions about art and art history. Winner is the first person to collect three clue cards all from the same painting, thus identifying the elusive "missing" picture. The game includes 12 postcard-size reproductions of famous artworks and 56 question-and-answer cards.

$24 from toy and game stores or
RB Walter Art and Craft Materials
Box 6231

Arlington, TX 76005
(800) 447-8787

4 *The National Gallery ABC Game*

Twenty-six pairs of beautiful alphabet cards, labeled on one side with a lower-case letter and a simple word, on the other with a picture from a painting in London's National Gallery. *A*, for example, is for a Cézanne apple; *R* for a Dürer rabbit.

$24 from toy and game stores or
Crystal Productions
Box 2159
Glenview, IL 60025-6159
(800) 255-8629

5 *Pablo*

A building set for budding modern artists. The set includes 120 laminated heavy cardboard pieces, all brightly colored and patterned, in a wide range of sizes and shapes: yellow-and-orange-striped circles, diamond-patterned blue rectangles, red-and-black triangles, squiggly half-circles. The pieces are fitted together with black plastic connectors to form wonderful three-dimensional sculptures.

$69 from toy and game stores or
Zephyr Press
3316 N. Chapel Ave.
Box 66006
Tucson, AZ 85728-6006
(800) 232-2187/fax (520) 323-9402
e-mail: neways2learn@zephyrpress.com
Web site: www.zephyrpress.com

13 *Philosophy & Art*

An "Aesthetics Game" for students in grade 9 and up intended to introduce kids to different aesthetic beliefs about art from western civilization. The game includes 20 color art reproductions, a teacher's guide, activity suggestions, and a collection of game cards with quotations and statements by philosophers and artists.

$45
Crizmac
Box 65928
Tucson, AZ 85728-5928
(800) 913-8555/fax (520) 323-6194
Web site: www.crizmac.com

Token Response

5+

Gets kids of all ages talking about art. The game includes student activity sheets, a teacher's guide, and 30 sets of eight "reaction tokens"—little colored symbols that represent different reactions to a given work of art. The game can be played with any art prints, postcards, or reproductions—or even while perched on a bench at the local art museum. Kids simply select the tokens that they feel best describes their opinion of the featured work of art; then participate in follow-up discussions. For 3 to 30 budding art critics, aged 5 and up.

$43.50

Crizmac

Box 65928

Tucson, AZ 85728-5928

(800) 913-8555/fax (520) 323-6194

Web site: www.crizmac.com

Where Art Thou?

5+

Four art games in one for persons of all ages. The game includes 36 pairs of 2¼-inch square art cards, each a color reproduction of a scene from a famous painting by such American artists as Winslow Homer, Mary Cassatt, Grant Wood, and Andrew Wyeth, a game sheet, and instructions for art versions of bingo, "Concentration," "Mix & Match," and "Art Trivia."

$20 from game stores or

Crizmac

Box 65928

Tucson, AZ 85728-5928

(800) 913-8555/fax (520) 323-6194

Web site: www.crizmac.com

Which Artist?

6+

Kids match color reproductions of the works of famous artists to the appropriate "Artist Card," which includes a short biography of the featured artist.

$14.95

Crizmac

Box 65928

Tucson, AZ 85728-5928

(800) 913-8555/fax (520) 323-6194

Web site: www.crizmac.com

Zolo

ALL

A marvelous high-quality building set for young sculptors from New York City's Museum of Modern Art.

The set includes over 50 hand-carved and painted wooden pieces that can be assembled into a near-infinite variety of zany, colorful, and dramatic works of art. Pieces include chunky rose-pink kidney beans, zebra-striped squiggles, turquoise and purple blocks, spirals, zigzags, curlicues, cylinders, balls, and blobs. Everything you build with it looks like a museum piece. The set comes in a nice wooden storage box. For sculptors of all ages, none of whom will be able to resist it.

$160 from game and art stores or

Flax Art & Design

240 Valley Dr.

Brisbane, CA 94005-1206

(800) 547-7778/fax (800) FLAX-123

e-mail: catalog@flaxart.com

Web site: www.flazart.com

VIDEOS

American Vision

12+

From PBS, a spectacular history of American art—and a history of America *through* art—from the colonial era to modern times. Titles in the series include "The Republic of Virtue," "The Promised Land," "The Wilderness and the West," "The Gilded Age," "A Wave from the Atlantic," "Streamlines and Breadlines," "The Empire of Signs," and "The Age of Anxiety."

The eight-video set (8 hours), $149.98

PBS Home Video

1320 Braddock Pl.

Alexandria, VA 22314-1698

(800) 645-4727/fax (703) 739-8131

Web site: www.pbs.org

See **Art On-Line: American Vision** (page 743).

Daniel and the Towers

8-12

Based on Patricia Zelver's *The Wonderful Towers of Watts* (see page 731), this is the story of 10-year-old Daniel, who collaborates with an Italian sculptor to save Los Angeles's Watts Towers. Part of the PBS Wonderworks collection.

$14.95

Knowledge Unlimited, Inc.

Box 52

Madison, WI 53701-0052

(608) 836-6660 or (800) 356-2303/fax (608) 831-1570 or (800) 618-1570

Web site: www.ku.com

Don't Eat the Pictures!

From Sesame Street Home Video, this is a delightful musical introduction to art and art museums for kids aged 3 and up. Big Bird and his *Sesame Street* pals spend the night in the Metropolitan Museum of Art, having been accidentally locked in at closing time. There, while exploring the galleries, they solve a mystery involving the ghost of a small Egyptian prince (and his invisible, but audible, pet cat)—and, incidentally, see many masterpieces of art. The "Don't eat the pictures!" warning is directed at the irrepressible Cookie Monster, who can't be trusted near still-life paintings of food.

$14.95

Movies Unlimited

3015 Darnell Rd.

Philadelphia, PA 19154

(215) 637-4444 or (800) 4-MOVIES

e-mail: movies@moviesunlimited.com

Web site: www.moviesunlimited.com

The Hideaways

Based on E. L. Konigsberg's *From the Mixed-Up Files of Mrs. Basil E. Frankweiler* (see page 729), this is the story of 12-year-old Claudia and 9-year-old Jamie, who run away from home to live—very inventively—in the Metropolitan Museum of Art. There, with the help of the crotchety Mrs. Basil E. Frankweiler (Ingrid Bergman), they solve a mystery about a beautiful little statue of an angel, believed to have been carved by Michelangelo.

$14.95

Movies Unlimited

3015 Darnell Rd.

Philadelphia, PA 19154

(215) 637-4444 or (800) 4-MOVIES

e-mail: movies@moviesunlimited.com

Web site: www.moviesunlimited.com

Linnea in Monet's Garden

The video version of the book by Christina Bjork (see page 726) which tells the story of the famous painter through a combination of charming animation

and actual film footage of Monet's house, garden, and studio. About 30 minutes long; recommended for kids in grades K–6.

$14.95

Crystal Productions

Box 2159

Glenview, IL 60025-6159

(800) 255-8629

e-mail: crystal@interaccess.com

The Life of Leonardo da Vinci

A five-part series on the life and times of Leonardo, from childhood (troubles with his stepmother) through his artistic apprenticeship and his wonderful and varied accomplishments in adulthood. Beautifully acted and filmed on location in Italy.

$59.95

Public Television Videofinders Collection

National Fulfillment Center

Box 27054

Glendale, CA 91225

(800) 799-1199

Sister Wendy's Story of Painting

Travel the world with art critic Sister Wendy Beckett, learning about the history of art from its most primitive beginnings through modern times. Five hours of art appreciation on five video cassettes, all spectacularly filmed on location.

$99.98

PBS Home Video

1320 Braddock Pl.

Alexandria, VA 22314-1698

(800) 645-4727/fax (703) 739-8131

Web site: www.pbs.org

Squiggles, Dots, and Lines

A 30-minute Ed Emberley video that shows kids how to take three basic shapes—the squiggle, the dot, and the line—and transform them into creative drawings.

$14.95

KIDVIDZ

618 Centre St.

Newton, MA 02158

(617) 965-3345

See *Ed Emberly Drawing Book Series* (page 734).

COMPUTER SOFTWARE

Escher Interactive

A multifaceted tour of Escher's art for kids aged 10 and up. "Gallery" contains over 860 of Escher's prints and drawings, each accompanied by descriptive information and quotations from the artist himself; in "Tessellation Workshop," kids can invent their own Escher-style tessellations; "Morphing" allows kids to morph one of 11 Escher animals (or one of their own); and "Concave and Convex" is a challenging game of spatial relationships based on the Escher print of the same name. On CD-ROM for Windows.

> $55
> Dale Seymour Publications
> Box 5026
> White Plains, NY 10602-5026
> (800) 872-1100 or (800) 237-0338/fax (914) 328-5487
> or (800) 551-RODS
> Web site: www.awl.com/dsp

Kid Pix Studio

Like the original "Kid Pix," a perennial favorite, "Kid Pix Studio" features a wacky and imaginative assortment of drawing and painting tools. Kids can sprinkle the screen with stars, grow a forest of fractal trees, or splatter a Jackson Pollock look-alike; make checkerboard, wallpaper, or broken-glass effects; or draw with pine needles, bubbles, or the northern lights. Or they can erase the whole thing with an exploding firecracker, a gulping black hole, a NASA-style countdown, or a slow fadeaway. To all this, the studio adds newer and fancier capabilities: with "Moopies" (moving pictures), kids can animate the painting tools, making the brush strokes wiggle, blink, and flash. With "Stampimator," they can animate any one of a library of 800 colorful stamps. "Digital Puppets" calls up a family of jointed marionettes (including a princess, a dragon, and an elf named Doofus), which, at the tap of a keyboard key, will kick, wink, walk, wiggle, or wave; "SlideShow" allows kids to string photographs, drawings, and sound effects into an animated presentation; and "Pick a Sound" provides an assortment of beeps, honks, squawks, and over 80 short musical selections. It's a blast. On CD-ROM for Mac or Windows.

> $39.95
> Broderbund
> Box 6125
> Novato, CA 94948-6125
> (800) 521-6263/fax (415) 382-4419
> Web site: www.broderbund.com

Leonardo the Inventor

A multimedia exploration of the life and inventions of Leonardo da Vinci. Players can read a biography of Leonardo, study his inventions in the fields of flight, water, music, civil engineering, and warfare, view a selection of his paintings, and play assorted interactive games. For kids aged 9 and up. On CD-ROM for Mac or Windows.

> $39.95
> Zenger Media
> 10200 Jefferson Blvd.
> Box 802
> Culver City, CA 90232-0802
> (310) 839-2436 or (800) 421-4246
> Web site: ZengerMedia.com
> e-mail: access@ZengerMedia.com
> fax (310) 839-2249 or (800) 944-5432

The Louvre for Kids

An innovative tour of the famous French museum. Kids can study 150 artworks from the Louvre collection—among them the famous *Mona Lisa*—in detail. Accompanying each is a text description and an audio narration. Also included are interactive maps and timelines, art-related games and puzzles, a slide show, a brief history of the Louvre, and a virtual tour of the museum. On CD-ROM for Mac or Windows.

> $29.95
> Learn Technologies Interactive
> Box 2284
> S. Burlington, VT 05407
> (888) 292-5584
> Web site: voyager.learntech.com

With Open Eyes

Great art for kids from the Art Institute of Chicago. The CD-ROM includes beautiful full-screen photographs of over 200 works of art, from African masks to Impressionist landscapes, pre-Columbian jewelry,

Picasso portraits, and Japanese prints. Each artwork is accompanied by an audio clip that provides information about the piece and its maker, an illustrated timeline showing when the work was made, a world map showing where the work was made, and a challenging game or puzzle. Kids can create their own slide shows, view artworks by time period or geographic location, or zero in—via magnifying glass—for close-up examinations of specific details. On CD-ROM for Mac or Windows.

$29.95

Learn Technologies Interactive

Box 2284

S. Burlington, VT 05407

(888) 292-5584

Web site: voyager.learntech.com

ART ON-LINE

A. Pintura, Art Detective

A clever art history adventure in which A. Pintura, Art Detective, solves "The Case of Grandpa's Painting," with help from the reader. Kids make artistic choices as the plot progresses, deciding which artist painted Grandpa's painting, and learning about perspective, style, color, composition, and subject.

www.eduweb.com/pintura

See **Inside Art** (page 745).

Activities for Kids: Hot Tips

A long list of creative activity suggestions for small children. Included are "Fingerpainting in the Bathtub," "Sand Art," and "Tie-Dye for Toddlers."

momsonline

African Art

An on-line exhibition of African artworks, with terrific color photographs, descriptions, and background information.

www.lib.virginia.edu/dic/exhib/93.ray.aa/African.html

American Vision

An on-line version of the PBS series (see page 740) on American history through art (or vice versa). The site includes an extensive gallery tour of artworks from the programs, with commentary by art critic Robert Hughes, plus over 100 links to related art and history sites.

pbs.org/wnet/americanvisions

Art Game

A game of matching art styles. A painting is shown in a central frame; players are challenged to find a stylistically similar painting by the same artist from one of many smaller pictures shown in the sidebars.

www.thru.com/art/game

Art Page

This site teaches all the basic elements of art (texture, color, shading, value) through text and illustrations. A pencil sketch of a duck, for example, is used to explain texture. Includes links to many other art-related sites for kids.

www.stemnet.nf.ca/~lstringe/art.htm

The Art Studio Chalkboard

An informational site for serious art students on the technical aspects of drawing and painting. Includes an explanation of the color wheel and color theory, an introduction to painting tools, instructions on how to stretch a canvas, and an overview of a typical artist's palette. Users can also submit their own questions.

www.saumag.edu/art/studio/chalkboard.html

The @rt-room

An excellent art site for kids, including creative games, projects, activities, information about famous artists (including a list of their birthdays), an art gallery, and an art-related book list.

www.arts.ufl.edu/art/rt_room/@rtroom_home.html

The Art Teacher Connection

Lesson plans for kids of all ages and over 200 links to good art-related sites.

www.primenet.com/~arted

The Barbie Chronicles: The Incomplete History of Art

Barbie as the featured character in famous works of art, among them *Whistler's Mother*, Wyeth's *Christina's World*, and Botticelli's *The Birth of Venus*.

743

Nothing is labeled; it's an added challenge to identify the originals.

www.erols.com/browndk/art.htm

Bio: Leonardo da Vinci

A detailed biography of Leonardo da Vinci, all encyclopedia-style text.

www.yawp.com/cjackson/vinci/vinci_bio.htm

Crayola

Everything any young artist could possibly want to know about crayons. The site includes games and activities, crayon trivia quizzes (how many crayons laid end to end would it take to reach the moon?), information on crayon history, and an explanation of how crayons are made. Also included are hints for getting crayon stains off carpets, couches, and wallpaper.

www.crayola.com/crayola/home.html

The Da Vinci Project

An innovative site linking art and chemistry. Included is biographical information about Leonardo da Vinci and a detailed list of suggested projects, based, for example, on atoms, crystals, elements and compounds, the periodic table, and chemical reactions. Kids studying the periodic table learn about general systems of organization, the structure and function of the table, study selected elements, and produce a painting or model based on an alternative periodic table organization. The site includes many color examples of student work.

educ.iastate.edu/projects/davinci/homepage.html

Diego Rivera Web Museum

A biography of Diego Rivera, a gallery tour of his paintings, views of his murals, and links to related sites and resources.

www.diegorivera.com/diego_home_eng.html

Exploring Leonardo

An excellent site for kids from the Museum of Science, Boston. Users can learn about Leonardo's paintings and drawings in "Leonardo's Perspective"; explore Leonardo's machines and inventions in "Inventors Workshop"; view samples of his handwriting in "Leonardo: Right to Left"; and click on a city on a colorful map of Italy to discover just what Leonardo was doing there and when. The site includes a lot of supplementary information and detailed suggestions for related classroom activities.

www.mos.org/sln/Leonardo

Eyes on Art Quiz

The site pictures 15 pairs of eyes as seen in famous paintings; the challenge is to study each image and then identify the artist.

www.kn.pacbell.com/wired/art/artquiz.html

Fine Arts On-Line

Games and puzzles variously based on fiber arts, graphic arts, paintings, and sculptures. Under "Painting," for example, kids choose an artist, read a short biography and view a sample of the artist's work, and then attempt to pick a painting by the featured artist from a selection of color reproductions. Under "Fiber Arts," they try to match a sample of textile art to its country or region of origin.

www.hbschool.com/harcourtpages/justforkids/
reading/grade_5/art_line

The First Impressionist Exhibition, 1874

A beautiful on-line re-creation of the landmark first Impressionist exhibition, held in Paris in 1874. Users click on the artist's name—Renoir, Monet, Pissarro, Morisot, Degas, Sisley, Boudin, or Cézanne—to see a selection of paintings.

lonestar.texas.net/~mharden/74nadar.htm

Fun Crafts for Kids

A series of projects and art recipes for kids, with illustrations, instructions, and patterns to print. Included are instructions for making homemade play clay, colored sand, and paint.

tac.shopnetmall.com/www.funroom.com/
craftindex.html

Fun Stuff

Users can make their own toys, based on exhibits at the Public Museum of Grand Rapids. Included, for example, are instructions for making an Odawa canoe, a whale flip-book, a tumbling acrobat, and a Victorian paper doll.

www.grmuseum.org/fun-stuff.htm

Georgia O'Keeffe Gallery

ALL The paintings of Georgia O'Keeffe on-line; click on the title for a view of the work.

webpages.marshall.edu/~smith82/okeef.html

Gupit-Gupit Paper Snakes

6+ How to make paper snake sculptures, with print-out patterns, step-by-step instructions, and color photographs of student work.

www.tiac.net/users/gneils/gupit-gupit.html

Idea Box

3 7 Art projects, crafts, recipes, on-line stories, games, and seasonal activities, all targeted at preschool and early elementary–aged kids.

www.worldvillage.com/ideabox/index.html

The Incredible Art Department

ALL A list of favorite art lesson plans for kids, listed by age group from early childhood through college, an on-line "Art Site of the Week," a multiple-choice art test ("The artist who painted the *Mona Lisa* was . . ."), and links to many other art-related sites.

www.artswire.org/kenroar

Inside Art

8+ An exciting adventure in art history. Players are trapped inside a famous painting and must discover what it is and who painted it in order to escape back into the real world. Wonderful color reproductions.

www.eduweb.com/insideart/index.html

See *A. Pintura, Art Detective* (page 743).

Kids Craft

5 12 Craft projects, games, and recipes for kids aged 5–12. Projects include masks, sculptures, juggling balls, stained-glass windows, bookmarks, and beanbag creatures.

www.ozemail.com.au/~teasdale/craft.html

Kodak K–12 Lesson Plans

ALL Lesson plans for kids, listed either by academic subject or by age group, from preschool to college. The "Art" page includes a long list of project suggestions involving photography.

www.kodak.com/customers/education/LessonPlans/LessonPlans.shtml

Learn Computer Art

8+ On-line lessons in computer graphics for kids.

www.sillybilly.com/draw95.html

Masterprints Gallery Shop

ALL Users click on thumbnail-size paintings to see close-ups of many of the world's most famous artworks.

www.rams.com/masterprints

Michael's Kids Club

5+ Includes the "Electric Canvas," an on-line coloring book, and a long list of simple arts and crafts projects for kids, with instructions, illustrations, and patterns.

www.michaels.com/kids/kid-main.html

Monet Gallery

ALL The paintings of Monet on-line, indexed by title.

webpages.marshall.edu/~smith82.monet.html

Museum of Art: Rembrandt

ALL A museum gallery of Rembrandt paintings; click on the picture on the wall for a close-up view of the artwork.

lonestar.texas.net/~mharden/rembrandt/rembrandt.html

My Many Colored Days

3 7 Rainy day art projects for kids, based the Dr. Seuss book *My Many Colored Days.*

randomhouse.com/seussville

Native Tech: Native American Technology and Art

History, descriptions, and illustrations of American Indian arts and crafts, variously listed under "Beadwork," "Clay and Pottery," "Leather and Clothes," "Plants and Trees," "Porcupine Quills," and more. Many of the pages include instructions for arts and crafts projects, among them making a corn-husk doll and a pine needle basket. The site includes links to American Indian poems and stories.

www.lib.uconn.edu/NativeTech

Recipes for Playdough, Etc.
Recipes for all sorts of arts and crafts materials for kids, including cinnamon ornaments, homemade silly putty, finger paint, and play dough.

ucunix.san.uc.edu/~edavic/kids-list

Shakespeare Illustrated
A large collection of paintings based on the plays of William Shakespeare. Paintings are listed by play; click on the title to view related paintings. Each artwork is accompanied by a description and information about the artist.

www.cc.emory.edu/ENGLISH/classes

Teachers Helping Teachers: The Arts
Lesson plans for kids in grades K–12, centering around art techniques, craft projects, famous artists, art appreciation, and theater arts. Lessons include an age recommendation, a materials list, and step-by-step instructions.

www.pacificnet/~mandel//The Arts.html

Tessellations Project
A fifth-grade math project involving M. C. Escher–style tessellations, with examples of student work.

www.inform.umd.edu/UMS+State/UMD
Projects/MCTP/Technology

Vincent Van Gogh Information Gallery
Information on over 900 of van Gogh's paintings, an overview of his work illustrated with thumbnail reproductions, a van Gogh biography, and a world map, pinpointing the location of the artist's works in museums and galleries.

www.interlog.com/~vangogh

Virtual Jack-o'-Lantern
A great computer art project for Halloween. Kids select jack-o'-lantern features from a multiple-choice list; then generate their own computer-carved pumpkin.

www.netmud.com/~glenn/jack

Warner Bros. Kids Page
Games, activities, animation, and interesting information on how cartoons are made.

www.kids.warnerbros.com

World Art Treasures
An eclectic collection of links to "world art treasures," among them archaeological and multicultural artifacts, sculptures, paintings, architectural monuments, and Renaissance gardens.

sgwww.epfl.ch/BERGER/index.html

World of Escher
Biographical information about M. C. Escher, an extensive gallery of his artwork, and an on-line tessellation contest.

lonestar.texas.net/~escher

The Worlds of M. C. Escher
Many links to Escher picture archives and on-line resources.

math1.vibk.ac.at/escher.html

ART MUSEUMS ON-LINE

American Treasures

Sketches, paintings, maps, letters, and artifacts from the collection of the Library of Congress. Entries are categorized under "Memories," "Reasoning," or "Imagination," which, the site introduction explains, is the way Thomas Jefferson categorized his books. A wonderful source for American history and art.

lcweb.loc.gov/exhibits/treasures/trupscale

Art Institute of Chicago
View color reproductions of paintings from the museum collections. Included is a kids' site, with games and puzzles.

www.artic.edu/aic/firstpage.html

Fine Arts Museums of San Francisco
Virtual art galleries, information about the museum collections, and educational resources.

www.thinker.org/index.shtml

Metropolitan Museum of Art
View hundreds of thousands of artworks from the museum's immense collection.

www.metmuseum.org

Museum Computer Network
ALL Links to over 500 museums on the web.
world.std.com/~mcn

The Museum of Modern Art (MoMA), New York
ALL A tour of the collections, general information, resources.
www.moma.org

National Gallery of Art
ALL A virtual tour of the museum, a descriptive list of the museum collections, and educational resources.
www.nga.com

The Vatican
ALL A virtual tour of the Vatican's impressive art museum.
www.christusrex.org/www1/vaticano/0-Musei.html

WebLouvre
ALL A virtual tour of the Louvre in Paris, with a view of Leonardo da Vinci's *Mona Lisa.*
mistral.culture.fr/louvre

WebMuseum, Paris
ALL A tour of Paul Cézanne's work, a medieval art exhibit, collections of famous paintings, and a tour of Paris.
sunsite.unc.edu/wm

World Wide Web Virtual Library: Museums
Hundred of links to museums worldwide.
www.comlab.ox.ac.uk/archive/other/museums.html

MUSIC

Our boys, to a person, are intense lovers of classical music. This love—though we would, of course, like to take total credit for their elevated tastes—is somewhat in spite of their parents: my husband is a fan of country music; and I come from a long line of people so musically challenged that they can barely hum. The kids, however, wear Bach T-shirts and sneak off to their bedrooms to play Vivaldi.

The boys' exposure to classical music began when they were very young, with Prokofiev's enchanting *Peter and the Wolf,* in which the grandfather's theme is played by a bassoon—the boys adored that bassoon—then Saint-Saëns's *Carnival of the Animals,* Tchaikovsky's *Nutcracker Suite,* and Grieg's *Peer Gynt Suite,* in which they were much taken with "In the Hall of the Mountain King." They began music lessons at home, with a trio of recorders—I play, weakly, the recorder—and then moved on to the violin, with a professional teacher. The choice of the violin was clinched, interestingly enough, not by Prokofiev, Bach, or Beethoven, but by Appalachian fiddler Jay Ungar. After listening, repeatedly, to Ungar's "Ashokan Farewell," the haunting piece that accompanied Ken Burns's *Civil War* documentary (see page 550), the boys determined to learn the violin, solely in order to play that song. Two of them succeeded; Josh, after a two-year struggle, decided that the violin was not for him and gave it up.

Which brings us to another familiar obstacle in the rocky road of parenting: when do you support a child's decision to abandon something and when do you, equally supportively, insist that he/she stick with it? Is this, you agonize, a mature, well-thought-out decision on the part of a young person whose interests simply lie elsewhere? Or is this premature quitting on the part of a kid who needs to learn that rewards come only through hard work and perseverance? Fifteen years from today, is our son going to turn to us and say, "I'd be a better person today if *you* had only made me practice!"? My husband and I, after much behind-closed-bedroom-doors debate, decided to take the mature-decision approach. Josh quit, and we sold his three-quarter-size violin to a little girl down the road. Last year, after a long hiatus, Josh asked for piano lessons, which he is now taking, weekly. He's enjoying it; we hear him in the back room, cheerfully plunking out Mozart minuets.

Sometimes the hardest part of parenting, homeschooling, and daily life is knowing when to leave people alone.

Music, these days, is a major force in the boys' lives. There are violin lessons, piano lessons, and—recently—talk of bassoon lessons. The two violin players belong to the local youth orchestra, an active and public-spirited group that practices weekly and gives several yearly performances. They also attend a local summer music camp, run by the orchestra director, who somehow manages to combine violin lessons, ensemble playing, chamber music, and orchestra, with swimming, kickball, crafts, and caving.

And they all love to listen. We comb the local papers for recitals and concerts, and look forward to the Vermont Symphony Orchestra's visits to nearby towns. Musically interested kids also—almost without trying—make interesting musical connections. Ethan, while pawing through selections in the music department in the local bookstore (in search of bassoon music), discovered that the head of the department plays string bass; Caleb made friends with a teacher at camp, a cellist who plays in a chamber orchestra. The gentleman who sold the boys their violins plays old-time country fiddle. He milked cows to pay for his violin lessons 60 years ago; today he repairs violins and plays jigs and reels with a country band.

Ethan recently discovered a decrepit violin at a flea market and bought it, announcing his intentions to learn to repair—even build—violins. About three miles down the road from us, at the bottom of the hill, there's a woodworker who, with a partner in New York, builds violins. We took Ethan to visit him a few weeks back. He showed us the storage shed behind his barn, stacked with slices of sugar maple, tiger maple, and spruce—the raw material of violins, violas, and cellos. Ethan's eyes lit up as he reached for his notebook; and Randy and I—who sometimes have our doubts—realized once again just why we homeschool.

From my homeschool journal:

◆ **April 25, 1991. Josh is nine; Ethan, eight; Caleb, six.**

We're still studying sound. This morning discussed the speed of sound and how sound waves travel. Read an episode in one of the Einstein Anderson books (see page 233) in which Einstein solves a mystery having to do with sound on the moon. Discussed why there is no sound on the moon, and the boys promptly invented and drew a number of devices to allow people to hear on the moon. (Ethan's: a conglomeration of air-filled tubes.)

The boys spent some time dropping pebbles in water to watch wave propagation; we discussed the propagation of sound in water and air, and debated the question of whether sound travels faster through warm air or cold air.

We discussed string instruments and how they work, and the boys built simple string instruments of their own, using blocks of wood, nails, and rubber bands. We then got out the boy's grandfather's banjo, which simply fascinated them: banjo investigations occupied the rest of the school day. The kids quickly figured out that thick strings make lower-pitched sounds than thin strings; and that short strings make higher sounds than long strings. They also discovered that tight strings make higher sounds than loose strings, which was a real revelation—"So that's what these little screw pegs are for!" They experimented with finger picks, fooled around with strumming—"Listen to what happens when you use all the strings at once!"—and generally had a wonderful time.

CATALOGS

Anyone Can Whistle

ALL A "Catalogue of Musical Discovery" filled with whistles, recorders, kazoos, panpipes, rain sticks, birdcalls, and wind chimes. Also available: kid-size guitars and harps, an Australian digeridoo, a queen conch shell horn, and sets of "CatPaws" and "FishStix," which mesh the fun of spoons with the resonant sound of castanets. Small users simply clack them together to play along with any song, any time.

Anyone Can Whistle
Box 4407
Kingston, NY 12401
(800) 435-8863

Educational Record Center

ALL A plump catalog of educational cassettes, CDs, videos, filmstrips, and computer software. Included is a large assortment of materials for teaching music appreciation and skills, variously appropriate for kids of all ages. An excellent resource.

Educational Record Center, Inc.
3233 Burnt Mill Dr., Suite 100
Wilmington, NC 28403-2698

(800) 438-1637/fax (888) 438-1637

e-mail: erc-inc@worldnet.att.net

Web site: www.erc-inc.com

Homespun Tapes

A catalog of music instruction videos, books, and tapes for those who want to teach themselves at home. Selections cover folk-rock, country, and blues. This is not a source for classical French horn or bassoon hopefuls, but there's a lot available for beginning players of the guitar, piano/keyboard, banjo, drums, harmonica, mandolin, and fiddle. Most "beginner" tapes and videos are aimed at adult beginners, but motivated kids should be able to handle them. There's also a small selection of instructional videos specifically targeted at children.

> Homespun Tapes
>
> Box 325
>
> Woodstock, NY 12498
>
> (800) 33-TAPES

Lark in the Morning

A large collection of unusual musical instruments, kits, music, and instructional materials, ranging in price from the readily affordable to the extremely expensive. Included, at the affordable end, are children's bodhrans (Irish drums), bones (musical clappers made of ox bone, with instructional book and cassette tape), an African "tongue drum" kit, pennywhistles and bamboo flutes, aeolian wind harp kits, recorders, a "Learn to Play the Bagpipe Kit," a "Greek Lyre Kit," and a "Little Picker" build-your-own-stringed-instrument kit, with which beginners (with help) can make a 12-stringed psaltery. More expensive items include a build-your-own harp, harpsichord, viola, or Renaissance lute. A fascinating catalog for creative musicians.

> Catalog, $3
>
> Lark in the Morning
>
> Box 1176
>
> Mendocino, CA 95460
>
> (707) 964-5569/fax (707) 964-1979

Music for Little People

An excellent and wide-ranging selection of musical instruments, videos, tapes, sing-along books, and toys for kids of all ages.

> Music for Little People
>
> 4320 Marine Ave.
>
> Box 1720
>
> Lawndale, CA 90260
>
> (800) 346-4445

Opera World

Videotapes and CDs of full-length operas and opera excerpts and selections. Included are the "Very Model of a Modern Major Series," six videotapes of Gilbert and Sullivan operettas, including *The Mikado, H.M.S. Pinafore, The Pirates of Penzance, Iolanthe, Patience,* and *The Gondoliers,* and a small selection of classics specifically arranged for young listeners.

> Opera World
>
> Box 800
>
> Concord, MA 01742
>
> (978) 263-9271 or (800) 99-OPERA/
>
> fax (978) 263-8075
>
> e-mail: opera@operaworld.com
>
> Web site: www.operaworld.com

Rhythm Band Instruments

The catalog carries a wide selection of instruments, from rhythm sticks, jingle bells, and kazoos for the very small to more sophisticated xylophones, glockenspiels, keyboards, and chromaharps for older players. RBI is also an excellent source for recorders. The catalog carries a complete line of high-quality Aulos recorders: sopranino, soprano, alto, tenor, and bass. The Aulos recorders are made of a durable plastic resin—they feel good, they're next to unbreakable, and they have beautiful, sweet tones. The common recorder for beginners is the soprano, available in one, two, or three pieces, with or without a built-in thumb rest to help new players keep their hands in the right position.

Also available from RBI: instruction and music books (there are pages of selections just for recorders), and music posters, teaching aids, computer software, and games. Games include "Musopoly," designed by Michiko Yurko of "Music Mind Games" (see page 754), a board game of music reading and theory for two to six players aged 6 and up, and "Music Bingo."

> Rhythm Band Instruments
>
> Box 126
>
> Fort Worth, TX 76101-0126

(800) 424-4724/fax (800) 784-9401

Web site: www.rhythmband.com

West Music

ALL Recorders of all kinds (including a "Bare Bones" C soprano model that costs a mere $2.50), xylophones, autoharps, guitars, keyboards, and a large assortment of out-of-the-ordinary percussion instruments, among them zube tubes and cowbells, buffalo drums and temple blocks, kalimbas, gongs, and thunder sheets, musical washboards, whistles, and a lot of colored plastic eggs that rattle when you shake them.

The catalog also includes a large list of music instruction, activity, and song books, posters, games, videos, teaching aids, computer software, and a terrific collection of multicultural recordings, including selections of African and African American music, and music and songs from Asia, Europe and the British Isles, Hawaii, the Caribbean, Latin America, the Middle East, and North America.

Games include "Composer Bingo," in which players learn to identify 24 composers from the Baroque period through modern times, and "Music Listening Bingo," in which kids learn to identify 24 famous composers by their musical themes. The game is accompanied by a cassette or CD. An excellent resource for music education.

West Music

1212 Fifth St.

Box 5521

Coralille, IA 52241

(319) 351-0482 or (800) 397-9378/fax (888) 470-3942

e-mail: service@westmusic.com

Web site: www.westmusic.com

MAGAZINES

Clavier's Piano Explorer

8 13 An excellent monthly magazine for musicians aged 8–13. Issues include profiles of famous musicians and composers, articles on musical instruments and music theory, musical pieces by young composers, kids' poems and letters, and puzzles and quizzes.

Annual subscription (10 issues), $8 or $4

(five copies or more)

Clavier's Piano Explorer

200 Northfield Rd.

Northfield, IL 60093

(847) 446-8550

8 *Pipsqueaks*

12 An on-line music magazine for kids. Includes music-related activities and games, music reviews, song lyrics, stories about young composers, and information about kids' radio programs.

www.childrensmusic.org/Pipsqueaks.html

12 *Strings*

+ For players of classical stringed instruments. The magazine includes feature articles about musicians, instruments, and music, "shoptalk" about instrument structure and repair, and music reviews. It is intended for adult readers but is of interest to all serious string players.

Strings

Box 767

San Anselmo, CA 94979-0767

(415) 485-6946 or (800) 827-6837

e-mail: subs.st@stringletter.com

MUSIC HISTORY AND MUSIC APPRECIATION

12 *88 Keys: The Making of a Steinway Piano*

+ Miles Chapin; Clarkson N. Potter, 1997

The piano, Chapin explains, is the most complicated piece of machinery made by hand in the world today. This wonderful 144-page account of the making of a piano covers the history of the piano, materials used for building a piano, how the instrument works, and how it is put together. A fascinating read, with many precise color and black-and-white illustrations.

8 *Alligators and Music*

 12 Donald Elliott; Harvard Common Press, 1984

A humorous introduction to the four main classes of musical instruments—strings, woodwinds, brass, and percussion—and their place in the orchestra.

Also see *Lambs' Tales from Great Operas* (page 761) and *Frogs and the Ballet* (page 789).

Bach, Beethoven, and the Boys: Music History as It Ought to be Taught

David W. Barber; Sound and Vision, 1996

Music history ought to be taught, according to David Barber, with a rich sense of humor and a tongue-in-cheek twist. *Bach, Beethoven, and the Boys* approaches music history through the biographies of famous composers. A companion book, *If It Ain't Baroque . . . : More Music History as It Ought to Be Taught* (1992), covers developing musical genres, from "Really Early Music" through the Gregorian chant, the passion, the oratorio, the madrigal, the concerto, and the symphony. (If you don't know the difference between *motet* and *minuet,* this is the book for you.) Each book is about 140 pages long, arranged in short, informational, and hilarious chapters.

Be a Friend: The Story of African American Music in Song, Words, and Pictures

Leotha Stanley; Zino Press Children's Books, 1995

A book, audiocassette, and teacher's guide set for kids aged 8 and up. The book, in five illustrated chapters, covers spirituals, blues, jazz, gospel, and rap; the accompanying cassette includes original songs by Stanley in each of these five musical styles.

Also see *A Drawing in the Sand: The Story of African American Art* (page 720) and *Sweet Words So Brave: The Story of African American Literature.*

Classical Music: An Introduction to Classical Music Through the Great Composers and Their Masterworks

John Stanley; Reader's Digest, 1997

A hefty history of classical music from the Middle Ages to the present day, covering music styles, prominent composers, and orchestral instruments and performances. Includes maps, illustrations, and over 300 full-color photographs.

The Complete Idiot's Guide to Classical Music

Robert Sherman, Philip Seldon, and Bob Sherman; Alpha Books, 1997

For families of classical novices, 352 reader-friendly pages packed with useful information. (Chapter one is titled "If You Know Nothing About Classical Music, Start Here . . .") The book covers everything from concert hall etiquette to the instruments of the orchestra, musical terms and styles, famous composers, and opera, with clever anecdotes, simple explanations, and many helpful hints.

A Cry From the Earth: Music of North American Indians

John Bierhorst; Ancient City Press, 1992

The story of American Indian music and dance, with information about native instruments and the importance of music to Indian culture.

Duke Ellington Education Kit

Developed by the Smithsonian Institution's National Museum of American History. The kit is a multidisciplinary approach to the life and music of Duke Ellington for kids in grades 6 and up. It includes an illustrated teacher's guide, with an annotated bibliography and a glossary of jazz terms, a collection of black-and-white photographs of Ellington, reproductions of newpapers from 1919, and audiocassettes of Ellington's music. There are also a number of activities based on Ellington and Shakespeare: Duke Ellington, who became fascinated with William Shakespeare in the 1950s, wrote a number of pieces based on the plays, including the Shakespearean suite "Such Sweet Thunder."

$98.50

Dale Seymour Publications

Box 5026

White Plains, NY 10602-5026

(800) 872-1100 or (800) 237-0338/fax (914) 328-5487

or (800) 551-RODS

Web site: www.awl.com/dsp

The First Book of Jazz

Langston Hughes; Ecco Press, 1997

A brief history of jazz, with capsule biographies of its foremost musicians, among them Louis Armstrong and Bix Beiderbecke.

Great Composers

Piero Ventura; Putnam, 1990

A beautifully illustrated 124-page history of music, from the very first primitive musicians to the great classic composers to the Beatles.

Also see *Great Painters* (page 720).

How to Grow a Young Music Lover: Helping Your Child Discover and Enjoy the World of Music

Cheri Fuller; Harold Shaw Publishing, 1994

Strategies and activities for introducing kids of all ages to the joys of music.

The Kingfisher Young People's Book of Music

Clive Wilson, ed.; Kingfisher Books, 1996

A lushly illustrated history of music, from medieval times to the present, covering the basics of music theory, historical and multicultural music styles, and different types of instruments worldwide, from the double bass to the digeridoo. Also included is a dictionary of composers, with portraits and capsule biographies. For readers aged 9–12.

Long Live Music!

Massin; Creative Editions, 1996

A history of music from the primitive bone flute through the Chinese mouth organ, the Greek lyre, the great operas and symphonies, blues and jazz, and rock and roll. Information is supplemented with cartoon-style illustrations and a simple plot: on each page, Silence the antimusical Giant, threatens to quash all music but never succeeds.

Marsalis on Music

Wynton Marsalis; W. W. Norton, 1995

A terrific introduction to music, illustrated with color photographs. Chapters include "Why Toes Tap: Rhythm," "Listening for Clues: Form," "From Sousa to Satchmo: The Wind Band and the Jazz Band," and "Tackling the Monster: Practice." Also included is a glossary of music terms, a CD of music examples to accompany the explanations in the book, with selections by such composers as Brahms, Tchaikovsky, Ellington, Gershwin, and Ives, and a detailed "Listening Guide."

See **Audiovisual Resources: Marsalis on Music** (page 766) and **Music On-Line: Marsalis on Music** (page 769).

The Mozart Effect

Don Campbell; Avon Books, 1997

Music appreciation may have additional intellectual rewards. In 1993, a pair of researchers at the University of California, Irvine, showed that school children exposed to as little as 10 daily minutes' worth of classical music—the scientists favored Mozart piano sonatas—showed significant gains in spatial-temporal reasoning abilities, which is the sort of intelligence that allows people to solve geometry problems and do jigsaw puzzles. This phenomenon, dubbed the "Mozart effect," is now the subject of Campbell's book of the same name. Baroque music, the author claims, has a positive effect on almost everything, from dyslexia to postsurgical recovery rates; it also boosts the IQ, enhances math and reading skills, and increases the ability to memorize prose, poetry, spelling lists, and foreign-language vocabulary.

For those interested in testing the Mozart effect at home or in the classroom, Campbell has also published a three-volume CD or cassette pack of music selections collectively titled *The Mozart Effect Music for Children.* Individual titles include "Tune Up Your Mind" (pieces especially selected "to improve intelligence and increase IQ"), "Relax, Daydream & Draw ("to inspire creativity and relaxation"), and "Mozart in Motion" ("to explore body movement, motion, and motivation"). Lovely to listen to whether they boost brain power or not.

The Children's Group
1400 Bayly St., Suite 7
Pickering, Ontario L1W 3R2, Canada
(905) 831-1142

Music

Neil Ardley; Alfred A. Knopf, 1989

A book of music history and musical instruments in the Eyewitness series, heavily illustrated with color photographs. Each double-page spread covers a different musical topic, among them "Pipes and flutes," "Beginning of brass," "The violin family," "From gourd to board," "Grand and upright," "Rhythm and ritual," and "Electrifying music."

The Music Pack

Ron Van der Meer and Michael Berkeley; Alfred A. Knopf, 1994

This looks like a book, but it's actually a spectacular kit, filled with imaginative paper manipulatives, models, and pop-ups. There's something astonishing on every page: a working model of the human larynx, an inset illustrated booklet on the history of musical notation, a Russian doll–style foldout of the four major bowed stringed instruments (double bass to violin), a playable set of strings (with included bow), a whole pop-up piano with working model of keys and hammers, a pop-up set of drums with miniature drumsticks, and an entire elegantly clad pop-up orchestra. Also included is a foldout timeline of musical styles and composers, a world map of musical styles (a pull tab simultaneously highlights geographical location and style description), a dictionary of "Music Words," and a 75-minute CD, "Twenty Masterpieces," with an accompanying descriptive booklet. Included on the CD are selections from Monteverdi, Purcell, Handel, Bach, Haydn, Mozart, Schubert, Berlioz, Chopin, Wagner, Brahms, and Debussy. Marvelous, which is why the list price is high.

$50

Available from bookstores

Music Smart! Ready-to-Use Listening Tapes and Activities for Teaching Music Appreciation

Gwen Hotchkiss; Parker, 1990

A complete music appreciation program for kids in grades K–8, including teaching strategies, student activities and games, reproducible worksheets, and background information on each composer and musical selection. The program, designed to occupy "21 great weeks" of class time, includes a teaching manual and three audiocassettes.

The NPR Guide to Building a Classical CD Collection

Ted Libbey; Workman, 1994

You want to assemble a family classical music library, but you don't know what to buy? The *NPR Guide* supplies basic information on over 300 "essential" symphonies, concertos, and operas, with a short list of recommended recordings for each.

A Very Young Musician

Jill Krementz; Simon & Schuster, 1991

A short photo essay about the daily life of a talented 10-year-old trumpet player. Readers follow the boy to music lessons, music camp, and to a very special meeting with Wynton Marsalis.

The Young People's Book of Music

Keith Spence; Millbrook Press, 1995

A 144-page overview of music history from its beginnings to the present day. The book covers basic definitions of music, types and histories of musical instruments, the various forms of music, classical and church music, opera and ballet, popular music, and national music. Included are color illustrations, photographs, and many sidebars and boxes of interesting facts, capsule biographies of composers, and lists of musical works. For readers aged 10 and up.

A Young Person's Guide to Music: A Listener's Guide

Neil Ardley; Dorling Kindersley, 1995

A beautifully illustrated book covering the instruments of the orchestra, their characteristics and histories, and the lives and works of famous composers. An accompanying CD provides musical illustrations for the discussion in the text.

The Young Person's Guide to the Orchestra: Benjamin Britten's Composition on CD

Anita Ganeri; Harcourt Brace, 1996

An overview of the instrumental families of the orchestra, through narration and music. Kids listen to the sounds of each orchestral instrument, from flute to trumpet, and take an audio tour of the orchestra's woodwind, string, brass, and percussion sections. The 56-page book is illustrated with excellent color photographs.

ACTIVITY BOOKS

The Homeschool Music Course

The Homeschool Music Course is a 102-page wire-bound book, with accompanying audiocassette tape, providing "easy self-instructiion" for the keyboard and piano, written by music teacher (player and composer) Mark Kapner. This is a great idea for those who want to experiment on their own before committing to costly piano lessons, plus it looks like fun. The book begins by teaching students the names of the keys—there are nice, big black-and-white diagrams of the piano keyboard—and by the end of chapter one, new musicians are already playing not only the inevitable "Mary Had a Little Lamb" but also "London Bridge," "Skip to My Lou," "Down in the Valley," and several more. Lessons proceed through sharps and flats, reading music (for right and left hands), musical notation, chords, and lots and lots of songs.

$24.95 (plus $3 shipping/handling)

Eight Winds Music Co.

26425 104th Ave. SE, Suite F-101

Kent, WA 98031

(206) 854-3878

Kids Make Music: Clapping and Tapping to Bach and Rock

Avery Hart and Paul Mantell; Williamson, 1993

All kinds of music activities for kids aged 3 to 9. Kids play rhythm games and learn folk songs, perform a "Little Red Riding Hood" opera, participate in a "kitchen cabaret," learn the instruments of the orchestra and make some of their own, and learn the five basic ballet positions, make a tutu, and invent their own ballet.

Let's Make Music: An Interactive Musical Trip Around the World

Jessica Baron Turner and Ronny Susan Schiff; Hal Leonard Publishing, 1995

A book-and-tape (or CD) set. The tape/CD is a collection of songs from around the world; the book includes directions for making simple instruments from different countries, such as a Chilean rain stick or a set of Spanish castanets.

Make Mine Music!

Tom Walther; Little, Brown, 1981

One of the Brown Paper School Book series for young musicians. The book covers the science of sound, the history and structure of the many different classes of instruments, from the lyre to the French horn, and an explanation of musical notation, along with instructions for many different musical hands-on projects. Readers, for example, can make a spike fiddle, an aeolian harp, a tubular glockenspiel, a thumb piano, bongo drums, a bull roarer, panpipes, a sliding trumpet, and a working model of the human vocal tract.

Music Mind Games

Michiko Yurko; CPP/Belwin, 1992

A fat (430 pages) and thorough resource book for music educators. The book is divided into two sections: the first explains philosophies and methods of music teaching; the second includes detailed instructions for over 200 games, designed to teach kids of all ages music theory and reading. The games variously teach the names of the notes of the grand staff; scales and key signatures; signs, symbols, and tempos; rhythm, melodic, and harmonic dictation; chords; and sight-reading.

Packets of game materials and manipulatives to accompany the book are available at three levels: elementary, intermediate, and advanced. Each level includes materials for six to eight games, variously including color-keyed flash cards, puzzles, game boards, bingo cards, cardboard keyboards, grand staff cards, game playing pieces and counters, and dictation slates.

Book, $24.95; game packets, $129.95 to $159.95

West Music

Box 5521

1212 Fifth St.

Coralville, IA 52241

(319) 351-0482 or (800) 397-9378/fax (888) 470-3942

Rabbit-Man Music Books

Julie Albright and Vincent Fago; Diversity Press

This simple interactive workbook series is designed to teach just-beginning musicians how to read music. The books are 32 pages long, filled with matching games, exercises, and simple puzzles, and illustrated with fat little cartoon rabbits (of both sexes). Book One covers the symbols for notes and staffs, bass and treble clefs, and the notes F and G. Book Two moves on to the letter names of the notes of the grand staff; Books Three and Four continue to reinforce note names, while introducing note values. The books provide enough repetition so that young users learn to read music, with enough imagination and variety so that they don't get bored out of their skulls in the process—and, as the publisher points out, if your small musician likes to color, Rabbit-Man doubles as a dandy coloring book.

Vincent Fago, the illustrator of the Rabbit-Man series, is a cartoonist famed in the annals of rabbits: a former editor of Marvel Comics, he drew the Peter Rabbit comic strip for *The New York Herald Tribune* in the 1950s. Collaborator Julie Albright is a music teacher.

$5.95 each
Diversity Press
Box 376
Bethel, VT 05032
(802) 234-9179/fax (802) 234-6334

Rubber-Band Banjos and Java-Jive Bass: Projects and Activities on the Science of Music and Sound
Alex Sabbeth; John Wiley & Sons, 1997

This 128-page book, filled with information and activities, covers the science of music and sound, how the ear hears, how different musical instruments are made, and how they make the sounds they do. Kids make their own saxophones, banjos, drums, and wind chimes using ordinary materials.

Usborne Music Book Series
Most kids love the Usborne books, with their pleasantly presented information and their many colorful and busy little illustrations. The series includes how-to books for beginners illustrated with pudgy cartoon characters (*The First Book of the Recorder, The First Book of the Piano, The First Book of the Keyboard*), children's songbooks (*Nursery Rhyme Songbook, Round the World Songbook, French Songbook for Beginners*), collections of easy-to-play tunes for many instruments, hands-on introductions to classical composers (*Learn to Play Beethoven, Learn to Play Mozart, Learn to Play Opera Tunes*), and music theory books (*First Book of Music, Music Theory for Beginners*).

EDC Publishing
10302 E. 55th Pl.
Tulsa, OK 74146
(800) 475-4522
Web site: www.edcpub.com

World Explorer Books Series
A series of 22-page story-and-activity books for 5–9-year-olds. Each book includes a simple musical story, plus assorted flaps, pull tabs, maps, and stickers, and the materials for making a musical instrument. Titles include *Shake It,* with which kids can make an American Indian rattle; *Drum,* which comes with sets of drumsticks and mallets; and *String,* which includes materials for making a simple zither.

$18 apiece
Museum of Fine Arts
Boston Box 244
Avon, MA 02322-0244
(800) 225-5592/fax (508) 588-9678
Web site: www.mfa.org

COLORING BOOKS

A Musical Alphabet
Bellerophon Books publishes several informational coloring books for young musicians, among them *A Coloring Book of Early Composers, A Coloring Book of Great Composers: Bach to Berlioz, A Coloring Book of Great Composers: Chopin to Tchaikovsky, A Coloring Book of Great Composers: Mahler to Stravinsky, Woman Composers,* and *A Musical Alphabet,* which includes portraits and brief descriptions of 150 composers, in alphabetical order from *A* to *Z.* (*X* is for Xenakis.) Each book includes pages of ready-to-color black-line drawings, plus brief biographical information.

Individual biographical coloring books include *Wolfgang Amadeus Mozart* and *Ludwig van Beethoven;* in each, illustrations of scenes from the composer's life are accompanied by an informational text.

$3.95 each
Bellerophon Books
36 Ancapa St.
Santa Barbara, CA 93101
(800) 253-9943/fax (800) 965-8286

Musical Instruments Coloring Book

Ellen J. McHenry; Dover Publications

A collection of 44 black-line drawings picturing the instruments of the orchestra (and some not ordinarily found in the orchestra), among them the violin, cello, bagpipes, saxophone, trumpet, French horn, and guitar.

$2.95

Dover Publications, Inc.

31 East Second St.

Mineola, NY 11501

SONGBOOKS

From Sea to Shining Sea: A Treasury of American Folklore and Folk Songs

Amy L. Cohn; Scholastic, 1994

A gorgeously illustrated 400-page tour of American history through folktales and songs, featuring such perennial favorites as "Yankee Doodle," "Johnny Has Gone for a Soldier," "Let My People Go," "Follow the Drinking Gourd," and "I've Been Working on the Railroad."

See **American History** (page 452).

Go In and Out the Window: An Illustrated Songbook for Young People

Dan Fox; Metropolitan Museum of Art/Henry Holt, 1987

Words and music to 61 traditional folk songs, each illustrated with an exquisite full-color reproduction of a painting, print, or sculpture from the Metropolitan Museum of Art.

Gonna Sing My Head Off!: American Folk Songs for Children

Kathleen Krull; Alfred A. Knopf, 1995

The words and music to 62 well-known American folk songs, arranged in alphabetical order, from "Acres of Clams" and "Arkansas Traveler" through "Will the Circle Be Unbroken" and "Yankee Doodle." State, city, or area of origin is listed for each song—an excellent connection for young geography students—along with an introductory paragraph of historical information. Color illustrations.

Just Listen to This Song I'm Singing: African-American History Through Song

Jerry Silverman; Millbrook Press, 1996

The music and lyrics of 13 African American songs serve as jumping-off points for an explanation of the events of black history. For readers aged 9–12.

Songs to Sing and Picture

Lillian L. Dudley and Harriet R. Kinghorn; Teacher Ideas Press, 1996

Fifty-four simple songs for kids in preschool through grade 2, each with an accompanying activity and a suggestion for a related book to read. Piano and guitar music are included for all the songs. The songs are about a wide range of topics, among them apples, balloons, butterflies, hats, healthy snacks, pen pals, the ocean, the five senses, rainbows, seasons, trains, and the zoo. Activities cover several academic disciplines: art, science, math, social studies, and language arts. Along with the song "Balloons," for example, kids color a bunch of color-name-labeled balloons and read Albert Lamorisse's *The Red Balloon;* with the song "A Rainbow," they paint a rainbow, experiment with color mixing, and read Don Freeman's *A Rainbow of My Own;* with "Shapes" ("There are three sides on a triangle, and three wheels on a trike/A circle's round just like the sun or two wheels on a bike") they play a shape-matching game and read *The Shape Game* by Paul Rogers. Music and activity sheets are reproducible, so you can make copies, if need be, for each kid.

$17.50

Libraries Unlimited

Box 6633

Englewood, CO 80155-6633

(303) 770-1220 or (800) 237-6124/fax (303) 220-8843

e-mail: lu-books@lu.com

Web site: www.lu.com

Wee Sing Series

Price Stern Sloan

A popular series of cassette tapes and accompanying sing-along books for kids aged 3–9. Titles include *Wee Sing Around the World, Wee Sing Dinosaurs, Wee Sing Songs & Fingerplays, Wee Sing and Play, Wee Sing*

Silly Songs, Wee Sing Singalong, Wee Sing Nursery Rhymes and Lullabies, Wee Sing Bible Songs, Wee Sing America, Wee Sing Fun 'n Folk Songs, and *Wee Sing for Christmas.*

> Book-and-tape sets, $9.95
> Available from book and music stores or
> Educational Record Center, Inc.
> 3233 Burnt Mill Dr., Suite 100
> Wilmington, NC 28403-2698
> (800) 438-1637/fax (888) 438-1637
> e-mail: erc-inc@worldnet.att.net
> Web site: www.erc-inc.com

BIOGRAPHIES: GENERAL

Famous Children Series
Ann Rachlin; Barron's

Charmingly illustrated picture-book stories of famous composers as children, plus, at the very end, a brief account of their accomplishments in later life. Titles include *Bach, Brahms, Chopin, Handel, Haydn, Mozart, Schumann,* and *Tchaikovsky.*

Famous Composers Series
Roland Vernon; Silver Burdett, 1996

A series of short biographies for readers aged 9–12, creatively illustrated with period works of art, fact sidebars, and timelines. Titles include *Introducing Beethoven, Introducing Chopin, Introducing Gershwin, Introducing Mozart, Introducing Stravinsky, Introducing Verdi,* and *Introducing Vivaldi.*

Getting to Know the World's Greatest Composers Series
Mike Venezia; Children's Press

A delightful series of 32-page biographies for readers aged 5–10, illustrated with hilarious little cartoons and full-color photographs. Titles include *Aaron Copland* (1995), *The Beatles* (1997), *Leonard Bernstein* (1997), *Duke Ellington* (1995), *George Gershwin* (1994), *George Handel* (1995), *Igor Stravinsky* (1996), *Ludwig van Beethoven* (1996), *Peter Tchaikovsky* (1994), and *Wolfgang Amadeus Mozart* (1995).

Also see **Getting to Know the World's Greatest Artists Series** (page 722).

Lives of the Musicians: Good Times, Bad Times (And What the Neighbors Thought)
Kathleen Krull; Harcourt Brace, 1993

Irresistibly interesting short biographies of 19 famous musicians, in chronological order, from Antonio Vivaldi ("The Red Priest") and Johann Sebastian Bach ("Twenty Children and 1,200 Compositions") through Woody Guthrie ("Traveling Troubador"). Also included: Mozart, Beethoven, Chopin, Verdi, Clara Schumann, Stephen Foster, Brahms, Tchaikovsky, Gilbert and Sullivan, Erik Satie, Scott Joplin, Charles Ives, Igor Stravinsky, Nadia Boulanger, Sergei Prokofiev, and George Gershwin. Each biography is accompanied by a color portrait by Kathryn Hewitt and a short list of "Musical Notes": additional fascinating facts about each musician. Readers learn, for example, that Bach wrote the *Goldberg Variations* to relax an insomniac count; that Beethoven's *Ode to Joy* was played during the 1990 dismantling of the Berlin Wall; and that Igor Stravinsky once wrote a polka for 50 elephants wearing ballet tutus.

Women Music Makers: An Introduction to Women Composers
Janet Nichols; Walker & Company, 1992

Biographies of 10 women who struggled to succeed in a male-dominated profession, among them Clara Schumann, Florence Price, and Ethel Smyth. An appendix includes short profiles of an additional 24 women composers.

BIOGRAPHIES: INDIVIDUAL

America, I Hear You: A Story About George Gershwin
Barbara Mitchell; Carolrhoda, 1987

A Creative Minds biography for readers in grades 3–6.

Beethoven Lives Upstairs
Barbara Nichols; Orchard Books, 1994

An illustrated story of Ludwig van Beethoven, told in a series of letters written by his landlady's 10-year-

old son to an uncle in Vienna. Young Christoph is puzzled and embarrassed by the strange tenant, who writes in pencil on the walls and pounds a piano while lying on the floor. Eventually, however, he learns to appreciate Beethoven's great talent.
See **Classical Kids Series** (page 764).

The Boy Who Loved Music
David Lasker; Viking, 1979

Joseph Haydn and his fellow musicians at the court of Prince Esterhazy are stuck: the prince refuses to allow them to return to Vienna at the end of the summer. Haydn gets around the problem by composing the *Farewell* Symphony in which the musicians, one at a time, get up and leave the stage. And the court.

Charlie Parker Played Be Bop
Chris Raschka; Orchard Books, 1992

The picture-book story of Charlie Parker, his music, his saxophone, and his pet cat.

Handel and the Famous Sword Swallower of Halle
Bryna Stevens; Philomel Books, 1990

The humorous picture-book tale of how young Handel managed to get organ lessons despite his father's objections to music. For readers aged 5–9.

Her Piano Sang: A Story About Clara Schumann
Barbara Allman; Carolrhoda, 1996

A biography of the talented pianist who gave her first public concert at the age of nine, and later formed friendships with many famous composers and musicians, among them Felix Mendelssohn, Niccolò Paganini, and Jenny Lind. For readers in grades 3–6.

If I Only Had a Horn: Young Louis Armstrong
Roxanne Orgill; Houghton Mifflin, 1997

A 32-page picture-book biography of Louis Armstrong that tells how he got his first horn: it was a bugle given to him at the reform school where he was sent for firing a gun on the streets of New York City on New Year's Eve.

Letters to Horseface, Being the Story of Wolfgang Amadeus Mozart's Journey to Italy 1769–1770, When He Was a Boy of Fourteen
F. N. Monjo; Viking, 1975

The story of Mozart's musical tour of Italy through 12 letters to his sister, whom Mozart calls "Nannerl-the-Horseface." He describes his music, his visits to the Italian court, and the food, clothes, and customs of Italy. Included are pencil-sketch illustrations and a map showing the extent of his travels. For readers aged 9–13.

Mozart: Scenes from the Childhood of the Great Composer
Catherine Brighton; Doubleday, 1990

Mozart's life from age 4 to 11, as told by his older sister, Nannerl, illustrated with elaborate full-page paintings. For readers aged 5–9.

Mozart Tonight
Julie Downing; Aladdin, 1994

Mozart, on the eve of the first performance of his opera *Don Giovanni*, tells the story of his life. With full-color illustrations, for kids aged 5–9.

Tchaikovsky Discovers America
Esther Kalman; Orchard Books, 1995

The story of Tchaikovsky's visit to America as told through the diary of 11-year-old Jenny, who meets the composer on a train journey.
See **Classical Kids Series** (page 764).

Wolferl: The First Six Years in the Life of Wolfgang Amadeus Mozart
Lisl Weil; Holiday House, 1991

A biography of the composer as a very precocious child, illustrated with clever line drawings.

MUSIC AND LITERATURE LINKS FOR PARENTS AND TEACHERS

Music Through Children's Literature: Theme and Variations
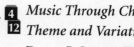
Donna B. Levene; Teacher Ideas Press, 1993

The book pairs illustrated folk songs and stories with musical themes with a large number of music-related activities for kids in preschool through grade 6. Topics covered include all the musical basics: rhythm, melody, instruments, music history, and dance.

Libraries Unlimited

Box 6633

Englewood, CO 80155-6633

(303) 770-1220 or (800) 237-6124/fax (303) 220-8843

e-mail: lu-books@lu.com

Web site: www.lu.com

MUSIC AND LITERATURE LINKS FOR KIDS

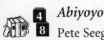

Abiyoyo

Pete Seeger; Aladdin, 1994

A story-song based on a South African folktale in which a ukelele-playing boy and his father defeat the giant Abiyoyo.

All of You Was Singing

Richard Lewis; Atheneum, 1991

A picture-book version of an Aztec creation myth that explains how music came to the earth.

Arion and the Dolphins

John Lonzo Anderson; Charles Scribner's Sons, 1978

A picture-book version of a Greek legend in which a young lute player, thrown off a ship into the sea, is rescued by the dolphins, who love his beautiful music.

Ben's Trumpet

Rachel Isadora; Mulberry, 1991

Ben sits on his city fire escape listening to the music at the nearby Zig Zag Jazz Club and dreaming of playing a trumpet of his own. A kind musician notices him and makes the dream come true.

Berlioz the Bear

Jan Brett; Paper Star, 1996

Berlioz, the bass-playing bear, has a number of disruptive adventures with an angry bumblebee on the way to the concert—where he is scheduled to play "The Flight of the Bumblebee." For readers aged 5–8.

The Facts and Fictions of Minna Pratt

Patricia MacLachlan; HarperTrophy, 1990

Minna, a talented young cellist, and her chamber group enter a challenging competition that brings Minna her first romantic involvement. For readers aged 10–13.

Georgia Music

Helen V. Griffith; Mulberry, 1990

A little girl visiting her grandfather in rural Georgia sits on the porch and listens to the rhythms and songs of summer evenings; back home in the city she remembers and re-creates Georgia music on the harmonica.

Mama Don't Allow

Thatcher Hurd; HarperTrophy, 1985

Despite all the things that Mama don't allow, the Swamp Band entertains a riotous gang of partying alligators. The book includes words and music to the foot-stomping title song.

The Mozart Season

Virginia Euwer Wolff; Henry Holt, 1991

The story of a talented 12-year-old violinist, Allegra, and her journey of self-discovery as she prepares to enter a music competition. For readers aged 10–13.

Pages of Music

Tony Johnston; Putnam, 1988

When Paolo was a little boy growing up on the island of Sardinia, a shepherd once shared a meal of bread (called "pages of music") with him and played a beautiful song on his pipes. Paolo, now a composer, has written a musical composition based on that remembered song. As a special Christmas gift, he brings a symphony orchestra to the island to play a concert of his music for the villagers.

The Philharmonic Gets Dressed

Karla Kuskin; HarperTrophy, 1986

All 105 members of the Philharmonic wiggle into their clothes and leave for work, to meet onstage for a performance of the orchestra.

Rachel's Recital

4–8 Melinda Green; Little, Brown, 1979

Rachel hates to practice the piano, which means that she isn't prepared for her big piano recital. Set in New York City's Lower East Side.

Raffi Songs to Read Series

3–7 Raffi; Crown

Brightly illustrated versions of favorite songs by the popular children's musician Raffi. The simple text of the familiar songs is an easy bridge to reading.

Titles in the series include *Wheels on the Bus, Tingalaya, Like Me and You, Five Little Ducks, Everything Grows, Down By the Bay, Rise and Shine, Baby Beluga, Shake My Sillies Out, Spider on the Floor,* and *One Light, One Sun.*

Rondo in C

9–12 Paul Fleischman; Harper & Row, 1988

As a piano student plays Beethoven's *Rondo in C,* each member of the audience conjures up different memories.

Stradivari's Singing Violin

5–8 Catherine Deverell; Carolrhoda, 1992

An On My Own History book for readers in grades K–3 that tells the tale of the wonderful Stradivarius violins.

Ty's One-Man Band

4–8 Mildred Pitts Walter; Scholastic, 1984

A little boy tells the story of the summer night when Ty's one-man band came to town, bringing with him a magical gift of music and dance.

The Voice of the Wood

6–9 Claude Clement, Dial, 1989

A magic cello, made from the wood of an old instrument maker's very special tree, can be played only by an honest musician who plays from the heart.

OPERA RESOURCES

See also **Catalogs:** *Opera World* (page 749).

Amahl and the Night Visitors

ALL Giancarlo Menotti's exquisite Christmas opera, the story of the little crippled shepherd boy, Amahl, who shelters the Three Kings on their way to Bethlehem. The music is marvelous; the story is beautiful and moving; and the third King, Gaspar, who is very deaf and always travels with a box of licorice, is irresistible. You might introduce—or follow—the opera with the illustrated storybook version: *Amahl and the Night Visitors* (Giancarlo Menotti; Morrow Junior Books, 1986).

> $19.99
> Movies Unlimited
> 3015 Darnell Rd.
> Philadelphia, PA 19154
> (215) 637-4444 or (800) 4-MOVIES
> e-mail: movies@moviesunlimited.com
> Web site: http://www.moviesunlimited.com

Composers' Specials Series: Opera

7–12 Two titles from the *Composers' Specials* series, a collection of beautifully done videos that introduce kids aged 7–12 to the lives and work of famous composers, feature operas. *Rossini's Ghost* centers around the opera *The Barber of Seville; Bizet's Dream* is a story involving the opera *Carmen.*

> $19.95 each
> West Music
> Box 5521
> 1212 5th St.
> Coralville, IA 52241
> (319) 351-0482 or (800) 397-9378/fax (888) 470-3942
> e-mail: service@westmusic.com
> Web site: www.westmusic.com

See **The Composers' Specials** (see page 764).

Hansel and Gretel: An Opera Fantasy

6+ Puppets, animation, and opera combine in an hourlong version of the old tale about the children lost in the woods, the cottage made of gingerbread, and the wicked witch.

> $19.99
> Movies Unlimited
> 3015 Darnell Rd.
> Philadelphia, PA 19154
> (215) 637-4444 or (800) 4-MOVIES
> e-mail: movies@moviesunlimited.com
> Web site: www.moviesunlimited.com

How to Listen to and Understand Opera

A 32-lesson lecture-and-listening course presented by Professor Robert Greenberg of the San Francisco Conservatory of Music. The course is divided into four parts, each consisting of eight 45-minute lessons, combining information and illustrative musical excerpts. Part I covers the origins of opera and the works of Monteverdi; Part II, the development of Italian opera, the rise of opera buffa, and Mozart; Part III, Rossini, Verdi, and French opera; and Part IV, German opera, Russian opera, Wagner, Verismo, and Puccini. For teenagers and adults.

> Available in audio and video versions. Audio series, $199.95; video series, $299.95
> The Teaching Co.
> 7405 Alban Station Ct., Suite A107
> Springfield, VA 22150-2318
> (800) 832-2412; fax (703) 912-7756

See *How to Listen to and Understand Great Music* (page 766) and *Concert Masterworks* (page 765).

Lambs' Tales from Great Operas

Donald Elliott; Harvard Common Press, 1984

Abbreviated stories of the great operas, cleverly presented by a series of perfectly delightful lambs. For readers aged 9 and up.

The Magic Flute

Anne Gatti; Chronicle Books, 1997.

A short picture-book version of Mozart's opera, in which Prince Tamino saves Princess Pamina from the Queen of the Night in a magical land filled with giant butterflies, spectacular flowers, and a monster serpent. The book is accompanied by a CD with selections from *The Magic Flute.*

Mozart's Magic Fantasy

On audiocassette or CD from the *Classical Kids* collection (see page 764), this is the story of a little girl who enters the magical world of Mozart's *The Magic Flute,* meets a talking dragon, and listens to a lot of glorious music.

> $10.95 (cassette) or $16.95 (CD)
> The Children's Group
> 1400 Bayly St., Suite 7

Pickering, Ontario L1W 3R2, Canada
(905) 831-1142
or
West Music
1212 5th St.
Box 5521
Coralville, IA 52241
(319) 351-0482 or (800) 397-9378; fax (888) 470-3942
e-mail: service@westmusic.com
Web site: www.westmusic.com

Mozart's The Magic Flute Story

An abbreviated (42 minutes) video of Mozart's famous comic opera for kids aged 6 and up. The production, gorgeously staged and costumed, is the tale of a Prince, a Princess, and a wonderful magic flute. Sung in the original German, with English narration.

> Movies Unlimited
> 3015 Darnell Rd.
> Philadelphia, PA 19154
> (212) 637-4444 or (800) 4-MOVIES
> e-mail: movies@moviesunlimited.com
> Web site: www.moviesunlimited.com
> or
> Educational Record Center, Inc.
> 3233 Burnt Mill Dr., Suite 100
> Wilmington, NC 28403-2698
> (800) 438-1637

Music! Words! Opera!

 A curriculum designed for introducing opera to kids, available at two levels. Level I is targeted at kids in grades K–2; Level II, at kids in grades 3–6. (Level III, for grades 7–12, is forthcoming.) Level I covers the operas *Hansel and Gretel, The Magic Flute,* and *The Child and the Enchantments;* Level II, *The Barber of Seville, Aïda,* and *Madame Butterfly.* Programs begin with a "Learn and Discover" section, in which the students are introduced to the music and story of the operas, followed by a "Create and Produce" section, in which the kids have a try at creating an opera of their own. Curriculum materials include a detailed teacher's manual, a cassette tape with musical selections from the operas, and student workbooks.

> Level I program, about $65; Level II program, about $80; student workbooks (one is needed for each

opera), $3.50 apiece

West Music

1212 Fifth St.

Box 5521

Coralville, IA 52241

(319) 351-0482 or (800) 397-9378/fax (888) 470-3942

e-mail: service@westmusic.com

Web site: www.westmusic.com

My Favorite Opera for Children

Eighteen songs chosen just for their appeal to young listeners by Luciano Pavarotti. Included are the "Song of the Gingerbread Children" and "Humming Chorus Lullaby" from *Hansel and Gretel*, and the thrilling "Ride of the Valkyries." Available on cassette or CD, with an accompanying booklet describing the stories behind each opera.

$8.95 (cassette) or $13.95 (CD)

Music for Little People

Box 1720

Lawndale, CA 90260

(800) 346-4445

A Night at the Opera: An Irreverent Guide to the Plots, the Singers, the Composers, the Recordings

Denis Forman; Random House, 1995

Descriptive summaries of 10 great operas, including *Aïda*, *La Bohème*, and *Carmen*. A comprehensive (and funny) reference book.

Opera for Dummies

David Pogue and Scott Speck; IDG Books, 1997

A fat volume in the familiar yellow-and-black series from IDG Books, this covers all the operatic basics. The information is serious; the presentation isn't. A light-hearted read for interested teenagers and adults. The book includes a CD with samples of works of the great composers, among them Puccini and Mozart.

When the Fat Lady Sings: Opera History as It Ought to be Taught

David W. Barber; Sound and Vision, 1990

"If you're looking for someone to blame for this whole opera business," writes Barber cheerfully, "look

no further than Claudio Monteverdi (1567–1643), a musician at the court of Duke Vincenzo Gonzaga of Mantua." The book begins with a short history of opera in general, followed by accounts of famous operatic composers and their operas, categorized by country. Included are "French Bred" (Lully, Rameau, Gluck, and Bizet), "The English Channel" (Handel), "Teutonic Tunesmiths" (Haydn, Mozart, and Beethoven), "Russian Into Things" (Glinka, Balakirev, Cui, Borodin, Rimsky-Korsakov, Moussorgsky, and Tchaikovsky), "Ulterior Leitmotifs" (Wagner), "Italian Sausage Machines" (Vivaldi, Rossini, Bellini, Donizetti, Verdi, and Puccini), and "20th-Century Leftovers" (including mention of the world's shortest opera, which is seven minutes long). Funny, factual, and unforgettable.

GAMES AND HANDS-ON ACTIVITIES

Composers Card Game

An illustrated rummy game, featuring 13 famous composers.

$6

U.S. Games Systems, Inc.

179 Ludlow St.

Stamford, CT 06902

(203) 353-8400 or (800) 544-2637

Music Maestro II

An award-winning "game of musical instruments past and present" for players aged 4 to adult. The board, which fits together puzzle-fashion, depicts 48 instruments, from the medieval shawm and rebec to the very modern electric guitar and synthesizer. Game materials include three packs of cards: "Instrument Cards," each illustrated with a color picture of an instrument on the playing board; "Conductor Cards," each with the name of an instrument and a series of three clues about its identity; and "Ensemble Cards," which picture instruments in "Ensemble Groups" (melodic percussion instruments, brass instruments, bluegrass instruments, woodwinds, jazz instruments).

Instructions are included for five games, appropriate for players of different ages and skill levels. In the simplest of these, players simply match instruments by name and picture. In a more difficult version, players identify instruments by responding to the clues on the "Conductor Cards." The three clues on each card are categorized under "Form," "Function," or "Fact." For example:

Form: "I am a bowed instrument with four strings, a shallow body, shoulders at right angles to my neck, and a fairly curved bridge."
Function: "Pegs on my head are used to tune my strings. I produce sound when my strings are pressed against my neck and bowed to resonate sound from my body."
Fact: "I was invented in the early 1500s in Italy where Amati and Stradivari were masters at my construction. More music has been written for me than for any other instrument."

The answer is *violin;* if you get it right, you collect the matching "Instrument Card" from the playing board. Player with the most cards at the end of the game wins.

In an audio version of the game, players attempt to identify the sounds of the instruments, as played on the included "Sound Off" audiocassette tapes. Each side of the two tapes features a different group of instruments: modern instruments, early instruments, more modern instruments, and ensembles of modern instruments. All the "Instrument Cards" are dealt to the players; as each instrument sounds on the tape, the player with the corresponding "Instrument Card" places it faceup in the appropriate space on the playing board. (Answers, for those who cannot agree on the source of a given tootle or beep, are listed in the instruction manual.)

$25
Aristoplay
450 S. Wagner St.
Ann Arbor, MI 48107
(800) 634-7738 or (888) GR8-GAME/fax (734) 995-4611
Web site: www.aristoplay.com

Music Maestro Parade

"Musical Bingo" for small fry. The game includes a cassette tape featuring the music of 32 instruments. On side one, each instrument demonstrates its sound and tells about itself and its history; side two includes the sounds of the instruments alone. Kids match sounds to labeled picture cards of the instruments, using these to play four games, all variants on bingo.

$15
Aristoplay
450 S. Wagner Rd.
Ann Arbor, MI 48107
(800) 634-7738 or (888) GR8-GAME
fax (734) 995-4611
Web site: www.aristoplay.com

Music Math Cards

A card game with which players simultaneously learn musical notes and math. The cards, patterned with mice and cats, come in sets of three, at three levels of difficulty. (Cards with only one mouse or cat are the simplest; cards with three mice or cats, the hardest.) The game, at each level, involves pairing a mouse card with the appropriate cat card. This requires matching musical notes and mathematical operations. For example, at the one-mouse level, four quarter notes (a mouse card) equals one whole note (a cat card); or a quarter note × 2 (mouse) equals a half note (cat). By the three-mouse level, kids are dealing with trickier problems, trying to find matches for a half note minus four sixteenth notes or a quarter note times 6.

$7.95
Diversity Press
Box 376
Bethel, VT 05032
(802) 234-9179/fax (802) 234-6334

Thumb Piano Kit

Kids build and paint a $6\frac{1}{2} \times 5$-inch African mbira, using precut wood pieces and bamboo sticks. The kit includes playing instructions, a beginner's guide to reading music, and several song sheets that allow thumb piano makers to play such tunes as "London Bridge" and "Twinkle Twinkle Little Star" on their new instrument.

$13.50 from toy and game stores; for a local source, contact
Curiosity Kits
Box 811

Cockeysville, MD 21030

(410) 584-2605 or (800) 584-KITS/fax (410) 584-1247

e-mail: CKitsinc@aol.com

AUDIOVISUAL RESOURCES

Carnival of the Animals

A favorite selection for introducing young listeners to classical music is Camille Saint-Saëns's *Carnival of the Animals,* written in 1886, in which each short musical piece represents a different animal. Many versions are available, including a video production by puppeteer Jim Gamble—the animals are marvelous marionettes—and an animation and live-action video featuring real live animals and the kids of the Los Angeles Youth Orchestra. For kids aged 3 and up.

Music for Little People

4320 Marine Ave.

Box 1720

Lawndale, CA 90260

(800) 727-2233

or

Educational Record Center, Inc.

3233 Burnt Mill Dr., Suite 100

Wilmington, NC 28403-2698

(800) 438-1637/fax (888) 438-1637

e-mail: erc-inc@worldnet.att.net

Web site: www.erc-inc.com

Classical Kids Series

Susan Hammond's *Classical Kids* series is simply superb. The audio series, available on audiocassette or CD, combines information about the lives of famous composers with imaginative stories and music from the featured composer's best-known works. The stories are delightful; the historical information is fascinatingly presented; and the music is, of course, wonderful. In "Beethoven Lives Upstairs" (also see page 757), impressions of the peculiar composer are narrated by the young boy who lives downstairs, Christoph, in letters to his uncle in Vienna; included are excerpts from the *Moonlight* Sonata, and from Symphonies nos. 5, 6, 7, 8, and 9. "Mr. Bach Comes to Call"—our favorite; the boys are Bach fans—features a little girl named

Elizabeth who is resentfully practicing the piano when Bach himself drops by, accompanied by an entire boys' choir. Bach tells the story of his life—which included 20 children and a stint in jail—and plays excerpts from the Brandenburg Concertos, the Goldberg Variations, and "Jesu, Joy of Man's Desiring." "Tchaikovsky Visits America" (also see page 758) tells of the composer's visit to New York in 1891, through the eyes of a little girl who meets him on a train trip to Niagara Falls. In "Mozart's Magic Fantasy," Sarah stumbles into the world of Mozart's opera and meets with a talking dragon; in Vivaldi's "Ring of Mystery," a young girl comes to the orphanage in Venice where Vivaldi serves as music director, and participates in a musical Venetian Carnival, complete with excerpts from the *Four Seasons, The Double Trumpet Concerto,* and *La Notte;* and in "Hallelujah Handel!," a young orphan boy living behind the London Opera House meets the famous composer and is found to have a truly extraordinary talent. All are marvelous; your kids will listen to these time and again.

For an enhanced educational experience, "Classical Kids Teacher's Notes" are available to accompany each recording, with suggestions for presenting the music to children, background musical and historical information, sheet music, student activities and projects, a glossary, and a bibliography of related readings. "Beethoven Lives Upstairs" is also available on video and on an interactive CD-ROM (Mac or PC).

The Children's Group

1400 Bayly St., Suite 7

Pickering, Ontario L1W 3R2, Canada

(905) 831-1142

or

West Music

1212 5th St.

Box 5521

Coralville, IA 52241

(319) 351-0482 or (800) 397-9378/fax (888) 470-3942

e-mail: service@westmusic.com

Web site: www.westmusic.com

The Composers' Specials Series

A series of six beautifully done videos intended to introduce kids to the lives and music of classical composers. In each, the story centers around a child who is paired with a famous composer in the telling of an exciting story. The action in each case proceeds against a background of the featured composer's best-known works.

"Rossini's Ghost," for example, set in 1862, begins with a little girl, Reliana, in the kitchen helping her grandmother with the cooking and listening to her stories about her life in the theater, back in the days when she knew the composer Rossini. Reliana, fascinated, tries on one of her grandmother's old stage costumes and is magically transported back in time to 1816, the year of the opening of Rossini's opera *The Barber of Seville*. Reliana, invisible to everyone but Rossini himself, is able to help when one of the singers puts a curse on the production and disasters begin to strike.

In "Liszt's Rhapsody," Franz Liszt, the world's greatest concert pianist, meets Josy, a young Gypsy street performer, and wagers that he can turn him into a world-class musician; in "Bizet's Dream," 12-year-old Michelle dislikes her cantankerous music teacher, M. Bizet—until he tells her the marvelous tale of his new opera, *Carmen;* and in "Handel's Last Chance," set in Dublin in 1742, the composer gets 10-year-old Jamie O'Flaherty out of jail—he was caught stealing in an attempt to help his poverty-stricken family—and Jamie, who sings like an angel, participates in the first performance of Handel's *Messiah*. Other titles include "Strauss: The King of Three-Quarter Time" and "Bach's Fight for Freedom." Each video is about 50 minutes long; all are intended for kids aged 7–11.

The set (6 videos), $99.95; single titles, $19.95

West Music

1212 5th St.

Box 5521

Coralville, IA 52241

(319) 351-0482 or (800) 397-9378/fax (888) 470-3942

e-mail: service@westmusic.com

Web site: www.westmusic.com

Concert Masterworks

A 32-lesson lecture and listening series by Professor Robert Greenberg of the San Francisco Conservatory of Music. The course is divided into four parts, each covering two musical "masterworks." Part I includes pieces by Mozart and Beethoven; Part II, Dvorák and Strauss; Part III, Beethoven and Brahms; and Part IV, Mendelssohn and Liszt. Each lecture covers the life, times, and musical style of the composers, with detailed analyses of the featured musical compositions, and a musical presentation, accompanied by a "WordScore Guide," which allows students to visualize the technical structure of the piece while listening to the music. For teenagers and adults.

Available in audio and video versions. Audio series, $199.95; video series, $299.95

The Teaching Co.

7405 Alban Station Ct., Suite A107

Springfield, VA 22150-2318

(800) 832-2412/fax (703) 912-7756

See *How to Understand and Listen to Great Music* (page 766) and *How to Listen to and Understand Opera* (page 761).

Elements of Jazz: From Cakewalks to Fusion

An eight-part lecture and listening series by Bill Messenger of the Peabody Conservatory of Music. The lessons combine lectures and music, including piano playing by Messenger himself. Lesson titles include "Plantation Beginnings," "The Rise and Fall of Ragtime," "The Jazz Age," "Blues," "The Swing Era," "Boogie, Big Band Blues, and Bop," "Modern Jazz," and "The ABC's of Jazz Improvisation." Each lesson is 45 minutes long. For teenagers and adults.

Available in audio and video versions. Audio series, $69.95; video series, $109.95.

The Teaching Co.

7405 Alban Station Ct., Suite A107

Springfield, VA 22150-2318

(800) 832-2412/fax (703) 912-7756

Fantasia

Disney's famous 1940 animation and classical-music combo, featuring dancing mushrooms, dinosaurs, balletic hippos, and Mickey Mouse as a disobedient sorcerer's apprentice, all to selections by Bach, Beethoven, Tchaikovsky, Stravinsky, and others.

$29.95

Movies Unlimited

3015 Darnell Rd.

Philadelphia, PA 19154

(215) 637-4444 or (800) 4-MOVIES

e-mail: movies@moviesunlimited.com

Web site: www.moviesunlimited.com

How to Understand and Listen to Great Music: The Greenberg Lectures

A 48-lesson lecture and guided listening series on the history of music, for older teenagers and adults. The course, taught by Professor Robert Greenberg of the San Francisco Conservatory of Music, is divided into six parts: "Sources: The Ancient World Through the Early Baroque," "The High Baroque," "The Classical Era I," "The Classical Era II and the Age of Revolution," "Nineteenth-Century Romanticism," and "From Romanticism to Modernism." Each part includes eight 45-minute lecture-and-listening sessions.

> Available in audio or video versions. Audio series, $249.95; video series, $549.95
> The Teaching Co.
> 7405 Alban Station Ct., Suite A107
> Springfield, VA 22150-2318
> (800) 832-2412/fax (703) 912-7756

See *Concert Masterworks* (page 765) and *How to Listen to and Understand Opera* (page 761).

The Life, Times, and Music Series
Friedman/Fairfax

A book-and-CD series designed to introduce novices to different styles of music and the historical context in which the music was played. "Strike Up the Orchestra: A Child's Guide to Classical Music," for example, includes the "William Tell Overture," the "March of the Toreadors" from *Carmen*, "Spring" from Vivaldi's *Four Seasons*, "The Sorcerer's Apprentice," and the first movement of Bach's *Brandenburg Concerto no. 4*. The accompanying short, illustrated book includes information on history of classical music and the lives of the composers.

Other titles in the series include "Dixieland: The Birth of Jazz," with selections by Louis Armstrong, Bix Beiderbecke, and Jelly Roll Morton; "Folk," with songs by Woody Guthrie, Burl Ives, Pete Seeger, and Joan Baez; "Big Bands," with selections by Benny Goodman, Duke Ellington, Tommy Dorsey, and Woody Herman; "*The Baroque Era*," "*The Story of the Blues*," "*Singing Cowboys*," "*Bluegrass*," "*The Romantic Era*," and "*Mozart*."

The Living Instrument Series
Barrie Carson Turner; Alfred A. Knopf, 1996

A terrific series of 48-page books, each featuring a separate instrument, with accompanying full-length CD. The books, beautifully illustrated with color photographs and paintings, include short biographies of composers and detailed information about the history and structure of the featured instrument. CDs each contain 10 musical selections. Titles include *The Living Clarinet*, *The Living Flute*, *The Living Piano*, and *The Living Violin*.

Making and Playing Homemade Instruments

By musicians Cathy Fink and Marcy Marxer, this 60-minute videotape, which looks like a kick for 5–10-year-olds, shows kids how to make and play nine musical instruments, mostly from household junk. Watchers learn how to recycle oatmeal boxes and bleach bottles into banjos, soup cans into maracas, and bottle caps and rubber bands into castanets. The first instrument on the tape is the "mouthbow"—the "simplest instrument in the whole wide world"—which Fink and Marxer whip together using nylon fishing line and plain old sticks (the outside version) or store-bought yardsticks (the inside version). Last are those down-home classics, the washtub bass and washboard; and the tape ends with a rousing rendition of "Mama Don't Allow."

Fink and Marxer also reveal the elusive trick of playing the spoons, which happy piece of instruction emptied our silverware drawer and had everybody clacking enthusiastically for days.

> $19.95
> Homespun Tapes
> Box 694
> Woodstock, NY 12498
> (914) 246-2550 or (800) 33-TAPES

See *Mama Don't Allow* (page 759).

Marsalis on Music

A four-part video series from the television miniseries/book featuring jazz musician and classical trumpeter Wynton Marsalis. Titles include "Why Toes Tap," "Listening for Clues," "From Sousa to Satchmo," and "Tackling the Monster." A terrific introduction to the joys of music for kids and families.

Set of 4 videotapes, $72; single videos, $19.95

West Music

1212 5th St.

Box 5521

Coralville, IA 52241

(319) 351-0482 or (800) 397-9378/fax (888) 470-3942

e-mail: service@westmusic.com

Web site: www.westmusic.com

See **Marsalis on Music** (pages 752 and 769).

The Lives and Music of the Great Masters Series

Moss Music Group

There are three sets in this audio series, each covering seven composers on six cassette tapes or CDs. Set I includes Bach, Mozart, Chopin, Mendelssohn, Schubert, Schumann, and Grieg; Set II, Handel, Beethoven, Haydn, Wagner, Dvořák, Vivaldi, and Corelli; and Set III, Tchaikovsky, Brahms, Strauss, Berlioz, Verdi, Foster, and Sousa. On each tape, selections of music by the composer alternate with narrated biographical segments. The tapes are about 40 minutes long and include about 25 musical selections, which means listeners only hear snippets of each. Our boys found this annoyingly choppy—"Just as you start listening to the music, somebody starts talking!"—but the Michael Olaf catalog (see page 26), which sells them, explains that the effect is that of a story set to music.

$24.95 per set (cassettes) or $35 (CDs)

Educational Record Center, Inc.

3233 Burnt Mill Dr., Suite 100

Wilmington, NC 28403-2698

(800) 438-1637/fax (888) 438-1637

e-mail: erc-inc@worldnet.att.net

Web site: www.erc-inc.com

The Orchestra

This award-winning recording, warmly narrated by Peter Ustinov, introduces young listeners to the wonderful and varied sounds of music and to the four major instrument families of the orchestra: strings, woodwinds, brass, and percussion. Excerpts from famous classical pieces are used as musical illustrations.

Cassette, $10.95; CD, $15.98

Educational Record Center, Inc.

3233 Burnt Mill Dr., Suite 100

Wilmington, NC 28403-2698

(800) 438-1637/fax (888) 438-1637

e-mail: erc-inc@worldnet.att.net

Web site: www.erc-inc.com

Peter and the Wolf

An enchanting and kid-appealing classic by Prokofiev. Many versions are available, among them a puppet production on video, starring Jim Gamble's marionettes; animated performances on video, including a "Storyteller's Classic" production narrated by Dudley Moore; and a version narrated by Sting, with life-size puppets, live actors, and music by the Chamber Orchestra of Europe.

Educational Record Center, Inc.

3233 Burnt Mill Dr., Suite 100

Wilmington, NC 28403-2698

(800) 438-1637/fax (888) 438-1637

e-mail: erc-inc@worldnet.att.net

Web site: www.erc-inc.com

or

Movies Unlimited

3015 Darnell Rd.

Philadelphia, PA 19154

(212) 637-4444 or (800) 4-MOVIES

e-mail: movies@moviesunlimited.com

Web site: www.moviesunlimited.com

COMPUTER SOFTWARE

Apple Pie Music: History of American Music

A historical survey of American music, from American Indian chants through Pilgrim psalms, African tribal music, slave spirituals, ragtime, the Big Band era, and rock and roll. Kids can hear over 400 classic songs, accompanied by period artwork, photographs, biographies of composers, and an explanatory text. On CD-ROM for Mac or Windows.

$75

Zenger Media

10200 Jefferson Blvd.

Box 802

Culver City, CA 90232-0802

(310) 839-2436 or (800) 421-4246/fax (310) 839-2249

or (800) 944-5432

e-mail: access@ZengerMedia.com

Web site: www.ZengerMedia.com/Zenger

Making Music

Musical composition for kids. Users enter notes by "painting" them on the screen; then they modify volume, tempo, and instrumentation, and play back the end result. Also included is a "Melody and Rhythm Maker"; "Building Blocks," with which kids can rearrange, transpose, and restructure six simple tunes; and "Mix 'n' Match," with which kids can combine a range of melodies, rhythms, and instrument groups, choosing from a musical flip-book of possibilities. On CD-ROM for Mac or Windows.

$29.95

Learn Technologies Interactive

Box 2284

S. Burlington, VT 05407

(888) 292-5584

Web site: voyager.learntech.com

Music Ace

A 24-lesson introduction to music for beginners of all ages, under the tutelage of Maestro Max and his animated choir of singing notes. Users learn all the basics, including staff and keyboard relationships, note reading and the notes of the grand staff, scales and octaves, sharps, flats, and key signatures. Each lesson includes a creative (and challenging) game, and kids also get to compose their own music, using a variety of instrumental sounds, on the "Music Doodle Pad." On CD-ROM for Mac or Windows.

$49.95

Harmonic Vision

906 University Pl.

Evanston, IL 60201

(800) 644-4994

Web site: www.harmonicvision.com

MUSIC ON-LINE

America's Shrine to Music Museum

The Shrine to Music Museum is dedicated to the study of the history of musical instruments. The site includes a virtual gallery tour of musical instruments from many cultures and historical periods. Each entry is accompanied by descriptive background information.

www.usd.edu/smm

Big Ears

The "original on-line ear trainer" for listeners of all ages. Having a "good ear," the introduction explains, is a teachable skill, necessary for such activities as sight-singing, aural recognition, and playing a musical instrument "by ear." The program is an interval driller: a random interval is played, over a range of two octaves; listeners are challenged to identify the sound.

www.pageplus.com/~bigears/index.html

Children's Music List

A large list of links to music-related sites for kids, including music reviews, performance calendars, educational resources, on-line fun and games, songbooks, and music stores.

www.cowboy.net/~mharper/Chmusiclist.html

Children's Music Web

A large index of children's music sites on the Web, a kid's concert calendar, information about favorite kids' artists with accompanying audio clips, music organizations for kids, educational resources, and an on-line kid's music magazine.

www.childrensmusic.org

CISV (Children's International Summer Village) Songbook

The words to 170 children's songs, many in foreign language versions, some with accompanying guitar chords. "Brother John," for example, is listed in English, Icelandic, Italian, Spanish, French, Finnish, Swedish, Thai, Romanian, Portuguese, Turkish, German, Dutch, Danish, Norwegian, Chinese, and Japanese.

antenna.nl/~wwwcisv/songs.html

Classical Composer Biographies

Portraits, brief biographies, and many links to related sites.

www.cl.cam.ac.uk/users/mn200/music/composers.html

Classical Composer Listings
A featured "Today's Birthday Composer" with portrait and biography, as well as pictures, biographies, and timelines of many many classical composers.

spight.physics.univ.edu/picgalr2.html

Classical World: Opera
Includes general information on opera, detailed synopses of the plots of famous operas with audio clips, and lists of recommended recordings.

classicalmus.com/opera

Internet Resources for Music Teachers
An immense list of resources for kids in grades K–12, categorized under "Band," "Orchestra," "Vocal," "Classroom," and "All Music."

www.isd77.k12.mn.us/resources/staffpages/shirks/music.html

J. S. Bach Home Page
A biography and portrait of Bach, a complete list of his works, reviews of modern Bach recordings, and links to other Bach-related sites.

www.jsbach.org

John Philip Sousa Page
A biography of the King of Marching Bands, with audio clips of Sousa marches to download.

www.dws.org/sousa/about.htm

Lullabies and Other Songs for Children
This colorful site decorated with cheerful teddy bears lists the lyrics to over 300 kids' songs, indexed alphabetically.

www.stairway.org/kidsongs

Marsalis on Music
Color photographs, audio clips, interactive games, and the text from the book (see page 752) in four segments: "Why Toes Tap," "Listening for Clues," "From Sousa to Satchmo," and "Tackling the Monster." There's also a "Music Educator's Guide," with suggestions for supplementary activities and a list of links to on-line music discussion groups.

www.wnet.org/archive/mom/index.html

Music: The Universal Language!
Links to articles on music education, classroom lesson plans, and "Fun Music Ideas," a collection of music-related activities for kids of all ages. Included are suggestions for study units about individual composers, listening lessons, finger plays, and instructions for making homemade instruments.

www.jumpoint.com/bluesman

Online Antique Phonograph Gallery
Many examples of antique phonographs, with color photographs, historical background information, and audio clips.

www.inkyfingers.com/Record.html

Piano on the Net
Piano lessons on-line, for beginning, intermediate, and advanced players. Lessons include a detailed text, piano keyboard diagrams, and music; students need to supply their own pianos or practice keyboards.

www.artdsm.com/music.html

Pitter Patter Music
An on-line music store for kids. Selections are categorized under "Country/Blues," "Lullabies," "Classical," "Rock 'n' Roll," and "Toddler." Each selection is accompanied by a description or brief review; many include sample audio clips.

www.asis.com/pitter

Ray Dretske's Computers in Music Online
A site devoted to the use of computers for teaching and composing music. Included are hints for would-be composers, teacher resources and information, software and hardware recommendations, a dictionary of Music Technology Terms (in alphabetical order, beginning with *amplifier*), a Music Technology Quiz ("What is a sequencer?"), and a multiple-choice "Test Your Musical Knowledge Quiz" ("Which of the following is *not* a famous jazz trumpet player?").

utg.org/cimonline

Sesame Street Lyrics Archive
All the songs from the children's PBS series, many with accompanying audio.

globalserve.net/~rhonda/sesame1.html

Virtual Keyboard
🌐 **ALL** The site features a diagram of the piano keyboard. Click on a key and hear the note.
www.xmission.com/~mgm/misc/keyboard.html

DRAMA

Our kids like plays. They loved children's theater performances when they were small—I remember taking them to a riotous production of *The Emperor's New Clothes* and an even more hilarious performance of *Greek Myths*, which they talked about for months. Now, as teenagers, they enjoy more challenging theater. We're lucky to have access to a number of local playhouses and drama-supporting colleges. Last year we saw *The Devil's Disciple*, *Our Town*, and a stunningly imaginative performance of *Hamlet* by a visiting Shakespeare company.

The boys also—at least two of them—love to perform. A family tradition in our house is the annual Christmas Eve play, put on for an audience of two parents, since the boys were toddlers. That first year they did a very short version of "Rudolph the Red-Nosed Reindeer," in which Ethan played Santa Claus, Caleb—who wasn't talking yet—played a very unpredictable elf, and Josh, outfitted in felt antlers and a red-paper nose, played Rudolph. They then ran through several home-grown and hilarious variations on familiar Christmas stories: "The Bear Who Slept Through Christmas," "The Polar Express" (with a wonderful train made out of cardboard boxes by Ethan), "Granny Glittens and Her Amazing Mittens," "Giant Grummer's Christmas," and (with everybody playing multiple characters) "A Christmas Carol." At first I did most of the writing of the plays and the inventing of the costumes; as time went by, however, the boys took over. We then had—among others—"Fractured Christmas Carols," "The Mistletoe Bandit" (which featured a chain saw), and the saga of the Political Correctness Elf, who goes from house to house on Christmas morning snatching politically incorrect gifts out of the hands of happy little children.

Last year on public radio we heard David Mamet's *Deer Dogs*, which lasted a mere five minutes from beginning to end. Josh was so entranced by the thought of a five-minute play that he proceeded to write a series of his own, co-opting his brothers as supporting actors. They then moved on to recording their performances on cassette tape (with Ethan, who is shy, doing the sound effects) or on video (with Ethan running the camera). Now there's talk of joining a young people's theater group this summer. Josh wants to write; Caleb wants to act; and Ethan says he'll paint scenery.

From my homeschool journal:

◆ **February 3, 1992. Josh is ten; Ethan, nine; Caleb, seven.**

For Josh, who has developed a passion for Shakespeare, I've just written a personal "Shakespeare Activity Book," centered around his two favorite plays, Macbeth *and* Hamlet. *He's decided to do a bit every day and is tickled to have a private project. First project: he reread the story of "Macbeth" in Leon Garfield's* Shakespeare Stories *(see page 93). Then, using the encyclopedia, he figured out who was the ruler of England when Shakespeare wrote the play (King James I). James, he discovered, inherited the throne from Elizabeth I, Good Queen Bess. He read a short biography of Elizabeth and drew a color portrait of her, complete with spectacular red wig. He then roped his brothers into reenacting scenes from* Macbeth, *with Josh as Macbeth, Ethan as Macduff, and Caleb as all the foot soldiers and Birnam Wood.*

◆ **February 4, 1992**

Josh memorized the famous witches' speech ("Double, double, toil and trouble . . .") from Macbeth *and we recorded him on cassette tape, sounding positively evil. Much general interest in the ingredients in the witches' spell: "What's a howlet?" "Are bats really woolly?" "What's a blindworm? Are they poisonous?"*

Josh then located Scotland on the world map and learned a bit about the battles between the Romans and the Picts and the reason for Hadrian's Wall.

◆ **February 5, 1992**

Josh still working through his Macbeth book. He read a short story about the Scottish king Robert the

Bruce and his lucky escape from the English soldiers because a spider had spun a web across the mouth of the cave where he was hiding. Project: Josh researched interesting spiders and drew a spider diagram, labeling all body parts.

◆ **February 6, 1992**

Josh tackled Macbeth's castle. Shakespeare never described it, so Josh read two books about castles, then designed one of his own, complete with boiling oil barrels on the upper walls. If Macbeth had simply stayed inside it, says Josh, Macduff wouldn't have stood a chance.

◆ **February 7, 1992**

So what did Macbeth wear? We discussed clans and tartans and looked at pictures of some representative plaids. Josh designed an "Official Macbeth Tartan."

◆ **February 10, 1992**

More Scottish geography. Josh looked through a collection of picture books on Scotland; located the Firth of Forth and Loch Ness on the map, learning about the importance of each. Josh drew some impressive pictures of the Loch Ness monster, and Ethan designed a machine for sensing its presence underwater.

◆ **February 11, 1992**

Josh memorized Macbeth's "Tomorrow and tomorrow and tomorrow . . ." speech and we discussed its meaning. Josh prefers the witches.

◆ **February 12, 1992**

Macbeth and math. Josh and I read aloud an essay by John McPhee about a visit to Birnam Wood ("From Birnam Wood to Dunsinane" in Pieces of the Frame), in which the McPhee family visited an oak said to have been standing in the days of Macbeth. Six people could just get their arms around it. We managed to determine the circumference and diameter of Macbeth's last tree.

◆ **February 13, 1992**

Listened to a tape of Scottish bagpipe music and looked up bagpipes in assorted reference books.

◆ **February 14, 1992**

A brief overview of "Other Famous People From Scotland Besides Macbeth." Josh read poems by Robert Burns and Robert Louis Stevenson (Treasure Island, Josh says, was much better), and read short accounts of the lives and work of James Watt and Alexander Fleming. In honor of Fleming, the boys started growing some penicillium mold: they dampened slices of bread, covered them with plastic wrap, and set them in a warm corner of the kitchen. We're now waiting for them to turn blue-green.

◆ **February 15, 1992**

Josh memorized Macbeth's speech delivered just before his fatal fight with Macduff, with gleeful emphasis on the "and damned be him that first cries 'Hold, enough!'"

I made the boys a trio of plaid sashes for Macbeth reenactments.

◆ **February 19, 1992**

Josh has moved on to Hamlet. Today he read a prose version of the play and began making a model human skull (from a biology kit). He'll need it, he says, for the Yorick scene.

Catalogs

Pioneer Drama Service

ALL A catalog of over 350 plays for performers and audiences of all ages, including full-length plays, one-act plays, musicals, melodramas, and seasonal plays. For each, the catalog lists cast size, set description, playing time, royalty price (per public performance), and a brief summary of the plot. Of particular interest for young actors may be the "Storyteller & Participation

Theatre" plays, in which kids from the audience participate in the performances, joining Alice, for example, at the Mad Hatter's Tea Party and on the Queen of Hearts' croquet lawn; becoming Munchkins in the wonderful land of Oz; and assisting the Pied Piper and the Mayor of Hamelin Town (in this version, the Piper gets rid of the rats but doesn't steal the kids). The catalog also carries "The Globe Theatre Series," a selection of Shakespearean plays abridged for young actors, among them *A Midsummer Night's Dream, Much Ado About Nothing, The Taming of the Shrew,* and *Romeo and Juliet.*

> Pioneer Drama Service, Inc.
> Box 22555
> Denver, CO 80222-0555
> (303) 759-4297/fax (303) 759-0475

Shakespeare: The Writing Company

A large catalog of Shakespeare resources for kids of all ages, including many materials for young actors: collections of plays, complete and abridged, collections of Shakespearean scenes and monologues, books on Shakespearean make-up, costumes, and stage production, a scale cardboard model of Shakespeare's Globe Theatre, and collections of dramatic games and activities. An excellent resource.

> The Writing Co./Social Studies School Service
> 10200 Jefferson Blvd.
> Box 802
> Culver City, CA 90232-0802
> (310) 839-2436 or (800) 421-4246/fax (310) 839-2249
> or (800) 944-5432
> e-mail: access@WritingCo.com
> Web site: WritingCo.com/Shakespeare

Smith and Kraus, Inc.

Smith and Kraus publishes an excellent line of drama-related books for kids, including plays, monologues, and drama workbooks for children of all ages.

> Smith and Kraus, Inc.
> 1 Main St.
> Box 127
> Lyme, NH 03768
> (603) 922-5118 or (800) 895-4331

MAGAZINES

Plays: The Drama Magazine for Young People

Plays, Inc., the publisher of *Plays* magazines, does not send out sample copies of their magazine. They do, however, provide a descriptive flier. *Plays* is published seven times a year, October through May. Each issue contains 8 to 10 plays, in order by appropriate age level, for kids in elementary through high school. The plays cover a wide range of themes and topics, including national and traditional holidays, American history, science fiction, fairy and folktales, readings and recitations, choral readings, and puppet productions.

> Annual subscription, $28
> Plays, Inc.
> 120 Boylston St.
> Boston, MA 02116-4615
> (617) 423-3157/fax (617) 423-2168

BOOKS

Center Stage: A Curriculum for the Performing Arts

Wayne D. Cook; Dale Seymour Publications

A large collection of activity-based lessons in creative dramatics for kids in grades K–6. The lessons attempt to approach drama through aesthetic perception, historical and cultural background topics, and creative expression, which encourages kids to invent, perform, and interpret stories through language and movement.

Supplementary materials are available to accompany the curriculum guide, including posters, an instructional book, *Dramatizing Aesop's Fables* (Louise Thistle), audiocassettes with readings of eight folktales suitable for dramatization, and *Story Scripts,* a booklet of the stories on the cassettes.

> *Center Stage,* $28.95
> Cuisenaire/Dale Seymour Publications
> Box 5026
> White Plains, NY 10602-5026
> (800) 872-1100 or (800) 237-3142/fax (914) 328-5487
> Web site: www.aw.com/dsp

THE ARTS

Costume

L. Rowland-Warne; Alfred A. Knopf, 1992

The Eyewitness history of costume, from the earliest origins of clothing to the present day. The book is illustrated with color photographs, many of history reenactors in elaborate period garb. Included are a winter-bundled Viking, a Roman aristocrat, a 14th-century lady, a 16th-century courtier in ruff and doublet, and an 18th-century "Macaroni" in powdered wig and patches.

Dazzling Disguises and Clever Costumes

Angela Wilkes; Dorling Kindersley, 1997

Instructions and templates for over 50 kids' costumes to make, paint, and sew, among them a pirate, a knight, Robin Hood, a Hawaiian dancer, and a robot. Illustrated with color photographs.

KidVid

Kaye Black; Zephyr Press

If you are the owner of an underused home video camera, this may be the resource for you. *KidVid* by Kaye Black is an illustrated 96-page "Fundamentals of Video Instruction" manual, which tells film-minded kids everything they need to know about making their very own video movie. Included are information and instructions about script writing and set design, production techniques (camera shots, lighting, sound, production cues, editing), and operation of the equipment. Recommended for film directors in grades 4–12.

$25
Zephyr Press
3316 N. Chapel Ave.
Box 66006
Tucson, AZ 85728-6006
(800) 232-2187/fax (520) 323-9402
e-mail: neways2learn@zephyrpress.com
Web site: www.zephyrpress.com

Live On Stage!

Carla Blank and Jody Roberts; Dale Seymour Publications

Games and activities for theater arts and dance, intended to develop student "self-image and social relationships" and to teach kids about the different cultures and periods in which various styles of drama and dance originated. The 253-page *Teacher Resource Book* includes suggestions for incorporating the performing arts into the curriculum, with scripts and background information; the 260-page *Student Edition* lists drama- and dance-associated student activities, such as keeping a theater journal and researching various periods and genres in theater history.

Teacher Resource Book, $35; *Student Edition,* $24.95
Cuisenaire/Dale Seymour Publications
Box 5026
White Plains, NY 10602-5026
(800) 872-1100 or (800) 237-3142
fax (914) 328-5487
Web site: www.awl.com/dsp

Make Costumes!

Priscilla Hershberger; North Light Books, 1992

Patterns and instructions for imaginative costumes for kids aged 6–11. Users can turn out assorted animal head masks, capes, armor, and truly unusual hats, plus a wonderful variety of finished costumes, among them an angel, American Indian, ballerina, bumblebee, clown, devil, dragon, knight, mermaid, pirate, Robin Hood, turtle, vampire, witch, and wizard.

On Stage: Theater Games and Activities for Kids

Lisa Bany-Winters; Chicago Review Press, 1997

Games, activities, and ready-to-use scripts for kids aged 7–12. Readers make puppets, build sets, and experiment with makeup, try some improvisational exercises, and perform monologues, scenes, and short plays. Possibilities include *Rip Van Winkle, Rapunzel,* and *The Cat Who Walked by Himself.*

Playbuilding Shakespeare

Wendy Michaels; Cambridge University Press, 1997

The Bard onstage for teenagers. Kids study five of Shakespeare's plays, preparing to stage a version of their own. Background information and activity suggestions are included. The book covers *Midsummer Night's Dream, Merchant of Venice, Julius Caesar, Romeo and Juliet,* and *Macbeth.*

Putting on a Play: The Young Playwright's Guide to Scripting, Directing, and Performing

Nancy Bentley and Donna Guthrie; Millbrook Press, 1996

A 64-page how-to guide for dramatists aged 8–11. The book covers several types of plays, the essential elements in writing a play, and the various stages of play production. Includes excerpts from sample scripts.

PLAYS FOR KIDS

 Childsplay: A Collection of Scenes and Monologues for Children

Kerry Muir, ed.; Limelight Editions, 1995

A 260-page collection of scenes and monologues from many varied sources, including plays, movies, teleplays, poems, and diaries, for kids of all ages.

Easy-to-Read Folk and Fairy Tale Plays

Carol Pugliano and Carolyn Croll; Scholastic, 1997

A collection of short simple plays based on familiar stories for early elementary students.

Famous Americans: 22 Short Plays for the Classroom

Liza Schafer; Scholastic, 1995

A collection of short fact-based plays for performers in grades 4–8, each centering around a famous American historical figure. Featured subjects include Benjamin Franklin, Harriet Tubman, Susan B. Anthony, Lewis and Clark, Abraham Lincoln, Rosa Parks, Alexander Graham Bell, the Wright brothers, Jackie Robinson, and Nelly Bly.

Five Plays: For Girls and Boys to Perform

Pleasant Company, 1995

Five plays, each based on one of the characters in the historical American Girls collection, with historical background information, production tips, and preparatory drama exercises and activities.

See **Pleasant Company** (page 448).

Monologues for Kids

Ruth Mae Roddy; Dramaline Productions, 1995

A collection of 28 one-page monologues for young actors (14 for girls, 14 for boys). For each, there's space in the book for notes and comments by the reader. By the same author: *Kids' Stuff: 30 Great Audition Pieces for Children* (Dramaline Productions, 1993).

Out of the Bag: The Paperbag Players Book of Plays

Judith Martin; Disney Press, 1997

A 48-page book of short plays for kids aged 8–12, all using props and costumes made from simple everyday materials such as paper bags and cardboard boxes.

Plays Around the Year

Liza Schafer; Scholastic, 1995

Over 20 simple thematic plays for kids in grades 1–3. Topics include butterfly life cycles, George Washington, Martin Luther King Jr., the weather, Chinese New Year, and a reenactment of Hans Christian Andersen's "The Ugly Duckling." Associated cross-curricular activities and book links are listed for each play.

Princess, Cowboy, Pirate, Elf

Liz Boyd; Hyperion, 1995

Fourteen very short two-person plays for actors aged 4–8, with nine full-color hats to be used as costumes.

Readers Theatre Series

 Teacher Ideas Press

A series of reproducible scripts with performance guidelines, variously suitable for kids in grades 1–12. Titles include *Fifty Fabulous Fables: Beginning Readers Theatre* (Suzanne I. Barchers; 1997); *Readers Theatre for Children* (Mildred Knight Laughlin and Kathy Howard Latrobe; 1990); and *Readers Theatre for Young Adults* (Kathy Howard Latrobe and Mildred Knight Laughlin; 1989). *Readers Theatre for Children,* for example, recommended for kids in grades 4–6, includes complete scripts based on children's classics, among them *Little Women* and *The Secret Garden,* plus scenes from popular novels such as *Tuck Everlasting, The Wish Giver,* and *Stone Fox,* to be used as starting points for kids writing their own scripts. *Social Studies*

Readers Theatre for Children (Mildred Knight Laughlin, Peggy Tubbs Black, and Margery Kibby Loberg; 1991) includes scripts based on American tall-tale characters such as Paul Bunyan and Pecos Bill, a unit based on the Laura Ingalls Wilder *Little House* books, and 60 script starters for young writers. *Great Moments in Science: Experiments and Readers Theatre* (Kendall Haven; 1996) contains 12 scripts for kids in grades 4–9 dramatizing important events in the history of science.

> Libraries Unlimited
> Box 6633
> Englewood, CO 80155-6633
> (303) 770-1220 or (800) 237-6124/fax (303) 220-8843
> e-mail: lu-books@lu.com
> Web site: www.lu.com

DRAMA AND LITERATURE

5 9 *Arthur's Thanksgiving*

Marc Brown; Little, Brown, 1984

Nobody wants to play the turkey in the class Thanksgiving play, so finally Arthur decides to do it himself.

4 8 *The Berenstain Bears Get Stage Fright*

Stan and Jan Berenstain; Random House, 1986

Brother and Sister Bear are starring in a school play; Sister Bear worries about learning her lines and suffers from stage fright. (But it's Brother, who claimed to know his part forward, backward, and upside down, who dries up onstage.) For readers aged 4–8.

7 + *The Best Christmas Pageant Ever*

Barbara Robinson; HarperTrophy, 1988

This funny and touching short chapter book tells the story of the truly horrible Herdman children who take over the annual church Christmas play, changing themselves and all around them in the process. A delight for all ages.

4 8 *The Bionic Bunny Show*

Marc Brown and Laurie Krasny Brown; Little, Brown, 1985

Wilbur plays the Bionic Bunny, star of a television superhero show. The book follows the production of a Bionic Bunny episode. Funny and informational. This book was a "Reading Rainbow" selection.

4 8 *Hattie the Backstage Bat*

Don Freeman; Viking, 1988

Hattie, who lives in the rafters of the theater, makes a hit in a new mystery play. For readers aged 4–8.

5 9 *Mother, Mother, I Feel Sick, Send for the Doctor Quick, Quick, Quick*

Remy Charlip and Burton Supree; Buccaneer Books, 1993

A shadow play based on the traditional rhyme, in which a little boy swallows everything from apples, a ball, and a birthday cake to the dishes on the table. The book includes instructions for hanging up a bedsheet and putting on a shadow performance of your own.

8 11 *The Mystery on Stage*

Gertrude Chandler Warner; Albert Whitman, 1994

A volume in the extensive Boxcar Children series (see page 103), in which the kids solve a mystery involving backstage sabotage during the community theater's staging of *The Wizard of Oz*. For readers aged 8–11.

4 8 *Onstage and Backstage: At the Night Owl Theater*

Ann Hayes; Harcourt Brace, 1997

The animals of the Night Owl Theater are staging *Cinderella*. This 36-page picture book takes young readers through the whole process of putting on a play, from casting through dress rehearsal and final triumphant performance. For readers aged 4–8.

7 10 *Secondhand Star*

Maryann MacDonald; Disney Press, 1997

Francie helps her friend Stella win the lead in the school play *The Wizard of Oz*. Francie herself gets the role of Toto, which she finds humiliating. When Stella comes down with the chickenpox, however, Francie, who knows all her lines, becomes a secondhand star. For readers aged 7–10.

4 8 *Starring First Grade*

Miriam Cohen; Picture Yearling, 1996

Jim wants to be the troll in the first-grade production of the play *The Three Billy Goats Gruff*. Instead, he's playing a tree, and his friend Paul is the troll. When Paul gets stage fright, Jim saves the day. For readers aged 4–8.

Theater Shoes

Noel Streatfeild; Bullseye Books, 1994

Streatfeild's *Shoes* series, originally published in the 1940s and 50s, includes 12 titles, all starring artistically gifted children. *Theater Shoes* is the story of Sorrel, Mark, and Holly, sent to London during World War II to live with their grandmother, a noted actress. Their grandmother enrolls them in the Children's Academy of Dance and Stage Training where, after some initial difficulties, their talents flourish. For readers aged 9–13. Also see *Dancing Shoes* (page 791).

Wombat Divine

Mem Fox; Harcourt Brace, 1996

A lovely Christmas story about Wombat, who has always wanted to be in the Christmas Nativity play but never seems to be chosen for a part. For readers aged 5–9.

GAMES AND HANDS-ON ACTIVITIES

Cut & Assemble Toy Theaters

Each book includes a colorful toy cardboard theater, complete with backdrops, scenery, props, and cutout costumed characters. Titles include *The Wizard of Oz Toy Theater, A Peter Rabbit Toy Theater, A Peter Pan Toy Theater,* and *A Fairy Tale Toy Theater,* which includes scenery and characters for three small plays, *Little Red Riding Hood, Hansel and Gretel,* and *Jack and the Beanstalk.*

$6.95 each
Dover Publications, Inc.
31 East Second St.
Mineola, NY 11501

Kids on Stage

A board game of dramatic charades for kids aged 3–8. As players hop their pieces around the board, they take turns drawing illustrated topic cards. Each card,

illustrated with a line drawing and a descriptive word, contains a "topic" for kids to act out, while the audience guesses what's on the card. Young actors variously pretend to skate or take a bath, or to be an airplane, a duck, a pig, or a rabbit.

$16 from toy and game stores or
University Games
1633 Adrian Rd.
Burlingame, CA 94010
(415) 692-2500/fax (415) 692-2770

Let's Pretend Series

A collection of kits for imaginative and dramatic play from Creativity for Kids, for actors aged 4 and up. Among the kits in the series are "Let's Pretend Fairy Princess," with materials for making ribbon-and-star-trimmed magic wands and jeweled crowns; "Let's Pretend Magic Show," with materials for making your own top hat, cape, and wand, plus posters and tickets for performances; "Let's Pretend Pirate," with a ready-to-decorate treasure chest, plus gold coins, treasure maps, a spyglass, gold earrings, a parrot, and a skull-and-crossbones-patterned hat; and "Let's Pretend Restaurant," with fake food, a red-checkered tablecloth, chef's hat, menus, an order pad, and—for the customers—paper money and credit cards.

Available from toy and game stores or
Creativity for Kids
1802 Central Ave.
Cleveland, OH 44115
(216) 589-4800 or (800) 642-2288
Web site: www.creativityforkids.com

The Play's the Thing

An attractive and enjoyable board game based on the Shakespearean theater. The playing board represents the Globe Theatre; the basic game includes three packs of playing cards, each based on a different Shakespearean play (*Hamlet, Romeo and Juliet,* and *Julius Caesar*). Players move around the board attempting to collect plot, quotation, and character cards; then perform brief scenes from the featured play. For players aged 12 and up.

$30
Aristoplay

450 S. Wagner Rd.

Ann Arbor, MI 48107

(800) 634-7738 or (888) GR8-GAME

fax (734) 995-4611

Web site: www.aristoplay.com

The Ultimate Costume Sticker Book

Dorling Kindersley, 1994

Over 60 reusable color stickers picturing reenactors in historical costumes from ancient times through the present day. Users match the stickers to their proper place in the descriptive text. Costume categories include "Men," "Women," "Children," "Warriors," "Hats," and "Shoes and Boots."

$6.95

Dorling Kindersley Publishing

1224 Heil Quaker Blvd.

LaVergne, TN 37086

(888) DIALDKP

Web site: www.dk.com

Computer Software

American Girls Collection

Put on a play with one of the American Girls: Felicity of colonial Williamsburg; Kirsten, growing up on the 19th-century frontier; Addy, a free black girl in Philadelphia at the time of the Civil War; Samantha, in turn-of-the-century New York City; and Molly, growing up on the homefront during World War II. Kids can choose a cast, props, and scenery; reenact scenes from the American Girls books (see Pleasant Company, page 448), or create and perform their own plays. On CD-ROM for Mac or Windows.

$34.99

The Learning Company

6160 Summit Dr. N

Minneapolis, MN 55430-4003

(800) 622-3390/fax (612) 589-1151

Web site: www.learningco.com

Opening Night

Players design and stage their own mystery play. In each scene, by a process of click-and-drag, kids arrange actors and props, select costumes, sound effects, and background music, and embellish or alter the preset script, or write their own. Kids can choose from among 40 different costumed characters, 110 backgrounds, and hundreds of props and sound effects. Once established, the production can be played back and viewed as a finished performance. Scripts can be printed for live reenactments. The program also includes video clips of interviews with theater professionals. On CD-ROM for Mac or Windows.

$44.95

The Learning Company

6160 Summit Dr. N

Minneapolis, MN 55430-4003

(800) 622-3390/fax (612) 589-1151

Web site: www.learningco.com

Drama On-Line

Emma's Dramatic Homepage

Resources for teaching drama to primary and secondary students, plus links to on-line plays, drama schools, and current theater news and events.

www.cream.une.edu.au/StudentFiles/ HomePages/372_96/Emma.html

Kids Rule! Drama

Links to many kids' theater sites on-line.

hukilau.com/kidsrule/dbkids/drama.html

World Wide Virtual Library: Theatre and Drama

Many links to theater companies, theater studies, academic journals, a calendar of events, and plays on-line, listed by author.

www.brookes.ac.uk/VL/theatre/index.htm

PUPPETS

Puppets are a delightful introduction to drama for kids of all ages, available in a wide range of home-style or commercial makes and models, from paper bag hand puppets to paper figures pasted on Popsicle sticks to elaborately jointed and costumed marionettes.

Our favorite puppet projects have always been homemade, up to and including the puppet theaters, which in our hands are usually ramshackle affairs cut from cardboard boxes. (Sometimes the puppeteers simply squeeze down behind the living room couch.)

PUPPET KITS AND SUPPLIES

People Shapes Project Kit & Storybook Characters Project Kit

One good source for potential puppet makers is Lakeshore Learning Materials, which sells project kits stuffed with puppet-making materials. The "People Shapes Project Kit," for example, includes 24 gingerbread-person-like chipboard "people shapes" in 12 "people colors," from pale cream to dark chocolate; 24 cutout felt costumes in bright colors; a large assortment of trims and decorating materials, including buttons, pom-poms, feathers, sequins, beads, sticky shapes, wiggly eyes, shiny lips, and yarn; and 24 craft sticks, for mounting.

The "Storybook Characters Project Kit" is similar, but the chipboard characters include not only people but wolves, bears, pink pigs, and green frogs (six of each). "The Puppet Factory Kit" contains all the necessary materials for making 16 decorated sock puppets: colored socks, pom-poms, colored pipe cleaners and foam shapes, feathers, felt, curly "hair," wiggly eyes, and patterns.

Kits, $22 to $30
Lakeshore Learning Materials
2695 E. Dominguez St.
Box 6261
Carson, CA 90749
(310) 537-8600 or (800) 421-5354/fax (310) 537-5403
Web site: www.lakeshorelearning.com

Puppets: Pretend and Play

Make 10 colorful paper bag puppets, decorated with googly plastic eyes, paper fringe, construction paper, feathers, pompoms, buttons, and felt-tipped markers. All materials are included in this kit for kids aged 3 and up.

$14.95 from toy and game stores or
Creativity for Kids

1802 Central Ave.
Cleveland, OH 44115
(216) 589-4800 or (800) 642-2288
Web site: www.creativityforkids.com

Shadow Puppets

The kit includes materials for two gorgeous colored-foil-and-sequin puppets, jointed and mounted on sticks, illustrated step-by-step instructions, and an informational booklet on the history of shadow puppets.

$20 from toy and game stores; for a local source,
contact
Curiosity Kits
Box 811
Cockeysville, MD 21030
(410) 584-2605 or (800) 584-KITS/fax (410) 584-1247
e-mail: Ckitsinc@aol.com

BOOKS ABOUT PUPPETS

Hand Puppets: How to Make and Use Them

Laura Ross; Dover Publications, 1990

Nearly 200 pages of puppet information, including instructions for making puppets and puppet costumes, designing puppet theaters, and writing puppet plays.

I Can Make Puppets

Mary Wallace; Firefly Books, 1994

Puppet making for kids aged 4–8 using socks, bottle caps, and old clothes. Instructions are also included for making a simple puppet stage.

The Most Excellent Book on How to Be a Puppeteer

Roger Lade; Copper Beech Books, 1996

Instructions for making and operating many different kinds of puppets, from the simple sock puppet to the jointed marionette. For kids aged 9–12.

Puppet Plays: From Workshop to Performance

Toni A. Schramm; Teacher Ideas Press, 1993

Detailed instructions for making several kinds of puppets, including stick puppets, felt hand puppets, and Styrofoam-headed puppets, plus eight puppet show scripts, for kids aged 6–12.

4 8 *Simple Puppets from Everyday Materials*

Barbara MacDonald Buetter; Sterling Publications, 1996

Directions for making puppets from all sorts of materials found around the house, such as socks, paper towel rolls, boxes, and spools.

5 12 *Worlds of Shadow: Teaching With Shadow Puppetry*

David Wisniewski and Donna Wisniewski; Teacher Ideas Press, 1996

A step-by-step guide for making shadow puppets, with patterns, scripts, scenery and staging suggestions.

PUPPETS ON-LINE

4 + *Michaels Kids Club*

Many arts and crafts activities for kids, including instructions for making spoon puppets and "Puppets in the Bag."

michaels.com/kids/kid-main.html

6 + *Stage Hands Puppets*

The site includes an on-line puppet theater, for which kids can design puppets and write a puppet play, and detailed instructions for making many kinds of puppets, including finger puppets, paper puppets, origami puppets, and scrap puppets. There are also directions for putting on a hand-shadow performance.

fox.nstn.ca/~puppets/activity.html

ARCHITECTURE

Our kids have always liked building things. Their introduction to architecture was thus both early and hands-on, through blocks, both wooden and Lego. From small boys building castles, caves, forts, towers, houses, and—once—the Great Wall of China in their bedroom, our homeschool program expanded for older boys to study architecture through history, geography, science, math, and art.

As with all the arts, we found that architecture could be easily and interestingly integrated into all academic subjects. Studies of different historical periods and worldwide cultures, for example, always involved investigations of characteristic styles of architecture. While learning about ancient Greece, the boys built scale models of the Parthenon; while studying ancient Rome, they built models of Roman arches; while studying the Middle Ages, they learned about the architecture of castles and cathedrals. (Of particular interest: gargoyles.) A unit on the science of light involved a number of projects with the camera: in one, we prowled surrounding towns, taking photographs of buildings with outstanding architectural features. A home renovation project led to practice in making scale drawings and a meeting with a professional architect who, as it turned out, lives just over the hill from us. He and his wife have two children, aged eight and ten. They're thinking about homeschooling.

From my homeschool journal:

◆ **January 20, 1992. Josh is ten; Ethan, nine; Caleb, seven.**

Today we started studying the state of Maine, using homemade workbooks that cover such multidisciplinary Maine-related topics as lighthouses and Victorian houses (architecture), lobsters (biology), Paul Bunyan (literature), potatoes and pine trees (botany), the Missouri Compromise (history), and sea chanties (music). We began by reading assorted books about lobsters (defining such useful terms as invertebrate, crustacean, *and* decapod*); then the boys colored lobsters in pictures copied from the* Marine Biology Coloring Book *(see page 321), identifying major anatomical features. Ethan, interested in lobsters, then put on an impromptu lobster play (titled* Claws*) and drew an accompanying lobster comic strip.*

We next read about Maine architecture, looking at pictures of Victorian houses complete with widow's walks ("What were those for?") and lighthouses. The boys were thoroughly intrigued with lighthouses. Read Keep the Lights Burning, Abbie! *(see page 100), a (mostly true) lighthouse story by Peter and Connie Roop.*

The boys spent the entire morning building model lighthouses. They studied pictures and photographs in assorted books; then built wonderful foot-tall versions of their own. Ethan's lights up; he wired the thing, using a flashlight bulb and holder, bell wire, batteries, and alligator clips. Josh's is lit by a tinfoil lantern with a birthday candle in it; Caleb's is elaborately landscaped and sits on a rock in a blue paper ocean, complete with clay boulders, clay seagulls, and a little cardboard boat. The models all look terrific—and the boys built them entirely by themselves.

Books

Amazing Buildings
Philip Wilkinson; Dorling Kindersley, 1993

Twenty-one enormous cutaway illustrations of famous architectural structures, among them the Taj Mahal, the Statue of Liberty, and the Roman Colosseum. In each, the dissected drawing shows both the exterior and structural details of the interior of the building; the accompanying text provides historical background information.

American Architecture
Cobblestone; August 1988

The August 1988 issue of *Cobblestone* magazine (see page 449) is centered around American architecture. Features include nonfiction articles on native American architecture ("From Teepees to Igloos"); brief biographies of famous architects, including Thomas Jefferson, Frank Lloyd Wright, and Julia Morgan; an "Architectural Tour of the United States," illustrated with black-and-white photographs; articles on architectural styles and historical preservation; and a "Saltbox House Model" building activity.

> Back issues available at most libraries or for $4.50 from
> Cobblestone Publishing, Inc.
> 30 Grove St.
> Peterborough, NH 03458-1454
> (603) 924-7209 or (800) 821-0015/fax (603) 924-7380
> e-mail: custsvc@cobblestone.mv.com
> Web site: www.cobblestonepub.com

Archabet: An Architectural Alphabet
Balthazar Korab; Preservation Press, 1995

Black-and-white photographs show all 26 letters of the alphabet as their shapes appear in architectural structures (from the old-fashioned to the very modern). Each photo is accompanied by quotations about buildings and architecture.

Architects Make Zigzags: Looking at Architecture From A to Z
Roxie Munro; Preservation Press, 1986

Architectural terms in alphabetical order, from architect, bracket, and column to zigzag, each illustrated with wonderful detailed pen-and-ink drawings. Many of the drawings show features of famous buildings: *G* (for gable) is illustrated with Nathaniel Hawthorne's House of Seven Gables in Salem, Massachusetts; *L* (landscaping), with a bird's-eye view of George Washington's Mount Vernon; and *E* (eaves), with Frank Lloyd Wright's Robie House in Chicago, Illinois.

Architecture: The World's Greatest Buildings Explored and Explained
Neil Stevenson; Dorling Kindersley, 1997

An "annotated guide" to 50 of the world's greatest buildings—among them the Taj Mahal, the Parthenon, and the Empire State Building—marvelously illustrated with color photographs, diagrams, cross-sections, and hundreds of informative labels. The text describes the history behind each building, along with details of style, structure, and construction.

Architecture Board Books
Michael J. Crosbie and Steve Rosenthal; Preservation Press

This series of small, simple books for the very youngest architects is illustrated with wonderful color photographs. Titles are *Architecture Animals* (1995), which includes pictures of the golden grasshopper weather vane that tops Boston's Faneuil Hall, and a great stone squirrel; *Architecture Colors* (1993), which includes orange bricks, green roofs, and a bright red barn; *Architecture Shapes* (1993), which includes round, square, and semicircular windows; and *Architecture Counts* (1993), in which kids can count from 1 skyscraper and 2 brackets up to 10 marble columns.

Architecture and Construction: Building Pyramids, Log Cabins, Castles, Igloos, Bridges, and Skyscrapers

Scholastic, 1995

A multifaceted introduction to architecture for kids aged 9–12. The book includes information on igloos, yurts, and Egyptian pyramids, a foldout Colisseum, a minibook on castles, and a tracing page of Frank Lloyd Wright's Fallingwater.

Architecture Is Elementary

Nathan B. Winters; Gibbs Smith, 1986

An instruction book on architectural principles for kids in grades 4–12; includes 50 lessons on seven different levels.

The Architecture Pack

Ron Van Der Meer and Deyan Sudjic; Alfred A. Knopf, 1996

A fabulous three-dimensional tour of the world of architecture with Ron Van Der Meer, the innovative paper engineer who designed *The Art Pack* (see page 719) and *The Music Pack* (see page 753), and architecture historian Deyan Sudjic. The book is crammed with clever illustrations, detailed diagrams, and spectacular paper pop-ups, among them re-creations of a Plains Indian tepee, Chartres Cathedral, and the Sydney Opera House. There are working models of a Roman arch, a Gothic vault, and a modern elevator; capsule profiles of such architectural innovators as Michelangelo, Palladio, Frank Lloyd Wright, and Le Corbusier; and a build-it-yourself Bauhaus. A gorgeous and fascinating architectural resource.

The Art of Construction: Projects and Principles for Beginning Engineers and Architects

Mario Salvadori, Saralinda Hooker, and Christopher Ragus; Chicago Review Press, 1990

Basic information on the building of houses, bridges, and skyscrapers, with instructions for many projects for budding engineers, in which kids build model houses, stadiums, and bridges, all with readily available materials. For teenagers.

Barmi: A Mediterranean City Through the Ages

Xavier Hernandez and Pilar Comes; Houghton Mifflin, 1990

Detailed line drawings and a short text trace changes in history, architecture, and culture from ancient times to the present day. Also see *Lebek: A City of Northern Europe Through the Ages* (Xavier Hernandez and Jordi Ballonga; Houghton Mifflin, 1991) and *San Rafael: A Central American City Through the Ages* (Xavier Hernandez and Jordi Ballonga; Houghton Mifflin, 1992).

Bridges Go From Here to There

Forrest Wilson; Preservation Press, 1993

An informative picture book all about the structure and function of bridges, for readers aged 6–12.

City: A Story of Roman Planning and Construction

David Macauley; Houghton Mifflin, 1983

David Macauley has written a superb collection of architectural histories for young readers. In each, Macauley traces the building process step by step, with marvelously detailed drawings, from the initial selection of the building site to project completion. *City* explores the design and construction of a Roman city. Also see *Castle* (1982), the story of the building of a 13th-century Welsh castle; *Cathedral* (1981), on the construction of a 14th-century French cathedral; *Mill*, (1989) on the building of a 19th-century water-powered spinning mill; and *Pyramid* (1982), on the design and construction of an ancient Egyptian pyramid. For a new and different take on architecture, see *Great Moments in Architecture* (1989), a hilarious collection of architectural follies, fantasies, and disasters rendered in Macauley's exquisitely detailed style (the famous Arc de Triomphe is shown upside down). *Unbuilding* (1987) is a startling look at architecture in reverse, as Macauley dismantles the Empire State Building; and *Underground* (1976) is a fascinating look at the world beneath our feet, as Macauley leads readers on a journey down a manhole and through the depths of a city.

Castle, Cathedral, City, and *Pyramid* are also available on **video** (see page 618).

Frank Lloyd Wright for Kids
Kathleen Thorne-Thomsen; Chicago Review Press, 1994

A 138-page biography-and-activity book for architects aged 9 and up. The first half of the book is biography, heavily illustrated with terrific black-and-white photographs of Frank and his family (he and his wife had six children), and of his buildings, inside and out. The second half is an assortment of multidisciplinary activities, based (sometimes very loosely) on Frank Lloyd Wright's life and work. Readers are encouraged to cook the architect's favorite breakfast (oatmeal), to sprout bean seeds and make careful drawings of each stage in their development (Frank liked nature), to learn basic geometric shapes, to design a Wright-style stained-glass window, to study house styles in their neighborhoods (there are three helpful pages of sample photographs), to build a model of Wright's most famous house—Fallingwater—out of graham crackers, to make a model textile block from plaster, and to throw a Wright-type seasonal festival (Frank liked parties).

Frank Lloyd Wright: Maverick Architect
Frances A. Davis; Lerner, 1996

A biography of the innovative American architect for readers in grade 5 and up. Illustrated with photographs.

Handmade Houses

Art Boericke; A & W Publishing, 1985

A wonderful collection of color photographs of creative handmade houses, including some terrific tree houses and a concrete house stuck full of colored bottles.

The Homes We Live In
Sally Hewitt; Raintree/Steck-Vaughn, 1997

The hows and whys of houses. The book explains why walls, roofs, windows, walls, and floors are made the way they are, why specific types of materials are used, and why they are built in certain shapes. For readers aged 4–9.

The House I Live In: At Home in America
Isadore Seltzer; Atheneum, 1992

A simple introduction to American architecture for kids of all ages through a tour of 12 very different homes, among them an adobe pueblo, a Pennsylvania Dutch farmhouse, a gingerbread-laden Victorian, and a houseboat.

Houses and Homes
Ann Morris; Mulberry, 1995

Photographs of houses from different regions and cultures around the world, accompanied by a simple explanatory text. Everything from Buckingham Palace to straw huts. For readers ages 4–8.

Houses and Homes
Tim Wood; Viking, 1997

A tour of houses and homes through history and around the world. Readers peel back an acetate overlay to see inside each structure. The book includes illustrations of Zulu homes, a Maori *pa*, the French palace of Chambord, the Assyrian palace of the Emperor Sargon II, a Mongol yurt, and a Roman villa.

Houses: Structures, Methods, and Ways of Living
Piero Ventura; Houghton Mifflin, 1993

A 64-page history of human houses, from huts to high-rise apartment buildings, with delightful illustrations. Included are descriptions of Roman villages, Viking longhouses, and medieval castles.

How a House Is Built
Gail Gibbons; Holiday House, 1990

The picture-book story of the building of a house, explaining the work of surveyors, heavy-machinery operators, carpenters, plumbers, and electricians. For readers aged 4–8.

I Know That Building!: Discovering Architecture with Activities and Games
Jane D'Alelio; Preservation Press, 1989

A beautiful and creative collection of activities, models, and games designed to introduce kids to architecture. Users, for example, make a manhole cover rubbing (there's an embossed manhole in miniature on the back cover of the book); color a Victorian garden, a Morris design, and a Frank Lloyd Wright window; solve architectural puzzles; build a model Woolworth Building, Queen Anne house, covered bridge, and 19th-century schoolhouse; design a Pennsylvania Dutch hex sign; and play a game of "Go Build!" in which they match portraits of famous architects to photographs of their best-known buildings. Wonderful color illustrations.

Julia Morgan: Architect of Dreams
Ginger Wadsworth; Lerner, 1990.

A biography of architect Julia Morgan, designer of California's Hearst Castle. Illustrated with color photographs. For readers in grade 5 and up.

Old House, New House: A Child's Exploration of American Architectural Styles
Michael Gaughenbaugh; Preservation Press, 1993

When his parents decide to restore a run-down Victorian house, a young boy learns firsthand about the history of American architecture and the process of historical restoration. He also views architectural styles around the country, in visits to friends and relatives. For readers aged 9–12.

Raising the Roof: Children's Stories and Activities on Houses
Jan Irving and Robin Currie; Teacher Ideas Press, 1993

Creative multidisciplinary activities based on children's picture books about houses. Activities cover a wide range of cultures and historical periods. Kids make masks and puppets, stage plays, sing songs, and much more. For students in preschool through grade 3.

Round Buildings, Square Buildings, & Buildings That Wiggle Like a Fish
Philip M. Isaacson; Alfred A. Knopf, 1988

A round-the-world tour of architecture, visiting bridges, castles, lighthouses, tombs, and cliff dwellings. Illustrated with photographs.

Stephen Biesty's Incredible Cross-Sections
Richard Platt; Alfred A. Knopf, 1992

Precisely labeled and incredibly detailed cross-sectional views of 18 structures, among them a medieval castle, an opera house, an oil rig, a coal mine, and the *Queen Mary.*

Also see *Stephen Biesty's Incredible Explosions* (1996), which contains equally incredible cross-sectional diagrams of a windmill, a steam engine, an airport, a space station, and the Grand Canyon.

The Story of a Castle
John S. Goodall; Atheneum, 1986

Lovely detailed watercolors trace the architectural and cultural evolution of a castle, from medieval times to the present day. In similar format, also see *The Story of a Farm* (1989), *The Story of a Main Street* (1987), and *The Story of an English Village* (1978).

Structures: The Way Things Are Built
Nigel Hawkes; Macmillan, 1993

An entertaining text explains the way buildings, monuments, bridges, dams, and towers are (or were) built, with many illustrations, including color photographs, diagrams, blueprints, and cutaway drawings revealing the innards of such structures as the Golden Gate Bridge and the Statue of Liberty.

This Is My House
Arthur Dorros; Scholastic, 1992

An overview of the different kinds of houses lived in by kids all over the world. Readers learn how to say "This is my house" in 19 languages.

Under Every Roof: A Kid's Style and Field Guide to the Architecture of American Houses
Patricia Brown Glenn; Preservation Press, 1993

A history of American architecture combined with a pictorial field guide, for readers aged 9 and up. The guide features 60 homes and contains 170 color illustrations, which allow users to identify a wealth of different architectural details.

Up Goes the Skyscraper!

4 8 Gail Gibbons; Simon & Schuster, 1986

A brightly illustrated picture-book account of the building of a skyscraper, from the clearing of the site through the details of construction to the day the first tenants move in.

The Visual Dictionary of Buildings

9 + Fiona Courtney-Thompson, ed.; Dorling Kindersley, 1993

An Eyewitness Visual Dictionary, filled with heavily labeled color photographs. The book covers historical and contemporary buildings of all kinds, identifying architectural elements and building components. See *Eyewitness Visual Dictionary Series* (page 132).

What It Feels Like to Be a Building

6 + Forrest Wilson; National Trust for Historic Preservation Press, 1988

An innovative picture book explaining what the parts of a building (columns, walls, beams, arches, buttresses) would feel like if they were people (squashed, squeezed, pulled, stretched). Readers get a personal feel for the functions of architectural structures.

The World of Architectural Wonders

8 + Mike Corbishley; Peter Bedrick Books, 1997

Color photographs and illustrations of 14 world architectural wonders, among them the Taj Mahal, Hoover Dam, Chartres Cathedral, the Great Wall of China, and the Pyramids of Giza. Includes information on historical background and construction techniques.

COLORING BOOKS

Famous Buildings of Frank Lloyd Wright Coloring Book

6 + Dover publishes a number of coloring books of architectural interest, each with detailed black-line drawings to color, plus an informational background text. *Famous Buildings of Frank Lloyd Wright* includes pictures of Wright's home, studio, and most famous buildings, among them the Guggenheim Museum, the Robie House, and Fallingwater. Also see *Bridges of the*

World Coloring Book, Cathedrals of the World Coloring Book, Historic Houses of New England Coloring Book, Historic Houses of New York State Coloring Book, and *North American Lighthouses Coloring Book.*

$2.95 each

Dover Publications, Inc.

31 E. Second St.

Mineola, NY 11501

Stained Glass Windows of Frank Lloyd Wright

6 + Dennis Casey; Dover Publications

Sixteen full-page window designs to color, each taken from one of Wright's well-known buildings. The designs are printed on translucent paper: color, cut out, and hang in the window for a glowing stained-glass effect.

$2.95

Dover Publications, Inc.

31 E. Second St.

Mineola, NY 11501

GAMES AND HANDS-ON ACTIVITIES

3-D Home Kit

10 + The kit includes enough material to build a ¼-inch scale model of one enormous (6,200 square feet) home or several smaller houses. Building materials, all cardboard, include simulated brick and stone, siding, roofing, windows, doors, decking, interior walls, stairs, kitchen cabinets and appliances, plumbing fixtures, and skylights—even scale landscaping, people, and pets. Also included: a floor plan grid, furniture symbols, and a detailed instruction booklet.

$29.95

Cuisenaire/Dale Seymour Publications

Box 5026

White Plains, NY 10602-5026

(800) 872-1100 or (800) 237-3142/fax (914) 328-5487

Web site: www.awl.com/dsp or www.cuisenaire.com

Archiblocks

ALL Sets of much better than average blocks for young architects. The blocks are available in different thematic sets, including Greek, Roman, Islamic, Gothic, Renaissance, and Post-Modern. Each set contains 50 to 75 finished maple blocks, and, along with conventionally blocklike beams and cubes, appropriately proportioned columns, arches, lintels, pediments, and gables.

$59 each from toy and game stores or

Zephyr Press

3316 N. Chapel Ave.

Box 66006

Tucson, AZ 85732-6006

(800) 232-2187/fax (520) 323-9402

e-mail: neways2learn@zephyrpress.com

Web site: www.zephyrpress.com

Architek Game

The game includes 18 geometric blocks of assorted shapes and 90 cards picturing 120 three-dimensional construction puzzles. The trick is to stack the blocks so as to reproduce the structure on the puzzle card. A spatial skill builder for kids aged 4 and up.

$29.95 from toy and game stores

Art Bits Architecture Card Games

The cards are illustrated with careful pen-and-ink drawings of famous buildings and architectural styles from all over the world. The "Apprentice" and "Journeyman" card sets each include 17 pairs of architectural cards, each labeled with the name of the building or style and its location or region of origin. The "Master" set combines both "Apprentice" and "Journeyman" sets, without the helpful labels. The cards can be used to play a concentration-type matching/memory game or an architectural version of old maid.

"Apprentice" and "Journeyman" sets, about $9.95; "Master" set, $15.95

Sax Arts & Crafts

Box 510710

New Berlin, WI 53151

(800) 558-6696

Block Building for Children: Making Buildings of the World With the Ultimate Construction Toy

Les Walker; Overlook Press, 1995

Detailed instructions, photographs, diagrams, and background information for an impressive series of 18 architectural projects using plain old building blocks. Among the projects are a bridge, a skyscraper, a castle, a Greek temple, and the Emerald City of Oz. For builders aged 9 and up on their own; younger kids will probably need some help.

A Blueprint for Geometry

Bill Lombard and Brad Fulton; Dale Seymour Publications

A unit in down-to-earth architecture for kids in grades 5–8. Users read and design floor plans, calculate materials and business costs, and build a scale model. The 96-page book includes 17 plans drawn by an architect, plus instructions and reproducible worksheets.

$16.95

Cuisenaire/Dale Seymour Publications

Box 5026

White Plains, NY 10602-5026

(800) 872-1100 or (800) 237-3142/fax (914) 328-5487

Web site: www.awl.com/dsp or www.cuisenaire.com

Box City

A community planning project for kids of all ages. The program includes a 160-page curriculum guide, an instructional video, and all the materials for building Box City: 40 white cardboard boxes in three sizes, to be assembled and decorated by the kids, and a 42 × 78-inch "Box City Grid Plan," scaled to match the sizes of the boxes, on which the completed boxes—as houses, factories, stores, and civic buildings—are arranged to form an ideal city. The result takes up a lot of space, but it's interesting, educationally mind-expanding, and fun to play with afterward.

Entire program, $79.95

Crystal Productions

Box 2159

Glenview, IL 60025-6159

(800) 255-8629

e-mail: crystal@interaccess.com

Building Toothpick Bridges

Jeanne Pollard; Dale Seymour Publications

A group project in which "companies" of students attempt to build a bridge that both stays within the budget and bears a required load. Materials—toothpicks—are ordered from the central warehouse; a project accountant pays for them by check and maintains financial records. A challenging combination of math, science, and architecture for kids aged 8–13.

$10.95

Cuisenaire/Dale Seymour Publications

Box 5026

White Plains, NY 10602-5026

(800) 872-1100 or (800) 237-3142/fax (914) 328-5487

Web site: www.awl.com/dsp or www.cuisenaire.com

Also see *Economics for Kids* (page 207).

Cardboard Creations

Prefabricated cardboard houses for kids to assemble and decorate. The houses include doors and window holes, are made of recycled materials, and fold flat for storage. Available in two versions: a castle (with drawbridge) and a town house. For kids aged 2–11.

$45

Cardboard Creations

1119 Stanford Ave.

Redondo Beach, CA 90278

(310) 318-3680

Web site: www.inventionconnection.com/BOOTHS/ booth162.html

Connections: Architecture

An architectural card game. The game includes two 55-card decks, each card with a wonderful full-color photograph of an architectural building, monument, or feature from around the world on one side, descriptive information on the other. The trick is to make imaginative connections between images. A helpful instruction booklet is included.

$18.95

Cuisenaire/Dale Seymour Publications

Box 5026

White Plains, NY 10602-5026

(800) 872-1100 or (800) 237-3142/fax (914) 328-5487

Web site: www.awl.com/dsp or www.cuisenaire.com

Cut & Assemble Buildings

Dover publishes a large collection of sturdy and colorful paper architectural models, assembled in 16-page $9\frac{1}{4} \times 12\frac{1}{4}$-inch booklets. Titles include *Cut & Assemble Frank Lloyd Wright's Robie House;* instructions and pieces for a full-color two-foot-long model of Wright's Robie House, a classic of prairie-style architecture; *Cut & Assemble a Victorian Gothic Cottage,* a detailed model of the 1844 Delamater House; *Cut & Assemble Colonial Houses; Cut & Assemble Victorian Houses;* and many more.

Each booklet, $6.95

Dover Publications, Inc.

31 E. Second St.

Mineola, NY 11501

Frank Lloyd Wright Prairie House Building Block Set

A set 68 of maple blocks with which kids can build houses in Wright's "prairie style."

$50 from toy and game stores or

Zephyr Press

3316 N. Chapel Ave.

Box 66006

Tucson, AZ 85732-6006

(800) 232-2187/fax (520) 323-9402

e-mail: neways2learn@zephyrpress.com

Web site: www.zephyrpress.com

Fun With Architecture

David Eisen; The Metropolitan Museum of Art/Viking, 1992

A high-quality kit of architectural rubber stamps with which kids can stamp out anything from the Taj Mahal to a medieval cathedral to the Brooklyn Bridge. The kit contains 35 rubber stamps, a (black) ink pad, and an 80-page booklet of information, instructions, and ideas, including directions for stamping out a Mayan ziggurat, a Greek temple, and a very modern city filled with towering skyscrapers.

$22.50 from book stores or

Zephyr Press

3316 N. Chapel Ave.

Box 66006

Tucson, AZ 85728-6006

(800) 232-2187/fax (520) 323-9402

e-mail: neways2learn@zephyrpress.com

Web site: www.zephyrpress.com

Great Buildings Model Kit

Julian Bicknell and Steve Chapman; Clarkson N. Potter, 1995

The kit includes materials for making scale models of four famous buildings: the Parthenon, the Leaning Tower of Pisa, the Taj Mahal, and Thomas Jefferson's Monticello. Each building is assembled from precut full-color card-stock pieces—no scissors needed. An accompanying 24-page book, illustrated with color photographs of the actual buildings, includes historical information and complete instructions.

It's a Gingerbread House: Bake It, Build It, Eat It!

Vera B. Williams; Mulberry, 1996

Edible architecture. The book includes step-by-step instructions for house bakers aged 5 and up.

Wonderboard: Architecture Magnet Set

Over 150 magnetic architectural shapes in black, a 9 × 12-inch white magnetic "Wonderboard," and a selection of activity cards, showing kids how to assemble Greek Classical, Gothic, Renaissance, or Modern architectural masterpieces.

$12.95 from toy and game stores or
Sax Arts & Crafts
Box 510710
New Berlin, WI 53151
(800) 558-6696

Young Architects

A reusable design and building set for architects aged 10 and up, with which kids can transform their two-dimensional designs into impressive three-dimensional models. The kit includes an 18 × 24-inch acrylic work mat, drafting paper, nine room templates, three furniture-tracing guides, and a collection of 30 clear acrylic exterior walls, 50 corner blocks, and peel-off vinyl doors and windows.

$75
Zephyr Press
3316 N. Chapel Ave.
Box 66006
Tucson, AZ 85732-6006
(800) 232-2187/fax (520) 323-9402
e-mail: neways2learn@zephyrpress.com
Web site: www.zephyrpress.com
or
Creative Learning Systems
16510 Via Esprillo

San Diego, CA 92127
(800) 458-2880/fax (619) 675-7707
Web site: www.clsinc.com

COMPUTER SOFTWARE

Frank Lloyd Wright Companion

A survey of all of Frank Lloyd Wright's nearly 500 works with background text, photographs, floor plans, and walk-through simulations. On CD-ROM for Mac or Windows.

$41.99
Educorp
12B W. Main St.
Elmsford, NY 10523
(914) 347-2464 or (800) 843-9497/fax (914) 347-0217
e-mail: service@educorp.com
Web site: www.educorp.com

Fun With Architecture

A CD-ROM based on the Fun With Architecture rubber stamp set (see page 786). Kids can create thousands of different buildings using a collection of 45 architectural shapes in a range of different colors and textures (including stone, steel, and wood). Included are scenic backgrounds and templates for many varied structures, including temples, castles (with drawbridges), and buildings by Frank Lloyd Wright and Le Corbusier.

$19.95
Learn Technologies Interactive
Box 2284
S. Burlington, VT 05407
(888) 292-5584
Web site: voyager.learntech.com

Gryphon Bricks

An on-screen 3-D building kit, with which kids create imaginative structures of all kinds using colorful Lego-like electronic blocks that slide into place with a satisfying click. On CD-ROM for Mac or Windows.

$39.95
Davidson
19840 Pioneer Ave.
Torrance, CA 90503

(800) 545-7677/fax (310) 793-0601

Web site: www.davd.com or www.education.com

SimCity 2000

Users design a city, complete with power lines, sewer systems, roads, railroads, airports, houses, factories, shopping districts, schools, hospitals, parks, and office buildings, all funded by an urban population of taxpayers, and then set it in motion, watching it grow and develop at four different speeds. They can also—sadly, popular with our children—subject their city to 10 disasters, among them an earthquake, a volcanic eruption, a monstrous fire, and an all-encompassing electrical blackout. Complex and continually challenging. On CD-ROM for Mac or Windows.

Also see "SimTower," with which young architects can design a skyscraper up to 100 stories tall (coping with cockroaches, fire, terrorist attacks, and structural stresses).

"SimCity," $59.95; "SimTower," $21.95

Zenger Media

10200 Jefferson Blvd.

Box 802

Culver City, CA 90232-0802

(310) 839-2436 or (800) 421-4246/fax (310) 839-2249

or (800) 944-5432

e-mail: access@ZengerMedia.com

Web site: www.ZengerMedia.com/Zenger

ARCHITECTURE ON-LINE

The Ancient City of Athens

A photo archive and virtual tour of archaeological and architectural sites and monuments.

www.indiana.edu/~kglowack/Athens/Athens.html

ArchKIDecture

An on-line game about architecture for kids.

www.childmmc.edu/cmhweb/kidshome.html

Castles on the Web

Virtual tours of castles, links to castle photo collections and resources, and a "Castles for Kids" page, with general information about castles and their history, a book list, an on-line castle-drawing contest, and links to other castle-related sites of interest to kids.

www.fox.nstn.ca/~tmonk/castle/castle.html

Castles of the World

Historical background information and color photographs of castles all over the world, a "Castle Site of the Week," and links to other castle sites.

www.castles.org

WebAcropolis

A virtual tour of the Acropolis, with explanatory text. An excellent introduction to ancient Greek architecture.

www.mechan.ntua.gr/webacropol

World's Tallest Buildings

See them all, in color photographs: the John Hancock Center, the Sears Tower, and many more.

www.dcircle.com/wtb/94.html

Also see **Carpentry/Woodworking** (pages 813–815).

DANCE

The boys' initial exposure to dance consisted of several annual Christmas treks to performances of *The Nutcracker,* where Caleb (aged four, five, and six) inevitably became terminally restless by the appearance of the Sugarplum Fairy. A friend, who had danced with a professional ballet company, gave the boys a sample lesson in ballet, demonstrating basic positions, exercises, and steps. They found this fun, but nobody was interested in pursuing dance. Gymnastics, yes; dance, no.

As part of a recent study of Ireland, however, the boys viewed the video of Michael Flatley's *Riverdance* (see page 794), a spectacular performance based on traditional Celtic dances. All three were impressed. Ethan, a devout classicist, has begun listening to Irish fiddle music; and Caleb, who now enters rooms with *Riverdance*-style leaps, has expressed a possible interest in dancing school.

Books

Ballet
7–12
Kate Castle; Kingfisher Books, 1996

A 64-page picture book about ballet, covering basic steps, choreography, costumes, rehearsals and performances, the history of ballet, and favorite ballet stories. The book includes assorted activities for young dancers, including hints on how to practice and suggestions for staging a simple ballet.

Ballet for Beginners
5–10
Marie-Louise Medora; Sterling Publications, 1995

The basic ballet positions, steps, and exercises, illustrated with color photographs of young dancers.

Behind the Scenes at the Ballet: Rehearsing and Performing the Sleeping Beauty
8–12
Leslie E. Spatt; Puffin, 1997

A 48-page account of what goes on backstage at the ballet, covering rehearsals, costumes, stage makeup, and the preperformance commotion in the dressing rooms. Illustrated with color photographs.

Dance
9–12
Angela Shelf Medearis and Michael R. Medearis; Twenty-First Century Books, 1997

A history of black dance traditions, from the days of slavery through modern jazz, tap dancing, and ballet.

Dance Me a Story: Twelve Tales from the Classic Ballets
9–12
Jane Rosenberg; Hudson Annex, 1993

The illustrated stories of 12 ballets, including *Giselle* and *Sleeping Beauty*.

Dancers
9–12
Peggy Roalf; Hyperion, 1992

A volume in the Looking at Paintings Series, this 49-page book traces art history through paintings of dancers by such artists as Rubens, Blake, Toulouse-Lautrec, and Botero.
See the **Looking at Paintings Series** (page 721).

Frogs and the Ballet
8–12

Donald Elliott; Harvard Common Press, 1984

An introduction to ballet history and technique, with humorous illustrations of some very graceful frogs.

I Want to Be a Dancer
8–12
Stephanie Maze and Catherine O'Neill Grace; Harcourt Brace, 1997

A 48-page picture book illustrated with color photographs about the many kinds of dance and the process of becoming a professional dancer.

The Illustrated Book of Ballet Stories
8–12
Barbara Newman; Dorling Kindersley, 1997

A 64-page color-illustrated collection of tales from famous ballets, among them *The Nutcracker, Giselle, Swan Lake, Sleeping Beauty,* and *Coppelia,* with historical background information and notes on choreography. The book is also available with an accompanying CD, which features music excerpts from each ballet.

Of Swans, Sugarplums, and Satin Slippers: Ballet Stories for Children
8–12

Violette Verdy; Scholastic, 1996

The illustrated stories of six famous ballets: *Swan Lake, Giselle, The Firebird, Coppelia, Sleeping Beauty,* and *The Nutcracker.*

On Wings of Joy: The Story of Ballet from the 16th Century to Today
9–+

Trudy Garfunkel; Little, Brown, 1994

Ballet from its beginnings in the French court of Catherine de Medicis to the present day. Readers learn that the first dancers were members of the court of Louis XIV, as well as the king. (Louis founded the Royal Academy of Dance only after he became too old and fat to dance himself.) The book includes capsule biographies of famous dancers and choreographers, and information about prominent ballet troupes. A thoroughly interesting read for kids aged 12 and up.

Petrouchka: The Story of the Ballet

Vivian Werner; Viking/Penguin, 1992

The picture-book story of the ballet by Igor Stravinsky, in which the clown puppet Petrouchka falls in love with a beautiful ballerina.

The Random House Book of Stories of the Ballet

Geraldine McCaughrean; Random House, 1995

Retellings of 10 ballet stories: *Swan Lake, Sleeping Beauty, Petrouchka, The Nutcracker, Coppelia, Giselle, Cinderella, Romeo and Juliet, La Sylphide,* and *The Firebird.*

Shoes of Satin, Ribbons of Silk: Tales from the Ballet

Antonia Barber; Kingfisher Books, 1995

A lavishly illustrated 96-page collection of nine ballet stories, among them *Swan Lake, The Nutcracker, Giselle,* and *The Firebird,* with notes on the performances.

The World of Ballet

Judy Tatchell; EDC Publishing, 1994

A guide to the world of ballet, illustrated with full-color photographs of the dancers of the Royal Birmingham Ballet Company. The book includes a who's who of famous dancers and a glossary of ballet terms. For readers aged 10 and up.

The Young Dancer

Darcey Bussell; Dorling Kindersley, 1994

Illustrated with wonderful color photographs, this is a 66-page tour of the ballet world through the students at London's Royal Ballet School. The book pictures and describes basic ballet positions and steps and how to practice each, and explains the ins and outs of stage performances.

BOOKS ABOUT DANCERS

Alvin Ailey

Andrea Davis Pinkney; Hyperion, 1995

A picture-book biography of the famous dancer.

Anna Pavlova: Genius of the Dance

Ellen Levine; Scholastic, 1995

A 130+-page biography of the great Russian ballerina, illustrated with black-and-white photographs.

Barefoot Dancer: The Story of Isadora Duncan

Barbara O'Connor; Carolrhoda, 1994

The story of the flamboyant inventor of modern dance, for readers in grades 4–7. Illustrated with photographs.

Dancing Rainbows: A Pueblo Boy's Story

Evelyn Clarke Mott; Cobblehill, 1996

The story of a Tewa Indian boy and his grandfather preparing for a feast-day dance, illustrated with color photographs.

George Balanchine: American Ballet Master

Davida Kristy; Lerner, 1996

A biography of George Balanchine, from his childhood in tsarist Russia through the Russian Revolution, and his life in Europe and America, with an emphasis on his creative choreography and his influence on American ballet. Illustrated with photographs. For readers aged 9–12.

Ragtime Tumpie

Alan Schroeder; Little, Brown, 1989

A fictionalized account of the childhood of Josephine Baker, who overcame a life of poverty to become a famous dancer.

A Very Young Dancer

Jill Krementz; Dell, 1986

The story of the daily life of a 10-year-old ballerina, dancing in the New York City Ballet's production of *The Nutcracker.* Illustrated with photographs.

DANCE AND LITERATURE

Angelina Ballerina

Katharine Holabird; Crown, 1983

Angelina, an enchanting young mouse, does nothing but dance. Finally her exasperated parents send her to ballet school.

Sequels include *Angelina and the Princess* (Crown, 1984), in which Angelina dances the star role in *The Princess of Mouseland;* and *Angelina Ice Skates* (Crown, 1993), in which Angelina convinces a pair of bullies to join her ice-skating ballet.

Barn Dance!
Bill Martin Jr. and John Archambault; Henry Holt, 1986

In catchy rhyme, the story of a farm boy who sneaks out one night to watch the animals square-dance in the barn.

Degas and the Little Dancer: A Story About Edgar Degas
Laurence Anholt; Barron's Juveniles, 1996

The story of Marie, who wants to be a famous ballerina, but her parents are too poor to pay her ballet school fees. Marie begins to model for a painter at the school to pay her way, and the result—the lovely statue of *The Little Dancer*—makes Marie a very famous ballerina. Illustrations include reproductions of Degas's paintings of dancers.
See **Degas** (page 724).

Dance With Me
Barbara Juster Ebensen; HarperCollins, 1995

A 32-page collection of poems about dance for readers aged 4–9. Subjects include both traditional dances such as the waltz, tap dancing, and ballet, and such imaginative variations as dancing with the wind.

Dancing Shoes
Noel Streatfeild; Dell, 1984

After her mother's death, Rachel and her adopted sister, Hilary, are sent to London to live with their Aunt Cora, who runs a London dancing school. There, as both girls develop their talents, they learn to adjust to their new life and to cope with Dulcie, the school's difficult star pupil. For readers aged 9–12.
Also see *Theater Shoes* (page 776).

The Hokey-Pokey
Sheila Hamanaka; Simon & Schuster, 1997

An upbeat song-and-dance picture book for kids aged 3–7, based on the words of the traditional song:

"You put your right foot in, you put your right foot out . . ."

Lili at Ballet
Rachel Isadora; Paper Star, 1996

The book details the life of a serious young ballet student, practicing at home with her cat, warming up before class, demonstrating the five basic ballet positions and classic ballet steps, and dancing in a school performance as a flower fairy. Lili also gets a glimpse of a professional ballet onstage. For readers aged 4–9.

Also see *Lili on Stage* (Putnam, 1995), in which Lili dances the part of a guest in a production of *The Nutcracker,* and *Lili Backstage* (Putnam, 1997), in which Lili explores the backstage world of the ballet, visits her grandfather in the orchestra pit, and watches a performance from the wings.

Listen to the Nightingale
Rumer Godden; Puffin, 1994

Lottie, a talented orphan raised by the costume mistress at a small London ballet school, is offered a prestigious dance scholarship and must make difficult choices about her art and home. For readers aged 9–13.

Other ballet stories by Godden for readers aged 12 and up include *A Candle for St. Jude* and *Thursday's Children.*

Max
Rachel Isadora; Aladdin, 1984

Ballet for boys. Max warms up at his sister's ballet class on his way to baseball practice; eventually he decides to participate in both. For readers aged 5–9.

Mirandy and Brother Wind
Patricia C. McKissack; Dragonfly, 1997

Mirandy captures the wind himself to be her partner is the cakewalk dance contest, but she ends up winning the prize with her best friend, Ezel. For readers aged 6–9.

Nutcracker Noel
Kate H. McMullan; HarperCrest, 1993

Noel longs to be the star of a real ballet, but in her ballet class production, she has to play a tree, while

Mia, her biggest rival, dances the part of a gingerbread doll. On the night of the performance, however, Noel discovers that the tree wears a beautiful snow-white costume lit with candles, while Mia has to wear an uncomfortable gingerbread mask. Noel generously comforts Mia, the show goes on, and all ends well.

Also see *Noel the First,* in which Noel struggles to maintain her place in ballet class as the dancers prepare for a production of *Cinderella.*

Ribbons
Laurence Yep; Paper Star, 1997

Robin Lee, a dedicated young dancer, must give up her ballet lessons so that her family can pay her grandmother's fare from Hong Kong to America. When her grandmother arrives, she is disapproving and old-fashioned; and Robin must deal with her own ambitions and disappointments, as well as conflicts between cultures and generations. For readers aged 9–13.

Song and Dance Man
Karen Ackerman; Alfred A. Knopf, 1992

Grandfather, complete with costume, top hat, and twirling gold-headed cane, performs his wonderful act as a vaudeville song-and-dance man for his fascinated grandchildren. For readers aged 4–8.

Song and Dance: Poems
Lee Bennett Hopkins, ed.; Simon & Schuster, 1997

An illustrated anthology of poems about dance and music by well-known poets, among them Carl Sandburg, Langston Hughes, Eve Merriam, and Charlotte Zolotow.

Tanya Steps Out
Patricia Lee Gauch; Putnam, 1996

Tanya, a beginning ballerina, learns new dance positions by imitating a long list of animals, among them a flamingo, a cat, an antelope, and a frog. For readers aged 4–8.

There are several other books about Tanya, among them *Bravo, Tanya* (Philomel Books, 1992) in which Tanya overcomes her difficulties in ballet class with the help of a kindly piano teacher; and *Tanya and the Magic Wardrobe* (Philomel Books, 1997), in which Tanya has an adventure at a performance of the ballet *Coppelia.*

The Twelve Dancing Princesses
Jacob Grimm; North South Books, 1995

The classic tale of the clever soldier who solves the mystery of why the princesses disappear each night and return with their shoes worn out—and then marries the loveliest of the 12. For readers aged 5–10.

COLORING BOOKS

Ballet
Trudy Garfunkel; Running Press

A fact-filled coloring book in the Start Exploring series, with 60 black-line illustrations to color, plus—on facing pages—an interestingly informative text. The book covers the basics of ballet—pictures of the five positions and a close-up of toe shoes—along with the history of ballet, famous ballets and dancers, and major modern-day dance companies.

$8.95 from bookstores or
Running Press Book Publishers
125 South 22nd St.
Philadelphia, PA 19103
(215) 567-5080 (800) 345-5359/fax (800) 453-2884

A Coloring Book of Great Dancers
Bellerophon Books publishes several coloring books on dance themes. *A Coloring Book of Great Dancers* is a collection of portraits of famous dancers in their greatest roles, among them Anna Pavlova as the Swan. Also see *A Coloring Book of the Sleeping Beauty Ballet,* which pictures the dancers in Leon Bakst's beautiful and elaborate costumes; *A Coloring Book of Peter and the Wolf Ballet,* which includes scenes from the ballet as well as pictures of the orchestral instruments; and *The Nutcracker Ballet,* which tells the story of the ballet and includes pictures of dancers in various *Nutcracker* productions.

$3.95 each
Bellerophon Books
36 Ancapa St.
Santa Barbara, CA 93101
(800) 253-9943/fax (800) 965-8286

HANDS-ON ACTIVITIES

6+ *Cut & Assemble Nutcracker Theater*

Tom Tierney; Dover Publications

A full-color cardboard theater to cut, fold, and assemble, complete with six backdrops—among them a towering Christmas tree—and dozens of costumed characters.

$5.95

Dover Publications, Inc.

31 E. Second St.

Mineola, NY 11501

4+ *Let's Pretend Ballerina*

Make your own ballet costume for dancers aged 4 and up. The kit includes material for making a pink tulle tutu with matching hairpiece, along with toe shoe–style pink satin ribbons.

$14.95 from toy and game stores or

Creativity for Kids

1802 Central Ave.

Cleveland, OH 44115

(216) 589-4800 or (800) 642-2288

Web site: www.creativityforkids.com

6+ *Paper Dolls*

Dover publishes several books of famous dancer paper dolls. *Pavlova and Nijinsky Paper Dolls* includes the two dancers, plus reproductions of 30 gorgeously colored costumes; *Ballet Stars of the Romantic Period Paper Dolls* includes eight famous dancers—among them Marie Taglioni, Carlotta Grisi, and Lola Montez—each with three costumes; *Isadora Duncan, Martha Graham and Other Stars of the Modern Dance Paper Dolls* includes eight dolls and 21 costumes; and *Diaghilev's Ballets Russe Paper Dolls* includes eight dolls and 32 costumes, from 20 different ballet productions. All by Tom Tierney.

$4.95

Dover Publications, Inc.

31 E. Second St.

Mineola, NY 11501

VIDEO RESOURCES

Celtic Feet

ALL Step-by-step lessons in Irish dancing on video, under the direction of Colin Dunne, a featured dancer in *Riverdance* (page 794). For kids (and families) of all ages.

$19.95

PBS Home Video

1320 Braddock Pl.

Alexandria, VA 22314-1698

(800) 645-4727

Web site: www.pbs.org

4–12 *The Children's Cultural Collection*

This highly recommended series was designed to introduce kids aged 4–12 to classical music and the performing arts. Each tape is 30 to 40 minutes long. Ballet titles include "Alice in Wonderland," "Cinderella, Daisy and her Garden," and "The Swan Lake Story." "The Swan Lake Story," for example, begins with a grandfather telling his little granddaughter a magical fairy tale as they sit by the fire. The narration blends into dance sequences performed by the Oregon State Ballet, against a background of beautiful outdoor scenery, with music by the London Philharmonic Orchestra.

$19.95 each

Movies Unlimited

3015 Darnell Rd.

Philadelphia, PA 19154

(214) 637-4444 or (800) 4-MOVIES

e-mail: movies@moviesunlimited.com

Web site: www.moviesunlimited.com

or

Educational Record Center, Inc.

3233 Burnt Mill Dr., Suite 100

Wilmington, NC 28403-2655

(800) 438-1637/fax (888) 438-1637

e-mail: erc-inc@worldnet.att.net

Web site: www.erc-inc.com

3–10 *Dance Along at Home With Miss Linda*

A 25-minute introduction to dance on video for kids aged 3–10. The action begins at the barre, where a company of little girls helps Miss Linda demonstrate the five ballet positions and basic steps. Subsequent exercises involve rhythm games, and jumps and stretches. Finally Miss Linda, glitteringly costumed as the Blue Fairy, leads the class in a fantasy ballet.

$19.95

Artistic Dance, Inc.

Box 120

Throgs Neck Station, NY 10465

(800) 270-7727

Fantasy Garden Ballet Class Series

The *Fantasy Garden* and *Fantasy Garden II* videos are designed to teach the basics of ballet to very young beginners, aged 2–6. The action takes place in a flower garden, where Rosemary Boross—Metropolitan Opera Ballet performer and Alvin Ailey instructor—leads a class of pink-clad preschoolers through their first steps. To help kids remember their lessons, Boross pairs each step with a flower or garden animal, such as a springing frog or leaping ladybug. Each video is 40 minutes long; young viewers can dance right along.

$19.95 each

Music for Little People

Box 1720

Lawndale, CA 90260-6620

(800) 346-4445

The Nutcracker

The Nutcracker is *the* classic ballet for children, and there are many versions available on video. *George Balanchine's The Nutcracker* (1993), narrated by Kevin Kline, features the dancers of the New York City Ballet; *Nutcracker: The Motion Picture* (1986) is performed by the Pacific Northwest Ballet Company, using designs by children's author and illustrator Maurice Sendak; and *The Nutcracker* (1977) stars Mikhail Baryshnikov, Gelsey Kirkland, and the American Ballet Theatre Company.

Movies Unlimited

3015 Darnell Rd.

Philadelphia, PA 19154

(215) 637-4444 or (800) 4-MOVIES

e-mail: movies@moviesunlimited.com

Web site: www.moviesunlimited.com

Riverdance

Riverdance is a spectacular celebration of Irish music and dance, starring dancer Michael Flatley. The video lasts about an hour and a half; you and your kids will be enthralled (and out of breath) by the end of it.

Also see *Lord of the Dance,* based on an Irish folk legend, in which Michael Flatley presents another wonderful Celtic dance and music production.

$24.95 each

PBS Home Video

1320 Braddock Pl.

Alexandria, VA 22314-1698

(800) 645-4727

Web site: www.pbs.org

DANCE ON-LINE

American Ballet Theatre

Biographies of famous dancers, a photo gallery of performers, and a ballet dictionary, as well as general information about the American Ballet Theatre.

www.abt.org

Dance Links

Links to dance schools, an events and competitions calendar, news groups, and dance publications, along with a long list of links categorized by dance type, from ballet and ballroom to Western square dancing.

artswire.org/Artswire/www/dance/dance.html

The History of Ballet

A complete text on-line. The site also includes an on-line bookstore of books about dance.

www.haas.berkeley.edu/~schladen/ballet_html/history.html

Sapphire Swan Dance Directory

A list of dance resources on the Web, categorized by dance styles.

www.SapphireSwan.com/dance

ETHICS, RELIGION, AND PHILOSOPHY

There are now-a-days professors of philosophy but not philosophers.

HENRY DAVID THOREAU

Philosophy, religion, and ethics: this interrelated trio doubtless generates more individual opinion and controversy than the rest of the academic curriculum combined.
None is heavily emphasized in the public schools. Most school systems, in judiciously
balanced fashion, do teach some comparative religion—usually as a subset of world history and geography programs—and many attempt to provide a cross-curricular grounding in ethics, now commonly called "values" or "character" education. Philosophy, as a
formal academic subject, is rarely taught in primary or secondary schools; most students
first encounter it in college.

Our children's homeschool introduction to all of the above began informally. Character education, at first glance, seems straightforward in content: a simple list of desirable virtues, the necessary prerequisites for what used to be called a proper upbringing. A moral child, for example, is honest, tolerant, and compassionate, hard-working and unselfish, courageous, trustworthy, and responsible. (Or else.) When the boys were small, character education was largely conducted according to the contingencies of the moment. How should you behave, for example, when your little brother snatches your toy fire truck? (No hitting or screaming.) When there aren't enough cookies to go around? (Share cheerfully.) When you throw a baseball through the kitchen window? (Own up.) Is it all right to pull the cat's tail? (Definitely not.) To call people mean names? (Ditto.)

As the boys grew older, however, the small experiences of everyday life gradually led to broader questions. Ethics ceased to be a matter of disaster control and began to take shape as an intellectual discipline.

From my homeschool journal:

◆ **June 3, 1991. Josh is almost ten; Ethan, eight; Caleb, six.**

We've been reading about George Washington as part of our ongoing study of the Revolutionary War. Today: George Washington's Breakfast *by Jean Fritz (see page 493) and* The Adventures of George Washington *by Margaret Davidson (see page 493). We discussed the famous (but untrue) story of Washington and his father's cherry tree, with its attendant moral, "I cannot tell a lie." Caleb was interested in the mechanics of the evil deed: "How big is a cherry tree? How long does it take to chop one down? How old was George Washington when he chopped down the tree? Can I have a hatchet?" Josh and Ethan, however, soon took off into more complex ethical territory.*

"It's wrong to tell a lie—but is lying always *wrong?" "What if you lie to keep from hurting someone's feelings?" "What about the conductors on the Underground Railroad? They lied to protect the escaping slaves. That wasn't wrong." "What about spies in wartime?" "What about Nathan Hale? If he had lied about what he was doing, maybe the British wouldn't have hanged him. Is it wrong to lie to save your life?"*

We found that character education, home-style, involved continual questions and answers, discussions and debates. Group or individual readings often served as jumping-off points: "Was it right for Jack to climb up the beanstalk and steal from the giant?" "How could Thomas Jefferson write 'All men are created equal' and then keep slaves?"

My homeschool journals turn up fragments of past family talk fests: "Are there some things that are always good or evil, or does it just depend on when and where you live?" "Is there a God? If there is a God, why do so many terrible things happen?" "What happens after we die?" "If it's wrong to kill people, why isn't it wrong to kill animals? What about bugs and plants?" "Is it sometimes right to break a law?" "Is abortion right or wrong? What about euthanasia?" "Should you have to go fight for your country if you don't think the war is right?"

In our household, these were not easily answerable questions. The quest for answers led, inevitably, to an interest in how other people and cultures have dealt with such questions—and eventually to studies of comparative religion, political science, and philosophy. Joshua, interested in classical philosophy, read Plato (and formed unshakably negative opinions about Socrates); then moved on to Jostein Gaarder's *Sophie's World* (see page 808), a creative overview of Western philosophy for teenagers and older readers. Interest still ran high, so we subscribed to an audiocassette series titled "The Giants of Philosophy" (see page 809), and Josh began listening his way from Plato to Jean-Paul Sartre.

ETHICS

CATALOGS

The Global Classroom

ALL A comprehensive catalog of materials for character and values education for kids of all ages. Included are parent/teacher books, lesson plans, curricula, activity books, storybooks, audiocassettes, and videos.

The Global Classroom
Box 584
Williston, VT 05495-0584

MAGAZINES

Teaching Tolerance

P/T A semiannual magazine published by the education department of the Southern Poverty Law Center, it aims to promote "intercultural understanding" in the elementary and secondary classrooms. Each issue includes articles on multicultural themes, the history of racial prejudice, and methods for teaching tolerance, along with lists of multicultural teaching resources: book reviews, addresses of helpful organizations, games, videos, and computer software. Copies of *Teaching Tolerance* are free to educators.

Teaching Tolerance

400 Washington Ave.

Montgomery, Al 36104

(205) 334-0286/fax (334) 264-3121

BOOKS: ABOUT CHARACTER EDUCATION

Educating for Character: How Our Schools Can Teach Respect and Responsibility

P/T Thomas Lickona; Bantam Books, 1991

The book describes a multifaceted approach to teaching good moral values in the classroom, variously by creating a "moral environment" in the school community, by establishing "democratic" classrooms, by including the teaching of ethical values in the academic subjects (for example, "Art and music instructors can examine the lives of great artists and composers as models of self-discipline"), by encouraging cooperative learning, by promoting moral discussions, and by teaching conflict resolution strategies. The schools should attempt to recruit parents as partners in this endeavor, Lickona suggests, pointing out that how effectively children are taught to respect parental authority is a determining factor for fruitful moral growth. The ideal parent is "authoritative"—requiring obedience, but for clearly defined and logical reasons—as opposed to "permissive" (wimpy about rules and confrontations) or "authoritarian" ("Mind me because I said so!").

Raising Peaceful Children in a Violent World

P/T Nancy Lee Cecil; LuraMedia, 1995

The book is divided into three parts: "Peaceful Communication," "Peaceful Entertainment," and "Peaceful Relationships." The first covers suggestions and activities for resolving family conflicts; the second discusses ways to combat the negative effects of the media and proposes alternatives to warlike toys and games; and the third presents suggestions and activities for forging peaceful social relationships. Kids, for example, are encouraged to keep "Dialogue Notebooks" in which they write about how they feel and their parents write (nonjudgmental) replies.

The book includes many reading suggestions and book lists for both children and adults.

Teaching Peace: How to Raise Children to Live in Harmony—Without Fear, Without Prejudice, Without Violence

P/T Jan Arnow; Berkley Publishing Group, 1995

The book is divided into three major sections. In Part One, "The Home," the author discusses the kids' everyday exposure to violence. Sale of war toys, for example, is a billion-dollar business; many video games are violent and battle oriented; and television is now near legendary: a child who watches two to four hours of television a day will have seen 8,000 homicides by the time he/she reaches junior high school. Included are addresses for parents who wish to protest or voice concerns, and guidelines for evaluating children's literature on the basis of violence, sexism, racism, and stereotyping. Part Two, "Home to School," discusses school programs designed to promote harmonious living. Arnow, for example, favors multicultural education, stating that the traditional "melting pot" analogy that once bound people together is now obsolete. Also covered are conflict resolution programs, methods for evaluating classroom literature (most, Arnow points out, is still written by Western white males), gender fairness in teaching, and suggestions for families on becoming school involved. Finally, Part Three, "Home to School to Community," covers wider social prob-

PHILOSOPHY

lems, hate crimes, gangs, and means of taking preventive community action.

Why Johnny Can't Tell Right from Wrong

P/T William K. Kirkpatrick; Simon & Schuster, 1992

Our current crisis in moral values among the young, explains Kirkpatrick, stems from the modern approach to values education: parents and teachers tend to stress feelings rather than good behavior. The author explains what's being done wrong and suggests how to fix it.

BOOKS: VALUES FOR KIDS AND FAMILIES

The Book of American Values and Virtues

ALL Erik A. Bruun and Robin Getzen, eds.; Black Dog & Leventhal Publishers, 1996

Over a thousand quotations and excerpts from stories, poems, speeches, and documents that celebrate "the rich diversity of thoughts and opinions, hopes and dreams that have shaped our country." Chapter titles include "A More Perfect Union," "All Men Are Created Equal," "Domestic Tranquility," and "Secure the Blessings of Liberty." Contributors include Samuel Adams, Black Elk, Ralph Ellison, Betty Friedan, Garrison Keillor, Abraham Lincoln, Rosa Parks, Eleanor Roosevelt, Babe Ruth, Maya Angelou, Mark Twain, and many more.

The Book of Virtues for Young People

9 12 William Bennett, ed.; Silver Burdett, 1995

A truncated version of *The Book of Virtues* (below) for readers aged 9–12. The book includes a varied assortment of fables, folktales, and short stories by such authors as Aesop, Charles Dickens, Leo Tolstoy, and James Baldwin.

The Book of Virtues: A Treasury of Great Moral Stories

ALL William Bennett, ed.; Simon & Schuster, 1993

Hundreds of stories, fables, and poems variously illustrating the virtues of self-discipline, compassion, responsibility, friendship, work, courage, perseverance, honesty, loyalty, and faith, from many varied sources. Included are stories from the Bible, tales from American history, Greek myths, and fairy tales. Contributors include Thomas Jefferson, Martin Luther King Jr., Robert Frost, O. Henry, Hans Christian Andersen, Leo Tolstoy, F. Scott Fitzgerald, and Rudyard Kipling. Some of the selections are great, some are heavy-handed, and some are awful. Our boys, who like their virtue with a sense of humor, were definitely unimpressed by the schmaltzy (but virtuous) poetry of Sam Walter Foss, Joy Allison, and Ella Wheeler Wilcox.

See *The Book of Virtues for Young People* (left), *The Children's Book of Virtues* (below), and *The Children's Book of Heroes* (below).

A Call to Character

ALL Colin Greer and Herbert Kohl, eds.; HarperCollins, 1995

The subtitle is "A Family Treasury of Stories, Poems, Plays, Proverbs, and Fables to Guide the Development of Values for You and Your Family," which pretty much says it all. The book has been described as a liberal alternative to Bennett's *The Book of Virtues*. The selections emphasize such exemplary character traits as courage, self-discipline, integrity, creativity, playfulness, loyalty, generosity, empathy, honesty, adaptability, idealism, compassion, responsibility, balance, fairness, and love, by authors as varied as Boris Pasternak, Charlotte Brontë, William Golding, and A. A. Milne.

The Children's Book of Heroes

4 8 William Bennett, ed.; Simon & Schuster, 1997

Role models for kids aged 4–8. The book is a collection of stories about admirable people and characters, among them Helen Keller, Jackie Robinson, Mother Teresa, and the indefatigable Little Engine That Could.

The Children's Book of Virtues

4 8 William Bennett, ed.; Simon & Schuster, 1995

Stories from *The Book of Virtues* (left) for young readers, with color illustrations by Michael Hague. Also available in a Spanish version.

If You Had to Choose, What Would You Do?

Sandra McLeod Humphrey; Prometheus Books, 1995

A collection of ethical dilemmas for 9–12-year-olds, in which the readers are asked to decide what they would do.

You Can't Sell Your Brother at the Garage Sale: The Kids' Book of Values

Beth Brainard; Dell, 1992

A picture book about right, wrong, and the process of thinking things through, for kids aged 4–12.

GAMES AND HANDS-ON ACTIVITIES

The Game of Dilemmas

The heart of the game is the softcover *Dilemmas* book—the full title is "Controversial Solutions to Some Devastating Dilemmas"—which contains over 150 ethical or intellectual dilemmas, problem scenarios to be solved by the players. For group play, each player in turn reads a dilemma aloud and must describe his/her solution to the problem within 10 minutes. The other players act as judges, voting to determine the deserved score. The game designer's solution to each dilemma is printed upside down in italics at the end of each selection. The dilemmas are sorted into 11 (somewhat overlapping) categories: "Self Preservation," "Ethics and Morals," "Crime," "Strange Encounters," "Working," "Embarrassing Moments," "Legal Matters," "Unusual Situations," "Romance," "Medicine," and "Family Affairs."

Try this sample dilemma:

A friend gives you things to be held in trust, to be returned upon request. Some time later the friend wants to reclaim what you are holding for him. He explains he requires what you are holding for the purpose of wreaking great damage to other people—people you know and admire. Evil as his plan is, it is not illegal. What can you do?

If you solve all your dilemmas, a sequel is available: "Dilemmas II." For older kids and adults.

$12

Avalon Hill Game Co.
4517 Harford Rd.
Baltimore, MD 21214
(410) 254-9200 or (800) 999-3222
e-mail: AHGAMES@aol.com
Web site: www.avalonhill.com

AUDIOVISUAL RESOURCES

Adventures from the Book of Virtues

A PBS television series for young children based on William Bennett's *Book of Virtues* (see page 798), in which young Annie and Zach learn such values as honesty, courage, responsibility, and compassion through animated folktales, fables, and Bible stories. Selections from the series are available on videotape. Episodes include "Honesty" ("The Indian Cinderella"), "Work" ("Tom Sawyer"), "Responsibility" ("King Alfred and the Cakes"), "Self-Discipline" ("The Magic Thread"), "Courage" ("William Tell"), and "Compassion" ("Androcles and the Lion"). Some episodes from the series are also available as picture books, among them *Honesty: Zach's Tall Tale* and *Courage: Annie's Race*, both by Shelagh Canning (Simon Spotlight, 1996).

A 6-tape set, $59.98
PBS Home Video
1320 Braddock Pl.
Alexandria, VA 22314-1698
(800) 645-4727
Web site: www.pbs.org

Morality in Our Age

A 13-part program on audiocassettes on the major moral issues of modern times. Titles of the two-cassette selections, narrated by Cliff Robertson and Robert Guillaume, include "Thinking About Moral Issues," "The Family," "Love and Sexuality," "Lying, Secrecy, and Privacy," "Punishment," "Property," "Drugs and Alcohol," "The Moral Standing of Animals and Plants," "Unity in Diversity," "Community and Civility," "Abortion and Euthanasia," "War, Terrorism, and Violence," and "Human Rights and Civil Rights." For teenagers and older listeners.

Series, $194; individual 2-tape sets, $17.95 (plus $3 shipping/handling). The series can also be purchased

by monthly subscription
Knowledge Products
Box 305151
Nashville, TN 37230
(800) 876-4332

RELIGION

Books

Adam and Eve: The Bible Story
Warwick Hutton; Margaret K. McElderry, 1987

A picture-book retelling of the Old Testament tale of Adam, Eve, and the Garden of Eden, illustrated with watercolor paintings. Also see *Jonah and the Great Fish* (Margaret K. McElderry, 1984), *Moses in the Bulrushes* (Aladdin, 1992), and *Noah and the Great Flood* (Atheneum, 1977).

Beliefs & Cultures Series
Children's Press

Each book in the series explains the tenets of a different world religion, covering history, cultural background, sacred texts, traditions, and holidays. The books are 32 pages long, illustrated with color photographs, and recommended for readers in grades 4–6. Titles include *Hindu* (Anita Ganeri; 1996), *Jewish* (Monica Stoppleman; 1996), *Muslim* (Richard Tames; 1996), and *Sikh* (Catherine Chambers; 1996).

Buddha
Susan L. Roth; Doubleday, 1994

A picture-book story of Siddhartha, the wealthy prince who, seeing the pain and suffering in the world around him, embarked on a spiritual quest, eventually attaining great wisdom and enlightenment. Illustrated with collages.

Buddha Stories
Demi; Henry Holt, 1997

A picture-book collection of Buddha's stories, each a parable with a moral, exquisitely illustrated in deep blue and gold.

Catherine Marshall's Story Bible
Catherine Marshall; Avon Books, 1987

There are numerous collections of Bible stories for children, but this version is distinguished by its wonderful full-color illustrations, all by kids. The book includes 37 stories from the Old and New Testaments, in chronological order, retold in simplified (but not too simplified) language for young readers.
See *The Kingfisher Children's Bible* (page 801).

Cobblestone: World Religions
Several issues of *Calliope,* the kids' world history magazine from Cobblestone Publishing (see page 597), center around world religions. Titles include *Buddhism* (March 1995), *Early Christianity* (March 1996), *Hinduism* (March 1993), *Judaism* (March 1994), and *Islam* (January 1997). The *Islam* issue, for example, includes a brief biography of Muhammad, nonfiction articles on the Islamic faith, the Koran, Islamic traditions and festivals, mosques, the Islamic calendar, and the hajj, the religious pilgrimage to Mecca that every Muslim is expected to make at least once in a lifetime. The magazine also includes a map, a timeline, instructions for an Islamic calligraphy project, and recipes for a Ramadan meal.

Back issues of *Calliope* are generally available from libraries or for $4.50 from
Cobblestone Publishing, Inc.
30 Grove St.
Peterborough, NH 03458-1454
(603) 924-7209 or (800) 821-0115
e-mail: custsvc@cobblestone.mv.com
Web site: www.cobblestonepub.com.

Comparing Religions Series
Thomson Learning, 1993

A series of 32-page books for readers aged 9–12, in which the customs of major world religions are described. Each book centers around a specific religious theme and compares the rituals, practices, and beliefs of six religions. Titles include *Birth Customs* (Lucy Rushton), *Marriage Customs* (Anita Compton), and *Death Customs* (Lucy Rushton).

Days of Awe: Stories for Rosh Hashanah and Yom Kippur

Eric A. Kimmel; Viking, 1991

Three traditional stories for young readers exemplifying the virtues of charity, prayer, and forgiveness, variously set in Russia, Moorish Spain, and Israel.

Hershel and the Hanukkah Goblins

Eric Kimmel; Holiday House, 1994

Clever Hershel outwits the goblins who have taken over the village synagogue and kept the people from celebrating Hanukkah.

How Do You Know It's True?: Discovering the Difference Between Science and Superstition

Hyman Ruchlis; Prometheus Books, 1991

An explanation of critical thinking and the use of the scientific method for young readers. The book includes discussion of the dangers of superstition, as witnessed in the witch-hunts of the 16th and 17th centuries, and the consequences of the religious repression of free thought.

How Do You Spell God?: Answers to the Big Questions From Around the World

Marc Gellman and Thomas Hartman; William Morrow, 1995

An excellent introduction to comparative religion for kids in grades 6–9. The book, written by a Jewish rabbi and a Catholic monsignor, explains how all world religions attempt to answer the "big questions" about ethical living, the existence of God, the afterlife, the effectiveness of prayer, and the place of the individual in the world. Each chapter—for example "Can I Talk to God?" and "What Happens After We Die?"—describes how each religion deals with these questions. The book covers Judaism, Christianity, Islam, Buddhism, and Hinduism.

Nothing, the authors explain, is perfect (except God): one chapter covers the bad things in religions (the Hindu caste system, religious fanatics, televangelists, hate); another covers the "terrific things" (weddings, the Ten Commandments, meditation, muezzins, Mahatma Gandhi, the Dalai Lama).

The essence of How Do You Spell God?, however, is summed up by an old story that the authors repeat in chapter one: A king has died and left a gift of three rings, one for each of his three sons. With the rings is a note explaining that only one of the rings is real—and the way to identify it is through the behavior of its owner, who will spend his life being kind and generous to all. Each of the sons then spends the rest of his life being kind and generous, each convinced that he has the real ring.

"So they were really all the same," said Caleb. "They were all real rings."

How We Saw the World: Nine Native Stories of the Way Things Began

C. J. Taylor; Tundra Books, 1996

An illustrated collection of creation legends from North American Indian tribes, among them the Cheyenne, Oneida, Algonquin, Micmac, Kiowa, Blackfoot, Mohawk, and Bella Coola.

Iblis

Shulamith Levy Oppenheim; Harcourt Brace, 1994

The Islamic version of the story of Adam and Eve, in picture-book form. Iblis (Satan) tricks the peacock and the serpent and manages to sneak into Eden where he persuades Eve to eat the fruit of the forbidden "wheat tree."

In the Beginning: Creation Myths from Around the World

Virginia Hamilton; Harcourt Brace, 1991

Twenty-five stories from around the globe about the creation of the world and its people, with 42 lovely color illustrations.

The Kingfisher Children's Bible: Stories From the Old and New Testaments

Ann Pilling; Kingfisher Books, 1993

Over 100 stories from the Old and New Testaments, lushly illustrated with watercolor paintings.

The Little Lama of Tibet

Lois Raimondo; Scholastic, 1994

An account of the daily life of 6-year-old Ling Rinpoche, believed to be the reincarnation of the Dalai Lama. Illustrated with color photographs.

9 12 *Maybe Yes, Maybe No:* *A Guide for Young Skeptics*

Dan Barker; Prometheus Books, 1990

An excellent explanation of the practical uses of critical thinking. The author, using a background story of kids hunting for ghosts, shows why it is unwise to believe everything you hear. He offers, as an alternative, a means of exercising rational skepticism: how to determine what constitutes proof, how to ask questions, and how to use the scientific method to check things out. These methods, Barker explains, can be used to come to a balanced conclusion about such phenomena as UFO reports, astrological predictions, and faith healing. The final answer depends on the evidence: sometimes yes, sometimes no.

9 12 *Menorahs, Mezuzas, and* *Other Jewish Symbols*

Mariam Chaikin; Clarion, 1990

An illustrated account of the history and significance of Jewish religious symbols, including the Star of David, the menorah, and the doorway mezuza.

5 9 *The Mountains of Tibet*

Mordicai Gerstein; HarperTrophy, 1989

A Tibetan woodcutter dies and is offered a choice between heaven and reincarnation. He chooses reincarnation and must then decide what sort of life to live.

12 + *My Friend's Beliefs: A Young Reader's* *Guide to World Religions*

Hiley Ward; Walker & Company, 1991

A tour of world religions for readers aged 12 and up. The book covers five religions in depth—Jewish, Hindu, Buddhist, Islamic, and Christian—and a host of others more briefly, among them the Jehovah's Witnesses, the Christian Scientists, and the Unitarians. For each, the author covers major historical and modern figures, rituals, commandments, scriptures, and tenets of belief. Illustrated with black-and-white photographs.

9 12 *One World, Many Religions:* *The Way We Worship*

Mary Pope Osborne; Alfred A. Knopf, 1996

Six short chapters on the beliefs and practices of Judaism, Christianity, Islam, Hinduism, Buddhism, Confucianism, and Taoism, illustrated with color photographs.

9 12 *The Passover Journey: A Seder Companion*

Barbara Diamond Goldin; Puffin, 1997

An illustrated retelling of the tale of the Israelites' escape from slavery in Egypt, with a detailed explanation of the 14 symbolic steps of the traditional Passover Seder as it is celebrated today.

9 12 *Religion*

Myrtle Langley; Alfred A. Knopf, 1996

An Eyewitness book, heavily and beautifully illustrated with color photographs of religious figures, relics, buildings, and rituals from around the world.

7 10 *Religion Explained: A Beginner's* *Guide to World Faiths*

Anita Ganeri; Henry Holt, 1996

A 68-page introduction to the world's major faiths for readers in grades 3–5, heavily illustrated with artwork and photographs.

9 12 *Religions of the World: Using* *and Understanding Maps*

Scott E. Morris, ed.; Chelsea House, 1993

Comparative religion and geography. The book includes 18 colorful maps showing the geographic distribution of world religions.

7 12 *The Story of Religion*

Betsy Maestro; Clarion, 1996

A simple history of religious beliefs for young readers, explaining both the differences among the world's many religions and the fundamentals that all share. The book covers the first primitive religions, the religions of the ancient Egyptians, Greeks, and Mayans, Taoism and Confucianism, Hinduism, Buddhism, Judaism, Christianity, and Islam. Illustrated with wonderfully colored paintings by Giulio Maestro.

12 + *The Tao of Pooh*

Benjamin Hoff; Penguin, 1983

Taoist philosophy, as exemplified by Winnie-the-Pooh. The book is clever and reader-friendly, but the concepts are for mature readers. Also see *The Te of Piglet* (Dutton, 1992).

Tomie de Paola's Book of Bible Stories
5 9

Tomie de Paola; Putnam, 1990

A collection of beautifully illustrated stories from both Old and New Testaments, from the creation to the Resurrection. Also see *The Parables of Jesus* (Holiday House, 1987) and *The Miracles of Jesus* (Holiday House, 1987).

The Wailing Wall
8 12

Leonard Everett Fisher; Macmillan, 1989

A short illustrated history of the Jewish people from the time of the First and Second Temples, the site of the present-day Wailing Wall.

The Way to Start a Day
4 8

Byrd Baylor; Aladdin, 1986

An illustrated account of how people throughout the world, past and present, greet the sunrise. This is a simple introduction to comparative religion.

What Is God?
4 8

Etan Boritzer; Firefly Books, 1990

A gentle picture-book introduction to the concept of "God" for the very young. The book explains how people may experience God—". . . maybe God is what you feel when you see a million stars at night and you feel very small looking up at them." It also discusses how different religious groups have special beliefs about God and how, though these differences in belief have led historically to fighting, most religions are really very similar at heart.

World Religions Series
12 +

A series of 128-page books from Facts on File for young adults, each covering a specific world religion or group of related religions. Titles include *Hinduism* (Madhu Bazaz Wangu; 1991), *Islam* (Matthew S. Gordon; 1991), *Judaism* (Martha Morrison and Stephen F. Brown; 1991), *Native American Religions* (Paula Hartz; 1997), *Shinto* (Paula Hartz; 1997), *Sikhism* (Nikky-Guninder Kaur Singh; 1993), and *Taoism* (Paula Hartz; 1993).

COLORING BOOKS

A Coloring Book of the Old Testament
6 +

Elegantly illustrated with black-line drawings of Biblical scenes from medieval manuscripts, with an explanatory text. In the same format, also see *A Coloring Book of the New Testament*.

$3.95

Bellerophon Books

36 Ancapa St.

Santa Barbara, CA 93101

(800) 253-9943/fax (800) 965-8286

Make Your Own Jewish Calendar Coloring Book
6 +

Chaya Burstein; Dover Publications

Twelve illustrations to color, plus a ready-to-complete calendar with which kids can learn the names of the Hebrew months and the dates of Jewish holidays. Also see the *Jewish Holidays and Traditions Coloring Book*, which contains 41 illustrations of Jewish rituals, traditions, and celebrations—a picture of a group of kids spinning a dreidel at Hanukkah, for example. Both books include informational picture captions.

$2.95

Dover Publications, Inc.

31 E. Second St.

Mineola, NY 11501

GAMES AND HANDS-ON ACTIVITIES

BibleTalk
ALL

There are two decks of "BibleTalk" cards, one based on the Old Testament, the other on the New. Each deck is a collection of conversation starters: individual cards present a short paragraph of interesting information, followed by an open-ended discussion-provoking question. A sample:

When King Xerxes was ruler of the Persian empire, he married a beautiful woman named Esther. King Xerxes did not know Esther was Jewish. When the prime minister, Haman, designed a plot to murder all Jews, Queen Esther risked her life by revealing her her-

itage and asking the king to save her people. What is the bravest thing you have ever done or seen someone else do?

$5.95
TableTalk
Box 31703
St. Louis, MO 63131
(314) 997-5676 or (800) 997-5676
Web site: www.tbltalk.com

See **TableTalk** cards (pages 67).

✋ 12 + *Islam*

A creative simulation of Islamic history and culture for kids in grades 6–12. The unit is divided into five main parts. During the "Introductory Phase," kids read about the history of Islam, are given a Muslim name, and study Muslim everyday life. In "Caravan Days," they study early trade routes and compete in a race to Mecca, advancing and earning dirhems (Arab money) by answering Quiz Cards; in "Oasis Days," they study Middle Eastern geography, learn about Muhammad and the Islamic faith, and role-play historical caliphs; and in "Festival Days," they complete a project involving Middle Eastern food, art, music, dance, architecture, or some other aspect of Islamic culture. Finally, in "Islamic Bowl," they compete in a "College Bowl"–style quiz game, summarizing all they have learned. Simulation materials are packaged in a looseleaf notebook, with five tabbed sections; included are background information, daily lesson plans, and reproducible student handouts and worksheets.

$43
Interact
1825 Gillespie Way, #101
El Cajon, CA 92020-1095
(619) 448-1474 or (800) 359-0961/fax (619) 448-6722
or (800) 700-5093
Web site: www.interact-simulations.com

✋ 13 + *Martin Luther*

Martin Luther, nailing his 95 Theses to the door of Wittenburg Cathedral, ushered in the upheaval of the Protestant Reformation, with its sweeping implications for Western history. The "Martin Luther" portfolio contains six historical "Broadsheet Essays," nine historical document reproductions from the early days

of the Reformation, and a detailed study guide with reproducible student worksheets. Essay titles include "Luther's World," "Martin Luther," "The Sale of Indulgences," "The Diet of Worms," "The Reformation Spreads," and "The Counter-Reformation." Among the historical documents are a copy of Luther's Ninety-five Theses, a portrait of Luther, period woodcuts satirizing the established church and comparing "true and false" religion, a handbill attacking John Calvin, and a page from a 1533 Lutheran hymnal.

$37
Jackdaw Publications
Box 503
Amawalk, NY 10501
(914) 962-6911 or (800) 789-0022/fax (800) 962-9101

♟ 7 + *Old Testament Stories*

A Bible story card game played like rummy: players attempt to collect four-card sets, each representing one of 13 Old Testament stories. The cards are beautifully illustrated in color and include a short, simple text. For 2 to 4 players, aged 7 and up. Also see *New Testament Stories,* a card game based on the New Testament.

$7
Aristoplay
Box 7529
Ann Arbor, MI 48107
(800) 634-7738/fax (313) 995-4611

✋ 13 + *Religion*

Designed as an "Independent Learning Project" (ILP), this study unit consists of a student guide booklet with instructions for nine learning activities centering around world religions. The unit is intended to expose kids in grades 7–12 to the history and development of religious thought and the place of religion in modern society. Young researchers study Hinduism, Buddhism, Judaism, Christianity, Islam, Shinto, humanism, existentialism, transcendental meditation, and "self-improvement" psychologies. Activities involve background reading assignments, essay writing, interviewing assorted subjects, participating in a role-playing activity, and completing a personal research project.

P
H
I
L
O
S
O
P
H
Y

$10

Interact

1825 Gillespie Way, #101

El Cajon, CA 92020-1095

(619) 448-1474 or (800) 359-0961/fax (619) 448-6722

or (800) 700-5093

Web site: www.interact-simulations.com

The World of Islam

A portfolio of materials covering the history, intellectual achievements, and religious beliefs of the world of Islam. Included are background historical essays (readers learn, for example, about the invention of algebra and the celebration of Ramadan, and find out what tabby cats have to do with Baghdad), nine historical document reproductions, and a study guide with reproducible student worksheets. Historical documents include a color reproduction of a page from a medieval edition of the Koran, illustrations of mosques, a survey of famous Islamic cities, a souvenir brochure from a hajj pilgrimage, and a collection of brief biographies of famous Muslim rulers, mystics, and writers.

$37

Jackdaw Publications

Box 503

Amawalk, NY 10501

(914) 962-6911 or (800) 789-0022/fax (800) 962-9101

AUDIOVISUAL RESOURCES

Genesis: A Living Conversation

Bill Moyers tackles the Book of Genesis and its meaning for modern society in a series of 10 creative debates and conversations with an opinionated group of scholars, historians, and writers of many faiths, philosophies, and viewpoints. Episode titles include "In God's Image," "Temptation," "The First Murder," "Apocalypse," "Call and Promise," "A Family Affair," "The Test," "Blessed Deception," "God Wrestling," and "Exile." Each episode runs about one hour.

About $120

PBS Home Video

1320 Braddock Pl.

Alexandria, VA 22314-1698

(800) 645-4PBS

Web site: www.pbs.org

The Greatest Stories Ever Told Series

A series of beautifully drawn animations of classical Bible tales from Rabbit Ears video, with excellent narration and musical scores. Titles include *David and Goliath, The Savior is Born, Noah and the Ark, Jonah and the Whale, The Creation, Joseph and His Brothers, Moses in Egypt,* and *Moses the Lawgiver.* Each runs about 30 minutes.

$14.95 each

Movies Unlimited

3015 Darnell Rd.

Philadelphia, PA 19154

(215) 637-4444 or (800) 4-MOVIES

e-mail: movies@moviesunlimited.com

Web site: www.moviesunlimited.com

Religion, Scriptures, & Spirituality

A 13-part audiocassette series on the histories and philosophies of world religions. Titles in the series, all narrated by Ben Kingsley, include "Orthodox and Roman Catholic Christianity," "Protestant Christianity," "Judaism," "Islam," "Hinduism," "Buddhism," "Shinto and Japanese New Religions," "Confucianism and Taoism," "The Religion of Small Societies," "Classical Religions and Myths of the Mediterranean Basin," "African and African-American Religions," "Native Religions of the Americas," and "Skepticism and Religious Relativism." Each title consists of two cassettes.

Series, $194; individual 2-tape sets, $17.95. Can also be purchased by monthly subscription

Knowledge Products

Box 305151

Nashville, TN 37230

(800) 876-4332

Tales From the Old Testament

Seven Old Testament stories, beautifully told by master storyteller Jim Weiss. Included are the stories of Abraham, Ruth, Noah and the Ark, Queen Esther, David and Goliath, and King Solomon.

CD, $14.95; audiocassette, $9.95

Greathall Productions

Box 5061

Charlottesville, VA 22905-5061

(800) 477-6234

The Ten Commandments

Cecil B. DeMille's 1956 epic to end all epics, with a cast of what does indeed look like thousands, Charlton Heston as Moses, Yul Brynner as the stubborn pharaoh, and some spectacular scenes of pyramid building. The movie traces the story of Moses from the basket in the bulrushes through the crossing of the Red Sea and the receiving of the Ten Commandments.

$29.95

Movies Unlimited

3015 Darnell Rd.

Philadelphia, PA 19154

(215) 637-4444 or (800) 4-MOVIES

e-mail: movies@moviesunlimited.com

Web site: www.moviesunlimited.com

Testament

A superb seven-part survey of the Bible as history, narrated by archaeologist John Romer. The series begins with the beginnings of monotheism in the ancient Middle East, and continues through the rise and fall of ancient Israel, the life and times of the historical Jesus, the origins of the Christian Bible, the conversion of the Roman Empire, the Middle Ages, and the Protestant Reformation, ending with the status of present-day biblical research.

$179.95

Films for the Humanities & Sciences, Inc.

Box 2053

Princeton, NJ 08543-2053

(800) 257-5126

Web site: www.films.com

ON-LINE RESOURCES

The Amish, the Mennonites, and "The Plain People"

Questions and answers about the history and lifestyle of the Amish, Mennonites, and related religious groups, illustrated with color photographs.

www.800padutch.com/amish.html

ARTFL Project: Bibles

The Bible on-line in several language editions, including French, German (Martin Luther's *Die Bibel*), Latin Vulgate, and King James English.

estragon.uchicago.edu/Bibles

Bible Gateway

From this site, users can search for specific Bible passages (by book, chapter, and verse) or individual words in a number of different editions of the Bible.

bible.gospelcom.net/bible?

Children's Corner: Muslims not Mohammadans

A detailed informational site all about Islam. The text—which lists, for example, the basic tenets of Islam, tells the life story of the prophet Muhammad, and explains how Muslims pray—is interspersed with short quizzes.

www.alislam.org/ram/articles/00000220.htm

Christian Kids Links

Devotional, educational, literary, and "just plain fun" sites for Christians.

netministries.org/kids.htmls

Cross Search

Links to Christian resources on the Internet by subject category, including education, history, music, media, theology, on-line forums, and children's resources. The children's link includes a long alphabetical listing of Christian materials and sites for and about children.

www.crosssearch.com

The Jewish Children's Web Site

Links to stories, songs, activities, educational sites, newsletters, chat lines, and quizzes with Jewish themes.

www.geocities.com/Heartland/Plains/7613

Kachina

A brief explanation of the religion of the Hopi of the American Southwest, along with a colorful photo gallery of kachina dolls.

www.aquila.com/jester/kachina.htm

Minerals of the Bible

The site lists all biblical passages that mention minerals. Click on the highlighted mineral name for a wealth of scientific information, links to related Web sites, and a color photograph. Among the mentioned minerals: topaz, emerald, sapphire, gold, silver, diamond, and chrysolite.

mineral.galleries.com/bible.htm

Also see **Geology** (pages 358–369).

Religion and Philosophy Gopher

Links to an immense number of on-line resources, among them the Atheist Manifesto, a biblical timeline, the Book of Mormon, the Dead Sea Scrolls exhibit, on-line religious texts, and Jewish, Buddhist, and Taoist sites.

gopher://riceinfo.rice.edu:70/11/Subject/RelPhil

The Web of Culture: World Religions

An alphabetical list of major world religions, from Atheism and Baha'i to Voodoo and Zoroastrianism. Click on the name for a description of the religion, plus links to other related Web sites. The site also includes a continent-by-continent list of all the world's countries, with the major religions practiced in each.

www.worldculture.com/religion.htm

PHILOSOPHY

BOOKS

Animal Farm

George Orwell; New American Library, 1996

A now classic political fable in which the animals of Manor Farm rebel against their owner and set up a state of their own—"Animal Farm"—under the leadership of the two pigs, Napoleon and Snowball. As time passes, however, Animal Farm evolves slowly into a restrictive totalitarian state, with a single ominous commandment: "All animals are equal but some animals are more equal than others."

The Giver

Lois Lowry; Houghton Mifflin, 1993

A fascinating and thought-provoking book. We read it aloud to each other, all in one sitting—no one could bear to put it down—and the boys talked about it for days afterward. The main character of *The Giver* is a young boy named Jonas, just entering adolescence.

Jonas lives in an apparently Utopian world, perfectly engineered to ensure peace, plenty, and happiness for all its inhabitants. Each citizen of the community is carefully studied and assessed by the all-knowing Elders to determine his or her optimal education, mate, career—children are even assigned to families according to predetermined criteria.

When Jonas reaches the age to be given his future job assignment, however, he is suddenly singled out from his peers: he is to become the community's Receiver, the keeper of all memories, good and bad, glorious and terrible, from the days before the community began. As Jonas assimilates these memories, absorbing them one by one from the previous Receiver, he learns about a new and unimagined world, filled with love and war, happiness and sorrow, bright colors, storms and sunshine, anger, hope, death. Each new revelation causes Jonas to think more and more deeply about the values of the society he lives in, the nature of human freedoms, and the importance of individual choice. Finally he makes a decision that changes the world. *The Giver* is also available in unabridged form on four cassette tapes, read by Ron Rifkin (Bantam Books Audio, 1995).

Great Ideas: A Lexicon of Western Thought

Mortimer Adler; Macmillan, 1992

There are 102 great ideas, presented in alphabetical order, from angel, animal, and aristocracy to will, wisdom, and world. (In between: beauty, democracy, education, fate, God, good and evil, justice, love, mind, progress, slavery, soul, state, and truth.) For each idea, Adler writes an explanatory essay, covering the history of thought on the subject as expressed by philosophers, scientists, historians, and writers. Challenging and thought-provoking reading for motivated teenagers.

Ishmael

Daniel Quinn; Bantam Doubleday Dell, 1995

The narrator of this engrossing book answers an ad: "TEACHER seeks student. Must have earnest desire to save the world. Apply in person." The teacher is Ishmael—a very wise gorilla—who leads his new pupil to consider mankind's destiny. His subject: captivity. People, Ishmael explains, are captives of their civilization, just as zoo animals are kept captive in cages. A mind-broadening, fascinating, and highly readable journey through many of life's greater questions. Also see *My Ishmael* (1997).

Looking At Philosophy: The Unbearable Heaviness of Philosophy Made Lighter

Donald Palmer; Mayfield Publishing Company, 1988

A humorously illustrated and humorously readable history of Western philosophy from the ancient Greeks to the existentialists. The author explains difficult concepts in a friendly and understandable fashion. For teenagers and up.

Philosophy for Children Series

Children are natural philosophers. Even the very young are intrigued by philosophical questions: What are right and wrong? Good and evil? What is death? How did the world begin? Philosophical debate, explains the spokesperson for the Institute for the Advancement of Philosophy for Children (IAPC), broadens the participants' views of the world and teaches kids to reason, reflect, evaluate, and develop their critical thinking skills.

The "Philosophy for Children" curriculum is a series of readers and teacher's manuals designed to encourage kids in grades K–12 to identify and analyze philosophical problems. Titles for elementary-level students include *Pixie, Elfie,* and *Kio and Gus;* for middle school students, *Harry Stottlemeier's Discovery* and *Lisa;* and for secondary-level students, *Suki* and *Mark. Pixie,* for example, leads young readers to discuss such concepts as the complexities of "meaning," analogies and reasoning, and the distinctions among "mind," "brain," and "soul." *Lisa* encourages kids to debate ethical issues such as "Do good intentions compensate for bad consequences?" and "What is the difference between right and fair?" Detailed and enormous (most are over 400 pages long) teacher's manuals accompany the books, each filled with lesson plans, discussion questions, reasoning exercises, and activities.

Student books, $10; teacher's manuals, $45
Institute for the Advancement of Philosophy
for Children
Montclair State University
Upper Montclair, NJ 07043
(201) 655-4277

Pooh and the Philosophers

John Tyerman Williams; E. P. Dutton, 1995

Examples from *Winnie-the-Pooh* are used to illustrate the ideas of the great philosophers, from "Pooh in Ancient Greece" through "Pooh and the Seventeenth-Century Rationalists" to "Pooh and Existentialism." Despite the friendly bear, the book is for older readers.

See *The Tao of Pooh* (page 802).

Sophie's World: A Novel About the History of Philosophy

Jostein Gaarder; Berkley Publishing Group, 1997

This book, originally intended as a vehicle for introducing young people to Western philosophy, is the story of almost-15-year-old Sophie Amundsen, who comes home from school one day to find two mysterious questions in the mailbox: "Who are you?" and "Where does the world come from?" Sophie begins to wonder—and thus embarks on a journey through the history of philosophy, under the guidance of the elusive Alberto Knox (and his dog, Hermes).

Sophie's philosophical education begins with a series of letters ("Course in Philosophy. Handle With Care") which she reads in her secret hiding place in the hedge in the backyard garden. By letter, Sophie learns about the ancient Greeks, including Democritus, Socrates, Plato, and Aristotle, the Semites, and the roots of Christianity. Then at last she meets Alberto in person—at first, he's disguised as a monk—and continues her philosophical education through the great thinkers of the Middle Ages and Renaissance, the ideas of Descartes, Spinoza, Locke, Hume, and Berkeley, the late 18th-century French Enlightenment, and the philosophies of Kant, Hegel, Kierkegaard, Marx, Darwin, and Freud.

Sophie's introduction to philosophy is interspersed with a real-life mystery: she is receiving postcards sent to a girl just her own age named Hilde, from her father, the mysteriously all-knowing major. As the book continues, it becomes increasingly uncertain how the stories of the two girls fit together. The conclusion is philosophically apt and startlingly unexpected. Intellectually challenging and fuel for endless discussions.

See **Sophie's World** on CD-ROM (page 810).

The Table Where Rich People Sit

6 / 9

Byrd Baylor; Atheneum, 1994

In this lovely picture book, Mountain Girl tackles one of the big philosophical questions: What is important in life? Her family has little in the way of material wealth, but they are rich in love for each other and for the natural world around them. How much money is it worth, Mountain Girl's parents ask her, to be able to smell the rain, listen to birdsong, watch the colors of the changing leaves on the mountainside?

What Does It All Mean?: A Very Short Introduction to Philosophy

12 +

Thomas Nagel; Oxford University Press, 1987

Ten very short chapters in 112 pages on the major questions of philosophy, for those "who know little or nothing of the discipline." Nagel covers such philosophical mind bogglers as the mind-body problem (What's the relationship between consciousness and the brain?), free will, right and wrong, justice, death, and the meaning of life. Simply and clearly written.

GAMES

Strange Bedfellows

13 +

Politics may make for strange bedfellows, but so, according to this game, do philosophers, writers, and religions. The game includes 10 example sheets, on which are printed a short list of philosophers, political figures, writers, political systems, or religions. Sheet I, for example, lists Karl Marx, Abraham Lincoln, Sigmund Freud, Henry David Thoreau, Mark Twain, and Benjamin Franklin; Sheet IV, Thoreau, Nietzsche, Aristotle, Confucius, Socrates, and Voltaire; Sheet VII, Hinduism, Judaism, Confucianism, Buddhism, Christianity, and Islam. The example sheets also each list 20 different statements or quotations—taken out of context, the game rules emphasize—made by or about each of the listed individuals or belief systems. Players listen to the quotation or statement, and then, using the included scorecards, vote on which of the listed persons/belief systems made the statement and, if possible, where.

Here's a sample of how it works:

QUOTATION: "How does it become a man to behave toward the American government today? I answered that he cannot without disgrace be associated with it."

PLAYER ONE: I vote for Sigmund Freud. He was always very critical of the American government.

PLAYER TWO: No, I think that's Thoreau. That sounds like his views on civil disobedience.

PLAYER THREE: I vote for Karl Marx. That was part of his famous argument against capitalism.

Upon checking the answers, it turns out that Player Three was right; he/she scores a point. Interesting, and often surprising. For teenagers to adults.

$25

Wff'n Proof Learning Games

1490 South Blvd.

Ann Arbor, MI 48104

(313) 665-2269

AUDIOVISUAL RESOURCES

The Giants of Philosophy

13 +

The Giants of Philosophy, narrated by Charlton Heston, is a 13-part series on audiocassettes covering the thought of 13 great philosophers: Plato, Aristotle, St. Augustine, St. Thomas Aquinas, Spinoza, Hume, Kant, Hegel, Schopenhauer, Kierkegaard, Nietzsche, John Dewey, and John-Paul Sartre. Each philosopher's ideas are presented on two cassettes, in very adult-lecture style.

Individual titles (two cassettes), $17.95 (plus shipping/handling); the entire program, $200.

Also available by subscription

Knowledge Products

Box 305151

Nashville, TN 37230

(800) 876-4332

The Giants of Political Thought

15 +

The Giants of Political Thought series consists of 12 two-cassette sets on great political thinkers and their philosophies. Featured political philosophers include Thomas Paine, Thomas Jefferson, Henry David Thoreau, William Lloyd Garrison, Adam Smith, John Stuart Mill, Mary Wollstonecraft, Niccolò Machiavelli, Etienne de la Boetie, Karl Marx and Friedrich Engels, Jean-Jacques

Rousseau, Edmund Burke, Alexander Hamilton, James Madison, and John Jay (*The Federalist Papers*), Thomas Hobbes, John Locke, and Alexis de Tocqueville.

The program, $200; individual selections (2 cassettes), $17.95 (plus shipping/handling). Also available by subscription
Knowledge Products
Box 305151
Nashville, TN 37230
(800) 876-4332

[15] The Great Ideas of Philosophy

A 50-lecture "supercourse" on audiocassettes or videotapes covering over 2,000 years of philosophical thought. Lectures, by philosophy professor Daniel Robinson of Georgetown University, are organized in seven sections. "Ancient Foundations" (15 lectures) covers the beginnings of philosophy through the ancient Greeks and Romans, featuring Pythagoras, Herodotus, Socrates, Plato, and Aristotle. "Early Modern Thought" (4 lectures) covers the Stoics, the early Christians, and Islam; "From Feudalism to Urbanity: Two Renaissances" (5 lectures) covers Roger Bacon, Thomas Aquinas, Petrarch, Erasmus, and Luther. "The Dawn of the New: The Foundations of the Scientific World View" (5 lectures) covers Descartes, Newton, Hobbes, and Locke; "Enlightenment" (8 lectures) covers Berkeley, Hume, 18th-century French philosophers, and Kant; "Romanticism" (4 lectures) includes Hegel, the Aesthetic movement, and Nietzsche. Finally, "Science and Scientism" (9 lectures) covers Mill, Darwin, Marx, Freud, William James, Wittgenstein, and Alan Turing. An intellectual challenge for older teenagers and adults.

Audio series, $199.95; video series, $299.95
The Teaching Co.
7405 Alban Station Court, Suite A107
Springfield, VA 22150-2318
(800) 832-2412/fax (703) 912-7756

[15] The World of Philosophy

The World of Philosophy, narrated by Lynn Redgrave, is a 13-part audiocassette series covering both individual philosophers and world philosophical traditions. Titles in the series (two audiocassettes per title) include "Socrates," "Stoicism and Epicureanism,"

"Confucius, Lao Tzu and the Chinese Philosophical Tradition," "Moses Maimonides and Medieval Jewish Philosophy," "Avicenna and Medieval Muslim Philosophy," "Duns Scotus and Medieval Christian Philosophy," "Descartes, Bacon, and the Beginnings of Modern Philosophy," "Rousseau and Voltaire," "The Philosophies of India," "William James, Charles Peirce, and American Pragmatism," "Bertrand Russell and A. N. Whitehead," "Simone de Beauvoir," and "20th Century European Philosophy."

Program, $200; individual titles (2 cassettes), $17.95 (plus shipping/handling). Also available by subscription
Knowledge Products
Box 305151
Nashville, TN 37230
(800) 876-4332

COMPUTER SOFTWARE

[12] Sophie's World

An interactive philosophy adventure in which players cover over 3,000 years of philosophical thought. The game moves through 20 "virtual environments" in which kids play games, solve puzzles, and participate in debates (by e-mail) with a range of philosophers from Socrates to Sartre. The program also includes a timeline of philosophers and a reference section of the "Big Questions," such as "What is time?" and "Where does the world come from?," with a list of the responses made by various prominent thinkers.

$39.95
Learn Technologies Interactive
Box 2284
S. Burlington, VT 05417
(888) 292-5584
Web site: voyager.learntech.com

Also see the book of the same name (page 808).

ON-LINE RESOURCES

[13] The Argument Clinic

How well can you frame a philosophical argument? Choose your topic, frame your argument, and submit; the Clinic will evaluate your reasoning and reply.

www.univnorthco.edu/philosophy/clinic.html

Hopkins Philosophy Pages

Links to a long list of philosophical topics by subject, plus connections to related Web sites, institutions and organizations, journals, and electronic texts.

www.jhu.edu/~phil/philhome.html

Internet Encyclopedia of Philosophers

The site includes links to a timeline of Western philosophy, to on-line philosophical texts, and to the works and biographies of philosophers, listed alphabetically.

www.utm.edu/research/iep

Philosophical Debates

A bibliographic guide to some of the greatest philosophical questions, among them "What is knowledge?," "What is the nature of reality?," and "Is there a God?"

www.mindspring.com/~mfpatton/debates.htm

Philosophy for Children on the World Wide Web

A work in progress. The portrait of a featured philosopher is linked to many associated sites. Under Archimedes, for example, are a biography, a timeline, individual stories about his inventions and discoveries, information about the royal family of Syracuse, and a description of the Archimedes Crater on the moon.

www.deakin.edu.au/arts/SSI/PStud/p4c.html

Philosophy in Cyberspace

An index of over 1,500 philosophy-related sites, arranged by subject.

www-personal.monash.edu.au/~dey/phil/index.htm

The Ultimate Philosophy Page

Many links to associations, university philosophy departments, research projects, discussion forums, on-line philosophical texts, professional journals, and some unclassifiable, but interesting, pseudophilosophical stuff.

www.rpi.edu/~cearls/phil.html

LIFE SKILLS

Carpentry/Woodworking, Cooking, Etiquette, Gardening, Gender Issues, Sex Education, Sewing/Fabric Crafts, Sports/Physical Fitness, Travel, and Work/Community Service

Oh, what a day-to-day business life is.

JULES LaFORGUE

CARPENTRY/ WOODWORKING

When we lived in California, there was a small alternative school down the road at which—every year, during the first week of school—the students built their own desks and chairs. I always thought this a wonderful idea, but our plans to do likewise never came to anything; somehow we always have more wonderful ideas than time. The boys do, however, build. Projects in our past include birdhouses and feeders; a never quite completed tree house; a house for the cats, painted bright blue, which the cats adamantly refused to so much as enter; an enormous raft, duly christened *The Minnow*, which, upon launching, sank dismally to the bottom of the lake; and—with the help of their father—a backyard swing, a set of bunk beds, innumerable bookcases, two chicken coops, and part of a barn. None of these projects, I must admit, was ever started with formal education in mind—though, on the other hand, it's hard to envision a project that doesn't involve some form of learning. Carpentry promotes a battery of practical and mathematical skills ("Measure twice; cut once"), to say nothing of all the miscellaneous information acquired during the building process. Kids constructing birdhouses are bound to pepper you with questions about birds' nesting habits; kids choosing boards for bookcases will discover how to tell one wood from another or find out what causes knotholes; and kids watching the demise of *The Minnow* will learn about Archimedes' principle and the inordinate weight of green logs.

BOOKS

Carpentry for Children
Lester Walker; Viking, 1985

Plans and instructions for 14 simple carpentry projects, among them a (small) boat, a birdhouse, a puppet theater, and a coaster car, for kids aged 8 and up (with a little adult help).

Handmade Secret Hiding Places
Nonny Hogrogian; Overlook Press, 1990

Easy-to-follow instructions for houses, forts, and hideouts, from the cardboard box house to the lean-to.

Housebuilding for Children
Lester Walker; Overlook Press, 1988

Written by an architect, with the hands-on help of a crew of kids, aged 7–10, the book includes plans and instructions for building six different kids' houses, with helpful diagrams and photographs showing the young builders in action.

In Christina's Toolbox
Dianne Homan and Maria Antonia Salgado; Lollipop Power, 1994

Tools aren't just for boys. In this picture book, a little girl, armed with her own toolbox, competently fixes things.

A Kids' Guide to Building Forts
Tom Birdseye; Roberts Rinehart Publishers, 1993

Instructions for building several kinds of appealing indoor and outdoor forts.

Tool Book
Gail Gibbons; Holiday House, 1982

A simple, brightly illustrated picture book showing the different kinds of tools used in carpentry and explaining just what they're used for.

Toolchest
Jan Adkins; Walker & Company, 1973

A basic illustrated introduction to woodworking tools. Adkins first explains various features of wood, defining grain, comparing different kinds of woods, and explaining what each is used for. The book then covers measuring, cutting, shaping, boring, and dowelling tools, and nails, screws, and glue—all with detailed pen-and-ink drawings.

The Treehouse Book
David Stiles; Avon Books, 1979

An illustrated guide to building tree houses, covering four basic designs, depending on whether you have one, two, three, or four trees. Also included: designs for ladders, rope bridges, and tree-house furniture.

Woodlore

Cameron Miller and Dominique Falla; Ticknor & Fields, 1995

A history of wood and woodworking for kids aged 7–11. Poems and color illustrations—each picture bordered with a frame of the featured wood—combine to describe a range of different woods and their traditional uses. Readers learn, for example, the yew was used to make medieval longbows.

See *Red Oaks and Black Birches* (page 278).

Woodworking for Kids

Kevin McGuire; Sterling/Lark, 1994

McGuire covers basic tools and techniques used in woodworking and describes 40 projects for kids to make—starting with a toolbox and workbench. For each project a materials and tools list is included, plus step-by-step instructions with detailed diagrams, and a full-page color photograph of the finished product. Projects include stilts, a tic-tac-toe game, bookshelf, rope ladder, pet bed, birdhouse, magazine rack, doll cradle, and puppet theater.

HANDS-ON ACTIVITIES

Bluebird House

A woodworking kit for kids aged 8 and up. The kit contains all necessary materials, including precut wood pieces, hardware, and glue. Also see the Insect House Kit for the same age group, with which young builders can turn out a screened box for bugs.

$14.95 from toy and craft stores; for a local source, contact Curiosity Kits
Box 811
Cockeysville, MD 21030
(410) 584-2605 or (800) 584-KITS/fax (410) 584-1247
e-mail: CKitsinc@aol.com

Build-It-Yourself Woodworking Kit

Over 80 pieces of pine in different sizes and shapes packed in a wooden "carpenter's box," plus sandpaper, nails, glue, a hammer, a ruler, and a project guide.

$24.95
Lakeshore Learning Materials

2695 E. Dominguez St.
Box 6261
Carson, CA 90749
(310) 537-8600 or (800) 421-5354/fax (310) 537-5403
Web site: www.lakeshorelearning.com

Crank It Kits

Especially interesting kits for young woodworkers. Kids assemble the kits from precut pieces, then turn the wooden cranks and watch them work. Our favorite was the "Crank It! Wave," which creates an up-and-down wave effect with moving wood pieces. There's also a "Dog" that barks (silently) when cranked, a "Birdwatcher" who tracks a circling bird, and an undulating "Caterpillar."

$19.95 from toy or craft stores or
The Great Kids Co.
Box 609
Lewisville, NC 27023-0609
(800) 533-2166

Tools

Our kids had small-size hammers; otherwise they had to make do with their parents' tools which—for person with very little hands—were often awkward. Sources for genuine child-size tools, such as saws, hammers, hand drills, mitre boxes, and clamps, include Lakeshore Learning Materials

2695 E. Dominguez St.
Carson, CA 90749
(310) 537-8600 or (800) 421-5354
fax (310) 537-5403
Web site: www.lakeshorelearning.com
or
Toad's Tools,
Box 173
Oberlin, OH 44074

Treasure Chest Kit

Build a pirate-style treasure chest with a rounded top, 12 × 10 by 9½ inches, suitable for storing a whole lot of treasures. The kit includes precut wood pieces, nails, screws, hinges, latch, rope (for handles), and detailed instructions.

$29.95
HearthSong
6519 N. Galena Rd.

LIFE SKILLS

Box 1773

Peoria, IL 61656-1773

(309) 689-3838 or (800) 325-2502/fax (309) 689-3857

Whirligigs

Kits for all skill levels, available as "uncut kits" (you do all necessary sawing and drilling) or "precut kits," ready to be sanded, assembled, and painted. Especially nice for young woodworkers are the bird whirligigs: 11 different birds are available, among them a whirling cardinal, woodpecker, blue jay, and goldfinch.

$15.95 (uncut kits) or $19.95 (precut kits)

Cherry Tree Toys, Inc.

Box 369

Belmont, OH 43718

(800) 848-4363

Wood Scraps

Three- to 18-pound packets of wood in random shapes and sizes for wood sculpture, collage, carving, or construction projects.

$6 to $24

Sax Arts & Crafts

Box 510710

New Berlin, WI 53151

(800) 558-6696

COOKING

Our boys have always liked to cook. The family recipe book—a fat and tattered notebook with a slightly charred spine, where someone (who shall remain nameless) once unwisely set it down on an active stove burner—includes Josh's very first recipe, written down in staggering printing at the age of four. It's for Bananas Joshua, a dish that involves frying sliced bananas in butter with a bit of lemon and brown sugar. Cooking, according to the educational literature, enhances a wide range of academic skills, among them science and math. Recipes, which require measurements, familiarity with fractions, and—occasionally—multiplication and division, are inherently mathematical; and the adroit parent/teacher can also

usually manage to throw a little science into the mix, discussing, for example, the biochemistry of bread-rising, the antiscurvy properties of lemon juice, and the reason that Jell-O gels.

Most of the boys' cooking is unplanned fun, of the serendipitous "I think I'll go make some oatmeal cookies now" variety. However, we also integrate cooking projects into academics. A study of Johnny Appleseed, for example, is paired to a batch of applesauce, apple bread, or apple pie; an investigation of American Indian lifestyles to preparing a pot of succotash; a study of China to rice, stir-fry, and learning to manipulate chopsticks.

From my homeschool journal:

◆ **December 13, 1989. Josh is eight; Ethan, seven; Caleb, five.**

Today is St. Lucia Day, celebrated in Sweden at Christmastime. I began the morning reading stacks of picture books with Caleb, who got up very early: he had cocoa with a marshmallow ("Where do marshmallows come from?") and we cuddled up next to the woodstove. After breakfast, Ethan and Caleb spent some time playing "Rockets," a card game played like "War," based on comparing numbers from one to ten (high card wins). Then, in honor of St. Lucia Day, we did a series of projects on Sweden and its Christmas holiday. Located Sweden on the world map, briefly discussed its climate and history, and colored pictures of the Swedish flag. We made St. Lucia Day–style "Star Boy" hats and star-tipped wands for all the boys and baked a batch of (perfectly delicious) Swedish cookies called "Lucia cats." The boys arranged their Lucia cats on decorated plates, learned how to say "Merry Christmas" in Swedish, and made a "Happy St. Lucia Day" sign for the table: they're planning a celebration, in Star Boy regalia, when their father gets home.

Then back to the woodstove to eat Lucia cats and read Barbara Robinson's The Best Christmas Pageant Ever.

◆ **September 29, 1993. Josh is twelve; Ethan, ten; Caleb, nine.**

We're studying apples—always a good fall topic— using homemade workbooks and a stack of supplementary reference materials. We read "Johnny Appleseed," a biography by Edward Hoagland in A Sense of History (American Heritage/Houghton Mifflin, 1985), following Johnny's travels on a map of the United States. The boys were interested: "If the last person who knew Johnny Appleseed died around World War II, that means Grandma could have known somebody who saw him!" We made pioneer-style dried apple rings—a messy and hilarious process; we need an apple corer—and hung them up across the kitchen. Reviewed the science of apple drying—why dried apples don't spoil—and moved from there into a discussion of microorganisms. Covered the three basic types of bacteria—cocci, bacilli, and spirilla—referring to assorted biology books; looked at samples of each in photomicrographs using the Microslide Viewer (see National Teaching Aids, page 223), and the boys drew and labeled pictures in their lab notebooks. We compared bacterial cells to animal cells, in detail, reviewing the parts of a cell. The boys had lots of related (and unrelated) questions, ranging over nitrogen fixation, fermentation, Egyptian beer, vinegar, black plague, Lyme disease, pneumonia, antibiotics, and what would happen if you tried to make dried watermelon.

◆ September, 30, 1993

Read about bacterial culture; defined nutrient media and agar. The boys mixed up some agar and poured it into sterile petri plates; then started a number of bacterial/fungal cultures, variously in the petri plates and on assorted food samples (damp bread, cottage cheese). Defined and read about fungi, referring to several sources: covered hyphae, spores, mycelium, fungal reproduction, mushrooms and toadstools.

Set up an apple browning experiment (with and without lemon juice), explaining the biochemical basis of browning, referring to Lehninger's Biochemistry and Harold McGee's On Food and Cooking (see page 819). The boys were interested: "What if you bred a really acidic apple—would it never turn brown?" "What if you add the lemon juice after the apple turns brown—can it reverse the reaction?" We then read about how interest in browning reactions led to the discovery of vitamin C, with an associated discussion of how vitamin C works, how many vitamins have been discovered, and why vitamin K is "K" and not "F."

◆ October 1, 1993

The boys collaborated on making apple pancakes for breakfast. We used the pancakes—with a little maternal nudging and the help of the Guinness Book of World Records—as jumping-off points into math. We covered the geometry of circles, calculating—among other things—the circumference and area of the world's largest pancake, crepe, cherry pie, and pizza, based on the diameters quoted in Guinness.

◆ October 4, 1993

We read The Apple and the Arrow, an account of the story of William Tell, pointing out Switzerland, Austria, and the Alps on the map, and locating Tell and his nemesis, Gessler, on timelines. The boys then made a series of elaborate archery targets—including one based on William Tell's son, with balanced apple—taped them to cardboard cartons, and took them out in the yard to practice with bows and arrows.

Made and canned two big batches of applesauce, calculating the number of apples per quart of sauce, and discussing the science of the canning process.

◆ October 5, 1993

Read several chapters in All About Great Medical Discoveries about the early days of bacteriology, with accounts of the accomplishments of Louis Pasteur and Robert Koch. Discussed "Koch's Postulates" and—at great length—rabies. Observed all our growing bacterial/fungal samples from last week, and the boys took photographs for their lab notebooks. They then took samples of each and studied them under the microscope. Especially popular: fungi.

So we made a cheese-and-mushroom pizza for lunch.

BOOKS

Acorn Pancakes, Dandelion Salad, and 38 Other Wild Recipes

Jean Craighead George; HarperCollins, 1995

A cookbook for nature lovers. "Learn your plants and then go foraging," says George. The book includes recipes for Acorn Pancakes, Indian Cattail Spoon-bread, Weedy Lawn Salad, Lemon Day Lilies, and Sugared Violets.

The Amazing Milk Book
Catherine Ross and Susan Wallace; Addison-Wesley, 1991

All about milk, plus science, art, and cooking projects for kids aged 7–11. Included are milk myths and legends, a dairy cow quiz, a scientific explanation of how milk is made (in the cow) and processed (in the dairy), histories of yogurt, cheese, and ice cream, and recipes for milk glue, butter, cottage cheese, and yogurt, plus instructions for making a milk-carton bird feeder. In the same series, see *The Amazing Apple Book* (Paulette Bourgeois), *The Amazing Egg Book* (Margaret Griffin and Deborath Seed; see page 330), and *The Amazing Potato Book* (Paulette Bourgeois; see page 825).

The American Girls Cookbooks
Jodi Evert, ed.; Pleasant Company, 1994

From Pleasant Company (see page 448), cookbooks are available for each "American Girl." The American Girls, each featured in a popular book series, include Addy, a black girl in pre–Civil War Philadelphia; Felicity, in colonial Williamsburg; Kirsten, on the western frontier; Molly, on the home front during World War II; and Samantha, living with a wealthy grandmother in turn-of-the-century New York. Cookbooks, each subtitled "A Peek at Dining in the Past with Meals You Can Cook Today," include *Addy's Cookbook, Felicity's Cookbook, Kirsten's Cookbook, Molly's Cookbook,* and *Samantha's Cookbook.* Each is 44 pages long, illustrated with color photographs, and includes, along with the recipes, plans for a historical party, among them a Victorian tea party with Samantha.

American Grub: Eats for Kids from All Fifty States
Lynn Kuntz and Jan Fleming; Gibbs Smith, 1998

Cooking and combined with U.S. geography. The book includes a representative recipe from each of the 50 states, plus accompanying food facts and state history.

The Apple Pie Tree
Zoe Hall; Scholastic, 1996

Two sisters follow an apple tree through the seasons of the year, from snowy bare branches in winter, through spring flowers, developing fruit, and apple-picking time. A recipe is included for an (autumn) apple pie.

Cooking Art: Easy Edible Art for Young Children
MaryAnn F. Kohl and Jean Porter; Gryphon House, 1997

A fat collection of artistic cooking projects for kids aged 4–10. Projects are grouped under such subheadings as "Shapes and Forms," "Colors and Design," "Flowers and Trees," and "Animals and Creatures." There's also a month-by-month list of special seasonal projects. Sample projects include making potato ghosts, number pretzels, cucumber airplanes, and flowerpot salad.

Cooking Up U.S. History: Recipes and Research to Share With Children
Suzanne I. Barchers and Patricia C. Marden; Teacher Ideas Press, 1991

Recipes for such all-American standards as porridge, pudding, and sourdough bread, coupled with discussion questions, research projects, and supplementary readings for kids in grades 1–6.

$22

Libraries Unlimited

Box 6633

Englewood, CO 80155-6633

(303) 770-1220 or (800) 237-6124/fax (303) 220-8843

e-mail: lu-books@lu.com

Web site: www.lu.com

Cooking Up World History: Multicultural Recipes and Resources
Patricia C. Marden and Suzanne I. Barchers; Teacher Ideas Press, 1994

A culinary trip around the world for kids in grades K–6. The book covers 20 countries or world regions, each with five or six ethnic recipes, discussion questions that connect regional culture and history to food, and an annotated bibliography of related readings.

$23.50

Libraries Unlimited

Box 6633

Englewood, CO 80155-6633

(303) 770-1220 or (800) 237-6124/fax (303) 220-8843

e-mail: lu-books@lu.com

Web site: www.lu.com

Cooking Wizardry for Kids
Margaret Kenda and Phyllis S. Williams; Barron's, 1990

A large and marvelous collection of recipes, science experiments, crafts projects, and information for kids of all ages. Kids make pretzels, rock candy, popcorn balls, mayonnaise, a rabbit-shaped cake, Hanukkah latkes, "elephant's ears," a rainbow salad, and a basket made of bread; they also learn the histories of graham crackers and hamburgers, find out how bees make honey, and discover why onions make your eyes water.

Easy Menu Ethnic Cookbooks
Lerner

A series of short, informative books about the food and cooking of other countries, each about 50 pages long, illustrated with lucious color photographs. Each of the 30 books in the series features a different country or cooking style. Titles include *Cooking the African Way, Cooking the German Way, Cooking the South American Way, Cooking the Mexican Way, Holiday Cooking Around the World,* and *How to Cook a Gooseberry Fool: Unusual Recipes from Around the World.* A terrific supplement to geography studies.

Eating Fractions
Bruce Macmillan; Scholastic, 1991

A picture book of beginning fractions. Kids learn about halves, thirds, and quarters by slicing bananas, pizza, and strawberry pie. Simple recipes are included.

Foodworks
Ontario Science Centre; Addison-Wesley, 1987

Over 100 science experiments and projects and a lot of interesting information based on food. There's a pictorial representation of the amount of food the average North American eats in a year (1 ton, or about 18 full shopping carts), explanations of why stomachs growl and burp, diagrams of teeth and taste buds, food histories, quizzes, a board game called "The Wheat Game" in which players must manage to move their pieces from plowed field to finished flour, and recipes for chocolate bars, cheese, ice cream, ginger ale, banana chips, and a Chinese breakfast.

Good For Me!: All About Food in 32 Bites
Marilyn Burns; Little, Brown, 1978

A creative collection of interesting information, appealing science and math projects, clever quizzes, and funny illustrations. *Good For Me!* covers the chemistry of food, the biology of digestion, and the basics of nutrition, as well as the stories of sugar, soda pop, noodles, hamburgers, and breakfast cereals, and the scoop on food additives, vegetarianism, and fat.

How To Make an Apple Pie and See the World
Marjorie Priceman; Dragonfly, 1996

A little girl takes a picture-book trip around the world to find out where the ingredients for an apple pie come from: wheat from Italy, eggs from France, cinnamon from Sri Lanka, sugar from Jamaica, apples from Vermont. A recipe is included for a delicious apple pie.

Incredible Edible Science
Tina L. Seelig; W. H. Freeman & Company, 1994

An 80-page mixture of science and recipes for kids aged 9–13. The book discusses solutions and boiling points and the science of curds and whey, explains why popcorn pops and bread rises, and elucidates the difference between light and dark meat. Each chapter is followed by a recipe that illustrates the scientific principle covered.

Kids Cook! Fabulous Food for the Whole Family
Sarah Williamson and Zachary Williamson; Williamson, 1992

Recipes for all three meals of the day, plus snacks and desserts, with clever illustrations. The book was written and the recipes tested by two kids, so you know they're all good bets.

LIFE SKILLS

The Little House Cookbook
Barbara M. Walker; HarperTrophy, 1995

Instructions for making the meals Laura and her family ate in Laura Ingalls Wilder's *Little House* books (see page 527), including recipes for cornbread and pumpkin pie.

Loaves of Fun
Elizabeth M. Harbison; Chicago Review Press, 1997

A timeline history of bread, from its earliest beginnings to the present day, with accompanying recipes and activities. Mixing crushed grain with water, then baking the batter on a rock next to the fire, Harbison explains, is "How the Cavemen Cooked"; kids can follow this up by making a batch of drop biscuits. An explanation of baking in the ancient Middle East is accompanied by a recipe for pita bread; a discussion of medieval baking is followed by recipes for pretzels and bread bowls for soup; a description of baking in colonial America includes recipes for cornbread and johnnycake. Also included: how to blow up a balloon with yeast, make flour-based poster paint, and construct your own baguette pans. History, geography, science, and a lot of good food.

The Math Chef: Over 60 Math Activities and Recipes for Kids
Joan D'Amico and Karen Eich Drummond; John Wiley & Sons, 1997

Math through applesauce, waffles, homemade animal crackers, banana muffins, and more. The book is divided into four main parts, each devoted to a different mathematical concept: "Measuring," "Arithmetic," "Fractions and Percents," and "Geometry." Kids discover, for example, how many grams are in a pound of potatoes, how to triple a sandwich recipe, and how to determine the area of a brownie, the diameter of a cupcake, and the circumference of a pie.
Also see *The Science Chef* (page 820) and *The Science Chef Travels Around the World* (page 820).

On Food and Cooking: The Science and Lore of the Kitchen
Harold McGee; Collier Books, 1997

An excellent reference for the scientific cook. This marvelous (and very thorough) volume explains—among much else—the chemistry involved in making cheese, lemon meringue pie, and charbroiled steak, the biological differences between fruits and nuts, the science of ripening (and spoiling), the history of flour, the nature of the four basic food molecules, and the processes of making tofu, cocoa, and beer. Written for adults, but the information will fascinate persons of all ages. Also see *The Curious Cook: More Science and Kitchen Lore* (1990).

Passport on a Plate: A Round-the-World Cookbook for Children
Diane Simone Vezza; Simon & Schuster, 1997

The book is divided into 12 chapters, each featuring a different country or geographical region, among them Africa, the Caribbean, China, France, India, the Middle East, and Russia. Young cooks get background information on each region and over 100 recipes, rated by level of difficulty, among them Caribbean Callaloo Soup, Kenyan Crunchy Bananas, Mexican fajitas, and Japanese sushi.

Peas and Honey: Recipes for Kids (With a Pinch of Poetry)
Kimberley Cohen; Boyd's Mills Press, 1995

Recipes (from breakfast through dinner and dessert) paired with poems by such kid-friendly poets as Jack Prelutsky, David McCord, and Aileen Fisher.

Pretend Soup and Other Real Recipes
Mollie Katzen and Ann Henderson; Tricycle Press, 1994

A cookbook for preschoolers (and up). Each recipe is written both in conventional adult form, with tips for supervising grown-ups, and in illustrated comic strip–style form for kids, with bright-colored drawings, just a few simple words, and numbered boxes. The book includes 19 kid-tested recipes, among them Bagel Faces, Green Spaghetti, Carrot Pennies, and, of course, Pretend Soup (orange juice, honey, yogurt, and fruit).

Roald Dahl's Revolting Recipes
Roald Dahl and Felicity Dahl; Viking, 1997

Food for fans of Roald Dahl. Kids can make Lickable Wallpaper from *Charlie and the Chocolate Factory,*

Snozzcumbers and Frobscottle from *The BFG*, Bruce Bogtrotter's Cake from *Matilda*, Hot Frogs from *James and the Giant Peach*, and a replica of the Enormous Crocodile himself, out of a baguette and frozen spinach, with spiky almond teeth.

The Science Chef: 100 Fun Food Experiments and Recipes for Kids

Joan D'Amico and Karen Eich Drummond; John Wiley & Sons, 1994

Recipes linked to science concepts. Kids learn why popcorn pops, why toast turns brown, and the chemical composition of baking powder, and find out how to make their own salad dressing, pasta sauce, cheese, butter, and pudding mix. There's also a section on "Science in the Supermarket," in which scientifically minded cooks investigate real fat versus fake fat, determine which cereal has more fiber, and compare white and brown rice.

Also see *The Math Chef* (page 819).

The Science Chef Travels Around the World: Fun Food Experiments and Recipes for Kids

Joan D'Amico and Karen Eich Drummond; John Wiley & Sons, 1996

The authors tour 14 countries: Mexico, Canada, Brazil, Italy, France, Spain, Germany, Israel, China, Japan, India, Thailand, Morocco, and Ghana. For each there's a science experiment based on a typical ethnic food or food ingredient—for example, readers study viscosity with honey (Egypt) and osmosis with pickled cucumbers (France)—along with a recipe for a complete ethnic meal.

Also see *The Math Chef* (page 819) and *The Science Chef* (above).

Science Experiments You Can Eat

Vicki Cobb; HarperCrest, 1994

Irresistible recipes paired with interesting explanations of science principles. For example, kids make rock candy, grape jelly, caramel, and popcorn while learning about crystallization, polymerization, and steam pressure. Also see *More Science Experiments You Can Eat* (1994).

The Scoop on Ice Cream

Vicki Cobb; Little, Brown, 1985

The history and science of ice cream in five short illustrated chapters, including an analytical ice-cream taste test and a recipe for Still-Frozen Ice Cream (made in the freezer, without an ice-cream maker).

Slumps, Grunts, and Snickerdoodles: What Colonial America Ate and Why

Lila Perl; Clarion, 1979

American history plus recipes. Slumps, grunts, and snickerdoodles are all a lot better than they sound.

LITERATURE LINKS TO FOOD FOR ADULTS

Storybook Stew: Cooking With Books Kids Love

Suzanne I. Barchers and Peter J. Rauen; Fulcrum, 1996

A large collection of recipes and hands-on science, math, and art activities to complement favorite children's picture books, among them *One Hundred Hungry Ants, Blueberries for Sal, Jack and the Beanstalk, A Medieval Feast,* and *The Story of Johnny Appleseed.* With *The Story of of Johnny Appleseed,* for example, kids make apple prints and apple butter.

LITERATURE LINKS TO FOOD FOR KIDS

The Berenstain Bears and Too Much Junk Food

Stan and Jan Berenstain; Random House, 1985

Brother and Sister Bear are getting pudgy from eating too much junk; they get a healthful lesson in diet and exercise.

Bread and Jam for Frances

Russell Hoban; HarperTrophy, 1993

Frances, an adorable little badger, decides to eat nothing but her favorite bread and jam. Her parents go along with it and finally, after bread and jam, morning, noon, and night, Frances finds herself becoming very sick of jam.

 8 11 *The Chocolate Touch*
Patrick Skene Catling; Dell, 1996

A King Midas story with a new twist: everything John touches turns to chocolate.

 4 8 *Cloudy With a Chance of Meatballs*
Judi Barrett; Aladdin, 1982

In the land of Chewandswallow, food falls like rain from the sky. It rains orange juice and snows mashed potatoes.

 4 8 *Cranberry Thanksgiving*
Wende and Harry Devlin; Aladdin, 1990

A picture-book tale of the little town of Cranberryport, including the recipe for Maggie's grandmother's family-secret cranberry bread.

 4 9 *Everybody Cooks Rice*
Norah Dooley; First Avenue Editions, 1992

A little girl travels about her neighborhood at dinnertime, discovering the many ways that people from different cultures cook rice.

 4 8 *The Giant Jam Sandwich*
John Vernon Lord; Houghton Mifflin, 1975

The unlucky residents of the little village of Itching Down have been infested by a swarm of four million wasps. They decide to capture the invaders with an enormous, sweet, and very sticky trap.

 4 8 *Gregory the Terrible Eater*
Mitchell Sharmat; Scholastic, 1989

Gregory, a small goat, wants only healthful fruits and vegetables: no tin cans, no rubber tires, no newspapers. His worried parents take him to the doctor.

 6 + *Poem Stew*
William Cole; HarperTrophy, 1983

An illustrated collection of poems on food, including works on soda pop, muffins, onions, prunes, potato chips, celery, bananas, liver, and artichokes by such poets as Ogden Nash, Shel Silverstein, John Ciardi, and Jack Prelutsky.

 4 8 *Stone Soup*
Marcia Brown; Atheneum, 1989

There are many versions of this old tale of the three hungry soldiers on their way home from the war and the villagers who don't want to feed them. The soldiers, who are kind and clever, then teach the villagers how to make "stone soup."

 4 8 *Thunder Cake*
Patricia Polacco; Paper Star, 1997

If you're afraid of a thunderstorm, a little girl's Russian grandmother explains, the thing to do is bake a cake—but a very special cake, which must be in the oven before the rain starts to fall.

GAMES AND HANDS-ON ACTIVITIES

 4 8 *Alphabake*
Debora Pearson; Dutton Children's Books, 1985

A kit for young bakers containing 26 letter-shaped plastic cookie cutters, a cookie sheet, and an illustrated cookbook of cookie recipes. Also see, by the same author, *Cookie Count & Bake* (1996), a similar kit with cookie cutters in the shape of numbers.

5 + *Eatonlya*
A board game designed to teach kids aged 5 and up the basics of good nutrition. The board centers around a big green-and-yellow diagram of the food pyramid, picturing six food groups: breads and cereals, vegetables, fruits, milk and cheese, meats and eggs, and, at the very top, fats and sugars. Before starting the game, players (or their parents) are told to prepare five snack bowls of real foods based on the first five groups (no fats or sugars). The bread/cereal bowl, for example, for example, could contain crackers, Cheerios, or slices of bagels; the vegetable bowl, carrot or celery sticks; and so on. Players then move their pieces around the food pyramid. On each food group square, they attempt to answer a question about foods and nutrition. A correct

answer earns the player a food allowance token from that food group and a corresponding snack from the appropriate snack bowl. First player to win all his/her daily food allowances wins the game. Sample questions:

"Fruits and vegetables which are orange in color are usually full of what vitamin?"

"Chang had fish and rice for lunch. What food groups do they belong to?"

Performance Education Technologies, Inc.
514 N. Third St., Suite 107
Minneapolis, MN 55401

Let's Pretend Restaurant

A kit for imaginative food-oriented play. The boxed set contains an assortment of plastic food (including a hamburger, a slice of pizza, and a pink-frosted doughnut), a red-checkered tablecloth, a chef's hat, order pads, menu sheets, signs, play money and credit cards. For kids aged 4 and up.

$14.95 from game stores or
Creativity for Kids
1802 Central Ave.
Cleveland, OH 44115
(216) 589-4800 or (800) 642-2288
Web site: www.creativityforkids.com

VIDEOS

Kids Get Cooking!

This 30-minute video from KIDVIDZ features two culinary puppets, four kids, one recipe, and a lot of information about eggs. The busy half hour includes the basics of nutrition, a visit to a poultry farm, a view of Fabergé's spectacular jeweled eggs, instructions for egg decorating, egg jokes, magic tricks, silly songs, and a recipe for Muffin Tin Eggs that kids can make themselves. Recommended for kids aged 4–10.

$19.95
KIDVIDZ
618 Centre St.
Newton, MA 02158
(800) 637-6772

ETIQUETTE

"Your boys," says the waitress at the breakfast restaurant, "are so polite. How did you do it?" Comments like that warm the cockles of a parent's heart—even a parent who knows perfectly well that, in the privacy of the home, the boys occasionally fight like weasels, complain about doing chores, make reprehensible statements about the quality of dinner, have to be viciously threatened before writing thank-you notes, leave half-empty cups all over the living room, and yell. Caleb has a devastating tendency toward social honesty ("It was nice of you to ask us, but my parents think those dinners are really boring") and Ethan, who is shy, flatly refuses to answer the telephone, though this may actually be a behavioral improvement, since he used to pick up the receiver and growl "What?" Still, it's nice to know that our sons can pull themselves up by their bootstraps in public. They *are* polite. We did it by prodding them persistently—"It's called nagging," says Josh, bitterly—for years and years. Manners, I'm convinced, cannot be taught in bulk. They must be ingrained Chinese-water-torture-style, drip by drip, interminably, until eventually they catch on. This is time-consuming and requires constant vigilance, but the end result is worth it.

BOOKS

The Bad Good Manners Book
Babette Cole; Dial, 1996

Zany pop-eyed illustrations demonstrate the real basis of good manners: always mind one's own business, do as one would be done by, and understand that—when things go disastrously wrong—there are dispensations for good intentions. Among the "don'ts": don't skateboard on the stairs, don't turn the bathtub into a snorkeling pond, and don't tell your mom that she's fat.

The Berenstain Bears Forget Their Manners
Stan and Jan Berenstain; Random House, 1985

Brother and Sister Bear have been rude, so Mama Bear institutes a Family Politeness Plan, complete with chart and list of penalties for such no-nos as name-calling, yelling, and neglecting to say "please" and "thank you."

Don't Do That! A Child's Guide to Bad Manners, Ridiculous Rules, and Inadequate Etiquette

Barry Louis Polisar; Rainbow Morning, 1995

A humorous and backward look at manners, covering such topics as "How to Play With Your Food" and "Rules for Scaring Your Grandparents."

Elbert's Bad Word

Audrey Wood; Harcourt Brace, 1996

Elbert, whacked on the great toe by a croquet mallet at a very upper-class garden party, utters a perfectly dreadful word. Elbert's outraged mother washes his mouth with soap, but the dreadful word—a giggling ratlike little creature—refuses to leave. Elbert is finally cured of the word by the estate gardener, who just happens to be a magician. A delightful picture book, especially for kids afflicted with forbidden words.

Elbows Off the Table, Napkin in the Lap, No Video Games During Dinner: The Modern Guide to Teaching Children Good Manners

Carol McD. Wallace; St. Martin's Press, 1996

The book is roughly divided into three parts: "Basic Training," which covers manners for 3–5-year-olds; "The Age of Reason," for ages 6–9; and "Young Sophisticates," for kids aged 10 and up. Wallace covers the etiquette of meeting new people, table manners, visiting, telephone behavior, party manners (six-year-olds get extra credit for saying that they had a good time), thank-you notes, good sportsmanship, and car and audience behavior. Expectations are nicely keyed to age: audience manners for 3-year-olds, for example, mean "Don't kick the back of the seat;" 12-year-olds are told not to applaud between musical movements and not to fool with their braces in public.

From Hand to Mouth, Or How We Invented Knives, Forks, Spoons, and Chopsticks, and the Manners to Go With Them

James Cross Giblin; HarperCrest, 1987

An interesting history of manners, from ancient times to the present, for readers aged 9–12.

George Washington's Rules of Civility and Decent Behavior in Company and Conversation

George Washington; Applewood Books, 1994

Etiquette and American history. George Washington, somewhere between the ages of 10 and 13, recorded in a notebook a list of 110 rules of etiquette, among them "In the presence of others, sing not to yourself with a humming noise nor drum with your fingers or feet" and "Spit not in the fire."

Goops and How to Be Them: A Manual of Manners for Polite Infants Inculcating Many Juvenile Virtues Both by Precept and Example, with 90 Drawings

Gelett Burgess; Dover Publications, 1968

Manners for kids through the cartoonish Goops, by humorist Gelett Burgess, famed for his writing of the immortal poem "I Never Saw a Purple Cow."

Hello! Good-bye!

Aliki; Greenwillow, 1996

A brightly illustrated picture book about the many ways people say "Hello" and "Good-bye" (including "Howdy" and "Toodle-oo"). For readers aged 4–8.

It's a Spoon, Not a Shovel

Caralyn Buehner; Dial Books for Young Readers, 1995

A humorous multiple-choice quiz on proper manners in 20 different social situations, with zany illustrations. (When a young cobra's mother is talking to a neighbor and he wants to get her attention, should he (1) hiss, (2) eat a rabbit, or (3) wait quietly? You pick.)

Letitia Baldrige's More Than Manners!: Raising Today's Kids to Have Kind Manners and Good Hearts

Letitia Baldrige; Charles Scribner's Sons, 1997

Kindness, according to Letitia Baldrige, is the basis of all good manners. Her prescription for raising well-mannered children includes not only the standards of good behavior but also the real reasons for it. It's rude to be a loudmouth, for example, but the worst part of sounding off is the insensitivity it shows toward the feelings of others. The book covers all the fundamentals of etiquette, including proper behavior at school, at restaurants, in church, and at parties; how to answer and take messages over the telephone; and how to use e-mail.

4 7 *Manners*

Aliki; Greenwillow, 1990

A very simple explanation of good and bad manners for beginners, with lovely illustrations. "Manners," the author begins, "are the way people behave."

P/T *Miss Manners' Guide to Rearing Perfect Children*

Judith Martin; Atheneum, 1997

Over 400 pages of good advice, in response to letters from concerned parents and kids, from the delightful, acerbic, wise, and incomparable Miss Manners.

5 9 *Perfect Pigs: An Introduction to Manners*

Marc Brown and Stephen Krensky; Little, Brown, 1983

A simple picture-book explanation of good manners in everyday situations, with family and friends, at school, at the table, on the telephone, and in public places. Illustrated with perfectly behaved pigs.

GARDENING

Our boys all started their gardening careers in the corner of the backyard, armed with tablespoons and packets of radish seeds—an ideal start for just-beginners, since radishes sprout fast, survive being stepped or sat upon, and are in general nearly foolproof. Their success rate, in fact, almost guarantees a prolific harvest: once the kids embark on such a project, the supportive parent must be prepared to eat lots and lots of radishes.

Gardening, if you've got the space for it, is an education in itself. Kids absorb an amazing amount of information in the course of raising their own carrots, potatoes, and pumpkins: the ins and outs of seed germination, soil pH, watering and weeding, garden insects (good and bad), flowers, fruits, and harvests. The process also lends itself to explorations in a range of academic disciplines: history, science, geography, literature, math. Grubbing around in the dirt inevitably sprouts a lush crop of questions. "Where do potatoes

come from anyway?" will take you to the Incas of Peru; "How many seeds are in a sunflower?" will introduce you to Fibonacci numbers; and a wail of "My seeds are *never* going to come up!" will send you comfortingly to storybooks in which various impatient characters had the very same problem.

Our boys' gardens, predictably, steered them off in assorted unpredictable directions. Josh, determinedly entomological, became more interested in potato bugs than potatoes—he's surely one of the few gardeners to express unqualified delight in their arrival—and moved happily into the study of beetles. Ethan developed an intense preoccupation with the weather and ended up compiling a scrapbook stuffed with carefully labeled photographs of cloud formations. Caleb, whose lettuce was eaten by rabbits, decided perversely that he wanted one as a pet and embarked upon an investigation of rabbit breeds, rabbit hutches, and all things rabbit. He has not, so far, acquired a rabbit. (Child-led learning is one thing; rabbits are another.) Still, it's clear that gardening generates a wealth of mind-broadening possibilities.

ORGANIZATIONS AND PROGRAMS

Gardens for Growing People

ALL Resources for "garden-based education" for kids of all ages, including kid-size gardening tools, fiction and nonfiction books about gardening, crafts, activities, and cookbooks, games, audiocassettes, and posters. The company also packages an assortment of "Heirloom Seed Collections" of special interest to kids, including seeds for a Rainbow Garden, a Colonial Garden, a Native American Garden, a Bird Garden, and a Butterfly Garden.

Gardens for Growing People
Box 630
Point Reyes, CA 94956-0630
(415) 663-9433
e-mail: growpepl@nbn.com

Growing Ideas

ALL *Growing Ideas,* from the National Gardening Association, is both a catalog of garden-based "teaching tools" and a newsletter—*Growing Ideas: A Journal of Garden-Based Learning*—a 12-page collection of how-to articles on teaching with gardens. The catalog includes books, activity books, and classroom-targeted garden supplies, notably the GrowLab indoor gardens. The GrowLab gardens, available in four models (one- or two-tier; with or without wheels) are aluminum racks equipped with plastic plant trays, fluorescent lights, and climate control tents. Prices range from $200 to $700. (For home learners, a sunny windowsill works just about as well.) GrowLab manuals—including a student activity book with background information, multidisciplinary project suggestions, reproducible record-keeping sheets, and an informational teacher's guide—are available separately.

Annual subscription to the newsletter, $6. A sample
issue and a copy of the catalog, free
National Gardening Association
180 Flynn Ave.
Burlington, VT 05401
(800) LETSGRO/fax (800) 863-5962
Web site: www.garden.org

Kids in Bloom

Many varieties of old-fashioned open-pollinated heirloom seeds are vanishing as modern strains of hybrid seed, produced by major seed companies, have come to dominate the seed market. Lately, however, concerned gardeners have begun to preserve these endangered varieties, growing heirloom plants in their gardens and saving the seeds to share with others. Without their efforts, we might not still have such garden rarities as Hopi Blue Flint corn, Moon and Stars watermelons, or Persimmon tomatoes. Heirloom plants are unusual, interesting, and fun to grow—and young gardeners can also participate in seed-saving programs.

Kids in Bloom
Seed Guardian Project
Box 344
Zionsville, IN 46077
(317) 290-6996

BOOKS

The Amazing Potato Book
Paulette Bourgeois; Addison-Wesley, 1991

Interesting potato information, recipes, and art, science, and gardening projects for kids aged 7–11.

Readers learn how to turn a potato green, make potato prints, create their own all-vegetable versions of Mr. Potato Head, whip up a batch of potato salad, and raise potatoes in the garden.

Backyard Scientist: Exploring Earthworms With Me
Jane Hoffman; Backyard Scientist, 1994

A collection of simple hands-on experiments exploring the science and ecology of the garden-friendly earthworm, for kids aged 4–12. The experiments are short and straightforward and require only inexpensive, readily available materials. Young researchers answer a number of worm-related questions: "Can earthworms hear?" "How many earthworms are in a patch of grass?" "Are earthworms sensitive to different colors of light?" "Are earthworms beneficial to our soil and for growing plants?" Experimenters also learn how to find earthworms, measure earthworms, and sneakily observe earthworms underground.

$10
Backyard Scientist
Box 16966
Irvine, CA 92713
(714) 551-2392
See *The Backyard Scientist Series* (page 233).

Beyond the Bean Seed: Gardening Activities for Grades K–6
Nancy Allen Jurenka and Rosanne J. Blass; Teacher Ideas Press, 1996

A creative 195-page resource for parents and teachers, divided into 11 chapters, among them "Flowers," "Vegetables," "Gardening Gadgets," and "Garden Inhabitants: Friend or Foe?" Each includes brief descriptions of related garden books, suggestions for in-the-garden activities, language arts and crafts activities, recipes, poems, puzzles, and supplementary reading lists. Under "Butterfly Habitats," for example, to accompany the book *The Butterfly Garden* by Jerry Sedenko (Villard, 1991), kids are encouraged to plant butterfly-attracting plants in the garden, read Rudyard Kipling's "The Butterfly That Stamped," make painted egg-carton caterpillars, sample honeysuckle nectar, read Roscoe Williams's poem "The Butterfly's Ball," and discuss the common phrase "butterflies in the stomach." Includes a large annotated bibliography.

$26
Libraries Unlimited
Box 6633
Englewood, CO 80155-6633
(303) 770-1220 or (800) 237-6124/fax (303) 220-8843
e-mail: lu-books@lu.com
Web site: www.lu.com

Blue Corn and Square Tomatoes

Rebecca Rupp; Storey Communications, 1987

Twenty chapters, each on the science and history of a different common garden vegetable. The book covers the science of how tomatoes ripen, why carrots are orange, and what makes peppers hot, as well as giving readers the scoop on what killed England's nasty King John (peas), what Ulysses S. Grant liked best for breakfast (cucumbers), and why the followers of Pythagoras wouldn't eat beans.

Corn Is Maize

Aliki; HarperTrophy, 1986

A picture-book history of corn, with instructions for a simple corn-husk craft project.

Eat the Fruit, Plant the Seed

Millicent Selsam; William Morrow, 1980

Plants that kids can grow from the seeds left over after eating the fruit, among them the avocado, the mango, and the papaya.

Gardening With Peter Rabbit

Jennie Walters; Frederick Warne & Co., 1992

Four seasons' worth of gardening activities for children, with illustrations from the Beatrix Potter books. See *The Tale of Peter Rabbit* (page 829) and **The Game of Peter Rabbit** (**Reading**, page 82).

Gardening Wizardry for Kids

L. Patricia Kite; Barron's, 1995

The subtitle is "Green Thumb Magic for the Great Indoors"; this is gardening wizardry that can be enjoyed in the unseasonable dead of winter or by eighth-floor apartment dwellers whose garden space is confined to a few coffee cans on the kitchen windowsill. The book is divided into five major sections. "History and Folklore of Common Fruits and Vegetables" covers everything from the apple to the watermelon, with detours into Indian bean games, the citrus solution to scurvy, and the invention of the potato chip. "Fun With Kitchen Fruits and Vegetables" shows kids how to plant practically everything from the refrigerator, from the avocado and the carrot to the pineapple and the potato. "Indoor Plant-Growing Experiments With Food Seeds" plunges young gardeners into science: armed with assorted seeds (catalog sources are listed at the back of the book), kids answer such questions as "How does water get from carrot roots into stems?," "Do all lima bean seeds of the same size grow at the same rate?," and "Do radish seedlings always grow toward the light?" After that, if there's still room on the windowsills, they can move on to garden fauna and try "Raising Earthworms, Pillbugs, and Snails." "Herb History, Folklore, and Growing Instructions" introduces young botanists to herbs, from basil to thyme; and "Easy Plant Craft Projects" includes instructions for drying and pressing flowers, making herbal bathwater and corn-husk dolls, decorating gourds, designing seed pictures, making pomander balls and potpourri, and stringing an herb wreath.

The book is 220 pages long, filled with big bright illustrations. It features a red spiral binding, which means that the book stays open flat on the kitchen counter—useful when referring repeatedly to directions. A terrific resource.

$14.95 from bookstores or
Barron's Educational Series, Inc.
250 Wireless Blvd.
Hauppauge, NY 11788
(516) 434-3311 or (800) 645-3476/fax (516) 434-3217

Green Thumbs: A Kid's Activity Guide to Indoor and Outdoor Gardening

Laurie Carlson; Chicago Review Press, 1995

Eighty garden-related hands-on projects for kids aged 3–9. Kids learn how to start houseplants from leaves, sprout seeds, and hatch praying mantises.

Growing Vegetable Soup

Lois Ehlert; Harcourt Brace, 1990

A simple picture-book account of a father and child planting a vegetable garden, plus a recipe for vegetable soup.

See *Planting a Rainbow* (right).

In a Pumpkin Shell

Jennifer Storey Gillis; Storey Communications, 1992

Instructions for growing your very own pumpkins, plus pumpkin crafts, projects, and recipes, among them making a pumpkin-seed necklace, a pumpkin-seed tambourine, a pumpkin pillow, pumpkin cookies, and pumpkin soup. Also see *From Seed to Jack O'Lantern* by Hannah Johnson (Lothrop, Lee & Shepard, 1974), a photo-essay on growing a pumpkin patch. Included is a recipe for roasted pumpkin seeds.

Kids Garden! The Anytime, Anyplace Guide to Sowing and Growing Fun

Avery Hart and Paul Mantell; Williamson, 1996

Many gardening activities for kids aged 4 and up, including making a plant person (from a nylon stocking, sawdust, and a handful of grass seed), building your own greenhouse, making garden markers, a scarecrow, and a pressed-flower bookmark, planting a rain forest in a bottle, growing a "dish garden," planting a salsa garden, a cactus garden, or a scented garden, and making a beanpole tepee.

Linnea's Windowsill Garden

Christina Bjork and Lena Andersen; Farrar, Straus & Giroux, 1988

Fifty-nine pages of information and plant projects for young gardeners, charmingly illustrated in black and white and green (the leaves). Activities include growing an orange tree, sprouting bulbs, holding a "Plant Olympics," and making a model of the water cycle.

Also see *Linnea in Monet's Garden* (pages 726 and 829).

The Magic School Bus Plants Seeds

Joanna Cole; Scholastic, 1995

Ms. Frizzle's class heads for the garden, where the Magic Schoolbus, transformed into a ladybug, tours the parts of a plant. The startled class learns about pollination, seed development, and seed dispersal.

See *The Magic School Bus Series* (page 227).

Native American Gardens

Michael Caduto and Joseph Bruchac; Fulcrum, 1996

American Indian legends, lore, history, and garden projects.

Planting a Rainbow

Lois Ehlert; Harcourt Brace Jovanovich, 1988

Simple picture-book instructions for planting a flower garden in all the colors of the rainbow.

See *Growing Vegetable Soup* (left).

Ready, Set, Grow! A Kid's Guide to Gardening

Rebecca Hershey; Good Year Books, 1995

How-tos of gardening indoors and out, plus a section of plant-based crafts, projects, and recipes. Each activity is accompanied by a reading list.

Slugs, Bugs, and Salamanders: Discovering Animals in Your Garden

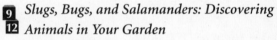

Sally Kneidel; Fulcrum, 1997

All about the different animals—some helpful, some harmful—found in the garden, plus information on how best to care for your garden plants.

Sunflower

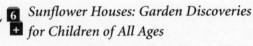

Miela Ford; Greenwillow, 1995

A short picture book for beginning readers/gardeners about growing a sunflower. Also see *Backyard Sunflower* (Elizabeth King; E. P. Dutton, 1993), which shows sunflower growing in color photographs.

Sunflower Houses: Garden Discoveries for Children of All Ages

Sharon Lovejoy; Interweave Press, 1991

A charmingly illustrated collection of old-fashioned garden lore, projects, stories, and poems for imaginative young gardeners. Kids make firefly lanterns and plant morning-glory tepees, design an all-blue garden, weave a clover chain, tell time by the four-o'clocks, and make a hollyhock doll. Also see *Hollyhock Days* (1994).

L I F E   S K I L L S

Literature Links to Gardening for Adults

Cultivating a Child's Imagination Through Gardening

Nancy Allen Jurenka and Rosanne J. Blass; Teacher Ideas Press, 1996

A collection of 45 lessons for kids in grades K–6, each centering around a book about some aspect of gardening. Books are grouped into nine chapters: "Dreaming of Gardens," "Dreaming in Technicolor," "Specialty Gardens," "Vegetable Gardens," "Nature's Gardens," "Plants Around the World," "Legendary Plants," "Fictional Gardeners," and "Famous Gardeners," this last including George Washington Carver, Johnny Appleseed, Beatrix Potter, and Rachel Carson. For each featured book there's a gardening, language arts, and craft activity; a recipe; a related poem; suggestions for a "word play" discussion; and a bibliography of associated reading suggestions.

$19.50

Libraries Unlimited

Box 6633

Englewood, CO 80155-6633

(303) 770-1220 or (800) 237-6124/fax (303) 220-8843

e-mail: lu-books@lu.com

Web site: www.lu.com

Also see *Beyond the Bean Seed* (page 825).

Literature Links to Gardening for Kids

The Biggest Pumpkin Ever

Steven Kroll; Cartwheel Books, 1993

Two young mice, unaware of each other, nurture a truly spectacular pumpkin, feeding it with sugar water and covering it with blankets at night. One has plans for winning the pumpkin-growing contest at the county fair; the other hopes to carve a gigantic Halloween jack-o'-lantern. When they finally meet each other, they figure out a way to do both.

The Carrot Seed

Ruth Krauss; HarperTrophy, 1989

An enchanting little picture book in which a hopeful and determined small boy manages to grow a marvelous carrot the size of a wheelbarrow.

The Empty Pot

Demi; Henry Holt, 1996

A picture-book tale of gardening, with a moral. The emperor offers a prize to the child who can grow the most beautiful flowers from his flower seeds. There's a trick to the contest, though: the emperor has boiled the seeds before passing them out, so that they cannot grow. Nonetheless all the children appear at the palace with pots of beautiful flowers—except for little Ping, who thereby shows himself to be truthful and honest.

An Episode of Sparrows

Rumer Godden; Viking, 1989

The story of 10-year-old Lovejoy Mason, a scrappy little London street child who plants a secret garden. The garden eventually changes the lives of all about her. A beautiful and heartwarming story for readers aged 12 and up.

The Garden of Abdul Gasazi

Chris Van Allsburg; Houghton Mifflin, 1979

Alan's naughty dog scampers into the forbidden garden of a magician. Magical and mysterious illustrations.

The Gardener

Sarah Stewart; Farrar, Straus & Giroux, 1997

In the days of the Great Depression, young Lydia Grace is sent off to the city to live with her uncle Jim, who runs a bakery. Uncle Jim never smiles—until Lydia Grace works a small miracle with her grandmother's garden seeds, planting a glorious roof garden as a surprise for her uncle on the Fourth of July. With lovely illustrations. For readers aged 5–8.

Grandpa's Too-Good Garden

James Stevenson; Greenwillow, 1989

Louie and Mary Ann's tale-telling grandpa tells of the terrible day when *his* grandfather's hair tonic spilled into the family garden, producing a phenomenal crop of enormous vegetables.

The Great Big Enormous Turnip

4 8 Alexei Tolstoy; Franklin Watts, 1968

An old Russian folktale about a gigantic turnip that nobody can seem to pull up: it finally takes a long line of pullers, including the farmer and his family, neighbors, and all the barnyard animals.

Jack and the Beanstalk

4 8 Steven Kellogg; William Morrow, 1991

The old tale of the boy, the cow, the magic beans, and the giant, with Steven Kellogg's colorful illustrations.

Linnea in Monet's Garden

9 12 Christina Bjork; Farrar, Straus & Giroux, 1987

Linnea visits the painter Claude Monet's wonderful flower garden and learns about the painter's life and work. Illustrations include photographs of Monet and color reproductions of his paintings. A video version of the book is also available.

Miss Rumphius

5 9 Barbara Cooney; Viking, 1985

The beautifully illustrated story of Miss Rumphius, who first travels around the world, and then, home again, plans to do something to make the world more beautiful. She decides to plant beautiful blue lupines wherever she goes.

The Secret Garden

9 + Frances Hodgson Burnett; Dell, 1990

A gardening classic, first published in 1911. Cross, skinny, 12-year-old Mary Lennox is sent from India to live with her uncle at gloomy Misselthwaite Manor on the moors of Yorkshire. There she meets the crusty old gardener Ben Weatherstaff and the boy Dickon, who has a magical way with wild things—and discovers the long-lost key to the mysterious secret garden. As Mary works to bring the garden back to life, miracles blossom and lead to a very happy ending. For readers aged 9 and up. A video version of the book is also available.

The Tale of Peter Rabbit

3 7 Beatrix Potter; Penguin, 1989

The classic tale of the bad little rabbit who—even though his mother told him not to—sneaks into Mr. McGregor's garden and gets into a great deal of trouble.

GAMES

The Farming Game

6 + "Used as an educational tool in thousands of schools," says one description. Players of "The Farming Game" have just inherited 20 acres of land from their grandpa that they plan to farm. Livestock and equipment, however, are costly, so while trying to accumulate enough assets to get the farm up and running, they have to hold down part-time jobs in town. Players move their pieces—overworked little plastic farmers—around a hay-colored playing board representing a map of the local farmland. As they proceed, they try to acquire enough seed, feed, cattle, and machinery to equip the farm, all the while struggling with real-life problems (dealt out in "Farmer's Fate" cards), operating expenses, and bank loans. For two to six players, aged 6 to adult.

> $32 from game stores or
> Turn Off the TV
> Box 4162
> Bellevue, WA 98009
> (800) 949-8688/fax (425) 558-7564
> Web site: www.turnoffthetv.com

The Garden Game

8 + "A Celebration of Cultivation for All Seasons" from Ampersand Press. The board is an exquisite garden (with flowers, fruit, vegetables, and a lily pond) around which players move their playing pieces (pebbles), step by step, upon a flagstone path. The game includes 100 "Garden" cards, illustrated with color paintings of vegetables, flowers, and insect pollinators, 121 "Gardener's Almanac" cards with helpful advice ("Weeds Take Over! Your seedlings can't get enough water and light. Take the time to pull weeds and then mulch. Pay one Garden card to the Community Compost for mulching material"), and a weather spinner, which deals out everything from hot sunny days to hurricanes. Players attempt to collect Garden cards and to provide their plants with pollinators. The player with the most cards—and the biggest, lushest garden—at the end of the game wins. All the gardens, however, are winners. For two to six players, aged 8 and up.

> $26.95 from game stores or
> Ampersand Press

750 Lake St.

Port Townsend, WA 98368

(800) 624-4263

3 7 *Harvest Time*

A delightful cooperative board game for gardeners aged 3–7. The board is illustrated with pictures of four gardens, each planted with corn, peas, carrots, and fat red tomatoes. At the beginning of the game, each veggie in the garden plot is covered by a colored plastic marker. On each turn, players roll a color-coded die that allows them to remove one marker from their gardens—that is, "harvest a crop"—or, if they roll white, has them add a piece to the snowy winter picture puzzle in the center of the board. The aim of the game is to harvest all the garden vegetables before the puzzle is completed, indicating the arrival of winter.

$18

Animal Town

Box 757

Greenland, NH 03840

(800) 445-8642/fax (603) 430-0334

GARDENS ON-LINE

5 + *KinderGarden*

Many creative links and activities for young gardeners. Visitors to the site can access garden poems or an art gallery of kids' garden pictures; there's also a list of kids' books about gardens, instructions for planting a Butterfly Garden, a list of edible flowers, and links to other kid-friendly plant sites.

aggie-horticulture.tamu.edu/kinder/index.html

Mr. Potato Head Home Page

ALL A biography of Mr. Potato Head, a gallery of "Funny Faces," among them a Picasso-style Potato Head and an ancient Egyptian Potato Head, and assorted creative Potato Head graphics.

www.cyberstreet.com/users/lynn

9 + *The Telegarden*

Visitors to the site can use a remote control robot arm and camera to look into the garden, plant seeds, and water the developing plants.

www.usc.edu/dept/garden

GENDER ISSUES

The "gender gap," in recent years, has been a focus of concern among educators, primarily as a result of a 1991 study commissioned by the American Association of University Women titled "Shortchanging Girls, Shortchanging America." The study, based largely on interviews with schoolchildren, found a marked drop in self-esteem among girls as they enter adolescence. Some psychologists argue that this drop in self-esteem explains the decreased academic test scores and increased emotional problems observed in high school–aged girls—and may ultimately be the reason that relatively low numbers of women enter technologically challenging professions.

Others counter that the gender gap gapes the other way: boys receive more discipline, drop out of school in greater numbers, and suffer more learning disabilities than girls. They do surpass girls in math and science, according to scores on standardized tests; girls, however, dramatically outperform boys in verbal (reading and writing) skills. The educator Thomas Sowell, in *Inside American Education: The Decline, The Deception, The Dogmas* (see page 15), points out that self-esteem is a poor predictor of academic performance. Self-esteem, argues Sowell, develops with the satisfaction of a job well done; to demand that self-esteem necessarily precede accomplishment is putting the cart before the horse.

Gender gap and self-esteem issues at present are unresolved; and the eventual outcome may be more a matter of politics than science. Perhaps just now the best we can do is to take it one kid at a time—supplying, if need be, additional math and science materials for our daughters, extra trips to the library for our sons.

MAGAZINES

13 *Blue Jean Magazine*

+ A magazine written and produced by young women. The theme, rather than the beauty and fashion topics often featured in women's magazines, is young women changing the world.

Annual subscription (6 issues), $29

Blue Jean Magazine

7353 Pittsford-Victor Rd.

Victor, NY 14564-9790

(716) 924-4080 or (888) 4-258-5326

fax (716) 924-4133

Web site: www.bluejeanmag.com

 New Moon

A bimonthly magazine for girls aged 8–14 that is intended to bolster female self-esteem, build resistance to gender inequities, provide supportive feminist role models, and offer a sense of female community—all in a manner appealing to young readers. The editorial staff includes a long list of girls, and the magazine contains contributions—letters, essays, opinions, poems, drawings, and cartoons—from girls all over the world. My sample issue includes an article about a 13-year-old Vietnamese girl and her country; a biographical piece on artist Georgia O'Keeffe; an account of up-and-coming female Olympic athletes; an interview with naturalist Diane Boyd, who studies wolves in Montana; articles on kids' environmental organizations and projects; and a piece titled "A Different Way of Learning" by 14-year-old homeschooler Sunshine Lewis of Pensacola, Florida.

Annual subscription (6 issues), $29

New Moon

Box 3587

Duluth, MN 55803-3587

(218) 728-5507 or (800) 381-4743

Web site: www.newmoon.org

Books for Adults

Failing at Fairness: How America's Schools Cheat Girls

David and Myra Sadker; Touchstone Books, 1995

This book, based on years of observations in classrooms, claims that the present school system and curriculum are heavily slanted in favor of boys. Boys talk more than girls in class; they are more likely to receive teacher attention and constructive criticism; they are asked more challenging questions. Teaching materials are similarly biased: kids read six times more biographies of males than biographies of females; textbooks picture seven times more males than females.

Great Books for Girls

Kathleen Odean; Ballantine, 1997

A list of over 600 books with plot summaries and descriptions, each selected for its ability to support and inspire girls. Also see, by the same author, *Great Books for Boys* (1998).

Let's Hear It for the Girls: 375 Great Books from Readers 2–14

Erica Baumeister and Holly Smith; Penguin, 1997

Books with themes and protagonists that provide good female role models, with plot summaries and descriptions.

 Reviving Ophelia: Saving the Selves of Adolescent Girls

Mary Pipher; Ballantine, 1995

Girls entering adolescence, explains Pipher, "crash and burn in a social and developmental Bermuda Triangle." The book discusses the reported abrupt drop in self-esteem and concommitant psychological stresses that bedevil teenage girls and suggests means of combatting the problem.

Books for Kids

Girl Power: Making Choices and Taking Control

Patty Ellis; Momentum Books, 1994

A self-help guide for teenage girls, with straightforward advice on such difficult issues as peer pressure, self-esteem, sex, and emotional abuse.

 Tatterhood and Other Tales

Ethel Johnston Phelps, ed.; Feminist Press, 1989

A collection of 27 folktales from around the world, all starring courageous, clever, and independent women. If your daughter is sick of playing the maiden in distress while her brother gets to battle the dragon, these might be the fairy tales for her. Good reading for both sexes; appropriate for ages 4–10.

Wise Women: Folk and Fairy Tales from Around the World

Suzanne I. Barchers; Teacher Ideas Press, 1990

A collection of tales all featuring strong women, who win out through their own intelligence, resourcefulness, or courage. For readers of all ages.

$18

Libraries Unlimited

Box 6633

Englewood, CO 80155-6633

(303) 770-1220 or (800) 237-6124/fax (303) 220-8842

e-mail: lu-books@lu.com

Web site: www.lu.com

AUDIO RESOURCES

The Wise Little Girl: Tales of the Feminine

On audiocassette, three multicultural stories narrated by Odds Bodkins that feature brave and resourceful young girls. One is a Russian folktale, one an American Indian legend, and the third is based on a story by the Brothers Grimm. The tape is 47 minutes long, appropriate for listeners aged 6 and up.

$9.95

Rivertree Productions, Inc.

Box 410

Bradford, NH 03221

(603) 938-5120

e-mail: rivertreeAconknet.com

Web site: www.oddsbodkin.com

ON-LINE RESOURCES

Girls Incorporated

A site devoted to "Helping Girls Become Strong, Smart, and Bold."

www.girlsinc.org

Ms. Foundation for Women

Information, articles on women's issues, and on-line links from the sponsors of "Take Our Daughters to Work" Day.

www.sherryart.com/daughters/ms.html

SEX EDUCATION

I learned about sex in seventh grade from my best friend's big sister, Charlene, who broke the news to both of us during a weekend sleep-over, using a dramatic example based on cocker spaniels. While this presentation was not precisely damaging, neither was it the way my husband and I wanted to present the facts of life to our sons—all of whom, as the inevitable age of curiosity approached, remained resolutely determined not to discuss such intimate issues with their parents. Josh, at the age of eleven, informed us firmly that he knew it all, as a result of broad-based and uncensored reading, and did not want to hear *one word* about it, the implication being that whatever disgraceful process had served to bring him into the world was better left in the dark. My husband and I were uncomfortable with this sweep-it-under-the-rug attitude, feeling that avoidance, accompanied by a perusal of miscellaneous novels, might not be the ideal means of acquiring an understanding of human reproduction. ("Knowing it all," after all, is a phrase with a wide range of definitions.) As it turned out, our approach to sex education was threefold. We tried to provide each kid, individually, with a concise explanation of the basics. We did our best to answer all questions clearly and matter-of-factly when they surfaced—"What's does 'homosexual' mean?" "What's a condom?" "What's AIDS?"—keeping all definitions accurate and brief, which was all our kids would stay still for. And we bought good informative books. Which they read, cover to cover.

BOOKS

Asking About Sex and Growing Up: A Question-and-Answer Book for Boys and Girls

Joanna Cole; William Morrow, 1988

A straightforward explanation in question-and-answer format for kids aged 7–12.

Girltalk: All the Stuff Your Sister Never Told You

Carol Weston; HarperPerennial, 1997

The nitty-gritty in 352 pages for girls aged 11–18 on such sensitive issues as changing bodies, sex, birth

LIFE SKILLS

control, pregnancy, and sexually transmitted diseases, as well as many of the other difficult choices modern kids have to tackle: drugs, alcohol, family conflicts, peer pressure, love and friendship, money. The style is direct, chatty, and practical—Weston leaves values up to the parents—and includes queries and comments from concerned teenagers.

5 8 *How You Were Born*

Joanna Cole; Mulberry, 1994

A clear and simple explanation of how a baby develops and is born, illustrated with black-and-white photographs and drawings. Cole explains how sperm and egg unite to form the "special cell" that divides to form an embryo, and there's a cutaway diagram of a woman and man, showing the locations of ovaries and testes. Cole does not explain here how sperm and egg get together—the young readers at whom this book is targeted (ages 5–8) generally aren't interested in this, she explains in her introduction—but she does provide suggestions and a brief bibliography for the curious.

11 13 *It's Perfectly Normal: Changing Bodies, Growing Up, Sex and Sexual Health*

Robie Harris; Candlewick, 1994

The facts, clearly presented and tastefully illustrated, with a little comic help from a cartoon-style bird and bee. The book covers puberty (boys and girls), sex organs, masturbation and sexual intercourse, birth control, pregnancy, homosexuality and heterosexuality, and sexually transmitted diseases. Appropriate for 11–13-year-olds.

4 8 *Mommy Laid An Egg! or Where Do Babies Come From?*

Babette Cole; Chronicle Books, 1996

A simple, humorously illustrated 40-page explanation of conception and childbirth for kids aged 4–8. The story has a clever twist: the parents are offering the kids fanciful explanations of where babies come from ("Sometimes you just find them under stones"); the kids take matters in hand and explain the whole business.

9 12 *The Period Book: Everything You Don't Want to Ask (But Need to Know)*

Karen Gravelle and Jennifer Gravelle; Walker & Company, 1996

An explanation of menstruation and the other physical and emotional aspects of female puberty, with cheerful cartoon illustrations.

9 15 *The What's Happening to My Body? Book for Girls*

Lynda Madaras; Newmarket Press, 1987

A thorough coverage of puberty and sex, for kids aged 9–15. *Girls,* in just over 300 pages, covers physical changes in puberty, reproductive organs, the menstrual cycle, and—so that readers will understand what the opposite sex is going through—puberty in boys. The companion book, *The What's Happening to My Body? Book for Boys* (1987), aimed at male readers, concentrates on the male half of the process, with an explanation of puberty in girls.

SEWING/FABRIC CRAFTS

Sewing projects in our past have included pillows, pot holders, Christmas ornaments, capes in assorted sizes and colors, three pairs of beaded felt moccasins, a latch-hook rug, and a very small quilt. I taught all the boys the basics of hand sewing—seams, hems, and buttons—and Randy taught them how to use his grandmother's treadle sewing machine. I taught everybody how to knit, more or less—including Ethan, who is left-handed—and they all experimented with weaving, using two kinds of homemade looms.

BOOKS

9 12 *Friendship Bands: Braiding, Weaving, and Knotting*

Marlies Busch, ed.; Sterling Publications, 1997

Easy step-by-step instructions for making many kinds of friendship bands and bracelets, for kids aged 9–12.

Knitting From Start to Finish: An Usborne Guide

An illustrated instruction book for beginners aged 11 and up, with directions for simple projects.

$7.95
EDC Publishing
Box 470663
Tulsa, OK 74147-0663
(800) 331-4418

My First Patchwork Book: Hand and Machine Sewing

Winky Cherry; Palmer Pletsch Publishing, 1997

Simple instructions paired with color photographs. In *My First Patchwork Book,* kids learn how to make an easy four-square patchwork block. Also see *My First Quilt Book* (1997), in which kids learn about the history of quilting and the structure of a quilt, and make an easy nine-block quilt of their own. For kids aged 9–12.

My Little House Sewing Book: 8 Projects from Laura Ingalls Wilder's Classic Stories

Margaret Irwin; HarperCollins, 1997

Illustrated step-by-step instructions for projects that Laura herself might have made in the *Little House* books, among them a sunbonnet, an embroidered sampler, and a nine-patch quilt.

See *Little House in the Big Woods* and sequels (page 527).

Sewing by Hand

Christine Hoffman and Harriett Barton; Harper-Collins, 1994

A very simple illustrated introduction to hand sewing for kids aged 5–8. Includes step-by-step instructions for making a pillow, a beanbag cat, and a flower girl doll.

Sewing Machine Fun

Nancy J. Smith and Lynda Milligan; Possibilities, 1993

Simple projects, puzzles, and instructions that teach kids aged 7 and up the basics of using a sewing machine. The book is intended for kids teaching themselves, which means that very little adult supervision is needed. Also available as a kit, including enough material for one kid to complete all the sewing projects.

Book, $15.95; kit, $29.95. From bookstores or Timberdoodle Co.
E. 1510 Spencer Lake Rd.
Shelton, WA 98584
(360) 426-0672

Also see **American History: Quilts** (pages 515–516).

SEWING/FABRIC ARTS AND LITERATURE

Angela Weaves a Dream

Michele Sola; Disney Press, 1997

The story of a 10-year-old Maya weaver and her craft, illustrated with color photographs. Readers learn about Angela's life and village, and about the entire process of traditional weaving, from the carding, spinning, and dyeing of the wool through the finished product. For readers aged 8–12.

Bruno the Tailor

Lars Klinting; Henry Holt, 1996

Bruno, a beaver, is making a blue apron. Readers follow the entire process, from choosing the fabric to cutting the pattern, basting the pieces together, and stitching the apron on the sewing machine. For kids aged 4–8.

Charlie Needs a Cloak

Tomie de Paola; Aladdin, 1988

The tale of a little shepherd boy who needs a new cloak, with particularly adorable illustrations of sheep, for readers aged 4–8.

The Empress and the Silkworm

Lily Toy Hong; Albert Whitman, 1995

A Chinese legend explaining the origin of silk. The wife of the Yellow Emperor is having tea and mooncakes in the garden when a silkworm's cocoon falls from a nearby mulberry tree into her cup and unwinds into a long, shimmering thread. For readers aged 5–9.

Grandpa Bear's Fantastic Scarf

Gillian Heal; Beyond Words Publishing, 1997

Grandpa Bear's wonderful long woven scarf is the story of his life: the different colors and textures each represent something about his feelings and experi-

LIFE SKILLS

ences. The threads of the warp, Grandpa explains to his little grandson, are fixed, but each weaver chooses whatever he or she wishes for the yarns of the weft. As they talk, the small bear begins to choose colors for his own life scarf: honey yellow, apple red, and sometimes, for sadness, a dark, dark gray. For readers aged 4–8.

Knitwits
William Taylor; Apple, 1994

Nine-year-old Charlie has made a bet—that he can knit a sweater for his new baby brother or sister—and is racing to finish the project in time to win the wager without his buddies on the hockey team finding out what he's doing. The hilarious trials of a secret knitter, for readers aged 9–12.

The Magic Weaver of Rugs
Jerrie Oughton; Houghton Mifflin, 1994

A Navajo legend about how people learned to weave. Long ago, in a time of great hunger and cold, two women pray for help. The Spider Woman hears them, makes them a giant loom, and shows them how to prepare wool, gather colors from the earth to dye the yarn, and weave a beautiful blanket. For readers aged 5–10.

Pelle's New Suit
Elsa Beskow; Gryphon House, 1989

The story of a little Swedish boy's new suit of clothes, from woolly sheep to jacket and trousers, for readers aged 4–8.

The Weaving of a Dream
Marilee Heyer; Viking, 1989

A Chinese folktale about a weaver whose beautiful tapestry is stolen by fairies. Her three sons set out on a journey to get it back. For readers aged 4–8.

HANDS-ON ACTIVITIES

American Sampler
Cross-stitch an old-fashioned 9 × 11½-inch alphabet sampler. The kit includes embroidery thread and needle, mesh for counted cross-stitch and muslin backing, and complete instructions. Recommended for kids aged 9 and up.

$14.95 from toy and craft stores; for a local source, contact
Curiosity Kits
Box 811
Cockeysville, MD 21030
(410) 584-2605 or (800) 584-KITS/fax (410) 584-1247
e-mail: CKitsinc@aol.com

Folk Art Rabbit
All the materials for stitching a six-inch-tall floppy-eared muslin bunny, with button eyes, a pink thread nose, and a flowered shawl. The kit includes pattern, cloth, thread, buttons, stuffing, and complete instructions.

$14.95 from toy and craft stores; for a local source, contact
Curiosity Kits
Box 811
Cockeysville, MD 21030
(410) 584-2605 or (800) 584-KITS/fax (410) 584-1247
e-mail: CKitsinc@aol.com

Inchworm Kits
This clever little device is essentially a hollow wooden cylinder with four pegs surrounding the hole on top. Kids loop yarn from peg to peg, thus producing long skinny knitted tubes that can be used to make belts and bows, or coiled up to make coasters, pot holders, and useful little mats. It's simple and fun. Clear instructions are included with the kits.

Available as a pack of two, in plain wood, for $18 from
Lark Books
50 College St.
Asheville, NC 28801
(800) 284-3388
Or shaped and painted to looked like a mushroom ("Jumbo Knitting Mushroom"), $9.95 from
HearthSong
6519 N. Galena Rd.
Box 1773
Peoria, IL 61656-1773
(800) 325-2502

Starting Needlecraft Kit
Everything a beginner needs for four simple sewing projects: needles, colored threads, scissors, fab-

ric, and a brightly illustrated instruction book that explains everything from threading a needle to quilting and cross-stitch. Kids make a sleeping bag for a stuffed animal, juggling bags, a frog pincushion, and a pocket mouse. Recommended for kids aged 5 and up.

$13.95
EDC Publishing
10302 E. 55 Pl.
Tulsa, OK 74147
(800) 475-4522
Web site: www.edcpub.com

Tie-Dye Kits
Squinch up your T-shirt, fasten it with rubber bands, and squirt it with colored dyes. The finished product is a rainbow-hued artwork, covered with circles, spirals, and spectacular designs. Kits, which are available from most arts and crafts suppliers, include procion (natural-fiber) dye powders, color fixative, plastic applicator bottles, rubber gloves, rubber bands, and a detailed instruction booklet. You supply your own T-shirts, socks, sweatpants, etc.

$11.95 to $19.95
Sax Arts & Crafts
Box 510710
New Berlin, WI 53151
(800) 558-6696
or
HearthSong
6519 N. Galena Rd.
Box 1773
Peoria, IL 61656-1773
(800) 325-2502

LOOMS

Available in many sizes and models, from the simple and inexpensive to the costly and complex. Available through most arts and crafts catalogs. Examples include:

Flat Loom
Notched wooden frames, available in various sizes; similar to the lap top loom (above). These are good looms for beginning weavers, simple to set up and use.

$11.50 to $32.95
Sax Arts & Crafts
Box 510710
New Berlin, WI 53151
(800) 558-6696

Inkle Loom
Used for weaving bands, strips, or belts, generally—depending on the size of the loom—from 2 to 12 inches wide and up to 8 feet long. Inkle looms are more complex to assemble and set up than the flat looms (see above) but are not difficult to master.

$17.95 to $56.50
Sax Arts & Crafts
Box 510710
New Berlin, WI 53151
(800) 558-6696
or
Lark Books
50 College St.
Asheville, NC 28801
(800) 284-3388

Lap Top Weaving Loom Kit
A packaged kit including the pieces for a 15 × 20-inch flat wooden lap loom, a shuttle, shed sticks, colored yarn, and instructions. Kids can make place mats, scarves, and wall hangings. Recommended for weavers aged 9 and up.

$19.95 from toy and craft stores; for a local source, contact
Curiosity Kits
Box 811
Cockeysville, MD 21030
(410) 584-2605 or (800) 584-KITS/fax (410) 584-1247
e-mail: CKitsinc@aol.com

Potholder Loom
For weavers aged 6 and up. These are small square metal looms upon which kids can weave pot holders using colorful cotton loops. Usually available as a kit, including a loom, a weaving hook, and a big bag of loops.

$10 from toy stores or
HearthSong
6519 N. Galena Rd.

Box 1773

Peoria, IL 61656-1773

(800) 325-2502

or

Lark Books

50 College St.

Asheville, NC 28801

(800) 284-3388

or

Sax Arts & Crafts

Box 510710

New Berlin, WI 53151

(800) 558-6696

SPORTS/PHYSICAL FITNESS

The question we get the most about homeschooling is "What do you do about socialization?" Runner-up is "How do the boys play team sports?" The answer to the first is "All sorts of things"; the answer to the second is "They don't." Organized sports, America's favorite extracurricular activity, has never been a part of our homeschool curriculum. When the boys were small, of the age to begin participating in group sports activities, we lived so far out in the boonies that it was difficult to transport them to continual practices; later nobody showed any interest. This doesn't mean that they're all lumpish couch potatoes. As younger kids, they took weekly gymnastics and swimming lessons. They all bicycle, hike, rollerblade, and ice skate; they participate, each winter, in a weekly downhill ski program. Two of them play racquetball. One of them jogs.

The bottom line, though, is that we're not a particularly sports-oriented household. This, as it turns out, is lucky for us, since our local school district is unwilling to allow homeschooled kids to participate in school-sponsored team sports. Sports—more so than math, science, or English literature—is often a major bone of contention between public and home schools, homeschoolers arguing that their payment of school taxes surely entitles them to the use of school facilities and participation in programs; school administrators countering that the school is solely for the use of offi-

cially enrolled and attending students. Some homeschoolers have managed to surmount this problem through creative negotiation and compromise: some school districts, for example, will allow homeschooled sports enthusiasts to enroll in a single school class, thus making them eligible for school sports teams. Alternatively, some homeschooled kids form teams of their own, or find non-school-affiliated teams through a local Y.M.C.A./Y.W.C.A. or health club.

CATALOGS

Collage Video

ALL A catalog of exercise videos for persons of all ages. Most selections are geared toward teenagers and adults; a kid's section contains videos for kids aged 2–12.

Collage Video

5390 Main St. NE

Minneapolis, MN 55421-1128

(612) 571-5840 or (800) 433-6769/fax (612) 571-5906

The Training Camp

ALL Sports books, games, videos, and equipment for kids of all ages. The catalog carries resources and gear for baseball, golf, swimming, skating, basketball, soccer, tennis, and more.

The Training Camp

Box 1602

Secaucus, NJ 07096-1602

(800) 284-5383/fax (201) 867-1112

Web site: www.thetrainingcamp.com

MAGAZINES

Sports Illustrated for Kids

7 14 A monthly magazine for young sports lovers, featuring general information on a wide range of sports, interviews with prominent athletes, comics, puzzles, and lots of color photographs.

Annual subscription (12 issues), $27.95

Sports Illustrated for Kids

Box 830609

Birmingham, AL 35283-0609

(205) 877-6152 or (800) 462-5154

Web site: www.pathfinder.com/SIFK

BOOKS

6 **10** *Albert the Running Bear's Exercise Book*
Barbara Isenberg and Marjorie Jaffe; Clarion, 1984

A 64-page book that explains the advantages of keeping in shape and shows kids how to do exercises the right way, along with Albert and his friend Violet, a very fit bear who wears purple leg warmers. The book discusses exercises that affect the hamstring, pectoral, and abdominal muscles, shows kids how to warm up before exercising, and demonstrates 12 basic exercises, among them sit-ups, leapfrogs, and push-ups. Also included is a section on aerobic exercises, in which Albert and Violet demonstrate a series of fun-to-imitate activities, including Giraffe Rolls, Hippo Bumps, the Camel Walk, and the Armadillo Curl.

9 **13** *Everybody's a Winner: A Kid's Guide to New Sports and Fitness*
Tom Schneider; Little, Brown, 1976

All about sports and physical fitness, for kids aged 9–13. Included are suggestions for inventing new games, descriptions of basic exercises, and instructions for determining what kind of shape your body is in, including evaluating your body type—are you an ectomorph, endomorph, or mesomorph?—and tests of various fitness skills, among them endurance, agility, speed, and strength. There's also a chapter on "handmade sports," with instructions on how to make your own weights, bungee cord exerciser, and superslide, and plans for holding a neighborhood bicycle gymkhana.

4 **18** *Home School Family Fitness: A Practical Curriculum Guide*
Bruce C. Whitney; Home School Family Fitness Institute, 1995

A physical fitness program for kids aged 4–18: advice, how-tos, lesson plans, record charts, and games, all packaged in one handy volume. First, writes Whitney, kids should be motivated to participate in a regular exercise program. This is accomplished by providing positive parental role models (you jog; they jog) and inspiring examples of professional athletes through books and videos, rewarding kids for accomplishing agreed-upon exercise goals, scheduling regular exercise periods, and exposing kids to a variety of sports and athletic activities. Book chapters include "Muscular Strength, Endurance and Flexibility" and "Aerobic Fitness," each with lists and descriptions of effective exercises; "Modified Fitness Games," with descriptions of active indoor and outdoor games—no. 1 among "Snow Games," I pointed out gleefully to the boys, is "Snow Shoveling"—and "Fitness Tests," a series of charts listing optimal performance levels for a variety of exercises according to age.

$15
Home School Family Fitness Institute
159 Oakwood Dr.
New Brighton, MN 55112
(612) 636-7738
e-mail: whitn003@maroon.tc.umn.edu

5 **13** *Hooked on Fitness! Fun Physical Conditioning Games and Activities for Grades K–8*
James C. Harrison; Parker Publishing, 1993

Many, many games, ranging from not so active to extremely active, among them aerobic warm-ups, running activities, active games (tag, throwing and catching games, dodgeball), strength-building activities, and exercise challenges. Also included are reproducible timer's sheets and instructions for game-related things to make, such as your own basketball basket.

9 **12** *Lives of the Athletes: Thrills, Spills (and What the Neighbors Thought)*
Kathleen Krull; Harcourt Brace, 1997

Engaging biographies of 20 athletes, among them Babe Ruth, Red Grange, Johnny Weissmuller, Sonja Henie, Jackie Robinson, Babe Didrikson Zaharias, Wilma Rudolph, and Arthur Ashe. Readers not only learn the basics but also discover that Babe Ruth liked pickled eels and that Johnny Weismuller's chest-pounding Tarzan yell—remember it?—was based on prizewinning performances of Austrian yodelers. With terrific illustrations by Kathryn Hewitt.

13 **+** *Newton at the Bat: The Science in Sports*
Eric W. Schrier and William F. Allman, eds.; Charles Scribner's Sons, 1984

A collection of throroughly fascinating essays on the science of various aspects of sports. The book is divided into four major parts: "Balls and Other Flying Objects," including the physics of curveballs, boomerangs, and Frisbees; "Gear," on the science of sneakers, tennis rackets, and cross-country ski wax; "The Body," which explains the physiology of keeping cool and the anatomy of the vulnerable knee; and "Form," which covers the physics of the high dive, the biomechanics of pole vaulting, and the science of darts. And much more. For teenagers.

Pretend You're a Cat
Jean Marzollo; Dial Books for Young Readers, 1990

An active rhyming picture book for toddlers, encouraging young readers to leap like a cat, fly (well, flap) like a bird, buzz like a bee, and imitate many other favorite animals, including fish, chickens, cows, and bears. Exercise for the body and the imagination.

Sports
Tim Hammond; Alfred A. Knopf, 1988

A volume in the Eyewitness series, filled with color photographs and diagrams. Each double-page spread features a different sport or sports topic, from soccer, football, and basketball through fencing, bowling, and golf. Readers learn how soccer balls and cricket bats are made, view a diagram of a football field, and study a pictorial history of tennis rackets.

Sportsworks
Ontario Science Center; National Science Teachers Association, 1989

A collection of over 50 sports-oriented science experiments for kids aged 9–12.

Toddlerobics
Zita Newcome; Candlewick, 1996

Eight cheerful and multicultural toddlers flap their arms, touch the sky, shake rattles, clap, stamp, dance, zoom like airplanes, tiptoe, spin, crawl, rub noses, and generally have a wonderful time at the "toddler gym." Your toddlers will want to exercise right along with the rest.

Yoga for Children
Mary Stewart and Kathy Phillips; Fireside, 1993

Stretching, breathing, moving, and relaxing techniques that help kids build strong, flexible bodies through noncompetitive exercise, illustrated with photographs and diagrams. For kids aged 3 and up. Also see *Yoga for Children* (Stella Waller; HarperCollins, 1996): the history of yoga, warm-ups, postures, and breathing exercises, for kids aged 5–15.

GAMES

Better Sports Through Science Cards/Kits
Kits, designed in collaboration with the Massachusetts Institute of Technology, are based on four sports: baseball, basketball, football, and soccer. Each kit includes 10 cards with instructions for sports-related scientific experiments, plus all necessary materials (except balls and bats).

$10.95 apiece
Edmund Scientific Co.
101 E. Gloucester Pike
Barrington, NJ 08007-1380
(609) 547-8880 or (800) 728-6999/fax (609) 573-3292
e-mail: scientifics@edsci.com
Web site: www.edsci.com

Footloose
If it's been raining for four days and the kids are bouncing off the walls, try "Footloose," a very active board game from Ravensburger for kids aged 3–8. Kids hop their playing pieces—shaped like sneakers—around the board, attempting to collect 10 "activity coins." To earn each coin, players must perform different simple physical activities, among them such energy users as jumping jacks, arm circles, sit-ups, and bunny hops.

$21.95 from toy and game stores

SportsTalk
A pack of conversation cards, guaranteed to start persons of all ages debating sports topics. Samples include:

> *Muhammad Ali repeatedly insisted, "I am the greatest." Who in your opinion is the greatest athlete of the twentieth century?*

> *The rules governing football change more frequently than do those of any other major sport. If you could change one sports rule, what would it be?*

$5.95

TableTalk

Box 31703

St. Louis, MO 63131

(314) 997-5676 or (800) 997-5676/fax (314) 997-3602

Web site: www.tbltalk.com

See also *TableTalk* (page 67).

EXERCISE VIDEOS

Elmocize

Half an hour of musical exercise with *Sesame Street*'s Elmo and Cyndi Lauper, for kids aged 3 and up. Lots of cute little tunes, bending Muppets, and an accompanying 10-page activities booklet.

$12.95

Music for Little People

Box 1720

Lawndale, CA 90260

(800) 727-2233

or

Collage Video

5390 Main St. NE

Minneapolis, MN 55421-1128

(612) 571-5840 or (800) 433-6769/fax (612) 571-5906

Funhouse Fitness Series

"Funhouse Funk" is a 40-minute music, dance, and exercise session for kids aged 8–12; "Swamp Stomp" includes 28 minutes of music, dance, and active make-believe for kids aged 4–8.

$12.95 each

Collage Video

5390 Main St. NE

Minneapolis, MN 55421-1128

(612) 571-5840 or (800) 433-6769/fax (612) 571-5906

Strength & Shape: A Teenage Workout

A 40-minute fitness workout on video, emphasizing strength, flexibility, and endurance for kids aged 10–16.

$14.95

Earth Smart, Inc.

Box 115

Lincroft, NJ 07738-0115

(908) 389-3679 or (800) EXERCI-4

Workout With Mommy & Me

Half an hour of exercises for mothers to do with their toddlers on the living room floor, while touring imaginary jungles or rainbow-filled skies, hopping on pretend pogo sticks, or pedaling imaginary bicycles. Also see *Workout With Daddy & Me.*

$12.99

Movies Unlimited

3015 Darnell Rd.

Philadelphia, PA 19154

(215) 637-4444 or (800) 4-MOVIES

e-mail: movies@moviesunlimited.com

Web site: www.moviesunlimited.com

TRAVEL

CATALOGS

The Family Travel Guides Catalog

A 32-page catalog of books, activity books, games, and travel guides for families. Included are handbooks detailing places to go and sights to see with vacationing kids (listed by region of the United States or Europe) and an eye-catching assortment of general guides for plan-your-own specialty vacations. Included among these last are *Adventure Holidays,* a list of vacations in over 100 countries, featuring such activities as gorilla tracking, pony trekking, and hang gliding; *Dinosaur Dig: Places Where You Can Discover Prehistoric Creatures;* and *The Zoo Book: A Guide to America's Best.* A particular plus for families may be *Books On the Move: A Read-About-It Go-There Guide to America's Best Family Destinations,* which pairs vacation destination suggestions with lists of topic- or area-related kids' books.

Catalog, $1

Carousel Press

Box 6061

Albany, CA 94706-0061

BOOKS

Family Travel: Terrific New Vacations for Today's Families

Evelyn Kaye; Blue Penguin Publications, 1993

A collection of unique alternatives to the run-of-the-mill family vacation, including information on ecology treks, river rafting, houseboats, art tours, dinosaur digs, dude ranches, family skiing expeditions, and bicycle tours.

Kids Camp! Activities for the Backyard or Wilderness

Laurie Carlson and Judith Dammel; Chicago Review Press, 1995

Over 100 learning activities and projects for kids on camping expeditions. Kids identify animal tracks, start a rock collection, weave a cattail mat, and press flowers. Also includes games and recipes.

Kids on the Go: Activity Logs for Young Travelers

John Haberberger; Teacher Ideas Press, 1994

Questions and activities for each of the 50 states and many major U.S. cities, as well as suggested lessons and activities for general travel, foreign travel, and local field trips. For kids in grades K–6.

$17.50
Libraries Unlimited
Box 6633
Englewood, CO 80153-6633
(303) 770-1220 or (800) 237-6124/fax (303) 220-8843
e-mail: lu-books@lu.com
Web site: www.lu.com

Smart Vacations: The Traveler's Guide to Learning Vacations Abroad

Priscilla Tovey, ed.; St. Martin's Press, 1993

From the Council on International Educational Exchange, a listing of over 200 one- to six-week educational vacations throughout the world, including study tours, outdoor adventure vacations, archaeological digs, art programs, language immersion courses, photography expeditions, cooking schools, and volunteer projects.

The Teenager's Guide to Study, Travel, Adventure Abroad

Council on International Educational Exchange

General information about travel and living abroad, and an extensive overview of foreign programs and opportunities for teenagers, among them educational exchange programs, language institutes, art programs, organized tours, work/volunteer programs, outdoor activities, and homestays. Updated periodically.

Weird and Wonderful America

Laura A. Bergheim; Macmillan, 1988

"The Nation's Most Offbeat and Off-the-Beaten-Path Tourist Attractions." Bergheim lists over 200 of these, among them the Nut Museum in Old Lyme, Conn., the Paper House (*all* paper) in Pigeon Cove, Mass., the Trumpet Museum in Pottstown, Pa., the Sponge Museum in Tarpon Springs, Fla., the Roller Skating Museum in Lincoln, Nebr., and the Checkers Hall of Fame in Petal, Mich.

WORK/COMMUNITY SERVICE

MAGAZINES

Better Than a Lemonade Stand! Small Business Ideas for Kids

Daryl Bernstein; Beyond Words Publishing, 1992

A collection of 51 good business ideas for kids, written by an experienced teenage entrepreneur. (He compares business to a trek through the jungle.)

Beyond Words
13950 N.W. Pumpkin Ridge Rd.
Hillsboro, OR 97123

Center for Teen Entrepreneurs

An organization for business-oriented kids. Publishes information and a newsletter.

Center for Teen Entrepreneurs
Box 3967
New York, NY 10163-6027
(800) 438-8336

Earning Our Own Money: Homeschoolers 13 and Under Tell Their Stories

Holt Associates, 1991

Stories by kids about the innovative ways in which they make money, among them collecting trash, hauling scrap metal, baby-sitting, making greeting cards, picking blueberries, breeding hamsters, baking cookies, assisting at ice-skating classes, and giving banjo lessons.

$4.50

John Holt's Book Store

2269 Massachusetts Ave.

Cambridge, MA 02140-1226

(617) 864-3100/fax (617) 864-9235

e-mail: holtgws@aol.com

Web site: www.holtgws.com

Turned On Business

An on-line business newsletter for teen women sponsored by "An Income of Her Own." Articles include how-tos, ideas, and interviews with teen entrepreneurs.

www.anincomeofherown.com/aioho_tob2.html

See **"An Income of Her Own"** game (page 843).

Fast Cash for Kids

Bonnie and Noel Drew; Career Press, 1995

Dozens of clever moneymaking ideas for ambitious kids, including how-tos, lists of necessary materials, suggested supplementary reading, and uplifting anecdotes about kids who succeeded. Suggestions include raising pet animals, watering lawns, planning children's parties, starting a home bakery, publishing a newsletter, and growing and selling fresh vegetables. Additional chapters cover turning ideas into viable businesses, attracting customers, and handling money.

$13.99

Career Press

3 Tice Rd.

Box 687

Franklin Lake, NJ 07417

(800) CAREER-1

Jobs for Kids: The Guide to Having Fun and Making Money

Carol Barkin and Elizabeth James; Lothrop, Lee & Shepard, 1990

The how-tos of finding and holding down a job, from a pitch for the pluses of working, through suggestions on how to determine what sort of job you should have, behaving responsibly, coping with emergencies, and setting prices.

Kid's Career Connection

A monthly career education periodical targeted at kids in grades 4–6. Each eight-page illustrated issue features an interview with a person in a different profession, plus a series of student activities based on the described job. Included are math challenges, vocabulary puzzles, and brainteasers.

Annual subscription (12 issues), $18

R.E.A.L. Success, Inc.

726 E. Main St., Suite F

Lebanon, OH 45036

(513) 933-0887/fax (513) 933-9083

The Kid's Guide to Service Projects

Barbara A. Lewis; Free Spirit Publishing, 1996

Over 500 public-service ideas and projects for kids "who want to make a difference."

The Kid's Guide to Social Action

Barbara A. Lewis; Free Spirit Publishing, 1998

For kids who want to be part of the solution, not part of the problem. Lewis includes examples of kids who have effectively participated in social causes and campaigns, and she describes many ways of furthering a cause: "power" telephoning, "power" letter-writing, interviews, surveys, petitions, proposals, and fundraising drives. She also explains how to contact a member of Congress and how to send a message to the president, and includes a list of addresses of activist groups.

The Lemonade Stand: A Guide to Encouraging the Entrepreneur in Your Child

Emmanuelle Medu; Gateway Publishers, 1996

Over 300 pages of how-to information for young businesspersons, plus lists of contests and supportive organizations.

Making Cents: Every Kid's Guide to Money

Elizabeth Wilkinson; Little, Brown 1989

A clever 128-page guide to money, its history, uses, and creative ways to earn it, for readers aged 9–12.

LIFE SKILLS

Money Doesn't Grow on Trees:
A Parent's Guide to Raising
Financially Responsible Children

Neale S. Godfrey and Carolina Edwards; Fireside, 1994

The book opens with a series of "Financial Personality Type" quizzes for adults and kids: lists of revealing questions on spending habits and attitudes toward money. Once you've discovered whether you and your kids are spendthrifts or Scrooges, the authors propose ways for improving or modifying financial behaviors, outlining a progressive financial program for kids from preschool age through young adulthood. They stress the importance of saving, urging that each child be provided with a savings account; they also suggest encouragements and incentives for reluctant savers; explain how allowances should be linked to chores; describe the "S.O.S." (Saving/Offering/Spending) system of money management; and show kids how to set up a successful budget.

Reaching Out Through Reading: Service
Learning Adventures Through Literature

Carrie Duits and Adelle Dorman; Teacher Ideas Press, 1998

Reviews of 20 popular kids' books with related discussion questions and suggestions for community service projects for kids in grades 4–6.

$23
Libraries Unlimited
Box 6633
Englewood, CO 80155-6633
(303) 770-1220 or (800) 237-6124/fax (303) 220-8843
e-mail: lu-books@lu.com
Web site: www.lu.com

The Teenage Entrepreneur's Guide
Sarah L. Riehm; Surrey Books, 1990

Business ideas for teenagers, with detailed descriptions.

GAMES

Careers for Kids

A series of conversation-promoting card decks, designed to encourage kids to discover and discuss the many career possibilities in different fields. Titles in the series to date include *Art, Music, Technology,* and *Sports.* (In preparation: *Medicine, Science, Construction,* and *Media.*) Each card in a deck covers one career. In the field of music, for example, career possibilities include music teacher, piano tuner, songwriter, and conductor; "Art" cards include everything from art historian to cake decorator; and "Technology" cards, careers from microchip engineer and virtual reality programmer to air traffic controller. Each card includes descriptive information about the featured career, an interesting fact about the job in practice, a discussion question, and an activity suggestion. The satellite engineer card (Technology), for example, lists a few facts and figures about satellites, asks kids to discuss what type of data they would like to record or transmit from a satellite, and suggests a research project based on the first communication satellites.

Each deck, $5.95
TableTalk
Box 31703
St. Louis, MO 63131
(314) 997-5676 or (800) 997-5676/fax (314) 997-3602
Web site: www.tbltalk.com

An Income of Her Own

A board game of business practices and money management targeted at girls.

$38
Independent Means, Inc.
Box 987
Santa Barbara, CA 93102
(805) 646-1215 or (800) 350-2978
Web site: www.anincomeofherown.com

See **Economics for Kids** (page 207).

INDEX

software, 668–69
videos, 668
ASL (American Sign Language). *See*
sign language
Astro-Dots game, 258
astronauts, 687–89
astronomers, biographies, 254–55
Astronomical Society of the Pacific,
249
astronomy, 247
activities, 4–5, 247
activity books, 256–58
audiocassettes, 263–64
books about, 252–55
equipment, 247–50
games and hands-on activities,
258–63
links to history, 542
literature links, 255–56
magazines, 251–52
on-line resources, 266–67
rockets, 261–62
software, 264–66
star maps and guides, 250–51
stencils, 263
videos, 264
Astronomy magazine, 251
Astroslides game, 258
Athenaze Series, 704
athletes
biographies, 838
See also physical fitness; sports
atlases, 408–9
Atlas-in-a-Box game, 426
atomic bomb, 576, 680, 681–82, 684,
685
Atom magazine, 218
A to Zap software, 62
AtoZebra magazine, 69
AudioEditions catalog, 83
Audio-Forum, 691–92
audio resources
American history, 459–60, 494
astronomy tapes, 263–64
birdcalls and songs, 337
books on tape, 83–84
dinosaur songs, 386
environmental science-related,
301–2
ethical issues, 799–800
folktales, 832
geography songs, 433–34
grammar songs, 127–28
high school and college courses, 17
King Arthur legends, 637
mathematics-related, 195–96
music tapes, 756–57, 761, 762, 764,
766
myth recordings, 91
news magazines, 159
philosophy recordings, 809–10
religion recordings, 805

Robin Hood stories, 638
science, general, 242
science songs, 328
Shakespeare recordings, 96
speeches, American, 459–60
Supreme Court recordings, 588–89
weather songs, 376
Western American music, 534
whale songs, 324
zoology-related, 346–47
Audubon, John James, 332, 334, 336
Audubon Society. *See* National
Audubon Society
Austen, Jane, 674, 676–77
authors. *See* writers
*The Autobiography of Miss Jane
Pittman*, 540
automobiles
books, 561–62
hands-on activities, 562–63
videos, 563
Avalon Hill Game Company, 444
Aves Science Kit Company, 221, 274,
280, 349, 353
Aztecs, 463, 657, 658, 659, 661
See also pre-Columbian American
history

B

Babybug magazine, 78
Bach, Johann Sebastian, 769
bacteria. *See* microbiology
Baker, Josephine, 790
Balanchine, George, 790
ballet. *See* dance
Ball-Stick-Bird, 52–53
Banneker, Benjamin, 255, 537, 555,
556, 558
A Beautiful Place game, 299
Beaver Tooth game, 509
Becket, 643
bees, 288–89, 293
See also entomology
Beethoven, Ludwig van, 757–58
Bell, Alexander Graham, 565
Bellerophon Books, 89, 444
Ben-Hur, 624
Ben and Me, 493
Bethump'd with Words game, 122
Bible, 800, 803–4, 805–7
games, 66
videos, 605
See also religion
BibleTalk game, 803–4
Big Bird in China, 434, 668
Big Dipper, 252, 542
A Bigger World, 17–18
binoculars, 248
biographies
American historical figures, 450,
451, 453, 491–97
in ancient history, 610

architects, 782, 784
artists, 722–28
astronomers, 254–55
athletes, 838
botanists, 279
composers, 757–58
dancers, 790
economists, 214
environmentalists, 298–99
explorers, 464–66, 653–55
inventors, 555–57
on-line resources, 446, 460
oral, of family members, 590
ornithologists, 332
paleontologists, 379–80
plays, 774
scientists, 230, 231, 327–28
women in history, 568, 569
world history figures, 416, 597, 599,
610
writers, 86–88
zoologists, 341
biology, 268–69
botany, 276–84
cell, 284–86
dissection, 275–76, 338–39
entomology, 286–94
environmental science, 294–302
evolution, 303–6, 339
genetics, 306–10
human body, 310–17
kits, 274–75
marine, 317–26
micro-, 326–28
microscopes, 269–74
on-line resources, 275–76, 286, 338
ornithology, 329–38
zoology, 338–47
bird feeders, 335
birdhouses, 335, 814
birds. *See* ornithology
Birds of North America software, 337–38
Black Heritage Brain Quest, 579
Black history. *See* African Americans
Black History Playing Cards, 579
Blind Justice game, 588
blood, typing, 315
Blue Jean Magazine, 830–31
The Blue Max, 679
Blue Planet, 368
Bluestocking Press, 447
Bob Books, 46, 59
Boggle game, 130
Bolchazy-Carducci Publishers, 703
Boodle magazine, 144
Book Links magazine, 69–70, 411, 718
books
buying, 75–78
electronic, 62–63
history of, 145–46, 645, 646
libraries, 161–63
making, 146

The Road to Ancient Egypt software, 619

The Road to Ancient Greece software, 625–26

Robin Hood, 637–38

robots, 399

rockets, 256, 261

Rock and Gem magazine, 359

rock paintings, 462, 463

rocks. *See* geology

rock tumblers, 365–66

Rocky Bingo game, 368

Rocky Mountain Beaver Pond, 535

Roman City, 625

Rome, ancient
    cities, 625, 781
    coloring and paper-crafts books, 622–23
    fiction books, 622
    games and hands-on activities, 611, 623–24
    myths. *See* classical mythology
    nonfiction books, 620–21
    number system, 182, 706
    on-line resources, 626
    videos, 624–25

Romeo and Juliet (Shakespeare), 646–47

Roosevelt, Eleanor, 571, 573, 574

Roosevelt, Franklin D., 571, 574

Roots, 541

Roots and Wings, 502

Rousseau, Henri, 727

Russia
    folktales and legends, 685–86
    history, 685, 686–87
    See also Soviet Union

Russian language, 708

S

S & S Arts & Crafts, 717

Sagan, Carl, 264

Saint-Saëns, Camille, 764

Salem witch trials, 470, 471, 472, 475–76, 478

Sammy's Science House software, 243–44

Santa Fe Trail, 528
    See also Westward movement, history of

Save the Whales game, 322–23, 514

Sax Arts & Crafts, 115–16, 717–18

Saxon Math, 177

Say It By Signing, 709

The Scarlet Pimpernel, 677

Scattergories game, 124

Scholastic New Media, 32

Schoolhouse Rock: America Rock, 490

Schoolmasters Science, 223, 270

Schoolmasters Video, 43, 84–85

schools
    correspondence, 15–17
    high schools, 16, 17

public, 14–15
    sports programs, 837

Schumann, Clara, 758

science, 215–17
    activities, 5–6
    activity books, 233–38, 425, 755
    audiovisual resources, 241–43
    books on general, 226–29
    catalogs, 221–25
    cooking activities, 815, 816, 818, 819, 820
    fairs, 245, 328, 343
    games and hands-on activities, 238–41, 623, 666
    gardening activities, 825
    history of, 229–32, 623
    literature links, 232–33
    magazines, 218–21
    museums, 246, 267
    national standards, 227
    on-line resources, 244–46
    organizations, 217–18
    software, 243–44
    See also astronomy; biology; chemistry; earth science; physics

Science-by-Mail, 240

Science Court software, 244

Science Kit and Boreal Laboratories, 223

Science Museum of Minnesota, 246

Science News magazine, 220

Science Sleuth software, 244

The Sciences magazine, 220

ScienceTalk Cards, 240

Science Weekly magazine, 220

Science World magazine, 220

Scientific American magazine, 220–21

Scientific Explorer, 223–24

scientific method, 217

scientists' biographies, 230, 231, 327–28
    astronomers, 254–55
    botanists, 279
    environmentalists, 298–99
    ornithologists, 332
    paleontologists, 379–80
    zoologists, 341

Scientists Card Game, 240

Scopes, John, 304, 305

Scrabble, 130–31

self-esteem, 830

Senet game, 617

Sergeant York, 679

service projects, 842, 843

Set game, 192

Seven Alone, 535

1776, 489

sewing and fabric crafts, 833
    books, 833–34
    hands-on activities, 835–36
    literature links, 834–35

sex education, 832–33

Shakespeare, William
    activity and coloring books, 94–95
    audio and video recordings, 96–97
    books, 92–94, 646–47, 773
    catalogs, 92, 772
    games and hands-on activities, 95–96, 776–77
    on-line resources, 97, 746
    study of, 770–71

Shello game, 323–24

Shoofly magazine, 79

The Sierra Club, 295

sign language
    American Indian, 503, 504
    books, 708–9
    on-line resources, 709
    videos, 709

silhouettes, cutting, 482

The Silk Road, 434, 668

The Silk Road software, 668–69

SimAnt software, 293

SimCity 2000 software, 788

SimEarth software, 302

SimIsle software, 302

Sing, Spell, Read, and Write (SSRW) program, 47, 54

Sister Wendy's Story of Painting, 722, 741

The Six Wives of Henry VIII, 651

The Skeptical Inquirer magazine, 221

Skipping Stones magazine, 157, 412, 693, 711

Sky & Telescope magazine, 251–52

The Sky Astronomy Software, 265

Sky Publishing Corporation, 249

Skytrip America software, 459

slavery
    emancipation, 548, 551
    fiction books, 538–39
    games and hands-on activities, 539–40
    history, 446
    nonfiction books, 536–38
    Underground Railroad, 537, 538–39, 540, 542
    videos, 540–41
    See also Civil War

Smith and Kraus, Inc., 772

Smithsonian Dreams of Flight, 561

Smithsonian Institution, 246, 369, 386, 449–50, 511, 585

Snowstorm game, 375

Social Studies School Service, 411, 446, 586, 596

software
    African history, 673
    American history, 29, 458–59, 524, 536
    ancient civilizations, 611–12, 619, 625–26
    archaeology, 609